Houghton Mifflin Company

Boston

DALLAS   GENEVA, ILLINOIS

HOPEWELL, NEW JERSEY

PALO ALTO   LONDON

INTRODUCTION TO

Personality and Psychotherapy

A THEORY-CONSTRUCTION

APPROACH

INTRODUCTION TO

Personality and Psychotherapy

A THEORY-CONSTRUCTION

APPROACH   SECOND EDITION

Joseph F. Rychlak

PURDUE UNIVERSITY

TO LENORE

Library of Congress Catalog Card Number: 80–68141

ISBN: 0–395–29736–2

Acknowledgment is made for permission to reprint the following materials:

From *Principles of Behavior Modification* by Albert Bandura. Copyright © 1969 by Holt, Rinehart and Winston, Inc. Reprinted by permission of Holt, Rinehart and Winston.

From Albert Bandura, *Aggression: A Social Analysis,* © 1973. Reprinted by permission of Prentice-Hall, Inc., Englewood Cliffs, N.J.

From Albert Bandura, *Social Learning Theory,* © 1977. Reprinted by permission of Prentice-Hall Inc., Englewood Cliffs, N.J.

From *B. F. Skinner: The Man and His Ideas* by Richard I. Evans, Copyright © 1969 by Richard I. Evans. Reprinted by permission of the publisher, E. P. Dutton.

From *Jean Piaget: The Man and His Ideas* by Richard I. Evans, translated by Eleanor Duckworth, Copyright © 1973 by Richard I. Evans. Reprinted by permission of the publisher, E. P. Dutton.

From *The Collected Works of C. G. Jung,* trans. R. F. C. Hull, Bollingen Series XX. Vol. 7: *Two Essays on Analytical Psychology,* Copyright 1953, © 1966 by Princeton University Press; Vol. 8: *The Structure and Dynamics of the Psyche,* copyright © 1960, 1969 by Princeton University Press; Vol. 16: *The Practice of Psychotherapy,* copyright 1954, © 1966 by Princeton University Press. Excerpts reprinted by permission.

From *The Psychology of Personal Constructs,* Volumes One and Two, by George A. Kelly, Ph.D. Reprinted with the permission of W. W. Norton & Company, Inc. Copyright 1955 by George A. Kelly.

From *Counseling and Psychotherapy,* by Carl R. Rogers, Houghton Mifflin Company, 1942, 1970. Reprinted by permission of the publisher and Constable & Company.

From *Client-Centered Therapy,* by Carl R. Rogers, Houghton Mifflin Company, 1951, 1979. Reprinted by permission of the publisher and Constable & Company.

From *On Becoming a Person,* © 1961 Carl R. Rogers. Reprinted by permission of Houghton Mifflin Company and Constable & Company.

Specified material from *Carl Rogers on Encounter Groups* by Carl R. Rogers, Ph.D. Copyright © 1970 by Carl R. Rogers. Reprinted by permission of Harper & Row, Publishers, Inc., and Penguin Books Ltd.

Contents

Chapter 2
The Individual Psychology
of Alfred Adler 116

Chapter 3
The Analytical Psychology
of Carl Jung 176

Chapter 4
Theory-Construction
Issues in Classical
Psychoanalysis 261

Part II
Lockean Models
in American Psychiatry
and Behaviorism

Chapter 5
An "American" Psychology:
The Interpersonal Theory
of Harry Stack Sullivan   323

Chapter 8
Theory Construction in
the Empirico-Behavioristic
Tradition 500

Part III
Kantian Models in the
Phenomenological Outlook

Chapter 9
Applied Phenomenology:
The Client-Centered
Psychology of
Carl R. Rogers 565

Chapter 10
Existential Analysis
or Daseinsanalysis:
Binswanger and Boss   619

Preface

Roughly eight years have passed since I first asked teachers of personality to try this text out in their classrooms. I am gratified that many have done so, and even more pleased by the number of users who regularly adopt the volume in their courses. Over the years, *Introduction to Personality and Psychotherapy: A Theory-Construction Approach* has been evaluated along four or five pedagogical dimensions, and I have taken all such considerations into account in laying plans for the present revision. I stand by the aspirations expressed in my original preface (see following), but I have also tried to improve the book in the following ways:

Reading Level

In the process of completely rewriting the text for this revision, I have gone through the contents, paragraph by paragraph, replacing difficult words with easier words and defining others for the reader. Naturally, I could not change technical terms or statements that have been quoted from a theorist's original writings. Many paragraphs have been rewritten in an effort to make them more conversational—less "text-booky" —in style. These revisions I have submitted to my undergraduate students with positive results. Repeated samplings of the book's contents that have been submitted to Flesch-count analysis suggest that the reading level is now equivalent to that which can be found in the typical weekly news magazines.

Depth of Coverage

This is still the most comprehensive, in-depth textbook available in the field of personality theory. I could not bring myself to reduce this coverage, but have instead tried to make the theoretical terminology easier to locate and review, and hence to learn than it was in the first edition. Each chapter now closes with a summary that touches on the lion's share of a theorist's primary constructs, pulling them together succinctly for the student and in a slightly different way than the chapter content did. Following this summary, the student will find an outline of the chapter, with each section heading listed and underneath this heading all of the important theoretical constructs taken up in that section. This means a student can quickly locate where in Chapter 1 Freud's notion of fixation is discussed or where in Chapter 9 Rogers's concept of unconditional positive regard is taken up. The instructor may alert the student to this outline at the outset of study, as it can be used as a parallel-structure teaching aid (first survey, then read, review, and so on). Also, if the instructor wishes to limit the theoretical constructs a student will be held accountable for, the class can be taken through these outlines and told specifically which constructs will be covered in the course. This allows the student to gain a comprehensive sense of the theory even as he or she focuses on specific concepts for course credit.

Use of Examples

It was clear from surveys of users that more examples of the book's concepts were desirable. Owing to space limitations, I could not include detailed case histories or typescripts from psychotherapy interviews. But I have made it a point in the revising of each chapter to add up to two dozen specific examples of the theoretical constructs. I found in my pretesting of students that it often helped to use the first names of people in illustrating a point (for example, "John finds that he cannot . . ." or "Britt fears that she may . . ."). This seems to encourage identification in the reading, resulting in better understanding. I have used this tactic sparingly in the revision.

Theoretical Coverage

Our surveys reveal that instructors have their favorites for inclusion in a volume of this sort. There was no great sentiment for excluding any of the theorists of the first edition, so I have not done so. Two theorists have been added—Bandura and Piaget: Bandura's inclusion is understandable, as he has written on psychotherapy; but Piaget's inclusion is debatable. I felt that Piaget's per-

sonality theory—not his developmental stages, but his actual *theory* of behavior—is not clearly presented in any current text, and that his use of "construction" is today being confounded with Kelly's notion under the same name. Hence I decided to include Piaget in the Kelly chapter. I also included a section on Oriental philosophy, hoping thereby to show how Oriental philosophy parallels existentialistic approaches to personality and psychotherapy. Finally, I added a discussion of the nature of projective versus psychometric assessment of personality.

Theory Construction

I have dropped the "basic meaning constructs" in favor of referring directly to the Aristotelian causes. Colleagues informed me that I was simply compounding the difficulty in understanding, since in any case they had to reason back to the causal meanings. The theory-construction sections of the text (the Introduction and Chapters 4, 8, and 12) have been completely redrafted. The above-mentioned spirit of easier reading, more examples, and the direct involvement of the reader through concrete issues faced by "real" people has been employed in the theory-construction chapters as well. The format throughout involves advancing questions having direct relevance to personality description and then providing an answer—or, at least, a better understanding of what is involved in the question. Examples of these questions would include "How is behavior determined?" or "If we predict and/or control the course of behavior, does this mean we necessarily understand it?" When relevant, comments made by the theorists of the volume are introduced. The effect of this approach is to make the reading of the theory-construction chapters more salient than they were in the first edition. An instructor may select one or two of these questions to enlarge upon in classroom discussion. Finally, a very detailed glossary has been included in the revision, covering all of the theory-construction terms employed in the text. This means that the student can quickly refresh his or her memory of some concept (realism, determinism, introspective perspective, or whatever) by flipping to the back of the text.

I hope that these measures will make the Second Edition a more useful, instructive textbook than was the First Edition.

J. F. R.

Preface

TO FIRST EDITION

Introduction to Personality and Psychotherapy: A Theory-Construction Approach surveys the major schools of personality and psychotherapy according to a standard outline per chapter, and then evaluates the content of these outlooks in terms of theory construction. Each theory is presented historically, with an effort to capture its development, the reasons for any changes in its content, and a detailed understanding of its full range of meaning. To promote this depth of understanding the theoretical rubrics of personality are extended to psychotherapy, where the student can see why they were initially advanced: to function helpfully in a living circumstance for both client and therapist. Finally, a comparative scheme of theory-construction issues drawn from the history of philosophy and science is offered to round out the student's grasp of the schools of thought, contrasting strengths and weaknesses of variations therein.

The area of personality theory is immense and confusing, and even the great thinkers in the field do not have a clear picture of one another. This multiplicity in outlook is compounded by the fact that many of the heavily used secondary sources were written before the better, more thorough translations of Freud, Adler, and Jung were available

and arrayed in proper sequence across the theorists' life spans, permitting a proper overview of developments and changes in their thought. Relying on secondary sources can confound the restricted and often slightly biased views of others with those of the original theorists. Thus in reporting from the original sources, I have tried to be meticulous in the citations, so that the serious student could look into the primary sources for more detail. The reader will find this book thoroughly referenced and well indexed.

Years of experience have taught me that the student really cannot understand the classical personality theorists without also understanding their theories of psychotherapy. The ideas of people like Freud and Jung are easily misconstrued as simply titillating or mystical interpretations of the human condition when presented in the classroom without an opportunity for the student to see why such conceptions were considered essential in the consulting room. Though there has been a tradition of concern lest students being told about psychotherapy might begin practicing without adequate training and supervision, the complexity of modern times seems to negate this line of argument. If anything, a well-presented discussion of *several* theories of personality and psychotherapy can only help to sophisticate the college student so that he or she is not an easy target for some one, saving theory of mental health. This broadening, after all, is the purpose of education.

The conceptual scheme I offer has scholarly credentials and content recognizable to other sciences which might be applied to the teaching of this course. Modern psychology must be able to provide generalizations which coalesce with the thinking in other sciences if it is to be successful in its struggle to become an undisputed science. The best scheme and series of issues to unify personality theory would seem to be drawn from the history of philosophy and science. Thus, I give a detailed account of each theory and then consider it in light of a set number of theory-construction issues that all personality theorists have wrestled with at varying levels of clarity and sophistication.

Though I am committed to raising the status of personality theory and would like to develop an area of specialization in psychology which might be termed "theory construction," I am not so naive as to assume that all instructors will want to frame their courses around this emphasis. Many will want to use this volume in an introductory personality theory course, or an introductory psychotherapy course, and no more. And so, the reader will find that he can skip the theory-construction considerations altogether. These issues are set off in independent chapters so that *Introduction to Personality and Psychotherapy* is actually a theory-construction book within a personality and psychotherapy book. I would prefer that the instructor-reader see things my way and help to establish this emphasis, but only time will tell how accurately I have diagnosed psychology's needs on this score.

I have tried to make the non-theory construction chapters clear and straightforward. Each chapter is written according to a common framework; the student will always know where he or she stands in relation to the point of view under presentation. There are enough details and examples that the student is not likely to feel that he or she is simply memorizing a string of terminology. I have also included diagrams of the more difficult concepts.

The theorists were selected for this volume on the basis of two criteria. First, they had to be major contributors to personality and psychotherapy. Second, they had to be an outstanding example of the various philosophical lines of development found in psychology. Fortunately, the combining criteria worked out to cover the most widely cited people in the area. Though some might quarrel with the inclusion of Kelly's constructive alternativism as a major school of thought, no one can question that his approach is a marvelous application of what I call a Kantian theoretical model.

Questions of space always nag the text writer, and since I wanted to emphasize the specific theorists' writings I eliminated any forays into side issues or attempts to bring a school of thought up to date. An instructor may cover such topics in lecture. The present effort is devoted to theory *as written* by the founder over the years. We study his thought and try to do justice to its development.

I find that undergraduates genuinely want to learn what this book has to offer. *This* is what they think psychology is all about. They are not disturbed by the fact that psychology lacks empirical facts to back up everything it proposes. The undergraduates today are unusually insightful on the question of implacable scientific truth. They know from reading newspapers that modern scientists almost daily raise new objections to Darwin's evolutionary theory or Einstein's theory of relativity. They are already schooled in the attitude that scientific facts are never "true" for all time but only for as long as they describe and explain phenomena needing such conceptualization better than any other.

J. F. R.

Acknowledgments

I would like to thank several people for their help and encouragement during the various stages of producing this volume. I am greatly appreciative of the biographical information provided by Gladys Kelly and Joseph Wolpe. Tom Stampfl not only gave me a candid overview of his life but helped immensely in making theoretical points clear. Carl Rogers generously provided me with material in pre-publication form which facilitated bringing his still active and creative viewpoints up to date. Before his death, Carl G. Jung made available valuable information concerning certain influences on his thinking. George Kelly, my teacher and personal friend, exchanged letters with me over the years dealing with the theory-construction questions which so fascinated me. His was a great and generous intellect. Heinz Ansbacher not only substantially contributed to the structure my study of Adler would take, but he has continued to audit its progress over the years.

I would like to thank Jim Naylor for helping me find the time to do this book. Marvelous colleagues and friends like Jim Mancuso, Bob Hogan, Mark Stephens, and Dick Ingwell played an inestimable role in making me feel that this effort was worthwhile. I thank them for their bent ears and critical assessments. My students have probably done more to inspire me than anyone, and I would like in particular to thank Nguyen Duc Tuan for his scholarly support and personal friendship.

Clare Thompson, Dan Levinson, and Heinz Ansbacher kindly read portions of the manuscript, and I thank them for their valuable comments. I greatly appreciate the typing assistance of Carol Vester, Lorna Stewart, Joyce Von Dielingen, and Mary Sue Burkhardt. Finally, this book like my first book would never have seen print without the devoted assistance of my wonderful wife Lenore, not to mention the forbearance and sacrifice of my children, Steph and Ron.

Introduction

A Framework for the Study of Personality

What Is Personality?

This question probably arises from the basic interest we all have in "What makes people different from each other?" Perhaps we are interested in knowing why we, personally, behave as we do. The issue of personality differences seems to impress us most when we have the opportunity to see people's behavior together. We attend a class in school or a meeting at our job and observe John, Bill, Ann, and Sarah interacting. John is a quiet, easy-going sort of person. Bill seems to be much more tense and "pushy." Ann is secretive; you never quite know what she is thinking about. Sarah is very competent and usually ends up leading the groups of which she is a member. Do these four individuals have different personalities? Not every psychologist would agree that the answer is yes.

Some psychologists believe that to speak of *a* personality is to *reify** (make real)

* The practice is followed throughout this text of italicizing new constructs as these terms are introduced. Subsequent uses are not italicized.

something that does not exist. The person under observation (John, Bill, Ann, or Sarah) does not have *a* personality, but rather is simply behaving in a predictable fashion. All living animals, from the lowest forms to the highest, behave. Are we therefore to say that birds and snakes and cows have personalities? No, answer these psychologists; the only scientific way to describe what animals do is to say that they behave in certain routine ways. They acquire *habits* that allow us to recognize them and to distinguish them from other animals, but this does not mean they have personalities. The same argument applies to the human animal.

Other psychologists believe that the word *habit* implies a kind of automatic or mechanical pattern of behavior, whereas often a person is clearly trying to present himself or herself to others with an aim in view. For example, Ann's secretiveness has been pointed out to her by many friends, but she goes on acting like this out of what seems to be a deep-seated preference. These psychologists also argue that what a person is "really" like does not always come through in the way the person behaves openly. Deep down, John knows that his easy-going manner is a front, and that underneath he is as tense as a wound spring. Examples like this impress the personality psychologist—sometimes called a *personologist*—with the ability that human beings have to influence their own behavior, to change or not change, to hide or be open about what they do, and to seek interpersonal advantages at every turn in life.

This seeking of advantage is called *motivation*. People have many kinds of motives, including those of which they may be unaware. Some personologists suggest that we have unconscious minds that direct us to some end as surely as do our conscious minds, but that we do not admit that we want these

unconscious ends. The reason we do not admit unconscious motives is that for some reason we are ashamed of what they mean or imply about ourselves. Those psychologists who reject the concept of personality usually dismiss all such talk of unconscious intentions. Out of consciousness, for these psychologists, is out of mind altogether.

In light of such disagreements about the very idea of personality, it is difficult to answer the question posed at the beginning of this section. Students must accept the fact that there is a lot more to the study of personality than they originally believed would be involved. No textbook of personality can honestly present a *single* approach to the subject. The present volume offers a means of arraying and analyzing many *different* theories of personality and the many issues that go along with their study. We can, however, define this area of interest as follows: *The study of personality is concerned with the various styles of behavior that different organisms habitually reflect.* Since we rarely assign personality labels to lower animals, we might modify the word *organisms* with *human,* but this would prejudice the case against those psychologists who find the personality concept of questionable value. As phrased, the definition probably encompasses all views held by psychologists today. The next suggested question is, What causes personality and personality differences in the first place?

What Is a Cause?

If we ask the average person today "What is a cause?" the answers we get usually stress such things as how events are brought about, what makes things happen, or how something is assembled. We think of causes as the impetus, thrust, or motion in events. But the concept of cause was not so restricted when the philosopher Aristotle (384–322 B.C.) first proposed the term. The Greek word that Aristotle used for *cause* was *aitiá*, which has the meaning of "responsibility," so that, if following his usage, we would, when assigning a cause, be trying to assign responsibility —and even blame!—for why something existed or an event took place. This is an odd way of talking about causes, judging from to-day's usage. We do not say that the wind is "responsible" for blowing leaves from trees in autumn.

But Aristotle would have talked this way, suggesting that all events in experience were to some extent *intending* to bring about a given result or end. For example, in his *Physics,* Aristotle theorized that leaves exist for the sake of providing shade for the fruit on trees, and he concluded from this that "nature is a cause, a cause that operates for a purpose." [1] Since we are now concerned with how Aristotle theorized, it would be helpful if we got clearly in mind what a *theory* is. As we shall learn, when we theorize we are always relating one idea to another, forming some kind of relational tie between a concept like "nature" and another like "purpose," as in the quote from Aristotle. If we say "Sarah is competent," we are theorizing by tying together this person with an adjective that supposedly captures her style of behavior (that is, her personality). So let us define *theory* as follows: *A theory is a series of two or more schematic labels (words, visual images that we name, and so on) that have been hypothesized, presumed, or even factually demonstrated to bear a meaningful relationship, one with the other(s).*

Note that in this definition we claim that even a factually demonstrated meaningful tie of one label (Sarah) to another (competency) is a theory. The word *theory* is often interpreted as meaning something that is unfounded or speculative, not accurately tied down to reality. We say "That's only a theory," meaning that it is subject to doubt and challenge by alternative theories. And we also say "This is a fact," meaning it is not to be doubted or challenged by alternative theories. Though it may be all right to distinguish between *theory* and *fact* this way in common language, the greater *fact* of the matter is that in science we have learned to accept the likelihood that two or more theories can account for the *same* pattern of observed facts (often called *laws*). We can prove as facts both that light is a series of particles and that it is a series of waves. Given such alternative explanations, it is proper for us to call everything that we understand mentally a theory, thereby recognizing that *theory* and *thought* are two ways of describing the same thing. It is impossible to theorize without thinking, and thinking is always a theoretical process. What we *think* is factual today, that is, our current theory, may on new evidence, or simply through re-analysis of existing evidence, turn out to be an error tomorrow.

In framing his concept of causation, Aristotle was therefore proposing a *theory* of how we can go about explaining our world. We can explain the many things and events of this world by finding out what is responsible for their existence or occurrence. Philosophers (our first scientists) before Aristotle had begun this process of theorizing by suggesting three general principles of explanation. The first principle was introduced by Thales of Miletus (640?–546 B.C.) and his students. It suggested that the world was made up entirely of water in various guises, or, as this universal substance was later named by Anaximander (611–547 B.C.), the *boundless.* (Today we would call it *matter.*) The principle of explanation here is: *To account for something, describe the substance of which it consists.*

The second principle of explanation brings the theme of action or movement into play. There was a famous debate between Heraclitus (540–480 B.C.) and Parmenides (515–456 B.C.) about whether anything really changes in life. Parmenides argued that there was no such thing as change, and Heraclitus argued that there was a constant flux of change within the overlaying order of events. We might summarize the principle implicit in this debate as follows: *To account for something, describe it in terms of the motions that it takes on over time, bringing it to be what it now is.*

As suggested in his argument, Heraclitus stressed the pattern that we see over and above the constant flux of events. He liked to point out that we never step in the "same" river twice. The river looks the same, it has a constant pattern, but the water flowing through it is *also* constant in change. Heraclitus called this tendency for things and events to take on a pattern the *logos* of nature. We derive our concept of logic—the study of patterned meanings—from this word root. Patterns are fundamental to all knowledge. We see our friend's body outline down the street, recognize thereby who it is, and call hello. The principle here would be something like this: *To account for something, describe it according to the reliable pattern it takes on.*

Aristotle had these three principles to build on as he formulated his theory of knowledge, that is, a theory that tried to explain how we can know anything. He did not call them *principles of explanation,* as he might have, but rather brought in his concept of *aitiá* ("cause") to suggest that we have a knowledge of something when we can explain it *in terms of* those causes that are responsible for its occurrence or existence.

And Aristotle was quick to add, there are *four* causes—four causal explanations—that can be used to show that we do have knowledge of things or events.

We have knowledge to the extent that we can assign a *material* cause to things, which is what Thales and Anaximander were relying on in their use of a substance concept like water or the boundless. Things are made up of different kinds of substances, and they might also share a common substance (like matter). In explaining the nature of a chair we can say we know it is a chair because like most chairs it is made of wood or iron or marble; not many chairs are made of cotton or of ice cream. Another cause of the chair is the fact that someone or some machine made it, or put it together. This motile and constitutive aspect of explanation Aristotle called the *efficient* cause, and we can see here the possibility of flux and change that so interested Parmenides and Heraclitus. Events move along, they change, get done or fail to get done, thanks to some kind of thrust or push or a lack thereof. Chairs also take on certain patterned outlines; they meet our blueprint ideas of what chairs look like. Chairs look more like chairs than they look like tricycles or apple trees. This usage, based on the logos idea of Heraclitus and our third principle, Aristotle called the *formal* cause. Each of these factors—material, efficient, and formal—*bore a responsibility* in accounting for the nature of the thing we call a chair.

Note that we are using more than one cause to describe a single item (that is, the chair). It is very important to remember that Aristotle's theory of knowledge favored using as many of the causes to explain (describe, account for) anything as we possibly could. This is like cutting and polishing facets on a rough diamond. The more facets we can cut the more the diamond will sparkle, increasing its value. Similarly, Aristotle believed that the more *different* causes we could put into our theories, the richer they would become. It is possible to have formless substances, such as a blob of mud, and even formless movements, such as the wafting of a breeze against our face. But mud can be shaped and baked into statues or dinnerware, and breezes can be elevated and patterned into an easily recognizable tornado. In like fashion, Aristotle believed, the physical scientist can bring to bear more and more causes to enrich his account of *natural* (that is, nature's) objects and events.

Aristotle rounded out his theory of causation by proposing a fourth meaning, one that was even more directly tied to the idea of responsibility, blame, or reason for something existing or taking place than were the other three causes. Aristotle called this fourth and last concept of his theory the *final* cause, which he defined as "that for the sake of which" something exists or takes place. We can just as readily call this the reason, purpose, or intention of an object or event in existence. The principle here would be: *To account for something, describe it in terms of that reason it has for being, or the end (goal, purpose) toward which it is intending.* The sake (reason) for which a chair is constructed might be termed "a person's comfort" or "laziness" or "utility in eating, writing," and so forth.

Of course, the chair does not *itself* decide to *come about* or *to be*. The human being who obtained the wood (material cause) and made it into a chair (efficient cause), matching his or her physical outline (formal cause) so that a more comfortable lifestyle might result (final cause), may be said to have a purpose or intention in the creation of a chair. However, as we noted above, Aristotle was not above assigning purpose to nature and his physics is full of examples in which inanimate objects like rocks and rivers are described in terms of the purpose they fulfilled in existence. The Greek word for *end* or purpose is *telos,* and hence we call those theories that employ the meaning of final causation to account for events *telic* theories or *teleologies.* A teleology is therefore any theory that uses one or more of the other causes *in addition to* the final cause. There are three general forms of telic theory. One may describe nature telically (*natural teleology*), or a god directing nature (*deity teleology*). And even if one does not accept these two views of natural events, it is still possible to interpret human behavior telically (*human teleology*).

As we shall see repeatedly throughout this volume, it is the final cause that has been most troubling to science, and, in particular, to the science of psychology. Even so, the four causes can comprise a very helpful *metatheory* (a "theory of theorizing") on the basis of which it will be possible to study what various theoretical accounts of personality are trying to say. As a simple example, let us return to the personality differences of John, Bill, Ann, and Sarah. What caused these differences? A theorist who would say "People have different hereditary influences and this is probably what accounts for why they differ" would be putting major emphasis on a *material*-cause explanation. Someone who argued "These four individuals were reared in very different environments and therefore they were shaped by these external circumstances into behaving as they do now" would be stressing *efficient* causation in the theoretical account.

Another theorist who suggested "It is God's plan that we all will have our own individuality during our lives on earth" would be falling back primarily on the *formal* cause in accounting for the observed differences. Finally, a theorist who said "People always strategize to get what they want in social relations, but they choose different ways of getting to their ends" would be framing a teleological account, putting major emphasis on the *final* cause to explain the observed behavioral differences. Note that the formal and final causes tend to be used together. That is, in speaking of God's plan (formal cause) the theorist necessarily suggests that the deity puts this into action—or creates life "for the sake of" (final cause) this plan. Since the plan encompasses the deity's end (purpose, intention), this would be a form of deity teleology. Similarly, when we say that people strategize in social relations we imply that they have some kind of plan (formal cause) "for the sake of which" (final cause) they are trying to get what they want (that is, their end, purpose, intention). In this case we would have a human teleology, which could be believed regardless of whether the deity teleology was believed.

The reader may find it difficult at first to be theoretical about causation. We Westerners are so used to thinking of causes as *only* efficient in nature that it seems to fly in the face of common sense to divide our thinking on causation into four piles. Eastern peoples have traditionally been open to explanations using a broader range of causation. With the rise of interest in Oriental philosophies among Westerners in recent years, it may be getting easier to accept a broadened view of "what causes what?" in explanations of natural phenomena. Probably the first hurdle to be leaped is that of acceptance. We must first believe that it was decided in our Western history what would or would not be considered *a* cause of anything (we take this up below). Earlier there were four causes and now we tend to think in terms of one or two. But since the rules can always be changed again, we can "back up" and begin to sort out our understanding in terms of these four

theoretical causes. As we then proceed through the theory-construction chapters of this volume (4, 8, and 12), the analyses of the theories in light of the four causes will help make their meanings routine. In the meantime, Table 1 lists the four causal meanings with examples for ready reference. (See also the glossary of theory-construction terms beginning on p. 810.)

What Does Meaning Mean?

Thus far we have defined *personality* as the habitual *style* of behavior that people reflect, and have seen how in capturing this style we can make use of four general principles of explanation. We have also defined the word *theory* as a series of two or more schematic labels that we bring together or relate hypothetically and even prove factually to be the case. Would our theory of four causes qualify under this definition? Table 1 suggests that it surely would. The four words used to capture the four meanings listed in the table (left-hand side) are schematic labels that we have related to the four definitions (right-hand side). It is the practice to call such schematic labels *constructs* (in certain instances they might be termed *abstractions*). We will call all terms that serve a theoretical role in this volume *theoretical constructs*. A *construct* is a schematic label that captures some meaningful relation to other idea-units or constructs that the theorist is trying to express. The four causes are constructs. We are always theorizing in terms of these causes, whether we understand this fact or not. As noted above, theorizing and thinking are two ways of referring to the same process of meaning-extension in coming to know anything. This is what the noted chemist and educator, James B. Conant, was getting at when he said "that what the scientist does in his laboratory is simply to carry over, into

MATERIAL CAUSE:	The presumed underlying, unchanging essence of a thing at any given point in time. *Examples:* wood, cloth, flesh, genes, carbon, ectoplasm, electron, or matter.
EFFICIENT CAUSE:	The succession of events over time that are believed to originate or sustain motion. *Examples:* push, move, activate, make happen, energize, fall, explode, expend, thrust, or impel.
FORMAL CAUSE:	The framework, style of organization, or internal consistency of an object or event in experience. *Examples:* design, logical consistency, personality type, blueprint, shape, or outline.
FINAL CAUSE:	The reason (end, purpose, goal) why a line of behavior is being carried out, or an object is under creation. *Examples:* intentions, plans, hopes, wishes, desires, expectations, aims, and even "just for the heck of it."

Table 1   The Four Causes

another frame of reference, habits that go back to the caveman." [2]

As any dictionary will verify, the word *meaning* derives from the Anglo-Saxon roots of "to wish" and "to intend." Meaning is therefore a telic conception. When we ask someone "What do you mean by that?" we are trying to clarify the relational ties he or she is putting together mentally so that we can understand the point being made (driven at, trying to get across). Let us call the ends of the relational ties in meaning the *poles* of meaning. Thus, in Table 1 a causal construct is at one pole (left-hand side) and the constructs defining and exemplifying the causes are at the other pole (right-hand side). *Meaning* can therefore be defined as the *relational tie existing between two or more poles,* each of which focuses on a construct. The constructs (schematic labels) may be even further related to other meanings extending outward to more and more complexes of meaning. For example, we might have a construct like *mother* defined by relational ties to constructs like *a female parent.* This does not mean each of the constructs involved (*mother, female, parent*) would lack addi-

tional meaning relations attaching to them. When the relational tie is clear and widely accepted, we call this a *denotative* meaning relation. Denotations are the kinds of definitions we find in the dictionary or in Table 1. But we also find words taking on unique, private, and even bizarre meaning relations. A woman might think of *bread* when she thinks of her mother. A man might think of *oil* when he thinks of his father. Such unique meaning relations are called *connotative.* We have many such connotations in the words (constructs) that we use.

It is therefore incorrect to think of meanings as being limited to just two poles in a single relational tie. But for analytical reasons we can do so, and we want to do so because there is a fundamental issue that comes up once we appreciate the relational nature of meaning. The question arises: are the poles of meaning always *joined* from two independent points of reference—such as the left- and right-hand sides of Table 1—or are they sometimes *pulled apart* in opposite directions from a common core of meaning? The word *house,* for example, has an independence about it that does not immediately suggest to us an opposite meaning (except for *no house,* which refers more to existence-nonexistence than to *house* per se). We define *house* by assigning relational ties to it from other constructs like *walls, ceiling, building, familial residence,* and so on. Each of these meanings stands separately and distinctly as *unipolar* designations now joined into *multipolarity.* The prefix *uni* means one or single, and the prefix *multi* means many or more than one.

But now, there are other nouns like *morality* or adjectives like *good* that do not quite fit this joining of unipolarities into multipolarities. That is, in order to define and hence know what *morality* means we must already understand its opposite designation of *immorality.* We can never, not even *in principle,* know just one pole in this relation. We cannot know *good* unless we know *bad,* or know *left* without understanding what *right* means. In all such cases one pole of the meaning relation is literally being defined by the other. The basic feature of such meanings is that they are *oppositional.* We are dealing in bipolarities that are implicitly related or "pulled apart" from a common core.

We can now introduce two constructs that capture the distinction just drawn and that will help us in our analysis of the personality theories of this volume. These constructs are taken from Aristotle,[3] but the ideas they represent have a much broader application in the history of both Eastern and Western thought than simply being a topic of philosophy.[4] Meaning relations occurring between terms that are unipolar (nonoppositional) are called *demonstrative.* When a thinker reasons demonstratively the emphasis is put on singularity, clarity, and unidirectionality in meaning-extension. There is a rule of thumb for demonstrative reasoning called the *law of contradiction* (or noncontradiction). It states that "A is not non-A" or "something cannot both be and not be." We have a popular expression of this law in the saying "you can't have your cake and eat it too." The stress on singularity and realistic acceptance of what *is* in demonstrative reasoning is what makes it tough-minded. The individual who asks us to "stick to the facts" or who says "I only believe in what I can see, touch, or smell" is emphasizing demonstrative reasoning. We must *demonstrate* in the hard facts of reality what we are talking or theorizing about. The relational ties are put together out there, in the observed reality.

Despite this rigorous attitude, however, this person like anyone can at times deal in meanings that have implicit relational ties that are not demonstrable. We refer here to *dialectical* meaning relations, which have the characteristics of oppositionality, duality, and even contradiction. Opposites are sometimes joined according to a process of combining a *thesis* (one pole) with its *antithesis* (the other pole) into a new *synthesis* (the totality). The rule of thumb here is called the *one and many* principle, although it is often referred to as the *one in many* or *many in one* principle. The basic idea is that at some level all meaning relations are tied together or they can be brought into a common core of meaning. The popular expression of this rule is that "the more things change (many), the more they remain the same (one)." But dialectical reasoning is far more complex than this, and at times it is even paradoxical. An example of this type might be the Oriental sage's challenging question (*koan*), "What is the sound of one hand, clapping?"

In drawing the distinction between demonstrative and dialectical reasoning, we have moved from single word meanings to complete sentences, a line of thought that is reflected therein, and so on. Nothing in human reason (theorizing) is too complex for consideration in light of our two kinds of meaning-extension in reasoning. The demonstrative reasoner says at a scientific convention, "I intend to deal with A and only A in my comments" and the dialectician in the audience rises to say, "But there are important implications in non-A, and why are you avoiding them?" It is clear that even as a demonstrative line of thought is being worked out and expressed, the person taking a dialectical stance is defining an alternative point of view in opposition to what is being expressed. This alternative is not always hostile or destructive, though it is contradictory. A father might say to his wife, "We're going to have to get even tougher on our kids if they are ever going to behave properly," only to have the mother respond with "Maybe we should let up on them for a time and see if that won't help?" As he was framing one meaning she was working in opposite meanings. What makes any interaction dialectical is the fact that the meaning being expressed by one person in an interaction conveys bipolarity and the second person in the exchange responds with the opposite meaning(s) implied.[5]

We will continue with this demonstrative versus dialectical-reasoning distinction in the next section as we consider the rise of scientific description in Western history. But we want to emphasize now that Aristotle and many of the *early* (pre-seventeenth-century) philosophers in this historical line believed that human beings could reason *both* dialectically and demonstratively. Even when they were critical of dialectical reasoning, these philosophers admitted that human beings did have this two-pronged type of reasoning capacity. They found dialectical reasoning to be the source of much error, but also of much that is creative. As we will learn in the chap-

ters to follow, whether or not a theorist accepts the possibility of dialectical reasoning in his or her theory dramatically affects the image of humanity that the theory will reflect.

What Is a Scientific Explanation?

Although there have been theories of human behavior since the earliest myths and religions of human history, modern theories of behavior in psychology have usually been put forward as a *science*. But it happens that scientific theory has certain restrictions placed on it. A scientific account is different from a common sense account. We may say that "Mr. Thompson died of old age," but if the precise reasons for his death were outlined, the description would have quite a different rendering, including talk of arteriosclerotic blood vessels, failure of certain heart valves to function, and so on. If we said, "Old man Thompson was called by his maker," we would be even less faithful to science, for this would imply that he died to fulfill an intention (albeit a divine one). Modern medicine recognizes that a person's desire to live enters into the likelihood of recovery from illness, but the classic theory of how our physical bodies work does *not* include purpose or intention. This is due to an involved historical precedent which we will now sketch in outline fashion.

Recall that Aristotle and those who followed his example in later centuries used final causes to describe the universe. In medicine this was to be seen in the writings of Galen (*c.* A.D. 175), who spoke of "vital spirits" that filled the body to give human beings their self-directing, morally responsible, free-will characteristics. Even today, *vitalism* signifies a theory of behavior that relies on spiritual forces in its explanations. It is not difficult to understand why a final-cause theory of the universe brings God (deity teleology) into its explanations. If nature is a cause that operates for a purpose, as Aristotle suggested, then the implication clearly follows that there is a superintelligence directing this purpose down the road of time. For centuries, religious philosophers or *theologians* reasoned according to deity teleologies in describing the nature of things.

A common form of argument used by theologians in the Middle Ages was to ask "What did God intend when He . . ." or "What is the intention of this natural act, as created by God?" [6] This style of theorizing put emphasis first on God's presumed divine plan (formal cause) "for the sake of which" (final cause) events in the universe were now being directed. It followed that, since God was by definition a perfect being, the universe He created would be perfect. This meant, for example, that the course of movement across the skies by the sun and the stars as they, it was erroneously thought, encircled the earth followed the path of a circle. Why a circle? Because this is the most perfect of geometrical forms, and since God is perfection, He would naturally select the circle for His design.

It was during the sixteenth and seventeenth centuries that the "new scientists," who relied on precise observation, mathematical calculation, and empirical demonstration of what they claimed, began seriously countering the plausible but unproven physical theories of the theologians. Copernicus (1473–1543) showed that the sun did not go around the earth (heliocentric theory), but rather that the earth went around the sun (geocentric theory). Because he defended this view, Galileo (1564–1642) was put under house arrest during the Inquisition and was forced to withdraw the *literal* Copernican claim, although he was permitted to express it as a "mathematical fiction." At about the same time Kepler (1571–1630) proved that the motion of planets was elliptical and not circular, thereby destroying another conviction that made sense rationally but did not stand up to empirical demonstration (demonstrative reasoning!). An *empiricist* is a theoretician who insists that ideas be based on what is clearly observable, hence provable scientifically. A *rationalist* believes that only through use of our understanding can we generate knowledge, even knowledge that is observed. In the seventeenth century, which was probably the most important period in the emergence of modern science, empiricism was clearly winning ascendancy over rationalism.

Because of the repressive excesses of the Inquisition, as well as the basically poor science which had resulted from mixing theology with physics and medicine, the philosophers of the seventeenth century began to attack the use of final causes in scientific descriptions. Sir Francis Bacon (1561–1626) was one of the leading critics of teleology in science. He did *not* deny that a final-cause account was appropriate for certain areas of human knowledge. Although nothing like modern psychology existed at this time, psychological issues arose in what Bacon would have considered *metaphysics* (a term used originally by Aristotle, which means "after physics" or "taking up philosophical assumptions about the physical world"). If a philosopher mulled over the problem of existence, for example, speculating on the metaphysical question "What is the reason for life?" Bacon agreed that a final cause might be employed in framing an answer. But in the *strictly* scientific sphere of *physical* description (explanation), there was no place for final-cause meanings. It was wrong to say, as Aristotle did, that leaves exist "for the sake of" shading the fruit on trees. A proper analysis of nature would reveal that it is always the material and especially the efficient cause that creates things or brings events about.[7] The form or shape of things is also determined by the underlying material and efficient causes that go to make them up.

Today we refer to this as *reductionism* in science. A reductive explanation brings the formal and seeming final causes of anything down to what are presumed to be the underlying "real" causes—that is, material and efficient causes. We might say, "I ate something that disagrees with me," but this common sense statement of why we now have a stomachache implies a humanlike judgment of either the food we ate or our digestive processes. Food and digestive processes *never* agree or disagree, which implies the meanings of formal-final causes in judgment. Digestion is a completely mechanical and chemical process of breaking down foodstuffs into assimilable blood sugars, minerals, vitamins, and so on. This more technical, reductive explanation of why a stomachache exists involves purely material- and efficient-cause meanings. Some combination of chemicals have irritated a tissue or generated intestinal gas that has distended the bowels painfully. There is nothing humanlike in this process, nothing recognizable as a decision or a disagreement. To describe physical events of this sort in humanlike terms is to *anthropomorphize* (from *anthrop-,* meaning "human being"). Bacon therefore suggested that the Aristotelians of history were anthropomorphizing nature by assigning purposes to it. From this time forward in the history of science, it has been considered poor explanation to rest with either a final- or a formal-cause description (though formal causes are occasionally acceptable).

Sir Francis Bacon was a philosopher in what has been called the school of British Empiricism. This style of philosophy emphasized that knowledge must be based on observable things and events. There were two other philosophers in this school whom we should consider, because they helped fix a certain view of mentality that is still very influential in academic psychology. They were Thomas Hobbes (1588–1679) and John Locke (1632–1704). Hobbes was fascinated by mathematics, so when he began to theorize about the workings of the mind he analogized from the latter to the former. He suggested that the human being's power of reason is "nothing but reckoning (that is, adding and subtracting) of the consequences of general names agreed upon for the marking and signifying of our thoughts."[8] We could use this kind of definition today to describe how a modern computer "reasons." But note: this is an exclusively *demonstrative* definition of the thinking process. Mathematics is one of the purest forms of demonstrative reasoning, for the meaning of any "given" is unipolar, and all of the elements are entered together into totals that are internally consistent. *One* never means *non-one*. To base our image of humanity exclusively on an analogy to mathematics means that we are willing to forget about dialectical meanings and dialectical logic altogether. This, both Hobbes and Locke were prepared to do.

Locke suggested that a person's ideas are mental models of experienced reality, imprinted as "primary and true" copies of what exists independent of mind. At birth, the human mind is a *tabula rasa* ("a blank tablet") on which external experience etches copies of what is to be known to the person. Our minds are like cabinets that are filled with input ideas over time thanks to experiences we have after birth. Locke's concept of the *idea* was demonstrative. He considered ideas to be built up from simple to more complex combinations in a unidirectional sense, that is, we first learn letters, then words; then sentences, and so on. Our minds are founded on a series of discrete, simple ideas which then act as building blocks to constitute or make up the more complex ideas of our knowledge. Locke's demonstrative theory is beautifully exemplified by the fact that he viewed these simple ideas as *indivisible* singularities. We might even call them atomic ideas. He therefore insisted that "it is not in the power of the most exalted wit, or enlarged understanding, by any quickness or variety of thought, to *invent* or *frame* one new simple idea in the mind . . . nor can any force of the understanding *destroy* those that are there." [9]

Now, no dialectician worthy of the name could go along with this unipolar view of the idea. No matter how simple a unit of meaning might be, the dialectician would suggest that oppositional meanings would enter into the learning at some point, even if only by connotation. For example, assume a child is being taught the letter *A* preliminary to learning how to spell. If the teacher now points to a letter and says *"A"* to the child— even though because of the trust between teacher and student the child accepts this figure as an *A*—there is always the implication of not-*A* in the pointing. (We discussed a similar case in the use of *house* on p. 8.) Assume that at some point an older *sibling* (brother or sister) points to some letter and says *"A,"* will the child necessarily agree and accept the meaning relation indicated? Brothers and sisters have been known to have doubts about each other's abilities or intentions; in such cases, dialectically generated alternatives arise like "I'll bet he doesn't really know" or "She's probably trying to fool me." The person has framed or invented a thought in opposition to the simple idea that was presented. Dialecticians therefore believe that the mathematical analogy is false,

particularly when we get into more intricate ideas and their potential opposites, as discussed above.

In addition to seeing simple ideas as unipolar building blocks, Locke began to think of these as efficiently caused "effects," placed into mind as one might place china into a dinnerware cabinet. The source of all meaning being in the person's experience, all mind can do is accept what is placed in it and then collate or rearrange the meanings that are housed there. Indeed, the processes of mentation (thinking, perceiving, and so on) are also of an efficient-cause nature. There is never a true "that, for the sake of which" (final cause) decision-making process going on.

Human beings, when made to feel uneasy by some biological need (material cause), can suspend their unidirectional course of efficient-cause behavior and in the process throw their weight toward one course of behavior or another. For example, a hungry couple out to dine can keep their (efficient-cause) motion temporarily in check as they deliberate which of two restaurants to eat in. But the way in which they eventually behave depends on the "primary and true" input influences that past experience has pressed upon them. A Lockean organism never really chooses *against* the probabilities it concocts based on past input etchings from experience. Though they have halted briefly, our hungry couple predictably will choose the Western steak house in which to dine over the Oriental restaurant, because it is a demonstrable fact that they have had more good dinners in the former than in the latter. Though they seem to be making a decision, they are in fact allowing time for mental calculations to take place. They go along with the final tabulations, just as any cybernetic computing machine does when it "reasons" (see p. 11). Seemingly free-will mental activities like doubt or indecision—or even oppositional reasoning—were accounted for by Locke by noting that sometimes the probabilities in a course of action facing a person are about even. In such cases we can observe the person wavering over what to do, but this is still the result of what has "factually" happened to the person in the past. It is never due to a dialectical reversal, a nonfactual selection of alternatives that were *never* input at all![10]

Although telic description and the dialectic had dropped out of the human image in the philosophy of British Empiricism, both of these features of human description were kept alive in Continental Philosophy. Immanuel Kant (1724–1804), a German philosopher, was immensely important in this regard. Kant began with a concept of mind (mentation, reason, and so on) that is the *creator* of meaning rather than a receptacle of input meanings. He believed that human beings are not tabula rasa at birth, but rather that they have a *pro forma* capacity to lend order to their experience according to what he called the *categories of the understanding.* These are like templets or frames of reference that turn incoming stimulations from the environment into something meaningful. A pro forma intelligence brings order to bear, it does not take order in. Kant was suggesting that human beings could not possibly learn the way Locke and other British Empiricists (or Associationists) claimed they learned, because only *after* the person organizes the input according to space and time considerations and *then* brings to bear the categories does meaning develop.

The Kantian categories were framed dialectically. For example, there was the category of quantity, which consisted of unity (thesis), plurality (antithesis), and totality (synthesis). A newborn child is taught the words for one thing as against several (two, three) things, but no one has to teach the child to understand when he or she confronts one piece of candy as opposed to four pieces of candy. Locke would say this difference is simply a difference in perception (in this case, seeing), brought into mind directly as a simple idea. But Kant argued that the mind *orders* such perceptions through applying the categories and that, although children are taught the words to stand for one thing as opposed to many things, this learning is only possible because of the child's preliminary understanding of such differences thanks to the innate nature of mind. Just as the stomach or liver "works" in certain ways, so too does the mind of the human being "work" to organize experience *from birth!* There were other categories, such as quality, relation, and modality, but for our purposes it is not necessary to discuss them.

Note that the categories are like meaning-creating ideas. We could express them as such, but, strictly speaking, in Kantian philosophy an idea is a *conception of reason* that can and often does transcend (rise above or go beyond) experience.[11] Kant suggested that when we pass through life, encountering this and that type of experience, we formulate ideas of what has happened to us. We have memories, as Locke contended, but we can *also* think up ideas in opposition to reality or totally outside of reality. This occurs because in speculative reasoning we rely on a *transcendental dialectic,* which permits us to go beyond or rise above what we already know in order to explore the other side of things. We can even turn back on what we usually believe and dialectically challenge everything including the categories of understanding. We can (as Einstein did) keep space and time considerations out of our beliefs and begin to theorize about our common sense conceptions of experience in a totally uncommon fashion. Kant was suspicious of the dialectical reasoning capacity, feeling that it is wrong to give free reign to our imagination, because just thinking of something does not make it so. But he did retain in his conception of mind a dialectic, and when he said that we reason "for the sake of" the frames of reference called categories, he gave us a telic conception of mind as well.

In the early years of modern science until about the late nineteenth century, the Lockean philosophy was dominant. Sir Isaac Newton (1642–1727) was a friend of Locke, and Newton's influence on the rise of science was immense. Indeed, it is probably correct to say that science was Newtonian until the present century. By this, we mean it was demonstrative, oriented to material- and efficient-cause reductionism, and totally empirical. However, twentieth-century physics was to challenge this complete reliance on empirical "reality" as the source of all knowledge. Mach, Einstein, Bohr, and Heisenberg have demonstrated to the modern world that something like a Kantian contribution to the observations made on reality influences what we can learn from it.[12]

There are a handful of terms we should introduce at this point. They describe how theorists view the sources and generality of the knowledge they try to capture in framing theories. We will have use for these terms in later chapters. A theorist is said to be a *realist* when he or she believes that the constructs being used are mapped from a reality that truly exists independent of mind. Empiricists tend to be realistic in outlook—Locke was a realist and so was Newton—but we should not equate the meanings of these two terms. The source of meaning relations (see p. 7) is "out there," in the (presumed) solid foundations of what can be seen, touched, smelled, and so on.

But sometimes a theorist doubts the complete accuracy of the senses. He or she may argue that what we *think* we see, touch, or smell is really a kind of illusion. Or the theorist might agree that there are things "out there" in perceived experience, but these things only have meaning because we thinking human beings lend it to them. The reader has probably heard the old philosophical question, "Does a tree falling in the midst of the forest with no animals around make a noise?" The point of this seemingly foolish question is that "noise" is a form of experience that only the living organisms called animals can experience. If we had recording equipment in the vicinity, the tree would surely be shown to have made a noise. But this would only occur when a human being listened to the recording! The theorist is an *idealist* to the extent that he or she says that meanings in life are framed (created, brought about) by the intelligence of living organisms with the greatest knowledge possible occurring in the conceptions of human reason.

Kant is therefore generally said to be an idealistic philosopher, because, in his view, mind (categories) lends meaning to experience and not the other way around. Even so, Kant called himself a *critical realist,* meaning that he believed there was a reality of things in existence (which he called *noumena*), but that he could never know them directly. All he knew about reality was what his senses and the categories of his understanding made it possible for him to know (he called such indirect experience *phenomena*). Hence, reality never enters our mind's eye in its naive form (that is, exactly as it "is"), but always through the translations of sensations and the organizations of our categories. When we look, touch, and smell a flower, we are not experiencing this "thing, in itself" (noumenal realm) but only our *own* mental construction of it (phenomenal realm). Kant admitted that his very assumption that reality existed independently of his phenomenal experience was based on an act of faith. But he was not a naive realist as were the British Empiricists. He was a sophisticated or critical realist. Since he did call reality into question, many of Kant's interpreters have considered him to be a type of idealistic theorist, and we follow in this tradition in the present volume.

There are two terms that are often confused with realism and idealism. We refer here to *objective* and *subjective*. An *objective theoretical construct* is one that is capable of being understood by all those persons who have spent time familiarizing themselves with the theory in question. For example, when considering a wave theory of light, the scientist would prepare himself or herself by studying the theory and seeing exactly how it has been proven empirically. If the assumptions of the theory and the steps to be taken to prove it are recorded clearly for all to understand, then the wave construct is an objective one. A *subjective theoretical construct* is one that is somehow private, is difficult to communicate even to those persons who have spent time familiarizing themselves with the theory in question, or is not generalizable beyond the single instance in which it was supposedly observed. If a theorist tells us of the discovery of a remarkable healing substance called "zerxo," but then cannot define it clearly or explain how the substance is extracted or precisely how it is thought to work, we would have to consider these speculations to be subjective. If a theorist claims that each subject in a psychological experiment is so unique that it is impossible to find a common tendency or at least a nearly common tendency among the people under study, we would have a subjective theory under development.

To be objective in our theoretical developments we must be able to generalize our constructs across situations and other people. But this does *not* mean that we are forced into taking a realistic position. Returning to the example of a theory of light, it would be possible to frame this natural phenomena as involving a series of particles rather than waves. We could present the particle theory in a thoroughly objective fashion, right alongside the wave theory. We could also prove our particle theory in completely objective experimentation. If this is the case, then which theory is *the* right one? A modern physicist could at this point easily take a Kantian position and say: "So long as both theories have been framed objectively and proven empirically they both are true. The only reason you are bothered by this result is because you assume that reality has only one possible theoretical rendering. But since we know that what we learn depends on assumptions made in the testing of our knowledge, we now accept as routine that it is possible to hold to and prove more than one set of theoretical assumptions about the *same* world of observed experience." This has been the outlook of modern physics beginning with the writings of Ernst Mach[13] in the late nineteenth century, and it is readily characterized as an *objective-idealism!* The other side of the coin is that even if a theorist believes that reality exists as directly experienced, there is still no guarantee that the theorist's rendering of it will be completely understood by others. Obviously, a theorist can be both realistic and subjective.

In order to focus the contrasting approaches to theoretical description in this section, we can frame two different *models* of general explanation. We can call one a Lockean and the other a Kantian model. This suggests that they are of relatively modern origin (post-seventeenth century), but the

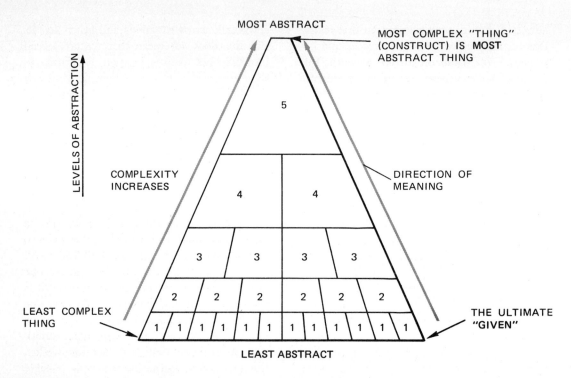

Figure 1   The Lockean Model

truth is that there has *always* been a division of this sort in the history of thought. For example, in ancient Western history, we could contrast Plato (à la Kantian) and Democritus (à la Lockean) on similar grounds. Even in ancient Eastern (Oriental) history, it is possible to find a parallel distinction in the views of Confucius (à la Lockean) and Mo Ti (à la Kantian). Down through Eastern and Western history, this distinction in the explanations of the nature of anything has been apparent. We select the names Lockean and Kantian only for convenience and because the differences in outlook they suggest are probably more familiar than any other set of terms to modern theoreticians in related physical and social sciences.

Figure 1 presents the Lockean or *constitu-*

tive model of theoretical explanation. Note that we have a triangle of increasing levels from low to high, 1 through 5 (there could be any number). The levels refer to meaningful points at which a theoretical construct could be used, except that in this case we might better call them theoretical *abstracts* or *abstractions*. Since Locke was a realist who believed that meaning relations existed as "input" from reality, it is right to think of all higher-level concepts as having been abstracted from the initial input, level 1. (To *abstract* is to leave out details in the naming or description of something.)

For example, if we see a building ahead we might call it a house. This word is or may be thought of as an abstraction, one that has within its definitional meaning many other meanings such as walls, roof, rooms, basement, stairways, and so on (see our discussion of meaning-complexes, pp. 6–7). In using the single term *house,* we leave out specific reference to these details for convenience. Realists would believe that all of their concepts are abstracted from the details of the separately existing "reality." Idealists, on the other hand, would put their emphasis on the mental act of construing or conceptualizing; hence, they more properly view their terms as constructs—as something created by mind or "constructed." In this volume we shall only use the term *construct* to refer to schematic labels employed by our theorists, but we can now appreciate that a realism-idealism issue is being masked for the sake of efficiency in the presentation.

Since the term *house* can itself be *subsumed* by (included in the definition of) terms like *neighborhood* and *city* and even *country,* we need some way of picturing that as our terms become more abstract they leave out more and more details. This is why the Lockean and Kantian models are presented as triangles. The more abstract our theories become, the more details are left out There probably is no real top to the triangle, of the theoretical terms used, and the narrower the apex of the triangle becomes. because it is always possible to make an abstraction of an abstraction. When we find theories operating at these extremely abstract levels, they are likely to be called *metaphysical,* which, as we may recall (see p. 10), means that they are far removed from simple, empirical demonstration.

Note that in the Lockean model all of the numbers at any one level of abstraction are the same. The basic-level units (where Locke placed the "simple ideas") are numbered 1; and these combine to form larger units (the beginnings of "complex ideas") like 2; and then 2 and 1 are both combined into the still more complex 3; adding another level gives us 4; and so forth. We consider this a constitutive model because little things add up to or literally are the nature of bigger things in this unidirectional, demonstrative-reasoning sense of "one and one makes two" (see p. 11). If we begin our theorizing on the assumption that larger things consist of smaller things, it follows that to account for the nature of anything we should break it down into its constituent parts. To clarify the meaning of a theoretical construct at level 4, we would be required to spell out clearly the 3, 2, and 1 constructs that make it up. And when we got down to the 1-level in our theoretical analysis and could go no farther, we would have come to the ultimate "given," or the fundamental building block on which the whole business rests. As we noted in discussing Locke, the atomic (and even subatomic) models of traditional science have followed this explanatory reductionism in accounting for physical events. The classical medical model is also constitutive in that chemicals and minerals are said to make up portions of the tissues in cells, which in turn make up organs, which in turn make up the complete body. Biology, physiology, and anatomy have all placed major emphasis on the Lockean view of theoretical explanation.

There are three important technical points that most clearly typify the Lockean model and along which we can contrast it with the Kantian model of Figure 2. Note that on the Lockean model (a) meaning always begins in and proceeds from the lowest level of abstraction upward. We can learn the meanings of a theoretical term at one level only by breaking it down into the levels beneath it (4 is broken down into 3, 2, and 1). (b) The ultimate "given" in meaning (where theoretical analysis ends) is that point at which a level must be taken for what it is—an indivisible, irreducible, noncontradictory, unipolar substrate to all else. (c) Increasing the

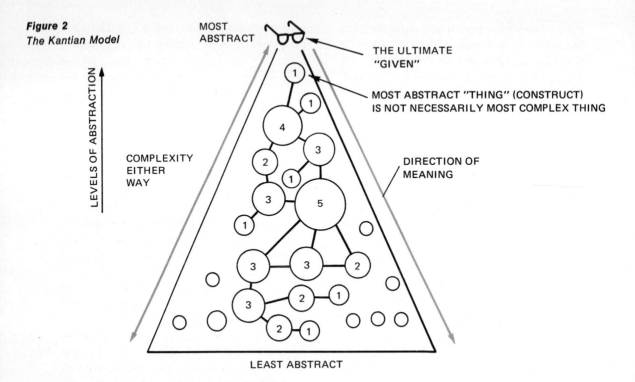

Figure 2
The Kantian Model

LEVELS OF ABSTRACTION

MOST ABSTRACT

THE ULTIMATE "GIVEN"

MOST ABSTRACT "THING" (CONSTRUCT) IS NOT NECESSARILY MOST COMPLEX THING

COMPLEXITY EITHER WAY

DIRECTION OF MEANING

LEAST ABSTRACT

LEGEND: 1,2,3,4,5 = COMPLEXITY OF CONSTRUCTS
(COUNT THE NUMBER OF CONNECTING LINKS)

Figure 2   The Kantian Model

levels of abstraction (from low to high) *always* increases the presumed level of complexity of the theoretical term being employed. Level 4 is always more complex than level 3 and yet 4 is always less complex than 5. There is a commonality between rising and falling complexity and rising and falling abstractness on the Lockean model.

Figure 2 is a triangular schematization of the Kantian or *conceptual* model. Note that the categories of the understanding are symbolized by a pair of conceptual spectacles. We do *not* suggest vision here, but rather the formative, active process of organizing and

bringing to bear a mental frame of reference *to* experience. All sensory data, from eye, ear, nose, the touch receptors, and so on, are organized by the conceptual glasses at the apex of the Kantian model. Our mental understanding resides on the "inside" portion of the glasses (phenomenal realm), whereas the sources of our sensations are on the "outside" portion as "things in themselves" (noumenal realm). We cannot pass through our glasses to experience things directly, but we can infer that noumenal items do literally exist independently of our understanding. The phenomenal glasses exist *a priori,* which means "at or even before literal birth." They are influenced by experiences had over a lifetime, of course, but then there is never a period in life when that "pure input" symbolized by level 1 on the Lockean model enters into mind. For the Kantian, even level-1 inputs are conceptualized (that is, framed in by a pro forma or form-lending intelligence).

We have already given an example of a Kantian interpretation of the nature of light on p. 15. Another example of Kantian theorizing might be a theory of the stock market, in which it is suggested that as investors take confidence in the outlook of their country's economy, they will invest their money in the stock market. Even if the economic noumenal reality is not so good at the outset (assuming that there is such a thing!), once people begin investing their money stock prices will rise. Confidence and profits go together, so as long as the majority of investors look through what we might now call "rose-colored" Kantian spectacles, there will be found "in reality" what was predicated (premised, assumed, believed in) from the outset. We have, in a sense, a self-fulfilling prophecy taking place. Let us now assume that the economy really begins to strengthen, thanks in part to the great confidence the rising stock market has generated. Even with this basically sound economy, if for some reason a new pair of conceptual glasses is put on by the investors, things could change dramatically. A pessimistic forecast by political leaders at the right moment can turn the stock market down, which in turn will lead to financial losses, and, who knows, in the long run this reversal from a bull to a bear market could adversely affect the basic economy of the country as well.

Returning to the three technical points along which we can contrast our models, note that on the Kantian model (a) meaning always begins and proceeds from the highest levels of abstraction downward. Before we can know what a theory means, we have to know what point of view (symbolized by the spectacles) is being taken in arranging the constructs below into some kind of order. (Thus, the spectacles are not "filters" of what comes in but rather arrange or "color" the meaning of what goes out.) (b) The ultimate "given" in meaning (where analysis ends) resides in the unique nature of the spectacles that frame the point of view from the outset. We cannot find the essential "facts" at the lowest level of abstraction in the Kantian model (which is what gives it an idealistic flavor). (c) Increasing the levels of abstraction (from low to high) does not necessarily mean that the theoretical account is becoming more complex. Complexity and abstractness are not uniform. To tell how complex a construct is in Figure 2, we have to count the number of connecting links (meaningful ties between the poles of meaning) that a given numbered construct makes with other numbered constructs. This would mean that a 1-construct has only one meaning-creating connection, a 2-construct has two connections, and so forth. At just what level of abstraction these interconnections take place is irrelevant to the question of construct complexity.

For example, a complex theory of gene transmission in the germ plasm of animals might include *human beings* as one of its necessary constructs. Men and women are influenced by genetic inheritance, but so are other animals. The gene theory we have subsumes both humans and lower animals, which would put it—let us say—at level 5 in Figure 2. The theory of human behavior we have would represent a level-4 theoretical scheme in this instance. To a Lockean theorist, this order might seem reversed. Since human beings are made up of many chemicobiological substances, including those that go to make up a gene, it would seem logical to the Lockean that the gene theory should be *less* abstract than the theory of human behavior. The Kantian model rejects this constitutive approach in stressing that the complexity and abstractness of a theory need not be the same. We must study the particular theory and see just what is being proposed before we can say what the significance is of one theory (gene) for the other (human being). On the Kantian model, we can only understand the complexity in terms of the constellation of meaningful ties—the connecting links of Figure 2—that are thought up in order to achieve some descriptive purpose.

If a Kantian theorist were to employ a dialectical construct, where would it come into play? This could occur as a theory within any of the collections of meaningful ties to be seen on the "outside" of the spectacles. But as a standard aspect of the Kantian model, we would place the *transcendental dialectic* on the "inside" of the spectacles, riding above the entire model, so to speak, at the apex of the triangle. This is where what Kant called *free thought* might be said to take place. It is free because at this level it is not "framed" by the spectacles, and in fact the person can reason to the opposite of the meanings the spectacles express. Human reason is always capable of turning back on itself this way, says the Kantian theorist. This turning back is called *reflexivity,* and when we think or theorize reflexively, we can challenge our very thought, or reconceptualize our conceptualizations. Ultimately, this says that we can always make an abstraction of an abstraction, which is why there will never be a true and final apex to the triangle.

Sometimes this ability to think about our ideas at different levels of abstraction changes

the meaning of a construct we are using (this is called *multiordinality*). Take the word *theory* itself. A lower-level, less abstract theory does not have the richness of meaning that a highly abstract "metaphysical" theory would have. There are psychologists who use the term *theory* in a very narrow sense, and they would never agree to the parallel we have drawn between theory and thought. It is a good idea when this word comes up in a discussion for everyone involved to give their own definitions, because of the different meanings the word acquires depending on the level of abstraction being expressed.

Are All Theories Written from the Same Meaningful Perspective?

We have all had the experience of being examined for an illness by a physician (M.D.) in general practice. After listening to our symptoms and performing an examination, the doctor might tell any one of us: "You have a 'strep' throat. I will give you a penicillin shot and then you will take some pills. Everything should be back to normal with you in a few days." Our only responsibility here is to follow the prescription, and, sure enough, within a few days we are our old selves again. On the other hand, were we to be seeing a doctor because of a psychological problem, the exchange would prove quite different. At some point the psychiatrist (M.D.) or psychologist (Ph.D.) might say to us: "You seem always to express hostility for your father, although you cover it up pretty well. How long have you been making such 'jokes' about your father's business?" In this case, our responsibility for whether a cure results is considerable. We had never realized how our little jokes about our father's business had been a veil for hostility. And now the psychotherapist is suggesting that our feelings for father enter somehow into the fact that we feel so depressed all the time and suffer from headaches. What in the world is the doctor driving at?

There are obviously two different kinds of theories going on in the interactions we have with a general practitioner or a psychotherapist. We may not even realize that the general practitioner has a diagnostic "theory." This doctor is very sure of the trouble: the streptococcal bacteria have been identified under a microscope, and penicillin is a proven medication. Yet, in the sense used in this volume, even these well-established meanings as to what brings on and what removes the symptoms of a throat infection involve theories of illness and cure. We will make this even clearer, when we take up the fallacy of "affirming the consequent" in validating theories (see p. 26).

What is important at this point is for us to recognize the differences in slant between the strep-throat and the father-hostility theories. The first theory asks nothing of us but to follow orders. We are not in any direct sense responsible for getting sick. A foreign organism entered our body and caused the illness in a purely material- and efficient-cause sense. The second theory implies that we are somehow responsible for the fact that today we have headaches and feel chronically depressed. There is at least the suggestion here of an intentional contribution on our part, something to do with how we feel about our father. There could well be a formal-final cause involvement in this theory. Setting aside the matter of what kind of causal constructs the doctors are using in treating us, we can sense immediately that the general practitioner is thinking about us as "something over there, to be treated." We are, in a sense, a "bag" of chemicals, fluids, and cellular tissues, and the doctor has identified something in the bag that needs to be removed if health is to be restored. This doctor thinks about our illness as an observer

looking *at* us rather than trying to get *into* our heads and peer out at the world the way we typically do. The psychotherapist doctor, on the other hand, is thinking about us as we *are* individually, seemingly asking, "If I were saying what this person is saying, what would that secretly mean to me?" This kind of doctor *is* trying to get into our heads and therefore we jokingly (semihostilely?) call the therapist a "head shrinker."

We now want to introduce some terms to capture this contrast in the way our two kinds of doctors are framing their theories. The technical term for this slant is *perspective*, which may be defined as the stance a theorist takes in capturing that which he or she intends to explain. If the stance or angle is third-person so that the emerging theory is written *about that item* under observation, we have an *extraspective* perspective. Our general practitioner was theorizing in extraspective terms as he or she studied us physicalistically. As our earlier survey demonstrated, the style of scientific explanation since the seventeenth century has been extraspective. When we as natural scientists account for the motion of the planets across the heavens, we do not try to "get into the heads" of the planets. We do not wonder if Mars has contributed to the path of its orbit in some way that is independent of the forces of gravity acting on it. This would represent an unwarranted anthropomorphization of our scientific account. But now, what do we make of the Machian insight in physics that postulates that how the physicist *as a human being* thinks about an object of study influences the kinds of theories he or she is likely to come up with (see p. 15)? In order to follow *this* kind of theory, we do have to get into the physicist's head and study the assumptions he or she makes in framing scientific explanations.

When we do this our perspective changes. If the stance a theorist takes is first-person, so that the emerging theory is written from the *point of view of the item* under observation (I, me, a personal outlook on the world) we have an *introspective* perspective. We may be able to account for the inanimate world extraspectively, but can we account for the thinking of physicists about the world extraspectively? The answer seems clearly to be no. One of the most important developments in the history of science took place in the present century: the rise of introspective theories. There had been introspective theories before this century, of course, but they were of a theological or literary nature. Shakespeare, for example, helps us understand the reasoning processes of Hamlet in the famous soliloquy. But science was not oriented to a study of introspective theories until Freud and others initiated the study of psychology as one aspect of the scientific quest. We are still in the historical epoch of trying to sort out what all of this means. Some would argue that science cannot be introspective, because theories written from this slant are always subjective and science must be totally objective. Others take the view of this volume, which is that we can and must have scientific studies of theories written from an introspective perspective. This is the point of view from which human beings come at life, and only by objectively examining the human experience from the introspective as well as the extraspective slant can psychology hope to remain a viable, relevant science.

There are some personality terms relating to the question of theoretical perspective that we should familiarize ourselves with. The first set of terms relates to a distinction between *types* and *traits* in the description of personality. When we typologize we try to capture the total person all at once. We do this informally in our framing of social *stereotypes*.[14] The images of aggressive, money-grubbing Jews, lazy and sensual black people, or stupid and impractical Polish people are all stereotypes, which have been used in recent American society to characterize not only a person but an entire people in one, formal-cause totality. A stereotype takes one item that may have a certain validity among a minority of a group in question and generalizes it unfairly to all members of the group. This is obviously *bad* theorizing, but the fact that it goes on merely teaches us something about our personal natures. We are easily drawn into the fixing of a set frame of reference, and this stereotyping tendency can influence us adversely when stereotypes are used to propagandize.

But a more sophisticated, professional tendency to characterize certain individuals (not whole peoples) surely goes on when a psychologist studies the behavior of others. The cultural belief that fat people are jolly is a stereotype, but Freud's *oral personality* which in some ways touches on this fat-person stereotype is not to be identified with it (see Chapter 1). In the case of Freudian theory we have a less rigid, factually based effort to characterize a total personality in light of a clearly thought-out personality theory. In fact, it would be proper to consider the Freudian construct a *theorotype* rather than a stereotype. A theorotype is a global description of the total personality in light of a generally accepted personality theory. Although theorotypes can be written from either the extraspective or introspective perspective, they are more likely to take on the introspective formulation. Modern personality theory was born in the efforts made by Freud, Jung, and Adler to help individuals understand themselves as total personalities through the use of such theorotypes.

Rather than trying to be descriptively global, it is also possible to account for behavior by seeing it as being constituted of a series of *traits*. A trait construct assumes that everyone has more or less of the same *general* characteristics that make up all personalities. For example, when studying people on the basis of their intelligence or their dominance tendencies, we would not type them globally as either intelligent or not intelligent, dominant or not dominant. We would probably want to classify people along a scale of the relative degrees of dominance and intelligence they manifest in a given situation or, as is usually the case in the studies of traits, on some test we have devised to measure these traits. Whether these traits are believed to *really exist* in the personalities under study depends on the particular theory under development. Some theorists believe that intelligence and dominance tendencies are reflections of a certain gene structure built into the biological apparatus of the individual. Others look at trait terms as simply convenient test constructs to be used in the prediction of behavior. In either case, there is a tendency for trait theories to be framed extraspectively rather than introspectively. Even Freud's concept of the oral personality has since been interpreted as a trait of orality, which everyone has to a greater or lesser extent. History therefore teaches us that *typologies move to trait theories.*

The final set of theoretical terms we want to consider in light of perspective were popularized by the famous personologist Gordon Allport, although they were introduced by the philosopher and social analyst Wilhelm Windelband.[15] Windelband was drawing a difference between the study of history and the study of a science like astronomy or biology. If we study the structure of body cells or the workings of the planets in a solar system, the historical past is of only remote interest. All we need do is collect a satisfactory sample of cellular tissues or take a sampling of measurements of the heavenly bodies through our

telescopes, and we can write a theory of the nature of cellular structures or the organization of the heavens. Windelband called this approach to science *nomothetic* (*nomos* = "law"), meaning that it sought to describe general laws applicable to every item (cell, planet) of the type studied *for all time*. A study of history, on the other hand, looks at the unique course of events that unfolded during a given period of time. The history of France, for example, cannot be generalized to the history of England, although there may be some commonalities across the two countries like their developing economies, the formation of cities, the kinds of leadership they accepted, and so on. But an essential feature of historical analysis is that it is *idiographic* (*idios* = "one's own"), tending to find what is distinctive and unique about a single country rather than what is common to all countries.

Allport found that Windelband's terms were useful in the study of personality. Some personality theorists like the trait theorists enjoy studying large numbers of people, cutting across them with a test of some type in order to find general laws applicable to everyone, more or less. These theorists, who often take an extraspective perspective, are nomothetic in their approach to the study of personality. Other personality theorists are drawn to what is unique about the individual. They like to study a single person, often in a psychotherapy context, and they give us the more introspective accounts we expect from the typologist. These latter theorists Allport considered to be idiographic in approach. Note that in singling out a distinction like idiographic-nomothetic in personality study, we have effectively applied a *typology* to the styles of theorizing used by different psychologists.

Why Do We Believe in a Theory?

So far, we have been taking the process of theorizing and the constructs they generate pretty much at face value. Obviously, there has to be more to this process, because we not only tend to select one theory over another as our favorite but we often put our theories to test by making predictions based on them in an actual life situation. Our golf game is suffering, and based on a theory of how to swing our clubs that we have learned from a professional, we drive some golf balls to see if we are in fact "jerking" our swing erratically as the theory suggests happens when we stand a certain way. Though we do not think of ourselves at the time as seeking proof for a theory, this is actually what our behavior comes down to. Returning to Conant's observation (pp. 6–7), we might say that one of the habits that goes back to the caveman and is still practiced in science today is that of finding a proper means or *method* of proving a theoretical proposition to be true or false.

Aristotle was actually getting into this question of proof when he first drew the distinction between dialectical and demonstrative reasoning. Aristotle is given credit for introducing the *syllogism* to logic. Most of us have at one time or another heard of the syllogism in its familiar sequence of "All men are mortal (*major premise*). This is a man (*minor premise*). Therefore, this man is mortal (*conclusion*)." But the syllogism can also be framed in an "if . . . , then . . ." form, as follows: "If a man, then a mortal. There is a man. Therefore, there is a mortal." In drawing our attention to the syllogism, Aristotle was proposing the psychological insight that when we grant certain things in reasoning, other things follow quite necessarily. If

we really believe that "all fat people are jolly," then upon seeing a fat person standing before us, we are sure to believe (conclude) that "this person is jolly." What we therefore believe depends on what we assume, presume, accept, and so on, in our most fundamental beliefs or major premises.

In order to be a proper scientist, Aristotle said, we have to base our theories on premises that are as "primary and true" as we can make them. We have to find iron-clad presumptions and we must not do what dialecticians tend to do, that is, base their reasoning on mere opinion. One type of the "primary and true" major premise is a definition of terms, as when we say "All bachelors are unmarried males." The meaning of one construct (*bachelor*) is tautological (identical) with the meaning of the other construct (*unmarried male*). A second type of the "primary and true" major premise occurs when we base our statement on *observed empirical* events. We do not accept the opinion that "all people are basically selfish (or moral, and so on)." Instead we go out and seek empirical evidence for or against this premise based on a careful, systematic observation of people's behavior.

This distinction between opinion and a factual basis for the belief in some theory sets the scene for two kinds of method that all scientists use in framing knowledge. First, we need to define *method: A method is the means taken by a theorist to prove the content of his or her theory as either true or false, sound or unsound, believable or unbelievable.* Method is concerned with the grounds for accepting or rejecting theoretical propositions. When we speak of evidence, we are getting into the question of a method. There are two general methods employed in the testing of theories. The first we can call a *cognitive* or *conceptual* method, in that the theorist bases his or her belief in a theoretical proposition on its consistency with common sense knowledge or understanding. When a proposition is self-evident to us, so that it "makes sense" implicitly, we are testing this proposition conceptually. We call this form of evidence *procedural,* because it frames in our understanding and permits us to proceed in thought that is based on this initial grounding. We may be right or we may be wrong, but we can at least proceed because the line of thought "looks" correct based on our best judgment. This is the sort of evidence Aristotle called *opinion,* but of course sometimes the opinion is so generally plausible to everyone that we do not think of it as being this arbitrary. Fundamental mathematical propositions are accepted through procedural evidence. A proposition, such as "life is precious and should be furthered in every human endeavor," is also something we are likely to take as implicitly true based on our procedural evidence through a conceptual test ("Yes, that makes sense! Who would argue with this?"). And let us not forget that stereotypes, such as a belief that fat people are jolly, are nurtured by procedural evidence.

The second type of method followed in proving theoretical propositions is called the *research* method. In this case we accept or reject a theoretical proposition on the basis of observed consequences that follow a prescribed (predicted) succession of events that have been specifically designed to test the proposition. We call this *validating evidence* in science. The predicted succession of events in validation encompasses what is called an *experiment,* or experimental design, in which certain so-called *variables* are controlled and a prediction is made about the outcome. If we wanted to test the proposition that "all fat people are jolly" through research, we would begin by isolating a number of subjects varying in body weight relative to their general size. This manipulation is called the *independent variable.* We would rule out

people who are overweight or underweight because of transitory influences like illness and try to get a broad sampling of individuals from all walks of life. Factors like these are called *control variables;* they are held constant or randomized across experimental conditions. When we have a good sampling of both fat and slender people, we can begin thinking about some measure of "jolliness," which is our *dependent variable.* We might have our subjects look at comic films and record their sensitivity to humor on an electric "laugh meter" of some sort. If our hypothesis is correct, we should find more fat people than slender getting high scores on the measured dependent variable. This simplified, semihumorous example does capture the general logic of scientific validation.

It is the ideal of science to move from procedural to validating evidence whenever possible. Scientists realize that they have to base their theories on plausibilities—especially those of mathematics—but once they arrive at a formulation that can be experimented on, they do so. In fact, what makes scientists "scientific" is not the kind of theories they are favoring, but rather the methods used to test the theories. Of course, as our review of the causes taught us, it is also true that a nontelic convention in scientific description has come about. Yet many modern physical scientists recognize the need for formal and final causes in the description of human beings. The famous physicist, Robert Oppenheimer, once spoke directly to psychologists and encouraged them to begin accounting for behavior theoretically in terms of purpose.[16] Since our theoretical descriptions do not influence the logic of "control and prediction" we must follow in experimenting, it really does not matter what causal meanings we employ. The scientific research method is theoretically uncommitted. Even so, the historical prejudice against telic theory continues in psychology and we will find that some of the personality theorists of this volume have had to wrestle with this opposition in framing their theories of human behavior.

What Is the Point of Studying Theories Which Have Not Been Completely Validated?

It is not unusual for some psychologists to dismiss "mere" theory as an unimportant part of their scientific work, which should presumably deal only with validation. These psychologists are likely to oppose the *facts* of personality to *theories* of personality and then ask, "Why are you studying all of these invalid or partially valid *theories* when you ought to be studying the *facts* of behavior?" A question like this has many answers, but the best one involves a more sophisticated look at the nature of science and what those who raise such questions are presuming to be facts. Are we to believe that facts, once established scientifically, lose all touch with theory? Our discussion up to this point would surely not support this view. Recall that in our definition of theory (p. 3), we included even those constructs that have been "factually demonstrated to bear a meaningful relationship, one with the other." This inclusion of *factual* was done for good reason, because it so happens that the logic of scienced is *flawed,* and if we are to be consistent, we must appreciate that even after we have put our ideas to test via the research method, we are still in the realm of theory. Our ideas are still open to replacement by other, more comprehensive theories, which might even reconstrue things and account

for our factual findings in a *totally different manner*.

What is this logical error in science? It is called *affirming the consequent* of an "if, then" proposition when following through on a syllogistic line of reasoning (see p. 24). *Affirming* refers to what meaning is emphasized in the major premise by stating the minor premise. For example, when we first say, "If a man, then a mortal" and then add, "There is a man," we have affirmed one of the related construct meanings of the major premise (in this case, *man*). When we break down the constructs of the major premise, we call the one modified by *if* the *antecedent* (first in order) and the one modified by *then* the *consequent* (following in order). Aristotle pointed out centuries ago that to reach a sound conclusion the minor premise must affirm the antecedent, as follows: "If a man, then a mortal. There is a man. Therefore, there is a mortal." On the other hand, when the consequent is affirmed, we end up with a conclusion that could be erroneous, as follows: "If a man, then a mortal. There is a mortal. Therefore, there is a man." Just because we see a mortal before us does not mean that it is a man or woman, for there are many mortal animals.

Now, the logical sequence of scientific theorizing-to-experimental-testing goes as follows: "If my theory is correct, then the research method will give me experimental findings A, B, and C. The findings of my experiment *are* A, B, and C. Therefore, my theory is correct." Obviously, we have affirmed the consequent of an "if, then" line of syllogistic reasoning here and though our theory might indeed be the best explanation for the experimental observations, *we can never be certain* that this is the case. No matter how much our tough-minded, empirical psychologist would like to claim that the empirical findings of his or her experiments are immutable facts, the truth is: *There are* N (*unlimited*) *potential theories to explain any fact pattern*. Of course, we do not ordinarily get an unlimited number of theoretical ideas about a fact pattern under observation. Usually, the evidence of experimentation is consistent with only a handful of explanations, and each scientist gravitates to one or two of these. The "affirming the consequent" fallacy does not mean the end of science, of course, because there is still no better way of putting one's ideas to test than the control-and-prediction strictures of the experimental method.

Though it may seem odd to suggest this, scientific theories are really not accepted or rejected solely on the evidence, because in the first place it is difficult to tell when sufficient evidence exists to make a final judgment. This is why we find so much argument going on among scientists over the effects of air pollution, population expansion, and dietary practices on the ultimate viability of human life. Scientists always seem to find evidence in support of their views, which often conflict with those of a colleague. And further, the scientist's pet theory has a heuristic (organizing, making sense) role to play in his or her activity. This means that a theory will be defended so long as it remains instructive to the scientist in question. As Thomas S. Kuhn has shown, scientists rarely accept a new theory simply because it has empirical evidence to support it.[17] It is not until a pet theory begins to bog down while a newer one seems to carry on, answering questions that the favorite cannot, that we see the scientist changing in outlook. The history of science suggests that most scientists stick with the theory they began their careers defending, so that revolutions in science are likely to be brought about by the younger men and women who enter these professions.

And so, it pays for us as psychological scientists to become as used to thinking about theory as we are now used to thinking about the proof of our theories. We can use the classic personality theories covered in this book to gain an appreciation of the many issues that must be dealt with in coming to understand the human being. As truly sophisticated psychologists, we will be just as suspicious of the evidential facts as we now are of the theories being advanced to account for these observed regularities. This is the proper scientific attitude for a twentieth century psychological scientist. It is tough-minded without being narrow-minded.

What Is Psychotherapy and Why Is It Relevant to Personality Study?

If it is difficult answering "What is personality?" then it is doubly so answering "What is psychotherapy?" The two questions are not unrelated, however, since it is true that many of our major personality theorists have come from the medical profession, or they have taken considerable interest in people's level of psychological health even as they were proposing theories of temperament, character, or personality. These are the three words most frequently used to account for a person's style of behavior (see our definition of personality on p. 2). *Temperamental* theories put their emphasis on the material cause, as when we say, "She is a Smith, and is easygoing like all the Smiths." The assumption here is that something genetic is at play in behavior—a biochemical determinant of some sort. *Character* takes on the meaning of an evaluation of a person's usual behavior, as when we say "You can count on good old Charlie; he is a trusted and true member of the community." In a sense, in making this judgment we reflect *our own* telic capacities because we are evaluating Charlie "for the sake of" (final cause) some standard that we have chosen as important.

When we speak about how this family behaves temperamentally and how that person can be counted on in a crisis, we enter into what is called *individual differences*. We want to write theories about what makes some people differ from other people. Not all scientists have this interest; many view themselves as writing theories at a general or *vehicular* level. Vehicular theories tend to be abstract, and they aim at explanations that take on many different forms of lower-level content. So-called stimulus-response psychology is a vehicular form of theory, because its principles of explanation—reinforcement, generalization, extinction, and so on—subsume many different kinds of explanations. For example, a stimulus-response theory might account for both the display of hostility *or* a display of affection by the same person as due to "elicited responses to stimuli which led to reinforcement." Behavior is viewed as lawful, and the aim of stimulus-response psychology is to explain events extraspectively on the basis of vehicular theoretical constructs that manifest themselves in common across many diverse circumstances (see Chapter 6).

Psychologists drawn to individual differences tend to propose *discriminal* theories, which seek to distinguish between *certain* behavioral sequences and other behavioral sequences. In this case the specific *content* of the behavior is all-important, and the discriminal theoretical construct does not have the abstract, broad range of application that the vehicular construct has. When Freud proposed his theory of fixation and regression, in which the personality of an adult is based on the time of life in which certain unresolved problems took place, he was proposing a discriminal theory of psychosexual stages. Though fixation and regression have vehicular features, the psychosexual stages are clearly aimed at capturing differences in behavior.

Many of those who took the first steps in modern science as personality theorists were members of the medical profession, men like Freud, Jung, Adler, Sullivan, Binswanger, and Boss. Others, like Rogers and Kelly, were clinical psychologists, a professional wing of psychology initially patterned to meet the needs of psychiatry. Though these men were healers, they did not confine their comments on personality to the abnormal individual. How could they? A well-rounded theory of human behavior was required if there was to be a place for the sick or abnormal person within the picture. The theories of Dollard and Miller, Skinner, Wolpe, and Stampfl are interesting extensions of vehicular theory into the consulting room. The contribution that these theories make to personality theory of a discriminal nature is consequently a lesser one than that of the traditionalists. This will all be made explicit in the chapters to follow, but for now two points can be made: first, it is not possible to grasp the full meaning of classic personality theory without also understanding the theories of psychopathology (mental illness) and psychotherapy within which they were framed; second, not all psychotherapists (nor their clients) are drawn to the therapeutic context for the *same* reason.

There are three general motives for entering into psychotherapy. The first is what we might call a *scholarly* motive. By taking his client's memories in the therapy situation as grist for his interpretative mill, Freud began the modern era of personality theorizing while at the same time establishing the medical practice of psychoanalysis. Today, aside from their desire to earn money, just as many people enter the profession of psychoanalysis because of an interest in personality as because of a desire to heal the sick. Indeed, many clients who enter psychoanalysis do not think of themselves as seriously maladjusted, and many more would enter if they could afford it financially. Such clients say, "I just wanted to get to know more about myself," or words to that effect. This is clearly a scholarly motive, relating more to personality than to psychopathology per se.

Another motive we are likely to see in psychotherapy is *ethical*. The study of ethics has to do with those aspects of life and behavior that are considered *good,* or valued by human beings.[18] Theology deals with the absolute good as embodied in the belief in God. Though *moral* has been used as the theological equivalent of *ethical*, in common practice these words are interchangeable. There are undoubtedly many therapists who practice psychotherapy out of what can only be considered an ethical interest. They may tie mental illness to various ethical injustices which some people suffer in a complex society. They may stress the positive role of self-realization, heightened experiences, or new levels of ethical living following some therapeutic involvement. Or they may see in the therapeutic relationship itself a source of ethical strength for one or both participants. In recent decades there has been a growing emphasis on group or communal therapies with such ethical overtones.

There is little doubt today that people frequently enter psychotherapy or even quasi-psychotherapy relationships in order to improve, to reform, and to grow better. They may seek a nonthreatening environment in which to examine themselves in the company of a sensitive and genuine listener who takes a certain ethical stance in relating with them aimed at furthering this goal of self-realization. The client occasionally begins therapy with a definite problem, but in time this need for specific help evolves into something quite different. At this point the client does not want to be interpreted so much as he or she wants to be appreciated and accepted "as a person." Once such an atmosphere is made available to them, certain clients begin to change and grow under the weight of their own potential. Still other clients come to therapy to find a substitute for religion: a new faith, a different orientation from which they can find new meaning in life.

The final and probably still the most important motive of all for both therapists and clients is the *curative*. People come to doctors to be cured of illness. When the illness is in their "minds" (translated by certain psychotherapists into "behavior"), then it is only natural that they analogize to physical illness and expect some kind of concrete assistance. They come into therapy as *patients* in the true sense of that word, as passive recipients of a service that works on them the same way that penicillin worked on the throat infection (see p. 20). Many people would no doubt love to submit to thought control from a competent physician, who would, through some kind of medical device, cure them of a psychological problem.

The insight therapies like psychoanalysis greatly lengthen the time considered necessary to arrive at a cure. Is this not a strike against them? Relationship therapies seem to modify a person's life outlook, but is there really a fundamental change in behavior involved or is all of this just "talk"? Curative therapies are tailored to efficiency and concrete change, but they often leave the client wondering *why* they got into difficulty or they may still feel somewhat empty in their life context. There are obviously strong and weak points for any one therapeutic approach. We do not intend to settle the question of which motive or treatment is best in the present volume, nor could we do so if we tried. But in order to grasp the total personality theory involved, we do want to look at how these constructs were advanced in light of explanations in abnormal psychology. As for a definition of *psychotherapy,* we will have to settle for the following: *Psychotherapy is an interpersonal relationship involving two or more people in which the motives of the participants touch on scholarly, ethical, and curative issues.*

The Plan of the Book

There are essentially three historical traditions in the field of personality and psychotherapy, and the present volume is organized around them. In Part One we begin with the first tradition of psychoanalytic thought, though the term *psychoanalysis* properly belongs only to Freud. Although they were not exactly his students, Adler and Jung followed to alter psychoanalysis in their own unique ways. In terms of our major models, the analytical tradition must be considered a mixed Lockean-Kantian one, with Freud retaining a middle position throughout his life. Adler moved from an early Kantian to a clearly Lockean emphasis in organic evolution, and Jung retained the most obvious Kantian approach of the "founding fathers" of personality theory.

In Part Two we take up the second major tradition, which emphasized the empirical, observable facets of behavior and a clearly Lockean view of explanation. Harry Stack Sullivan nicely bridges the distance between classic psychoanalysis and this tradition, moving as he did from an early analytical influence to what might be termed an eventual Americanization of his thought. In the be-

havioristic tradition of American academic circles, we are then brought decidedly into an almost nonpersonality-style of explanation in the work of Dollard and Miller, Skinner, Wolpe, Stampfl and Bandura. That is, in the vehicular psychology of behaviorism, the subtleties of internal dynamics as described in psychoanalysis give way to the view that "behavior is behavior and *observed behavior* is all."

Finally, in Part Three we take up the third major force in personality and psychotherapy, which we will call the phenomenological outlook. This view returns to the more Continental line of explanation and is clearly Kantian in emphasis. At least, Rogers, Binswanger, and Kelly are decidedly Kantian. Piaget has some complexities needing special consideration, and Boss has consciously tried to remove his identity from a strictly Kantian model. But the spirit of all these theorists is surely in opposition to British Empiricism and therefore friendly to the Kantian line of descent.

We noted in the opening section that though there is no single theory of personality to study in the present volume, we do offer a single frame of theory-construction constructs. This frame may help the student to compare and contrast the many theories surveyed, as well as to analyze their basic meanings in light of the historic terminology of causation, demonstrative versus dialectical reasoning, and Lockean versus Kantian models. As our study of meaning revealed, to "know" something we have to relate it to something else, an already known and generally applicable point of understanding. It is hoped that the theory-construction terms offered in this volume will serve as one pole of a meaning relation in terms of which the student's understanding will be furthered. We next review under three headings the structural frame to be followed in presenting the personality theories: personality, psychotherapy, and theory construction.

Personality Theory

A personality theory must answer four basic questions: (1) What is the essential structure of personality? Or if structure is to be disregarded, what are we to substitute? (2) On what basis does this structure act or behave? (3) Does this structure change over time, and if so, in what way? (4) How do we account for the variety of human behavior among different individuals? If we can answer these four questions, then we have pretty well exhausted the kinds of things people ask about themselves and other people. Each section dealing with personality shall therefore take up these questions in four different sections presented in the following order:

Structural Constructs

How does the personality theorist speak about the framework of personality? What theoretical analogies and metaphors are used in creating the outline of consistent behavior enabling us to speak of a personality? Is the human being a machine, a collection of unconscious identities, or a self-expressive animal on the lookout for a better future? What is the *structure* of personality?

Motivational Constructs

How does the personality structure get underway in behavior, and why? Are there internal conflicts preventing behavior, and how do they arise? Are there truly mental motives, or does all reduce to a bodily thrust of some type? Can there be unconscious motives, or is "out of consciousness" the same as "out of mind"?

Time-Perspective Constructs

Does the personality theory consider reasons for change in behavior over time, from birth through adulthood and on into old age? What implications are there for personality here?

Individual-Differences Constructs

Since personality theories often are written to frame discriminal constructs, what efforts are made to do so in the theory under consideration? Are any theorotypes suggested?

Psychopathology and Psychotherapy

When the review of the personality theory has been completed, we shall move on to a consideration of psychopathology and psychotherapy. There are three questions that must be answered at this point: (1) How does a personality "get sick" or "become maladjusted" or "begin behaving in an unrewarding fashion"? (2) How does the therapist go about curing, resolving, or controlling this condition? And (3) does the therapist have any unique procedures that are distinct from those of other psychotherapists? In order to answer each of these questions, we shall organize the second half of each chapter around the following three subheadings:

Theory of Illness

By using *illness* here, we do not imply that every psychotherapist will consider behavioral maladjustment to be a sickness on the order of a physical malady. Traditionally, people who entered psychotherapy were viewed as somehow out of sorts, short of potential, or lacking in sufficient insight or ability to perform at their maximum potential. To that extent all our theories can come under an *illness* label, even though few psychotherapists believe that they relate to sicknesses in the conventional sense. Hence, under this subheading we will be reviewing the explanation of mental illness in light of the personality theory that has gone before it.

Theory of Cure

Here again, by using *cure* we do not mean to draw a direct parallel to physical cures. The purpose of this section will be to review the ways in which a theorist claims or implies that a personality is righted following the onset of some process consistent with the personality theory and aimed at rectifying the maladjustment. What would a "therapeutic intervention" consist of?

Therapeutic Techniques

This section takes up the specific and often unique procedures followed by a theorist in readjusting the disordered personality.

Theory-Construction Questions

The Introduction to the text has been framed around eight questions (What is personality?, What is a cause?, and so on), and we shall continue in this question-answer format in the theory-construction Chapters 4, 8, and 12. Each of these chapters comes at the close of a book part, and it takes up important questions that are rarely dealt with directly by the theorists under consideration. For example, we will be considering what it means to say that behavior is determined (Chapter 4), wondering whether we necessarily understand behavior simply because we can control and/or predict it (Chapter 8), and asking whether it is possible to know anything without first making an assumption about it (Chapter 12). The answers to these questions will be elaborate and will make use of the theory-construction terminology of the Intro-

duction. These questions and answers can form the basis of classroom discussions or simply assist the individual reader to think more broadly about the implications of the theories under presentation. None of these theory-construction chapters intrudes on the integrity of the other chapters of this volume. Indeed, Chapters 4, 8, and 12 may be left out of a course offering, but it is hoped that many readers and instructors will want to go beyond a survey of theories to consider such basic issues in the study of humanity as well.

Summaries, Chapter Outlines, and Glossary

There are three other aspects of this text's organization that the reader may find useful. First, each chapter closes with a summary. Though major constructs will be mentioned in these summaries, they are not simply overviews of a chapter's contents. Interpretations and evaluations of the theory in the context of what it sought to accomplish will be a major feature of the summaries. For a reader who seeks to review *all* of the constructs mentioned, we have provided outlines at the close of each chapter. These outlines follow the chapter exactly, so it is a simple matter to find, for example, the section of Chapter 1 in which Freud's repetition-compulsion construct is discussed. This is helpful for study purposes, of course, because it gives the reader a sense of the context within which repetition compulsion was discussed (something that a subject index cannot provide). Finally, in order to encourage and facilitate the study of theory construction, a glossary of important terms used in the Introduction and Chapters 4, 8, and 12 begins on p. 810. An effort has been made to be very thorough in this theory-construction glossary, so that if at any point a term such as *empiricism* or *discriminal theory* cannot be recalled, a quick check with the alphabetized glossary can refresh the reader's memory.

Summary

The Introduction alerts us to the fact that there is more to the study of personality than we had probably bargained for. As the style of behavior manifested by a person, personality is not necessarily described in the same causal terminology that psychologists use to describe the behavior of lower animals. Traditional behavioristic theory in psychology has relied exclusively on material- and efficient-cause description, but the modern personologist is increasingly aware that formal- and final-cause descriptions may be necessary to capture the styles of behavior that human beings take on. The latter descriptions are teleological (or telic) in nature. Though a personologist may not employ a natural or deity teleology to describe behavior, it is not unlikely that a human teleology will be introduced into his or her personality theorizing. This puts the personologist in a bad light because there has been a tradition in the "hard sciences" for almost four hundred years to avoid anthropomorphizing descriptions of "natural" events. The question arising for the personologist is, can we anthropomorphize the *anthrop,* that is, the human person?

There are several problems that arise when the personologist sets about explaining the human being in humanlike (anthropomorphic) terms. First and foremost, of course, is the matter of having to say what human behavior probably involves, and whether it can be understood as a complex extension of the behavior of lower animals. Final causality seems basic to these issues, but there is also the question of what *meaning* means to the behaving person. Is meaning a fundamentally unipolar or a bipolar relationship between (and among) constructs? The inanimate, machinelike things in nature are easily described in unipolar, that is, demonstrative terms, but the living beings whom we try to capture in personality study may require a more involved, bipolar, internally contradictory interpretation of meaning. This dialectical interpretation of meaning and the style of description it makes possible has never been used in the hard sciences (biology, chemistry, astronomy, and so on). Final-cause constructs have traditionally been reduced to underlying material- and efficient-cause constructs, all of which are seen as totalling-up in a quasi-mathematical fashion to the patterns (formal-cause concepts) of events we witness taking place empirically, including that behavior of people known as personality.

This has been the style of natural-science description. Telic accounts of nature were called *vitalisms* and were considered theological and not scientific descriptions of events. The philosophy of British Empiricism was very influential in restricting the Aristotelian causes to two (material and efficient causation) in the reductive explanation of natural events. Psychology followed this lead, adopting what we have called the Lockean model in the description and analysis of behavior. This model is a constitutive conception of things, in which it is assumed that the real world orders events demonstratively (using unipolar meanings), and that whatever exists does so because of its make-up, the underlying atomic substances that make it what it *is.* Human behavior is thus viewed as a complex assemblage of "lower-level" patterns of behavior that have been etched upon tabula rasa intelligence by the environment, and shaped and wound into ever-increasing complexities known as "higher-level" behavioral habits. Patterns of behavior that seem to be intentional (telic) are in fact merely the results of these lower-level influences occurring quite automatically, moved along by silent natural laws that in one context direct the falling of raindrops and in another the behaviors of people.

Reacting against such mechanistic accounts stemming from Lockean influences, a number of personologists have fallen back on the Kantian model. In this case a certain idealism enters the account, for it is claimed that human beings are not entirely understood by the constitutive forces that go to make them up. People have a point of view on life, which they bring forward from out of a phenomenal realm to order and understand the noumenal realm of experience. Noumenal reality is not capable of solely creating meaning for the individual. Meaning must be ordered by the pro forma intelligence of a person acting as conceptualizer. The Kantian model is therefore a conceptual model, viewing meaning as being placed upon, rather than taken in from, the independent reality. In addition, the Kantian model embraces dialectical reasoning and the transcendent self-reflexivity it makes possible, whereas the Lockean model has no place for dialectical-meaning processing. Kantian theories draw our attention to the point of view of that which we are observing—to the first-person or introspective perspective. Lockean models retain the advantages of remaining exclusively extraspective, that is, of looking *at* that which is observed and describing events in a third-person fashion. The hard sciences have all been extraspective in theoretical perspective, explaining things in a nonanthropomorphic, nontelic manner. Per-

sonality theory has for the first time claimed scientific status while also getting—or trying to get—into the heads of "those people, over there" and explaining things from the introspective vantage of *I, me, us.*

This has led to additional problems. Can we have an introspectively framed theory in science? Is it possible to be objective about such constructs? Objectivity demands that we be able to convey our ideas to others and be capable of proving them true or false in some way. The Introduction draws an important distinction between a theory on one hand and the method of proving it true or false on the other. Although everyone begins in the procedural evidence of a cognitive or conceptual method, the unique thing about science is that it moves to validate its hypotheses through the research method. What makes an area of study into a science is not the topics studied or the kind of constructs used, but rather the nature of the evidence that is advanced. Validating evidence is scientific evidence, and here is where traditional personality theories have had their difficulties; it is not easy putting some of the constructs framed in therapy consulting rooms to test in an experimental laboratory. Freudian typologies have been transformed into traits measured by objective tests, but the resulting nomothetic efforts have not always captured what Freud meant idiographically in his theorotypes.

To further complicate matters, we have also learned in the Introduction that the knowledge-generating sequence used in science—from theoretical hypothesis to experimental test—necessitates that the scientist commit the logical error known as "affirming the consequent" (of an "if, then" proposition). Even when we frame an objective experiment and prove something empirically, there is always the possibility *in principle* that an alternative theory might account for the same fact pattern. This does not mean that the scientific (research) method is useless in resolving differences between theories, of course, because often one theory does indeed stand up to more of the evidence than another, providing us with a greater range of validated knowledge. What this built-in fallacy means to science is that scientists are never completely free of the responsibility to consider their theories as something a bit different from their methods of proving hypotheses true or false.

Psychology has to date placed almost its total emphasis on objectivity, empirical demonstration, and experimental validation. The resulting attitude has developed in our science that this is all we need concern ourselves with because the facts must "speak for themselves." We now understand that this naively empiricistic attitude is erroneous. We must devote at least as much time to our theoretical assumptions as to our accrual of factual data, for our assumptions will be reflected in both what we select for study and what conclusions we draw from the data observed. Hence, we need not apologize for studying in this volume personality conceptions that have not yet been put to empirical test in a properly scientific context. We study traditional personality theory not because we accept it untested—beyond procedural-evidence testing, that is—but because we are trying to understand the image of humanity that classic personologists have found useful in their psychotherapeutic work.

This is why it is so important to delve into the theory of illness and cure that traditional personologists have devised to understand human behavior. Whereas the laboratory scientist can take a vehicular theoretical view of behavior, seeing all that differs individually as variations around a common central tendency, the clinician working with the individual is prone to devise a discriminal form of theory, hoping to explain why the individual differences in behavioral style (per-

sonality) come about in the first place. Though many therapists and their clients enter into this relationship out of strictly curative motives, many do so out of a scholarly and/or an ethical interest—hoping to enrich their understanding of the human condition whether or not a "cure" is achieved. Personality theory received its greatest impetus out of these latter motives. The biologically based theories of temperament gradually gave way to the more psychologically framed theories of character or personality. Today, we have a rich field of study in personality, which touches on all of the fascinating problems of psychology as a science of the human being.

Outline of Important Theoretical Constructs

What is personality?
    personologist · motivation

What is a cause?
    theory · material cause · efficient cause
    · formal cause (logos) · final cause
    · teleology (natural, deity, human)

What does meaning mean?
    construct · meaning · denotative versus
    connotative · unipolar versus bipolar
    (multipolar) · oppositional meaning
    · demonstrative meaning (reasoning)
    · law of contradiction · dialectical
    meaning (reasoning) · thesis, antithesis,
    synthesis · one and many .

What is a scientific explanation?
    scientific description · vitalism
    · empiricism versus rationalism
    · metaphysics · reductionism · anthro-
    pomorphize · British Empiricism

• tabula rasa • pro forma • categories of the understanding • transcendental dialectic • realism versus idealism • critical realism • noumena versus phenomena • objective versus subjective theory • Lockean model (constitutive) • subsume • Kantian model (conceptual) • reflexivity of theory • multiordinality

Are all theories written from the same meaningful perspective?
perspective (theoretical slant) • extraspective • introspective • type • trait • stereotype • theorotype • nomothetic • idiographic

Why do we believe in a theory?
method • syllogism • cognitive (conceptual) method • procedural evidence • research method • validating evidence • experiment • independent variable • control variable • dependent variable

What is the point of studying theories which have not been completely validated?

• affirming the consequent • antecedent (first in order) • consequent (following in order) • N theories for any one fact pattern

What is psychotherapy and why is it relevant to personality study?
temperament • character • individual differences • vehicular versus discriminal theory • motives (scholarly, ethical, curative) • psychotherapy

Notes

1. Aristotle, 1952a, pp. 276–277. **2.** Conant, 1952, p. 40. **3.** Aristotle, 1952b, p. 143. **4.** Rychlak, 1968. **5.** Rychlak, 1976. **6.** Leff, 1958. **7.** Bacon, 1952, p. 44. **8.** Hobbes, 1952, p. 58. **9.** Locke, 1952, p. 128. **10.** Locke, 1952, p. 369. **11.** Kant, 1952, p. 115. **12.** Rychlak, 1977, pp. 240–241. **13.** Bradley, 1971, p. 83. **14.** Lippmann, 1946. **15.** Cassirer, 1944, p. 235. **16.** Oppenheimer, 1956. **17.** Kuhn, 1970. **18.** Sidgwick, 1960, Ch. 1.

Part I

Mixed Kantian-Lockean Models in Classical Psychoanalysis

Chapter 1

The Beginnings of Psychoanalysis: Sigmund Freud

Biographical Overview

Sigmund Freud was born 6 May 1856 in the small town of Freiberg, Moravia (Czechoslovakia). He was of Jewish extraction and proud of his heritage but never practiced the religion. His father, a merchant and a freethinker, had been widowed, and Sigmund was the first child of the father's second wife. She was twenty-one years old at the time, and it is not surprising that Sigmund grew to be the apple of his mother's eye. He was a well-behaved son, and he tells us in later years that he stood at the head of his grammar school class for the full seven years.[1] When he was about four or five years old, his family relocated in Vienna, Austria, a more cosmopolitan environment and the city in which Freud was to live and work for the majority of his eighty-three years. As an adult he was critical of Vienna, but he also seems to have loved the city, for he would not leave his residence at Berggasse 19 until forced to do so by the threat of hostility after the Nazis entered Austria in 1939. He finally

Sigmund Freud

gave in to the urgings of friends and emigrated to England where, on 23 September 1939, he died after suffering for almost two decades with cancer of the mouth and jaw.

As a young man Freud was undecided about what career he would pursue. He was more drawn to human than to natural science problems,[2] and for a time he gave serious consideration to the study of law. Thanks to inspiration from Darwin and Goethe, Freud eventually settled on medicine, but he was the first to admit that he was never a doctor in the usual sense of the term.[3] After entering premedicine at the University of Vienna in 1873, Freud found himself greatly attracted to the career of a basic scientist. This attraction was based on the model

provided him by a tough-minded physiology professor named Ernst Brücke. Brücke, whom Freud grew to admire greatly, once swore to follow the scientific canon that "no other forces than the common physical-chemical ones are active within the organism." [4] As we shall see, this traditional Newtonian view of science was to stay with Freud and end up in a much-disguised form as his theories of instincts and libido.

Working in Brücke's laboratory, Freud did many studies on the structure of the nervous system and devised a method of staining cells for microscopic study that in its own right earned him a minor reputation. Freud never experimented successfully, in the sense of validation through the design of a study (see Introduction). His view of science stressed careful observation. But events were to make a career as university scholar impossible for Freud. Only a limited number of positions were available, and Brücke had two excellent assistants ahead of Freud. Time had slipped by, and Freud's medical class had already graduated. He had also, in the meantime, met and fallen in love with Martha Bernays, the young woman who was to become his wife. Since income was now more than ever an important consideration, Freud talked things over with Brücke and decided to go on, complete his medical degree, and enter medical practice as a neurologist (specialist in the nervous system).

Before doing so he was fortunate enough—with the help of Brücke—to obtain a small traveling grant, which permitted him to spend a year (1885) in Paris studying under the famous neurologist Jean Charcot at the Salpêtrière (mental hospital). In 1889 he again returned to France to observe the work of Bernheim in Nancy. Both Charcot and Bernheim were conducting experiments on hysterics with the use of hypnotism. *Hysteria* is a mental disorder (neurosis) in which patients believe they have lost some sensory (like vision) or motor (like walking) function, although they have not. Under hypnosis the patient suffering from hysterical blindness or lameness can often be made to see or walk again. Students of Freud have noted that his contact with the French helped support him years later, when he began to deviate from the kinds of chemical-mathematical theories to which Brücke had limited his scientific explanations.[5]

After a short stay in Berlin, where Freud served a medical residency in neurology (which included the direction of a children's ward), he returned to Vienna to marry and to take up the practice of neurology. Today, his medical specialty would come under the heading of neuropsychiatry, or simply psychiatry. Even before he had traveled to France, Freud had made the acquaintance of

Joseph Breuer, a neurologist like himself but an older, more settled and successful practitioner in the Vienna area. Later, Breuer was instrumental in helping Freud to establish a practice in Vienna. He was important in the evolution of psychoanalysis as well, and we shall turn to Freud's professional relations with him in the next section.

Another important friend of Freud's in his early years as practitioner was Wilhelm Fliess, who had apparently been introduced to Freud by Breuer. Fliess was a successful nose-throat specialist who practiced in Berlin, thus accounting for the need to correspond through the mails with his friend in Vienna (though they also met fairly regularly to exchange scientific points of view). Fortunately, Fliess kept all of his letters from Freud, and this correspondence reveals the remarkable fact that virtually all of Freud's theoretical ideas had been sketched in during the period of 1887 through just after the turn of the twentieth century; the 1890s were especially important: Freud observed that the "secret of dreams" was revealed to him on 24 July 1895.[6] His father died in October 1896, which seems to have increased certain anxiety tendencies and psychosomatic problems (colitis) which troubled Freud throughout his life. Having by this time worked out a general approach to the study and treatment of neuroses, Freud began in 1897 his celebrated self-analysis, from which we trace the personality theory and psychotherapy procedure now called *psychoanalysis*. In the 1900–1901 period Freud published his two great initial works, *The Interpretation of Dreams* (Volumes IV and V) and *The Psychopathology of Everyday Life* (Volume VI). These books mark Freud's beginnings as the father of modern personality theory.

Freud was soon to attract a group of supporters, among whom the more famous were Alfred Adler, Carl Jung, Sandor Ferenczi, Otto Rank, Karl Abraham, and Ernest Jones. He was not to hold the friendship of all these men, however; in fact, Freud's life is the story of a man with a tendency (if not a weakness) to reject or be rejected by those colleagues whose views opposed his own. Breuer, Fliess, Adler, Jung, Ferenczi, and Rank—not to mention others—were to separate from Freud on more or less friendly terms; the separation with Adler was probably the most bitter.

Freud made one trip to the United States in 1909 at the invitation of G. Stanley Hall, who invited him and Jung to speak at Clark University. As he grew in stature and reputation he was also active in helping to establish the International Psycho-Analytic Association with an accompanying journal; it began as a small group of friends in Vienna and then spread throughout the world.

The Breuer Period

Around 1880, while Freud was still in medical school, Breuer undertook the treatment of a twenty-one-year-old woman who was bedridden, suffering from a series of hysterical symptoms like headache, loss of speech, inability to understand when spoken to, visual distortions, and in particular, a pronounced loss of function and feeling in her right arm.[7] This woman was to become the patient in the celebrated case of Anna O. (a pseudonym), which in a way is the very first psychoanalytical case history. On a hunch, Breuer decided to use the hypnotic tactic that Freud later observed Charcot using. Breuer found that when Anna was put under light hypnosis and taken back through time (time regression), she could recall the onset of each hysterical symptom (taken in turn). The common factor in all these recollected beginnings was that Anna was feeling some kind of strong emotion at the time, which for various reasons she could not express. For example, she was feeling anger toward her father, but as a good daughter she refrained from expressing her growing rage. Instead, she found herself unable to understand her native German tongue when her father spoke to her, though she could still communicate in English! Gradually, her inability to understand German spread to contacts with others as well.

Breuer encouraged Anna to express her formerly unexpressed emotions while under hypnosis and reliving the old situation, and to his complete surprise he found that as she worked through each symptom in this fashion it disappeared. Breuer called the situation out of the past in which Anna had not reacted emotionally the *pathognomic situation* and the emotion that she did not express, the *strangulated affect*. (It is common for the words *affect* and *emotion* to be used interchangeably in psychology.)

The central symptom of the immobile right arm provided the most dramatic hypnotic recollection. Anna recalled sitting in a chair next to the bed of her father, who was terminally ill (he later died). Her mother was out of the house and the servants were dismissed for the evening, so doubtlessly Anna felt frightened at the responsibility of looking after someone so close to death. Suffering from fatigue and prone to what she called *absences* (momentary blackouts like sleepwalking), Anna seems to have had what Breuer called a *waking dream*.[8] She "saw" a black snake coming from the wall next to her father's bed, ready to bite the dying man. Anna tried to fend the snake off, moving her right arm from the back of her chair where it had been resting. Apparently it had become slightly numb due to the lack of proper blood circulation, for when she tried to move it, she could not. Glancing at her hand, Anna was further startled to see that her fingers had turned into little snakes with her fingernails appearing to be like "death's heads."

Though she was unable to scream or otherwise express the terror she felt at the time (pathognomic situation), Anna *did* do so under hypnosis, and as we have noted, this release led to an improvement in her condition. After several such relivings of the pathognomic situation in which she now gave vent to screaming and flailing about, Anna's right arm returned to normal. Breuer and Freud were later to call this *mental* reliving of a situation out of the past an *abreaction.* The physical expression of emotion was called *catharsis.* These terms have since been used interchangeably by psychoanalysts, but strictly speaking there is a mind (abreaction) versus body (catharsis) issue involved here.[9] Now Breuer was a conventional medical theorist, who favored Brücke's approach to science. He saw illness as being due to hereditary-biological influences, as being brought on by purely biochemical processes. He suggested that Anna suffered from a hereditary disorder which he called the *hypnoid state.* He believed that some people are born with this tendency to "split consciousness" in a way that allows a set of ideas with strong emotional coloring to continue to influence behavior outside of the person's self-control. Freud never really accepted this line of theory.

In 1893 Breuer and Freud coauthored *Studies on Hysteria* (Volume II), in which they presented various cases of hysteria and two theories of its etiology (causes). Freud was finding in his practice that invariably there was some unknown (by the patient) *reason* for the splitting of consciousness. What he saw at work was not simply some in-herited, automatic hypnoid state. Rather, there was what he termed a kind of *defense hysteria,* in which the person invariably rejected a sexual implication in some behavior in question. As Freud's later case histories were to demonstrate, at least *some* of the emotion that Anna never expressed in relation to her father was lust. He would call this the Oedipal complex one day. Though he is polite enough in the *Studies,* accepting in theory that hysteria may take two forms, Freud wryly observes: "Strangely enough, I have never in my own experience met with a genuine hypnoid hysteria. Any that I took in hand has turned into a defence hysteria."[10] In thus turning his attention away from the strangulated affect to the *strangulator* of the affect—the defensive counter to whatever was trying to reach expression initially—Freud made himself over into a new kind of physician. He was not *only* a healer, but a student of the workings of mind.

Personality Theory

Structural Constructs

Dualism of Mind versus Body

Freudian psychology is a *dualism,* meaning that it builds on the assumption that there are two interacting spheres of behavior—the *psyche* (mind) and the *soma* (body). Brücke's science would explain everything in terms of bodily constructs, thereby reducing mental to physical processes. Freud began with a preference for theorizing about people the way his beloved professor wanted, and he received additional promptings in this direction from both Breuer and Fliess. In fact, he once started but did not finish a theory of psychology based exclusively on biology (a *monism*), but he found after a few months that he simply could not fit this mechanistic view of behavior to his understanding of abnormal behavior (see the *Project* [11]). Freud later said that physical explanations were useless for the proper understanding of the psychological side of human behavior.[12]

Even though he relied less and less on physicomedical models of human behavior and turned to the writings of anthropologists, archaeologists, and sociologists for understanding, Freud continued to admit and even to stress a necessary tie-in of purely biological factors to human behavior.[13] There is disagreement among those who have studied Freud as to his actual reliance on biological or physical explanation. Since he always kept the door open to such explanations, we cannot claim that he was a purely psychological theorist. Yet his theory, including its energy conceptions, was always kept *exclusively* in the realm of the psyche once the body-mind dualism had been bridged by the instinct construct (see below).

The Early Mental Structural Constructs: Depth Emphasis

In his pursuit of the strangulator of affection, Freud first put together a model emphasizing the *depth* features of the mind or the psyche. He broke down the sphere of mind into three regions: *conscious, unconscious,* and *preconscious.* In order to appreciate why he did this, we will have to consider what is actually a motivational construct, the *censorship,* for it is this mechanism of defense that plays the role of strangulator in Freud's first model. His first patients—most of whom were upper-socio-economic-class women—were invariably defending themselves against the

recall of a memory out of the past that was *still active* in mind, but in a deeper region outside of awareness. What is more, these were almost always memories of a sexual or hostile nature. Figure 3 provides us with a schematization of Freud's early mental structural constructs. Note the stylized dotted arc, moving an arrow from left to right across points 1 through 9, both originating and ending in the external world.

This arc traces a perception that might be taken in at point 1 through an action at point 9 that the person might perform in relation to what was perceived. For example, the person might see a water fountain (point 1), and assuming that all went well through the mind, would end up at the fountain, taking a drink to satisfy thirst (point 9). This scheme is actually based on the reflex-arc concept, which was a popular style of explanation in 1900 when Freud framed this model.[14] The important thing to remember, however, is that Figure 3 is a model of *mind.* Reflexes are biological units, built into the body (soma). Hence, in framing this model Freud was *analogizing* to the body but he was referring exclusively to mind. If we now follow a mental perception (stimulus) from its entry at point 1, note that it passes through consciousness into the second region of preconsciousness and down into the lowest level of mind, the unconscious, before returning upward again through points 7 and 8 (censorship points) and issuing into motor action at point 9.

Freud defined *consciousness* as a "sense organ for the apprehension of psychical qualities,"[15] through which the individual is aware of sensory input (seeing, smelling, thinking about things seen) and also of pleasurable or painful experiences. Consciousness does *not* rule the mind in Freudian psychology. It does not even retain memories, which are kept down below the level of conscious awareness. Freud considered mental contents

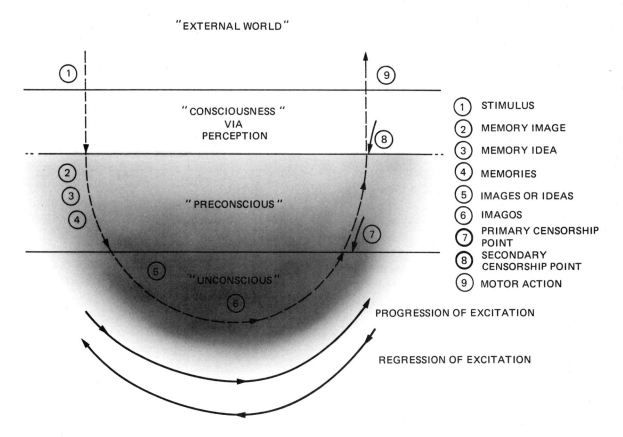

Figure 3   Freud's Early Mental Structural Constructs

to be in consciousness only if we are *presently* aware of them.[16] Thoughts do *not* originate in consciousness. For centuries, philosophers had identified ideas in awareness with thought, but Freud broadened the concept of mind when he said that "every psychical act begins as an unconscious one, and it may either remain so or go on developing into consciousness, according as it meets with resistance or not."[17]

To understand what Freud called the person's "true psychical reality," we have to understand the unconscious.[18] Sense impressions as perceptions may be taken in at point 1, but *ideas* are put together somewhere around point 6. Freud used the construct

of *unconscious* in a general and a specific sense. In its general sense, *unconscious* merely meant all those psychic contents like thoughts, ideas, and images that are not conscious at the moment but might become so at any time (he sometimes included preconscious contents in this general usage).[19] More specifically, however, Freud considered the *unconscious* to be an actual region of mind, one that was much larger than consciousness and that lived a mental life of its own. The analogy of an iceberg is often drawn. The portion we see above the water line is merely the tip of the iceberg; the vast majority is below the water line. Consciousness is like the tip of an iceberg, and unconsciousness is the vast area below. We can never appreciate psychoanalysis if we fail to understand the importance of the unconscious to behavior. As Freud observed, "the unconscious is a particular realm of the mind with its own wishful impulses, its own mode of expression and its peculiar mental mechanisms which are not in force elsewhere." [20] We can only get in touch with the unconscious by interpreting what it seems to be indicating in our dreams, waking fantasies, "slips of the tongue," and so on.[21]

Freud accepted Darwinian theory, which holds that human beings have evolved from lower animal forms. Freud believed that the unconscious was more in touch with this basic animalistic nature than was consciousness. We are all more primitive as unconscious identities. Unconscious ideas are totally *hedonistic,* which means they are aimed solely at providing pleasure for the individual. Consciousness has to take reality into consideration, and hence it is more oriented to the needs of others. The unconscious "never forgets" because it literally does not weaken its hold on ideas over the passage of time.[22] What we call *forgetting* is actually the disappearance of conscious ideas into the unconscious, where they remain perfectly clear for all time. Indeed, every person now alive carries around in the unconscious a memory of everything that ever happened to him or her. What is more, these memories can form into a body of ideas having complete autonomy and independence from the typical style of thinking in consciousness.

Then, when the unconscious wants to make known something to consciousness, it can do so directly—that is, in a waking state —by way of what Freud called *unconscious derivatives.*[23] We can use the example of Anna's snake and the death heads she saw on her fingers. These hallucinated (imagined) derivatives were communicating something that Anna did not want to admit consciously —possibly a wish that her father would die! Before something this dramatic takes place there has to be a long period of censorship. Sometimes when the unconscious breaks through like this in the waking state, the person may be astonished by the illogical things that take place. The unconscious does not worry about logic and often wants both to have its cake and to eat it too.[24] People with severe mental illness may feel they have been possessed by a devil who forces them to do strange things. A less dramatic possibility in the waking state occurs when two people actually communicate at a completely unconscious level.[25] Freud believed that two people could be relating at one level in consciousness and yet *also* be relating in their mannerisms and bodily postures at a totally different level outside of awareness. For example, two men may talk business consciously and yet carry on an unconscious homosexual flirtation at the same time.

Since emotions are revealed to us through consciousness, is it correct to speak of unconscious emotions? Strictly speaking, Freud would say no. There are no unconscious emotions per se, but there are unconscious ideas that in themselves relate to emotions. If these ideas begin to traverse our dotted arc in Figure 3 and threaten to seek motor action, then conscious awareness would reflect an emerging emotion to the personality.[26] Assume that a person has an unconscious desire to kill a loved one (a seeming contradiction, but remember: the unconscious is not logical!). As this idea drifts forward in mind from point 6 to point 7 and especially 8, considerable emotion is generated because it is terrifying to think that one would want to hurt a beloved person. It is the idea that causes the emotion here, and what we censor in holding back potentially emotional circumstances is always a mental and not an emotional factor in our mind.

Another often-raised issue concerns the possibility of unconscious ideas coming down to us from our evolutionary ancestors. Did Freud think of the unconscious *only* as a receptacle for ideas or images fed into the mind from external reality and then kept from conscious awareness by the censor? Although this was surely his major emphasis, the truth is that Freud was influenced on this point by his famous associate C. G. Jung (see Chapter 3) and held open the possibility of hereditary transmission of psychic contents.[27] If human beings were to receive mental influences from racial heredity, then such ideas or images would make themselves known in the unconscious (by way of the id[28]).

To account for that region of unawareness over which we often *do* have some control, Freud proposed the term *preconscious*. The *preconscious region* is made up of contributions from *both* the conscious and the unconscious, and it is the area of mind where censorship takes place.[29] The conscious and unconscious never communicate directly, but only by way of this intermediate level of preconsciousness. When we forget something like the telephone number of a friend only to recall it after an effort of concentration, we have dealt exclusively with a preconscious content. Since the telephone number returns to our consciousness in time (an unconscious psychic content like a death wish would not do this), we can refer to the forgotten number as unconscious only in that general sense to which we referred above.

Notice that Figure 3 has two different censorship points. As we shall see in other aspects of his theory, Freud was likely to speak of primary and secondary mental func-

tions (this will come up in his theory of repression, for example). The primary point of censorship occurs at the region between unconsciousness and preconsciousness. As long as a mental content (idea, image) is held below this level, there is no threat to the personality. This would be a basic strangulation. But if we move up now to the region between consciousness and preconsciousness (point 8), here is where severe threat arises, for the person might now be prompted to *act out* his or her unconscious ideas.[30] In other words, Freud's model assumes that if mental contents get into consciousness, they *will* be carried out, or at least the *intent* of the idea will be known. A person might realize "I know now that I really *do* want to kill my father." Censorship seeks to avoid these literal acts as well as the necessity of having to face up to them at all. Here is where Freud brought in his idea of unconscious derivatives to tilt the direction of excitation from progression to regression.

Note in Figure 3 that moving from left to right, from stimulus to motor action along the dotted arc, was termed *progression* of mental excitation, whereas moving in the reverse direction was called *regression*. This is clearly a Freudian addition to the reflex-arc concept, because our bodily reflex arcs—as witnessed in the action of the patellar knee tap—always move in the progressive direction (stimulus to response). In proposing a reversal to this direction, Freud was trying to account for the fact that sometimes ideas originating in the unconscious are experienced by the individual as literal stimuli in the environment—as visions or hallucinations (seeing, feeling, smelling things that do not exist). Anna's snake and death's heads reflected such a regression of an unconscious image moving in the reverse direction. She did not experience this image as the internal stimulus that it was but as an external perception.

What determines which way a mental excitation will move? This selection is up to the censor. If it blocks the progressive flow very aggressively, the process can be tilted in reverse, and then if in addition the unconscious very much desires to fulfill a wish, this reverse trend can culminate in a false input at the stimulus end of the dotted arc (point 1).[31] These regressive states are not always abnormal, since all dreaming depends on them. This concept of regression in mental life is to play a very important role in Freudian developmental theory (see below). The concept of a progression is for all practical purposes dropped after its appearance in *The Interpretation of Dreams,* which appeared in 1900, and we shall have no further need of it.

The Final Mental Structural Constructs: Dynamic Emphasis

The depth model is all right for describing interactions *across* levels of mind, as between unconscious and preconscious contents, but what about those mental interactions that seem to go on *within* as well as across levels? Freud found that he needed more complexity in his model of mind if he wanted to account for all of the psychic dynamics that seemed to be taking place in his patients. He therefore modified the depth model by combining it with what he called a *topographical* model. Topography is the science of graphing or mapping a region that is capable of being divided into different kinds of terrain. Freud therefore introduced a series of three constructs, some of which stretched *across* the depth levels of unconscious, preconscious, and

conscious as if these were different sorts of terrain. This meant that all three identities could function at the same topographical level and work out certain mental defenses among them. Unconscious or preconscious mind no longer opposed conscious mind, but certain identities within and across these regions now opposed one another. This clash-and-compromise model fixed once and for all the *dynamic* quality of Freudian psychology.

Figure 4 presents a schematization of the final structural model of mind employed by Freud. In order to maintain a continuity with our discussion above, assume that we have placed the egg-shaped structure of Figure 4 as a transparent template *over* the levels of mind of Figure 3. Note that now our combined schematization has an id (completely in the unconscious region), an ego, and a superego stretching across all three levels, and an area of repressed content at about the spot of our primary censorship. The term *repression* now replaces *censorship* as a motivational construct, but it is the same general idea of strangulation first used by Breuer.

Down at the very depths of the mental structure in Figure 4 we find the *id,* which now is taken as that animalistic, hedonistic side to our natures that we discussed above as true of the unconscious mental contents. The id never leaves the unconscious realm of mind, and it is the identity point at which instinctual promptings which begin in the bodily sphere first make contact with mind. The id seeks satisfaction or pleasure in all things; it is entirely amoral and incapable of making judgments like good versus bad or just versus unjust. The id in everyone is greedy, envious, and thoroughly selfish. As Freud poetically defined it, "we call it a chaos, a cauldron of seething excitations." [32] The id is not concerned with realistic evaluation of the demands of society, much less of logic. It often has illogical wishes, as for ex-

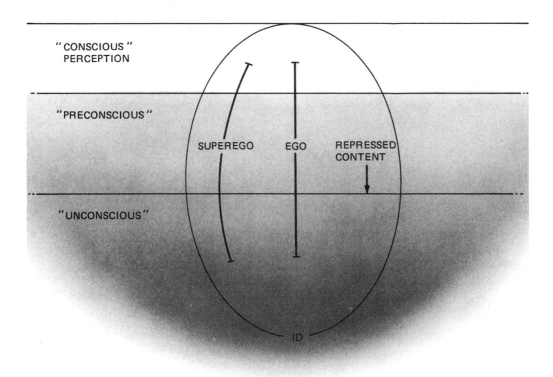

Figure 4   Freud's Final Mental Structural Constructs

ample to both lust after and want to kill the same person.[33] The id is full of such contradictions and never bothers to iron out inconsistency.[34] The id is not concerned with the passage of time or of changes that may take place; but it never forgets as it never forgoes anything it wants.[35]

Out of this unorganized, self-serving heritage from nature there develops a portion of mind devoted to reason, the realistic evaluation of external conditions, and self-identity. It does not exist at birth,[36] but as conscious awareness progresses over the first few months of life, the *ego* begins to be identified as an unchanging permanent component of the personality structure.[37] The role of muscular sensations in this developmental process is important, as the newborn

child begins to identify a difference between "over here" (self-identity) in the movements of the body and the external world "over there." [38] Although the ego has contact across all three levels of mind, its sphere is predominantly that of consciousness.[39] What we superficially consider to be our personality is usually the style of behavior taken on by our egos in contact and negotiation with the external world.[40]

The ego has a commitment to the external world, but it is also directly tied to the id. In fact, since it develops out of the id, Freud once referred to the ego as the "organized portion of the id." [41] It is in this organization and order that the ego becomes useful, because the id is totally lacking in these qualities. Other definitions of the ego used by Freud were a "dominant mass of ideas" [42] and a "coherent organization of mental processes." [43] We see Freud's Darwinianism emerging in his theory once again. That is, he assumed that what is first or earliest on the scene in life is basic to and determinative of all that is to follow. Thus, since the ego develops from the id, the id is primary; and an ego would not evolve if this ego did not further the hedonistic goals of the id. We must never forget that the ego wants to get the same pleasurable things out of life that the id wants. They differ only over the means to the ends sought. As Freud said, "the ego stands for reason and good sense while the id stands for the untamed passions." [44]

Freud also expressed this difference between the id and the ego in terms of what he called the *primary* versus the *secondary* process in mind. [45] The id, coming earlier in development, operates according to a primitive (primary) mental process, which seeks immediate gratification through what in Figure 3 we called progression to motor action or, if checked, resorts to regression in order to hallucinate what is desired (see Figure 3). A baby might react in this way during the first weeks of life, grabbing out for whatever it wants or possibly even hallucinating a desired mother's breast as if it were within view when it is not. It is the ego's (secondary) process in reasoning that helps check in time these impulsive and make-believe tendencies in the child's behavior. The ego is that part of the personality that learns to cry and show signs of needing attention when the mother is actually within view or presumed to be within earshot. But of course, in this process there is a lot of immediate gratification that goes unfulfilled as the baby matures. This checking of the id is, accord-

ing to Freud, the reason why most of our unconscious contents consist of unsatisfied wishes. [46]

In working out a proper strategy for need satisfaction, the ego must actually serve *three* masters: the id (which may lust and want to kill someone), the demands of external reality (where society frowns on such acts of murder), and the final identity of the topographical model, the *superego*. [47] We all realize that a certain "voice within" us—which we call our conscience—may well disturb us as we plan to do something wrong, even though nobody else may know about it. In 1914 Freud said this "judgment from within" was due to a standard of how we ought to behave called the *ego ideal*. [48] When he later introduced the id construct (1923), Freud referred to the ego ideal as the *superego*. He did not make any real distinction between these terms, and we can view them as synonymous. [49] The main point is that, as the id is organizing into the ego, a portion of this ego-organization is forming into a superego— that is, an identity point in mind that is ego but is also beyond or above it as a built-in ideal.

Since the superego has developed from the same mental beginnings as the ego, it too is basically a product of the id. [50] It is easy for us to forget this, because the contents of the superego are often so clearly in opposition to the id. [51] The id wishes to take something, even if it is stealing. The superego wishes that the id would be punished for thinking such thoughts or for bringing them about if the person actually does steal. Rather than confronting the id directly, the superego makes its wishes known to the ego. In some of Freud's writings it is clear that he thought the id might even occasionally stir up or irritate the superego with extreme indecencies so that it will nag at the ego all the more. In this way, the id can sometimes get back at the ego if too many repressions are being put on the personality. These "negotiations" between id, ego, and superego take place in the region of mind known as the unconscious. The ego unfortunately always ends up as the one in the middle, having to restore harmony in the personality while keeping "one eye" open to reality considerations.

The superego is just as unbending and unreasonable as the id. It has, like the id, received a kind of inheritance from the past in the sense of ethicomoral principles (like the Ten Commandments). It sticks to these rigidly and can never see exceptions to the rule. The id's inheritance is physical and hedonistic, and the superego's is sociocultural, but both of these identities in mind try to dictate to the ego. The superego dictates in a dual sense, for it not only tells the ego what it "ought to be like," but it also tells the ego what it "may not be like." [52] The seat of reason, common sense, and good judgment in changing circumstances is thus found only in the ego.

Motivational Constructs

Instinct and Energy

Freud did not make much use of an instinct construct in his earliest writings. It was not until about 1905, following his major work on dreams, that he began employing the instincts as a major theoretical tool. [53] By that time Freud was beginning to attract colleagues and students who met with him weekly at his home, a group that became in 1906 the Vienna Psycho-Analytical Society. [54] These discussions with colleagues had brought up the question of the relation between mind (psyche) and body (soma). Freud found that the *instinct* construct could help him here, and he eventually made three definite points concerning instincts: (1) they are based on a stimulation taking place within the body and not in the external world; (2) they provide a *constant* level of stimulation that we cannot run away from as we can run away from pressing stimulations (like cold or heat) in our external environment; [55] and (3) they seem always to function "on the frontier between the mental and the somatic," [56] acting therefore as bridges between the mind and body. Figure 5 schematizes this bridge function of the instinct, originating in the body but leading to the mind; it also lists the four characteristics that Freud attributed to any instinct (source, aim, pressure, object).

Each instinct is said to have the *aim* of satisfaction, or removing the *pressure* (extent of stimulation) from its *source* (the point in the internal body area from which it originates). If we have a great need for something, a given instinctual stimulus is exerting great pressure on us with the aim of achieving satisfaction, and the particular nature of the instinct (let us say it is to eat when hungry) determines just how we act (look for something to eat). Now, "the thing in regard to which the instinct is able to achieve its aim" is the *object*. [57] This is a widely used technical term in psychoanalysis which can refer to a person, an item of food, or a general desired state of affairs. It can even refer to one's own person. Literally *anything* that might conceivably lead to the satisfaction of an instinct is an object.

The instinct theory is also a different way of talking about hedonism. Pleasure consists in removing the pressure of an instinctive prompting in the body. Re-establishing the harmony of the body and keeping all tension at a low level is known in biology as *homeostasis*. Freud's concept of pleasure is therefore a homeostatic construct. But how do we explain this balancing out of tensions in the

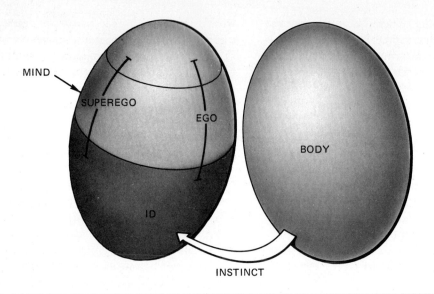

SOURCE:	LOCUS OF STIMULATION IN THE BODY.
AIM:	SATISFACTION OF STIMULATION OR NEED.
PRESSURE:	HOW MUCH DEMAND THE INSTINCTUAL STIMULUS IS MAKING UPON US AT THE MOMENT.
OBJECT:	THE PERSON, PLACE, OR THING IN THE ENVIRONMENT WHICH WILL SATISFY THE NEED (I.E., THE INSTINCTUAL STIMULATION).

Figure 5   Freudian Instinct as a Mind-Body "Bridge"

body so that the individual no longer feels hunger, thirst, sexual lust, and so on? Here is where we can see the influence on Freud of his former teacher and mentor, because Ernst Brücke had emphasized that all natural actions followed the *principle of constancy*. This principle was first proposed by Robert Mayer in 1842; it was later popularized by a student friend of Brücke's, named Hermann von Helmholtz.[58]

The basic idea of the constancy principle is that energies or forces within a closed system tend to redistribute themselves if for any reason there has been a disruption or unequal distribution of energy in different parts of the system. For example, weather patterns are influenced by high and low pressure points in the earth's atmosphere. When the barometer falls, we know that a "low" is moving into our area, and that there will probably be clouds, rain, or snow in the picture for us pretty soon. High pressure areas, on the other hand, send the barometer upward and signify that a clearing trend is on the way. But why do these changes in weather take place? Because, Helmholtz and Brücke would have said, something like a principle of constancy is at work in the total earth's atmosphere, redistributing the pressures in order to seek a kind of balance. There is a *constant* tendency to equalize, forcing the high pressure points to press outward and replace the lows so that in the end the total amount of energy in the earth's atmosphere will be evenly distributed. For various reasons, this total balance is never achieved and so we have our varying weather patterns.

When Freud and Breuer were collaborating on the *Studies on Hysteria,* they actually made use of the constancy-principle idea in what they called the *principle of neuronic inertia,* as follows: "If a person experiences a psychical impression, something in his nervous system which we will for the moment call the sum of excitation is increased. Now in every individual there exists a tendency to diminish this sum of excitation once more, in order to preserve his health." [59] In other words, just as a high pressure point in the atmosphere presses outward to dissipate itself into low pressure areas, so too do the excitations of the nervous system press outward to re-establish an even level of sensation (nervous impulses) throughout this bodily system. If, for some reason, this sum of excitation is not run off and a homeostasis achieved, then there would be trouble developing. Anna's pathognomic situation was a "sum of excitation" (in memory) like this that never quite got released (or worked over) and therefore resulted in her hysterical symptoms. The manner in which the mind succeeds—however effectively—in ridding itself of these states of heightened excitation is called the *vicissitudes* of the instincts. [60] A vicissitude is a regular or irregular state of change in something (like the weather!), and this is the pattern of change we see in our instinctive promptings as we get hungry and eat, only to get hungry again and eat once more. Sexual instincts are somewhat more difficult to satisfy.

Most psychologists would define *motivation* as the "activation of behavior due to a need deficit in relation to a goal (object)." Freud's *object* was usually an item in the person's experience that could satisfy such a need, but the *aim* of instinctual satisfaction

was *pleasure* (the hedonistic issue once again). Freud even spoke of a *pleasure principle* in mental life, as follows: "It seems as though our total mental activity is directed towards achieving pleasure and avoiding unpleasure—that it is automatically regulated by the *pleasure principle*." [61] It would be proper to identify the constancy principle with the pleasure principle as a homeostatic mechanism in mind seeking an even keel. [62] Freud did not believe that human beings have an instinct to feel *pain*. At best, pain is a "pseudo-instinct" which has as its aim "simply the cessation of the change in the organ and of the unpleasure accompanying it." [63] *Pain* is thus merely another way of saying *loss of pleasure,* and Freud has assigned the role of pleasure seeker (balancer) to the instinct construct. How many instincts (needs) do human beings have? Before we speak of Freud's theory of instincts as a whole, we must consider the *one* instinct (and need) he could never forgo in his view of the human being.

Freud's Promethean Insight: The Sexual Instinct

Freud's lifelong conviction was that he had found the basic reason for all neuroses, as well as the major motivator of all human behavior, in the human being's sexual instinct. He had a rather stubborn attitude about the use of the term *sex* in his theory. Though its meaning seemed stretched out of proportion at times and he broke with colleagues rather than rename this instinct (Jung being the most famous example), Freud steadfastly refused to change this precise usage.

Freud believed that the strangulator in defense hysteria was *always* an unwillingness to accept into consciousness a sexual thought or impulse. He repeatedly found evidence for this in his early clients, and we also have reason to believe that during his self-analysis Freud recalled his own sexual urges for his mother, whom he once saw in the nude when he was very young.[64] But over the years, the meaning of *sex* broadened tremendously in his writings, so that at times it is impossible to distinguish this meaning from the meaning of *pleasure*. Thus, Freud noted that in "man the sexual instinct does not originally serve the purpose of reproduction at all, but has as its aims the gaining of particular kinds of pleasure."[65] Sucking in a baby may be compared to other behaviors like masturbation as *identical* forms of what Freud called *autoerotic* activities. The term *autoerotic* means that the person uses the instinctual source of pleasure (mouth area, penis, and so on) as the *object* of pleasure. This gaining of pleasure from areas other than the genital regions of the body is sometimes referred to as *organ pleasure,* but Freud was quick to point out that the *reason* various organs have pleasure attached to them is because they satisfy a sexual instinct. Hence, regions of the body other than genital regions are sources of sexual instinctual stimulation.[66]

Freud called a region of the body giving rise to the sexual instinct at any point in time an *erotogenic zone*. Literally *any* part of the skin can become an erotogenic zone, stimulating the person to seek pleasure in some way. It can be the mouth area (pleasure in sucking) or the anal area (pleasure in defecation); even the eye can serve as a sexual stimulant (pleasure in pornographic viewing).[67] In line with his view that there are a number of erotogenic zones, Freud made perfectly clear that he believed there are *many* sexual instincts, each contributing its

components to the overall state we think of as "sexual excitation."[68] There are also other than sexual instincts in the body, a theoretical view that Freud was never to reject. Thought of as a bridge concept, the instinct originates in the body but it has its ultimate effect in the mind. Freud contended that the *physically* based instincts stimulate or set loose a *psychic* energy in the mind (symbolized by the arrow in Figure 5). Precisely how this takes place was never clarified, because of course this would mean Freud had solved the mind-body problem (that is, how can the physical and the mental interact?).

Despite this multiplicity of instincts in his theory, Freud gave a name to only *one* energy in mind, so that whenever he would describe a patient's behavior based on his structural model (id, ego, superego), he would frame the description exclusively in terms of this single mental energy. This energy was called *libido,* and it was defined variously as *"psychical desire,"*[69] all of the person's "erotic tendencies,"[70] "sexual desire in the broadest sense,"[71] and "the motive forces of sexual life."[72] But probably the most complete statement of libido in his writings, and one that also gives us a good picture of Freud's use of *love,* may be found in the following quote:

Libido is an expression taken from the theory of the emotions. We call by that name the energy, regarded as a quantitative magnitude (though not at present actually measurable), of those instincts which have to do with all that may be comprised under the word "love." The nucleus of what we mean by love naturally consists (and this is what is commonly called love, and what the poets sing of) in sexual love with sexual union as its aim. But we do not separate from this— what in any case has a share in the name "love" on the one hand, self-love, and on the other, love for parents and children, friend-

ship and love for humanity in general, and also devotion to concrete objects and to abstract ideas.[73]

With an energy this all-encompassing there was probably no need for naming alternatives. Nevertheless, since there *are* other instincts than the sexual, one would have thought that Freud might have named an energy for at least one more such instinct. The fact that he never did is mute testimony that he continued to base his major motivational theories on sexual factors in the human personality. One of the most common errors made in studying Freud is to equate libido with emotion, with the "good feeling" experienced in genital release and so on. As noted above, since emotions are not directly "in mind" any more than the pain we feel when we stub our toes is "in mind," the mental energy known as libido is not directly comparable to feelings or emotions. Emotions are rooted in the body and are made known to us mentally. We are aware of the pain of a stubbed toe, but we do not equate our awareness with the locus of our pain (the toe area). In like fashion, sexual pleasures emanate from the genital region of the body and are central in our emotional life. But libido is in the mind, orienting behavior in terms of these bodily based needs yet separate and distinct from them as well.

Libido is the *psychic* energy of the sexual instincts, and Freud now required an additional term to describe how this worked, how it oriented the person to seek a sexually desirable object. The term he settled on was *cathexis.* Freud first used this construct in his *Project* (see p. 44) as a physical concept, and noting his original usage helps us to understand what he means in his later psychological theorizing. In the *Project,* Freud said that a physical neurone (which is a "cell" in the nervous system) was *cathected* when it was filled with a certain quantum of phys-

ical energy.[74] This is related to the principle of neuronic inertia, because what happens when a "sum of excitation" is increased is that a neurone "fills up" with physical energy (see p. 53 for discussion of neuronic inertia).

This idea of filling up or occupying something is what Freud retained when he later used cathexis in relation to libido as a *mental* energy. Thus, if a man were to fall in love with a woman, he would mentally "fill" her image in his mind's eye with libido![75] *Cathexis* now has the meaning of a thrust, an entering, an occupation of a mental image, or a fixing of interest on some *given object* by attaching libido to it or engulfing it with libidinal energies.[76] Motives are therefore concerned with the libidinal cathexis of this or that object. The next step is to attain the cathected object (in our example, for the man to win the woman's love in return). However, simply cathecting an object does not mean the individual will always seek to attain it in the external world (that is, external to the contents of mind). For example, if the id lusts for some object—let us assume it is a parent—then the ego can *anticathect* this investment of libido in the image of the parent by opposing its own supply of libido to the id's cathexis.[77] Anticathexis, therefore, is another way of talking about strangulation, censorship, or repression.

One last point must be made concerning Freud's views on sex. He always held to the position that humans were *bisexual.* This theory was favored by Fliess, and Freud never rejected the notion, even though he did not develop it very much in his formal theories. Fliess made use of the concept in a physical sense, arguing that both men and women are guided by a natural constitutional cycle of influence. Women show this in their menstrual cycles, and men can be shown to experience something comparable in the fact that the blood vessels in certain tissues of their nasal region engorge with blood periodically. Both sexes are thus governed by periodic cycles of physical influence.[78] Fliess's theory was similar to what are called biological-clock theories, which attempt to show that behavior is based on natural rhythms built right into the physical structures of the body.

Freud, on the other hand, gave his construct of bisexuality a *psychological* interpretation, viewing masculinity as akin to *activity* and femininity to *passivity*.[79] He even thought of libido as masculine in nature, because it was such an active agent of mental life.[80] Freud made the greatest use of bisexuality in his analysis of President Woodrow Wilson, but most of his descriptions here were centered around Wilson's activity versus his passivity toward his father.[81] Hence though we have here a bisexual theory, biological in tone, it is actually a psychological theory of how the mind thrusts and parries in interpersonal situations—in either an active or a passive manner.

History of Freud's Instinct Theories

Now that we have an understanding of some basic terms, let us review the history of Freud's thinking on the role of instincts in human behavior. The first question that arises is, just how many instincts are in the human animal? Freud believed that this was unknown and that the only way the question could be answered was to study the problem empirically by tracing each instinct in turn to its ultimate *source* in the body.[82] The problem here, Freud noted, was that one is tempted to think up too many instincts to describe behavior. For example, to explain

playfulness, we might propose that human beings have an instinct to play. Yet, if we were to break this activity down into its components, we might find that an underlying instinct entered into this activity in combination with one or possibly two other *more basic* instincts, so that playfulness was not a true instinct at all. Freud therefore suggested that we probably need think of only a small number of underlying instincts to explain all kinds of behavior at more complex levels.

Freud called these underlying instincts *primal instincts,* and the instincts made up of these he called *compound instincts.* Now, it is very important to keep in mind that, as a general theoretical strategy, *Freud was always to base psychoanalytical theory on the interplay of two primal instincts, even though he implied that more than two were in effect.* He changed the names of these primal instincts over the years, but the fundamental opposition of two basic forces in the personality remains constant in Freudian thought. In fact, Freud maintained that instincts occurred in pairs of opposites, usually—as we have seen in the case of bisexuality—taking an active and a passive opposition.[83]

Freud's first opposition of instincts was that of the *self-preservative instincts* (or *ego instincts*[84]) and the *sexual instincts* (or *object instincts*[85]). Recall that the ego was seen as the seat of reason in the personality. Whereas the id was guided initially by the pleasure principle, Freud now said that the ego comes to be guided by the *reality principle.* "This latter principle does not abandon the intention of ultimately obtaining pleasure, but it nevertheless demands and carries into effect the postponement of satisfaction, the abandonment of a number of possibilities of gaining satisfaction and the temporary toleration of unpleasure as a step on the long indirect road to pleasure." [86] Rather than permit the id to act out (motor action) its cathexes overtly (in real life), the ego opposes itself to these impulses (anticathects) and seeks a pleasurable gratification in more acceptable ways. For example, the married woman who works as a secretary to an employer she lusts after might still refrain from being seduced by him, thanks to the anticathexes of the ego in union with the superego, which hold her sexual motives below consciousness (point 7 of Figure 3). However, in the evenings when this woman makes love with her husband, the id might hallucinate her boss in place of the husband—all going on still at the unconscious level! Since the marital vows have not been broken, this type of solution would be generally acceptable to all identities concerned, id, ego, and superego.

As we have already noted, Freud never coined an energy for the self-preservative instinct, even though he continually spoke of *energies,* implying that something other than libido was involved in moving the mental apparatus. But in actual practice, theoretical explanations were primarily based on the libido. With further experience and some challenges on certain points from his critics, Freud was eventually to change his theory of instincts. In place of self-preservation, he introduced the construct of a death instinct. This addition was part of a masterful piece of theorizing, and the way in which he accomplished it was to base the Death-Instinct theory on two preliminary ideas: *narcissism* and the *repetition compulsion.* We will work our way into this change by way of these preliminary constructs.

Narcissism. In Greek myth, Narcissus, the beautiful son of the river-god Cephissus, was supposedly the embodiment of self-conceit. Many nymphs wanted to be his lover, but he rejected their flirtations. One such rejected maiden prayed to the deity that he might know what it meant to love and not be loved

in return. A curse was put on his head and one day, leaning over a river bank for a drink of water, Narcissus was doomed to fall in love with his own reflection. He talked to it, tried to embrace it, lusted after it, and pined away until he died without ever achieving satisfaction.[87] Freud was to take this theme of self-love and use it to alter his instinct theory. Problems were mounting because of the challenges of his detractors, some of whom—like Adler—wanted Freud to give a more central role in the personality to conscious, reasonable, ego functions. Others—like Jung—felt that he was redefining the meaning of libido, making it into an *élan vital,* a general life force subsuming sexuality and many other functions as well.[88] What Freud had to do was (1) explain ego functions (self-preservation) as a special case of the sexual instincts, yet (2) avoid making the sexual instinct the *only* primal instinct of his theory. In short, he deliberately set out to remove self-preservation from the list of *primal* instincts and to replace it with some other opposing force in the personality.

His first step was accomplished through his use of *narcissism,* a term that had been used by Paul Näcke and Havelock Ellis to describe a person who treats his or her own body as if it were a sexual object.[89] Rather than saying that the ego looks after self-preservation because of a *primal* (basic, underlying) instinct of this nature, Freud now claimed that the *ego is itself cathected* with libido from the outset. Thus, in developing out of the id, the ego takes over its share of libido in the mental structure and acts like a special instance of love—that is, self-love (narcissism). We can now draw a parallel between autoerotism (see p. 54) and narcissism because they both refer to gaining sexual pleasure from an investment of libido in our own bodies as objects (ego-cathexes).[90]

Freud referred to the libido invested in the ego as *ego libido* or as *narcissistic libido* and the libido eventually sent outward to others as *object libido*. It is the sign of a more mature person that libido is being sent outward (object libido) rather than being invested inwardly (ego libido) in narcissistic fashion. But by the same token, everyone begins life and wishes to sustain it only because there *is* this initial self-love or self-cathexis.

Freud had now successfully done away with self-preservation as a *primal* instinct, even though the same kinds of self-preservative actions that the ego carries on continue as a secondary (component) instinctual pattern. The person looks out for himself or herself, avoiding injury whenever possible. Self-care is self-love. But what do we now oppose to the sexual instinct and its pleasure principle? At this point, Freud went "Beyond the Pleasure Principle" (Volume XVIII) and introduced one of his most controversial theoretical constructs as opponent to pleasure —the Death Instinct.

Repetition compulsion. Not until roughly 1920 did Freud decide to drop the pleasure principle as a major concept and to substitute in its place an entirely new concept of mental functioning, the *repetition compulsion*. He had been observing for decades that neurotics in psychoanalysis seemed to have a compulsion (uncontrollable urge) to repeat the dynamics of their past life in therapy, bringing him as therapist into their conflicts as if he were their parent in the re-enactment. He was also struck by the fact that children are ever willing to repeat the same game or to hear the same fairy tale over and over again. It was as if they were working through some anxious concern that preoccupied them,

like the mystery of birth in their hide-and-go-seek amusements. There are repetitive dreams and repetitive fantasies that everyone experiences occasionally, and even historians have noted that history tends to repeat itself.

Basing his argument on such points, Freud then concluded that in addition to the pleasure principle, "there really does exist in the mind a compulsion to repeat." [91] Note that this is a mental principle, whereas, if we recall, Fliess's periodic cycle theory had suggested something of the sort in the biological realm. Freud now brings his two final primal principles together by a stroke of genius that ties them both back to Brücke's constancy idea. He observes that *"an instinct is an urge inherent in organic life to restore an earlier state of things* which the living entity has been obliged to abandon under the pressure of external disturbing forces; that is, it is a kind of organic elasticity, or to put it another way, the expression of the inertia inherent in organic life." [92] Instincts do not make new things happen so much as they cause things happening to return to an earlier state (the conservative nature of instincts). As in the case of the pleasure principle, a state of quiescence is achieved through sexual activity, thereby returning the organism to its even, homeostatic level. Life is a rhythm—expressed initially by Freud in the construct of vicissitudes of the instincts (see p. 53). But the ultimate state of quiescence is death itself!

If we consider the issue biologically, even physical matter has a way of returning to a common inorganic state, as the Biblical reference of "dust to dust" reminds us. Thus, Freud can say, in a biological manner of speaking, *"the aim of all life is death."* [93] This now permits us to oppose our two instincts and view life as a vacillating rhythm of self-destruction (death) and self-perpetuation (life). He called the life-propelling instincts *Eros,* and they now take over the role of the older sexual instincts, including self-preservation by way of narcissism. Eros ensures that the final quiescence (death) will not come about too quickly. We love ourselves, so we look out for ourselves and try to extend our stay on this planet. Eros also ensures that there will be offspring to perpetuate the race as a by-product of pleasurable copulation between the sexes.[94] Opposed to Eros we now have another collection of instincts that have as their *aim* the restoring of living human beings to an inorganic state from which they presumably sprung during centuries past. This collective name is the *Death Instinct* (Freud did not like the term Thanatos, which some of his advocates have used since). Grisly though they may be, the aims of death are the satisfactions of the grave—repose, rest, and organic constancy.

As when he seemed to be identifying libido with pleasure (see p. 54), Freud here again seems to be identifying death with (pleasurable) satisfaction. He referred to this ultimate reduction in tension into the quiescence of death as the *Nirvana principle,*[95] but for all practical purposes as a theoretical device this is nothing more than a rephrase of the constancy principle and identical to the pleasure principle in a theoretically technical sense. Thus, in his final theory of instincts, Freud has Eros and Death as the two primary instincts entering together into all kinds of secondary or component instincts found in the personality (that is, the interactions of id, ego, and superego). This was sometimes called a *fusion of instincts.*[96] For example, sadism (receiving pleasure from inflicting pain on others) would be termed a component instinct in which there has been a fusion of hostility (Death) and sex (Eros).[97] Even something as simple as looking out for one's self, being willing to fight if necessary to retain one's integrity as a person, could be

seen as a fusion of self-love (Eros) and hostility (Death). In fact, Freud once said that the Life and Death Instincts hardly ever appear in their pure form in human behavior; there is almost always some fusion of the two.[98]

We might finally ask, since Freud named libido as the energy of Eros in this final formulation of his instinct theory, did he ever name an energy in opposition to it? No, this was never to be the case. Even though he said that the Death Instinct can turn into a destructive instinct during wartime and thus send out its hostile influences toward objects in the external world, Freud never sent a theoretical—to coin a word—"lobodo" outward to cathect such objects.[99] In his analysis of President Woodrow Wilson, he actually referred to the mixture of life and death energies without naming one of them, as follows: ". . . and the charge [that is, quantum] of mingled libido and Death Instinct was again without outlet and remained repressed."[100] It seems certain that he *did* have an energy in mind for the Death Instinct, and his theory surely called for it, but Freud was not moved to raise other energies into the prominence he had assigned to libido.

Defense Mechanisms or Mental Mechanisms

Over the years, Freud introduced a number of constructs that helped him to describe the dynamics of personality. Since in most instances he was describing the behavior of abnormals, we have come to think of these as *defense mechanisms.* However, as the extension was made to normals and what Freud called the "psychopathology of everyday life," we have come to think of them as simply *adjustment* or *mental mechanisms.* They are often defined in terms of energy expenditure, the blocking or rerouting of mental energies, and so forth. However, there is a clear meaning for each mechanism, which is easily grasped by anyone who lacks knowledge of libido theory.

Repression. We have already introduced this construct as the historical descendant of the strangulator and the censorship. Repression was Freud's most basic mental mechanism on which all of the other mechanisms are predicated. As Freud said, repression is "the corner-stone on which the whole structure of psycho-analysis rests." [101] We can define *repression* in two ways: (1) it is a countering of one cathexis by an anticathexis, or (2) it is the opposing of one idea in mind by an opposing idea. These are two ways of saying the same thing. We really cannot understand why one energy cathexis is opposed by a countercathexis without knowing the content of the ideas. The ideas act as *intentions,* preparations for action which come into conflict with one another. One aspect of the personality structure (id) intends to do one thing, and another aspect of the structure (ego-superego) intends another. [102] Though it is popular today for a person to say "I have repressed that" in referring to something that is annoying to think about, actually this is a misuse of the term. If we *know* that we have put something out of mind because it is annoying, then we have not repressed but *suppressed* a mental content. It is possible to suppress and remove mental contents from consciousness to the preconscious. However, true repression is *always* done unconsciously. We are unaware of our repressions, unless of course we have been

psychoanalyzed and thereby informed of what they are by the analyst.

There are actually two stages in repression (Freud's dichotomizing tendency again; see p. 46). The first, or *primal repression,* takes place during the time of the original conflict between ideas. This results in what Freud called a *fixation,* a mental mechanism that we will take up in the next section, which deals with the stages of psychosexual development. Then later, when certain mental *derivatives* (vague recollections or symbolical manifestations like Anna's death's heads; see p. 43) begin slipping by the primal censorship (repression), a *repression proper* is carried on by the mind. This has to be kept up, and it proves taxing to the mind.

Displacement. Freud introduced *displacement* to describe how it is possible to fool the censor and, in a dream formulation, to displace the true meaning of a dream content onto an unrelated event or happening. [103] If we have an unconscious hatred for our brother, for example, we might displace this hatred in our dream onto a bobcat, which we track down and kill after a satisfying hunt. We never actually realize *consciously* that our victim is Bob, which is short for our brother's name, Robert. Unconsciously we have killed our brother, but consciously only an unconscious derivative symbolized by a game animal has been done in.

Substitution. Humans can often find alternate objects in life. We can redirect our interests, for example, and find a new libidinal object if we are blocked from getting our first sexual preference. Freud suggested that when an aging unmarried woman dotes over a pet dog, or when an old bachelor collects snuff boxes, the former has found a substitute for the marital partner she never acquired, and the latter has substituted a series of pretty boxes for the succession of beautiful women he never conquered.[104] *Substitution* thus specifically refers to the replacing of one object by another.

Sublimation. Freud defined this as follows: "The most important vicissitude which an instinct can undergo seems to be *sublimation;* here both object and aim are changed, so that what was originally a sexual instinct finds satisfaction in some achievement which is no longer sexual but has a higher social or ethical valuation."[105] Sublimation thus goes beyond substitution, to change *both* the object and the aim of the instinct. The cited definition makes it appear that a person cannot sublimate hostility or the Death Instinct. Actually, most of the instances which Freud uses to demonstrate sublimation *do* deal with sex or Eros, but it seems clear that he meant that *any* (primal or component) instinct that is unacceptable to the superego could be sublimated.[106] An example might be the young man who considers his sexual promptings to be "dirty" (due to severe superego), and therefore turns to art and becomes a talented painter. The paintings are changed objects, but there is no longer a sexual instinctual aim in the painting activity.

Projection. Freud often noted that his patients—particularly the paranoiac (extremely suspicious tendencies)—would behave like a dreamer and attribute internal fantasies to the external world in the way reviewed in Figure 3 (regression of mental excitation back to the stimulus). For example, the id might prompt the patient to feel hostility toward another person, but the superego would negate any expression of this anger in overt behavior. At this point, the patient could *project* her own hostility onto the disliked person and say, "I'm not hostile to her, but she is very irritated with me." Notice that the *nature* of the projected instinct remains the same—it is still hostility that we are

dealing with.[107] Freud believed that the capacity to project internal perceptions outward was a very primitive tendency in humans, and that in point of fact, projection "normally plays a very large part in determining the form taken by our external world."[108]

Reaction-Formation. Freud introduced the construct of reaction-formation to account for those instances in which people seem to be arguing or favoring some action, point of view, or intention in diametric opposition to what they *really* wish would occur. The pregnant young woman who unconsciously wishes that her forthcoming child would miscarry may profess consciously that she wants the child "very, very much."[109]

Rationalization. Freud's student and biographer, Ernest Jones, introduced the term *rationalization,* which refers to the fact that a person often finds an acceptable (plausible, rational) reason to justify some action that is really prompted by a completely different (usually irrational, emotional) motive.[110] Thus, an otherwise gracious and friendly woman who unconsciously dislikes another woman in her circle of friends may find all manner of reasons for avoiding contact with this particular person. Her real reason is unconscious hatred (Death-Instinct components), but her consciously stated reasons (rationalizations) may include that she is too busy to call the woman on a telephone, she is never free on the afternoons when this woman has a tea party, she was sick on the occasion when they were to travel together, and so on.

Isolation. A disturbed person may sometimes be able to keep a rather horrible or frightening idea in mind. In order to account for this feature of mental life, Freud introduced the construct of *isolation,* by which he meant separating an idea from its emotion.[111] Thus, a psychotic person might have a delusional belief that his stomach had turned into a huge snake and that it was eating him alive, or some such. The normal person would be horrified—on the order of Anna O.'s reaction —but this psychotic individual might continue to think about the delusion without showing a sign of emotion. Normals might occasionally isolate, such as in times of war when killing is required, or when a parent tries to remove a child's badly mangled finger from a wire fencing where it had become impaled in an act of play. We cannot always let our emotions get the better of us and must sometimes carry out a difficult task with a cool head even though it may appear unnatural to others.

The mental mechanisms of *introjection, identification, fixation,* and *regression* will be taken up in the next section, as we outline the stages of psychosexual development.

Time-Perspective Constructs

Psychosexual Stages

Freud first suggested that four life stages covered the period from birth to adulthood.[112] He told Fliess in 1896 that each stage must build on the earlier one, and that measurable amounts of psychic energy probably pass along from an earlier to a later developmental level. If the proper amount of psychic energy does *not* move up from level A (ages 8 to 10) to level B (ages 13 to 17), then "the excitation is dealt with in accordance with the psychological laws in force in the earlier psychical period and along the paths open at that time. Thus . . . *fueros* are still in

force, we are in the presence of 'survivals.' " [113] A *fuero* is an ancient Spanish law or decree made by a ruler, which is given to a province for some reason and can at some later date be exercised or used. For example, a king might give a province exemption from paying taxes or the right to avoid contributing manpower to the military forces. A fuero is thus a claim on the head of state for privileges.

In like fashion, said Freud, we have personal fueros that dictate to us from out of our own past (recall that the unconscious is timeless!). They arise when we do not pass smoothly through one developmental stage to another. A primal repression at one stage will surely mean that a fuero has been established there, forever afterward placing demands on the personality structure to—in a sense—return and resolve the issue that led to the conflict of cathexis and countercathexis. As time went by, Freud not only worked out a detailed series of psychosexual stages in human development, but he provided many theoretical explanations for why certain of these stages are not passed through satisfactorily. This became an important part of psychoanalysis, allowing Freud to account for everything from minor personality differences to neurotic and even psychotic disorders.

The term *psychosexual* reflects Freud's dualism. We must appreciate that the developmental stages occur in *mind* (psyche), even though they are given their unique coloring by the region of the *body* from which Eros, or the life instinct (sexual), is being most active at the time. Freud called these bodily regions through which the pleasure principle is primarily active at any one point in development the *erotogenic zones.* Sucking, a pleasurable activity to the infant, receives its libidinal component from the erotogenic zone of the mouth. If for some reason the developing baby does not move on psychologically to the next erotogenic zone, then the resulting fuero in mind would have mouthlike or oral dictates to make on the total personality structure.

Freud was to drop his first model of four levels in mind, and over the years we can actually count six or seven stages (sometimes called *phases*) in the development of the human being from birth to maturity. However, the first four, which are called the *pregenital stages,* are the most important in personality formation. Freud meant by *genital* the capacity to reproduce, so that pregenital levels are those in which, although sexuality is active, the genital (procreative) potential is not yet realized and no offspring can result from sexual intercourse. These psychosexual stages, to which we now turn, should not be thought of as fixed rigidly to age level. There can be several months' variation in age between any two people passing through the same psychosexual stage.

Oral Psychosexual Stage

At birth the person is all id, because there is no real consciousness and the ego-superego elaborations of the personality structure have not yet taken place. Infants are said to have an *oceanic feeling* of power, for the world is their oyster.[114] Desire is centered around *oral erotism* or the seeking of pleasure in activities of the mouth (which is the erotogenic zone of this stage). Food sources like the mother's breast or a milk bottle are "attacked" and devoured as a cannibal might attack and devour another person.[115] Freud called this taking something physical into our body from an outside source *incorporation.* The oral stage is typified by such *takings-in,* both from the external and the internal world of experience. In fact, this is how it is possible for the ego to begin developing. In the same way that the total person takes in milk as nourishment, what will become the

ego within the personality takes in libido from the id to build its alternative, a more reality-oriented outlook on life.

The child in the first few months of life is said to be in a state of *primary narcissism* (autoerotic), living only on the basis of the pleasure principle. If a bodily tension arises, the infant removes it automatically through internal reflex actions like urination or defecation. But if in order to remove the tension some external object is necessary—like mother's breast—the child can resort to *wish fulfillment* and literally see (that is, hallucinate) what he or she desires in an act of fantasy (primary process thought). Wish fulfillments through fantasy are identical to the mechanisms of dream formation (both follow the model presented in Figure 3). Since there are no superego wishes to be met with this early in life, the wish fulfillments of a baby in the oral stage are *all* pleasant.[116]

Gradually, the taking-in tendencies of the oral stage bring about *identification*, a mental-mechanism process that is not completed until the phallic stage of development (as we discuss later in this chapter). To identify is to take over the behavioral styles, attitudes, and belief systems of other people as our own. Freud considered identification to be a more primitive mechanism than object choice. To choose an object means that the person has sent libidinal cathexes outward, away from the self-identity. But to identify is to send libido inward, forming the internal life of the psyche in what is essentially a narcissistic way. Recall that in narcissism the person's own identity is the object. Psychoanalysis recognizes that narcissism always precedes object choice in human development. The id is totally narcissistic, and even as the ego is forming, it does so on this basis. For this reason Freud occasionally referred to the oral period as the *stage of narcissism*.[117] His student Ferenczi coined the term *introjection* to describe the specific act of taking into the personal identity characteristics of others.[118]

Anal Psychosexual Stage

Sometime around the close of the first year of life, when the child is first confronted with the need to meet the demands of polite society and learn to control his or her sphincters (urination, defecation), Freud viewed a shift in erotogenic zones from the mouth area to the anus (and also to the urethra, our next stage). Whereas experience up to this time had allowed the child to take in (introject, incorporate), he or she is now called upon to delay certain gratifications (secondary process in thought), to live more along the lines of a reality principle. By this time the ego is being differentiated out of the mass that was the oceanic total of psychic events, and as such the ego is confronted with certain problems in living. Freud said that when an instinct is not satisfied, the person experiences a *frustration;* the rules and restrictions put on the child by parents that cause this frustration he called a *prohibition;* and the resulting psychological state of affairs in general he called a *privation*.[119] The anal stage begins a lifelong process of having to put up with privations and trying to live up to the prohibitions of one's elders, who ultimately represent the values of the broader culture. The little girl therefore bears up with frustrations in order to obey her mother ("Don't soil yourself"). Often punishments follow if the child does not meet parental prohibitions. This is therefore a difficult time for the child, who has to move from the passive-receptive coloring of the oral stage to a more aggressive and as-

saultive stage of development (Death Instinct more prominent now!). In fact, Freud first referred to the personality in this phase as the *"sadistic-anal* organization, in which the *anal* zone and the component instinct of *sadism* are particularly prominent."[120] Sadism involves taking (sexual) pleasure from the infliction of pain (see p. 59).

The anal stage is still pregenital; but as the child is toilet-trained by the mother, there is an ever-increasing source of potential difficulty in the clash of wills, both individuals desiring to fulfill their own ends. The child finds that the mucous membranes of the anal region are a source of pleasure and might even physically manipulate this region or play with fecal matter through retention, then rapid expulsion in defecation, and so forth. The mother may find such "games" disgusting and punish the child; of course, another mother might be more permissive and allow the child to make extensive manipulations of this sort.

Urethral Psychosexual Stage

The *urethra* is the canal that carries urine from the bladder to the male's penis or to the vestibule of the female's vagina. Although he did not draw a hard and fast line between the anal and urethral stages, Freud did feel that an erotogenic-zone contribution is made to pleasure (sex in the broader sense) from the urethra. We probably all pass through a phase where the anus is uppermost as contributor of libido and then another, briefer period in which the urethra takes the center stage in this role as source. This stage is still pregenital, and we are therefore speaking about the life period of roughly the third year. Children at this time often take pleasure in manipulating urination along the lines of retention-and-release "games," which they play with themselves or even other children. For example, two boys may have competitive exchanges in a kind of urinary combat, or they may try to see who can send a stream of urine the farthest from a fixed point. Obviously, such activities greatly upset parents when they are uncovered.

Phallic Psychosexual Stage

We come now to the stage in which infantile sexuality takes a heterosexual turn, as object cathexes are directed outwardly toward a parent. This is still a pregenital stage because the child is not yet able to reproduce. The term *phallus* refers specifically to the male penis or female clitoris being engorged with blood. This can occur even before the reproductive (genital) organs have fully matured, of course, and in naming this level the phallic stage Freud wanted to stress that it was based on "not a primacy of the genitals, but a primacy of the *phallus*."[121] We begin now to see that Freudian psychology places the masculine above the feminine as an ideal for *both* sexes. Freud has been much criticized as a masculine chauvinist, but he believed this is what the clinical findings were *in fact* and that therefore it would be uncourageous to deny that in early life *both* boys and girls highly value the *penis* (when erect, *phallus*).

The phallic stage begins late in the second or third year of life.[122] Differences between the sexes at this point are nonexistent, and for all practical purposes "the little girl is a little man."[123] The boy discovers his pleasurable organ as the erotogenic zone shifts away from the anus-urethra to the penis, and he begins masturbating in order to capitalize on this new libidinal source; the girl does precisely the same thing with her "small penis," the clitoris.[124] In fact, the girl senses a loss or a lack and very much envies her brother and other boys (called *penis envy*) for their superior organ, which un-

doubtedly exudes more pleasure as an erotogenic zone because of its size.[125] Often the first reaction of the girl is to *deny* or *disavow* that she lacks a penis, but in time her psychology is greatly influenced by this fact.[126]

Ontogeny Recapitulates Phylogeny and the Origin of Society. Before going into what are called the Oedipal complexes of children, we will review Freud's theories on the origin of society, culture, or civilization (he did not make fine distinctions among these terms). First of all, we must understand the Darwinian-Lamarckian theoretical rule that *ontogeny recapitulates phylogeny*. This rule suggests that in its *in utero* ("prebirth") development from a fertilized egg (one cell) to a highly complex anthropoid, the human being re-enacts the evolution of the entire animal kingdom. The human fetus passes through a state in which it has a gill structure, suggesting a fishlike animal; later it develops a tail, and during the early stages of gestation it is hard to tell a human fetus from a pig fetus. This theory is rejected by many biological scientists today, but Freud was much taken by it and seems to have used it to buttress his theory of the repetition compulsion.[127] By 1913 he was arguing that we had to see this principle in operation mentally as well as physically.[128] Freud therefore contended that not only did people re-enact their *physical history* before birth, but they also re-enacted their *psychological history* after birth! The family setting, with its relations between parents and children, is to be seen analogically to the *origin of society*. Each family re-enacts what took place in the "first" family, or social unit.

Theories of societal origin fall into two broad categories: those that stress the aggressive conquering of one people by another, and those that stress the more reasonable, cooperative, even loving side of human behavior.[129] Freud succeeded in using both views at different points in his theory. Basing his main argument on Darwin's theory of a *primal horde,* he argued that in the dawn of human society people lived in small groups under the complete dominance of a single male. This "primal father" owned all of the horde's property, and the women of the group were his most prized possessions for they brought him sexual pleasure. He had unlimited power and exerted it sadistically, keeping all of his sons from the pleasures of sexual contact with the women in the group (privation). If a son violated this prohibition, the father would either kill, castrate, or send him off into the wilderness to fend for himself. This naturally led to the practice of *exogamy* (seeking sexual objects as mates from outside one's kinship group), as the sons raided other groups and kidnapped their own women.

However, one group of sons eventually violated this pattern. A number of them who had been run off by the primal father returned as a smaller group of attackers with a common hatred. They were fearful of the old man, but through the strength of their numbers they succeeded in killing him off. Then, as many primitive groups are known to have done, they *literally* incorporated his physical identity. They ate him (or a goodly portion of him) in cannibalistic fashion, just as the baby now eats mother's milk in the oral stage. The reason for eating the father was that they hoped to take in or introject his strength. We might say that in killing him the sons cathected their father's body with the energy of the Death Instinct, but they *also* cathected him with libido in desiring his power. Hence, rather than taking him as a sexual object (object choice), they reverted

to the more *primitive identification* (incorporation) in the narcissistic oral fashion that we have already discussed.[130]

The shock of having killed and eaten the old man sobered the sons up enough to realize that hostility breeds a return in kind and that no one profits if the killing continues. Hence, they succeeded in doing what the primal father could not bring himself to do: they struck a rational bargain (sometimes called a social contract). They agreed to found what we now think of as families within the society, to have sexual intercourse with only their specific group of wives (this was a polygamous society), and that *their sons* should limit their selection of wives from outside the family (taboo of exogamy). Hence, sons and daughters could not properly expect to have sexual gratification (Eros) within their own family units. As the generations slipped by, the memory of having killed an actual human being was repressed, and the father's image was replaced by a totemic animal of some sort. Ordinarily, the animal could not be eaten except on certain ceremonial occasions, such as that of a sacrifice to God. And this now heavenly God-image was also a projection of the primal father. Religious myths were then thought up to change the meaning of early events in the history of society. For example, the true original sin was not violating orders from God about whether or not to eat certain fruit; the true sin was killing the primal father (God) in order to get the forbidden fruits of sexuality.[131] With a common totemic animal and a common God, the families that were organized into a culture (commonly identified with a leader) would drain off hostility stimulated within the group (Death Instinct) by directing it outward in wars on other societies that also had evolved in the manner we have outlined.[132]

To weld this social theory to a single family, Freud now once again drew on

Greek mythology in the tale of Oedipus. This famous myth runs as follows: Laĭus, king of Thebes, having been warned by the oracle that his newborn son would destroy him, had the child sent off to be murdered by a herdsman. Emotionally unable to kill the child, the herdsman merely pierced his feet and left him on a mountain to die in the elements. However, a shepherd rescued the boy and carried him to another region where he was reared by a noble family, who named him *Oedipus* which means "swollen foot" (the foot is a penis symbol in Freudian thought). In time, as he grew to manhood, Oedipus was to hear from the oracle that he would someday slay his father. Thinking his stepfather was his natural father, he left the region by chariot only to meet Laĭus on a narrow road. After a disagreement over the right of way, Oedipus unknowingly killed his real father. Later, thanks to the heroic act of solving the riddle of the Sphinx, Oedipus was made king of Thebes and thereby took Jocasta, his mother, as wifely queen. Years passed, and eventually the oracle made known the true relationship of mother and son to the two priniciples of our drama. Jocasta put an end to her life by hanging herself, and Oedipus blinded himself by puncturing the pupils of both eyes.[133] Freud used the term *Oedipus* to describe a *complex* (an ideational content or collection of ideas[134]) that both males and females carry about within their unconscious minds, and that they actually lived through in the sense of ontogeny recapitulating phylogeny as follows:

Male Oedipus Complex. In the case of the boy, along about his third year of life in the phallic stage, we find a re-enactment (repetition) of the primordial lusting for the female in the home (the mother). The boy senses pleasurable stimulations from his penis erotogenic zone, and he also has some hunch that this region is tied to mother in a physical

way. Thus, said Freud, ". . . he becomes his mother's lover. He wishes to possess her physically in such ways as he has divined from his observations and intuitions about sexual life. . . ."[135] This talk of intuition reminds us of the Jungian influence on Freud concerning the possibility of inheriting mental contents from antiquity in the unconscious (see p. 181). The law of *talion* (animalistic retribution in kind, as in "dog eat dog") is one such possible sense of intuition that everyone might generate via unconscious promptings. It is precisely at this time that the son is lusting after the mother in the primitive-horde re-enactment. He therefore senses the early prohibition of this ancient drama with its threat of castration for those who break the father's commands.[136] This *castration fear* establishes what Freud called the *castration complex* as an aspect of the broader Oedipus complex.[137] The four-year-old boy literally believes that his father will cut off his testicles, penis, or both! With each rise in the level of mother cathexis (the more libido invested in her image as an object choice), the boy feels a parallel rise in anxiety as he senses the inevitable castration (this idea is coming up from unconsciousness to consciousness). The ego is the most intimidated portion of the personality. It tries to head off the id, but as we know, the latter's needs are unreasonably insatiable. Things look increasingly bad for the boy.

When things are darkest and the fear is greatest, a solution is found by the boy who essentially sells out his interest in his mother, reverts from object choice to identification, and rather than continuing his lust for mother, takes in (introjects) the father's superego standards. Since the father's ideals also represent the cultural norm, the boy gets "civilized." The male conscience is thus born of fear. Although the son had had a warm feeling for his father before the phallic period, and he had doubtlessly begun to identify with the father somewhat out of this love, the final act of *paternal identification* is a matter of self-defense, born of extreme anxiety. "Conform or be castrated" is the civilizing rule. This is why Freud said that the superego is the "heir of the Oedipus complex."[138] In terms of libido theory, what supposedly happens is that a great wave of *anticathexis* sets in, which turns the boy's interest away not only from the mother (repressing his lustful id prompting), but from *all* members of the opposite sex (bringing on the latency period; see below). Men do not recall their earlier lustful desires (cathexes) for their mothers because out of castration fear they have succeeded in putting this all down into the darkest regions of their unconscious mind. The ego triumphs by giving birth to the superego, but this is rarely a total victory. Virtually every man suffers some remnant of his Oedipal conflict. But if he does not resolve this complex pretty much as outlined, acquiring a reasonably effective superego in place of the castration anxiety, he will surely be doomed to a life of neurosis.

Female Oedipus Complex. Some of his students have called this the *Electra complex*, basing their analogy on the mythological tale of a slaying of a mother that was instigated and abetted by a revengeful daughter (Electra), but Freud specifically rejected this usage and its mythological parallel.[139] We continue now with the fact noted above that psychoanalysis is more a masculine than a feminine theory of personality. Freud was definitely uncertain in his theory of female sexuality. He did not believe that girls experience the great fear of the mother as boys do of the father. The prephallic attachment of a daughter to her mother is far more important in the development of a girl, and it is only much later that hostility and competitiveness with the mother might set in. Put another way, girls do not have a castration fear of the same-sex parent because of course they lack the testicles or penis to fear for. What they do have is a *penis envy* and a basic sense of inferiority because they assume that they have *already been* castrated—either by nature or by one of their parents (the mother is usually seen as the guilty party after a period of time).[140]

The course of feminine development is now seen as the girl working out the substitutes and sublimations of her "lost penis." The healthiest solution in the Freudian view is simply that the little girl find in her father's penis an adequate substitute, cathect it with libido, and thereby come in time to identify with her mother's role in the family. This gives us a certain parallel with masculine psychology, because this makes the little girl her father's lover. Many Freudians use this framework today and say that there is a hostile competitiveness between the maturing girl and the mother over who will *really* be the father's genital partner. They surmise that Freud believed this competition set up a comparable level of fear to the boy's castration anxiety, and that in this way the anticathexes of latency set in with roughly equivalent force for both sexes. Actually, though Freud *did* feel feminine identification was furthered in the competition with mother,[141] he *did not* propose such a neat parallel with masculine identification.

Freud's theoretical problem was that he did not have this mounting level of anxiety on which to base the final formation of the superego for the girl. He vacillated about how much trouble this affords the female, noting in one context that it does little harm if she does not fully resolve her Oedipal attitudes,[142] but stressing in others that she really has a more difficult Oedipal matura-tion than the boy.[143] Both heterosexual desire and motherly love spring from the root of penis envy. The normal, healthy progression for the girl is thus: castration acceptance *to* penis envy *to* cathect father's penis and identify with mother *to* desire for a father-substitute's penis (husband) *to* desire for a baby.[144]

But what about the superego as heir to the Oedipal complex? If girls do not have castra-tion fear, how can they get their superegos firmly in place? Well, they really cannot, and in Freudian psychology they do not. Speaking of women, Freud observes:

Their super-ego is never so inexorable, so impersonal, so independent of its emotional origins as we require it to be in men. Char-acter-traits which critics of every epoch have brought up against women—that they show less sense of justice than men, that they are less ready to submit to the great exigencies of life, that they are more often influenced in their judgements by feelings of affection or hostility—all these would be amply ac-counted for by the modification in the forma-tion of their super-ego which we have in-ferred above.[145]

Women sublimate less often than do men,[146] which would account for the fact that it is the man who has been the prime mover of civilization. It is easy to see why the modern feminist finds Freudian psy-chology so offensive. Women are undoubtedly painted as lesser human creatures by psy-choanalysis (although there have been fe-male analysts who countered these portions of Freudian theory).

Latency Psychosexual Stage

Both sexes eventually do forget (repress) their parental Oedipal attractions.[147] Thus,

at about age six to eight and lasting until sexual pubescence at age ten to as late as fourteen, there is a dramatic decline in the sexual interests of maturing children. Freud called this span of years the *latency* period.[148] The child substitutes a feeling of affection for the former emotion of lust, which suggested to Freud that the sexual instincts become "inhibited in their aim" [149] during the latency period. The child begins turning now to imaginative play with members of his or her own sex (sublimated libido, projected onto other humans "who look like me").[150] We can also see the phenomenon of reverting to identification from object choice here (see p. 66), as little boys solidify their identities as *males* and little girls as *females;* they may say at this time that they hate the other sex (reaction formation) and wish only to play and be with members of their own sex, which essentially means "with myself" (autoerotic use of libido). Object choice has been success-fully eclipsed for the time being.

Freud did not believe that latency was inevitable in every person's life. He notes that in some life histories the latency period has been skipped entirely. He also stressed that the course of the latency period is not always uniform, and the cessation of sexual promptings might not be observed at every point along the way.[151] Some children, de-pending particularly on their environmental stimulation, have incidents of overt sexual play during this time of life. However, by and large, the principle of aim-inhibited sexuality is the case for children in this age span. One last point concerning latency: there is always the clear implication in psy-choanalysis that a contribution is made to the onset and ending of latency by sheer bio-logical factors. Freud referred to sexual development as a two-stage or *diphasic* process, which begins very early in life and is then interrupted by latency before surging forth again at pubescence. This diphasic process he referred to as a "biological peculiarity" of the human species,[152] but one that did not function unless it was nurtured in a certain sociocultural climate. "The period of latency is a physiological phenomenon. It can, however, only give rise to a complete interruption of sexual life in cultural organizations which have made the suppression of infantile sexuality a part of their system. This is not the case with the majority of primitive peoples."[153]

Pubescence and Adolescence

Pubescence is the period of maturation when humans begin to take on the mature physical characteristics of sexuality, including pubic hair, the production of semen in the male, and menstruation and enlarged breasts in the female. The period heralds the onset of genitality—true reproduction is now possible —and when this transformation in the body is completed, humans enter the adolescent period, which is usually considered to fall between the ages of twelve and twenty years. Primitive peoples often have puberty rites, which ceremonially introduce the child into adulthood with much fanfare and recognition. Often this is tied to a religious theme, as in the bas/bar mitzvah of the modern Hebrew religion. But in the main the adolescent period is a time of uncertainty and stress for most individuals because of the rapidly changing demands being put on the growing young adult, who sometimes feels neither fish nor fowl as he or she tries to work out a place in the scheme of things. Freud did not devote very much of his writings to adolescence per se, doubtlessly because he

felt that the personality is already established by the time of puberty. One must always go back to the first five years to really understand a personality system in Freudian terms.[154]

Puberty, said Freud, initiates the second step in the diphasic human sexual development. The sexual instinct now makes known the full strength of its demands.[155] Due to the changes in internal physical secretions of the various sexual hormones associated with pubescence, the actual amount of libido "accumulated" in the cathexes and anti-cathexes of the Oedipal resolution is increased.[156] This serves to enliven the repressed Oedipal conflict, which flares up again but in a somewhat modified form.[157] Unless a neuroticism is involved, the usual course of this flare-up is that the adolescent falls in love with an older person of the opposite sex (crush):[158] a teacher, a cinema star, or a political figure. Adolescents are also noted for their sense of emotional commitment, and Freud would have viewed this characteristic as sublimation of libido into political causes, public demonstrations, or the desire to make this a better world.

In addition to the sublimation of libido (Eros) in the sociopolitical criticisms of adolescence, we can also see a Death-Instinct component in the *hostility* that adolescents sometimes express. They are angry young men and women. Their hostility can also be channeled into antisocial behaviors like delinquency or revolutionary activities.[159] The opposite can be seen in that sometimes all instinctual promptings are repressed out of sight, even to the point of reaction-formations like the pursuit of asceticism, vows of celibacy, the need to be alone, and the attraction to mystical philosophies, religions, and esoteric cults—literally, a total rejection of the sensory or material world. But the average adolescent will, in time, find a substitute for his or her parental objects in the heterosexual partners of the "dating and petting" years. The adolescent will thus fall in love—probably several times—and eventually marry one of these heterosexual partners as he or she achieves adulthood.

Most modern theorists who have studied the adolescent stress the latter's reliance on a peer group or gang. Although he did not address himself directly to the question of adolescence, Freud *did* place great stress on the role of group factors in human behavior. Freud described the human being as "a horde animal, an individual creature in a horde led by a chief." [160] In developing a group interest, the adolescent is therefore merely reflecting the in-group identification tendency that will be carried on for the rest of his or her life.

Adulthood and Genitality

Adulthood or the *genital phase* of psychosexual development implies not only the ability to reproduce, but also to obtain satisfactory *heterosexual* physical gratification in lovemaking. Freud therefore did not see a homosexual adjustment as fully adult or satisfactorily genital (see our discussion. below, p. 79). He also emphasized that the female's *second* phase in the diphasic sexual development had to be a feminine one, whereas initially she had been a "little man." To accomplish this shift, the girl's erotogenic zone moves from the clitoris ("little penis") to the vaginal area proper, which occurs during and following pubescence. [161] As this takes place the maturing woman becomes increasingly passive (feminine) and receptive to the sexual advances of the male, finding personal satisfaction in the penis of her lover and also in the bearing of a child.

Freud realized that mere sexual activity would never bring happiness in adulthood. In his view, people who are "sexually liberated" and therefore promiscuous by con-

ventional standards are also likely to be immature and narcissistic. If two people marry and feel *only* sexual lust for one another, this union will probably not last. To be sexually gratified through lovemaking is, after all, to satisfy the instinctive promptings of lust. [162] Romantic love or a "passing affair" are based on such immediate sexual passions; but if a man and woman are to remain committed to each other, something must be added to the relationship in addition to lustful passion. Freud therefore suggested that to last, a mature love must consist of *both* lustful desire *and* the aim-inhibited lust of "feelings of affection," like those we have for our parents during latency. [163] Marriages are often begun under the original drive of lust, but in time a growing sense of affection (aim-inhibited lust) partially replaces this exclusively sensual zeal. The marital partners say "I not only love my mate, I *like* him (her)." If only aim-inhibited ties of affection are involved in the marriage (no lust), then the love is platonic. Freud did not favor the platonic relationship for most people because instincts should be satisfied and a complete lack of sexual activity in marriage would not meet this natural need of the human organism.

Fixation and Regression

Freud based his explanations of personality differences and mental illness on the various ways in which people pass through the psychosexual stages. By *pass through,* we mean in the psychic realm. Someone who does not grow up mentally we consider psychologically immature. In this sense, Freudian theory has all of us more or less immature. This is what gives us our different personality tendencies. Since the libido theory plays a central role in this explanation of how we mature, it is a good point at which to consider this construct in more detail. What did Freud have in mind when he spoke of this mental energy? What analogies or metaphors did he use as his model of psychic energy? We have already gotten the impression of libido as similar to an electrical charge of some type, as when Freud first spoke of a neuron as cathected when it was filled with an electrical charge (see p. 55). Even though he later switched to the mental-energy usage, we are left with the clear impression of an analogy to electricity. But now in some of the most important passages on the fixation and regression of libido, Freud *also* analogizes to a stream of water or a riverbed.[164] He was fond of using the phrase *psychical damming-up,* which he took from Lipps,[165] and the reader will find the modern Freudian referring to *dammed-up libido* as one way of talking about repression (cathexis dammed-up by anticathexis).

We conclude that Freud's libido construct comes down somewhere between a charge of electricity being carried along and a hydraulic force of the type we associate with a liquid in its fluid or a steamlike state. Actually, since libido is a construct that has no measurable referent in observed experience, it is impossible to get a clear picture of what it is "really" like. In reading him over the years, one can easily get the impression that Freud initially thought of libido as an energizer that might someday be discovered and measured; but in time this view seems to have weakened and in the end it is obvious that he is simply using the term *libido* to organize his thoughts as a metaphor. Jung tried valiantly to get Freud to clarify the concept, but without success. What makes it all the more difficult for the student of Freud

is that he seems to have relied on libido as a construct more and more over the years.

When Freud put stress on the hydraulic meaning of libido, he usually spoke in terms of what he called its *quantitative factors* in behavior. Any single person has just so much libido available to the total personality at any given point in time. That aspect of the personality structure that has relatively the most of this precious mental fuel can accomplish the most, get its needs answered the most, or keep mentally active the most.[166] The artist who sublimates libido into his or her art form must take it away from something else, and therefore the heterosexual drive will be to some extent reduced. Moreover, if libido is dammed-up over time in the development of personality, then the psychosexual stage that pocketed this libido must necessarily have more to say about the ultimate coloring of that particular personality structure, in the sense of influencing the style of behavior it will engage in. Another way of putting this is that the fuero of a psychosexual stage at which libido has been dammed-up makes the major claims on the style of behavior that this given personality will emphasize (see our discussion of the fuero, p. 62). We are mixing metaphors now, but the truth is, so did Freud over the years of his theoretical efforts.

This trapping or pocketing of libido during any given stage of psychosexual development is called *fixation*. Freud noted that the pathway to adulthood through the psychosexual stages is never without problems—today we might call these hang-ups—and it is such frustrations that lead to a psychical damming-up of libido.[167] Such fixations can take place at any point in psychosexual development, and even repeatedly so.[168] Figure 6 presents a schematization of libido as a "river" beginning its flow at the top *from birth* and continuing downward through the various psychosexual stages (which are

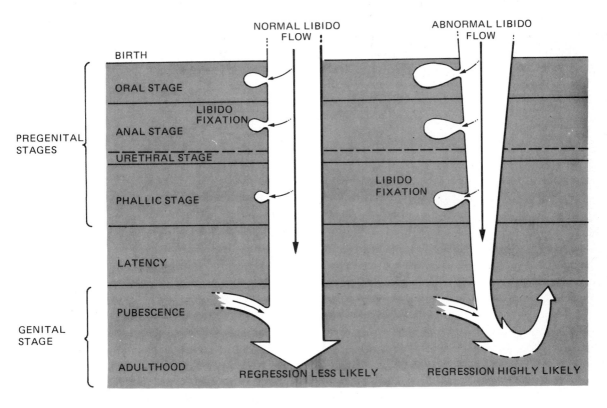

Figure 6   Fixation of Libido and Regression

listed on the left-hand side of the figure and further divided into pregenital and genital levels). Note that, as the river flows down through these stages, it has three pockets of libido running off to one side, as when a river forms small ponds or larger lakes as tributaries when it flows along the land. (To enrich the metaphor, try to think of this river as flowing down a sloping mountain.) These pockets of libido can be thought of as having been dammed-up, brought about artificially by draining off libido from the mainstream and then trapping it with a dam. Each of these reserves of dammed-up libido is a *fixation*. We could also describe the fixation pockets as being due to primal repressions (see p. 60), and by going back even further to Breuer, we could call them

pockets of *strangulated affect* (see p. 42). There is a common thread running through all of these models.

Why does fixation take place? Here is where Freud has been severely criticized, because he has used almost any reason possible to account for this adjustment mechanism. We see a remnant of the medical model in the fact that Freud said certain hereditary or constitutional factors might make it more likely for a person to fixate in development than another.[169] Sometimes a fixation occurs because the child is so pleased with one level that he or she becomes frustrated when it comes time to move on to the next level.[170]

A baby receiving considerable oral gratification in sensual sucking does not want to move on to the demands of the anal stage when toilet-training comes on, and therefore fixates libido (builds a dam mentally!) at the oral stage. A fuero is framed that says essentially "But I don't want to leave this nice life. Let me be. Come back and let me focus on my sucking pleasures." The request to "come back" is being made to the total personality structure, so that even in adulthood a person fixated orally has this unconscious desire to *act out* oral needs. It is unconscious because, of course, it would be the id pressing for continued orality, and the ego-superego would have in the meantime countercathected (or anticathected) the id's cathexis of mother's breast leading to the fixation.

The most common reason for fixating is probably thought to be some continuing *dissatisfaction* while living through a given psychosexual level. Instead of being orally gratified, what if a baby had been continually frustrated by a mother who did not allow sufficient sucking? Then, rather than being frustrated at the point of having to move on to the anal stage (leaving a "good" period of life), the baby would be miserably frustrated throughout the oral period itself (living a "bad" period of life).[171] This would doubtlessly result in even *more* libido being fixated than in the first case, resulting in a more severe fixation.[172] The fuero-claims might be even more dramatically put, as follows: "I was cheated. You must come back and help me get restitution. I demand fair play. This was a terrible time for me and I have many claims needing settling." Like anyone who is dealt an unfair blow in life, particularly if it seems arbitrary and unnecessary, the fixated portions of the personality seek retribution and restitution. Mother must be made to pay! Things cannot be simply swept under the rug and forgotten. We can see now more clearly how the repetition compulsion works. Fixation is a part of it, calling the personality back to repeat something that happened in the past or that did not happen but should have happened.[173] Things need correcting, or at least, evening up (eye for an eye!).

There are three pockets of fixated libido in Figure 6, because it is possible to have—and in most cases we all do have—more than one fixation point in the same personality. Usually, there is a major fixation (it is the oral stage in Figure 6), which lends coloring via fuero-claims to the personality, and then others provide secondary hues. Note also that Figure 6 has two rivers of libido, one labeled *normal* and the other *abnormal*. The obvious difference is that in the case of an abnormal sequence of fixations there is considerably *more* libido being fixated along the way (Freud's quantitative emphasis). This heavy concentration of nonflowing libido results in a narrowing of the abnormal river. Since this means that the personality structure (id, ego, superego) has less and less active libido to use in current behavior, the abnormal personality is doomed to break down at some point. All of the abnormal's mental energy is being shunted off to keep something that happened a long time ago enlivened at the unconscious level. Like an animal with inadequate food supplies or a machine without fuel, the person destined to be abnormal staggers and sputters along in life with a weak defensive system, a weak ego, and a lot of personal pressure from the internal fueros, which like bills of credit need to be met someday.

Note also in Figure 6 that we have placed a large tributary coming into the main course of libido, as when a smaller river joins a larger one. This occurs at pubescence and is the second step of the diphasic sexual development in humans (see p. 69). As we may recall, there is a quantitative increase of libido at this time. Since the Oedipal conflict is stimulated by this increase, the abnormal libidinal development of Figure 6 is in great danger of suffering a breakdown of some sort, because all of its troubles will be greatly multiplied simply because of the greater quantities of libido that must be dealt with. The normal libidinal development can absorb the influx of libido at puberty without much strain, although the adolescent behavioral patterns we discussed above are brought on by this elevation in level of mental energy. There are two rules of thumb we can cite concerning fixation: (1) virtually no one gets through development without *some* minor fixations taking place; and (2) the greater the amount of libido fixated and the earlier these serious fixations take place, the more abnormal is a person's later life adjustment going to be.

Are the fuero-claims ever answered? Does the personality system ever go back and try to recoup some of the libido that has been pocketed, working through the problems of that level in the process? Yes, the personality does indeed revert at times and, as if the river could turn back on its course, returns to the psychosexual levels where fixation occurred. This reversion of libido Freud called *regression*.[174] It happens when the maturing personality—possibly in adulthood —receives additional frustrations. For example, the orally fixated adult might be fired from a job or confront an unhappy love affair. At such frustrating points in life, said Freud, as when a "stream of water . . . meets with an obstacle in the river-bed,"[175] there is a reversion of the flow back into old channels.

When this happens, all of the fuero-complaints and claims may be enacted in behavior. The orally fixated man may go off on a drinking binge, which regressively create the oral preoccupation (taking in) of his major fixation point. A woman who cries easily and needs constant reassurance from her friends may be regressing to oral passive-dependencies on a regular basis. The slightest life challenge may send her into one of her crying spells. Though we have not referred to Death-Instinct fixations, the model represented in Figure 6 could work here as well. Because of its more aggressive features we could think of the anal level as relating to hostile regressions. The teen-aged "tough guy" who has a reputation for hotheadedness and is ready to fight at the drop of a hat may in fact be regressing in the face of social frustrations. Being easily intimidated and basically afraid of relating to people, this young man is essentially re-enacting the hostility he feels toward parents who frustrated him when he should have been learning the first lessons of social propriety (toilet-training demands); now, instead of feeling at ease socially, he is constantly on edge and ready to fight at the slightest provocation. His conscious reasons for fighting are foolish, but unconsciously there is a serious battle being waged, a fuero-claim is being settled, again and again, as he tries to get back at his parents (repetition compulsion).

Freud was fond of using as an analogy to mind the stratified levels of Rome, the "eternal city," which is constructed of layer upon layer, city ruin upon city ruin, open to all manner of archaeological excavation.[176] So too with the mind. No matter when something has taken place in the past, it is open to study today because "the primitive mind is, in the fullest meaning of the word, imperishable."[177] Freud used the term *topographical* for these spatial layers in mind (see p. 48), and he spoke of *topographical regression*

... the return of libido ... an adult returns com- ... psychical state and be- ... whole person, the case ... nporal regression. And if ... tive behavior styles re-place the ... ... ure styles that we should be using in the present, then this would be called *formal regression.* A psychotic person who literally becomes babylike in total behavior would be experiencing a temporal regression, whereas an occasional reversion to childishness by an otherwise mature adult would be formal regression.

Individual-Differences Constructs

Adult Character or Personality Styles

We have been considering the adjustment mechanisms of fixation and regression in terms of how they color the personality—or as Freud called it, the *character*—structure of a given person. Now we take an additional step in this direction to say that *all* personality styles are analyzable in terms of the particular fixation levels and mechanisms employed by people to deal with their past life experiences.[178] Hence, by *personality* Freud means the working out of conflicts among the id, superego, and ego,[179] involving the repressions, sublimations, and reaction-formations of instinctual pressures,[180] and the resultant compromises that can be worked out across the topographical levels of mind. Let us now review some typologies that Freud suggested might be observed among all peoples. Each of these discussions follows the pattern we referred to in the Introduction (see p. 23) of first being cited as a typology and then moving to a trait description (from

the "anal personality" to "anal tendencies in all people, more or less").

Oral Personality

Since the mood of the oral stage is predominantly *passive* and *receptive* (taking-in), it follows that an adult with major fixations at this level tends to be passive, dependent, and subservient in personality. This person is more likely to be a follower than a leader. Since the oral period is a fairly care-free time of life (toilet-training demands not yet placed on the child), the oral personality is prone to be optimistic, trusting, and accepting—even a little gullible. The smiling, congenial, easy going young person who is always open to influence from others is reflecting an oral-personality style. Since love is equated with the ingesting of food in the oral stage, these personality types tend to be heavy eaters—and often therefore overweight. Any oral personality might also enjoy other mouth-related activities, such as gum-chewing, drinking, smoking, or simply talking and laughing with others. The stereotype of the cheery, chubby fat person whom everybody loves stems from the oral behaviors it subsumes. Think of how the Santa Claus image would suffer with each pound of weight the jolly little fat man shed!

When things go wrong, the oral personality tends to feel blue, but is not too likely to become irritable or hostile. If we were to stress the cannibalistic potentials of this phase (eating mother's milk), an oral type might be called hostile or even sadistic,[181] but by and large the *main* suggestion of orality is passivity and acceptance of what the world has to offer. These individuals are more likely to be "lovers" than "haters." They also tend to identify with the people from whom they receive what are sometimes called *external supplies* of affection, attention, and respect. Show our congenial young man that you are interested in him and he begins to take an interest in your hobbies, dresses a bit like you, and seeks your advice on many of his life's problems.

Anal Personality

Freud named three characteristics of the anal personality, and we can see in each of these a persistence of a fuero-attitude associated with bowel training. Freud said anal personalities have the characteristics of *orderliness* (concern over having cleaned the anus following a bowel movement, not soiling one's underclothes), *parsimoniousness* (wanting to hoard money and other valuable items, just as the child once wanted autoerotically to hoard and cherish its own fecal matter), and *obstinacy* (negativism stemming from early conflicts with parents over whether or not to "go potty" when expected).[182] Recall also that the toilet situation is the first time our external world places definite requirements on us, intruding on our autoerotic satisfactions, and asking that we begin laying down the outline of a superego in our personality. Fecal matter is, in a manner of speaking, the first *gift* that the child has for the parent, something which he or she has created entirely through personal effort.[183] It is not unusual for children to "save" their fecal matter after "going potty" until everyone in the family has had a chance to observe and admire this personal "creation."

In fact, feces can become a kind of economic barter between parent and child. If mother loves baby, baby gives feces when coaxed to do so on the potty; if mother rejects baby, baby withholds feces in retribution. For this reason, Freud took fecal content in dreams as symbolizing something very valuable like money,[184] or in the case of females, as symbolizing a baby.[185] Misers are anal adults, for they want to retain money (derivative of feces). People who hoard just

about anything have traits of anality. The woman who expects her husband and children to live "only for her" is exhibiting an anal trait of hoarding affection and allegiance in interpersonal relations. The anal personality is not as loving or passive as the oral personality. Anality can be a helpful personality tendency for those professions that demand an orderly approach, such as lawyers who must track down every last detail in making their case presentations. But in a less positive vein, anality can lead to excessive efforts for perfection. Some highly religious people are overly guilty about everything they do, reading in sins where none exist because of their anal tendencies. The anal housekeeper gets on our nerves, as he or she constantly jumps up to straighten pictures we would never have noticed were crooked or picking up minute specks of lint from the furniture.

The anal personality is often asocial and selfish, but to that extent it is also self-sufficient; whereas the oral person, who is usually socially engaging and unselfish, can become a clinging, dependent individual. The anal person is thus more likely to emerge as a leader than the oral type. Of course, excessive anality can lead to a narrow, constricted view of life and a hostile suspiciousness of the other person's point of view, which we can identify in the Scrooge character in Dickens' *Christmas Carol*.

Urethral Personality

Freud noted that certain of his clients who had suffered the humiliation of enuresis as a child acquired a burning *ambition* to succeed in life.[186] Rather than fighting through life's annoyances in the head-on manner of the anal personality, urethral characters are likely secretly to envy the success of others and to look for quick successes of their own. If they cannot attain easy success on the first attempt, they find it difficult to try again.[187] Thus, urethral personalities have built their competitiveness on a strong underlying sense of inferiority ("You can't even keep from wetting your pants"). Though they strive to overcome personal doubt (react-formate), their bid to achieve something is usually unsuccessful because they crumble when the going gets rough or they are placed on the spot in having to perform as their manner suggested they could perform. Males of this personality type never really feel heterosexually potent.[188] The man who becomes sexually excited only when flirting with and fantasying the seduction of other men's wives is reflecting urethal competitiveness in these flirtations. Actually, he has protected himself because these are all women he cannot have anyway. Should one of the married women with whom he flirts respond and seek to carry the relationship forward, he would find some reason to break it off; or he might make the contact only to fail in some way as a sexual partner (impotence, crudeness, selfishness, and so on).

Phallic Personality

The Oedipal complex takes place during this stage and fixations at the phallic level therefore take on the dynamic characteristics of this most important of all triangles in the life of every person. If the Oedipal complex has not been satisfactorily resolved, the adult person *will* develop a neurosis (see p. 67). However, more restricted fixations and the female's rather subdued working through of the Oedipal result in distinctive personality styles that are not in themselves neurotic (see

discussion of male-female differences, pp. 67–69). We therefore expect to see a sexualized pattern in the phallic personality. This adult might be concerned with looking sexually attractive to the opposite sex. He or she may be very *self-centered* and egotistical. The "glamour-girl" stereotype fits here. Unlike the urethral character discussed above, the phallic character not only flirts but carries through on sexual liaisons with a vengeance. The "Don Juan" type of man, who presumably goes from one love affair to another seeking mother substitutes, is fixated at this level. For the phallic personality, heterosexual love is more colored by lust than affection (aim-inhibited lust). These people may masturbate when tense or upset.

Male phallic personalities are often driven by unconscious remnants of their castration anxiety. In some cases a male will reactformate and strive to be revolutionary rather than accepting the paternal superego (as heir to the Oedipal).[189] We may then find the person taking up the banners of social movements to overthrow the system currently in power. Often sexual promiscuity is a major feature of such antisocial acting-out, which can also take a criminal turn. Freudians are not surprised to learn that many famous criminals of history were sons of ministers or highly religious fathers. It would follow from Freudian theory that when the Oedipal does not "take," such male offspring would be more likely than other men to live totally at variance with the conventional superego values.

Another type of phallic personality is the female who never resolves her Oedipal by accepting that she lacks a penis. This attitude frames her fixation at the phallic level with what Freud called a *masculinity complex.* Such a maturing girl goes on acting like a boy, retaining her aggressive clitoral pleasure and renouncing the passive vaginal pleasures of femininity.[190] As an adult, she might be the career woman who seeks her place in a man's world. Such women are often called *castrating females,* because the suggestion is that they wish to take a man's penis for their own (show him up at the office, defeat him in a court case, and so forth). If the masculine identification is extreme, we might even witness a homosexual tie, so that a greatly masculinized woman might well find her sensual pleasure in playing husband to another female.[191] Here again, we find Freud's theory generating hostility among those women today who consider themselves feminists. Obviously, there are present-day women who wish to compete equally with men in professional careers who are not castrating or seeking a penis of their "own." Freud would not wish to apply his theory indiscriminately against all women who are part of the feminist social movement. Yet this does not invalidate his views for any one individual currently active in this movement. Obviously, only a clinical case history framed from the psychoanalytical perspective would settle the issue for any individual woman.

Another controversial area in which Freudian theory is being challenged today is that of *homosexuality.* As we noted above (p. 71), homosexual behavior was *not* considered a healthy alternative to normal heterosexual behavior in the Freudian outlook. Homosexuals are one type of phallic personality. Freud's psychological explanations of the origins of homosexuality varied over the years, and he was always careful to note that genetic or hereditary factors probably contributed to the likelihood of a person becoming a homosexual. His theory of female homosexuality is particularly unclear, but we might take a look at the most common homosexual theory Freud advanced.

Homosexuality begins in the phallic phase for the boy, even though his actual decision for a lasting homosexual adjustment is presumably not made until around the onset of pubescence.[192] In order to explain homosexuality in the male, Freud made use of the now-familiar theoretical device of reversion from object-choice to identification (see discussion on p. 66 and p. 69). The homosexual boy is one who has been very close to and presumably pampered, doted over, greatly protected by a maternal figure (mother or mother-substitute). Rather than taking this mother as object in the phallic stage, thereby initiating the Oedipal complex, the male invert reverts from object choice and *identifies* with his mother. He thereby not only becomes feminized in his outlook, but he also seeks to re-enact the mother-son love pattern that he had enjoyed, playing the mother's part himself and using other boys as *his* substitute.[193] As he moves into latency, therefore, his sexual instincts may be less aim-inhibited than those of normal boys. Other males are really projections of himself, and he seeks to cathect them with libido as stand-ins *for himself*—also a variation on the identification process. Homosexuality and narcissism are therefore related phenomena, because what the homosexual is seeking is a narcissistic self-love through loving himself in other males.[194]

This was an important theoretical point: although homosexual acts in earlier maturation are often a normal feature of sexual education, Freud questioned homosexuality as a satisfactory adjustment beyond the teen-age years because it was a more primitive, identification-based, narcissistic pattern of adult behavior than heterosexuality. Modern homosexuals may dispute this view, and in time the gay community may even alter the dynamics of homosexuality. But for the present we should merely be cognizant of the grounds for Freud's clinical judgments.

t, and

ies

...ality structure is finalized by ...ency—approximately age six years ˙ ˙ ˙ ˙ ˙ had no need to frame a latency or adolescent personality type. The important figures in our lives, our parents, brothers and sisters, and related family members who dealt with us in the formative years, now act as *imagoes* against which we will be measuring the behavior of everyone we meet throughout life. An *imago* is thus a kind of "person prototype" (original scheme), and Freud observed that all of the person's later friendship and love choices "follow upon the basis of the memory-traces left behind by these first prototypes." [196] We thus re-enact (repetition compulsion of instincts) our very earliest patterns throughout life.

Some psychoanalysts do speak about the *genital character organization,* but this too is one of those uncertain constructs in Freudian theory. All this means, really, is that the person is finally capable of reproduction and presumably can find in sexual relations the satisfactions that he or she had obtained earlier from the pregenital erogenous zones. Of course, not all humans pass through the earlier levels smoothly enough to find sexual relations gratifying. Many women in particular find sex degrading and "dirty" because of the contents of their superego instruction as children. Interestingly enough, Freud viewed the sexual organs as *animalistic*—that part of human physiognomy that had not altered in evolution from its original shape in the state of lower existence. [197] Even so, he felt that heterosexual intercourse was an important aspect of human self-realization. Freud simply could not see the value of celibacy, [198] and he looked upon the supposed love of mankind (altruism) that religious or socialistic political leaders often voiced as a convenient smokescreen for an underlying hatred of an outgroup. [199] He viewed altruistic love as *entirely* aim-inhibited, derived basically from genital lust but not really a natural solution to the instinctual prompting. Freud once said that he could not see universal love as man's highest form of behavior, and then he added dourly, "A love that does not discriminate seems to me to forfeit a part of its own value, by doing an injustice to its object; and secondly, not all men are worthy of love." [200]

Psychopathology and Psychotherapy

Theory of Illness

Antithetic Ideas and Counterwill

At about the time of his first publication with Breuer, and in fact, even before the Breuer-Freud "Preliminary Communication" on hysteria (1893) made its appearance, Freud put out a small paper under his name alone, entitled "A Case of Successful Treatment by Hypnotism." [201] In what seems to be his first attempt at explaining how a hysterical symptom like Anna O.'s right arm might arise, Freud made use of a psychological theory without employing mental energies at all. He began by noting that there are two kinds of ideas that have an emotion connected with them: (1) *intentions* to do something in the future that might be challenging or threatening, and (2) *expectations proper,* which are estimates of what might actually take place given the threat or challenge. It is the worry involved in our expectations proper that causes us to have strong emotions about the future. Can we really do what we intend to do?

Because of such personal uncertainties, we tend to frame what Freud called *distressing antithetic ideas* about our upcoming performance, whether we want to do so or not.[202] To quote Freud's example of a distressing antithetic idea, "I shall not succeed in carrying out my intention because this or that is too difficult for me and I am unfit to do it; I know, too, that certain other people have also failed in a similar situation."[203] We all have such antithetic ideas as we undertake life's challenges. We are about to be interviewed for a job that we very much want yet deep down are certain we will not get because others are more capable. Highly competent people have such doubts, but as long as they are normal they can keep them suppressed thanks to the "self-confidence of health."[204] Unfortunately, the neurotic person has lost this confidence and begins to give in to the influence of his or her distressing antithetic ideas. It is almost as if a *counterwill* within the personality were taking over and forcing the person to do the opposite of what his or her original intention was framed to accomplish.[205]

Freud gave as an example the case history of a woman (Frau Emmy von N.) who uncontrollably made a clacking sound with her tongue and lips (hysterical tic). He traced the origin of this symptom to a time when, exhausted with worry and fatigue while nursing her sick child, the woman had told herself that she must not make any noise lest she disturb the sleep into which the child had fallen. But in her exhausted state the antithetic idea that she *would* make a noise took the upper hand and in spite of her attempts to suppress it, she began to clack her tongue. In time, the symptom generalized, so that to her extreme embarrassment she began clacking her tongue at inopportune times in the company of others. Freud said that the symptom had thus become fixated in her behavior for many

years.[206] Charcot's famous student Pierre Janet had used a concept of the *fixed idea,* which is obviously similar to Freud's construct of the antithetic idea. Janet's theory was primarily biological, akin to Breuer's hypnoid state theory (see p. 43). Thus, Janet suggested that probably because of some as yet undiscovered physiological mechanism, certain people *dissociate* or split off an idea from the rest of their mind's contents, and this fixed idea then operates on its own without any possibility of influence from the rest of mind.[207] A woman gets the idea that she is going blind. As this idea dissociates from the rest of her common sense understanding, she gradually *does* go blind, even though there is no biological reason for her illness (hysterical blindness); it is the fixed idea alone that causes the illness. Freud may well have been influenced by the French during his studies in Paris, but his concept added the important psychological explanation of how such ideas arise—namely, as *antitheses to intentions*. Freud would therefore be drawn to the question: "What did this woman intend to see in the first place? Was it something she considered improper, antisocial, or disgusting?"

We all have such unacceptable promptings from time to time which we consciously refrain from acting out, thanks to the healthy state of our ego control. Are these antithetic inclinations over a life span ever lost from the mind? Freud answered no, they are not, ". . . they are stored up and enjoy an unsuspected existence in a sort of shadow kingdom, till they emerge like bad spirits and take control of the body, which is as a rule under the orders of the predominant ego-consciousness."[208] We recognize the "shadow kingdom" of this quote as what Freud would someday call the unconscious mind. Thus, Freud continued, mass hysteria among the clergy in the Middle Ages seemed to be possessions by the Devil for monks and nuns would from time to time shout out blasphemies and erotic language that they had been successfully suppressing for years. The triggering mechanism seemed to be a form of mass hypnosis in which there was a release of the suppressed material allowing the counterwill to be expressed.

Coitus Interruptus and Childhood Molestation

Since antithetical ideas are *reverse intentions,* that is, intentions that we *do not* wish to carry out, they must bear some meaningful import in opposition to what we consider proper or acceptable behavior. They must be at odds with our conscious ego structures. Freud was fully aware of this conflict, and as we have seen, in time he was to find that invariably a sexual experience was somehow involved in the mental dynamic. Two of his earliest sexual theories of illness are of historical interest because they were really somewhat more physically based than we ordinarily expect from Freud. Freud was searching about for a straightforward physical explanation of the possible relationship between the sexualized memories his patients were recalling and the nature of the neurotic illness that had prompted them to seek treatment.

One of the complaints he often heard, especially from patients suffering an anxiety neurosis, was that they could not obtain gratification in sexual intercourse. A female patient could not achieve climax because she feared having children. A male patient became hysterically ill during a period when his wife was physically ill and sexual intercourse had to be suspended.[209] Freud referred to this sexual frustration as *coitus interruptus* (interrupted sexual intercourse), and he felt that possibly a kind of *sexual noxa* (a harmful physical substance) was physiologically generated in the body during the time when a pressing sexual need (he did not speak of instincts at this time) was not being gratified.[210] He did not always try to trace the psychic factors that might have led to an inability on the part of some people to copulate successfully. Just *any* interruption was taken as a potentially harmful event, and he thought of this process in fairly mechanical, automatic terms. Though he believed that coitus interruptus was invariably a factor in certain neuroses, he was cautious enough to suggest that possibly a predisposing hereditary factor was also involved (an obvious remnant of the medical model in Freud's theorizing at this point).[211]

The second biosexual theory that Freud entertained early in his career centered around the belief that neurotics had been molested or seduced into sexual activity before their physical apparatus had matured.[212] He had a series of patients who could recall an early childhood experience of having been either raped or at least sexually fondled by a parent, sibling, relative (uncle, aunt), or possibly, a household servant.[213] Accepting these memories as factual, Freud felt that the premature introduction to sexuality might well have acted like a precipitator of the maladjustment he was then observing in coitus interruptus. Here again, the weight of explanation was on what had happened to the individual in the past. It was just an unhappy accident that the neurotic was molested as a very young child, and his or her present disturbance was therefore in large measure independent of a directly *personal* involvement. Something bad had happened to the neurotic, who was not in any way at fault.

The corrected *infantile sexual theory* was a remarkable example of how to win by losing, and it fixed for all time Freud's commitment to what we have called his Promethean insight. He could make this turnabout because, as one sees in his speculations, he was giving a growing weight to the purely psychological role of fantasy (wish fulfillment) in behavior.[214] In his reformulation, the individual was no longer portrayed as an innocent bystander in life's sexual misfortunes. Freud now claimed that recollections of seduction scenes are not copies of a past reality but rather the memories of *fantasies* indulged in during what we now call the early phallic phase.[215] While masturbating at this stage, the child has fantasied the sexual rape or molestation, then has repressed the entire affair following the Oedipal resolution. The memory of a fantasy is subsequently recovered while the patient is in treatment and taken as fact. Sometimes this experience is indeed a factual recollection, but more often fantasy is confused with reality. The difference between fantasy and fact in the memory of patients is always difficult to distinguish,[216] but this confusion makes no difference because psychical reality is what counts in behavior and not what may or may not have *factually* happened outside of mind.[217] Thus, rather than rejecting his retrospective method of personality study because it had generated false memories, Freud now made a virtue of the error, and through the concepts of fantasy and wish fulfillment, took as *convincing evidence* of sexuality the fact that his patients "remembered" so many *untrue* instances of sexual aberration in their early lives.

Three-Stage Compromise Model of Mental Illness

Freud eventually settled on what we would like to call a *three-stage compromise model* of mental illness. His mature view of mental illness retained the kernel ideas of both

coitus interruptus and the seduction-to-fantasy theory, added them to the original antithetic-idea theory, and then proposed a *deflection* concept which could account for how abnormal symptoms might arise. The coitus-interruptus theory gradually evolved into what Freud called the *actual neuroses—* which were in turn then opposed to the *psychoneuroses proper.* The actual neuroses (neurasthenia, anxiety, and hypochondria) were presumed to be caused by a somatic (bodily) toxic factor, a *physical noxa* much like the one he had earlier attributed to frustrated copulation.[218] The psychoneuroses proper were those disorders (hysterias) that were due to purely psychological causes (via the compromise model). Since they were due to a physical toxic factor, Freud said the actual neuroses could not be treated by purely verbal psychoanalysis; the physician had to prescribe definite changes in sexual routine in order to cure them.[219] Thus, despite his distinction between a physical (constitutional or hereditary) and a psychological cause of neuroses, Freud was still explaining *all* abnormal behavior exclusively on the basis of sexual difficulties. The somatic (bodily) toxic substance was not a foreign blood protein of undetermined origin nor was it set loose by some unknown irregularity in the bodily structure. It was strictly a *sexual* function that led to the toxic substance being set loose, and we can see in this the earlier imprint of the coitus-interruptus theory.[220]

The major difference between the original seduction theory and the fantasy-recollection theory was that the abnormal person moved from the role of an innocent victim to that of a central and willing actor in a re-enactment of the Oedipal situation. Freud was emphatic in calling the Oedipal the nuclear complex of every neurosis.[221] *All neurotics have unresolved Oedipal complexes.* In their present abnormal states the neurotics are re-enacting family situations that have never been properly sublimated, anticathected, or otherwise resolved (repetition compulsion). Recall that Freud referred to the initial stage of repression as *primal* (see p. 60). Then later on, the individual is forced to keep repressed material down through a continuing repression proper (sometimes called *after-repression* by his students). Neurotics find it impossible to keep Oedipal and other content-memories out of consciousness without also making it known overtly in a symptom. We will now review this process, using the schematization in Figure 7 as a point of reference for the three-stage compromise model of mental illness.

Figure 7 retains the dualism of Freudian theory: the mind is schematized by the figures on the left and the body by those on the right In Figure 5 (p. 52), we confronted the theoretical problem of how to think about a bodily influence (instinct) on mind. Figure 7 represents the opposite problem, for now we want to picture how it is that a purely mental conflict can be reflected in a bodily symptom (like Anna O.'s arm).

Beginning at the top of Figure 7 and working downward, stage I takes place in the pregenital life period. A hostile idea might have occurred to a little boy concerning his father ("I will kill him") during the phallic psychosexual stage, along with an Oedipal idea concerning the mother as sexual object ("I want to steal her for my sexual pleasure alone"). We see here the Oedipal re-enactment of society's origins (see p. 67). In trying to resolve the Oedipal conflict and also reduce the castration anxiety it generates, the little boy represses such id (Life- and Death-Instinct) wishes by using energy (libido plus "lobodo") from the ego and whatever superego is formed by now as anti-

cathexes. In Figure 7 we have symbolized this repressive process by inserting two steps under stage I: step A (black arrow) would be the id wishes (kill, steal, sex) and step B (white arrow) would be the countering defensive wishes (avoid castration, conform) of the ego-superego tandem. Two sets of mental intentions are opposed, checkmating one another for the time being. We have symbolized this clash in the meeting of the black and white arrows of stage I, which confront each other in an unconscious region, probably at the primary censorship point of Figure 3 (see p. 45). Stage I thus resolves itself into a *primal* repression, and if things have not been worked out smoothly at this period of life (unresolved Oedipal), there would of course have been a fixation developing during this phallic psychosexual stage (earlier fixations may also have occurred; see p. 71).

Let us assume that the boy we have been considering does not satisfactorily resolve his Oedipal complex. Trouble would develop for him at the close of latency, brought on by the quantitative increase of libido following pubescence (diphasic theory of sexual maturation).[222] This is schematized as stage II in Figure 7. Note that the inadequately repressed id promptings (kill, steal, sex) symbolized by the black arrow come dangerously close to entering consciousness. The anticathexes symbolized by the white arrow have been pushed back to the brink of awareness (point 8 or the "secondary censorship point" of Figure 3, p. 45). We have symbolized the danger here by the stressed appearance of the black and white arrows at stage II, as the cathexes and anticathexes strain against one another. The pubescent boy is about to know consciously what he already knows unconsciously—that he is at heart a rapacious murderer who would kill his father and sexually assault his mother! Freud referred to this dangerous circumstance as the *return of the repressed memories,* caused by

STEP A: Id Prompting (Wish)　　　　　STEP B: Ego Defends (Counterwish)

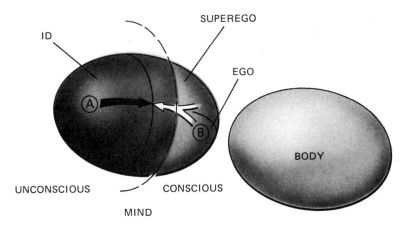

STAGE II: RETURN OF THE REPRESSED CONTENT FOLLOWING PUBESCENCE

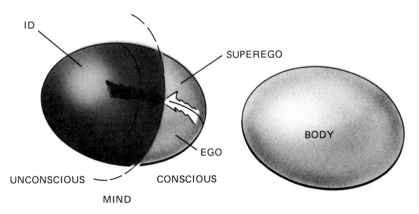

STAGE III: COMPROMISE DEFLECTION (CONVERSION) TO "SYMPTOMS"

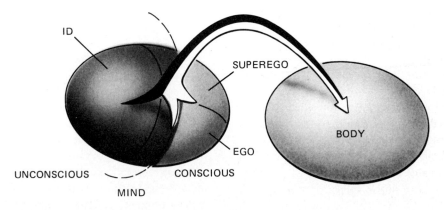

Figure 7 Freud's Three-Stage Compromise Model of Mental Illness

a breakdown in the defense system.[223] Desperate efforts are made at this point to keep up a repression proper, but without real success. Things have gone too far, and a more drastic maneuver is called for. The problem now facing the personality is how to "show" the mental conflict in a way that is not consciously understandable even though it is, in a sense, out in the open at last.

To accomplish this feat, said Freud, humans are able to substitute one form of overt expression (physical) for another (psychological), thereby deflecting the course of an intention by way of a compromise that satisfies all sides (id, ego, superego) in the conflict. The two wishes (black and white arrows) strike a bargain and find some mutually expressive way to make themselves known in a physical symptom of some sort. Stage III of Figure 7 symbolizes this compromise process. Note that the combined black and white arrows are deflected now as one interfused arrow pointing back into a bodily symptom of neurotic illness that always expresses the conflict overtly if we could but understand the subtleties. Thus, in addition to being compromises,[224] symptoms are always wish fulfillments.[225] The unconscious mind knows what symptoms mean, but even though they are observable, the conscious mind remains ignorant. In the case of our boy, we might find him developing a severe stammer, which immediately disgusts his father, an excellent public speaker, and brings out all of the maternal instincts of his mother. His id wishes which are fulfilled here are to frustrate the father (Death Instinct) and to get physically close to mother whenever possible (Eros). Mother smothers him with affection each time he has one of his stuttering episodes. Father storms out of the room in a rage. The ego wish would be

satisfied here thanks to the fact that no real murder or carnal display, much less a castration, takes place. And the superego's wish is also granted because the boy does, after all, suffer from a vocal disturbance. He has been punished for the illicit intentions that the id entertained!

Precisely how this deflection takes place cannot be stated, nor can we say exactly how the instinct turns mental energy free in the mind (see Figure 5). Freud called this stage-III process *conversion,* which he defined as "the translation of a purely psychical excitation into physical terms." [226] As our example demonstrates, neuroses are actually begun in childhood, but they do not show themselves until the second wave of libido comes on at pubescence or possibly after years of failing repression efforts.[227] Freud's definition of the neurotic symptom was as follows: "A symptom is a sign of, and a substitute for, an instinctual satisfaction which has remained in abeyance; it is a consequence of the process of repression." [228] The symptom is, in a very real sense, a communication to the environment of the person from the unconscious. It literally says something (expresses meaning) though the person is not consciously aware of what it is saying. Freud even referred to the *organ speech* of a hypochondriacal symptom.[229]

We might have considered our model in Figure 7 a four-stage model, since we have two "wish" steps in stage I; or we might have considered stage II identical to stage III because Freud virtually identified "return of the repressed" with "symptom formation." [230] However, the alignment chosen meshes best with our earlier presentations of the Breuer model and the diphasic theory of sexual development. Freud once speculated that this diphasic onset of sexual maturation in human beings—its onset in two waves with latency intervening—might perhaps be the biological determinant of our predisposition to neuroses.[231] It is interesting to note that Freud retained the core of his early antithetical-idea theory in this final model of symptom formation. In every neurotic disturbance he diagnosed, Freud considered the likelihood that there were dual wishes or intentions reflected in the single symptom of the disorder.[232] As he once expressed it, at least certain "illnesses . . . *are* the result of intention." [233] The intention is not to be sick, of course, but to let sickness express the antithetical intentions (wishes) that have been compromised and converted into the symptom picture. This is a far cry from his constancy-principle days. It represents a major break with the medical model. Sickness takes on intelligence; it expresses an intended meaning for all to know if we but understand the method of expression being employed.

Differential Diagnosis

There is a certain advantage to be gained from illness: the individual can usually expect to be cared for by others or at least to be worried about thanks to his or her *flight into illness.*[234] It is uncomfortable having a symptom, but this advantage has long been noted in medicine and is often called *secondary gain.* For example, a daughter who has just faced the introduction into her home of a baby brother may regress for a period of time into some uncertain "illness," taking the spotlight off her sibling for a while.[235] Freud once compared neurosis to a monastery, as a place of refuge where people can flee when they feel too weak to face life's frustrations.[236]

Freud has a quantitative as opposed to a qualitative view of mental illness. He did not draw a hard and fast line between normal and abnormal or between neurosis and psychosis within the abnormal disorders.[237] People fall ill from the same frustrations that normals bear up under.[238] How then does abnormality arise? Well, first of all we must recall that instinctual promptings cannot be avoided (p. 51). They exist within our psychosomatic identity, and unlike other stimuli in the environment, we cannot flee from the stimulations of the instincts.[239] Hence, if at some point early in life we fixate libido because of a frustration and then later as adults suffer a frustration and regress even as we are evolving a mental illness, the nature of the illness will be colored by (1) the initial stage of fixation, (2) the amount of libido fixated initially, and (3) the extent of libido regressed following the second frustration in adulthood.

Thus, as with differences in personality, we fall back on the fixation-regression model to understand differences in abnormal behavioral styles.[240] Someone who as an adult is behaviorally abnormal enough to be called psychotic (insane, crazy) would therefore have fixated a large amount of libido at one of the pregenital levels or a moderate amount very early in the oral stage (weakening the developing personality in the process; see p. 73). Neurotic fixations are not so libidinously profound nor do they occur so early in life as the psychotic fixations. Neurotic symptoms of *obsessive-compulsivity,* in which the patient is afraid to touch anything for fear of germs or must follow a rigid routine in life without variation, would be traced to anal fixations. *Hysterical* patients, who are very suggestible and easily swayed by others, would likely be fixated at the oral psychosexual level. *Psychosomatic* problems follow suit: *ulcers* are oral; *colitis* (constipation, diarrhea) are anal; and so on.

Just as Freud could find unlimited numbers of differences in personality based on the partial fixations and regressions of a lifestyle, so too could he find ways of distinguishing between clinical syndromes in the re-enactment of earlier fixations (see stage I of Figure 7) of the more severe variety. Since this fixation-depth-of-regression explanation is used to cover both normal and abnormal behavior, it is almost better to distinguish between normal, neurotic, and psychotic adjustments on the basis of how the individual handles reality than on the basis of how deep or extensive the regressions are. Everyone must confront frustration in life. We also all regress occasionally, and thus any of us might reveal in our regressive behavior the levels at which we have fixated (more or less) libido. But the difference between normal and abnormal regression centers around what the person is trying to accomplish in the process.

Freud believed that the *neurotic* does *not reject* reality or try to change reality as he or she understands it to be; the neurotic merely flees into illness through a regressive symptom-formation. The *psychotic,* on the other hand, *rejects* perceived reality in the regressive process and then seeks to reconstruct it in fantasy according to how he or she would prefer (wish) that it be. Thus, psychotics concoct *delusions* (unrealistically false beliefs) and *hallucinations* (seeing, hearing things that are not there), whereas neurotics retain a better contact with perceived reality. Freud then suggested that the *normal* personality combines the best, most constructive features of both clinical syndromes. "We call behaviour 'normal' or 'healthy,' if it combines certain features of both reactions— if it disavows the reality as little as does a neurosis, but if it then exerts itself, as does a psychosis, to effect an alteration of that reality." [241] In short, the normal person fights to keep in contact and to effect a constructive outcome, a change in the external state of things. Normals neither run away from a

challenge nor do they settle for a dream-world solution, even though they might regress and even act childlike from time to time.

Anxiety Theory

Freud experienced some major difficulties getting his theory of anxiety stated clearly over his long career. Problems arose when anxiety seemed for a time to be taking over the energizing role that Freud had assigned to libido (and, by implication, to the energy of the Death Instinct as well). It seems clear that Freud viewed anxiety as he did any emotion (see p. 46), that is, as a feeling-tone that takes place in the *physical* realm. Anxiety is something felt in the body. It is *not* something that runs the mind, particularly the unconscious mind! But for a long time, thanks to a way he had of referring to anxiety, it seemed as though Freud really meant for anxiety—a feeling rooted in the body—to be the main motivator of the personality. We want in the present section to review Freud's developing views on anxiety.

His first theory of anxiety was strictly physical in nature, based on a daring analogy between the similarities in bodily responses during an acute anxiety attack and those to be seen during sexual intercourse! Freud proposed this theory around 1894 as an off-shoot of his coitus interruptus theory (see p. 82). The construct of libido was not even being used at this time. He described anxiety as a physical-release mechanism, in which we use primarily the breathing apparatus of the body to rid ourselves of physical stimuli that cannot themselves be worked over mentally. By *working over mentally,* Freud meant something like the principle of neuronic inertia (see p. 53), in which a mounting energy dissipates itself by being carried throughout the mind (in the constancy-principle sense). For example, if because of her prudish attitudes a woman cannot gain full sexual release in copulation, then there will be a mounting sexual tension generated in her physical (bodily) apparatus. She will be experiencing *biological emotions* which she is *psychologically* unprepared to accept. Were she able to accept the meanings involved in sexual intercourse, then even if her climax (release) were not always attained, she could at least take some satisfaction in the foreplay and the mental understanding of what such displays from her lover signify in their relationship.

But she cannot mentally confront the meanings of sex, and since she also cannot gain release in the sexual act, there is no place for the rising sexual tension—the *emotion* of sex in her bodily apparatus—to go. In such a case, an anxiety neurosis is likely to show itself in this woman's behavior (fixation point would probably be the phallic, reflecting poor Oedipal-conflict resolution). As Freud put it, *"anxiety* has arisen by *transformation* out of accumulated sexual tension. . . ." [242] Thus, in her anxiety attack, this neurotic woman will show the clinical appearance of sexual intercourse—heavy breathing, shortness of breath, heart palpitation—because she is draining off her physical sexual tension through a common autonomic-nervous-system pathway in the body. [243]

An indirect release is therefore attained solely at a physical level without any intervention of the mind at all. Freud said very clearly that, whereas hysterics convert a psychical excitation (fellatio fantasy) into a physical symptom (cough or sore throat), anxiety neurotics convert one physical excitation (sexual tension) into another physical manifestation (anxiety attack). [244] Of course, we are referring now to the case of anxiety in an *actual* neurosis. In the case of *anxiety hysteria* (psychoneurosis proper), the individual transforms a psychical excitation (libido) into physical manifestations (symp-

toms) along the lines of the compromise model in Figure 7.

It was this latter use of anxiety that Freud turned to. He dropped the solely physical interpretation of anxiety after about three years and then for about thirty years referred to anxiety simply as *transformed libido.* [245] This usage follows the conversion model of Figure 7. A person represses libidinal cathexes made by the id via anticathexes put up by the ego and superego, and then in time this combined libido is transformed (converted) into an anxiety dream [246] or a symptom of neurosis (stage III of Figure 7). [247] This second theory of anxiety presented a few theoretical problems, which Freud had eventually to deal with. First of all, it was difficult to explain the type of traumatic neurosis (sometimes called *shell shock*) that developed in many soldiers following World War I as being due supposedly to transformed libido. [248] Such men often had repetitive nightmares regarding the battlefield from which they awakened in a state of absolute panic. The construct of repetition compulsion (see p. 58), as a need to repeat a traumatic situation out of the past as part of the striving to master it seemed a more accurate description of what took place in these war neuroses than did an explanation based on libidinal factors alone.

Secondly, and more importantly, a theoretical conflict arose because of the tendency to substitute anxiety for libido in explanations of behavior. Freud had a number of students —Otto Rank was the foremost example (see p. 574)—who seemed too ready to consider anxiety the prime motivator of the personality. This would mean that Freud's Promethean insight (sexuality is what moves personality) would be theoretically engulfed by a desexualized account. It is vital to appreciate that in the Freudian view, the abnormal person (as well as the normal person) does *not* behave symptomatically in order to avoid anxiety. Indeed, as we have seen, anxiety is often itself a symptom of "something else" in the personality. Abnormal behavior is defensive and regressive because it is seeking to avoid confronting the repressed mental content, which in turn is moved about in the psyche (mind) by libido (mental energy) as well as by the energy of the Death Instinct. Anxiety is a physical emotion, "felt" mentally as all sensations including sight and hearing are experienced mentally. But anxiety no more runs the personality than vision or hearing.

In order to clear up such problems, in 1925, some thirty-odd years after proposing his first (entirely physical) theory of anxiety to Fliess in their exchange, Freud settled on a more general definition of *anxiety* as simply "a reaction to a situation of danger." [249] Anxiety symptoms occurring at stage III of Figure 7 are therefore seen as *substitutes,* as the means whereby the individual can avoid facing up to the return of the repressed. Rather than being a major motivator, anxiety is merely an *instrumentality* or a *signal* of the real danger that is yet to come. As Freud said: ". . . the ego subjects itself to anxiety as a sort of inoculation, submitting to a slight attack of the illness in order to escape its full strength. It vividly imagines the danger-situation, as it were, with the unmistakable purpose of restricting that distressing experience to a mere indication, a signal." [250] In speaking of the ego subjecting itself to anxiety, Freud meant that the unconscious portion of the ego, which knows what the "danger-situation" is, submits itself including its *conscious* portion to anxiety, thereby offsetting a complete confrontation or "facing-

up-to" of the Oedipal themes that are bringing on the danger.

Freud now specifically removed anxiety from being *only* transformed libido. [251] Literally any situation of danger—real or imagined—could generate anxiety. Since the id is unable to evaluate situations, it does not even "feel" this emotion. In fact, neither does the superego "feel" anxiety, which is why it can wish for such harsh self-punishments as people inflict on themselves—as when someone cuts off a finger or a hand to "pay for" the past sins committed by this appendage (the realization of a superego wish in overt behavior!). Only the ego is said to produce and feel anxiety that is based on id and superego promptings, but is done in order to self-deceive and avoid doing what the id and superego want done directly. [252] In fact, Freud's final types of anxiety paralleled what he had earlier called the "three tyrannical masters" of the ego, namely "the external world, the super-ego, and the id." [253] Each of these sources of influence has its own intentions (wishes) that it would like the ego as personality executive (arbitrator, decision maker, identity in the middle) to do, to be, to act out overtly. The pressured ego is thus in a constant state of diplomatic relations, trying to see that all sides get some form of satisfaction in the transactions and negotiations.

In his final theory, Freud spoke of three forms of anxiety paralleling the harsh masters of the ego, [254] but he also emphasized their basic similarity in signaling the ego of an impending situation of danger. [255] Freud did not always draw a hard and fast distinction between anxiety and fear. The convention today is to suggest that we are anxious when the worry we have is uncertain or unclear, but we are fearful when the point of our worry is clear. We are anxious about going to the dentist because we may have a cavity or we may not, but once the diagnosis is made and the dentist prepares to drill our infected tooth, we become fearful. Freud's first form of anxiety probably always touches on the emotion of fear at some point. He called this *realistic* anxiety, because it points to a factual challenge in the external world (the first of the three harsh masters). Realistic anxiety is experienced by a young man who knows that he is to go into battle tomorrow; he is safe for the night, but what of tomorrow? It is this kind of fear that many of the traumatic neurotics (shell-shocked) have, for any of a number of reasons, failed to master. Freud said that the very first (prototypical) form of this anxiety occurs at birth, which is the first traumatic situation we all face.[256] Simply growing up and taking leave of one's parents can also be seen as involving realistic anxieties in living.[257]

The second form of anxiety relates to the compromise model (Figure 7) and was termed *neurotic* anxiety. If a person has an inadequately resolved Oedipal complex, then the id-wishes that have not been properly repressed by the ego (and superego) continually threaten to return to consciousness following puberty (stage II of Figure 7).[258] The thought, "I wish mother were dead," might come dangerously close to conscious awareness in the teen-aged girl, who might at this point use the defense of anxiety by developing fainting spells (stage III of Figure 7). She is now completely preoccupied with anxiety over her fainting (conversion) and no longer in danger of confronting the true mental state. Note that it would be incorrect to say that this girl's behavior is "motivated by anxiety." The girl is no more determined by anxiety than we would be determined by anxiety (or fear) as we stood on a railroad track with a freight train bearing down on us, roaring and whistling our imminent destruction. We would surely be anxious in this realistic situation. But why exactly would

we jump off the track bed? Would we jump because we wanted to remove the signs of anxiety, the heart palpitation, rapid breath, and knotting up of our stomach? If we could take a pill that instantly removed these uncomfortable symptoms, would we go on standing on the tracks and watch, knowing that in a second or two the train would most surely crunch our bodies into a lifeless pulp of flesh and bone?

Obviously, though the warning sign of anxiety is uncomfortable, what is *really* motivating our behavior—as well as the instrumentality of anxiety—is the *knowledge* that the train is there, and closing and we are here, in its path and unmoving. In like fashion, the girl with the fainting spells has an unacceptable weight of knowledge bearing down on her. She knows what this is unconsciously (the unconscious portion of her ego knows!). She does *not* want to be "hit" with this unacceptable wish for her mother's death bearing down on consciousness (stage II of Figure 7). Hence, the anxiety and the fainting are her means of "jumping off the track" without really knowing consciously why she is doing so. But these are merely the *symptoms* of her problem and as such do not cause her behavior to take place. What causes her behavior is a totally unacceptable picture of herself as harboring an unconscious wish she cannot accept into consciousness; there is possibly an additional concern lest she actually do something to bring about her mother's death. Behavior is caused by all these *meanings*, by the psychological circumstance of her existence, and *not* by the biological complex of her feelings.

Freud termed the final type of anxiety *moral*, tying it to the superego of the personality. Recall that in Freudian terms, the superego is formed out of fear (see p. 68).

In the father's castration threat to the son, there is a form of anxiety that serves as the initial pattern (prototype) of the conscience the boy later forms. Freud said that castration anxiety develops into moral or *social anxiety*.[259] Hence, all of the moralistic teachings that are introjected by the child in framing the superego (the heir of the Oedipal complex!) can later serve as grounds for calling down the ego as acting sinfully.[260] This is actually what we mean by *guilt;* as Freud put it, ". . . the sense of guilt is at bottom nothing else but a topographical variety of anxiety; in its later phases it coincides completely with *fear of the super-ego*."[261] Note here again that it is the poor ego that is always made to feel anxiety, or its derivative, guilt. The id and superego are often extreme in their demands because they do not have to suffer these biologically based feelings. There is another truism of Freudian psychology to be noted here. Quite often Freud found the cause of a neurotic symptom in the too-harsh, too-demanding superego, which serves as the handmaiden of cultural taboos and prohibitions. This takes us to the final topic of this section.

Culture as a Prime Agent of Abnormality

Freud's theory of society and the ways in which we become socialized through anxiety made him inevitably base the major cause of mental illness on the demands of civilization.[262] Culture advances thanks to the sublimations of sexual impulse, but people are forced by this same culture to keep their animalistic behaviors relating to hostility and lust in check.[263] Freud once said that he could not form a very high opinion of the way in which society attempts to regulate the problems of sexual life.[264] In most instances, he felt that the individual's superego is overly severe and does not appreciate the strength of the id promptings that the ego has to bear up under; more generally, the *cultural superego* (common beliefs, norms, and values of the group) is too rigid and unrealistic, issuing commands people find impossible to obey.[265] Thus, society, civilization, culture, and religion *all* melt into one at this point, constricting people by imposing unattainable standards on them. Freud's attitude toward the Golden Rule is interesting in this regard: " 'Love thy neighbour as thyself' is the strongest defence against human aggressiveness and an excellent example of the unpsychological proceedings of the cultural super-ego. The commandment is impossible to fulfill; such an enormous inflation of love can only lower its value, not get rid of the difficulty."[266]

The reason the superego can become so cruel and literally wish to destroy the ego is, that as the individual checks his or her outwardly directed hostility, the ego ideal becomes ever more *severe*. There is a continually higher standard set. Freud noted that even ordinary morality has a rather harshly restraining, cruelly prohibiting quality about it in the thou-shalt-nots of formalized religion. Hence, to the extent that we *do not* express our basic human natures (including hostility and lust), our ego ideals must be elevated and made more demanding, seeking a higher and higher standard by which to live in almost a snowballing manner.[267] And the higher these standards the less likely we are to achieve them, which in turn means that the superego (ego ideal) has a greater sense of the disparity between where behavior ought to be and where it actually is. This disparity generates hostility for the ego because it is, after all, the executive of the personality. Freud's analysis of President

Woodrow Wilson's character, including his eventual depression and nervous breakdown, was based in large measure on such an elevated superego, with the attendant tie to the father as a representative of—and, in fact identifiable with—God, who is now carried within as ego ideal.[268]

It follows, therefore, that Freud would favor a relaxation of the strict rules of religion and other social taboos. Not that he was in any way an advocate of sexual licentiousness and unrestrained hostility. His own life was a model of mature conformity to the niceties of polite society. Psychoanalysis as a world view is anything but a philosophy of revelry and instinctual release, which in most instances would be viewed as abnormally narcissistic and regressive in tone.[269] But Freud did argue for more insight into the nature of mental illness as a preventive measure, so that child-rearing practices might be better gauged to human nature as we honestly find it and not according to unrealistic overidealizations that foredoom the person to feelings of worthlessness and sinfulness.

Theory of Cure

The Role of Insight

If we believe that a neurotic is suffering from certain meanings buried (repressed) deep in the unconscious, then our tactic of cure should be to provide the person with an understanding of these hidden meanings (which *are* known to the unconscious, of course). Thus Freud's first theory of cure after his separation from Breuer stressed what has come to be called the *insight* of the client. As Freud then phrased it: "The principal point is that I should guess the secret and tell it to the patient straight out; and he is then as a rule obliged to abandon his rejection of it."[270] The general steps in providing client insight include (1) determining which decision for the flight into illness was made and why; (2) assuring the patient that a different pathway in life is possible and worthwhile; and (3) stressing all the changes of a positive nature that have taken place in the patient's life since his or her act of primal repression.[271]

Freud viewed insight therapy as something different from traditional medical therapies. A physical therapy that could remove symptoms of illness through the use of chemical agents (pills, drugs), he termed a *causal therapy* (meaning, of course, material and efficient causes were being used; see Introduction, pp. 4, 7).[272] Freud did not claim that psychoanalysis was a causal therapy. There are no chemical agents to give the patient in psychoanalysis, and so Freud said that he worked at symptom-removal from a more distant point of origin.[273] Even if a chemical were someday discovered that could alter levels of libido and therefore make a truly causal therapy possible, Freud believed that psychoanalysis would have already clarified how it was that the libido became abnormally distributed (fixated, cathected, and so on) in the first place. A physical or causal therapy would *not* therefore invalidate his theory of illness.

Fundamental Rule of Psychoanalysis, and Free Association

To facilitate insight, Freud asked his clients to be as free and open in their dealings with him as was humanly possible. He was, of course, trying to relax the level of client censorship, loosening the grip of the anti-cathexes. One day, a female client criticized him for talking too much during the hour, asking questions of her, and so Freud simply sat back in his chair and let her speak. He found that he could gain as much insight into her condition by letting her do all of the talking during the hour as he could gain through questioning her directly. The main factor of importance was that she say everything that occurred to her, no matter how irrelevant or silly it might appear to her conscious judgment. Thus, open verbal expression and complete honesty are the hallmarks of the *fundamental rule* of psychoanalysis, and the procedure followed by the client is termed *free association*.[274]

The usual free-association procedure is to have the client report what comes to mind spontaneously, no matter how irrelevant or even foolish it may appear to common sense. A female client might say "I don't know, for some stupid reason the idea of 'face cream' just popped into my head. Now, I can see my jar of face cream when I close my eyes. What has that to do with my problems?" The analyst need not answer at this point, merely recording what is freely associated and waiting until the full picture begins falling into place. Gradually, the client will probably drift off into a recollection of past life events, trailing back to childhood times. If the client cannot get started during any one therapy session, the therapist may cue him or her by returning to material that has been mentioned earlier, or possibly by taking an image or an idea from a dream or fantasy (like the face cream) and asking the client to focus on this for a time to see what ideas or images occur next.

Although we refer to *free* association, the fact that Freud believed he could in time come to guess or discern his client's repressed mental contents reflected his belief in *psychic determinism* (see discussion of determinism in Chapter 4, p. 262). Incidental ideas like "face cream" were not irrelevant or chance affairs to Freud. As he said, "I cherished a high opinion of the strictness with which mental processes are determined, and I found it impossible to believe that an idea produced by a patient while his attention was on the stretch could be an arbitrary one and unrelated to the idea we were in search of."[275] Freud said that he believed in chance only in the realm of external events; in the internal world of psychical events, he was an uncompromising determinist.[276] It is fundamental to the Freudian view that mental events press on to expression. The unconscious is said to have an "'upward drive' and desires nothing better than to press forward across its settled frontiers into the ego and so to consciousness" (see Figure 7).[277]

Resistance and Transference

From the first, when he was using hypnotism, Freud noted that neurotics disliked having to look into themselves.[278] They tried in countless ways to end or at least alter the course of therapy, in hopes of retaining the status quo in their lives. According to Freud's later theory of defense, any neurotic has two motives for beginning therapy—one to be cured and one to avoid being cured (discovered, uncovered).[279] He called these defensive efforts during therapy *resistance,* which in its broadest phrasing refers to "*whatever interrupts the progress of analytic work.*"[280] Literally anything the client does to disrupt or even detract from the validity of analysis is considered resistance, no matter how innocent it appears on the face of things. Asking for a change in the appointment hour is resistance. Telling the analyst a joke in which psychoanalysis is made to appear a hoax is resistance. In fact, even when the client miraculously loses his or her presenting symptoms after a brief period of analysis, this "sudden cure" is resistance.[281] There can be a "flight into health" in order to avoid confronting (resisting) the details of the Oedipal repressions.

Freud had some interesting things to say about regression in resistance. Sometimes, in reaction to the frustration of being analyzed by the therapist, the ego of a client regresses in hopes of recreating a life period that was more pleasant than the present.[282] The analyst can actually see the psychosexual level at which fixation occurred being reflected in the nature of this resistance.[283] For example, a man with an anal personality might begin going into extreme detail (pedantism) on each freely associated memory, stalling, through his obsessiveness, any chance the therapist has to pull things together into a coherent picture. The resultant confusion of details acts as a smokescreen. A woman with an oral personality might regress to a state of childlike dependency and "yes doctor" the therapist, letting insightful comments go over her head by agreeing to everything the analyst says without *really* letting the insights register and thereby have an impact on her personality.

Another way in which the client can resist is to change the nature of the relationship, from analyst-*analysand* (the latter is the person being analyzed) to one of father-son or father-daughter or two brothers or two lovers. Freud found that several of his female clients began relating to him in a most unprofessional and often amorous manner. They asked him questions about his personal life, they wanted to know what kinds of books he read, or what he did with his free time. If he gave in to any of these diversions by answering such questions, he found his therapeutic effectiveness declining. In one session a woman threw her arms around his neck in an erotic gesture, and as Freud later said, the "unexpected entrance of a servant relieved us from a painful discussion."[284] Freud did not attribute these love feelings

to his personal charm. He saw in these maneuvers the re-enactment of *earlier* paternal affections (Oedipal feelings for the father).

By projecting her lust from father to therapist, the patient achieved two results: (1) she could re-enact her past dynamic, thereby repeating attitudes and emotional displays from her fixation point (repetition compulsion),[285] and (2) she could establish the possibility that therapy would have to be ended like a broken love affair, because how can the analyst—a married man, with many other patients to treat daily—return such love?[286] Freud called this emotional involvement with the therapist *transference,* by which he meant ". . . transference of feelings on to the person of the doctor, since we do not believe that the situation in the treatment could justify the development of such feelings."[287] The female patient was *acting out* her repressed images and ideas, now coming to consciousness and diverted into sexual feelings for the therapist by way of a *father-imago.* An *imago* is someone we have known in the past (see p. 80), whose image we can press onto other people, turning someone in the present (therapist) into someone in the past (father). Considered in light of libido theory, transference always involves cathecting the therapist with mental energy (libido, but also Death-Instinct energies) that has been withdrawn from the imago and put onto the therapist as stand-in. The emotional feelings for the imago *then* follow as the client re-enacts the earlier dynamic (that is, libido is *not* feeling, but feelings are generated in the repeated dynamic just as Anna O. relived emotionally what was pathognomic in her memory under hypnosis).

Thus, through use of the imago the patient can "replace some earlier person by the person of the physician."[288] Re-enactments of this sort, in which present-day people are substituted for early people, go on all of the time in the neurotic's life as a result of the repetition compulsion.[289] A man or woman working as a machinist turns the supervisor into a father-or-mother-imago and begins to act very strangely toward this person. As we have already indicated in citing the variety of relationships that can be attempted, the imagoes being projected onto the therapist by the client need not be *only* those of the parents. Brother, sister, and literally any figure of importance out of the client's past can serve as an imago-projection.[290] The therapist often finds himself or herself a composite of *many* people (including both sexes!) over the course of psychoanalysis with a single client.

The feelings transferred onto the therapist are not always *positive* in tone, of course. In fact, Freud said that it was virtually impossible for a patient to remain in psychoanalysis and continue in a positive state of transference throughout.[291] This is due to the fact that the feelings (evaluations) generated by the dynamic interaction with imagoes are never one way, but are always *ambivalent* (from *ambi,* meaning "both," hence both positive and negative evaluations); inevitably the therapist sees both sides to the feelings being expressed concerning an imago-figure. In addition to this unrealistic factor, there is the course of therapy itself to consider. As the client reveals more of his or her unconscious conflicts in the ongoing analysis, there is sure to be a sense of threat generated by this *uncovering process.* This threat invariably brings on resistance, which shows up as what Freud called *negative transference.*

Precisely when the negative transference will emerge is hard to say. Freud believed he could sense it beginning when a client's free associations began to fail (called *blocks*), or there were no dreams to report; any prolonged period of silence in the therapy hour suggested the possibility of negative transference.[292] The analyst begins at this point to *interpret* the nature of these positive or negative transferences. To interpret is to "find hidden sense in something," [293] and in providing insight through analysis of the transference, the therapist is trying to *overcome the client's resistance.* This move on the therapist's part is all the more threatening, and hence it is not unusual for the client to go through some very difficult therapy sessions at this point in the series, suffering high levels of neurotic anxiety at the challenge of having to face up to the return of the repressed. The therapist is present to assist the client, but this does not make it much easier and the person of the therapist often becomes a scapegoat for irritation and hostility.

It is therefore no surprise that, as time went by, Freud began to think of overcoming resistance as the most difficult and yet crucial aspect of psychotherapy. He once defined psychoanalytic treatment as "a *re-education in overcoming internal resistances.*" [294] Clients can become quite hostile and abusive during this period of analysis. Freud summed up the hard work of analyzing resistance (negative transference) as follows:

Resistance, which finally brings work to a halt, is nothing other than the child's past character, his degenerate character. . . . I dig it out by my work, it struggles; and what was to begin with such an excellent, honest fellow, becomes low, untruthful or defiant, and a malingerer—till I tell him so and thus make it possible to overcome this character.[295]

Although it need not always proceed in step fashion—sometimes both sides of the ambivalence emerge in the early sessions—the usual course of transference is from a positive to a negative *stage*. Freud believed that successful therapy calls for a complete resolution of the transference phenomenon. The full implications of the transference onto the therapist must be made clear to the patient, who through insight gains an understanding of his or her dynamics. As Freud put it, "At the end of an analytic treatment the transference must itself be cleared away; and if success is then obtained or continues, it rests, not on suggestion, but on the achievement by its means of an overcoming of internal resistances, on the internal change that has been brought about in the patient." [296] Many ex-patients who leave their therapists during the stage of negative transference are highly critical of the procedure and give psychoanalysis an undeservedly bad name. [297] Even so, Freud did not favor avoiding such —what he took to be—necessities of the therapeutic procedure; he did not think it advisable to use the transference-love to manipulate clients and thereby allow the hostile repressions to escape examination. [298]

The therapist must also be careful about forming a *countertransference,* which involves the unconscious motives that the therapist might have acted out in relations with the client. [299] If the therapist has not developed adequate insight into his or her own personality dynamics, then very possibly there will be a reversal of the usual procedure, in which the therapist uses the client as a "blank screen" on which to project imagoes. This is why Freud believed that a psychoanalyst should first be analyzed before personally undertaking the role of therapist. [300] Indeed, as we shall see below, he even favored a kind of continuing, periodic psychoanalysis for therapists (as patients!) to keep them growing and in command of their mental and emotional faculties. A therapist who actually engages in sexual relations with a client would not only be doing something that is professionally unethical, he or she would literally be bringing the client into what are *personal* neurotic dynamics. Therapy ends when there is such a turn of events, and indeed, clients can be made worse.

Final Theory of Cure

Thus far we have been considering the general terminology that evolved in Freud's thinking about the nature of cure. His final formulation brought in libido as well (which we mentioned only in passing above) as fundamental to transference. The final theory of cure may be summarized in six points.

1. The neurotic is a person with significant primal repressions (Figure 6), including those surrounding the unresolved Oedipal complex. Due to the repetition compulsion, the neurotic seeks in interpersonal relations to re-enact these Oedipal themes, trying to find that sense of love that he or she never adequately repressed, substituted, or sublimated. Freud termed this seeking of love in relations with others a *libidinal anticipatory idea* (that is, looking forward in anticipation of recapturing the Oedipal cathexes by projecting the imago onto others). [301] This libidinal idea, which encompasses the fuero-demand (see p. 62), is in operation unconsciously and it might be something like "Won't you give me your love and sexual commitment?" or "Maybe now I can smooth things over and experience that love that was denied me earlier." These libidinal anticipatory ideas influence the neurotic's behavior in his or her everyday routine, bringing about those transferences onto others whom the person must deal with daily (see p. 95). It is this re-enactment with others that eventually drives the neurotic

into therapy, because all sorts of interpersonal problems arise as the acting-out process distorts normal social relations.[302]

2. In therapy this same acting-out process occurs in the transference of feelings onto the therapist. There are three aspects to transference, two of which are positive and one negative. First, a neurotic transfers affectionate, friendly feelings for the therapist *as a person*—a helper with the power and authority to cure a sickness or solve a problem. Second, there are the positive transferences of an erotic, sexually lustful nature that are actually aimed at the imago. Third, there are the negative transferences of a hostile, death-wishing variety that are also aimed at the imago rather than the person of the therapist. Freud candidly admitted that it is on the basis of the first factor in transference that the relationship between patient and doctor is built and out of which the therapist gains a certain power of suggestion to influence the neurotic to change. But it is the neurotic who must do the hard work of facing up to the repressed contents if therapy is to work. As Freud put it:

We readily admit that the results of psychoanalysis rest upon suggestion; by suggestion, however, we must understand . . . the influencing of a person by means of the transference phenomena which are possible in his case. We take care of the patient's final independence by employing suggestion in order to get him to accomplish a piece of psychical work which has as its necessary result a permanent improvement in his psychical situation.[303]

3. Neuroses stem from a personal dynamic, and it is only the neurotic who can directly confront his or her own unconscious and

try to end the lack of communication between the private realms of mind. Freud measured his success as a psychoanalyst according to the extent that he could remove amnesias dating from roughly the second to the fifth year of the client's life when the Oedipal complex was active.[304] Because it brings out the dynamics of such Oedipal fixations, Freud called transference the *"true vehicle of therapeutic influence."* [305] We must also keep in mind that transference has its resistance components to hinder therapy, and that such duality is common to neurotics who are generally ambivalent in behavior.[306] Recall that every neurotic symptom means *at least* two things (repressed wish plus repressing wish!).

4. As the neurotic client moves through psychoanalysis, he or she develops an *artificial* or *transformed neurosis* within the four walls of the consulting room.[307] This is a miniature replica of the neurotic dynamics then being acted out in everyday life. It is prompted by the repetition-compulsion nature of the instincts, so that the neurotic cannot help but reflect the Oedipal dynamics in the therapeutic relationship. Freud occasionally referred to this miniature reenactment as the *transference illness,*[308] a usage that has led to some confusion, because the artificial or transformed neurosis has since been called the *transference neurosis* by some of his followers. Actually, the latter phrase is better reserved for a distinction that Freud made between those mentally disturbed individuals who can profit from therapy and those who cannot.

5. Put in mental-energy terms, when we speak of positive or negative feelings being transferred to the therapist via imagoes, we are *also* saying that libidinal or hostile cathexes are taking place (Eros and/or the Death Instinct is active). This is another way of speaking about the li-

bidinal anticipatory idea. Recall that feelings are generated bodily, but the imago and fuero dynamics occur *exclusively* in the mental sphere. Shifting our emphasis to the energic type of Freudian explanation, we might say that psychoanalysis as a therapeutic method requires that the client be able *in fact* to cathect objects. If an individual cannot cathect objects, he or she will be unable to develop a transformed neurosis within the transference relationship; how then can we hope to provide such a client with insight? We cannot, really. We need the dynamic play staged by the acting-out in order to interpret for the client what is going on in his or her life.

Based on this capacity for cathexis to occur or not, Freud distinguished between those people who can profit from psychoanalysis and those who cannot. People, he said, suffer from two basic kinds of neuroses: (1) the *transference neuroses,* which include anxiety neurosis, hysteria, and obsessive-compulsive disorders; and (2) the *narcissistic neuroses,* which include the schizophrenias and the more serious affective disorders like manic-depression. Today we consider the latter disorders to be psychoses (insanity). The point Freud was making, however, is that any mental disorder taking on a narcissistic feature means that the individual has removed all libidinal cathexes from the external world and affixed them onto his or her own personality structure (taking self as object).

The woman who has regressed to the severe psychotic state of hebephrenia (a form of schizophrenia)—doing nothing all day but making faces and giggling a lot, sucking her thumb, and soiling herself without concern—is no longer in libidinal contact with the outer world. She has built her dream world in her narcissistic neurosis (psychosis) and now lives completely

within it as a baby, and no psychoanalyst can hope to break into her delusions as a significant part of her daily life.[309] The man who goes through life with all kinds of physical symptoms, expecting to be worried over and cared for by others, *does* experience libidinal anticipatory ideas, meaning he *does* cathect others in his transference neurosis, and therefore he *would* be a proper candidate for psychoanalysis. We could as therapists expect him to re-enact his dynamics in the transformed neurosis of the therapy hour. Using this fascinating replay of the Oedipal situation, said Freud, "we oblige him to transform his repetition into a memory" which is *insight.*[310]

6. In more precise libido terms, the patient in psychoanalysis comes gradually to remove libido from object cathexes in the environment and from the symptoms manifested in the body and to redirect this free libido onto the relationship with the therapist. This is why the therapist becomes so important to the client; he or she is now an object in which very much libido is invested. The therapist's tactic is to make this additional libido available to the conscious aspects of the client's ego and thereby to further a strengthening of the ego, thanks to its added quota of energy. How is this accomplished? By having the therapist support and encourage the client's ego to study its total personality. As the conscious portion of ego confronts the return of the repressed and finds it possible to live with what this all means, an increasing amount of the libido initially invested in the therapist returns to the control of the ego and strengthens it.

The therapist must watch out lest this reinvestment in the conscious ego becomes narcissistic. It may begin this way, but in time a client should begin extending his or her growing feeling of competence to interpersonal relations with others, building a realm of cathected objects including aim-inhibited contacts of a friendly nature. It is also important to prevent a client from forming additional repressions. When this happens the ego has to use libido to form anticathexes, and this simply wastes energies which could be better used in adapting to the external world. Gradually, the "ego is enlarged at the cost of this unconscious."[311] The man who had before shrunk from people and regressed to states of physical self-concern now begins to meet others, to entertain and be entertained by them. He finds a woman companion and begins to mature into love relationships which until this time had been impossible due to the unproductive use of libido in the past. Assuming that this man also has a good idea of the role of transference in his change of behavior, we would consider his case to have reached a successful therapeutic outcome.

Extent and Permanence of Cure

Experience with clients was in time to suggest that psychoanalysis was not a cure-all. In a paper entitled "Analysis Terminable and Interminable," written in 1937 a few years before his death, Freud made some rather limited claims for the effectiveness of psychoanalysis. He had found that only those instinctual conflicts that were *literally* being acted out in the transformed neurosis could be helped through providing insight of the dynamics involved.[312] If some *other* problem exists in the psyche but does not come alive in the therapy hour, then simply talking

about it in post hoc (after-the-fact) fashion will not result in a cure. Assume that a young man has authority problems in everyday life, projecting a father imago onto others. In therapy he acts out this problem with the therapist in the transformed neurosis. He at some point is literally alive with the hostility feelings he once had in relations with his father, projected now onto the therapist. The therapist waits for the right moment, and when these feelings are clearly active, makes an interpretation to the young man. The resultant insight works, even though there may still be a degree of resistance to work through. But now, a related problem in this case might be this young man's inability to compete with other men. The therapist might include this fear of competition in the broader interpretation of the young man's personality conflicts. But since the young man has not brought this conflict into the transformed neurosis—for example, by awkwardly trying to compete with the therapist in the use of language, only to abruptly switch and ridicule all those who use "big words"—no interpretation made by the therapist based on past life competitions with other men will work. In order to *really understand* this personality dynamic, the young man has to be feeling in a competitive mood "right now," when the therapist makes the interpretation.

This phenomenon has come to be known as the difference between intellectual and emotional understanding in psychotherapy. It shows up in all insight approaches, where the experienced therapist soon learns that intellectual insight is not enough. There has to be fundamental feeling involved in the client's understanding at the time insight is provided, or it will just not take hold. The fascinating thing about this is that it takes us back to the abreactive-cathartic method first used by Breuer and Freud (see p. 43). If we think of hypnotic time regression as going back to the pathognomic situation and being recalled at that point and now acted out (abreacted), then the emotional release (catharsis) signifies that a legitimate recollection is being made. This is not simply an intellectual memory. The emotional display could not be faked. This memory is the real thing! Anna O. could never have intellectually dreamed up the emotion-laden circumstance Breuer observed her reliving. In his closing years Freud claimed that in order for his therapy to work, there had to be a similar, genuine reliving of a past emotion in combination with an intellectual understanding (insight) putting this feeling into perspective. We are back where psychoanalysis started!

Freud believed a patient can never bring *all* of his or her past conflicts into the transference relationship as a transformed neurosis.[313] Nor can the therapist artificially stimulate them by using theatrical tricks, such as acting like a parent in order to bring out the client's death wishes for this parent.[314] Here again, fakery is less than useless to the curative process. The backbone of psychoanalysis remains truthfulness and genuineness. All the therapist can hope for is to end a psychoanalysis on the best terms possible. As Freud put it:

Our aim will not be to rub off every peculiarity of human character for the sake of a schematic "normality," nor yet to demand that the person who has been "thoroughly analysed" shall feel no passions and develop no internal conflicts. The business of the analysis is to secure the best possible psychological conditions for the functions of the ego; with that it has discharged its task.[315]

Because of this likelihood that certain conflicts have not been experienced emotionally in the transformed neurosis, Freud advocated periodic reanalyses for even practicing psy-

choanalysts. He felt that a practitioner should go back into analysis every five years or so, as a kind of continuing prophylactic against the menace of countertransference.[316] This is why psychoanalyses never seem to end. They *do* end for one problem, but then begin again (in a sense) to consider another problem.

Social Revision

Freud was a "proper" man, and in no sense a revolutionary. His hope for the future emphasized not sexual license, but a life based on the insights of science and the *rule of reason*.[317] We are not to give ourselves over to base emotions at every turn. In the final analysis, Freud's therapy is more *preventive* than anything else. If humankind is instructed by the insights of psychoanalysis—as a "student body" or a "patient" en masse—then just possibly it will no longer need to bring on those harmful repressions that it now bears up under. Oedipal conflicts need not be so severe, superegos need not be so rigid, human understanding and mutual acceptance based on something more honest and true than even brotherly love can be brought about in human relations. A gradual revision in the social structure is clearly implied in Freud's writings.[318] Sometimes, in removing repressions during analysis, a patient's life situation is actually made worse. The resulting frustration at having to give up a symptom picture that provided a secondary gain may lead to the patient acting out against the society. Even so, said Freud:

The unhappiness that our work of enlightenment may cause will after all only affect some individuals. The change-over to a more realistic and creditable attitude on the part of society will not be bought too dearly by these sacrifices. But above all, all the energies which are to-day consumed in the production of neurotic symptoms serving the purposes of a world of phantasy isolated from reality, will, even if they cannot at once be put to uses in life, help to strengthen the clamour for the changes in our civilization through which alone we can look for the well-being of future generations.[319]

This is the ultimate therapeutic message of Freudian psychoanalysis. Freud is not a doctor "in the proper sense"[320] of being a physician for the individual. He is the doctor of the body politic, and his cures through insight transcend the individual or even an individual generation of human beings.

Therapeutic Techniques

The relationship between therapist and client is commonly referred to as a *method* of therapy. Though we have occasionally employed this usage earlier in the chapter, at this point we will keep more strictly within our definition of *method* (see Introduction) as the vehicle for the exercise of evidence, and refrain from using *method* in the present section, which deals with therapeutic techniques. The evidential usage would be appropriate for Freud, because he believed that psychoanalysis is a scientific investigation in addition to a curative process. But not all of the therapists who practice psychoanalysis today agree, and many therapy orientations never propose to do the work of science within the four walls of the consulting room. We will refer to factors like the nature of the relationship and the various devices used to further

therapy as *techniques,* recognizing that this does not imply any commitment by the therapist to use of a manipulative approach in dealings with clients. Just as many styles of behavior are subsumed by the term *personality,* so too we can refer to various styles of relating to clients as *techniques.*

Evolution of the Relationship

Freud began his career like most neurologists of his day, using various physical remedies for the treatment of mental illness, including sedatives, rest, massage, hydrotherapy (for example, baths or stimulating showers), diet control, and change of routine. Freud's clients were predominantly of the upper socioeconomic classes,[321] and therefore he could send them off for a period of rest at a local resort spa. Of course, in extremely disturbed (psychotic) cases, he hospitalized the patient. Freud gradually defined a new doctor-patient relationship as he evolved the psychoanalytical technique.[322]

As we recall, Freud began his search for the pathognomic (repressed) memory through the technique of *hypnotic* age or time regression. The patient was asked to relax in a reclining or semireclining position on a sofa, and hypnosis was induced through the usual suggestions of drowsiness, falling off to sleep, and so forth. As he used this technique with more clients, Freud found that not all of them could be put under a sufficiently deep hypnotic state to bring about time regression. In fact, several could not be hypnotized at all. Freud recalled that Bernheim (one of the French doctors he had studied with) could get subjects to remember what had gone on during a previous hypnotic trance by taking their heads in his hands and essentially ordering them (strong suggestion) to do so. When one day a difficult patient was not responding to the hypnosis instructions, Freud took her head in his hands, asked her to concentrate, and while applying a slight pressure he confidently asserted that she *would* recall when her symptoms had begun. Sure enough, the patient remembered the pathognomic situation and obtained a certain cathartic release in reliving it.[323]

Freud called this the *pressure technique,* and he used it successfully for several years, feeling that it had definite advantages over hypnosis because the client was conscious of the thought processes as he or she made the mental search. The therapist did not have to retrace these steps later after the client came out of hypnosis, when the added problem now arose of trying to remember what went on in the hypnotic trance. Freud had surpassed Bernheim! Even so, the focus of psychoanalysis was still on symptom removal during this period of its development. It was only a matter of time until Freud noted a strange and annoying tendency in the client's efforts to recall the past while not under hypnosis. He found them recalling all manner of trivia, apparently unrelated scraps of information that had no bearing on their neurotic symptoms. He did not dismiss these apparent irrelevancies; instead, drawing on a theory of psychic determinism (see Chapter 4, p. 264), he considered them to be *screen memories* or *screen associations.*[324] These supposedly random memories were covering up a more deep-seated complex of memories clustering around the pathognomic situation. Freud began to question his clients about these screen memories, taking them even further back in time, until he hit upon the technique of free association. For a time, Freud used both the pressure technique and free association in combination, but by 1905 he had stopped touching the client entirely (a dangerous procedure, considering the matter of transferences). Thus today free association has emerged as the exclusive technique of the classic psychoanalyst (see p. 94 for a discussion of this technique).

View of Therapeutic Change

Freud was aware of the historic relationship psychoanalysis had with hypnosis, and by way of this tie, the possible criticism that he had cured people exclusively through suggestion. He defined *suggestion* as uncritically accepting an idea implanted in one's mind by another,[325] but he did *not* accept that this is what went on during psychoanalysis. He felt that the id promptings which lay at the root of a neurosis could not be so easily influenced, thanks to the counterweight influence of the superego and the compromise effected by the ego. The id, after all, is illogical and refuses to evaluate any of its anticipatory ideas realistically. The therapist can use a little suggestion because the client likes him or her as a person (see p. 98), but this kind of suggestion is directed to the ego and it might not help at all with the id! Freud loved to point out that anyone who works with clients in therapy soon learns that they do not swallow whole every idea the therapist offers them.[326]

He also critically observed that those who use the concept of suggestion never say what it *is*. According to Freud, suggestion is based on sexual forces in operation between two people. Its power in therapy results from the childlike dependency—the re-enactment of an infantile relationship—on the person of the therapist as a stand-in for others. To understand the nature of suggestion we must first understand the nature of transference. Thus Freud's goal in therapy was to provide a certain type of relationship and thereby to learn something of the client's past history. He was not out to prove some obscure theoretical point in each case, and he observed, ". . . the most successful cases are those in which one proceeds, as it were, without any purpose in view, allows oneself to be taken by surprise by any turn in them, and always meets them with an open mind, free from any presuppositions." [327] Freud said that he refused emphatically to make a patient into his private property, to force his own ideals on the patient "and with the pride of a Creator to form him in our own image." [328]

The point is: *a neurotic is not a free person*. He or she is locked into the past like a character in a play. The past forces the neurotic person to re-enact the unresolved Oedipal complex again and again. Thus, says Freud, "analysis sets the neurotic free from the chains of his sexuality." [329]

Client Prognosis and Trial Analyses

Freud once suggested (half jokingly) that the ideal client for psychoanalysis is a person suffering considerably from an inner conflict that he or she cannot solve alone. This person would therefore come to analysis literally begging for help.[330] Anything short of this ideal circumstance—which is probably never realized, we might add—detracts from the *prognosis* (likelihood of cure) in a given case. If a man is forced into analysis by relatives, this is *not* a good prognostic sign. If a woman is using psychoanalysis as a way of getting back at her husband through making him pay for large doctor bills, this is *not* a good prognostic sign. As we know from our discussion of the narcissistic neurosis (see p. 99), psychotic individuals are not good bets for psychoanalysis nor are the mentally retarded, the brain damaged, or the senile members of our society.

Children present a special difficulty, and in truth Freud was not much attracted to the role of child therapist. His famous case of Little Hans (Volume X) was based on the work of an intermediary therapist—the boy's

father—who saw Freud privately and then carried the sexual interpretations to his five-year-old son in a most open and straightforward manner. In general, Freud thought it was best for the parent and child to enter into therapy together. Children externalize their problems in their current parental relations and therefore it is not too helpful to search about in their internal psychic lives for solutions. The best bet is simply to try to improve the parent-child relationship in the ongoing present.[331]

When a therapist takes a patient, usually he or she is "buying a pig in a poke." [332] Freud favored a trial period of diagnostic assessment of from a few weeks to a few (or even several) months during which the therapist can make the decisions so important to prognosis, such as whether a relationship can be formed, whether we have here a narcissistic or a transference neurosis, and so on. This trial period is quite flexible, and when it is extended, the reputation of psychoanalysis suffers because these rejected clients are considered failures by critics who do not understand or accept the principle of a trial analysis. Freud admitted that psychoanalysis takes a long time, in some cases many years, but he could see no other way of curing neurosis short of the superficial, suggestive cures that relied on manipulation and the authority of positive transference to suppress a symptom.[333]

Interpretative Techniques in Dreams and Parapraxes

Freud once said that he based the entire science of psychoanalysis on the *foundation stone of dream interpretation*.[334] As totally mental phenomena, dreams express a meaning, they say something, and though we think we do not know what their content is getting at, in the unconscious regions of mind *we know full well*.[335] While asleep, all of those anticipatory libidinal ideas that we cannot consciously express because of their repression by the ego and superego—which combined might be thought of as the censoring agency of mind—are given expression. Of course, in order to get around the censorship, these ideas must be distorted in various ways so that their content is expressed through symbols which must be deciphered. Dreams have a *manifest* (apparent, evident) content or story line which often appears foreign and even odd to us because we do not understand the meaning. For example, we may dream that we are walking upside down on the ceiling and that our hair is falling out, but it drops upward to the ceiling instead of to the floor. Each of these dream concepts would be taken as a potential content for hidden meaning. Freud's technique involved translating this manifest content into what he called the *latent* (hidden, potential) content, which gets at the real meaning of the dream.[336] If we free-associate to our dream contents (ceiling, hair, upside down, and so on), what translations might occur to us or the therapist as several related meanings are associated? A stable translation, one that invariably means the same thing no matter who dreams it, Freud termed a *symbol*.[337] Thus, in general, elongated objects are taken to be masculine (penis symbols) and enclosed objects are likely to be more feminine (vaginal or uterine symbols). Humankind's use of symbols traces back to its most primitive thought forms, and they can be seen in the various myths and religions of antiquity.[338]

A dream is put together by the unconscious mind from *day residues,* which are the little bits and pieces of experience during the sleep day (day before night of dream) on which we have probably not fixed our conscious attention.[339] The dream is prompted by a wish fulfillment, of course, but we must keep in mind that this can be a lustful wish of the id, or it can be the self-punishing wish

of the superego. We must not make the error of assuming that by claiming every dream is a wish fulfillment Freud necessarily referred to a pleasurable outcome.[340] Freud relented on the idea that all dreams have to have a sexual content, but his wish fulfillment construct was retained to the end. This wish-fulfilling aspect of dreaming is achieved by way of what he called *dream work,* and its fundamental way of expression is through imagery. We do not dream in ideas (words, sentences), but in images, so that dreaming is like thinking in pictures. Freud once put it well when he observed that "a dream is a picture-puzzle."[341] Dreaming also bears a psychological tie to the process of hallucination in psychosis.[342] Recall that Freud spoke of a regression of excitation to the stimulus-end in Figure 3 (see p. 45). This process is fundamental to both dreaming and hallucinating. In fact, Freud was to say that "a dream . . . is a psychosis, with all the absurdities, delusions, and illusions of a psychosis." [343]

Since dreaming follows primary-process thought, Freud suggested that the rules of conventional logic are suspended when we dream. Thus, we can *condense* many concerns or even different people in our lives into a single dream image and often *displace* the resultant combination onto a seemingly unrelated activity.[344] For example, a young man, with doubts about his ability to succeed independently in life because he has been kept immature by a dominant but loving father who makes all the family's decisions, drives past an amusement park one afternoon. Snatching scenes from the park as day residue, the young man dreams that night that he is riding round and round on a carousel; instead of the usual horse, however, he is sitting on a bull which—free association later establishes—has the heavy torso of his father.

Though it is an amusement ride, the young man recalls clearly that he is *not* having a good time on the carousel. The dream is about important life issues and the feeling of domination by a parent (latent content), but the young man recalls only that he had a rather strange time at an amusement park (manifest content).

A more general case of this human ability to combine several factors into one dream content is *overdetermination*. Freud believed that many dream images are more pregnant with meaning than is minimally necessary to make them occur in the first place.[345] Many more wishes squeeze into the same dream image than are required to express this content in the dream. Hence, it follows that no *single* interpretation of the manifest content can capture all of the latent content that is actually being expressed.[346]

Dreams are actually the *guardians* of sleep, because if we could not express our unconscious mental concerns in some form, we would probably toss and turn all night long. If these concerns occasionally disturb our rest, we must appreciate that they are merely carrying out a noisy duty for a good end, "just as the night-watchman often cannot help making a little noise while he chases away the disturbers of the peace who seek to waken us with their noise."[347] Since dreams always deal with our more important mental concerns, the interpretation of dreams provides the analyst with a *"royal road to a knowledge of the unconscious activities of the mind."*[348] Freud gave the following rules of thumb for analyzing a dream:

1. Do not take the manifest content of a dream literally, because it never reflects the unconscious meaning intended.

2. Present various portions of the dream contents to the client as a prompt for free association, and do not worry about how far this line of investigation takes you from the original dream story.

3. Never lead or suggest things about the dream to the client; wait until several dreams and/or free associations to dream contents suggest the direction to be taken in making interpretations.[349]

Freud made many practical hints for dream interpretation over the years. The following are examples. Dreams produce logical connections by simultaneity in time, so that things happening together are probably seen by the dreamer as somehow related. When a cause-effect relationship is suggested, then the dream content is changed or distorted, as by a sudden shift in scene or the distortion of a face from one person into another's. If we dream that our parent's face changes into our spouse's, then it is likely that we see an influence stemming from the former to the latter. We cannot express *either/or* in a dream, but instead link such alternatives with an *and* so that opposites can be combined into single images or actions. Any time there is a condensation of dream figures, we must always suspect that the dreamer sees a similarity, identity, or possession of common attributes between the figures (father and bulls are *both* strong, if also a bit too demanding). A popular device used by the dreamer is *reversal,* or the turning into its opposite of some latent wish or image in the manifest content. For example, the business man or woman recalls dreaming that a competitor scored a major financial gain and wonders why he or she should be dreaming such an unhappy theme. All of these devices Freud referred to as the *means of representation* in dreams.[350]

In addition to the content of free associations and dreams, Freud found that he could gain insights into the motives of others through what he called *parapraxes,* or errors in behavior, "misactions" in which the person does something he or she is not intending to do. When a man intends to say to his wife "please sit down" and says instead "please fall down," he is actually substituting the opposite of his intention—in this case, hostility for affection.[351] Here again, the censoring agency is circumvented for a fleeting moment when our attention is caught off guard. The new bride writes a letter to her mother-in-law, beginning with "dead mother" instead of "dear mother," and the cat is out of the bag. Whether in spoken or written word, these are the notorious *Freudian slips* which tell us something of our unconscious wishes. The reason they are often humorous to uninvolved people observing us is that they know intuitively what our true feelings are.[352]

Some Procedural Details

Although such techniques have been altered considerably today by psychoanalysts, Freud had a patient lie on a sofa while he sat behind the head of the patient, out of direct sight.[353] This position reflected the influence of his earlier hypnotic and pressure techniques, but Freud believed, too, that it was wise to eliminate feedback to the client from his facial expressions. Also, he frankly admitted that he could not stand being stared at by other people for eight hours or more per day. He felt it advisable to tell the patient that therapy would take a long time—a year or more at the very least. His clients assumed a heavy burden in time commitment, for he met them several times a week—anywhere from two or three to five or six sessions weekly. As therapy wore on, the number of sessions might be reduced, depending on how well the client was progressing. Another important burden to the client was financial. Freud stressed that analysts must treat money

matters as frankly as they treat sensitive personal topics. Money can be a tool of resistance for the client, who can use this excuse to terminate the contacts—particularly because the practice followed by Freud (and since by his followers) was to charge for *every* scheduled session, including those that a client missed (except under highly unusual circumstances). The only recourse, Freud thought, is simply to state things clearly to the client at the outset and then to carry on without any further embarrassment. As Freud summed it up, in any case, "nothing in life is so expensive as illness—and stupidity."[354]

Freud saw his patients for the classic fifty-minute hour. He was not much attracted to taking notes during the hour, preferring to do this sort of record keeping between patient appointments and at the close of the day. In the very earliest—including the first—sessions, Freud would simply turn the lead in the conversation over to the client and say, "Before I can say anything to you I must know a great deal about you; please tell me what you know about yourself."[355] Many of these early sessions undoubtedly were spent in going over details of the illness that had prompted the client to seek assistance. Gradually, they would turn their attention to dreams and other materials emerging in the free associations. Freud would begin instructing the client in the basics of psychoanalysis, even as early as the fifth or sixth session,[356] but he was decidedly opposed to the patient's independent reading and studying of psychoanalysis from books.[357]

Freud advised his patients not to make important decisions during the course of treatment—such as choosing a profession or selecting a marital partner.[358] His reason was to limit the patient's chances of making important errors in life decisions through the acting-out of unconscious impulses during the transformed neurosis. This suggestion may appear inconsistent with Freud's desire to avoid living the patient's life, but he viewed this request to *delay* important decisions as something quite different from the making of decisions *for* the client. In the lesser of life's decisions, he definitely favored a hands-off policy for the therapist.

When he first began treating clients, Freud went quickly into an interpretation of their personality dynamics, but later in his career he cautioned against rushing the client. He favored having the therapist wait on an interpretation until the client is "one step short" of making it himself or herself.[359] Freud also dabbled in setting time limits to a therapy series—particularly since one of his students (Rank; see p. 574) made this a major technique variation. He admitted that at times if a client is told that there will be only so many more sessions, this can act as a prompt to get around the client's resistance. But Freud felt that one has to use this time-setting technique sparingly, and his reference to it as a "blackmailing device" obviously suggests that Freud did not think highly of it in any case.[360] Freud said analysis ends when the analyst and patient mutually decide to stop seeing one another. From the therapist's point of view, two general conditions have to be met before an ending to therapy is called for:

. . . first, that the patient shall no longer be suffering from his symptoms and shall have overcome his anxieties and his inhibitions; and secondly, that the analyst shall judge that so much repressed material had been made conscious, so much that was unintelligible has been explained, and so much internal resistance conquered, that there is no need to *fear a repetition of the pathological processes concerned.*[361]

Summary

Freud came on the historical scene at the height of traditional natural-science explanation. He was encouraged by his teachers and colleagues to explain behavior monistically, according to the principle of constancy. Realizing that he could not capture the behavior of his clients without a dualism, Freud bravely argued for both a psychic and a somatic realm of behavior, linking the two through his concept of the instinct. Instincts have an aim, pressure, source, and object which must be satisfied if homeostasis is to be attained, and it is through the vicissitudes of the instincts that the person experiences pleasure. That is, when the instincts rise in pressure they have to be eased, and in this return to normalcy a feeling of pleasure arises. However, the vicissitudes (rising and falling) of the instincts is not simply automatic, for people can intentionally bring on increased pressure of an instinct, as when they wish for sexual excitement or think about favorite foods. The psyche has an innate capacity to frame experiences that in turn influence the instinctive drives to change their level and even the way in which they will be enacted overtly. Much of this framing of experience goes on at an unconscious level. Indeed, conscious thought arises from unconsciousness in the course of development and is never more than a small portion of the total mind (psyche).

Certain unconscious thoughts which frame wishes for external objects cannot be enacted overtly because of their hostile and/or sexual nature. Parents and other family members are the first objects of these culturally unacceptable wishes. Indeed, Freud believed that in the Oedipal conflict the person re-enacts the patricidal beginnings of the social order, moving from the primal horde to the rules of monogamy currently practiced by civilized peoples. When a wish cannot be enacted, it is counteracted by another wish, leading to what Freud called repression—and thereby, any of a number of defense mechanisms can be brought to bear in order to fulfill the intentions of the wish. When he began attributing such intentional, self-directing behavior to human beings, Freud ran into trouble with colleagues like Breuer and Fliess, who preferred to remain with the biological reductive explanations of natural science. Thus, whereas Freud traced the strangulations of affect to be seen in hysteria to defensiveness, Breuer claimed it was due to an inherited physical condition which he called the hypnoid state.

Freud was not completely insensitive to the criticisms of his telic, anthropomorphic style of explanation, so he began to analogize to physical energies by introducing a conception of psychic energies which supposedly propelled the mind along on the order of physical energy. He always admitted that psychoanalysis did not provide the evidence for this energy conception, but that biology seemed to demand it, and he was, after all, a physician. The chief energy he used in his explanations and the only one he ever named was libido, the energy of the sexual instinct. As his theory developed, Freud always found it possible to explain things in either a strictly psychological manner *or* in an energic manner. Thus, his topographical model of the psyche, which enlarged on his initial depth model, effectively broke down the personality into three somewhat distinct identity points— that is, the id, ego, and superego. The id was viewed as the basic animalistic, selfish, completely amoral side of the personality. We all enter life as id creatures in a state of primary narcissism, which gradually gives way to a less selfish, more realistic approach to life—

one in which we consider the feelings and attitudes of others with whom we identify. Much of this identification is out of fear, as in the boy's castration anxiety prompting identification with the father during the Oedipal conflict.

As a result of such identifications, the person begins to put down what Freud called the ego, and its closely related aspect, the superego. Freud did not always distinguish clearly between these two aspects of the personality, so that the fundamental break-down of the psyche is oppositional (id versus ego states). When he filled in this picture of opposed psychic identities representing different aspects of life—the id our organic-animalistic side, the ego and superego our sociocultural side—Freud employed psychic energies as kinds of "precious material" that the three identities maneuver over to command and to use. A wish becomes a cathexis or a fixing of libido upon a desired object's image in the mind—literally occupying this image with precious energy that then orients the psychic structure to attain this end. A repression of this wish becomes a counter-cathexis, or an application of one psychic force against the other. Sublimation involves raising the sociocultural levels of the ends sought, so that, say, rather than engaging in copulation the artist expends libido to produce a painting. Projection involves disowning one's wishes by attributing them to others. Rationalization means finding a psychic explanation other than the real reason for why one is doing something relating to the wished-for end (object). Reaction-formation is doing something directly opposite to the real end being sought, and so forth.

In time, Freud's complete theory of psychosexual development was expressed in terms of instinct theory. The basic theory always contrasted two instincts, each of which presumably had its own energies to bring to bear. Initially, the sexual was opposed to the self-preservative instincts. Later, Life was opposed to the Death Instinct. It was also possible to fuse instincts from each of these sides into a kind of (dialectical?) synthesis. Freud never coined a name other than libido for his instinctive energy. Development was therefore explained in terms of psychosexual stages framed around the progression and/or fixation and regression of libido. Everyone moves through a course of psychosexual development in the oral stage and then passes consecutively through the anal, urethral, and phallic stages until latency holds the psychic structure in abeyance for a time. With the onset of puberty, the progression of psychosexual development continues, and in the ideal case, terminates in full development at the genital stage.

Developmental progression through the stages is never perfect and hence a series of more or less pronounced fixations occur, explained by Freud as pockets of libidinal retention that can, later in life, be recouped thanks to the operation of regression. Individual differences in personality are accounted for by the nature and extent of fixation, so that personality styles are analogized to the predominant concerns of the psychosexual stages. Thus, the adult oral personality is most likely to be passively receptive, the anal personality orderly, the urethral personality ambitious, and the phallic personality narcissistic. Male-female differences are explained in light of the dynamics of the Oedipal situation, which supposedly leaves females with a less well-formulated superego than males.

Freud's theory of illness moved through several formulations but settled finally on a three-stage compromise formulation that combined his diphasic model of sexual mat-

uration with his fixation-regression thesis. Though he always accepted the possibility of biologically based (actual) neuroses, he viewed the majority of illnesses seen by psychiatrists as caused by the return of memories once repressed to avoid acting them out or even facing up to the fact that they were entertained. For example, as an infant the neurotic may have wished to kill a same-sexed parent and copulate with the opposite-sexed parent. All neurosis begins, Freud thought, in an unresolved or poorly resolved Oedipal conflict. Psychosis is merely a more extensive type of mental deterioration, one in which the fixations have begun earlier in life and have involved more extensive pocketing of libido than is true in neurosis. Pathological symptoms are always the result of *two* wishes—both the repressed and the repressing —so that we can speak of them as transforming the libidinal cathexes into a symbolical manifestation of the meaning mental illness has for the person.

Though he had arrived at his theory through analogies to physical energy, Freud obviously retained his telic emphasis. He spoke of symptoms as conversions of libido, but these signs of illness have an "organ speech," in that they can express the reasons for the illness. Psychosomatic symptoms tell us what is bothering the person. An ulcer patient wants to be fed and cared for even though there may be a facade of independence in his or her behavior. A constipated person is holding back not simply fecal matter but the love that he or she feels has been withheld in turn by others. Neurotics continue trying to adjust to their external world of real interpersonal relations. Psychotics, on the other hand, regress and never return to reality, because their delusions and hallucinations serve as substitutes for real living. Both neurotics and psychotics avoid looking into themselves. They want to retain the status quo of their lives and use anxiety as a kind of instrumental means of avoiding insight into what must be done.

In his theory of cure, Freud suggested that only those patients who can form an artificial neurosis in the therapeutic relationship can be treated by psychoanalysis. Psychotics who have what Freud termed a very severe form of narcissistic neurosis cannot be treated because, in order for psychoanalysis to work, the client must be capable of removing libido from all other aspects of life and fixing it onto the person of the psychoanalyst. This is the core of the artificial neurosis, and if the person is too narcissistic, this becomes impossible. Once the libido is removed from outside the therapy room and fixed upon the therapist, it becomes possible for the client to redirect it inwardly, to restructure his or her ego by way of the transference reactions to the therapist. This all takes place as insights are provided and resistances worked through. The analyst uses various means, such as free association, dream interpretation, and the analysis of both positive and negative transference, to provide the client with insight.

Thus, as a transitional figure in the history of thought, Freud seems to have done a remarkable job of retaining the shell of natural-science description even as he framed an image of the person as more self-directing (telic) than his colleagues would ordinarily accept. Although he would have liked to comply with the demands of traditional science, Freud had the courageous skill to describe human behavior in a way that was helpful to the understanding of his patients. He seems to have achieved this remarkable feat by winding biological and psychological metaphors together into a mix which the modern personologist still puzzles over, wondering "Was Freud a psychological teleologist or a biological reductionist?" This debate will doubtlessly continue unresolved in the future, but there can be no debate over

Freud's genius as the fath sonality theory.

Outline of Important Theoretical Constructs

Biographical overview

The Breuer period
pathognomic situation · strangulated affect · absences, waking dreams · abreaction · catharsis · hypnoid state · defense hysteria

Personality theory

Structural constructs

Dualism of mind versus body
dualism · psyche · soma

The early mental structural constructs: depth emphasis
conscious · unconscious · preconscious · censorship · hedonism · unconscious derivatives · act out · progression versus regression

The final mental structural constructs: dynamic emphasis
topographical model · dynamic · repression · id · ego · primary versus secondary process · superego · ego ideal

Motivational constructs

Instinct and energy
instinct · aim · pressure · source · object · homeostasis · principle of constancy · principle of neuronic inertia · vicissitudes · pleasure principle

Freud's Promethean insight: the sexual instinct
autoerotic · organ pleasure · erotogenic

zone · libido · cathexis · anticathexis
(countercathexis) · bisexuality

History of Freud's instinct theories
primal instinct · compound instinct
· self-preservative instinct (ego instinct)
· sexual instinct (object instinct)
· narcissism (ego-cathexis) · ego
libido · object libido · repetition compulsion · Eros (Life Instinct) · Death
Instinct (Thanatos) · fusion of instincts

Defense mechanisms or mental mechanisms
repression · primal repression (see fixation) · derivatives · repression proper
· displacement · substitution · sublimation · projection · reaction-formation
· rationalization · isolation

Time-perspective constructs

Psychosexual stages
fueros · psychosexual · pregenital stages

Oral psychosexual stage
oceanic feeling · oral erotism · incorporation · primary narcissism · wish
fulfillment · identification · introjection

Anal psychosexual stage
frustration · prohibition · privation
· sadistic-anal

Urethral psychosexual stage
urethra

Phallic psychosexual stage
phallus · ontogeny recapitulates phylogeny · origin of society · primal horde
· exogamy · complex · male Oedipus
complex · law of talion · castration fear
(anxiety, complex) · female Oedipus
complex (Electra) · penis envy

Latency psychosexual stage
latency · diphasic sexual development

Pubescence and adolescence

Adulthood and genitality
genital

Fixation and regression
fixation · regression · topographical
regression · temporal regression
· formal regression

Individual-differences constructs

Adult character or personality styles
character · personality

Oral personality
passive · receptive · external supplies

Anal personality
orderliness · parsimoniousness
· obstinacy

Urethral personality
ambition

Phallic personality
self-centered · masculinity complex
· homosexuality

Latency, adolescent and genital personalities
imago · genital character

Psychopathology and psychotherapy

Theory of illness

Antithetic ideas and counterwill
intention · expectation proper · distressing antithetic idea · counterwill
· fixed idea (Charcot) · dissociate

Coitus interruptus and childhood molestation
coitus interruptus · sexual noxa
· sexualized fantasy · infantile
sexuality

*Three-stage compromise model of
mental illness*
three-stage compromise model · deflection · actual neuroses · psychoneuroses
proper · after-repression · return of the

repressed memories · conversion
· organ speech

Differential diagnosis
flight into illness · secondary gain
· obsessive-compulsivity · hysteria
· psychosomatic · neurosis · psychosis
· delusion · hallucination

Anxiety theory
biological emotion · transformed libido
· instrumental role of anxiety · realistic
anxiety · neurotic anxiety · moral
anxiety · guilt

Culture as a prime agent of abnormality
severity of ego ideal or superego

Theory of cure

The role of insight
insight · causal therapy

*Fundamental rule of psychoanalysis,
and free association*
fundamental rule · free association
· psychic determinism

Resistance and transference
resistance · transference · imago
· positive transference · ambivalence
· uncovering process · negative transference · re-education · overcoming
resistance · countertransference

Final theory of cure
libidinal anticipatory idea · transformed
(artificial) neurosis · transference illness
· transference neurosis · narcissistic
neurosis · insight

Extent and permanence of cure

Social revision

Therapeutic techniques

Evolution of the relationship
hypnosis · pressure technique · screen
memories (associations)

View of therapeutic change

Client prognosis and trial analyses
prognosis

*Interpretative techniques in dreams
and parapraxes*
dream interpretation · manifest content
· latent content · symbol · day residues
· wish fulfillment · dream work
· condensation of dream image · displacement of dream image · overdetermination · reversal · means of
representation · parapraxes · Freudian
slips

Some procedural details

Notes

1. Freud, Vol. XX, p. 8. **2.** Ibid. **3.** Jones, 1953, p.
28. **4.** Ibid., p. 40. **5.** Wittels, 1924, pp. 29, 31. **6.**
Freud, 1954, p. 322. **7.** Freud, Vol. II, pp. 38–39.
8. Ibid., p. 38. **9.** Ibid., p. 8. **10.** Ibid., p. 286. **11.**
Freud, Vol. I, pp. 281–397. **12.** Freud, Vol. III, p.
234; Vol. XIV, p. 168. **13.** Freud, Vol. XIV, pp.
78–79. **14.** Freud, Vol. V, p. 538. **15.** Ibid., p. 574.
16. Freud, Vol. XII, p. 260. **17.** Ibid., p. 264. **18.**
Freud, Vol. V, p. 613. **19.** Freud, Vol. XV, p. 113.
20. Ibid., p. 212. **21.** Freud, Vol. XXII, p. 70. **22.**
Freud, Vol. XVII, p. 28. **23.** Freud, Vol. XIV, p.
149. **24.** Freud, Vol. XII, p. 266. **25.** Freud, Vol.
XIV, p. 194. **26.** Ibid., p. 80. **27.** Freud, Vol. XXIII,
p. 240. **28.** Freud, Vol. XIX, p. 55. **29.** Freud, Vol.
XIV, p. 187. **30.** Freud, Vol. V, p. 617. **31.** Ibid.,
p. 542. **32.** Freud, Vol. XXII, p. 73. **33.** Ibid. **34.**
Ibid. **35.** Ibid., p. 74. **36.** Freud, Vol. XXIII, p.
240. **37.** Freud, Vol. I, p. 323. **38.** Freud, Vol.
XXII, pp. 66–67. **39.** Freud, Vol. XIX, p. 18. **40.**
Ibid., p. 40. **41.** Freud, Vol. XX, p. 97. **42.** Freud,
Vol. II, p. 116. **43.** Freud, Vol. XIX, p. 17. **44.**
Freud, Vol. XXII, p. 76. **45.** Freud, Vol. V, pp.
601–603. **46.** Ibid., p. 603. **47.** Freud, Vol. XXII,
p. 78. **48.** Freud, Vol. XIV, pp. 93–94. **49.** Freud,
Vol. XIX, p. 28. **50.** Ibid., p. 36. **51.** Ibid., p. 55.

52. Ibid., p. 34. 53. Freud, Vol. XIV, p. 113. 54. Nunberg and Federn, 1962. 55. Freud, Vol. XIV, pp. 118–120. 56. Ibid., pp. 121–122. 57. Ibid., p. 122. 58. Jones, 1953, p. 41. 59. Freud, Vol. III, p. 36. 60. Freud, Vol. XIV, p. 126. 61. Freud, Vol. XVI, p. 356. 62. Freud, Vol. XVIII, p. 9. 63. Freud, Vol. XIV, p. 146. 64. Freud, 1954, p. 219. 65. Freud, Vol. IX, p. 188. 66. Freud, Vol. XVI, p. 323. 67. Freud, Vol. VIII, pp. 168–183. 68. Freud, Vol. IX, p. 187. 69. Freud, Vol. III, p. 107. 70. Freud, Vol. XVII, p. 139. 71. Freud, Vol. XI, p. 101. 72. Freud, Vol. XXII, p. 131. 73. Freud, Vol. XVIII, p. 90. 74. Freud, Vol. I, p. 298. 75. Freud, Vol. XII, p. 74. 76. Freud, Vol. XIV, p. 234. 77. Freud, Vol. V, p. 605. 78. Freud, 1954, p. 324. 79. Freud, Vol. VII, pp. 219–220. 80. Ibid., p. 219. 81. Freud and Bullitt, 1967. 82. Freud, Vol. XV, p. 123. 83. Freud, Vol. XI, p. 44. 84. Freud, Vol. XVII, p. 137. 85. Freud, Vol. XXI, p. 117. 86. Freud, Vol. XVIII, p. 10. 87. Gayley, 1965, pp. 188–189. 88. Freud, Vol. XXI, p. 118. 89. Freud, Vol. XIV, p. 73. 90. Ibid., p. 134. 91. Freud, Vol. XVIII, p. 22. 92. Ibid., p. 36. 93. Ibid., p. 38. 94. Ibid., p. 56. 95. From Barbara Low, in Freud, Vol. XVIII, pp. 55–56. 96. Freud, Vol. XIX, p. 41. 97. Freud, Vol. XVIII, p. 53. 98. Freud, Vol. XXI, p. 138. 99. Freud, Vol. XXII, p. 211. 100. Freud and Bullitt, 1967, p. 279. 101. Freud, Vol. XIV, p. 16. 102. Freud, Vol. VIII, p. 5. 103. Freud, Vol. IV, pp. 307–308; Vol. XIV, p. 305. 104. Freud, Vol. I, p. 209. 105. Freud, Vol. XVIII, p. 256. 106. Freud and Bullitt, 1967, p. 43. 107. Freud, Vol. XII, p. 66. 108. Freud, Vol. XIII, p. 64. 109. Freud, Vol. XII, p. 299. 110. Ibid., p. 49. 111. Freud, Vol. III, p. 58. 112. Freud, Vol. I, p. 229. 113. Ibid., p. 235. 114. Freud, Vol. XXI, pp. 67–72. 115. Freud, Vol. VII, p. 198. 116. Freud, Vol. V, p. 471. 117. Freud, Vol. XXII, pp. 60–62. 118. Freud, Vol. XVIII, p. 113. 119. Freud, Vol. XX, p. 10. 120. Freud, Vol. XVIII, p. 245; also see Vol. VII, p. 198. 121. Freud, Vol, XIX, p. 142. 122. Freud, Vol. XXIII, p. 189. 123. Freud, Vol. XXII, p 118. 124. Ibid., p. 118. 125. Freud, Vol. VIII, p. 218. 126. Freud, Vol. XXII, p. 118. 127. Freud, Vol. XI, p. 97; Vol. XII, p. 82. 128. Freud, Vol. XIII, p. 184. 129. Becker and Barnes, 1952, Ch. V. 130. Freud, Vol. XIII, pp. 141–143. 131. Ibid., p. 153. 132. Ibid., pp. 144–150. 133. Gayley, 1965, pp. 261–263. 134. Freud, Vol. IV, p. 104. 135. Freud, Vol. XXIII, p. 189. 136. Freud, Vol. XIII, p. 153. 137. Freud, Vol. XIX, p. 144. 138. Ibid., p. 36.

139. Freud, Vol. XXI, p. 229. 140. Ibid., pp. 229, 234. 141. Freud, Vol. XXII, p. 134. 142. Freud, Vol. XXIII, p. 194. 143. Freud, Vol. XIX, p. 251; Vol. XXII, p. 117. 144. Freud, Vol. XIX, p. 178. 145. Ibid., pp. 257–258. 146. Freud, Vol. IX, p. 195. 147. Freud, Vol. XIX, pp. 177–178. 148. Freud, Vol. IX, p. 171. 149. Freud, Vol. XVIII, p. 111. 150. Freud, Vol. XII, p. 222. 151. Freud, Vol. XVI, p. 326. 152. Freud, Vol. XVIII, p. 246. 153. Freud, Vol. XX, p. 37. 154. Freud, Vol. XXII, p. 147. 155. Freud, Vol. XVI, p. 336. 156. Freud and Bullitt, 1967, p. 74. 157. Freud, Vol. XVIII, p. 246. 158. Freud and Bullitt, 1967, p. 74. 159. Ibid. 160. Freud, Vol. XVIII, p. 121. 161. Freud, Vol. XXI, p. 228. 162. Freud, Vol. XVIII, p. 115. 163. Ibid., p. 142. 164. Freud, Vol. II, pp. 50–51, 170, 237. 165. Freud, Vol. VIII, p. 118. 166. Freud, Vol. XXI, pp. 103–104. 167. Freud, Vol. VII, p. 235; Vol. XII, pp. 317–318. 168. Freud, Vol. XVIII, p. 184. 169. Freud, Vol. VII, p. 235. 170. Freud, Vol. III, p. 163. 171. Freud, Vol. XI, pp. 98–99. 172. Freud, Vol. VII, p. 30. 173. Freud, Vol. XII, pp. 61–62. 174. Freud, Vol. XIV, p. 286. 175. Freud, Vol. VII, pp. 50–51. 176. Freud, Vol. XXI, p. 69. 177. Freud, Vol. XIV, p. 286. 178. Freud, Vol. XIII, p. 184. 179. Freud and Bullitt, 1967, p. 43. 180. Freud, Vol. IX, p. 175; Vol. XII, p. 190. 181. Freud, Vol. XXII, p. 99. 182. Freud, Vol. IX, pp. 169–170. 183. Freud, Vol. XVII, p. 81. 184. Freud, Vol. IX, p. 173. 185. Freud, Vol. XVII, p. 82. 186. Freud, Vol. IX, p. 175. 187. Freud, Vol. XIII, p. 196. 188. Freud, Vol. XXI, p. 90. 189. Freud, Vol. XIX, pp. 91–92. 190. Freud, Vol. XXII, pp 129–130. 191. Ibid., p. 1. 192. Freud, Vol. XI, p. 121. 193. Freud, Vol. VI, p. 145. 194. Freud, Vol. XII, p. 72; Vol. XIV, p. 96. 195. Freud, Vol. XIII, p. 243. 196. Ibid., pp. 243–244. 197. Freud, Vol. XI, p. 188. 198. Ibid., p. 133. 199. Freud, Vol. XVIII, p. 110. 200. Freud, Vol. XXI, p. 102. 201. Freud, Vol I, p. 116. 202. Ibid., p. 121. 203. Ibid. 204. Ibid., pp. 121–122. 205. Ibid., p. 124. 206. Ibid., p. 125. 207. Janet, 1920, p. 324. 208. Freud, Vol. I, p. 127. 209. Ibid., p. 185. 210. Ibid., p. 183. 211. Ibid. 212. Freud, Vol. III, p. 203. 213. Freud, Vol. VII, p. 274. 214. Freud, 1954, p. 193. 215. Freud, Vol. VII, pp. 264–276. 216. Freud, Vol. III, p. 168. 217. Freud, Vol. XIII, p. 159. 218. Freud, Vol. VII, pp. 278–279. 219. Freud, Vol. XII, pp. 248–249. 220. Freud, Vol. XI, p. 218. 221. Ibid., p. 46; Vol. XVII, p. 204. 222. Freud, Vol. XII, p. 236. 223. Freud, Vol. III, p. 169. 224. Freud, Vol. I, pp. 249–251. 225. Ibid., p. 256. 226. Freud, Vol. VII, p. 53. 227.

Freud, Vol. XXIII, p. 184. **228.** Freud, Vol. XX, p. 91. **229.** Freud, Vol. XIV, p. 199. **230.** Freud, Vol. XII, p. 76. **231.** Freud, Vol. XX, p. 37. **232.** Freud, Vol. VII, p. 51. **233.** Ibid., p. 45, **234.** Ibid., p. 43. **235.** Ibid., p. 44. **236.** Freud, Vol. XI, p. 50. **237.** Freud, Vol. XIX, p. 204. **238.** Freud, Vol. XI, p. 50. **239.** Freud, Vol. XX, p. 156. **240.** Nunberg and Federn, 1962, pp. 100–101. **241.** Freud, Vol. XIX, p. 185. **242.** Freud, Vol. I, p. 191. **243.** Ibid., pp. 192–193. **244.** Ibid., p. 193. **245.** Ibid., p. 257. **246.** Freud, Vol. IX, pp. 60–61. **247.** Freud, Vol. X, pp. 114–115. **248.** Freud, Vol. XVII, p. 210. **249.** Freud, Vol. XX, p. 128. **250.** Ibid., p. 162. **251.** Ibid. **252.** Freud, Vol. XXII, p. 85. **253.** Freud, Vol. XII, p. 77. **254.** Freud, Vol. XXII, p. 85. **255.** Freud, Vol. XX, p. 144. **256.** Ibid., p. 93. **257.** Ibid., p. 130. **258.** Freud, Vol. XI, p. 37. **259.** Freud. Vol. XX, p. 139. **260.** Freud, Vol. XXII, p. 62. **261.** Freud, Vol. XXI, p. 135. **262.** Ibid., p. 124. **263.** Freud, Vol. IX, p. 203. **264.** Freud, Vol. XVI, p. 434. **265.** Freud, Vol. XXI, pp. 142–143. **266.** Ibid., p. 143. **267.** Freud, Vol. XIX, p. 54. **268.** Freud and Bullitt, 1967, p. 42. **269.** Freud, Vol. XIV, p. 312. **270.** Freud, Vol. II, p. 281. **271.** Freud, Vol. XVI, p. 438. **272.** Freud, Vol. I, p. 100; Freud, 1954, p. 151. **273.** Freud, Vol. XVI, p. 436. **274.** Freud, Vol. XII, p. 134. **275.** Freud, Vol. XI, p. 29. **276.** Freud, Vol. VI, p. 257. **277.** Freud, Vol. XXIII, p. 179. **278.** Freud, Vol. I, p. 217. **279.** Freud, Vol. II, p. 268. **280.** Freud, Vol. V, p. 517. **281.** Freud, Vol. XVI, p. 291. **282.** Freud, Vol. XI, p. 49. **283.** Freud, Vol. I, p. 266; Vol. XIV, p. 311. **284.** Freud, Vol. XX, p. 27. **285.** Freud, Vol. XVI, p. 290. **286.** Freud, Vol. XII, p. 167. **287.** Freud, Vol. XVI, p. 442. **288.** Freud, Vol. VII, p. 116. **289.** Freud, Vol. XII, p. 101. **290.** Ibid., p. 100. **291.** Freud, Vol. XVI, p. 440. **292.** Freud, Vol. XII, p. 139. **293.** Freud, Vol. XV, p. 87. **294.** Freud, Vol. VII, p. 267. **295.** Freud, Vol. I, p. 266. **296.** Freud, Vol. XVI, p. 453. **297.** Freud, Vol. XXII, p. 156. **298.** Freud, Vol. XII, p. 166. **299.** Freud, Vol. XI, pp. 144–145; Vol. XII, pp. 117–118, 164. **300.** Freud, Vol. XXII, p. 150. **301.** Freud, Vol. XII, p. 100. **302.** Nunberg and Federn, 1962, p. 102. **303.** Freud, Vol. XII, p. 106. **304.** Freud, Vol. XVII, p. 183. **305.** Freud, Vol. XI, p. 51. **306.** Freud, Vol. XII, p. 107. **307.** Freud, Vol. XVI, p. 444. **308.** Ibid., p. 454. **309.** Ibid., pp. 444–447. **310.** Ibid., p. 444. **311.** Ibid., p. 455. **312.** Freud, Vol. XXIII, p. 231. **313.** Ibid., p. 233. **314.** Ibid., pp. 232–233. **315.** Ibid., p. 250. **316.** Ibid., p. 249. **317.** Freud, Vol. XVI, p. 435. **318.** Freud, Vol. XI, pp. 144–150. **319.** Ibid., p. 150. **320.** Jones, 1953, p. 28. **321.** Ansbacher, 1959. **322.** Freud, Vol. XI, p. 144. **323.** Ibid., pp. 22–26. **324.** Freud, Vol. VI, p. 43. **325.** Freud, Vol. I, p. 82. **326.** Freud, Vol. XVII, pp. 51–52. **327.** Freud, Vol. XII, p. 114. **328.** Freud, Vol. XVII, p. 164. **329.** Freud, Vol. XVIII, p. 252. **330.** Ibid., p. 150. **331.** Freud, Vol. XXII, p. 148. **332.** Ibid., p. 155. **333.** Ibid., p. 156. **334.** Freud, Vol. XII, p. 170. **335.** Freud, Vol. XV, p. 100. **336.** Freud, Vol. IV, p. 121. **337.** Freud, Vol. XV, p. 150. **338.** Freud, Vol. V, p. 345. **339.** Freud, Vol. IV, p. 228. **340.** Freud, Vol. XXII, p. 27. **341.** Freud, Vol. IV, p. 278. **342.** Freud, Vol. XV, p. 129. **343.** Freud, Vol. XXIII, p. 172. **344.** Freud, Vol. IV, p. 279. **345.** Freud, Vol. II, p. 263. **346.** Freud, Vol. XIX, p. 130. **347.** Freud, Vol. XV, p. 129. **348.** Freud, Vol. V, p. 608. **349.** Freud, Vol. XV, p. 114. **350.** Freud, Vol. IV, pp. 314–327. **351.** Freud, Vol. VI, p. 59. **352.** Ibid., p. 94. **353.** Freud, Vol. XII, pp. 133–134. **354.** Ibid., p. 133. **355.** Ibid., p. 134. **356.** Freud, Vol. X, p. 180. **357.** Freud, Vol. XII, pp. 119–120. **358.** Ibid., p. 153. **359.** Ibid., pp. 140–141. **360.** Freud, Vol. XIII, p. 218. **361.** Freud, Vol. XXIII, p. 219.

Chapter 2

The Individual Psychology of Alfred Adler

Although Sigmund Freud wrestled with identical issues, no theorist in the history of personality study met the problems of physical versus psychological explanation more directly than Alfred Adler. In order to appreciate the form of medical models that preceded his appearance on the historical scene—and against which he reacted—we will survey a handful of theorists, most of whom Adler referred to in his own writings. Individual psychology will then appear against the backdrop of this earlier means of explaining human behavior.

Medical–Physical Models of Human Behavior

Hippocrates (c. 400 B.C.)

Hippocrates, the Greek "father of medicine," completely rejected earlier Babylonian and Egyptian theories of illness which held that disease was a punishment sent by a god, who infected the sick person with a worm or possibly a small stone. Diseases are due to natural causes, Hippocrates said, such as improper diet or poor climate. There are also, he said, four types of body fluids or *humors* which combine in various ways to result not only in illness but in temperamental variations as well: black bile, blood, yellow bile, and phlegm. When these humors are mixed in the right proportions by the natural functioning of the body, a person is healthy. But if an imbalance develops, then the person can easily suffer from what today we would call a mental (or physical) illness. For example, an excess of black bile can result in depression (*melancholia*) and too much yellow bile can make the person irritable and hostile (*choleric*).

A healthy, energetic person was said to have blood in ascendance, and an easygoing, slow individual would have phlegm as the major humor active in the body. Hippocrates based his humoral theory on clinical observations: a sickly, cranky individual might indeed exude a yellow fluid at some point—such as pus from a sore or mixed in sputum from a cough—whereas a healthy individual with ruddy skin color surely appears quite saturated with health-giving red blood. Hippocrates also proposed a structural model of body type which he felt bore a relationship to physical and mental health. People, he said, tend to have two basic types of *physique*: on the one hand, a thick, muscular, physically strong body (*habitus apoplecticus*) and on the other, a thin, delicate, physically weak body (*habitus phthisicus*). When illness strikes these body types, the former is more likely to suffer from a cerebral stroke (*apoplexy*) and the latter from tuberculosis (*phthisis*).[1]

Hippocrates' theories were extremely influential over the centuries as the science and profession of medicine evolved. In the interests of space, we must pass over several centuries and ignore many details relevant to the study of behavior in order to arrive at the eighteenth and nineteenth centuries where we find the specific physical theories against which Adler was to react.

Franz Joseph Gall (1758–1828)

Theories of physical and psychological evolution were widely discussed in the eighteenth century. A French naturalist, Jean Baptiste de Lamarck (1744–1829) proposed that one generation could pass on to its offspring the bodily characteristics it had acquired during the course of life. For example, a man and woman who train themselves into magnificent physical condition and then have a child would transmit the fruits of their training to their child. Thanks to heredity, this child would have a superior physique from birth. The German anatomist and physiologist Franz Joseph Gall extended this kind of theorizing to the explanation of personality differences.

Gall's theoretical system is known as *phrenology* (from the Greek *phrenos,* meaning "heart of mind," hence, "study of the mind"). His idea was that personality characteristics are subject to direction from the physical workings of the brain. Gall believed that an enlargement of the brain's physical size at any one point on its surface (whether due to inheritance or continued practice of some given personality trait called a *faculty* of the mind) could be studied by examining the convolutions of the skull. In the same way that an arm muscle becomes enlarged with exercise from lifting weights, a brain region that is the seat of a personality tendency would enlarge through use—or tend to become larger through hereditary influences—and press against the skull as the person matured, thereby forming a bump which could be detected by a phrenologist using a special set of calipers. Gall claimed to have proven empirically a number of such relationships between personality tendencies and the bumps on people's heads.

For example, the faculty of "combativeness" was said to exist back and upward from the ear, along the side of the head. Gall claimed that he found that members of the lower social classes, masculine females, and hostile males have bulgings of the skull in this region. Gall and his students became notorious for their efforts to measure the bumps on people's heads, and in time they claimed to have proven that over two dozen faculties enter into behavior, including such regions as "secretiveness" and "desire."[2] In the same way that Hippocrates' clumsy beginnings were to influence the medical studies of nutrition, blood circulation, and anatomical structure, so too did Gall's primitive efforts contribute to the modern study of brain localization. We no longer seek to localize "self-esteem" as he did, but we are aware that visual processes are mediated by the occipital regions of the brain, auditory by the temporal regions, and so forth. There is a pattern of distribution in the physical structure of the body, all right, but is this in any direct way related to personality factors of behavior?

Charles Robert Darwin (1809–1882)

The most important evolutionary theorist of history was the British naturalist, Charles Darwin (1952b). It took centuries for the philosophers and scientists of Europe to believe that natural forms of life on earth were actually progressing in some way, rather than declining from an ancient Golden Age (Greek mythology) or Garden of Eden (Christianity).[3] Without knowledge of genetic (Mendelian) transmission, Darwin worked out a way of describing how there could be progress in the physical bodies and behavioral adaptations of succeeding generations of animals and plants. The human being, like any creature of nature, advances biologically and psychologically because only those species of animals who are well adapted to their environment survive to live on. There is a *natural selection* process going on across generations of living things and the reward for a species of animal or plant life is "survival of the fittest" (a phrase that Darwin borrowed from Herbert Spencer). Animals with heavier coats of fur live on in frigid environments and those with lighter coats die off. There is no divine guidance here, no God's hand at play in nature; it is a blind process of continuing change leading to improvement at the expense of many failures in the test of survival.

What about human choice and the interpersonal evaluations that are manifested as ethics or morality? Darwin was uncertain when it came to answering such questions. For example, in *The Descent of Man* (1952a) he argued that morality was probably retained by social organizations because a tribe whose members had the spirit of helping one another would be more courageous, obedient, and sympathetic.[4] During times of threat, as when under attack or confronting a famine, this unselfish concern for fellow human beings would doubtlessly aid in meeting the communal challenge. Hence, morality—the Golden Rule—would have *survival value* in natural selection. Yet a few paragraphs later in the same book, Darwin acknowledged the opposite side of the moral coin when he observed:

We civilised men . . . do our utmost to check the process of elimination; we build asylums for the imbecile, the maimed, and the sick; we institute poor-laws; and our medical men exert their utmost skill to save the life of every one to the last moment. There is reason to believe that vaccination has preserved thousands, who from a weak constitution would formerly have succumbed to small-pox. Thus the weak members of civilised societies propagate their kind. No one who has attended to the breeding of domestic animals will doubt that this must be highly injurious to the race of man.[5]

The potential benefits of brotherly love to natural selection are not so clear in this case. Maybe it would be better for nature if only the strong were to survive. Actually, there have been as many "Darwinian" arguments advanced in favor of rugged individualism as there have for the survival value of communal protectionism.[6] As we shall see, Adler used a Darwinian rationale to support a communal theory of fellow-love and concern. Darwin rested his personal case with the "morality has vitality through natural selection" argument, basing his belief in morality on this justification. He therefore rejected supernatural explanations altogether—although he had once considered becoming a clergyman—and ended his days an agnostic humanist.

Cesare Lombroso (1836–1909)

Combining Gall's thought with the newer insights of organic evolution, the Italian criminologist Cesare Lombroso argued that criminal populations contain more people with physical irregularities than do normal populations. Criminals were said to have *atavistic* (throwback to animal form) physical signs, signifying that a degenerative process or a reversion to earlier evolutionary stages have been at work in their bodily develop-

ment. Signs, such as low foreheads, jaws that jut out beyond the upper face, or small, beady eyes set well back into the skull, were supposedly indicative of an animalistic mentality leading to criminality. By 1900 the Mendelian laws of genetic transmission had been rediscovered and popularized. This theory of dominant and recessive genes permitting an occasional return of older forms to manifestation in a current population—as when some children are born with a vestigial "tail"—offered a ring of plausibility to the atavistic conception of heredity. Lombrosian theory has not stood up well under the weight of subsequent evidence, and it is generally rejected today.

Ernst Kretschmer (1888–1964)

It remained for the German psychiatrist Ernst Kretschmer to adapt certain earlier body-build typologies (of Rostan in France and Viola in Italy) and to elevate this approach to an empirical science. Kretschmer defined three basic body types: *pyknics* (rotund, large visceral mass, portly physiques), *athletics* (large bones, heavy musculature, robust individuals), and *asthenic* (thin, linear, delicate types). Kretschmer also reflected the tendency discussed in the Introduction (see p. 22) to move from pure type to traits in that he had mixed typologies in his classificatory scheme (for example, having the torso of an athletic type and the long, linear legs of an asthenic).

The point of this typology was to help find out whether or not there is a relationship between body build and mental illness. Kretschmer conducted a number of empirical studies in which he compared a mental patient's body type to independent diagnoses of his or her psychosis. An elaborate check list was used to categorize the body type of a patient standing nude before a trained observer. Kretschmer found in general that pyknic types were prone to cyclothymic temperaments (moodiness, feeling "up" and then feeling "down" or blue), and when they became emotionally upset, they developed a manic-depressive psychosis. Asthenic types, on the other hand, were shy personalities who developed schizophrenia (retreat from reality, secretiveness, muteness) if they became ill.

Critics have since argued that if a person has a slight physical build, he or she was probably a "late bloomer" in adolescence; hence, there is a greater probability that such a person will be shy and a loner in interpersonal relations. The corpulent child, on the other hand, may be relatively more likely to enter into interpersonal relationships, if only as a follower and part-time group member. Once mentally ill, a shy person is more likely to be called schizophrenic by the diagnosing physician, because that is the presumed "nature" of schizophrenia—to be split off from reality and live in a world of one's own. And since a sample of more outgoing individuals is likely to reflect mood variations, manic-depressive diagnoses will be more prevalent among such a group of patients. Hence, it may not be the common genetic factors of body build and mental illness that Kretschmer has found signs of, but merely the social learning processes that take place, given two kinds of potentials for living.

Emil Kraepelin (1856-1926)

This German neuropsychiatrist might be called the "father of modern psychiatric diagnosis." In 1883 Kraepelin took a number of clinical *syndromes* (a collection of symptoms) identified and named by others, and combining these with his own observations, proposed a scheme that has survived in general outline to the present. Clinical typing is no longer considered vitally important in modern psychiatry, but thanks in part to the weight of convention—and in many instances to legal statutes requiring the typing of patients—the practice of Kraepelinian diagnosis in mental disturbance has survived.

The classic Kraepelinian scheme is essentially as follows: the *schizophrenic psychosis* breaks down into four types: *simple* (distracted, deadened emotions, asocial tendencies); *paranoid* (suspiciousness, delusions of persecution); *catatonic* (rigid and mute, or highly excited and assaultive); and *hebephrenic* ("silly," most deteriorated in personality of all subgroups).

William H. Sheldon (1899–   )

Although he was never referred to by Adler, we could not do better than devote a section to William H. Sheldon, whose *constitutional psychology* is the clearest and most complete statement of the body build-temperament relationship. No student of personality should overlook his unique contribution to the field. Sheldon was an American psychologist-psychiatrist who began theorizing with a reliance on hereditary factors by postulating a *morphogenotype* (gene-induced body form).[7] This genetic factor is what causes both the kind of body build a person will have as an adult and the kind of temperament he or she will display. In order to classify a person as to body build, Sheldon said it was necessary to consider the three *primary components of physique*. Here he relied on a brilliant analogy to the *in utero* (within the womb) development of the human embryo. During cell division and multiplication as the developing organism enlarges through the blastula and gastrula stages, three levels of cells can eventually be distinguished: the *ectodermal* or outer layer of the embryo, which eventually develops into the nervous system, sense organs, skin, and hair; the *endodermal* or inner layer of cells, which develops into the digestive system and other visceral organs; and the *mesodermal* or intermediate layer of cells, which develops into the muscles, bones, blood vessels, and sex glands of the body.

What Sheldon did was to parallel this tripartite breakdown of *in utero* embryonic dermal (skin) layers with a tripartite breakdown of the Kretschmerian variety, thereby uniting internal with external factors.[8] Thus, each person is assessed in terms of primary components of physique as follows: *endomorphy* (digestive tract well developed, so that physique is rounded, soft, and often corpulent, similar to pyknic); *mesomorphy* (muscular, strong, big-boned, tough, similar to athletic); and *ectomorphy* (thin, lightly muscled, fragile, similar to asthenic). The theory holds that everyone is influenced along all three dimensions thanks to his or her morphogenotypic inheritance, and that what we type someone as being is merely an overriding impression of all three factors at once.

Improving on Kretschmer's check-list rating procedure, Sheldon introduced the practice of having a subject photographed against a standard background in the nude, with pictures of him or her taken from the side, front, and back. He then worked out a reliable method of measuring the primary components of physique—using ratios of one body part to another, height to girth, and so on. Several indices for each component of physique are then collapsed into a single number along a seven-point scale, with "1" a low and "7" a high score on the component in question. Hence, any given individual's combined ratings on all three components

would read something like 7—3—1 or 2—1—6. Since the first number always refers to endomorphy, the second to mesomorphy, and the third to ectomorphy, we would have here an endomorphic and an ectomorphic body type, in that order. We make this judgment by naming the three components in terms of the most prominent score. If all three scores were "4," we could not name any *one* tendency of physique. This succession of three scores is called the *somatotype* (*soma* is Greek for "body," hence "body type").

Sheldon also made ratings of the person photographed which he called the *secondary components of physique*. One such component is *dysplasia,* which is an inconsistent or uneven mixture of the primary components, similar to Kretschmer's mixed rating. Another is *gynandromorphy* (or the *g*-index), which is a rating of how many characteristics of the opposite sex a person has. Feminized men and masculinized women would thus have scores of 6 or 7.[9] Finally, the *textural* component (or *t*-index) deals with the coarseness of skin and hair, and the proportions of body build combined in an aesthetically pleasant or unpleasant fashion.

Following an extensive review of the literature on personality, Sheldon next proposed three *primary components of temperament* which he believed covered the major differences between people, as follows: *viscerotonia* (people who love physical comfort; are socially outgoing, self-satisfied, agreeable, tolerant of others, and relaxed; enjoy eating and the company of others in social relations); *somatotonia* (assertive, physically active people, who love risk-taking, competition, and the taking of a leader role in social relations; can be disagreeable and hostile); and *cerebrotonia* (people who are restrained and timid in behavior, emotionally low-keyed; love privacy; have tendencies to impulsivity and unpredictability on occasion; are hypersensitive to pain). Sheldon found a significant relationship between (1) endomorphy and viscerotonia (reminding us of Freud's oral type, Chapter 1); (2) mesomorphy and somatotonia; and (3) ectomorphy and cerebrotonia. He also found some support for Kretschmer's thesis about the relation of body build to abnormality.[10] The same questions come to mind when reading Sheldon as arose in reaction to the theory of Kretschmer. That is, does the morphogenotype really *cause* the personality or can we not account for observed personality differences on the basis of social influences?

Modern Trends in Biochemistry and Psychopharmacology

We see from our review of history that the biological approach to personality description follows Hippocrates' body-type explanations more than his body-fluid (humoral) theories. Even so, at some level of explanation these two approaches become one, because it is assumed that there is some underlying physiological-chemical reaction that brings the body type around in physical maturation. The study of biochemistry has always been very influential in the thinking of psychologists.[11] For example, early in this century deficiencies of vitamin B were shown to lead to physical illnesses like pellagra and beriberi, which in turn lead to psychotic disorders because of their harmful effects on brain metabolism. Work with the mentally retarded, in which administration of thyroid extract (an endocrine substance) led to improvement in cretinism (a form of mental retardation), spurred all manner of chemical

investigations into the nature of mental functioning.[12]

Because of the relative success of certain organic cures in mental illness, such as insulin-, Metrazol-, and electro-convulsive treatments, a continuing series of investigations have been made in this area, based on organic-model theories, such as correcting misfiring circuits in the brain or wiping out unpleasant "memory banks" so that a patient can start life afresh. Another popular organic theory suggests that because of hereditary influences or some disease process after birth, the individual's body malfunctions in some way, producing a harmful substance which then brings on abnormal behavior chemically much as certain drugs do.[13] Foreign proteins in the blood are often cited, and some theorists have even spoken of a "schizophrenic serum."[14] It makes good sense that if abnormal behavior is due to serums and blood chemistry, then personality itself may have such biological roots. The chemical breakthrough, however, that will isolate a physiological *cause* for mental illness has yet to happen, although we already have seen a chemical breakthrough in the *treatment* of mental disorders.

We refer here to the remarkable success of relaxant or *psychotropic* drugs (tranquilizers, antidepressants). The number of beds occupied by mental patients has been drastically reduced, thanks to the self-control achieved by those who take these "miracle" drugs, which we will not attempt to list because they multiply in number yearly.[15] There seems little doubt about the significant contribution to the treatment of the mentally ill made by such drugs. Yet how much this has to do with personality factors per se is debatable. A more directly related drug issue that has come to the fore dramatically in recent decades involves the use of hallucinogenic drugs, such as *mescaline* and *lysergic acid diethylamide* (LSD). Since the users of such drugs often cite as their reason the expanding of consciousness or some related mystical experience of a quasi-religious nature, we must recognize a potential role for drug-induced states in personality theory.

Biographical Overview

Alfred Adler was born on 7 February 1870 in a suburb of Vienna, the son of Hungarian-Jewish parents. Few Jews lived in his community, and so Adler never acquired a strong cultural identity. Although he attended synagogue as a boy, as an adult he considered himself a Christian.[16] Adler's father was a grain merchant, and though the family went through a period of financial setback, his earliest years were not made difficult by material want. He was the second son and third child in a family of six children (four boys and two girls). This proved highly significant in his life (and eventual personality theory) for he always seemed to live in the shadow of his older (first-born) brother's successes. Though he was apparently fairly popular, a good singer, and a physically active child, Adler did not think of his childhood as a particularly happy time of life.[17]

He suffered from rickets in infancy, and his choice of a medical career stemmed from a near-fatal bout with pneumonia at the age of five.[18] After he miraculously recovered, Adler resolved someday to become a physician. For the rest of his life, Adler believed that young people should be encouraged to make their career or occupational choices early, before fifteen years of age.[19]

Adler was clearly his "father's son," and although he was to look back at his mother with understanding and acceptance in later years, he was never very close to her. He disliked staying home and spent many hours outdoors, trying to set records of accomplishment in children's games and related play activities which might compare favorably with his older brother's. Adler admitted that he brought much of his childhood misery on himself as a result of his great ambition to stand out among his peers.[20] He was only an average student, however. In 1895, true to his aspiration, Adler earned the medical degree from the University of Vienna, but he seems to have lacked a close mentor-student relationship with a professor to match Freud's tie to Brücke (Chapter 1) or Jung's tie to Bleuler (Chapter 3).[21] He joined a group of student socialists in college, some of whom were Marxian, and Adler seems to have met his wife in this group.[22] Raissa Adler was from a wealthy Russian family, and she was much the enlightened, intellectual revolutionary of her time.[23] They were married in 1897 and eventually reared a family of three daughters and one son.

Adler opened his first office as medical general practitioner in a neighborhood near the Prater, Vienna's famous amusement park. His patients were primarily of the lower social classes, and significantly, several of them were performers, artists, and acrobats from the nearby amusement stands. Adler found that these physically skillful and often exceedingly strong performers had developed their outstanding abilities in reaction to a physical weakness or accident in childhood.[24] Although it is not documented with certainty, the initial contact with Freud apparently stemmed from a defense Adler made of Freudian theory in the public press. In line with his socialistic leanings, Adler was a tireless champion of the underdog. In 1902 he was invited by Freud along with others to begin a series of weekly meetings dealing with psychoanalysis. This is the group that eventually

Alfred Adler

mushroomed into the Vienna and then International Psycho-Analytic Association. He was made the first president of the Vienna group in 1910. By the close of 1911 he had resigned his position and broken permanently with Freud.

The split with Freud can be credited to many factors, not the least of which was that Adler simply rejected the domination of a second "older brother." In 1907 he published his first book, the study of *Organ Inferiority and Its Psychical Compensation*.[25] There were many physical conceptions in this work, and we shall consider it below. Shortly thereafter, he published a paper in which he introduced the concept of an *aggressive drive*. But as the years slipped by, Adler became increasingly reluctant to think of human behavior in drive terms. He was developing a more self-determined, truly psychological conception of human behavior. Adler was particularly dissatisfied with Freud's insistence on the omnipresent sexual instinct, and apparently the issue that brought their theoretical differences to a point of no return was the Oedipal complex.[26] An unfortunate situation developed in which opposing camps formed, and Freud was apparently prompted by his supporters to force Adler's hand in some way. Freud therefore wrote to a psychoanalytical journal which both men edited, saying that his name could no longer remain on the title page unless Adler's name was removed. Adler immediately resigned, and though Freud tried in a subsequent meeting of the association to find some middle ground, the split could not be repaired. This was the most bitter parting of the ways Freud ever had with a former associate.

Nine other members of the Vienna Psycho-Analytic Association left the organization with Adler.[27] Individuals from this core established an Adlerian group which was initially called the Society for Free Psycho-Analytic Research, an obvious jibe at Freud's authoritarianism.[28] Eventually they were to establish their own journal, and Adler's supporters were to increase and form into organizations all over the world. Shortly after the break with Freud, Adler discontinued his general practice and took up psychiatry as a full-time profession. It was 1911, and he was clearly his own man.

One of the first important influences on Adler's thought following the Freud period was a book published in 1911 by Hans Vaihinger, entitled *The Philosophy of "As If"*.[29] Vaihinger was a neo-Kantian admirer of Nietzsche, who took the spirit of Kant's ethical doctrine to "behave *as if* a God exists" and developed it into a concept of "fictions" of which Adler was to make use. Yet over time, we can see a drifting away from fictionalism in Adlerian thought to what he took to be the lessons of Darwinian evolutionary theory. He discussed evolution in a correspondence with Jan Christian Smuts, whose book *Holism and Evolution* appeared in

1926.[30] Adler's last book, *Social Interest: A Challenge to Mankind* (1964, published first in 1933), is heavily colored with evolutionary themes.

It is actually possible to identify the period in his life when this concept of *social interest* (*Gemeinschaftsgefühl*) tipped the theoretical scales for Adler and literally recast his outlook. It was immediately following World War I. Adler had spent two years as a doctor near the Russian front. He was later in charge of a hospital ward which treated Russian prisoners suffering from typhus. He then returned to Vienna and worked in a military hospital setting. He also visited a children's hospital and saw the pitiful effects of war from this heart-rending perspective. Returning to his followers after discharge, a definite change had come over Adler. He was always a good mixer and an optimistic, convivial, and affectionate friend. But now his energies were directed toward a single purpose: his theoretical approach was to be dedicated to the further development of "social interest" among humankind. Human beings must fulfill the potential that evolution was nurturing within their very bosoms and cultivate a sense of responsibility and care for their fellow human beings.[31]

This shift in emphasis, combined with Adler's unwillingness to associate his movement with a specific socialist political philosophy, was greeted with outcries of protest by many of his followers. The strong moralistic flavor of his social-interest concept seemed to wash away the earlier emphasis on subjectivity and relativism in the Vaihinger period. By 1925 considerable internal dissension had developed over these and other issues—resulting in an "old guard" versus "young Turks" confrontation which re-enacted the Freudian drama like a haunting replay of the past. At a heated meeting in which the younger Adlerians clashed with the old guard, Adler was moved, if not actively to support, then at least to do nothing that might contradict his more rabid young advocates. His older, influential followers, frustrated by his unwillingness to defend their point of view, left the auditorium and broke off from him much as he had broken off from Freud years before.[32] Undoubtedly, Adler's personal nonauthoritarianism and sympathy with the underdog played a role in his actions, which cost him dearly for he lost the theoretical support in the Viennese academic circles that individual psychology might otherwise have enjoyed.

Meanwhile, the practical effects of individual psychology were being felt throughout Vienna. Following the war Adler held a minor political post as a vice-chairman of a workers committee, and through such contacts he made friends with certain officials of the Social Democratic Party, which had come to power. Through one of these associates, Adler succeeded in having an individual psychology clinic attached to each of more than thirty of the state schools of Vienna.[33] These advisory councils were essentially child guidance clinics in which the entire family participated for counseling. Between 1921 and 1934, Adler and his students ran these clinics with such success that a noticeable drop in delinquency was recorded in the Vienna area.

In one sense, the loss of his older, scholarly, even bookish followers spurred Adler to implement the kind of psychology he really favored, a psychology of *use* which today might be called applied psychology. Adler devoted himself to adult education, lecturing to groups of teachers and parents in a very down-to-earth manner. His psychology has ever since been viewed by some as nontechnical and even superficial. Of course, nothing could have upset Adler less than this charge.

Unlike Freud, whose patients were predominantly from the upper social classes, Adler prided himself in being a psychologist for the common person of the lower social classes.[34]

In 1926 Adler made his first trip to the United States and later spent one year (1929–1930) as lecturer on the temporary faculty of Columbia University. He then became visiting professor for medical psychology at the Long Island College of Medicine—a position he held until his death. The situation in Vienna was deteriorating during this period because of the rise of fascism.[35] In 1934, after the Austro-fascists had come to power (they later closed his clinics), Adler left Vienna permanently and lived in New York with his wife.[36] His death came unexpectedly on a European speaking tour. Adler was in the midst of delivering a series of lectures at Aberdeen University in Scotland and they were going extremely well. Following breakfast on 28 May 1937, Adler went for his accustomed stroll during which he suffered a heart attack (degeneration of the heart muscle) and died. He had lived sixty-seven years.

Personality Theory

Structural Constructs

Dualism, Holism, and the "Law of Movement"

Adler viewed the human being as a *holistic* organism that behaves as a totality of mind and body;[37] we should never separate the two. What distinguishes mentalistic from nonmentalistic creatures? The factor of *movement,* answered Adler. Plants, for example, are *rooted* products of nature. Even if a plant could see that it was about to be ground underfoot by a stroller, it could do nothing to deflect the fatal end. "All moving beings, however, can foresee and reckon up the direction in which to move; and this fact makes it necessary to postulate that they have minds or souls. . . . This foreseeing the direction of movement is the central principle of the mind." [38]

Mind and body are united through what Adler liked to call the *law of movement*.[39] He argued that mentality may be seen in both physical *and* psychological actions of people. Adlerian structural constructs are thus intimately related to motivational (movement) constructs. As he once phrased it: "Movement becomes moulded movement— [that is] form. Thus it is possible to gain a knowledge of mankind from form, if we recognize in it the movement that shapes it." [40] A human being is not a machinelike structure first and a moving system second, as when pushed by libido or some such. People appear to have *set* structures only because their behavioral movements take on a consistent style (form) of what we have come to call personality.

Adler was thus historically important in the development of what is called *nonverbal communication* or *expressive movement* in interpersonal relations. He proposed that an *organ dialect* (*organ jargon*) could be seen as a kind of "communication through body movement" in the way a man carries himself or in the thrust of a woman's jaw and the steadiness of her gaze.[41] People speak out to us through nonverbal behavior, telling us of their confidence, timidity, deviousness, and so on, even though they may not state anything aloud.[42] We do not need a depth psychology to understand this expressive language. Freud erred when he saw in the childlike behavior of the adult—bed-wetting or retention of feces—a *regression* to earlier times prompted by unconscious mental forces. This is rather a continuing and unchanging physical expression, a communication through

organ dialect that has been said before and will continue to be said.[43]

Movements in human behavior therefore reflect *both body and mind*. There is a difference to be noted between body and mind in that psychic movements always take on a *direction* whereas physical movements need not. A digestive process in the body or a leaf blowing in the wind lacks the goal direction that we see when people communicate their personal attitudes in organ dialect or tell us literally of their outlooks on life. In 1914 Adler put into words the most basic law his thinking was to retain throughout his mature years as theorist. "If we look at the matter more closely, we shall find the following law holding in the development of all psychic happenings: *we cannot think, feel, will, or act without the perception of some goal.*" [44] Since this principle of goal direction clearly distinguishes psychic (mind) from physical (body) actions, Adler cannot be labeled *monistic*. The monist would place emphasis on the *similarity* between mental and physical events.

Goal Orientation in All Psychic Living

The *psyche* or *soul* (Greek root of *psyche*), as he sometimes referred to it,[45] was for Adler merely the *locus of movement*, set in the context of interpersonal relations, as well as the individual's unique striving for advantages in life.[46] A brother maneuvers to outwit his sister and get the last piece of cake for himself, thus reflecting in his personal (locus of) movement the cleverness of a *goal-oriented, psychic* act. Adler's definitions of the psyche were likely to be framed in functional, useful terms, as when he spoke of the psychic organ as ". . . the evolution of a hereditary capability . . . for offense and defense with which the living organism responds according to the situation in which it finds itself." [47] Although this definition recognizes the role heredity plays in evolving the psyche, Adler was quick to point out that hereditary explanations fail to capture the true nature of the human soul (psyche). [48] Arguments from heredity turn our attention backward, to the fixedness of the physical past, rather than forward, to the uniqueness of the future. Hence, "it seems hardly possible to recognize in the psychic organ, the soul, anything but a force acting toward a goal, and Individual Psychology considers all the manifestations of the human soul as though they were directed toward a goal." [49]

Human beings are not only goal-directed in psychic living, they never work at cross-purposes with themselves as Freudian psychology would have it. As mind and body can move in unison, conscious and unconscious psychic factors strive for the *same* ends. [50] Of course, consciousness may conflict with unconsciousness over the means to these ends. [51] Unconsciously we may want to steal something while consciously we insist on earning it, but the desired object is still a common goal for both regions of mind. So-called unconscious psychic contents are poorly formulated intentions; they are "parts of our consciousness of which we have not fully understood the significance." [52] Consciousness is important to life because this is how we make certain of our goals and in turn strategize to achieve them. [53] An animal that lacks consciousness is more at the mercy of chance events than an animal that can effectively think around obstacles to goal attainment. The aim of individual psychology is to teach people how to assess their total (holistic) behavior in light of their goals and to learn

thereby that when it comes to ultimate goals, the psyche never wages war against itself. [54]

Style of Life

Adler believed that the human being is an animal who needs to frame its personal existence with meanings. But meanings do not simply exist independently of the person's ideas about existence. [55] Jane's meaningful understanding of an event is never precisely what John's meaningful understanding is, because each of these persons comes at life from a different body of predicating ideas. Sometimes the meanings we ascribe to our life situation are wrong, and errors in living are the result. [56] Jane could misunderstand John's intentions and unfairly think less of him. Whether a person's actions stem from accurate or inaccurate assumptions, the wise psychologist knows that "*a person's behaviour springs from his idea.*" [57] One of the earliest and most important guiding ideas the person formulates is the *prototype,* defined by Adler as the "original form of an individual's adaptation to life." [58]

At a very early age, roughly between three and five years, the child assesses his or her life circumstance and then lays down a prototypical life plan of action. [59] This plan is rarely understood completely in consciousness, so most often one's prototype is unconscious, consisting always of (1) a goal and (2) a relevant strategy for achieving that goal. In fact, Adler once referred to the prototype as the *complete goal* of the life style. [60]

Once the child has framed a prototype, for the rest of his or her life everything that takes place will be carried out for its sake. We all therefore make our own law of movement by behaving according to the pattern dictated by our unique strategy. Adler used several different terms to refer to the uniquely individual strategy each person uses in trying to realize the goal contained in the prototype.

In 1913 he spoke of it as an *ego line.*[61] By 1914 he was speaking of the course of life as a *life line,* and then a *life plan.*[62] He later spoke of the graph of life as a running path of development being carried on by the prototype.[63] It was not until the middle 1920s that he finally coined the phrase that has come to be most widely known in his writings, *style of life.*[64]

The style of life (or life style) is therefore Adler's most comprehensive description of personality. At times he would also use the term *ego* which he defined as the "personality as a whole."[65] He meant by this that we tend to characterize a person by some limited feature of that person's life style, as in Freud's typology of the anal character. Anality does not tell us all there is to know about this person's behavior, but it does convey a quick impression having some validity.[66] In order to get a comprehensive understanding of personality, we have to consider the person's early life setting, the prototype he or she puts down, the resultant law of movement, and the success or failure of this strategy in pursuit of the projected goal.[67] When we add up all of these factors and refer to them collectively, we are concerned with the life style. There is also a strong suggestion in Adlerian writings that the ego is concerned with the more understood (conscious) aspects of the psyche, whereas the life style always involves the not-understood (unconscious) aspects as well!

Adler also used a concept of the *self,* but this was not precisely a structural construct. It enters into his theory more properly as a motivational construct, and we shall be taking it up below. When a theorist uses a self-construct structurally, he or she ordinarily refers to a self-image or possibly a self-identity. However, Adler specifically rejected the approach that reduces behavior to an individual's self-conception. Even though he viewed people as being moved by the ideas they bring to bear in life, Adler preferred to base a personality description on what people actually do in their behavior rather than on what they say about themselves in a "self-concept." As he summed it up: "The only thing we can evaluate are his [the person's] actions. Thus, a person may consider himself an egoist, whereas we may find that he is capable of altruism and working with others. On the other hand, many people may consider themselves as real 'fellow men,' but a closer examination may show us, unfortunately, that such is not the case."[68] Note here the obvious stress Adler put on the conscious self-image. One gets rather light treatment of the unconscious in Adlerian psychology. It is not a major concept since it is interpreted as the *lack* of something (understanding) rather than the positive assertion of a behavioral pattern.

In order to clarify our thinking on the major structural terms of this section, Figure 8 presents a schematization of the style of life. Note that an abscissa labeled *span of life* runs from birth to maturity. The ordinate symbolizes increasing life experience, as the little boy pictured moves from cradle out to the world. By roughly age five, he has formulated a prototype that frames his law of movement and shapes his goals as a continuing life plan. Let us say that the boy of Figure 8 has adopted the prototype of being a "Peck's bad boy." For whatever reason, he has decided to aspire to naughtiness. The prototype is symbolized as a scroll with wavy lines running through it as if we were looking at a partly unfurled road map. The idea here, of course, is that the road map points out the various moves our individual child must make in order to retain his particular life style of being a "bad boy." As the individual in fact behaves according to his

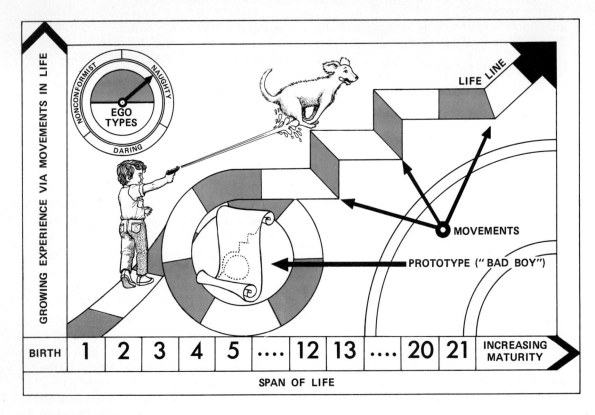

Figure 8   Style of Life

prototype, the wavy lines over the years act out the plan proposed by the prototype (labeled the *life line*). Adler was fond of referring to these life-line moves or strategies as the *games* people play in life.[69]

As an adult, the individual pictured would naturally continue his life plan (prototype) by being a nonconformist, possibly a practical joker, or even an asocial individualist. If at any point along the way to maturity, we type him in some such fashion, considering his personality as a totality, then this characterization would be an *ego* reference. His ego designations might thus change over

time—as from naughty child to daring teen-ager to nonconforming adult. But the basic prototype would remain unchanged, even as he might shift to a new, previously unused strategy in the game of life. Indeed, Adler once observed: "Very few individuals have ever been able to change the behavior pattern of their childhood, though in adult life they have found themselves in entirely different situations. A change of attitude in adult life need not necessarily signify a change of behavior pattern. . . . [The] goal in life is also unaltered."[70] Hence, when we step back and view the entire process—past, present, and future, prototype and law of movement, ego and life line—we capture the totality of Figure 8 in the phrase, *style of life*.

The Meaning of Individual:
Subjectivity and Uniqueness

In 1914 Adler summed up individual psychology as follows:

. . . I have called [my approach] "comparative individual psychology." By starting with the assumption of the unity of the individual, *an attempt is made to obtain a picture of this unified personality regarded as a variant of individual life-manifestations and forms of expression. The individual traits are then compared with one another, brought into a common plane, and finally fused together to form a composite portrait that is, in turn, individualized.*[71]

These traits of personality are *not* inherited, but are laid down by the person as he or she enacts the prototype strategies.[72]

It would not be wrong to equate Adler's use of *individual* with *subjective.* In referring to the development and education of the school child, he said: "There is always something subjective in the development of a child and it is this individuality which pedagogues [teachers] must investigate. It is this individuality which prevents the application of general rules in the education of groups of children."[73] It is important to appreciate this subjectivity meaning of *individual,* because Alder also made frequent reference to social or group factors in his theory. Since he felt it is impossible to get the individual's subjective point of view without having proper knowledge of the possibilities the social environment affords the person, Adler clearly stated that "Individual Psychology comes into contact with sociology."[74] But the focus of Adlerian psychology is always on the subjective life style, the totality of factors that go to make up the unique individual, rather than group influences as such. People do not strive for *sameness.*[75]

Every life pattern we see before our eyes *could* be different.[76] If Emily blames her chronic shoplifting on the fact that she was reared in a tough neighborhood where everyone was encouraged to steal, Adler would *not* accept this social-influence argument as an explanation of her current behavior, but merely as an *excuse* for it.

Vaihinger's concept of *mental fiction* gave Adler the theoretical foundation for his view of subjectivity in behavior. *Fictio* derives from the Latin root meaning "to invent, shape, form, or construct."[77] Hence, the concept of a *prototype* is a direct translation of the fiction, though Adler also specifically used the terms *fictions* or *fictive goals* before he used the *prototype* phrasing to convey the same meaning.[78] Further, just as Vaihinger had claimed that the "real" world is not real, but merely appears *as if* it were the way we want it to be, Adler argued that individuals behave *as if* their life experiences were as the (fictional) prototypes spelled them out to be.

Prototypes formulate the meridians and parallels of personal life maps, but maps can be wrong. A map that is in error as to the lay of the land is not only useless, it is dangerous. As he developed his theory of personality and especially psychotherapy, Adler became increasingly prone to refer to fictions disparagingly,[79] as when he referred to the neurotic as being "nailed to the cross of his fiction."[80] Normals do not *lack* fictions, of course. We all have them; for instance, we believe that our country is the "best"—or the "worst"—on earth. Such consciously expressed beliefs are likely to be *fictive* and hence erroneous.

For Vaihinger, *all* beliefs are fictions—relativistic "concepts"—so that one person's "error" is only an error because another person's "error" somehow has gained the upper hand and convinced the first party that he or she is wrong. There is no "real world" on which to base absolutes, so that convention decides which fiction is "true" and which is "false." Adler, who was not so relativistic as Vaihinger, first thought of fictions as prototypes, then incorporated the prototype notion into his formal theory and subsequently referred to fictions as *discernible* errors. For a time, Adler even proposed a *counterfiction* construct which balanced the excessive or erroneous claims that a given fiction might make. As he said: "The counterfiction consists of ever-present corrective factors and brings about the change of form of the guiding fiction [that is, the basic prototype]. This counterfiction forces considerations upon the guiding fiction, takes social and ethical demands of the future in account with their real weight, and, in doing so, insures reasonableness." [81] This reference to "social and ethical demands" should be kept in mind, for at this point in 1912, Adler was willing to call these *counterfictions*. Following his return from World War I, however, he was not so ready to agree that all social demands are fictional. As we shall see, Adler was to find his absolutes in evolutionary theory.

Motivational Constructs

Adler's Early Use of Organic Constructs

Adler's first book, *Study of Organ Inferiority* (1907), was based largely on a medical model of abnormal behavior. The central thesis of the book was a kind of Achilles'-heel argument in which Adler suggested that congenital or developmentally retarded (physical) *organ inferiorities* could lead to "a special tension in the psychical apparatus." [82] By *organ* Adler meant any physically identifiable part of the human body, like the eyes,

the leg muscles, or even the nerve tracts leading from the kidneys to the urinary apparatus. In fact, Adler made a special study of the latter type of organ inferiority in children in which he found that when such individuals became physically ill, they were more likely to develop enuresis (bed-wetting) than migraine headaches. [83] A person breaks down at his or her weakest physical point. Adler cited over fifty cases in this study, tracing the tendency to enuresis to hereditary causes—a style of theorizing that he later rejected. [84] At the same time that various organic inferiorities of the body show up as symptoms (like enuresis), Adler suggested that there is also a parallel tendency for people who develop neuroses to suffer a physical *inferiority of the brain*. [85] This brain inferiority is a multiplying factor, since the combination of a heightened tension in the nervous system and a brain that lacks the capacity to adjust to such rises in tension surely make a neurotic breakdown likely.

Even so, Adler found that not all children whom he suspected of having the necessary organic inferiorities (brain and related urinary weakness) actually developed enuresis. Some exhibited this symptom only during certain times of the day or night. Others did not stay enuretic but developed neuroses. [86] It was this discovery of the variety of individual reactions to inferiority that gave Adler his first inkling that the patient as an intentional *person* contributes something to the life situation to which he or she has to adjust. [87]

Compensation

In order to explain the varied reaction to organic inferiorities, Adler proposed one of his most important early concepts, *compensation*. Initially, he described this process in organic terms.

As soon as the equilibrium, which must be assumed to govern the economy of the in-

dividual organ or the whole organism, appears to be disturbed due to inadequacy of form or function, a certain biological process is initiated in the inferior organs. The unsatisfied demands increase until the deficit is made up through growth of the inferior organ, of the paired organ, or of some other organ which can serve as a substitute completely or in part.[88]

For example, a small girl might be likely to get inner-ear infections. Having suffered through several of these illnesses—and assuming there was no permanent damage to her hearing—she might develop such sensitivity to sound and rhythm that she could turn this initial weakness into a strength. In time, she might become a talented musician.[89] Compensation could also be seen in the case of a man who develops a keen sense of hearing following the loss of his eyesight.

To account for the variety of reactions to enuresis, Adler introduced interpersonal explanations to this theory of compensation.[90] He came to see that some children compensated their physical problem in a nonphysical way. A little girl with enuresis became very babylike and dependent on her parents who were totally involved in helping her to overcome this seemingly incurable "sickness." A little boy with enuresis seemed to be gaining satisfaction from the irritation his domineering father suffered whenever the boy wet the bed. Adler could see that both of these children had turned an initially completely physical minus into what was now a psychological plus of sorts, and in coming to this insight he became a psychologist as well as a medical doctor.

This development in Adler's theoretical style was a gradual one. Initially, any kind of psychological maneuver by the compensating person was said to be due to organic changes taking place in the brain itself. In other words, Adler suggested, in the same way that an arm muscle increases in size because of exercise, so too does the brain of a compensating person increase in size because of the effort to overcome the organ's inferiority. In time, thanks to the larger brain size, some alternative is hit upon to compensate the weakness. We have here a theory of physical changes in the brain itself making psychological changes possible rather than psychological changes in strategy being made by the same brain. Here is how Adler captured this mechanical form of brain compensation in 1907:

. . . compensation is due to overperformance and increased growth of the brain. This strengthening of the psychological superstructure is shown by the successful outcome; its relation to steady exercise is easily guessed. . . . The psychological manifestations of such an organ may be more plentiful and better developed as far as drive, sensitivity, attention, memory, apperception, empathy, and consciousness are concerned.[91]

This organic style of theorizing is not very original. It departs little from the theories we reviewed at the outset of this chapter, and in time Adler was to drop this style of explanation entirely.

Adler's Shift from Organic to Sociopsychological Explanation

Whether because of the influence of his student days or simply because of his growing experience as clinician, between roughly 1910 and 1918 Adler's writings reflected a continuing move away from biological to sociopsychological explanations. He drew parallels between his theory and Marx's social (not economic) theories.[92] He came to speak against such historically important physical models as those of Hippocrates[93] and Lombroso.[94] He spoke positively of Kretschmer's brilliance[95] but dimissed his efforts to reduce human personality to internal chemistry.[96]

Adler noted that a child born with a poor digestive system will probably receive a certain amount of pampering from his or her parents. The likelihood of this child becoming spoiled by the parents, of learning to give up in the face of life's challenges, is doubtlessly greater than for a child born with healthy internal organs.[97] Yet what is at work here? Is this child's personality *due* to the weak stomach, or is it the combined result of the parental attitudes (they might have avoided overprotecting their offspring), the child's assessment of the familial situation in light of these attitudes, and the compensating possibilities in *other* aspects of life? Adler concluded that organ inferiorities are only *one* of many factors in the child's total life situation. Further, by now introducing the prototype construct, Adler shifted the source of influence in a child's life from the *past* (heredity, humors, body types) to the *future* (the goal of the life plan framed by the prototype).

We can see how this developing change in Adler's thought came into conflict with Freud's thought. Adler was denying the importance of instincts and drives.[98] Although he flirted with drive theory at one point, even speaking of a "confluence of drives" and a "transformation of drives" into their opposite, only a few years later he began to reject all such concepts.[99] By shifting his emphasis forward to the *goal* of behavior, Adler could no longer see the value of energic systems or pleasure principles which impelled the person willy-nilly.[100] Pleasure and dis-

pleasure are secondary factors, ways we talk about the individual's psychic state as he or she advances along the pathways of life in search of various goals. Rather than being determined by a physical state from the past, Adler now said, "*the psychic life of man is determined by his goal.*"[101] This goal was framed by the prototype, and the person behaves according to it determinately, changing his or her life style only when the prototype and its attendant goal is changed.

Adler assumed that *life itself is motion*. Though he used a homeostatic model in his initial theory of organ inferiority, he came to reject the conservation-of-energy model that Freud had used as the *constancy principle* (see p. 52). A mechanical balancing of forces will never capture the maneuvering and strategizing that takes place in human behavior, which is *teleological* or goal-seeking.[102] Hence, said Adler: "We do not think of conservation of psychological energy because we know that the causality which we seem to meet was actually placed into the situation by the given individual himself. Man makes one thing the cause and another thing the effect. . . . The most important question of the healthy and the diseased mental life is not whence?, but whither?"[103]

This view is a direct rejection of the Freudian libido theory, though as we noted in Chapter 1, libido does play a directional role in psychoanalysis that is not unlike Adlerian goal concepts (cathexes fix goals for the individual; see p. 55). Although Adler made passing reference to libido in his earlier publications,[104] it was not long before all mention of a presumed underlying energy disappeared from his writings on personality. What he substituted was a reference to the *creative power* of the individual.[105] Although Adler did not make this power a central *formal* construct of his theory, he considered creativity to be an aspect of compensation; the prototype is also a way of describing the individual's creative power, since we all continually create our own existence in light of it each day that we live.

Creativity, unlike *libido,* is a psychological construct with *no* physical analogue. When we observe an artist painting a landscape, we can ask two kinds of questions about the product taking form. We can wonder about the artist's physical coordination or the expenditure of caloric energy in getting the job done. But we can ignore such mechanical questions and consider the painting as an intended end product. Why this interpretation of the scene and not another? What was the artist striving to communicate? What goal (*telos*) did he or she have in mind? This latter interest is precisely the interest Adler had in personality as a *style* of movement created by the person each lived moment for the sake of an intended goal. The *psychological* question was not the "how" of motion but the "why" of one style of movement rather than another.

The Role of Feelings in Motivation

A child's first creative act was said to be spurred by compensation,[106] leading to the framing of the prototype. But what triggers this compensatory reaction in the first place? Initially Adler thought of compensation in organic, mechanical terms, but what about his later thinking, when the more psychological motivations might have been said to be operating?

Here Adler wrestled with varying motivational constructs before working out his mature point of view. While still under Freud's influence he toyed with drive theory; in fact, he proposed two contradictory drives that were not so different from Freud's Life and Death Instincts. Thus, Adler spoke of an *aggression* and an *affection drive.*[107] People must try to dominate others, push them around, and even let off steam occasionally

by being hostile; but people also have a need to love and be loved by others, to trust them, and to care for them. This *drive* or *need* terminology did not last long, and at about the time he was writing of fictions, Adler substituted the concept of a *will to power* for that of the aggression drive. Vaihinger was an admirer of the philosopher Friedrich Nietzsche, and Adler specifically mentions that his will-to-power construct was related to Nietzsche's.[108] Whether he really understood Nietzsche on this issue of power-seeking is another matter.

Nietzsche's will to power and will to seem (not unlike Vaihinger's "as if") were *not* to be interpreted as a hostile, selfish exertion of one's individuality.[109] In the same way that Vaihinger's fictions were used positively and without an implied error connotation, Nietzsche's will to power was simply a reflection of the person's will to grow and to self-realize (improve, be better than now). The general drift of Nietzsche's philosophy was that each person has to develop and express his or her own identity because God is dead (as a concept worth cultivating), and therefore we can no longer continue shifting our human responsibility for what happens in this world onto a superhuman power. As we shall note in Chapter 10, Nietzsche is one of the fathers of existentialistic philosophy, which puts great emphasis on this theme of assuming responsibility for one's personal behavior. Even though Adler would have agreed with this view, we find him using the will to power in a somewhat negative tone, as if it were heir to the old aggression-drive concept.[110] In fact, he saw it as based in a reflexive response, as follows:

When not more than six months old the child is known to reach out for all objects and is unwilling to return them. Shortly after that, under the pressure of a will-to-power, it seizes hold of people who take an interest in him. Jealousy is the safe-guarding tendency accompanying this desire for possession.[111]

Adler did not think it desirable to cultivate this will to power in children, since he believed it to be a remnant of humanity's lower nature that might best be lived without. In the same way that he had opposed the affection drive to the aggression drive earlier, he now placed most of his emphasis on something in human nature that might offset the uglier aspects of power striving. He spoke of the will to power as a "guiding fiction" (in a negative sense) and then noted that only when this is tempered by a *will to cooperate* can the individual avoid gross mistakes in living.[112] A child who always seeks to lord it over others is doomed to adjustment problems in time, because life is not only competition in goal attainment, but cooperation in goal attainment. The concept of will was an improvement over instinct, since it emphasized self-direction and the goal sought by the person, but a full understanding of how this behavioral process might be initiated seemed to evade Adler for some time.

Not until he had brought the emotions into central focus in his theory did Adler speak with greater clarity on the actual mechanics of compensation.[113] The purpose of emotions is to create an advantage for the person in any situation that is about to involve him or her. Emotions compress the life style into a more active, insistent movement toward the goal. The young man whom we say has quite a temper tells us in his very loss of control how important the goal he is trying to gain is to him. If things do not go his way, he becomes very angry, shouts and curses, and through the resultant intimidation of those with whom he relates, gets his own way after all.[114] A person's feelings put his or her body into shape to meet a challenging situation in life. We steel ourselves with the emotional mood of determination ("I can do it!") in order to get the job done. Even so, Adler rejected the notion that emotions are *produced* by the person's body. "To a great extent, though they rule his body, they do not depend on his body: they will always depend primarily on his [a person's] goal and his consequent style of life." [115] Adler firmly believed that a person's emotions never contradict his or her life style.

Fixing now on those emotional feelings that might operate at the outset of a compensation, Adler proposed a duality which was reminiscent of his earlier opposition of aggression and affection needs. He named these emotions, which often work in opposition to each other, *inferiority feelings* and *social feelings*. The feeling of inferiority is a conscious or unconscious recognition of physical or psychological shortcomings.[116] It may be based on an actual organ inferiority (as the enuretics), or it may be prompted by a misjudgment of personal worth. A teen-aged girl might think of herself as ugly when in fact she is *not* unattractive.[117] Such misjudgments usually stem from childhood feelings of inferiority, which everyone has—and legitimately so because we are then incompetent in many ways—but which are outgrown through winning friends, achieving success in at least some of our efforts, and so on.[118] Some people are never quite able to get this feeling of competence for any of a number of unique reasons. Adler liked to point out that to feel inferior is to be human,[119] and that this basic feeling is what provides the psychic motivation for both normal and abnormal individuals.[120] He could now make the blanket statement that the single spur to action in compensation is a *subjective sensation of inferiority*.[121]

This feeling of inferiority results in a compensation leading to selfish power strivings in the individual's behavior. That is, such a negative form of compensation results if there is no counterweight emotion occurring. Adler thought of social feelings[122] as a natural counterweight to offset this selfishness, much in the way he had earlier opposed affection to aggression in his drive theory, or the will to cooperate as a counter to the will to power. The terms change, but the single theoretical idea Adler was trying to get across was that a person who simply lets his or her feelings of inferiority run loose and even multiplies them can become an overbearing, self-seeking, thoroughly unsocial human being. Fortunately, nature has provided the inborn capacity to feel tender toward others, to empathize with them, and to promote contact with them.[123] We call this *social feeling* when we focus specifically on the felt emotion. However, when we want to describe the conscious effort people can make to bring on these feelings in themselves and in others, we should use the more inclusive term, *social interest (Gemeinschaftsgefühl)*. Actually, Adler used the terms *social interest* and *social feeling* interchangeably so that practically speaking they are synonymous.[124] Probably the best definition of *social interest* is the following: "Social interest means . . . feeling with the whole . . . *under the aspect of eternity*. It means striving for a form of community which must be thought of as everlasting, as it could be thought of if mankind had reached the goal of perfection."[125]

From Overcoming to Fulfilling Compensation

Adler's original meaning of *compensation* was as an automatic, act-react mechanism. Some physical or psychological minus serves as a signal for a plus reaction. As such, a good catchword for early Adlerian theory would be *overcoming*.[126] One does not give in to misfortune but overcomes deficiencies precisely because they are there for the overcoming. Adler once put this in the form of a law to parallel his basic law of compensation. *"The fundamental law of life . . . is that of overcoming."*[127] Deficiencies can be overcome in either a positive (affectionate, socially concerned) way or in a more negative (power seeking, aggressively selfish) way. The ruthless businessman who seeks every shady advantage within the law may lack an admirable character, but we cannot overlook the fact that his merciless moves in the game of life could well be compensating any hint of being a failure in life. On the other hand, the saintly woman who gives her life to good works could well be compensating for her misspent selfish youth.

Adler tried to find some common way of describing such different forms of compensation. He suggested that in compensating for inferiority, we always set the highest goals for ourselves to overcome our greatest weaknesses. We therefore *strive for superiority;* we not only try to make up for our greatest weakness, but we try to go "one up" in this or a related area of life. The businessman and the saintly community-working woman both in their own ways are striving for superiority. Originally, Adler applied the striving-for-superiority construct to all people as a natural tendency, but gradually it began to take on a negative connotation (similar to the will to power), as when he observed: "This goal of complete superiority, with its strange appearance at times, does not come from the world of reality. Inherently we must place it under 'fictions' and 'imaginations.'"[128]

Striving for superiority is thus one of those guiding fictions we have already considered.

This is why those who strive for superiority often strike us as going too far in their (positive or negative) efforts to overcome their weaknesses. Adler suggested that we can even guess at how severe a person's feelings of inferiority are by the extent of the countereffort being made to compensate it. Someone who is excessively moved by feelings of inferiority is said to be suffering from an *inferiority complex,* which Adler defined as "the gulf between an individual and his supernaturally high goal." [129] When this gulf between what one is and the outstanding or unusual person one is striving to become (goal) is lessened, we are likely to witness *overcompensation*.[180] To overcompensate is to carry compensation too far. The weakling adolescent boy who begins a Spartan regime of body exercises, spending most of his time weightlifting to the exclusion of other activities, would be overcompensating an inferiority. This would still be a positive overcompensation because he does not injure anyone or intrude on their lives. Had this boy begun a series of antisocial acts, such as armed robbery or car theft, he would have overcompensated his feelings of weakness in a negative direction by supposedly overpowering or outwitting the law.

Not only is the counterbalancing compensation overdone in such unusual or abnormal strivings for superiority, but there is also a rigidity and compulsiveness about it. Normal striving for superiority retains a degree of flexibility so that if one avenue is blocked another can be substituted for it.[131] Once the boy realized how much time it would take to acquire a muscular body in the extreme degree he had in mind, he should have (if this were a normal superiority-striving effort) tapered off his goal and sought alternative goals. He might have settled for a well-toned body and engaged in school activities designed to get him recognition in other ways. He might have become a worker on the school paper, for example. In some cases, the inferior individual may live out his or her superiority strivings so actively as a life style that it would be possible to speak of this person as having a *superiority complex*.[132] Such people constantly want to be singled out as somebody special, and they make exaggerated claims on others as well as on themselves to be superior in every way. They carry a "Do you realize who I am?" emotional attitude (pride) into every social contact. Superiority and inferiority complexes are really two reactions to the same thing.

Adler's continuing problem as theoretician was how to distinguish between superiority strivings of an acceptable and those of an unacceptable nature. He thus brought in the constructs of social feeling and social interest —as well as the self construct—to round out his final theoretical formulation. That is, he began seeing the cultivation of social feeling through active social interest as the natural antidote to the more negative, selfish, and overcompens tory ways of striving for superiority. If people would only cultivate social interest, then social feelings would be multiplied, and a kind of spontaneous caring for each other would take place, thereby negating the reasons for overcompensation in the first place because no one would be made to feel excessively inferior! Even though he had named his approach *individual* psychology, the net result was that Adler placed himself firmly on the side of *social* factors in human relations. "That which we call social feeling in Individual Psychology is the true and inevitable compensation for all the natural weaknesses of individual human beings." [133] Community feeling had to be cultivated, for it was not so much an inborn instinct as it was an innate potentiality.[134]

Adler had returned from World War I heartsick at the devastation it had wrought. The only antidote to this madness was social interest (*Gemeinschaftsgefühl*), which is a worthy goal because humanity strives not only for superiority but ultimately for *perfection*. Adler's final theory thus placed the *striving for perfection* as the general case in all compensatory moves, with either selfish or altruistic (unselfish) strivings as variations of this *single* motivation in life.[135] In his final years of life Adler contended that the power-grabbing and predatory actions of our fellow human beings are due to an overcompensated inferiority complex transferred into a kind of misdirected striving for perfection. Such individuals have taken their *innate* prompting to perfect themselves and perverted it to selfish ends. To clarify what he meant by *innate,* Adler reached back to his early interest in the physical side of behavior and emphasized concepts taken from the Darwinian theory of natural evolution.

Human beings are by nature and through nature evolving to a higher state of living. By cultivating social feeling as a goal for humankind (social interest), we are not therefore cultivating just another sociocultural *fiction* nor even a counterfiction, but an *absolute truth*.[136] As we noted previously, Adler did not retain the complete relativism of Vaihinger's "as if" philosophy. One is not behaving *as if* social feeling could be experienced or *as if* social interest could be cultivated. The superiority and power strivings are the fictions of humankind. Social feeling is a *fact* of life, one not to be taken lightly if humanity is to survive.

With this growing emphasis on the striving for perfection, late Adlerian thought began to take on a different coloring. The catchword became *fulfilling* or *becoming*. People are still overcoming feelings of inferiority, but they are doing so as *one family,* rather than as *one person*. The family of humanity is evolving to a higher state, and each individual human being has the moral responsibility to further this end, to raise the level of ultimate human perfection that nature began in organic evolution. The individual cultivates the total by improving himself or herself as a single representative of that totality. The *self* therefore means the uniquely individualistic goal we all have open to us as a potentiality. Each of us must fulfill the potentials of humanity in our unique life style; hence "it is the self which grows into life, which we recognize later on as creative power."[137] To be truly human we must project as a goal our selfhood as an evolving human being trying to create individually a better (social) totality. We must grow and fulfill our human potential by moving toward and in time literally creating our *self*.[138] This fulfilling rather than overcoming emphasis in later Adlerian theory is demonstrated in the closing lines of his last book, *Social Interest* (published posthumously in 1939).

Our present-day burdens are the result of the lack of a thorough social education. It is the pent-up social feeling in us that urges us to reach a higher stage and to rid ourselves of the errors that mark our public life and our own personality. This social feeling exists within us and endeavours to carry out its purpose; it does not seem strong enough to hold its own against all opposing forces. The justified expectation persists that in a far-off age, if mankind is given enough time, the power of social feeling will triumph over all that opposes it. Then it will be as natural to man as breathing. For the present the only alternative is to understand and to teach that this will inevitably happen.[139]

The Growing Reliance on Darwinian Evolution

In a curious, roundabout fashion, the final formulation of Adlerian theory returned to its initial emphasis on the person's physical stature by stressing organic evolution. Evolution was taking humanity someplace, and though Adler now put his emphasis on the evolution of social interest, he still did not quite become a full-fledged sociologist, a *supra-individual* theorist. He always stressed the individual physical being, as when he defined *culture*: "The changes which the human race has made in its environment. . . . our culture is the result of all the movements which the minds of men have initiated for their bodies." [140]

What is really significant about Adler's Darwinism is that he always seemed to consider it in teleological (intentional, final-cause) terms. We know from his biographer and personal friend Phyllis Bottome that Adler's belief in organic teleology was so basic to his thought that he took progressive evolution to be a proven scientific fact.[141] Evolution of new forms follows the aim and the will of the animal concerned. In 1910, for example, Adler argued that ". . . a nutritive organ has followed the will and need of assimilation; touch, auditory, and visual organs have followed the will and necessity to feel, hear, and see; a procreative organ followed the will and necessity for progeny [offspring]." [142] Adler rejected the survival-of-the-fittest aspects of Darwinism, scoffing at those who believed in a talion (dog-eat-dog) principle (as did Freud) or even a self-preservation principle.[143] The lessons of history proved that human beings were pack animals;[144] they had to be part of a group because of their weak physical structure, as Darwin had explained. Hence, the natural compensation for individual weaknesses was the evolution of society.[145]

Adler suggested that social feelings per se had probably evolved when human beings were made aware of this weakness, particularly as typified by the helplessness of their newborn offspring.[146] Thus *motherly love* plays an extremely important role in Adlerian psychology, because the mother is the first to respond to her child's weakness and must instruct the offspring in social interest as he or she matures. So imbued was Adler with evolutionary theory that he came to define his entire approach in such terms. "The talking about social interest as belonging to the evolution of man, as part of human life, and the awakening of the corresponding understanding is today being attended to by Individual Psychology. This is its fundamental significance, its claim to existence, and this is what represents its strength." [147]

The great confidence that Adler came to place in his interpretation of Darwinian thought in his later years is nicely exemplified in the following quote. Overlooking Darwin's celebrated antiteleological theme of natural selection, Adler said in 1933:

The originators of the concept of evolution in the field of general organic life, such as Darwin and Lamarck, have pointed out that life must be understood as movement toward a goal, *and that this goal—the preservation of the individual and the species—is attained through the overcoming of resistances with which the environment confronts the organism. Thus* mastery of the environment *appears to be inseparably connected with the concept of evolution. If this striving were not innate to the organism, no form of life could preserve itself.*[148]

Having cast Darwin in a teleological light, Adler went on to argue against survival-of-the-fittest doctrine by claiming that the "striving to *master one's fellow man*" has been shown by individual psychology to be erroneous, "contradicting the concept of evolution."[149] People who justify selfish, predatory acts based on a survival-of-the-fittest argument are not reading the lessons of evolutionary history correctly. Social organisms (societies) pass through stages of evolution much like physical organisms do.[150] Just as the physical body of the human being reacted to a situation of weakness and evolved into a higher form, the body of all humanity must now react to its social weaknesses (selfishness, hostility) and evolve to a higher form. Adler realized that he was describing a utopia. He was not referring to any present-day society nor to any given form of political or religious practice.[151] God concepts and religious beliefs merely reflect the fact that all people *have* been made aware of what a perfect state of humanity might be—a "heavenly" state of interpersonal relationships.[152]

The good sense which evolution gave us tells us that what we must do is strive to create that ideal here on earth; we must appreciate that this insight is itself a product of evolution. We must be socially useful, for to act in opposition to the community is literally to *oppose* evolution.[153] It was this confident reliance on the lessons of organic evolution that gave Adler his basis for whatever socialistic commitments he had. His socialism was *loving* in contrast to the *angry,* class-warfare socialism of Marxian communism. He tells us,

The honest psychologist must therefore talk and work also against poorly understood nationalism if it harms the community of all men; against wars of conquest, revenge, and prestige; against the drowning of the people in hopelessness due to widespread unemployment; and against all other disturbances of the spreading of social interest in the family, the school and the social life.[154]

Moralistic Tones in Adlerian Psychology

Adler held what might be called a *natural ethic,* in that he believed people were naturally good and the direction evolution was taking humankind was positive.[155] Though he was always prepared to blame a person for "errors" in living, Adler did not wish to judge people so much as he thought it best to call a spade a spade. A person's character reflected his or her outlook on life, and the psychologist who must deal with the person must therefore take a position on this question of how to describe behavior.[156] It does not make sense to speak of character except in a social context of how the person's behavior affects other people.[157] It follows that if a person has no concern for others but expects everyone to contribute to his or her life satisfactions, then psychology would fail in its duty if the selfishness of this mistaken life style were not pointed out openly and honestly. Such a person is literally in violation of the further evolution of the group! Adler therefore took the viewpoint of the total social context as his point of reference, as follows: "And so Individual Psychology stands on firm ground when it regards as 'right' that which is useful for the community. It realizes that every departure from the social standard is an offense against right and brings with it a conflict with the objective laws and objective necessities of reality."[158]

Adler was no apologist for the status quo. He made it quite clear that, though social structures rely on social feelings among individuals, the social institution must exist for the sake of the individual and not vice versa.[159] Courageous people, who feel themselves to be part of a whole community,[160] are also the ones who take on progressive values because they naturally want things to improve.[161] People who strive for personal satisfactions without concern for others are *failures* in living.[162] The middle-aged person who shuns town meetings, believing such co-operative efforts cannot solve a town's problems, reflects the life style of a failure.[163] Paradoxically, the father of Individual Psychology called people who compensated in a selfish—and completely individualistic—manner *cowards*. The coward is "like a person living in an enemy country."[164] How is it that such cowardice and selfishness arise in people? Adler usually traced these personality tendencies to the *errors* of his clients and others whom he considered to have lost *courage* (feeling with the total), or possibly who had never learned to feel courageous in the first place.

Sometimes a mistaken life style can spur the evolutionary advance of mankind. This happens when the harmful effects of an antisocial person, a selfish person, or a spoiled (pampered) person generate some kind of countering effort on the part of others to offset his or her negative influence.[165] The excesses of a selfish political leader like Adolf Hitler might have elevated the common social consciousness—social interest hence social feeling—of the peoples on earth ever after. Yet it would be well if such errors were not made. The lesson of evolution is that those aspects of life that are mistakes, hence ill-adapted to the environment, do not survive.[166] Thus Adler honestly believed that if we could educate people concerning their mistakes, they would respond and rectify them. The problem is one of making it clear to others, for "if a man understood how he erred, stepping out of the way of evolution, he would leave this course and join general humanity."[167]

Defense Mechanisms or Mental Mechanisms

In 1913 Adler used the term *repression* to describe how a person might be working toward some goal but not be entirely clear on the means being used to attain it.[168] Sometimes these poorly understood movements reveal themselves in dreams.[169] An efficient secretary, for example, does not realize that her high level of competence is actually a reflection of her striving for superiority over men until one night she dreams of her boss as the only male file clerk among many women. She dominates the boss unmercifully and ridicules him in the dream by comparing him to the female file clerks under her charge. The emotional satisfaction she gets from this domination tells her something about the meaning of her job competence when she examines the dream content upon wakening. Though Adler was to retain this style of dream interpretation, as time went by he felt less need for a concept of repression in his theory. He objected to the presumed split in the psyche that the repression construct in the Freudian sense relied on, and so in time Adler was to reject this construct altogether.[170]

Adler interpreted *identification* as being due to the empathy that one person always feels for another, based on social feeling.[171] Identification continues in our behavior throughout life and is one of the bases for group formation. Sympathy is a partial expression of identification. In Adlerian terms, a boy identifies with his father only out of love and never out of castration fears, as Freud had suggested.[172] The same applies to the girl, who identifies with her mother out of love. Adler felt it was wrong to draw analogies from physics to explain behavior, such as claiming that energies flow back to infantile pathways, and so on. Thus he made no use of the *regression* construct—which he felt favored a post hoc explanation of human behavior rather than a forward-looking, telic explanation.[173]

The most fundamental and widely used defense mechanisms in Adlerian psychology are *compensation* and *overcompensation,* related concepts which we have already covered. The actual maneuvers (movements) in the game of life compensating for inferiority feelings account for the kinds of individualized reactions that Freudian mechanisms tried to explain. One of the first analyses Adler made of an excessive form of compensation (or overcompensation) concerned what he called the *safeguarding mechanisms (or tendencies)* employed by people suffering an inferiority complex. He meant specifically their tendency to be overly fearful of failure even in minor things, to be hypersensitive to criticism, and to view any setback as a fictionalized "disgrace" in life.[174] Such a person might become habitually ill in order to avoid people or possibly shrink about in a character structure of submission and defeat. Adler eventually renamed the safeguarding tendency, fixing more on the goal confronting a person and the methods used to avoid meeting it. For example, a person who feels too inferior to meet the goal of being with others socially can become a chronic grumbler, thereby ensuring that people will *not* wish to associate with him or her. The challenging goal of having to relate to others can then be avoided. This avoidance mechanism, which Adler called *distance,* indicated the disparity between where one is and where the beckoning goal is.[175]

A graphic example of distance was cited by Adler's case of the woman who suffered from incontinence of urine and stool because she feared the responsibilities of marriage. When she was a child her mother had told her that such illnesses would surely make marriage impossible. When she reached adulthood and had to confront the possi-

bilities of marriage, she fell back on these "sicknesses" and placed a distance between herself and the dreaded marital goal that most of her girlfriends were achieving.[176]

Another term used by Adler was *protest,* which relates to the construct of overcompensation. To *protest* means that individuals who feel unprepared for some desired goal in life overreact to their feeling of being denied by talking about the goal too much or trying in some way to carry it off in any case.[177] Although anything occurring in life might be protested against, Adler's major usage of this concept centered on the *masculine protest*. We shall return to this construct when we take up Adler's theory of neurosis, but for now let us think of it as a form of power struggle between the sexes.[178] Historically, in most cultures the man has been considered superior to the woman. Usually, anything associated with masculinity thus has certain advantages guaranteed by right of sex. Not until recent decades have women had the sexual freedom of men, who usually are permitted a double-standard sexual morality in that they need not restrict their sexual liaisons to one partner, whereas they expect their wives to do so. Speaking during the 1920s and 1930s, Adler therefore noted how some women express masculine protest by taking on the values, manners, careers, and even attire of men. In Adlerian terms, the career-woman type who studies law, wears business suits, and refuses to be subordinated to any man is likely to be protesting masculinity. Of course, in the 1970s and 1980s we find a broadly based *feminism* taking shape in many countries of the world. Whether Adler would want to call such a major social development protest or not is open to question. As we shall see, he was a champion of women's equality during an age of male superiority. But at the same time, he was a champion of the home and family and undoubtedly would have been disappointed by the frequent denunciations of home life, motherly duties, and so on, that often accompany feminist arguments.

Adler first wrote of masculine protest in girls, but then noted later that boys could be infected with this "poison" as well.[179] The "man's man" who thinks of women as silly little playthings to be put on a domestic shelf until needed sexually would also be expressing masculine protest. The main symptom of masculine protest is: ". . . a needlessly domineering attitude towards the opposite sex. It is always noticeably connected with a very ambitious style of life, with a goal of super-man or of a very much pampered woman."[180] The modern feminist would refer to such a man as a male chauvinist. Not all masculine-protesting women lack feminine mannerisms or heterosexual interests, though Adler considered lesbianism (female homosexuality) to be one form of masculine protest.[181] Often one can find a highly feminine woman expressing masculine protest in her pampered and petted relationship with a harassed husband who finds himself continually under the thumb of his "sweet little tyrant." The pre-twentieth-century mechanism for the woman's masculine protest was in fact to make of her man a "gallant" slave, who bowed and scraped and catered to her every whim. Yet Adler was much concerned about what he took to be the masculinizing trends of the women of his time. In a quaint pre-1928 observation he may have proven himself the prophet of our time, albeit in a disdainful sense, when he wrote, "At the present time, the masculine protest is rampant and widely displayed by women of all ages, who smoke, wear short skirts and short hair and do everything possible to approximate to masculine manners."[182]

Time-Perspective Constructs

Growth and the Three Problems of Life

Adler viewed the newborn child as a reflexive organism to whom environmental experiences happen automatically and mechanically. Since the infant has no ego identity and no goal toward which he or she is striving, these very early life experiences are not especially important to the style of life eventually adopted. Somewhere beyond the first year, about the time the child begins to speak of himself or herself in the first-person pronoun *I* we can expect the prototype to begin being formed.[183] This means that ego-identity is taking shape, and now the child can tell that a life situation is acting *to* and *for* him or her. Strategizing for advantage begins with this recognition. Hence, Adler's view of development reverses what many feel happens to us as we mature. Rather than being victim to experience: *nobody really permits experiences as such to form, without their possessing some purpose*. Indeed, experiences are moulded by him [a person]. That simply means that he gives them a definite character, being guided by the way in which he thinks they are going to aid or hinder him in the attainment of his final goal."[184]

No two children grow up under precisely the same circumstances nor do they make the same evaluation of their life situation once their I (ego) awareness forms. One characteristic that all children do share, however, is the tendency to divide everything they become aware of into opposites, such as good or bad.[185] This *antithetic scheme* of mentation (thought) is carried on into adulthood but is particularly strong in childhood, so that children are prone to go to extremes in personal evaluation. If they find someone else attractive, they are likely to consider themselves ugly because they presume things to be "either-or" in their antithetic scheme. They are not sensitive to midpoints nor do they appreciate the relativism in most judgments. It is thus very important to provide opportunities for the child to see that *everyone* has strong and weak points. Sexual identities should be established as quickly after ego identity as possible, particularly for the girl, whose inferior role in our culture excites her wish to become a boy and hence makes her more vulnerable to masculine protest.[186] The child should be told at the age of two that he is a boy, or she is a girl, and that little boys grow up to be men and little girls to be women.[187]

Sexual development undoubtedly begins early in life, and therefore the child may begin fondling his or her sexual organs because this is pleasurable. However, this does not mean that children literally seek to copulate with their parents, nor are they masturbating in the same sense that an adult does. Since this fondling is culturally inappropriate and a selfish indulgence, Adler favored discouraging the baby from this practice with as little show of concern or distaste as possible. Children who sense that we are overly concerned with sexual play will be more likely to continue these habits in order to gain attention.[188]

The prototype is finalized around the age of four or five, but the child's ego identity is still not well established at this time. This means that many of the experiences and subsequent strategies incorporated into the life style are poorly articulated or possibly not verbalized by the child at all. They would be *not understood* in Adlerian terms, hence unconscious. Adler felt that Freud and Jung had misunderstood these *wordless impressions* of childhood, attributing to them the properties of instincts or inheritances from a racial unconscious.[189] Children are extremely dependent on the parent for adequate preparation for life, and the parental challenge is to make a highly dependent creature independent yet considerate of others.[190]

Whenever Adler spoke of the problems or challenges of life which people confront he framed them in terms of three problem areas: *occupational*, *social*, and *sexual*.[191] He felt that any problem of living could be traced to these sources, because human beings have certain inevitable ties. We are tied to the earth and in order to exist we must produce the necessities of life from natural products through work; we are tied to others in society as fellow creatures seeking common satisfactions in unique ways; and we are tied to our history and the future of our kind by way of sexual reproduction.[192]

Family Constellation and Birth Order

Since everything hinges on a child's life situation and the evaluations made of this situation when framing the prototype, the kind of character a child will develop must take root in the nature of the parental family constellation.[193] Such factors as the size of the family, the position of the child in the succession of brothers and/or sisters, or the sex of siblings must necessarily influence the kind of prototype a person is likely to form.[194] We should never be routine about the study of birth order, but there are noticeable trends to be seen in people that depend on their order of birth.[195] In a multiple-child family, for example, the *eldest* or *first-born* child often looks after his or her younger brothers and sisters, thereby becoming an extension of parental authority.[196] The first-born child not only becomes a great believer in power, but as an adult he or she is more likely than other children in the home to have a conservative, conforming outlook, to be a "regular citizen" and a conventional individual.[197]

The *second-born* child is likely to feel a sense of challenge in the family constellation. The older sibling is more competent in games that children play, setting standards of winning that the second-born would like to surpass but may be unable to. The second-born child is also the one who is looked after and bossed by the older brother or sister, and he or she is also removed from the limelight role of being the baby of the family as younger offspring arrive. Adler said that if a second-born child has any talent, we are more likely to see this offspring develop it than the others because of the child's probable life style of trying to excel in some way.[198] Unfortunately, this birth order can also foster an extremely ambitious and even jealous personality. In any case, we expect to see a lot of drive in the second-born and less authority-proneness than in a first-born child. The reckless kid brother, who is willing to "take any dare" and likes to break the rules, nicely meets the picture of a second-born child. Later children must be examined in terms of a combination of factors. What opportunities do they have to share a bit of the family spotlight? Are there older sisters, brothers, or both to outshine and compete with, and what are their particular skills?

It is not the number of children or the specific order so much as it is the *total* situation facing the child that must be understood if we are to gain an insight into his or her personality. If the eldest child is mentally retarded, or for some other reason has adopted a very repressed personality, the second-born might acquire the authority-proneness that is thus left open for the more normal sibling to acquire. If the time between birth of sets of children is long, with one couplet

of children much younger than an older couplet, two separate eldest-versus-second-born dynamics might emerge in the same family.[199] In some ways the *last-born* or youngest child of the family has the most serious handicap of all to overcome in life, for he or she is the continuing baby of the family and thus most likely to be *pampered*.[200] Pampered children grow up to be selfish adults, who expect to have everything handed to them in life. The *only child* is also likely to have been given everything he or she wanted in life without having to share and hence is likely to grow to maturity as a pampered child.[201] Even if he or she escapes this selfish character, the only child is more likely to be an individualist as an adult than is a child with siblings.[202] Since Adler valued social interest, his writings make clear that he much favored families with more than one child. He felt it was excellent training to be brought up in a home with siblings where one learned the give-and-take so essential to communal living in general.

Adler once said that proper mothering demands two things: winning the child's trust through a show of love and redirecting this trust to other persons.[203] He believed that we can always see the harmful effects of bad mothering in the lives of failures, the neurotics, criminals, drunkards, and prostitutes of society.[204] There is no special skill or mystical power to the art of mothering. It demands interest and effort and is more likely if the woman in question has had a childhood in which such attitudes were passed on to her from her own mother.[205] But even if they were not, personal effort can make up for an unhappy childhood caused by a bad mother. In his final theory, Adler spoke of motherly love as the product of evolution, that is, as a special case of social interest.[206] He suggested that this love is probably triggered emotionally in the mother initially by the baby's obvious helplessness and then develops further by the baby's crying insistence to be cared for.[207]

Adler was not trying to fix guilt on one person by pointing to the harmful effects of *bad mothering*.[208] He was aware that there are many reasons for this failure including the relationship with the husband. "Moreover, it is not the child's experiences which dictate his actions; it is the conclusions which he draws from his experiences. . . . We cannot say, for example, that if a child is badly nourished he will become a criminal. We must see what conclusion he has drawn." [209] Adler was always careful to assign the individual child a major source of the blame—or credit—for his or her eventual style of life.

The father plays a secondary, enlarging role in the socialization of the child. He is secondary because his influence starts later, but he is still very important to the child's eventual success in living.[210] As Adler put it, "The task of the father can be summed up in a few words. He must prove himself a good fellow man to his wife, to his children and to society." [211] Adler was strongly opposed to the authoritarian role for the father.[212] In fact, he was opposed to authoritarian family structures of any sort. The father, he felt, does not have any special authority even for being the breadwinner because as a totality the family has common claims on the money earned by any of its members. Mothers should not pressure their husbands into being the family enforcer or disciplinarian. If they do, then they are admitting that they have failed to win their children through social interest (motherly love).

Adler spoke rather informally of stages or *epochs* in development, and he did not name explicit stages through which the individual supposedly moves in growing up.[213] He looked at this maturing process in somewhat more fluid, individualistic terms than Freud. In line with his emphasis on the moves in the game of life, Adler stressed the useful role of *play* as a preparation for life. Making an analogy to lower animals who sharpen their hunting skills in playful activities as cubs or pups, Adler noted that humans as well cultivate their interpersonal skills through play.[214] He favored games that require cooperative skills, or make-believe activities that foster a productive goal with social interest. In fact, Adler was none too sympathetic with the telling of fairy tales to children. It must be emphasized that fairy tales are make-believe stories lest the child grow up hoping for the magic of these stories to provide an easy way out of life's problems.[215]

Adler's view of the universal *Oedipal complex* was as an extension of the preparation-for-future-life tendency we see in the games of children. He said that this is simply an attempt on the child's part to play at being fathers and mothers.[216] If a child does *in fact* develop an Oedipus complex in the Freudian sense, Adler would consider it an abnormal condition. One could not say that *everyone* goes through a literal Oedipal situation in development. Of course, the pampered child, who has been coddled and petted by the parents, might well end up with the dynamics of a classic Oedipal complex.[217] For example, an indulgent mother can literally stimulate the sexual appetites and fantasies of a son by her frequent hugging, kissing, and massaging of the boy.[218] The Oedipal pattern can also be seen in an offspring who uses it as a means of distance. A daughter who has incestuous wishes for her father can attach herself to him, dominate him in time, and thereby use this supposed sexual fixation not only to receive many favors from the father but to avoid meeting other males—men who could in fact fulfill the sexual promptings that she is really terrified to confront in a mature fashion.[219]

In rejecting the literal Oedipal complex, Adler also rejected the Darwinian-Lamarckian theme of "ontogeny recapitulates phylogeny" on which it was based in Freudian theory (see p. 65). Here again, Adler proved selective in his acceptance of evolutionary concepts. For him a true Oedipal complex is essentially a mistaken life style, seen in the behavior of neurotics who have not been adequately prepared to meet one of the three major problems of life, the sexual.[220]

Sometimes mistaken life styles are prompted by the competitive relationships established with brothers and sisters in the home. Adler called this *sibling rivalry,* by which he meant the striving for the family spotlight among the children, taking into consideration as well such factors as birth order, organ inferiorities, and parental attitudes toward the children.[221] Sibling rivalry is a natural extension of the need for each child to feel uniquely worthwhile, but it can get out of hand in families lacking social interest. Some family settings become a battleground on which children wage a running warfare, one trying to outdo the other in any way possible. An occasional outcome of sibling rivalry is a sort of striving for naughtiness in one or more of the children. If a first-born, for example, is especially good, then the only avenue open to the second-born in the antithetical scheme of good or bad is to try to be as naughty as possible.[222]

Adler felt that one could always judge the nature and adequacy of a child's life style from behavior during the transition periods of life, as when a family structure suddenly alters with the birth of a new child, or the father has to shift jobs, or the family moves to a new location.[223] Well-prepared children make these transitions smoothly and without overcompensation. Poorly prepared children are thrown into a crisis by such changes in routine.

The Roles of the School and Teacher in Maturation

By the time a child leaves home to begin school, his or her prototype has been put down. Of course, school experiences can help alter a prototype or at least add some features of more appropriate socialization by cultivating the child's social interest. Adler was one of the first theoreticians to point out that school failures are often life failures as well.[224] Few school failures suffer from a physical problem like mental retardation, so when a child begins to receive failing grades, we can be fairly certain that he or she is beginning to give up on the problems of life. The child would like to be removed from the challenge of school studies (distance), even if this means being labeled *slow and uneducable.* Often, a boy or girl substitutes naughtiness for academic effort in a distancing maneuver because teachers then begin to ignore them. The school's responsibility is to help all children retain hope of overcoming their inferiorities.[225] Each child has a strong point that must be identified and given an opportunity to grow, thus bringing the person some degree of success so that overcompensatory moves will not be necessary.

Adler's emphasis on the values of equality led him to criticize certain teaching practices, such as the track system in school where children are grouped according to their intelligence or supposed ability to learn.[226] Children from homes with more material advantages have had more experiences in travel, have been exposed to more educational aids like books and magazines, wear better clothes, and probably speak better than children from poorer homes. As a result of these factors, the wealthier children end up in the upper tracks of a grouped system and receive a better education than their poorer classmates. Adler was also opposed to children skipping classes because they are considered gifted.[227] The child who skips something and is therefore ahead of his or her natural peers adopts the psychology of wanting to skip and to achieve unreasonable goals in the future. Finally, Adler criticized use of the intelligence quotient (IQ) to categorize children as normal, subnormal, and so on. At the very least, neither the child nor the parents should be told the exact IQ score lest they use this knowledge to inflate or injure the child's ego identity.[228] As with the track systems that use them, Adler felt that intelligence tests greatly favor children from the upper social classes.[229]

Children should learn as much as possible from their actual experience of doing things in school. They should learn the logic of life, not memorize information in rote fashion.[230] Adler favored letting children work along at their own rate rather than insisting they try to meet arbitrary standards, because they are individuals. "It is this individuality which prevents the application of general rules in the education of groups of children." [231] Not all children are suited to the standard programs of basic education. Some children learn most effectively in coordination with their eyes, ears, and hands as they acquire occupational skills.[232] Adler therefore favored the use of manual training education, particularly for the child approaching adolescence.[233] Any form of discrimination, whether of race, creed, or social class, negates a good education for the children involved. The effective teacher should see that student rivalries and personal ambitions are kept within bounds, and that each child has an occasional turn in the classroom spotlight.

One of the recurring controversies in education, especially around the time of pubescence, is whether or not the school should provide children with sex education on a routine, formal basis. Based on his individualized approach to personality, Adler did *not* favor the teaching of sex as an academic subject. Children are so different in their needs to know about sex that the teacher can never really know what sex education means to a specific child when presenting the topic to the class as a whole.[234] If a child asks a particular question, then the teacher should deal with it in individual instruction. Otherwise, the home is the proper place for sex education.

Adolescence

Adler did not wish to make anything special of adolescence, feeling that it would be too easy to emphasize the physiological changes and resultant dramatic changes in the body.

In fact adolescence is, for Individual Psychology, simply a stage of development through which all individuals must pass. We do not believe that any state of development, or any situation, can change a person. But it does act as a test—as a new situation, which brings out the character traits developed in the past.[235]

At no other time in life is a person's life style so apparent as it is in adolescence. The challenge here is to become a finished person, to come up to the front of life's development and take on a pattern for one's occupation, marriage, and social life throughout maturity. The child naturally feels this period is a test, a time of gnawing need to prove that one really is adult material.[236]

Adler felt that more concern should be shown in adolescence to the problem of occupational choice. We let sexual adjustment completely replace the far more pressing problem of "What shall I do with my life?"

As we noted in the biographical overview, Adler believed that each person should settle on an occupational or career goal early in life—surely by early adolescence and preferably before the age of fifteen.[237] This bias followed from his view that only the individual who works toward a meaningful goal can find satisfaction in life. Occupationally disjointed people or people with no given job aspiration can hardly live socially useful lives. Adler felt that some people avoid career decisions because they fear the challenge of setting an aspiration; others secretly dream of having good fortune fall their way without personal effort.[238] The high school girl who dreams of being discovered as a movie star and the boy who hopes for a lucky break to move him ahead in life are courting disaster. The schools must therefore provide help with career decisions.

Adulthood and Old Age

Once into the twenties, the individual as an adult has the task of harmonizing occupational goals with family and social goals. If sex was a preoccupation and concern in adolescence, it is doubly important to life now. Adler had to take a clear stand on the question of physical love or sex, because Freud's sexual orientation continually stood in contrast to the social-interest emphasis of individual psychology. In the following quote, Adler gives us a good picture of what he took *love* to mean:

"Love," with its fulfillment, marriage, is the most intimate devotion towards a partner of the other sex, expressed in physical attraction, in comradeship, and in the decision to have children. It can easily be shown that love and marriage are one side of cooperation —not a cooperation for the welfare of two persons only, but a cooperation also for the welfare of mankind.[239]

Sex is not a power play, a domination of one sex (feminine) by the other (masculine).[240] It irritated Adler to hear people speak of marriage as an acceptable outlet for the satisfaction of a sexual "instinct." This was a drive psychology, a mechanistic interpretation of sex, and he felt it grossly underestimated the importance of love to humanity. He was opposed to premarital sexual relations; he had seen too many unhappy outcomes from relationships founded on what was later recalled (especially by the male) as "easy virtue."[241]

The only way for a marriage to succeed is for each mate to be more interested in promoting the happiness of the other than in securing personal gratification. Adler also believed that for a full solution to the problem of love and marriage children are necessary. "A good marriage is the best means we know for bringing up the future generation of mankind, and marriage should always have this in view."[242] Since the intimacy required for a rich marital life must be regularly cultivated, the proper marriage custom for human beings is monogamy.[243] People who enter into marriage with possible escapes in mind, such as promiscuity or divorce, are often those who have been pampered as children. Marital breaks occur "because the partners are not collecting all their powers; they are not creating the marriage; they are only waiting to receive something."[244]

Old age brings on special problems. The older person must step aside and allow new ideas and new directions to replace the old. Unfortunately, the older person tends to be inflexible in outlook. He or she becomes stubborn and loses the will to cooperate which is so essential to effective social living.[245] Even so, Adler felt that our civilization has not sufficiently considered the problems of the elderly. Too often we simply retire people to a drab existence, one offering nothing but death as its final goal. We must care enough for our elderly to offer them a place in society. Religions, of course, provide the very old person with the hope for a life hereafter, which is a worthy goal if the individual has a faith. Actually, of course, religious beliefs are an extension of social interest in the Adlerian view.[246] The older person without a religious concept of the hereafter can achieve a related sense of working toward some lasting end by helping others in the continued growth of humankind.

Individual-Differences Constructs

Although his fluid view of living made typing according to some fixed scheme of development difficult, and in one sense, contrary to his major emphasis, Adler was aware of the need for personality theorists to generalize their insights. He therefore admitted to being a typologist of sorts.[247] Over the years Adler had occasion to type personality, sometimes in a technical but more often in an informal sense. He usually did so in the context of a clinical analysis, so that many of his suggested typologies were best suited to a psychotherapy or diagnostic scheme. However, we will combine Adlerian typologies of all sorts into our individual-differences section in the interests of organization.

Three Types of Women
Who Flee Femininity

Adler once suggested that there are three types of women who really do not believe that woman can be equal to man. The first type is similar to Freud's conception of the castrating female. She spends her life proving that she is the equal or the better of any man. She "wears the pants" in the marriage, if indeed she ever does marry, and her interests are always in the direction of the masculine culture—to have a career, enter politics, and so forth. A second type goes through life as a kind of slave to the opposite sex—obedient and humble in relations with men, entirely resigned to the fact that she is a member of the "weaker" sex. The third type is like the second, except that she is unable to accept this lesser role. She cannot fight like our first type, but rather drags herself through life appearing on the surface to be resigned, yet constantly irritated that she must play a second-class role.[248]

Two Approaches to
Problem Solution

Adler respected the person who feels confident enough to speak his or her mind, to exert enough independence and aggression to find solutions to problems in a direct fashion. Those who use devious methods of getting their ideas across or speak in a halting and uncertain manner, he found, are habitually frustrating to both themselves and others. He called the former type the *optimists* in life, the latter were *pessimists*. Pessimists always look for the darker side of things because of an underlying inferiority complex; they cannot meet life head on, so they never manage to solve their problems.[249]

Two Styles of Failing in Life

Adler's preference for the direct, aggressive manner of the optimist did not blind him to the fact that often a person with something like this pattern of behavior can nevertheless fail in life. He once proposed to classify failures in terms of an active-passive dimension.

I have proposed a classification of difficult children which proves useful in many respects: into the more passive children, such as the lazy, indolent, obedient but dependent, timid, anxious, and untruthful, and children with similar traits; and into a more active type such as those who are domineering, impatient, excitable, and inclined to affects, troublesome, cruel, boastful, liable to run away, thievish, easily excited sexually, etc.[250]

Three Types of Children Likely to Overcompensate

Although he spoke of compensation rather than overcompensation, Adler once typified three kinds of childhood situations that are likely to generate pronounced reactions in the individual facing them. We think it best to call this a typology for the tendency to overcompensate, given Adler's eventual stress on the fulfilling aspects of compensation. Those most likely to overcompensate are "children who come into the world with weak or imperfect organs; children who are treated with severity and with no affection; and, finally, children who receive too much pampering."[251] Adler believed that neurotics are prone to be passive failures in life, retreating as they do to symptoms that might then be used as excuses for not confronting life (distance). Criminals, on the other hand, would be considered active failures because they aggressively seek to achieve their goals by taking, pushing others aside, hurting, and so forth. Regardless of the style chosen, all failures in life are due to a lack of social interest.

Four Approaches to Reality

Adler also typed the behavior of people in interpersonal relations. Some individuals take a dominant or *ruling* approach. We always know we are in their presence because they have something in mind for us to do—with them, for them, or directed by them. A sec-

ond, which might be termed the *getting* type, is constantly leaning on us, borrowing or begging, asking us to help rather than ordering, but in one way or another managing to have us provide them with something they want. A third type is the individual who is unavailable when problems arise. Adler called this the *avoiding* type of person, who simplifies existence by withdrawing from any challenge that threatens defeat. Thus far we have a series of rather unsuccessful life styles. Fortunately there is also a fourth type, the *socially useful* person who does not forget us when we are in trouble, but actively tries to help us overcome our problem. We all can think of certain people in our lives who think more about giving than receiving, and who never put themselves above us but relate in a friendly manner as our equal.[252] These are the courageous human beings, the true heroes of individual psychology.

The Various Types of Complexes

In 1935 Adler published a paper on the nature of complexes which stands as his most thorough attempt to name types or traits of personality. Adler said that a *complex* was a simplified expression of the goal contained in the prototype. Someone with a *power complex,* for example, has had a goal of domination over others since childhood when he or she first framed the prototype. Complexes tell us what the individual is trying to get or bring about in life. There are thousands of complexes possible and again as many variations of these basic life styles.[253]

As if to show that he could describe an unending series of complexes, Adler pointed to several examples which we can recognize as further descriptions of the life style.[254] Thus, an individual with an *inferiority complex* is telling us that he or she does not feel strong enough to solve life's problems. The child with an *Oedipus complex* has been pampered and lets us know that the parent is the goal that cannot be let go. Some people have *redeemer complexes,* going through life trying to convert others from one life style to another whether they want to be converted or not. Others have a *proof complex,* because they are terrified of committing errors and therefore want to frighten us as well by constantly asking for immediate proof of anything we say.

Some people go through life with a *pre-destination complex,* either fearing nothing because they believe nothing can happen to them or failing to plan adequately because "it is all the same in the end anyhow." There is also the *leader complex,* frequently noted among geniuses and highly ambitious people. They stick to their guns and go their own ways because they see themselves as out front in life. If their actual talent lags behind their life goal, they can become pitiful specimens. Many people go through life with a *spectator complex.* They want to be near the action of life, but they do not wish to stick their necks out and really participate. Finally, there are those who oppose all change, so we may describe them as having a *"no" complex.* Such people are either highly conservative and fearful of change or they must simply contradict whatever is said in their presence. It is as if they see something extremely advantageous and even important in disagreeing with others.

Psychopathology and Psychotherapy

Theory of Illness

Achilles' Heel and Psychological-Tension Theory

Recall that Adler had begun by proposing an Achilles'-heel theory, with a paralleling in-feriority-of-the-brain concept, which implied that a *psychic tension* was set up because of the weak point of the physical body (see p. 132). Then as the brain compensated by increasing in size and proficiency, there developed a capacity to overcome the body weakness (see p. 133). This purely biological and mechanical explanation did not last long because Adler found that there was always a psychological contribution made to this internal, psychic tension.[255] A little boy might have some hereditary weak link in his body making him prone to enuresis—Adler called these *segment inferiorities*—but the fact that he *does* develop enuresis depends more on the interpersonal tension he feels in relation to unloving parents than it does to the physical weakness per se. In his final theory, we therefore find Adler saying that interpersonal tensions that reflect themselves internally as psychic tensions are a major cause of neurosis. The specific symptom the neurotic then suffers is also due to certain hereditary segmental inferiorities of the body (that is, the Achilles' heel or weak link).

Psychic Hermaphrodism and Neurotic-Reversal Tendencies

Children use *antithetic schemes* to order reality, splitting their experience into black-white alternatives in what Adler considered to be a primitive way of thinking. Neurotics continue to reason as children throughout life. They first see the world as a power play of winners versus losers, and then they strategize in their prototype to avoid losing. Casting male-female relations as such a contest, neurotics have strict prescriptions of an either-or nature for the sexes. All of those traits of personality that appear weak—passivity, obedience, softness, fright, ignorance, tenderness—are relegated to the *feminine* role. And all of those traits appearing strong—greatness, riches, knowledge, victory, coarseness, cruelty, violence, activity—are elevated to the *masculine* role (which is the winner role). We can see *masculine protest* in this division and recall that either a man or a woman can reflect this form of overcompensation.[256] But Adler thought of this split between masculine and feminine in an even more complex fashion than *just* masculine protest.

He viewed it as a deep-seated tendency on the part of certain neurotics and labeled it *psychic hermaphrodism*.[257] An animal that is physically *hermaphroditic* is one having both sexual reproductive organs (penis as well as uterus). Psychologically, certain neurotics are threatened by the thought of behaving in both a masculine and a feminine way (*androgynous* behavior). Since the masculine role is dominant, this is the one they identify with. A normal man may be willing to admit that he is sensitive, cries easily, and likes to have tender interpersonal friendships with other men. He is not threatened by these personality traits because he feels basically secure, has a satisfying job, is appreciated by his family and neighbors, and so on. A neurotic man, on the other hand, may find it impossible to admit to having what he considers soft tendencies in his personality. He behaves like a man, not like a woman! Rejecting any hint of androgynous behavior on his part, this neurotic man will strive all the more to be tough, even though fundamentally he may be a weakling. He is as upset about being psychologically hermaphroditic as he would be about being physically hermaphroditic. He fails to understand that everyone has the potential to behave like everyone else.

Falsehood, Fictions, and Life Lies

The basic difference between normals and neurotics is how they design their style of life. Adler occasionally referred to the life style as a *life line,* as the course of movement over the years, which we have already discussed in the sections on personality. The neurotic, however, is someone who lives a *life lie.*[258] Having divided his or her world into simple opposites, the person destined to be neurotic now plays one side against the other, using cowardly excuses to gain advantage. "Act 'as if' you were lost, 'as if' you were the biggest, 'as if' you were the most hated." [259] If a little girl finds life too much of a challenge, she can always cultivate the feeling of being hated by her parents—particularly if there is a fleeting element of truth in this assessment. Probably all parents go through a period when they tire of—and to that extent reject—their child to a greater or lesser degree. There is no one living who has not received this kind of negative response from a parent at some time or other, no matter how subtle its expression. But the neurotic life style capitalizes on this and uses it as an excuse for not confronting life's challenges. The girl can now go through life blaming her parents for the fact that she is not successful in solving the problems of living.

The truth is, her parents neither hate the girl completely nor feel love for her at every moment. She has simply capitalized on a passing mood of irritation to frame a coward's prototype. Adler considered this *if maneuver* a common neurotic excuse. "The discussion [in therapy] invariably reveals an accented 'if'. 'I would marry *if*'; 'I would resume my work *if*'; or 'I would sit for my examination *if*'; and so on. The neurotic has always collected some more or less plausible reasons to justify his escape from the challenge of life, but he does not realize what he is doing." [260] Life lies as life lines remain *not understood* or unconscious. Neurotics live by their fictions more firmly than normals, elevating themselves into godlike figures and then, by skillfully avoiding challenges, keeping up their self-deception. Whereas the normal never loses complete sight of reality, the abnormal exists in a kind of dream state, hypnotized by the fictional importance of the life lie. The neurotic is thus "nailed to the cross of his fiction." [261] There are many imagined conflicts and cheap victories concocted in this fictionalized reality. People are set up as imaginary opponents, or having lost out in one sphere, there is sometimes a *fictitious triumph* won in another. [262] For example, a neurotic businessman might correct his friend's grammar after the friend has got the better of him in a business dealing or in a friendly golf match, for that matter. Losing in one sphere, this man must come off as the final winner in another (antithetical scheme).

As a reflection of their selfishness, neurotics tend to see today's life circumstances as continuations or extensions of yesterday. Adler called this *analogical thinking*. The argument they have with us today is "just like" the arguments they used to have with their father. Hence, they react to the present *as if* it were the past. We are suddenly in a drama not of our choosing, taking on attributes we never would assume if allowed to be ourselves instead of a stand-in for the father. [263] This is another example of the neurotic's errors in living which serve to keep a life lie going over the years. [264]

One thing is certain, "every neurotic has an inferiority complex." [265] Differential diagnoses of neurosis are based on the life style adapted by the person to compensate (overcompensate, protest) this inferiority. Since there is *always* a fictionalized idealization of the ego in this compensation, Adler said that it is equally true to say that every neurotic

also has a superiority complex! The neurotic individual tries above all else to preserve his or her godlike fiction. [266]

Symptoms are the means by which the neurotic avoids solving life's problems without taking blame for the resultant failure. [267] As Adler graphically expressed it, "The symptoms are a big heap of rubbish on which the [neurotic] patient builds in order to hide himself." [268] The most apparent and important neurotic symptom is what Adler called the *advance backward*. The neurotic gives us a flurry of activity to hide his or her retreat. "Neurosis is the patient's automatic, unknowing exploitation of the symptoms resulting from the effects of a shock. This exploitation is more feasible for those persons who have a great dread of losing their prestige and who have been tempted, in most cases by being pampered, to take this course." [269] Note in this quote Adler's emphasis on the *pampered* individual. He was to take an increasingly critical view of pampering as a major source of neurotic behavior over his years as therapist.

Diagnostic Distinctions in Individual Psychology

According to individual psychology, the problem of diagnosis is to determine where a symptom is helping to take the individual. It is not a question of "where from" but "whither" the symptom leads. [270] Adler did not particularly favor diagnosing patients before taking them into therapy, but he did seem to feel that his psychology should be able to account for the major clinical syndromes.

Neurosis Versus Psychosis. Adler took a quantitative view of abnormal behavior; that is, normality shades into neurotic behavior which in turn can go over into psychosis by quantitative steps of increasing maladjustment. The neurotic is a person who has a history of the life lie, seeking fictional goals, but he or she continues to meet a few of life's challenges. The psychotic, on the other hand, has completely failed in the three problem areas of life (work, love, society).[271] Psychotics greatly elaborate their fictional life style, making it into a full-blown delusional system to which they can withdraw, and see and hear things that are imaginary (hallucinations), thereby ending up being cared for on a full-time basis.[272] Although symptoms and hallucinations are painful in the short term, in the longer term an abnormal person's suffering brings more gain than loss. Anxiety, for example, can be used by the person to stimulate sympathy in others. The anxiety patient is so pathetic, constantly anguishing over some upcoming but unidentified disaster, that we all feel sympathetic and extend our help without realizing that this is like giving a drink to an alcoholic.[273]

Mania. People who develop manic reactions are those who have some very important and pressing decision to make, but because of their underlying inferiority are unable to make it. Rather than accept this fact, they try to devalue and trivialize the problem even as they keep up some type of fictional superiority in their manic episode.[274] For example, a stock-market analyst must decide whether to sell or keep a large block of stocks which he has managed for a client. The decision is due immediately, but a note from our expert tells us that he has left his office for the racetrack. A hurried search at the track locates him, and we learn that he has been investing huge sums of money on the horse races based on some foolproof system he has suddenly come up with. The

stock decision is said to be minor by comparison, and he not only jokes about it but says that he cannot be bothered by such menial matters. His excited mood, loud talking, and eccentric money manipulations all indicate that he has broken down into a manic episode. As he is led off forcibly to the hospital, he curses his back-stabbing associates who are jealous of his ability to make money at the racetrack. The heavy losses he has already sustained, he says, are "merely the first step" in his system, which will surely pay off in time.

Melancholia or Depression. People who develop melancholia or depression are those who have lived a life of distrust and criticism. We can see a general lack of social interest in their hesitating attitude. A woman who is prone to attacks of depression tends to avoid helping out with chores in most social situations; she holds back from meeting and talking to others, and is blue a good deal of the time. Underneath this pitiful exterior, she feels a continuing sense of rage and blames others for her miserable existence.[275] As with all cases of depression, this woman feels that someone has failed her in the past. She may say discrediting things about herself during an attack of depression—that she is no good for anything, that she does not deserve to live—but in actuality there is someone else whom she is calling down. Since childhood she has blamed her mother for all her dissatisfactions. To get back at her mother, she used to "get sick" and demand attention, later she was accident prone, and now when depressed she has attempted suicide. Adler found that suicide in depressed patients "always represents an act of revenge" aimed at the opponent, the supposed wrongdoing party.[276] Rather than cooperate with others, which for the depressed patient would be an act of defeat, he or she leaves the scene of fictive conflict altogether and tries to make the wrongdoer bear the guilt of the suicide. If this woman succeeds in killing herself, it will "be her mother's fault," not hers.

Schizophrenia. This is one of the most severe forms of psychosis in which the individual has completely given up all hope of a victory in the real world. In the delusional belief that he is Jesus Christ, we see the fictive goal that splits a man off from reality.[277] Actually, he has never in his life achieved the social feeling that Jesus Christ attained. This man pretended to be humble and accepting of others in a Christian way. But underneath he pictured himself in a fictionalized role as someone very special, who should be admired and even adored for his goodness. When others became irritated with his meddlesome tendency to find fault with their sinful behavior, he was isolated from social contact. After spending his late teen years in solitary dreaming and pretending to be various important Biblical figures, he finally settles on the most perfect of all human beings that ever lived.

Paranoia. This disorder, often combined with schizophrenic symptoms, is typified by extreme suspiciousness and hostility. Adler felt that these individuals probably advance toward their place (goal) in society for a time, but then, out of inferiority feelings and a complete disregard for the status of others, they begin to concoct imaginary schemes (fictions) that supposedly were the cause of their lack of courage to continue toward the fulfillment of their aspiration.[278] The paranoid attack is likely to appear when the individual feels his or her social position is threatened. A woman who for some years has managed the church social single-handedly begins acting strangely when the pastor assigns two women to assist her one year. Rather than accepting this aid in a sense of communal sharing and cooperation, she begins to withdraw from contact with other parishioners, writes unsigned notes to the pastor complaining of "evil forces" at work in the church, and on one occasion threatens the lives of her two assistants.

Sexual Perversions. Those who practice sexual perversions show in their behavior that they cannot face the challenges of love. Rather than conducting themselves in the common fashion, they *reverse* the customary morality, or the roles of their sexual partners. Adler saw this as a case of "when you cannot meet the goal, change it." Basically, all sexual perverts are highly selfish (lacking social interest). Personal gratification of lust is put above a tender regard for the pleasure of a partner, so that in one sense, perversions such as peeping, child molestation, and rape are variant forms of (selfish) masturbation.[279] Adler once defined *masturbation* as "the style of sexual life adapted to confirm isolation and to avoid love and marriage."[280] Exhibitionists are visual types who want to look or be seen at a distance rather than to confront sexual objects directly. The sadist achieves a feeling of superiority by sexualizing hostility (lack of social feeling), and the willing masochist sexually revels in the power he or she can wield over the sadist.[281] The lesbian is expressing the ultimate of masculine protest,[282] and the male homosexual is often encouraged to take this role by a strong identification with a mother who gave him feelings of being different by dressing him in girl's clothing, and so on.[283] Though, as we noted in our discussion of Freud, modern trends are currently underway to consider homosexuality a normal life style, Adler could not accept this point of view. He was family-oriented, and any sexual activity that threatened the integrity of the family was therefore *not* considered a healthy solution to the problem of love.

Alcoholism and Criminality. Adler had the unique distinction among personality theorists of pointing to the many gains that supposed losers in life might actually be seeking to achieve through what he once termed "a cheap success of notoriety." [284] People were self-defeating, but not because of a death instinct or a wish for self-destruction. They were self-defeating as one of the moves in the life game, seeking a distinctiveness even if on the negative side of life. [285] The "town drunk," for example, gains a certain distinction by having achieved the goal of being a monumental drinker. He becomes the butt of jokes, but this also means he is the center of attention. He can also use this curse as a convenient excuse for not having done something with his life. This strategy is designed to win by losing in life. [286] The egocentric pattern among criminals is documented by the fact that so many of them delight in composing autobiographies. [287] They play at being Robin Hoods, but they merely delude themselves into overlooking the strong inferiority that lies at the root of their cowardice. Adler laid much of the blame for prostitution on a society in which the major sexual emphasis is on the male obtaining satisfaction. The women who take up prostitution do not relish the feminine sexual role. They express their masculine protest by bartering with men for the highest dollar even as they despise their customers and take no satisfaction from the sexual union itself. [288]

Obsessive-Compulsivity. This disorder is often found among second-born family members, due to their drive to succeed. [289] They have a compulsive need to be perfect, to keep clean, to get ahead, to escape criticism, and so on, and when a neurosis develops, we witness these tendencies in their symptoms. Occasionally, a symptom, such as the obsessive fear of germs, may be used as a device to escape the necessity of being with people. [290] A hand-washing compulsion is "always used as a means of avoiding sexual relations, and invariably gives the fantastic compensation of feeling cleaner than everybody else." [291]

Stuttering. The fact that a person who stutters does so on a selective basis, often losing the symptom when reciting, singing, or speaking to loved ones, led Adler to conclude that this disorder was in large measure interpersonal in nature. For some reason, the individual has settled on this symptom to achieve the questionable but excuse-providing distinction of being somebody special. Possibly a girl's parents were overly concerned about her speech when she was a child, and she thus found it easy to gain their undivided attention by stumbling over her words. [292] This is often found in the life history of a pampered child. Maybe this girl also found that she could irritate or otherwise get back at her parents for imagined injuries by stuttering.

Sleep Disturbance. Adler was a firm believer that "an individual who cannot sleep well has developed but a poor technique of living." [293] It therefore followed that any sleep disturbance would diagnose a life-style problem. Nervous insomniacs, for example, were seen as people who overvalue success yet lack the confidence to achieve their highly ambitious goals. [294] They cannot relax and sleep because they are so intensely worried over getting what they want in life. Adler saw a kind of *body language* (variant of *organ dialect*) in the sleep postures of his clients. One man slept on his side with his arms drawn up tightly against his body; Adler found that this man intensely disliked his profession.[295] Defeated people without initiative in life are prone to sleep with their bodies pulled up into a ball, like the fetal position, and they also pull the covers over their head.

Theory of Cure

Some General Considerations

Adler said that the first rule in treatment is to win the confidence of the patient completely, and the second is not to worry about success. The therapist who is constantly worried about his or her success will invariably forfeit it.[296] The aim of Adlerian psychotherapy is twofold. It proceeds from the assumption that the neurotic or psychotic has framed a *mistaken style of life,* which continually distorts reality. The therapist must first help the person to correct this view of reality and to strengthen his or her confidence to live a genuine life line rather than a life lie. Secondly, the therapist has to confront the superiority mechanisms being used by the neurotic and encourage their replacement by a self-cultivated sense of social interest.[297] In this way, selfish idealization will be replaced by social feeling. This dual strategy takes us into the matters of self-study (insight) and client-therapist relationships (transference).

First, however, we should consider briefly the general framework of the psychotherapeutic contact, as practiced by the individual psychologist. Adler believed that those who know enough about human nature to see the mistakes being made by others with unproductive life styles have a *duty* to help the self-destructive individual correct these errors.[298] This is not to say that the therapist should force corrective aid on others; the responsibility for a lasting change is placed

squarely on the client's shoulders with the therapist acting as skillful coparticipant.[299] Therapists should never promise a sure cure to their patients.[300] However, Adler found that sometimes a prospective client had heard of extended analytical treatments lasting up to eight years, only to end in failure. It is only fair to give such a person some idea of how long therapy might take. Adler was therefore in the habit of saying to his clients that, though length of therapy varied based in part on the person's willingness to cooperate, he did feel that at the end of three months they should note signs of improvement. He often added to the client, "If you are not convinced after one or two weeks that we are on the right path, I will stop the treatment." [301]

The Role of Insight

Adler believed most strongly in the importance of providing the neurotic client with insight into his or her condition. As he once summed it up, "The cure can only be effected by intellectual means, by the patient's growing insight into his mistake, by the development of his social feeling." [302] What Adler was emphasizing here is the fact that even social feelings must be cultivated by conscious intellectual effort, by making the decision to look out for and be interested in others. The strategy of the individual psychologist is to begin with the present life pattern of the patient and then to work backward until it is clear to both therapist and client what the latter's superiority goal entails.[303]

Adler's close association with teachers in adult education and his founding of individual psychology clinics in Vienna combined with his emphasis on intellectual insights to give his theory of cure a kind of educational flavor. He was likely to speak of the therapeutic task as a re-education of the neurotic in the art of living.[304] He did not refer to a formalized education procedure, of course, but rather a kind of corrective mothering to be administered wih curative goals in view. The neurotic has not been made to feel in empathy with a mother figure, who then could successfully transfer this community feeling outward to others. Hence, the therapist's role is literally "a belated assumption of the maternal function." [305] As therapists, we must teach the neurotic the evils of striving on the useless side of life even as we somehow regain the neurotic's commitment to the community (foster social interest). This is not easy to achieve because not only have neurotics lived according to a mistaken life style for some years but, even when they begin to grasp the nature of their errors, they can always make use of their symptoms to confuse and demoralize our therapeutic efforts.[306]

A typical neurotic ploy is to have a symptom flare-up when therapy gets too threatening. For example, as the life lie is being made clear by the therapist's interpretations, a patient's hand-washing compulsion or fear of height suddenly becomes "worse." An inexperienced therapist can be thrown off the track by such maneuvers. Rather than be alarmed by this apparent setback, Adler proved a genius at minimizing the importance of the symptom. He often used humor, told little jokes, or made light of the symptom complaint with his attitude and expression.[307] By acting this way, Adler was fixing his attention on the *goal* of the neurotic maneuver. Like the experienced mother who does not simply buckle under when the child

begins to act up in a temper tantrum or pretended illness, Adler was not allowing the client to obtain a fictional triumph. He did not reject the client, he simply refused to let neurotic manipulations prevent him from doing his job.

Adler once referred to psychotherapy as an artistic profession.[308] He meant that one could not cite routine rules of thumb for its practice, but had to develop spontaneity as well as a sense of discipline through experience. The best therapists are those who can "see with the other person's eyes, hear with his ears, and feel with his heart: one must identify with him." [309] It also helps if a therapist has known the neurotic state personally. As the saying goes, "It takes one to know one," and a therapist who has successfully come through a neurosis is therefore less likely to be misled by neurotic maneuvers that he or she has also tried to use in the past.[310]

Adler realized that his first interpretations in a therapy series could turn out to be wrong as the sessions slipped by. This realization did not disturb him, for he pictured himself: "in the same position as a painter or sculptor, who at the outset does whatever is suggested to him by experiences and skill. Only later on does he check his work, strengthening, softening and changing the features to bring out the correct image." [311] The *cardinal rule of interpretation* is that "a real explanation must be so clear that the patient knows and feels his own experience in it instantly." [312] The emphasis on feeling is of great importance here, because Adler believed that an insight that is correct *always arouses affect* (emotion).[313]

The Role of the Therapist-Client Relationship

Unless completely psychotic to the point of being in a stupor, all clients in psychotherapy retain a minimum amount of social feeling or *group consciousness.*[314] By confronting the client as an equal, by showing him or her the interest of one human being toward another, the therapist can begin to kindle this group consciousness and cause it to rise.[315] Concern for others breeds a return in kind. Adler once called this showing of concern (social feeling) for others *pedagogical tact,* by which he meant "the attitude of one man toward another, which is determined by a desire to raise the level of the other's feeling in a kind manner." [316]

Adler reversed the Freudian tables by having his concept of transference work in an opposite direction to that of classic psychoanalysis (see p. 95). Rather than therapy transferring unhealthy features of the life style onto the therapist (transformed neurosis), Adler believed that it works through the process of transferring healthy features of the relationship with the therapist back into the life style of the patient. Hence "the task of the physician or psychologist is to give the patient the experience of contact with a fellow-man, and then to enable him to transfer this awakened social feeling to others." [317] The therapist thus acts as a mediator between the selfish, secretive goal of superiority clung to by the neurotic and the broader community of fellow human beings.[318] Adler believed that many therapeutic approaches and even quacks gain their successes through this simple device of providing a disturbed person with a good human relationship and then encouraging (mothering) him or her to approach life once again. Doubtlessly, this is how some of the "miraculous" cures of the saints, Christian Science, or visits to Lourdes take place—by cementing the errant individual back to the group.[319] Even so, Adler refused to see the relationship per se as the vehicle of cure: ". . . we remain convinced that the cure of all mental disorder lies in the simpler if more laborious process of making the patient understand his own mistakes." [320] In-

sight was always to remain the *primary* vehicle of cure in individual psychology.

Insofar as one can speak of *transference* as a feeling of warmth toward the therapist by the client, Adler claimed it was merely another term for *social interest.*[321] But the notion that transference of sexual feelings onto the therapist is a necessary ingredient of therapy, leading to a positive and then a negative or resistive stage in the process, struck Adler as preposterous. If a female client were to dream of having sexual relations with him, Adler took this as a caricature of the real emotion. This woman would be running away from the genuine problems of love and marriage through distance, by forming an impossible alternative to the real goals beckoning her.[322] To see this as a "positive" love transference, as a literal sexual intention on her part, was to misunderstand the client's motivation.

It was Adler's view that classic psychoanalysis fosters sexual expressions by the client because of the analyst's willingness to see everything in the client's behavior as sexual from the outset.[323] As for individual-psychology therapy, he felt that a *sexualized* positive transference is to be avoided at all costs.[324] Not only does the positive transference of this type reinforce the patient's feelings of inferiority—because this sexual love has to be rejected—but it also robs the patient of independence and self-direction. We can understand the great length of classic analyses when we appreciate the fact that the patient is made to feel dependent and inferior—literally infantile—for long periods of time, as the supposed result of a "positive" transference.[325]

All neurotics behave stubbornly (negatively) in therapy from time to time. One of Adler's female patients constantly nagged him to rearrange her therapy hour to suit her schedule.[326] He accepted this ploy along with her clinical picture generally as a reflection of her masculine protest (bossing the analyst). But when a client resisted in the sense of refusing to examine and admit to the life lie, Adler considered this a lack of courage. The neurotic lacks the courage to return to the useful side of life, and hence he or she strikes us as resisting therapy.[327] A certain amount of this behavior is to be expected. However, any therapist who constantly has problems of client resistance or so-called negative transference is bringing this on in the relationship. Such therapists are always found to take on an authoritarian role in therapy. Adler, of course, did not favor such authoritarian approaches, and he thus considered it wrong to call every client a resister when it was the therapeutic style that was to blame.

The Role of Social Factors

Adler did not blame society for mental illness. Societies were not sick or in error; only people were. If people took care of their individual lives properly with social interest, all of the social ills would take care of themselves. When community leaders capitalize on social interest as a collective phenomenon (many people with a common identity) rather than encouraging it as an interpersonal phenomenon (two people in face-to-face relations as fellow human beings), we always see the rise of nationalistic and imperialistic interests. Adler's socialism strained at power grabbing and dismissed the presumed boundary lines of class or national origin. This also prompted him to reject the communism he saw forming in the world. "The rule of Bolshevism is based on the possession of power. Thus its fate is based on the possession of power. Thus its fate is sealed. While this party and its friends seek ultimate goals which are the same as ours, the intoxication of power has seduced them." [328]

The point is, collective solutions—by definition—seek to manipulate people. The group is a fiction. What we need are *individual solutions* to humanity's problems with a collective aspiration in mind—even if this aspiration is never literally achieved! We are to be as the utopianist: individually working for idealized goals beyond actual attainment.[329] After all, once goals have been achieved progress stops, and it was in the *creativity* of an unfolding life that Adler put his faith. The neurotic has fixed a goal and now tries to make it real, literal, actual. The healthy person accepts the fluid nature of life, looks to a goal of perfection for all people, and constantly works to make it come true in his or her *individual* life while realizing that it is beyond achievement.

Therapeutic Techniques

The Strategy of the Relationship

Adler was opposed to hypnotism as a technique because it takes a patient's responsibility away.[330] A neurotic can use hypnotism as an excuse for not directing his or her own life. Hypnotism seems to cure individual symptoms but it does not further insight and this is what the basic job of a therapist is supposed to be.[331] Adler disliked the authoritarianism of hypnotism, wherein the therapist plays at being a superhuman healer who can dictate what will or will not be. It was this unwillingness to put the client in a subservient role that led Adler to reject that psychoanalytical remnant of the hypnotic method— the *couch*. His patients were free to sit, stand, or even to move about the consulting room if they wished.[332]

The therapist must keep three goals in view: (1) see things from the client's perspective on life; (2) understand why a client behaves the way he or she does; and (3) instruct the client in this understanding by interpreting the prototype and its resultant life style (life lie, and so on).[333] If these three steps are followed, a therapist does not have to worry about "What do I do next?" The mistaken moves of a neurotic life style are fairly easy to see and then to convey to the client, who will then occasionally maneuver to avoid accepting some insights but will also begin to see the good sense of what is being outlined. After all, whatever the therapist says in the interpretation is aimed specifically at helping *current* problems in living. Clients gain immediate benefit, because once they know the mistake, the corrective direction is implied. Cultivating social feeling is another important part of therapy. Like an effective mother, the therapist must encourage the client to advance on life with a confidence and a trust in others. Simply doing so becomes therapeutic as the client begins to find a completely different, satisfying experience in social relations.

The Technique of Comparison

Adler recommended a *technique of comparison* in coming to understand the client.[334] The therapist can compare himself or herself to the client and ask, "What goal would I be seeking if I behaved like this person?" Adler would be putting this question to himself as the client entered the consulting room for the first time. Could he detect signs of an organ dialect in the client's manner as he or she entered the room (erect, slouching, haughty), shook hands (demanding, tremulous), and took a seat (close by or far away)?[335] What was being communicated here? Though he made mistakes, Adler said it was not unusual for him to determine accurately the neurotic's life style on the first day of psychotherapy.[336] Sometimes the dy-

namics of a family problem—as between a mother and daughter—are so obvious that the clinician can be completely clear about essentials in ten minutes of contact with the principals.[337] Another form of comparison is aimed at determining the degree of community feeling a patient has. We do this by comparing the amount of time spent in social relations, religious activities, political works, and so on, with the amount spent in solitary pursuits. This can even be seen in the recreational outlets of the person, as in comparing the amount of time devoted to fishing (solitary) versus dancing (social).

The next major step is to take the patient back in time, drawing out those psychological attitudes and physical handicaps that have in some way been wound into the prototype. The reason for calling this a comparison technique is that the therapist continually weighs the implications of each bit of information against each other—the presenting complaint against the handshake, the outside activities against the memories of the past, and the combined effects of all four factors at once—until a single, overall prototype regularity is suggested.[338] If such an overview convinces the therapist that the client is really suffering from a neurosis, therapy moves into the *interpretive* phase. By this time, thanks to *pedagogical tact,* the therapist should have established a relationship of trust with the client. A continuing comparison of life-history data is now made with contemporary events in the client's life, and if the life-style interpretation of the therapist is correct, the insight afforded the client will be accepted because of its usefulness in actual life.[339] The woman who has been avoiding challenges by using the distance maneuver of illness goes forward, makes an effort to achieve the goals that beckon her, does achieve some, feels better about herself, stops running away from life, and so on. She also relies more on others now and gives her time to others whenever they seek help to gain their goals in life.

Early Recollections

Another technique used by Adler was to ask the client for his or her earliest or first memory. He was convinced that "memories can never run counter to the style of life." [340] The only reason we have recollections of anything is because we are trying to keep in mind those things that justify our ongoing life style. Hence, the recollections from our earliest years are especially important, because they give the individual psychologist a picture of why we framed our particular prototype in the first place. A client's earliest recollections helped Adler understand the ground rule or game plan (prototype) that the client was *still using* (see Figure 8, p. 130). Adler occasionally predicted what certain life styles would recall, as when he once said, ". . . if I suspect the life-style of a pampered child, I can invariably guess that the patient will recall something about his mother." [341] The solitary, defeated individual might well recall being lost and alone in some large department store as a child. The timid adult would be likely to remember a great fright experienced during childhood play, and so forth.

Dreams

Adler also used dream analysis, because he felt that dreams reflect most clearly the goal-oriented nature of the psyche. Dreams present us with our future goals *now*. In the same way that the neurotic tries to make future goals true in the present, our dreams encourage us to believe that we can see into the future and make our desires into reali-

ties. [342] The dream is always stimulated by some frustration in life. We sense or know clearly that what we want is slipping from our grasp, so the dream either short-circuits our striving attempts by making it seem that our desired goal is already realized, or it suggests possible moves we might make in order to increase the chances of getting the goal in the future. [343]

An example of the first type is the dream of a shop owner who was once Adler's client. This neurotic woman suffered from a physical illness for a time, necessitating that she leave the shop under the direction of hired employees. One night she dreamed, "I enter a shop and find the girls playing cards." [344] Adler interpreted this dream as evidence that this woman literally hoped to find the hired help taking advantage of her absence in the same way. She wanted to make this future real in her dream because she was a dictatorial employer who had the fictional belief that the business could not go on without her presence. [345] An example of the second type of dream was the case of a jealous wife who dreamed that she saw a cat snatch a fish and run off with it. A woman then ran after the cat and recovered the fish. Adler interpreted this to show the jealous housewife that she was preparing herself for such a theft so that when the occasion arose she would be ready to recover her husband (the "fish"). [346]

Adler believed that an acceptable psychology must account for dreams, since this is such a large part of mental life. [347] At the same time, he was careful to add, "The dream tells us nothing more than can be inferred from the other expressive forms as well." [348] Daydreams have the same self-deceptive quality as night dreams. Fantasy is an escape precisely because it allows us to paint a future state to our liking, one that denies the reality we are likely to face. [349]

Dreams suggest the mood we want to feel. "Dreaming is a process of turning away, in sleep, from reality and common sense towards the individual's goal of superiority." [350] Freud was very wrong to presume that dreams could somehow tell us about a past reality.[351] The dream is a fiction, "a dress rehearsal, a trial performance of a step towards the fictive goal." [352] An adult male who dreams—or who fantasizes, for that matter—that he has had sexual relations with his mother is rarely stating a genuine sexual prompting from the past *or* the present. He is demonstrating by way of a metaphorical expression that he wishes to subdue his mother, to possess her completely and command her complete attention and emotional efforts. The parent may even stand as metaphor for someone else, as for authority in general or possibly for all of humanity—whom this man wishes to bend to his will.

We call these metaphorical devices *symbols,* said Adler, and he was none too pleased with the necessity of using them. "Metaphors are used for beauty, for imagination and fantasy. We must insist, however, that the use of metaphors and symbols is always dangerous in the hands of an individual who has a mistaken style of life." [353] Take the case of a boy faced with a school examination. The challenge is there, the problem is clear. He must study and prepare himself for the task and then face it squarely and courageously. But if his style of life encourages retreat, then he might well dream some night that he is in a war. He pictures the straightforward problem of an upcoming examination (the beckoning goal) in a heightened metaphor—fear of death in war—and thus creates the mood he wishes to have, one that might enable him to flee the challenge that awaits on the morrow.[354] In the morning he develops a "sickness" and fails to attend school (distance).

The fact that dreams are designed to intoxicate us with power accounts for their obscurity. If we really understood the reason for a dream, we would destroy the reason for having it. "The dream is a bridge between the present real problem and the style of life; but the style of life should need no reinforcement." [355] That is, only those styles of life that are selfish, devious, and unwilling to take a straightforward approach to life require dreaming as a supporting deception. If a person meets his or her responsibilities, there is no need for dreaming. "Very courageous people dream rarely, for they deal adequately with their situation in the daytime." [356] Courageous people meet life with social interest and cooperation. One aspect of cooperation is seeing things the way most people do—in other words, with common sense. If people live according to common sense, they do not need to dream, for "dreaming is the adversary of common sense" and vice versa.[357]

Although he carefully noted that one could not make easy generalities about dream interpretations, over the years Adler proposed a number of ideas on the likely meaning of dream patterns. Sometimes a neurotic person does *not* dream. The absence of dreams in this case indicates that the individual has established a neurotic situation he or she does not wish to change.[358] Short dreams suggest that the dreamer wants to find a short cut between the present life situation and the desired goal. Longer, more involved dreams reflect a hesitating attitude in the life style, where security needs are uppermost and the person delays facing up to a beckoning goal.[359] Dreams about dead people suggest that the dreamer has not yet buried his or her dead and hence is still under the influence of the lost ones.[360]

Dreams of falling, which Adler found to be the most common theme reported, invariably deal with the anxiety sensed by the individual who is losing a sense of worth. This dream content also implies a superiority feeling, the raising of the self above others.[361] Dreams of flying occur with regularity among highly ambitious types, who also want to raise their status above the crowd. Dreams in which the person is improperly clothed or naked reflect a concern about some personal imperfection or possibly a fear of being detected in some fraud. Sexual dreams may be seen in many lights. Sometimes they clearly suggest a poor preparation for sexual intercourse. At other times they reveal a retreat from the partner and a withdrawal to oneself.[362] They often have power overtones which transcend sexuality, as the dream mentioned above in which a parent is selected (metaphorically) as love object. We can never be certain what a dream means until we use a broad base of comparison within the unique life history of a single person. "The interpretation of dreams is therefore always individual. It is impossible to interpret symbols and metaphors by formula; for the dream is a creation of the style of life, drawn from the individual's own interpretation of his own peculiar circumstances."[363]

Before leaving this topic, we should observe that modern research on "rapid eye movements" during sleep establish that everyone dreams each night. Subjects awakened during this eye-movement period (as picked up by electrical equipment affixed to their eye region) are found to be dreaming. Though we do not wish to speak for Adler, who did not have the benefit of such research evidence, it should be noted that what he said about early recollections would apply here as well. That is, Adler would simply contend that he was referring to *recalled*

dreams. The unique selection from a range of many dreams to remember would tell us about the person's prototype. Straightforward people say they dream little or not at all because they have no need of recalling such short cuts to the goal. They do not need supporting fictions, hence do not make the recollection.

Gamesmanship Tactics

Knowing as he did that neurotics seek to manipulate by their moves in the game of therapy, Adler was always alert to such maneuvers. He would not allow the neurotic to reinforce his or her power strivings by gaining an easy victory in the therapy relationship. We have chosen to call these techniques *gamesmanship tactics,* referring now to the approach he used in countering the moves of the client. For example, Adler once told of a twenty-seven-year-old woman who came to see him after five years of neurotic suffering and various unsuccessful attempts at previous therapy. She opened their first conference with "I have seen so many doctors that you are my last hope in life."[364] Realizing that this neurotic woman was *daring* him not to cure her, so as to make him feel bound in duty to do so, Adler countered her superiority tactic with: "No . . . not the last hope. Perhaps the last but one. There may be others who can help you too."[365]

Another interesting gamesmanship tactic Adler discussed concerned his handling of a melancholic (depressed) patient. Such individuals are often difficult to work with because they have retreated from life and seem very ill-disposed to make any new efforts at contacting others. Put another way, their social interest needs considerable rejuvenation, even if it has to be pump-primed mechanically. Adler felt that occasionally the therapist had to use an indirect tactic with the melancholic, although it would be slightly devious and manipulative. For example, he might open his approach to a man complaining of depression by saying, "Don't tax yourself, do only what you find interesting and agreeable these days." If the melancholic now says, "But doctor, nothing is agreeable to me," Adler counters with, "Then at least . . . do not exert yourself to do what is disagreeable." [366] This has a certain novelty about it, which usually catches the patient unaware and sets the stage for Adler's next move in the game—which is to encourage a development of social interest.

Looking rather thoughtfully and a little doubtfully at the patient, Adler then suggests that he has a second rule he would like to recommend, but he is not certain that the man can obey it. Nevertheless, if he could follow the rule, Adler feels sure that he could be free of his melancholic symptoms in fourteen days. Naturally, the patient now wants to know the second rule, which is: " . . . to consider from time to time how you can give another person pleasure. It would very soon enable you to sleep and would chase away all your sad thoughts. You would feel yourself to be useful and worthwhile." [367] If the man then responds with something like "But how can you expect me to give others pleasure when I have none myself?" Adler counters directly with "I see, then you will probably need four weeks to get back to your old self." If the patient instead responds "But who in this world gives pleasure to me that I should worry about them?" Adler applies what he considers the strongest move open to him, by saying, "Perhaps you had better train yourself a little thus: do not actually *do* anything to please anyone else, but just think out how you *could* do it." [368] Adler also would occasionally ask the melancholic to bring the therapist pleasure by recalling and reciting his or her dreams during the therapy hour.

What is Adler doing here? We must not think of these as routine exercises or gimmicks to train a client's behavior mechanically. Adler sincerely believed that by encouraging clients to take an interest in others—combined with insight—a therapeutic outcome would be likely to take place. Social interest is a natural potential within each person's breast, so to speak, and therefore all we have to do as therapists is get it started and it will eventually take over by itself. The insight obtained from therapy provides the client with a frame within which this rising sense of social feeling can be understood. The client begins to take over personally in time, so that we no longer have to make concrete suggestions. The improved success in living ensures that the client will want to act on the insights afforded by individual psychology.

Some Procedural Details

Adler believed that a therapist should present a hopeful attitude to the patient, even when uncertain about the eventual success of the therapy.[369] Only when there is obvious physical damage, such as certain forms of mental deficiency, should the therapist hesitate to make an effort at curing the client. We can always terminate therapy if things are going poorly after a few weeks. There is nothing to be gained by demoralizing the client at the outset. Adler had some definite ideas on how his followers were to behave. "The Individual Psychologist, unlike other psychotherapeutists, will avoid being sleepy, or going to sleep or yawning, showing a want of interest in the patient, using harsh words, giving premature advice, letting himself be looked upon as the last resort, being unpunctual, getting into a dispute, or declaring that there is no prospect of a cure." [370]

It is important to get all questions of procedure cleared up and settled with the client from the very beginning. This would include such things as fees, the physician's pledge to secrecy, and the scheduling of appointments over the weeks.[371] The frequency of contacts will vary according to the needs of the client, from daily through weekly or even monthly contacts. Adler believed that therapists should contribute some time without pay, and he stressed that the client who cannot pay should never be made to feel inferior because of this arrangement. Payments would be best made on a weekly or monthly basis, and Adler did not favor prepayment schemes.[372] Gifts from the client should be declined in a friendly manner or at least put off until the end of therapy. In no case should the therapist and a client mix socially during the run of therapy.

We have already mentioned that Adler could always detract from the overestimation of a neurotic symptom by his manner of relating with the client. This same attitude of confident steadiness should typify the relationship with the client, because effective therapists cannot become too preoccupied with their clients. "You must be as unprepossessed as possible toward the patient; avoid everything which could make him believe that you are sacrificing yourself for him."[373] Never appear confused, accept everything in a calm and friendly manner, and devote yourself completely to the investigation of the life style. Finally, Adler believed in the advisability of using a series of fairly dramatic examples in drawing out an interpretation for the client. If the therapist is too academic or too sober, it can actually worry a client as well as ensure that an authoritarian relationship will be established. The therapist should never make light of the

client, of course, but the proper mood Adler sought was that of spontaneous cooperation in a joint effort of therapist and client which had a good chance of success if they did not take themselves too seriously. A hopeful person is not without a sense of happiness and lightheartedness, even in the face of some rather agonizing challenges.

Summary

Alfred Adler is often presented as a social psychologist in courses on personality theory, but we have not found him to be so in Chapter 2. Adler stressed social interest in human relations, and in pulling away from the medical model, he placed emphasis on the role of a person's life situation in individual psychology. Because he said a situation is interpersonal and social interest must be demonstrated in relation to others seems to have led to the conclusion that Adler was a social psychologist. Actually, Adler, more than any other personologist in this volume, devoted paragraphs of writing to specifically denying the individual the excuse as he considered it, of saying "I behave as I do because of the influence of my family upbringing, my social class, the people I associated with in my neighborhood, and so on." Social interest is a product of organic evolution. Hence it is carried in our individual natures and we must each—individually!—cultivate it in order for humanity as a totality to develop to a higher form of interpersonal living.

Rejecting Freud's reductive efforts to explain everything in terms of sexual fixations, Adler stressed the law of movement in life behaviors. Movements occur toward ends. Life *is* goal-orientation and the psyche is at heart a teleological process of moving with purpose and intention. The prototype or life plan fixes the style of life a person takes on, hence, the personality (style) is created by the individual. It is sometimes said by personologists that the life plan gets put down at about age five because it takes that long for parental influences to mold the child. This is diametrically opposite to what Adler believed. The child settles on a life plan (prototype) at about age five because this is usually how long it takes to grasp the family situation in which he or she is living. At this time in life a plan can be created. This is why a child's birth order is important. The first-born child has the opportunity to become mother's or father's "little helper" simply by being the eldest. And the last-born child has a built-in possibility of becoming babylike through pampering. However, it is not the situation that then decides these roles for the individual, for some first-borns are lifelong babies and some last-borns are reliably helpful throughout life. But the potential scenario is always a relatively common possibility for a child born into one or the other of these life situations.

In breaking with Freud, Adler relied heavily on Vaihinger's idealism and the relativism of the "as if" philosophy. He was, in a sense, trapped into being more relativistic than he would have preferred. Vaihinger's fiction construct suited his purposes when he was reacting to Freud's authoritarianism or explaining the life lies that neurotics enact. But to call every belief including social interest a fiction was too much for him. He first spoke of counterfictions that supposedly correct the errors made by neurotics in their fictional outlooks—something that would never have occurred to Vaihinger. Later Adler argued that social interest is a *fact* and hence in no way a convenient fiction or counterfiction. In his final theory he held that fictionalized constructions of life would be unnecessary if social interest were only more pronounced in human behavior. This ideal of growing social interest cannot be manipulated into people

from outside their individual identities. Everyone must sincerely and consciously strive to develop social interest "biologically." Evolutionary advances can occur only through such individual efforts of all members of the human species.

Adler's reliance on evolutionary theory was great, but unlike Darwinian theory, the Adlerian view of evolution is teleological. His original motivational theory of organ inferiorities prompting through strictly biological means a compensation of some type was to change over the years to a more psychological view of compensation as growth. He moved from an overcoming to a fulfilling interpretation of compensation. There is some confusion among personologists concerning the relationship between creativity and the self-concept employed by Adlerian theory. The important concept for Adler was *creative power,* a phrase he used from his earliest days as theorist. The concept of a self was brought in later to signify that creative power is effected by the individual, who makes certain ends come about by way of will. The self-concept as such is not to be overemphasized, and indeed, Adler frequently cautioned lest we make our *self* psychologies into *selfish* psychologies. Social interest must always take precedence to considerations of the self.

Although he used the Nietzschian phrase of *will to power,* Adler was interpreting this in a negative sense, and he framed an opposite *will to cooperate* in an effort to offset the selfishness of power motives in human relations. Social interest is ultimately the compensation of choice in which all human beings, acting as individuals, help redress the wrongs that life sends to all of us. Though it is natural for human beings to seek advantages in moving toward their life goals, Adler did not believe that this competitive striving had to be as vicious as it often is. People strive to be superior to others only because they already feel a deep inner sense of inferiority. Inferiority complexes breed superiority complexes. Rejecting Freudian explanations of male-female psychology, Adler argued that only in those cultures that repress women do we find something like a penis envy coming about. The female in such a culture does not want a penis, she wants the power that having a penis symbolizes. Adler called this desire for power masculine protest, and he pointed out that both men and women can express it in trying to gain the competitive edge in a masculine-dominated culture.

In place of such unhealthy compensations —overcompensations, actually—Adler called for a striving for perfection in human affairs. We must change the rules by having the courage to care for others. Only cowards refuse to admit their errors in living. Freudian defense mechanisms are, by and large, ways in which people try to excuse their selfishness and predatory efforts to gain superiority over their fellows. Rather than meet the challenge of social interest, such individuals put distance between themselves and the goal which we all know must be worked for. There are three problems in life which we must all answer: the occupation we will follow, our relationship to others in social contacts, and the sexual issues relating to marriage and ultimate familial responsibilities. How the person meets these or runs away from them (distance), determines the overall personality style and level of adjustment.

Adler's theory of illness follows the fictive goal, falsehoods, and the resultant use of distance to deny the lie that the person is living

out. For example, a pampered person not wishing to assume responsibility in life might develop a psychosomatic illness, which he or she then uses as the reason (excuse) for living in the parental home beyond the normal age level. Adler did not put the stress on unconscious behavior that we find in Freudian or Jungian theory. The goal that is being sought or avoided (through distance) is identical across levels of consciousness. The means for attaining this goal is what differs. In the unconscious state, as when we are dreaming, our highly selfish motivations to excel may become apparent in a heightened metaphor, as when we picture ourselves as heroes or geniuses. We want such recognition consciously as well, but would never pretend to actually be one of these exalted figures in our waking state. Neurotics follow the same process of putting up imaginary goals, pretending at life, or enacting little scenes in life that enable them to fictitiously triumph over others. Adler believed that every neurotic has an inferiority complex. The young man who feels inferior in relation to a sibling may pick on a subordinate coworker on the job, dominating this person as he would like to dominate his sib. He is not "conscious" of the parallel, but he can be made to see it in psychotherapy.

Neurotics are persons who have been living a life lie, seeking fictional goals, but they continue to at least meet a few of life's challenges. Psychotics, on the other hand, have completely failed in the three problem areas of life (work, love, society). In their delusions and hallucinations, psychotic people make their fictive goals into a "reality." Whether under threat or simply "endowed" with some superhuman power, they achieve a sense of importance in mental illness that life has denied them—or, more properly, that they have never courageously pursued in life.

In Adler's theory of cure, the mistaken style of life must be pointed out to the therapy client, beginning in the behaviors manifested in the consulting room and then extending outward into life. Following this, the client must be encouraged to return to the more productive side of life and to stimulate a growing feeling of social interest by thinking of others, helping others, earning some of that feeling of belonging that he or she so desperately wants from others. Adler analogized to the maternal role in describing therapist behavior. He spoke of therapy as a re-education of the neurotic in the art of living, as a kind of corrective mothering. His cardinal rule was to always interpret a patient's behavior clearly, so that the point of the interpretation is immediately felt and known. We do not need a fanciful, high-blown theory for such explanations. Adler believed that Freud had misunderstood and overtheorized the clinical phenomenon of transference. *Transference* is simply another term for *social interest*. In re-establishing contact with others, the neurotic is bound to enact both positive and negative feelings with the therapist. Adler often referred to client maneuvers and the countering maneuvers of the therapist as *moves in the game* of therapy.

As to specific techniques, Adler favored taking what the client brings to therapy spontaneously, but he would often ask the client to report the earliest life recollection. This first memory can give us an insight into the life plan that was put down by the person early in life. Dreams were used by Adler quite regularly, but unlike psychoanalysis, the individual psychology of dreams stresses global themes rather than specific symbols of supposedly sexualized contents. Dreams are usually blatant reflections of the goals being sought by the person, short-circuits that place us at the (feared or desired) goals that move us about. Adler was ever the teleologist in his study of humanity. He has left us with a more common sense theory of personality, in which people are not so internally wrought with contradictions and hidden identities as

in the Freudian or Jungian views. Adler's impact on child psychology has been great.

Outline of Important Theoretical Constructs

Medical-physical models of human behavior

Hippocrates: humors

Franz Joseph Gall: phrenology

Charles Darwin: natural selection

Cesare Lombroso: atavism

Ernst Kretschmer:
  Body types: pyknic, athletic, asthenic

Emil Kraepelin:
  syndromes · schizophrenia: simple, paranoid, catatonic, hebephrenic

William H. Sheldon:
  constitutional psychology · morphogenotype · primary components of physique (*endomorphy, mesomorphy, ectomorphy*) · somatotype · secondary components of physique (*dysplasia, gynandromorphy, textural*) · primary components of temperament (*viscerotonia, somatotonia, cerebrotonia*)

Biographical overview of Alfred Adler

Personality theory

Structural constructs

Dualism, holism, and the "Law of Movement"
  holistic organism · law of movement · organ dialect · movement in mind and body

Goal orientation in all psychic living
  psyche as "locus" of movement · goal-orientation of all psychic acts

Style of life
  prototype · ego line · life line (moves in "game" of life) · life plan · style of life · (self)

The meaning of individual: subjectivity and uniqueness
  comparative individual psychology · unity of the individual · mental fiction (prototype) · fictions, fictive goals · counterfiction

Motivational constructs

Adler's early use of organic constructs
  organ inferiority · inferiority of the brain

Compensation
  compensation

Adler's shift from organic to socio-psychological explanation
  teleological behavior · creative power · style of movement

The role of feelings in motivation
  aggression and affection drives · will to power · will to cooperate · inferiority feeling · social feeling · subjective sensation of inferiority · social interest (Gemeinschaftsgefühl)

From overcoming to fulfilling compensation
  overcoming · strive for superiority · inferiority complex · overcompensation · superiority complex · striving for perfection (self)

The growing reliance on Darwinian evolution
  motherly love · movement toward a goal · mastery of the environment · master one's fellow man

Moralistic tones in Adlerian psychology
  natural ethic · failures in living · cowards · errors in living · loss of courage

Defense mechanisms or mental mechanisms
  repression · identification · regression · compensation · overcompensation · safeguarding mechanisms (tendencies) · distance · protest · masculine protest

Time perspective constructs

Growth and the three problems of life
  purpose in all experience · antithetic scheme · not understood · wordless impression · three problem areas of life (*occupational, social, sexual*)

Family constellation and birth order
  first born · second born · last born · pampering · only child · bad mothering · Oedipal complex · sibling rivalry

The roles of the school and teacher in maturation

Adolescence

Adulthood and old age

Individual differences constructs

Three types of women who flee femininity

Two approaches to problem solution
  optimism vs. pessimism

Two styles of failing in life
  passive versus active

Three types of children likely to over-compensate

Four approaches to reality
  ruling, getting, avoiding, socially useful

The various types of complexes
  inferiority, Oedipus, redeemer, proof, predestination, leader, spectator, "no"

Notes

1. Sheldon, 1944, p. 526. **2.** Combe, 1851. **3.** Becker and Barnes, 1952, Ch. 13. **4.** Darwin, 1952a, p. 322. **5.** Ibid., p. 323. **6.** Hofstadter, 1955. **7.** Sheldon, Dupertuis, and McDermott, 1954, p. 19. **8.** Sheldon, Stevens, and Tucker, 1940; Sheldon and Stevens, 1942. **9.** Sheldon, Hartl, and McDermott, 1949. **10.** Ibid. **11.** Shock, 1944. **12.** Alexander and Selesnick, 1966, Ch. 18. **13.** Kety, 1960. **14.** Bercel, 1960. **15.** Alexander and Selesnick, 1966, Ch. 18. **16.** Bottome, 1957, p. 26. **17.** Ibid., p. 27. **18.** Ibid., pp. 32–33. **19.** Adler, 1964a, p. 148. **20.** Bottome, 1957, p. 27. **21.** Furtmüller, 1964, p. 331. **22.** Ibid., p. 333. **23.** Bottome, 1957, pp. 46–49. **24.** Furtmüller, 1964, p. 334. **25.** Ibid., p. 341. **26.** Bottome, 1957, p. 75. **27.** Ansbacher and Ansbacher, 1956, pp. 73–74. **28.** Furtmüller, 1964, p. 345. **29.** Ansbacher and Ansbacher, 1956, pp. 77–87. **30.** Bottome, 1957, p. 84. **31.** Ibid., p. 121. **32.** Ibid., pp. 169–171. **33.** Ibid., p. 128. **34.** Ansbacher, 1959. **35.** Bottome, 1957, p. 224. **36.** Ibid., pp. 45–49. **37.** Adler, 1958, p. 25. **38.** Ibid., p. 26. **39.** Adler, 1964b, p. 74. **40.** Ibid., p. 95. **41.** Adler, 1964a, p. 156. **42.** Adler, 1958, p. 57. **43.** Adler, 1964b, p. 47. **44.** Adler, 1968, p. 3. **45.** Ibid. **46.** Adler, 1963, p. 166. **47.** Adler, 1954, pp. 27–28. **48.** Ibid., p. 31. **49.** Ibid., p. 29. **50.** Adler, 1964a, p. 163. **51.** Adler, 1968, p. 229. **52.** Ansbacher and Ansbacher, 1964, p. 93. **53.** Adler, 1968, p. 229. **54.** Ibid., p. 228. **55.** Adler, 1958, pp. 12–13. **56.** Ibid., p. 14. **57.** Adler, 1964b, p. 19. **58.** Adler, 1964a, p. 46. **59.** Adler, 1964b, p. 229. **60.** Adler, 1958, p. 59. **61.** Adler, 1968, p. 126. **62.** Ibid., pp. 3, 6. **63.** Adler, 1954, p. 73. **64.** Adler, 1964a, p. 7. **65.** Adler, 1964b, p. 244. **66.** Ansbacher and Ansbacher, 1964, p. 216. **67.** Adler, 1964b, p. 49. **68.** Adler, 1963, p. xiii. **69.** Adler, 1954, p. 86. **70.** Ibid., p. 18. **71.** Adler, 1968, p. 2. **72.** Adler, 1964b, p. 49. **73.** Adler, 1930, p. 138. **74.** Adler, 1964b, p. 42. **75.** Ansbacher and Ansbacher, 1956, p. 180. **76.** Ibid., p. 194. **77.** Ibid., p. 78. **78.** Adler, 1968, p. 229. **79.** Ansbacher and Ansbacher, 1956, p. 98. **80.** Ibid., p. 246. **81.** Ibid., p. 144. **82.** Adler, 1964b, p. 92. **83.** Adler, 1958, p. 37. **84.** Adler, 1968, p. 307. **85.** Ibid., p. 313. **86.** Adler, 1958, p. 37. **87.** Adler, 1968, p. 3. **88.** Ansbacher and Ansbacher, 1956, p. 25. **89.** Adler, 1963, p. 76. **90.** Adler, 1958, p. 37. **91.** Ansbacher and Ansbacher, 1956, p. 26. **92.** Adler, 1954, pp. 34–35. **93.** Ibid., p. 147. **94.** Adler, 1968, p. 336. **95.** Adler, 1964b, p. 93. **96.** Adler, 1954, p. 148. **97.** Adler, 1968, p. 318. **98.** Adler, 1964a, p. 47. **99.** Ansbacher and Ansbacher, 1956, pp. 30, 38. **100.** Ibid., p. 121. **101.** Adler, 1954, p. 29. **102.** Adler, 1968, p. 41. **103.** Adler, 1956, p. 91. **104.** Adler, 1968, p. 143. **105.** Adler, 1964b, p. 219. **106.** Ibid., p. 103. **107.** Ansbacher and Ansbacher, 1956, pp. 34, 143. **108.** Ibid., p. 111. **109.** Kaufmann, 1956. **110.** Adler, 1968, p. 5; Adler, 1954, p. 128. **111.** Adler, 1968, p. 150. **112.** Adler, 1964b, p. 147. **113.** Adler, 1954, pp. 133, 209. **114.** Ibid., p. 212. **115.** Adler, 1958, pp. 29–30. **116.** Adler, 1964b, p. 96. **117.** Adler, 1954, p. 69. **118.** Ibid., p. 65. **119.** Adler, 1964b, p. 98. **120.** Adler, 1968, p. 100. **121.** Ibid., p. 81. **122.** Ibid., p. 9. **123.** Adler, 1954, pp. 136–137. **124.** Ansbacher and Ansbacher, 1964, p. 35. **125.** Ibid., pp. 34–35. **126.** Adler, 1958, p. 15. **127.** Adler, 1964b, p. 71. **128.** Adler, 1968, p. 8. **129.** Adler, 1954, p. 178. **130.** Ibid., p. 69. **131.** Adler, 1958, p. 60. **132.** Adler, 1964b, pp. 117–122. **133.** Adler, 1964a, p. 31. **134.** Ibid. **135.** Ansbacher and Ansbacher, 1964, p. 30. **136.** Adler, 1964b, p. 277. **137.** Ansbacher and Ansbacher, 1956, p. 177. **138.** Ibid., pp. 177–178. **139.** Adler, 1964b, p. 285. **140.** Adler, 1958, p. 29. **141.** Bottome, 1957, p. 122. **142.** Ansbacher and Ansbacher, 1956, p. 57. **143.** Ibid., p. 121. **144.** Adler, 1930, p. 117. **145.** Adler, 1954, p. 35; Adler, 1963, p. xi; Adler, 1958, pp. 263–264. **146.** Adler, 1930, p. 118. **147.** Ansbacher and Ansbacher, 1964, p. 38. **148.** Ibid., p. 39. **149.** Ibid. **150.** Adler, 1964b, pp. 72, 103. **151.** Ibid., p. 275. **152.** Ibid., pp. 272–273. **153.** Ansbacher and Ansbacher, 1964, pp. 38, 69. **154.** Ibid., p. 65. **155.** Adler, 1964b, p. 48. **156.** Adler, 1954, p. 153. **157.** Ibid., p. 133. **158.** Adler, 1930, p. 21. **159.** Ibid., pp. 34–35. **160.** Adler, 1963, p. x. **161.** Adler, 1964b, p. 110. **162.** Ansbacher and Ansbacher, 1964, p. 56. **163.** Adler, 1958, p. 8. **164.** Adler, 1930, pp. 82–83. **165.** Adler, 1964b, pp. 103–104. **166.** Ibid., p. 274. **167.** Ansbacher and Ansbacher, 1964, p. 37. **168.** Adler, 1968, p. 60. **169.** Ibid., p. 223. **170.** Adler, 1964b, p. 16. **171.** Adler, 1954, p. 60. **172.** Ansbacher and Ansbacher, 1964, p. 42. **173.** Ansbacher and Ansbacher, 1956, p. 60. **174.** Ibid., p. 109. **175.** Adler, 1968, p. 167. **176.** Ibid., p. 118. **177.** Adler, 1964b, p. 192. **178.** Adler, 1954, p. 107. **179.** Adler, 1968, p. 72. **180.** Adler, 1964a, p. 42. **181.** Adler, 1964b, p. 64. **182.** Adler, 1964a, p. 68. **183.** Adler, 1954, pp. 73–74. **184.** Adler, 1968, p. 62. **185.** Adler, 1930, p. 144. **186.** Ibid., p. 161. **187.** Ibid., p. 221. **188.** Ibid., p. 224. **189.** Adler, 1964b, p. 232. **190.** Adler, 1958, p. 59. **191.** Ibid., p. 7. **192.** Adler, 1964b, p. 42. **193.** Ibid., p. 149. **194.** Adler, 1954, p. 128. **195.** Adler, 1964a, p. 117. **196.** Ibid., p. 101. **197.** Adler, 1968, p. 321. **198.** Ibid., p. 322. **199.** Adler, 1964a, p. 96. **200.** Adler, 1968, p. 322. **201.** Adler, 1954, p. 127. **202.** Adler, 1968, p. 321. **203.** Adler, 1964a, p. 77. **204.** Adler, 1958, p. 123. **205.** Ibid., p. 121. **206.** Adler, 1964b, pp. 44–45. **207.** Ibid., p. 221. **208.** Adler, 1958, p. 123. **209.** Ibid., pp. 123–124. **210.** Ibid., p. 132. **211.** Ibid., p. 134. **212.** Ibid., p. 135. **213.** Adler, 1968, p. 62. **214.** Adler, 1954, pp. 81–82. **215.** Adler, 1930, p. 206. **216.** Adler, 1964b, p. 51. **217.** Ibid., p. 21. **218.** Adler, 1930, p. 225. **219.** Adler, 1968, p. 11. **220.** Adler, 1958, pp. 54, 126. **221.** Adler, 1954, p. 127. **222.** Adler, 1930, p. 140. **223.** Ibid., p. 150. **224.** Ibid., pp. 12–13. **225.** Adler, 1963, p. 172. **226.** Adler, 1930, p. 104. **227.** Ibid., p. 182. **228.** Ibid., p. 171. **229.** Adler, 1954, pp. 100–101. **230.** Adler, 1930, pp. 112–113. **231.** Ibid., p. 138. **232.** Ibid., pp. 185–186. **233.** Ibid., p. 173. **234.** Ibid., p. 184. **235.** Ibid., p. 209. **236.** Adler, 1958, p. 182. **237.** Ibid., p. 243. **238.** Ibid., p. 244. **239.** Ibid., p. 263. **240.** Adler, 1954, p. 105. **241.** Adler, 1958, p. 277. **242.** Ibid., p. 280. **243.** Ibid. **244.** Ibid., p. 281. **245.** Adler, 1964b, p. 67. **246.** Ansbacher and Ansbacher, 1956, p. 461. **247.** Adler, 1964b, p. 127. **248.** Adler, 1954, pp. 112–113. **249.** Ibid., pp. 142–143. **250.** Adler, 1964b, p. 129. **251.** Adler, 1930, p. 8. **252.** Ansbacher and Ansbacher 1956, pp. 167–168. **253.** Ansbacher and Ansbacher, 1964, p. 72. **254.** Ibid., pp. 74–79. **255.** Adler, 1968, p. 307. **256.** Ibid., p. 22. **257.** Ibid. **258.** Ibid., Ch. XX. **259.** Ansbacher and Ansbacher, 1956, p. 246. **260.** Adler, 1964a, p. 72. **261.** Ansbacher and Ansbacher, 1956, p. 247. **262.** Adler, 1968, p. 45. **263.** Adler, 1964a, p. 81. **264.** Ansbacher and Ansbacher 1964, p. 302. **265.** Adler, 1958, p. 49. **266.** Adler, 1968, p. 30. **267.** Adler, 1958, p. 186. **268.** Ansbacher and Ansbacher, 1964, p. 198. **269.** Adler, 1964b, p. 180. **270.** Adler, 1968, p. 244. **271.** Adler, 1964b, pp. 13–14. **272.** Adler, 1968, p. 56. **273.** Ansbacher and Ansbacher, 1964, p. 303. **274.** Adler, 1968, p. 243. **275.** Adler, 1958, p. 259. **276.** Adler, 1968, p. 254. **277.** Adler, 1964a, p. 128. **278.** Adler, 1968, p. 255. **279.** Adler, 1964b, p. 201. **280.** Adler, 1964a, p. 75. **281.** Ibid., p. 130. **282.** Adler, 1964b, p. 64. **283.** Adler, 1968, p. 188. **284.** Adler, 1964a, p. 39. **285.** Adler,

1958, p. 61. **286.** Ibid., p. 62. **287.** Ibid., p. 226. **288.** Adler, 1968, p. 336. **289.** Ibid., p. 203. **290.** Ibid., p. 207. **291.** Adler, 1964a, p. 105. **292.** Adler, 1930, p. 73. **293.** Adler, 1954, p. 143. **294.** Adler, 1968, pp. 166–167. **295.** Ibid., p. 170. **296.** Adler, 1964a, p. 73. **297.** Adler, 1968, p. 15. **298.** Ibid., p. 23. **299.** Adler, 1964b, p. 294. **300.** Adler, 1968, p. 43. **301.** Adler, 1964b, p. 294. **302.** Ibid., p. 181. **303.** Adler, 1968, p. 13. **304.** Adler, 1964a, p. 20. **305.** Ibid., p. 73. **306.** Adler, 1968, p. 228. **307.** Ansbacher and Ansbacher, 1964, pp. 192–193. **308.** Adler, 1968, p. 227. **309.** Adler, 1963, p. 162. **310.** Adler, 1968, p. 22. **311.** Adler, 1963, p. 1. **312.** Adler, 1964a, p. 74. **313.** Ansbacher and Ansbacher, 1964, p. 299. **314.** Adler, 1968, p. 152. **315.** Adler, 1958, p. 72. **316.** Adler, 1963, p. 162. **317.** Adler, 1964a, p. 20. **318.** Ibid., pp. 73–74. **319.** Ibid., pp. 40–41. **320.** Ibid., p. 41. **321.** Ibid., p. 73. **322.** Adler, 1968, p. 151. **323.** Ansbacher and Ansbacher, 1964, p. 217. **324.** Adler, 1964b, p. 289. **325.** Adler, 1958, pp. 72–73. **326.** Adler, 1968, p. 144. **327.** Adler, 1964a, p. 73. **328.** Ansbacher and Ansbacher, 1956, p. 457. **329.** Ansbacher and Ansbacher, 1964,

p. 40. **330.** Adler, 1964a, p. 162. **331.** Adler, 1958, p. 47. **332.** Adler, 1964a, p. 88. **333.** Adler, 1968, p. 25. **334.** Ibid. **335.** Adler, 1964b, p. 287. **336.** Adler, 1968, p. 43. **337.** Adler, 1963, p. 165. **338.** Adler, 1964a, p. 72. **339.** Ibid., p. 72. **340.** Adler, 1958, p. 74. **341.** Adler, 1964a, p. 122. **342.** Adler, 1968, p. 214. **343.** Ibid., pp. 219–220. **344.** Ibid., p. 217. **345.** Ibid., pp. 217–218. **346.** Adler, 1964b, p. 84. **347.** Adler, 1964a, p. 15. **348.** Adler, 1964b, p. 262. **349.** Ibid., p. 242. **350.** Adler, 1964a, p. 16. **351.** Adler 1968, p. 116. **352.** Adler, 1964a, p. 16. **353.** Adler, 1958, p. 103. **354.** Ibid., pp. 103–104. **355.** Ibid., p. 107. **356.** Adler, 1964a, p. 164. **357.** Adler, 1958, p. 101. **358.** Adler, 1964a, p. 164. **359.** Ibid. **360.** Adler, 1964b, p. 263. **361.** Ibid. **362.** Ibid., p. 264. **363.** Adler, 1958, p. 107. **364.** Adler, 1964a, p. 8. **365.** Ibid. **366.** Ibid., p. 25. **367.** Ibid. **368.** Ibid., pp. 25–26. **369.** Adler, 1964b, p. 288. **370.** Ibid. **371.** Adler, 1968, p. 43. **372.** Adler, 1964b, p. 295. **373.** Ansbacher and Ansbacher, 1964, p. 192.

Chapter 3

The Analytical Psychology of Carl Jung

Biographical Overview

Carl Gustav Jung was born in 1875 in a small Swiss village (Kesswil) but was relocated while an infant to the Rhine Fall near Schaffhaused where he spent his boyhood as the only child of a country parson. There were churchmen on both sides of Jung's parental family—six parson uncles on the mother's side, and two paternal uncles as well—but his own father was really more attracted to philology and classical studies than to the ministry.[1] Economic necessity forced him to enter the ministry, and he married the daughter of his former Hebrew professor. Jung seems to have been his father's son.[2] Though his mother was the stronger parental personality, he found her puzzling and even eccentric in manner.[3]

Jung's classical education began early in life, for when he was six his father introduced him to the study of Latin. Throughout later life Jung could read ancient texts, and this training doubtless helps to account for his historical approach to humankind. In a real sense he was a classical scholar. When Jung was roughly twelve years old, his family moved from the Rhine Fall to the more urban community of Basel. He had developed into a physically large, solitary person, active, yet secretive and self-reliant. Going to school was never a particular joy for him; he disliked athletics, mathematics, and the competition for grades among classmates. Jung tells us that he deliberately settled for a second-in-the-class standing which he found "considerably more enjoyable" [4] than competing for first. Even so, his father's tutoring had put him ahead of the urban classmates he confronted in Basel, and this superiority led to a rather difficult hazing. He was kidded as a country bumpkin, teacher's pet, and so on. He came to despise school, using sickness as an excuse to avoid attending, and for a time he actually experienced a period of neurotic fainting spells of which he eventually cured himself through self-discipline.[5]

When he grew to young manhood Jung attended the University of Basel. He was interested in historical, classical, anthropological, and philosophical subjects, but decided on medicine because it was a distinguished profession offering various alternatives for a career. Thanks to a selection he read by Krafft-Ebing, the famous German neurologist, Jung settled on psychiatry as a specialty that could combine his more humanistic and his scientific interests.[6] Following graduation from medical school, Jung took a position at the Burgholzli Hospital in Zürich, Switzerland, serving under Eugen Bleuler, the noted psychiatrist who had coined the term *schizophrenia*. Bleuler was a professor of psychiatry at the University of Zürich, and Jung was also to hold a lectureship there while he conducted studies on the nature of schizophrenia. It was at the Burgholzli Hospital (from 1900–1909) that Jung reached maturity as a scientist and became a world authority

on the psychology of the abnormal and the normal individual. He furthered the technique of *word association* there, coined a term, *complex,* that played a central role in all of his later theorizing, and published his first book.

Jung recognized Freud's genius from the outset, and he felt that his own studies had confirmed the undoubted existence of an unconscious sphere in the human being's mind. Their first meeting took place in Vienna in 1907, and it was memorable because Freud and Jung talked for thirteen consecutive hours. In using the method of word association, Jung would ask a patient to respond to a stimulus word with the first word coming to mind. For example, Jung would say *garden,* and the patient would be free to say anything. Jung then noted certain disturbances in the patient's word associations, such as taking a long time to speak, blocking on a word and not thinking of anything, or thinking only of a repetition of the stimulus word.[7] By going over a series of words several times, Jung gradually established that certain of these words hung together, interlaced in the patient's associations, and formed a *complex* of ideas with a common core of meaning. Since these *idea masses* were always tied to emotional concerns of the person, Jung called them *feeling-toned complexes.*[8] The repressed memories and conflicts of the Freudian school were thus experimentally verified by the word-association method.

Jung did not come to Freud as a psychiatric novice. He was a man who had made his own reputation, one that in academic circles was even more important (because of its acceptability) than Freud's. Furthermore, Jung was too much of a loner and an independent thinker ever to play a submerged student role to Freud. It is clear from early

Carl Jung

reactions that Jung, like Adler before him, was never completely accepting of Freud's views, especially those on sex.[9] In 1909 they made their famous trip to Clark University in Massachusetts and it was this extended contact that led to their break.

There were three major reasons for this split. First, Jung was unable to accept the concept of libido as limited to sexual energy. As we shall see, Jung based his energizing theory on a *principle of opposites,* and at one point he urged Freud to suggest an opposite balancing energy to libido.[10] Since this

criticism was necessarily a threat to the sexuality thesis, as we can recall from Chapter 1, Freud could not comply. Related to this matter was the question of how sex was to be interpreted symbolically. Did every unconscious dream symbol refer to a lustful interpersonal memory in *this* person's life, or was there something far more profound and even extraindividual about certain symbols? Drawing on his classical studies, Jung argued that a mother imago (motherly image) cannot be tied to a single patient's life, for such mother symbols have made their appearance in too many cultural myths to be seen as the reflection of a *personal* conflict.[11]

Jung wanted to include a *collective* aspect to the unconscious, and though Freud held to this view in principle, he could not revise his theory to formalize this idea. The collective aspect of the unconscious would require a theory of inherited racial influences, and Freud felt that he could not let this obviously controversial suggestion take further attention away from his already notorious sexuality thesis. When Jung formalized these views on a collective psyche in his book *The Psychology of the Unconscious,* he sealed his fate, for by his own admission this work cost him Freud's friendship.[12] The final major cause of their split stemmed from an incident on the trip to Clark University. Apparently the two men fell into analyzing one another's dreams—possibly as an exercise in mutual learning, although Jung hints that Freud actually referred to personal problems.[13] At one point, Freud stopped free-associating with the observation that were he to continue, he would lose his authority in their relationship. This attitude surprised Jung, who had been relating to Freud out of respect but *not* as the lesser authority. Jung felt they were equals.

The relationship between the two cooled noticeably after the trip to America, even though Jung was by then president of the International Psycho-Analytical Association (thanks to Freud's direct influence). Following a stormy convention of the association in Munich in 1913 when Jung's "heretical views" on the (collective) unconscious were the focus of debate, Freud and Jung went their separate ways. Though Jung was re-elected to a two-year term as president, future conventions during his tenure were made impossible by the developing World War I, and the two men never faced one another again. There followed a very difficult period for Jung, during which he analyzed himself much as Freud had done (see Chapter 1). His only satisfactions at this time came from

his wife's emotional support and their growing family. He describes this period, from roughly 1913 to 1917, as one of inner uncertainty and disorientation.[14]

It was as if he were being assaulted by fantasies from his unconscious, and he tried to hold them in check through yoga and other means. He began to record these fantasies and eventually to work out a means of communication with his unconscious. He literally came to talk to a "person" within his identity, one he was to call the anima.[15] In a manner reminiscent of his childhood, he once again found that he had to conquer the hold this person had on his psyche, and by way of regaining his self-command, to single out or individuate a new personality more representative of what he was really like than the original.

After World War I Jung continued to attract a wide circle of followers. He once studied a group of Navajo Indians in America. He canvassed various tribes in field trips to North, East, and Central Africa. He spent time in the Sudan as well as Egypt and India. What Jung sought in each of these trips was further confirmation of his views on mankind. He thus not only saw his own patients in psychotherapy and read widely, but he actually did the work of an archaeologist-anthropologist when the opportunity presented itself. On one occasion, while in America, he made a special study of black patients at St. Elizabeth's Hospital in Washington, D.C. He became recognized as a scholar of the first rank, was awarded honorary degrees by eight universities, and was made an honorary fellow of the Royal Society in England.

Although he had actually spoken out against the rise of a war psychology in Germany as early as 1936,[16] some misunderstandings of his other writings and his acceptance in 1933 of an editorship of a German journal of psychotherapy resulted in Jung being criticized as a Nazi sympathizer.[17] Yet as Jung himself noted, his books were burned by the Nazis, and he had it on good authority that he was on the Nazi blacklist.[18] In time, it was established that not only was Jung unsympathetic to the Nazi cause, he provided significant aid to Jewish psychiatrists and psychologists who had fled the Nazis to settle in England. A thorough study of the entire matter cleared Jung's name without question, if any such exoneration was necessary.[19]

In addition to his academic appointment at Zürich, Jung once served as professor of medical psychology at the University of Basel. He remained a productive worker and writer throughout his life, and his collected works are second in size only to Freud's. He spent the years following World War II putting together his finished autobiography and meeting the requests of students and interested laypeople to make his thoughts known. His students organized an institute, and for a time his approach was referred to as *complex psychology*. However, the name Jung preferred and the one we shall use is *analytical psychology*. He died at Küsnacht, Zürich, in 1961.

Personality Theory

Structural Constructs

Dualism of Mind versus Body

In the *Psychology of Dementia Praecox* (Volume 3), published before his meeting with Freud, Jung proposed that "the affect in dementia praecox [schizophrenia] favours the appearance of anomalies in the metabolism—toxins, perhaps, which injure the brain in a more or less irreparable manner, so that the highest psychic functions become paralysed." [20] This view was advanced very tentatively while under the influence of Bleuler and other medical colleagues, but even so it has convinced many that Jung was a theorist who favored physical explanations of abnormal and, therefore, possibly all behavior. Actually, if we review what he said about this speculation over a lifetime, it seems clear that Jung was highly ambivalent if not actually embarrassed about it altogether. In what is probably his final (1957) statement on the matter, he took a moderate position, saying:

I consider the aetiology of schizophrenia to be a dual one: namely, up to a certain point psychology is indispensable in explaining the nature and the causes of the initial emotions which give rise to metabolic alterations. These emotions seem to be accompanied by chemical processes that cause specific temporary or chronic disturbances or lesions.[21]

Jung was in fact highly critical of his medical peers for their exclusive reliance on physical explanations. He complained that too many of his colleagues presumed that just because the psyche relies on brain physiology it can be understood and explained in physical terms.[22] It cannot, anymore than dancing can be explained by examining the biological structure of the leg on which dancing depends. Physical explanations cannot ensure us an understanding of mental life.[23] In the above quotes Jung gave emotional factors a prominent position in speaking about what might be termed "mental" illness. Unlike Freud, who theorized that mind qua mind is free of emotional content (see p.

46), Jung's psychology lumped both affective (emotional) and rational intellectual contents into the mind from the outset. According to Jung, primitive people were moved to behave not by intellect but by emotional "projections" of images and moods which they attributed to the world around them.[24] Rather than bringing them on personally, thoughts simply "happened" to a primitive individual, who, like a modern person caught up in emotions, could not tell an idea prompted by feelings and projected onto reality from an idea prompted by independent facts of reality.[25] When primitives began to recognize the contribution to experience made by their emotions, they moved from being exclusively part of a collective identity to being *also* a single identity. Personal consciousness was born, and the person could then direct his or her thinking apart from influence solely by the group (via the emotions). We could even say that rather than *being thought* the person could *think* (*directed thinking*).[26]

Psyche as a Region

In Freud's theory the structures of mind are fixed in relation to the levels of mind, so that, for example, the id is constantly in an unconscious segment of the psyche. The id never leaves the realm of unconsciousness to take a self-directed turn around consciousness. It sends its derivatives (ideas or images) into consciousness by way of cathexes which are themselves often symbolized to fool the conscious side of the ego; but the "id as an identity" remains rooted in the depths of the mind. For Jung, the psyche is a *region*, a kind of multidirectional and multitemporal housing within which identities of the personality like the ego can move about. In this case an id-like structure (complex) *can* move up into the conscious realm out of the unconscious and initiate behavior to suit its

own purposes (that is, outside of the control of consciousness!).

Though Jung did not stress physical explanations of human behavior, he did emphasize hereditary factors. However, his meaning here was more historical (idiographic) than physical (nomothetic) (see p. 23 of Introduction for a discussion of this distinction). Humanity's heredity is psychic as well as physical in nature, and psychic heredity is not identical to the physical development of the body in evolution. The mind-body distinction is too often used as an excuse for the theorist who wants to detract from the importance of the psyche by saying "Oh, that's only a mental phenomenon, it's not real." Jung was always quick to point out that the psyche has as much validity and reality as the (physical) body events on which it is based.[27] The person begins life with *both* a physically ordered structure (hands work much the same for all people) and a psychically ordered structure (people think and create meanings in much the same way). The psyche has also developed in a purposeful or *teleological* line.[28] This is one reason why Jung found it wrong to speak of behavior in *only* biological-instinctive terms. If we were only instinctual creatures we would have no need of a psyche, because the essence of mentality is that it *modifies* such exclusively reflexive responses.[29] The human is an intentional animal which infuses life with meaning *from birth* even as it takes into consideration the strictly environmental influences located in the facts of reality.[30]

Jung once said: "The psyche is not of today: its ancestry goes back many millions of years. Individual consciousness is only the flower and the fruit of a season, sprung from the perennial rhizome [root system] beneath the earth. . . ."[31] There are potentials for almost any kind of meaning to be expressed in the psyche, including those that according to a traditional logic would strike us as inconsistent and contradictory. We can make sense of this seeming confusion if we realize that the psyche operates according to a *principle of opposites*, which means that for any tendency in one direction there is a countering tendency. For any meaning that we might think up or that pops into our minds, the opposite meaning *also* has validity in a psychological sense.[32] If a person says "I hate lilacs," it is psychologically true that at another level of mind he or she is saying "I love lilacs." We just have to appreciate the inevitability of this mental process. As psychologists we cannot let the rules of traditional logic blind us to the fact that meanings expressed mentally are bipolar and hence one mind can entertain *both* ends of such a dimension of meaning—in this case, love-hate (see p. 8 of the Introduction for a discussion of dialectical meaning).

Figure 9 is a schematization of Jung's model of the psyche. There are essentially three points to consider in Figure 9, separated by two arrow bands—a double-headed arrow between points 1 and 2, and a single-headed arrow between points 2 and 3. Note that a directionality from out of the past is suggested by presenting the psyche as a vortex (point 1). The *primordial past* refers to our roots in a primitive state, evolving as we did from a lower animal both physically and psychologically. The purposiveness of humanity's psychic descent is symbolized in the teleological line of advance from the vortex, going "this" way and then "that" down through time: human intellect has selected *alternatives* in the directions taken. The region of the psyche at which Jung framed

his personality constructs is the open-ended front of the vortex. Assume that a membrane (dotted portion offset at point 1) stretched across this open end and that we can slide it off to give an egg-shaped diagram of the psyche at point 2. Note that the psyche is now divided into halves, an upper half labeled *consciousness* and a lower half labeled *unconsciousness*.[33] Recall from the biographical overview that Jung believed each of these two major subdivisions of the psyche (mind) could be said to have a collective and a personal aspect. This is what we have schematized at point 3 by a double set of egg halves, one of which (collective) can slide over the other, making for a combined collective psyche and a combined personal psyche laying one over the other. These are not mutually exclusive regions, however. The contents of one can interpenetrate and interfuse with the contents of the other. In other words, if we snapped the overlaying halves of the egg shut over the core beneath at point 3, we would have the same figure as at point 2, with the exception that now the upper and lower halves of the egg would combine collective *and* personal mental contents.

Even though we have allowed for the *collective conscious* at point 3 of Figure 9, Jung never used this precise phrase. He did speak of a *collective psyche*[34] which combined unconscious and conscious features, and he also referred to the *empirical psyche*[35] when considering aspects of the personality one might think of as involving a collective consciousness. Jung introduced the phrase *collective unconscious,* but he never seemed to need a paralleling collective term in the conscious sphere of psychic life, preferring to cover ground in consciousness under the *ego* and especially the *persona* constructs, both of which we will be taking up in the next section. For this reason, we have put the term *persona* in brackets within the egg-

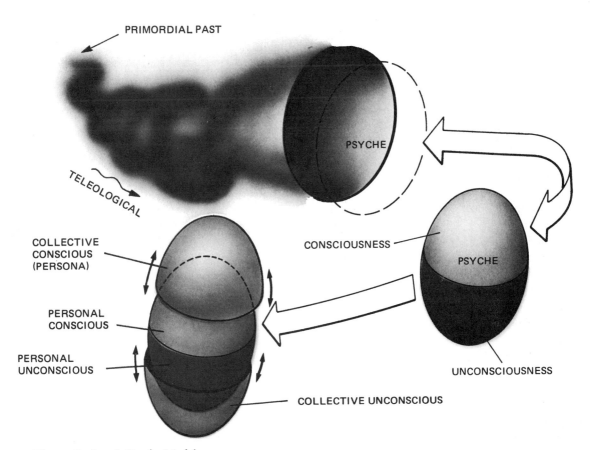

PRIMORDIAL PAST

TELEOLOGICAL

PSYCHE

CONSCIOUSNESS

PSYCHE

COLLECTIVE
CONSCIOUS
(PERSONA)

PERSONAL
CONSCIOUS

PERSONAL
UNCONSCIOUS

COLLECTIVE UNCONSCIOUS

UNCONSCIOUSNESS

Figure 9 Jung's Psyche Model

half labeled *collective conscious*. For all practical purposes these two are one.

According to Jung, during the descent of humanity as our brain evolved physically, a parallel evolution of the psyche was also taking place.[36] As subhumans we were totally instinctual creatures, responding mechanically and without the ability to decide for ourselves through use of a personal will. There was no personal aspect to the psyche at this time because we were immersed in a collective psyche which was for all practical purposes completely unconscious. That is, people were awake. They moved about and did the chores necessary to keep alive. But their actions were entirely communal because subjectivity did

not exist. People had common instincts like seeking food or sexual release, and they also had common mental experiences. They had ideas, but these were not their own ideas. They banded together and did things together but they never really knew why or that things could be otherwise than what they were. This is what we mean by *unconsciousness*. This form of unconsciousness was *impersonal* because it was common to everyone—it was therefore an *objective unconscious*.[37] The objectivity arises from the fact that all members of the human species shared *common* meanings (see p. 15 of Introduction for a discussion of subjective versus objective).

Primitives see nature as an undifferentiated mass of which they are a part.[38] Things happen to them that they sense but cannot explain. They feel awe when looking at a mountain and therefore ascribe a godlike quality to it; they see witches and devils in thunderstorms or earthquakes, which frighten them.[39] Primitives turn nature into human form (anthropomorphize) because they have not yet distinguished between *me* and *it*. Everything in nature has equal validity and integrity to the primitive. This is another way in which Jung approached the definition of *unconsciousness,* as a mental condition in which all things are possible and distinctions have not yet been made between, for example, good and evil. The opposition principle has not yet begun to generate either-or splits in mind. It is from this broad psychic background of collective unconsciousness that consciousness (and by way of it, personal unconsciousness) must eventually emerge.[40]

Consciousness formed through what Jung called *differentiation,* or the development of differences by separating the whole into parts, the one into the many by way of dividing experience into opposites.[41] Occasionally the word *discrimination* is used to describe this process. Jung theorized that consciousness first arose when the human being either had a very intense emotional experience leading to a differentiation of "*I* am having a feeling now that the others are not," or when a collectively prompted mental event passed through the mind and the person contemplated, "Say, that is such a powerful notion that *I* want to mull it over for a time." In

either case, the impression made by an emotional or intellectual impact jolted the person into realizing that there is a bipolar dimension of *I* in relation to *non-I* (that, them, it, and so on).[42] The principle of opposition had come into play, and with the newly found identity, the newly born individual began to differentiate (discriminate) a consciousness.

This process of breaking up the unity into relations by way of opposition has continued. It continued across the history of the psyche resulting in the gradual evolution of a collective consciousness (point 1 of Figure 9), and it continues across at least the first half of the life span for every one of us as a personal consciousness. This is how we *know,* by expanding consciousness.[43] With the rise in knowledge human beings also stop projecting personal attributes and attitudes onto the environment.[44] Consciousness cannot project feelings or experiences, and it has little appreciation for the role of projection in life generally. In fact, widening consciousness invariably results in a downgrading of the unconscious; as Jung put it, "Because of its youthfulness and vulnerability, our consciousness tends to make light of the unconscious."[45] Yet as, in a sense, the offspring of the unconscious, our consciousness must always remain the smaller identity within the larger,[46] just as an island sits within the expanse of the sea from which it emerged.[47] In fact, if we would only appreciate that the unconscious remains the ever-creative principle in life[48] and that it can help us solve our problems of existence in the same way that our automatic (physically unconscious) instincts (to eat, to flee, and so on) help us survive, we would be far better off.[49]

As consciousness arises and a subjective awareness is made possible, mental contents can be assigned to this personal awareness. Material once conscious in the Freudian sense can now be repressed. This is the *personal unconscious* realm at points 2 and 3 of

Figure 9, and we can equate this completely with Freud's theory of the unconscious (see Chapter 1). But contents of the collective unconscious are never repressed. How could they be pushed back from experience when they have never *been* in the individual's experience at all? Just as in the case of Freudian theory, Jung would place the personal unconscious somewhat less deep in the realm of psychic unconsciousness than is the collective unconsciousness.[50] But we have indicated at point 3 in Figure 9 that a complete parallel of the two realms of unconsciousness is possible because Jung always has the contents of one mixing or uniting with the other. Even so, the reason we have the collective unconscious as the outer shell of our egg-shaped figure is so that, as in Figure 10 below (p. 190), we can drop it down deeper in unconsciousness to show that here, in closest union with the primordial past, we have contents of the collective unconscious residing.

The Adhesive Model of Psychic Structure

In order to understand how Jung describes the workings of various "identities" within mind (psyche), we have first to understand an *adhesive model* of mental events that he used. Recall that Jung spoke of *feeling-toned complexes* in mind. He meant that various ideas, attitudes, opinions, and so on, which occur in mind tend to accumulate and combine around a core of emotion. In a sense, these mental contents adhere or stick to this emotional core, they *agglutinate* like so many red blood cells forming clumps to fight off antibodies. This agglutination of mental contents in the psyche is not only a defensive maneuver, of course. This is a process through which we form idea-positions, points of view, and even (one or more) identities in mind. If we have a strong religious commitment, the beliefs maintained by our faith would

combine (agglutinate) into our very identity as a person, resulting in an identifiable totality within the psyche known as the *complex*.

Jung first made use of this adhesive model in his dissertation for the medical degree in 1902 when he was trying to explain the "psychology and pathology of so-called occult phenomena." [51] How does it happen that a medium—a person who mediates between death and life—can seem to have a deceased loved one speaking through his or her (the medium's) vocal cords in conversation with the surviving relatives? Jung did not believe there was always a conscious intent to deceive on the part of the medium. Drawing on the thought of both Bleuler and Pierre Janet, he equated such occult reactions with the dissociative reactions of hysterics and schizophrenics.[52]

Jung noted that mediums often begin by calling out to a presence they sense during an emotionally charged trance state. It is not unusual for the medium to ask this presence, "Who is there?" and then, of course, to allow a reply by way of the medium's voice, which may change noticeably in tone and inflection. In asking this suggestive question while in an emotional state, Jung argued, an *automatism* formed just as such automatic actions are formed in cases of hysteria. This identity or presence is not from the grave but rather from within the medium's own psyche. It is, in short, a *feeling-toned complex* (sometimes called *feeling-toned train of thought*).[53] The dynamics of all complexes are as follows: emotions stimulate mental thoughts (the medium felt close to the dead person, experienced emotions toward the dead person) which then agglutinate around this core of feeling (the dead person's attributes are formed into a total identity combining the medium's identity as well).[54] The life of a complex depends on the emotional core, for when this feeling extinguishes so too does the complex.[55] Returning to the example of a religious faith, the person who loses a feeling for God loses the total meaning this faith has signified in the past. He or she might recall the principles of the faith and possibly even go on attending church services. But this complex of mental attitudes and outlooks no longer exists as a living complex in the psyche.

Jung believed that most complexes formed in life quickly sink back with decreasing feeling tone into the memories we all carry about in our personal unconscious. However, if a complex should encounter some related complex, it can adhere to it, and then, thanks to the added size and importance of this larger agglutination, the older mental contents can begin to return to consciousness as a "new" totality. There is a snowball effect to be seen in complex formation, because the stronger the complex is, the more it will assimilate other contents in the psyche.[56] As it grows in size and strength, it takes on directive powers in mind, and we begin to notice its influence in dreams, slips of the tongue, and, as Jung first determined (see p. 177), in our association of ideas generally. Whereas Freud believed the dream to be his royal road to the unconscious, Jung concluded, "The *via regia* to the unconscious . . . is not the dream . . . but the complex, which is the architect of dreams and of symptoms." [57]

Because Jung so often discussed complexes which have been formed around emotional upsets,[58] many people today think incorrectly that every complex is something "bad." Actually, the complex-formation process is simply one of the major ways in which the psyche expresses itself, and a complex can have either a positive or a negative role in the person-

ality.[59] We next turn to a series of important personality constructs which Jung employed, each of which is a complex within the psyche. Keep in mind that Jung did not believe the psyche had to be logically consistent. Unlike Adler (Chapter 2), who saw the totality of mind working for a common end, Jung's teleology included the possibility of cross-purposes within mind. Two separate mental referent points or identities (complexes) could be seeking to bring about quite different ends in the same personality. We now review four such points of identity before arriving at Jung's specific definition of personality.

Ego. One of the first major complexes Jung named was the *ego complex,* which is usually shortened to simply *ego.* The ego's major region of activity in the personality is consciousness,[60] but, as we shall see, it is not the only complex in consciousness. The ego is that part of our personality that we usually think of as ourselves, containing more of our strong than our weak points.[61] We tend to think of our weak points as mistakes rather than as genuine parts of our personality. The ego is also without front or phoniness, so when we are being fairly genuine and sincere we are expressing attitudes of the ego. The person that we talk to when we are alone, as in driving a car, quietly ("under our breath") is the ego; that is, the ego does the talking and the answering. The contents agglutinated into the ego complex stem from our personal experience with our physical body, its strengths and weaknesses, and also from interpersonal relations as we mature.[62] An important factor in ego development is that feeling of success following an achievement. The little girl who wins an award for a poem she wrote achieves a sense of ego development (complex formation) in the good feeling (emotional core) of "I did that." [63]

The ego can sometimes be the butt of projections which are sent outward from identities in the unconscious and mirrored in the ego.[64] We can think our personality is becoming accident prone because we begin breaking things or injuring ourselves in minor accidents. In Jungian psychology, rather than this thought being some kind of Freudian compromise among ego-superego-id, we would instead be witnessing a projection from the unconscious onto the ego—possibly as an effort to make the ego "look bad." Why should the ego look bad? We will answer this more fully below when we discuss the balancing of personality, but for now we can just suggest that maybe the ego has been looking "too good." So, by way of the principle of opposites, now the unconscious side of the personality wants to even up the sides a bit. The main point here is that the ego's influence is kept *primarily* in consciousness in Jungian psychology. It is not free to do unconscious bargaining (compromising) and is more the *moved-by* than the *mover of* unconscious processes.[65] The ego in Jungian psychology therefore plays a lesser role in the personality than it plays in the personality theory of Freudian psychology.

Persona. The word *persona* is taken from the Greek meaning "mask." [66] In ancient Greek drama, actors held masks up to their faces in portraying a part, and this struck Jung as very descriptive of what we all do in social relations. We have our cheery-person face which we put on in the morning as we greet friends. We have our hard-working face as we get down to our jobs in the presence of our boss. There are sad faces too, as when we must show proper sympathy for others who have suffered a setback whether we think they deserve it or not. Though the persona is our cover or front in social relations, we always recognize something else as more representative of our true

identity (usually, we think of this as our ego). The reason we equated the persona with collective unconsciousness at point 3 in Figure 9 is because social masks are defined for us by our group to apply across the board in everyone's behavior. As Jung himself observed, ". . . what we said of the collective unconscious is also true of the persona's contents, that is, they are of a general [objective] character." [67]

It is virtually impossible to avoid forming some masks in life, at least during our childhood and youth. There are so many socially prescribed behaviors to be proper about, or demands to meet the expectancies of others as they look for certain behaviors from us ("Please try to be pleasant!"), we are constantly falling back on these stylized patterns. Our parents, particularly fathers,[68] help to model many of these masks for us. Our masks are essentially adjustment devices, because they help us get along with others in life.[69] As with the ego, the persona can take on unconscious projections and even serve as a model for the ego to identify with. When we say of a movie queen that "she believes her press clippings," we imply that this person's ego has identified with her persona (that is, public image). Phony, superficial people often do the same thing. Jung explained the tendency for fads to occur in terms of the persona, which takes on the latest dress, food preference, entertainment style, and even sexual practice.[70] Although it need not always happen, there is the continuing danger that one's ego will identify with the group-manipulated persona.[71] Jung favored more balanced personalities which could resist such group manipulations or at least be more selective in the behavior to be manifested.

Shadow. There is a side to our personality that we are likely to ignore, because it represents all those attitudes, temptations, fears of failing, and even immoral and uncivilized inclinations that we have rejected and kept from doing in the past. The emotional core of such complexes is often of a negative sort, such as envy ("I want that wristwatch he's wearing badly enough to steal it") or hostility ("If she frustrates me again I swear I'll beat her skull in"). The ego considers such feelings and ideas but rejects them by not furthering them only to have them form into a complex on the darker side of the personality. Jung called this complex of nondeveloped feelings and ideas the *shadow* or the *alter ego*,[72] defining it as follows: "By shadow I mean the 'negative' side of the personality, the sum of all those unpleasant qualities we like to hide, together with the insufficiently developed functions and the contents of the personal unconscious." [73]

The shadow is like an inferior personality within the broader personality, a repressed, usually guilt-laden collection of behaviors located in the uppermost layers of the personal unconscious.[74] We say it is in the personal unconscious, because any person's actual shadow is formed by being the opposite of those behaviors that have entered into consciousness as a part of the ego and the persona complexes. But there *is* knowledge of shadow tendencies in the collective unconscious as well (that is, the shadow is an archetype; see Table 2 below). The shadow is not as finely differentiated as the ego and persona, making it an agglutination of crude, bumbling, even confused behaviors which would shame us and alarm our friends if it made itself known in consciousness. When we see people change overnight, so that we say "Good old Charlie isn't himself

lately—messing up everything he does, and cranky as the very devil," we may be referring to someone who is indeed under the influence of a kind of devil. The shadow may have increased its role in Charlie's personality, bringing out all those things he is *not* like consciously (principle of opposites). Even so, Jung believed it was important for us to understand our shadows. If we get in touch with our darker side consciously, we do not have to be like it. But if we repress our darker side (like Charlie did!), it can in time get hold of our behavior within consciousness and change us completely.

Having presented the shadow as the negative side of our personality, in his typical oppositional fashion Jung added that occasionally the shadow has a *positive* role to play in the personality. The rarer of the two possible situations occurs when the individual is living a conscious life of crime and/or immorality. In this case, the urges for behaving in a socially acceptable way, caring for the feelings of others, and so on, would be repressed and formed into a good type of shadow.[75] Thus, even the sinner has a potentially good side, because every time in the past when he or she opted for evil, there was this other course in life that might have been followed. It is such other behaviors that agglutinate into shadow complexes, and they can return to influence how even an evil person behaves via the principle of opposition.

The second way in which a shadow can be said to have positive features is through a more sophisticated understanding of what factors go into evaluations like success, good versus evil, or socially acceptable versus socially unacceptable. Surely these are often biased and shortsighted judgments pressed on the individual by the group. Take the Victorian repression of sexuality, for example. Was this not an unnecessarily harsh judgment being placed upon a perfectly natural human urge? If the shadow of a Victorian person therefore contained strong sexual urges, would this not be a reflection of honest, even necessary, human needs? In like fashion, Jung claimed, our shadows often contain the germ of "good qualities, such as normal instincts, appropriate reactions, realistic insights, creative impulses, etc." [76]

Self. The final identity point of Jungian theory is a potential complex not formed by every personality system. If we want to locate the meaning of *self* in everyone's personality, we have to begin looking into the collective unconscious, where we will find this *potential for unity* which the self means as a psychic content (that is, the self like the shadow is an archetype as well as an actual identity point in certain personalities; see Table 2 below). Jung viewed the self as the ultimate stage of personality growth, in which the contents of the ego, persona, and shadow are completely acknowledged and dealt with by the self. A person who has developed a self knows that he or she is *both* loving (ego) yet hateful (shadow), socially concerned (ego) as well as selfish (shadow), and energetic (ego) but also lazy (shadow). Jung used terms like *totality,* the *center of personality,* and *wholeness* to capture the basic meaning of selfhood.[77]

Jung once analogized to the ego in defining the self. He said that just as the ego is the subjective point of reference for consciousness, so too is the self the subjective point of reference for the totality of the psyche.[78] As such, the self is an ideal, something that not all people come to realize in their lifetime. This is why it is only a potential identity point in the personality. We cannot become a complete *individual* unless we have first combined the influences of the historical past with the potentials and aspirations of the future. The point of subjective identity within the flow of time is the self.[79] The self

is that which unites all opposites in the psyche, so that the self-realized person finds it impossible to overlook any aspect of his or her nature, confusing persona with ego or rejecting the shadow as nonexistent. To quote Jung, "In the end we have to acknowledge that the self is a *complexio oppositorum* [collection of opposites] precisely because there can be no reality without polarity." [80]

Personality. We now have four constructs all of which have something to say about the structure of personality. How do we put them together, and is some comprehensive definition of personality now possible? Figure 10 presents a schematization of Jung's view of personality. It is based on and further elaborates the egg-shaped top of the vortex at point 1 of Figure 9. We have dropped the collective-conscious half of the egg in lieu of the complex of masks we now know to be the persona. The ego is set in the conscious sphere, the shadow sits near the line dividing consciousness and unconsciousness, in what we know as the personal unconscious. And the self is sketched in as a dotted circle down more deeply as *in potentia,* ready to emerge into a definite entity if the conditions are right.

When Jung actually used the word *personality,* his meaning was similar to what we know as the self; for example: "I have suggested calling the total personality which, though present, cannot be fully known, the self. The ego is, by definition, subordinate to the self and is related to it like a part to the whole." [81] It would follow that if a self were to emerge from potentiality to actuality, this subjective point of reference for the entire psyche would then contain much of the meaning of *personality.* The question, therefore, is not what is *the* (single) personality in Jungian psychology. We all have several

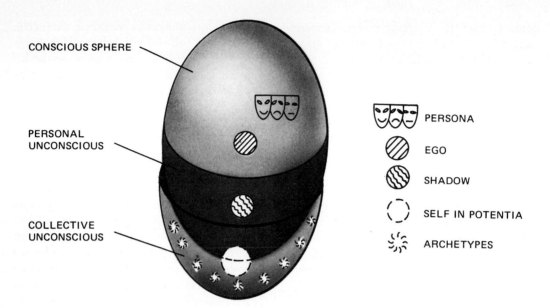

CONSCIOUS SPHERE

PERSONAL
UNCONSCIOUS

COLLECTIVE
UNCONSCIOUS

PERSONA

EGO

SHADOW

SELF IN POTENTIA

ARCHETYPES

Figure 10   The Psyche as Personality

personalities within our psyche, taking *psyche* to mean the functioning of part personalities like the ego, shadow, and persona.[82] A completely integrated (highly differentiated) personality, a total human being, would be a self-realized human being.

The Stylized-Meaning-Expression Model

In addition to the adhesive quality of psychic contents forming around an emotive core, Jung constantly utilized what we might call the *stylized-meaning-expression* model of mental events. The psyche is intentional by nature, and just as primitive humans might anthropomorphize a rock by projecting their subjectively generated images and beliefs onto it, so too does the modern person express unconscious-to-conscious mental contents as *symbols*. The human being is a symbolizing

animal, which for Jung meant that people always create meanings that express, say, or intend something (see p. 7 of Introduction for a discussion of meaning). Psychic expressions of meaning take on styles, so that in time we can come to know what is being expressed by recognizing the various patterns or forms of the meanings intended.

Symbolism. Jung made a strong point of differentiating between a symbol and a sign, arguing that Freud had blurred this important distinction. A *sign* is a mental content (image, idea) that acts as a surrogate or stand-in for some other mental intention. When we use the word or character for the number 7 as a sign, we intend a shorthand designation for *seven things*. The hardware salesperson counts out seven shovels now in stock and records 7 in the proper slot on an inventory form for such construction tools. Signs are translations of meanings; they are not active agents in the creation of meanings. However, if we now use the number 7 to express an alternate meaning, a meaning not originally intended by the mathematician in selecting this sign as a shorthand, we begin to get the idea of what symbolizing is all about. The number 7 might now symbolize *luck*.

The most important source of symbolic expression is the unconscious and particularly the collective unconscious. The human's capacity to symbolize is probably based on some physical capability.[83] That is, we are simply organisms with this physically based ability, just as our walking is based on the physically based leg structure we have. Symbols are less likely to appear in our psyche as ideas; they are usually images that point beyond themselves to meanings that are still out of our grasp.[84] A symbolic image can combine with idea thoughts from the personal unconscious, of course, but when we consider it strictly, the symbol is on the side of a picture rather than a collection of words. Symbols are usually analogues,[85] bearing a relation of similarity to what they are pointing toward. Thus, a symbolic expression flowing from something like a flower conveys a more pleasant meaning than a symbolic expression flowing from a thunder cloud. Symbols can also express more than one intention, even if they are contradictory, and so we have to study an individual for some time before we can get the drift of his or her symbolic expressions.[86]

Dreaming is one of the ways in which a symbol is likely to make its first appearance. Since this symbolic manifestation is likely to have a collective influence behind it, a symbol can even express itself among large masses of people simultaneously. Our myths probably originate as extensions of dream reports or as daydream fantasies which capitalize on an inspirational prompting from the collective unconscious. Myths are never made up consciously; they arise from our collective unconscious.[87] In the primitive state, be-

cause *thinking* was just *happening* to human beings, a myth was nothing more than the recounting of this dreamlike experience.[88] In this sense, primitive thinking is similar to hallucinating. Myths can hold great truths for humanity, or they can mislead us entirely because they frequently convey meanings that are two-pronged or oppositional.

In his study of the dream symbols of his patients, Jung first began seeing parallels with mythological motifs. For example, a very young child would recite a dream to Jung that exactly paralleled some ancient Persian myth. The child could not have been taught the myth, for very few people even knew of it who were not classical scholars. Further, in his travels and studies of primitive peoples in America or Africa, Jung found that, though the content of a specific myth might change, the general story line was identical across cultural heritages which had no possible chance of contact. A common, almost instinctual, necessity for all peoples—including civilized peoples—to symbolize the very same theme in their myths seemed to exist. A good example is the masculine hero-figure who comes from out of nowhere to save a tribe or a civilization during a time of drought, moral decay, and so on. Though the specific content of the redeemer figure might vary—he could have been a fish, lizard, man, man-bird, or God-man—the commonalities of the myths were striking in story line.[89] After considerable study and deliberation, and after he found such common themes spontaneously arising in his own fantasies and dreams during his self-analysis, Jung adapted the Platonic-Augustinian term *archetype* in 1919 to account for such presumed expressions of a collective psyche.[90]

Many people incorrectly conclude that

Jung believed in a fixed or *universal symbolism*. What he actually believed in was a reflection of *universal archetypes* in the psyche of all peoples. Though he admitted that symbols have to take on a relatively fixed content in order for us to grasp their meaning and to recognize them in different contexts—that symbols are relatively objective[91]—Jung was careful to point out that this necessity does *not* suggest a universal symbolism. He was very critical of Freud's tendency to ascribe a sexual significance to all elongated objects (male symbol) or enclosed places (female symbol).[92] Jung believed that "you get caught in your own net if you believe in fixed, unalterable symbols."[93] A sign can have fixed meaning, but never a symbol.

Symbols are what we come to know in consciousness as images (possibly set within a complex of ideas as well). They are what dimly shines through the veil of historical dust from out of our collective past. The archetype, on the other hand, though recognized after much study by its theme, is *never* seen as an image. It stands behind the light in the darkest reaches of the unconscious and expresses its meaning by somehow directing the light thrown symbolically upon our conscious understanding. Hence, the symbolic contents may vary, but the theme or motif (archetype) under expression remains the same. We might dream of a wheel, a cross, or a circle of dancing people; none of these symbols are universal, yet the archetype being expressed from behind such pictorial images (that is, self) would be one and the same, and even universally expressed. That is, in another culture than our own this archetype might tend to appear in dreams as a water lily, a joining of two rivers, or the sun.

Archetypes. We will take up Jung's concept of instinct below in the presentation of his motivational constructs, but it must be recalled at this point that the use of instincts to explain human behavior was very common at the turn of the twentieth century. Jung was no less attracted to this tactic than was Freud. If it is possible to think of the physical body as having evolved certain stylized ways of automatic behavior—called instincts to do this or that in a certain manner—then why is it not also possible for an evolving psyche to have its instinctual counterpart? And so Jung came to think of the recurring dream and mythological motifs as analogous to and based on the instincts. He defined the *instincts* as *typical modes of action* and then added that the archetype might suitably be described as the "*instinct's perception of itself,* or as the self-portrait of the instinct."[94] Archetypes are thus typical ways the psyche has of understanding existence; they are stylized psychic behaviors reflecting the very essence of what the psyche intends to bring about, to learn, accomplish, or express.[95]

Since they come from the deepest regions of the collective unconscious, the archetypes are also called *primordial images*.[96] Jung meant by this that archetypes are just like those collective thoughts that a primitive (primordial) human being had happen outside of directed thought. There is some problem at this point in distinguishing the concept of archetype from that of symbol, and universal from fixed-and-unchanging. That is, Jung at times used definitions of the archetype as innate "pre-existent imagoes"[97] or inherited "form determinants."[98] Yet, he always insisted that, because they lack the language structure within which an idea must be framed (put into words), the archetypes cannot be *inherited ideas*.[99] Now, it is easy to confuse idea (word content) with image (pictorial content) and to forget Jung's stress on the distinction between symbol and sign. Jung is saying that in having evolved and differentiated over the centuries, the psyche has become a process in which *symbolizing* takes place. This is the most fundamental nature of mind, as a teleological, symbolizing process. Ideas are framed within those signs that our culture teaches us as we grow up. Hence, the archetypes are at the root of that meaning that is symbolized *through* cultural names for certain images. We name a flower a water lily, but it is the image of this flower through which the archetype expresses meaning and *not* through the words (signs) *water* combined with *lily*. Language terms (signs) are used by mind, but they do not reveal the basic nature of mind, any more than what a hand *does* tells us about the hand's nature or its potentials for expression.

After all, hands are constructed in a certain way, with definite restrictions but also with innate potentials for expression. This hand paints a beautiful picture, and the delicacy of its movements gives us some idea of what its owner's life has been like, while that hand is preoccupied with stealing from others, thereby revealing an alternative possibility for the hand which might have been that of an artist's. Now, if we come upon a hand that steals, would we be justified in concluding that this is what the hand's basic nature *is*—a stealing organ? Hardly, for other hands paint. Clearly, what is inherited by the hand is its grasping and manipulating capacity, but we cannot find this capacity by looking at what the hand has learned to accomplish since birth. In fact, the hand's manipulative capacity is what made this learning possible. In the same way, by looking at the product of the mind's symbolizing nature—the fact that a language framing ideas is learned—we do *not* address the mind's basic nature. The mind uses ideas and is influenced by cultural factors as

people mature. But mind *is* a framer of meanings, and since it begins this process *from birth,* some potential for expressing meanings (archetypes) exists even before cultural influences like learning the alphabet and how to read have been undertaken. The mind does not have to wait on ideas to express meaning. Asking why the mind expresses meaning in the first place is like asking why the hand grasps in the first place.

Continuing our parallel, in the evolution of hands, the precise nature of fingers, how they work, and so on, depended on the use made of these appendages by the animals that possessed them. It would not be too wrong to say that hands mirror the past achievements of the animals possessing them, basing their form on the challenges and threats to survival that were overcome. The same goes for mind. The evolving psyche has had to confront, again and again, certain universal themes or motifs in human experience. These are the most basic themes of life, such as the fact that sexual identities differ in male-female relations, the awe sensed in confronting a superhuman essence (God), or the realization of a darker side to our personality. As the hand brings with it a manipulating capacity from birth, the mind brings a capacity to express the past meaningful concerns and preoccupations of those animals who were fortunate enough to have evolved such higher mentalities. The mind, or psyche as Jung called it, lacks specific contents for these archetypal thematic meanings. The culture within which a psyche meets experience will provide the items (and the words naming them) on the basis of which a symbolical analogy can be drawn—such things as water lilies, the sun, or people dancing in a circle—but it is the nature of the psyche to make such symbolizing possible.[100] And this symbolizing capacity has a remnant of its past reflected in its very expressions; that is, it has meanings to express *from birth* but *not* ideas!

What then determines when an archetypal meaning will be expressed? Jung said that they must be beckoned forth by circumstances a particular person is facing, so that different archetypes operate in different lives.[101] Jung once used the metaphor of a deep riverbed to explain what he meant by the archetype.[102] Though past evolution washed such beds into each of our psyches, not all of us experience their influence. Not until a mental thunderstorm—a challenge, fascination, some problem—empties its contents into all of the available channels will this deepened pocket make itself known, as the shallow stream of mental activity swells into a mighty river, rumbling deep and quite out of its usual character. Possibly the most appropriate phrase Jung used to capture the meaning of archetypes was "*a priori* categories of possible functioning."[103] They are a priori because they come to us through inheritance before birth, and are already there for possible but not necessary functioning *at birth.*

Over the years, thanks to his study of dreams, mythologies, legends, religions, and even alchemy, Jung came to classify two broad categories of archetypes. First, there were the *personifying archetypes,*[104] which naturally took on a humanlike identity when they functioned in the psyche. For example, there is the *anima* in man and its counterpart in woman, the *animus.* The anima represents all of man's ancestral experiences with woman, and the animus represents all of woman's ancestral experiences with man.[105] Jung believed that the most direct way in which the unconscious can influence us is through an act of *personification* (turning objects, moods, things into persons).[106] When

a primitive man anthropomorphized a rock, projecting unconsciously his subjective mental contents onto objective reality, this was personification; and when we now dream of a "wise old man," that too is the personification of all of our inherited psychic experiences with wisdom, authority, cunning, and so forth.

The other category of primordial images Jung termed *transforming archetypes.* These are not necessarily personalities, but include typical situations, geometric figures, places, and ways and means that express the kind of transformation that might be taking place within the personality. We will be dealing with transforming archetypes when we take up Jung's psychotherapy; some examples are the circle, quaternity (a set of four), and most important of all, the *self.* By and large, transforming archetypes emerge when the personality is moving for change and particularly that balancing change that will result in a total personality. Table 2 presents a list of Jungian archetypes.

Note that the shadow is an archetype. It will play an important role in psychotherapy, along with the anima. The ego and persona are not listed in the table because most of their content is conscious. As complexes framed within the unconscious, the shadow and the self are naturally more likely to express themselves (via symbols) archetypally. Jung always insisted that he had *discovered* the archetypes of Table 2. They were not *thought up* by him—as indeed it would be impossible to do—but rather identified and tentatively named only after years of painstaking research. One of the reasons he did not think it wise to memorize a list of archetypes was because new archetypes obviously might be discovered at any moment. Nor are the archetypes mutually exclusive designations. The Wise Old Man might appear in a dream as a wise old cockroach (Animal), or a clever clown (Trickster) who

Anima (including Soul, Life, Goddess, Witch)
Animal (various, as Horse, Snake, etc., including Theriomorphic Gods)
Animus
Child (including Child-God, Child-Hero)
Family
Father
God
Hermaphrodite (including Union of Opposites)
Hero (including Redeemer Figure, Mana Personality)
Hostile Brothers (or Brethren)
Maiden
Mother (including Earth Mother, Primordial Mother)
Order (or Number, Numbers 3, 4)
Original Man
Self (including Christ, Circle, Quaternity, Unity)
Shadow
Soul (including Mana)
Trickster (including Clown)
Wise Old Man (including Lucifer, Meaning)
Wotan (including Daemonic Power)

"It is no use at all to learn a list of archetypes by heart.
Archetypes are complexes of experience that come upon us like
fate, and their effects are felt in our most personal life." [107]

Table 2   A List of Jungian Archetypes

teaches us the clue to some puzzling problem. Fairy tales usually have interesting combinations of archetypal identities, and Jung often used such children's stories as examples of his theoretical outlook.

The best approach to an understanding of the archetypes is to take up these constructs as they emerge naturally in the Jungian topic under consideration. One term that we should know at this point is *dominant(s)*. In some of his writings Jung seemed to use this term as synonymous with *archetype*,[108] but with this usage he also had in mind a special instance of archetypal manifestation. He seemed to use it when stressing the actual functioning, the bringing to bear of an archetype into the stream of mental fantasy—as during a dream, reverie, or other form of imagination. Thus, when archetypes are no longer potentialities but actualities underway as mental influencers, we may speak of them

as dominants.[109] It is possible for such an engaged archetype to influence an entire group of people communally. The Nazi swastika, for example, served as a symbolic intermediary for a dominant. Since all who fell under its sway were subject to the meaning it was expressing, we might even think of this as a kind of "daemonic" power of the symbol (the dominant Wotan lying beneath; see Table 2).

Motivational Constructs

Instinct and Energy

Though constructs like *instinct* and *energy* strike many people as mechanical terms and thus nonteleological, for Jung these meanings were quite otherwise. Jung thought of life itself as an energy process, one that was always directed toward some goal. He said, "Life is teleology *par excellence;* it is the intrinsic striving towards a goal, and the living organism is a system of directed aims which seek to fulfill themselves." [110] Energies are therefore expended in relation to goals, presumably even in the physical sphere, but unquestionably so in the psychic sphere. Self-direction or subjective direction implies a capacity for conscious, willful choice. [111] Jung saw this as an ego function in the personality, [112] and in opposition to the *will* he suggested an *instinct* concept. "According to my view, all those psychic processes over whose energies the conscious has no disposal come within the concept of the instincts." [113] We say that our behavior is instinctive when our ego does not willfully direct it, so that it appears to be happening automatically. [114] It rarely occurs to us that there may be *other* complexes with their own intentions bringing this "automatic" behavior about.

Jung rejected Freud's narrow definition of *libido* as the psychic energy of a sexual instinct. He acknowledged that medicine typically used the term *libido* to refer to sex, particularly to sexual lust; but Jung preferred to think of it in the sense first used by Cicero, as capturing "passionate desire, want, wish, or excited longing." [115] In some of his writings Jung even used the term *hormé* (rather than *libido*), which is the Greek word for "attack, impetuosity, urgency, and zeal." [116] All of these usages are highly telic in meaning. Even though he occasionally fell into this usage, [117] Jung stated quite explicitly that libido was not to be hypostatized (made into a physical reality) and considered a psychic force. [118] Admitting that he was at fault for seeming to use it in this sense on occasion,

Jung tried to clarify matters by noting that "technically, we should express the general tension in the *energic* sense as *libido,* while in the *psychological sense relating to consciousness, we should refer to it as value.*" [119] Thus, if we value something highly, it may be said to have a high concentration of libido attached to it. A woman who loves to knit, for example, has invested this activity with much libido. This is not to say that libido really exists as a physical or quasi-physical (psychic) energy, but it may be called an energy to help us understand the workings of the psyche. We have schematized Jung's views on psychical versus physical energy in Figure 11.

Note the mind-body dualism in Figure 11. Issuing from the mental region there is a psychic energy (libido) which in turn is experienced by the individual as a value intensity (desire) which in turn goes into the mental activities of symbol formation, thinking, willing, and so forth. Issuing from the body region there is a physical energy which in turn exerts a certain force intensity on the formation of actions we call behavior, the doing of things physically (including internal processes like digestion or breathing). At the extreme left side of Figure 11, we have the instinct that—as in all psychoanalytical theories—unites the mutual influence of mind and body within the personality. Jung makes it plain that instincts are partly psychic and partly physiological in nature. [120] But unlike Freud, who set libido loose in the mind by way of the sexual instinct and then explained all behavior on the vicissitudes of that libido, Jung has his instinctive counterpart (archetypes) built *directly* into the mind from the outset. Here is the heart of Jung's position.

Instinct is not an isolated thing, nor can it be isolated in practice. It always brings in its train archetypal contents of a spiritual nature,

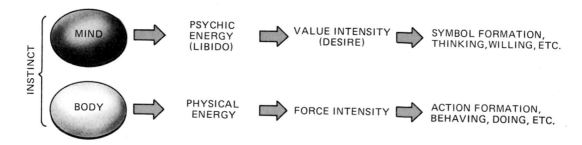

Figure 11   Jung's Views on Psychical versus Physical Energy

which are at once its foundation and its limitation. In other words, an instinct is always and inevitably coupled with something like a philosophy of life, however archaic, unclear, and hazy this may be. Instinct stimulates thought, and if a man does not think of his own free will, then you get the compulsive thinking, for the two poles of the psyche, the physiological and the mental, are indissolubly connected. ... . Not that the tie between mind and instinct is necessarily a harmonious one. On the contrary it is full of conflict and means suffering.[121]

What instincts *really* are we shall never know, for they are in large measure nothing but convenient labels for organic and psychic factors about which we must honestly claim ignorance.[122] But insofar as there is a tie between the physical and the mental, Jung called upon the theorist to admit of more than simply one or two instincts at play in human behavior. There is a sexual instinct, but even before it might come into play, there is surely also a nutritive instinct in operation.[123] There are probably also self- and species-preservative instincts to be seen in human behavior.[124] Jung did not accept the validity of a death instinct as such.

The psychic energy of libido can now be said to reflect itself in *any* of the instinctual ways.[125] An interest in cooking relates to our hunger, desiring protection from the elements

results from an instinctive wish to live out our days, and so forth; all such human behaviors are goal-directed or teleological. Bergson's concept of *élan vital* and Schopenhauer's concept of *Will* have much the same teleological meaning and it is therefore not surprising to find that Jung equated his concept of libido with these more philosophical notions.[126] Jung believed that we could get a relative idea of our personal (subjective) libidinal investments by asking ourselves how we *feel*—positively or negatively—about some aspect of life.[127] If we happen to like some one activity, person, or place more than another, the reason is because there is more libido potentially available for the former than for the latter.[128] Unconscious value preferences also exist, but our egos cannot put themselves in touch with them. To get at the deeper preference values, we must rely on dream analyses, parapraxes, free (word) associations, and so forth.[129]

If our unconscious psyche begins to form complexes around a core of emotions that have value preferences included thanks to libido, it is possible for our egos in consciousness to be influenced by these values. A person's ego (I, me) can sense this value source as part of the internal psyche or project it outwardly. This is how Jung believed religions were born. Primitive peoples sensed large concentrations of libido at the unconscious levels of the psyche as *mana*. Jung occasionally used this word as a synonym for *libido*.[130] To the primitive, *mana* means "extraordinarily potent" in the sense of supernatural or even divine power. A primitive person sensing mana (libido) issuing from the unconscious might therefore project it as coming from a mountain, which through personification is turned into a god; or the mana might be interpreted as either good or evil spirits (possibly both) that have taken possession of the individual from within.[131]

The Principle of Opposites

Jung once observed,

I see in all that happens the play of opposites, and derive from this conception my idea of psychic energy. I hold that psychic energy involves the play of opposites in much the same way as physical energy involves a difference of potential, that is to say the existence of opposites such as warm and cold, high and low, etc.[132]

It is difficult to overstate the importance of the *principle of opposites* in Jungian psychology. If repression was the cornerstone construct of Freudian psychoanalysis, then Jung's most basic conception was that of opposition. In fact, Jung believed that repression was a product of the psyche's oppositional tendencies. For any given intention or wish, there is always and immediately an *opposite* wish suggested. Since every good intention has a corresponding bad one, it is only natural that certain of these intentions will have to be repressed.[133]

Although the principle of opposites remains the basic mover of behavior, by slightly modifying two physical science principles, Jung made it appear—as Freud had before him—that libido behaves something like physical energy. The two principles borrowed from physical science were *equivalence* and *entropy*. Jung's theory did not initially contain these principles. He introduced them later and devoted a minimal amount of space to them, but in an interesting manner he capitalized on their meaning for his own purposes. Both equivalence and entropy are related to the principle of constancy, which Freud found useful as a theoretical device to unite the psychological and the physical (see p. 52). The *principle of equivalence* states that ". . . for a given quantity of energy expended or consumed in bringing about a certain condition, an equal quantity of the same or another form of energy will appear elsewhere."[134]

Jung then added significantly to this conception by claiming that as *opposite intentions* (wishes) are conceived in the psyche, pontential energy is put at the disposal of *either* alternative. If we repress some bad intention, then the libido of the rejected alternative is not simply lost to the psyche when repression takes place. The repressed alternative has set loose a certain amount of free libido in the mind, even as the chosen (good) alternative puts its libido to work by framing a conscious intention (we usually do what we think is right or good to do). For example, a woman must attend a meeting of an organization and present a report. She would like to avoid this responsibility, and for a fleeting second she imagines herself pretending sickness or quitting the organization. But quickly repressing this negative inclination, she attends the meeting and presents the report. This is the right or good thing to do. But her rejected (repressed) alternative of getting out of the duty has turned loose free libido in her unconscious like some aimless intention which has potential for directing behavior later on.

This free libido can *constellate* (agglutinate) a complex in the psyche à la the adhesive model. It therefore happens that the more we deny our bad intentions and repress their contents without accepting them as having occurred to us, the more likely it is that free libido will flood the psyche with potential constellating power. By the *principle of entropy,* Jung meant an "equalization of differences" in the psyche, a tendency to vacillate more or less violently between the poles of opposition until a state of equilibrium or balance is reached.[185] Entropy thus served as a homeostatic rationale for the psychic energy of Jungian psychology. Like the constancy principle, entropy implied that energies seek a common level, but before they equalize there often is a burst of energy release, depending on how far apart the original split of the two opposites (intentions, attitudes, biases, and so on) has been. Jung referred to the extent of disbalance in the psyche as *one-sidedness.*[186]

Note what has happened here: libido is seen to be generated by way of differentiation! As the teleological psyche frames an intention, differentiating the desired alternative ("I am going to help him with his work") from its opposite alternative ("I wouldn't help that bum out of this spot for anything"), libido is literally under spontaneous creation thanks to the act of discriminating between opposites. As we pull psychic opposites into independent contents, we turn psychic energy loose as if we had split a mental atom. Freudian libido is not generated in this way, except in the sense of a certain rejuvenation that takes place at puberty (see p. 70). This is an often-cited distinction made between the theories of Freud and Jung. But the more important points to keep in mind are that Jung based his energy on the principle of opposites, and that teleology (intentional behavior) played a very important role in his view of mind. The *physical* principles of equivalence and entropy were certainly not based on teleology, nor did they require that opposites be involved in the generation or dispersion of any energy that might have arisen.

Complex Formation

Jung felt that the unconscious bears a *compensatory* or counterbalancing relationship with the conscious.[137] This is yet another reflection of the role of opposition in the psyche—to balance off what has become one-sided by bringing such mental contents into relation with their contradictions. Figure 12 presents Jung's complex-formation model, broken down into five steps. Note first of all (step 1) that the unconscious should properly balance the conscious in what Jung sometimes called a *reciprocal relativity.* In other words, as the arrows indicate by being aimed in both directions, there is a mutual give-and-take across the levels of mind. A person like this listens to the promptings from his or her unconscious, takes the theme of a dream seriously enough to consider what it might be saying about personal attitudes and behaviors now manifest in consciousness, and so on. Furthermore, this person is openly accepting *all* of those attitudes and intentions which have been considered, those enacted overtly in behavior *and also* those turned aside as unworthy. Rather than repressing these latter, bad alternatives, the individual is accepting responsibility for having considered them. He or she *did* create these possibilities just as surely as the more acceptable ones. By keeping all alternatives

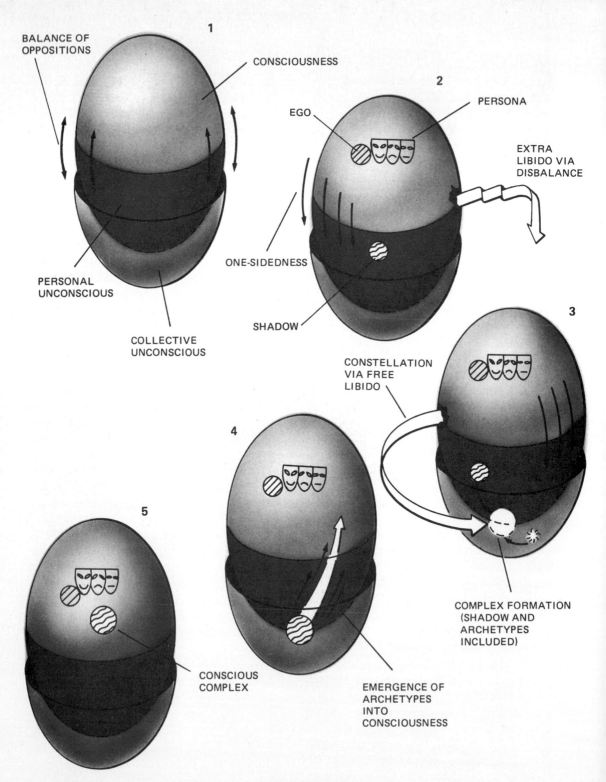

Figure 12 Jung's Complex-Formation Model

in consciousness like this, the person is able to use the free libido from the rejected alternative to shore up the ego. More importantly, this use of free libido consciously *prevents* formation of a complex at the unconscious level.

Formation of a complex would begin with the one-sided development and conscious recognition of only *certain* attitudes and intentions; that is, a person who is likely to develop a complex begins immediately repressing or denying the bad alternatives as if they had never really been considered. This could take place over many years in the development of the personality. Assume that as the ego was developing, the socially acceptable behaviors were being organized (agglutinated via adhesive model) into this ego complex. Over this same period of development, all of those pleasant mannerisms we put on in public—the politeness and cheeriness when we feel rotten, the pretended concern about the health of people whom we basically dislike—would be going to form our persona complex (masks). Since each of the good and stronger aspects of behavior has its opposite possibility, we can think of several behavior potentials which have *not* been incorporated into consciousness. We have symbolized this (step 2) by arrows pointing down into unconsciousness, with no counterbalancing arrows pointing back into consciousness. Many of these behaviors would of course go down and form into our shadow.

Now, unless we are aware that we do indeed *have* a shadow, and that those immoral and unfair behaviors we see in others are actually *in us too* (as rejected alternatives under projection), we will begin to develop a one-sidedness in our psyches. Another type of one-sidedness occurs when we identify our egos with our masks, when we think that the superficial face we show to others is *really* who we are. This also makes us likely to be manipulated by the group (see p. 195),

because the group sets the styles incorporated by the persona complex. We might now believe ourselves to be one of the "in-people" or the "beautiful" ("chic," "cool," and so on) people to be admired and accepted by all. At this point, the unconscious as a compensatory—oppositional, balancing—process takes steps to call up our *other* side.[138] This is not a mechanical but an intentional (telic) process.

On the night of our greatest triumph as an actor or an athlete, we might have a dream in which we suffer stage fright or cause our team to lose in an athletic contest. The next morning we might remark to our friend how strange it is that we should dream of failure at precisely the time when everything is going so well for us. If only we knew! This dream could be an oppositional-meaning expression, warning us like an alarm bell from the unconscious that says, "Look, don't go overboard and think you are extra special because you had this great triumph. You aren't so perfect, there is a side to your nature that is anything but admirable."

If some such change in mental attitude does not occur, greater one-sidedness continues to develop, which means that more and more free libido is set loose in the psyche. The additional libido set loose by this vicious cycle is symbolized at step 2 by the phrase "extra libido via disbalance." Now, all of this free libido is eventually drawn into the unconscious, because the intentions to which it has been attached have not and are not consciously acknowledged. It is important to stress that Jung never said all psychic intentions must be overtly *acted out* by the individual. If we have a socially inappropriate prompting, he is not saying that we must actually do the immoral thing that has occurred to us. What we must do to avoid complex formations of an abnormal type (using these very intentions!) is consciously to recognize that we have created them, been tempted by them, and put them aside for reasons we value above them. This keeps their libido in consciousness where it can be used constructively, rather than going into unconscious-complex formations. Consciousness can always use free libido, as to lend support to the ego when the person occasionally tries to "go at reality" *without* persona masks. It takes courage (feelings drawing on libido) to "be your own person" or to "know who you really are."

If we do not have some means for becoming aware of and admitting consciously to our shadow or alter ego, and if we continue to repress and ignore the warning signs contained in our dreams or parapraxes (slips of tongue, and so on), then in time the free libido that constellates unconscious contents must necessarily form a large, potent complex of some sort. We have symbolized this at step 3. Note that as the complex forms, as the contents of the unconscious agglutinate, all kinds of mental contents may go to make it up. Thus, a complex might include not only those things we never were—never did before —but also various archetypal identities can form into the complex by way of symbolical expression. The archetype at step 3 is the small star-burst moving up from the collective unconscious to agglutinate with the other contents of the complex. We will have more to say of how archetypes do this when we take up Jung's theory of psychopathology (see especially Figure 15). The shadow does not always combine into the complex, but usually it does and so we present it this way for simplification. Since the newly forming com-

plex has considerable libido at its disposal, thanks to the extensive repressions and the one-sidedness of the individual, it can now emerge into consciousness under its own power (step 4). This is what we were alluding to above (p. 188), in referring to the sudden change that came over "good old Charlie." When the shadow-in-combination with other unconscious factors comes into consciousness, it presents the *other side* of the personality. At this point the actor may indeed suffer a case of stage fright or an athlete might in fact perform some uncharacteristic error to lose a contest for the team. We are no longer in the dream world but in reality, but even so the unconscious is still attempting to compensate the conscious. The complex would in this case still be trying to bring the person down from the inflated level.

Step 5 completes the schematization of Table 12, showing the complex now fully established within consciousness but outside of the control of consciousness. Neither the ego nor the persona have any control over the complex. Things are not necessarily in a very bad way as yet for the personality. There is still time to rectify what we might now call a mild neurosis. The former man's man (mask) may cry easily now, or the mild-mannered schoolteacher (mask) might begin losing her temper rather frequently. If such behaviors can be accepted by these individuals, all may go reasonably well for their personalities, which now have color if not eccentricity. A final word: we have sketched the course of complex formation around the nondevelopment and repression of conventionally negative behaviors. But in theory, a subcultural deviant, like a delinquent or criminal who denies his or her better promptings, could also form a good or guilt-laden complex in time. The model should work with any coupling of behaviors, as long as those behaviors are oppositional.

Psychic Determinism:
Causality versus Synchronicity

Surely the complex that emerges into consciousness, popping up from below as a cork might break water level if released from one's grasp beneath the sea, must be thought of as a completely self-contained, *determined* entity. Jung cautioned against the naive view that we humans are what we consciously think we are as a personality. "The truth is that we do not enjoy masterless freedom; we are continually threatened by psychic factors which, in the guise of 'natural phenomena,' may take possession of us at any moment." [139] Not only are we influenced by unconscious personal forces in Jungian psychology, but the psychic inheritance from antiquity enters in to direct our fate to some degree. Racial-historical promptings within the collective unconscious that have been differentiated but denied consciousness *also* may form into a complex. Regardless of how a complex arises in consciousness, once it is there we can confront it and deal with it as if it were another personality within our personality.

We do not *have* to submit to our complexes any more than we have to be only one sort of conscious person in the first place. We can understand and admit to all of our attitudes, even the less desirable ones, yet ultimately direct our own fate by coming to know the unconscious ground plan written for us collectively—and then *modifying* it to suit our unique purposes. As Jung once said of himself: "I had to obey an inner law which was imposed on me and left me no freedom of choice. Of course I did not always obey it. How can anyone live without inconsistency?" [140] This paradoxical outlook makes Jung a *hard determinist* in the psychic sphere, but a *soft determinist* in the sphere of overt behavior. A hard determinist believes that everything takes place as it *had to* happen, and that events could not have gone

otherwise than they did. A soft determinist claims that although many things *had to* happen as they did, at least some of the events that took place could have gone otherwise (see Chapter 4, p. 262 for a discussion of determinism).

Even better evidence justifies the claim that Jung actively rejected the hard determinist's position. Probably more than any other psychoanalyst, Jung wrestled with the problems of whether or not it is possible for the cause-effect principle to explain all that we know of human behavior. When Jung used *cause-effect* here, he referred to *efficient* causation (see p. 2 of the Introduction for a discussion of the various forms of causation). How can this deterministic view explain the strange and eerie experiences we know as "psychic phenomena," like telepathy, clairvoyance, or extrasensory perception? For example, what do we say when a train ticket purchased in the morning on our way into the city bears the identical six-digit number that a theater ticket purchased in the afternoon bears? And then, upon returning home in the evening, we find a message to return a telephone call—once again, with the same six numbers! [141]

We probably call such events chance occurrences, yet they have such meaningful impact that they can be among the most important determiners of our life's style. Take the case of a daughter who dreams of her mother's death at the exact hour this parent is killed in an automobile accident. The impact of this chance experience is of monumental importance to the daughter's life thereafter, yet cause-effect theories of physical science must dismiss these coincidences as happenstance and hence of no theoretical importance. Jung could not accept this shortsighted view, and as if to give such paranormal

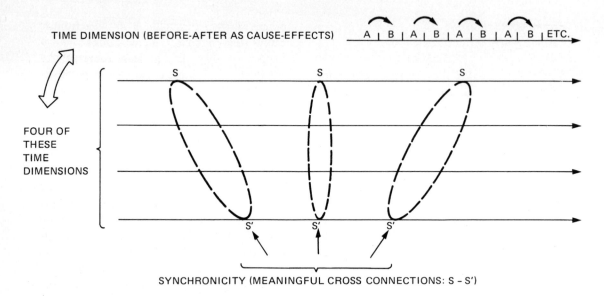

Figure 13 Jung's View of Synchronicity

happenings acceptability, he coined a term to cover them.

The term he selected was *synchronicity,* a concept stressing the fact that meanings can emerge in the patterning of events when we disregard the before-after determiners of actions in (efficient) causation. Thus, Jung referred to synchronicity as *meaningful co-incidence, acausal orderliness,* or *meaningful cross-connection.*[142] These cross-connections are not cause-effects, but rather a kind of falling into pattern which cuts across the antecedent-consequent succession of events over time. Indeed, synchronicity is an effort to explain events with time left out of the explanation as a cause of anything. Such causes are going on, and time can be said to be slipping by, but the patterning within time that is synchronicity has nothing specifically to do with time. We have tried to get this idea across in Figure 13. Note that there are four arrows running from left to right:

these represent a chain of cause-effect lines over time. The "time dimension" heading at the top of the figure represents a series of before-after, A-to-B causal connections over time. The inscription on the extreme left indicates a series of four such A-to-B causal connections running over time. These four time dimensions can be thought of as running along, parallel to each other but without affecting each other in the A-to-B causal sense.

Think of these as four lines of events taking place over time. These could be the life events of four different people. Or two lines could represent people's lives and the other two could refer to inanimate events like the passage of the sun across the sky during the day and the passage of the moon at night (actually, both planets continuing their passage throughout the lives of these people). Anything at all might be represented as long as these are seemingly four independent series of causal events (A-to-B, A-to-B, and so on). Using *S* to symbolize *synchronicity,* we can now demonstrate that this refers to the cross-connections between any two (or more) time dimensions: S-to-S' or vice versa. Rather than cause-effects, these interrelated and highly meaningful patterns emerge within the time series but not in a space-time sense. One happening (S) interlaces meaningfully with another happening (S'), neither of which can possibly be explained on the basis of before-after or proximity (closeness) to one another.

We have symbolized the synchronistic pattern by showing three dotted circles. Suppose a young woman experiences a sudden sense of alarm at 9:10 A.M. (S) on a certain day, only to learn subsequently that at precisely that instant (accounting for time changes) her fiancé had sustained a battle wound (S') halfway around the earth from her. This would be a perfect example of synchronicity that occurred simultaneously at two different points in space. We can think of this as the center circle of Figure 13, because the girl's life (top line) touched her fiancé's life (bottom line) at a precise moment of danger and injury, creating a meaningful cross-connection. However, it is not necessary for synchronous events to occur at the identical time like this.[143] Time is not germane to the explanation. We might dream of a friend's good fortune after he or she had experienced some great success but had not yet found the time to contact us by telephone. Or we might also dream of something that had not yet happened, but that will in fact take place some time later. In either of these cases, the S and S' connections of Figure 13 might vary over time, and tilting the dotted circle backward and then forward in time is our attempt to illustrate this conception of a pattern entirely beyond time factors. It is immaterial which way we think of the S and S' occurrences, but we do not believe that one *causes* the other in any case. Nor is it a matter of one S predicting the S',

because the issue is not A-to-B (efficient) causality.

Adjustment Mechanisms

Repression versus Suppression. Jung believed that *repressions* start as voluntary *suppressions,* that we actively try to keep something disliked (bad) out of consciousness, and then in time the boundary between consciousness and unconsciousness is crossed by the negative mental content and a repression results.[144] The reasons for repression were as varied for Jung as they were for Freud (see Chapter 1), but of course, Jung did not find quite so many sexual involvements in repressed material as Freud did. Sometimes we might dislike feeling guilt over our behavior and actually repress a *moral* impulse to do the right thing for past sins and take our medicine. In this case, the right impulses become a bad alternative because we do not want to be punished, so we end up repressing our better side.

Projection versus Introjection. We have already seen that Jung made extensive use of the *projection* construct. He viewed this as unconscious and automatic,[145] in most cases resulting when one individual transfers psychic contents onto another.[146] Only the unconscious can project, and this mechanism is one of the oldest in the history of humanity.[147] What we actually do in projection is to blur the distinction between subjective and objective experience. The "in here" becomes the "out there" as we attribute our subjective beliefs to objective reality. *Introjection* is the other side of the coin, since it blurs or fails to differentiate between object and subject; in this case the "out there" becomes the "in here" as we accept the beliefs or behavioral patterns of others as our own.[148]

Compensation, Balance, and Wholeness. Jung admitted that he had borrowed the idea of *compensation* from Alfred Adler, who had introduced the concept (see Chapter 2).[149] As we noted in the discussion of complex formation above, the unconscious is said to compensate and help *balance* off the personality. Once the personality is balanced Jung spoke of it as having achieved *wholeness,* so that all three of these meanings interrelate. Jung also used the term *compensate* in a special way, as when he suggested that the anima could compensate the persona.[150] We will take up this usage below, when we discuss Jung's approach to psychotherapy.

Differentiation (Discrimination) and Opposition. Since Jung used these terms to explain the adjustment mechanisms, we should consider them as such. Repression was further explained as a loss in *differentiation* between the conscious and unconscious, or projection was said to be a failure in discrimination between subjective and objective experience. Jung believed that the human being's ability to make such differentiations is due to the principle of opposites. Since we can readily see duality in experience, we can always split it up into *that* and *not-that,* many times over. A period of time in the bathtub is enjoyable, but when the water is too hot the experience *is not* what it *is* otherwise. As infants and children, we break up our experience through such *oppositional contrasts* even before we have words to name things hot or cold.

Identification, Possession, Numinous, Assimilation, and Inflation. In the classic psychoanalytical sense, Jung would accept *identification* as one type of introjection, and he even referred to it as *unconscious imitation*

—as when we take in (introject) a parental attitude and make it our own.[151] However, when Jung used this term in the context of analytical psychology, he was usually referring to imitations of one aspect of the personality by another. We have already seen this above, where we said that the ego could identify with the persona (see p. 187). It is also common in Jungian psychology to hear of the ego identifying with a potent complex that has emerged from unconsciousness into consciousness (combining the shadow).[152] Since this complex might also bring an archetype into its constellation, Jung occasionally referred to an *identification with the archetype.*[153] When this happens, Jung would say that a *possession* has taken place, in that now the personality is under direction by unconscious meanings which have fixed on a symbol to almost hypnotize the person. To capture this idea of a power under which the individual falls, Jung borrowed a term from Rudolf Otto: *numinosum.*[154] A numinous mental content occurs to the person as an idea, hunch, or even an image of what something is or is about to become in some really important sense. Something *big* is always taking place in a numinous mental event, so that it is sensed as containing a power beyond reason. These are superhuman conceptions which often imply that something divine is being expressed. The idea, which arose in ancient Jerusalem, that "God is born on earth" was an example of such a numinous idea. A less-benign example was the one mentioned above (p. 195), of how a community fell under the dominant in the Nazi swastika. This symbol had a numinous quality about it. Almost always, when we have a numinous experience developing in a single personality or in a collective group, there is an archetype involved.

If the ego identifies with the complex or the archetype contained within it, an *inflation* of the personality can take place.[155] In other words, the ego can presume that it has the superhuman power (numinosity) of the complex causing it to inflate its importance.[156] Assume that a man has the idea that he is the son of Satan. Jung would say that this man had, upon forming a complex through the steps of Figure 12, constellated a daemonic power (Lucifer) archetype in it and now has identified with these contents to presume that he is an offspring of the devil (or is the devil himself). The same would go for a woman who thinks she is the Blessed Virgin Mary (that is, a variation of the Earth Mother archetype; see Table 2). Another term that Jung sometimes used to describe a special type of identification—really a unification —was *assimilation*. By this he meant the enveloping of one psychic identity by another, so that the engulfed identity is literally no longer differentiated in the personality. Thus, Jung said the self could assimilate the ego in toto, which would *not* be a good thing for the personality.[157]

Progression versus Regression. Jung took these terms from Freud but modified them to suit his own purposes (see p. 47). *Progression* was interpreted teleologically "as the daily advance of the process of psychological adaptation."[158] *Regression,* on the other hand, was the "backward movement of libido" that takes place when the person is trying to recapture something important in his or her past.[159] Although he referred to something like it in a few of his writings, Jung did not really make use of the concept of *fixation*. Regressions happen all right, and libido (life energy) is blocked resulting in a re-experience of early memories—even reaching back into the racial history—but this is seen differently from Freud due to Jung's teleological interpretation of libido. Something that is telic works forward, as a reason that is being expressed or an end (telos) toward which life is progressing. If libido flowed

backward at some point, it would seem to be reversing the usual course of telic advance.

Why then does regression take place? The reason for the return of libido is not to recapture pockets of fixated libido as Freud would have it; rather, the individual in regressing is attempting to rekindle a self-awareness that he or she lost in the past.[160] Regression is a compensatory attempt on the part of the personality to return (regress) to that point in time when healthy progression was forsaken and a one-sided development began. The going back is only the first step in a total effort to reinstate more balanced progression. The perfectionist now admits to occasional errors and laziness, the pessimist now confesses having a spark of optimism from time to time, and so on. Life's progression is now more whole than before.

Constellation and Mobilization. By *constellation* Jung meant: ". . . the fact that the outward situation [external life circumstance] releases a psychic process in which certain [psychic] contents gather together and prepare for action. . . . The constellated contents are definite complexes possessing their own specific energy."[161] This definition stresses the energic potential, the fact that a significant amount of libido is made available for an organizing of psychic contents. In terms of our adhesive model, however, we can say that the psychic meanings that are constellated have been *mobilized* into a single body of importance or significance.[162] This is so because Jung did in fact speak of the mobilization of complexes like the shadow, for example, or he referred to the mobilization of one's psychic virtues as a first step toward self-realization.[163]

Individuation and Transcendence. These mental mechanisms will be considered in great detail under the psychotherapy headings. But we will now simply observe that in Jungian psychology the process of self-realization involves differentiating a totality called the self from the different parts of the personality, including the collective unconscious. This process of differentiating the self is termed *individuation*.[164] Life is teleological, and its most treasured goal is this final emergence of a completely total individuality. To accomplish this desired end, we must *transcend* (rise above) what we are, consider what we are not (opposition), evaluate the pressures put on us by the collective to follow its dictates, and then emerge as a uniquely individuated totality. Jung used this concept of transcendence to describe the process whereby all of the opposites and group pressures are finally united in the personality.[165]

Time-Perspective Constructs

Jung did not work out the elaborate psychosexual levels that we find in Freud (Chapter 1). He was critical of Freud's efforts to explain behavior by tracing it to early fixation points. This criticism stems from his telic interpretation of progression, libido, and so on.[166] If life is oriented toward goals in a purposive sense, then what does it add to retrace our theoretical steps in order to find the presumed meanings of the past? Even so, Jung did outline some general periods in the life cycle.

Presexual Period

Jung accepted as Freud had the Darwinian-Lamarckian principle that ontogeny recapitulates phylogeny (see Chapter 1, p. 65). He thus believed that children re-enacted in their growth of consciousness after birth the prehistoric development of consciousness by humanity.[167] He stressed the influence of our racial history enough to suggest that our true fathers and mothers are not our parents but our grandparents.[168] Children are not born empty-headed or tabula rasa, said Jung (see p. 11 of the Introduction for a discussion of this concept). We find mythological themes in the dreams of three- and four-year-olds which belong more properly in the dreams of grown-ups.[169] Of course, in the very early days and months of life, children cannot report their dreams to us because they lack consciousness as well as language.

Recall that consciousness begins in the child's differentiation of *I* or *me* (subjective identity) from *that* or *it* (objective reality). This is the first step in acquiring knowledge, and it occurs through the principle of opposites. But the second step in acquiring knowledge takes place when the infant puts two psychic contents into a (meaningful) relation, such as tying the visual image of mother to the sensations of satisfaction from taking in nourishment (drinking milk).[170] The child learns "mother brings milk to me" even before this insight can be put into actual words. For the rest of life, knowledge continues on this basis of first drawing oppositional discriminations and then uniting delineated items into meaningful relationship in consciousness. Jung did not believe that the sexual instinct is active in the presexual stage. This period of life is characterized almost entirely by the processes of nutrition and (both physical and psychological) growth.[171] It is a time of no real problems for the person, because serious contradictions have not yet arisen in consciousness.[172]

Prepubertal Period

This period sets in around ages three to five, depending on the particular child's tempo of development. The sexual instinct begins to develop in this period, and it is a time of rapidly expanding consciousness because the child will be entering school. Education is a major means of extending consciousness.[173] The prepubertal period remains a fairly carefree time of life, because the child is still heavily identified with the parental family and many of the problems in life are thus answered for him or her, thanks to what might be termed dependency.[174]

Jung could never bring himself to believe in the legitimacy of incestuous desires on the part of all children, as Freud's theory called for. Jung felt the word *incest* has a definite meaning, describing an individual who cannot direct sexual promptings to a proper object. But to use this term to describe a child who has not yet attained mature sexual functioning was for Jung a gross misuse of language.[175] He did not deny that cases of incestuous desire for parents could be found in any clinical practice. He merely pointed out that in such actual cases of incest the child was brought into an abnormal relationship through the attitudes of his or her parents.[176] As to the normal person who might "recall" having fantasied sexual relations with a parent, Jung said these reminiscences were merely the repressed half of an intention that passed through the individual's mind while he or she was learning about sex. When we learn about sexual intercourse around pubescence, it is only natural for us to think of this act in relation to our opposite-sex parent as well as other potential objects. A fleeting "possible intention" of this sort is repressed because of its inappropriateness; later in life it might come back as a "memory." Actually, we had never fantasied sexual copulation with our parent in infancy at all. Jung stressed that we should not feel guilty about an incest memory when it arises; we should merely accept it as the mind's ever-ready capacity to suggest possibilities, even unacceptable ones.[177]

Pubertal Period

Puberty, of course, has its onset sometime between the tenth and the thirteenth year of life. Jung felt that most females leave their pubertal phase around age nineteen or twenty. Males were said to continue on to age twenty-five before they have seen the last of their pubertal phase.[178] Physiologically speaking, the estimates of a completed puberty are usually much earlier (ending in the middle teens). We note here a tendency on Jung's part to stretch out the life span considerably, so that a person is not psychologically "complete" in life nearly as early as the infantile bias of psychoanalysis would suggest.

Because of the many challenges facing the individual in this period, Jung felt that "true psychic birth" takes place in the pubertal time of life.[179] Not only does the sexual instinct mature to place a major burden on the person for gratification, but also there is the problem of having to settle on a work or career goal. The range of social relations also extends, so that there are all sorts of problems concerned with establishing a proper identity among gang peers. Although this shift to peers aids in the differentiation from family ties, there is sometimes a too-great reliance put on the persona at this time. There is always the threat of identification with the persona. Parents may object to friends, proposed marital partners, or the choice of an occupation. Decisions have to be made and put into effect, and loyalties have to be decided upon. For the first time in life, the person is seriously threatened by the likelihood of a one-sided development.[180]

Youth

The next period sets in at roughly twenty to twenty-five and runs to about thirty-five or forty. By this time the separation (differentiation) from family dependency should have been completed, or the person is in for serious psychological trouble. For example, Jung felt that a problem like male homosexuality is crystallized during this period, because of the fact that a man is unable "to free himself from the anima fascination of his mother."[181] But for most of us youth is the time of marriage, the rearing of offspring, the purchase and establishment of a home, and the striving for a modicum of success in a career or occupation. In short, it is a time of increasing responsibilities and increasing consciousness (meanings, knowledge).

Middle Life

At about age forty we enter the second half of life, and now there is an entirely new psychic challenge for the individual, based in part on the fact that he or she has already lived this long, and in part on the fact that the meaning of life is not *only* on the side of consciousness. That is, in line with his opposition principle, Jung believed that people spend this first half of life enlarging consciousness by way of learning, acquiring possessions (including offspring) and experiences, investing themselves in the world of affairs, and so forth. This is right and proper, but as we are fashioning this one side of our psyche, we must necessarily be slighting the other side, *unconsciousness*. Thus, without turning his back on the realities of consciousness, Jung said that the individual past middle life must *also* now further the knowledge of that inner nature that he or she has been neglecting. And the proper time to begin it is now, in middle life, when the rewards of

an active growth to this point begin to bear fruit. Children are now grown and leaving home to fashion their own lives. Work has begun to pay off with positions of responsibility allowing for some delegation of the actual work load to other, younger people. Social demands are lessened. This is the beginning of a new life order.

Old Age

Once past sixty or sixty-five we have to accept a time of life in which the term *old age* is appropriate simply because this is the reality of the life cycle. Jung took more interest in the psychology of the aged than any other major personality theorist. He believed that the older person must live by different ground rules than he or she had thus far been observing. The older person must never look back, but rather "look inward." People at this age have a marvelous chance for individuation because they have now lived long enough to experience many different situations as well as their opposites. Jung believed that it was necessary for a balancing counterweight to express itself in the latter half of life because "man's values, and even his body, do tend to change into their opposites."[182] Physiologically, the male becomes more feminine and the female masculine, and psychologically too there is a counterbalancing of psychic attitude by the anima or animus between the sexes.

Jung believed that a life directed toward a goal is in general one that is better, richer, and healthier than an aimless life, or one that is discouraged about the future. As he expressed it, "I am convinced that it is hygienic—if I may use the word—to discover in death a goal towards which one can strive, and that shrinking away from it is something unhealthy and abnormal which robs the second half of life of its purpose."[183] This is where the primordial image of a life after death plays such an important role in humanity's existence, as a goal reaching beyond the grave. If an older person were to consult Jung and complain of a depression or an anxious emptiness (loss of identity), Jung might well say after a period of studying the patient, "Your picture of God or your idea of immortality is atrophied [wasting way], consequently your psychic metabolism is out of gear." [184] The individual's archetypal prompting was being denied, and he or she had to pay the penalty of such repression. Thus it is that in Jungian psychology religious expressions are not taken lightly, as sublimated parental dependencies or the like, but rather are considered extremely important manifestations of the collective unconscious. In continuing the teleology which is life into an afterlife, these archetypal symbolisms are to be cultivated, personified, and understood as important psychic necessities.

Immaturity Rather than Fixation

Jung admitted that there is a tendency for people at all ages to look back to an earlier time in life when things seemed to be working out better for them. The teen-aged boy wishes that he could have that feeling of simple certainty and security that the protection of the parental home had given him. The married woman of thirty wishes she had the freedom of her teen-age years. The aging man of sixty wishes he had the vigor of his thirties. All of these natural desires for a replay of the life cycle are normal enough. Life is challenging, there are constant decisions and commitments to be made, and one might easily sentimentalize about a bygone day.

If the individual has not actually become free from the childhood environment with its dependency upon parents and other adults, leading to an immature outlook on life in adulthood, Jung would call this *immaturity*

rather than *fixation*.[185] It is a failure on the part of the individual to develop rather than a damming-up of libido into pockets of fixation. How can something that never was underway become blocked? Hence, as we noted above, the phenomenon of regression was for Jung a teleological attempt to return to an earlier time in life and thereby rekindle that opportunity for self-growth (progression) that had been overlooked or shunted aside by the individual.

Individual-Differences Constructs

Jung was very sensitive to the problems of typing people, and he undertook the task with some reluctance. He felt that when we name a type, we are speaking about statistical averages and not about people.[186] The danger in this is that the theorist may force his conceptions onto others in an arbitrary way, more to justify a point of view than to capture the accuracy of the individual case. For his part, Jung wanted a scheme that could capture the obvious complexity of behavior yet also not lose the open-ended features of the psyche. He was interested in the general problem of how it was that we came to type personalities in the first place. Jung therefore turned to history, and he studied a number of earlier typologies to find some common thread among them. Thanks to his scholarly approach, Jung moves us in his book *Psychological Types* (1946, first published circa 1920) over the ages from the early Greeks like Plato and Aristotle, through the thought of churchmen like Tertullian and Origen, down to the more recent views of psychologists like Friedrich Nietzsche and William James.

Running through this history of personality description, Jung found that a common dimension of opposition was suggested. He named this bipolar dimension the *introversion versus extraversion* polarity in psychic attitude. Thus, for example, Nietzsche's Apollonian and James's tenderminded types were introverted in psychic attitude, and the opposite types of Dionysian and toughminded were extraverted.[187] This classification was helpful, but Jung also needed a way of explaining how the various psychic behaviors we know of as thinking, seeing, or feeling were ordered mentally even before we could speak of them as taking place in an introverted or extraverted manner. Basing his line of theoretical development on the nature of the psyche as an active agent, Jung then named a series of what he called *functions*.

Basic Functions of the Psyche

Jung's construct of *function* can be thought of in two ways: as a psychological *or* an energic (libidinal) tendency to remain constant in order to judge the changing conditions of experience. Judgment always calls for a fixed standard or frame of reference against or within which to relate what we are considering. For example, we use a standard measuring unit (ruler) to judge whether one fish is really longer than another. Knowing that our finances are fixed by a certain level of income, we can judge whether some desirable item (like an imported sports car) is to be considered a potential purchase or not. The psyche needs its set of fixed coordinates within which to evaluate and order the many sensations, feelings, hunches, and ideas that arise in the course of life. That is, as consciousness is expanding through differentiation and the drawing of relationships between items in experience, a few fixed frames of reference permit the (unconscious

as well as conscious) psyche to judge what is taking place, whether events change, what the potentials of any item are for the future of the person, and so on.

As Freud could do (see p. 44), Jung occasionally gave his constructs both a psychological and an energic interpretation. Thus, Jung defined the *function* psychologically as "a certain form of psychic activity that remains theoretically the same under varying circumstances." [188] Considered energically, a *function* was a constant libido expenditure, a means of keeping libido channeled into a fixed activity. If we need some basic continuity in the psyche so that we can recognize changes by way of contrasts to these regularities, then how many such functions are necessary to cover our psychic needs? Since these needs are like structural features of the mind, we might have taken them up under our structural-construct discussion. We did not do so because they were written specifically for individual differences. Jung felt that four functions could properly account for the basic psychic equipment of human beings, as follows:

There are four aspects of psychological orientation, beyond which nothing fundamental remains to be said. In order to orient ourselves, we must have a function which ascertains that something is there (sensation); a second function which establishes what it is (thinking); a third function which states whether it suits us or not, whether we wish to accept it or not (feeling); and a fourth function which indicates where it came from and where it is going (intuition).[189]

The functions are part and parcel of the psyche. In one sense they define the psyche in action. In theory, all four functions begin as conscious psychic activities,[190] but in short order we begin to rely on one or two in consciousness rather than all four. Before we take up this question of function selection, let us give more extensive consideration to the functions as such. Note first of all that they are paired opposites, and two such pairs make up the total model. Thinking is the opposite of feeling, and sensation is the opposite of intuition. *Thinking* is the function that allows for thought to take a direction, to begin with a premise then follow it through to a conclusion only to infer another premise, and so forth, in what we call *reasoning*.[191] Thinking therefore permits us to understand the nature of things, to assess their meaning, and to infer their usefulness. Its opposite, *feeling,* can also be brought to bear in assessment. However, unlike directed thought, feeling is a process that takes place between the subjective ego and another mental content based on *value*.[192] Does the ego like or dislike the item under consideration? If liked, then more libido is involved and an idea might be taken on without thinking it through logically. Thought demands evaluation by way of clear-cut statements, but feeling tones allow us to settle questions without deliberation. In buying a house, the thinker-type person evaluates the construction of the building, interest charges, the neighborhool and so on, whereas the feeling-type person walks through the door and "knows" whether it is suitable or not. In this sense, thinking and feeling must always contradict each other.

Even so, Jung considered both thinking and feeling to be *rational functions*.[193] We tend to think of emotional decisions as prone to be illogical and to that extent nonrational. But Jung was driving at the fact that both thinking and feeling are concerned with judging the worth, truth value, significance, or import of a mental content. This always involves a subjective factor, because what is valuable to one person may not be valuable to another. Thinking emphasizes truth versus falsity or plausible versus implausible, and

feeling emphasizes like versus dislike or attraction versus repulsion, but in either case the *point* of the function is to judge or assess, and the very essence of rationality is judgment, the making of decisions, or the choosing of an alternative.

The other set of opposites Jung called the *irrational functions*. He did not mean that they are contrary to reason but merely outside of the province of reason. They are not psychic functions that have as their role the directed judgment and assessment of mental contents, but rather they make psychic material available so that such reasoning processes can be carried out. They are to that extent more on the automatic, reflexive side of mental life. *Sensation* is that psychological function that transmits physical stimuli to psychic awareness.[194] We can think of this as meaning "conscious perception," that is, being directly aware of objective reality as sensed by our organs designed to register such incoming stimuli from the environment. Seeing, hearing, touching—all of those psychic activities that put us in touch with the objective world are aspects of the sensation function.

In contrast to this way of knowing experience, Jung defined the *intuition* function as "unconscious perception."[195] Just as consciousness takes in sensory data, so too can the unconscious automatically perceive the inherent possibilities of a situation as a kind of unconscious perception.[196] The intuitive-type person buys a house that the sensation-type individual has "seen" to be very plain and uninteresting, but with a few structural changes and some exciting color combinations on renovation, turns the place into a beautiful home. The intuitive person perceived what the sensation person did not—the possibilities inherent in this house! Sometimes the intuited input goes contrary to the sensory input of the same person, so that even though we might consciously perceive no danger in a situation, our intuition tells us that something "bad" is going to happen. The fact that Jung accepted an intuitive function in human behavior places him in a unique position among personality theorists, most of whom would attempt to reduce this intuitive knowledge to something else in the psyche. Jung took intuition at face value, recognizing that yet undiscovered stimuli may account for these reactions which do seem to occur to people.

We come back now to the question of function selection. This arises because we have to keep our conscious style of behavior consistent in interpersonal relations.[197] It would not do to jump about in consciousness from a thinking to a feeling to a sensation to an intuitive style of behavior. Not only would we be confused about ourselves, but our social relations would be strained to the limit; people would find us maddening. Thus only one function can be uppermost in consciousness at a time, and thanks to our unique experiences in living, we differentiate the particular function to emphasize what has proven most effective in the past. We develop the one that works best for us, and Jung called this the *primary* or principal function.[198] He occasionally referred to it less formally as "the most differentiated function"[199] or "the more favoured function."[200] The ego identifies with this primary function and it comes to color our consciousness, which in turn makes it possible for a clinician to typologize the typical personality style.[201] In the meantime, the function in opposition to the primary function is removed from open display by repressing it into the unconscious. Jung named this undesired opposite the *inferior function*.[202]

Speaking in this depth fashion, of con-

scious versus unconscious functions, we can now consider the primary (favored) function the *superior function* of the personality.[203] This gives us a superior-inferior contrast, which is another reflection of the principle of opposites active in the psyche. The less-preferred psychic tendencies that are repressed constellate (agglutinate, combine) into the shadow complex, and so the shadow identity takes on the character of our inferior function. What has happened to the remaining two functions as the superior versus inferior functions are being differentiated across the levels of consciousness?

Since they are not diametrically opposed to the most differentiated (primary, superior) function, these functions drop into an intermediate level of differentiated consciousness. They settle as poles of opposition just below consciousness in a kind of twilight position where they can come into play as complementary functions for *either* the superior or the inferior function.[204] Jung called these the *auxiliary functions*.[205] Usually, *one* of the auxiliary functions is used in consciousness as a supplementary way of knowing reality. It can be thought of as assisting the primary function and Jung viewed it as a *secondary function* in the apparent personality which people display consciously. The other auxiliary function may or may not then be repressed further into the unconscious to supplement the inferior function by constellating into the shadow complex. In order to help the reader visualize the rather intricate relationships now under presentation, Figure 14 schematizes the four functions.[206]

Note in Figure 14 that the primary function of thinking is at the highest point of differentiation, dominating consciousness. We have not put the ego in here, but someone with this psychic arrangement would surely be described as a thinking type. The inferior function of feeling is shown down in the personal unconscious, where of course it

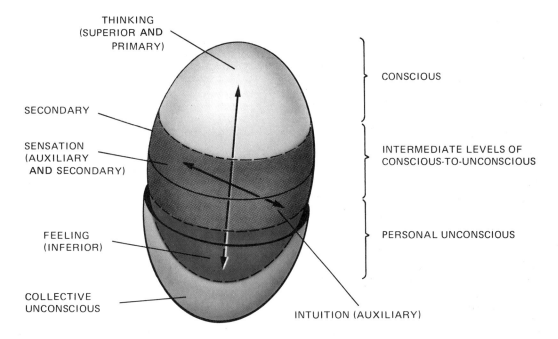

THINKING
(SUPERIOR AND
PRIMARY)

SECONDARY

SENSATION
(AUXILIARY
AND SECONDARY)

FEELING
(INFERIOR)

COLLECTIVE
UNCONSCIOUS

CONSCIOUS

INTERMEDIATE LEVELS OF
CONSCIOUS-TO-UNCONSCIOUS

PERSONAL UNCONSCIOUS

INTUITION (AUXILIARY)

Figure 14 The Four Basic Functions of the Psyche

could form into complexes with the archetypes and other unconscious contents. The shadow is not a part of the figure, but as we have already suggested, it would be identified with the inferior function. Across the intermediate levels of decreasing consciousness (which means decreasing levels of differentiation), we have our two auxiliary functions. Sensation is tilted up toward a higher level of consciousness to symbolize the fact that it has come to serve as a supplementary function to the primary function in the personality. As such it can now be referred to as the secondary function. The tandem of thinking-sensation would now represent what we might call the *conscious personality* of this psyche. An individual with a primary function of thinking and a secondary function of sensation would surely have a precisely ordered, logical, and efficiently running mental style of coming upon the world. For example, we might consider the

person here who likes to think things through carefully, to weigh arguments by spelling out details and repeatedly checking logic, referring to "the facts" at every turn and possibly using statistics to project the best probabilities discernible. This conscious-personality type might make a good detective, lawyer, or stock-market analyst.

At the same time, depending on how one-sidedly (repressively) the conscious personality is developed, this individual could have a tremendous impulse at times to cast logic to the winds and play a hunch which, it is "felt," cannot miss. This would tell us that the feeling-intuition functions were trying to compensate the conscious style. This impulse might first appear in a dream. If the person does not respond to these promptings, then of course he or she might end up acting impulsively, amazed with such foolishness yet unable to do otherwise (in consciousness the complex operates under its own direction; see Figure 12). In Jungian psychology the principle of opposites must always be satisfied.

Since either auxiliary can serve as the secondary function (we can have a thinking-intuition type rather than a thinking-sensation type), it is theoretically possible to classify people into eight distinct conscious-personality types on the basis of Figure 14. Jung had something to say about these eight possibilities, but we could carry this out even further because any one of these primary functions and its secondary (auxiliary) function can orient itself toward life in either an extraverted or an introverted attitudinal manner. This raises the possibilities of cataloging people into sixteen different conscious-personality types on the Jungian model. Jung did not go this far in his writings, and in fact nothing would have interested him less than hanging such labels on people.

Introversion versus Extraversion and the Psychological Types

We have already noted how Jung came to identify the two major constructs of extraversion and introversion in his review of history. Here again, we can think of these constructs in either psychological (attitude) or energy (libido) terms. The latter is the simplest in that extraversion may be considered an outward flow of libido and introversion an inward flow of libido.[207] This does not tell us much, actually, since it is the practical effect of the supposed libidinal flow that gives the concepts meaning.

The introversion-extraversion dimension ties into what Jung called the subject-object dichotomy in developing consciousness. As the person is differentiating and relating items in the growth of consciousness, he or she can take an interest in the subjective (the "I" pole) or the objective (the "that" pole) side of life. This is a more psychological interpretation of introversion-extraversion, and Jung called this the *attitude* taken toward subjectivity or objectivity. How much choice the person has in this attitude tendency is debatable. Jung hints that nature may supply the psyche with one or the other of these attitudes and that an underlying physiological tempo may be the actual determiner of the course any one person will follow in the psyche.[208] In fact, Jung felt that to try and change one's natural attitude into its opposite could be physically dangerous. At least, he found that in those few cases where people did try to exchange attitude styles they suffered from extreme physical exhaustion.[209]

Turning to the specific psychological behaviors of the *extraverted* type, Jung noted that such individuals fix their attention on people and things in their external environment.[210] A woman of this type would be seen giving her time and interest to projects in the community, such as working with a political action group or trying to raise funds for an art gallery. Her thinking would be practical and realistic, so that her interest in political causes or art would not be so much philosophical or aesthetic but rather devoted to getting things accomplished in the world. She would find her greatest sense of worth in interacting with concrete, no-nonsense, solid happenings. She would know current events well and keep up on the latest developments in the news; her view of history would be as the dead past. Her general outlook on life and morality would be quite conventional.

This woman's husband, on the other hand, is an *introvert*. He is a loner rather than an activist, who prefers to conserve himself and find within his own identity satisfactions comparable to those his wife gains by moving her libido outward.[211] He is interested in her efforts to fund an art gallery because he loves to contemplate paintings and experience the effects they have on him. This man likes to abstract and play with ideas; his wife finds them to be unreasonable and extreme. In social situations he strikes others as shy or egg-headed (intellectual). This man tends to forget appointments, and he has to count on his wife to keep the bills paid on time. He can be stubborn at times and is not always worried about what others think when he gets this way. His impractical ideas often give his behavior a childlike quality, but here again he is not upset when others consider him to be eccentric in any way. As we might recall from his biographical overview, Jung was himself an introverted type, and he believed the twentieth century is an age of extraversion, a difficult time for the introvert to live.

By claiming introversion or extraversion is fixed by nature, Jung may appear to have built a one-sidedness into his theory. This is not really correct, however, because the principle of opposites is used in the case of the attitudes as in the case of the functions. Thus, if the superior function—whether by nature's prompting hand or otherwise—adopts an extraverted attitude, then the inferior function offsets the tendency by adopting an introverted attitude.

Reaching back through history, Jung contrasted Plato (introvert) with Aristotle (extravert) and then later Kant (introvert) and Darwin (extravert).[212] Aristotle and Darwin surely placed considerable emphasis on the importance of external fact-finding, whereas Plato and Kant were more concerned with the internal workings of mind per se. Jung also gave examples of personality types that combined his functions and the extraversion-introversion attitudes, and we will next survey a number of these observations.

Good leaders would be extraverted thinking types, and this personality is found more often among men.[213] Women are more likely to be extraverted feeling types; this personality reflects considerable reasonableness and a concern for good manners.[214] The most reality-oriented personality of all is the extraverted sensation type; found most often among males, one might consider this personality hedonistic, for there is a great attraction to receiving pleasures through the senses, such as eating, drinking, viewing liked objects, mixing with others socially, and so forth.[215] Politicians, businessmen and women, and clubpeople are likely to have the extraverted intuitive personality, for this type is excellent at anticipating the politics of a situation and capitalizing on them for personal prestige, power, or advantage.[216] The absent-minded professor would be an introverted thinking type; these persons can think individually, hence either reach genius status or fumble miserably into a quack status.[217] When we use the phrase "still waters run deep," we capture the style of an introverted feeling type—found most often among women.[218] The childlike, innocent person, responding almost impulsively to felt emotions is the introverted sensation type.[219] Finally, the introverted intuitive type can range from the mystical seer at one extreme to the social crank or creative artist at the other.[220] Keep in mind that when we typologize a personality in this fashion, we are doing so on the basis of its superior function. Obviously, all of these personality types have other personality potentials as well.

Transcendental Function and the Mana Personality

We have already seen how Jung spoke of transcendence in connection with his concept of individuation (see p. 207). He also viewed transcendence as an actual function of the psyche, along the lines of the four basic functions we have just discussed. The *transcendental function* is concerned with the human being's tendency to combine consciousness and unconsciousness into a balanced totality,[221] and to that extent it stands for all unions of opposites within the psyche.[222] Jung referred to it as a "process of coming to terms with the unconscious"[223] or a "process of getting to know the counterposition in the unconscious."[224] As we have seen in the discussion of the four basic functions, though we might live by them, they do not prevent the development of one-sidedness in the total personality. In order to balance off any tendency to one-sidedness, we have to confront the other side of our conscious personality and see that we are also what we *are not!* We accomplish this balanced overview by way of the transcendental function.

How do we achieve this confrontation with the unconscious? The transcendental functional process involves "a sequence of fantasy-occurrences which appear spontaneously in dreams and visions,"[225] which act as pacers of the individuation process in psychotherapy. If we were to take this discussion further, it would carry us into Jungian psychotherapy, so let us now put the concept of transcendence aside until we once again pick it up in the relevant section. However, this would be the appropriate point at which to introduce another personality term that Jung uses and that we will also take up in the general context of individuation during psychotherapy. The *mana personality* is a kind of inflation of the conscious personality. Consciousness becomes puffed up when a mana personality forms, and there is a decided rejection of unconscious factors at this time

because the person mistakenly assumes that he or she knows all there is to know about the psyche. In actuality, consciousness has been possessed by this very unconsciousness.

Primitives often acquire this sense of personal power in their tribal rites.[226] In a war dance the primitive man can work himself into a state of frenzy and literally feel the surge of power (mana) taking over his consciousness as he dashes off to do battle. Jung argued that even the modern individual can lose his or her identity in the reality of the moment as a crowd member, and then in response to the collective promptings (archetypes), swell up into a self-proclaimed superperson. In fact, this is what occurred during the rise of Nazi Germany, when crowds not only fell under the sway of a Wotan (war god) archetype but the mana personality dominant as well (see p. 195).[227] Another time when an individual is likely to develop a mana personality is when the individuation process misfires.

Individual as Collective Identity

Jung made it clear that he could not think of the life of a people as in any way different from the life of an individual. "In some way or other we are part of a single, all-embracing psyche, a single 'greatest man,' the *homo maximus,* to quote Swedenborg."[228] This collective identity has a history, one that is "written in the blood" but also shows itself through individual behavior, so that it is the person who moves history rather than vice versa.[229] To differentiate between individual people, we must at times differentiate between the groups of people to which they are historically related. Personality constructs cannot be limited to individual referents, even when speaking of one person's behavior. The term *race* for Jung had a very broad meaning, combining not only physical (blood line) factors, but historical, sociocultural, climatic, and even theological considerations as well. For Jung, Christianity was just as much a part of European "races" as were their skin color and the shape of their skulls.[230]

This is the reason Jung claimed that a Jewish psychology could not fully appreciate the psychology of a European. He did not say that a Jew (or any Semite) is incapable of understanding Europeans. He merely claimed that in order to do so, the Jew would have to make use of a psychology written specifically for the European's unique history. Jung's supposed anti-Semitism stems from a misunderstanding of what he was claiming about the psychology of collectives. Thus, Jung made the point that the Jewish people —because of a history of suppression by other "races" (nationalities, and so on)—had never acquired that tie to the land that the European had achieved. The Jews were unable to own land in many of the countries where they were allowed entry, making them fluid and mobile in both the economic and the psychological spheres of life. Even as they moved about without ties to the land, the Jewish people were acquiring a high level of culture, so that Jung said they are more civilized as a people than are Europeans. Now here is the point of confrontation between Freud and what Jung considered his Jewish psychology. Since the Jew is not as barbaric as the European, he can look into his unconscious with less threat of a dangerous upheaval than can the European.[231]

Whether Jung was correct in his claims about the Jewish character and its supposed weakened tie to the land—particularly since the establishment of the state of Israel—is not nearly so important for our purposes as the recognition that Jung was applying a construct to a people in the same way that we are accustomed to apply such constructs to an individual. Jung was prone to do this in many of his writings. For example, he was critical of the tendency of the European person to ape the mental exercises of Eastern peoples. Many people wrongly think that Jung advocated the study of yoga or Zen Buddhism as a balancing tactic in their lives. Actually, Jung was opposed to the practice of yoga for a European, because the latter's problem is not one that will respond to a greater control over consciousness—which is yoga[232]—or to the utter submission to the unconscious promptings of nature—which is Zen Buddhism.[233] Europeans must find their own "way" (Tao), because they have evolved a certain history, one that stamps their peculiar nature, and one that cannot be borrowed from another historical tradition.

Therefore it is sad indeed when the European departs from his own nature and imitates the East or "affects" it in any way. The possibilities open to him would be so much greater if he would remain true to himself and evolve out of his own nature all that the East has brought forth in the course of the millennia.[234]

The most serious problem facing modern humanity is its one-sidedness. Not only was Jung a man of the West, but two savage world wars seemed to convince him that the problem of disregarding unconscious forces was becoming severe in the West. The rise of Nazism, the decline of moral fiber, even the conflicting schools of modern art were seen by him as early signs of the unconscious upheaval closing in on the one-sided materialism of Western society. Jung was not opposed to one-sidedness in principle, since only through complete commitments of this sort are great achievements brought about.[235] However, he also believed that it is a sign of advanced culture for diversities in out-look to balance one another. It is not good for everyone in a civilization to develop an *identical* one-sidedness,[236] which seems to be happening in modern society, according to Jung. By denying our darker side on a massive scale, we ensure that retaliations from the unconscious in the form of collective complexes—including mana-personality inflations—will take place. Jung even referred to this modern plight as the "sickness of dissociation."[237] This development is not irretrievably negative, however, since the beckoning counterbalance of modern complexes suggests a rebirth impulse. Modern Western humanity still has time to turn its attention inward and thereby not only recoup lost possibilities but extend its level of self-realization.[238]

Male versus Female Psychology

The final individual-difference constructs to which we might refer in Jungian psychology concern masculinity and femininity. Considering the conscious personality first of all, Jung claimed that women are ruled by the *principle of Eros* (Love), whereas men are ruled by the *principle of Logos* (Logic). Women are thus guided as conscious personalities by a capacity for relating to others. Eros relates to the binding, uniting, and also loosening and separating of portions from the whole. This includes not only life-giving (birth) activities, but interpersonal contacts as well. Marital love for the woman is a union, not a sexual contract. "For her, marriage is a relationship with sex thrown in as an accompaniment."[239] A man's consciousness, however, is ruled by logical objectivity, interest in specifics, discrimination,

judgment, and insight (which is why the thinking function is more often superior in the male). Logos relates to thought, confidence in finding solutions, and certainty in drawing conclusions.[240] Judging from these conscious principles, it would follow that as a compensating manifestation, the unconscious should present us with a contrasting psychological picture. And so it does.

Jung found rather early in his studies that male patients often reported feminine-like moods in their dream symbols, and conversely, women reflected opinionated masculine styles of symbolic expression. He viewed these as tied to the archetypal manifestations of the *animus* (Latin for "mind") and the *anima* (Latin for "soul" or "life-giving principle"). The animus, which is therefore found in the unconscious of the female, arises at times in symbols to compensate for the female's conscious attitude as usually manifested in the principle of Eros. This is why women seem so puzzling to men. Though obviously reasoning on vague (unconscious) grounds, the woman seems perfectly certain in her animus-based conclusions.[241]

The man, on the other hand, is likely to develop a *mood* (rather than an opinion) of some sort when under the compensating activity of the anima.[242] When the he-man Army sergeant breaks down and "cries like a woman" under severe stress, he is paying the price of one-sidedness and reflecting the anima possession under which he suffers at the same time. The anima plays a very important role in Jungian psychology, because not only is it an archetype that represents man's historical relationships with women and to that extent compensates for his conscious-personality principle of Logos, but it is involved in spiritualizing and life-giving symbolism as well. The symbols of life, birth, rebirth, rejuvenation, and so forth, are all likely to take on anima colorings.[243]

Psychopathology and Psychotherapy

Theory of Illness

Incompatible Opposites, Complex Formation, and Assimilation-Dissociation

The fundamental theory of illness used by Jung follows the model of complex formation we already outlined in Figure 12. Jung once said that he considered *normal behavior* to mean that an individual can somehow exist under all circumstances in life, even those that provide a minimum of need satisfaction.[244] Of course, few of us are this competent. The real truth is, we all develop more or less one-sidedly. The extent of disturbance we eventually suffer from will depend on the number of incompatible opposites we generate in living, and how soon it is before we attempt to compensate for our lack of balance. According to Jung, "the vast majority of mental illnesses (except those of a direct organic nature) are due to a disintegration of consciousness caused by the irresistible invasion of unconscious contents."[245] He never totally rejected his early theory that certain mental disorders—particularly those in the family of schizophrenias—might someday be traced to a metabolic toxin of some sort.[246] But Jung's unique theoretical contribution lay, as had Freud's, in the explanation of the functional disorders.

Jung traced the autonomy of complexes to their emotional core (feeling tone). He emphasized that emotions behave as the more primitive thought processes once had for early humanity; that is, they are not willfully produced by people but simply happen to them. We can even see this happen to us if we are under a great deal of emotional stress, as when character traits that shock us emerge against our will. We later say, "I don't know what came over me," as we recall behaving in an excessively jealous, spiteful, or self-pitying manner following a frustration in life.[247] If this sudden change takes place in our normal behavior, imagine what it must be like for the abnormal person. No wonder paranoid schizophrenics feel they are under the control of people from another planet! We find the psychotic paranoid saying, "Someone has me under electronic control, trying to force me to do things I don't want to do." Insanity is thus an invasion from the unconscious of contents that are flatly incompatible with the intentions of the ego. Therefore, the intentions of these shadow contents (complexes) cannot be *assimilated* into consciousness. By assimilation, Jung meant accepting and integrating (constellating) these formerly repressed contents with the more familiar elements of consciousness.[248] The opposite of assimilation is *dissociation,* which is another way of expressing the fact that the personality is being split apart by conflicting intentions.

When a complex is active within consciousness, we are as if in a dream state, with conscious and unconscious factors mixing together without assimilating each other. A dramatic example of this would be the multiple personality forms of hysteria, in which two or more personalities seem to take over consciousness in turn; actually, the original conscious personality (the one fashioned before the illness) remains out of direct contact with the emergent personalities (the ones formed via the illness). The latter, secondary personalities (complexes) invade consciousness and push the original personality aside, keeping it therefore in the dark as in the Jekyll-Hyde conflict of the classic tale. In the same way, lesser complexes as part-personalities within consciousness can make themselves known to the ego even though the ego may feel they are not part of its identity. The person may say, "I know that at times I lose control and do some pretty crazy things. But I am not myself at those times. Something 'clicks' in my head and I can't control myself." At other times, the ego may not even be aware of the operation of a complex within consciousness side by side with its very routine behavior. Such a person may blackout for brief periods and not recall his or her atypical behavior during this time.

One sure way in which the ego *can* be made aware of a complex is through the mechanism of projection. Recall that only the unconscious can project! By putting its contents onto the external world, where the ego now takes them to be properties of "that" rather than "me," the complex finally opens an avenue for its own defeat. That is, by putting its constellated contents onto the world, the complex makes it possible for the ego to enter into a relationship with the meanings of these contents. Take a dream, for example, which is a simple type of projection: by putting its contents into the dream, the unconscious makes it possible for the ego (consciousness) to learn—with the help of the therapist—what "that" dream means to "me." In time, through such study, the ego may be able to assimilate the incompatibilities of the complex as projected into the dream. The ego learns that the meanings of the dream are not foreign to the personality, but merely represent another side to the personality. As we shall see in discussing Jungian therapy techniques below, other means of projection include artistic representations.

Role of Morals, Evasion, and Denial

In trying to understand the nature of mental illness, the analytical psychologist asks, "What is the task which the patient does not want to fulfil? What difficulty is he trying to avoid?"[249] Jung viewed the Freudian superego as a collective body of ethical beliefs, similar to what Lévy-Bruhl meant by "collective representations"; he believed that such collective views, although not infallible and not always to be routinely followed, can often allow us to discover the basis for our judgments and decisions in life. If we were to reflect on the problem of "how ought we to treat one another?" for example, our collective symbols would help provide the answer if given a chance to express themselves—as by way of a dream analysis.

When an individual for any of a number of reasons no longer attends to the promptings of the collective (superego) to balance, let us say, a one-sided pattern of selfish behavior, serious consequences are likely to develop. This person is essentially saying, "I know what I am doing is wrong by conventional standards, but I don't give a damn." Maybe, were he or she to examine the behavior further, only modest changes would be called for. But by refusing to look into the question, the selfishness can only increase, and in time a complex will form à la the steps of Figure 12.[250] We note an interesting duality in Jung's theory of the collective here. Though he was suspicious of the collective mentality and did not want the individual to be easily swayed by it, he also believed that there was much wisdom in certain collective promptings born of past ages in meeting life's challenges. Though we do not have to give in to every collective prompt or conventional standard, we had better listen to our conscience when it calls us down in order to see just what is implied.

Jung even described clients who developed their neurosis for *want of a conscience*.[251] Denying a superego admonition was no small thing for Jung. For example, he considered the rigidly stylized behavior of some obsessive-compulsives as merely the surface appearance of a profound moral problem. These obsessive-compulsive patients are meticulous and ceremonial in behavior because there is an internal struggle with evil underway in their psyche.[252] A bad conscience can be a heaven-sent compensation, if used in the interests of higher self-criticism.[253] It balances our natures and puts us back on the track of life.

Jung was critical of both Freud and Adler for downgrading the spiritual needs of human beings. He felt that they had too readily accepted the premises of nineteenth-century science and thus had become overly materialistic in outlook.[254] Human beings are morally responsible, they have an intellect which evaluates and strives for a *better* purpose in life, no matter what that judgment of *better* is based on.[255] In fact, Jung drew a parallel between the conception of *sin* and that of *repression*. Once the human mind had invented a sin concept, people had no alternative but to conceal or repress their sinful promptings.[256] And since they invariably see alternatives open to behavior which are sinful, a psychic division into conscious good and unconscious bad choices is possible. These latter, repressed contents take on the coloring of a *secret*, which of course means that the individual nursing secrets is likely to be cut off from the support of other people.[257] Secrets are divisive mechanisms which permit individuals to shrink back from external reality and remove themselves even further from the ethical tenets of their society. Evasion always plays a role in neurosis. "If we follow the history of neurosis with attention, we regularly find a critical moment when some problem emerged that was evaded."[258]

In addition to suggesting that people may fall ill for lack of a conscience, Jung said also that some people develop neuroses because they fail to live up to their potentials. He said these are usually people of a higher type,

who simply have never gotten themselves underway in life so that they have much more to give than they now reveal.[259] For example, a young person with exceptional intellectual skills gradually loses interest in college, drops out, and drifts into a period of living aimlessly, relying heavily on alcohol and drugs to get through the day. The individual eventually conquers this addiction, but from then on lives a simple life of menial work, never thinking about anything. Gradually, the person begins to feel uneasy and complains of nightmares in which he or she is being given the "weight of the world" to shoulder. The person also questions everything to be done and cannot seem to make the simplest decisions anymore. Jung would say this complex formation was due to the young person's "retarded maturation of personality."[260] People like this need to achieve self-realization so that their above-average potential may be realized. Average people can live average lives successfully, but a naturally superior person is living one-sidedly at the average level.

Meaning Creation and Symbols in Illness

One of the reasons why some people develop a neurosis is because they have no proper symbol through which an archetype can express meaning in consciousness and thereby facilitate a balancing of the personality. Symbols are like *bridges* between the conscious and unconscious portions of the psyche. Recall that for Jung a symbol was something in psychic life that expresses meaning, even helping to formulate—put into a meaningful form—what is at first inexpressible. Figure 15 is a schematization of Jung's symbolic-meaning-expression model, framed in libido terms.

Symbols Create Meaning from Stored Libido (Numen)

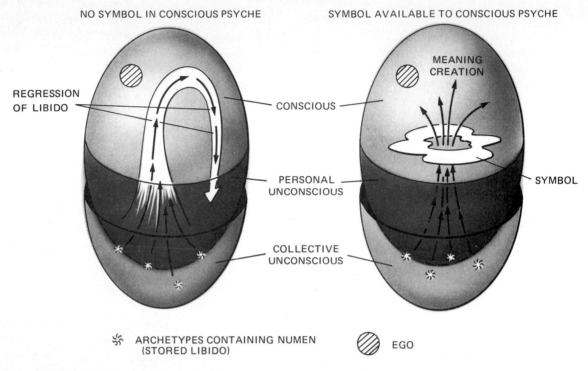

Figure 15   Symbols Create Meaning from Stored Libido (Numen)

Note that the archetypes are presented as star-bursts located in the collective unconscious (this is the same as in Figure 12, step 3; see p. 200). This is meant to suggest that the archetype has no exact form in its natural psychic location (star-bursts are flashes of indefinite shape). But the archetypes *do* signify that a store of libido is present at their location in the collective unconscious. This stored-up unit of libido is called *numen*.[261] It has a potentiality for being used in the psyche, so it can be thought of as a reserve of life energy.

Figure 15 shows archetypes with numen nestled in the collective unconscious. Assuming that the conscious portion of the psyche—where we find the ego at the top of the egg-

shaped figures—has developed one-sidedly because of a "retarded maturation of personality," how then might we hope for a balancing compensation to come about? If it were possible for an archetype to seize upon some *given* symbol (recall that archetypes take on various specific symbolic contents), then in expressing their meaning by way of a dream or fantasy symbol, the ego could come to grips with the unconscious prompting and possibly begin an offsetting counterbalance. Thus, if a young woman asks "What is the point of life?" or "Why was I born?" she might conceivably receive an answer to this question from out of her own psyche. That is, she could know the answer if she had a symbol to cloak it in.

Two possibilities are represented in Figure 15, each of which could take place in her case. On the left, we have archetypal identities with stored libido (numen) releasing this libido in the act of compensation with the goal of answering the question posed ("Why was I born?"). However, since no symbol in consciousness is available through which archetypal promptings in the form of libido release are expressible, the only alternative is for the libido to reflow or *regress*. Regression is not giving up the compensation, but rather cycling back again to the roots of the collective in hopes of achieving a rebirth.[262] On the right-hand side of Figure 15, we have the other possibility in which a bridging symbol is available, so that now the libido released by the archetypes (numen) *does* achieve a conscious-meaning expression. The woman can now communicate with her unconscious, assuming that she has the insights of analytical psychology to help her. Her collective unconscious has something to say about why she is living and what is to be expected of her as a member of the human race.

Symbols that act in the way just outlined were termed *symbols of transformation,* because they transformed the libido from a potential (numen) to an actual expression of meaning.[263] Jung believed that human beings need to symbolize like this just as much as they need to eat and drink.[264] If we can no longer find meaning in the symbols of our forefathers, then we must find new symbols or risk falling out of touch with our roots— as embodied in our primordial images which define for us the very nature of our humanity.[265] This can be very dangerous.

Not all symbols are of the transforming variety, of course. As we can recall from our discussion of complex formation, an archetype can constellate into a complex which is forming and then make its effects known in consciousness, even though it is, strictly speaking, of the unconscious. This occurs when the ego identifies with the complex active in consciousness. In a manner of speaking, the ego slips into unconsciousness by way

of identification. Jung referred to this as *identification with the archetype.*[266] This invariably produces an inflation of the ego for either good or evil in the life of the personality. The archetype comes to direct the ego, which is itself then said to be *possessed* by the archetype. For example, the psychotic young man who thinks himself a great savior of mankind by senselessly killing a popular political figure might have fallen under the numinosity of a hero archetype, possibly constellated (agglutinated) with the wizard archetype because of the supposed cunning involved in laying his murderous ambush. In this instance, the poor deluded ego would have no understanding of the meaning of its actions. It would have been the tool of a shadow complex dominated by the archetypal themes of salvation, retribution, and deviousness. Of course, not all outcomes of numinous experiences are so horrible. Anything that acts on the individual ego with a great intensity and urgency is numinous.[267]

Neurosis versus Psychosis

Precisely *when* a neurosis will appear depends on the degree of one-sidedness evolved in living and the consequent possibility of keeping the constellated complexes under repression. Jung did not feel that all neuroses have their beginning in the first five years of life. He approached each neurotic patient with the following question in mind: "What is this person attempting to avoid in his or her development or general life responsibility at *this* point in time?" Neuroses have a role to play in the present, and we must not allow the patient to flee into the past and remain there safely in preference to confronting life in the present.[268]

Jung believed that the Freudians had been taken in by the maneuvers of an *adult* personality which, in its attempts to avoid responsibility and because of its infantile character generally, had concocted absurd sexual fantasies and projected these onto the past in an effort to evade the counterbalancing changes called for by the neurosis in the present. For example, after one of his female patients had "recalled" that her father once had supposedly stood at her bedside in an obscene pose, Jung remarked coolly: "Nothing is less probable than that the father really did this. It is only a fantasy, presumably constructed in the course of the analysis. . . ."[269] Yet even as the neurotic is retreating into regressive fantasy, the teleologically oriented search for health has begun. The *neurosis* is two-pronged, consisting of both an "infantile unwillingness and the will to adapt."[270] Through regression a rebirth, a fresh start, is always possible. Thus neuroses do cleanse us, and they are not in themselves undesirable or meaningless diseases of the mind.

We should not try to "get rid" of a neurosis, but rather to experience what it means, what it has to teach, what its purpose is. . . . We do not cure it—it cures us. A man is ill, but the illness is nature's attempt to heal him. . . . in the long run nobody can dodge his shadow unless he lives in eternal darkness.[271]

There is a decided advantage in being neurotic.[272] If nothing else, this inner cleavage can prompt a balancing of one-sidedness before a more serious, total invasion of the conscious by unconscious forces takes place.[273] Recall that there can be more than one complex forming in the same personality. Com-

plexes can also be larger depending on what enters into them—as, for example, the number of archetypes. When a complete flooding of consciousness by complexes takes place, we have a *psychosis* taking place.[274] Jung's theory of psychopathology was clouded by the fact that he did speculate on the possibility of a toxin in schizophrenia, suggesting that psychoses might be qualitatively different from neuroses. However, because of his psychological explanations of all mental illness based on the stylized-meaning-expression model (complexes, dissociations), Jung must actually be counted as holding to the quantitative view as regards neurosis and psychosis (see p. 87 of Chapter 1 for a discussion of this issue). Jung saw many patients move from neurotic to psychotic states in their lives, and he rejected the suggestion that they might have been latently psychotic all of the time.[275]

Psychosis is therefore an extension of the division of personality that begins in complex formation as a neurosis. A term like *dissociation* is used more often in describing psychotic than neurotic conditions. The neurotic patient finds himself or herself acting strangely, but the psychotic is completely dissociated from the other side of familiar reality. Hence, the neurotic patient can still understand his or her predicament, because it has some rational ties to what is going on in the personality otherwise.[276] The psychotic, on the other hand, is like a sleepwalker, living out the most bizarre kind of dream which has been put together by promptings from the darkest levels of the unconscious psyche. The contents of a psychosis can never really be completely understood, not even by a psychiatrist.

Neurotics are therefore likely to have a better prognosis, because they can acquire insight (meaningful understanding) whereas psychotics cannot. Jung was a great believer in the benefits of insight, even when dealing with the most severe clinical syndromes.[277] He found that insight often softens the total impact of the psychosis. At the same time, he did not place much stock in the finer points of differential diagnosis for the functional disorders. He said that we are "not dealing with clinical diseases but with psychological ones."[278] The major discrimination to make is that of the clearly organic versus functional disorder, but after that it seemed pointless to go on categorizing patients.

Theory of Cure

Growth, Balance, and Symbolic Assimilation of Opposites

Over the years, Jung found that a certain percentage of his patients simply outgrew their problems. Even though he realized that time heals some wounds, what was unique in these cases was the fact that these people seemed to have evolved a new level of consciousness.[279] They somehow learned to live within life's inner contradictions, and they did not assume that it was possible to solve every one of life's problems in any case. Sometimes all we can do is recognize their existence. Life depends on *polarities,* and the major problems of living stem from the need to decide or choose (differentiate) one side of a future course rather than the other.[280] We take a job far from our home town because it is a tremendous promotion and a sign of success, which means we now have the problem of how to keep in contact with our family and friends. Had we decided to stay close to our loved ones in the home town, we would always have the realization that we could have been more successful and happy in our work. Either way, we have a problem! In fact, every time we decide something in life, we solve one problem only to create another. But this is not a cause for

worry or regret, because such differentiations are what create libido which then gives life its power and zest. All we have to do is understand both sides of all that we do and in that way we avoid one-sidedness. Thus, the *wrong* thing to do would be to deny our dependency on friends and family when we move, or should we stay, to deny our great desire to be successful in our work.

It is the polarization of seemingly incompatible opposites in the personality that brings on mental illness, so what therapists must do is to bring the two halves of the client's psyche back together again. This goal is very difficult to achieve because the two halves (conscious and unconscious) cannot easily make themselves known to one another. In a situation like this *any* communication— whether hostile and erratic or controlled and reasoned—is better than none. As Jung put it, "Every form of communication with the split-off part of the psyche is therapeutically effective."[281] Thus, the main strategy of analytical therapy is to bring about a *confrontation with the unconscious.* This permits the individual to get to know aspects of his or her nature that have previously been denied, and therefore are at the root of the one-sidedness. Once such factors are admitted, a state of *wholeness* is possible.[282] If we can personify the shadow half of our psyche and come to terms with it, then an assimilation is possible.[283] We would have to first engage the personified complex in some kind of dialogue, and then win out in the discussion and debate to follow. Jung referred to the defeat of the personified complex as a *depotentiation*—a depowerizing—of the unconscious (daemonic) forces of psychic life.[284]

Jung cautioned that merely providing the client with an intellectualized insight would not result in a cure.[285] We cannot simply outline for the client the steps of his or her

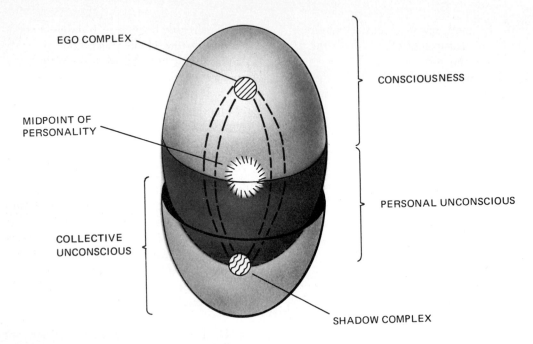

Figure 16   Centering of the Personality

neurotic complex formation and expect this insight to result in cure. The only way consciousness can be liberated from its possession by the unconscious forces is through a painful recognition and an experiencing of the feelings that initially prompted the complex formation. This is no easy matter, and a risk is involved because we can lose our conscious ego identity in a confrontation with the unconscious.[286] This happens when the ego loses out in the discussion and debate with the personified (neurotic) complex. As we shall see, even the psychotherapist runs the risk of losing his or her mental health in the great effort which coming to, terms with the unconscious demands. This is so because, though the confrontation begins with the shadow features of the personal unconscious, in time the client descends into the collective unconscious with tremendous effort not un-

like a Faustian descent into the underworld.[287] All manner of fearful possibilities emerge as we come face to face with our primordial past and hence admit to the influence it has exerted in our supposedly consciously directed lives.

The aim of psychotherapy is to convince the patient to give up the naive belief that life is exclusively directed by consciousness and to find a new midpoint in the personality halfway between consciousness and unconsciousness. This process begins with a recognition of the ego-versus-shadow polarity and settles into an eventual balance at what we have labeled in Figure 16 as the *midpoint of the personality*. The ego is not given preference in this balancing assimilation nor is the shadow. As Jung said, "Assimilation is never a question of 'this *or* that,' but always of 'this *and* that.' "[288] One grows only by becoming whole.

To accomplish the balancing of opposites,

Jung relied on two general tactics: (1) symbol creation and (2) verbal confrontation with the personified complex. Jung called this therapy a form of *hermeneutic* treatment.[289] The root of this word is from Hermes, the messenger of the Greek gods. Hermes thus brought meanings (information, messages) to the gods from various places. During the Middle Ages, theologians adopted the term *hermeneutics* to convey what they were doing in the Holy Scriptures. That is, they were trying to find every bit of information that was presumably there, including semihidden meanings in symbols and the import of things that might *not* have been said when they should have. In like fashion, the Jungian therapist helps a patient extract from his or her unconscious all of those meanings that are potentially there, seeking expression through symbols of transformation in compensation for the one-sidedness of consciousness (see Figure 15). Symbols therefore "compensate an unadapted attitude of consciousness."[290] They are an essential ingredient of the curative process, but they can cure only when experienced as a living phenomenon in psychic life.[291]

It is not enough to know the meaning of our dream and other fantasied symbols. We must confront the implications of the symbol and make a decision as to which side of the question we will live on, preferably accomplished by turning the complex that troubles us into a person (personification). For example, if the person discussed earlier had *failed* to move to a better job location and denied that this was due to a strong dependency on family and friends, the neurotic complex that might then have developed would have dependency as a central theme. The conscious ego would consider itself success-oriented and independent, but when the neurotic complex appeared, it would have definite signs of dependency and fearfulness involved. In order to clear up this split in the personality, it would be best if the neurotic complex could be turned into a person (personification) with whom consciousness (ego) could openly debate and discuss the course of life to be followed (confrontation with the unconscious). By personifying our other half, we can speak with it and hash out all of the attitudes it represents and come to some form of balanced overview which takes both sides into consideration and accepts them more or less. This solution is not always completely satisfying to either consciousness or unconsciousness; but then, that is the nature of life! Jung once referred to the course of analytical treatment as "rather like a running conversation with the unconscious."[292]

The Stages of Psychotherapy

In order to help the client achieve a state of psychic balance, Jung encouraged the analytical therapist to promote a kind of dialectical process in the therapeutic relationship (see p. 8 of the Introduction for a discussion of dialectic).[293] By permitting a completely free and equal climate to emerge in the relationship between therapist and client, spontaneous and open confrontations should emerge between participants. Not only does the relationship take on dialectical coloring, but the internal dialogue between conscious and unconscious contents are also viewed as dialectical in nature.[294] Jung insisted that the prime rule of his therapy was to consider each case uniquely and to give a patient completely equal status in the two-person encounter.[295] Indeed, the therapist is constantly in therapy with each client and can therefore make no claims to superiority except in the sense that he or she has devoted more hours to personal insight and therefore may be somewhat more balanced than the average person. But this experience is never to be used as a club over the client's head.

The course of analytical psychotherapy can be broken down into four stages. These are not clear-cut, nor is it necessary for a person to carry out all four steps in order to get a positive outcome from therapy. In the opening sessions with a client, the therapist finds the stage of *confession* developing quite spontaneously. Jung said this was the goal of the cathartic method introduced by Breuer and Freud (see Chapter 1). Cathartic release proves that a neurosis is more than just an intellectual problem. To clear it up there must be some involvement of the emotions as well. Doubtlessly catharsis—making confessions—was the means employed by people for centuries to balance. A sin is really the beginning act in a move to split the personality between what ought and what ought not be done in life. In then repressing the guilt over sinning, we ensure that a complex will someday arise around these very denials. Confession alone will not serve to balance the personality of everyone, but Jung felt that certain rather uncomplicated personalities can actually gain full therapeutic benefit from regular use of the confessional (for example, the Catholic sacrament).

As the sessions slip by, the therapist will find the client moving out of a confessional mood and wanting to explore his or her past life. This gradual change signifies that the second stage of therapy, called *elucidation,* is beginning. To elucidate is to make clear or explain something, and this is what the therapist begins doing. This explanatory process stirs up the client's psyche and in short order he or she begins projecting (positive and/or negative) unconscious contents onto the therapist. This is *transference,* and a therapist

knows for certain that elucidation has begun when such projections appear.[296] Jung had many things to say about transference over the years. He began his theorizing rather traditionally, viewing transference as a special type of projection in which parental (maternal or paternal) *imagoes* are attributed to the therapist.[297] He also spoke of libido cathexes which had been fixed on the therapist and needed to be removed and reinvested in the patient's personality after transference had been resolved.[298] This is all very similar to traditional Freudian theory (see Chapter 1). However, Jung was to expand on the construct of transference, and in time, he even dismissed its importance in cure. As we know from Chapter 1, for Freud a transference was the sine qua non of psychotherapy. Jung, on the other hand, eventually said that he did not think transference onto the doctor was a necessary precondition for therapy to take place.[299] Other forms of projection could serve the course of therapeutic insight equally well.

Jung viewed the client's sexualized efforts to relate with the therapist as a gross distortion of the fundamental social bond uniting all people.[300] Neurotics do not want sex with the therapist, but rather a true social relationship which they cannot take responsibility for establishing. In the positive transference, we therefore see neurotics giving love in hopes of receiving direction in their lives as children do. Because they are adults, they sexualize this love. The patient submits to the therapist as a slave to the master. Since regression also accompanies the projection of unconscious contents, there is often considerable infantile acting-out in the relationship. The therapist can be made into a father, mother, or even a combination of parental figures. In the Jungian view, it is even possible for a patient to project himself or herself as an *imago* onto the therapist.[301] This intensified tie to the doctor thus acts as a compensation for the patient's faulty attitude toward reality.[302]

The aim of transference is clearly the reestablishment of rapport with reality, the uniting of the split in the personality that has forced the neurotic into a continuing retreat from life. If the doctor and the patient lack mutual understanding, the break from life is not likely to be restored. Once the patient realizes that he or she has been projecting onto the therapist, the transference is resolved, and the stage of elucidation comes to an end. Before this can happen, however, any *countertransferences* which may exist must also be resolved. It is inevitable that countertransferences will develop in the relationship because *"all projections provoke counter-projections."* [303] This is why Jung claimed that the therapist is constantly working at his or her own therapeutic advance with each client seen. Jung once observed that "a therapist with a neurosis is a contradiction in terms." [304] This must be the case, because a sick therapist would have no ability to sense the unconscious projections likely to pass between doctor and patient. Incidentally, in Jungian therapy a patient has as much right to identify (interpret) countertransference as the doctor has to identify transference.[305]

The third stage is that of *education,* in which the therapist helps the client to learn about all of those personal and extrapersonal things he or she has found lacking as knowledge or behavioral alternatives in the past. The emphasis shifts now to the present, where concrete efforts are made to change behavior. Naturally, such changes are dependent on value judgments, and the client has as much to say about what will be changed as does the therapist.[306] Jung believed that Adler actually began his therapy at about this stage of education, whereas Freud had been content with ending his therapy at the close of elucidation. Since Jung believed that we seldom get rid of an unhealthy psychic state by simply

understanding it, he felt it was necessary to train the client to live a more satisfying life after we had provided insight about the past.[307] Jung did not offer any set recipe of training aids at this point. Whatever needs doing in the unique life history will have been made plain by this time. The selfish or timid person will make concrete efforts to meet and lend aid to others. The narrow person will begin reading more widely, earning a broader perspective on life. The too interpersonal activist will learn to enjoy solitude, and so on. The therapist will have to lend moral support to the client at this time, encouraging him or her as a person would coax any friend to develop more fully.

For many clients these first three stages will suffice, and therapy will normally be ended. However, occasionally a therapist will discover a special client whose problem is not curable by a therapy that aims at normalizing people. These individuals have potentials beyond the average, and hence, "that it should enter anyone's head to educate them to normality is a nightmare . . . because their deepest need is really to be able to lead 'abnormal' lives." [308] When a client of this type appears, the therapist has to move to the fourth and highest stage of therapy, *transformation.*

Selfhood and Individuation via the Transcendental Function

The stage of *transformation* is a completely unique view of the therapeutic process, which no other major therapy has ever quite captured. It demands that we bring together many of the terms learned above to describe the process of self-realization or self-emergence. The general process by which we accomplish this self-realization Jung called *individuation.* It is the first conscious inkling that we *do have* a shadow complex which brings he individuation process on.[309] In order to assimilate and integrate these shadow contents, we have first to bring them into consciousness in a form that will allow us to confront them meaningfully and in time defeat them as rejected alternatives which should not be given the chance to take over the personality.[310] But we do not want to destroy the shadow complex for all time, because in the first place, this is impossible due to the polarity in psychic events, and second, the shadow plays a necessary role in the psychic economy. Thanks to the libido generated by the tension of opposites between shadow factors and consciousness (ego sphere), there is an enlivening of psychic processes.[311] It does no good to try to destroy the shadow completely or to project it off onto others. We must learn to live with our shadow and even take strength and direction from an interpersonal association with it by way of personification.[312]

One might reasonably expect Jung now to claim that the shadow must be personified and confronted in the process of transformation. Yet, this is not precisely how the confrontation with the unconscious comes about. Rather, it is the anima, standing directly behind the shadow, so to speak, and directing the shadow's actions in the psyche, that must be confronted in personified form.[313] Jung's usage of the term *anima* in this sense is captured in the following: "I have defined the anima as a personification of the unconscious in general, and have taken it as a bridge to the unconscious, in other words, as a function of relationship to the unconscious." [314]

Why does the anima complex now take on the meaning of our entire unconscious life in place of the shadow? There are two reasons for this technical adjustment. First of all, Jung did not want the ego confronting

and defeating the shadow during transformation because—in line with his view of its utility—the shadow must continue to have a role in the psyche *following* individuation. Second, and doubtlessly more important, Jung had the anima stand as representative for the unconscious during transformation because this is what he discovered happened in his own case, during his personal self-analysis. In describing his self-analysis, Jung said that he was prone, when under a state of tension, to do something with his hands—to paint a picture, hew a stone, or record something (a fantasy) in writing. This creative urge made his moods concrete, for he literally made them come alive in this seeming artistic activity. One day, while he was writing down some fantasies which had been actively pressing upon his consciousness, Jung was prompted to ask himself a question. Something happened then which brought home his theory of complex formation in a most dramatic and uniquely personal way; that is, a voice independent of his conscious control answered his query, as follows:

When I was writing down these fantasies, I once asked myself, "What am I really doing? Certainly this has nothing to do with science. But then what is it?" Whereupon a voice within me said, "It is art." I was astonished. It had never entered my head that what I was writing had any connection with art. Then I thought, "Perhaps my unconscious is forming a personality that is not me, but which is insisting on coming through to expression." I knew for a certainty that the voice had come from a woman. I recognized it as the voice of a patient, a talented psychopath who had a strong transference to me. She had become a living figure within my mind.

Obviously what I was doing wasn't science. What then could it be but art? It was as though these were the only alternatives in the world. That is the way a woman's mind works.

I said very emphatically to this voice that my fantasies had nothing to do with art, and I felt a great inner resistance. No voice came through, however, and I kept on writing. Then came the next assault, and again the same assertion: "That is art." This time I caught her and said, "No, it is not art! On the contrary, it is nature," and prepared myself for an argument. When nothing of the sort occurred, I reflected that the "woman within me" did not have the speech centers I had. And so I suggested that she use mine. She did so and came through with a long statement.

I was greatly intrigued by the fact that a woman should interfere with me from within. My conclusion was that she must be the "soul," in the primitive sense, and I began to speculate on the reasons why the name "anima" was given to the soul. Why was it thought of as feminine? Later I came to see that this inner feminine figure plays a typical, or archetypal, role in the unconscious of a man, and I called her the "anima." The corresponding figure in the unconscious of woman I called the "animus." [315]

This remarkably candid account of his personal analysis gives us some firsthand knowledge of how Jung arrived at his finished theory and terminology. When adult males confront their unconscious, what better figure to stand in as representative for the unconscious than the other half of their sexual identity? It is obviously the animus a female patient would confront in personification during the transformation stage of therapy. Note also that it was a question— "What am I really doing?"—that first prompted the personified anima to make her appearance. This is similar to the theory of complex formation that Jung had used to explain the appearance of spirits in the voices

of mediums whom he had studied for his medical degree. Just as the medium called up a voice by posing the question "Who is with us?" or some such, so too did Jung encourage a personification of a living complex within his identity. Once out in the open of consciousness, the anima was found to have decided opinions in opposition to those of Jung—that is, his *ego*. She told Jung that he was doing something "arty," an aesthetic exercise which had no real significance except possibly as a kind of pleasurable pastime.

Jung did not accept this view. If all he was doing was "art," then the balancing process would have no personal significance. In other words, the anima was resisting individuation by detracting from its importance. And since the anima *was* Jung—that personality which he *was* unconsciously—what we see here is one part of Jung resisting therapy. His conscious personality, his ego, would have no part of this resistance and countered with an argument of its own. In time, the anima accepted Jung's vocal cords and responded to his counter with the logic of the female. And so it goes—the constant struggle of opposites, separated into polarized identities over the years and now coming to a confrontation by way of an internal debate of the attitudes to be taken toward life.

The anima is a great threat to consciousness because in this internal debate she *could* emerge the victor. If consciousness is to win out, then it must press its case unflinchingly. Very often the shadow side of such arguments are illogical and therefore because of such inconsistency they can be shown to be impractical. Even so, the conscious viewpoint (of the ego) must accept the fact that these *are* arguments of the personality system, coming back today because they were rejected and unrecognized earlier. Take Jung's anima attitudes, for example. Since the anima discredited Jung's psychological efforts to balance as art, we might surmise that she was returning all of those nonscientific attitudes that Jung may have rejected in the past. Jung may have, as a younger man, been so anxious to appear the perfect scientist that he repressed any suggestion that his analytical psychology was even slightly "tainted" by art. Now, when the complex that had formed around this and other attitudes returned, it had *precisely* this formerly rejected point of view to express. He was doing art and not true science after all! [316]

Many of the anima's arguments hit home, and they alter our conscious attitude (speaking now from the perspective of a male client) toward our parents, our careers, our very selves. But since the anima is at this point necessarily one-sided, we cannot submit to her pronouncements completely. We must depotentiate her lest we simply move from one type of one-sidedness (conscious) to another type of one-sidedness (unconscious) by identifying with her value system (be possessed by her). What we need is a balancing wholeness and therefore transformation is always concerned with educating the anima (or the animus for the female).[317]

How does Jung get the individuation process underway? He tells us that he asks a patient to take some aspect of a dream or possibly just any fantasied image which has occurred to him or her and then to elaborate or develop it spontaneously. "This, according to individual taste and talent, could be done in any number of ways, dramatic, dialectic, visual, acoustic, or in the form of dancing, painting, drawing, or modelling." [318] For example, a client might take an image of a mountain which keeps coming into his or her dreams, and then paint it or sculpt it, or try to capture its monumental impact by

writing about it or dancing about it in some spontaneous fashion. Quite often this reduces the frequency and vividness of the mountain image in dreams. Why? Because now the meaning coming through this symbol of the mountain (hermeneutically) is being dealt with *directly*. By creating the "artistic" production, we are creating the meaning that presses on our consciousness from the other side of consciousness. The mountain is that symbol of the right-hand side of Figure 15 that creates meaning. In time, we will be able to personify the anima or animus, and then the balancing effort to depotentiate it begins and hopefully ends with totality rather than further one-sidedness. When this totality is achieved we have successfully individuated, that is, become a new individual! Thus Jung referred to *individuation* as a "process of differentiation," [319] or as the "process by which a person becomes a psychological 'in-divid-ual.'" [320] Since it balances all sides including potentialities not yet realized, we can also think of it as the process "in which the patient becomes what he really is." [321]

The purpose of the dialectical process of confronting the anima is to bring these contents into consciousness, but then we must also break up these personifications for they are autonomous complexes with their own supply of libido (numen).[322] If we can break them up, then we can make use of their libido stores in a healthy, balancing way. Libido is set free by the anima or animus (and other archetypes constellated into the complex) which can then be used to form a connecting link between the conscious and unconscious regions of the psyche. It is the *transcendental function* that makes this connecting link possible, and it is the *self* as the symbol of unity that permits the libido to be constantly at the disposal of consciousness. We transcend what we had been, we unite all sides, and then we enter into a new personality constellation by way of the self-

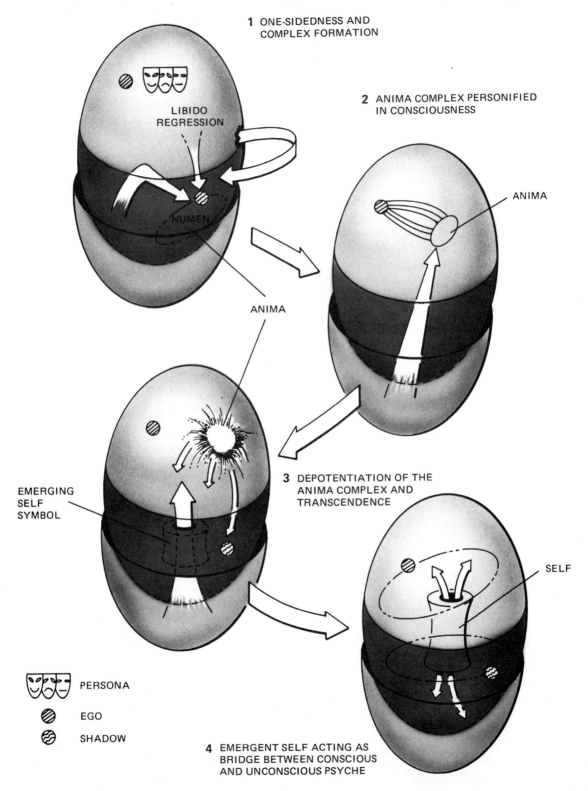

1 ONE-SIDEDNESS AND COMPLEX FORMATION

LIBIDO REGRESSION

NUMEN

ANIMA

2 ANIMA COMPLEX PERSONIFIED IN CONSCIOUSNESS

ANIMA

EMERGING SELF SYMBOL

3 DEPOTENTIATION OF THE ANIMA COMPLEX AND TRANSCENDENCE

SELF

PERSONA

EGO

SHADOW

4 EMERGENT SELF ACTING AS BRIDGE BETWEEN CONSCIOUS AND UNCONSCIOUS PSYCHE

Figure 17 The Individuation Process

emergence. To demonstrate this process of individuation we must build on the model for symbolic-meaning creation in Figure 15 and the centering of the personality of Figure 16. Figure 17 combines these two features into a schematization of the individuation process.

We have our familiar egg-shaped psyche in Figure 17. Note that at point 1 we show libido regressing into unconsciousness where the shadow is being joined by the anima archetype with its numen (stored libido) to constellate into a potentially autonomous complex. The more one-sided the personality becomes the larger is this unconscious complex (which could include other archetypes as well as the anima archetype and the shadow). When this unconscious complex gets large enough, it will emerge into the conscious realm, particularly when prompted to show itself as by Jung's question or by a symbol of transformation like the mountain image. In the latter case, the mountain image might be personified via the Wise Old Man of the Mountain, such as a leprechaun or a gnome from a children's fable (see Table 2). This is what we have pictured at point 2 of Figure 17. Now, the anima and the ego confront each other as opposites. The series of six lines looping between the ego and anima at point 2 signify the tension of dialectical exchange as these opposites wrestle for control of the personality.

At point 2 the shadow is for all practical purposes included within the anima archetype. The anima is actually now equated with unconscious contents and the ego is equated with conscious contents of the psyche. By the time we reach the stage of transformation, most of the persona factors would have been confronted and removed during

elucidation and so forth, so we have not included the persona complex at point 2. The task now facing the ego, which has essentially invited the anima to a confrontation by asking it to assume a personified form, is to depotentiate the anima and thus balance the personality. The dialectical confrontation (debate, discussion, feeling-toned expressions of preference, and so on) between these two identities continues over points 2 and 3.

Note that at point 3 we show the self beginning to take form, emerging as an archetypal symbol from the collective unconscious. But before the self can really emerge (be realized) as an actual point of identity, the anima will have to be depotentiated. If the anima *is* depotentiated, then its numen will be used by the emerging self archetype to form an identity point at the very center of the personality (à la Figure 16). If the anima is *not* displaced, then of course a self-bridge would not form to center the personality. We show at point 3 that a depotentiation has indeed occurred by having a kind of bursting of the anima complex, with its energy gravitating to the emerging self which now is actually constellated into an identity. At the same time the shadow leaves to return to its customary level of unconsciousness. Point 4 is then a schematized version of a successfully individuated personality.

Note at point 4 that the self acts as a bridging pipeline through which libido can now flow in *both* directions. Instead of having free libido regressing as at point 1 into the unconscious each time the conscious personality opts in favor of one behavior pattern over its opposite, we now have formed a major identity which can accept both sides to the personality. We have retained the polarity of the personality. There is still an ego in consciousness enacting the good behaviors (that is, the chosen alternatives we show to others) and a shadow in the unconscious constellating the bad behaviors (those only we know about ourselves completely). The self looks in both directions, accepts both sides, takes strength from the multiplicity and contradictions of the personality which both "is" and "is not" at the same time. Note also that the individuated person no longer needs to use a persona complex. The individuated person is a genuine human being who no longer hides behind masks.

The emergence of the self presents some problems for the ego, which is in many ways displaced and itself defeated by the arrival of a new focal point for the personality.[323] The self is closer to the inferior than the superior function on the basis of which the ego has been operating; with this shift in emphasis the ego is threatened.[324] Similarly, if the ego-dominated consciousness has taken on an extraverted coloring it must now find meaning in the introverted characteristics brought to light by self-emergence.[325] This is all very upsetting to the ego, which in fact does not always give up its important position without a fight. There is often a dialectic carried on between the ego and the self, except that in this case there is no depotentiation and in fact the self always prevails.[326] The point is, our ego is a very biased, shortsighted psychic complex. It has no proper appreciation of the historical antecedents of humanity.

The self, on the other hand, takes a much larger view of things. In fact, Jung once referred to it as an objective ego, meaning that the self has a more universal character.[327] The self originates in an archetypal prompting and then emerges into consciousness by way of a symbol, or else the libido, set free by the depotentiation of the anima, and the numen of the self archetype will not be put at the disposal of consciousness to solidify the self-bridge. Jung called a symbol that converts energy in this fashion a *libido analogue*.[328] The libido analogue is thus a special case of the symbol of transformation, which emphasizes the role of self-emergence in the personality. Libido analogues channel libido and change the form it takes from the form of the anima to the form of the self. We refer to libido analogues when we are concerned with symbols of the self, which we will take up below.

Another benefit of individuation, in addition to balancing the personality, is the widening of consciousness that occurs, even though the individual now appreciates the import of unconscious factors in his or her life.[329] This is a typical Jungian paradox: we enlarge consciousness through recognizing the importance of the unconscious (especially the collective factors). Jung once defined the *transcendental function* as "getting to know the counterposition in the unconscious" and he gave an example of how some such insight could be mentally helpful in the following comment: "A Christian of today, for instance, no longer ought to cling obstinately to a one-sided credo, but should face the fact that Christianity has been in a state of schism for four hundred years, with the result that every single Christian has a split in his psyche."[330] Thus, someone with a religious problem is not out of step with history. The collective schism for all Christians would simply be making itself known in his or her life and time.

The anima is not always unseated so easily in its battle with the ego as we have made it appear. Sometimes, when it is near defeat the anima can deceive the ego by appearing to depotentiate, only to have at this precise point in time a substitute archetype take its place with the express purpose of so fascinating the ego with its power of insight that the ego will be possessed (that is, identify with the substitute). By doing so, the anima succeeds in having the unconscious direct the conscious after all. Jung called this replacement for the anima the *mana personality* (see Table 12 where *mana* is listed as an archetype). Recall that mana conveyed extraordinary potency (numinosity) to the primitive intellect. The ego inflation resulting would usually come about as follows: at the point when the anima seems to be depotentiated several insights are achieved by the ego. The ego has benefited from the creative efforts during the fourth stage of therapy. It now feels as if it had conquered the unconscious and that it now knows a great deal about all aspects of the psyche. Sometimes these insights are frightening, so that Jung speaks of a positive or a negative type of inflation.[331] But the point is: the ego becomes drunk with power over its success in forcing the anima to withdraw and seeming even to depotentiate.

What may *really* be happening is that in taking credit for the defeat of the anima, the ego has actually identified with a mana archetype and slipped into a state of the mana personality. This is most likely to happen if the ego has become deeply involved in mythological themes, which hold great fascination (numinosity) for human beings.[332] Tales in which a person is said to have made a pact with the devil in order to acquire daemonic power are essentially based on this dynamic of an identification with the combined mana and devil archetypes. Manics or paranoids who try to convince us that they have unusual talent in business or political leadership might seem very convincing—since they are, after all, speaking from an unusual perspective (out of the unconscious)—yet something smacks of the extreme, the excessive, and the overly pat in their urgent requests for our money or votes, and we instinctively draw back from them. Some people do not. They follow such mana personalities believing them to be *charismatic* leaders.

If the mana personality evolves in therapy, the client begins once again to make projections onto the therapist, thereby reviving transference. This is one of the signs the therapist uses to recognize this setback in therapy.[333] The client might begin to idealize the therapist as a magical healer (positive transference) or criticize the therapist in any of a number of ways (negative transference). Sometimes this criticism seems warranted, so that in either case, if the therapist is unfamiliar with the mana personality dynamic, he or she may be fooled into believing that the neurosis has been cured. Sometimes these mana personalities profess to be analytical therapists and extend the Jungian therapy to lengths that offended the founder of analytical psychology. In several of his writings, Jung expressed concern over these supposedly enlightened healers, many of whom have a social action program in mind to "make this a better world." They are *not* conscious of their unconscious direction (possession), and hence it is a case of the blind leading the blind.

The correct way to handle a mana personality is first, to recognize it, and second, to repeat the process already outlined in Figure 17, only this time with the aim of depotentiating the mana personality rather than the anima. The best defense here is simply to admit that there will always be promptings from the collective unconscious in our lives.[334] In this way, we differentiate the ego from the mana personality by way of personifying the latter and simply recognize its numinous qualities. As Jung observed,

The mana-personality is on one side a being of superior wisdom, on the other a being of superior will. By making conscious the con-

tents that underlie this personality, we find ourselves obliged to face the fact that we both know more and want more than other people. . . . Thus the dissolution of the mana-personality through conscious assimilation of its contents leads us, by a natural route, back to ourselves as an actual, living something, poised between two world-pictures and their darkly discerned potencies.[335]

The reference to a poised balance between two world pictures is to the self, which has now once again emerged according to the Figure 17 dynamic. The ego falls to the background with this new focus of the personality. When conscious insights occur to it as lucky ideas, the ego no longer takes direct credit for them, but realizes how dangerously close it has come to an unresolvable inflation.[336] The ego can no longer claim the central place of the personality, but must be satisfied with the position of a planet revolving about the sun.[337] Figure 17 presents both the ego and the shadow as equal counterparts of conscious and unconscious psychic living, circling about the self at point 4 as if they were planets revolving about the sun. This representation is true to Jung's principle of opposites, which continues to operate after individuation is completed. As noted above, having depotentiated the anima—and possibly also the mana personality—the ego still needs its polar opposite against which libido may be generated. The self acts as the continuing vehicle (bridge, pipeline) for the balancing of this dialectically generated libido, and the contrast provided actually vitalizes the personality as a whole.[338]

The question remains: is it possible to individuate the personality in other than an analytical setting? Could a person self-realize in a general life setting, for example? Jung felt this was possible. In fact, he thought of the individuation process as *quickened maturation,* a term he borrowed from G. Stanley

Hall.[339] He meant that just as many people mature into a far-reaching wisdom over their life span, particularly in the latter half of the life cycle, so too does the individuated patient in analytical therapy acquire a vision of life beyond his or her years. Such people mature before their time, but they might have done so in any case.

Symbols of Transformation in Mythology, Religion, and Alchemy

We come now to a part of analytical psychology that has probably done more to give Jung the reputation of being mystical than any other aspect of his theory. Believing as he did that symbols cured through their molding of insight by way of transforming libido,[340] Jung was fascinated by the many ways in which he found humanity trying to correct for its collective one-sidedness through the manipulation of archetypal symbols— that is, symbols through which an archetype may be seen expressing its particular meaning. The main archetypes of transformation discussed by Jung are the *quaternity* and the *mandala,* and we shall limit our consideration to these two because not only are they in a sense identical, but they include in their meaning virtually all of the organizing, unifying, or balancing symbols he discussed.

The word *mandala* is Sanskrit for "circle," [341] and *quaternity* (from the Latin *quatre,* meaning "four") refers to geometrical figures having the property of being divisible by four, having four sides or four directions, and so on. If we consider a circle or a four-pointed (-sided, and so on) figure, it is easy to see that analogies to totality or wholeness are relatively easy to come by. Circles impel us to consider their centers, as we draw our attention within the circumference, hence inward to the heart of the figure, very naturally. Assuming now that a personality needs to symbolize a centering tendency, as stylized in Figure 16, for example, what more appropriate image could we select than a circle? And so it is that in analytical psychology any circular, spherical, or egg-shaped formation which appears in dream or waking fantasies is considered a mandala symbol. Some common examples of mandalas are wheels of various sorts, eyes, flowers, the sun, a star, rotation (including a swastika!), snakes holding their tails, enclosed places like courtyards, and whirling about centrifugally (like the dervish dances). Bringing mandala and quaternity symbols together, Jung said the most common forms of mandalas are the flower symbol (twelve or sixteen petals focusing our attention on the pistil) and the wheel symbol (eight or twelve spokes focusing attention on the hub), but he also noted that a frequent symbol for the mandala was the cross (focusing attention on the union point of the four-sided structure).

The number four is a common quaternity symbol, of course, including all numbers divisible by four (as the flower and wheel examples just cited). Thus if a patient dreams of four ugly witches mixing a pot of some sort, we might interpret it as a quaternity (four) and a mandala (the round pot) constellated into one dream theme. The fourth point is said to express a balancing tendency in the psyche. One is single, two is only half-complete, three adds a tension calling for a complete coverage, but only four gives us that well-rounded, spatially complete image as the four points of a compass (direction), the four sides of a box (complete enclosure), and so forth. Jung claimed that the primary colors of red, blue, green, and yellow reflect a quaternity, as did the early speculations on the nature of the universe in terms of the supposed basic elements of earth, fire, water, and air.[342] It is no accident that Jung has four steps in his therapy, with the fourth being the one during which balance occurs.

Jung reminded us that primitive peoples often insist on a more fantastic explanation of birth than their own good sense would suggest. For example, they might go on claiming that sexual intercourse has nothing to do with pregnancy, even in the face of their personal experience or the proof being given them by civilized peoples. Jung also underscored a tendency that any mother might find true of her child. That is, children not only seem to prefer a mythological explanation to a scientific or a truthful one, but they often simply "forget" the scientific explanation when it is forced on them. A seven-year-old child will not always give up his or her belief in the stork or Santa Claus simply because a modern parent does not want the child to believe in fairy tales and therefore informs the offspring about the facts of life. Jung believed that this fascination with myth is basic to the human being's capacity for abstraction. People are not really organisms designed to fit their thought to the facts of life. Besides, if we must someday realize a self that is not itself real (factual) but merely a possibility, then we have to develop a background of experience with mythologies of various sorts so that we can transform when the opportunity arises. This is a vital human process, one that needs practice, and one that might be termed *spiritual* because it is not involved with reality at all. As Jung summed its importance up, "Side by side with the biological, the spiritual, too, has its inviolable rights."[343] Hence the gremlin was a symbol of a modern myth, but the archetypes that went into its fashioning might have included the Trickster, Daemonic Power, and possibly even the Devil (Lucifer) (see Table 2).

Thus myths have a compensating role just

as dreams do. Myths arise from our unconscious, and they often make their first appearance in the form of a dream.[344] Jung defined this feature of his theory as follows: "Mythology is a pronouncing of a series of images that formulate the life of archetypes."[345] Since archetypes express meaning about all kinds of experience, it is possible to have mythologies reflected in science, religion, or political ideologies, that is, literally anything humanity finds itself doing. We do not make up myths, they are like the primitive thought forms that simply happen to us independently of our conscious will.[346] The compensating balance that results when they make their appearance can actually be thought of as an elongated individuation process.[347] Interpreting the mythological symbol is thus an important part of individuation in this sense. Jung did precisely this with flying saucers, a post–World War II phenomenon which he interpreted as the emergence of a modern myth.[348] Flying saucers were viewed as projected mandalas, put up in the sky by people needing a new balance within their psyches. In this age of science, when the old symbols (myths, religions) are losing their capacity to transform libido and thus balance the personality, a new symbol and its underlying myth is taking form. Since there is often a religious twist given to the saucer myth, Jung took this to mean that people's spiritual needs are being projected in an effort to find a new relevance for the nonmaterial side of life in this materialistic age.

Jung said on several occasions that the Roman Catholic church, with its wealth of symbolic rites and its liturgical dogma, holds a decided advantage over the Protestant sects (of which he was once a member) when it comes to promoting individuated balance.[349] Religious belief systems excel the more rationalistic systems of thought because they alone consider *both* the outer and the inner person.[350] The appearance of a papal bull (an official document issued by the pope) was for Jung a happy development, because this suggested that some of the older religious symbols might not be dying away completely.[351] Nothing is more dangerous to modern humanity than the disappearance of such symbols, for they act as the media for compensating archetypal themes. Furthermore Jung held that people who deny the patent fact that they *are* often moved by what can only be called a religious prompting are just as likely to slip into a one-sided neurosis as those individuals who refuse to admit that their religious faiths are occasionally shaken by doubt.[352]

As to specific religious beliefs, Jung suggested that the concept of an eternal *soul* serves a good purpose. In the first place, by believing in a hereafter, the individual retains his or her teleological approach to life and thus maintains a sense of personal advance throughout the years on earth. Secondly, the average person's belief in a soul reflects the underlying possibility he or she entertains that a unity can be achieved in the personality.[353] In this sense, the soul is the bridge we can utilize to achieve that totality of personal being most people refer to when they speak of *God* (an archetype signifying unity).[354]

Since, as we know, individuation calls for the emergence of a self symbol, religions might be expected to have created a self-symbol. And so they have: *Christ* is the symbol of selfhood, combining such opposites as God and man, inner and outer, divine and corporeal.[355] Christ also meshes with the Hero archetype,[356] balanced by the opposite fact that he was also a victim. We can see in the myth of a man made into God the rise of the self, the realization of the most noble aspects of our human nature now personified in the figure of Christ. The symbolism of the

Catholic mass captures this in *transubstantiation*, which refers to the turning of bread and wine into the body and blood of Christ. In the same way that a man was transformed into God, a priest now transforms material of one sort into material of another, higher sort. The resultant sharing of this body by all the faithful in the act of communion brings about a totality which is in all essentials a direct parallel to individuation in psychotherapy. Thus Jung can say, "In this sense . . . we can speak of the Mass as the *rite of the individuation process*." [357]

Jung had some very interesting, unusual views on the nature of religion and its mythology. He did not appreciate the decline in ritual and dogmatic symbolism that had set in among the Protestant sects and was eventually to extend to the Catholic church. But there were aspects of dogma he could *not* appreciate as well. One of these was the Augustinian view of the trinity (three persons in God),[358] which falls one short of a quaternity; Jung believed that for a complete totality we must have four identities represented in a God concept. Related to this was the issue of evil. Is evil an active principle in the world, as one might say that goodness is? If so, what is the relationship between God and the obvious existence of evil? The early Gnostics (theologians) had speculated on this problem, and they had accepted the fact that God was *both* good and evil in His impact on human beings. Later, St. Augustine and others defined *evil* in the negative sense as the "absence of good," but Jung could not accept this definition because it seemed an obvious denial of what we know to be the case.

Writing in his autobiography, Jung tells us that as a very young man he had the following insight regarding the God concept: "God is not human . . . that is His greatness, that nothing human impinges upon Him. He is kind and terrible—both at once—and is therefore a great peril from which everyone naturally tries to save himself." [359] Jung was thus prone to refer to the "dark deeds of God," [360] and his interpretation of the biblical account of Job, who suffered though he was a good man, was that God simply had no appreciation of the supposed evil He was inflicting upon Job. God gives and He takes away, and from His vantage point there was no real understanding of why Job complained so. Thanks to His confrontation with Job, God decided to become human—that is, He sent His Son down to earth in the form of a man. This action provided God with a view of things from the human being's slant. Job thus served as a vehicle for God's Self-conscious development—in a sense, for God's individuation.[361]

Coming back to the fourth point of the quaternity, if we now think about a complete totality in the God concept, we might oppose the Son to the Father, and in opposition to the Holy Spirit, it would be appropriate to oppose the active principle of evil as personified by Lucifer.[362] The Devil should round out our quaternity, but thanks to the Augustinian influence, neither evil nor Satan are acceptable counterparts of the theological God concept. Yet there was a time when theologians did speak of Christ as the brother of—and in some texts as even identical to—the Devil. It is probable that, at a very early stage in the church, the real man named Christ vanished behind the emotions and projections that swarmed about him from peoples all over the world. It is often true in history that a given personality will act out in life the unconscious promptings of an entire people. In the case of Christ, the historical man became the religious myth because it was *necessary* for such a projection to take place as a compensation from the collective unconscious.[363] Initially, the projection of a self symbol (Christ) had the archetype of the Devil combined with it, but in time the opposites were made a bit clearer, and then two figures emerged.[364]

The early churchmen commonly spoke of an *Antichrist* coming to life, and Jung took this to stand for the shadow of Christ.[365] Gradually, thanks to the drift of theology, the Devil and Antichrist symbols fell from potency (lost their numinosity), and the concept of the Holy Trinity was fixed ever more rigidly in the Western mind. However, as must inevitably take place in the act of individuation, a tripartite identity was simply not satisfying because it did not fulfill all sides as a quaternity symbol would. Jung believed that, in dropping the Devil as one of the quaternity, it was only a question of time before the substitution of the Blessed Virgin was accomplished as the new "fourth."[366] Thus, the trend to what is sometimes called Marianism (after Mary) in the Catholic church Jung took as evidence that a quaternity symbol of totality was not to be denied. Yet, for his part, Jung would have preferred the retention of the Devil as the fourth identity of the religious quaternity. He liked to point out that even Jesus taught us to pray the Lord's Prayer in the most quizzical fashion, and said, " 'Lead us not into temptation'—for is not this really the business of the *tempter,* the devil himself?"[367]

Because he viewed religion as an important part of human living, and he was also willing to talk about religious beliefs in the way that he did, many people honestly feel that Jung believed in the existence of God as a *formal* hypothesis within his theory. Others think that he was deviously trying to bring psychology back to the older religious beliefs. Neither view is correct. Jung made it quite plain that God is not real, for nowhere can He directly touch our lives. He is

sensed as a power within, but as we have already noted, such a numinosity could just as well be considered daemonic as divine.[368] Psychology is in no position to make metaphysical statements of this nature in any case. Analytical psychology can establish that the symbolism of psychic wholeness coincides with the God archetype, but it can never prove the existence or lack of existence of a true God.[369] Jung stated flatly that "it would be a regrettable mistake if anybody should take my observations as a kind of proof of the existence of God."[370] Jung regarded the psyche as real, *not* the God-image as such.

In addition to his writings on mythological and religious symbols, the charge of mysticism has been leveled at Jung because he tried to explain the nature of alchemy. He often dealt metaphorically with the symbols of alchemy, leading critics to think that he had developed an esoteric view of some sort. Actually, boiled down to its essentials, the Jungian interpretation of alchemy is identical with the individuation theory we have been reviewing in terms of mythologies and religions. Alchemy drew its roots from pagan beliefs, supplemented by borrowings from the Gnostics as well as from the more conventional church dogma of Western history.[371] The alchemists are sometimes said to be the first scientists, because they stressed the pursuit of empirical evidence rather than faith in the A.D. world.[372] However, Jung was to show rather clearly that in its early history alchemy was predominantly a religious movement. One could say that its prototype was something akin to transubstantiation. The alchemists drew an analogy to the transmutation of a natural, soiled, imperfect material state (bread and wine) into a spiritual state of perfection (body and blood of God) and claimed that they too sought to convert something baser (lead) into something higher and more valuable (gold).[373] Occasionally this higher substance was taken to be quicksilver (mercury) because this remarkable "liquid-metal" readily symbolized a union of opposites. Alchemists also searched for the basic substance that went to make up all things, thinking of this physical matter as a kind of divine prison in which the God spirit was confined; this was called *lapis* or the *stone,* or sometimes combined as the *lapis stone.*

Alchemists thus set out to find the secrets of matter, which they believed contained the divine soul (self symbol) as a captive waiting for release. As Jung said of the alchemist, "His attention is not directed to his own salvation through God's grace, but to the liberation of God from the darkness of matter." [374] These men were extremely devout, and the aim of changing lesser metals into gold or quicksilver was not to acquire riches. If such a discovery could be made, then we would have an empirical demonstration of the existence of God! During their pseudo-chemical work, alchemists often had hallucinations and other hysteroid states in which complexes of various sorts would emerge and confront them in personified form. They projected their unconscious contents onto matter to such a degree that the product to be extracted from matter as a divine essence was called *cogitatio* (having to do with thought).[375] A clear indication that an individuated self was being sought in the symbols of alchemy can be seen in the statement of Dorn, one of the famous alchemists Jung studied, who once urged his peers to "transmute yourself from dead stones into living philosophical stones!" [376] In short, just as the patient in psychotherapy works through art forms to individuate, so too did the alchemist

work at his experiments in an effort (unknown by him) to find his unique self-identity. He looked outward to matter in an effort to find what was really going on within him psychically.

Alchemy as a spiritual practice flowered through the Middle Ages until roughly the seventeenth century when it began its decline, thanks to the offsetting rise of modern natural science. The alchemists began to make a distinction between the psychological (*mystica*) and the material (*physica*) aspects of their study.[377] The older symbols lost their fascination (numinosity), and men calling themselves alchemists were no longer seeking individuation so much as they were literally trying to turn lead into gold. Materialism replaced spiritualism, and this unfortunate distortion of the original aims of alchemy brought on its current decline and disgrace.

Mental Health and Modern Times

Beginning around World War I and running through the rest of his life, we note a mounting concern in the writings of Jung with what he called the *sickness of dissociation* in the twentieth century.[378] One can see this splitting-up in the political and social conditions, the fragmentation of religion and philosophy, and even in the contending schools of modern art. Since he believed that art reflected the psychic state of humanity, Jung was alarmed by the detached quality of modern art. The creations of a Pablo Picasso or a James Joyce did not enthrall him.[379] He felt the meaninglessness and the deliberate aloofness from the spectator or the reader in such art products express only too well what is taking place in the psyche of modern humanity.[380] Symbols are no more alive in modern art than they are in modern religion. And for Jung, when we lose our symbols, we have lost the potential for balancing any one-sided state that may develop in our personality. The irony of modern times is that, though we profess an almost religious conviction that consciousness is all there is to psychic living, we are steadily falling more and more under the direction of unconscious collective forces.[381]

As his example, Jung took the horrors of two world wars in his lifetime.

Nobody realized that European man was possessed by something that robbed him of all free will. And this state of unconscious possession will continue undeterred until we Europeans become scared of our "god-almightiness" [inflated convictions]. *Such a change can begin only with individuals, for the masses are blind brutes, as we know to our cost.*[382]

If the vast majority of people suffer dissociation from their darker side, which in turn leads to possession, inflation, and the projection of these problems onto others, then the stage is set for *external* solutions when *internal* solutions are called for. Such external solutions tend to be collective in nature, which means they will be ineffective because the problem is an internal, *individual* one. Though Jung favored listening to the collective promptings of the unconscious, to learn from what these group symbols had to say, he rejected the reliance on collective solutions so many people advocate in modern times. He once observed, "The steady growth of the Welfare State is no doubt a very fine thing from one point of view, but from another it is a doubtful blessing, as it robs people of their individual responsibility and turns them into infants and sheep."[383]

Lest Jung seem an archconservative and reactionary, we should add that he had an ethical view of how people ought to behave which, if followed, would lead to a social order in which variations and even contradictions in personal behavior would be welcome

as uniqueness and individuality. Jung called behavior that is accepted from the group without a personally reasoned basis *moral behavior.* As we are growing, our parents and other important social influencers provide us with the mores of the group, and we accept these principles emotively, based entirely on the feeling-toned fact that they are considered appropriate by everyone we know. In a sense, moral behavior is automatic. *Ethical behavior,* on the other hand, comes into play when we *reflect* upon our moral inclinations. Sometimes our automatic moral tendencies come into conflict with one another, and when we do not think about it we might overlook an inconsistency of this sort in our morally conflicting behaviors. At other times a conflict between our moral duties ushers in a severe test of our ethical judgment or character.[384] It was Jung's firm belief that unconscious promptings, taken seriously and studied for what they suggest, could function by way of our conscience to help us settle such ethical questions, and even more basically, to know precisely who we are in relation to them.[385]

Unfortunately, we moderns are too busy doing things to take time for contemplation and introspection of this sort. We wait on science to solve our problems and adjust us psychologically. But only we, as individuals, can through meditation and fantasy-production stop the tendency so rampant today to project our shadows onto others.[386] If we confronted the personified evil that exists below awareness and assimilated it as *our self* (individuation), there would obviously be little need for the social reformers, because everyone would see things more clearly and work to further rather than to hinder the adaptations of community life.

Therapeutic Techniques

Dialectical Equality
in the Relationship

The prime rule of analytical psychotherapy is that it is a *dialectical* procedure, in which the individuality of the sufferer has as much right to existence as do the theories and individuality of the doctor.[387] The analytical procedure is dialectical in two ways: (1) the patient and therapist have equal rights in the dialogue,[388] and (2) the conscious and the unconscious square off on equal terms in their confrontation.[389] Real change demands openness and equality with an opportunity for either side to express a point of view.

As an exercise, Jung once showed how the theories of either Freud or Adler could be used satisfactorily to explain the dynamics of the same patient.[390] This admission has implications for client *resistance,* of course, because if the therapist admits that any of a number of theories can account for the client's problems, then when the client rejects a given interpretation, how can the therapist call this an act of resistance? Jung therefore concluded that analysts make entirely too much of resistance, which places him quite opposite to Freud, who stressed the overcoming of resistance as a major job of the analyst.[391] Jung insisted that his students take a self-critical attitude and wear their theoretical prejudices lightly by not dismissing all patient objections as resistance.[392] Of his own practice, Jung stated, "I am inclined to take deep-seated resistances seriously at first, paradoxical as this may sound, for I am convinced that the doctor does not necessarily know better than the patient's own psychic constitution, of which the patient himself may be quite unconscious."[393]

Jung borrowed his dialectical procedure from the ancient Greeks, who called it the Socratic method. He felt that its strength lay in the fact that it encourages new points of view to emerge as a synthesis of the views expressed by the client (thesis) and the therapist (antithesis).[394] Furthermore, in a dialectical exchange the analytical therapist does not have to worry about what to do or where to go next, because the client has equal responsibility for direction and in fact always sets the stage for what will be considered. Jung admitted that suggestion plays a certain role in all therapies, but he distinguished between conscious and unconscious suggestion. *Conscious suggestion* he took to mean following out a preconceived line of development or argument in making interpretations to the client.[395] Though the therapist cannot entirely avoid making unconscious suggestions to the client, he or she can and should avoid all such conscious forms of suggestion.

The therapist must be the model of a balanced individual if he or she is going to help the client. Clients do not make themselves similar to the therapist in a specific sense. They do not take on the likes and dislikes of the therapist in food, art, politics, and so on. But on the issue of wholeness and totality, there will be an identity between client and therapist, for this is what *self-realization* means. The therapist must show the way in his or her own adaptation, and Jung can thus say, "The great healing factor in psychotherapy is the doctor's [balanced] personality."[396] The so-called transference relationship is nothing more than a running series of projections sent the therapist's way from the unconscious of the client. Interpreting the origins of these imago projections is helpful, but this alone can never produce an attitude of healthy adaptation toward life in a teleological sense. By reducing today's relationship attempts to yesterday's imagoes (see p. 230), we constantly frustrate that which the patient needs most—a feeling of rapport with people in the present.[397] And so Jung once again uses his bridge metaphor to say that in the human ties of the therapeutic relationship, the abnormal individual can find the way back to the corpus of humanity. The neurotic person does not have to deny, lie, sin, keep secrets, or fight the mores of the group anymore, because the path from which he or she had strayed so long ago has been rediscovered.

Hermeneutic Techniques of Amplification and Active Imagination

Jung always believed that the free-association procedure used by Freud led to the uncovering of the same type of complex that he had discovered in his association experiments.[398] He therefore used various kinds of association techniques in therapy, at times giving the client clue-words or images to respond to and also adapting the completely free associative approach in which the client says whatever comes to mind spontaneously. In time he came to the conclusion that free association is not enough for a complete elaboration of the complex through the symbols involved. We can get at the repressed complex through free association all right, because mental events are linked together in the mind with 100 percent necessity (see Chapter 4, p. 266 for a discussion of hard determinism).[399] In fact, we could probably start the association procedure with a line taken from a newspaper.[400] All roads lead to the complex in the psyche. But what we want in addition to this identification of the complex is a means of understanding what it is the unconscious wants us to do about the client's problems, the kinds of compensations to be made, and the change in conscious attitudes called for.

What the therapist needs is some way of understanding messages being sent from out of the unconscious to consciousness. Here is where we now appreciate what Jung meant by the "hermeneutic treatment of imaginative ideas." [401] Symbols are not to be thought of as defensive maneuvers on the part of a client. Rather than covering up or hiding unconscious meanings, the symbol tries—as Hermes did for the gods—to convey this meaning. Freud was wrong to distinguish between manifest and latent dream content, because: "The 'manifest' dream-picture is the dream itself and contains the whole meaning of the dream. When I find sugar in the urine, it is sugar and not just a facade for albumen. What Freud calls the 'dream-facade' is the dream's obscurity, and this is really only a projection of our own lack of understanding." [402] Dreams are not only or even primarily defensively constructed false fronts, hiding what they really mean to say. Dreams are full of symbols, and we must devise hermeneutic techniques not only to recognize the collective meaning they embody but also to make this assimilatable to the client's consciousness.[403]

There are two, somewhat related, hermeneutic techniques used in analytical psychotherapy. The first, tied more closely to free association, Jung called *amplification*. He took this term from alchemy, where it referred to the fact that an alchemist would often let flow a series of psychic images and analogies while concentrating on his chemical studies.[404] Though he failed to appreciate what was occurring, the alchemist was in fact enlarging upon the context of some archetypal symbol which was expressing itself in his ritualized experiments and the theory he was following to justify them. This process of "taking up the context" is what Jung meant by amplification.[405] The client takes up each prominent point of his or her dream, and then lets a spontaneous flow of imagery occur while focusing on it—essentially amplifying or enlarging the meanings therein. This is not the same thing as free association, because the client is not allowed to go from dream image to thought and then ramble on away from the dream images as such. For example, if as Jung's patient we dreamed of a mountain scene, and then by concentrating on this dream image we were reminded of a vacation last summer during which time we had a dreadful argument with our spouse, Jung would not consider it proper amplification if we were to go off and rehash our marital problems—letting the dream per se slip from view. This would be a freely associated identification of a complex or problem area, but what he would hope to do in having us amplify is find out what the unconscious is saying to us. Jung would therefore encourage us as follows: "Concentrate on the mountain scene. What is happening? What comes to mind? Describe it all in full detail, including any changes that might occur as you experience the succession of images."

If we were to follow Jung's instruction, we might be surprised that our mind's eye will indeed begin to witness a scene of some sort, either limited to the dream as recalled or possibly even extending beyond it. The mountain might change its shape. Someone might begin falling down the mountain. We might find that from behind the mountain the sun was beginning to emerge, and so forth. Based on the recall of the dream and any additional action that might occur in the reactivated scene, Jung could now help us learn the broader meaning of the dream symbols that have emerged. He might draw a parallel with the fantasied mountain scene and some relatively obscure Norse legend about mountain folk who had great strength of will.[406] This may strike us as very odd

because not only are we rather timid and unable to get hold of our life, but we have always been somehow ashamed of our Scandinavian lineage. In time, Jung would show us that this is precisely what our collective unconscious is trying to cure through compensated dreaming. It is telling us essentially to balance attitudes, to drop the one-sided timidity and advance on life even as we take pride in our national roots (the pride we could have taken years back but did not). The meaning of the dream is right there in the manifest story line. One dream of this sort might not convince us, but if we were to have a number of them like this, all relating in some way to our personality problems and making the same point through dream symbols, we might begin taking our unconscious seriously. This is what Jung meant by hermeneutics, and in time he was to extend this technique to go beyond simply a dream context as such.

This broader hermeneutic application is *active imagination,* which Jung defined as "a sequence of fantasies produced by deliberate concentration." [407] In a sense, this is a highly sophisticated form of daydreaming, which is what Jung was doing when he stumbled upon his own complex (see p. 232). Once a theme emerges in active imagination it can continue for weeks and even months or years, possibly falling from view only to return again. The medium used to fantasize differs, of course, so that some patients use paintings and put on canvas what preoccupies them, others put their fantasied symbols into written form. Themes might include painting certain scenes (for example, mother-daughter relations) with variations, or recording in writing thoughts or images that arise spontaneously about anything from interpersonal relations between peoples to an examination of the anxieties of loneliness. Jung taught his patients to use this technique as a kind of barometer for the psychic state of balance, and he was known to diagnose the follow-up adjustments of his clients based on the kinds of paintings they continued to come up with in active imagination after they had left him.[408] Jung believed that when we concentrate on our unconscious content productions in this fashion, we literally charge them with more psychic energy and thus vitalize their symbolism.[409] In this way, we ensure that symbols of transformation will solidify and effect a cure through balance.

Insight, Symbols, and the Strategy of Interpretation

Jung once said that the psyche needs to know just like the body needs food—and not just any food or knowledge but that which is appropriate and necessary for existence.[410] The symbol is the groping means by which the mind comes to know its new meanings.[411] Symbols are made up of cultural contents used as analogies and metaphors through which they can express meanings never stated before. It is as if the archetypes were by nature dumb, and in order to express their compensating significance, they had to reach out and fix on whatever it was that the mind had learned in its particular culture. For example, if the theme of birth or rebirth is being pressed by the Self archetype during individuation, a fish image may be used symbolically in the dream as an analogy to a fetus *in utero* (both organisms surrounded by water; see Table 3, p. 250). The dream would be about fishes, but the archetypal theme involved would be (re)birth (individuation). The cultural contents change and hence there are no fixed, unalterable meanings to be found in true symbolical expression.[412] Yet surely within a given culture for a given period of time, common symbolic meanings might emerge, recognized as meaningful by the entire collective.[413]

The important point to keep in mind is that "every symbol has at least two meanings."[414] One *never* exhausts the meaning of a symbol with a single interpretation. Take the supposed sexual meaning of a dream, for example. Must we assume that every sexual theme is aimed at a literal wish fulfillment of a sexual prompting, or can there be other meanings to the *union* formed in copulation? Jung felt that there could indeed be, as in the frank eroticism of many coital symbols found in the otherwise reserved symbolism of the Middle Ages, where kings and queens were occasionally pictured copulating in artistic sketches.[415] The symbolism here was not sexual lust, but the unity of the nation (or two different nations joining through marriage)—a form of totality and wholeness. In like fashion, it is often true that human beings symbolize their need for a return to social intercourse (relationship) with others by dreaming of sexual intercourse. The latter serves an analogical function for the former, so to speak.

Over the years Jung had many opportunities to make interpretations of symbolic content—both in dreams and other mythological, religious, and alchemical contexts. In order to give the reader some flavor of his style of symbolical interpretation, we have listed a number of symbols taken from his works in Table 3. Note the decided lack of sexual interpretations.

Coming now to the practical style of interpretation, Jung would usually begin by having his clients free-associate to a dream image on the order of Freud's approach, to whom he gave credit as his teacher.[416] He departed from the classic free-association procedure by voicing his own free associations in the dialogue to supplement the thinking of the client's.[417] Since the therapist is in therapy and many symbols have a collective

Symbol	Interpretation
Albedo (Light)	consciousness [418]
Animal(s), Aggressive	untamed libido [419]
Ascent, Climbing	sublimation, transformation [420]
Dark, Darkness	chthonic, i.e., concrete and earthy [421]
Descent	psychic setback, confrontation with unconscious [422]
Eye	consciousness [423]
Fish	unborn child (in utero) [424]
Gold	union of opposites [425]
Leftward Movement	moving to the unconscious [426]
Lightning	sudden, unexpected, overpowering psychic change [427]
Mercury, Quicksilver	uniting all opposites [428]
Moon	in man, unconscious; in woman, conscious [429]
Nigredo	unconscious [430]
Sun	in man, conscious; in woman, unconscious [431]
Theriomorphic Snake, Dove	male vs. female [432]
Tree	personality, especially growth of [433]
Water	unconscious or wisdom [434]

Table 3 Some Jungian Symbolical Interpretations

implication, his or her spontaneous ideas are just as legitimate as the client's. Furthermore, the Jungian analyst knows more about mythological and other historical symbols than the client, and we must bring out all such information from the objective psyche, if possible. Jung was also prone to report his own dreams to the client, particularly if these seemed relevant to their relationship. He once had a dream in which one of his female patients was standing at the balustrade of a castle. He had to look up at her, for she was standing high in the air because of the rise of the castle walls, and he felt a crick in his neck as he fixed his gaze upward. This therapy series was not going well, and the next day he told the client that probably the reason it was not moving along was his fault. He had been thinking less of her than of other people, and his unconscious was now trying to compensate for his conscious attitude of looking *down* on her by forcing him to strain in the opposite direction of looking *up* at her. The client admitted that she had felt this countertransference attitude on his part, and from then on the therapeutic relationship improved considerably.[435]

Jung agreed with Freud that no permanent harm results if a therapist makes an incorrect interpretation at any given point during therapy. Soon enough, the continuing flow of unconscious influences will make the error known. The therapist should use several dream contents before settling on a given interpretation, and Jung frequently based his insights on a dream series extending into the hundreds.[436] He told of a patient whose dreams reflected the water motif twenty-six times over a two-month period.[437] Though suggestion may operate, the therapist ensures by giving enough leeway and opportunity for self-expression that only those suggestions the patient is ready to accept in any case will be assimilated by consciousness.[438] Hence,

Jung did not lose sleep over the accuracy of individual interpretations. As he summed it up, "I do not need to prove that my interpretation of the dream is right (a pretty hopeless undertaking anyway), but must simply try to discover, with the patient, what *acts* for him—I am almost tempted to say, what is actual." [439]

Jung defined *dreams* in various ways, as "impartial, spontaneous products of the unconscious psyche, outside the control of the will," [440] as "the hallucinations of normal life," [441] or even as free associations, taking place without consciousness. [442] The emphasis here is obviously on spontaneity and autonomy. Basically, dreams have two functions: a *prospective* function, in that they help to prepare the dreamer for the following day, [443] and a *compensatory* function in that they balance off one-sided conscious attitudes, such as Jung's condescension toward the client at the balustrade. [444] Jung took each dream as a kind of self-portrayal, giving us in the conscious sphere of the psyche a look—through symbols—at the state of our psyche *as a whole*. For this reason Jung believed *every* dream actor is representative of some aspect of the dreamer's personality needing balancing. A dream might compensate the conscious attitude without conscious awareness (by the ego), but ordinarily people need conscious understanding for a compensating balance to take place. [445] Jung also spoke of *big dreams*, analogizing to the highly significant dreams that primitives report to their group as visions. The biblical story of Jacob's dream in which he saw the staircase to heaven would be an example of a big dream, for the significance of this imagery on his life—and hence on the life of other people—was monumental.

In approaching an interpretation of some dream, the analyst should ordinarily consider two points. [446] First of all, enlarge on and come to know the context of the dream:

Where is it set? What seems to be going on now? How does the action proceed? Second, establish what compensation is being suggested by the unconscious. In studying the symbolical manifestations of the dream, Jung once observed, "Our position is more like that of an archaeologist deciphering an unknown script." [447] We will now review three dreams which Jung used as examples of his interpretation technique. They will provide an opportunity to see how his approach differed from that of Freud.

A favored example of a prospective dream mentioned by Jung in several of his writings [448] was told to Jung by a male colleague who used to chide him about making up interpretations of dreams. One day the two friends met in the street and Jung was told the following dream: His friend is climbing a particularly steep mountain precipice. At first the ascent is very exhausting, but as he moves upward he seems to be drawn to the summit with increasing ease. Faster and faster he climbs, in a state now of ecstasy, until it feels as if he is actually soaring to the top on wings. When he reaches the top of the mountain he seems to weigh nothing at all, and the dream ends as he steps off lightly into space. Jung advised his friend to be especially careful in his future expeditions because this was a rather ominous dream (particularly since the truth was that the man's marriage was going poorly and his conscious outlook was not a happy one at that time). The friend scoffed at this advice and rejected any thought that the dream was a message from his unconscious. A few months later he was observed to have actually stepped out onto space while descending a rock face, taking himself and a friend to their deaths below. The dream had him ascending and stepping up, the life actuality had him descending and stepping down. A Jungian could not dismiss this grim reflection of the principle of opposites as merely a coincidental happening.

Jung provided an excellent example of a compensatory dream in his case accounts. This dream was told to him by a young adult male. The dreamer and his father are preparing to leave their home by way of a new family automobile. The father takes the wheel of the car but begins to drive in a very clumsy fashion. He moves the car forward with a jerk, then backward, zigs to the left and zags to the right until finally he crashes the machine into a wall, damaging it rather badly. The dreamer is highly irritated with his father's behavior, and he begins to scold the parent only to find that his father is laughing—and obviously very drunk, a condition he had not noticed until after the accident. A classic Freudian interpretation of this dream would involve an Oedipal theme of some sort. In fact, the automobile as an enclosed place might actually symbolize mother, and the dream theme could be something like "this no-good bum is mistreating my mother, and he feels no remorse." In making this interpretation, we would naturally be relying on the manifest versus latent content distinction. Jung, on the other hand, took this dream at face value. The dream was aimed at taking the father down a peg or two. ". . . The unconscious resorts to a kind of artificial blasphemy so as to lower the father and elevate the son." [449] Knowing something about the client helps us to make this interpretation, of course, and in point of fact, this young man did tend to put his father on a pedestal. The dream was simply compensating for

this attitude and asking that the conscious attitude be given more balance in outlook.

The final example of Jung's dream-interpretation approach is the report of a ten-year-old girl who, Jung cautioned, had absolutely no possibility of ever hearing about the quaternity of God. This is important, because Jung here drew an archetypal parallel with biblical themes and thus presents us with the sort of evidence he accepted as an indication that an objective collective unconscious exists in portions of the psyche. The little girl wrote the dream as presented in italics, and then Jung's comment follows to close the section.

Once in a dream I saw an animal that had lots of horns. It spiked up other little animals with them. It wriggled like a snake and that was how it lived. Then a blue fog came out of all the four corners, and it stopped eating. Then God came, but there were really four Gods in the four corners. Then the animal died, and all the animals it had eaten came out alive again.

This dream describes an unconscious individuation process: all the animals are eaten by the one animal. Then comes the enantiodromia [running to the opposite]: the dragon [matter] changes into pneuma [fog, spirit], which stands for a divine quaternity. Thereupon follows the apocatastasis [restoration], a resurrection of the dead. This exceedingly "unchildish" fantasy can hardly be termed anything but archetypal.[450]

Some Procedural Details

Jung did not believe in taking a detailed case history of the client from the outset, feeling that through free association one would get at the problem soon enough.[451] By and large, Jung's view of therapy techniques was broad. He felt that all therapists are eventually forced to borrow from each other, because no one will go on using that which is less effective than an alternative technique just to be a purist in outlook.[452] Any one of a number of theoretical outlooks (Freudian, Adlerian, and so on) can provide the rationale for understanding a patient's dynamics. Jung therefore played down the specific technique a therapist might use,[453] suggesting as we have already seen that the doctor's personality is more important than his or her particular therapeutic gimmick. He cautioned against trying to live the patient's life.[454] Jung approved of the patient modelling himself or herself after the therapist, who has come to a higher level of adjustment by way of individuation. But if a therapist who has not individuated wants to manipulate the life of a client, a crisis will soon develop because in this case a therapist might in fact be identified with and directed by a mana personality. Similarly, Jung was not attracted to group therapy approaches. He felt that group interactions merely prevent the individual from a painful confrontation with the unconscious.[455] In the Jungian world view, all of our troubles flow from within, so it is merely a furtherance of the one-sidedness to pretend that we can rectify the situation by focusing on the outward, interpersonal situation.

Since he believed it to be a means for individuation, Jung was not above sending his Catholic clients off to the confessional where they might cleanse their souls through recognition of their shadow side.[456] By the same token, once balance of a sort was restored through communion, Jung would not necessarily enter into a dialectical procedure with such a client. Anything that would aid in providing a meaningful balance for the individual would be acceptable to Jung. "If he [the client] can find the meaning of his life and the cure for his disquiet and disunity within the framework of an existing credo—including a political credo—that

should be enough for the doctor. After all, the doctor's main concern is the sick, not the cured." [457] Of course, with the more sophisticated client, it would be essential to carry on therapy through a dialectical tactic on into transformation by way of individuation.

At the outset of therapy Jung saw his clients four times weekly.[458] As time slipped by and he moved ever more into the hermeneutic phase, he began cutting back the appointments to one or two hours per week. As this reduction in contacts was taking place, Jung would be encouraging the client to analyze dreams for himself or herself. He acted as consultant to the client's self-analyses. As long as proper assimilation was taking place, there was no need for sessions more often than once weekly. Regarding the kind of patient he saw in therapy, Jung observed: "About a third of my cases are not suffering from any clinically definable neurosis, but from the senselessness and aimlessness of their lives; I should not object if this were called the general neurosis of our age. Fully two-thirds of my patients are in the second half of life." [459] This is in striking contrast to the general characteristics of Freud's patients, who were considerably younger as far as we can judge. It seems clear that Jung's outlook on life was much different than Freud's, and his entire view of balance and of self-realization doubtlessly made it likely that he would carry a message well suited to the older person.

Summary

Jung is known in psychology for his introduction of a *collective unconscious* construct, but we have found in Chapter 3 that his concept of the persona is a *collective consciousness* notion as well. Jung's principle of opposition, through which he always seemed able to find one contrasting or contradicting mental content to offset another, is reflected in this division of the psyche. We also have the ego opposed by the alter ego or the shadow, and every type of behavioral style manifested on one side of the psyche has its opposition on the other side. If the ego is introverted, the shadow is extraverted, and if the thinking-sensation functions predominate in consciousness, the feeling-intuition functions color unconscious life with a style quite the opposite. It is out of this totality of opposites that Jung could eventually weave a balancing nodal point in the emergence of the self, that unifying identity of the complicated psychic realm, the *one* among the *many.*

Jung's adhesive model of the psychic structure was prompted by his early work in free association, in which he felt that he had proven the existence of feeling-toned complexes. This theoretical notion of a complexity of mental contents—a complex—was then to provide the basis for all of his mental conceptions. Complexes were said to function psychically under their own direction, and they could form anew over the life span of an individual. Some complexes like the ego, persona, and shadow seemed to form quite readily, thanks to the very fact of living. In living, we have to affirm certain behaviors (ego, persona) and deny others (shadow). The denied behaviors never simply go away. The difficult thing in life is to somehow bring about an understanding and even a communication between the affirmed and the denied sides. This is what the self complex affords because it acts as a go-between and a representative of both sides

of the psyche—the conscious and the unconscious. As Jungians, we always stress both sides of the psyche, because there is a sense in which the person begins life totally under the sway of unconscious thought, but not only a *personal* realm of unconsciousness.

Here is where Jung built on the concept of the unconscious that Freud and Adler had employed. Keeping his principle of opposition in mind, Jung essentially said that just as we have group influences on our conscious thought so too do we have group influences on our unconscious thought. Our family, social order, and civilization influence what we think about the world we now live in. But so too does our historical heritage of others who have "thought before us" influence how we think today. This objective, impersonal style of thought is just as much a part of our natural make-up as the fact that everyone's hands work in a certain way, with fingers bending and closing to form the same essential fist for everyone when they are clenched tightly. The working of the hand and the working of the psychic apparatus have this common influence from out of the past. Hence, in the collective aspects of our psyche there are general forms of expression, vaguely framed archetypes, which can be brought to bear in expressing some needed thought—a bright idea, a stroke of insight—at the right time. These primordial images are a priori categories of possible functioning. We can personify them, turning them into living figures in our mind, or we can get to understand them through other forms of symbolical mediation. For example, in an overly masculine man the anima archetype may enter into a dream calling him back to his feminine possibilities; in an overly feminine woman the animus archetype can provide the opposite (masculine) balancing outcome for her. The difficult aspect of such internal balancing is finding the common tongue—a symbol of some type—through which one side of the personality (unconscious) can make itself known to the other (conscious).

Just as Freud was able to describe his theory in both psychological and energic terms, so too was Jung able to move back and forth between such contrasting types of explanation. Jung, however, disliked Freud's limitation of the libido conception to the sexual instincts. He viewed libido more broadly, as a hormic life energy, an impulse the human being has to move toward valued goals of both a sexual and nonsexual nature. Jung's libido is teleological, a life-giving force directing the psyche which primitive peoples referred to as mana. Libido is that constellating force in the psyche that makes the formation of complexes possible. It works through the basic functions of the psyche to organize personality along both rational and irrational lines. Extraversion can either be thought of as the outward flow of libido, or in psychological terms, it can be described as the person's valuing external over internal life experiences. A reverse theoretical statement is possible for introversion. Jung's conception of the life stages was much more extended than Freud's, in the sense that he viewed developmental changes as taking place right through maturity. Youth is a longer span of time in Jungian than Freudian psychology. Jung did not accept the Adlerian claim that a life plan was fixed into place by age five. There is a grand play of opposites over the life span in analytical psychology, a counterbalancing of the one-sidedness of youth by the greater vision and understanding of midlife and old age.

Jung dismissed the Freudian fixation-regression hypothesis, preferring to believe that so-called fixated individuals have simply stopped moving forward in development. Hence, they are immature and can be brought forward again through a progression in development. One of the major things to avoid in life is the development of one-sidedness. When this occurs for any of a number of reasons, libido that is generated through the tension of opposition created by the one-sidedness drops into the unconscious to form complexes. This is the theory of illness that Jung worked out to account for abnormal behaviors of various sorts, that is, the emergence of complexes that function in consciousness outside of the control of consciousness. The natural balance of the psyche is disturbed accordingly, and the extent of this disruption defines for us whether we are speaking of neurosis or psychosis. Though Jung did speculate at one point on the possibility of schizophrenia as being due to a toxin in the blood, his primary view of psychosis was as a complete flooding of consciousness by the contents of the unconscious. Neuroses begin in an effort by the personality to rectify its one-sidedness, so that when libido surges forth from the unconscious, taking an additional source from the numen of the archetypes, it is aiming to express something useful to consciousness (the archetypal theme). It is at this point that a transforming symbol must be gleaned or the free libido will simply regress again to unconsciousness.

If a transforming symbol is found, a balancing of opposites in the personality can begin. If this balancing is successful and a complete individuation occurs in time, this always means that a self will emerge. The self individuates from all sides of the personality, once the primary neurotic (or psychotic) complex has been depotentiated. Jung called this major-problem complex the anima complex, thanks to its appearance in his self-analysis. But a comparable complex in the female would be called the animus complex. The complete process of analytical therapy moves through four stages: confession, elucidation, education, and transformation. Individuation occurs in the last of these four stages, and not everyone who enters analytical therapy necessarily individuates. When individuation does occur it is due to the transcendental function, for now the person can rise above all sides (the *many*) of his or her psyche to form a unifying centering point (the *one*) in the personality. This is a sensitive period in psychotherapy, for it is possible that the mana personality will deviously assume command of the personality if the anima complex is not depotentiated properly.

When individuation begins, we witness the appearance of mandala or quaternity symbols in the dreams or free fantasies of patients in Jungian analysis. Cultivation of these symbolical expressions is all-important to the curative process. The Jungian techniques of amplification and active imagination are designed to promote the formation of symbols. Jung stressed that effective therapy demands equality in the relationship between the participants. He believed that the Freudians had made entirely too much of resistance. The client ultimately knows what is best. Transference, which arises during the second stage of elucidation, is not to be misunderstood as a true genital effort on the part of the client toward the therapist. Transference behaviors are caricatures of the social bonds that hold peoples together. The client behaves in this way because he or she is trying to regain a sense of rapport with reality, not to re-enact an Oedipal complex from out of the past. Indeed, Oedipal themes are transpersonal manifestations, mythical motifs that take their force of meaning from archetypal materials. Jung underscored the dialectical nature of the therapeutic relationship as well as the dialectical nature of individuation, in which the split in the personality caused by one-sidedness is confronted and allowed to play itself out.

Jung was very concerned about the sickness of dissociation which he saw developing in modern times. People are being cut off from their unconscious side of the psyche thanks to the idolatrization of science, which can admit of no true psyche, much less of an unconscious psyche. The more we deny the darker forces at play in our nature, the more we project these factors onto others, and in turn, fall under their sway as neurotic complexes. Jung hoped that modern culture could become sufficiently enriched to accept what might be called an irrational component of human nature. In the final analysis, the serious problems of humanity are not "out there," in some kind of hard fact pattern. The serious problems of humanity are "in here," within our very identities as teleological animals who create our own circumstances. We have to learn more about the unknowable, and that most difficult task of all, learn to take direction from our unconscious. If not, the outlook for humanity is ominously self-dissociative if not self-destructive.

Outline of Important Theoretical Constructs

Biographical overview

Personality theory

Structural constructs

Dualism of mind versus body
  directed thinking

Psyche as a region
  teleological direction · principle of opposites · primordial past · consciousness

versus unconsciousness · empirical psyche as collective conscious · collective unconscious · persona · objective unconscious · differentiation (discrimination) · personal unconscious

The "adhesive model" of psychic structure
adhesive model · agglutinate · complex · automatism · feeling-toned complex · ego (ego-complex) · persona (persona-complex) · shadow (shadow-complex) · (*alter-ego*) · self (self-complex) · (*complexio oppositorum*) · personality

The "stylized meaning expression" model
symbolism · (*symbol versus sign*) · archetype · universal symbolism · universal archetypes · instincts as typical modes of action · archetypes as instinct's perception of itself · primordial image · archetypes not inherited ideas but meanings · *a priori* categories of possible functioning · personifying archetypes: anima versus animus · personification · transforming archetypes: self · dominant

Motivational constructs

Instinct and energy
instinct · libido as life energy or value estimates · instinct and archetype · telic nature of libido · mana

The principle of opposites
principle of opposites · principle of equivalence · constellate (agglutinate) · principle of entropy · one-sidedness

Complex formation
compensation (counterbalance) · compensation of consciousness by unconsciousness

Psychic determinism: causality versus synchronicity

hard versus soft determinism · synchronicity

Adjustment mechanisms
repression versus suppression · projection versus introjection · compensation, balance, and wholeness · differentiation (discrimination) and opposition · identification, possession, numinous, assimilation and inflation · (*identification with the archetype*) · progression versus regression · (*view of "fixation"*) · constellation and mobilization · individuation and transcendence

Time perspective constructs

Presexual period

Prepubertal period

Pubertal period

Youth

Middle life

Old age

Immaturity rather than fixation

Individual differences constructs

Basic functions of the psyche
function · thinking · feeling · rational functions · irrational functions · sensation · intuition · primary function · inferior function · superior function · auxiliary function · secondary function

Introversion versus extraversion and the psychological types
attitude · extraverted attitude · introverted attitude

Transcendental function and the mana personality
transcendental function · mana personality (inflation)

Individual as collective identity

Male versus female psychology
principle of Eros · principle of Logos
· anima · animus

Psychopathology and Psychotherapy

Theory of illness

Incompatible opposites, complex formation, and assimilation-dissociation

Role of morals, evasion, and denial
conscience · secret

Meaning creation and symbols in illness
symbols as bridges · numen · regression
of libido · symbols of transformation
· possessed by archetype (identified with
archetype)

Neurosis versus psychosis
neurosis as two-pronged · psychosis as
flooding of consciousness

Theory of cure

Growth, balance, and symbolic assimilation of opposites
polarities of life · confrontation with the
unconscious · wholeness · depotentiation
(depowerize) · midpoint of the personality · hermeneutic techniques in
treatment

The stages of psychotherapy
confession · elucidation · (*transference,
imago, countertransference*) · education
· transformation

*Selfhood and individuation via the transcen-
dental function*
transformed into selfhood · individuation
· transcendental function · libido
analogue · mana personality (via anima
or animus maneuver) · depotentiate
mana personality (if not anima or animus
initially)

*Symbols of transformation in mythology,
religion, and alchemy*
quaternity · mandala

Mental health and modern times
sickness of dissociation · moral versus
ethical behavior

Therapeutic techniques

Dialectical equality in the relationship
dialectical procedure · resistance

*Hermeneutic techniques of amplification
and active imagination*
amplification · active imagination

*Insight, symbols, and the strategy of
interpretation*
symbol formation · prospective dream
· compensatory dream

Notes

1. Jung, 1963, p. 76. 2. Ibid., pp. 24–25. 3. Bennet, 1961, p. 14. 4. Jung, 1963, p. 43. 5. Ibid., p. 31. 6. Bennet, 1961, p. 147. 7. Jung, Vol. 1, p. 166. 8. Jung, Vol. 8, p. 96. 9. Jung, Vol. 3, pp. 3–4. 10. Bennet, 1961, p. 43. 11. Jung, Vol. 5, p. xxiv. 12. Evans, 1964, p. 89. 13. Bennet, 1961, p. 40. 14. Jung, 1963, p. 171. 15. Ibid., pp. 185–186. 16. Jung, Vol. 9i, p. 48. 17. Fromm, 1963. 18. Bennet, 1961, pp. 58–60. 19. Harms, 1946. 20. Jung, Vol. 3, pp. 36–37. 21. Ibid., p. 272. 22. Jung, Vol. 8, p. 8. 23. Ibid., p. 7. 24. Jung, Vol. 11, p. 312. 25. Ibid., p. 83. 26. Harms, 1946, p. 566. 27. Jung, Vol. 8, p. 325. 28. Jung, Vol. 5, p. 58. 29. Jung, Vol. 9ii, p. 4. 30. Jung, Vol. 4, p. 287. 31. Jung, Vol. 5, p. xxiv. 32. Jung, Vol. 16, p. 77. 33. Ibid., p. 90. 34. Jung, Vol. 7, p. 279. 35. Jung, Vol. 9i, p. 43. 36. Jung, Vol. 5, p. xxix. 37. Jung, Vol. 7, pp. 269–270. 38. Ibid., p. 204. 39. Jung, Vol. 13, p. 45. 40. Jung, Vol. 16, p. 170. 41. Jung, 1946, p. 539. 42. Jung, Vol. 16, p. 155. 43. Jung, Vol. 8, p. 390. 44. Jung, Vol. 13, p. 92. 45. Jung, Vol. 9i, p. 280. 46. Jung, Vol. 16, p. 177. 47. Jung, Vol. 17, p. 52. 48. Ibid., p. 115. 49. Jung, Vol. 7, p. 183. 50. Jung, Vol. 15, p. 80. 51. Jung, Vol. 1, pp. 3–92. 52. Ibid., p. 44. 53. Ibid., p. 97. 54. Jung, Vol. 3, p. 67. 55. Ibid., p. 43. 56. Ibid.,

p. 63. **57.** Jung, Vol. 8, p. 101. **58.** Ibid., p. 98.
59. Ibid., p. 101. **60.** Ibid., p. 323. **61.** Jung, Vol.
9i, p. 276. **62.** Jung, Vol. 9ii, p. 3. **63.** Ibid., p. 6.
64. Jung, Vol. 14, p. 107. **65.** Jung, Vol. 11, p.
259. **66.** Jung, Vol. 7, p. 155. **67.** Ibid. **68.** Ibid.,
p. 195. **69.** Jung, Vol. 9i, p. 122. **70.** Jung, Vol.
7, p. 291. **71.** Ibid., p. 191. **72.** Jung, Vol. 10,
p. 215. **73.** Jung, Vol. 7, p. 65. **74.** Jung, Vol. 9ii,
pp. 233, 266; Vol. 16, p. 124. **75.** Jung, Vol. 9ii, p.
8. **76.** Ibid., pp. 266–267. **77.** Jung, Vol. 11, p. 82;
Vol. 12, pp. 41, 103. **78.** Jung, 1946, p. 540. **79.**
Jung, Vol. 7, p. 190. **80.** Jung, Vol. 9ii, p. 267.
81. Ibid., p. 5. **82.** Jung, Vol. 7, p. 194. **83.** Jung,
1946, p. 294. **84.** Ibid., p. 336. **85.** Jung, Vol. 14,
p. 468. **86.** Jung, Vol. 15, p. 104. **87.** Jung, Vol.
4, p. 210. **88.** Jung, Vol. 9i, p. 154. **89.** Jung,
Vol. 16, p. 124. **90.** Jung, Vol. 11, p. 518. **91.** Jung,
Vol. 16, p. 156. **92.** Ibid. **93.** Jung, Vol. 4, p. 279.
94. Jung, Vol. 8, pp. 136, 137. **95.** Ibid., p. 137.
96. Jung, Vol. 7, p. 65. **97.** Jung, Vol. 4, p. 315.
98. Jung, 1946, p. 368. **99.** Jung, Vol. 5, p. 102.
100. Jung, Vol. 9i, p. 48. **101.** Jung, Vol. 5, p.
181. **102.** Jung, Vol. 15, p. 81. **103.** Jung, Vol. 16,
p. 34. **104.** Jung, Vol. 9i, p. 37. **105.** Jung, Vol.
7, p. 207. **106.** Jung, Vol. 14, p. 106. **107.** Jung,
Vol. 9i, p. 30. **108.** Jung, Vol. 5, pp. 390–391. **109.**
Jung, Vol. 8, p. 204. **110.** Ibid., pp. 405–406. **111.**
Ibid., p. 182. **112.** Jung, Vol. 9i, p. 319. **113.** Jung,
1946, p. 565. **114.** Jung, Vol. 8, p. 206. **115.** Jung,
Vol. 4, p. 111; Vol. 5, p. 130. **116.** Jung, Vol. 3,
p. 190. **117.** Jung, Vol. 5, p. 328. **118.** Jung, 1946,
p. 571. **119.** Ibid., p. 356. **120.** Jung, Vol. 5, p. 139.
121. Jung, Vol. 16, p. 81. **122.** Jung, Vol. 17, pp.
191–192. **123.** Jung, Vol. 4, p. 127. **124.** Jung, Vol.
7, p. 31. **125.** Jung, Vol. 5, p. 431. **126.** Jung,
Vol. 10, p. 147. **127.** Jung, Vol. 7, p. 46. **128.**
Jung, Vol. 8, p. 9. **129.** Jung, Vol. 9ii, p. 10.
130. Jung, Vol. 5, p. 165. **131.** Jung, Vol. 16,
p. 6. **132.** Jung, Vol. 4, p. 337. **133.** Jung, Vol. 15,
pp. 36–37. **134.** Jung, Vol. 8, p. 18. **135.** Ibid., p.
25. **136.** Jung, Vol. 3, p. 207. **137.** Jung, Vol. 7,
p. 175. **138.** Jung, Vol. 9ii, p. 24. **139.** Jung, Vol.
11, p. 87. **140.** Bennet, 1961, p. 357. **141.** Jung,
Vol. 8, p. 424. **142.** Ibid., pp. 426, 427, 516. **143.**
Ibid., p. 443. **144.** Jung, Vol. 5, p. 58. **145.** Ibid.,
p. 59. **146.** Jung, Vol. 10, p. 25. **147.** Jung, Vol.
14, p. 107. **148.** Harms, 1946, pp. 294, 582. **149.**
Ibid., p. 531. **150.** Jung, Vol. 7, p. 190. **151.** Jung,
1946, p. 551. **152.** Jung, Vol. ·8, p. 98. **153.**
Jung, Vol. 9i, p. 351. **154.** Jung, Vol. 11, p. 7.
155. Jung, Vol. 16, p. 15. **156.** Ibid., p. 262. **157.**
Jung, Vol. 9ii, p. 24. **158.** Jung, Vol. 8, p. 32.
159. Ibid., p. 33. **160.** Jung, Vol. 16, p. 33. **161.**
Jung, Vol. 8, p. 94. **162.** Jung, Vol. 9i, p. 267.

163. Jung, Vol. 9ii, p. 25. **164.** Jung, 1946, p. 561.
165. Jung, Vol. 9i, p. 289. **166.** Jung, Vol. 3,
p. 187. **167.** Jung, Vol. 10, p. 32. **168.** Jung, Vol.
17, p. 44. **169.** Ibid., pp. 44–45. **170.** Jung, Vol. 8,
p. 390. **171.** Jung, Vol. 4, pp. 116–117. **172.** Jung,
Vol. 8, p. 390. **173.** Jung, Vol. 17, p. 52. **174.**
Jung, Vol. 8, p. 390. **175.** Jung, Vol. 17, p. 75.
176. Ibid., p. 16. **177.** Jung, Vol. 7, p. 25. **178.**
Jung, Vol. 17, p. 52. **179.** Jung, Vol. 8, p. 391.
180. Ibid. **181.** Jung, Vol. 9i, p. 71. **182.** Jung,
Vol. 8, p. 398. **183.** Ibid., p. 402. **184.** Ibid., p.
403. **185.** Jung, Vol. 5, p. 284. **186.** Jung, Vol. 9i,
p. 87. **187.** Jung, 1946, pp. 172, 374. **188.** Ibid.,
p. 547. **189.** Jung, Vol. 11, p. 167. **190.** Jung,
1946, p. 564. **191.** Ibid., p. 428. **192.** Ibid., p. 543.
193. Ibid., p. 452. **194.** Ibid., p. 585. **195.** Ibid.,
p. 587. **196.** Jung, Vol. 8, p. 141. **197.** Jung,
1946, p. 514. **198.** Ibid. **199.** Jung, Vol. 12, p. 102.
200. Jung, 1946, p. 564. **201.** Jung, Vol. 12, p.
102. **202.** Jung, 1946, p. 563. **203.** Ibid., p. 426.
204. Jung, Vol. 12, p. 102. **205.** Jung, 1946, p.
514. **206.** Based in part on the Jacobi stylization,
see Vol. 12, p. 102. **207.** Jung, 1946, pp. 542, 567.
208. Ibid., pp. 414–416. **209.** Ibid., p. 416. **210.**
Ibid., pp. 417–419. **211.** Ibid., p. 414. **212.** Ibid.,
pp. 53, 389–390. **213.** Ibid., p. 436. **214.** Ibid., p. 466.
215. Ibid., p. 457. **216.** Ibid., p. 464. **217.** Ibid., p.
484. **218.** Ibid., p. 492. **219.** Ibid., pp. 500–503. **220.**
Ibid., pp. 508–509. **221.** Jung, Vol. 7, p. 79. **222.** Jung,
Vol. 8, p. 90. **223.** Jung, Vol. 7, p. 79. **224.**
Jung, Vol. 14, p. 200. **225.** Jung, Vol. 7, p. 79.
226. Ibid., p. 231. **227.** Jung, Vol. 8, p. 225. **228.**
Jung, Vol. 10, p. 86. **229.** Ibid., p. 149. **230.** Jung,
Vol. 9ii, p. 97. **231.** Jung, Vol. 10, pp. 13–14. **232.**
Jung, Vol. 11, p. 534. **233.** Ibid., p. 549. **234.** Jung,
Vol. 13, pp. 9–10. **235.** Jung, Vol. 11, p. 493. **236.**
Jung, Vol. 13, p. 9. **237.** Jung, Vol. 10, p. 140.
238. Ibid., p. 141. **239.** Ibid., p. 123. **240.** Jung,
Vol. 14, p. 179. **241.** Jung, Vol. 7, p. 205. **242.**
Ibid. **243.** Jung, Vol. 9ii, p. 11. **244.** Jung, Vol.
7, p. 55. **245.** Jung, Vol. 17, p. 153. **246.** Jung,
Vol. 3, p. 253. **247.** Jung, Vol. 9i, pp. 278–279.
248. Jung, Vol. 13, pp. 36–37. **249.** Jung, Vol. 4,
p. 182. **250.** Jung, Vol. 16, p. 120. **251.** Jung, Vol.
8, pp. 355–356. **252.** Jung, Vol. 7, p. 179. **253.**
Jung, Vol. 11, p. 49. **254.** Ibid., p. 330. **255.** Jung,
Vol. 8, p. 244. **256.** Jung, Vol. 16, p. 55. **257.**
Jung, Vol. 5, p. 207. **258.** Jung, Vol. 7, p. 23.
259. Ibid., p. 182. **260.** Ibid. **261.** Jung, Vol. 5,
p. 232. **262.** Ibid., p. 398. **263.** Ibid., p. 232. **264.**
Jung, Vol. 13, p. 346. **265.** Ibid., p. 12. **266.** Jung,

Vol. 9i, p. 351. **267.** Jung, Vol. 10, p. 462. **268.** Jung, Vol. 4, p. 166. **269.** Ibid., p. 173. **270.** Jung, Vol. 10, p. 169. **271.** Ibid., p. 170. **272.** Jung, Vol. 11, p. 43. **273.** Ibid., p. 340. **274.** Jung, Vol. 5, p. 370. **275.** Jung, Vol. 3, p. 239. **276.** Jung, Vol. 9i, p. 278. **277.** Jung, Vol. 3, p. 247. **278.** Jung, Vol. 16, p. 86. **279.** Jung, Vol. 13, pp. 14–15. **280.** Ibid., p. 15. **281.** Ibid., p. 342. **282.** Jung, Vol. 14, p. xv. **283.** Jung, Vol. 9ii, p. 33. **284.** Jung, Vol. 13, p. 38. **285.** Ibid., pp. 327–328. **286.** Jung, Vol. 11, p. 157. **287.** Jung, Vol. 13, p. 348. **288.** Jung, Vol. 16, p. 156. **289.** Jung, Vol. 7, p. 287. **290.** Jung, Vol. 13, p. 302. **291.** Jung, Vol. 16, p. 123. **292.** Jung, Vol. 7, p. 109. **293.** Jung, Vol. 16, p. 3. **294.** Jung, Vol. 12, p. 4. **295.** Jung, Vol. 10, p. 168; Vol. 16, p. 10. **296.** Jung, Vol. 16, pp. 61–62. **297.** Jung, Vol. 9i, p. 60. **298.** Jung, Vol. 4, p. 200. **299.** Jung, Vol. 7, p. 62. **300.** Jung, Vol. 4, p. 199. **301.** Jung, Vol. 7, p. 90. **302.** Jung, Vol. 16, p. 136. **303.** Jung, Vol. 8, p. 273. **304.** Jung, Vol. 16, p. 78. **305.** Ibid., pp. 137–138. **306.** Jung, Vol. 7, p. 62. **307.** Jung, Vol. 16, p. 68. **308.** Ibid., p. 70. **309.** Jung, Vol. 11, pp. 197–198. **310.** Jung, Vol. 9i, p. 20. **311.** Jung, Vol. 14, p. 497. **312.** Ibid., p. 168. **313.** Ibid., p. 452. **314.** Jung, Vol. 13, p. 42. **315.** Jung, 1963, pp. 185–186. **316.** Jung, Vol. 13, p. 42. **317.** Jung, Vol. 7, p. 201. **318.** Jung, Vol. 8, p. 202. **319.** Jung, Vol. 7, p. 152. **320.** Jung, Vol. 9i, p. 275. **321.** Jung, Vol. 16, p. 10. **322.** Jung, Vol. 7, p. 209. **323.** Jung, Vol. 13, p. 45. **324.** Jung, Vol. 12, p. 26. **325.** Jung, Vol. 11, p. 501. **326.** Jung, Vol. 14, pp. 544–546. **327.** Jung, Vol. 16, p. 199. **328.** Jung, Vol. 8, p. 48. **329.** Ibid., p. 91. **330.** Jung, Vol. 14, p. 200. **331.** Jung, Vol. 16, p. 262. **332.** Ibid., p. 15. **333.** Ibid., p. 321. **334.** Jung, Vol. 7, p. 232. **335.** Ibid., p. 235. **336.** Jung, Vol. 14, pp. 370–371. **337.** Jung, Vol. 12, p. 131. **338.** Jung, Vol. 8, p. 224. **339.** Ibid., p. 290. **340.** Jung, Vol. 5, p. 141. **341.** Jung, Vol. 9i, p. 355. **342.** Jung, Vol. 11, p. 189. **343.** Jung, Vol. 17, p. 34. **344.** Jung, Vol. 5, p. 390. **345.** Evans, 1964, p. 48. **346.** Jung, Vol. 10, p. 443. **347.** Jung, Vol. 11, p. 196. **348.** Jung, Vol. 10, pp. 325–327. **349.** See Jung, Vol. 5, p. 441; Vol. 11, p. 353. **350.** Jung, Vol. 12, pp. 6–7. **351.** Jung, Vol. 9ii, pp. 174–175. **352.** Jung, Vol. 16, p. 46. **353.** Ibid., p. 265. **354.** Jung, Vol. 9ii, p. 31. **355.** Jung, Vol. 11, p. 432. **356.** Jung, Vol. 9ii, p. 36; Vol. 11, p. 88. **357.** Jung, Vol. 11, p. 273. **358.**

Ibid., p. 59. **359.** Jung, 1963, p. 55. **360.** Ibid., p. 62. **361.** Jung, Vol. 11, p. 406. **362.** Ibid., p. 196. **363.** Ibid., pp. 154, 432. **364.** Jung, Vol. 9ii, p. 72. **365.** Ibid., p. 42. **366.** Jung, Vol. 11, p. 161. **367.** Jung, Vol. 9i, p. 214. **368.** Jung, Vol. 7, p. 237. **369.** Jung, Vol. 9i, p. 108. **370.** Jung, Vol. 11, pp. 58–59. **371.** Jung, Vol. 12, p. 343. **372.** Ibid., p. 35. **373.** Ibid., p. 297. **374.** Ibid., p. 299. **375.** Ibid., p. 254. **376.** Jung, Vol. 9ii, p. 170. **377.** Jung, Vol. 12, pp. 403–404. **378.** Jung, Vol. 10, p. 140. **379.** Jung, Vol. 15, pp. 135–137. **380.** Jung, Vol. 10, p. 383. **381.** Jung, Vol. 13, p. 36. **382.** Jung, Vol. 12, p. 461. **383.** Jung, Vol. 10, pp. 200–201. **384.** Ibid., pp. 454–455. **385.** Jung, Vol. 14, p. 498. **386.** Ibid., p. 168. **387.** Jung, Vol. 16, p. 10. **388.** Jung, Vol. 11, p. 554. **389.** Jung, Vol. 12, p. 4. **390.** Jung, Vol. 16, pp. 113–114. **391.** Jung, Vol. 9i, p. 61. **392.** Jung, Vol. 16, p. 115. **393.** Ibid., pp. 39–40. **394.** Ibid., p. 3. **395.** Ibid., p. 147. **396.** Ibid., p. 88. **397.** Ibid., p. 135. **398.** Jung, Vol 4, p. 29. **399.** Ibid., p. 16. **400.** Jung, Vol. 16, p. 149. **401.** Jung, Vol. 7, p. 288. **402.** Jung, Vol. 16, p. 149. **403.** Jung, Vol. 7, p. 80. **404.** Jung, Vol. 12, p. 277. **405.** Jung, Vol. 8, p. 285. **406.** Jung, Vol. 13, p. 348. **407.** Jung, Vol. 9i, p. 49. **408.** Ibid., pp. 292–354. **409.** Jung, Vol. 11, p. 496. **410.** Jung, Vol. 13, p. 346. **411.** Jung, Vol. 14, p. 468. **412.** Jung, Vol. 4, p. 279. **413.** Jung, Vol. 16, p. 156. **414.** Jung, Vol. 4, p. 237. **415.** Jung, Vol. 16, p. 250. **416.** Ibid., pp. 46–47. **417.** Ibid., p. 44. **418.** Jung, Vol. 14, p. 77. **419.** Jung, Vol. 5, p. 328. **420.** Jung, Vol. 12, pp. 55, 60. **421.** Ibid., p. 167. **422.** Ibid., p. 60. **423.** Jung, Vol. 14, p. 53. **424.** Jung, Vol. 5, p. 198. **425.** Jung, Vol. 14, p. 111. **426.** Jung, Vol. 12, p. 184. **427.** Jung, Vol. 9i, p. 295. **428.** Jung, Vol. 12, p. 282. **429.** Jung, Vol. 14, pp. 53, 135. **430.** Ibid., p. 77. **431.** Ibid., pp. 53, 135. **432.** Ibid., p. 76. **433.** Jung, Vol. 13, p. 194. **434.** Jung, Vol. 9i, p. 18. **435.** Jung, Vol. 7, p. 111. **436.** Jung, Vol. 8, p. 289. **437.** Jung, Vol. 16, p. 12. **438.** Ibid., p. 47. **439.** Ibid., p. 45. **440.** Jung, Vol. 10, p. 149. **441.** Jung, Vol. 3, p. 148. **442.** Jung, Vol. 4, p. 234. **443.** Jung, Vol. 5, p. 7. **444.** Jung, Vol. 8, p. 255. **445.** Jung, Vol. 10, p. 388. **446.** Jung, Vol. 16, pp. 152–154. **447.** Jung, Vol. 17, p. 154. **448.** Jung, Vol. 8, p. 81; Vol. 16, pp. 150–151; Vol. 17, p. 60. **449.** Jung, Vol. 16, p. 155. **450.** Jung, Vol. 9i, p. 353. **451.** Jung, Vol. 4, p. 29. **452.** Jung, Vol. 16, p. 88. **453.** Jung, Vol. 10, p. 159. **454.** Ibid., pp. 456, 459. **455.** Ibid., p. 471. **456.** Jung, Vol. 16, p. 16. **457.** Ibid., pp. 16–17. **458.** Ibid., p. 20. **459.** Ibid., p. 41.

Chapter 4

Theory-Construction Issues in Classical Psychoanalysis

Now that we have devoted three chapters to a study of personality as interpreted by the psychoanalysts, it is about time for us to consider a series of important questions that always come up in the study of human behavior. We will direct the questions and present the answers in light of the psychoanalytical tradition of Part I, but the issues discussed will relate equally to the traditions of Part II (behavioristic) and Part III (phenomenological). Here are the questions to be considered in Chapter 4:

How is behavior determined?
How is behavior changed?
Can the mind-body problem be solved?
According to psychoanalysis, how does the mind "work"?
What motives to therapy are primary in psychoanalysis?

In answering these questions, we will make use of the theory-construction terminology we learned in the Introduction, with particular emphasis given to the four causes, dialectical versus demonstrative meanings, and the Lockean versus Kantian theoretical models. In Chapters 8 and 12, we will be asking further questions along the line of those above, and in order to be "up" with the whole series of questions, it is a good idea to review the Introduction and theory-construction chapters in order as each new question is encountered. Thus, at this point the Introduction should be reviewed, and when Chapter 8 is arrived at, review the Introduction and Chapter 4, and so on. Recall that for quick reference to specific theory-construction terminology, there is a complete glossary at the end of the text (p. 810).

How Is Behavior Determined?

Psychologists typically believe that "behavior is determined." But what does the word *determine* mean, precisely? Are we really clear on its usage? For example, let us say that we are passing through a deteriorating section of a large city, a place frequented by panhandlers, and drunks are seen loitering about the streets or sleeping it off in the doorways of buildings. One man in particular attracts our attention, because he is rather distinguished looking in a tattered sort of way, with an intelligent face and an expression that suggests competence and a sense of humor, despite the alcoholic haze through which he contemplates experience. He is middle-aged, graying, with a ruddy complexion, and still in reasonably good physical condition. We cannot help asking ourselves, "I wonder how a man like that ends up here on the streets, drinking his life away with seeming abandon?"

Without realizing it, we have posed a question concerning behavioral determination. If we try to answer it at all, we will find that our speculations fall along the familiar lines of causal explanation. Thus, we might propose that he was doomed to the life of alcoholism by heredity, or having tasted alcohol for the first time, his unique physiology put him on a one-way track toward drunkenness (material cause). We might put our emphasis on certain environmental circumstances out of his control, such as having been reared in a home where alcohol was used as an escape by his parents. When, later in life, he suffered through an unhappy marriage and/or a tension-laden job he automatically used the behavioral pattern that had been modeled for him by his parents (efficient cause). We might simply check this man off as a victim of chance. That is, in any population of human beings, there are a certain number who contract cancer, have serious automobile accidents, or become alcoholics. He happens to fall in one of these categories and that is too bad, but we could probably have predicted this from certain tendencies he showed as a young man if we had studied him statistically (formal cause). Lastly, we might consider that this man arrived at where he is today thanks to a series of intentional decisions, times in his life when he submitted to direction from others rather than standing up to them, or when he could have said no to certain temptations but gave in to them with a self-serving excuse (final cause).

Of course, our explanation could involve any combination of or even *all four* of these factors taken together. Moreover, to the extent that we put our emphasis on one or the other causal meanings, we are setting limits on the alternatives open to our eventual description of this man's behavior. Interestingly, the word *determine* has Latin roots with precisely this meaning, that is, to "set a limit" on something. To the extent that alternatives are limited in anything, we have increasing determination taking place. If we were ordered by an authority to use only material- and efficient-cause meanings in accounting for this man's behavior, our explanation would itself be *determined* beforehand. It would necessarily be true that no real formal- or final-cause meaning would be given serious emphasis in our explanation of why this man seems to be ending his days on skid row. *But note:* since someone has ordered us to use only material and efficient causes, we could still say that our behavior is under a formal- and final-cause determination. That is, we have accepted this order from authority, and using it as a guiding assumption (formal-cause pattern), behaved "for its sake" (final cause).

Whether we look at things this more telic way or not is up to us. Most psychologists today—possibly as many as 90 percent—specifically avoid using final-cause meanings in their scientific theories. They follow the restrictions placed on scientific description that began in the seventeenth century (see p. 11 of the Introduction for a discussion of this historical development). This is not exactly an order handed down, but there is at least some weight of authority put behind today's admonitions to avoid Galenic vitalism or the anthropomorphizing of human description. Psychologists are taught to describe events in terms of *antecedents* which necessarily determine *consequents* in one way and one way only. A perfect example of this type appears in the writings of the famous experimental psychologist, Clark L. Hull (1937), who drew the following analogy between animate human beings and inanimate raindrops (the analogy was first made by Albert P. Weiss):

We may start with the assumption that every drop of rain in some way or other gets to the ocean. . . . Anthropomorphizing this condition we may say that it is the purpose *of every drop of rain to get to the ocean. Of*

course, this only means that virtually every drop does *get there eventually. . . . Falling from the cloud it may strike the leaf of a tree, and drop from one leaf to another until it reaches the ground. From here it may pass under or on the surface of the soil to a rill, then to a brook, river, and finally to the sea. Each stage, each fall from one leaf to the next, may be designated as a* means *toward the final end, the sea. . . . Human behavior is merely a complication of the same factors.*[1]

By the *same factors,* Hull, of course, meant the material- and efficient-causes which thrust our man to skid row just as determinately (certainly, necessarily) as they thrust the raindrop to the ocean *entirely without purpose* (nontelically). But now, what of Hull's behavior as a reasoner using analogies to make a point? Recall the discussion of a sign versus symbol and the creation of meaning through analogy or metaphor in Jungian psychology (see p. 190). Jung would surely have said that Hull *the human being* had symbolized, had created a meaning by drawing this analogy between the patterning of a raindrop's behavior and the patterning of a human's behavior. Only a telic organism can do this, Jung would say, and it is noteworthy that Hull's efficient-cause theory is unable to subsume the specific meaning of analogical symbolization—of creating meaning by drawing a parallel to make a (purposive!) point.

Hull would undoubtedly have said that Jung was being tenderminded and nonscientific in wanting to explain natural events in one way (nontelically) and human events another way (telically). We can get a better insight into this debate between the mechanistic and telic psychological theorists if we consider the breakdown of determinism into the antecedent-consequent sequence already indicated. It is common today for the mechanistic psychologist to reason as follows: Behavior is set in a context of antecedent-to-consequent events. Given an antecedent, the consequent to which it relates (is attached, is a determiner of, and so on) *must* follow. Hence, to speak of non-determined behavior is nonscientific.

What often goes unrecognized in this line of reasoning is that we can agree that "all behavior is determined via antecedents leading to consequents" without agreeing that a *reduction* to material- and/or efficient-cause determinism is required. For example, in the Introduction to the text (p. 26), we discussed the role of antecedents and consequents in a line of logical reasoning, as flowing in an "if, then" sequence. The conclusion we arrive at in the following example is completely determined by the antecedent meanings of our major and minor premises: "If a man, then mortal [major premise]. There is a man [minor premise]. Therefore, there is a mortal [conclusion]." However, we *cannot* capture the determinism involved in this logical sequence by using either a material- or an efficient-cause meaning. The major and minor premises do not "impregnate" each other, "giving birth" to the conclusion. Nor does the major premise thrust the minor premise along, determining the conclusion in the same way that Hull's raindrop got to the ocean. We have in the patterning of the syllogism, as is true of *all* logic and mathematics, a clear indication of formal-cause determination.[2]

The final cause comes in here when we realize that a thinking organism could take on (affirm) a major premise of this sort *or not*. For example, what if a person, basing his or her objections on a precedent religious belief, would challenge our major premise by saying: "I disagree with you in at least one instance. Jesus Christ was not *only* a mortal,

but was also divine. Hence, any conclusion suggesting that he was *only* mortal must be wrong." Arguments of this sort, which are common in human discourse, are called *arguments from definition*. How do we define the terms of our basic assumptions, those that frame our major premise(s)? Mathematical equations or logical statements *never* define themselves. We have to introduce a final-cause concept here and say that a thinking, reasoning organism can align or not align (formal-cause) patterns "for the sake of which" sequences of meaning are developed (patterned) into conclusions, deductions, inferences, and so on. Table 4 brings this discussion to a focus by presenting the four types of antecedent determinants of behavior, arrayed according to the four causes which make them up (that is, the metaconstructs which subsume them).

The key word in Table 4 is *limit*. To determine is to limit alternatives in some way, and the ways possible fall into our four causal meanings. We have not put the consequents of the four types of antecedent determiners into Table 4, but these would be easy to imagine based on the examples listed on the right-hand side. We will touch on this issue of consequents by now taking up three somewhat different ways in which the concept of determinism has been used in the study of behavior.

Physical versus Psychic Determinism

The theories that dominated science before the twentieth century were based on material- and efficient-cause interpretations of determinism, with some consideration given to formal causation as a kind of secondary factor. In describing a physical illness, the physicians of the nineteenth century would propose the likelihood that a genetic factor brought on the sickness, or after Pasteur had proven the role of microorganisms in

Causal Meanings	Nature of Determining Antecedent	Examples
Material	A substance having certain qualities that set limits on behavior.	Genes, drives as chemical agents, sensory experience, organic development, etc.
Efficient	A thrust, push, unidirectional action, or necessary inducement limiting one line of behavior in regard to another.	Stimuli, signals, cues, reflexes, motions, etc.
Formal	A pattern, form, or style of behavior that limits what will be expressed, recognized, or expected.	Type, logical order, mathematical derivation, game plan, norm, etc.
Final	A precedent "that for the sake of which" certain alternatives are limited in preference to others.	Reason, premise, belief, assumption, bias, implication, conviction, etc.

Table 4 Four Types of Antecedent Determinants

illness, that some kind of invasion of the body by a germ had brought it about. The clinical syndrome of a disease like smallpox or tuberculosis could be said to take meaning from the formal cause, but the *basic causes* of these diseases were still said to be material and efficient in type. When Freud's colleagues in neurophysiology at the close of the nineteenth century began to describe mental illness, they employed this same theoretical style. They claimed that microorganisms or genetic factors (material causes) triggered (efficient causes) biological-physiological processes which resulted in neurosis and/or psychosis. This explanation relied on a *physical determinism* that was identical to the determinisms being used at the time in all of the so-called natural sciences, such as physics, astronomy, and so on. This unity in outlook is often expressed by the statement that "all natural objects obey [are determined by] the same physical laws."

Now, although he did not specifically set out to do so, Freud challenged this unity of description in the sciences even though he continued to believe in behavioral determination. Thus, in describing the dynamics of neurotic disorders, Freud was to say, "What characterizes neurotics is that they prefer psychical to factual reality and react just as seriously to thoughts as normal people do to realities."[3] If this is true, where in Table 4 can we put this determination of behavior? Physical antecedents *are* factual, they exist as external realities to bring events about. If as Hull contends a person follows the same laws of nature as the raindrop, then Freud must be wrong when he says that a neurotic illness can be based on mere thoughts—because raindrops *never* think! What Freud has done, of course, is to shift his determinism from the physical to the *psychical* realm of explanation. Jung agreed with Freud, as did Adler; in fact, using a falling stone as his analogy, Adler essentially rejected Hull's physical determinism as follows:

It may be asserted that when a stone falls to the ground, it must fall in a certain direction and with a certain speed. But the investigations made by Individual Psychology give it the right to claim that in a psychic "fall" strict causality does not play a role—only bigger or smaller mistakes which, after they are made, affect the future development of the individual.[4]

By *strict causality,* Adler means material-efficient causality, and in rejecting physical determinism as inadequate for the description of psychic life, he reflects the fundamental attitude of all three founding fathers. To capture the meanings of a psychic determinism, we have to look at the lower half of Table 4, where we see formal- and final-cause determinations listed. This leads into our second point concerning the uses of determinism.

Hard versus Soft Determinism

It is possible for two theorists to call themselves *determinists* and yet mean different things by this label. We might first note that no one is ever a complete "indeterminist" because this would mean that a theorist believed there was never any limitations put onto anything in experience. We could not count on any regularity or fixed patterning in an indeterminate world, where a person might open his or her automobile door and step into an airplane or a submarine. There are theorists who believe that unless we hold to strict determinism we *must* be indeterminists. These are the *hard* determinists. A hard determinist believes that everything that has occurred took place *exactly* the way it had to happen. Determinism is 100 percent or it is indeterminism.

Probably the most famous hard determinist of history was Pierre Simon Laplace (1749–1827), who believed that all of the atomic particles (material cause) of the universe were in place and working to move things along with perfection (efficient cause), so "that a superhuman intelligence acquainted with the position and motions of the atoms at any moment could predict the whole course of future events." [5] In other words, the universe was like a clock that had been wound with all of its parts interconnecting in perfect coordination; it would run its eternal and inflexible course exactly as determined by these material and efficient causes.

Not all hard determinists would express things in exactly these terms, of course, but their common outlook is that what occurs in the world or in behavior is precisely what must have occurred. Things could not have gone otherwise. And here is where Freud's psychic determinism enters to change things because he introduced what is called a *soft determinism* in drawing his explanation of psychic behavior. A soft determinist believes that events are determined, but not in a Laplacian or 100 percent sense. The soft determinist believes that things could have gone otherwise than they did. Actually, Freud's theory combined *both* a soft and a hard determinism, and in order to make this clear, we have to take up the final use of determinism. Once again, both Adler and Jung followed Freud in his acceptance of soft determinism to describe behavior.

Conscious versus Unconscious Determinism

It is not uncommon for students of psychoanalysis to think of Freud as a hard determinist. We can find some places in his writings where this belief seems to be well founded. For example, in discussing the validity of ideas which might have occurred to a person, Freud said to his reader:

. . . when you are faced with the psychical fact that a particular thing occurred to the mind of the person . . . you will not allow the fact's validity: something else might have occurred to him! You nourish the illusion of there being such a thing as psychical freedom, and you will not give it up. I am sorry

to say I disagree with you categorically over this.[6]

This seems to be the challenge of a hard determinist, but actually, Freud is discussing parapraxes in this paper, and when he refers to the lack of psychic freedom, he means in the *unconscious* realm of mind. We have no freedom from unconscious thoughts which simply happen to us or are sent our way as messages via slips of our tongue, misactions we perform, and so on (see p. 46). At the outset of this paper, Freud raised the question of what such parapraxes can mean, what their sense is to the person who experiences them. "We mean nothing other by it [that is, a parapraxis] than the intention it serves and its position in a psychical continuity. In most of our researches we can replace 'sense' by 'intention' or 'purpose.'"[7]

In other words, there is an intended meaning being expressed by these parapraxes. In an effort to be polite, we say to someone whom we are not too fond of, "Why not drop out . . . er . . . over, sometime?" In fact, we may even slip up this way in speaking to a person whom we (consciously) believe that we like. But our unconscious here *determinately* expresses the opposite attitude. These are *not* chance occurrences in behavior, according to Freud, who once said, "I believe in external (real) chance . . . but not in internal (psychical) accidental events."[8] We would actually prefer *not* to see the person whom we have just invited to visit us. Freud is therefore taking a position of hard determinism when he considers unconscious motivations of this sort. But having now understood what the parapraxes have indicated in our conscious state, we can *do something about them.* Why do we seem to dislike this person? Is it his or her fault, or are we to blame? Depending on what we then consciously decide to believe, we can then take steps to either break off contact with the person or sincerely try to develop better interpersonal relations.

It is right here, in the realm of conscious insight and decision making, that Freud becomes a soft determinist. As he puts it in the closing lines of his paper on the parapraxes:

All those of us who can look back on a comparatively long experience of life will probably admit that we should have spared ourselves many disappointments and painful surprises if we had found the courage and determination to interpret small parapraxes experienced in our human contacts as auguries [omens, telltale clues] and to make use of them as indications of intentions that were still concealed.[9]

Freud is obviously contending that things in the past *could* have gone another way if we had only been willing to admit to intentions (purposes) which one side of our mind (unconsciousness) was expressing for us in a completely determined way. This is 100 percent psychic determinism, but the other side of mind (consciousness) *also* has the capacity to think and project intentions. In this case, the determination is soft because the way in which we use the information sent to us by the parapraxes is *not* limited to one and only one alternative (that is, it is less than 100 percent). The same applies to dream analysis or any fantasy in which material looms up from the unconscious as grist for Freud's interpretative mill.[10] If Freud tells us that our dream symbolizes an incest wish, this does *not* mean we will necessarily be propelled into a sexual contact with our parent. The insight is what counts, because we are unable to correct our behavior without it. The theme expressed by the dream is 100 percent determined, but our behavior following the insight is at least partially up to us.

The same theoretical approach is taken in Jungian theory, where not only do we have messages sent to consciousness by way of parapraxes or dream symbols, but we have the archetypal themes as well. These themes come on us, press upon consciousness in 100 percent fashion once they have formed into a significant complex. But even when they appear within consciousness, the ego does not *have* to be controlled by them. It is only when the ego identifies with the unconscious complex that we might say a direct, hard psychic determinism takes place. Jung's efforts are given over completely to helping the person *avoid* such unyielding possession by unconscious forces. As Jung says of himself: "I had to obey an inner law which was imposed on me and left me no freedom of choice. Of course I did not always obey it." [11]

Adlerian psychology puts its emphasis on the holistic nature of psychic life. The dualism of a conscious and unconscious is more apparent than real since both sides of mind seek the same goals. There is a fixing of behavior in the prototype, and although framed in consciousness, it can gradually slip into the unconscious. Since the person loses touch with the fact that he or she actually framed the prototype, it might appear that a hard determinism is underway in the psyche. However, Adlerian theory is definitely a soft determinism in which the aim is to bring a person to realize what his or her prototype involves. Dream and fantasy productions, body dialect, and so on, reveal the life plan framed by the prototype. Once the person is made conscious of the unconscious strategies underway to achieve a life goal, adaptations and changes can be made. But then, even if the person has always been fully

conscious of the prototype, the mistaken behaviors mentioned above in Adler's quote will still call for correction. There is nothing special about the unconscious locus of self-direction here. [12]

How Is Behavior Changed?

As the present volume surely demonstrates, the classic theories of personality were proposed in the context of therapeutic healing or change of behavior. Even if Freud, Adler, and Jung had not been therapists, their theories of personality would have needed a concept of change. In fact, the Latin word *natura* from which we derive *natural* had the original meaning of "the changing features of everyday experience." Natural science therefore seeks explanations for the daily changes in events which inevitably touch on the questions of determinism. Just as we now know that to say "behavior is determined" does not mean *one* source of causal limitation, so too will we now discover that there is more than one way in which to describe change taking place.

To gain a better understanding of what change means, we can return to the writings of Aristotle, who was very influential in this area. He found that it was first necessary to speak of motion before one could talk about change, and as a teleologist, Aristotle believed that motions always occurred in relation to certain *ends* (goals, that is, final causes). [13] For example, a rock rolling down a hill to the valley below was said to have this end—to *be* in the valley—as a potentiality which could be actualized. Motion occurred as the rock was actualizing this potential, but once it settled into place at the bottom of the hill, all motion ceased. In Aristotelian terms, there is a state of existence in which things are in their place, motionless and unchanging (that is, not realizing a potential). Euclid combined this idea of a fixed place into his geometry, where a straight line is the shortest distance between two points (places) or a circle is a series of points (places) equidistant from a center point (place).

Aristotle next broke motion down into three major classes, each of which had something different to say about change: (1) *local motion,* or the movement from one place to another, as in our example of a rock; in time, this was shortened to our common word *locomotion;* (2) *qualitative motion,* or the alteration of a thing's attributes, as when the leaves turn color in the fall; and (3) *quantitative motion,* or the alteration in size (mass, bulk) to be noted when things either develop or decline in physical appearance, such as the developing grapes on the vine which become plump but if left unpicked, shrivel and drop to the ground noticeably reduced in size. These motions defined types of change that Aristotle considered *accidental* because they occur by degrees; the passage of time may be used as a standard against which their change can be measured (we can clock accidental changes as they are taking place). There is a fourth type of change that does not take place as a motion but rather "instantaneously," as when a living body passes into an inert mass at the time of death. Aristotle called this *generation and corruption,* and we shall have no need of discussing it further. We will confine our study to the changes of locomotion, quality, and quantity because these are the ones that have come down to us over the centuries in our theories of behavior.

Note that it is relatively easy to see the causal meanings in Aristotle's theory of change through motion. Locomotion is readily subsumed by the meaning of efficient causality. In behavior, we would see a person moving from "here" to "there" and say that he or she has "behaved." A qualitative motion takes its meaning from the formal cause because there is always an altered pattern in changes of this type. Tree leaves that change color in the fall define a completely different pattern for us, giving our outdoor experience an aesthetic *quality* which it did not have in the summer. In describing behavior, a qualitative change would be something like a mood shift in the expression of a person. There is no change of location but we can tell in the person's demeanor (organ dialect) that either optimism or pessimism has set in.

Quantitative changes would of course suggest a material cause in that something is changing in volume or substance. When children grow to adulthood, we see a quantitative increase in size. And in the closing years of the life cycle, we might actually witness a decline in physical stature as the person deteriorates into senility. Physical explanations of behavior relying on levels of energy (for example, blood sugar in the hunger drive) also put their emphasis on quantitative motion and change. Aristotle's belief in the potential of a thing to be that which it is presently *not* would of course be subsumed by the meaning of final causation. We *only* have motion because something is realizing its potential.[14] Bronze is potentially a statue, but this potential may or may not be actualized. It depends on the combined factors of an artist's locomotions, the qualitative and quantitative changes having to do with the use of this metal in art work, and the aesthetic goals the artist has projected in attaining his or her own ends.

In other words, as with the causes, Aristotle would combine all three (or four) of his types of change into a description of anything. He did say that locomotion is probably the most general form of motion in experience, but it never occurred to him that this one or even two of his change concepts would be able to explain *everything* in experience. Recall from the Introduction (p. 11) that, with the onset of modern scientific description in the seventeenth century, causal description was limited by *reductionism*. The four causes were no longer considered equal, as the material and especially the efficient cause began to be used exclusively in scientific accounts. Well, something like this also happened to the concepts of change.

Beginning in the works of Rene Descartes (1596–1650) and continuing thereafter in the writings of British Empiricism as well as in all subsequent scientific theories, the idea of change was confined to that of locomotion. Descartes was a brilliant mathematician as well as a renowned philosopher, and he concluded that there was no other motion in nature except what had come to be known as locomotion. He specifically rejected Aristotle's telic interpretation of motion.[15] Furthermore, Descartes brought this bias of locomotion into his geometry, where it is held that points are *not* fixed into place as Euclid presumed in framing his geometry but are always moving—moving by definition, so to speak. Thus, rather than being the shortest distance between two points, a straight line for Descartes becomes a *moving* point tracing this level of direction, or a circle is a *moving* point keeping a constant distance between it and a center point.

Cartesian analytical geometry paved the way for Sir Isaac Newton (1642–1727) to write the differential calculus, which in turn provided the grounds for the mechanistic views of the universe like those of Laplace.[16] The ideal of Newtonian science becomes the accurate *tracking* and *predicting* of bodies moving in relation to each other. Change is

motion through space (locomotion), and the concept of a fixed place is no longer required. *To be at rest* in modern scientific description is to be in a constant state of motion relative to some other moving object that provides a standard of comparison. When we take our seat on a subway train, we are "in place" only relative to the surroundings provided by this vehicle—which is itself moving along relative to the "fixed" tracks. If we compared our train to another, running along parallel to it at an identical speed, we might say that our train is now motionless (in place) if we did not realize that both trains were moving along on tracks. For similar reasons, in outer space where nothing "fixed" as a point of reference exists, it is impossible to decide which of two planets seen coming together is moving. We might therefore select a third planet as our "fixed" standard and then render a judgment as to which of the two planets is in motion relative to it or whether both planets coming together are in motion. Note, however, that a different reference point could reverse this conclusion in some way. This element of *arbitrariness* in scientific description, whereby what we conclude depends on what we presume to begin with, is what Albert Einstein (1879–1955) formalized into his brilliant theory of relativity.

With this general introduction to the concepts of change, we can now take up some representative ideas from each of our psychoanalytical founders to show that they really could not limit their theories to locomotion and be true to the human characteristics they were trying to describe theoretically.

Project for a Scientific Psychology

We can now appreciate that when Freud's medical colleagues were relying on physical determinism to explain the behavior of abnormals, they were adapting the style of using quantitative change and locomotion in scientific explanation that had been widely accepted by the Newtonians. Thomas Sydenham (1624–1689), a colleague of both Isaac Newton and John Locke, promoted what he called empirical medicine, and the essential idea here was that the physical body could be understood in terms precisely like those used to account for the universe.[17] A germ is a quantitative mass of protoplasm, something that can be seen and removed from the body to effect a change. If the body too consists of swirling substances called atoms, locomoting about in patterns under physical determinism, then just possibly sickness occurs when these patterns get out of alignment. Chemical interventions of various sorts might put the atoms back into proper alignment through an alternative form of physical determinism, thereby bringing about a cure. Chemical or physiological processes in the body can be thought of as different (quantitative) levels of energy which push atomic patterns around through the force of locomotion. The *Principle of Constancy,* which Brücke encouraged Freud to use, was such an idea of locomotion and quantitative changes in the distribution of force throughout a closed system (see p. 52).

There is one marvelous example of Freud attempting to write a psychology based exclusively on quantitative change and locomotion. This was undertaken thanks to the immediate pressure of Wilhelm Fliess, who, as we noted in Chapter 1 (p. 43), was something of a scientific conscience for Freud at one point; that is, Fliess urged Freud to express psychoanalysis in the more acceptable biological terminology of that time. Recall (p. 41) that Fliess was a conventionally extraspective medical theorist who proposed one of the early biological-clock theories. That is, he believed a human being's physical and mental health depends on the regularity with which a certain *periodic cycle* of blood flow through the body takes place. We see this

clearly in the menstruation of the female, but Fliess had found evidence in his medical practice to suggest that even men live according to cycles of fluctuating levels of blood flow in the body. The blood vessels of the nasal region of the male engorge on a twenty-three- or twenty-eight-day cycle, paralleling the female's menstrual cycle. In a nutshell, Fliess's theory held that when these cycles of biological change get out of kilter, the person becomes physically and/or mentally sick (the biological clock is out of order).

Freud gave this theory credence, even though he did not adopt it directly into psychoanalysis.[18] More importantly, he early in his career seems to have envied the biological explanation that Fliess accomplished. Following a lengthy discussion with Fliess in 1895, Freud set about writing what he was to call his *Project for a Scientific Psychology.* The fact that he emphasized *scientific* in this title clearly implies that Freud was making an effort to meet conventional Newtonian principles of explanation. Although he was never to finish this book, and later remarked that he could not understand why he started it in the first place, it is fascinating to learn that Freud knew that a "proper" scientific account of that time called for quantitative change and locomotion. Thus, in the *opening paragraph* of this unfinished manuscript we read:

The intention [of the Project] *is to furnish a psychology that shall be a natural science: that is, to represent psychical processes as quantitatively determinate states of specifiable material particles, thus making those processes perspicuous and free from contradiction. Two principal ideas are involved: (1) What distinguishes activity from rest is to be regarded as Q, subject to the general laws of motion. (2) The neurones are to be taken as the material particles.*[19]

This is clearly the most Lockean (-Newtonian) statement in all of Freud's writings, an effort on his part to build a completely extraspective theory relying only on locomotion (*Q,* efficient causation) and quantitative change (neurons, material causes) to describe the flow of behavior. Thus, if behavior were to change abnormally, Freud could ascribe this to the workings of his *Q* construct along the lines of the constancy principle. People are moved to behave or not to behave depending on energies available to propel them, and the effectiveness of their behavior depends in part on the number and working order of their neurons. Abnormality could thus be seen to be due to a loss of neuronic structures through disease (quantitative change) or the excessive pressures and counterpressures put onto the organism by the energies exchanged (locomotion). Disease processes like syphillis are known to destroy brain tissues which cannot then be regenerated. Why not other, as yet undiscovered diseases like this? Why not blood disorders in which insufficient oxygen is carried to the nerve cells which then die off? And why not abnormal bodily chemical reactions that might increase *Q* so that a person is thrust into a manic or anxiety state because of this excessive motility in the central nervous system? This is the kind of explanation Fliess (also Brücke and Breuer) would have preferred to hear from Freud.

That he gave this extraspective, efficient- and material-cause style of theorizing an honest effort is to Freud's credit. But he was working in relationships with clients who constantly reflected intentionality and purposiveness in their behavior. To understand them, Freud was required to take an introspective, formal- and final-cause approach in his therapeutic contacts. It is therefore also a credit to his integrity that Freud *did not stay* with the language of the *Project* but devised a series of terms that met the challenge he had encountered interpersonally. He eventually told Fliess on more than one occasion that he simply found it impossible to understand the neuroses based solely on the presumptions of a physical-chemical medical model.[20] As we have seen in Chapter 1, he was in time (around 1900) to bring the libido theory in as a quasi-energy, that is, one that seemed to be like the physical energies that (quantitatively) measured the extent and rate of locomotion at all levels of nature. But Freud did not actually think about the person in these mechanistic, reductive terms. His concepts of change gave primary emphasis to qualitative change and relied heavily on a telic image of the person. We will return to this issue below when we consider the matter of insight in psychoanalytic therapy.

Synchronicity

We can see now that in proposing his concept of synchronicity, Jung was trying to go beyond simply locomotion to explain behavior. People occasionally seem to know things that have happened miles away before they hear the news of this event from others —an injury to or a turn of good fortune for a loved one. Is this to be dismissed as chance or do we have a *paranormal*—beyond conventional explanation—type of event occurring? Jung took these occurrences seriously. But how to explain them? He began by distinguishing between what he called a *causal-mechanistic* and a *final-energic* explanation.[21] The causal-mechanistic explanation has things happening by being "bumped" from behind, much as a row of dominoes is toppled when the initial one of a series is pushed thereby conveying this force along a line of moving objects. Freud's *Q* construct was aimed at measuring this force in the nervous system, reflected in the electrical impulses moving across the tissues of the neurons. We are obviously referring to locomotion in Jung's example of the causal-mechanistic explanation. If we now refer back to Figure 13 of Chapter 3 (p. 204), we can see that the time dimension of A-to-B units pictured are examples of causal mechanism. These are each efficient-cause units of time, depicting locomotion.

In his concept of synchronicity, Jung wanted to show how changes might take place entirely within these time lines, cutting across and interrelating them as meaningful cross-connections. He therefore said that in a final-energic explanation of change, there is a rearranging of events *all at once,* so that the total amount of energy is constant and never gets used up. Energy is consumed in changes that take place over time, but changes occurring without regard for time rearrange the distribution of energy rather than consume it. It is clear that Jung was seeking here to introduce a qualitative change to supplement changes caused over time in the sense of locomotion, which demands a movement in place along the A-to-B sequence of Figure 13. Since he took time out of the explanation in favor of complete reliance on pattern (formal causality), Jung's concept reminds us of Aristotle's generation and corruption. But, the essential point is that he found it impossible to "reduce" paranormal events to the explanations relying on quantitative change and locomotion. He needed a (formal-cause) concept of qualitative change as well.

It might appear to some that Jung was being nonscientific in this daring theoretical effort. The critic might ask if any physical scientists have used qualitative change to explain inanimate nature? This question Jung could answer with a confident yes. He wrote his paper on synchronicity around 1951,[22] but as early as 1929 the famous physicist Niels Bohr had proposed an atomic theory which can also be seen as an effort to capture qualitative changes in pattern without relying on locomotion across time. Atoms have electrons which move in a global orbit around the atomic nucleus, much as the planets of our solar system move around the sun. It so happens that the electrons within the atom can change orbits from time to time. The orbits have different radius values, so they define somewhat different global pathways around the nucleus. If nothing but locomotion is involved in these changing orbits, it should follow according to Newtonian principles that an electron would move to *any* orbit (any radius distance from the nucleus). Though this makes sense based on locomotion, the fact is that this is *not* the way a change of orbit works at the subatomic level.

What Bohr's theory explained is the fact that the atom's electrons change from one *total* organized pattern of orbits to another in a most selective fashion. At one point the atom will have a given arrangement of electrons, and then following a sudden shift in orbits, the atom will take on a totally different arrangement. Bohr called these set configurations that occur between pattern changes the *stationary state* of the total atom. What is stationary here is the overall pattern of the orbits and not the electrons which continue to move within these orbits.

Although the circulating electron is properly described as locomoting, problems arise when we try to describe the change in orbits as also due to locomotion. Why? First of all, because there is *no* continuing trajectory to be tracked when an electron jumps from one orbit to another (when there is a move from one stationary state to another). Locomotion breaks down as a description of change because the electrons shift *all at once,* changing the pattern but not moving over from one orbit to another (sometimes called the *quantum leap*). This is precisely what Jung meant by the final-energic explanation, and doubtlessly he was influenced here to some extent by Bohr's writings. Newtonian theory presumes a traceable motion across orbit changes, and it also holds that an electron could move to any of an infinity of possible orbits around the nucleus. And here is the second drawback to locomotion, because the fact is that electrons avoid certain orbits *in preference to* others! We can predict the successive patterns through statistical probabilities by considering many electrons at once, but this merely tracks a collection (sampling) of *qualitative* changes going on within individual atoms. It is impossible to demonstrate locomotion in all of the changes going on within a single atom. Rather than taking the Newtonian position that we must "reduce" such pattern changes to locomotion (efficient causation), Bohr had this to say about the changes taking place in the sub-atomic world: "We are here so far removed from a[n efficiently] causal description that an atom in a stationary state may in general even be said to possess a free choice between various possible transitions to other stationary states." [23]

If an eminent physicist can speak this way about his subject of study, it seems especially unfair to call Jung unscientific or mystical simply because he was willing to forgo locomotion and describe changes in behavior according to qualitative change. Synchronicity is no more vague and difficult to entertain as a theory than is the stationary-state explanation. What is required of us is that we appreciate why such theories are proposed in the first place, and that we have a useful framework of theory-construction concepts within which to understand the steps being taken. Both Jung and Bohr moved away from an exclusive reliance on locomotion toward partial reliance on qualitative change.

Insight

The final example of qualitative change in psychoanalysis we will consider has to do with insight. As we know from the chapters on psychoanalytical therapy, all three founding fathers gave this major emphasis in their theories of cure. We can help to rectify neurosis by providing our clients with insight. But what kind of "change of behavior" is this? Assume that a woman comes to one of our three analysts to find out why she is getting increasingly irritated with her husband's mannerisms. He is easygoing, takes life as it comes, is never upset by sudden changes in routine, and readily overlooks messiness in the home. She, on the other hand, likes promptness and orderliness in her life. Earlier in their marriage, she was amused by his sloppiness and was willing to pick up after him, but recently their differences have been getting on her nerves. They have more squabbles now, and their sexual relations have been diminishing in frequency and satisfaction as a consequence. She has been getting various physical ailments because of the rising tension and frustration. Assume now that this woman is given a course of psychoanalysis by one of our founding fathers, and it proves successful. Whatever the dynamics of the insight provided—whether explained in terms of toilet-training, one-sidedness, or a striving for superiority—the woman *does* improve. She gains insight and sets her life in better order after the therapy series. What kind of change has taken place?

The analysts would *not* interpret this woman's improvement as being due to locomotion. To gain insight is to rearrange the order of one's understanding *altogether,* to shift the grounding patterns that lend meaning to experience *all at once.* As Adler expressed it, first we redefine the fictional life plan (qualitative change), and then the movements (locomotions) in the game of life are going to be noticeably different. The same applies to Jung's archetypal themes seeking expression. If the person really understands these meanings, they can act as the "that" or the *reason* (grounds, belief, assumption) "for the sake of which" a change can be accomplished. An archetype is thematic but lacking in form. It is like pure final causality, because, although it has something to convey, it cannot do so until a proper analogue is found (as in the symbolic image of a flower or a wheel). Once this symbol is caught onto by the person, the meaning is expressed; the symbol is the "that for the sake of which" the meaning is conveyed. Aristotle did not limit such a telic description to one or a few of his types of motion. He said *every* motion occurs in order to actualize an end (*telos*). Even so, it is clear that qualitative motion better captures the description Jung wanted to convey in his archetype construct than does quantitative motion or locomotion. As with Adlerian change, first we have the pattern (symbol, life plan) and *then* we have possible grounds on which to change overt behavior (locomote).

Pure final causality is extremely difficult to put into words or even to picture as a motion. This is why the archetype concept is so puzzling. We never really see final causes as we see substances (material causes), overt movements (efficient causes), or even patterns (formal causes) in events. We can only infer such intentions in the person's grounding plans (Adler) or parapraxes (Freud) or mandala dream symbol (Jung). A slip of the tongue tells us that the person does not really want his or her associate to "drop over" but to "drop out" of interpersonal contact altogether (see above). This gives us a new—that is, changed—insight into the *order* of interpersonal contacts that the unconscious would like to see come about. The unconscious wants this person who has slipped to rearrange his or her life and end the association. Once this new possibility is presented to the client as an alternative possibility, there is an *instantaneous* shift in meaning which reorients understanding *instantaneously,* on the order of Jung's final-energic conception. Even so, as we noted above, once we are aware of a distaste for an associate, we might drop this person as the unconscious intends, or we can work harder to improve relations.

Understanding our motives does not always tell us what to do about them. This is what therapists mean when they say "insight is not enough" to bring about therapeutic change. We can have insight without showing overt changes in our life—except at a purely verbal level. Our obsessive-compulsive wife might go on as before, being very meticulous and often frustrated with her husband's sloppiness. It would be hard to show a measurable difference in the routine of this household before and after therapy had been instituted. Even so, if asked, this woman would say, "I know things haven't changed much, but now I understand why he is the way he is and I am the way I am. I guess I have just learned to accept him and myself better. Whose life is perfect, anyhow?" Would this woman have been "changed" by psychotherapy? Those who accept qualitative change as a proper description of behavior would consider the woman changed. Those who do not, who wish to measure changes in actual, overt patterns of behavior—that is, see this woman locomoting less in house-cleaning behaviors or locomoting through manipulations of the husband to get him to pick up things —would say that therapy has *not* been effective except possibly at the verbal level (see Chapter 8, where the behaviorists are of this persuasion).

It is difficult trying to describe the workings (changes) of our mind in exclusively material- or efficient-cause terms, because what we tend to mean by *mind* is the ability to see orders (*logos*) in experience and to reorder and interrelate them in different ways to extend our range of understanding (recall that meaning is patterned order; see p. 7 of the Introduction). Freud's hard psychic determinism arose *not* from some efficiently caused thrust over time as in the causal-mechanistic explanation. He once said that the unconscious has "a natural 'upward drive,'" [24] meaning it pressed forward to express ideas. But this cannot be due to the force of energy "pushing" ideas to awareness. This drive is more like the logical necessity we have when we reason syllogistically. That is, given a certain major premise and a minor premise, there is *necessarily* a conclusion to be drawn. We cannot escape such conclusions because they emerge within the patternings of one meaning on another (psychic determinism). We cannot turn off

such implications, conclusions, or deductions because the overall order is there (qualitatively).

Freud used examples of a logical nature like this, as when he discussed paranoid projection developing from a propositional statement like "I (a man) *love him* (a man)." [25] If we were to now provide the backdrop major premise of "All homosexuals are mad" or "Only a filthy, degenerate subhuman could love a member of his own sex," we can see the *necessary* conclusion to follow if a man now senses "I love him." *This* patterned meaning is what drives ideas ever upward from the unconscious, and it is impossible to stop them because there is a kind of pure teleology here, similar to the upward thrust of the archetypal meaning in Jungian one-sidedness. Repressions never work to finish off an unconscious idea for all time because the meaning being ordered *has* to be expressed. Incidentally, when repression is given a libido interpretation, we have an analogy to clashing forces: a *locomotion* trying to account for what may be a qualitative motion. Repression interpreted in terms of the fuero is probably more consistent with the view of mentation (thought) as aligning patterns within patterns or orders within orders. The reason libido theory is so confusing is that it shifts the grounds of explanation like this from qualitative change to locomotion, and we are never certain which meaning of change Freud considered to be primary.

It can be shown that qualitative change, which demands that meanings be expressed *exactly* as ordered or reordered, is one of the historical reasons for believing in a Laplacian world of 100 percent determinism. That is, the Newtonian scientists of the seventeenth and eighteenth centuries tended to base their confidence in the complete predictability of physical events on a "God's Divine Plan" which worked *perfectly* because it was ordered by a perfect intelligence. Laplace's natural clock was not only made by God, it was wound into motion by God, who possessed the supernatural understanding of all the atoms, so that the future was perfectly known. Scientists today no longer base their confidence in 100 percent (hard) determinism on the working of a divine plan, but the historic tie to this conviction cannot be denied. As Newton himself once said: ". . . the motions, which the planets now have, could not spring from any natural [that is, efficient] cause alone, but were impressed by an intelligent agent." [26] Newton perceived the workings (locomotions) of the universe as cosmically identical with a supreme being's existence.

Bohr's reference to the atom's "freely willing" the next stationary state is not so different as a theoretical way of describing things from the freely selected decision of a god to create things according to "this" rather than "that" order of events. Bohr would be framing a *natural teleology,* but if we think of a god as making the selection of order, we would have a *deity teleology.* Teleological theories always put the idea of a pattern (plan, meaningful organization, intended goal, and so on) *before* actual [loco-]motion begins. As Newton said, first an intelligent agent puts down the order that will be followed, and *then* the natural causes of motion set in. The first move here to create is qualitative, and the second series of moves is pure locomotion. This same style of explanation can be applied to the more mundane example of a *human teleology.* Thus, a coach of some sport like football or soccer first imagines a game plan which he instructs the players in terms of, so that they might compete successfully. The coach sketches the game plan on the strategy board and the players observe and then practice their team positions before contesting a game with an opponent.

If this were God creating the plan of a universe on some divine strategy board, then when this order was put into [loco-]motion, we would have perfection (100 percent determinism). All our coach can do is draw circles and crosses on the board to represent the players and their opponents. Looked at from the coach's *fixed* plan, any given play should work to perfection if these symbols would only spring to life and play the game as intended by the coach's strategy. But the coach is not a god. The coach can be said to rely on qualitative change in creating first one pattern of play and then another— each representing a kind of stationary state of how things might go in the game to achieve victory. But the players actually locomote within the play—like the electrons during a stationary state—as they try however imperfectly to carry out the coach's intentions. We can now ask: which of these changes in the fluctuating course of behavior accounts for the actual athletic contest we observe on the field of competition? Surely *both* are important, but if we were to draw a theory-construction parallel to psychoanalysis, the qualitative changes of the coach's psychic activity would be primary! Pattern (insight) in this case is fundamental to motion.

In fact, patterns can retain their integrity even though there is much that changes within them. Heraclitus (*c.* 540–*c.* 480 B.C.) is often cited for having said that we can never step into the "same" river twice. This is usually interpreted to mean "nothing is permanent but change." What we fail to appreciate in this singular interpretation is that rivers continue looking like rivers even though they are constantly flowing along. Heraclitus was as interested in making this point of *permanence* in pattern (what he called *logos*) as he was of pointing to change.

Thanks to Cartesian geometry and Newtonian mechanics, the modern person equates motion with locomotion, just as cause means *only* efficient cause today. We see people moving about from here to there, airplanes flying overhead, raindrops falling from the sky and moving to the ocean (as in Hull's analogy), and so on. All of these movements can be measured across what we assume to be the flow of time. Locomotion is intrinsically tied to a concept of time's passage. It never occurs to us that it would be impossible to conceive of either [loco-]motion *or* time without some framing, fixed order which is not precisely either conception. Yet this is precisely what modern scientists were to conclude.

In putting down rules for his mechanics, Sir Isaac Newton proposed two laws of motion (we are equating *motion* with *locomotion* now). The first law (*inertia*) states that if no force acts on it, a body will remain at rest, or if in motion, this body will continue to move at a steady rate in a straight line indefinitely. The second law (*force*) states that a force acting on a body will equal the product of the mass of the body times the acceleration that force produces. Note that motion at a steady rate (first law) ties motion directly to the passage of time.

These laws (more properly, axioms or assumptions) were considered the most universal statements that science could make concerning the workings of the universe. And yet, in order to determine change through motion and to clock the steady rate at which an object moved, it was necessary to find an *unchanging* (fixed) standard of comparison. We have here precisely the problem referred to above (p. 270) in the example of two planets changing locations in space. In

his mathematical calculations, Newton accepted the concept of an absolute space, which as an unchanging given provided the standard required. As it was interpreted, the total constellation of the stars was considered this unchanging frame of reference.[27] Of course, scientists have since estimated that this framework is expanding, so that its dimensions are not absolute or fixed after all. But since the expansion is uniform, the *pattern* of the stars in constellation remains constant. Motion is judged against this fixed frame of reference, and time is estimated by the constant rotation of the earth in relation to—that is, patterned by the earth's relationship with—the sun.

If we take our lessons from the history of physical science, then we must be prepared to accept other kinds of changes than just those about locomotion. Since locomotion as a construct is itself dependent on the psychological assumptions of the scientist, who searches about for a patterned frame of reference within which to make statements in terms of this construct, we cannot as psychologists ignore this seeming qualitative ability to see things first "this" way and then "that" way depending on the frame of reference being employed. In modern physics the Newtonian laws of motion are considered arbitrary conventions rather than some ultimate statement of reality.[28] The famous philosopher of science Phillip Frank has said that in order to judge the usefulness of concepts like absolute space, time, or motion, we have to rely on more than the science of physics; we must employ psychology and even sociology as well.[29] The psychoanalysts would agree with this. It was their hope to write a psychology that would place pattern above motion, timelessness above the passage of time, and formal-final causation above material-efficient causation. In so doing, their frame of reference shifted from a Lockean to at least a partially Kantian one. This takes us to the next question of Chapter 4.

Can the Mind-Body Problem Be Solved?

The basic problem facing our founding fathers was how to meet the theoretical prejudices of the medical community and *also* put together a theory of behavior that permitted the client to develop insight. This involved them in the traditional mind-body problem, because insight is another way of talking about mental as opposed to physical (body) events. As we recall from the Introduction (p. 9), theories that put telic direction into physical explanations were called *vitalistic,* after Galenic medicine. Galen based his vitalism on a deity teleology, of course, but there is a tendency to lump all final-cause accounts together, so even though the analysts were concerned with human teleology, they ran the risk of being called vitalists. Furthermore, as trained physicians, the analysts knew factually that biological functioning had direct influences on the working of the brain. Jung's toxin theory of schizophrenia is a routine medical explanation. Adler's early speculations on organ inferiority and brain compensation were also strictly biological. Freud's efforts in the *Project* and later in his libido theory are similar attempts to bridge physical and psychical description.

Because of such writings there is much confusion today over just what the analysts were intending to emphasize in their theories. This is most true of Freud, whom many people today, including psychoanalysts, interpret as a biological reductionist. This interpretation is difficult to accept when we consider what Freud had to say on this matter over the years. He appreciated the importance of the body's biological structures to mental functioning, but in speaking of his topographical model of mind, Freud specifically cautioned his reader as follows:

> . . . I must beg you not to ask what material it is constructed of. That is not a subject of psychological interest. Psychology can be indifferent to it as, for instance, optics can be to the question of whether the walls of a telescope are made of metal or cardboard. We shall leave entirely on one side the material [-cause] line of approach, but not so the spatial [formal-cause] one.[30]

Freud believed that perverse sexual acts are potentials in everyone's behavior, so that it is wrong to attribute them to abnormal germ plasm when we find some person indulging in window-peeping or self-exposure.[31] He rather emphatically held that no physiological or other chemical process could account for the psychological findings of psychoanalysis.[32] This is why he did not see how the study of lower animals could hold any promise for the insights of psychoanalysis.[33] As for anatomical structures, Freud had done several dissections of the medulla oblongata (a part of the brain) while working in Brücke's laboratory. Even so, he had to admit, "I know nothing could be of less interest to me for the psychological understanding of anxiety than a knowledge of the path of the nerves along which its excitations pass." [34]

Freud recognized through his constructs of the "actual neuroses" as well as through obvious factors like brain damage and toxic infection that some types of mental illness—maybe as many as 50 percent—can be seen as biological in origin.[35] But what he objected to was the insistence by so many of his colleagues that this is *all* that there is to

Figure 18 The Pyramid of Life in Organic Evolution

mental illness. In a 1908 letter to Jung, he complained about these colleagues as follows:

I believe that if they were analysed it would turn out that they are still waiting for the discovery of the bacillus or protozoon of hysteria as for the messiah who must after all come some day to all true believers. When that happens a differential diagnosis from Dem. pr. [dementia praecox, that is, schizophrenia] ought to be a simple matter, since the hysteria parasite will no doubt have only one stiff whiplike appendage, while that of Dem. pr. will regularly show two and also take a different stain. Then we shall be able to leave psychology to the poets! [36]

Another reason why psychoanalytic theories probably receive so many biological interpretations is the use they all make of Darwinian themes. Freud's origin-of-society speculations were Darwinian-Lamarckian in style. Adler was very dependent on organic evolution in his later writings. And Jung's collective psyche was biologically based, even though he was thinking more historically than organically in his "racial" theories. As Figure 18 demonstrates, the Darwinian theory of evolution is almost a direct translation of the Lockean model (see Figure 1 on p. 16 of the Introduction for a schematization of the Lockean model). At the lowest levels of life in Figure 18, we have the one-celled animals. Above these amoebalike creatures, we have in ascending order the sea urchins, fishes, amphibia, land-crawling, and then flying creatures. We next move up to mammals and the higher apes until at the apex of our triangular hierarchy (the 5s of Figure 1) we find the highest, most complex anthropoid, a human being. To round out the picture, we should also include all of the extinct forms of life (such as the dinosaurs) as well as the presumed links between humans and apes (such as the Neanderthal man). But in broad outline, the course of evolution follows a Lockean constitutive theme of from simple to complex assemblages of material structures. There is also the suggestion of a linking genetic tie between earlier and later organisms, so that ontogeny is said always to recapitulate phylogeny (see p. 65 of Chapter 1).

Though the analysts did indeed make use of the hierarchical ordering of Figure 18 in their borrowings from Darwin, we should never forget that they significantly *altered* the way in which traditional biological science had interpreted organic evolution. This goes for Darwin himself! Adler essentially saw in the pyramid of life (Figure 18) a teleological direction taken by the organisms who evolved into higher levels only because they individually *willed* themselves to do so. This telic direction of intentional striving is literally "written in the form" of the animals considered higher and higher in evolution. As Adler put it:

One must assume . . . that organic evolution has led to developments which we must

regard as the differentiation of originally present potentialities of the cell. Thus a nutritive organ has followed the will and need of assimilation; touch, auditory, and visual organs have followed the will and necessity to feel, hear, and see; a procreative [sexual] organ followed the will and necessity for progeny [offspring].[37]

Harking back to our discussion of change above, evolutionary changes are qualitative, in that we intend some plan (patterned meaning) and *then* locomote to attain it. We have as human beings hands of a certain shape because in the past we manipulated our appendages to achieve certain ends. Our plans are like formal-cause *antecedents* (qualitative changers) of our behavior, and the resultant shape our hands take on after we work (locomote!) at this plan are like formal-cause *consequents*.

This is hardly standard "biological" theory. As we noted in Chapter 2 (p. 118), Darwin's construct of natural selection was designed in order to get away from such telic description. Darwin would say that insofar as we can see an increasing complexity in the evolution of organisms in Figure 18 this is purely "survival of the fittest"—an unintended benefit of blind luck. And although Jung talked a good deal about racial inheritances from evolutionary (historical) pasts, we must always remember that for him heredity was not only organic, but also psychic. Jung was thus unwilling to confound psychological with organic explanations of behavior; he once summarized this aspect of his outlook as follows: ". . . anyone who penetrates into the unconscious with purely biological assumptions will become stuck in the instinctual sphere and be unable to advance beyond it, for he will be pulled back again and again into physical existence." [38]

We see the psychoanalysts here mixing into the completely extraspective, realistic theory of evolution depicted in Figure 18 a significant amount of introspective, idealistic commentary. They were willing to say that behavior is determined not only by what is put into the body by heredity or infectious invasions, but also by how this biological-physiological structure meets and orders that which is called reality. The analysts did not only look *at* the course of organic evolution. They put themselves into the scheme. They stood at the apex of Figure 18 as a human person and looked out onto experience, which shifted their theoretical perspective to that of conceptualization (Kantian model) rather than constitution (Lockean model). What was that man at the top of Figure 18 thinking about? How did he come at life no matter what his body was made up of or what kind of germs may have infected his mechanism? We cannot dismiss heredity or the infections of microorganisms, but then we cannot dismiss the psychological side of life either.

As indicated, this shift in perspective brought the analysts more into a Kantian frame of reference—not completely, but enough so that we can call them *mixed-model theorists*. As Freud said:

Just as Kant warned us not to overlook the fact that our perceptions are subjectively conditioned and must not be regarded as identical with what is perceived though unknowable [that is, we never know things-in-themselves] so psycho-analysis warns us not to equate perceptions by means of consciousness with the unconscious mental processes which are their object. Like the physical, the psychical is not necessarily in reality what it appears to us to be. [39]

Adler's Kantian influence came through Vaihinger, and he was fully aware of the fact that in his model of mind the prototype acts much as the spectacles of the Kantian model (see Figure 2 in the Introduction, p. 18). [40] Jung was clearly the most Kantian of the founding fathers, and it would be correct to think of him as a bridge theorist to the phenomenologists of Chapters 9, 10, and 11. [41] Jung much preferred Kant's views on the mind as a pro forma influence *from birth* to the Lockean contention that we are born tabula rasa. [42]

This is the *core difference* between *Kantian* and *Lockean interpretations of mind*. Can the person from the very beginnings of knowledge—whether we call this at the point of birth, before birth, or some time after birth—*do something* about how that knowledge will be ordered, patterned, put to meaningful organization? The Lockean model says no and the Kantian model says yes. If order is meaning and meanings make up knowledge, then assuming that a human being has the biological capacity to lend experience order in some way, he or she would not simply behave on the *effect* side of material and efficient causality. The individual would be a *cause* of behavior, or to use the more technical term, an *agent*. Agency means that there is an identity factor (ego, self, I) in the creation of behavior, there is a point of view, a capacity to determine behavior psychically as well as physically. All three of the analysts believed in agency as a psychic capacity based on human biology. The human body has somehow evolved this capacity to transcend itself and through such psychic activity interpret what it wants to behave "for the sake of" in addition to or even in opposition to what the palpable (real, existing) facts are.

This Kantian theme does not seem overly extreme to us today, but the problem faced by the analysts was that the physical sciences in which they were educated lacked theoretical terminology to subsume theory conceptions. As Freud bitterly joked in the letter to Jung (see above), only poets (that is, artists) seemed to have an interest in and a language of psychological description. The physical sciences had for almost three hundred years been specifically trying to avoid describing things in a mental or anthropomorphic fashion. Freud was very aware of the fact that his analogies to physical description were just that, unneeded parallels that someday would hopefully tie into an organic substructure. As late as 1914 he could say, "I should like at this point expressly to admit that . . . the libido theory . . . rests scarcely at all upon a psychological basis, but derives its principal support from biology." [43] Jung complained that the reductive explanations of physical science overlook the fact that human knowledge is always influenced by an a priori point of view, similar to the spectacles of the Kantian model.[44] Though physical scientists make these predicating assumptions, they act as if the person whom they observe does not have the same ability. Adler addressed the same point when he said, "The study of instincts or urges [biological explanation] will never enable us to understand the structure of an individual psyche: and it is interesting to note that psychologists who endeavour to explain the mind's working from such observations instinctively presuppose a style of life [psychological explanation] without noticing that they have done so." [45]

Returning to the question of this section, we might now reframe it as follows: what are the descriptive terms necessary to solve the mind-body question? The analysts seemed to have doubted that traditional biological explanations of the medical model would really solve the problem. When we analyze this issue in theory-construction terms, we see that they were aware of the difference in meaning between formal-final causation on the one hand and material-efficient causation on the other. They could sense that a psychic event occurs more by qualitative motion than locomotion, and a person's reasoning power is due more to choosing the right issues to predicate and logically reason through than it is to the thrust of a physical energy being expended in the brain. Physical energy is important to the life of the body, but there has to be more than this to mentation. And so, having no real traditions of theoretical description from which to draw, the analysts did the best they could to frame their personality theories in a mixed, Lockean-Kantian way. Freud and Jung could shift back and forth between (1) the more properly "scientific" Lockeanism when they were delivering technical lectures to colleagues, and (2) a Kantianism when they spoke more popularly about the person. Adler was least moved of the three men to meet the needs of conventional science; he did, however, achieve an emphasis on Lockeanism in his later writings in which he raised organic evolution to such a central position.

So the answer to the question posed by this section is that a solution of the mind-body problem hinges on what sorts of theoretical constructs we will permit a theoretician to employ. If it is possible for a physical substance to behave in ways other than *just* material and efficient causation can describe, then we may be able to work out a satisfactory description. But if we are limited to language that cannot capture the common sense meaning of mentality, then no solution will be possible. This takes us to our next question.

According to Psychoanalysis, How Does Mind "Work"?

Critics of psychoanalysis often say that it relies on a *homunculus* view of mind—that is, it must assume that a "little person" exists within the psychic apparatus to direct the mental machinery much as we sit in and drive our automobiles around. Freud is said to have broken the personality down into three such little people in the id, ego, and superego conceptions. Jung has three or four constructs like this in the ego, shadow, persona, and self. Adler's prototype acts like a homunculus. There are two points that must be made concerning this criticism. First, it makes sense only if we consider mentation to be an *unintelligent* process. Intelligence suggests a process that is selective, evaluative, and directing in nature. We say "Roger is an intelligent person. Every time he faces a problem he seems to figure out what is involved and clears it up." Now, if by speaking about egos and alter egos a theorist must therefore be placing little people inside the mental machinery, then mind cannot be capable *in its essence* of making decisions or choosing intelligently. Roger's own mind cannot be in command of his behavior. In fact, the homunculus itself is considered as lacking in intelligence because it too is usually said to be run by an even smaller homunculus, and so on, ad infinitum. The second point regarding this criticism—which is actually another way of referring to the first—is that it pictures mind from an *extraspective* perspective. The homunculus is described introspectively, but the mind is thought of in third-person terms, as "that machinery over there" into which the homunculus gets in order to direct "it." The homunculus therefore has *identity* whereas

mind does not. Identity is "continuity in thought" which results in a consistent "point of view" regarding the world; it is impossible to capture identity in anything but an introspective description.

When we combine the idea of intelligence with identity, we arrive at what most philosophers mean by *agency,* a term we used above (p. 282). That is, a person is an agent when he or she can truly affect what takes place in behavior. To be an agent of our behavior, we must be able to behave according to formal-cause plans that *we* create or assumptions that *we* make, and then behave "for their sake." Our friend Roger impresses us with his intelligence because he seems to be in command of most situations, or at least he is in command of that part of the situation he can actually influence. He does not necessarily know more than we do, but he makes wise use of the information he possesses. He *acts* when we are *reacting,* he thinks ahead and gets things going, whereas we are always at the mercy of events as they come at us. He puts his finger on the right issues, whereas we tend to go off half-cocked and end up wasting much of our time.

Roger is clearly intelligent, but do we really know him? If we studied him closer, we might find that there are two (or more?) Rogers. There are times when he is quite disoriented and sloppy in his behavior. He does not keep his room in order, for example, so that he tends to misplace things. He seems unable to keep his checkbook in balance. He is an amateur artist, and when he gets off to paint a landscape he seems a completely different person, quite spontaneous and "arty." Well, maybe he is not so different here after all, because he always has a "point of view" concerning his art work. He knows when his painting is achieving the effect intended and when it is not. This ability to judge is not always a plus for Roger, because at times he suffers from a feeling of guilt for not doing better in something. He is often hard on himself, so that occasionally, in reaction to this sense of responsibility and high standards, he has an urge to chuck it all and drift easily with the stream of life. But then, he gets this inner feeling or whatever it is, deep down, to straighten up and meet the standards he knows really ought to be maintained.

This mildly conflict-laden, intellectual yet aesthetically sensitive young man epitomizes what the psychoanalysts thought mental activity is all about. Roger is an agent because he is—to some extent—an *originating source* of his own (psychic) determination. He is purposive, and even crosspurposive (conflicted) because he always sees more than one possible end toward which his life could be intended. Sometimes he sees too many possibilities for his own good. In fact, there may be ends toward which he is directed of which he is totally unaware. The multiplicity of such intended ends in mind is theoretically unsettling only if we presume that meanings can be framed from but *one* identity point. The analysts never limited the framing of ideas from just one identity point in mind. This is why they all accepted the concept of an unconscious, and even within the different realms of consciousness or unconsciousness, they were prepared to see more than one "point of view" expressing itself. Different viewpoints can generate different purposes, as Freud recognized in his psychoanalytical work. "We seek not merely to describe and to classify phenomena, but to understand them as signs of an interplay of forces in the mind, as a manifestation of purposeful intentions working concurrently or in mutual opposition. We are concerned with a *dynamic view* of mental phenomena." [46]

This is an excellent example of Freud mixing together words like *force,* which conveys to the mechanist a material-efficient cause meaning like locomotion, and *purposeful intention,* which conveys to the teleologist a formal-final cause meaning of qualitative change. Which meaning does Freud consider to be essential to a conception of mind? We have argued that he like Adler and Jung put the *telic* conception first. This does not mean that various forces cannot *also* be operating in mental activity. Brain cells might be working according to physiological processes in which a physical energy impels events along, just as in any part of the body, energy is metabolized through blood sugars measured in caloric units, and so on. Such locomotions can be going on, right down to the substrate atoms with their electrons going round the nucleus in efficient-cause fashion. But there is nothing to keep us from *also* postulating the force or weight of a logical argument, as when we say to a fellow discussant, "You made your point" ("Your meaning has had its impact on me"). In this case we are dealing in formal-final causation and qualitative changes in viewpoint. Freud could have been using the word *force* in either the strictly physical (body) sense or the more logical (mind) sense. He also could have been using it in *both* ways. We can employ all four of the causal meanings in any theory of behavior.

This general discussion of causality in relation to mind-body issues provides us with a springboard into three different but related topics of relevance to the question posed by this section. Though we will find our psychoanalysts disagreeing on the precise usage or emphasis to be given to each of these issues, we will see a definite unity in presentation, which distinguishes this school of thought from traditional medical-biological explanations of the mind.

Dialectical Alternatives

The first challenge that any theory of agency must meet is: *how does choice arise in behavior?* After all, if behavior is nothing more than a unidirectional, one-way locomotion from A-to-B in the sense of Jung's causal-mechanistic series (see Figure 13 in Chapter 3, p. 204), there would be no ·need for an *identity* to select from among alternatives. A would happen and then B would necessarily happen (physical determinism). If we are being pushed through life by antecedent instincts and physical energies that have been transmitted to us hereditarily, then to believe in agency would be an illusion. Add in influences by infection as through illness and we have here the general position of the medical models the analysts confronted at the turn of this century. How could they possibly see the individual as an agent of his or her behavior if all this behavior ever amounted to was a material- and efficient-cause succession of (extraspectively conceived) physical forces?

The way in which psychoanalysis solved the problem of agency was to fall back on *dialectical* theoretical constructions of behavior. The Lockean medical models were exclusively demonstrative in conceptions, but we find in all three of our founding theories a heavy emphasis on the antithetic, the contradictory, and the compensatory. This does not mean that all of the analysts considered themselves dialecticians. As we shall see below, two of them definitely objected to this label. But there can be no doubt that basic to their view of mind was a recognition that certain meanings are bipolar, that whenever something is stated or thought of, there is either a directly implied reversal of this meaning or at least an expectation established

in the person's mind of "so what?" or "what next?" or "what does that get at?"

For example, if Edith says to Sylvia, "I saw John last night," the effect of this communication on Sylvia is to have her respond with "Oh, where?" while possibly saying to herself, "Why is she bringing him up?" If Edith now says, "He talked with me for a time, at the train station," Sylvia is clued to ask "What did you talk about?" There is a necessary style in all such communications, with a speaker expressing an observation, belief, recollection, and so on, and a listener with the option of furthering the meaning being expressed or not. The *flow of meaning* is not unidirectional, but rather oppositional, by way of a *thesis* (I say) and an *antithesis* (you say). The content of the conversation between Edith and Sylvia has not been oppositional or contradictory. We see merely the opposite sides of a dialectical exchange here in the opposing persons, with the exchange of meanings left somewhat open. That is, Sylvia could have ignored Edith's opening statement altogether, saying "That's nice" to Edith while thinking to herself, "She wants me to ask about John again. Well, she can just 'forget it'!" In this case, Sylvia would have dialectically contradicted what Edith had indicated that she wanted to talk about. Another, more obvious contradiction would have arisen if Edith had said, "I saw that tremendously handsome John last night at the train station," and Sylvia had countered with "I fail to see why you find him so attractive."

The dialectical insight here is that nothing with meaning is entirely alone in the broader world of meaningful relations. Every meaning reaches out in some way to connect with the interlacing ties of other meanings. This many-in-one thesis is basic to any dialectical argument (see p. 8 of Introduction). If someone comes up to us and says "peanut," we simply cannot avoid asking ourselves or this person what this word could be driving at (its intention). We can, of course, ignore the person and say nothing in return, but could we completely ignore our fleeting sense of curiosity as to what is taking place? If this person had walked up and made a peculiar sign with his or her hands, waving them over our head in some way, we would have a similar reaction of "what is that all about?" Now, once we have caught onto the meaning being conveyed, we have the opportunity to accept it and possibly further it or to negate it by discoursing with the person facing us.

If "peanut" was a reference to the size of our brain, and therefore a slur on our intelligence, we might enter into a heated debate with this person in which we would contend the dialectical opposite to this intended meaning-communication. Whether we ignore the person or enter into a debate, the dialectical nature of our relationship is obvious. Finally, what if when the person had first said "peanut" there was no intention to relate this to our level of intelligence? What if this was merely a joke, a silly statement with no aim? Well, in this case we may or may not have found the interlude amusing. But the point is, we would through examinations of the type already mentioned try to set this communication into a context of understanding. And the dialectical nature of our examination would be obvious.

Suppose we had dreamed the word *peanut*, or it had just popped into our minds by itself. Would our reaction be anything like the case of having someone else use this word in relation to us? Probably so. We "talk" to ourselves because meanings that arise in our minds have this same tendency to imply a direction, a furtherance of what is intended, or a stopping, so that we can agree with the intention or contradict (dismiss, reject) it. No meaning just "sits" there in mind. In fact, even as we frame a meaning we are always at least dimly aware that the *reverse* intention of that which we say is capable of being expressed. Mother says to daughter, "Want to go to the movies?" and daughter says with a smile, "No." Mother knows that daughter wants to go and that the "no" is really an emphatic "yes." Father asks son, "Can you bring those grades up next semester?" and son says, "Yes," knowing full well that the answer could just as readily be "No." Father knows that son is worried and that he may be unable to pull up the grades, but the "yes" answer at least implies that an effort will be made. Both daughter and son know from their private (introspective) perspective—from inside their own skulls—that they are saying what they are not exactly intending, but that their messages got across to their parents who accepted them for what they really meant.

It is the *negative* duality of intentions that Freud relied on to begin his speculations on the nature of mental illness. His *very first* theoretical paper relied on the *antithetic ideas* and *counterwill* constructs (see p. 81 of Chapter 1). We should not conclude from this usage that Freud assigned this duality *only* to abnormal states. Actually, what he did here was to propose a new way of looking at the workings of the mind—yes, even of the brain-cell tissues which provide the underlying physiological basis of thought. Rather than *unidirectional* processes, brain actions were being construed by Freud as *bidirectional*. We see this in a physical way in Freud's reflex-arc model schematized in Figure 3 of Chapter 1 (see p. 45). Recall that he had nervous excitations locomoting in *both* a progressive and a regressive fashion. The antithetic-ideas construct captures this duality or reversal more psychologically. Freud asks: what if the locomotion of physiological processes "depends" on which of two contradictory directions in meaning an individual "accepts" as being intended?

When the young man speaking to his father says, "Yes, I will pull up my grades," he necessarily knows that he is *not* saying, "No, I cannot pull up my grades." He has to convey one or the other of these answers to the father's question. These are his major choices, though there are other choices as well (he could simply say, "I don't know if I can pull up my grades"). The counterwill operates to bring about the negative outcome in Freud's early theory, but in life we could just as easily think of examples in which it might operate to bring about a positive outcome. The weak-willed, unconfident person who has always said to others, "Yes, you are right," knowing full well that the opposite judgment was sometimes the greater truth, one day stands up to say, "No, you are quite wrong in what you say." This would be just as much a counterwill phenomenon as the unhealthy example that Freud focused on. His theory of mind implies both alternatives, and Jung was later to develop this same position in his suggestion that each time we affirm one side of an opposition, we generate a teleological force of intentionality. This psychic energy, this thrust of life is *not* like the push of physical energies. Rather, it is based on the weight of logic—both demonstrative and dialectical forms of logic. We affirm one side, and its reverse intention splits off to live as a potential alternative in another region of the mind (shadow).

The demonstrative medical models had placed all of the patterning of meaningfulness *outside* of mental processes per se. They held that we are given through heredity certain patterns of behavior called instincts, and then as we go through life, these instinctive patterns are altered through learning, thanks to physiological processes in our brains, or they are made abnormal by chemical reactions, senility, infectious germs, and so on. Meanings that we have in mind are not *themselves* open to alternatives, to changing patterns devised by the person, simply because meanings are constituted of *singular* (unipolar) "building blocks" (underlying material and efficient causes organized according to the Lockean model). Bipolarity is not intrinsic to meaning on the medical model. Rather bipolarity results when one unipolar meaning just happens to negate another unipolar meaning. We call this relationship *opposition,* but this does not imply anything intrinsic about the relationship between the two unipolarities. They are different points (poles) brought into a relationship and no more.

Freud and Jung now come along to suggest that some patterns arise as dualities right from the outset of mental understanding, as if two sides of the same coin. In 1910, some fifteen years after his paper on antithetic ideas was published, Freud returned to this topic in a work entitled "The Antithetical Meaning of Primal Words."[47] The text was based on the work of the philologist Karl Abel, which delighted Freud, for Abel's evidence suggested that in the earliest known examples of human language, such as Egyptian, "there are a fair number of words with two meanings, one of which is the exact opposite of the other."[48] Abel contended that the human being's earliest mental concepts emerged as a kind of undifferentiated total (one among many) which united many opposites, and only by guessing from the context could one person understand what another person was intending to communicate. The same word might signify *stay* or *flee,* and depending on inflection or the total circumstances, a speaker and a listener would get their often *opposite* meanings across using the *same* word. Freud wanted such justifications for a concept of "primitive" mentation because he was finding dual patterns of thought in the id, which he always took to be an archaic region of mind, a remnant of our ancient past in organic evolution. Thus he observed that "the logical laws of thought do not apply in the id, and this is true above all of the law of contradiction."[49] Recall that the law of contradiction is fundamental to demonstrative reasoning (see p. 8 of Introduction). In the id we always want to eat our cake and have it too.

Now, if words as meaningful organizations arise as dualities and even multiplicities, then possibly all meanings have this quality. Maybe awareness is not simply being aware of *a* single item in experience, but rather being aware that there are *alternatives* in experience. Perhaps as the antithetic-ideas theory suggests, to *know* requires from the outset a decision as to *what* to know or what to pursue further in a situation that does not leave any *one, single, clear* implication about it—anymore than *peanut* has one, clear implication about it when stated in our presence. What if the swirling motions of the subatomic particles in the brain cells define bipolarities as well as unipolarities in meaning, and it is up to the person as an identity to *opt* or *choose* or *decide* which of a series of alternatives should be enacted? A primitive man looked over a battlefield, saw enemies charging him menacingly, and in the situation knew that he would either stand or flee. One word captured the battle alternatives, and he voiced it to friends as he *also* chose to further one or the other of these possibilities. The locomotions of the subatomic particles of his brain may have been repatterned in this decision-making process, but the source of change—the real cause—was from the "decided upon" pattern *to* locomotion exactly as in our discussion of qualitative change (see above).

Although in modern times humanity has more words by which to express distinctive meanings, the duality of discourse remains the same. As one person is talking, expressing the meaning of A, another person is at *that very moment* framing the meanings of not-A, particularly if these two people are in disagreement over something. Even a friendly discussion can take on this dialectical quality. Bill says to Ed, "You know, I really get sick of this daily routine in school, study and take a test, study and take another test. It gets me down." Ed has the option of going along with the thrust of these comments even as he also knows that he could say something like, "Yeah, you're right, but I guess someday it'll all add up to something." In other words, as he frames the understanding of what Bill is communicating, Ed is *also* framing the position that Bill is *not* communicating. Even when he greatly agrees with Bill and responds, "Man, you are right, it is a big bore," Ed is fully aware of the more hopeful and encouraging stance he *could* be taking. Antithetical ideas are not limited to mental reasonings of the abnormal. Antithetical ideas are basic to all of our thoughts.

In this way agency becomes possible. For if oppositional meanings indicate "reverse directions" in the conversation, or if oppositional meanings occur to a person privately in thought, the individual has the option to reverse the course of meaning extension. Phyllis gets up in the morning and says to herself, "This is the day I begin my morning exercises. Ten push-ups every morning." Implied immediately is "I don't want to do these exercises. They really 'hurt' to do." As she reasons along, Phyllis may end up on the floor doing her push-ups or avoid them altogether for some flimsy excuse; or she might arrive at some kind of alternative of a less demanding nature. She might begin her daily exercise program with mild stretching exercises. Thinking as psychoanalysts, we could readily believe that Phyllis has compromised and created an alternative, thanks to her dialectical reasoning processes of thesis (push-ups), antithesis (nothing), and synthesis (stretching). The main point of this insight is that alternatives in behavior always evolve from the poles of opposition (opposite meanings). The person is never trapped between just the thesis *and* the antithesis. There is a range of things that can be done between these opposite poles, and this range results in the synthesis. Furthermore, the person can always think of an opposite to the opposite, or an opposite dimension of contrast to the initial dimension altogether. If Phyllis's goal is weight loss, she might reconsider exercising in favor of fasting (no eating for several days) or using steam baths, and so on.

What is the biological mechanism through which the physical brain cells perform this kind of dual thinking? Here is where psychoanalysis did not pretend knowledge. Freud learned in his efforts to write the *Project* that he could not limit himself to the material- and efficient-cause meanings that physical constructs demand. He had to devise his own style of explanation, free of these restrictions. Even so, he was willing to admit that "our provisional ideas in psychology will presumably some day be based on an organic substructure."[50] This did not mean we could reduce these ideas to the substructure, of course. In any case, he believed that psychoanalysis had its own job to do, and tying psychoanalysis to physical explanation could not really benefit either side. For psychoanalysis to be supported biologically would require that a medical scientist, working in human brain research, propose and prove that a dialectical process operates in the brain.

How might this take place? Well, we might begin here with Kant's concept of the *transcendental dialectic* (see p. 13 of the Introduction) as our model. If it is possible for brain activity (that is, locomotions of subatomic particles, and so on) to pattern a bipolar meaning, and if other cells in the brain have the capacity to dialectically transcend—know what meanings are under process in mind and their reverse implications—then possibly a biological process could require a contribution from the pure ordering of the direction thought will take. This pure ordering could be like the Jungian patterning of synchronicity or the rearrangements of Bohr's electrons within the atom. The central question here seems to be: can the brain transcend its unidirectional (demonstrative) processing of meanings by cognizing alternatives via (dialectical) opposites? There are growing indications in the research literature on the brain that the answer to this question may be yes.[51] Recall from the Introduction (p. 20) that this capacity for mind to turn back on itself and to know that it is in process and therefore open to alternative directions is called *self-reflexivity* or simply *reflexivity*. Human beings have reflexive minds because they know that they reason, they understand that they have a way of knowing; we might say that they "know that they know." And if an intelligence knows that it knows, then it also knows that it *could be* "knowing otherwise."

This is why there are multiple identities in Freudian and Jungian psychology. Psychoanalysis accepts the fact that there can be more than one point of view in mind. There are a number of different points of view that Phyllis takes concerning the benefits of exercise. Following Jung in oversimplified fashion for the sake of demonstration, we can think of Phyllis the persona, who is very interested in the modern vogue to keep trim and look good. Then there is Phyllis the ego, who has finally decided to get down to something concrete about managing her long-standing weight problem. Finally, we have Phyllis the shadow, who finds the whole business absurd. What is so important about physical appearance anyway? How many people kill themselves exercising every year? Surely there is a more sensible way to do things. We could have the same kind of multiple exchange in Freudian theory between id, ego, and superego. Freud and Jung do not populate their conceptions of the psyche with homunculi. They simply accept the fact that we all have the ability to take more than one position on the same life experience, thanks to our dialectical reasoning capacities. This means we are constantly making decisions with our minds. In time, it is even possible to identify consistent mental attitudes. And when we give these identifiable viewpoints names (id, ego, and so on), we have what the critics call homunculi running the mind. Actually, the psychoanalysts have devised a system of terms to describe how the mind runs *itself* through the diversity generated by dialectic.

It would be nice if we could now say that the analysts fully appreciated their dialectical approach to the description of mind. Unfortunately, only Jung did so. Freud understood *dialectic* to mean *sophistry,* or manipulative, insincere argumentation. He makes this attitude clear in the following: "I have never been able to convince myself of the truth of the maxim that strife is the father of all things. I believe it is derived from the Greek sophists and is at fault, like them, through overvaluing dialectics." [52] This does not deny that dialectical exchanges take place in life, but it does suggest that Freud did not appreciate the necessity of conflict and contradiction in events. These are strange words

from a man who fought the resistance of the censor, broke with many of his former colleagues, said of himself that he always needed an enemy to oppose as well as a close friend in whom to confide, stood against a generation of his fellow scientists confident in the belief that they were too threatened or constricted by their own sexual repressions to look objectively at the truth, and who spent the larger part of his life in dialectical exchanges, with patients, with students, and with the readers of his books.

Only Freud, the man who could give the simplest acts an oppositional twist to set one's head spinning, could also in 1937 dismiss the dialectic with a cool sentence in a letter to R. L. Worall concerning Marxian theory. "As to the 'dialectic', I am no clearer, even after your letter." [53] Since Freud viewed dialectical analysis as sophistry, could it be that he did not wish to find the obvious parallels between his method and this style of proving what one wants to prove by clever manipulation of the words people use to express themselves? We shall never know, but we *can* at least take the position that Freud was a dialectician of major proportions in the history of thought. [54]

Adler was equally distrustful of dialectical theoretical usages, and after he left the Freudian camp, he positively opposed any explanation that seemed to split up what he called the holistic nature of the psyche. In one sense, this rejection of the dialectic is all the more remarkable for Adler than it was for Freud, because the founder of individual psychology was admittedly influenced by neo-Marxists. For this and other reasons, there are those who would dispute our present claim that Adler was unfriendly to the dialectic. [55] It is not unusual to find Marxian phrasings in Adler's early papers, as in the 1913 reference to "inner contradictions." [56] Adler frankly acknowledged parallels between his assessment of society and the writings of Marx and Engels,[57] though as we saw in Chapter 2, he rejected communism as a totalitarian, unsuitable philosophy for the advance of society.

The early Adlerian constructs of a neurotic's reversal tendencies[58] or attraction to antithetic formulations[59] are clearly in the vein of dialectical theorizing—reminding us somewhat of Freud's antithetic-ideas paper. The basic meaning of compensation—as a reaction to felt inferiority—is also dialectical in tone. Adler seems to have been aware of this dialectical approach in his theories of compensation[60] as well as psychic hermaphroditism.[61] While presenting the latter theory in 1911, Adler reasoned aloud for the compensating male, "The thought, 'I wish to become a man,' is only made tenable and only becomes bearable when joined to the contrasting thought:—'I might also become a woman' or 'I do not wish to become a woman.'" [62] Adler's subsequent theories of male versus female protest can thus be viewed as stemming from this dialectical theme of a contradiction between opposites. However, as time went on Adler found that dialectical theories were unfruitful and even harmful.

*It is well known that it is difficult to rid ourselves of this manner of thinking; for instance, to regard hot and cold as opposites when we know scientifically that the only difference is a difference in degree of temperature. Not only do we find this antithetic scheme of apperception very frequently among children but we also find it in the beginnings of philosophical science. The early days of Greek philosophy are domi-*nated by this idea of opposites. Even to-day almost every amateur philosopher tries to measure values by means of opposites. Some of them have even established tables—life-death, above-below, and finally, man-woman. There is a significant similarity between the present childish and the old philosophic scheme of apperception [mentation], and we may assume that those people who are accustomed to divide the world into sharp contrasts have retained their childish way of thinking.*[63]

Dialectic led to error and hence was an unacceptable intellectual strategy, one which hopefully would be evolved out of existence in favor of a more straightforward, honest style of thought which did not require guile or trickery to twist reality into a selfish viewpoint. In the late 1920s Adler observed, "Individuals who do not regard their life's structure from a logical and objective point of view are for the most part unable to see the coherence and consistency of their behavior pattern." [64] This is a decided alteration in outlook for a man who had begun by championing the *subjective* reality of each individual. As he located his extra- or supra-individual standard for reality in the teleological direction of evolution, Adler found it increasingly easy to pass judgment on the supposed errors—dialectically arrived at, to be sure—of the individual human being.

Adler at no point in his theorizing denied that people *do*—after all—reason dialectically. Reminding us of Jung he said of his outlook:

Dialectics in the sense of thesis, antithesis, and synthesis is, of course, found in our view as in the other social sciences. It becomes apparent most often when we are dealing with persons who expect to be spoiled by others (thesis). When they do not receive such treatment, they fall into hate and resentment (antithesis), until they find their way through to contribution, to general humaneness (synthesis).[65]

Clearly, Adler was sensitive to the dialectical aspects of human behavior. He like the other founding fathers saw this convoluted style of reasoning in his clients, who invariably lived out a life of lies. But he also did not seem to believe that it is a human being's natural state to be caught up in internal contradictions and devious maneuvers like this. We only find contradiction when the individual is selfishly trying to maintain a life style in opposition to what he or she either knows or *can* know is the proper (realistic) way in which to strive (that is, via social interest).

This selfishness was first brought to attention by humanity's religions, and psychology would do well to reject it rather than to further it by acting as dialectical apologist for those who set themselves in opposition to the evolution of social interest.

. . . the "contradictory character" of man, as the deepest of Christian insights, first becomes evident, in our view, when the erring individual, on the road to initial improvement of his social interest, no longer can defend his error as strongly as before. The apparent contradiction in the neurotic does not lead to change in the neurotic attitude. As long as there is a contradiction, only one thing is certain: no change will set in.[66]

The seeming contradictory nature of the neurotic is merely an artifact of growing social interest, which at one point makes the neurotic person seem doubt-laden. But to misconstrue this condition and somehow reify such inner turbulence as a reflection of basic human nature is to confound the truth completely. This distaste for dialectical themes merges nicely with Adler's growing Lockeanism in his final theories. He clearly saw the course of evolution as unidirectional, pointing to the demonstrably "true" direction, and he was not about to provide rationalizations for those who would deviate in the name of their supposedly self-contradictory natures. Individual psychology is thus less dynamic in its formulations than psychoanalysis or analytical psychology.

Jung was without doubt the most conscious, thorough, and outspoken dialectician of the founding fathers. He was philosophically the most well-read and sophisticated scholar of the group, who liked to say, "I see in all that happens the play of opposites. . . ."[67] There is no premise that mind takes on that cannot also be countered with an opposite position. By affirming one point of view we *must* create its obverse, as an equally plausible alternative.[68] This is undoubtedly the nature of a human being's conceptualizing ability. "We name a thing, *from a certain point of view,* good or bad, high or low, right or left, light or dark, and so forth. Here the antithesis is just as factual and real as the thesis."[69] Note how well this quote meshes with our discussion of the multiplicity in identities within the Jungian conception of mind (refer above). Jung's commitment to the dialectic was great indeed. He even went so far as to say, "It is my belief that the problem of opposites . . . should be made the basis for a critical psychology."[70]

Will and Free Will

We can now appreciate that agency arises due to the dialectical alternatives that are always facing the individual in ongoing behavior. It is pointless to speak of purposes, intentions, or goals unless the individual *selects* these personally and then behaves for their sake *or not*—that is, behaves for the sake of *other* (dialectically generated) alternatives. The popular term for this capacity is *free will*. Even though we all use this phrase, as when we refer to doing things "against our will" or "freely deciding" to do what we want to do, few of us can describe how free will comes about. It has been said that even major religions, which routinely teach their congregations that human beings have free wills, fail to say how this ability is supposed to work.[71] Free will has been identified with religion for centuries, and it is another way of referring to *teleology*. But it is not exactly correct to say that religions, which are based on deity teleologies, always work to promote free-will decisions for individuals in the sense of a human teleology.

Many psychologists believe incorrectly that if a theorist argues for freedom of the will in behavior, this must necessarily be a pro-religion argument. A toughminded psychologist can be heard to say: "If we let 'free will' get back into the description of behavior we will have to let 'God' back in too. And, then 'there goes our science!'" This psychologist would be surprised to learn that many if not *most* religions argue against reliance on a personal free will in favor of giving one's self-direction over to (a presumed) God. If we survey the history of Western religion, we find major figures, such as St. Paul, St. Augustine, St. Thomas Aquinas, Luther, and Calvin, arguing *against* free will in favor of divine direction and assistance from God called *grace*.[72] It is when the Christian *freely* gives himself or herself to the deity (Jesus, God, and so on) and thereafter submits to direction by the deity that the benefits of religion take place.

In brief, the devout, "saved," "born-again" Christian has used personal free will (human teleology) to submit to divine direction (deity teleology) and from that point forward no longer relies on his or her free will to make *moral* decisions as a person. Other of life's decisions would presumably be made based on something akin to a free will, of course. Returning to our discussion above of divine plans and game plans (see p. 277), a Christian who accepts God (Jesus, and so on) as a personal savior conforms to the deity's plan as recorded in religious writings, such as the Bible. Such a person becomes like one of those sketched-in figures on a coach's strategy board—behaving *exactly* as God intended (we are speaking now of an ideal case, for the sake of presentation). The devout person never presumes to put himself or herself above the deity by opting for alternatives freely, but says always, "Thy will be done." Of course, it is possible to *reject* the deity, to refuse to submit to divine ordinance, and opt instead to "disobey" the divine plan. This too would be a form of dialectical negation by the person through exercise of free will.

Those psychologists who say that acceptance of a free-will construct will let religion return to psychology by the back door are definitely wrong. A human teleology could even be antireligious. Nietzsche, the philosopher who was called by some an antichrist and who said, "God is dead," was in his view of humanity a teleologist. Indeed, in earlier centuries it was common for humanistic philosophies that viewed people as the prime agent in their behavior to be called antireligious beliefs, because they seemed to be putting man above God. Obviously, psychologists must leave questions of *divine agency* to theology, but there is no reason why we cannot offer—indeed, must offer—a purely psychological explanation of *human agency*. The psychoanalysts did not set out to do so, but they could not avoid the question once their descriptions began to take on the final-cause meaning.

In our discussion of dialectical alternatives in meaning, we neglected to consider the difficulties facing a self-reflexive, qualitatively changing intellect as it comes at experience from moment to moment (note that we are employing the Kantian model exclusively now). The discussion of what *peanut* can mean alerted us to the fact that all meanings *reach out* in some way to designate *a* single meaning amidst a sea of many possible (alternative) meanings. The person walks up to us, says "peanut," and there we stand, looking into the next moment of our lives wondering which of several possible indications are implied here. When we *do* affirm one meaning rather than another, what is this psychological action to be called? Popular parlance has this an "act of will." This is always a dialectical process of saying "yes, *this* is the meaning intended" even as we dismiss several other possibilities (alternatives) by judging "no, this is *not* what is meant." *Peanut* does *not* mean "food" in this instance, it does *not* mean "shape of body," it does *not* mean "nothing," it *means* "my intelligence factor." We *will* a fixed alternative by affirming one and only one premise through a dialectical reasoning process of "this versus not this." Someone is calling us a "peanut brain" with little intelligence. And whether our interpretation is right or wrong from the point of view of the person who said the word *peanut does not matter.* What matters is our psychic understanding of the case, for as Freud has taught us, it is the psyche that takes precedence over external reality. Psychic determinism is what counts, and the aligning of meanings waited on our willful decision to affirm (take a stand on, take as a major premise) the meaning we sensed was being intended.

Sometimes we can entertain two or more alternative premises like this at the same time. We are not always sure about just what is taking place in our life. For example, we are buying tickets to the theater; we find them to be quite expensive so we are deliberating where to sit. The woman selling tickets drops a few jokes about the evils of the ticket-selling business as we are pondering our selection. Is she trying to make us look cheap because we have not considered the most expensive seats in the house? Or could it be that she is just acting this way to break the monotony of the day and even to be a bit friendly? We ponder *either* alternative (friendly-hostile) as we are also making our other choice, realizing that what we think of this interpersonal experience will depend upon which meaning we affirm. There are many times in life when we face a dilemma over what meaning to believe in. In fact, this is probably when we are most aware of our agency, because why else would we find it such misery having to make the "decisions, decisions" of life—and later to have remorse over some that we made— unless we really were agents in this process?

To *will* is therefore to opt, decide, affirm one meaning-alternative from among the many possible. We might now ask: is this willful reasoning process strictly conscious, or can it be unconscious as well? Here is where our founding fathers diverged somewhat in their treatments of will. Recall that in Freud's very first theoretical effort, he said that a *counterwill* [73] works in behavior to bring ideas that have earlier been suppressed back into actual, overt behavior (see p. 81 of Chapter 1). This dialectical treatment has the antithetic idea ("I can't do that") existing at the unconscious level with the conscious side of mind ("I must do that") attempting to keep it from being "made actual" in overt behavior (resulting in failure, neurotic symptoms, and so on). It would therefore follow that we can speak of a will operating at *both* the conscious and the unconscious levels of mind. We have a conflict of wills in this early theory, but Freud later translated this formal-final causal analysis (à la logic) into the pseudo-energic, material-efficient causal analysis of cathexes and countercathexes in his libido theory. Freud always stressed that unconscious mental states are identical to conscious mental states,[74] and that ideas always begin at an unconscious level to move forward to conscious awareness unless repressed.[75] The decision as to which premising idea the mind should take on—the one selected by the conscious will or the one selected by the unconscious counterwill—can be seen as a typical form of dialectical-reasoning process.

Interestingly, Jung placed willful behavior exclusively on the side of consciousness. He gave central importance to the will construct in mind, as follows: "I have . . . suggested that the term 'psychic' be used only where there is evidence of a will capable of modifying reflex or instinctual processes."[76] Archetypal themes were of the latter sort, occurring to the individual against his or her conscious will. This is a primitive form of mental action, as when people are "being thought" by the collective rather than doing their own thinking as individuals (see pp. 183–184 of Chapter 3). Willful behavior is more advanced, subject to conscious instruction and the cultivation of standards. As Jung put it, "A psychic process . . . which is conditioned by unconscious motivation I would not include under the concept of the will. Will is a psychological phenomenon that owes its existence to culture and moral education, and is, therefore, largely lacking in the primitive mentality."[77] Viewed in energy terms,

Jung would say that will refers to a "certain amount of energy freely disposable by the psyche."[78] It is the ego that employs this energy (libido), working in the sphere of consciousness. In fact, Jung even equated "conscious will" with "ego."[79]

Note that even though Jung limited will to consciousness, he like Freud provided a basis for the examination of *intrapersonal conflicts,* taking place across levels of the psyche. Freud had the will (ego-superego) and counterwill (id) in dialectical contradiction, and Jung had the ego-consciousness (will) and the shadow-unconsciousness (instinct) in dialectical contradiction. Adler, on the other hand, removed this internal contradiction factor by focusing on the "right or wrong" use of the *same* willful process. Adler based his concept of a *will to power* on Nietzsche's concept of the same name.[80] He properly understood that Nietzsche meant by this phrase a desire on the part of people not simply to survive, but also to transcend and perfect themselves during their lifetime.[81] But in our willful maneuvers to perfect ourselves, some of us exert the will to power in a mistaken way. We might say that instead of expressing this as a will to cooperate via social interest, we express it as a will to dominate others in a selfish way.[82] It is not that one will contradicts the other, because both of these cases reflect the *same* will. We do not suffer internal conflicts so much as we suffer external, interpersonal conflicts with those in whom we feel competition. Our willful manner must be corrected. We must change its manifestation from domination to cooperation. We thus observe that, as Adler drew more away from direct reliance on dialectical conceptions in the manner of Freud, he moved the locus of conflict from the intrapersonal to the interpersonal (social) context.

We move next to the possibility of free will. What can this mean and how did the analysts deal with this question? (For the behavioristic handling of this concept, see Chapter 8, pp. 530–538). Freedom is the opposite of determinism. If to determine behavior means setting limits upon it, then freedom in behavior means a lessening of such limitations, opening it up to more and more alternatives. We can now return to Table 4 (p. 265) and see that there are *four* kinds of freedom to parallel the four types of determinism. We can be free from certain organic or chemical substances that affect our behavior. We can be free of certain signals or stimuli that trigger our reflexive behavior. We can be free from the order of any one logical succession or game plan that forces us to assume a given style of behavior. And we can be free of reason itself by not taking on the usual assumptive beliefs as premises in our behavior.

Many times when "human freedom" is being discussed, the concept referred to bears an extraspective meaning, as in the examples of political liberty, independence, or rights. These are stipulations of what a human being supposedly can expect to be accorded by virtue of the fact that he or she has been born and is a citizen of a given country, or a member of the human race, for that matter. Although we often speak of the "will of the people" in deciding and enforcing such political rights, these are essentially valued grounds for collective behavior that each citizen or member of the human race is asked to affirm and behave for the sake of. As such, these prescriptions have no will and surely are not themselves free to change. Only the human beings who have advanced political freedoms in the first place can be expected to change them at a later time.

Looked at introspectively, the question of freedom or—now more properly—free will has to do with just how the person may be said to change such grounds "for the sake of which" behavior is intended (psychically

determined). The grounds *themselves* may relate to political freedom, as when we shift from a society having a managed press to one in which there is a free press. More alternatives hence freedom issue in the latter society. But this shift in grounds per se does not tell us how the individual has freedom to behave psychologically as an agent. Let us now think of a single person, shifting personal behavior from a plan A to a plan B in his or her individual behavior. Plan B is now determining the person's behavior, whereas earlier it had been Plan A, so where does psychological freedom or agency come in?

We must never forget that there are two words in our phrase "free will." The first is concerned with freedom but the second definitely has to do with determination. As we now study freedom in behavior from the introspective perspective, we see that free will is always concerned with *both* the freedom to select meanings (ideas) for the sake of which to behave *and* the resultant willful intention (psychic determinism) to enact them overtly in behavior. This is what we were driving at in discussing the relationship between God's free-will decision to create a certain type of world (frame the meanings of a plan as a grounds "for the sake of which" it could be made) *and then* to institute it by way of creating things perfectly (hard determinism). Looked at through God's eyes (that is, introspectively), there was complete freedom to shape human beings physically, to decide the arrangements to give to the heavens, to choose the kinds of foods possible, and so on, but once such decisions were made, there was *no* freedom for these details of the overall plan to vary. The laws of nature flowed with perfection because they were 100 percent determined via the divine plan.

We do not find such perfection in human beings, who lay down plans or simply make assumptions about what is to take place as they continually behave. As we all know from personal experience, such plans and/or assumptions are frequently wrong. But note: our behavior may still be said to have occurred through personal freedom *and* determination. For example, as we are leaving a large room with several doorways that we have only recently entered and are therefore unfamiliar with, we open what we take to be the door leading out and see that we have actually taken a step into a closet. We have affirmed an erroneous premise about the room's layout. At the precise moment of opening the closet door, we may be very embarrassed because there are several rather distinguished people watching us. We would like to walk through the closet's rear wall, but this is not possible. We are not "free" to do this except in our imagination, of course. So, we turn and with as much composure as we can muster, we begin contemplating alternative ways out of the room. The analysts would contend that we have been and still are under the control of a *psychic* determinism. There is a definite relationship between our ideas and our behavior.

The analysts would also not overlook our fleeting wish that we could just walk through the rear wall of the closet. What does this tell us about our psychic apparatus in which ideas are occurring? Obviously, our psyche is not limited by the demands of reality since it will contemplate impossible alternatives, however fleetingly. We can think ourselves into and out of literally any situation if we are prepared to forgo reality considerations (physical determinisms). Well, if we can do this and if there is a relationship to be noted between the person's ideas and his or her overt (observable) behavior,

then what *free will* must mean is some *ability to change the meaningful grounds (premise, belief, plan, and so on) for the sake of which behavior is being determined.* A normal person is embarrassed by opening the closet door, realizes that walking out through the closet is impossible, and returns to find an alternative exit. But an abnormal person might simply walk into the closet, sit down, and fantasize the outcome desired. Is this not an action sequence of freedom-determinism? Even the prisoner, locked in a cell, can dream of the outside world and find satisfaction in this fantasy equal to or greater than the satisfactions of prison life. Is this prisoner or the psychotic in the closet totally without freedom, if we mean now not political but *psychic* freedom?

In psychoanalysis, so long as the individual can influence in some way the grounds for the sake of which he or she is under determination, there *is* psychic freedom. Whether one wishes to call this free will or not depends on all of the religious, philosophical, and sociopolitical issues that have attached themselves to this ancient phrase. The analysts were not entirely comfortable with this phrase. After all, Freud had founded psychoanalysis and in a sense had sold it by claiming that we are all being determined by unconscious ideas. He was therefore prone to refer to the "illusion of Free Will"[83] as he placed his emphasis on psychic determinism from out of the unconscious. But what would be the point of insight, of having to assist clients to see things from within their own psychic reality (introspectively) if it were not *also* true that clients have the freedom to change personal meanings (qualitatively) based on such an examination? Freud was caught up in the duality of free will, wanting to point out on the "will" side of this phrase that our ideas do make a difference in our behavior, even those which we are not yet conscious of, and on the "free" side of this phrase that we can through personal study come to change these ideas in helpful ways. After much study he finally took a stand, combining, as is quite proper, both meanings of the free-will phrase, as follows:

According to our analyses it is not necessary to dispute the right to the feeling of conviction of having a free will. If the distinction between conscious and unconscious motivation is taken into account, our feeling of conviction informs us that conscious motivation does not extend to all our motor decisions. . . . But what is thus left free by the one side [consciousness] receives its motivation from the other side, from the unconscious; and in this way determination in the psychical sphere is still carried out without any gap.[84]

Note that Freud was placing free will into the psyche, suggesting that there is a freedom from the demands of reality (recall the psychotic in the closet!) or even from the controls of the body. But within mind, there are two equally determinate influences that first select an intention to be fulfilled and then seek to carry it out. Hence, mind is free but also completely (psychically) determined across levels of consciousness-unconsciousness. Jung too wished to point out that the personality is *both* free and determined. In line with his position that the ego is the willful portion of the personality, Jung placed freedom of willful behavior there as well, recognizing that there are also unconscious determinants of behavior. For those people who have achieved self-realization, both freedom and determinism exist side by side. Here is how Jung phrased things:

I have suggested calling the total personality which, though present, cannot be fully known, the self. The ego is, by definition, subordinate to the self and is related to it like a part to the whole. Inside the field of consciousness it has, as we say, free will. By this I do not mean anything philosophical, only the well-known psychological fact of "free choice," or rather the subjective feeling of freedom. But, just as our free will clashes with necessity in the outside world, so also it finds its limits outside the field of consciousness in the subjective inner world, where it comes into conflict with the facts of the self.*[85]

The self is broad enough to encompass determinations from the unconscious, for example, shadow tendencies, archetypal themes and the like—all of those instinctual promptings that take effect as unconscious forces in our behavior. Our ego has a narrow outlook compared to the self, and it can become inflated thanks to its free-will capacities, believing that what we think about is solely up to a conscious decision on our part. Jung said no to such one-sidedness, rejecting the "popular illusion" that everything in mind has been put there since birth and therefore could be completely otherwise.[86] Some things are already "in mind" as potentials at birth, and we are never free of their determinate influences. So once again employing the principle of opposites, Jung stood on a view of the mind as *both* free and determined. He had arrived at Freud's position, but his explanation differed significantly in that he did not have the direct parallel across levels of conscious-unconscious that Freud had. Freud had these levels working in the same way. Jung had these levels working in different ways.

Even though he did not postulate the internal conflict of Freud or Jung in his theory, Adler's teleology nicely reflects the two sides of our free-will phraseology. That is, early in life (at about age five) the person willfully affirms a prototype (plan) framing a goal (via qualitative change), and then as this gradually slips into unconsciousness, the person is under 100 percent psychic determinism in relation to the goal selected. Adler even spoke of the "pulling force" of such goals; this is what he meant by finalism.[87] Of course, if we look at the total life span, then when the individual was young and *before* he or she actually framed the prototype, there was a free-will capacity to put down whatever plan was most beneficial—including mistaken plans (life lies). This is what makes human beings different from rooted organisms, such as plants; we can move and thereby arrange our behavior in terms of intended goals.[88]

However, once the person has willfully decided on a prototype, he or she must enact it, and here is where the psychic determination comes in. We are all put in this position of having to be both coach and player, designing our game plans (life styles) and then bringing them to bear in our behavior. And since they invariably slip into our unconscious after a time, we are essentially unfree, "pulled forward" by our fictive goals. Since most of the clients whom Adler worked with already had these unconscious prototypes in place, he was reluctant to admit that they had free wills. He tells us that if someone were to accuse him of denying free will in behavior, his response would be:

So far as free will is concerned this accusation is true. Actually we see [that] this behavior pattern [life style via prototype], whose final configuration is subject to some few changes, but whose essential content, whose energy and meaning, remain un- *changed from earliest childhood, is the determining factor, even though the relations to the adult environment which follow the childhood situation may tend to modify it in some instances.*[89]

We therefore see that all three founders of psychoanalysis arrived in one way or another at a psychic determinism even though they each had the implicit view that a person does behave as an agent in behavior. They were soft determinists overall but hard determinists when strictly the unconscious was being considered. Denials of free will were made in terms of a denial of freedom from psychic forces (wishes, cathexes, goals, and so on) and never in terms of denial of freedom from physical forces. The psychoanalysts believed that occasionally mind can conquer matter in the determination of behavior, but behavior is never free of mental intentions once they have been framed. Is it then possible for us to speak of an unconscious teleology in psychoanalysis, a free will of the unconscious which decides *for* consciousness at least some of the time? This takes us to the final point of this section.

Unconscious Teleology

We want now to pull together a number of points and show how the analysts actually had self-directing hence telic behaviors issuing from the unconscious. To set the stage, we will first summarize eight points that have emerged from our study thus far. (1) Teleology is the theoretical view that events are predicated (premised, grounded) according to assumption, plan, or design, and therefore directed purposively (intentionally) toward the end (goal, wish, and so on) encompassed in the predication; (2) All teleologies rely on *final-cause* description, in which the predicating meaning frames a *formal-cause* pattern "for the sake of which" behavior is intended; (3) Since meanings are frequently bipolar, there are always *dialectical alternatives* to what will be predicated by the person; (4) *Will* is the opting, deciding, or affirming of one dialectical alternative rather than others, at which point behavior becomes 100 percent determined (discounting errors) by a fixed course to the end intended; (5) It is possible to will more than just one alternative at a time, so that different *points of view* can exist in mind together; (6) *Free will* arises from this multiplicity, and may be defined as "the capacity to change the predications (grounds) for the sake of which behavior is determined"; (7) When predications are changed, they follow qualitative change and not locomotion; (8) After the new predication has been affirmed, the person is again 100 percent determined to achieve the new end (wish, goal, and so on) framed by it.

We noted above that Freud helped sell psychoanalysis by showing how the mind plays tricks on us, how it can be saying things to us or controlling our behavior even when we think that we are in command of our own reasoning processes. Hypnotism, dream analysis, and the many types of parapraxes were all used as convincing examples in this popularizing of psychoanalysis. Many psychologists who did not consider the specifics of how this determination of behavior worked saw no real difference here between psychoanalysis and the medical model. The medical model's determinism suggested that mind was under influence from chemical-biological forces. We take a drug, and our mental processes are distorted "against our will." This is determination. Freud said our consciousness is also distorted "against our will" in the misactions of the parapraxes. This too is determination. Conclusion? Freud is a determinist in the traditions of medical-biological explanation. And since the medical model is nontelic, Freud too must

be nontelic. How could a telic theory admit to such manipulations of the mind as Freud was reporting having discovered?

We appreciate now that this is an erroneous conclusion based on a false paralleling of *psychic* with *physical* determinism. In Chapters 5 through 8 of the text, we will be surveying the psychologies which often draw an equally erroneous parallel between psychoanalysis and behaviorism. Behaviorism bases its hard determinism on efficient causation, precisely in that sense of Jung's causal-mechanistic explanation (see above). Here again, because both behaviorism and psychoanalysis have behavior strictly determined (at least, insofar as unconscious determinism is being considered), there are psychologists who believe they share a common outlook on the nature of human behavior. Freud's hard determinism was completely "within mind" and behaviorism's hard determinism is completely "outside of mind," yet because such psychologists fail to distinguish between our four types of causal determinisms, they lump these two *quite different* theoretical accounts together as one.

Even when we appreciate that Freud placed hard determinism *solely* in the mind, we can become confused over the fact that he gives mind different levels of consciousness and that within these he speaks of several different points of view (id, ego, superego). There are behavioral determinations coming forward from all of these sources at once. In the unconscious, we have the id reasoning in an illogical fashion—relying heavily on dialectical logic rather than demonstrative logic—but there is also plenty of sound reasoning going on, thanks to the unconscious portions of the ego. We also reason illogically in consciousness, so there is no fundamental difference between the structure of conscious and unconscious thoughts. What is different is the meaning being expressed. We keep some unconscious thoughts back from becoming conscious, but many more are brought into consciousness. As Freud said of latent thoughts in the unconscious, ". . . the only respect in which they differ from conscious ones is precisely in the absence of consciousness." [90] When ideas enter consciousness, we can speak of them as being in our *awareness,* which refers to the ongoing present knowledge that we have of the meaning in certain of our ideas.

As we noted above on p. 289, we are aware to the extent that we know there is more than one possibility or alternative open to us in (mental or overt) behavior. For example, when driving an automobile, we are fully aware of the road conditions and location of other automobiles in our path—where various threatening possibilities can always arise—but think nothing at all about the motions we go through in shifting the gears of our vehicle, applying the brakes, and so on. We say that the mechanics of operating the auto have become automatic, but what this means is that we carry them out without concern for alternative selection in an essentially mechanical manner. Of course, in the event of a breakdown in the workings of the automobile, our driving mechanics might quickly pop into awareness because then we would have to consider what alternative measures to take.

It would be a serious mistake to equate *awareness* with *known* in psychoanalytical theory. Some people think that when Freud said we are unaware—unconscious—of our motives we do not know what our motives in life are. This is wrong. Since ideas always begin in the unconscious, we are fully informed on that which we may not yet be aware of. Think of this as paralleling our automobile-driving mechanics. Surely we know how to shift the car's gears and apply its brakes, but we may not be aware of doing so at any one stretch of actual driving. In like fashion, we know all things mental in the unconscious, but are we necessarily aware of what we already know? Sometimes we are, sometimes we are not. When an idea is in the so-called preconscious, we are unaware of it but with effort can recall it. We forget a person's name for a time, but after searching our memory we come up with it. At other times, when an idea's meaning is especially reprehensible, we never are aware of it at all. A wish to kill our opposite-sex parent would be such an example. Sometimes we have an idea close enough to awareness, so that, as Freud said, we experience a "strange state of mind in which one knows and does not know a thing at the same time." [91]

Awareness in Freudian psychology borders on the meaning of *admission.* Do we admit to holding this or that *alternative* idea? We can deny that we have ever wished our father or mother dead, but what has this to say of the whole psychic truth? Only our unconscious may know the *id truth.* We are speaking from the narrow vantage point of the conscious *ego truth.* There are alternatives we are just not aware of, although if we pay attention to our dreams and everyday parapraxes, we might begin learning more about some of the other ideas we have contemplated. According to psychoanalysis, *meanings will out* one way or another, so that we cannot deceive ourselves for too long if we are sensitive to the ways we have of exposing our alternative intentions. Freud once said of himself in this regard: "Perhaps . . . my being scarcely able to tell lies any more is a consequence of my occupation with psychoanalysis. As often as I try to distort something I succumb to an error or some other parapraxis that betrays my insincerity. . . ." [92]

Why was Freud dishonest over what he lied about in the first place? Because, as we all know, as human reasoners we often have more than one point of view about things. We have reprehensible thoughts, but the reason we know them to be reprehensible is that we also judge these meanings and dialectically *oppose* them with a more humane alternative. We call the rash, improper, evil thoughts *id thoughts* (id promptings), but the point of view represented by the id is our own. And the opposing point of view represented by the ego (and superego) is also our own. We therefore have a *clash of intentions* or a *clash of wills* over what we should be considering, taking seriously, carrying out into behavior, and so on. Each of these identity points in mind is behaving "for the sake of" its preferred meaning, trying to get its ends made manifest in overt behavior or at least out into awareness, where they will have to be admitted and confronted.

It follows, then, that we can speak of unconscious free-will decisions because in negotiating and compromising, all three of the personality's identity points (id, ego, superego) reflect a typical final-cause approach to behavior. It is therefore entirely proper to speak of an *unconscious teleology* in psychoanalysis.[93] If it were not for the especially disgusting, frightening, or "crazy" contents of certain of the ideas being negotiated at the unconscious level, we would consider them openly in the conscious portion of mind. The telic nature of this thought process would then be clear. We only think that teleology is impossible in the unconscious because we somehow view unconscious thought processes as completely different from conscious processes. There are vast differences in the content of thought across these levels and also in the proportion of dialectical to demonstrative logic being used, but in the final analysis all human reasoning is the same no matter where it takes place. This is how Freud viewed things.

The reason that unconscious derivatives (dream themes, parapraxes, and so on) are so rigid and unyielding in their expression is because they reflect ideas about which we are unaware; they cannot take on an alternative expression but must be covered over by whatever defensive means is possible. We see the univocal expression of rigid ideas as presumptions when a person is hypnotized. Whatever is said to the person under hypnosis is taken as *the* and only *the* thought to be entertained, no matter how distorting it might be of reality. Thus, people will see what is *not there* and fail to see what is *actually there* before their eyes. Note also that the id thought is always direct and straightforward. The id never uses a euphemism; its thought or idea is "death" and the ego strikes a bargain to substitute "sleep" so that in recalling our dream, we picture our parent as soundly asleep rather than being dead. But then, in an unguarded moment, we say to our parent during a supposedly joking taunt, "I'll be the . . . er . . . you'll be the death of me yet." We know but are unaware of what one side of our personality is intending. Now, our parent may not show overt signs that he or she has caught onto our deadly wish (intention), and indeed there may be no awareness of our unconscious hostility. But there *could* be knowledge on the parent's part nevertheless. As Freud said of this possibility, "I have good reason for asserting that everyone possesses in his own unconscious an instrument with which he can interpret the utterances of the unconscious of other people."[94] Once again: awareness of and knowledge of are two different things!

Jung captured the rigidity of unconscious contents in his concept of one-sidedness. When the complex emerges from the unconscious to function within consciousness, it has one and only one intention, which is to enact the opposite of what has been enacted to that point. We must argue it away or submit to it. Since Jung placed willful behavior on the side of consciousness, how can we say that his theory embraces an unconscious teleology? Where is the free will of the unconscious paralleling the decisions made by the id to express *this* idea (death) and not *that* idea (sleep)? Jung's teleology begins in the initial decision of the person when an option is made consciously to behave one way rather than another. When a young woman decides to behave passively and to deny any aggressivity in her behavior whatever, she *at that point* initiates a process that can eventuate in a clash of intentions across levels of awareness. Her ego and persona build on passivity and her shadow builds on aggressivity. Both realms of identity use libido, which is like saying "the thrust of intentionality" because that is what libido meant to Jung.[95]

So, even as it forms, a complex like the ego or shadow is taking on a point of view "for the sake of which" it will behave. This means that the ego has intentions to fulfill and the shadow has intentions to fulfill. As was true of Freudian theory, each of these viewpoints *necessarily* (psychic, hard determinism) seeks expression. Unlike Freud, Jung did not have the ego and shadow confront each other in the unconscious, where a freely willed bargain might be struck. There may be some passing contact made during dreaming, but when there is a clear-cut squaring off between the two sides of the personality, we are witnessing a neurotic state *totally within consciousness*. But just

because the shadow—actually, anima or animus—complex is now in consciousness, this does not mean that full awareness exists in the personality. The ego cannot grasp what the anima or animus complex is driving at and vice versa. Only when the two viewpoints are transcended and a *self*-identity point emerges does awareness come about. From that point forward, the self acting as bridge between consciousness and unconsciousness keeps the personality system fully aware of the alternative points of view that the psyche must always generate. As Jung summed it up, "In the end we have to acknowledge that the self is a *complexio oppositorum* precisely because there can be no reality without polarity."[96]

It is easy to overlook precisely how Jung had the collective psyche express its point of view through archetypal themes and consequently erroneously think of these themes as inherited "givens" that must be expressed in efficient-cause fashion without any prompting teleology in mind. We can now see that in his so-called principle of opposites Jung was actually trying to account for the play of dialectical alternatives in all mentation. Archetypal themes are not triggered in efficient-cause fashion, as we might push the button of a computer and revive items that have been stored in a memory bank. Archetypes are stimulated into activity only when there is one-sidedness, when after a series of free-will decisions, the person has gone out of balance, or possibly after an entire group of people (a society or "race") has neglected some beckoning necessity, such as the need to be more well-rounded in attitudes. We *first* get this freely arrived at pattern of one-sidedness, unfulfilled promise, or dissociation, and *then* we get the archetypal theme being expressed.[97]

Adler's treatment of unconscious determination was closer to Freud's than Jung's, in that the prototype functions identically whether in consciousness or later, as it slips into the unconscious. Adler did not have the alternative points of view in the unconscious that Freud achieved via the id, ego, and superego. As a result, we do not get that conflict-laden sense of a psyche fraught with dialectical dispute and compromise (thesis, antithesis, synthesis). Adler did, however, point to a conflict between what people *say* they intend to do and what they actually *do* in behavior. The person whose prototype has become unconscious is unaware of the *actual* ends being sought in his or her behavior and may explain away or lie about what is taking place. Adler observed:

It is not that the patient deliberately wants to lie to us, but we have learned to recognize a vast gulf between a man's conscious thoughts and his unconscious motivations—a gulf which can best be bridged by a disinterested but sympathetic outsider. The outsider—whether he be the psychologist, or the parent or the teacher—should learn to interpret a personality on the basis of objective facts seen as the expression of the purposive, but more or less unconscious, strivings of the individual.[98]

Adler's second teleology—the supposed direction of organic evolution—may strike us as a supraindividual and therefore mechanical concept. Darwin's reference to the origin of *species* makes it clear that he was thinking about large numbers of organisms in a kind of statistical or probability sense. A fortunate turn of events for one species means the likelihood of survival is greater, and an unfortunate turn of events for another species means probable extinction. But this is *not* how Adler viewed the evolutionary process. He thought of it individually, and constantly emphasized that it was only through the striving toward a goal of perfection that the organic process could be brought about.[99] We do not improve if we just "sit there,"

and every single member of a species must be intending that something better come about in behavior or it will not come about. Put in terms of awareness, we must first consciously opt to have more social interest, and then in time, just as other reflexive habits become automatic (including automobile driving), so too will social interest become automatic (unconscious, unaware). Adler's theorizing is shot through with such telic conceptions.

We therefore conclude that to speak of a freely willed unconscious activity is *not* a contradiction in terms to the psychoanalyst. We make such decisions, we take such stands, including two or more contradictory stands on the same issue, at both the conscious and the unconscious level. When we want to deny something highly offensive to our personal values and self-image, we keep it out of awareness by repression, denial, and so on. We know what we want kept out of awareness, but since meanings have to be expressed if they are "there," it is always possible for someone with the insights of analysis to figure out what we are intending to convey, one way or another. If we do not slip up through a parapraxis, we reveal our hidden intentions in our dreams, body language, and so on. As dialectical organisms we are a bundle of contradictions held together by deceit, denial, and compromise. Psychoanalysis unravels the dualities by making us aware of what we already know is troubling us.

What Motives to Therapy Are Primary in Psychoanalysis?

Scholarly Motive

We can see a decided trend to this motive as being uppermost for Freud. In 1909 he spoke of the scientific insights as secondary to the therapeutic effects of psychoanalysis.[100] By 1916 he was saying that even if psychoanalysis proved to be an unsuccessful form of therapy, it would remain an irreplaceable instrument of scientific research.[101] In the mid 1920s he was admitting that the term *psychoanalysis* had changed in meaning from a primarily therapeutic approach to "the science of unconscious mental processes."[102] And by the late 1920s Freud was rather confidently asserting that "in point of fact psycho-analysis is a method of research, an impartial instrument, like the infinitesimal calculus, as it were."[103] Recall from the Introduction (p. 24) that a *method* is concerned with the means or manner of establishing proof, and that we have two primary forms of evidence issuing from two somewhat different methods—procedural evidence (via the cognitive method) and validating evidence (via the research method). What sort of method is psychoanalysis?

It is clear that Freud considered proof to be a matter of internal consistency. Just as long as a hypothesis hangs together internally and throws new light on old questions, we have good reason to accept its truth value.[104] Furthermore, if a client finds personal meaning in the interpretation (after resistances have been overcome) and obtains benefits, such as the loss of symptoms, this adds further evidence to the truth of the theory under development.[105] This approach to proof is usually termed a *coherence theory of truth* in opposition to the *correspondence theory of truth* advocated by the experimentalist who tries to array a hypothesis to meet an entirely independent series of prearranged empirical events leading to what we have called validating evidence (see p. 25 of Introduction

When we validate, we keep our methodological steps (experimental design) entirely independent from our *and the subject's* procedural evidence. What we think about the flow of methodological steps makes no difference to the outcome. Though Freud felt that anyone using his method would arrive at the same findings he did,[106] the record of departed colleagues belies this conviction. Accepting client improvement (cures) as *necessarily* proving the therapist's—admittedly plausible—insights are true remains a major weakness of the Freudian method.

Recall that the research method has a continuing error of logic built right into it— *affirming the consequent* of an "if, then" logical sequence (see p. 26 of the Introduction). All science must proceed with this recognition that just because empirical findings support the theory that prompted their collection, they never change the fact that an alternative theory might account for the data observed to an equal degree (see pp. 506–513 of Chapter 8 where a thorough discussion of this issue is presented). We can apply this same logical error to psychoanalysis, so that when Freud said something like "if my theoretical insight is correct, then the client believing in it will improve during therapy," he was subject to the same proviso as any scientist. Adler's theory or Jung's theory might have worked just as well to give the client an insight leading to a cure of the neurotic condition. There is an even *more serious* problem in the method of psychoanalysis, if we seriously want to parallel it with the research method of science. Validating evidence follows an efficient-cause sequence in which manipulations are made in the independent variable(s) and control variable(s) *by the experimenter* and the meaningful tie of these antecedent factors is then observed upon the consequent dependent variable(s). The one set of measurements (antecedents) is kept distinct from the other set (consequents). If there is direct information by the subjects of the study, who know what *ought* to be found—what is being predicted in the experiment—then they might bring about the expected findings intentionally.

For example, assume we were conducting a study in which the independent variable was the color of an automobile, and the dependent variable was the number of subjects who would select a color we predicted would be most popular by picking automobiles of this color as their favorite. Subjects would be given a stack of colored pictures in which all kinds of automobile body styles with varying colors were displayed. If the subjects are kept in the dark about our hypothesis, and we simply ask them to sort the pictures according to their preference, we might get a reasonably clear-cut test of our hypothesis. But if the subjects somehow learn about our expectation that one color will be preferred by all, it is not unusual to find that they will choose the expected color out of this knowledge alone. There is always a great danger in conducting research on human beings that their knowledge of the experimental hypothesis is sufficient to bring about the predicted outcome. Sometimes they reject our hypothesis and purposively do the (dialectical) opposite of our expectations (see p. 475 of Chapter 7), but this is merely the other side of the same coin. The point is: in validation, the person acting as subject must not be allowed to pass on the truth value of the hypothesis put to test, thereby intentionally making the outcome be as he or she intentionally prefers. In validation, the experimenter (who is *not* also a subject) arranges circumstances, predicts, and then steps back to see what the outcome is *independent* of his or her willful influence.

In psychoanalysis, a contamination takes place between the experimenter and the subject roles. Psychoanalysis follows an intro-

spective course, studying events through the eyes of the client who is essential to the process, helping to fill in the formal-cause outlines of a total life pattern. Once this pattern fits, the client acknowledges insight and essentially judges the theory filling in the details to be true. In other words, the client is acting as a coexperimenter in arranging the preliminary antecedents and then *also* acting as a subject who decides how well these antecedents fit the facts. Of course, precisely what are facts independent of a client's fantasy are never studied by the analytical method itself. Thus, psychoanalysis is unable to distinguish between *falsified recollections* of a sexual nature (fallaciously remembering fantasying a parent sexually fondling us), and the actual sexual fantasies supposedly concocted in the infantile years (the fact of having *actually had* this fantasy years past). This distinction might make no practical difference to the insight and therapeutic outcome, because as Freud taught us, fantasies cause illness and hence fantasies may cure illness. But as a method of science, we have to go beyond cure to say whether the grounds for cure were literal or imagined.

Psychoanalysis does not, in its clinical procedures, come up to the rigorous standards of validation. Psychoanalysis is obviously a cognitive method, in which the theory under development is put to test based solely on the *procedural evidence* of the client. The analyst uses procedural evidence as well and may even draw on the findings of validated (research) evidence to make interpretations. But the ultimate grounds for proof rest with the client, who either accepts the theory and improves based on such insights or does not. Thus, a woman with migraine headaches might be convinced, had she gone to a Freudian analyst, that her problems stemmed from an unresolved Oedipal complex. Had she gone to an Adlerian therapist, she would be just as convinced that her headaches took root in sibling rivalry. And had she gone to a Jungian analyst, she would now trace her difficulties to one-sidedness. It is not this multiplicity of explanation that makes psychoanalysis nonscientific. It is rather the fact that there is nothing in the method used by the psychoanalysts that can resolve such differences once they show up. Theoretical disputes must therefore be resolved by splitting up into different camps. There are camps in all science, of course, but scientists also share a *common* basis for resolving differences, one that moves beyond procedural to include validating evidence as well.

Jung made a spirited defense of the use of procedural evidence in proving theories true or false. He began his argument with the suggestion that personality psychology as we know it is made up of the personal confessions of many individuals, as when Freud incorporated his own dreams into his writings or Jung recorded his personal confrontations with the unconscious.[107] If Freud, Adler, and Jung were as individuals completely different from every other person in the world, then their respective insights would be limited to themselves as subjective observations and in no way objective statements about others.[108] We would need as many psychologists as there are people to account for the great diversity of personality styles. But, said Jung, such multiplicity or subjectivity does not occur because "individuality . . . is only relative, the complement of human conformity or likeness; and therefore it is possible to make statements of general validity, i. e., scientific statements."[109]

As we look around, broad ranges of hu-man experience overlap. The individualities of Freud, Adler, and Jung merge into the commonalities of large segments of other people. Some people find themselves entirely within Freudian psychology, others in Adlerian or Jungian psychologies. Still others find a mixture of two or even three theories fitting their personal experience. And since the personal experience has to rest on the common sense of procedural evidence, there is nothing wrong with accepting such evidence as proof of the theories in question. The subjective (procedural) always becomes the objective (validating) as the numbers swell, permitting us to apply a theory across the board.

Though he presented an interesting case, Jung surely minimized the possibility of an *incorrect* common belief which can be psychially held by many people (objectively). When all humanity believed the world was flat, their belief was objective. But if we think of science as an enterprise devoted to explaining the universe independent of the plausibilities of common sense, then this belief was false as well. Science has constantly worked to remove human biases from its *testing* procedures. In this way scientific truths have contradicted and negated the objectivities of the sort Jung was defending. In time, the newer scientific truths become absorbed into the common sense of people, and they once again serve to prejudice the psychic outlooks of all concerned. The scientist does not have to accept the preferred theories of other people—even if all people now alive agree on *a* theory on some subject. The scientist must conform to one type of (research) *method,* but the theories put to test by this method are unlimited and never subject to convention. Defending a theory as true because it is commonly (objectively) believed is to misunderstand the type of proof required by science.

Jung once conducted an empirical experiment on the horoscopes of 483 married couples, to see if astrology could predict successful combinations.[110] He failed to use an adequate control (comparison) group against which to judge his matched protocols, settling for a statistically determined chance estimate. What are the chances that these couples could have well-matched astrological charts (that is, compatible arrangements in the stars), and what do we actually find? What Jung found was not enough to exceed chance expectations; the pattern predicted by astrology was *not* confirmed. Undaunted, Jung went on to say that "the statistical view of the world is a mere abstraction and therefore incomplete and even fallacious, particularly so when it deals with man's psychology."[111]

He was, of course, correct in recognizing that mathematics rests upon a procedural-evidence base in the same way that other theories begin in such plausible abstractions. But this is still the accepted scientific avenue, and Jung had to swallow the verdict of an uncontaminated test in which what occurred as a dependent variable was separate and distinct from what any one subject thought ought to occur. After the initial setback, Jung fished about in the data and found that the three "most important" signs predicted by astrological theory *did* seem to come together in a very small number of marital unions, too small for proper statistical test yet synchronistically meaningful.[112] These chance occurrences were for Jung still important. "Inasmuch as chance maxima and minima occur, they are *facts* whose nature I set out to explore."[113] Though this is true, science is interested in what *reoccurs*. What was needed here was for Jung to conduct further empirical researches using the three "best" signs, along with better controls to see if these suggestive findings would continue to show up.

The scholarly motive did not play such a leading role in Adler's commitment to the consulting room as it did for the other founding fathers. As his biographical overview suggests, Adler lacked a scholar's temperament. He disliked having to write his theories down for publication, and he was not above purposefully leaving ambiguous meaning in written presentations so that he could not be pinned down to a fixed phrase or a catchword at some later date.[114] Adler wanted a "psychology of use," and he stressed that "we mustn't make our psychology too hard for people to understand."[115] He was not impressed by the Freudian and Jungian approaches, which made the patient a subject-collaborator in research.[116] Too often, he complained, the therapist lost sight of client needs as a result, and the scholarly motivation also multiplied beyond plausibility the number of supposed reasons for maladjustments. Adler was not in the business of finding excuses for neurotics, justifying their persistence in mistaken life styles.[117]

Adler did advocate the conducting of experiments along the lines of validating evidence, but he insisted that these be done in natural life settings.[118] Of what use was it for an experimental psychologist to design an apparatus to study some irrelevant point?[119] Although he did not concern himself with extensive controls, Adler did occasionally embark on empirical projects of his own. He tells of a survey tactic in the following: "I have occasionally attempted to make investigations in schools in such a tactful manner that no one could possibly be hurt. On a sheet of paper on which no names appeared, answers were to be written to the following question: Has anyone ever lied or stolen? The general results showed that all the children confessed to petty thefts. . . ."[120]

However, merely collecting data and submitting them to mathematical test did not constitute adequate science for Adler.[121] He felt that many investigators who were afraid of theoretical criticism fled to an artificial reliance on mathematical reductionism in an effort to feel certain and secure.[122]

Adler encouraged guessing at what the client might do next during a therapy series. If our guess is correct, then this would approximate the predictions made in experimental research.[123] Though plausible on first consideration, there are serious drawbacks to this parallel. In the research experiment, a scientist has prearranged things at the criterion end so that there is no changing the dependent variable after the experiment is underway. In the consulting room, the therapist has the option of deciding what is an example of the prediction being made. We might, for example, predict that our client will soon become hostile in the relationship. In fact, the client is seen to become jocular. But now, as analysts we can "interpret" this jocularity as veiled hostility and consider our prediction validated when it has *not* been. Humor is indeed a form of veiled hostility. But it is also other things, and we failed to stipulate objectively what *hostility* would mean in our prediction at the outset. As a result, we cannot take this sequence as properly validational. All we have done is use our own procedural evidence to rearrange the pattern of facts (qualitatively).

Ethical Motive

It is clear that Freud was a social revisionist and critic of civilization in general. He said that psychoanalysts are not social reformers, but the unrealistic way in which the culture suppresses sexuality forces them to speak out for greater acceptance of this natural func-

tion.[124] The morals of passivity that engendered the Golden Rule were interpreted as stemming from strong reaction-formations to the underlying cruelty and violence of human nature.[125] For this reason, Freud felt it necessary to align himself with the ego and try to soften the grip of the superego.[126] In fact, Freud thought of himself as the therapist of an entire culture; and his social criticism must be viewed in this light. He drew a parallel between the development of the individual and the development of the culture,[127] and he even spoke in terms of a cultural superego, handed down from past generations and operating very much like the superego of the individual.[128]

Freud was occasionally annoyed by those who, like Adler, wanted to account for human goodness. He lacked such an optimistic view of the march of civilization. Jung believed that Freud was almost neurotically pessimistic concerning human nature. Freud felt that we have to accept honestly the fact that a human being is a higher animal with id promptings that are quite beyond the ego's ability to control successfully, particularly since the ego is itself an extension of the id and "a separation of the ego from the id would be a hopeless undertaking."[129] However, if there is anything hopeful about us humans as being innately good, it seems to be in the fact that we cannot act out evil promptings without guilt, assuming that our superego has formed properly. Psychoanalysis confirms the Platonic saying that the good are those who are content to dream about the things that the bad really carry into action.[130] About as far as Freud ever went in agreeing to humanity's basic goodness is contained in the following quote, which also reminds us of his free-will conception of mind:

The ethical narcissism of humanity should rest content with the knowledge that the fact of distortion in dreams, as well as the existence of anxiety-dreams and punishment-dreams, afford just as clear evidence of his moral nature as dream-interpretation gives of the existence and strength of his evil nature. If anyone is dissatisfied with this and would like to be "better" than he was created, let him see whether he can attain anything more in life than hypocrisy and inhibition.[131]

In contrast to Freud's negative view of superego promptings, Adler felt that the only hope for humanity lay in the affectively based judgments of the right, the proper, the good way to behave interpersonally. Due to the human being's comparatively weak position in the animal kingdom, and as a natural compensation in the movement of organic evolution, a necessary feature of humanity is *collectivity,* the living in groups in which we care for one another. Adler felt that many of those individuals who transgress this naturalistic ethic turned up in his consulting room as patients.[132] Since their eventual recovery of mental health was dependent on a cultivation of that which they lacked—that is, social interest—it would be correct to say that Adlerian therapy tended heavily, if not primarily, toward an ethical motivation. An individual psychologist has a certain duty to perform. "When we find an individual whose behavior pattern has rendered him incapable of a happy life, there arises out of our knowledge of human nature the implicit duty to aid him in readjusting the false perspectives with which he wanders through his life."[133]

This intrinsically motivated ethic does not mean that the therapist should—or can—do anything for the client, except encourage a change in life style. Precisely what this change will involve is up to the client who must take responsibility for acting on the insight that therapy has afforded.[134] Adler tried to offset the harsher implications of his ethi-

cal approach by stressing *errors* (mistakes) rather than *sins*. He did not want to make people feel guilty when they behaved selfishly.[135] He believed that a human being is born neither good nor evil,[136] but is a product of the environmental circumstances into which he or she is born and—most importantly—the prototype put down personally and uniquely in light of these circumstances. Since the personality is self-created, it can only be changed by the individual person after a correction is indicated. Adler believed in a fairly simple rule of conduct, which could bring satisfaction for everyone if followed; that is, the individual must consider others and always adjust to the collective rather than the personal need. He once phrased his ethic succinctly as follows: "When we speak of virtue we mean that a person plays his part; when we speak of vice we mean that he interferes with co-operation."[137]

Arguing as he did for the common good led to charges by critics that Adler favored repressive measures in human affairs. It was as if he were saying that whenever a conflict arose between the individual and the group, regardless of the merits of the individual's case, the group must win out and be appeased. Adler took pains to answer this charge, noting that he did *not* advocate repression as a principle of adjustment, whether the individual's claim on the group is justified or unjustified.[138] When a person's claim is unjustifiable, Adler believed that this inequity could be easily determined by comparing it to the broader standard of community benefit. The individual who has such an unjustified (selfish) claim is not expected to repress anything, but to *cultivate* (as a compensating measure) the social interest he or she has potentially available as a human being. Adler felt that Freud's mistake was viewing humanity as selfish by nature.[139] We have to see in the march of organic evolution a different side to humanity, the side that is taking us above the animalistic tendencies subsumed by the concept of an id. The steady movement of creative evolution is away from selfishness, even though the specifics of an ethical code cannot be stated for all time. It is not some fixed ethical truth, but the striving upward that Adler emphasized as an ethical position. One need only look to his roots to see where he is going as an organic product. What we have *left* is precisely that side of our natures that Freud seemed so intent upon retaining in his image of humanity.[140]

As we recall from Chapter 3, Jung relied heavily on an ethical position in explaining maladjustment, as well as the steps one must take to overcome neurotic tendencies. If we would all look inward and admit to our shadow sides, then this world would be much better, projections would be minimized, and a sense of personal humility would be substituted for the impersonalisms and hostilities detracting from modern life.[141] Though he never put it precisely this way, Jung felt that the weight of alternatives in dialectical reasoning meant that we human beings constantly face a judgment in our ongoing behavior. Conscious living involves deciding, choosing, opting for the good as we saw it in preference to the bad. Although the dispreferred does not have to be the immoral or unethical in behavior, it frequently is and results in a shadow complex of this nature. Unless we are willing to search about and find these bad (evil, immoral) alternatives in our psyche, we can develop a neu-

rosis through one-sidedness. This is why religion is associated with cure in the Jungian view. Religions have aimed at restoring the balance through admissions of the shadow side to existence (weakness of character, wrongdoing, sin). Religions are evaluative and moralizing because they reflect our most fundamental ability to choose, then generate standards of how humans *ought* to behave, as well as criticism for those who fall short of such higher ends. Whereas Freud agreed with Shakespeare that conscience makes cowards of us all, Jung believed with Adler that conscience makes higher animals of us all, because it is only through our judgmental ability that we can submit our actions to a higher type of criticism.[142]

Jung once shocked a client by telling him that his problems stemmed from a lack of conscience.[143] Such an interpretation struck the client as not only too religious and non-scientific, but almost unprofessional as well. Jung was amused by this response, since it was his clear insight that if a man could become ill because of a harsh self-evaluation (Freud's rigid superego), it should be possible for him to fall ill because of a lack of that character that one ordinarily sees in people of high standards and good conscience. Jung felt that Adler had seen this side of humanity more clearly that Freud.[144] By being sensitive to our own weaknesses—even sins—Jung argued that we would balance our shadow factors and thus be less likely to project them onto others. Here is a good summary statement of Jung's basic ethic.

If men can be educated to see the shadow-side of their nature clearly, it may be hoped that they will also learn to understand and love their fellow men better. A little less hypocrisy and a little more self-knowledge can only have good results in respect for our neighbour; for we are all too prone to trans-

fer to our fellows the injustice and violence we inflict upon our own natures.[145]

Curative Motive

We have already indicated that Freud was—at best—a reluctant therapist. His delayed graduation from medical school, his interest in making "scientific" generalizations from his cases, his cautions about assuming responsibility for other people's lives in psychoanalysis, all testify to what Freud once said of himself: "You are perhaps aware that I have never been a therapeutic enthusiast. . . ."[146] After more than forty years as a psychoanalyst, Freud could say that he had "never really been a doctor in the proper sense."[147] Freud had larger goals in mind than simply putting out the individual flames of neurosis which are kindled by the clash between cultural demands and the human being's natural seeking for pleasure. Freud's "cure" was a long-range program of understanding, demanding an intellectual grasp and a sense of tolerance if not humor concerning our common human plight. Freud was distrustful of the overly enthusiastic revolutionary with a program for curing all of humanity's problems overnight. Revolutions breed reactions, and the inevitable outcome of such zeal on both sides is suppression—if not in the present, then surely in the future.[148]

Freud championed the individual person against the group, and argued for a new God for humanity: *reason*.[149] We must drop the superstitions and illusions of yesteryear, recognize that humanity slowly advances only through hard work and a willingness to face facts, and through rational efforts like science, there may yet be hope for the future. Though we might fault him for having an unworkable method of scientific investigation (see above), we must see in this late nineteenth-century rationalist whose thought could encompass human irrationality, a monumental bravery and sincere honesty as he tried to interpret for us what he took to be the facts of the human condition.

Closely aligned with the ethical motives of Adler were his curative motives. ". . . The practitioner should either pledge himself to bring about a cure or not accept payment."[150] Because he did not think of the therapeutic relationship as primarily a scientific activity, Adler was more prone to emphasize the necessity of effecting a cure. He placed emphasis on the specifics of *how* to do therapy, and his descriptions of the maneuvers in the relationship we called gamesmanship tactics (see p. 166) could have been put into a manual of techniques for the practitioner. This kind of "practical hint" is not spelled out for us by Freud or Jung. For example, Adler tells us at length how he notices and tells patients about their tendency to swallow gulps of air when anxious, giving them gastric disturbances of various sorts which only further their anxiety.[151] Therapy in this case is achieved by the simple instruction to the client to counter this gulping tendency when it begins. No behavior therapist (see Chapter 7) could do more for the client's symptom at this point.

Unlike Freud, Adler did not pin his hopes for the future of humanity on sociocultural advance but rather on the physically based advance that each *individual* person carries along by simply living. A typical ordering of Adlerian priorities can be seen in the following: "The miracle of evolution is manifest in the perpetual endeavor made by the body simultaneously to maintain, complete, and supplement all the parts that are vital to it. . . . Here, too, the association of men—society—has acted helpfully and successfully."[152] It is in this sense that society is a compensatory—and the most important compensatory—factor for human weakness.[153] A human being relies on another human, but the *reason* for this interpersonal concern is rooted in organic evolution. Cultural values then emerge, but social interest is *not* a cultural product, something derived from our reason and a decision to behave in a certain way. Adler did not wish to see social interest put in the category of a sociocultural fiction. Humanity's social ethic of community feeling is a *fact* to be accepted as a given just as it is a fact that humans breathe.

Hence, in the Adlerian view, nature and *not* nurture (sociocultural factors) is our teacher, showing us what direction we are already going in. Culture is itself a product of the organic basis of life which has already evolved to a certain level of development making social interest possible. The culture does not ride above this organic substrate to somehow influence its developmental direction. The human's direction on this earth is ready-made from out of a cultureless past. Hence, unlike Freud, Adler was no healer of society but of the *individual* person as a singular example of this organic progress. Treat the individual and the society will take care of itself.

We have already made the point that Jung was not primarily motivated by curative intentions. As he put it: "I should deceive myself if I thought I was a practising physician. I am above all an investigator, and this naturally gives me a different attitude to many problems. . . . I was a medical practitioner quite long enough to realize that practice obeys, and must obey, other laws than does the search for truth."[154] Jung stressed that analysis is not like a cure, to which the individual submits and is then discharged healed.[155] Nor did Jung appreciate views that failed to see the client as an independent entity—literally a coworker—in the relationship. "The patient is not an empty sack into which we can stuff whatever we like; he brings his own particular contents with him which stubbornly resist suggestion and push themselves again and again to the fore."[156] The best tactic is to avoid being directive and judgmental, and the therapist can help create such an atmosphere by adopting the Socratic dialectical approach we outlined in Chapter 3.[157] Probably the clearest indication that Jung was not attracted to the role of healer can be seen in his view of the nature of human problems. To have problems is part and parcel of existence. As he once put it so well: "In the last resort it is highly improbable that there could ever be a therapy that got rid of all difficulties. Man needs difficulties; they are necessary for health. What concerns us here as therapists is only an excessive amount of them."[158]

Summary

Chapter 4 takes up a number of issues that arise in any consideration of behavior. Few of these issues are directly confronted by psychologists, much less personologists. The problem seems to be that too many psychologists consider these issues either (1) settled, or at least agreed upon by the scientific community, or (2) essentially out of the domain of psychology and more directly related to philosophy. Take the question of behavioral determination, for example. No psychologist would deny that "behavior is determined." Yet, in what sense is this true? That is, are all determinations alike? Chapter 4 teaches us that to determine is to limit in some fashion the alternatives open to a course of action, including behavior. After clarifying the terms *antecedent* and *consequent*, we then learn that there are actually *four* ways in which to speak of determination, based on which causal meaning we give emphasis to in our definition. Material-cause determinations refer to substances, such as genes, that set limits on behavior. Efficient-cause determinations refer to unidirectional actions, such as stimuli or reflexes, that induce one line of responsive behavior and one alone. Formal-cause determinations rely on the patterns to be seen in events or logical orders of various types which encompass plans, syllogistic successions, and mathematical proofs. And final-cause determinations rely on putting such plans, reasonings, or proofs into intentional manifestation by behaving "for their sake" purposively.

When we now look at classic issues, such as the distinction between psychic and physical determinism, hard and soft determinism, or conscious and unconscious determinism, the contrasting types of determinism can be understood more clearly. For example, Freudian psychic determination is obviously of a final-cause nature, whereas traditional physical determinations are due to material- and especially efficient-cause constructs. Interestingly, hard determinisms including those that issue from the so-called unconscious realm of mind are readily understood in light of final causation. Thus, the Freudian slip (parapraxis) is a construct combining intentional (final cause) and hard determinism.

Another issue taken up in Chapter 4 has to do with the change of behavior. Here again, a causal analysis proves helpful as we find that historically the motions connected with change are not as singular as we might have thought. There is first local motion (locomotion), as in the movement of a body from one place to another. This meaning borrows from efficient causation. Next, there is qualitative motion, or the alteration of a thing's attributes or patterned appearance.

This meaning rests on formal causality. Finally, we have quantitative motion, or the alteration in size (mass, bulk) to be noted in the growth or deterioration of things. We obviously have a stress on material causation here. Chapter 4 next traces the fact that in the rise of natural science, wherein analytical geometry was predicated on locomotion in the sense of defining geometric figures on the basis of moving points rather than fixed (Euclidian) points, the convention arose of assuming that *all* change occurs through this single motoric process. Even when we witness qualitative changes taking place in events or the growth of things quantitatively, the reductionistic theorists argue that underlying this apparent change, there is a more basic locomotion taking place. Freud tried to use this style of explanation in his unsuccessful attempt to write a *Project for a Scientific Psychology*. Both Breuer (constancy principle) and Fliess (periodic cycles) favored this reductive-biological type of explanation. But Freud could not think in these terms and also understand his patients' psychic difficulties.

In Jung's concept of *synchronicity*, which he defined as "meaningful cross-connections," we witness an effort to understand change in a formal-cause, qualitative sense. Patterns change (qualitative motion) but without being thrust along through efficient-cause determinations (locomotion) over time's passage. This is what Jung tried to convey, and he was alert to the fact that he was dealing in teleology for he contrasted his style of explanation as a final-energic type with the more traditional causal-mechanistic type of explanation in natural science. In most instances, when the modern theorist speaks of a cause, he or she means efficient cause, and Jung in drawing this distinction is no exception to the rule. Chapter 4 next shows how in the rise of modern physics, subatomic theories like Bohr's stationary-state formulation fall back on a type of qualitative change in preference to locomotion. If we now extend this type of explanation to a description of the way in which people reason, we might argue that human beings can qualitatively change the patterned meanings they use as grounding reasons "for the sake of which" (final cause) they behave. This would give us a teleology for we would not have to "reduce" qualitative-motion types of changes to locomotion types of changes. In the same way that the atom's changing patterns are not due to underlying forces of a causal-mechanistic type (Bohr), so too would we now contend that people act as agents to influence their course of behavior entirely separate from, for example, stimulus-response locomotions.

Accepting a human teleology does not necessarily commit one to accepting a deity teleology. But in order to explain how telic behavior "works," it is necessary to depart from complete reliance on the tabula rasa conception of ideas the Lockean model embraces and move over to the pro forma conception of the idea subsumed by the Kantian model. Chapter 4 takes up this question of whether or not the mind-body problem can really be solved. Adler's unique interpretation of organic evolution is discussed, which holds that it occurs thanks only to the willful intentions of organisms seeking to do various things in terms of projected goals. This is not precisely a vitalism, a term devolving from Galen in which a deity teleology is assumed. Adler made no assumptions about the deity in his natural and human telic analyses. The reliance that all of the psychoanalysts had on Darwinian conceptions is

shown to be a major reason for interpreting this school of thought as more biological than it actually is.

Chapter 4 next takes up the question of how psychoanalysis actually saw the mind as working. It is found that Freud's dynamic interpretation of the mind rested on a dialectical formulation, in which one idea opposed another—translated in a quasi-reductive manner to read that one cathexis of libidinal energy was countered by another. Freud's very first theory of antithetic ideas and a counterwill in mind is therefore the clearest example of his dialectical theoretical strategy. Yet Freud did not wish to be identified with dialectical terminology, viewing this style of description as sophistical and confusing. Adler was equally distrustful of the dialectic, although he certainly had oppositional conceptions in his theory, such as compensation, fiction versus counterfiction, and so on. Jung was the most conscious, thorough, and outspoken dialectician of the psychoanalytical founding fathers. His principle of opposition was fundamentally a dialectical conception in which everything expressed by mind has its contradiction, with a valid meaning to be expressed albeit in a conflicting or self-negating way.

Chapter 4 then takes up the question of agency in some detail, analyzing the concepts of willful behavior and free will in behavior. It is shown how in behaving "for the sake of" grounded reasons (plans, the presumed divine intention of a god, and so on) the person is always affirming one of at least two (dialectical) possibilities. Psychoanalysis teaches that sometimes both possibilities—both lines of behavior—are affirmed, presumed, wished for, and so on, *at the same time*. The shadow contains many possible reasons and purposes that the ego would never entertain, never think about or enact. When the Jungian self emerges, it is a *complexio oppositorum,* a singularity combining what to now has been incompatible meanings. The compromises of an id, ego, and superego in Freudian theory can be viewed in this same dialectical fashion—as a combining of opposite intentions into a singular expression. Freud's theory of illness holds that there are always two meanings symbolized in any one symptom. An important point made in Chapter 4 is that simply because behavior is unconsciously determined it cannot also be telic in nature. Recalling that psychic hard determinism is readily framed in terms of final causation, the mere fact that we find people being rigidly determined by some unconscious wish does *not* mean they are under a blind (nonintentional) physical determination. Indeed, a free-will psychology is entirely compatible with a view of the mind as having both conscious and unconscious forms of agency in operation.

The final question taken up in Chapter 4 has to do with the motives to therapy that prompted the psychoanalysts. Freud's primary motive was surely the scholarly. This meant that he was forced to base his theory exclusively on the procedural evidence of the client—whose "insights" acted as evidence of the truth value of the interpretation framed by Freud. Psychoanalysis therefore rests on a coherence theory of truth, whereas scientific theories rely on a correspondence theory in their use of the research method with its validating evidence. This is a serious drawback to the theoretical fruits of psychoanalysis, a greater drawback to its acceptance than the sexuality thesis per se. Jung was also scholarly in outlook, but Adlerian therapy placed curative goals uppermost. Though Freud did not place ethical considerations as central to cure, he did point out that such experiences as punishment dreams often give evidence of the human being's moral (as well as evil) nature. Jung and Adler both felt that the human being's conscience is what

made people into "higher animals." Adler's effort to cultivate social interest in his theory of cure demonstrated his great reliance on ethical considerations. Jung tied his ethical interests more into scholarly than curative motives per se.

Outline of Important Theoretical Constructs

How is behavior determined?
determine, determined, determinism • antecedents • consequents • purpose • reduction • arguments from definition • four types of determinism • physical versus psychic determinism • hard versus soft determinism • conscious versus unconscious determinism

How is behavior changed?
local motion • qualitative motion • quantitative motion • accidental change • reductionism • Cartesian geometry and locomotion • tracking • predicting • arbitrariness • Freud's "Project for a Scientific Psychology" • Principle of Constancy • periodic cycle • synchronicity • causal-mechanistic versus final-energic • stationary state • insight • logic • natural teleology • deity teleology • human teleology

Can the mind-body problem be solved?
vitalistic theory, vitalism • will • mixed-model theories • pro forma versus tabula rasa • Kantian versus Lockean views of mind • agent, agency

According to psychoanalysis, how does mind "work"?
homunculus • identity, agency • dynamic mental phenomena • dialectical

alternatives and choice · thesis versus antithesis in meaning flow · antithetic ideas · counter-will · unidirectional versus bidirectional brain processes · opting for dialectical alternatives · transcendental dialectic · self-reflexivity, reflexivity · dialectic as sophistry · will and free will · grace · morality · divine versus human agency · psychic freedom · unconscious teleology · clash of wills · self as "complexio oppositorum"

What motives to therapy are primary in psychoanalysis?

Scholarly

coherence theory of truth · correspondence theory of truth · affirming the consequent · procedural evidence

Ethical Motive

Curative Motive

Notes

1. Hull, 1937, p. 2. 2. Whitehead and Russell, 1963. 3. Freud, Vol. XIII, p. 159. 4. Adler, 1930, p. 28. 5. Burtt, 1955, p. 96. 6. Freud, Vol. XV, p. 49. 7. Ibid., p. 40. 8. Freud, Vol. VI, p. 257. 9. Freud, Vol. XV, pp. 58–59. 10. Freud, Vol. XVI, p. 368. 11. Jung, 1963, p. 357. 12. Ansbacher and Ansbacher, 1964, p. 64. 13. Aristotle, *Physics,* 1952a, p. 270. 14. Ibid., p. 278. 15. Descartes, 1952, p. 24. 16. Simon, 1970, p. 75. 17. Cranston, 1957, p. 91. 18. Schur, 1972, p. 95. 19. Freud, Vol. I, p. 295. 20. Rychlak, 1968, p. 177. 21. Jung, Vol. 8, p. 31. 22. Ibid., p. 417. 23. Bohr, 1934, p. 109. 24. Freud, Vol XXIII, p. 179. 25. Freud, Vol. XII, p. 63. 26. Burtt, 1955, p. 289. 27. Frank, 1957, p. 105. 28. Ibid., p. 106. 29. Ibid., p. 144. 30. Freud, Vol. XX, p. 194. 31. Freud, Vol. VII, p. 171. 32. Freud, Vol. XIV, p. 168. 33. Ibid., p. 189. 34. Freud, Vol. XVI, p. 393. 35. Freud, Vol. XI, p. 224. 36. McGuire, 1974, pp. 115–116. 37. Ansbacher and Ansbacher, 1956, p. 57. 38. Jung, Vol. 11, p. 516. 39. Freud, Vol. XIV, p. 171. 40. Ansbacher and Ansbacher, 1964, p. 51. 41. Jung, Vol. 11, p. 5. 42. Jung, 1963, p. 70. 43. Freud, Vol. XIV, p. 79. 44. Jung, Vol. 9ii, p. 76. 45. Adler, 1964a, p. 47. 46. Freud, Vol. XV, p. 67. 47. Freud, Vol. XI, pp. 153–161. 48. Ibid., p. 156. 49. Freud, Vol. XXII, p. 73. 50. Freud, Vol. XIV, p. 78. 51. Granit, 1977; Penfield, 1975. 52. Freud, Vol. XVI, pp. 244–245. 53. Jones, 1957, p. 345. 54. See Rychlak, 1968, pp. 324–336 and Rychlak (ed.), 1976, pp. 34–35. 55. Ansbacher and Ansbacher, 1978; see esp. 292–301. 56. Adler, 1968, p. 227. 57. Adler, 1954, p. 23. 58. Adler, 1968, p. 143. 59. Ibid., p. 34. 60. Adler, 1930, p. 145. 61. Ansbacher and Ansbacher, 1956, p. 229. 62. Adler, 1968, p. 92. 63. Adler, 1930, p. 145. 64. Ibid., p. 63. 65. Ansbacher and Ansbacher, 1964, p. 287. 66. Ibid., p. 289. 67. Jung, Vol. 4, p. 337. 68. Jung, Vol. 9i, p. 109. 69. Jung, Vol. 11, p. 305. 70. Jung, Vol. 8, p. 125. 71. Rickaby, 1906, p. vj. 72. Horne, 1912, p. 43. 73. Freud, Vol. I, p. 122. 74. Freud, Vol. XIV, p. 168. 75. Freud, Vol. XII, p. 264. 76. Jung, Vol. 9ii, p. 4. 77. Jung, 1946, pp. 616–617. 78. Jung, Vol. 8, p. 182–183. 79. Jung, Vol. 9i, p. 319. 80. Ansbacher and Ansbacher, 1956, p. 11. 81. Kaufmann, 1956, p. 215. 82. Adler, 1964a, p. 147. 83. Freud, Vol. XVII, p. 236. 84. Freud, Vol. VI, p. 254. 85. Jung, Vol. 9ii, p. 5. 86. Jung, Vol. 17, p. 91. 87. Ansbacher and Ansbacher, 1956, p. 88. 88. Adler, 1954, p. 27. 89. Ibid., p. 73. 90. Freud, Vol. XIV, p. 168. 91. Freud, Vol. II, p. 117. 92. Freud, Vol. VI, p. 221. 93. Freud, Vol. II, p. 116. 94. Freud, Vol. XII, p. 320. 95. Jung, Vol. 4, p. 125. 96. Jung, Vol. 9ii, p. 267. 97. Jung, Vol. 7, p. 108. 98. Adler, 1930, p. 17. 99. Ansbacher and Ansbacher, 1964, p. 39. 100. Freud, Vol. X, p. 208. 101. Freud, Vol. XVI, p. 255. 102. Freud, Vol. XX, p. 70. 103. Freud, Vol. XXI, p. 36. 104. Freud, Vol. VIII, p. 178. 105. Freud, Vol. III, p. 104. 106. Freud, Vol. VII, p. 113. 107. Jung, Vol. 4, p. 334. 108. Jung, Vol. 7, pp. 40–41. 109. Jung, Vol. 16, p. 5. 110. Jung, Vol. 8, pp. 459–504. 111. Ibid., p. 463. 112. Ibid., p. 477. 113. Ibid., p. 463. 114. Bottome, 1957, p. 171. 115. Ibid. 116. Adler, 1968, p. 297. 117. Ibid. 118. Adler, 1964b, p. 188. 119. Adler, 1968, p. 1. 120. Ibid., p. 340. 121. Adler, 1964b, p. 86. 122. Ibid., pp. 154–155. 123. Adler, 1930, p. 7. 124. Freud, Vol. XVI, p. 434. 125. Freud, Vol. X, p. 112. 126. Freud, Vol. XXI, pp. 142–143. 127. Ibid., pp. 139–140. 128. Ibid., p. 141. 129. Freud, Vol. XIX, p. 133. 130. Freud, Vol. XV, p. 146. 131. Freud, Vol. XIX, p. 134. 132. Adler, 1964b, pp. 210–211. 133. Adler, 1954, p. 23. 134. Adler, 1964a, pp. 73–74. 135. Ans-

bacher and Ansbacher, 1964, p. 302. **136.** Ibid., p. 307. **137.** Adler, 1964b, p. 283. **138.** Ibid., p. 290. **139.** Ansbacher and Ansbacher, 1964, p. 210. **140.** Adler, 1964b, pp. 278–279. **141.** Jung, Vol. 14, p. 168. **142.** Jung, Vol. 11, p. 76. **143.** Jung, Vol. 8, pp. 355–356. **144.** Jung, Vol. 4, p. 87. **145.** Jung, Vol. 7, p. 25. **146.** Freud, Vol XXII, p. 151. **147.** Jones, 1953, p. 28. **148.** Freud, Vol. XXII, p. 151. **149.** Freud, Vol. XXI, p. 54. **150.** Adler, 1968, p. 297. **151.** Adler, 1964a, pp. 94–95. **152.** Adler, 1964b, p. 72. **153.** Ansbacher and Ansbacher, 1964, p. 213. **154.** Jung, Vol. 4, p. 262. **155.** Jung, Vol. 8, p. 72. **156.** Jung, Vol. 4, p. 280. **157.** Jung, Vol. 16, p. 5. **158.** Jung, Vol 8, p. 73.

Part II

Lockean Models in American Psychiatry and Behaviorism

Chapter 5

An "American" Psychology: The Interpersonal Theory of Harry Stack Sullivan

Biographical Overview

Harry Stack Sullivan was born on 21 February 1892, the son of poor Irish-American parents who scratched out a bare existence on a farm in central New York state; he died unexpectedly of a cerebral hemorrhage while traveling abroad, in Paris, France, on 14 January 1949. His childhood was not very happy. He was the only child to have survived in the family, others having died in infancy, and seems to have been a lonely figure who felt isolated from other boys in his early years.[1] His mother believed she had married beneath the Stack family and Sullivan seems to have been closer emotionally to his father. He was brought up in the Catholic faith but left the church in his adulthood.[2] Somehow, the family put away enough money to send their son to college, where he was a good student. After first considering physics as a career, Sullivan entered the Chicago College of Medicine and Surgery, where he took the M.D. degree in 1917.

Sullivan reports that in 1915, while in

medical school, he first studied psychoanalysis.[3] Apparently he also entered psychoanalysis as a patient in the winter of 1916–1917, receiving seventy-five hours of treatment or self-study.[4] Later Sullivan was to receive over three hundred hours of training analysis from Clara Thompson, an eminent psychoanalyst. Upon receiving his degree, Sullivan entered the U.S. Army during World War I. He worked at a public health institute for a time and later became a Veterans Bureau liaison officer at St. Elizabeth's Hospital in Washington, D.C.[5] It was here in the 1921–1922 period that he met and was greatly influenced by William Alanson White, superintendent of St. Elizabeth's and a leader in the "new psychiatry," along with others like Adolph Meyer who were trying to explain mental illness without primary emphasis on the medical model. White believed that psychiatry had much to learn from the social sciences of anthropology and sociology. Sullivan was eventually transferred from St. Elizabeth's to the Sheppard and Enoch Pratt Hospital in Towson, Maryland, where he also obtained an appointment as associate professor of psychiatry at the University of Maryland School of Medicine.[6] At the latter hospital, sometime in the 1922–1923 period, he began a new type of receiving service on an experimental basis. Through this work he became a leading authority on schizophrenia (particularly in the male).

By 1925 Sullivan was convinced that there was no satisfactory explanation of the schizophrenic process, even though he had read all of the major works on the subject, including those of Jung.[7] At about this time the American Psychiatric Association sponsored a series of meetings (funded by the Rockefellers) on personality investigation with William Alanson White as chairperson. By now, Sullivan had become White's protégé, and he was assigned the role of secretary to these meetings. The first gathering was held in December 1928, and it brought together a host of eminent social scientists, including Edward Sapir, W. I. Thomas, Gordon W. Allport, Harold D. Lasswell, Sheldon Glueck, L. K. Frank, Arnold Gesell, and David Levy.[8] The group of socioanthropological theories that dominated this gathering have been referred to collectively as the Chicago school of social science, with traditions taken from Cooley, Mead, James, and Dewey; the foremost advocates were Sapir, Lasswell, and Robert E. Park. A decided shift in Sullivan's thought began with these contacts. He found a style of thinking here that proved highly compatible with his own budding outlook on the *interpersonal* aspects of mental illness.

Finding the usual hospital routines nontherapeutic for schizophrenia, Sullivan made his experimental receiving service into a kind of subculture within the broader limits of the Sheppard and Enoch Pratt Hospital. He admitted only male patients to this ward and surrounded them with talented, well-trained male aides who acted as properly masculine models for the patients. Although he practiced individual therapy and even tried hypnosis with select patients, Sullivan's therapeutic efforts focused on altering the patient's social environment on a twenty-four-hour-per-day basis. Treatment was a full-time job that must be carried out within the framework of interpersonal relations and must emphasize the total personality of each patient within the context of the group. As he phrased it, "The mental hospital became a school for personality growth, rather than a custodian of personality failures."[9]

Sullivan's thinking continued to take on a more supraindividual coloring over the years, so that near the end of his life he actually called himself a social psychologist.[10] By 1929 the transformation from Freudian to

Harry Stack Sullivan

Sullivanian thought was apparently complete, but the specific theoretical constructs we now associate with interpersonal psychology were not framed for many more years. He seemed to accomplish his best theoretical integration under the demands of a speaking or lecture-series engagement. An important statement of his view of abnormality—*Personal Psychopathology,* written between 1929 and 1933—never reached print in his lifetime, at least partly because of Sullivan's fear that he might be "premature" in formulating his ideas.[11] Although Sullivan was to publish many articles, the only book to reach print during his lifetime was his *Conceptions of Modern Psychiatry* (1940). His other books and clari-

fications of his views—taken from lecture notes and electronic recordings of his talks—we owe to his students, particularly Helen Swick Perry, Mary Ladd Gawell, Martha Gibbon, Otto A. Will, Mabel Blake Cohen, and the foremost expert on Sullivanian thought, Patrick Mullahy.

In 1929 Sullivan left Maryland and moved to New York City, where he took up the private practice of psychiatry and psychoanalysis on Park Avenue. He had noted in his hospital studies that schizophrenia seemed to develop out of an obsessive personality structure, so he hoped to concentrate on the obsessive neuroses in his private practice. However, there was to be no report of this projected work. Sullivan's reputation continues to hinge on his initial competence in schizophrenia and the personality theory he devised based on his early work. He did much to advance psychiatry as a profession in the 1930s. Following White's death in 1933, Sullivan—with the help of Sapir and Lasswell—established and served as the first president of the William Alanson White Psychiatric Foundation.[12] The foundation was dedicated to an interdisciplinary approach to psychiatry, having training branches in both Washington, D.C., and New York City. Psychiatrists trained through this foundation are given a broad, sociocultural theoretical background in addition to their customary medical education. The resulting orientation has come to be called the Washington school of psychiatry, even though the spirit of Chicago is most evident. In 1938 Sullivan founded the journal *Psychiatry,* which he edited until his death.

In 1941 Sullivan dropped all other clinical work to act as consultant to the U.S. Selective Service Commission, which was then making plans for improved psychiatric evaluations of draftees.[13] This experience helped him formulate a series of lectures which we now have as the posthumous book, *The Psychiatric Interview* (1954). His basic ideas on personality can be found in *Clinical Studies in Psychiatry* (1956), which is taken from a series of electronically recorded lectures delivered to the staff of Chestnut Lodge, Rockville, Maryland, between 1942 and 1946. After World War II, Sullivan participated in the International Congress of Mental Health in London and the UNESCO Tensions Project which dealt with sources of international conflict and misunderstanding. In 1948, the year before his death, Sullivan was active in forming the World Federation for Mental Health. He was on the executive board of this organization, and it was while he was traveling in connection with the business of this body that his sudden death in Paris occurred. He never married.

Sullivan drew his personality theory from many sources. As we shall see, he used most of Freud's concepts, though he gave them significantly different meanings. His concept of dissociation goes back to Janet (1920) and others. Jung's influence on Sullivan is seen in concepts like personification and the multiplicity of identities that form within the personality. We know that Jung once did a study of Afro-American symbolism at St. Elizabeth's while visiting America, and he apparently was assisted by William Alanson White to make arrangements for this study.[14] Sullivan's concept of integration seems to have roots in the theories of Adolph Meyer (1910). The predominant line of sociocultural theory we see reflected in Sullivan comes from Charles H. Cooley (1864–1929) of the University of Michigan, and more directly, from George H. Mead (1863–1931) of the University of Chicago. Mead emphasized the role of language in his theory of behavior, proposing that the spoken language plays a major role in human development. Cooley emphasized the pliable nature of social customs, which in themselves cannot be reduced to physical explanations.[15] Both Mead and Cooley stressed the importance of the "other person" in defining our personality for us, that is, we behave and think of ourselves in light of how others relate to us. This *mirroring* action or "looking-glass self" emphasis can be traced to the concept of sympathy employed by the Scottish economist and social philosopher Adam Smith (1723–1790), and it is in line with the British Empiricist school of thought (see p. 11 of Introduction).[16]

Mead also coined the term *selective attention,* a variant of which Sullivan used. There was a common outlook between Mead and William James, the father of Pragmatism,[17] which is an American philosophy that follows the lead of British Empiricism; both Sapir and Lasswell followed its general tenets. Robert E. Park, the major empiricist of the Chicago school, contributed ideas to Sullivan that had to do with participant observation, operationalizing terms, the pursuit of empirical laws in behavior, and so on.[18] Sullivan even came to subtitle his journal *Psychiatry* as the "Journal for the Operational Statement of Interpersonal Relations."[19] To *operationalize* in science is to define one's theoretical construct in terms of some empirical measurement, entailing the use of independent and dependent variables in research (as when "jolliness" was measured by a laugh meter in the experiment discussed on p.   of the Introduction). W. I. Thomas (1951) provided grounds for speaking of behavioral patterns in terms of situations. Sullivan also cited the work of A. Korzybski (1921, 1924), and his mature theory is more compatible with Korzybski than with his lifelong friend Sapir (1921). Alfred Storch (1924) apparently provided background for Sullivan's theories of archaic and primitive thought forms, and the anthropologist W. H. R. Rivers (1920) actually used terms we see in Sullivan's work like *unwitting* and *diffuse.* Rivers also utilized a concept of the protopathic stage in thought. Dom. T. V. Moore (1921) was the first to use *parataxes,* though he limited this concept to the thinking of the abnormal.

In his later years as theorist, Sullivan began using the term *tension* which he adapted from A. M. Dunham, Jr. (1938), and he also made use of Lewinian (1935) field terminology, although he made it perfectly clear

that he was *no* Lewinian.[20] We have detailed the sources of Sullivanian theory because many people have the mistaken impression that he was more unique—almost eccentrically original—in his terminology than he actually was. Sullivan's style of theorizing was very much within the traditions of the Chicago school of thought. He more than any other theorist in the first half of the twentieth century moved the locus of personality description to *inter*personal rather than *intra*personal aspects of human behavior. Though Freud, Adler, and Jung had all touched on this aspect, they did not quite capture the *sociological* (supraindividual) meanings the way Sullivan did.

Personality Theory

Structural Constructs

Mind versus Body and the Organizing Role of Pattern

Sullivan was convinced that psychology had to be based on a view of behavior in which the human's cognitive (thought) processes are taken seriously. In one of his first publications (1924), he even flirted with a form of human vitalism (teleology). He was very critical at this point of the "materialistic twaddle" that results when the human's thought processes are reduced to the physical mechanisms of the medical model.[21] He was still primarily under the influence of psychoanalysis at this time, and he found it generally acceptable to embrace teleologies, dualisms, or even pluralisms if such theories would help us to understand behavior.[22] Beginning in the mid 1920s, however, we note a gradual change taking place, so that by the time he had worked out his mature outlook (*c.* 1940) there was no room for teleology or dualism in his accounts of behavior.

Sullivan needed a principle of explanation that could unite the physical with the psychic in human behavior. He found in the writings of Adolph Meyer[23] an analysis based on *pattern* which seemed to solve his theoretical problem. Meyer argued that the higher an organism rises in the scale of evolution, the more complexly organized or *patterned* is its behavior. In the case of human behavior, we find occurring the most complex organization of the animal kingdom, thanks in large measure to the patternings of language usage. Because of our language ability, we humans can name things and *conceptualize* (organize, pattern) broad areas of knowledge. We can even conceptualize *ourselves* as an identity—an ego or a self!

This patterning into complexity was extended by Sullivan to include *social unities* of an interpersonal nature as well. Think of the family unit as such a patterning, which then combines into even more complex patternings, such as religious or political identities, socioeconomic levels, and so on. Sullivan liked to define *pattern* as follows: "*A pattern is the envelope of insignificant particular differences.*"[24] When energic motion takes on a form, the result is a pattern. The swirl of air, clouds, and water that we categorize as a hurricane is actually a patterning of many different energic forces. The amount of difference between one hurricane and another is insignificant, because if we see one hurricane, we can pretty certainly know when we see another. It is at this point

—when we can slip all hurricane concepts into the same envelope (construct)—that we speak of a *pattern*.

In the case of higher living organisms, not only do we have a physical patterning into bodily parts from the basic unit of a cell to organs, but we have increasingly complex units of human experience dealing with speech functions, interpersonal relations, and so forth. Sullivan essentially asked why we call one sphere of patterned units the body and the other the mind? *Both* aspects of life share a common tendency to organize into patterns by way of identifiable energies or *an* energy. Sullivan first toyed with the idea of two energies (physical and hormic), but later he spoke in the singular. Patterned energy results in identifiable events that are more or less complex. Though some of his interpreters have taken this singular-energy construct as evidence that Sullivan considered himself a *monist,* actually he disliked this label. He thought of himself as a more dynamic, interactive, pluralistic thinker than the term *monistic* seemed to suggest was possible.

The emphasis on patterning appears in his definition of *memory* as "the relatively enduring record of all the momentary states of the organismic configuration."[25] *Thought* was defined as "organismic activity by the implicit functioning of symbols, themselves abstracts from the 'material' of life events."[26] Anything material that looks like "something" takes on a shape and to this extent is patterned; hence, Sullivan put his reference to such material in quotes. Even though Sullivan emphasized the role of language in thought, he did accept the possibility of "wordless thinking" through imagery.[27] His favorite construct was *referential processes,* by which he meant all those activities (energy transformations of a patterned sort) that we usually call our thoughts, mental pictures, or mind's-eye views.

The Patterning of Dynamisms and Personifications

Just as the term *structure* is not entirely appropriate for Alfred Adler, it is only relatively appropriate for Sullivan, because he too wanted to view human behavior in a fluid and patterned but ever-changing fashion. Sullivan carefully selected the term *dynamism* as his major structural term. He defined this construct as *"a relatively enduring configuration of energy which manifests itself in characterizable processes in interpersonal relations"* [28] and also as *"the relatively enduring pattern of energy transformations which recurrently characterize the organism in its duration as a living organism."* [29] The former definition emphasizes the human being's social side, but the latter could be used by any biologist or physiologist. The point of either of these definitions, however, was to stress that the flux and change of life fall into identifiable patterns. Because of a particular emphasis he was making in the context of defining *dynamism* on one occasion, some of Sullivan's interpreters believe that he meant *the* dynamism was the "smallest useful abstraction" for describing behavior or personality, no matter who was making the descriptive effort. This is not correct. Dynamisms or constructs can be very small relative to other dynamisms, or they can be vast conceptualizations.

For the biologist who is analyzing physical structures in behavior, a cell might prove to be the "smallest useful abstraction" he or she chooses to use in theory generation. Since the cell transforms energy for life processes, it is clearly a dynamism, though in relation to the total body we might consider it a *subdynamism*. Cells go to make up tissues and bones, which in turn constitute organs and skeletal frames, "totaling up to" the *dynamism* of a "person." A subdynamism can often carry on life even after the total dy-

namism comes to an end, as in the cases of hearts or kidneys which are transplanted from one body (dead) to another body (living). [30] Yet this explanation does not mean that in order to deal with dynamisms in a theory, we must think of a cell as *the* dynamism. We merely have to find some convenient level of abstraction from which to begin identifying our constructs of basic interest. The psychiatrist, for example, working on another theory—with different interests than the biologist—might propose as a basic unit something like the interpersonal situation. The interpersonal situation involves transformation of energy, and as long as we can conceptualize this patterned interchange as a unit of analysis in our theory, *it is a dynamism*. [31] Sullivan divided behavioral dynamisms into two broad groups: [32] (1) *zonal dynamisms,* associated with physical activities like eating, drinking, excretion, sexual gratification (lust dynamism), and so on, and (2) *interpersonal dynamisms,* which range all the way from a self dynamism [33] through two-person interactions, groups, social classes, and even entire nations. [34]

Many zonal dynamisms are patterned and in full operation at birth, but others, as well as the interpersonal dynamisms, mature after birth and are also subject to change through learning. [35] Language is an important interpersonal dynamism of this learned variety. [36] Thus far, in speaking about a dynamism as an identifiable, patterned unit of whatever we are looking at or theorizing about, we have made it appear that only an observer—like a biologist or a psychiatrist—can fix such dynamisms. Actually Sullivan did not intend this. He believed that *everyone* can fashion dynamisms, for this indeed is how self-dynamisms or many of the attitude dynamisms (political conservatism, let us say) arise. People pattern their experience all the time, and one of the *earliest* patternings we indulge in and continue throughout life is what is known as *personification.*

Dating from about the period of his contact with the Chicago school of social science, Sullivan mused over the difference between social and other forms of human experience. He concluded, "It is approximately correct to say that experience is distinguished as social rather than extrasocial when the 'external' objects which have important relation to it are invested by the experiencer with potentialities which are more or less human or anthropomorphic in character." [37] To anthropomorphize is, of course, to ascribe humanlike characteristics to inanimate nature like rocks and trees and to lower animals of all types (see p. 11 of the Introduction). Sullivan was using the term *anthropomorphic* in a more basic sense, however, in that he meant we also assign human characteristics to other people and to ourselves! This is the essence of a *social* relationship. In time, Sullivan was to call this widespread tendency for us to assign humanity to the inanimate *and* animate aspects of life *personifying* (the action or process), which then resulted in a *personification* (the patterned aspect of life).

What occasionally confuses the student of Sullivanian thought is the fact that our personifications are also dynamisms. [38] Dynamisms do not have to exist "in reality," they merely have to be under energy transformation in the heads of people—as in the fantasy products of a daydreamer. A personification can be entirely make-believe or *fantastic* (fantasied). Take, for example, the personification of a boogeyman, which so many of us as children have related to interpersonally ("He's out there, and he's gonna get me!") in our frightened retreats under

the bedsheets in a darkened bedroom. Or the fantastic but happier personification of Santa Claus. Sullivan held that God and related deity concepts are also *fantastic personifications* or *potent representations* of an anthropomorphized supreme being whom we can interact with and ask favors of. We personify our personal possessions, as when we name our automobile "Bessie" and even talk to it at times ("Come on, get started!"). Natural phenomena are personified, as when a hurricane is called "Alice." Stereotypes of all sorts are personifications of a group of people taken en masse. Finally, social institutions or national identities are also personified as "Mother Church" or "Uncle Sam." There is no doubt about the fact that the human being is a personifying animal.

Sullivan believed that personification begins with the child's personal recognition in infancy that "my body" exists. [39] This self-personification usually is distorted and at times even bizarre, but it begins the process which is then directed to others. [40] Personifications do not have to be consistent. We combine incompatible traits into a single, *complex personification* having both good and bad elements. As children we learn to think of ourselves in terms of a *me* but also a *good-me*, a *bad-me*, and even a *not-me* (all of those things we are "not like"). We also personify our parents into a breakdown of *good mother, good father, bad mother,* and *bad father.* [41] Each of these categories is due to the kinds of experiences we have with our parents as children, so that when mother is comforting and helpful, that is her good personification, and when she is punishing or distant, that is her bad personification. As children we do not see these as two different sides of the same person as much as we literally see two persons in one.

The division of our mother's personification in particular acts as the basis for a series of what Sullivan called *eidetic people* which are then retained in our memories through-out life. We can equate this term roughly with "imaginary people," [42] "illusory peo-ple," [43] or "past people." [44] We all have a storehouse of such personifications which we can dig out of our pasts and ascribe to things in the present in a fantasied interpersonal relationship. Often these eidetic people are based on the anxiety-provoking personifica-tions out of our past. Marvin, the angry young man, may be embroiled in an *inter-personal* struggle with the system of his social group because he has personified it as a bad mother or father based on childhood frustra-tions and anxieties. He claims to be fighting impersonal forces in the system, but in his fantasies he is literally trying to strike down a humanlike identity!

There is also something called a *subper-sonification* in Sullivanian theory,[45] which refers to a number of pretended roles and viewpoints we take on if they are to our benefit or just fun to play with. For example, as children we might pretend to be our parents, dress and talk like them and ex-press their attitudes. Yet we would not *really* be personifying ourselves as holding to these manners and points of view. Taking a page from Adler, Sullivan called these *as if per-formances* and *dramatizations*.[46] Sometimes we do such a good job of expressing parental attitudes that other people think we believe in them. If this is to our advantage, we may even cultivate the illusion in our public be-havior. These Jungianlike masks that Sullivan admitted might be called *personae*[47] were what he meant by *subpersonification*.

Interpersonal Relations, Personality, and Responsive Situationism

The next major dynamism of Sullivanian theory we must understand is what he called the *interpersonal relation*. As spokesman for the Washington school of psychiatry, Sullivan

could say (*c.* 1927), "The dynamisms of in-terest to the psychiatrist are the relatively enduring patterns of energy transformation which recurrently characterize the interper-sonal relations—the functional interplay of persons and personifications, personal signs, personal abstractions, and personal attribu-tions—which make up the distinctively hu-man sort of being." [48] The unit of study is now the patterned totality of all "in-between" relations going on between two different people or even within the head of one person. In other words, in *interpersonal* Sullivan in-cluded fantasied thoughts about relations be-tween people that other theorists might con-sider *intrapersonal* (that is, within the mind and not between people).[49] Sullivan would thus say that when Myra developed schizo-phrenia, she slipped into an inner or intra-personal world of fantasy in which she now carries on interpersonal relations with her fantastic personifications (hallucinated people drawn from the past, eidetic people).

Sullivan called the interacting unit of in-terpersonal relations the *situation,* referring most often to the *interpersonal situation* but occasionally to simply the *personal situation.* Situations always take on designs, so that they have purposes woven within their pat-tern of energy transformation. Whereas Sul-livan had earlier ascribed goal direction (teleology) to the human dynamism (the "per-son"), he began to move away from this to the dynamism of the situation as the source of goal direction, as follows: "The situation is not any old thing, it is you and someone else integrated in a particular fashion which can be converted in the alembic [filtering] of speech into a statement that 'A is striving to-ward so and so from B.'"[50] Situations in which interpersonal relations take place can be either *conjunctive,* in which there is harmony and a desire to come together, or *disjunctive*, in which case there is tension and a desire to separate.[51] The first life situation of a baby occurs in the me-you pattern of relating to the mother's breast. Sullivan suggested that the *good* and the *bad nipple* would be a more accurate description of our earliest personifications than *mother*.[52]

It was the recognition that human beings are *always* in a situation interacting with personifications of one sort or another that led Sullivan to drop the distinction between "person" and "situation." In the same way that he had brought together mind and body through patterned organization, Sullivan now (*c.* 1933) united the person and the social situation by considering *all* behavior fundamentally interpersonal. His definition of *personality* can be compared with the above definition of the interpersonal relation: ". . . personality is conceived as the hypothetical entity which manifests itself in interpersonal relations, the latter including interactions with other people, real or fancied, primarily or mediately integrated into dynamic complexes; and with traditions, customs, inventions, and institutions produced by man."[53]

Sullivan was now contending that personality as a *hypothetical entity* is abstracted from the basic interpersonal relations that bring behavior about. He therefore effectively dissolved personality into social relations. Critics were quick to accuse him of having lost the individual person in his social theory, pointing out that though we all participate in common social situations, we still retain our individuality. In response to such criticisms Sullivan began a lifelong denial that people *are* as individual as they flatter themselves to be. He liked to call this the *illusion of personal individuality*. Thus he observed,

For all I know every human being has as many personalities as he has interpersonal relations; and as a great many of our interpersonal relations are actual operations with imaginary people—that is, in-no-sense-materially-embodied people—and as they may have the same or greater validity and importance in life as have our operations with many materially-embodied people like the clerks in the corner store, you can see that even though "the illusion of personal individuality" sounds quite lunatic when first heard, there is at least food for thought in it.[54]

Sullivan is here using *individual* to mean *single*. Some theorists have emphasized individuality as an aspect or characteristic of *uniqueness*, and though he did not take this issue up directly, Sullivan accepted so-called uniqueness as the sum of interlacing factors in the situation for the individual (objective, subjective, fantasied, and so forth).

Modes of Experience, Language, and Awareness

As the child is born and then matures there is a different *mode* of experience to be had over the succeeding years of maturation. Life means different things to us at different points in our development. A mode is the particular style of interpersonal experience possible, based on the zonal and/or interpersonal dynamisms available to the growing person at the time.[55] In order to understand why a person behaves as he or she does, we must appreciate the inner mode through which experience is being patterned into enduring dynamisms.[56] Sullivan outlined three *modes of experience* through which he felt we all must pass—more or less—in the course of achieving adulthood: the *prototaxic, parataxic,* and *syntaxic.*

The raw feel of life is first revealed to us on the basis of our *prototaxic* mode,[57] which is based heavily on strictly zonal dynamisms. Our earliest memories are rooted in some crude infantile recollection of a momentary state in which a particular discomfort or a fleeting satisfaction took place. This would be a preverbal period of life, of course, in which significant experiences would be drawn from our bodily zones, such as the pleasure of sucking in the oral zone, or possibly the discomfort brought on from tactile sensations in the anal zone.

It is important to appreciate that Sullivan thought that the prototaxic mode—as well as the parataxic—would continue to intrude on our interpersonal relations at a somewhat lessened rate throughout life. Sometimes a highly important aspect of a social interaction is that our buttocks itch terribly but we cannot scratch in public for fear of being considered vulgar and impolite. We laugh about such experiences later, even as adults, but they do color our relations with others. A factor like this might be interpreted as a disjunctive force in the relationship by those with whom we are relating, because we do appear uneasy and ready to break off contact. By and large, all of those physiological reactions we sense throughout life as our bodily needs can be considered a form of prototaxic experience.[58] There are also initial attempts to conceptualize in the prototaxic mode. The earliest personifications like those of the good and bad nipples are formed at this time. Along about the eighth or ninth month of life, the child begins using baby talk, which signals the beginning of the *parataxic* mode of experience. In order to understand the parataxic and syntaxic modes more fully, we must now consider Sullivan's theory of *language*.

Sullivan said that we humans communicate with each other through use of gesture (nonverbal) as well as through language (verbal).[59] Nature provides us with the physical equipment to make vocal noises, but it is culture which evolves the basic sound units enabling us to express meanings in language.[60] As we grow to maturity we adapt our vocal sounds to those of our parents, who act as models for us. Sullivan stressed that words do not *carry* meaning in and of themselves but that they *evoke* meanings in the cognitive experience of the person who has been acculturated.[61] Language can be broken down into *signs* and *symbols*, each of which are patterns, hence dynamisms. A *sign* is defined as "a particular pattern in the experience of events which is differentiated from or within the general flux of experience."[62] Signs evoke meanings, as in the case of our seeing a road sign ahead that reflects a patterned organization of light which we recognize and interpret meaningfully. *We* experience the meaning, not the sign. This procedure of coming to know signs is increasingly complex, for the signs themselves combine into more and more complex (abstract) signs. Letters form into words, words into sentences, and sentences themselves are likely to be more or less intricate in the meanings they evoke. To capture this complexity factor, Sullivan suggested that: "Signs of signs we call symbols. Thus while signals [signs] are rather simply related to behavior, symbols are more complexly related, in that they refer to sundry signals which affect behavior."[63]

Signs and symbols (complex signs) are what make the human being's higher thought processes possible.[64] When we symbolize events, we relate them to other things, to thought forms, words, and other aspects of our experience, forming increasingly intricate webs of meaning.[65] To the extent that people rely on word symbols to frame higher level abstractions we can speak of them as behaving increasingly symbolically: ". . . the infant behaves non-symbolically when he is taking nourishment from the breast; and the child behaves symbolically when he calls an inanimate toy 'kitty.' . . . Thus it is quite obvious that a great deal of what goes on by the time one is a year old, even if it is inborn, is very highly symbolic." [66] Sullivan felt that it was extremely difficult to distinguish between what is symbolic and what is not symbolic in behavior.

This is not to say that we are free from nonsymbolized or poorly symbolized experience. Indeed, what Freud and the other analysts saw as an independent region of mind—the unconscious—Sullivan was to take as simply the remnants of our poorly symbolized prototaxic and parataxic experience. To the extent that we symbolize experience we are growing in awareness or consciousness, particularly if we follow the rules of logic culture designates as common sense. Our parents thus not only model sounds and words for us, but they reflect the cultural patterns of thinking that will now strike us as plausible. To the extent that a person is *not* following the culturally acceptable definitions and the logic advocated by the sociocultural climate we can speak of him or her as being *autistic*, which is ". . . an adjective by which we indicate a primary, unsocialized, unacculturated state of symbol activity, and later states pertaining more to this primary condition than to the conspicuously effective consensually validated symbol activities of more mature personality." [67]

By *consensual validation* Sullivan meant (1) the ability to discriminate in experience sufficiently well so as to be able to assess what is a fact and what is not, and (2) the capacity to formulate communicable knowledge, to make our thinking clear to others and in turn have them make their thoughts clear

to us. [68] Thus, as we come to adulthood, we move from a primary state of preverbal experience (prototaxic mode) to one in which our language terms (signs, symbols) begin taking on meaning for us. But is this communicable meaning? If it is not, then we are still at an autistic level and not yet capable of consensual validation. The schizophrenic patient who asks us to "please make them stop hypocrazing my gyrocycles" is expressing an autistic meaning lacking in consensual validation. The *parataxic distortion* of this request is too great for us to deal with.

Returning to our consideration of the parataxic mode, we can see now that all of the early words used by children have this uncertain quality about them. At some point in the latter half of the first year, a baby says something like "da da" and the happy father presumes this "word" refers to him when it may be meaningless or refer to something else entirely from the baby's viewpoint. In fact, we can even describe this autistic word as being a *private word*. [69] Of course, no word is private for long, so that in time the child learns through mother's influence the consensually valid meaning of "da da" (that is, it refers to a certain person). [70] Autistic words are generally nouns, and they continue through about the first half of the second year of life. Just as we never lose the prototaxic mode of experience entirely, so too we never lose the autistic (uncommunicative) language signs and symbols that we have concocted in our early years. Nor do we lose the capacity to assign new autisms to experience, as witnessed most clearly in our dreams. Sometimes a person will speak in his or her sleep and say something parataxic like "I see the bell top on the crop" and not be able to decipher it for a friend who has overheard this autistic statement. Autistic disturbances of thought can also be seen when people mix up their words and say things that don't quite make sense. A word that has a personal meaning to someone but is not communicable is sometimes referred to as a *neologism* (new word); in the example of psychotic speech cited above *gyrocycle* and *hypocraze* would be neologisms.

Sullivan believed that early human beings lived in a parataxic mode of experience. Rather than perceiving things accurately enough to achieve consensual validation, primitive peoples intuited or *prehended* their experience. They therefore approached life with a bias to expect this or that to happen in this or that way even before the happenings took place.[71] Prehensions are what we call our hunches, and as parataxic ways of coming to know life, they do help us to take a direction when we are uncertain. Sullivan believed that the infant even prehends the nipple-in-lips experience before he or she knows that maternal nipples actually exist.[72] Because it relies upon such intuitive and autistic processes which are in large measure nouns, we can say that parataxic thought is typified by "thinking in stereotypes."[73] We do not have the suppleness or flexibility of later, more abstract thought. Parataxic logic is often impractical and contradictory. Memory is also rudimentary; the parataxic reasoner is like a thinking machine with a poor memory bank.[74] Even so, the parataxic is a stage up the ladder of patterned organization from the prototaxic mode of experience.

Some time in the second year of life, probably around the eighteenth month, the child moves into the *syntaxic mode of experience*. The word *syntax* refers to an orderly arrangement of language terms, so that the child's understanding of experience is now ringed by consensual validation. As Sullivan put it: "I should stress that syntaxic symbols are best illustrated by words that have been consensually validated. A consensus has been reached when the infant or child has learned the precisely right word for a situation, a

word which means not only what it is thought to mean by the mothering one, but also means that to the infant."[75] Now *da da* really does mean *father,* which in turn designates a certain type of child-father interpersonal relationship.

The conscious-unconscious distinction of classic psychoanalysis also enters into this matter of presyntaxic versus postsyntaxic modes of experience. Consciousness is tied to the increasing role of consensual validation in behavior, as follows: "When we are conscious . . . we are more or less completely under the sway of the processes of consensually valid communicative thinking that we have had to learn."[76] Sullivan was eventually to drop the use of *unconscious* as a construct in favor of other terminology we will take up below. Sullivan said that Freudian symbolism, rather than being consensually valid expressions of meaning that could be interpreted by the analyst, merely traded on the eccentricities of parataxic distortion.[77] Or so-called unconscious behavior might be some preverbal remnants from a prototaxic memory containing a fantastic personification. It is important to keep in mind that by *fantastic* Sullivan did *not* mean *tremendous* or *super;* this word specifically means a fantasied, imagined, made-up personification of some type.

The Dynamisms of Personality

Sullivan believed that all personality descriptions are based on inferences a given observer makes while interacting with that which he or she is observing. "Persons (personalities) are the entities which we infer in order to explain interpersonal events and relations."[78] Just as the field anthropologist cannot go into a strange culture and interpret it meaningfully without admitting to personal cultural biases, so too the psychiatrist must appreciate that his or her *own* personality becomes a major tool of interpretation in the assessment of other people's personality. Freud's personality contributed to the interpretation of his client's personalities. This is what Sullivan was driving at when he said that his role as a psychiatrist was that of a *participant observer*.[79] He "observed," but his observations were not free of his own participation as a personality in the description of what was "seen."

Turning to Sullivan's own observations of personality, we find him drawing a major distinction between the "self system" and the "rest of the personality."[80] The terms *self, self system,* and *self dynamism* are used interchangeably by Sullivan, and occasionally he even referred to this identity concept as the *ego*. In 1931 he said that the self: ". . . is built up of all the factors of experience that we have in which significant other people 'respond' to us. In other words, our self is made up of the reflections of our personality that we have encountered mirrored in those with whom we deal."[81]

The self dynamism is the central and most important dynamism in the personality. Its functions are to (1) control awareness through whatever means it can, such as suppressing or repressing certain events;[82] (2) maintain interpersonal security and harmony so that the personality as a whole does not feel threatened or disintegrate entirely;[83] (3) control the direction of development the personality will take;[84] and (4) guard against change by forces outside of the personality which might disrupt its adjustment.[85] The self is, therefore, a kind of benign dictator and censor which restricts what will be seen

and therefore known by the personality, much as a microscope limits the range of inspection to the walls of its tubular channel.[86]

The self begins to form during the prototaxic mode, so that even though it is influenced by cultural factors as we mature, it always retains a degree of autistic distortion. This is complicated by the fact that when we personify ourselves, we never really capture our actual selves. That is, since the self dynamism is a censoring and protective agency of the personality, it will never personify the *total* range of behavior that ought to be included because some of these behaviors are upsetting to the person. The *personified self* is less inclusive than the self system.[87] Michael thinks of himself as "I, me," and so on, but he does not include in this self personification the fact that he is virtually an habitual liar. It would take someone else—a participant observer—to bring these less admirable behaviors to light with a more accurate description (personification) of Michael's total personality. None of us really ever includes all that should be included in our self personification as we think of the "I" we presume to be.

There are two broad types of personifications: (1) personifications of *ourselves* and (2) personifications of *other people*. Each of these types of personification can be thought of as examples of a structural construct. We have already mentioned the *good-me* and *bad-me* constructs. Combining these two into a single *self-image* would approximate what Sullivan meant by the personification of the self. We think that our relatively good and bad points make up the total of our self. Yet there are times when we come up against a *not-me personification*, which refers to emotional states that seem completely foreign to our natures. For example, we might be experiencing a dreadful situation (like a state of shock following the death of a loved one in an accident that was partly our fault) that makes us think "this is not happening to me." We may also sense a not-me personification while under the influence of alcohol or drugs.

Personifications of others include the good and bad nipple, mother, father, and so forth, as well as those fantastic personifications of institutions and inanimate objects we referred to earlier. There are a few more of these "other" personifications worth considering. Sullivan called an interesting one the *supervisory pattern*.[88] This is the imaginary and generalized-other person to whom we are speaking when we deliver a talk or write something down. We write or speak to someone; we choose our words and formulate our thoughts in order to make our intentions clear (consensually) as if we were communicating to a *specific* other. And, of course, not everyone in speaking or writing has the same image of what this other person is, so the choice of words, the level of argument, the clarity of presentation may vary. Sullivan made an effort to clarify his supervisory pattern, noting on one occasion that it was an "overprivileged juvenile."[89]

Another personification we all have of a generalized other is *thee,* which Sullivan employed in talking about what he called *me-you patterns.* We relate to others thinking in terms of "me and thee," but in point of fact no one is completely separate from his or her "thee."[90] The other person is always to some extent us (me), just as any personality conception we make of others is *also* reflective of our own personality. Furthermore, in coming together interpersonally, we bring to the relationship multiple me-you patterns from our past—which gets even more complicated because there are two or more people relating interpersonally, so the fantasy involved in any social situation proceeds at a geometric rate.[91] Edna is talking to Flo for the first time and is reminded of Karen. And Flo finds that Edna reminds her of a number of grade school teachers she has had in the past (eidetic people). Hence, in the conversation between Edna and Flo, we *also* have a conversation between Edna and Karen, and between Flo and her schoolteachers going on at the same time in a kind of mixed bag of personifications.

Sullivan liked to call the two-person interpersonal relation a *two-group,* which meant two *real* people interacting as opposed to one person interacting with fantasied others.[92] Sullivan put his emphasis on what social psychologists sometimes call the face-to-face group, or in the case of family members, the primary group. It was his belief that society is held together by the individual's overlapping memberships in such basic interpersonal groups.[93] But Sullivan went one step further than most social psychologists in demanding that we take the individual's fantasy productions into consideration as well.

Figure 19 presents a schematization of Sullivan's conception of personality in terms of a two-group interpersonal relation. Note that we have the entire interpersonal relation encircled, with the self and the other defining the extremes of the ellipse. On the left-hand side is a series of personifications, divided into self and other subgroupings. The self personification is made up of the good- and bad-me, and it is opposed to the not-me which lies over to the right-hand side of the interpersonal situation (relation). A series of other personifications are symbolized, running up the left-hand side of the interpersonal situation (relation), including for demonstration purposes good father, bad mother, thee, and a supervisory pattern. We must always keep in mind that the *same* scheme can be considered from the point of view of the other.

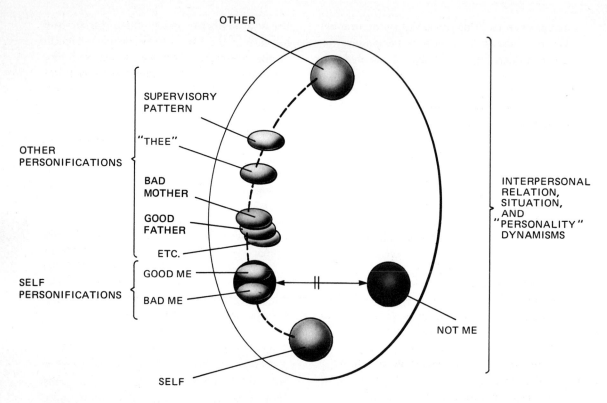

Figure 19 Sullivan's Conception of Personality

Motivational Constructs

Needs as Energy Transformations in Situational Integration

Since personality is abstracted from interpersonal relations, it is reasonable to expect Sullivan's theory of motivation to reflect this supraindividual flavor as well. He achieves this by speaking of the *integration* of a situation. We all have these *integrating tendencies,* based on biological or cultural factors in our make-up.[94] To become integrated with others is to involve ourselves with them emotionally, so that our existence means something to them and vice versa. In a sense, the action of integrating situations is synonymous with "interpersonal relations."[95] It means that we *do* relate to others,[96] that we cement our ties to others,[97] but it also means that we "pull ourselves together" in the sense of having a self-identity and good feeling about who we are.[98]

Sometimes a situation is integrated on the basis of negative feeling tones, so that interpersonal relations are then inharmonious, but as we shall see below, individuals have certain devices (dynamisms) that allow them to overlook unhappy aspects of the interpersonal situation.[99] There is usually more than one integrating tendency at work in cementing the relationship.[100] In the conversation between Edna and Flo cited above, each of these personalities had more than just one integrating tendency leading to the situation actually integrated. It is also possible for integrating tendencies to exert influence from outside of awareness—outside the self dynamism's range of vision.[101] Sullivan noted that the average person thinks of integrating tendencies as *needs*.[102] When we sense a personal need of hunger for food, or even a need to be liked by others, we are actually sensing a disequilibrium in our interpersonal situation. We are "out of integration" at the point of being in need, and therefore we are prompted to regain the equilibrium of energy transformation. It is this alternation of needs with their gratification that literally makes up our experience of life.

Needs are sensed by the individual as a *tension,* which Sullivan viewed as the "potential for energy expenditure."[103] There are *three* types of tension and changes in tension level likely to be experienced by any of us: (1) the tension of physical needs (hunger, thirst, lust); (2) the tension of interpersonal needs (security, intimacy, love); and (3) the altered levels of tension we know as sleep and waking.[104] Sullivan did not give an exhaustive list of needs for the human being, but he did give examples in both the physical and the interpersonal spheres. He spoke of the infant's needs to have oxygen, water, foodstuffs, a constant body temperature, freedom of movement, and an efficient organ system.[105] He also proposed a *power motive,* which he felt we are all born with and which generates needs to acquire, gather, collect, achieve—as in the poetic allusion to a babe in the crib who sees the moon for the first time and spontaneously reaches for it.[106] The interpersonal needs for security, intimacy, and love (combined with lust) also played prominent roles in Sullivanian thought.[107]

How do needs (integrating tendencies) actually work? We know they herald energy transformation by way of tension, but how can we say they carry over into actual be-

havior? It was in dealing with this question that Sullivan was prompted to speak of drives, forces, and vectors. A *drive* is just another way of referring to the needs we have, except now we are emphasizing the motion rather than simply the disequilibrium.[108] The *force* is another way of speaking about the tension, for it implies to the individual that not only is there a potential for energy transformation (that is, the tension) but that there is power to accomplish the changes once behavior is underway.[109] The concept of *vector* adds the idea of a magnitude and a direction that needs will take.[110] Needs are "more or less" in nature and they also suggest a direction to be taken in order to answer their prompting (integrating) tendencies. Since the vectors map the direction that force will take interpersonally, Sullivan was prone to speak of *field forces* in his final theoretical formulations.[111] Figure 20 contains the various terms in a schematization of the integration of a situation.

Notice in Figure 20 that we have two persons (A and B), beginning to integrate an interpersonal situation. Each person sends forward several arrows symbolizing needs (integrating tendencies) to hopefully connect with the other and thereby create a total field of energy transformation. Note at the bottom of Figure 20 that we have equated needs with the typical motivational concepts found in psychology, such as drives, motives, or tensions. All of these terms get at the same point in interpersonal relations, according to Sullivan. The arrows are labeled *vectors* in Figure 20 because they signify that a force of energy is being directed toward a specific person. We have basically the same two-group situation here as in Figure 19. But in Figure 20 we are now focusing on the mo-

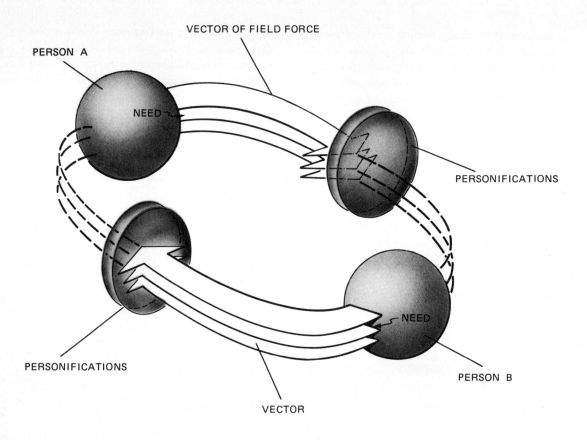

NEEDS = DRIVES, MOTIVES, TENSIONS — I.E., "ENERGY TRANSFORMATIONS"

Figure 20   Integration of a Situation

tivation aspect rather than on the various structural constructs in Sullivan's theory. We do have a few personifications (structural constructs) symbolized in Figure 20. This is to remind us that needs are always answered in part through what person A fantasies about person B and vice versa, regardless of what the complete truth of the situation may be. When we now back off and look at the total integration of the situation, we can see that it looks like a field in which energies from

spatially different points move to form a totality of transformations.

Emotion, Security, Satisfaction, and Anxiety

Emotional reactions—feelings—reflect the kinds of needs that are at play in the interpersonal situation. Sullivan held to what he called a theorem of reciprocal (two-way) emotions,[112] which meant that integration is a mutual process in which the complementary needs of the participants in a situation are either gratified or frustrated. If John has a need to be mothered and Mary, his girl-friend, has a need to mother, then the resulting two-group will probably be well integrated. However, if either Mary or John did not feel complementarily about this matter of mothering, then we would not witness a happy interpersonal situation. John would feel Mary did not appreciate him, or Mary would not understand why John feels that she is overly possessive, and so forth. If reciprocal patterns of behavior could not then be developed (some kind of altered relationship), then the two-group would become disjunctive and be dissolved.

If the level of emotion is too great in a situation, the integration will suffer as the person finds the tension impossible to direct properly.[113] There is a range of emotion to be considered in interpersonal relations. At one end of this range, we have an emotional state of utter well-being, which Sullivan named *euphoria*.[114] At the other end of the range, we have the utmost states of extreme anxiety which are literally foreign to experience, such as awe, dread, loathing, and horror. Sullivan named these the *uncanny emotions*.[115] Most of the time in life we spend between these two ends of the dimension in varying states of disequilibrium. Complete euphoria is an ideal rarely realized by the human being, but what we call "feeling good" or "pleasure" would surely approach this mood of satisfaction and security.[116] We also rarely feel the uncanny emotions, but when something happens to "shake us up" or "scare us to death," we are close to this end of the emotional range.

When the tension of an interpersonal situation is clearly physical in nature, Sullivan referred to the integration efforts as based on *satisfaction*.[117] Such things as meeting life's most basic needs to take in food, maintain oxygen, retain water, and so forth, are all tied to satisfactions. In feeling hunger, we personify the refrigerator and integrate

an interpersonal situation with it in order to relax the muscle tonus prompting us to seek the satisfaction of eating.[118] When we are seeking friendships and integrating situations with human beings, Sullivan would not always consider this to be due primarily to a satisfaction motivation. People are moved to integrate situations for other than strictly physical reasons. Of course, sometimes we can see both sides in a course of behavior. The *forbidding gesture* of a mother, frowning at her child's antics when visitors are in the home, might lead to a termination of the misbehavior. As the child stops acting up, he or she may indeed sense a feeling (emotion) of well-being as muscles relax now that mother is no longer irritated. But the main motivation of the child is what Sullivan called *security* or *security operations*, something more psychological and interpersonal than physical and intrapersonal.[119] Sullivan wanted to emphasize that in integrating situations with other people, we have a need for acceptance which cannot be reduced to some underlying physical condition.

This need for security shades into a need for *self-esteem* or *self-respect*, which is also more than a physical satisfaction. Sullivan even spoke of this as a "drive to maintain security," and essentially equated it with the power-motive construct we mentioned above.[120] It is our self dynamism that looks after the security operations, constantly trying to maintain our illusion of being better than we really are in every way imaginable. The stronger the self dynamism, the more likely it is that an individual will lack insight concerning his or her impact on others. This is why very successful people—captains of industry, movie stars, political figures, athletes—often have decidedly eccentric mannerisms. We think of them as great individualists because they do not adjust (reintegrate) their interpersonal patterns. They have a sufficiently powerful self dynamism to keep a sense of security in interpersonal relations despite their atypical styles of behavior. But it is not only the successful person who has a strong self dynamism. Even the psychotic can have a strong self, paradoxical as this may seem on first consideration.

Security as a construct tells us what a person desires in interpersonal relations, but it does not tell us what represents nonsecurity to the person. Over the years, Sullivan came increasingly to think of *anxiety* as the major indicant of nonsecurity in the personality. It is not always easy to distinguish between anxiety and *fear,* and Sullivan realized that in early life the infant probably cannot distinguish between these two emotions clearly.[121] However, the experience we call fear does have more specificity about it. We say we fear something when we have something specific in mind, which often permits us to plan action to counter the threatening object and possibly to destroy it.[122] If we fear a snake, we can avoid places where snakes are likely to be found; or if we see a snake unexpectedly and are unable to flee, we can crush it with a rock. Fear is thus a conjunctive force, and it often permits us to meet and solve our problems. Anxiety, on the other hand, is more diffuse and vague. When we are anxious, we do not always know why we feel as we do. Or if we become anxious in a situation, we might lose our head and actually become our own worst enemy. Rather than destroying the snake, the anxious person tries to flee in dangerous terrain and blindly runs off a cliff or stumbles into an entire nest of snakes just off the beaten path. Anxiety is thus a disjunctive force in interpersonal relations.

It is anxiety as an emotional reaction that takes us most directly into the theoretical explanation of interpersonal relations (personality). Anxiety is only gradually distinguished from fear by the child, probably because of its greater vagueness[123] and because it seems more oriented to his or her future expectations.[124] How is anxiety first generated? Sullivan put it very succinctly in his *anxiety-transmission theory,* as follows: *"The tension of anxiety, when present in the mothering one, induces anxiety in the infant."*[125] Anxiety is *always* triggered or evoked interpersonally (in the sense in which Sullivan used the term[126]). When an infant is held at arm's length and then given a slight drop through loss of support, he or she will stiffen up and show obvious signs of *fright*. This is a fear reaction. However, when the child becomes listless, cries pitifully, or even becomes apathetic because of a poorly integrated two-group of mother and child, we are witnessing the effects of anxiety.

The "mothering one" (actual mother, nurse, and so on) is thus the source of our first emotional awareness of anxiety. If she is relaxed and confident, loving and at ease in her contact with us, we have the feeling of euphoria. If she is in any way uncertain, unloving, or rejecting, we sense a *disphoric* state which Sullivan considered to be anxiety.[127] This combined "emotional linkage existing between the mother and infant" Sullivan called *empathy*.[128] Empathy would be like one of the vector arrows of Figure 20. Sullivan believed that empathy is a remnant of the very primitive way in which people probably first related interpersonally. It is like what the sociologists call *contagion,* that is, a direct emotional stimulus as in the hysterical responses of crowds that get whipped into a frenzy by a speaker. A child will feel in empathy with the feelings of its mother even before there is a language system or an awareness of other signs (forbidding gestures, for example) to influence his or her feelings. Even in the prototaxic mode of experience, emotions permit a child to evaluate his or her situation and to feel well integrated (conjunctive force) or poorly integrated (disjunctive force).

Some people retain this empathetic manner of integrating situations throughout life, but in most cases by the time the child is two years old, he or she no longer relies exclusively on empathy interpersonally.[129] It is probably most important in early childhood from roughly the sixth through about the twenty-seventh month of life or thereabouts. Since we are coming to know and define our selves at this time (good-me, bad-me, not-me), anxiety (loss of euphoria) has much to do with self-esteem. Sullivan came increasingly to define *anxiety* in terms of self-evaluations, as follows: ". . . anxiety is a signal of danger to self-respect, to one's standing in the eyes of the significant persons present, even if they are only ideal figures from childhood [eidetic people]; and this signal, other things being equal, leads to a change in the situation."[130]

Anxiety is often sensed by the person as some other kind of feeling. For example, we may dislike a man we know and find reasons for avoiding him, yet the real reason may be that in some region of our personality (outside awareness, unconscious) he provokes anxiety. Hence, our self dynamism very smoothly puts into effect the security operation of "I find him a bore" or "His personality annoys me" when *in fact* we should be aware of "He makes me anxious." Sullivan noted that anger is a frequent cover-up for anxiety because: ". . . anger is much more pleasant to experience than anxiety. The brute facts are that it is much more comfortable to feel angry than anxious."[131] This indirect use of the anxiety construct led some of Sullivan's critics to accuse him of calling everything that has a disjunctive effect on integration anxiety. He answered this charge by noting that several other emo-tions have equally harmful effects on integration as does anxiety, such as loneliness, envy, people's conventional prejudices, or doctrines of sin and atonement.[132]

Defensive Maneuvers, Self-Esteem, and the Socialization Process

Thanks to the growing sensations of euphoria and anxiety, the child can maneuver defensively in life. He or she can literally avoid noticing those behaviors that bring on feelings of anxiety (loss of security). This *selective inattention* permits the self dynamism to lift awareness above the level where we actually can say that we *know* this or that about ourselves.[133] Karl's shoes are not shined, and this will surely bring him a scolding if his mother notices. Even so, his self system selectively inattends and he somehow shows up once again with scuffed shoes. Strange, how Karl can put on his shoes and yet fail to notice their obviously sloppy condition until mother once again brings the matter up. Hence, Sullivan tells us that when he is talking about selective inattention he is "talking about things which you notice but never attend to—and they can be sentences or all sorts of things."[134]

If there is a defensive aspect to selective inattention, it is to avoid a lowering of self-esteem. But there is also a completely straightforward, nondefensive reason for this maneuver. Many of our activities demand rather complex, well-coordinated movements which would be impossible to carry off if we had to fix attention to every detail. A lathe operator can selectively inattend to the routine aspects of his job even as he focuses on the more difficult or dangerous aspects. A hostess looking after the affairs of a large party can selectively inattend irrelevancies to make certain that essentials get done. The important point for our long-term adjustment is just how smoothly selective inattention works and whether or not it excludes from awareness some rather important material we could well use in improving our work or social adjustment.[135]

There is a natural tendency to selectively inattend to aspects of our behavior that embarrass us.[136] Edna picks at her nose when tense, but "fails to notice" that she has this habit. Yet when it is pointed out to her—and after some soul-searching—Edna does find truth in the charge. She has selectively inattended, but there *is* a determinable tie between this nervous behavior and her self-image (self dynamism). Sometimes we selectively inattend in a period of heavy concentration or absorption, in what Sullivan called *brown studies*.[137] We are so immersed in our thought or a conversation that later, when someone tells us about a certain highly important aspect of the situation that we did not find significant to our line of thought, it amazes us to learn that we could have overlooked what took place. Earl and Barbara are having a serious discussion that is upsetting Barbara, but Earl never really notices the effects of his words on her. He is so absorbed in the point of the discussion that he selectively inattends her emotional response—leading, of course, to a disjunctive integration of the two-group.

A misperception of a situation is not clearly maladjustive until contents of experience have literally been *dissociated* from the self system. *Dissociation* means that things have been entirely cut off from identification with the self.[138] No amount of soul-searching is going to result in an awareness on the individual's part that he or she does indeed "do" this or "believe" that or "have"

such a desire. Sullivan did not make an either/or distinction between selective inattention and dissociation, viewing the entire procedure as being on a continuum, as follows: "It seems to me that the hierarchy of things that can happen about awareness of events begins with selective inattention and goes on to dissociation of events, with various degrees of awareness between, controlled largely by substitutive processes." [139]

The dissociative dynamism is always active and—a seeming contradiction—*vigilant*. It works by continuous alertness to all of those factors in awareness that might reveal its content.[140] When something in life is likely to reveal the dissociated contents, the self system is capable of changing the topic of conversation, shifting the locus of concern, or simply dismissing the newly emerging factor as "boring." These defensive maneuvers are what Sullivan meant in the above quote by *substitutive processes,* because they stand in for a healthier process in which the person would confront his or her not-me behaviors. We tend to think of a person with a strong self as necessarily being healthy, but Sullivan is saying quite the opposite. The stronger the self system is, the more smooth or *suave* (Sullivan's term) is dissociation carried out.[141] This is not unlike contrasting a child with an adult; the adult, who is more sophisticated, can cover up much more successfully than the child, who has not yet achieved a confident self-identity. The participant observer can sometimes get clues by watching the eyes of a patient for signs of *unobserved alertness*.[142] Thus, a man with dissociated homosexual impulses may take fleeting glances at the pants fly of another male. He would be shocked and revolted at the suggestion of a lustful intention toward men on his part, for he is not aware of his (dissociated) alertness. But the sensitive participant observer can literally see his suave performance.

Why are behaviors considered "wrong" by the person in the first place? Because, in maturing, we all define ourselves according to the *reflected appraisals* (judgments, preferences) of significant people with whom we have integrated situations; *they* convey the standards by which we will come to judge ourselves.[143] In appraising us, others are of course also *personifying* us and we then are capable of taking their personifications to heart in personifying ourselves and other people.[144] Our personalities are created interpersonally, and we also help create the personalities of others when we relate to them. If we therefore meet the expectations indicated in the reflected appraisals of others, we may selectively inattend but probably will not move to dissociation.[145] We personify behaviors that bring on euphoric feelings as our good-me.[146] Behaviors that will damage our self-esteem, if indulged in, we personify into our bad-me.[147] And all of the completely unacceptable behaviors or the bizarre events that result in uncanny emotions we personify into the not-me.[148] It is these behaviors, directly in opposition to the values of the self dynamism, that first call out dissociative processes.[149] Whereas the good-me and bad-me are within consciousness—we can recognize our stronger and weaker points—the not-me is always outside of awareness, though it can enter into personifications during dreaming or states of hallucination when the person is mentally ill.[150] The child's nightmare or the psychotic's seeing "evil people" both reflect dissociated, not-me dynamisms.

Sullivan liked to use the adjective *significant* to describe all those in a person's life who mediate cultural standards via reflected appraisals, whether he was referring to *parents*,[151] *people*,[152] *persons*,[153] or even *adults*.[154] Anyone who is thus important interpersonally "for us" and has to that extent "made us what we are today" is a *signifi-*

cant other. We usually carry our significant others along with us throughout life as eidetic people. Sullivan acknowledged that this was similar to Freud's introjection construct.[155] Therefore, much of the *guilt* we feel when we "misbehave" is due to these internally retained significant others out of our past, whom we have fantastically personified into bearers of the public morals.

The final point concerning Sullivan's view of socialization relates to his discussion of the *will* or *will power*. He found this concept to be outdated and unacceptable for modern psychiatry.[156] It is the self that guides and directs awareness via dynamisms, such as selective inattention and dissociation, relying in good measure on *foresight* to effect change.[157] Yet this does *not* mean that we as individuals have true freedom of choice to behave as we might choose.[158] This is an illusion used by parents and educators in a misguided effort to single out responsibility for *the* cause or *the* fault of an undesirable situation.[159] Great harm is done when a parent assumes that a son "has a will of his own," particularly when this is attributed to the boy in infancy before he has had a chance to develop a proper self dynamism. Just as no one is completely individual, so too no one is completely free from the demands of others, the situation, or the reflected appraisals in the present and those in the past. Assigning a locus of control to the individual was for Sullivan just as wrong as assigning a fixed structure to the mind. So we must ever look beyond the individual to the social milieu if we wish to know what is happening within—even a single—personality.

The Adjustment Mechanisms

Sullivan referred to almost every one of Freud's constructs over the years, and so we should examine his modifications. It is easy to see how what psychoanalysis considered *repression* or *repressed material* Sullivan considered dissociation or dissociated material.[160] He also felt that what was called repressed contents of mind were sometimes merely poorly formulated concepts and idea forms.[161] Recall that he believed thought without language is possible. Hence, it is equally possible to think of preverbal (parataxic) or nonverbal experience manifesting itself in dreams or other so-called parapraxes (Freudian slips). It is not that something has been pushed out of awareness so much as that something never had been properly framed for conscious expression to begin with. Sullivan simply could not accept a view of the mind turning in on itself via *antithetical* ideas in the way that Freud was so willing to conceptualize.[162] Whereas Freud was prone to see syntaxic meaning in mental blocks, slips of the tongue, neologistic words, and so forth, Sullivan questioned this antithetical strategy, claiming that parataxic distortions are syntactically *meaningless*.

Sullivan could find no evidence for *fixation* in his schizophrenic subjects.[163] He did think of human development in terms of stages, however. At certain crucial points along the way to maturity, while moving from one stage to another, a child might develop what Sullivan called a *malevolent transformation*.[164] This was a special form of dynamism, which crystallized some unhealthy pattern which then persisted in the person's behavior. Rather than being a fixation, the malevolent transformation would thus be a continuing pattern of maladaptive behavior. The teenaged girl who continues acting like a baby has not fixated; she has just malevolently—that is, with the aim of irritating her parents and others—transformed her behavior from

one level to another. Hence, though Sullivan does not speak of fixation, he does refer to the "arrest and deviation of personality development."[165] In line with this view of fixation, Sullivan thought of *regression* as the collapse of behaviors not yet fully learned, or as the perseverance of previous stages still active when they should already have been passed through.[166] Regression is thus a common occurrence: ". . . In the course of the life of any child, you can observe, practically at twenty-four-hour intervals, the collapse, when the child gets thoroughly tired, of patterns of behavior which are not very well stamped in. . . ."[167]

Sullivan defined *sublimation* as "the unwitting substitution, for a behavior pattern which encounters anxiety or collides with the self system, of a socially more acceptable activity pattern which satisfies part of the motivational system that caused trouble."[168] An acceptable motivation is thus deflected and given only partial gratification in sublimation, as in the case of a woman Sullivan described who had sexual promptings for every male she met, including some subliminal thoughts of being a prostitute. In time, through the mediation of a rather handsome preacher, she deflected her energies into "good works" aimed primarily at helping "fallen women."[169]

The concept of *identification* was handled by Sullivan in terms of a "feeling of familiarity" that exists between a mother and her daughter or a father and his son.[170] Parental interest and pleasure is stimulated when, for example, a mother sees her daughter excel at modern dance or a father observes his boy tossing a baseball around. The parents relive their own pasts in this way, and by applauding such efforts in their offspring, they ensure that the acceptable patterns will be culturally transmitted. Sullivan preferred the term *interiorization* to introjection.[171] We have already noted above how interiorized personifications of past significant others (eidetic people) act as the basis of conscience over our lifetime.

Projection was interpreted as a special case of foresight. Everyone projects in interpersonal situations because we all try to foresee what is about to happen.[172] But if we have a low sense of self-esteem, our projections will reflect this negativism as we always anticipate the worst, see our failures in everything we do, expect others to dislike us, and so forth. Another probable cause of seeming projections is the fact that some individuals simply have not made adequate discriminations or differentiations between people.[173] A rebellious teen-aged boy might not have discriminated properly between the authority-subordinate relationship he has been experiencing with his father and the analogical but still *different* relationship of this sort he has with his teacher. Hence, he seems to be projecting elements from the father relation to the teacher relation, but rather than projecting, he is simply failing to discriminate.

Sullivan's view of *compensation* was as a dynamism "by which simpler activities and implicit processes are substituted in lieu of difficult or impossible adjustment."[174] Going to the movies rather than doing homework would be a compensation. This is quite a different usage than we saw Adler develop in Chapter 2. Sullivan used *displacement* somewhat more conventionally as the deflection of an emotion from one context to another. For example, the schoolchild who picks a fight with a peer on the way home from the classroom in reaction to irritation with the teacher that day has displaced hostility from the latter to the former.[175] Finally, Sullivan also used *rationalization* in the familiar sense of "giving a plausible and often exceedingly inconsequential explanation" of some event rather than owning up to the real reasons prompting one's behavior.[176]

Time-Perspective Constructs

Sullivan named and outlined six preadult *eras* or *epochs* of development, and we will take them up in order.

Infancy: From Birth to the Maturation of Language Capacity

The newborn infant comes into the world in the parataxic mode of experience, with the major *zone of interaction* the oral activities of breathing, sucking to eat, and so forth. This is what fixes the infant's attention on the mother's breast and makes it likely that he or she will personify it in the first discriminatory act of life (good versus bad breast).[177] There are two ways in which anxiety now arises in the child: through a violent disturbance in a zone of contact (injury to the mouth, for example) or through a loss of empathy with the mother (moving from euphoria to anxiety).[178] Sullivan felt that the oral zone is the "main stream" for the evolution of the self, because it enters into so many of life's activities, from eating and drinking to speech and sexual play.[179] Zones are always tied into the person's needs, which, of course, represent integrating tendencies. Dynamisms can thus be identified in connection with zones, and something like an oral zone is *also* an oral dynamism. When we stress the particular location of a dynamism's influence, we are speaking of the *zone,* the region in which integration is literally being patterned. By knowing the zone involved in an integrating situation, we know the *basis* for the formation of a two-group like mother-child.

Zonal definitions are not limited to the specific body part after which they are named. For example, the oral zone includes the lower part of the face and the muscles of the mouth, throat, and larynx (voice box).[180] It also includes in the very young child the muscles controlling breathing, crying, and probably to an extent, the auditory channels as well.[181] As we mature, a number of zones act as the locus of our dynamisms, such as the retinal area, auditory apparatus, tactile receptors, kinesthetic apparatus, urethral and anal zones, and the genital zone.[182] Sullivan even stretched his concept of zonal need to include a kind of "capability" or "competence" pleasure (related to the power motive) in the delights of sheer growth. He once referred to a general concept of the *zonal need* as the "need to manifest every capability that matures—what we see as the child's pleasure in manifesting any ability that he has achieved."[183]

Early learning begins in *prehension* (primitive perception). By about the sixth to eighth month of life the infant makes facial expressions. In most instances, the child is rather well organized by the ninth month,[184] distinguishing between fear and anxiety by this time and responding to the changes in his or her anxiety level in order to meet parental expectations. Language training is also beginning near the end of the first year of life, and the child thus moves into the parataxic mode of experience in which autistic speech is the rule. It is very important for the child to acquire a sense of foresight in experience. "The comparatively great influence of foresight is one of the striking characteristics of human living in contrast to all other living."[185] Sullivanian theory emphasizes that a child can evaluate even *before* he or she has speech. The child can judge what is likely to be taking place in the upcoming situation based on how he or she *feels* emotionally about it.[186] Later, the child uses language to name and specify these foresightful judgments concerning what is likely to occur in experience.

Childhood: From Language to the Maturation of the Need for Playmates

Much of what we mean by socialization is the restriction of personal needs, the willingness to forgo and adapt to the demands of others, and the acceptance of partial satisfactions rather than full pleasures. This pretty well sums up what Sullivan meant by *sublimation,* and in his theory of development he saw this dynamism as taking shape during the first few months of life.[187] However, it is in the era of childhood that sublimation becomes a very prominent dynamism, thanks in large measure to the onset of language, the learning of "no, no" and "do this" or "don't do that." Mother and father are expanding their prohibitions, and the child must increasingly settle for less energic transformation than he or she would like to have in zonal needs.[188] Gradually, sublimation is joined by identification, as the child comes to play "as if" he or she were a parent (playing mommy and daddy).[189] The childhood era is a time of growing self-awareness, and the personifications of the self are increasing at a rapid pace (especially the good-me and bad-me). We are moving along now into the second and third years of life. Empathic controls are giving way to the controls of consensually validated language. Hence, the prototaxic mode is traversed, and early syntaxic experience is beginning.

Juvenile Era: From Playmates to the Maturation of the Need for Isophilic Intimacy

The next stage in development is defined broadly as "the years between entrance in school and the time when one actually finds a chum—the last landmark which ends the juvenile era, if it ever does end."[190] This is a time of continuing expansion in self-definition and knowledge for it covers much and sometimes all of our grammar school years. The personality really awakens for the first time in the juvenile era, and the self system confronts the world as something existing for its own sake and following its own rules.[191] Children gradually realize that if they are to find a place in this scheme of things, they will have to become involved in many things that never before occurred to them. The world is no longer their oyster. The "spoiled" child finds that on the playground he or she must be considerate of others or be rejected by them.[192] This would be very upsetting to the child of this era, because there is a growing need at this age to have playmates or *compeers*. The compeer is a friend who helps the child extend his or her range of capability in play and who acts as a buffer against the feelings of loneliness that might result if the child were isolated. There can be several compeers in the child's life at this time, but they do not assume the major importance that a very select person—the chum—will assume in our next stage of development.

Children in the juvenile era also learn the importance of *competition* in life. They find that status in the group hinges on how bright one is in the classroom, how daring on the playground, or how expert in the misadventures of childhood pranks. A child tries to establish a favorable *reputation* in one or more of these realms of activity, which means he or she must compete with compeers for the limelight. In fact, Sullivan used to equate the concept of a "juvenile person" with something like "habitually competitive" even if he were referring to an adult.[193] To make it more likely that they will have self-esteem, children in this era begin collecting into various in-groups with select compeers.

Identification with the age group is thus furthered, for the child quickly takes on the behavioral styles of those compeers he or she considers desirable—whether they be school achievers, delinquent groups, or those with expensive and attractive clothes. Children readily understand groupings of this sort, which makes them especially vulnerable to accepting social stereotypes of all sorts (honkie, nigger, kike, wop, and so on).[194]

We might note at this point that Sullivan put more stress on the ages beyond four or five than the classical analysts did. He once said quite specifically that personality development continues beyond the age of ten.[195] In fact, one can never really say in Sullivanian terms that a personality is fixed, for what one *is* depends on the social environment being integrated at the time. Commonalities and continuities in behavior are to be seen, but these are due more to the constancy of social forces than to some internally fixed structure called personality.

Presumably the *Oedipal complex* would take place around the late childhood to the early juvenile era of development (ages four through six). Sullivan did not deny that a seeming Oedipal situation exists in the male. He was not so certain about the female, and he once wrote a paper with the collaboration of his training analyst, Clara Thompson, in which the *Electra complex* was specifically denied.[196] In time, it seemed to Sullivan that so-called Oedipal factors probably were misunderstandings made by analysts of some rather common tendencies in human behavior. For example, we have the man who actively compares his wife with his mother. Hysteroid people are likely to do this, probably because they are dependent, suggestible, and likely to seek mother substitutes as marital partners.[197] But this comparison need not be taken as evidence that the grown man had literally desired his mother as he now desires his wife in the sexual (lustful) sense. Recognizing that *philos* is Greek for "love," Sullivan distinguished between this state and *eros,* which would refer more specifically to a genital factor in interpersonal relations. Lust (eros) is *not* identical to love (philos). "The tendencies to integrate lustful-erotic situations should not be confused with those which eventuate in love situations. The latter may survive indefinitely the loss of prospective sexual satisfactions or the integration of sexual situations with persons not in the love relationship."[198] The genital-lust dynamism is not even matured at the period of life in which the classic psychoanalytical theory would have children lusting after their parents.[199]

We can now add some prefixes to our eros-versus-philos distinction and speak about *autophilic* (self-love), *isophilic* (loving a member of the same sex), and *heterophilic* (loving a member of the opposite sex); or alternatively, *autoerotic* (self-lust), *isoerotic* (lusting for a member of the same sex), and *heteroerotic* (lusting for a member of the opposite sex).[200] The point of this breakdown is to make entirely certain that we distinguish between *love* and *lust,* as well as the sex of the "other" sought for either form of emotional integration. Early in life children doubtlessly pass through what might be called an *autophilic* stage in which, as a result of a poorly defined awareness, they invest all love emotions in themselves. Gradually, they extend these loving ties to parents as isophilic and heterophilic ties. But these emotional ties are not to be confused with erotic attachments of a so-called Oedipal situation.

From the vantage point of the parent, a child is also something to be loved (not lusted). In addition, we have already noted that parents have a "feeling of familiarity" for offspring of their same sex. It thus happens that a mother is probably less accepting of her daughter's antics or a father is more quick to paddle his son for misbehaving than either parent would be if they were dealing with an opposite-sex offspring.[201] The upshot is that children appear to be in conflict more often with the parent of their own sex.

Preadolescence: From Isophilic Intimacy to the Maturation of the Genital-Lust Dynamism

Sometime between the ages of 8½ and 12 years, a child moves into preadolescence—assuming that he or she *ever* does—and this period is typified by the development of a need for *isophilic intimacy.* Sullivan occasionally referred to this time as an isophilic stage of personality development,[202] and he was not above speaking of it as a homosexual age in some of his earliest theoretical papers.[203] But as he came to distinguish more definitely between lust and love, he dropped the reference to a homosexual stage per se. The point of isolating this life era is to underscore the growing need the young person has for an intimacy with someone, a bond of love (philos) that unites him or her to a member of the same sex on a far deeper level than is the case with compeers. As Sullivan said of the preadolescent, "We can picture him as driven by the need for intimacy—just as lust will drive one when sufficiently unsatisfied—to look at practically everyone he came in contact with who was anywhere near his age as a potential friend, intimate, or chum."[204]

The same-sex person the preadolescent settles on is technically referred to as the *chum.* Preadolescence is clearly the era of the chum, and it waits on the maturation of a "capacity for intimacy" which is the highest manifestation of love.[205] When we love someone, we care more about the other person's satisfactions and security than we do about our own.[206] The preadolescent comes to trust and rely on his or her chum and exchanges innermost secrets with this very significant other. This two-group integration provides the first truly social orientation of the person's life, because there is an intimacy never before achieved with anyone.[207] Sullivan defined *intimacy* as perfect equality in a two-group integration.[208] Up to this point in life the socialization process has depended on the anxiety versus euphoria contrasts provided by parents, or the predominantly autophilic pleasures attained in playing with compeers. But now the preadolescent is *giving* something to another and is entirely committed to the interpersonal gratifications of an other.

The chum acts as a realistic sounding board for the preadolescent. All of those autistic ideas and fantastic personifications about oneself or others can now be tested against the thinking and experience of the chum.[209] If there is a serious distortion of facts about growing up or some uncanny feeling about an emerging (for example, sexual) impulse, the chum can calm fears of being different by noting that he or she too has experienced the same thing. Sometimes, particularly in later preadolescence when the lust dynamism begins to mature, transitory homosexual behavior may take place between chums. This is ordinarily nothing to worry about and can actually prove a healthy experience since it teaches both participants something about themselves in a shared and less distorted sense than might otherwise be true.[210] Of course, if this form of sexual release is continued—if the preadolescent era is not passed through and forgone—then a

continuing homosexual pattern might well result.

Even when homosexuality is not practiced between chums this period of life can seem abnormal to parents who sometimes witness their daughters/sons having a terrible crush on another girl or boy and being concerned about this other person's every move, change of friendships, and so on. This situation is sometimes complicated by the presence of more than one intimate, though rarely do we find more than three people in a chum relationship. Preadolescence is also the expanding age of the gang, and patterns of being leader or follower are under formation.[211] When chums and other gang members are separated—because of vacations or squabbles, say—the parent must live through unhappy periods of their child being lonely. The wretchedness of loneliness, however, is the other side of intimacy.

Early Adolescence: From Genital Lust to the Patterning of Lustful Behavior

The time of puberty may vary considerably from person to person, but sooner or later the young person passes into pubescence and begins to feel definite promptings from a bodily zone that was formerly concerned with the elimination of wastes.[212] Sullivan called this prompting feeling *lust,* or the "felt aspect of the genital drive." [213] Just as he or she was previously driven by the need for intimacy, the adolescent is now driven by the need for lustful gratification. The problems that arise here are confounded by the fact that *erotic* is not necessarily *philic* love. Some adolescents, having been taught that sexual love is "dirty," shift their love style appropriately—from *isophilic* (same sex) to *heterophilic* (opposite sex)—yet cannot *also* acquire a *heteroerotic* tie to their loved one. They can fall deeply in love, eventually marry, and still have a problem in adjusting to the sexual side of marriage. Others shift love style and readily acquire erotic drives for the opposite sex as well. Often it is possible to satisfy the genital-lust dynamism without having *any* true sense of love for a sexual partner. If one partner in sexual intercourse is satisfying love and lust while the other is satisfying only lust, the outcome of this relationship is likely to be unhappy (disjunctive) for one of the participants, if not both.

Sullivan noted that some people engage in sexual intercourse yet really do not concern themselves with the satisfactions of the other. We witness people who, even as chronological adults, use other people's bodies rather than their own hands in what might be termed *autoerotic masturbation*.[214] Such an individual has not really matured properly nor patterned sexual integrations in a truly interpersonal, social sense. Such a person would surely not be "in love" and probably would have no particular need for intimacy. Sullivan felt that, as the last integrating tendency to mature, the lust dynamism was very powerful and could *not* be sublimated as easily as could other zonal needs (the zone here would be the genitals, of course).[215]

Late Adolescence and Maturity

Sullivan wrote that ". . . a person begins late adolescence when he discovers what he likes in the way of genital behavior and how to fit it into the rest of life."[216] There are many factors of educational and social class entering into a person's decisions to seek gratifications of this or that variety. In certain cultures homosexual relations are tolerated, and

as long as this is acceptable to the group and the individual is not otherwise immature, we cannot fault this level of adjustment. Not since the early years of its inception have we seen the rapid expansion of the syntaxic mode that we witness in late adolescence.[217] Higher education, marriage, and career occupations extend the person's horizons and bring him or her ever more centrally into the fold of consensual validation: the established practices of social man and woman that eventuate in families, homes, parenthood, and all of the ensuing responsibilities of citizenship. It is the lot of the mature personality to learn how to live by way of *sublimatory reformulations* which are ways of gaining a good deal of, yet not complete, satisfaction.[218] Complete satisfactions can be degrading and uncivilizing for the person, but if he or she has come through the years with a regard for others, the mature person should have learned enough to make life generally satisfying. It is essential that the mature personality reflect a need for intimacy and collaboration with at least *one*—and preferably many—others.[219]

Individual-Differences Constructs

One does not find many personality typologies or traits in interpersonal-relations theory, not the least of the reasons being that Sullivan had doubts about the validity of a fixed personality at play in behavior.[220] Personality was not the *cause* of behavior, but more the *effect* of social factors. For his part, Sullivan remarked, he would really rather typologize interpersonal relations than people's personalities.[221] At the same time, he recognized that there are variations in the ways in which people integrate situations. They reflect social class, race, and immigrants' national origins, as well as styles derived from the developmental eras.[222] There is really only one major attempt in Sullivan's writings to define a series of types or *developmental syndromes,* as he called them. In his 1940 book, *Conceptions of Modern Psychiatry,* he sketched a series of ten identifiable syndromes.[223] These were based on his "arrest and deviation" view of fixation and were really more appropriate to a theory of abnormality than to personality in general. We will not devote much space to their consideration but will survey them as an example of how Sullivan looked at human behavior.

The first five developmental syndromes were considered *autistic,* based on the fact that they set in very early in development. There are those persons who show a *lack of duration* in their interpersonal ties, who never become intimate or committed to others; they often are unable to profit from experience and can appear superficial and even psychopathic (shallow, manipulative) in behavior. There are *self-absorbed* people, who go through life in constant reverie (daydreaming); we call them escapists and idlers. The *incorrigible* person refuses to be educated and seeks out ineffectual people with whom to integrate situations so that he or she can feel superior without really being challenged. The *negativistic* person is the opposite of the self-absorbed; rather than turn inward this type constantly makes known to all who will listen that things are "just not right." Since this griping sometimes leads to change and reward ("the squeaky wheel gets the grease"), the negativistic person is socially more useful than the self-absorbed. There is the *stammerer* (stutterer), who uses this verbal failing in interpersonal relations to control others, who must wait until he or she decides when they may speak.

The next five syndromes are not considered autistic. They are the result of arrests and deviations in development, dating from roughly the juvenile period through late adolescence. Recall that a chronic juvenile is likely to be competitive throughout life; hence, it is fitting that the first nonautistic syndrome is the *ambition-ridden* person, who has to compete with everyone on every silly and unimportant dimension of life. The *asocial* person avoids intimacy, entering into two-group ties only when it is convenient and profitable to do so. The *inadequate* person integrates situations on the basis of dependency on another, or identifies with some worthy cause needing accomplishment. There is the *homosexual* person, who cannot integrate two-groups with members of the opposite sex; the degree of this inability varies from the routine "woman or man hater" to the more pronounced clinical syndromes in which lust can be satisfied only with members of the same sex. Finally, we have a rather broad category of behaviors that Sullivan lumped into the *chronically adolescent.* These individuals are driven by lust, and they never seem able to find the right sex object because, in fact, they lack the capacity for heterophilic relations and are consequently cynical in their frequent love affairs. Speaking of males, Sullivan called these the Don Juan or "hymen hunter" types, searching throughout life for a new sexual conquest in the misguided belief that lust can satisfy the need for love.[224]

Sullivan liked to refer to what he called a *one-genus hypothesis,* which held that the commonalities among people far outweigh their differences.[225] We have seen this tendency in his reluctance to emphasize individuality, as well as his dislike for typologizing people in general. But Sullivan claimed to be studying *all* people *all* of the time, even when psychotic individuals were subjects for his participant observation. Here is his final formulation of the one-genus hypothesis.

We shall assume that everyone is much more simply human than otherwise, *and that anomalous interpersonal situations, insofar as they do not arise from differences in language or custom, are a function of differences in relative maturity of the persons concerned. . . . I try to study the degrees and patterns of things which I assume to be ubiquitously [uniformly, commonly] human.*[226]

This provides us with a natural bridge for considering the next major aspect of Sullivan's thought—his theories of illness, cure, and therapy.

Psychopathology and Psychotherapy

Theory of Illness

The General Theory of Abnormal Behavior

In line with the theory of classic psychoanalysis, Sullivan felt that mental abnormality is tied to personality in that sick individuals are limited in the kinds of behavior they may exhibit.[227] These limitations are specifically concerned with the self dynamism, which for various reasons is not able to get some kind of biological satisfaction.[228] This inefficiency of the self dynamism can often be traced to the fact that one form of dynamism is used in attempts to relate interpersonally. Take the person who tries to agree with everyone, for example. Sullivan would call this agreeing tendency a *dynamism of difficulty*, because the individual

cannot be spontaneous or flexible interpersonally.[229] At times, we all must oppose others and form disjunctive relations. We will have more to say of this below, but the point of Sullivan's definition of mental illness is that a quantitative and continuous dimension extends from *normal* agreeableness to *abnormal* agreeableness. We can measure this tendency and draw a line on the scaled dimension beyond which we would call a person "abnormally agreeable," but all this means is that there is a region beyond which the society suffers if all people behave in this way.[230]

As in his approach to personality, Sullivan did not want to rely on organic, hereditary, or other constitutional factors to explain the nature of mental illness. He was attracted to the biological explanation only in the case of manic-depressive psychosis. But dating from his earliest contacts with schizophrenic patients, he was convinced that mental illness—insofar as we can use the term—stemmed from bad interpersonal relations.[231] He chose to speak of "difficulties of living" when referring to mental illness.[232]

In one of his first papers, Sullivan stressed what he called the *warp of personality* to be seen in the developing abnormal, usually occurring around the juvenile era.[233] He was later to revise upward the period of onset, as when he discussed the vital role of a chum during preadolescence. But the fundamental point here was that a maturing child needs to have his or her asocial or poorly socialized (autistic, fantastic) views of the world *corrected*, both by interactions with compeers and especially through the intimacy of a chum. The next point Sullivan used to explain abnormality concerned a person's self-esteem or confidence. Very often the individual withdraws into a dream world to cultivate unrealistic (autistic) views of life.[234] This lowered confidence and tendency to withdraw stems from a lack of parental empathy or negatively reflected appraisals from significant adults.

As the developing child feels confidence slipping away, he or she begins to selectively inattend to and then to dissociate important weak spots needing attention and correction.[235] Rather than meet challenges the self dynamism has set on a course of avoidance, building security on foundations of sand. Hence, "we may say . . . as a generality, that healthy development of personality is inversely proportionate to the amount, to the number, of tendencies which have come to exist in dissociation."[236] One of the major sources of lowered self-confidence in our culture is the stringent taboo on sexuality.[237] Too many young people—especially young girls—are made to feel that sex is a not-me experience. Since the lust dynamism is extremely difficult to sublimate, the wretched tensions put upon the personality through sexual taboos lead to eventual dissociation and the deterioration of adjustment.[238]

The Role of Social Factors

Considering Sullivan's one-genus hypothesis and his view in general of personality as a social phenomenon, we could easily ask him: is the *person* mentally ill, or is the interpersonal situation—and, by extension, the *society*—the actual locus of abnormality? In 1931 Sullivan would have answered this as follows: "Some ten years' rather close contact with sufferers of schizophrenic disorders culminated in the firm conviction that not sick individuals but complex, peculiarly characterized situations were the subject-matter of research and therapy."[239] By the late 1930s Sullivan had generalized this attitude to the social order as a whole.[240] And finally, during the period of World War II, he put this supraindividual view most graphically. "The Western world is a profoundly sick society in which each denizen, each person,

is sick to the extent that he is *of it,* of its blended vitality and debility, of its chances of dissolution or reorganization and recovering after a dangerous crisis."[241] We thus have Sullivan diagnosing an entire civilization at one historical moment, coining what was to become a major phrase—the *sick society!*—in the post–World War II writings of many social analysts as well as critics of Western culture in general.

The Symptoms of Mental Disorder

All psychiatric patients, like everyone, reveal certain signs in their behavior implying a possible maladjustment. But the psychiatrist cannot assume that all signs are true symptoms.[242] As participant observer the psychiatrist must pursue his or her diagnostic impressions until clarity is arrived at. Not everyone who likes to straighten pictures on the wall (sign) is an obsessive-compulsive neurotic (symptom). A true symptom usually appears when least expected, popping into view when the self dynamism for some reason has lost the ability to restrain the dissociated material. Symptoms appear in awareness as tics (involuntary muscle movements), seizures of emotions (uncanny emotions), or the more dramatic forms of delusions and hallucinations.

Material that has been dissociated in the personality does not just sit and wait in limbo, split off from awareness. It continues to integrate experience, to grow in influence as it increases in range and complexity.[243] This incubation phenomenon means that something that is dissociated as a fairly minor item can return as a major factor in the personality. Emily began to selectively inattend then dissociate minor worries about dark corners in the large, ramshackle farmhouse she inherited from her uncle. That was five years ago, but today she is a virtual recluse in her own home, afraid to leave her bedroom because she is certain there are evil spirits lurking about the place, a few of which she claims to have seen.

It sometimes happens that a symptom makes its appearance at that point in time when the individual can gain some advantage through its arrival.[244] A man who is afraid of responsibility can believe that he has an uncontrollable impulse to kill himself and thus keeps his wife dashing about looking after his affairs, because he must avoid all "risky" activities like crossing streets or driving a car.[245] The wife is made victim of the husband's symptom. This secondary-gain feature of symptoms should not be overrated, but it is often an important reason for the appearance of dissociated material. (See p. 87 for Freud's use of secondary gain.)

But the more serious form of symptom appearance occurs as what Sullivan called an *automatism*. In this case, the dissociated material is actively attempting to *integrate* a situation independent of awareness. Also personification is likely to take place as in the case of the woman "seeing" humanlike forms (evil spirits) in the shadows.[246] Hallucinatory symptoms usually begin with feelings of low self-esteem. The person may have been dissociating self-critical ideas, only to have them return in the form of "voices." The next step is to pattern these into personifications. "The hallucinated utterances come rather quickly to be statements of particular illusory persons or personifications— God, the Devil, the President, one's deceased mother, and the like."[247] Delusions follow the same pattern as they descend upon

awareness as if from some other power, usually during a time of crisis to solve some problem in living. Sullivan called these *autochthonous ideas,* by which he meant "a content of thought, a matter in mind, which seems literally to have come from outside one, as if put there—that is, one has no feeling of ownership or parentage."[248] The dissociated material is now on its own, having been personified into an identity with which the patient has integrated a two-group!

Note that hallucinations and delusions always have considerable parataxic and even prototaxic distortion about them. This is why they can appear so crazy to us; they reach beyond consensual validation. The psychotic person brings all manner of not-me experiences and eidetic people into these symptoms.[249] As the psychosis progresses, the autistic reveries are stimulated and the person's referential processes (thoughts) become even more primitive.[250] If the resulting complex of beliefs is poorly rationalized and autistic, we are likely to use the term *unsystematized* in describing this state of delusional mentality. *Systematized* delusions are better rationalized and hence are more consensually plausible.[251]

Sullivan was intrigued by the highly dramatic nature of many delusional and hallucinatory symptoms. Autistic revery is, after all, similar to a play in which we put ourselves on center stage to achieve some feeling of victory, revenge, depression, or sympathy. There is a rough analogy between the personal mythology of a psychotic—who is likely to see himself or herself as the emissary of good and the psychiatrist as the emissary of evil—and some of the great mythologies of mankind.[252] But an analogy is *all* that this can be. Sullivan refused to believe that these tragic fantasies come from some Jungian racial unconscious.[253] If there is anything universal about these dramas, it is the fact that all people—being essentially alike—find themselves struggling with the same sorts of things in life.[254]

The Syndrome of Schizophrenia

Sullivan distinguished between two broad types of schizophrenia: (1) an organic, degenerative disease of gradual and insidious onset (more serious than it at first appears), which was suggested by the Kraepelinian concept of *dementia praecox* (see p. 120); and (2) the disorder of *schizophrenia* proper, which is due to problems in living and comes on more abruptly although there are subtle signs of the abnormality in a person's behavior for years.[255] It was the second form of mental disorder that Sullivan took to be schizophrenia. He considered the Kraepelinian diagnostic category of simple schizophrenia to be dementia praecox and not a true schizophrenia.[256] In general, the more rapidly a schizophrenic disturbance arises, the better is the patient's prognosis for eventual recovery.[257] In other words, people who are getting along reasonably well and then suddenly "go crazy" are more likely to recover than people who have for years been slowly sinking into the world of autistic reverie.

In diagnosing the severity of any one illness, we take as our first clue the patient's *depth of regression* (inadequately developed behaviors which collapse; see p. 346). The deeper the reversion to earlier developmental levels, the more serious the illness. This is not an infallible sign, however. The *hebephrenic* schizophrenic, for example, who regresses to an infancy level, often smearing his or her excrement about the walls of the room while babbling incoherently, is probably not as deeply regressed as the *catatonic* schizophrenic, who assumes prenatal postures in what seems an intrauterine regression (with knees pulled up to chest, enveloped by the arms).[258] Yet the outlook for catatonia is more promising than it is for hebephrenia.

Despite this technical problem over the depth of regression in schizophrenia, it is generally true that the schizophrenic regresses below the level of socialization, which puts this person at least into the parataxic mode.[259] Schizophrenia usually begins between the fourteenth and twenty-seventh year of life.[260]

Sullivan believed that schizophrenia has two stages of development. In the first stage there is a rapid loss of faith in the self and the universe (in the worthwhileness of life itself), with great emphasis on dissociation to avoid resolving the immense threat involved. The second stage was described by Sullivan as follows:

The individual, with serious impairment of the dependability of his self and the universe progresses into a situation in which the dissociated parts of his personality are the effective integrating agencies. . . . The result is a condition which I cannot distinguish by any important characteristic from that undergone by an individual in attempting to orient himself on awakening in the midst of a vivid nightmare.[261]

This parallel between schizophrenia and sleep is central to Sullivan's theory. He noted as early as 1927 that the schizophrenic's thought patterns are like a normal's reverie or dream processes, and it was his view that increasing knowledge of the sleep process should help us understand the dynamics of schizophrenia.[262]

The sleep-theory aspects of schizophrenia might be considered the mechanics of the disease. It appears that a light sleep is the means through which a person moving into schizophrenia actually regresses. In a sense, this light sleep is a misfired attempt to dissociate. As Sullivan put it, "when you effect contact with the intimate history of markedly schizoid people, you learn that at times which we would ordinarily say were times of unusual stress, these people underwent for quite extended periods a life that was more than half—sometimes nearly all—spent in a kind of light sleep." [263] If a deeper sleep had been possible at this time, then a satisfactory dissociation might have taken place. But in the light sleep of an individual developing schizophrenia, what is happening is that the poorly dissociated dynamisms of disturbance (let us say homosexual cravings or hostile impulses) are not being taken out of (dissociated from) the realm of potential integration (where they can influence behavior as automatisms). The self dynamism begins to lose control over awareness (note the parallel here with Jungian theory; see p. 221). The poorly dissociated dynamisms thus begin to integrate more and more of the conscious life as the personality falls under their grip in the acute phase of the illness. As personifications, these dynamisms now run things so that the person responds not to his or her own mental products, but to the voice of God, or the devil, or people from another planet. The mythological drama has begun.

We can actually see such schizophrenic-like states in the normal person. "An individual manifesting behavior when not fully awake would thus be clearly schizophrenic." [264] We are at times like these struggling to distinguish between—dissociate!—the logical and the illogical, the reasonable and the bizarre. But in the case of a true *schizophrenic dynamism,* the dream state becomes habitual. The person literally lives in a dream state, a living nightmare, so to speak. The very dynamisms the schizophrenic wanted to dissociate now take over his or her life as automatisms,

and the way in which they (personified) do so is as difficult to understand as it is for the normal to understand a dream. [265] We can therefore view schizophrenia as a failure of the self system, "a failure to restrict the contents of consciousness to the higher referential processes [thoughts] that can be consensually validated." [266] A profound puzzlement is thus engendered, and from the stress of being unable to maintain dissociation comes a loss of control of great consequence; the self system is now totally at sea, adrift, without conscious direction. [267]

So much for the onset of schizophrenia, but why is the self system so inadequate in handling dissociations in the first place? Because schizoid personality types—personalities tending toward schizophrenic behaviors—are basically shy, sensitive individuals who have been made to feel less than adequate through the reflected appraisals of significant others in the past, especially those of the parents. [268] Sullivan gave the general example of a young man who has always been very dependent on his parents—especially his mother —who never really considered him to be capable. [269] Parents like these view the child's first few fumbling steps as errors (missteps) rather than as the beginnings of accomplishment. The sickness as such usually begins in the juvenile to preadolescent era, [270] and an important factor in this case is the lack of a chum in the maturing boy's life. Distortions grow because he has never had a chance to test his errors against the experience of a really close friend. Neither has he been able to get a reasonable perspective on his developing sexuality, so he carries the immature patterns of preadolescence and adolescence into adulthood. [271] It is correct to say that the schizoid personality has never really passed through adolescence completely. [272] If we now add to this the failure of intimacy with others in adulthood, so that personal fears cannot be talked over with a loved one, we can see how difficult it is for the schizophrenic to dissociate pressing personal problems.[273] Little wonder that when the break comes, it is like a "fragmentation of the mind."[274]

Sullivan acknowledged the different types of schizophrenia known as *hebephrenia* (grimacing, infantile behaviors), *catatonia* (posturing, muteness, rigidity versus motility), and *paranoia* (prominent use of fairly systematized delusions). He did not think of these as separate and distinct entities, but did not want to speak of mixed diagnoses either. Instead, he worked out a view of the progression of schizophrenia through a few of these subsyndromes, making one of them basic to the sequence. Sullivan thus argued that when a schizophrenic dynamism (illness) emerges, when the self has been countered by the poorly dissociated systems, there is a rush of highly frightening (uncanny emotions) or otherwise peculiar occurrences in awareness (automatisms appearing). The *first* reaction of the individual at this point is catatonic in nature. He or she simply suspends all social habits and communication centers (muteness). If this continues to the extreme, a collapse into the despair of hebephrenia may be the case. However, if there has been a history of at least some intimacy with a person (chum) in preadolescence, the course of the disorder will be more along the lines of a living nightmare, with all of the consequent delusions and anxieties that any of us know from our own dream states. If the self system is capable, it might formulate an explanation of the dissociated states. This would place the individual under the paranoid designation. The catatonic phase of muteness which initiates the whole sequence may be very brief, as it seems to be a defensive effort to cut off integration with others for a time. Of course, it can also become chronic, but there is always an underlying paranoia or hebephrenia to be seen if and

when we re-establish contact with the catatonic schizophrenic.

The catatonic state is thus pivotal, falling roughly between the hebephrenic and the paranoid conditions. As such, Sullivan concluded, "I would say that the catatonic is the essential schizophrenic picture."[275] The patient is considered increasingly "crazy" by family members and friends to the extent that his or her verbal statements go beyond the realms of consensual validation (reflect parataxic distortion). Telling others about the personified automatisms is what lands the schizophrenic in the hospital, and it is true that many patients learn to "keep their mouth shut" when doctors ask them if they are "hearing voices" or "seeing strange people." But often these poorly dissociated states are very frightening to the schizophrenic, and it is impossible to pretend that they do not exist. This would be like a normal person trying to ignore a nightmare while he or she was having one! Because of the parataxic distortion confronted in a schizophrenic break, the patient becomes increasingly puzzled and confused over "what is happening to me?" The truth is, much of schizophrenia is insolvable or uninterpretable for both the patient *and the psychiatrist*. All human beings have early in life organized autistic and therefore uncommunicable signs and symptoms. Sullivan thought it was vain to think that psychiatry could unsnarl every aspect of such prototaxic and parataxic remnants.

Many psychiatrists of his time spoke of a "pure" form of paranoia, in which the individual does not show the distortions of schizophrenia when presenting a highly systematized delusional belief—one that is so plausible we can easily believe it. However, Sullivan did not accept this as a significant possibility, remarking that in three thousand cases of paranoid schizophrenia, he had seen only one individual who might be considered a "pure" paranoiac.[276] Every paranoid individual has been schizophrenic in the sense discussed above, at least for a time. Paranoid individuals have a relatively strong self system for a schizophrenic, which is probably the reason that we never see this syndrome appearing before preadolescence.[277] The older the patient, the more likely it is that he or she will be capable of at least some dissociation—meaning that the more bizarre aspects of the illness will be fended off. The so-called true paranoid is simply a schizophrenic who is aware of his or her inferiority as a person, passes quickly through the muteness of catatonia, and then transfers the blame for this inadequacy onto various other people.[278] Occasionally such paranoids can make the necessary adjustments to society during all of their lifetime, and thus some schizophrenics remain unidentified and unhospitalized.[279]

Other Clinical Syndromes

As we may recall from earlier chapters, psychoses are broadly divisible into the family of the schizophrenias, which we have been considering, and the *manic-depressive* disorders (see p. 120). Sullivan did not treat the latter cases in his experimental ward, and he admitted that he really did not have a complete theory concerning them.[280] In fact, noting that he was departing from his usual script, he was even tempted to accept a biological explanation for such mental disorders.[281] Assuming that a biological theory was not forthcoming, Sullivan did offer a few tentative explanations for these—frequently called affective—disorders based on his theory of interpersonal relations.

It seemed to him that *manic* individuals

are those who try to sublimate extensively (dynamism of difficulty), until they eventually find it impossible to continue using this one dynamism as a cure-all.[282] Such an individual lacks the self-esteem to face an unhappy situation or to take setbacks in stride. Melissa is the kind of person who tries to see the good in everything that takes place as a manifestation of God's will. Each time she is spurned by her family, made to feel incompetent, she tells herself that this is the way God has found to strengthen her character, to develop her tolerance for suffering, and so on. Yet, she never seems to grow strong or competent. One day, under a sense of extreme pressure, Melissa begins frantic efforts to raise her self-esteem. She founds a new church, claims to have been visited by Jesus Christ, and sets about seeking followers for her fantastic (fantasized) "Religion of the Will." Her efforts are frantic, and as Sullivan noted of all manics, she seems to be one step ahead of a great wave of anxiety threatening to engulf her. Even so, the manic phase of this disorder is constructive in that integration is outward, toward others, and aimed at doing something about a miserable life situation.

In the case of *depression* we have quite another matter. "Depression is not a dynamism for the health-preserving release of integrative bonds which connect one to another. It is a chiefly destructive process. It cuts off impulses to integrate constructive situations with others."[283] Depression is thus always colored by divisive and even hostile emotions, and if the depressed patient directs this hostility inward, the result can be an act of suicide.[284] Melissa's new religion is based on sublimated hostility toward her parents, and if she concludes that it will not succeed, she may direct her hostility inward and end her life as damned for her failure by Jesus Christ. There is also revenge toward the parents reflected in such a suicidal act.[285]

It is, of course, possible for the same patient to pass through both phases of the affective disorder at different times of life. After her depression leaves, Melissa can once again swing upward into a manic phase, only to return again to the depressed state as her frustrations mount, and so on.

We now turn to the disorders that are considered subpsychotic because they are less likely to manifest delusional or hallucinatory dynamisms. As we noted in the biographical overview, Sullivan became convinced that schizophrenia and the *obsessive-compulsive* neuroses are etiologically connected. He often saw a preschizophrenic individual with obsessive symptoms slip into a schizophrenic break and then later return to a nonpsychotic obsessional level.[286] He felt that obsessives regress to a stage of autistic speech, as the schizophrenic does. This is why their symptoms often include magical phrases, neologisms, and peculiar stylized verbal tendencies.[287] Before driving an automobile or conducting a business deal, for example, the obsessive person may have to repeat meaningless phrases like "twenty-four, twenty-four, once more, twenty-four" one or more times. If this magical phrase is not expressed, the obsessive cannot accomplish the task.

This deep-seated inferiority is also reflected in what Sullivan called the *flypaper technique* of conversation used by the obsessive person.[288] Just as flypaper sticks to the hand, and when we try to remove it, it sticks to the other hand as well, so too the obsessive entangles us in a boggled mass of sticky confusion. Each time the conversation touches on a sensitive area, the obsessive person finds some way to misunderstand, go into great detail over some minor point, or pin us down to haggle over something we never wanted to consider in the first place. With each step we take to clarify things, we draw ourselves deeper into the side issues and irrelevancies. The obsessive, of course, is

successfully avoiding the dissociated material—until this avoidant maneuver leads to a full-blown schizophrenic episode. Sometimes an obsessive disturbance will forestall the development of a schizophrenic break, so that in one sense we could speak of obsessive-compulsivity as a defense against acquiring a schizophrenic disorder. But this is by no means a sure defense, as many times the obsessional neurosis is a guaranteed way station to schizophrenia. Sullivan did not feel that there is any real difference between the obsessional neurosis that progresses into schizophrenia and the one that does not.[289]

Sullivan considered *neurasthenia* to be a form of mild depression in which insomnia, physical complaints, and general exhaustion are prominent related symptoms.[290] Sometimes such patients are suffering from malnutrition or other physical deficiencies because of long periods of self-neglect. There is an element of hostility in these cases; patients nag others to death with their annoying, complaining manner. *Hypochondriacs* are individuals who try to integrate situations entirely on the basis of their supposedly failing state of physical health.[291] They have no other interests in life but will relate interpersonally if someone humors them and lets them talk about their fantastic (imagined) aches and pains. The *hysterics* also employ various sicknesses as the basis for interpersonal relations, but they are more likely to use these as excuses for why they do not live up to their potential.[292]

Sullivan did not seem to feel that hysterics have quite the profound dissociations that characterize the psychoses. A multiple personality is, of course, a rather dramatic dissociated dynamism, but these cases are rare. In most instances, the hysterical activation (tic, grimace, arm movement) or inactivation (blindness, lameness, amnesia) are easily corrected through hypnosis. This proved to Sullivan that these disorders are closer to awareness than we might at first suspect. As he once summed them up, "What you see in the hysteric is . . . not a high-grade conflict between ideal structures and unregenerated impulses, but just a happy idea of how to get away with something."[293] A *fugue* state is when the individual actually lives out a dream, taking on an alternate identity, much as we might do in a reverie, while not losing contact with reality.[294]

We might now close our consideration of Sullivan's theory of illness with a few words on the syndrome known as *psychopathy*. In some of his earliest formulations, Sullivan suggested that a psychopathic personality underlies schizophrenia.[295] The predominant characteristic of this disorder is an "inability to profit by experience,"[296] as well as a tendency to "say the right thing" and then presume that all is set right without having to prove oneself in actual performance.[297] Psychopaths are therefore extremely manipulative, insincere people who never really form an intimate relationship with others.[298] Psychopaths use language as the obsessive does— as a tool for self-defense. They will say anything to get out of a tight spot. They seem always to be expressing regrets about past misadventures and laying extensive plans for correcting things in the future, but somehow they are always unable to fulfill expectancies when the time comes to act. Sullivan occasionally used the term *sociopath* as a synonym for the psychopath.[299]

Theory of Cure

The Nature of Mental Health

Sullivan did not like to use the term *cure* because he felt this remnant of medical ter-

minology really had little meaning in the realm of personality.[300] Psychotherapy is closer to education than it is to the *medical* healing of sick individuals.[301] Sullivan said that in over twenty-five years of working with psychotherapy patients, he had never found himself called upon to "cure" anybody.[302] The steps to mental health must be taken by the client, who always reflects a corrective tendency as a type of dynamism, as a *"drive toward mental health."*[303]

What then is *mental health?* We know from our review thus far that two major problems arise in the lives of abnormals: (1) an extensive dissociation; and (2) failing interpersonal relations, as a result of the disjointed pattern of behavior occurring when aspects of experience are not *in* awareness yet show up in behavior. It is therefore not surprising to find Sullivan emphasizing balance in speaking of mental health.[304] The disintegrated or poorly integrated personality must thus be reintegrated—rebalanced—before it can be said to be mentally healthy.[305] This rebalancing results in improved interpersonal relations and, to that extent, the state of living we all accept as normal. Summing it up, Sullivan observed that *"one achieves mental health to the extent that one becomes aware of one's interpersonal relations. . . ."*[306]

The Role of Insight

Sullivanian therapy is an insight approach much like that of the classic analysts. Sullivan even used the Freudian-Jungian term *imago* to refer to the eidetic personifications of the therapist by the client, personifications that become the focus of interpretation over the course of therapy. Indeed, the psychiatrist will find that there are always three people in therapy: (1) the psychiatrist as imagined (personified) by the patient; (2) the patient; and (3) the psychiatrist as he or she really is, participantly observing and trying to get some clue as to what the imago to whom the patient is reacting may be like.[307] It is also possible for several imagoes to intrude on the two-group therapeutic relationship, either alternatively or at the same time. As parataxic distortions, they seriously detract from the proper functioning of memory in recalling the essentials of past experience.[308] The psychiatrist must convince the patient that these personifications are from the past and that they are at the root of many of his or her interpersonal problems. The patient must search and work hard to learn about these eidetic people. Therapy is thus an "uncovering process."[309] This is anxiety-provoking, and hence all of the interpersonal skills of the psychiatrist as an expert in human relations are required to reassure and support the patient in this soul-searching effort.[310]

The easiest course for the therapist to take as educator is to begin with a client's selectively inattended behaviors and attitudes, pointing them out in a supportive manner.[311] The patient therefore comes to see an alternative integrative possibility in the relationship to the one initially suggested by the imago. Gradually, the central aspects of a client's case history are uncovered and interpreted, bringing in more and more of the total life experience of the present and the past. Once the imagoes are understood, the client can see how past losses of empathy stemmed from a relationship with some such person, with consequent anxiety, overreliance on dissociation as defense mechanism, and an eventual breakdown in the inadequate self system permitting automatisms to emerge, and so forth. Hence, said Sullivan, "The goal of the treatment, including the ultimate complete resolution of the patient-physician relationship, dictates the gradual evolution of valid insight."[312]

Prognosis depends on support factors in the patient's broader life context. If there is a family that really wants the patient to return to the home setting, or a boss who is sensitive to the patient's illness and is willing to provide time for readjustment, then prognosis is favorable indeed.[313] If the interpersonal context is hostile or unsympathetic to the patient, then the chances for eventual recovery are naturally bleak. Therapy relies on communication between psychiatrist and patient, so obviously if for any reason there is a problem at this level, the prognosis suffers.[314] Extremely regressed patients may need time for rest and other forms of medical treatment before they are moved into the two-group relationship of psychotherapy.

Expansion of Self

The course of therapy brings material that has been removed from awareness back into awareness. In accomplishing this reintegration, the therapist must confront the patient's self dynamism as a major obstacle to change. It was the self, after all, that initiated the dissociative process in the first place. There is nothing in the present circumstances that makes it easy for the self dynamism to relax its vigilance and readmit into awareness what it considers unacceptable parts of its total personality (bad-me, not-me). Sometimes it is necessary to enfeeble the self in some way, and though he did not live to see the complete impact of the relaxant-drug therapies in the post–World War II period (see p. 122), Sullivan's theory of cure was completely consistent with such a development. In fact, Sullivan tells us that he sometimes used alcoholic intoxication to relax and inhibit the "dissociating power of the self."[315] Intoxication seemed especially helpful in the case of a highly excited schizophrenic, who could usually relax and feel less threatened when "under the influence." Anything that permits the individual to relax his or her guard in this way can serve a therapeutic goal. Often, a vacation that allows one to get away from it all relaxes the individual enough to permit reintegration to occur quite spontaneously, and more than one incipient psychosis has probably been checked in this natural fashion.[316]

The paradoxical outcome of inducing the self to relax and admit certain elements of past experience into awareness is that the self is strengthened. "Therapeutic results are the expansion of the self dynamism and the simplification of living which results from this." [317] The individual no longer needs to live a series of lies, to divert others from exposing him or her, or to withdraw from communication with others out of a sense of anxiety. Another way of saying this is that consciousness is widened.[318] The self really integrates the dissociated impulses, so that now the person can admit, "Yes, I feel extreme shame whenever I feel sexually stimulated." Rather than behaving defensively in reaction to diverse threats, the individual now assumes command of his or her life in a more confident manner. At this point we have the beginning of a psychiatric cure, but there still may be a long road back to normalcy in the sense of a social cure.

Social Factors in Therapeutic Change

Dating from his contact with the Chicago school of social science, Sullivan emphasized the need for *social* as well as *personal* adjustment.[319] It was not enough for the patient to understand some of the reasons for his or her unique motivations in life. Sometimes a patient will improve simply by being allowed to live for a time in a climate of acceptance and understanding. This sympathetic environment does more for an enhancement of self-esteem than any amount of "interpretation of patient dynamics" can hope to achieve. Sullivan called this approach a *sociopsychological treatment,* and though he did not say that all patients should be placed in this procedure, he did feel that considerably more emphasis should be given to it.[320] In fact, he came to analyze the climate of the mental hospital much as the anthropologist might analyze the culture of a country. He spoke of the fixed *castes* that develop, with the physician at the top of the social structure and the patients at the bottom. As for diagnosing patients, "hospital classification of patients is in theory the segregation of patients on the basis of similarity of signs and symptoms." [321]

Sullivan felt that we need *therapeutic communities,* and he argued that something along the lines of the Civilian Conservation Corps for mental patients would be helpful.[322] This would involve a community of people, all of whom are victims of their social environment, working together to cultivate better interpersonal adjustments. After spending some time in such a milieu, the person could pass on to the more usual life experience we all face. We see this half-way house philosophy in practice today in group efforts, such as Alcoholics Anonymous and organizations for ex-drug addicts, ex-gamblers, and so on. Sullivan can be thought of as one of the fathers of the *halfway-house* concept.

Therapeutic Techniques

The Two-Group Relationship and Psychotherapy

The same interpersonal factors that are part of *any* two-group integration make up the psychiatric relationship.[323] Of course, in time—thanks to the accepting attitude of the psychiatrist—the therapy situation takes on a special importance, because patients find they can say or think about anything they want to; in fact, they can do whatever they wish as long as they do not harm the therapist.[324] As a trained psychoanalyst, Sullivan was quite familiar with the workings of *transference*. We find him using this term in 1925, and he even noted how certain schizophrenics have been known to effect a transference cure.[325] Transference grows out of the need everyone has to gain intimacy in interpersonal relations.[326] The only difference between the relationship with a psychotherapist and the relationship with any other person is the intention of the two-group.

All patients begin psychotherapy as subordinate participants, because of the expertise of the therapist. An *expert* is someone who is well versed in a field—such as interpersonal relations—and who earns both money and status by dispensing information concerning this field for the benefit of others.[327] Clients have a right to expect help from therapists, which is why they begin therapy in what analysts call the state of *positive transference*.[328] Only later, after parataxic distortions enter into the relationship, do we see *negative transference* arising.[329] Negative transference is an interpersonal relationship with a negative eidetic person (imago), who is now personified into the image of the psychiatrist. The therapist works to make these interfering personifications known to the client (*interpretation*), which naturally provokes anxiety. Since anxiety can disorient memory and prove harmful to interpersonal communication, it is not unusual for a client to *block* mentally at this point in therapy. Sullivan charged that the psychoanalysts took such unavoidable blockings of memory as signs of an intentional *resistance* on the

client's part.[330] Rather than purposeful deception, the real culprit is anxiety. An interviewer must always be alert to the many ways in which anxiety enters into the therapeutic two-group.[331]

Clients also become dependent on the therapist, seeking advice and opinions on a range of topics. Sullivan felt that sometimes this very normal way of relating was overemphasized by the analysts in their theories of transference. If we study the client's behavior outside of the consulting room, we find that he or she has similar ties to other people. In other words, therapists are not always as special as they flatter themselves to be. Sullivan did not discuss *countertransference* as such, but he did recognize that a therapist might integrate into the two-group personifications from out of his or her past which are essentially nonprofessional because they are highly personal and distorting (eidetic). This is what analysts mean when they speak of projecting imagoes onto the client, and why they favor psychoanalysis for every analyst. Although he had himself submitted to psychoanalysis, Sullivan did not agree that every therapist should be forced into therapy. This is a basically personal decision to be made at the time of entering the profession by the aspiring psychotherapist.[332]

The Psychiatric-Interview Series

Sullivan defined the *psychiatric interview* as "a two-group in which there is an expert-client relationship, the expert being defined by the culture."[333] The therapist is a participant observer in this group, demonstrating his or her expertise by taking the client through four stages in the interview series: *inception, reconnaissance, detailed inquiry,* and *termination.*[334]

The *inception* includes the formal reception of the client in the initial contact, the seating arrangements, and the beginning inquiry into why the client is seeking help. Sullivan did not use the couch with his clients. He met them at the door, took a good look at their general appearance, indicated where they might sit, and then purposefully avoided staring at them.[335] Sullivan did not like to take notes during the interview, feeling it broke his concentration to be scribbling while the client was talking. We know that he was one of the first to experiment with electronic recording of interviews. In general, his approach to the client was very structured, in that he tried to focus on the problems that needed solving rather than to wander about in what he took to be freely associated irrelevancies. The client is present to learn about interpersonal problems, and the therapist is not being paid to putter about with a favorite theory. The effective psychiatrist must always keep three questions in mind: What is the client trying to say? How can we best phrase what it is we wish to say to the client in return? And what kind of pattern is emerging in the contents being discussed? [336]

The inception phase may require one interview or several, but at the point when the psychiatrist decides that the client really needs psychotherapy, we move into the *reconnaissance* phase of the interview series. The therapist needs more information and begins to survey the client's life, ranging from strictly factual points like educational experiences through highly personal material bearing on the presenting complaint. We are now moving along over several days of interviewing, and the psychiatrist takes a more active role without appearing to be a detective.[337] The deeper this phase of interviewing, the more it is true that an intensive psychotherapy series is underway. More and more of the client's life is brought under consideration in the process.

At this point the therapist may use free association, but Sullivan criticized those who make this technique the end-all of psychotherapy. Too often, the invitation to the client to say "every littlest thing that comes into mind" merely results in a string of autistic words having no usefulness for therapy at all.[338] Yet many therapists go on chasing these verbal rainbows. Though he did use free association, Sullivan often found it more helpful to throw out possible hypotheses as interpretations rather than sit back and listen to a purposeless course of talk by the client.[339] He felt that his psychiatric colleagues seemed to derive pleasure from "getting lost in the schizophrenic woods with their schizophrenic patients." [340] He did not respect therapists who become too dramatic during the sessions, pretending to enter the psychosis with the client, and so on. Too many psychiatrists have this juvenile desire to have "fun" in their work.[341]

Free association is best reserved for those times when a client hits a snag in his or her recollections of the past. At this point, the therapist may say something like "Well, if that seems to have escaped you, why not just tell we what *does* come to mind when you think about this question?" This natural transition permits the client to work at the blocked material without rousing further anxiety—as might happen if we were to make a big thing out of free association and go into involved instructions in how to do it.[342] The better one's relationship with the client and the more trust and interpersonal intimacy achieved in the two-group, the less likely it is that such blocks will arise. Free associations will therefore not be necessary.

As we continue searching the client's past recollections, and as we begin making instructive interpretations of how parataxic distortions may have arisen, we move into the *detailed inquiry* phase of the interview series (that is, psychotherapy). In line with his emphasis on clear structure, Sullivan recommended that we summarize for the client what the reconnaissance has taught us.[343] He was a great believer in keeping therapy on track. Occasionally he would interview a client for 1½-hour periods (rather than the usual fifty-minute hour), and he always spent the last fifteen minutes summarizing what they had learned. The client comes to appreciate the psychiatrist's expertise in organizing and bringing out the essential points being covered in the therapy sessions. From time to time Sullivan would ask a client to prepare a life chronology in writing, so that as material in the interviews emerged, it could be put into proper order, thereby avoiding fantastic distortions in time and place.[344]

As the early, tentative hypotheses and suggested interpretations begin taking on greater order and an overall understanding begins to take shape, we move into the *interpretation* phase of psychotherapy. It is vital to make this broader picture clear to the patient, because what he or she does not understand cannot be of benefit to a cure.[345] If we are too abstract and theoretical, our interpretations will go over the client's head. All interpretations should be based on concrete data obtained from the client and clarified thoroughly. Timing is an extremely important aspect of interpretation.[346] We must make certain the client is prepared to accept the interpretation before we make it. Since most insights arouse anxiety in the client, a second vital aspect of interpretation is providing *reassurance*. As Sullivan put it, "Any question, and in particular, any explanatory statement—interpretation—that arouses anxi-

ety is apt to prove worse than useless."[347] This is so because dissociative tendencies are triggered by the self when the anxiety level disturbs the client's euphoria.

Sullivan once said that there are roughly five different types of interpretation that we make as therapists.[348] There is the comment made on the nature of the relationship, including any parataxic distortion the client is integrating into the two-group. There is the clarification of such distortions in extratherapy relationships, as with superiors or marital partners. There is the description we make of the client's past, to show how eidetic people have been personified and brought forward into the present. There are also constructive attempts to be made for the future which we might help the client plan for. Finally, there are all kinds of emergencies that arise both in and outside of therapy which we can use as concrete examples of the client's personality tendencies. Sullivan liked to interpret according to what he called a *technique of small contexts*.[349] He would take a small but clear area of the client's life, such as the relationship a man had with his parents, or a woman's lifelong religious involvement. Once this delimited context had been interpreted, Sullivan would move on to another small piece of the client's life. Near the end of therapy, these various points could then be pulled together into a more overriding insight, particularly since there were commonalities across several of these interpretations.

Sullivan encouraged his patients to be sensitive to and report any changes taking place in their physical state, such as fluctuations of mood or increases in muscular tension.[350] He also encouraged them to notice and report any marginal thoughts they might have concerning the material covered in the interview. It is absolutely essential that a client feel comfortable enough to say anything he or she would like during the therapy series. As the therapist's formulation of the case becomes clearer and is being extended to more and more of the client's life, an improvement in adjustment can be expected. An expansion of the client's self occurs, because dissociation is no longer taking place and the person now knows himself or herself as others do. There is considerably less distortion going on in interpersonal relations (although it is doubtful that we can ever remove all distortion from the two-group integration).[351] This new balance of the personality is interpreted as mental health by the client, and quite properly so.

At about this point in the interview series, we move into the *termination* stage. This opens with a summary of what we have learned over the course of the interviews thus far. We then draw from this *final summary* a number of *prescriptions* for specific actions the client should carry out in the future. Actually, these tend to be more the "don't do" than the "do" form of prescription, because Sullivan felt that no one can tell a person how to "be happy." Based on his or her expertise, however, the psychiatrist can make some worthwhile estimates as to what the client should shun in the future if a recurrence of the illness is to be avoided.[352] Next, the therapist makes a *final assessment* of the probable effects the prescriptions might be expected to have on the client's future life. Finally, there is the *formal leave taking*. One has the distinct impression in reading Sullivan that his clients were thoroughly schooled and well rehearsed in a life strategy before he turned them loose to regain some semblance of life adjustment on their own.

Dream Analysis and Miscellaneous Factors

It follows from Sullivan's view of autism that so-called latent content of dreams is a highly debatable presumption made by the therapist who is taking parataxic material and translating it into consensually validated terminology.[353] Sullivan felt that this was another one of those games psychiatrists play with the lives of their patients to keep themselves amused.[354] He felt the therapist should be involved in more important and productive things than trying to guess what this or that dream symbol might mean to the client. He considered theories of dream symbolism to be farfetched speculations. Sullivan did not, however, dismiss dreams as irrelevant to interpretations made during the detailed inquiry. The key to understanding a dream lies in its interpersonal nature. "Dreams are interpersonal phenomena in which the other fellow is wholly illusory, wholly fantastic, a projection, if you please, of certain constructive impulses, or of certain destructiveness, or of certain genital motivations, or something of that kind." [355]

Impulses that in waking life are dissociated from awareness make their appearance in dreams. Dreams are literally portrayals of all that we are *not* in conscious life. We think of them as always concerning lust and hostility, but the principle can also be seen in the cases of those who dream very nice dreams. "Thus the dream processes of people who are full of hate [in awareness] will be found to include symbolic operations which actually have the purpose of releasing the tension of positive, constructive drive; this is one of the curious situations in which the nearest a person comes to warm human companionship is in his sleep." [356] Sometimes the dream of one person can serve as a presyntaxic expression of gratification, sublimation, or compensation for an entire group of people, who then personify it as a myth.[357]

Sullivan had occasionally relied on hypnotism in his work with psychotics,[358] but he seems to have eliminated this technique from his later work, and we do not hear anything about his using the tactic with neurotics. He believed that the sex of the therapist and the client should be the same.[359] In his work with male schizophrenics, he always emphasized the use of talented aides to work as assistants. He viewed these men as belated chums for his patients, who could help cultivate the intimacy and reality testing so necessary to proper development in the adult.[360] Sullivan placed great stress on reassuring the client, doing nothing to confuse, frighten, or demean the client as a person.[361] He had a kind of Yankee, cracker-barrel, nononsense approach to therapy in which practical, achievable goals were set and carried out, thanks to the psychiatrist's expertise. Sullivan's psychiatry was, as he intended, a uniquely American psychiatry.[362]

Summary

Sullivan was clearly a sociological thinker. Unlike Adler, Sullivan placed the ultimate source of behavioral direction in the supraindividual (social) situation of the person. Whereas Adler had viewed behavior as telically oriented to goals, Sullivan described behavior as a patterning of energic transformations under the direction of purely natural (nontelic) processes. He called such patterned transformations dynamisms, which came down to any of a number of constructs used by any theorist to capture the nature of a structure or action event. Thus, Sullivan would call dynamisms anything from the patterned reflexive processes of the stomach in digestion to the learned habits of people

behaving interpersonally. Dynamisms could also have partial orders, functioning as subdynamisms (patterns within patterns). The patterning of energies is the foundation construct in Sullivanian thought, permitting him to say how body and mind unite. Since everything is made up of the same energy, Sullivan suggested that dynamisms oriented to the satisfactions of a physical nature (eating, sleeping, and so on) are also often integrated with the more psychological security operations (interpersonal needs). Thus, how a mother treats her child (security) in feeding or toilet-training situations (satisfactions) combine to influence the child's self dynamism and the attendant self-esteem he or she incorporates into this personal definition.

Sullivan had a distinctive interpretation of what it means to speak of social or interpersonal behavior. One does not have literally to be relating to another human being in order to behave interpersonally. The basic posture of human behavior involves making everything we know more or less personlike. That is, we anthropomorphize or personify (make personlike) other people, other inanimate things like our automobile or our country, and we even personify ourselves. These personifications then enter into our behavior as an aspect of the social situation in which we position ourselves. Sullivan called these fantastic (fantasied) personifications. Personifications are often focused in terms of the situation that brings them on initially. If we have misbehaved as a child, this situational context is personified into a bad-me. We also have a good-me for those times when we behaved well in a situation. Finally, there is the not-me personification, derived from those times when we felt completely out of things. We also personify our parents into good and bad images in this fashion. As significant others in our lives, our parents can go on influencing us even after they have died. For example, what we call our conscience may in fact be our good-mother personification, looking over our shoulders and confronting us when we enact interpersonally as our bad-me. Mother enters into an interpersonal relation with us at this time, even though she has long since passed away.

Interpersonal relations are characterized by the nature of the child's personifications and the interpersonal dynamisms that establish the patterns of meeting and interacting with other people. Harmonious interpersonal relations are called conjunctive, and destructive interpersonal relations, disjunctive. Some of the earliest personifications of an interpersonal nature occur in the infant's contacts with the mother's breast during feeding. Evaluative assessments are noted even this early in life, for Sullivan claimed that children characterize the nipple as either good or bad depending on whether their relationship with their mother is conjunctive or disjunctive. Someone who carries forward a style of forming disjunctive interpersonal relations is courting personal maladjustment. Of course, *personal* does not mean *unique* in Sullivanian thought. He believed that we human beings have an illusion of personal individuality, and that the properly scientific definition of *personality* would be that it is a construct used by the personologist to characterize the sum total of all factors entering into any interpersonal relations (with real and imagined people, and so on). Once again, Sullivan and Adler are on opposite sides of the street when it comes to matters of individuality, uniqueness, and personal agency.

Sullivan placed considerable emphasis on the role of language in behavior. Life experience was seen as moving through various modes—prototaxic, parataxic, and syntaxic—in which the maturing child passes from an autistic existence to one having consensual validation, thanks in large measure to the understanding of language. Along this path of development, the child also personifies a self dynamism and acquires patterns of me-you relating to others, moving through the two-groups of the family and on into the larger interpersonal relations of everyday experience. The child is said to integrate experience, incorporating the reflected appraisals of significant others along the way. Human beings have such integrating tendencies through which they meet their needs by interpersonal means. It is sometimes difficult for the person to integrate feelings or habit patterns into a self system, which results in a form of disjunctive behavior that starts out as what Sullivan called selective inattention. The person simply does not recognize that aspect of the self dynamism that is unacceptable to him or her. Gradually, such bad feelings and habitual behaviors can become dissociated or cut off from the self dynamism altogether. Even though it is cut off, a dissociated dynamism is vigilant and can influence behavior—in much the same way that Jung contended complexes could function in an independent manner in consciousness. Sullivan reinterpreted Freudian mechanisms in light of his interpersonal constructs. For example, projection is viewed as a reflection of the fact that we must always anticipate through foresight what will be taking place as we integrate a situation. When we are upset or disturbed, we can anticipate (project) negative integrations in the upcoming interpersonal relationship with other people.

Sullivan spoke of an elaborate series of stages through which the person was said to develop in coming to maturity. He called them epochs and aligned them in the following order: infancy, childhood, juvenile era, preadolescence, early adolescence, late adolescence, and maturity. Sullivan did not accept Freud's sexual thesis, tracing the so-called Oedipal complex to the feelings of familiarity parents have for their same-sex offspring. Thus, a father knows all of the tricks used by his son to gain advantages in the family. Hence, he seems to be jealous of the boy or seems to be a threatening (castrating) figure, when the truth is the father is simply not permitting the son to integrate situations that are improperly advantageous. Sullivan carefully distinguished between love and lust and argued that Freud's confounding of these two emotions led him to attribute homosexuality to childhood ties between members of the same sex that are in fact isophilic. Sullivan did not believe in fixation, but he did say that through malevolent transformations from one epoch to another, some people retain inappropriate behaviors beyond their epochal time period. Regression is often simply these persistent dynamisms; or repression might stem from poorly integrated dynamisms that collapse under the tension of interpersonal relations. Personality styles are thus to be viewed as all of the varying factors entering into the integration of interpersonal relations.

Sullivan's theory of illness took root in his conception of dissociation. To the extent that the self dynamism avoids integrating aspects of behavior to the self, there is a growing reliance on one and only one pattern of behavior. This becomes a dynamism of difficulty because it lacks the adjustive capacity to meet with the alternatives life throws up to the person. A serious warp develops in the personality, leading to symptom formation as the dissociated material increases. Pretty soon the person develops automatisms in behavior and autochthonous ideas which in more familiar terms we call delusions and hallucinations. Sullivan was the first theorist

to speak of the sick society, within which all kinds of poorly integrated interpersonal relations are continually being manufactured. Here again, in direct opposition to Adlerian theory, Sullivan put the blame on supraindividual forces for the generating of abnormal behavior. In his famous theory of schizophrenia, Sullivan traced the various parataxic distortions and malevolent transformations that lead to the extreme dissociation of this mental disorder. The other clinical syndromes were analyzed along the same line. Sullivan also held to the medical view of his time that there is probably a form of schizophrenia that is due to an organic degenerative disease.

Even so, Sullivan did not like to think of his therapy as a cure in the classic medical sense. He viewed the process more as education than as medical treatment. People were said to have a drive toward mental health which the therapist can capitalize on in order to provide insight. One finds all of the dynamics of interpersonal relations popping up in the therapy relationship. Positive and negative transferences arise because of the play of eidetic people and potent representations from out of the past. People also seek intimacy in interpersonal relations which aids positive transference. The therapist gradually makes all of these factors known to the client and deals with the deceitful tendencies of the dynamisms of difficulty, as well as the anxiety that invariably arises. Sullivan worked out a series of phases through which every psychiatric-interview series naturally passes: inception, reconnaissance, detailed inquiry, and termination. He occasionally used free association, but in most cases simply presented the client with hypotheses concerning the dynamics of the case history and invited his or her reactions. Interpretations were made in a direct, clear manner, well timed and to the point. Sullivan liked to take up what he called the small contexts of a case history, which enabled the client to get a good understanding of the point being made. Dreams were used as indications of the person's parataxic distortions and fantasied projections, as well as the side of life the person wanted to further. Sullivan did not favor the symbolical interpretations of dreams.

Though Sullivan did not set out to do so, surely his style of thinking supported the rising behaviorisms of his era, for it suggested that human beings behave according to the habitual style (dynamism) their environments shape them into manifesting. The person can interact with this environment, can bring to bear influences out of his or her past (eidetic people, and so on). In the final analysis, however, there is no uniform self acting as agent in the psychology of interpersonal relations. The behaviorists were to find this style of explanation very compatible, and, indeed, in a sense it is correct to say that all behaviorists are social psychologists in the style of Sullivan. That is, the behaviorist must find a source of behavioral styling (shaping, modifying) outside of the personal identity of the actor. Whereas Freud indirectly, and Adler and Jung very directly, tried to frame behavior teleologically, the Yankee spirit moving Sullivan and the behaviorists was devotedly nontelic. Behavior was simply a manifestation of scientifically lawful motoric processes (locomotion), proven empirically to hold in the laboratory and used pragmatically to manipulate people's habits which through no fault of the people had been shaped into maladaptive habits.

Outline of Important Theoretical Constructs

Personality theory

Structural constructs

Mind versus body and the organizing role of pattern
> pattern = envelope of insignificant particular differences · monism · referential processes

The patterning of dynamisms and personifications
> dynamism · subdynamism · zonal dynamism · interpersonal dynamism · personification · fantastic = fantasied · fantastic personification · potent representation · complex personification · good-me, bad-me, not-me · good mother, good father, bad mother, bad father · eidetic people · subpersonification

Interpersonal relations, personality, and responsive situationism
> interpersonal relation · interpersonal situation · personal situation · conjunctive relations · disjunctive relations · good nipple, bad nipple · personality · illusion of personal individuality

Modes of experience, language, and awareness
> mode of experience · prototaxic mode · parataxic mode · sign · symbol · autism · consensual validation · parataxic distortion · neologism · syntaxic mode

The dynamisms of personality
> participant observer · self, self-system, self dynamism · personified self · good-me, bad-me, not-me · self versus other personifications · supervisory pattern · other · thee · me-you patterns · two-group

Motivational constructs

Needs as energy transformation in situational integration
integration of a situation · integrating tendencies · need · tension · power motive · drive · force · vector · field force

Emotion, security, satisfaction, and anxiety
euphoria · uncanny emotion · satisfaction · forbidding gesture · security, security operations · self-esteem, self-respect · anxiety versus fear · disphoria = anxiety · empathy

Defensive maneuvers, self-esteem, and the socialization process
selective inattention · brown studies · dissociation · vigilance · substitutive processes · suave · unobserved alertness · reflected appraisals · significant others = parents, people, persons · will, will power · foresight

The adjustment mechanisms
repression · fixation = malevolent transformation · regression · sublimation · identification = interiorization · projection · compensation · displacement · rationalization

Time perspective constructs

Infancy: from birth to the maturation of language capacity
zone of interaction · zonal need · prehension

Childhood: from language to the maturation of the need for playmates
sublimation

Juvenile era: from playmates to the maturation of the need for isophilic intimacy
compeers · competition · reputation · Oedipal Complex · Electra Complex · philos · eros · autophilic, isophilic,

heterophilic · autoerotic, isoerotic, heteroerotic · love · lust

Preadolescence: from isophilic intimacy to the maturation of the genital lust dynamism
isophilic intimacy · chum

Early adolescence: from genital lust to the patterning of lustful behavior
lust versus love conflict · autoerotic masturbation

Late adolescence and maturity
sublimatory reformulations

Individual differences constructs
developmental syndromes · autistic · lack of duration · self-absorbed · incorrigible · negativistic · stammerer · ambition ridden · inadequate · homosexual · chronically adolescent · one genus hypothesis

Psychopathology and psychotherapy

Theory of illness

The general theory of abnormal behavior
dynamism of difficulty · warp of personality

The role of social factors
the sick society

The symptoms of mental disorder
automatism · autochthonous ideas · systematized versus unsystematized delusions

The syndrome of schizophrenia
dementia praecox versus schizophrenia · depth of regression · schizophrenic dynamism · catatonia = pivotal syndrome · hebephrenia · paranoia · (simple)

Other clinical syndromes
manic-depressive · mania · depression

• obsessive-compulsive (and schizo-phrenia) • flypaper technique of conversation • neurasthenia • hypochondria • hysteria • fugue state • psychopathy

Theory of cure

The nature of mental health
drive toward mental health

The role of insight
imago = eidetic person

Expansion of self

Social factors in therapeutic change
sociopsychological treatment • therapeutic communities • halfway-house

Therapeutic techniques

The two-group relationship and psycho-therapy
transference • expert • positive transference • negative transference • interpretation • blocking = resistance • countertransference

The psychiatric interview series
inception phase • reconnaissance phase • detailed inquiry phase • interpretation • reassurance • technique of small contexts • termination phase • final summary • prescriptions • final assessment • formal leave taking

Dream analysis and miscellaneous factors

Notes

1. Sullivan, 1962, p. xxi. 2. Ibid., p. xxxiv. 3. Sullivan, 1940, p. 178. 4. Sullivan, 1962, p. 312. 5. Ibid., p. 5. 6. Ibid., p. xv. 7. Sullivan, 1940, pp. 178–179. 8. Sullivan, 1962, p. xxvi. 9. Ibid., p. 264. 10. Sullivan, 1964, p. xxxi. 11. Sullivan, 1962, p. 321. 12. Sullivan, 1964, p. xxviii. 13. Sullivan, 1956, p. xii. 14. Jung, Vol. 5, p. 102. 15. Hofstadter, 1955, p. 167. 16. Becker and Barnes, 1952, p. 536. 17. Sullivan, 1964, pp. xxii–xxiv. 18. Park and Burgess, 1921. 19. Sullivan, 1964, p. 196. 20. Sullivan, 1953, p. 35. 21. Sullivan, 1962, p. 142. 22. Ibid. 23. Ibid., pp. 30–31. 24. Sullivan, 1953, p. 104. 25. Sullivan, 1940, p. 105. 26. Sullivan, 1962, p. 83. 27. Sullivan, 1953, p. 185. 28. Sullivan, 1964, p. 35. 29. Sullivan, 1953, p. 103. 30. Ibid. 31. Ibid. 32. Ibid., p. 109. 33. Ibid., pp. 164–165. 34. Sullivan, 1964, p. 325. 35. Sullivan, 1953, pp. 280–281. 36. Ibid., p. 109. 37. Sullivan, 1962, p. 161. 38. Sullivan, 1964, p. 324. 39. Sullivan, 1953, p. 162. 40. Ibid., p. 302. 41. Ibid., p. 118. 42. Sullivan, 1964, p. 309. 43. Sullivan, 1940, p. 201. 44. Sullivan, 1954, p. 231. 45. Sullivan, 1953, p. 209. 46. Ibid. 47. Ibid. 48. Ibid., p. 103. 49. Sullivan, 1964, p. 239. 50. Sullivan, 1940, p. 51. 51. Sullivan, 1964, p. 243. 52. Sullivan, 1953, p. 90. 53. Sullivan, 1962, p. 302. 54. Sullivan, 1964, p. 221. 55. Sullivan, 1953, p. 26. 56. Ibid., p. 29. 57. Ibid., p. 38. 58. Ibid., p. 110. 59. Ibid., p. 178. 60. Ibid., p. 105. 61. Ibid., pp. 106, 184. 62. Ibid., p. 77. 63. Ibid., p. 87. 64. Sullivan, 1962, p. 31. 65. Sullivan, 1964, p. 202. 66. Sullivan, 1953, p. 186. 67. Sullivan, 1940, p. 17. 68. Sullivan, 1964, p. 163. 69. See Sullivan, 1956, p. 221. 70. Sullivan, 1953, p. 182. 71. Sullivan, 1964, p. 19. 72. Sullivan, 1953, p. 76. 73. Sullivan, 1964, p. 311. 74. Sullivan, 1940, p. 92. 75. Sullivan, 1953, pp. 183–184. 76. Sullivan, 1940, p. 70. 77. Sullivan, 1962, p. 32. 78. Sullivan, 1964, p. 64. 79. Sullivan, 1962, p. 149. 80. Sullivan, 1954, p. 138. 81. Sullivan, 1962, pp. 249–250. 82. Sullivan, 1956, p. 4. 83. Ibid., p. 92. 84. Sullivan, 1954, p. 142. 85. Sullivan, 1953, p. 192. 86. Sullivan, 1940, pp. 20–21. 87. Sullivan, 1954, p. 178. 88. Sullivan, 1953, p. 239. 89. Ibid. 90. Sullivan, 1956, p. 349. 91. Sullivan, 1964, p. 46. 92. Ibid., p. 39. 93. Ibid., p. 148. 94. Sullivan, 1956, p. 11. 95. Ibid., pp. 69–70. 96. Sullivan, 1964, p. 83. 97. Sullivan, 1940, p. 80. 98. Ibid., p. 224. 99. Ibid., p. 277. 100. Sullivan, 1964, p. 72. 101. Sullivan, 1956, pp. 8–9. 102. Sullivan, 1953, p. 97. 103. Ibid., p. 36. 104. Ibid., p. 59. 105. Ibid., p. 99. 106. Sullivan, 1940, p. 14. 107. Ibid., pp. 263–264. 108. Ibid., p. 47. 109. Sullivan, 1956, p. 7. 110. Sullivan, 1962, p. 5. 111. Sullivan, 1964, p. 244. 112. Sullivan, 1953, p. 198. 113. Sullivan, 1964, p. 234. 114. Sullivan, 1953, p. 34. 115. Ibid., p. 315. 116. Ibid., p. 37. 117. Sullivan, 1940, pp. 13–14. 118. Ibid., p. 88. 119. Sullivan, 1964, p. 218. 120. Sullivan, 1940, p. 47. 121. Sullivan, 1953, p. 9. 122. Sullivan, 1964, p. 235. 123. Ibid.,

p. 234. **124.** Sullivan, 1954, p. 218. **125.** Sullivan, 1953, p. 41. **126.** Sullivan, 1964, p. 238. **127.** Sullivan, 1956, p. 113. **128.** Sullivan, 1962, p. 249. **129.** Sullivan, 1940, p. 17. **130.** Sullivan, 1954, p. 218. **131.** Ibid., p. 109. **132.** Sullivan, 1964, p. 250. **133.** Sullivan, 1956, p. 60. **134.** Ibid., p. 64. **135.** Ibid., p. 43. **136.** Sullivan, 1964, p. 216. **137.** Sullivan, 1956, p. 55. **138.** Ibid., p. 166. **139.** Ibid., p. 63. **140.** Sullivan, 1953, p. 318. **141.** Sullivan, 1956, p. 73. **142.** Ibid., p. 178. **143.** Sullivan, 1940, p. 22. **144.** Ibid., p. 15. **145.** Sullivan, 1953, p. 351. **146.** Ibid., p. 316. **147.** Sullivan, 1964, p. 311. **148.** Ibid., p. 309. **149.** Sullivan, 1953, p. 314. **150.** Ibid., p. 316. **151.** Sullivan, 1962, p. 213. **152.** Sullivan, 1940, p. 78. **153.** Sullivan, 1964, p. 44. **154.** Sullivan, 1956, p. 230. **155.** Ibid., p. 232. **156.** Sullivan, 1940, p. 28. **157.** Sullivan, 1953, p. 359. **158.** Sullivan, 1940, p. 194. **159.** Sullivan, 1953, p. 173. **160.** Sullivan, 1956, p. 63. **161.** Sullivan, 1940, p. 185. **162.** Sullivan, 1956, p. 328. **163.** Sullivan, 1962, p. 283. **164.** Sullivan, 1964, p. 303. **165.** Sullivan, 1953, pp. 217–218. **166.** Sullivan, 1962, p. 196. **167.** Ibid., p. 100. **168.** Sullivan, 1956, p. 14. **169.** Sullivan, 1940, p. 126. **170.** Sullivan, 1953, p. 218. **171.** Sullivan, 1956, p. 232. **172.** Sullivan, 1953, pp. 358–359. **173.** Sullivan, 1956, p. 27. **174.** Sullivan, 1962, p. 195. **175.** Sullivan, 1940, p. 71. **176.** Sullivan, 1953, p. 113. **177.** Sullivan, 1964, p. 297. **178.** Sullivan, 1953, p. 9. **179.** Sullivan, 1940, p. 66. **180.** Sullivan, 1962, p. 97. **181.** Sullivan, 1953, pp. 122–123. **182.** Sullivan, 1940, pp. 64–65. **183.** Sullivan, 1953, p. 193. **184.** Ibid., p. 151. **185.** Ibid., p. 39. **186.** Ibid., p 89. **187.** Sullivan, 1964, p. 298. **188.** Sullivan, 1953, p. 193. **189.** Ibid., pp. 208–209. **190.** Ibid., p. 227. **191.** Sullivan, 1956, p. 123. **192.** Sullivan, 1953, p. 228. **193.** Ibid., p. 233. **194.** Ibid., p. 238. **195.** Sullivan, 1964, p. 265. **196.** Sullivan, 1962, p. 204. **197.** Sullivan, 1956, p. 215. **198.** Sullivan, 1964, p. 72. **199.** Sullivan, 1953, p. 294. **200.** Ibid., pp. 291–292. **201.** Ibid., pp. 218–219. **202.** Sullivan, 1956, p. 164. **203.** Sullivan, 1962, pp. 192–193. **204.** Sullivan, 1956, p. 153. **205.** Ibid., pp. 105–106. **206.** Sullivan, 1940, pp. 42–43. **207.** Ibid., p. 42. **208.** Sullivan, 1956, p. 157. **209.** Sullivan, 1953, p. 249. **210.** Ibid., p. 256. **211.** Ibid., pp. 250–251. **212.** Ibid., p. 263. **213.** Ibid., p. 295. **214.** Sullivan, 1954, p. 171. **215.** Sullivan, 1953, pp. 259–260. **216.** Ibid., p. 297. **217.** Ibid., p. 298. **218.** Ibid., p. 234. **219.** Ibid., p. 310. **220.** Sullivan, 1956, p. 193. **221.** Sullivan, 1962, p. 262. **222.** Sullivan, 1940, p. 77. **223.** Ibid., pp. 77–86. **224.** Sullivan, 1953, p. 280. **225.** Sullivan, 1962, p. 224. **226.** Sullivan, 1953, pp. 32–33. **227.** Sullivan, 1962, p. 297. **228.** Sullivan, 1940, p. 22. **229.** Sullivan, 1956, p. 359. **230.** Sullivan, 1953, p. 6. **231.** Sullivan, 1962, p. 261. **232.** Sullivan, 1953, p. 314. **233.** Sullivan, 1962, p. 190. **234.** Ibid., p. 221. **235.** Ibid., p. 279. **236.** Sullivan, 1940, p. 47. **237.** Sullivan, 1962, p. 206. **238.** Sullivan, 1956, p. 34. **239.** Sullivan, 1962, p. 261. **240.** Sullivan, 1940, p. 175. **241.** Sullivan, 1964, p. 155. **242.** Sullivan, 1954, p. 183. **243.** Sullivan, 1962, pp. 327–328. **244.** Ibid., p. 107. **245.** Sullivan, 1956, p. 258. **246.** Sullivan, 1940, p. 139. **247.** Ibid. **248.** Sullivan, 1953, p. 360. **249.** Ibid., p. 361. **250.** Sullivan, 1956, p. 337. **251.** Sullivan, 1940, p. 157. **252.** Sullivan, 1956, p. 332. **253.** Sullivan, 1940, p. 152. **254.** Sullivan, 1962, p. 99. **255.** Sullivan, 1940, pp. 148–149. **256.** Sullivan, 1956, p. 309. **257.** Sullivan, 1962, p. 239. **258.** Ibid., p. 165. **259.** Ibid., p. 164. **260.** Sullivan, 1953, p. 325. **261.** Sullivan, 1962, p. 243. **262.** Ibid., p. 149. **263.** Sullivan, 1956, p. 190. **264.** Sullivan, 1962, p. 278. **265.** Ibid., p. 218. **266.** Sullivan, 1956, p. 182. **267.** Ibid., p. 187. **268.** Sullivan, 1962, p. 219. **269.** Ibid., p. 327. **270.** Ibid., p. 190. **271.** Ibid., p. 327. **272.** Ibid., pp. 327–328. **273.** Ibid., p. 160. **274.** Sullivan, 1940, p. 142. **275.** Sullivan, 1956, p. 313. **276.** Ibid., p. 305. **277.** Ibid., p. 154. **278.** Ibid., p. 146. **279.** Ibid., p. 358. **280.** Ibid., p. 284. **281.** Ibid., pp. 287–288. **282.** Ibid., pp. 290–291. **283.** Sullivan, 1940, p. 102. **284.** Ibid., p. 25. **285.** Sullivan, 1956, p. 298. **286.** Sullivan, 1964, p. 231. **287.** Sullivan, 1956, p. 29. **288.** Ibid., p. 271. **289.** Ibid., p. 257. **290.** Sullivan, 1940, p. 104. **291.** Sullivan, 1956, p. 78. **292.** Ibid., p. 216. **293.** Ibid., p. 204. **294.** Sullivan, 1953, p. 323. **295.** Sullivan, 1962, p. 110. **296.** Ibid. **297.** Sullivan, 1956, p. 229. **298.** Ibid., p. 360. **299.** Sullivan, 1954, p. 196. **300.** Sullivan, 1956, p. 228. **301.** Sullivan, 1962, p. 281. **302.** Sullivan, 1954, p. 238. **303.** Ibid., p. 106. **304.** Sullivan, 1962, p. 280. **305.** Sullivan, 1956, p. 168. **306.** Sullivan, 1940, p. 207. **307.** Sullivan, 1954, p. 231. **308.** Sullivan, 1940, p. 115. **309.** Ibid., p. 94. **310.** Sullivan, 1964, p. 331. **311.** Sullivan, 1953, p. 346. **312.** Sullivan, 1940, p. 208. **313.** Sullivan, 1962, p. 158. **314.** Ibid., p. 183. **315.** Sullivan, 1940, p. 219. **316.** Ibid., p 224. **317.** Ibid., p. 98. **318.** Sullivan, 1956, p. 360. **319.** Sullivan, 1962, p. 348. **320.** Ibid., p. 269. **321.** Sullivan, 1940, p. 227. **322.** Ibid. **323.** Sullivan, 1954, p. 53. **324.** Sullivan, 1940, p. 206. **325.** Sullivan, 1962, pp. 37, 44. **326.** Ibid., p. 283. **327.** Sullivan, 1954, p. 11. **328.**

Ibid., p. 16. **329.** Sullivan, 1956, p. 200. **330.** Sullivan, 1954, p. 219. **331.** Ibid., p. 107. **332.** Sullivan, 1940, p. 214. **333.** Sullivan, 1954, p. 17. **334.** Ibid., pp. 39–41. **335.** Ibid., p. 60. **336.** Ibid., p. 50. **337.** Ibid., p. 78. **338.** Sullivan, 1940, p. 190. **339.** Sullivan, 1956, p. 48. **340.** Ibid., p. 328. **341.** Sullivan, 1953, p. 295. **342.** Sullivan, 1954, pp. 81–82. **343.** Ibid., pp. 85–87. **344.** Ibid., p. 89.

345. Sullivan, 1956, p. 370. **346.** Ibid., p. 225. **347.** Sullivan, 1940, p. 97. **348.** Ibid., p. 191. **349.** Sullivan, 1956, p. 244. **350.** Sullivan, 1940, pp. 200–202. **351.** Ibid., pp. 233–237. **352.** Sullivan, 1954, p. 213. **353.** Sullivan, 1962, p. 91. **354.** Sullivan, 1953, pp. 338–339. **355.** Sullivan, 1940, p. 69. **356.** Sullivan, 1956, p. 105. **357.** Sullivan, 1953, p. 339. **358.** Sullivan, 1962, p. 101. **359.** Ibid., p. 289. **360.** Ibid., p. 253. **361.** Sullivan, 1956, p. 366. **362.** Sullivan, 1940, p. 176.

Chapter 6

Behavioral Learning in Personality and Psychotherapy: Dollard and Miller

Before we can properly appreciate the theoretical approach of John Dollard and Neal E. Miller, we must survey the background positions of the leading historical figures in what is usually called learning theory—a branch of which is *behaviorism*.

Historical Overview of Learning Theory and Behaviorism

Ivan Petrovich Pavlov (1849–1936)

One of the fundamental constructs in this theoretical line is the *conditioned reflex,* or *conditioned response* as it has come to be known. It was the Russian physiologist Ivan P. Pavlov (1927) who first demonstrated that natural or spontaneous responses could be made conditional upon the appearance of an unnatural stimulus. When a light or bell (unnatural stimulus) is presented with or slightly before meat powder (food stimulus) is blown into a dog's mouth, the animal's salivating tendency becomes attached to the light or bell after several such pairings. The theoretical language that issued from this work labeled the meat powder an *unconditioned stimulus* and the natural tendency to salivate when food is present an *unconditioned response*. The arbitrary alternative stimulus of a light or bell is considered the *conditioned stimulus,* and when it reliably elicits salivation, the salivating behavior is called a *conditioned response*. Stimuli and responses that are conditioned are thus manipulated, controlled, or nonspontaneous alterations of a natural course of events.

This procedure, which was crystallized by 1902, has come to be known as *classical conditioning* (as well as *Pavlovian conditioning*). Pavlov believed that conditioning can be achieved only through physiological changes taking place in the brain. His theory of human behavior suggested that our higher nervous system has the capacity to form temporary nervous connections on purely physical grounds. The agent that can cement these connections was termed a *reinforcement*. Food, for example, is a natural *reinforcer* of such bonds, because it restores the body and re-energizes it through chemical action. The human organism will continue to perform a certain behavior if that behavior re-establishes the chemical balance that was disrupted earlier (for example, remove the disbalance we call hunger).

The Pavlovians discovered that both response and stimulus *generalization* take place in learning. For example, a dog conditioned to salivate to a bell of a certain level of cycles per second (for example, 1000) will *also* salivate, though perhaps to a lesser degree, to values approximating this level (for example, 500 to 1500). This would be an example of *stimulus generalization*. Similarly, other responses were found to develop in relation to the conditioned stimulus, responses not specifically reinforced (for example, blinking as well as salivating). This is called *response generalization*. It is possible, through repeated reinforced or nonreinforced trials in the classical conditioning procedure, to reduce the range within which such generalizations occur or to eliminate them entirely (so that in our example above, the animal would respond to 900–1100 cycles, or stop the blinking). This is called stimulus or response *differentiation* (or *discrimination*).

Another form of conditioning first studied by the Pavlovians has come to be called *instrumental conditioning* (named by Hilgard and Marquis, 1940). In classical conditioning, the animal does not have to carry out any contributory behavior in order for it to be reinforced. Some of Pavlov's associates modified this procedure so that after the bell was sounded or a light flashed (unconditioned stimulus), they flexed a dog's leg manually (unconditioned response) and *then* blew the meat powder into the dog's mouth (reinforcement). After a few presentations of the unconditioned stimulus, the dog began to flex its leg without the experimenter having to touch the animal. It therefore appeared that the dog was automatically anticipating the reward to follow leg flexion, and in a sense was doing something to ensure that it would come about. This is what *instrumental* means: an animal's behavior is a contributing factor (an instrumentality) in the sequence of conditioning.

Edward L. Thorndike (1874–1949)

Our next theorist Edward L. Thorndike is, as are all of the remaining psychologists we will consider, in the behavioristic tradition. Thorndike's early work on animals actually predated Pavlov's, and he drew a series of laws from his experiments that are of great importance to learning theory, although neither Thorndike nor Pavlov are behaviorists as such. Although we need not review all of his laws, the *law of effect* should be considered. This law suggested that certain responses get stamped in and others get stamped out of an animal's—or a human being's—supply of responses according to their consequences. In its first version, the law of effect held that responses are *connected* to the situations in which they appear if their consequences are satisfying to the organism.[1] If the consequences are annoying, the law of effect held that the connection between the situation and the response will be weakened. After conducting studies with humans, Thorndike revised the law of effect by noting that annoyance does not weaken the connections between a situation and a response as much as satisfaction strengthens it. Annoyance simply allows an alternative response to take place. For example, if our friends satisfy us by laughing at our party jokes, we will continue telling jokes at all the parties we attend. But if suddenly our friends annoy us by no longer laughing at our jokes, we will not necessarily stop telling them. We might simply switch the topics of our jokes. If we do stop telling jokes, we substitute doing magic tricks as the life of the party. But we never really lose the potential for joke telling, and given the right group of friends and a playful situation, our jokes are likely to reappear.

Thorndike added another major idea to this intellectual tradition, his *law of exercise* (also called *use and disuse*). It held that mere *frequency of repetitions* of a response in a given situation will strengthen the connection, whereas prolonged disuse of a response will weaken the connection. After some work with humans, Thorndike admitted that mere repetition strengthens a

person's response little, if at all. A simple example here is that of efforts to memorize something: no matter how often we repeat the material, it refuses to stick in our memory. Thorndike finally decided that repetition requires what he called a *confirmatory reaction* in order for a person to learn the connection between situation and response. The confirmatory reaction is the result of an individual establishing a set toward obtaining a particular goal and subsequently confirming it through reaching the goal.[2] To explain how satisfactions or confirming reactions work to cement a connecting link between situations and responses, Thorndike took a modified biological position.[3] He suggested that a physical satisfaction probably occurs as the confirmatory reaction, so that there is an ongoing sense of learning taking place.[4] As we go through the day establishing a set (expectancy) to respond in a certain way, our bodily tension rises. We get a little tense knowing that we must now drive our automobile through heavy traffic to get to the grocery market. Once there, our physical tension subsides which confirms the fact that we have arrived at our goal. On the way home the same physical tension and release confirms our return achievement.

John B. Watson (1879–1958)

Our next historical figure is clearly the father of *behaviorism*. John B. Watson coined this term and initiated this rigorous outlook on the nature of psychology while completing his doctoral studies and working as an instructor at the University of Chicago, where he studied with John Dewey, among others. Watson's call to a behavioral psychology was based on a rejection of the then-prevalent tendency to find psychological data within awareness. In a manner of speaking, behaviorism is the diametric opposite of awareness psychology. Watson argued that what counts is the observable behavior of organisms and not what these organisms are aware of or think about in making responses. For his part, Watson based his explanations on the following principle: "The rule, or measuring rod, which the behaviorist puts in front of him always is: Can I describe this bit of behavior I see in terms of 'stimulus and response'?"[5] It was this basic commitment to description of events in stimulus (S) and response (R) terminology that made behaviorism synonymous with *S-R psychology*. By limiting himself to observables, Watson could, in 1913, erase the distinctions between higher and lower animals that most philosophically inclined psychologists had accepted as obvious until that time. "The behaviorist, in his efforts to get a unitary scheme of animal response, recognizes no dividing line between man and brute."[6]

Although he made some effort to apply and extend Thorndike's laws of learning, Watson gradually relied almost exclusively on the conditioned response to explain behavior, which was based in turn on the biological structure known as the *reflex arc*. We can actually see an identity in the way behaviorists speak about the *response* and what they mean by *behavior*; that is, both conceptions are motile, under the control of a stimulus, subsuming all that can be said about animal or human psychology, and depending on reinforcements. Watson described psychology as a natural science, one needing no assumptions about consciousness or mental events to explain the succession of stimuli and responses that are the proper object of its study.[7] He introduced an important theoretical distinction between the *external response* and the *internal response*, suggesting that what we consider to be thought (mentation) is actually a form of subvocal speech in which we covertly manipulate the muscles of our speech apparatus and related structures.[8] We "think" with the motions of our voice box!

Watson helped fix the terms *shaping of behavior* and *habit* into the vocabulary of all psychologists.[9] He did not deny that physical equipment limits what one can do, given certain factors in the environment. As long as pianos are made according to a standard size, the person with a small hand will find it difficult to become a great pianist. Physiology is also important since, after all, we cannot behave effectively if what Watson called our *response repertoire* (total supply of responses available) is made inadequate by hereditary shortcomings or is otherwise diseased.[10] Even so, the *major* source of behavioral variety continues to be the influences that enter the life cycle following birth. This famous quote beautifully captures Watson's environmental determinism.

I should like to go one step further now and say, "Give me a dozen healthy infants, well-formed, and my own specified world to bring them up in and I'll guarantee to take any one at random and train him to become any type of specialist I might suggest—doctor, lawyer, artist, merchant-chief and, yes, even beggar-man and thief, regardless of his talents, penchants, tendencies, abilities, vocations, and the race of his ancestors."[11]

Human behavior involved aligning a series of stimulus-response sequences (considered now in the sense of numberless Thorndikian connections or Pavlovian associations) into *habits* (fixed sequences). Watson thus viewed the person as coming into the world as an *"assembled organic machine ready to run."* [12] The environment takes this machine and shapes it or molds it according to the particular responses that are positively or negatively reinforced into *habits.* It is the scientific duty of psychology to establish laws and principles for the *"control of human action."* [13] The human being is thus fundamentally a responder, not a creator of aspirations or goals toward which he or she can direct personal behavior. Watson believed that those psychologists who place a mentalistic control in people "get lost in the sophistry of 'foresight' and 'end.'" [14] What then is personality? It is the *"end product of our habit systems."* [15]

Edward Chace Tolman (1886–1961)

Not all psychologists who considered themselves behaviorists followed strict Watsonian lines. Edward C. Tolman became the foremost spokesman of his time for those behaviorists who would like to have seen a more complex formulation of behavior than the input-stimulus–output-response mechanism of Watsonian reflexology. Tolman spent time studying with the gestalt psychologist Kurt Koffka (see Chapter 9), and he became convinced that something more than a simple, unidirectional stimulus-to-response circuit is involvd in human learning. Drawing on the writings and inspiration of William McDougall (1923a, 1923b), a nonbehavioral social psychologist who had called for purposive descriptions of behavior,[16] Tolman named his approach to psychology *purposive behaviorism.* He did not mean to imply by this that animals, or human beings for that matter, are teleological organisms.[17] He felt that purpose can be directly observed, as when an animal, facing several trial-and-error alternatives relative to some end (such as a food box), is *observed by the experimenter* to follow the "more efficient of such

trials and errors with respect to getting to that end." [18]

Tolman argued that there must be a cognitive (knowing) process which *intervenes* or *mediates* between the stimulus input and the response output.[19] These coming-between variables, which Woodworth (1929) had termed *organismic* (O) variables—leading to an S-O-R and not simply an S-R sequence of behavior—are thus given a central role in purposive behaviorism. The organism does not simply respond to the environmental stimuli in an automatic fashion. It formulates a kind of cognitive map which it can later use in memory to direct its present behavior. The animal in the maze learns a *significate,* or a visual image, giving the general layout of the physical properties of the maze. In addition, as the animal runs across this recalled layout, a series of *signs* orient it in relation to the goal that is being purposively sought (the food box). Tolman then combined all of these features—the significates, the signs, the means-to-ends purposive behaviors that were thus made possible—into the single theoretical construct of the *sign-gestalt.*[20]

In the evolution of learning theories, Tolman's sign-gestalt sequences of means-to-ends have been incorporated under the global term of *expectancy.* Tolman frequently spoke of his *means-end-readiness* constructs as expectancies, held by the animal in probabilistic fashion toward one goal or another.[21] What is the probability that behavior A (run to the left in a maze) will lead to B (food) rather than to C (no food)? He also suggested, regarding expectancies, that "to some extent, rats, and to a large extent the higher animals, seem capable of expecting not merely simple, and single, direction-distance correlations but also successions or hierarchies of such correlations." [22] This concept of a *hierarchy* of expectancies—which probably flows from Watson's concept of a repertoire of response—has since been of central importance as a means of conceptualizing the sum of all behaviors going to make up habitual animal or human behavior.

Clark Leonard Hull (1884–1952)

It remained for Clark L. Hull to raise behaviorism and learning theory to what is probably its highest level of expression. In addition to the extensive and detailed experiments he and his students conducted, Hull provided a kind of philosophical-theoretical background for the thinkers who followed Watson's lead. Building on Tolman's intervening or mediating approach to learning, Hull formulated a highly sophisticated and intricate theoretical system to explain the nature of learning (1943, 1952). For our purposes, only a few aspects of this theory need consideration.

First of all, it is historically important to appreciate that Hullian theory rests on a *drive-reduction* interpretation of reinforcement. That is, learning is not held to take place unless a response, which has been continuously associated with a stimulus, is followed by some form of drive or need reduction. This is essentially identical with the Pavlovian-Watsonian tradition. In his first formulation, Hull (1943) spoke of this reinforcement as involving a definite drive reduction or drive gratification. For example, the animal learns in classical conditioning to make a response in relation to a stimulus because of the gratification of a food drive when powdered meat is blown into its mouth. After several years of study, Hull

modified the specific reference to a drive per se in favor of a *drive stimulus*. It takes time for drives to result in a bodily gratification, as in the case of hunger where several minutes elapse in the processes of ingestion, digestion, and absorption before the organism achieves a sense of revitalization. Obviously, reinforcement must follow a given response fairly quickly in order for a stimulus-response connection to be strengthened. It therefore seems plausible that a partial reduction in the stimulations that herald a drive's presence—not total drive reduction—might well account for how stimulus-response bonds are cemented (reinforced). Hence, once food is in the mouth of an animal, the stimulus value of a drive is doubtlessly reduced because the animal has learned that such slight changes of a drive stimulus (smell, taste) herald the certain gratification of a need. This pitched behavior toward the goals being sought rather than simply being due to automatic reflexes in the Watsonian sense.

In time, this goal orientation of behavior became a major feature of Hullian theory. Hull in no way implied a teleology, and indeed he was less attracted to expectancy constructs than Tolman. However, he did introduce a concept of the *fractional, antedating goal reaction* or *anticipatory goal response* which accounted for the fact that behaviors are often learned that are not specifically consummatory—directly reinforcing, such as eating, drinking—yet they *are* vital aspects of the total learning process. [23] For example, a rat running a maze in which it must turn left in order to reach the food box (goal) may begin running closer to the left-hand wall before making its turn; or it may begin a series of head-turnings to the left before coming to the point at which it must turn. Tolman would have considered these to be purposive moves on the animal's part, adapting to ongoing signs along its significate-expectations. Hull, however, preferred to consider these responses *fractions* of the eventual complete goal response (turn left and eat)—fractions that in turn provoked a further stimulus to register on behavior, the goal stimulus.

This theoretical innovation extended the mediation conception of Tolman and Woodworth to say that some stimuli intervene between an input and an output because they have literally been generated by a fraction of the total output. A fraction of the output (a response) thus can generate a type of new input (an intervening stimulus). These new stimuli, which have been produced by fractional responses, Hull called *pure stimulus acts*. They are pure in the sense that their only role is to guide the course of behavior along the route to eventual reinforcement. They cannot result in gratification through stimulating the consummatory responses. These latter, broader response patterns include the fractional antedating goal reactions (running to the left, head-turning) plus all of the physical behavioral responses needed to consummate the behavioral sequence (chewing, swallowing, and so forth).

Two important theoretical concepts flowed from Hull's treatment of fractional antedating goal reactions and their consequent goal stimuli. First of all, this characteristic accounts for *secondary reinforcement*. The *primary reinforcement* would imply a decided drive reduction, of course—or at the very least, a sense of immediacy as when we literally have food in our mouth. However, it is possible to see how goal stimuli more and more removed from the consummatory act can take on reinforcing properties of a secondary sort. Thus, the tendency to run along the left wall or the slight head-turning of the rat can themselves function as pure stimulus acts leading to the (primary) reinforcement. The animal has learned that this or that sequence of events antedates the goal attainment, hence its behavior is furthered

by the appearance of these secondary reinforcers. The very fact that the rat *is* turning its head at a certain point in its running signals (mediately) that it is just about to begin chewing and swallowing (consummatory behavior).

Second, picking up from where Tolman had begun, Hull acknowledged that animals learn *many* behaviors that might gain the achieved goal object in their series of learning trials. The organism never learns just one habit (stimulus-response regularity) but a host of such habits forming a *habit-family hierarchy*. The habit a given stimulus or complex of stimuli is most likely to evoke stands at the apex of this hierarchy as the most-probable response(s) to occur. However, given that this response could not be made, or given that this response were to be made several times without eventual reinforcement taking place, an alternative response, lower in the probability of occurrence at the outset, could move up the hierarchy to most-probable response. In our earlier example of the telling of jokes versus doing magic tricks, Hull would suggest that initially joke-telling was highest in the habit-family hierarchy having to do with being the life of the party. When the stimulus complex of a party occurred, the person told jokes and received a positive reinforcement in the laughter of peers. This person also knew how to do magic tricks, but rarely did so outside of the family or in a group of close friends. But, when the joke-telling response(s) no longer led to reinforcement, this magic-trick response(s) moved up the hierarchy to become a highly probable alternative. In the meantime, the joke-telling habit dropped in the hierarchy of probability, even though it was retained as a potential alternative for the future.

Burrhus Frederic Skinner (1904–   )

Having considered Hull's elegant attempts to raise behaviorism to the status of a theoretical science, we will end our review of prominent figures with a consideration of B. F. Skinner, a neobehaviorist who not only found the S-O-R model inappropriate for psychology but rejected all attempts to theorize about what is supposedly taking place inside the organism.[24] Skinner took the Watsonian empirical approach to its logical limit, even though he was not attracted to a reflex-arc psychology. In his now-classic *The Behavior of Organisms* (1938) and the papers that followed shortly thereafter, Skinner gradually turned attention away from classical conditioning to the form of behavioral control we discussed above as instrumental conditioning.

Skinner argued that classical conditioning was a stimulus-produced form of behavioral regularity. A specific and clearly known stimulus (for example, food powder) is paired with a response under conditions in which it serves as a reinforcer of the other stimulus (the bell or light) in relation to the spontaneous response (in this case, salivation). Knowing the specific stimulus, the experimenter can treat the behavior under his or her control in a physical reflex sense—that is, see that it is *elicited* (drawn out or evoked in a way that does not bring the animal's behavior into the picture at all). Nothing the animal might *do* will alter what eventually *happens*. The unconditioned stimulus (food) is also the reinforcer, so everything gets aligned automatically.

It was Skinner's belief that this form of conditioning is not typical of most of life's learned behaviors. Responses of animals or people are not elicited through such ironclad successions of events. Rather than being elic-

ited, most behavioral responses are actually *emitted* or sent forth by the organism in relation to certain consequent environmental factors which either reinforce the behavior emitted or fail to do so. In this case, what the animal does as a response is crucial to obtaining reinforcement. If a bear roaming the woods turns over a log and is rewarded thereby with a nest of insects, this consequence (insects as reinforcement) will ensure a subsequent repetition of log-turning (the response) by this particular animal. The behavior (log-turning) that operates on the environment to produce a reinforcing effect Skinner termed the *operant response* (or simply *operant*). Hence, *operant conditioning* focuses on the response and asserts that responses followed by reinforcers are likely to be carried out again, and the more we reinforce these responses (operants) the more likely will they be to appear. The classical conditioner of behavior had looked to the size of the response eventually conditioned (for example, the amount of saliva secreted), or the rapidity with which this response is made as conditioning is carried out (how quickly salivation begins following flashing of the light) as the measure of learning. The operant conditioner, on the other hand, focuses on the frequency of conditioned responses (the number of log-turnings over a fixed period of time) as the proper measure of learning.

Note what has happened here: Skinner dismissed as irrelevant for his purposes the time-honored behaviorist concern with *the* stimulation of a response (why did the bear roll the first log over?). This means that he also was not called upon to speculate about the nature of drives or needs, as Watson and Hull had done before him. Such speculations are risky at best, dealing with presumed factors going on within the organism. As Skinner once phrased it: "I don't see any reason to postulate a need anywhere along the line. . . . As far as I'm concerned, if a baby is reinforced by the sound made by a rattle, the sound is just as useful as a reinforcer in accounting for behavior as food in the baby's mouth." [25] Thus, we might characterize the position Skinner took on reinforcement as an *empirical law of effect.*

As we have already seen, Thorndike proposed the law of effect and subsequent developments were to tie this law to presumed drive reductions of various needs. Skinner then argued in opposition to this approach that whatever stimulus he can *empirically observe* following a response that increases the likelihood or rate of that response's subsequent emission he will accept as a reinforcement stimulus or a positive reinforcement on its face. Its reinforcing properties have been observed empirically because it *in fact* has increased the response rate, thanks to its appearance following the response. Thus, the baby shakes his or her hand, a rattle sounds, and we observe over time that this hand-shaking (rattling) increases. We conclude empirically that the rattle sound is a *positive reinforcement* or *reinforcer* of the response that produced it—hand-shaking. A *negative reinforcement,* on the other hand, occurs when an aversive (annoying, painful) stimulus is removed, leading *also* to an increase of responsivity, but in this case to whatever removed the aversion. For example, taking off a shoe when it pinches stops an aversive stimulation and therefore the likelihood increases that the next time the person's foot hurts he or she will take off a shoe. Strange as this may sound on first hearing, Skinner would call this control through *negative* reinforcement, even though there is a feeling of relief as the shoe is removed (which might be thought of as positive by the person).

By emphasizing the *subsequent effect* of a behavioral response in this fashion, Skinner picked up a theme introduced by Tolman.

That is, Skinner spoke of these subsequent affairs as *contingencies,* by which he meant "the conditions which prevail at any given time and which relate a bit of behavior to its consequences." [26] Skinner also emphasized that responses occur as *classes* rather than in a one-to-one sense.[27] An operant is thus a *class of responses,* and though he did not speak of hierarchies, Skinner clearly achieved the same multiplicity of behavioral description in this use of a class construct as Tolman and Hull had achieved in their hierarchy constructs. We do not learn a single response when we find that rummaging through the kitchen can lead to a tasty snack, we learn a host of potentially rewarding responses. It is thus the case that operant behavior is far ranging and greatly adaptive.

At the same time, precisely which way behavior will go and how specific it becomes is to be determined by the *response-reinforcement contingency.* Skinner extended Watson's concept of *shaping* behavior to include what he called the *method of successive approximations*—a method of behavioral control that is presumably at work in all of our lives each day. The idea here is gradually to arrive at a desired (or randomly decided) behavior in the organism by taking it in stages of shaping. Take the man who earns his living by training dogs to put on an act for circus performances. He patiently rewards his dogs as they approach a stool, until he has them up on the stool, then jumping from it, then through a hoop, and so forth. This man is using the method of successive approximations. With each movement toward the desired behavior, he slips his dog a bit of food as a reward, and the likelihood of the animal repeating this behavior is thereby increased, until the proper sequence is one day aligned and—at a signal—the dog will carry through the entire act before seeking his reward at the hand of the trainer. In the same way, Skinner argued, all of us are controlled by our environmental circumstances. We are shaped each day, behaving this way or that contingent on the reinforcements that originate in our environment. To change ourselves, we must first change our environment, for "men will never become originating centers of control, because their behavior will itself be controlled, but their role as mediators may be extended without limit."[28] Thus, *mediation theory* in behaviorism has been kept intact even though there are differing views of reinforcement based on either a classical or an instrumental view of conditioning. In all behavioristic views, we must look to sources outside the individual to find observable shaping circumstances for why people behave as they do.

Biographical Overview of John Dollard and Neal E. Miller

The two men we now turn to were uniquely equipped to achieve the task they set themselves—that is, to unite the physical and behavioral with the social and psychiatric sciences. It is rare to find the breadth of scope each man had personally achieved in theoretical outlook. Dollard brought the knowledge of ethnology, sociology, and anthropology to the partnership. Miller brought the knowledge of experimental psychology, physiology, and animal experimentation. Dollard was the field investigator, Miller, the laboratory experimenter. Dollard leaned in the direction of the social sciences, Miller, the natural sciences. Both men had firsthand experience with psychoanalysis. Dollard and

Miller are transitional figures in the history of personality theory. They paved the way for the behavioral therapy approaches of Chapter 7, though their stated objective and major achievement was to show how theories of human behavior might be brought together into an enriched overall picture.

John Dollard was born in Menasha, Wisconsin, on 29 August 1900 and grew up in this small town set in rural surroundings before attending the University of Wisconsin. He took his B.A. degree from Wisconsin and then did graduate work in sociology at the University of Chicago where he earned the M.A. (1930) and Ph.D. (1931) degrees. It is of some interest to note that Dollard's intellectual stimulation thus came from the same Chicago school of social thought that was infusing Harry Stack Sullivan with his outlook on humanity. During the 1931–1932 period Dollard was in Germany as a research fellow in social psychology, and it was there that he received training in Freudian psychoanalysis at the Berlin Psychoanalytic Institute. In 1932 he returned to America as assistant professor of anthropology at Yale University. In 1933 he moved into the newly formed Institute of Human Relations at Yale, where he was to begin his working collaboration with Neal E. Miller. Some appreciation of Dollard's versatility can be gained from the fact that he was carried on the staff rolls of three departments at Yale (anthropology, sociology, and psychology) before retiring in 1969. He died in October 1980.

Dollard's professional studies have ranged with his career interests. He did a classic field study in the 1930s dealing with the role of the black man in a southern community, which quickly established his talent for combining personality and sociocultural factors into an overall analysis.[29] He was a consultant to the secretary of war during World War II and published works on the psycho-

John Dollard

logical aspects of fear, including those associated with battle.[30] He seems to have become increasingly interested in psychotherapy during this time. Dollard did in fact train psychotherapists and for many years carried on a moderate private psychotherapy practice. In addition to his work with Miller, he has published books dealing with the practical aspects of psychotherapy as well as the assessment of human motivation.[31]

Neal E. Miller was also native to Wisconsin, born in the more metropolitan city of Milwaukee on 3 August 1909. He attended several universities, obtaining his B.S. from the University of Washington in 1931, an

M.A. from Stanford University in 1932, and his Ph.D. from Yale in 1935. During the period of 1932–1935, while completing his doctoral studies, Miller served as an assistant in psychology at the Institute of Human Relations. In the year following completion of his doctorate, Miller obtained a traveling fellowship which sent him to Vienna, where he studied psychoanalysis at the Vienna Institute of Psychoanalysis. Although his training and research interests were in animal study and Hullian neobehaviorism,

Neal E. Miller

this experience with psychoanalysis laid the groundwork for his eventual collaboration with Dollard.

Clark L. Hull was at Yale during this period, and during the year 1938–1939 he held a series of Monday night gatherings with members of the Institute of Human Relations and others. Miller was an active participant in this group. Indeed, in time Miller became an important influence on Hull, encouraging him to change his interpretation of reinforcement—from requiring that a drive be reduced to requiring that merely the drive stimulus be lessened (see p. 382).

Miller's excellently conceived researches were making this point increasingly clear to all those interested in Hullian theory.

Miller retained his academic affiliation with the Institute of Human Relations until 1942, when he left to direct a research project for the U.S. Army Air Force during World War II. He returned to Yale in 1946 and continued his distinguished work there until 1966, when he accepted an appointment as professor of psychology and head of the Laboratory of Physiological Psychology at Rockefeller University. As the latter appointment might suggest, Miller's interests in his maturing years as researcher and theorist centered more and more on the physiological aspects of behavioral reinforcement. Miller has published extensively and importantly for several years, in addition to his collaborative efforts with Dollard.[32] He was honored by his fellow psychologists who elected him president of the American Psychological Association in 1949, and in 1965 he was awarded the U.S. President's Medal of Science.

The collaboration of Dollard and Miller was the natural outgrowth of the spirit born of the Institute of Human Relations. In 1939, the Institute's staff combined to publish what has become a monumental example of interdisciplinary study, a monograph entitled *Frustration and Aggression*.[33] The point of this work was to analyze the general phenomena of frustration and aggression in terms of stimulus-response psychology, psychoanalytical theory, and the findings of sociology and anthropology. Following this, Dollard and Miller wrote two books together from which most of the material of Chapter 6 will be drawn, *Social Learning and Imitation*[34] and *Personality and Psychotherapy*.[35]

Personality Theory

Structural Constructs

Behavioral Monism and Mental Activities

True to their behavioristic tradition, Dollard and Miller rejected all telic descriptions in favor of what they took to be the superiority of the reinforcement principle.[36] Human beings can make *only* those responses they have learned and make them *necessarily* when the stimulus conditions are right.[37] Purposive behavior is not really possible, although by using more precise terms, we can account for what are popularly called mental activities.[38] Hence, to speak of a mind versus body

dualism in this neo-Hullian approach to personality is really beside the point. All behavior, whether inside the organism's skin or outside it, is essentially the *same* thing.[39] Dollard and Miller would therefore be called *monists* (one realm of description) in their theoretical approach. Actually, we do not find the mind-versus-body type of discussion in their writings that we have found in the works of the nonacademic therapists discussed so far. This is probably due to the fact that they came at the problem of behavioral description free of medical-model influences.

Dollard and Miller were distrustful of explaining behavior exclusively on the basis of hereditary principles. They were of the opinion that a scientist's inquisitiveness suffered to the extent that he or she settled on explanations based on hereditary instincts.[40] It is always tempting to simply say that "person X is different from person Y because they have different inborn instincts." The same applies to those theories that rely on principles of organic development.[41] Though they did not deny that physical limitations and physiological developments (for example, sexual promptings at puberty) enter into the range of behaviors we must consider in describing personality, Dollard and Miller stressed the great capacity of behavior to change and be shaped in countless directions by environmental influences. Their theoretical goal was to account for the Freudian regularities of personality in terms of more empirically derived learning principles. Dollard and Miller said they wanted "to combine the vitality of psychoanalysis, the rigor of the natural-science laboratory, and the facts of culture."[42] They hoped to clarify Freudian terminology in the process.[43]

*The Fundamental Organization of
Behavior: Attachments, Stimuli,
and Responses*

Given their stated goals, one might expect that the constructs of id, ego, and superego would be given prominence in Dollard and Miller's writings. Actually, this is not what we find. What are the basic structural constructs of personality? Though their 1950 book is entitled *Personality and Psychotherapy* and one can find several definitions of psychotherapy within its pages, there is no clear-cut definition of what a personality is, except that it is part and parcel of behavior, and behaviors always differ across people because of their environmental influences. If we look closely at what Dollard and Miller always relied on to discuss behavior, we can point to what are, in our terms, structural constructs of personality.

One such basic structuring concept was *attachment,* or the attaching of different elements of experience. Some examples would be attaching words to different features of the environment,[44] anxiety to certain sentences ("I am going to fail"),[45] specific physical responses to certain cues ("Run for your life"),[46] or correct emotional responses to certain habitual behaviors ("I meditate and always feel relaxed afterwards").[47] Dollard and Miller even suggested that higher-level thought processes are made possible by the attachments of words to words in an increasingly complex fashion.[48] We see in this hooking-up conception of attachment a theoretical descendant of the *association* or *connection* constructs, which have been used since Pavlov, Thorndike, and Watson to organize behavior into some kind of structural regularity.

Of course, the basic units that become attached in all behavioristic theories remain the *stimulus* and the *response*. Since stimuli cannot be stimuli unless they bring about responses, and, in turn, responses must occur in relation to stimuli, it would seem that these two terms form into a singular conception. That is, how could we call anything a stimulus unless it stimulated a response and vice versa? Though this is true, according to S-R theory a given stimulus can either now or through learning at some time in the future stimulate *any of a number* of responses. And thinking in the reverse direction, a given response can occur to *any of a number* of stimuli. Since we can think of stimuli on the one hand and their attached or detached responses on the other, it is therefore correct to construe these as independent theoretical terms.

In their 1941 book, Miller and Dollard made clear that they were not using the terms *stimulus* and *response* in the way that reflex psychology had used them earlier. Responses were not considered as *only* those muscular contractions or glandular secretions that the early associationists and behaviorists had sometimes made them out to be. Dollard and Miller defined their terms as follows: "A response is any activity within the individual which can become functionally connected with an antecedent event through learning; a stimulus is any event to which a response can be so connected."[49] They did not consider this definition circular because it rested on observably demonstrable facts. Hence, in their 1950 book they once again rested their case with "We shall call anything a stimulus that seems to have the functional properties of a stimulus and anything a response that seems to have the functional properties of a response."[50] By *functional properties,* they mean an observed role in behavior, so that when we see a person blink to a flashing light, we have literally seen a stimulus (light) and response (blink) in the state of attachment.

When some environmental antecedent A

is tied regularly to a behavioral consequent B, we have a stimulus-response regularity or *habit*.[51] If we now analyze how habits arise, we become involved in a study of *learning*. Theories of learning try to explain how habits are established, sustained, and often changed. Reverting to the language of Thorndike's connectionism, Miller and Dollard asked:

What . . . is learning theory? In its simplest form, it is the study of the circumstances under which a response and a cue stimulus become connected. After learning has been completed, response and cue are bound together in such a way that the appearance of the cue evokes the response. Everyone remembers to stop at a red light when driving an automobile.[52]

A *cue* is thus an antecedent event that takes on stimulus properties.[53] Cues determine when we will respond, where we will respond, and which particular response we will make.[54] Cues do not have to occur singly or in isolation. It is possible for a *patterning* of cues to take place, so that a complex network of stimulations can happen all at once, often giving qualitative differences to the stimulations of experience. Getting down to the specifics of their concept, Miller and Dollard noted that "stimuli may vary in two respects: in strength and in kind."[55] The cue of a flashing red light is different from the cue of a delicious aroma drifting out from the kitchen. Each signals a different kind of response.

What we *do* about the stimuli depends on the kinds of responses we have in our *repertoire* (store of responses). Behavioral responses are organized into a certain likelihood of occurrence, beginning at birth. Dollard and Miller spoke of an *innate hierarchy of response* which any living organism brings into the world. This concept of a hierarchy refers to the probability of an innate (unlearned) response being elicited by a given stimulus or stimulus-complex.[56] For example, babies have the cry as an innate response, and this is one of the most probable (called *dominant*) responses any baby will make in response to painful stimulation. If a diaper pin pricks the infant, crying occurs automatically. In time, other responses to such painful stimulation will be learned (the older child learns to remove the pin), yet this crying potential will always remain as a weaker response in the hierarchy (see our discussion of Hull above, p. 382).[57] There are certain selective environmental situations in which crying always remains a likely response, such as the deaths of loved ones, funerals, and even weddings. But in most cultural situations, as maturity increases, the acceptability of crying when injured or frustrated decreases.

Responses Become Stimuli: Mediation, Labeling, and Language

Dollard and Miller followed the *mediation model* of their predecessors in suggesting that behaving organisms not only attach stimuli to responses, in the Watsonian S-R sense of a direct hook-up, but they also make use of some of these earlier responses by retaining them in memory where they come to serve as special mediating stimuli (on the order of Tolman's sign-gestalt; see above). This led to a basic distinction in their response construct. Dollard and Miller suggested that organisms make two kinds of behavioral responses, *instrumental acts* (direct S-R sequence) on the one hand and *cue-producing responses* (mediated S-O-R sequence) on the other.

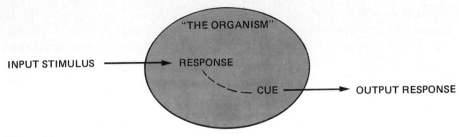

Figure 21

An instrumental act is one whose main function is to produce an immediate change in the relationship to the external environment. Opening a door, lifting a box, jumping back on the curb are examples of instrumental acts. A cue-producing response is one whose main function is to produce a cue that is part of the stimulus pattern leading to another response. Counting is a cue-producing response.[58]

We human organisms have the capacity to restimulate ourselves by making use of former responses which we now will call *cue-producing responses,* though the term *response-produced stimuli* conveys the same meaning and was used by Dollard and Miller in their first formulation.[59] We might conceptualize this *mediational process*—that is, one that comes between a former input and a current output—as shown in Figure 21.

The instrumental act or, as it is sometimes referred to, the instrumental response is obviously the actual, overt, *output response*. If we were nothing but instrumental organisms, then each stimulus input would go over directly into an output. Some behaviors do indeed work this way, such as the reflexive-type physical connection of a tap on the knee leading to a knee jerk (Patellar reflex). Even more psychological behaviors are of this type, as when we fly off the handle and say things without thinking or even

strike out at someone because of a real or imagined hurt. But human behavior is heavily influenced by mediational factors most of the time. There are two kinds of cue-producing responses: *verbal* (words, numbers) and *nonverbal* (sensory images, moods). We can mediate behavior by talking (words) to ourselves or by recalling something seen (sensory image) in the past. Something so simple as asking another person to bring us a glass of water would utilize both forms of cue-producing responses and, incidentally, save us the effort of making our own instrumental response.[60] Sometimes we rely almost exclusively on nonverbal cue-producing responses, as when we do not recall the name of a street in trying to locate a friend's house and, by simply driving along in our automobile, find the right place through familiar (recalled) visual-cues.

Instrumental responses aligned in a sequence of from stimulus-to-response and no more would mean that no alternatives would ever occur in behavior. But:

A series of cue-producing responses is not limited in this way. It is possible for certain cue-producing responses that have been associated with the goal to move forward in the sequence and provide cues that have a selective effect on subsequent responses. Hull . . . calls these anticipatory goal responses [fractional, antedating goal reactions; see our comments on Hull above] and presents a rigorous deduction of how they could make the adaptive combination of habits more likely to occur in a novel situation.[61]

This capacity for problem solving is a great improvement over the kind of learning known as *trial and error*,[62] wherein the organism cannot anticipate but fumbles along, learning always after the fact of having behaved incorrectly in the first place. Human beings can make *insightful* responses based on a preliminary use of cue-producing responses.[63] In fact, they can also make finer *discriminations* between patterns of stimulation in their environments and come thereby to a more refined pattern of learned responding.[64] In doing her homework (rehearsing), Nancy learns to tell when one type of mathematical solution is called for and not another. If she puts enough time into her studies, she will not make the wrong response and apply an erroneous solution to a problem in the classroom tomorrow (that is, *generalize* incorrectly).[65] She will have acquired discriminating ability, thanks to the cue-producing responses learned (attached to the mathematical stimuli through frequency of rehearsal).

Another possibility we see in human behavior is *transfer of training,* which refers to the fact that responses made in one context can be transferred to another because of the mediation of cue-producing responses.[66] We can recall that as children we realigned a skidding bicycle by turning into the direction of the skid; we apply the same principle to our automobile driving in adulthood. Visual cues might be all that would be necessary here, but obviously much of transfer is mediated by language. Dollard and Miller once said that "language is the human example *par excellence* of a cue-producing response."[67] From childhood on throughout our lives, we are learning to attach language signs to experience. Dollard and Miller called this process of language acquisition *labeling*

and defined the *label* as a "verbal cue-producing response."[68] We can also call labels *signs* or even *symbols* because there is no real distinction to be drawn between such cues, as far as Dollard and Miller were concerned.[69] Certain signs or symbols are nonverbal like a country's flag or the display of wealth in wearing expensive jewelry, but the verbal symbol—word-forms—plays the most important role in higher mental processes. Dollard and Miller observed that "most human thinking is done in words and sentences"[70] and "words and sentences play an exceedingly important role in human reasoning."[71]

As we mature, we learn to match words (signs, symbols) to important features of the physical and social environment.[72] Once we have attached it to the proper feeling state, the word *love* becomes a cue-producing response of major significance for most of us. Complexity is introduced through the patterning of these words into sentences and sentences into various thought forms known as *logic,* or the use of proper reason to eliminate contradictions and confusions.[73] Furthermore, language is the natural storehouse for all of those effective problem solutions that culture has discovered through experience from generations past.[74] The natural role of culture is to aid in the transmission of those artifacts and living styles that have proven successful across the span of time.[75]

Freudian Structural Constructs as Learning-Theory Terms

What have Dollard and Miller to say of the classic Freudian structural constructs? They never discussed the *id,* though we can infer that the hedonism of a reinforcement principle relying on drive reductions would touch on this construct. There is a fairly extensive treatment of the unconscious-versus-conscious aspects of experience, some of which has relevance for the id construct. That is, Dollard and Miller can see how an uneducated, uncultivated person lacking in a repertoire of the more civilizing labels (dos and don'ts of culture) might impulsively act out in an illogical and immoral way by going over directly to instrumental responses without mediating checks on behavior.[76] Such an uncouth person might be described as id-dominated, but this does not mean that personality is populated by a unique identity of this sort, directing it from out of an unconscious region of the mind.

All the *unconscious mind* amounts to is the total number of behaviors carried over into action without an intervening label of some sort making the sequence known or *conscious* to the person doing the acting.[77] These unverbalized (unlabeled) behaviors are often conditioned into the person's repertoire as an infant before language has been acquired. Stanley becomes unreasonably hostile whenever anyone begins to take an interest in anything he considers uniquely his own. This instrumentally hostile reaction dates back to his first few years of life when he had to give up his playthings to older siblings who simply took what they wanted from him. Stanley has only a very hazy, visual recollection of the source of his hostility, and without proper labels, he finds it difficult if not impossible to consciously understand his pattern of behavior.[78] Freud's well-known tendency to find the sources of unconscious behavioral tendencies in the early years of life depended on factors such as these. To the extent that the person has labels, consciousness increases and the fruits of higher mental processes can be achieved.

The *ego* was described by Dollard and Miller in terms of the capacity the person has to deal with life through higher mental processes.[79] Conscious, directed thinking implies *ego strength* because the individual is not simply at the mercy of environmental stimuli triggering those unexamined and primitive instrumental responses we noted above. Our egos are shaped by learning as we are prepared by parents and teachers to confront the realities of life. When this life preparation has been poor, Dollard and Miller would say that we have "a weak ego or a poor sense of reality."[80] If the consciousness is weak and there are many unlabeled aspects of experience entering behavior, it follows that the ego would be submerged and something like an id domination of the personality would result. Dollard and Miller, on at least one occasion,[81] used the phrase *unconscious wish* in describing a personality pattern. This usage is quite proper in classic psychoanalysis, but it is somewhat unclear how an unlabeled and unconscious stimulus could be a wish, unless of course we are dealing with unlabeled images of some sort, as in a dream. We might thus "see" ourselves visually in a dream, doing something we would like to do but have never actually put into words (labeled).

The *superego* is the result of cultural modeling and training. We are taught the rules of personal cleanliness, and then building on the conditioned traces of proper behavior first used to shape us in the toilet-training situation, we transfer to increasingly complex rules of civilized behavior.[82] All of those familiar emotions we experience when we transgress social boundaries, like guilt, fear, and anxiety, are controlling mechanisms to make us hew to the line valued by the culture. This is not meant in the sense of repression, of course, because *any* collective identity of people, from a gang of delinquents to an entire nation, must have its rules of conduct laid down if it is to survive.

Motivational Constructs

The Nature of Drive, Motivation, and Reinforcement

In order for S-R attachments to form into habits, they must be *reinforced*. Dollard and Miller replaced Freud's pleasure principle with the *principle of reinforcement*.[83] It is correct to speak of reinforcements as *rewards*, but the former term is used more generally and we shall follow this practice. Reinforcements depend on *drives* which motivate the organism in the first place.[84] A *drive* is defined as a strong stimulus that impels action; literally any stimulus can become a drive if it becomes strong enough.[85] To be *motivated* is to be under drive, ready to act, and there is really no clear distinction between these terms, except that a motive can probably combine several different drives into an overall state of readiness to behave.[86]

The two broad classes of drives are *primary* or *innate* and *secondary* or *learned*. Primary drives include such feelings as pain, the sexual urge, hunger, or the desire to take a breath of air.[87] Secondary drives occur when a previously neutral cue stimulus has gained the functional capacity to stimulate an organism to respond.[88] The middle-aged man who competes with his neighbors to have the nicest looking lawn (stimulus) in the neighborhood has acquired a secondary drive which never occurred to him in his younger years before he had bought a home of his own. Once a habit has been established, drives also increase the tendency for the habit to be performed.[89] A competitive neighbor might have our man out tending to the lawn daily, in hopes of retaining that satisfying sense of "My lawn is truly the best one of all." It is the reduction in the drive that originally motivates the behavior that cements (attaches) the S-R regularity we call a habit. And the continuing drive reduction that occurs as the S-R sequence is being carried out makes it certain that the habit will continue. Dollard and Miller had this to say about their principle of reinforcement:

. . . the following relationships between drive and reinforcement are clear: (1) a prompt reduction in the strength of the drive acts as a reinforcement; (2) reinforcement is impossible in the absence of drive because the strength of stimulation cannot be reduced when it is already at zero; and (3) the drive must inevitably be lower after the reinforcement so that unless something is done to increase it, it will eventually be reduced to zero, at which point further reinforcement is impossible.[90]

The heart of reinforcement is thus the occurrence of a "prompt reduction in the strength of a strong drive stimulus."[91] When the sun's glare becomes strong enough to motivate us to move into the shade, the reduction in the annoying stimulus that results is itself a reinforcement of the habitual movement being formed—that is, to seek the shade when annoyed by the sun. Dollard and Miller admitted that there may be other forms of reinforcement, but rather than haggle over the matter, they chose to say that as long as at least *some* reinforcements operate through sudden reductions in drive stimulation, their theory retains its integrity.[92] They wanted to further their theory without having to pass on the ultimate nature of all reinforcements.

Paralleling the drives with which they are associated, *reinforcements* can be considered *primary* or *secondary* in nature. The satisfaction gained by eating when hungry or the reduction of painful tensions in defecation are both examples of *primary reinforcement,* resting ultimately on innate response tendencies. But most of our motives and habit systems are taken from the secondary sources of the sociocultural environment. The drive for success can take on proportions far exceeding that necessary to keep up life and limb. Since wealth reflects power in the social hierarchy, all of the signs of *social status* (nice home, good clothes, automobiles, memberships in the better clubs) begin taking on secondary-drive properties which means they take on *secondary-reinforcement* potentials as well.

It takes a rather high-level animal to work for the distant reinforcements of a pay day. Several experiments on both lower animals and humans have shown that *immediate reinforcements*—given immediately following the response being rewarded—are more effective to habit formations than are *delayed reinforcements*. The greater the delay between a response and its reinforcement (called the *latency*) the more difficult it is to establish a stimulus-response connection. Folk wisdoms, such as "a bird in hand is worth two in the bush" and "don't count your chickens before they hatch," capture the idea that one is better off with reward *now* than dreaming about what might happen tomorrow. The principle that immediate reinforcements are more effective than delayed ones is called the *gradient of reinforcement*.[93] Another aspect of this principle, which accounts in a way for the cue-producing responses Hull had called the *anticipatory goal response,* is that there is a more active tendency to respond the closer one comes to goal reinforcement. The goal is ever more present as one gets closer to pay day, and

though a working woman may have felt down during the week, the day she receives her check, she is cheered by the prospect and works with renewed vigor.

Thus, thanks to our higher mental processes, we are capable of working toward the more distant or delayed reinforcements of life. Lower animals are lacking in this capacity (relatively speaking, since even chimpanzees have been trained to work for poker chips associated with food on earlier learning trials), and hence they cannot show the delay-of-reward potentials that human behavior constantly reflects. When we speak of learned drives that work by motivating an animal for the future, we are referring to *incentives*.[94] The *goal* is that cue-produced response or incentive the organism has learned to work toward after the fashion of a delayed reinforcement.[95]

Are we consciously aware of having been or now being reinforced? Dollard and Miller would respond, "According to our hypothesis, all reinforcements have a direct automatic strengthening effect on immediately preceding responses. Thus the primary effect of a reinforcement is always unconscious. In addition to this primary effect, it is possible for a reinforcement to have other effects that are mediated by verbal responses." [96] There are actually three levels of consciousness involved in reinforcement. First of all, there is the case of verbal labeling and mediation in which the person is conscious of his or her motivation. The boy who is cutting a lawn for pay and decides he has had enough of the hot sun sustains his drive level by reminding himself, "I'm getting ten dollars to do this job." Second, a nonverbal mediation may occur, such as in the pleasant visual fantasy the boy may have, seeing himself buying a desired motorcycle in the future without actually putting this intention into words. Finally, the drive and its goal response may be completely unlabeled and unmediated, so that a direct instrumental response is made with a following reinforcement occurring entirely outside of consciousness. The boy may be cutting the grass for reasons other than money; for example, a pretty daughter of the homeowner who employed him may be providing as yet unconscious (unlabeled and unimagined) motives of a totally different nature.

How is it possible for reinforcements to influence behavior at the unconscious level? To account for this influence, Dollard and Miller relied on the constructs of stimulus and/or response *generalization,* including *secondary* or *learned* generalization. For example, if the child is taught the word *sharp* in relation to kitchen utensils that can cut and injure a person (knives, slicers), he or she can later be taught to avoid other sharp objects as well (broken glass, sheared metal), thanks to the mediation of this language sign (label). But there is a *primary* or *innate* form of generalization as well. If a pattern of cues is learned as a stimulus to certain responses, closely related patterns of cues will spontaneously elicit the responses as if the original stimulus were calling forth the action. If on a mushroom hunt we strike a bonanza of mushrooms in a certain type of terrain, it is natural for our hunting responses to occur in a similar locale the next time we go out. In fact, the more a terrain matches our original "good-luck area"—even if we have not named it such (no verbal cue-producing responses are involved at all)—the more likely it will be that our hunting will begin again. The mushroom-hunting response will be *least* likely to occur in countryside that is highly *unlike* our bonanza area. This demonstrates the *gradient of generalization,* or the fact that the less similar a stimulus situation is to the original stimulus situation, the less probable it is that a transfer of response will take place. This is not to be confused with the response-hierarchy construct, in which we are speaking about different types of responses to the identical stimulus. The gradient of reinforcement refers to *changing stimuli* with the response held constant.

Of course, it is also possible to see responses generalize automatically, so that the organism makes more responses to a stimulus than are necessary. In learning to write (response), some children also learn to stick their tongue out of the side of their mouth (response) when they face the writing task (stimulus), as a kind of tension-sustaining mechanism. Later in life, remnants of this tongue response can generalize to all writing activities, so that some people even as adults make odd facial expressions (grimaces, lip-biting, and so on) when they write. There need be no significance attached to these mannerisms. They may merely be the result of response generalizations (from moving hand, to moving body, to moving tongue, and so on).

The relative permanence of a response that has been elicited by a stimulus situation is a function of the reinforcement that follows. If Bruce, a college freshman attending his first mixer, asks *every* available young woman for a dance, he may find that not all of his potential partners (cue stimuli) will agree to his request (response). In time he may learn that *certain* girls, with certain mannerisms as he approaches them, signal reasonably clearly that his chances for success are good (that is, reinforcement will follow). Unless Bruce has a very strong ego and does not mind being rejected, before long he will learn to *discriminate* between girls who are likely to dance with him and those who are not. Much of what goes on in the name of *rehearsal* or *practice* is this interlocking process of response generalization (any girl-stimulus elicits dance request) and discrimination (only certain girl-stimulus elicits dance request). Behavior is thus shaped to greater efficiency over time.[97]

If a habit continues without at least occasional reinforcement, it will gradually disappear or *extinguish* (also called *response extinction*). With 100 percent failure Bruce will be seen to give up (though he may not have mediated this consciously via a cue-producing label) and spend his time talking with male cronies at the mixer. Bruce might even stop attending dances altogether, particularly if this lack of popularity reflects itself in his dating behavior generally. It is not that he has forgotten how to dance or how to ask young women out. *Forgetting* is to lose a behavior as a result of spending a long interval of time during which the response is not practiced, such as when we do not recite a poem for months. But "extinction occurs when a response is practiced without reinforcement." [98] The rapidity of extinction depends on the level of drive stimulation experienced (how badly Bruce feels the drive for feminine company) and the number of times the habit has been reinforced during original learning (how many acceptances Bruce got when he first set out to ask girls to dance). Interestingly, even after a response has been extinguished, it can recur from out of the blue. One night, after several months of nonattendance at the mixers, Bruce shows up and tries again. Even he is surprised that he had this impulse to return at the last minute. This reappearance of an extinguished response after an interval of time is called *spontaneous recovery*.[99] The fact that it takes place demonstrates that extinction does not destroy a habit but merely *inhibits* it.

Unlike forgetting, where there seems to be a loss of the cue-to-response connection, in extinction the inhibited response seems to be replaced by an incompatible response in the hierarchy of response. When a mixer (stimulus situation) is announced, Bruce makes other plans (response). But the connection to the older habit (attending mixers) remains and can be activated after a period of time quite spontaneously. If a response is to be kept from reappearing, the incompatible response must be very effective—that is, reinforcing. In *not* going to dances Bruce must find greater pleasure than he did when he was attending. Since solitary hobbies are rarely that rewarding, it is easy to see how the older responses might spontaneously recur. For this reason extinction is ordinarily not the best way to remove a response from the most probable levels of the response hierarchy. More effective results, if more unpleasant, can be achieved through the use of *punishment*. If Bruce had not been simply politely declined when he asked girls to dance or accompany him on dates but was in addition ridiculed in some fashion, then his sudden reappearance at the Friday night mixer would be much less likely.

Even though reinforcement makes a response more likely to recur and punishment usually makes it less likely to recur, the two mechanisms are really not so different. It is the *end* of punishment that strengthens the avoidance response associated with it.[100] When a child is spanked for an improper act, the reason he or she continues to avoid that act is because anxiety mounts with each (verbal or nonverbal) cue-produced thought of it. The child knows that if the undesirable behavior continues, it will be followed by painful stimulations—which causes anxiety—but also that if proper behavior continues, everything will be all right—a thought that quickly removes this anxiety. Hence, punishment can be seen to be influential for long periods of time through a drive-reducing reinforcement (reduction of anxiety or fear).

It was O. H. Mowrer, one of Hull's more

brilliant students, who in 1939 worked out this theoretical description that suggested that certain drives—like fear—can both be stimuli to behavior (motivators) and also act as reinforcers of behavior once their level has been reduced. Fear was the most important drive construct employed by Dollard and Miller, probably because it adapts so well to the explanation of abnormal behavior. There is no real difference between their views of fear and anxiety. "When the source of fear is vague or obscured by repression, it is often called *anxiety*." [101] As a learnable drive, fear (anxiety) can be attached to previously neutral cues—including language labels. The ultimate source of fear is innately determined by the physiology and neurology of the body; but in human learning it is extremely difficult to separate the innate from the learned aspects of fear.[102] Fear is also highly resistant to extinction, and it easily becomes a drive forcing the organism into trial-and-error behavior.[103] As we may recall, straightforward trial-and-error learning is often unmediated or instrumental in nature. This is not a very effective form of learning and hence fear-motivated learning is not desirable. When under a fear drive, an animal is likely to do almost anything, just as long as this annoying reaction goes away—that is, is reduced to manageable levels. The resultant reinforcement then perpetuates whatever was done to reduce the fear drive, and as we shall see below, this is sometimes a maladaptive sequence of behavior.

A term often confused with drive is *need*. When we say there is a need in the organism, we usually imply that a drive needs reduction. However, not all organismic deficits are necessarily drive producing. Take the case of carbon monoxide poisoning, for example. Although we need to escape the inhaling of carbon monoxide, there is no innate drive to do so, and an individual can be accidentally killed if he or she inhales the gas.[104] The same goes for eating a well-rounded diet. Though we all need adequate vitamins and minerals, many people suffer from various deficiencies even though they eat large amounts of food. Dollard and Miller used many drive constructs to explain behavior, of course; fear is simply a major concept. Since drives are learnable, virtually anything that can be taught can take on drive value. Such learnable drives provided Dollard and Miller with their major tools for the explanation of sociocultural behaviors. They spoke of learned drives to connect (make meaningful ties in experience), to be logical, reasonable, and sensible, and to *not* fear things that are harmless.[105] But the major learned-drive construct in their outlook—the drive to imitate others—stemmed from their early theoretical collaboration.

The Role of Imitation in Human Learning

A major reason for people in a given sociocultural group behaving alike is *imitation*, which Miller and Dollard defined as follows:

Imitation is a process by which "matched," or similar, acts are evoked in two people and connected to appropriate cues. It can occur only under conditions which are favorable to learning these acts. If matching, or doing the same as others do, is regularly rewarded, a secondary tendency to match may be developed, and the process of imitation becomes the derived [learned] drive of imitativeness.[106]

The little girl who is given love and attention in the home when she matches her behavior to that of her parents—by coming to the dinner table on time, eating with the proper utensils, and so on—will acquire a drive to imitate others outside the home as well. This is what is meant by the *socialization process* which brings large numbers of people into a common behavioral style.

There are two major types of imitation to be seen in human behavior. One is simple *copying,* in which case individual A consciously tries to bring his or her behavior into line with a model, individual B. In this case, individual A has to have a certain amount of insight to know when personal responses are consistent with those of the model. Children consciously rehearse their language sounds (phonemes) with insight and thereby copy the verbal expressions of adults by design.[107] However, there is a type of imitation in which the model responds to environmental stimuli with insight but the imitator does not. This is called *matched-dependent* imitation, because the imitator is dependent on the model to carry out the correct instrumental response if reinforcement is to follow. Leaders emerge as leaders in life because they have insight into the behavioral sequences that bring rewards. And their followers often blindly imitate them in this behavior, behaving in a matched-dependent fashion because this is how they are most likely to be reinforced in life.

Children conform to the patterns of their parents, even before they understand why it is important to do so (matched-dependent). They accept parental religious views and come to have an outlook on life consistent with the social class in which they are reared. In time, a change in outlook can take place. The child in school may adopt the behavioral patterns of a different social class, and the direction this takes defines aspiration in terms of upward or downward *social mobility.* Ordinarily, there is a strong learned drive to strive upward in the social structure.[108] The ambitious daughter of a working-class

family wants to get ahead, to advance herself through education and become a professional person because, as she ascends the social hierarchy, the reinforcements of life are constantly more assured. Hence, we often find a form of in-group identity at certain social levels, which is expressed as being with one's own kind or not marrying beneath one's station. This furthers commonality in attitude and behavioral pattern. Social levels and, indeed, national identities seem to be the result of this tendency for people to imitate the best among their number—which means the most rewarded and successful models available.[109]

There is a form of behavioral similarity among people that is *not* imitation. Dollard and Miller referred to this as *same behavior,* by which they meant that two or more people can be stimulated by the same cue to behave in common *at the same time.* At a sporting contest, for example, people can be seen to behave much the same as everyone else, cheering on their favorites and waving their hands or shouting as the play unfolds. Although imitation may enter in here, much of the similarity would be noted even if these people were at home, watching the sporting event over their televisions. It is therefore possible to view certain behavioral regularities like these as merely same behavior, learned by everyone in the past without imitative aids.[110]

An interesting secondary motivation that springs from certain types of imitation is that of *competition* or *rivalry.* If person A not only imitates person B but tries to go one step better in what is being copied, person B may return this challenge with an escalation in kind. The young brother not only imitates his older sibling's dare-devilry by climbing the apple tree, but is seen shinning up most of the schoolyard flagpole as well. The next day finds his brother leaping from a garage roof top, and so on, as each boy now seeks to outdo the other. This competition can achieve drive status in these brothers, which can then generalize to lifelong competitive endeavors outside the family as well.[111] Human beings are probably the most competitive of animals because of their language ability, which permits them to make intricate anticipatory-goal responses as plans or aspirations. A *goal* is essentially a cue-producing response, a form of improvement in reinforcement mediated and hence generalized into the future.[112] We say to ourselves, "If I do this, then I can get that." Since there is a probability factor to consider, we sometimes call these anticipatory-goal responses our hopes, but the main point is that in making our future projections, we are trying to ensure that reinforcement will take place.[113] Without this eventual reinforcement we would not make plans or express hopes.

Finally, an important behavioral response in successful human relations known as *empathy* or *sympathy* is based on a special type of imitation. According to Dollard and Miller, we express empathy or sympathy with others when we copy their ongoing emotions or mood.[114] If Patty is depressed and Loretta is able to capture this mood and reflect it back properly, then Loretta would be expressing sympathy or empathy in the relationship. Here again, because we human beings can put ourselves in the place of others and feel with them, we engender a strong social bond between us—which makes us all the more likely to identify as one. We have little or no sympathy for the enemy, who is construed as being outside of our in-group identity.

Frustration and Conflict in Human Behavior

Life rarely goes along smoothly. Sometimes there is a high state of drive in the organism but the response called forth by this (innate or learned) drive is blocked. When this happens we speak of *frustration*.[115] The tired and hungry woman, arriving in town too late to find a restaurant open while on a business trip, encounters one of life's frustrations. The poorly educated, working-class man who is thrown into unemployment with each dip in the economic cycle suffers a lifelong round of frustrations as he loses economic power and can never see himself getting ahead. Frustrations can mount, one on another, so that the losers in life often are pressed into a drastic frame of mind by their string of bad luck. One of the predictable outcomes of a frustration, easily noted in researches on lower animals as well, is that frustration stimulates innate anger responses in living organisms. Block a child's approach to attractive toys and he or she will kick your legs trying to get around your obstructive body. Nature has seemingly provided an assertive response, high in the innate hierarchy, to attack and hence remove the *barriers* to goal attainment.

Sometimes this barrier arises from the fact that incompatible responses are being triggered at the same time in a given situation. This is called a *conflict*. In 1931, the (quasi-) gestalt psychologist Kurt Lewin (see Chapter 9, p. 571) described three types of conflict in which people are likely to find themselves.[116] Though he did not use stimulus-response terminology to make his case, Hull (1938) and Miller (1937) later translated these three types of conflict into learning-theory terminology. Considerable experimental work was then conducted by the Hullians, much of it by Miller (1944), to provide evidence in support of their terminology. Today, rather than a gestalt theory, the conflict theory is one of the bulwarks of S-R theory.

We have already noted that goals are often cue-producing responses that mediate a person's aspirations for upcoming reinforcements. If we drop this limited definition and simply consider any given stimulus or pattern of stimuli in the behavioral environment as possessing either a positive (reinforcing) or negative (punishing, fearful) quality, then we can consider these stimuli as goals. To sight a water fountain when thirsty is to see a goal with positive incentive properties. To avoid the drafty corner of a room is to withdraw from a goal having negative incentive properties.

Recall that the level of motivation exerted by an organism in relation to a goal is known as the *gradient of reinforcement* (see p. 396). The closer an animal is to a point (place) of reinforcement, or, as we can now call it, a *goal,* the greater is the level of motivation concerning this reinforcement. Miller was to prove in his laboratory research that— all other things being equal—rats would exert more effort to *get away* from a negative goal (negative reinforcement) when they were close to it than to *get toward* a positive goal that was nearby (positive reinforcement). Such findings can be extended to human behavior as well. Thus, granting that we have a high level of fright when walking by a graveyard at midnight and also a high level of delight when entering our favorite ice cream parlor, we are relatively *more* motivated to get away from the graveyard than we are to enter the ice cream parlor. Both of these goals are nearby. However, as Miller was to learn by having rats pull various weights toward positive and away from negative goals, the motivation to avoid a nearby disliked goal drops off fairly rapidly

as distance is put between this source of negative reinforcement and the behaving organism. The motivation to achieve the desired goal, on the other hand, drops off less abruptly with distance. In other words, were we to have left *both* graveyard and the ice cream parlor vicinity (without anything taking place in either locale), within a block or two our motivation to return to the ice cream parlor (positive reinforcement) would be greater than our motivation to continue running away from the graveyard.

The first of the three major conflicts analyzed by Dollard and Miller emphasized the contrasting influence of approach-and-avoidance gradients in relation to the *same* goal. This is called the *approach-avoidance conflict* (also called *ambivalence*), in which the same goal has both positive and negative incentives.[117] A good example is the necessity of our having to see the dentist for a toothache. In this case, we would be caught in the conflict of *approaching* the goal (dentist's office) out of a desire to end our pain, yet also suffering an *avoidance* motivation to flee the goal due to the undoubted pain and anxiety of the treatment procedure. Since the avoidance motivation is relatively lower than the approach motivation when we are far away from the dentist's office, it is not difficult to make the telephone call to arrange for an emergency appointment, to get into our automobile, and to begin our drive to the dentist's office. However, as we get closer and closer to the office, our avoidance motivation rises ever more rapidly, eventually surpassing our motivation to approach. By the time we park our automobile and begin climbing the stairs to the dentist's office, we are much more motivated to flee than we are to be treated.

What we actually do depends on several factors. One of the most important of these is how painful our toothache is (drive to avoid pain). Another motivation that can fuse with this one is the concern we have generally built up as a secondary drive to keep our physical appearance attractive and hence to avoid losing teeth through neglect. Such drive factors can summate and decide the outcome in favor of our seeking dental aid if they become strong enough. It is obvious that proper labels, acting as cue-producing responses, would be important here. One must be able to plan, to project desired goals, and to sustain an immediate pain for a longer-term, delayed reinforcement. Better a little pain today than toothlessness tomorrow! Sometimes there is considerable vacillation at some *choice point* or point of decision. We might be seen walking to and fro outside of the dentist's office on the sidewalk below, making up our mind. Strictly speaking, of course, according to this behavioristic theory, the human being does not determine his or her own fate. We can only do what the stimulus conditions make it possible for us to do, so what happens is up to the drive combinations already mentioned.

The second major conflict is the *avoidance-avoidance conflict.*[118] In this case, we face alternatives that are both negative, so that our motivation is like being "caught twixt the devil and the deep blue sea." The young man who has just been drafted and must now decide between the infantry or the field artillery and considers either alternative a horror of empty living faces the avoidance-avoidance conflict. There is an understandable tendency for people in avoidance-avoidance conflicts to run away. Mothers and fathers who desert their families, financially pressed businesspeople who drop from sight, or even the abnormal person who chooses to live in fantasy rather than reality are all demonstrating the same basic tendency to remove themselves from what they consider an intolerable and unsolvable set of life problems. Everything is negative. There is no way out.

The third major form of conflict is the *approach-approach conflict.*[119] In this instance, a person must select either of two goals, each of which has positive incentive value. Since there is no offsetting avoidance motivation in the picture, once a move is made off the choice point in the direction of either goal, the conflict is resolved. If we are standing on a street corner trying to decide which of two movies we should see that evening, and it really makes no difference to us since both are worth seeing and we will probably go to the one we do not see tonight another time, this would be an example of the approach-approach conflict. It is obviously a minor kind of frustration. Any whim or related motivation that would move us closer to one or the other of the movies would undoubtedly decide the issue. For example, suppose that we looked up the street and saw a candy shop a half-block from our street corner. If we now stroll the few steps to get our favorite chocolate, this slight distance advantage for one movie over the other would probably determine our choice for that evening, because our motivation would now be slightly higher for this movie than for that one.

We might question whether the approach-approach conflict is a frustration at all. We often settle such matters in life by simply tossing a coin! What is more true to life is the fact that decisions of this sort are usually like *double approach-avoidance conflicts,* in that each of the two goals has some positive *and* some negative incentive value. Rather than the single goal of a dentist's office, we now think in terms of each of our movie theaters having both an approach- and an avoidance-gradient feature. The negative incentive at this point is at least something like "well, if we see this movie we won't see that one."

Freudian Adjustment Mechanisms as Learning-Theory Terms

We now turn to a number of Freudian adjustment mechanisms to see how Dollard and Miller redefined them in terms of learning theory. The mechanisms of *fixation* and *regression* will be discussed in the time-perspective constructs section which follows.

Repression, Suppression, and Inhibition. Each of these terms relates to some form of nonresponding. In learning-theory terms, *inhibition* refers to the blocking of a response when its normal stimulation occurs. This could refer to either instrumental responding or cue-produced (mediated) responding. Dollard and Miller made a distinction between *overt inhibition* and what we might call the *inhibition of mediators,* defining the former as follows: "Overt inhibition will be used by us to refer to the prevention of instrumental responses by strong conflicting responses that are not under verbal control. Thus a patient is sexually inhibited when he is unable to perform normal sexual responses." [120] *Overt inhibitions* stop observable actions, whereas the mediational form of inhibition is limited to the realm of covert thoughts—that is, labels and other forms of cue-producing responses. The patient need not have thought about why he is unable to perform sexually; he is simply impotent and thus overtly inhibited (possibly even because of some physical cause).

When a person does need to think about something but lacks cue-producing responses (labels, mediational signs, language words, sentences), we have inhibition of mediators or *repression,* which Dollard and Miller defined as "the automatic tendency to stop thinking and avoid remembering." [121] There are three forms of such repression in behavior.[122] The first involves inhibition of the response labeling a drive. Agnes is frustrated and angry, but she has not labeled her emotional state correctly, so she claims to be "feeling strange" which could mean anything. A second form of repression occurs when the person inhibits the cue-produced responses that can help stimulate a drive. Agnes might have been taught as a child that it was wrong for a woman to display her anger. Hence, each time Agnes has felt anger coming on, she has stopped thought, which in turn has helped to keep this mood from continuing to well up in her behavior. But this can only work for a time and now she is paying the price of repression (inhibition of mediators).

Thus far we have been considering emotions that are generated by a life situation and *then* inhibited. The third type of repression considers the equally likely possibility that human beings can create a situation by labeling it in such a way as to bring on an entirely new emotion. For example, Ed and Bob are arguing but also controlling their more hostile impulses to fight. Ed seems to be especially insulting of Bob, who has to this point repressed—failed to label—Ed's apparent hostility. But now, should Bob think to himself, "Ed is trying to make a fool of me," there would be an entirely new situation emerging, one that could well end in fisticuffs. Bob has moved on from a mood of anger and competition to one of feeling insulted and desiring revenge. His relabeling of the argument has brought out these latter, more hostile tendencies in his behavior.

This teaches us something about repression: it need not always be a bad thing, and, in theory, it should occasionally work to the betterment of personal adjustment. Dollard and Miller took a more positive view of such inhibitory tactics in the handling of human affairs than had the classic psychoanalysts. Societies have always taught their members to avoid painful topics, to be civil, or to present themselves as socially mature and not impulsive in their relations with others.[123] When this process of stopping thought and avoiding remembering is done by conscious design, we can speak of *suppression*. Suppression is a normal human response, employed effectively by religious institutions and helpful to self-control for all humans as long as it is not used to deny reality.[124] Repression is, therefore, merely the automatic, unconscious counterpart of suppression.

Identification. This adjustment mechanism is an aspect of imitation, whether of the copying or the matched-dependent variety.[125] As children and later as adults, we tend to take on certain customary patterns of behavior through imitating our parents, friends, and other members of our society.

Projection. The attribution of personal motives to others is like its reverse, taking in such motives through identification.[126] Dollard and Miller noted that we all learn to expect fellow members of our society to react in roughly the same way that we do to different experiences (same behavior). This makes empathy and sympathy possible, and we help guide our interpersonal relations through such knowledge.

Reaction-Formation. The capacity to respond with opposites is probably the outgrowth of language learning. Dollard and Miller noted that many studies on word associations have found antonyms to be a frequent type of response to word stimuli (for example, left-right, up-down, in-out).[127] Both responses might therefore be high in

the person's habit hierarchy at the same time. And if for some reason the person knows that one response will lead to negative reinforcement in a given instance, its opposite response can be quickly substituted. Laurie asks Tammy, "Do you like my new hair style?" and Tammy automatically inhibits the "no" response which would be her honest reaction and substitutes, "Yes, very much." To react-formate is therefore to deal with motivations by moving to their opposite expression in the face of threat.

Rationalization. We are taught to have logical explanations for anything we do. The drive to be logical makes us feel uneasy when involved in a behavior that we cannot explain or that seems irregular by common standards. Hence, there is strong motivation to justify what we do, to find good reasons for our behavior, even though the actual motivation may be unconscious (unlabeled). This is rationalization.[128] The young man who feels driven to smoke a cigarette and frequently dashes off to buy a pack at the local tobacco store, overlooking the pack lying in clear view on his dresser top, may rationalize by saying he needs cigarettes. But we, knowing that an attractive young woman works in the nearby store, could suggest alternative motives for the frequent emergency trips.

Displacement. The displacing of emotions like love or hostility to sources other than the original stimulus pattern is explained in terms of generalization. For example, a woman who feels great hostility for her mother, though unable to recognize this source of her feeling because she has not labeled it properly, may express hostility toward all older women.[129]

Time-Perspective Constructs

Although Dollard and Miller did not present their developmental theory according to Freud's psychosexual stages (Chapter 1), we can see an influence stemming from psychoanalysis in their discussion of development. They speak of the four critical training situations in development as feeding, cleanliness, sex, and anger.[130] We shall take up their comments on these four situations and then turn to their views on fixation and regression.

The Feeding Situation

The newborn infant is completely dominated by desires for immediate (instrumental, pleasurable) reinforcement. Hunger, thirst, pain, and fatigue are the (primary) drives of importance, and the child's helplessness in the face of these stimuli makes early life a difficult experience. "Infancy, indeed, may be viewed as a period of transitory psychosis. Savage drives within the infant impel to action. . . . The higher mental processes (the Ego) cannot do their benign work of comforting, directing effort, and binding the world into a planful sequence." [131] As infants we are frustrated easily and, hence, the likelihood of conflict formation is great. Dollard and Miller favored highly permissive treatment of young children, until such time as they have the mental equipment (language terms) to deal with problem solutions.[132]

High in the innate hierarchy of response is the instinctive pattern to root for the mother's nipple, to suck, and to take in nourishment. This is the basis for a child's first social contact, and the feeding situation is the premiere learning situation in life. When reinforcement is not forthcoming, the child's innate response is to cry. If babies are left to cry themselves out, they may learn that there is nothing they can do about circumstances, hence the experience may foster a developing tendency to passivity and a distaste for trying something new in later development.[133] The mother or mother-surrogate is extremely important in establishing a child's basic outlook on life. She is the first representative of society.[134] A child who is generally ignored and given minimal care can grow into an adult who is compulsively driven to seek social contact; the person cannot stand being alone because of the anxiety that solitude generates.[135]

Since infants lack verbal cue-producing responses in the first year, they cannot label their conflicts, which then become unconscious influences in their later behavior.[136] Language learning probably stems from the matched-dependent imitative behavior of children.[137] Infants rehearse sounds, both their own crying patterns and the vocal patterns of their parents. How readily children learn to speak depends on the reinforcements received in this activity. Here is where a close relationship with the mother is vital. A mother who lovingly responds to the child's primary drives gains the child's attention and then can gradually bring his or her interest to bear on items in the environment through naming them and reacting positively when speech efforts are made.

Cleanliness Training

The toilet-training situation is potentially even more threatening to the child than the feeding situation. If there are any hidden feelings of rejection for the child in a parent's attitudes, they are sure to come out at this time. Parents become as frustrated as the child in this difficult training period, and frustration generates aggression. But often even a loving and accepting parent can forget that the child is learning a complex behavioral task without complete verbal skills to help in problem solution.[138] Dollard and Miller felt that it is pointless to begin toilet-training until a child can verbally make his or her needs known in this area. Since this is the first time the child may be feeling the weight of social pressure to conform, we want to generate positive emotions toward the weight of authority.

A well-managed relationship between child and parent begins in the feeding situation and then is carried over naturally to the toilet situation. Aided by maturing language skills—hence, increased understanding—a child can learn that social cooperation can be rewarding even though it is not always easy. If the child is punished for mistakes in toilet training, he or she can attach anxiety cues to the very presence of the parents and can thus become devious and secretive, trying at every opportunity to escape from the parent's sight.[139] The implications here for later character formation are obvious. It is also possible for the child to become too meticulous about personal hygiene and thereby generalize this pattern rigidly to all of life's concerns. This is what Freud presumably meant in his reference to a " 'Superego' or unconscious conscience." [140] Such individuals may grow into highly conforming, guilt-ridden adults.

Early Sex Training

Dollard and Miller pointed out that sex is far from our most important drive stimulus. As primary drives, pain, hunger, and fatigue outrank sex; and even secondary drives like anxiety, ambition, and pride can prove stronger motivations than sex in human behavior. Why then has sex been given such prominence in personality theories like Freud's? Dollard and Miller answered:

Sex seems to be so frequently implicated because it is the most severely attacked and inhibited of primary drives. Even though

relatively weaker, sex can exert a strong pressure which produces great activation in the organism and great misery if blocked for long periods. In no other case is the individual required to wait so many years while patiently bearing the goading drive.[141]

The taboos of religion and other sociocultural institutions, such as marriage and the family pattern, all combine to pressure the individual to bear up under a heightened sexual drive. Hence a relatively unimportant drive in the scheme of things—so far as the economy of the body is concerned—becomes a major source of human motivation.

So-called infantile sexuality would be for Dollard and Miller simply a natural outcome of the reinforcement achieved when, for example, an infant boy discovers that fondling his penis brings a pleasurable sensation. There need be no more significance attached to this act than the fact that this child tugs at his ear and, here too sensing a tickle or pulling feeling, continues to play with his ear for a longer period. If the parent sees the child fondling his penis and interprets this as sinful or dirty and punishes the child accordingly, anxiety can be attached to the genital sphere. In later years, when a prompting to masturbate may arise around pubescence, the conflict of sex versus anxiety can present a serious adjustment problem.[142] Such concerns may be carried on into adulthood and can adversely affect the individual's marital adjustment as well. The masturbatory taboo is the first of the important sex taboos our particular culture exerts on our behavior.

Another early taboo each of us experiences stems from the sanctions Dollard and Miller called *sex typing* of personality.[143] Historically, the *sex roles* have been apportioned so that men are expected to act in one way and women in another. The growing child soon learns what "boys do" and what "girls do" in the way of games, social activities, and interests. Clothes differ, and all of the training received aims ultimately to prepare the child of a given sex for the "proper" role he or she will someday fill as a man and husband or woman and wife. Mothers who baby and overprotect their male child may rear a timid, fearful, essentially effeminate young man. Rather than emphasizing the boy's masculine character, such a mother may keep his sexual identity uncertain. If a boy's sex typing is unclear, it is all the more probable that he will learn to relate his sexual impulses to a person of his own sex. It is in this way that sexual "deviation" (homosexuality) may be considered a product of learning.[144]

After sex has been typed and the proper taboos against masturbation and homosexuality have been learned, the child is vaguely led to expect that sexual reward is to be forthcoming from the opposite sex. If a male child has been severely punished for earlier masturbatory activity, each sexual prompting toward the mother or a sister will generalize his anxiety, and hence we can observe what Freud called *castration anxiety* and the *Oedipus complex*.[145] This matter is often complicated by the fact that the father may be jealous of the child who now seeks close contact with the mother, possibly even wanting to sleep with her.

Dollard and Miller's view of the *Oedipus complex* emphasized the contribution parents make to this interpersonal conflict. The father becomes jealous of his son's masturbatory attraction to the mother and makes a hostile projection onto the offspring, which is picked up by the child who can actually interpret it in terms of castration anxiety.[146] Occasionally, the tales of school friends about

parents emasculating their children reinforce the child's anxiety. The female Oedipal has similar roots: closeness to the father and a resulting jealous reaction by the mother. Dollard and Miller accepted the view that some little girls feel they have been castrated in life, probably by their mothers. The Oedipal conflict is eventually resolved as follows:

Anxiety which was once attached only to the masturbation impulse is now attached to the heterosexual approach situation [for example, toward mother in the boy]. If the anxiety is made very strong it can produce a certain relief in the intensity of the conflict. This is the so-called "resolution" of the Oedipal complex. When anxiety is greatly dominant over approach tendencies, the conflicted individual stays far from his goal and but few of the acquired elements in the sexual appetite are aroused.[147]

Since Dollard and Miller did not feel that everyone passes through the Oedipal complex in coming to maturity, their theory was not nearly so reliant on this construct as was Freud's.

Training in Anger Control

The final critical training situation relates to how a growing child manages the *anger* or *hostility* (these terms are used synonymously) that occur as responses to life's many frustrations. As infants, we have very low *frustration tolerance,* so that we easily scream, kick our feet, and flail our arms when under frustration of a drive state. The socialization process through which we all pass is concerned with teaching us how to manage these unproductive emotional outbursts. As already noted, the toilet-training situation stimulates anger responses, and we might even say that cleanliness training parallels the learning of anger controls. Dollard and Miller recall that the punishing of rebellious children is one of the oldest patriarchal codes in our culture, once incorporated into the early Connecticut blue laws to the extent that a father could even kill his disobedient son.[148]

It is important to know what stimulates anger in a child. If we know what the source is, we can probably do something about changing the stimulating conditions. Unfortunately, too many parents will punish their child without knowing exactly why anger is taking place. Dollard and Miller reminded us that anger is a healthy response in many instances, one that helps us mount aggressive behavior against some barrier to our drive reduction. Becoming a little irritated actually helps us jerk open a balky door leading to a goal we are seeking. There is also the righteous form of anger, which cultivates a sense of sympathy for minority members of our society who may be discriminated against in housing, employment, or education. If the parent overlooks this more positive role for anger and blindly represses all angry displays by the child, this can result in what Dollard and Miller called an *anger-anxiety conflict*.[149] The child may mature with inadequate social skills, since each time he or she feels anger there is also an inhibiting feeling of anxiety arising. Such individuals may fail to stick up for their rights and end up being bullied by others.

On the other side of the coin, a child who matures believing that it is all right to give free vent to anger in public and expects special consideration from others via temper tantrums would not be learning proper social skills either. We usually find that such individuals have a lifelong pattern of uncontrolled aggression, beginning as so-called spoiled brats and continuing on to become highly selfish and inconsiderate adults. There are many reasons why a child first feels anger in the family setting. Some children (rightly or wrongly!) sense parental indifference or rejection; anger is a way of demanding some kind of attention or consideration. Another common source is *sibling rivalry*,[150] with all of the related signs of jealousy and hatred for a brother or sister. Parents must be sensitive to these underlying causes of frustration and take measures whenever possible to stop them at their source rather than simply trying to suppress them through punishment after they arise.

Frustration will continue throughout life for all of us. Dollard and Miller noted that the most common source of frustration in maturing probably is the growing recognition that our life dreams (goals) will never be realized in quite the way we pictured them. The little boy grows up to learn that he lacks the ability to become a top professional athlete. The little girl matures into a pretty woman, but hardly the talented movie star she had dreamed of becoming. Middle-aged men and women come to see that they will never get the promotion or receive the invitation to join a country club that would indicate they had achieved the success they desperately want in life. Sometimes we cannot state the reasons for our lack of upward mobility; we blame it on luck or not knowing the right people, and this makes it all the more frustrating. Entire groups feel the grip of social prejudice and discrimination, which keep them "in their place" and forever outside the reward structure of the society.

Age Grading, Fixation, and Regression

A growing child's level of social maturity is gauged by certain common achievements, such as the first step, the attainment of bladder control, the use of language, and so on.

Cultures tend to *age grade* behavior,[151] and the practice continues into adulthood, so that "the first date" and "the first steady job" become important milestones in anyone's life. Dollard and Miller suggested that the drive to get ahead in life may be a generalization from the even earlier drive to grow up. Since behaviors can be rank-ordered from childhood to adolescence to maturity, Freudian conceptions of *fixation* can be thought of as the retention of a certain habit beyond the age-level when it should have been discontinued. A strongly reinforced habit, for example, which has never really been put far down in the hierarchy of response, can return at an inopportune moment and make the individual appear to have *regressed* in behavior to an earlier point in time (fixation). In order to make this process clearer, we would do well to review the usual course of learning in terms of the response hierarchy.

Recall that children come into the world with an *innate hierarchy of response* (see p. 391). We now know that this hierarchy is arranged and rearranged many times according to the history of reinforcement, extinction, and punishment in the individual's course of life. The innate hierarchy is thus eclipsed and altered, thanks to the new learning that goes on in development. We must think of the response hierarchy as something occurring and changing *over time*.

At any point, the individual's response repertoire is arrayed in what we may now call his or her *initial hierarchy of response*.[152] The first initial hierarchy was the innate hierarchy, and Dollard and Miller used the term *initial* to emphasize the constantly changing ordering of the response hierarchy. What changes this ordering is the organism encountering a *learning dilemma*.[153] Learning dilemmas arise when the most probable response of the hierarchy *fails* to result in reinforcement. The politician who finds his or her listeners uninterested in what has been a sure-fire issue—that is, has had the highest probability of occurrence in the politician's campaign-response hierarchy—will switch to some other issue that might perk up the interest of potential voters. If the switch works, we witness the birth of a new sure-fire issue as these responses move to the top of an ever-changing hierarchy. The new rank-ordering of probabilities in the hierarchy is called the *resultant hierarchy of response*.[154] The terms *initial* and *resultant* thus merely indicate which side of a changing hierarchy of response we are considering over the passage of time.

The point of *age grading* is that as we become mature, certain responses are less likely to be elicited by certain stimuli. Bladder control is a basic example. Because of years of effort we learn to inhibit urinating while wearing clothing, yet some situations may permit an adult to be forgiven if self-soiling occurs. Uncontrolled giggling in church is not ordinarily acceptable behavior, but it is far more understandable if the offenders are a pair of ten-year-olds rather than thirty-five-year-olds. The potential always exists for anyone to break up over some ridiculous issue and go into silly laughter. But when this occurs, we are likely to label it childishness and—in Freudian terms—*regression*. To regress is to return to an earlier habit, usually in response to the frustration of a current habit.[155] The earlier habit may be fixated, which means that it has been given enough reinforcement in the past to make it more likely to appear than some other, more appropriately age-graded response. Some people have been rewarded for being dependent on others when tensions arise and for showing respect for their benefactors who are naturally flattered. Thus, even as adults, these people will exhibit childlike patterns in personal relations when the slightest frustration arises. We meet such people on street corners in strange cities, unable to find the streets on which they stand despite the signposts above their heads. They seek assistance from others and are always very grateful for any help they receive.

Immature behavior can also be triggered impulsively as a direct instrumental response to a stimulus. Recall that infant behavior is of this sort; it goes directly from stimulation to response without any cue-producing responses mediating. The same can happen to an adult who faces extreme frustration and resorts to a flow of behavior that is by all standards childishly impulsive. These are the times when we throw things or say to loved ones things we do not mean. Sometimes we are even aware of our idiocy and wonder why we let ourselves fly off the handle this way. At other times we lose ourselves completely in these regressive behavioral setbacks. Hence, according to Dollard and Miller, regression takes place in two ways: (1) we return to earlier habits, and (2) these habits are age graded *much* below the point at which we ought to be functioning. When people become hysterical or act like animals when panicked, we are witnessing the most severe of all regressions—to directly triggered instrumental behavior of the most base variety.

Individual-Differences Constructs

There is really no place for trait or type constructs in S-R theory. All such behavioral regularities are habits. It was Dollard and Miller's view that Freud had settled too easily for a nonscientific explanation when he spoke of the defenses people supposedly throw up to fend off unconscious wishes.[156] What is unconscious is essentially out of mind, an instrumental line of responding that has no cue-producing responses intervening to dodge and select parapraxes for

expression the way Freud said they did. There is no room for such telic description in science. The behavior we see is behavior under determination by drive stimuli, discriminative stimuli, response elicitation, and the reinforcements that follow in this sequence. Freud, Adler, and Jung offered their own nonscientific explanations for the sequence, but learning theory was the only complete explanation. That is, we could just as easily subsume Adlerian or Jungian theory by S-R theory as we have subsumed Freudian theory.

Dollard and Miller did, of course, make certain general statements about behavior. We have already reviewed the sources of behavioral trends, such as hostility, passivity, the immature personality, and so forth. They were also not above using such phrases as the *affirmative personality,* when discussing the fact that children must be brought up with sufficient confidence to express appropriate aggressiveness.[157] But these were all merely examples and informal designations to make their thinking clear to us.

If there is any single theoretical device Dollard and Miller might have favored to account for individual differences, it would be the use of a social (including class-level) construct, along the lines we have already considered in the previous section. Culture accounts for such behaviors as social attitudes, dress, religious convictions, and so on. There is a fascinating complexity among the peoples of the world, as well as among the peoples within any given sociopolitical identity. Delinquent gangs have their normative style of behavior which influence the individual in certain predictable ways, and so do the religious callings of minister, priest, and rabbi. To find the *individual,* we must look at that intersection point where social roles and heritages—as well as biological factors—meet, adding a touch of accidental-habit formations that are due to the specific (unique) experiences of the person under observation. There is no internally directing trait or type of personality. There are only habits combining responses into a hierarchy of probabilities.

Psychopathology and Psychotherapy

Theory of Illness

The Stupidity-Misery-Symptom Cycle

Abnormal behavior is learned behavior, which means it has to be reducing a drive of some sort.[158] How did Dollard and Miller explain the fact that neurotics and psychotics continually suffer from anxiety or fear and yet *also* gain some form of drive-reduction (reduced anxiety) from their maladaptive behavior? How does self-defeating behavior arise in the first place and then go on recurring despite reinforcement? This seems to contradict Darwinian ideas of only the competent aspects of behavior surviving in nature—a kind of survival of the unfittest, so to speak. Dollard and Miller accepted the fact that a neurotic's misery is genuine. There can be no doubt that most people who present themselves to psychotherapists are living a nightmarish existence, made all the more frustrating by the fact that nothing they do seems to help them.[159] They are caught in some form of round-robin life

cycle which cannot be broken and seems ever worse with the passage of time. Dollard and Miller noted that a common factor here is that such individuals reflect a *stupidity* concerning the cause of their *misery* which brings on their eventual *symptom* picture. Since there is a circularity to this sequence, we will hyphenate their terms and present this aspect of their theory as the *stupidity-misery-symptom cycle*.[160]

In calling the neurotic person *stupid*, Dollard and Miller did not mean that he or she has lowered intelligence. The neurotic is a person with strong, unlabeled, emotional conflicts,[161] particularly of the approach-avoidance variety.[162] Such a person is motivated two ways, to *do* something (positive incentive) and *not* to do this very thing (negative incentive). As the conflicting drives increase, the person is made miserable, being torn apart from within by unresolvable impulsions. Indeed, the neurotic does not even have words to capture what is taking place within. Repression (stopping thought as a response) has long since removed the labels (cue-producing responses) that might have assisted in problem solution. This makes proper discrimination impossible, so that behavior is abnormally generalizing from one situation to another. A male patient treats all authority figures as if they were the father who earlier in life rejected him and thus acts out a learned pattern to inappropriate cues.[163] A female patient goes through life competing with all women who look even vaguely like the sister she used to constantly try to outdo (sibling rivalry).

Such symptoms, along with the misery they only partially or temporarily remove, are what usually bring the client into psychotherapy. Dollard and Miller did not feel that the symptoms are *the* neurotic disorder but merely the observed results of the underlying conflict needing a solution. "The symptoms do not solve the basic conflict in which the neurotic person is plunged, but they mitigate [lessen] it. They are responses which tend to reduce the conflict, and in part they succeed. When a successful symptom occurs it is reinforced because it reduces neurotic misery. The symptom is thus learned as a habit." [164] Although literally *any* repressed (unlabeled) emotion can cause a neurotic's misery, Dollard and Miller made greatest use of *anxiety* (vague fear) in their explanations. For example, they tell of a woman who was unable to walk or even stand because she could not flex her knees. Based on their study of the case history, they concluded that a severe approach-avoidance conflict over sexual intercourse was the basic reason for her symptom. She had learned earlier in life to attach an anxiety response (avoidance) to a sexual response (approach) (see section on sexual training, p. 407). Hence, when her legs stiffened up, this meant (1) she could not engage in sexual intercourse, which in turn (2) reduced her anxiety for the time being (reinforcement). [165]

Of course, in the long run this was a poor solution because the sexual drive was not reduced and it would simply return again at an equal or even greater level of stimulation (misery). [166] But because the woman had not labeled her conflict nor therefore recalled its origins (stupidity), the whole process recurred (cycle). Dollard and Miller believed that simply removing the symptom without confronting the underlying conflict would *not* result in a lasting cure. If a symptom is suppressed or inhibited by hypnotic suggestion, for example, the drive level being held back below the surface is going to rise in time, and this is bound to raise the misery level and eventuate in the learning of an entirely new symptom. [167] Usually, the neurotic settles on those few symptoms that bring the most consistent reduction to his or her drive levels, and hence we have the emerging patterns of so-called clinical *syndromes*. [168] There

is also an admitted *secondary gain* (secondary reinforcement) from neurotic illness, because we feel sorry for anyone in this condition. [169]

Why do certain people become neurotic? We do not find Dollard and Miller speculating on the likelihood of inherited biological factors in illness, but undoubtedly any handicap in life can provide a potential reason for the development of neurosis. The fact that a daughter is being reared by a father who very much wanted a son will doubtlessly increase the chances that a behavioral disorder will develop in the girl, especially if her mother cannot offset the paternal attitudes in relation to the child. Sexual identity is inherited, but it has nothing to do with built-in neurotic disposition. Hence, to the question of why certain people become neurotic, Dollard and Miller responded:

Our answer is that neurotic conflicts are taught by parents and learned by children.... Out of confused instructions to parents, combined with the character faults of parents themselves, arise the situations in which children are put in severe conflict....even if one granted the existence of a science of child rearing, it would still be necessary to get the correct rules into the habit systems of whole generations of parents. [170]

Dollard and Miller agreed with Freud on the harmful effects of a too harsh superego or conscience. "It is hard to say whether a morbid conscience is a worse enemy of life than a disease like cancer." [171] It would follow, therefore, that extremely high parental standards before adequate labeling is possible would be a bad sign for the future adjustment of a child. All children are vulnerable to conflict formation. They do not understand the world and cannot control their emotions.[172] Therefore, even the well-meaning parent may find that one of his or her children is taking on abnormal behavior. Some of this process is due to the unusual circumstances of early life, circumstances over which no one could hope to have control. Therefore, Dollard and Miller did not intend to blame parents in blanket fashion for the neurotic patterns of their children.

Frequently the person developing a neurosis has some glimpse of his or her problems. However, since these developing cues immediately trigger anxiety, the response to stop thought occurs and is reinforced by the resultant reduction of these vague fears. The individual literally knocks out connections that might have removed the stupidity.[173] Indeed, now the individual is even more stupid than before, is generalizing behavior even more inappropriately than before, which makes him or her even more miserable than before, because other people find these abnormal responses upsetting to interpersonal relations. Anxieties pile on anxieties, and the person feels caught up in a behavioral sickness that is "utterly mysterious and uncontrollable."[174] Dollard and Miller used the concept of *obstructive* or *aversive responses*[175] to describe all of those abnormal efforts made by the person, such as stopping thought, or triggering anxiety when a situation is frustrating, or even acting excessively dependently rather than taking responsibility. Rather than learn to solve conflicts, the neurotic person responds obstructively to dig an even deeper pit of misery in the long run.

Differential Diagnosis in Learning-Theory Terms

The *neurotic*'s basic approach-avoidance tendencies are between thinking and repression

on the one hand and goal responding and behavioral inhibition on the other.[176] Even though a neurotic person's behavioral capacities are equal to the problems confronted, the stupidity-misery-symptom cycle brings on a loss of courage to face up to life. "The neurotic starves in the midst of plenty; a beautiful woman cannot love; a capable man cannot fight; an intelligent student cannot pass his examinations. In every case the contrast is sharp between capacity to enjoy and opportunity to enjoy." [177] The *psychotic* person withdraws from reality to become completely preoccupied with internal cues.[178] Out of such internal fantasy are born the *delusions* and *hallucinations* of this most serious form of mental illness. The connection between cue-producing responses (mental responses) and the observable instrumental responses they mediate gradually weaken.[179] This means that in actual, overt behavior the psychotic behaves instrumentally (unconsciously), whereas internally he or she is living in a completely fantasized world of labels that have no tie to reality. In a manner of speaking, psychotics move about in our world, but they live in a dream world of behaviorally unattached, nonmediating, cue-producing responses. Since this fantasy realm is not reality oriented, it offers an inviting escape opportunity to the conflict-laden individual. Drive reduction is occurring for some especially strong drives (anxiety, and so on), and it is therefore difficult to break into this behavioral pattern.[180] Dollard and Miller did not consider the psychotic treatable by their approach to psychotherapy.

Delusional beliefs are explained along the lines of rationalization. In the same way that we find good reasons for our behavior we can—when extremely conflict laden—find a socially acceptable reason for why we are beginning to fail in life at a growing pace. At first it is that our schoolteachers do not like us; they seem to have it in for us. Later, our employers and then our friends are also against us. They are jealous of our attractiveness or of the fact that we are so honest in our relations with others, and so on. In time, we suspect that a grand plot has been laid against us, and the elaboration of this scheme might take on such vast implications it becomes obvious that we are one of the most important people in the world. Next, we search around to find why we are so important. Could it be that we are not whom we thought we were? Maybe our so-called parents really are not our parents after all. And so it is that psychotics enter the hospital with delusional beliefs of self-importance which seem bizarre distortions of the learning process. But this is possible because such beliefs have been hatched entirely within fantasy.

We all know that when under the heightened drive of fear it is not unusual to "see something move" or to "hear an unnatural sound" in a vacant house or along a pathway leading past a graveyard. There is undoubtedly some stimulus for our "normal" form of hallucination, like the rustling of leaves. But we interpret the cues differently as a result of our uneasiness (elevated drive level). It is the same with the psychotic, although in this case the cues are even more remote and possibly even entirely within fantasy. If the drive state is strong enough, an image retained in memory can easily be called into sight where it can compete with incompatible responses being elicited by cues in the external environment.[181] The psychotic individual sees the face of a deceased loved one talking to him or her from out of a mirror or a darkened window. Dollard and Miller pointed out that in societies where the expression of visions is more acceptable, the frequency of hallucination increases tremendously, which suggests that learning is at the heart of this phenomenon.[182]

Alcoholism and *drug addiction* are mal-

adaptive habits kept active by the temporary relief (drive-reduction) they provide from anxiety.[183] Dollard and Miller noted that alcohol is probably more effective in the removal of inhibitions (encouraging the doing of some act previously avoided) than it is in the removal of repressions (beginning to think about a previously avoided topic). Hence, alcohol does not aid in acquiring insight (labels, cue-producing responses).

The *phobia* or unnatural fear of some object, person, or situation is also a learned pattern of anxiety increase and reduction.[184] The housewife who has narrowly escaped death in an automobile accident might later find it impossible to drive the family automobile to the market. Soon *all* automobiles and (generalizing) even buses and bicycles cause her to break out in a cold sweat and breathe rapidly (anxiety). By avoiding the fear-producing cues she can keep her composure, and hence this phobia is learned as an obstructive habit.

The *anxiety attack* is a most dramatic symptom picture, in which anxiety mounts to an extreme degree and then stops abruptly following a swoon, a pseudo-heart attack, or complete loss of control through a fit of some sort.[185] The individual feels certain that his or her world is about to come apart, and the pressure of the anticipated terrifying climax is almost unbearable. The terror we witness in a panic of this sort is admittedly difficult to explain by a drive-reduction theory of reinforcement. How is it that the anxiety drive continues to mount so rapidly and painfully in the attack episode? Dollard and Miller frankly admitted that this was an unexplained process, but since they felt that no one really knows enough about the role of painful stimuli in the neuroses, they continued to apply their drive-reduction theory until forced to give it up by a better explanation.[186]

The *obsessions* (thoughts forcing themselves on the person) and *compulsions* (acts forcing themselves on the person) were explained very much like phobias.[187] That is, if we are forced to think something or to do something even though it is against our conscious desire, the fact that we *are* engaged in some activity means that we *are not* engaged in something else. The woman who has an unconscious approach-avoidance conflict over sexual promiscuity—she is drawn instrumentally toward the men she meets yet also repulsed by a sense of anxiety—can avoid thinking about it by counting her heartbeat five or ten times each hour of the day.[188] The clinical pictures of *hypochondria* and other so-called *psychosomatic* illnesses are doubtlessly related mechanisms. The man who is always worried about his health has probably succeeded in avoiding many other of life's frustrations ("You can't think about two things at the same time"). Although a little miserable, he is greatly sheltered by his physical preoccupations.

The avoidant response can also be seen in *hysteria*.[189] The conflict-laden person sometimes just forgets everything and develops hysterical amnesia. Without necessarily planning this move, the person may have thought initially, "Who can blame people for blanking out?" Later, when some approach-avoidant conflict arose, this mediating idea helped trigger the memory loss. Hysterical symptoms of blindness ("What you can't see, can't hurt you"), the loss of motility ("How can I do that when I can't even move?"), or the uncontrolled action, such as a tic or tremor ("See how hard I am trying? I am shaking to pieces trying to get

the job done"), may all be directly instrumental responses mediated initially by cue-producing responses which are then forgotten (via stopping thought as a response). In other words, the true hysterical patient is *not* conscious of such reasons for having a symptom. The *malingerer* (pretender) is still conscious of such reasons (retains cue-producing responses as mediators),[190] but the hysteric has long since forgotten the mediators and is behaving completely instrumentally.

Though Dollard and Miller did not take up the psychoses in detail, they did single out *paranoia* for consideration.[191] This mechanism is an extension of projection, and it often has a bit of reaction-formation involved. For example, the man with a homosexual urge may repress it because of the anxiety it arouses and then express overt disgust for all such, what he now considers, subhuman beings. In time, since the conflict is engendered by attractive individuals whom he meets or sees in the newspapers, he may attribute homosexual motives to all such people as a form of class or caste. For example, the claim that a government agency is being overrun and perverted by homosexual administrators may represent a kind of paranoid projection (delusion) of unconscious conflicts.

Theory of Cure

Psychotherapy as the Teaching of Labels and Discriminations

If neurotic behavior is learned, then it follows that psychotherapy is a matter of unlearning old habits and eventually learning new habits to take their place.[192] Dollard and Miller viewed the psychotherapist as a kind of teacher or coach who works to improve the client's pattern of living. "In the same way and by the same principles that bad tennis habits can be corrected by a good coach, so bad mental and emotional habits can be corrected by a psychotherapist." [193] Hence, to be successful, psychotherapy must first provide conditions under which neurotic habits can be examined, identified, and then unlearned; and second, it must facilitate the learning of more adaptive patterns of behavior which will extend beyond the consulting room into life generally.[194] This defines the two phases of psychotherapy. In the first, or *talking phase,* the therapist and client work to remove repressions and thus to restore the client's higher mental processes (mediators).[195] In the second, or *performing phase,* the client must be supported and encouraged to apply these new mediations to actual performance changes outside the therapy hour.[196]

Thus, the basic job to be accomplished by the therapist in the talking phase is to teach the client proper labels, so that conflicts can be identified and proper discriminations made. Since the client is reluctant to speak openly because of the threat of self-disclosure, therapy is itself a form of approach-avoidance conflict. The therapist must therefore remove as much of the negative incentive in the situation as possible. This is achieved by assuming an accepting, nonjudgmental manner.[197] In this atmosphere of freedom, the client can be helped to learn what has never been learned in the past.

The neurotic is a person who is in need of a stock of sentences that will match the events going on within and without him. The new sentences make possible an immense facilitation of higher mental processes. With their aid he can discriminate and generalize more accurately. . . . By labeling a formerly unlabeled emotional response he can represent this response in reasoning.[198]

The therapist can point out, for example, that the frigid wife is at least in part unre-

sponsive to her husband because she has failed to see a difference between him and her father. It has never occurred to her before, but the husband's behavior is often identical to that of her now deceased father. Over the years she has come to react to the husband in the cold manner that she had earlier reserved for her moralistic father, whom she had disliked. As the cues are rehearsed in the dialogue with the therapist, the woman begins to view her husband in a new light. If the therapist were now to add something like " 'Enjoying sex with your husband is expected and permitted,' the word 'permitted' could serve as a cue for all the responses that had already been attached to it and would tend to make [her] . . . free to respond to sex activity as she had previously responded to other 'permitted' activity." [199] This interplay of discrimination and generalization continues throughout the talking phase of psychotherapy.

Often certain key labels play an important role in this learning process. For example, if Nancy has always considered herself loyal and dependable, but is now told (relabeled) by the therapist that her seeming loyalty and dependability are really signs of an immature dependence on others, then she will see her entire behavioral pattern differently. Nancy can then generalize the usage of this label and better discriminate when she is being overly dependent in other social situations as well. She is the good old reliable helpmate to friends because she is too frightened to express her own desires when they conflict with others; she cannot risk losing their friendship. Hence she is constantly being taken advantage of and left to wonder why others are treating her so badly. If the relabeling is not instructive in this fashion, in time it will simply be ignored by the client with little positive or negative effect. Therapist *interpretations* (relabelings) must therefore lead to reinforcements in behavior or they will quickly extinguish.[200]

A useful verbal discrimination cue is the simple dichotomy of past versus present.[201] Sometimes a client could be cured rather easily if a first attempt were made to do that which is threatening. If Bob, a handsome young man who is terrified to ask a young woman for a date, were to make even a fumbling effort, he could surely be successful. Based on past failures in probably irrelevant circumstances—such as not having been selected as a member of athletic teams or elected to student government offices—Bob has come to be convinced that he lacks the masculinity and popularity to be considered attractive to females. But if the therapist were to emphasize that yesterday's failures are *not necessarily* relevant to today's successes, anxiety might be reduced, allowing the approach motivation to take over. Bob might be made to feel that this is a fresh start in a new life situation. With success in getting the first date—and the encouragement of the young woman to set Bob at ease—the avoidance responses that have kept him in conflict could easily extinguish and a cure would result. This example demonstrates a general rule Dollard and Miller recommended. Since the avoidance gradient rises more rapidly as we approach the goal (asking for a date) than does the approach gradient, it is better to encourage advancement toward the goal by *reducing the avoidance* motivation than it is by increasing the approach motivation.[202] To have encouraged Bob to "be a man" and "get in there and *make* the girl go out with you" would have been the wrong tactic, for it would have done little to reduce the avoidance motivation (probably would have raised

it) and instead would have threatened Bob's masculinity worries all the more by challenging him to prove himself.

One success leads to another, so the client who takes the first step acquires an anticipatory sense of hope, which can even be labeled so by the therapist.[203] There is hope in the future concerning the specific problem being dealt with and there is also hope for a general life of better adjustment in the future. As achievements continue, the power drives begin to take over for the anxiety drives that have been under reduction to that point. We have underway a positive rather than a negative line of drive reduction in the client's life. It is essential for the client to move into a performing phase, because "insight is not enough" for a cure to be achieved. "According to our theory of the matter, the matter of 'trying out something new' is quintessential to a therapeutic result. Mere verbal change will not suffice."[204] If generalization from relabeling to overt action does not occur, psychotherapy has not really been carried out.[205] As Dollard and Miller put it, "We conceive of therapeutic results . . . as strictly related to and dependent upon the external conditions of reinforcement in the life of the person."[206] It is not what one knows but what one *does* that counts.

The Nature of Insight

It is tempting to draw a direct parallel between the Dollard and Miller discussion of what is usually called insight in therapy and the kind of insightful interpretations Freud made. This is even furthered by the fact that Dollard and Miller said they were describing "essentially the psychoanalytic technique for adult neurotic patients."[207] Yet, the differences that emerge in their approach are so dramatic that they demand special consideration. The parallels to classic insight are clear, but the differences in outlook on the function and even necessity of insight outweigh the similarities.

First of all, insight begins in the understanding the therapist has of the client's conflicts. The therapist must identify the neurotic habits and then gradually label them for the client so that adjustments and changes may follow.[208] Classically, this has meant a kind of self-study, a review of the past in which the client describes his or her life to the therapist in great detail. In doing so, the client sometimes restimulates emotions that have occurred before, but were either unlabeled or improperly labeled. It is important to stress that labeling does include the identification of feelings, along with other promptings to instrumental (overt) action. "We emphatically do not take the stand that mere labeling can be important if it is not immediately linked with the emotional, instrumental, and other responses which are being manifested and *changed* in the relation between patient and therapist."[209]

If the therapist points out the neurotic conflict or suggests a more appropriate label and the resulting insight is helpful to the client, the potential for change in the latter's behavior is great. In fact, the procedure that is learned can take on drive properties, so that the client imitates the therapist as model and furthers the process personally. "In some cases the patient will know immediately that he has created a valuable new sentence because drive reduction (insight) occurs at once."[210] Clients find that they can predict their own behavior now.[211] They are no longer a slave to their emotions. Self-control and self-direction are finally possible.[212] This procedure is formalized into a habit in time, one we might call *learning to stop and think*.[213] Rather than immaturely responding instrumentally to an input stimulus, the client now properly mediates with cue-producing labels of greater relevance to self-direction. Edgar no longer flies off the handle but

mediates a generalization from therapy, such as "What am I really getting 'hot' about? Is there really enough going wrong here to justify my anger?" In most instances this self-examination is enough to depress Edgar's formerly hair-trigger temper and permit responses other than shouting and arm-flailing to take place.

Thus far, we have a fairly straightforward translation of classical psychoanalytical terminology into S-R theory. However, Dollard and Miller's great emphasis on change in observed behavior makes it clear that insight is not the client's understanding of personal behavior in terms of one *particular* theory of personality. It is not the theory but its practical effect that counts; as they express it, the "recovery of the past is not useful *per se* but only to the extent that past and present conditions are actually different and that the contrast between them is vividly made, either spontaneously by the patient or with the aid of the therapist."[214] In other words, whereas Freud thought of insight as an *end in itself,* Dollard and Miller thought of it as an *instrumentality* (means) for change. Freud was building his personality theory and took insight as evidence for his image of the person. Dollard and Miller were applying their theory which had already been proven to their satisfaction in the laboratory. Hence, insight is never a finding of the therapy procedure for Dollard and Miller. Insight is a tool which has value only if it works to bring about change.

In fact, Dollard and Miller were to call into question the necessity for using a case-history examination of the client's life in therapy. "While highly advantageous, we do not feel that the reconstruction of the past is an absolute necessity for therapeutic advance. The therapist may be able to set up a strong presumption that present-day neurotic habits have been learned without being able to specify the learning conditions in detail." [215] Clients gain a sense of conviction when they have the chance to take their past life and place it alongside their present life. But is the value of this historical survey the literal truth recalled from the past or merely the sense of conviction (positive reinforcement) that there is a meaningful connection between the two life periods under comparison? Dollard and Miller favored the latter explanation of insight.[216] Hence,

> . . . *it should be made perfectly clear that* significant therapeutic effects can also be produced in other ways without any improved labeling or "insight" *on the part of the patient. As has already been pointed out, we would expect the general reassuring and permissive attitude of the therapist to be able to produce a considerable reduction in fear. This reduction in fear should generalize from the therapeutic situation to the rest of the patient's life and thus reduce somewhat his conflict, misery, and motivation for symptoms.*[217]

It is this highly pragmatic view of insight as a kind of instrumentality in the therapeutic process that makes Dollard and Miller the *bridge theorists* to the behavioral theories of Chapter 7. Though still cloaked in the older terminology of therapist interpretation and client insight, theirs is a new vision in the history of psychotherapy. Change comes about in the present, and no matter what one *says* about why the initial or resultant patterns of behavior array themselves as they do, the processes of change have a relevance all their own. The next historical step was to drop the emphasis on the client's past entirely and focus attention only on what is taking place in the active present. Dollard

and Miller did not go quite this far, presumably because they were hoping to unite psychotherapy approaches under one theoretical language rather than trying to strike off on an approach entirely different from that known to their time. But the seeds were sown, and an even more action-oriented, pragmatic psychotherapy was to follow (see Chapter 7).

Relationship Factors

Dollard and Miller said that the therapist and the client are equally responsible for any cure achieved. Clients must not believe that the therapist will make them well by dispensing pills, advice, or reassurance.[218] Neither will the effective therapist make decisions for the client when it comes time to apply the insights gained from the talking phase.[219] Patients must work hard, beginning with a detailed review of their background, and the therapist must make it as easy as possible for them to review these anxiety-provoking memories. Dollard and Miller felt that mere catharsis, which presumably means telling others about past sins or mistakes, can rarely be therapeutic.[220] If the client makes guilt-laden confessions without being punished, then anxiety may be reduced. But for lasting benefit, the lengthy working through or *practicing* of relevant words and sentences (mediators) must be followed up by actual overt behavioral changes.[221]

The client constantly generalizes emotional responses to the therapist and the therapy situation. Since the therapist is comparable to former authority figures in the client's life history like parents and teachers, power-versus-submission behaviors may begin showing up in therapy. Freud called these generalizations *transference*, but Dollard and Miller did not make anything special of their occurrence.[222] Generalization is automatic, of course, and from the outset of therapy the client begins transferring both facilitative and obstructive responses to the therapist.[223] On the *positive* side, clients transfer training in being sensible, self-critical, orderly, and logical. The motive to please others, particularly those in authority, is also generalized to the therapist. Therapy could not proceed without these generalizations. On the *negative* side, clients transfer patterns of dependence and fearfulness which have remained fixated in their response hierarchy since childhood.

Not all of the feelings the client has toward the therapist are false generalizations from the past. "If the therapist is hasty, stupid, cruel, or uncontrolled, he will earn real emotional reactions from his patient."[224] If the therapist can achieve a warm and even loving relationship (positive transference) with the client, then this can be used as a kind of leverage in reinforcing desirable behaviors. The client can be encouraged and shown attention (positive reinforcement) when needed changes are made in the performing phase of therapy. If too much client dependence is built up by this use of a therapist's reinforcing capabilities, then near the very end of therapy the appropriate interpretations can be made to the client.[225]

Dollard and Miller did not accept the phenomena of *negative transference* and *resistance* in the same way that Freud did.

The therapist is frequently inclined to feel that there is something diabolically purposive in these emotional interruptions, that the patient is somehow cunningly "resisting" him. He should refuse to accept such a view of the phenomenon. He should, instead, understand that the emotional responses in question [arguing with therapist, missing sessions, and so on] are generalized automatically to the therapeutic situation because the strength of avoidance reactions to unconscious emotion has been reduced.[226]

As for the source of these resistive and critical tendencies, Dollard and Miller noted that most of us have learned a drive for independence and self-direction, so that when we seem to be submitting to the direction of another, we automatically respond with a degree of negativeness in our self-expressiveness.[227]

The therapist must be prepared to see these developing changes in the proper light. It would be a great mistake to punish the client for assuming responsibility. Although they did not discuss it in specific terms, Dollard and Miller made clear that *countertransference* (unconscious generalizations to client by therapist) works against successful psychotherapy.[228] The merits of client transference are thus to be seen in both phases of therapy. In the first (talking) phase, thanks to the automatic generalizations onto the therapist, a kind of ongoing staging of the neurotic's maladaptive habits occurs, allowing for immediate relabeling. In the second (performing) phase, the therapist can use the affection and respect achieved to become a direct influence in the client's life by positively reinforcing desirable behaviors.

Normal Behavior

Though *normality* is hard to define, Dollard and Miller suggested that a person who (1) is meeting his or her drive stimulations relatively well, (2) has not repressed (that is, *has* labeled) major areas of experience, and (3) is not suffering the misery of avoidance is what we mean by the *normal person.*[229] There are many reasons why people can fail to maintain this normal pattern, some of which lie far beyond any possible hope of their control—as in the social conditions surrounding them. Many times a therapist feels inadequate to help a client who may simply require so many preliminary interpersonal skills in order to adjust more satisfactorily that no amount of insight is going to help. "Perhaps the resources of schools where speech, manners, 'charm,' and [social] class traits are taught should, when needed, be added to those of the therapist's." [230]

One of the unfortunate realities of the psychoanalytical technique is that it is itself class-linked, a therapy for the wealthy, verbal, and sophisticated members of our culture. Too often a psychoanalyst begins to make interpretations of others from lower social-class levels or rural backgrounds and completely misses the mark because of an ignorance of sociocultural differences.[231] Dollard and Miller noted that there are two general errors made in the social sciences. The *sociologist's error* is to assume that a study of class and social situations per se can account for everything in behavior, thereby giving little thought to constitutional and other unique factors in personality. The *psychologist's error* is to place too much emphasis on constitutional and unique habitual patterns and to dismiss sociocultural factors as minor and secondary. Based on their experience, Dollard and Miller suggested that "the favorite error of therapists is *not* that of sociologists!" [232]

Therapeutic Techniques

The Selection of Patients

If psychotherapy is to be successful, then the therapist must be especially careful about the kind of patient accepted for contact. Dollard and Miller listed a series of points in this selection process.[233] Obviously, a first consideration is the nature of the presenting problem. It has to be one resulting from past learning and not based on organic deficiencies. The prospective client should also be suffering misery—the more the better!—because this is what motivates him or her to seek professional help and work for a cure. The history of a symptom or syndrome picture is important to evaluate, because the longer such habitual patterns have been reinforced the more difficult it is to alter them. An individual trapped in the repressed economic conditions of the lowest classes cannot be considered a good bet for successful behavioral change.

Prospective clients should also have certain minimum social skills, such as understandable speech, the capacity to relate to others in a fairly consistent manner, and so on. The therapist cannot be expected to take over the basic functions of a parent. Ordinarily, a person who can use language reasonably well has attained the minimal level of competence for therapy, assuming that he or she is not psychotic. This rules out the mentally retarded. Further, if the fundamental social training of trying to be reasonable and logical in discourse has not been achieved, then individual psychotherapy cannot be successfully carried out. Obstructive habits that deny the usefulness of psychotherapy would also be a negative indicator. The abnormal who does not recognize personal eccentricity, the rigid moralist who considers any talk of human motives sinful, or the social revolutionary who views psychotherapy as a way of repressing certain peoples are all examples of poor subjects for successful behavioral psychotherapy. Finally, practical matters like the physical health of the client or the ease with which he or she can meet therapy appointments must be considered in accepting patients.

Free Association, Interpretation, and Therapeutic Suppression

Dollard and Miller described the practical procedures in therapy much as any Freudian would. They used *free association* during the talking phase of therapy, interpreting it as a type of learning imposed on the client.

The rule of free association is not a mere invitation to speak freely. It is an absolute obligation which is the foundation of the therapeutic situation. It is a compulsion which has some of the rigor of any compulsion. This rule defines the "patient's work" which is to drive ruthlessly through to the pronouncement of sentences which may evoke sickening anxiety.[234]

The therapist learns much from the statements made during free association. Even if they wanted to, therapists could not ask the right questions to elicit the information that pops up automatically during free association. These associated meanings are never really free, but rather follow lawful regularities like any observed behavior.[235] Once again, there is no real strategizing or intentionality in free association as there is none in unconscious behavior generally. The client is under a compulsion to say what is associatively there for the saying.

The therapist is trained to listen to this flow of verbal material without in any way imposing an a priori hypothesis on what is being communicated. The therapist's goal, based upon learned drives to give a complete account, to be logical, and to judge the appropriateness of a response, is eventually to propose a thorough and rational verbal account of the patient's life.[236] Gradually, hypotheses based on what the client is saying in free association are put into words by the therapist. Commonly occurring cues like blocked associations or slips of the tongue

are all noted and taken into account in forming hypotheses. When these hypotheses have received considerable support from the client's verbalizations, the therapist advances them as his or her *interpretation*. Dollard and Miller spoke of using *successive approximations* in the interpretative technique, by which they meant the therapist must constantly refine his or her hypotheses to match a succession of facts which emerge over the course of therapy.[237]

Observations made in the situation of psychotherapy are a kind of natural history, even though they lack the controls of a purely scientific experiment.[238] The neurotic individual will transfer feelings in the transference relationship, and this focused dynamic can be observed by both the therapist and the client as it is actually taking place. It is important for the client to begin rehearsing the labels and sentences being proposed by the therapist as interpretations.[239] Often, the client will pick up this procedure of self-insight through a form of matched-dependent copying of the therapist. If this imitation does not come about, the therapist should fall back on *interpretative prompting*,[240] or the continued use of suggestions to the client, such as "Could this feeling you speak of really be anger and not fear?"

Though Dollard and Miller did not devote great space to *dream interpretation*, they acknowledged that dreams can be profitably used as a kind of extension of the processes involved in free association.[241] A dream involves: " . . . private, imageal responses which produce cues. These cues are what are 'seen' as the dream. Since they are private responses they are less likely to have strong anxiety attached to them and are likely to be 'franker.' "[242] In other words, we may see ourselves doing things in the dream that seem quite in contrast to our usual behavior. These deviations from the common pattern are entered into the successive approximations of the interpretation. These in turn can be rehearsed by the client and then used as cue-producing responses for later discriminations as repression drops off and the person gains increased control over his or her behavior.

In the performing phase of therapy the patient is expected to begin making actual behavioral changes. One of the sources of encouragement here is the therapist as a model to be imitated by the client. "Since he has a great deal of prestige, his calmness, courage, and reasonableness are imitated by the patient, who thus tends to become calmer, more courageous, and more reasonable." [243] One of the procedures recommended in bridging the gap between talking about behavior and doing new things is to use a series of graded tasks. [244] For example, a young man who is concerned about his masculinity and is not entirely certain that he has adequate heterosexual drives might be taken through a series of graded efforts, beginning with the practice of masturbation while contemplating intercourse with sensuous females (possibly using pictures of inviting women). In time, his interest in the opposite sex would be stimulated, and then he and the therapist would plan a series of strategies to begin dating women—possibly beginning with group activity so the responsibility for entertaining his companion would not fall entirely on the client's shoulders. Double-dating might be the next step. Finally, the young man would be brought along to dating on his own and complete sexual adjustment—culminating in sexual intercourse with a female either before or after engagement or marriage (a choice left for him and his cultural values to decide).

Dollard and Miller recognized that one of the major vehicles of cure in the later stages of psychotherapy must be *suppression,* or the conscious restriction of thoughts by the individual. [245] Whereas free association tended to open up recall and widen the range of mental processes, suppression must now close off the behavioral habits of compulsive self-examination. It works as follows:

In order to suppress a train of thought a person must take his attention off the stimuli which are producing this train of thought and turn his attention to some other cues which produce an incompatible train of thought. . . . As attention is turned to new cues, these cues produce different responses, and these responses in turn produce new and different motivation—that to accomplish the task to which the person is addressing himself. [246]

Dollard and Miller wisely recognized that individuals who constantly mull over memories, labels, and statements or presumed insight are the sort of people who will never change. They have acquired a secondary habit of thought that insulates them from overt action (in a manner analogous to the psychotic's withdrawal into a world of cue-producing responses unattached to overt, instrumental responses). They are, in a manner of speaking, "all talk and no action." Hence, suppression is particularly useful as a technique of cure *late* in therapy.

In psychotherapy, as elsewhere, suppression should be used when the patient knows what to do but lacks the ability to get into action. Suppression is particularly necessary in the phase of "trying out in the real world" the new plans that have been made in the period of free association. Eventually the patient must abandon brooding and reflection, form a dominant plan, make a decision to act, and put the plan at hazard. Only thus, as we have shown, can he achieve real reduction of the drives which have been producing misery.[247]

The Termination of Therapy

In discussing one case, Dollard and Miller referred to an interpretation that was framed in the *nineteenth hour;* it was therefore implied that they considered therapy to be a long-term affair—at least for some clients.[248] Surely there should be no effort to terminate the contacts until "the baneful effects of repression are lifted." [249] This would involve a weakening of fear in the avoidant motivation of the underlying conflict. Most importantly, the client should not be considered cured until he or she is trying out new responses in life outside the consulting room and getting significant rewards for them.

Dollard and Miller believed that if a good level of adjustment is to be maintained following termination of therapy, the client must form a habit of continuing *self-study.*[250] All ex-psychotherapy clients should set some time aside weekly to review their behavior and to head off any developing problems. They can do this by, for example, simply listing a series of points around some worries that might be developing. What seems to be the problem? Is this really the problem, or could it be something else? When did it start? What seem to be the factors involved? Questions like these are brought into the open and dealt with in turn. Plans are made to rectify the problems even as they are being framed openly. Dollard and Miller viewed this self-study as the logical heir to Freud's original self-analysis (see Chapter 1). It differs from ordinary reasoning in that the client makes use of the knowledge gained through psychotherapy.[251] Training in self-study should become a routine closing technique of psychotherapy. "It is theoretically possible that special practice in self-study might be given during the latter part of a course of therapeutic interviews. The patient might be asked to practice solving particular problems and the therapist could act as a kind of control." [252]

Summary

Chapter 6 begins with a review of learning theory in psychology. A distinction is drawn between classical or Pavlovian conditioning and operant or Skinnerian conditioning of behavior. Classical conditioning views responses as elicited, whereas operant conditioning interprets responses as being emitted. Operant conditioning assumes that the organism operates on the environment to produce contingent circumstances which are or are not rewarding. Hence, the organism in effect causes the reinforcement to come about. Classical conditioning does not view the organism as necessarily creating the reinforcer that turns an unconditioned stimulus-response regularity into a conditioned stimulus-response regularity. An important development in classical conditioning theory occurred when Tolman emphasized the role of mediation—former responses to environmental stimuli acting in the present as cue-stimuli to direct behavior. This concept plus the hierarchy of mediational cues has played a major role in the evolution of behaviorism. Another central issue in conditioning theory is whether a drive-reduction is necessary in order for a stimulus-response habit to be learned. Modern cognitive interpretations of learning have steadily reduced this emphasis on drive-reduction theory.

Chapter 6 next takes up the learning-theory adaptation of Freudian psychology by Dollard and Miller. This effort was based on Hullian learning theory, which rested on classical conditioning and mediational assumptions concerning behavior. Thus, Dollard and Miller viewed the fundamental organization of behavior as being due to the attachments of stimuli and responses, leading to habits and a repertoire of such behavioral patterns into a hierarchy of response. The response hierarchy is innately influenced because of certain reflexes an organism has at birth; but shortly afterwards, the precise nature of what sorts of responses will occur in relation to what sorts of stimuli results from the frequency and contiguity of succeeding events, flowing over time and leading or not to drive reduction. As life progresses, the ordering of this hierarchy, which dictates the most likely response to occur in relation to a given stimulus pattern (including social situations of various types), varies according to the success or failure in obtaining reinforcement. Responses that lead to reinforcement are kept high in the hierarchy of responses, while those that do not lead to reinforcement fall in their probability of elicitation.

Mediation is central to Dollard and Miller's learning theory. Behavior that is not mediated, that goes directly from stimulus to response, is termed *instrumental*. Behavior that is mediated has one or more cue-producing responses occurring between the stimulus (pattern) and the response(s). A cue-producing response is a former response acting in the present as a stimulus, and can be thought of as either a verbal (word, sentence) or a nonverbal (image, pictorial scene) behavioral action. Dollard and Miller placed the same emphasis on language in behavior as had Sullivan. Language terms (letters, words) are all cue-producing responses, or, they may be called, labels. Insightful learning, discrimination learning, and transfer of training can all be furthered through the use of mediated labels of this type. Dollard and Miller traced the basic source of motivation to primary or innate drives, promptings for food, sexual gratification, and so on, as well as to the secondary or learned drives, such as pursuing recognition from or power over others. Reinforcements follow in kind, because human beings can be conditioned on the basis of biological satisfactions like food (primary reinforcement) or purely social satisfactions like popularity (secondary reinforcement).

Behavior is also oriented to goals, so that an immediate goal is often more readily drive reducing than a more distant goal achievement (delayed reinforcement). The longer an organism lives and the more complexly mediated its behavior becomes, the more likely it is that it will work toward distant goals. Behaviors can also generalize as can learned drives. Responses extinguish and spontaneously recover. Punishment suppresses a response but can have harmful side effects. Picking up on the sociopsychological emphasis of Sullivan, Dollard and Miller made wide use of the role of imitation in behavior. There is a copying form of imitation, in which person A tries to match person B's behavior with some understanding of why this behavior is being enacted, but there is also a matched-dependent form of imitation in which one person acts like another without really understanding that this reproduction is taking place or why it might be occurring. Conflicts arise in behavior when goals having different valences (positive or negative qualities) begin to intrude on each other. We can have approach-avoidance, approach-approach, and avoidance-avoidance conflicts arising as well as the doubling of the approach-avoidance conflict. Finally, responses that are learned through social influence are age graded, so that what the person does at one level of development may not be considered appropriate at another. Critical learning situations in development include the feeding situation, cleanliness training, instruction in sex roles and sex typing, and the management of anger.

In accounting for Freudian constructs, Dollard and Miller began by viewing so-called unconscious behavior as instrumental (nonmediated) responsivity. They did not view the ego as an agent in the personality system, but were prepared to use this term to describe the capacity a person has to deal with life through higher mental (mediated) processes. Conscious, directed thinking implies ego strength. The superego is, of course, all those socially learned behaviors that others have modeled for the person. Libidinal promptings would be accounted for in terms of the sex drive. Repression is an automatic tendency to stop thinking and avoid remembering. When the person is instructed to consciously avoid thinking, this is suppression. Identification is described in terms of imitation, whether of the copying or the matched-dependent variety. Projection is the reverse of this, in the sense of attributing personal motives to others. Reaction-formation stems from linguistic mediations in which we learn to respond in terms of opposites and hence can easily substitute one response for another. Rationalization is considered a response style learned culturally, in that people are instructed to be consistent and logical in their behavior and hence can find sound reasons for behavior that is motivated by totally other reasons. Dollard and Miller stressed the contribution parents make to the so-called Oedipus complex, as when a father is jealous of the attention given to a son by the mother. The anxiety this stimulates in the son is not castration anxiety, but rather a realistic reaction to the social circumstances. Parents also sexualize their relations with cross-sex offspring. Fixation is the persistence of a habit beyond its age-graded level. Regression occurs when, because of some frustration, the person returns to an earlier response in his or her hierarchy, one that is age graded lower and may indeed appear to be a return to an earlier period of life. There were no efforts made to account for the Freudian personality types (oral, anal, and so on), except to suggest that these are habit patterns characterized by a personologist as global unities when in fact they are built up and shaped by social forces quite without choice or internal direction (that is, based exclusively on locomotion).

Dollard and Miller's theory of illness rested on the stupidity-misery-symptom cycle, in which, thanks to rising anxiety, the person stops thinking as a response, loses cues (labels) that might help in problem solution, suffers as a result, and develops a symptom in an effort to alleviate this misery. However, the cycle only reproduces itself again and again until serious maladjustment is the result. Factors like secondary gain enter to perpetuate abnormal habits. Neurotics and psychotics are caught up in various conflicts, but the psychotic person is much more instrumental in responding and in time withdraws from reality to deal almost exclusively with internal cues. Here is when delusions and hallucinations enter the picture. Phobias are learned patterns of behavior which enable the person to reduce anxiety by fleeing from certain situations. Obsessions and compulsions are much the same sort of mechanism, except that in this case a personal action (compulsion) or recurring thought (obsession) provides the means for fleeing from anxiety-provoking life circumstances. Hypochondria affords much positive reinforcement in secondary gain, as people feel sorry for the sick person. Hysterical patients gain advantages through their dependency or through simply forgetting (amnesia) their life challenges via the stopping-thought response.

Dollard and Miller's theory of cure framed the therapist's role as that of a teacher or coach, who strives to provide new labels (cue-producing responses) which can in turn facilitate discrimination and more accurate responsivity in the future. They viewed the therapy series as breaking down into a talking and a performing phase. In the initial, talking phase the client is taught to stop and think, and to frame more accurate cues of life's challenging situations. Insight comes down to learning labels. Interpretation is a relabeling of poorly labeled circumstances or offering the client a completely new label. Such interpretations and the insights they afford are only as good as the reinforcements they make possible. The therapist is not present simply to spin fanciful labels as a theory without direct benefit to the client. In the later, performing phase of psychotherapy, the client is encouraged to begin making positive steps outside the consulting room. Transference is interpreted as the positive or negative responses generalized to the therapist from out of the past learning of the client. Resistance is interpreted the same way, as generalized avoidant reactions. The therapist can also generalize responses to the client, which is tantamount to what Freud called countertransference. Dollard and Miller employed free association and dream materials as sources of data concerning the client's response hierarchy. A positive form of suppression was also advocated.

Dollard and Miller provided the transitional theory to modern behavioral therapies. Whereas they tried to bring the rigor of the laboratory to the descriptive theories of the psychoanalytical consulting room, the behavioral therapists who followed them found the need to retain the traditional personality terminology wanting. If the techniques of cure can be fashioned in strictly stimulus-response

terms, why bother with the translation into Freudian terminology? It was inevitable that the next step would be taken by therapists who saw no value in such translations and considerably more efficiency in the techniques of therapy flowing strictly from stimulus-response theory.

Outline of Important Theoretical Constructs

Historical overview of learning theory and behavior

Ivan Petrovich Pavlov
conditioned reflex · unconditioned stimulus · unconditioned response · conditioned stimulus · conditioned response · classical conditioning · reinforcement (reinforcer) · generalization · differentiation (discrimination) · instrumental conditioning

Edward L. Thorndike
law of effect · connection · law of exercise · frequency of repetition · confirmatory reaction

John B. Watson
behaviorism · S-R psychology · reflex arc · external versus internal response · shaping of behavior · habit · response repertoire · mechanism

Edward Chace Tolman
purposive behaviorism · intervening or organismic variables · mediation (mediator) · significate · sign · sign-gestalt · expectancy (means-end-readiness) · hierarchy

Clark Leonard Hull
drive-reduction reinforcement · drive stimulus · fractional, antedating goal reaction (anticipatory goal response)

• goal stimulus • pure stimulus act •
primary versus secondary reinforcement
• habit-family hierarchy

Burrhus Frederic Skinner
elicited versus emitted responses • operant response • operant conditioning
• empirical law of effect • positive versus
negative reinforcement • contingency
• class of response • response-reinforcement contingency • method of successive
approximations • mediation theory

Biographical overview of Dollard and Miller

Personality theory

Structural constructs

Behavioral monism and mental activities
monism

*The fundamental organization of behavior:
attachment, stimuli, and responses*
attachment • association (connection)
• stimulus and response • habit • learning • cue • patterning of cues • repertoire • innate hierarchy of response
• dominant response

*Responses become stimuli: mediation,
labeling, and language*
mediation model • instrumental acts
(instrumental responses) • cue-producing
responses (response-produced stimuli)
• output response (instrumental-response)
• verbal versus non-verbal cue-producing
responses • anticipatory goal responses
• trial and error learning • insightful
learning • discrimination • generalization • transfer of training • labeling
(label) • signs and symbols • logic as
thought forms

*Freudian structural constructs as learning
theory terms*
unconscious versus conscious behavior
• ego and ego strength • superego

Motivational constructs

*The nature of drive, motivation,
and reinforcement*
principle of reinforcement (reward)
• drive • primary (innate) drives
• secondary (learned) drives • primary
versus secondary reinforcement • immediate versus delayed reinforcement
(latency) • gradient of reinforcement
• anticipatory goal response • incentive
• goal • primary (innate) generalization • secondary (learned) generalization
• gradient of generalization • discrimination • rehearsal (practice) • response
extinction (extinguish) • forgetting
• spontaneous recovery • response inhibition (inhibit a habit) • punishment
• anxiety

The role of imitation in human learning
imitation • copying • matched-
dependent imitation • social mobility
• same behavior • competition (rivalry)
• goal • empathy (sympathy)

Frustration and conflict in human behavior
frustration • barrier • conflict • gradient of reinforcement • goal (positive
versus negative) • approach-avoidance
conflict • choice point • avoidance-
avoidance conflict • approach-approach
conflict • double approach-avoidance
conflict

*Freudian adjustment mechanisms as
learning theory terms*
inhibition • repression • suppression
• identification • projection • reaction-
formation • rationalization • displacement

Time perspective constructs

The feeding situation

Cleanliness training

Early sex training
sex typing · sex roles · castration anxiety · Oedipus complex

Training in anger control
anger (hostility) response · frustration tolerance · anger-anxiety conflict

Age grading, fixation, and regression
age grade · fixation · regression · innate hierarchy of response · initial hierarchy of response · learning dilemma · resultant hierarchy of response · regression in age grading level

Individual differences constructs

Psychopathology and psychotherapy

Theory of illness

The stupidity-misery-symptom cycle
stupidity · misery · symptom · stupidity-misery-symptom cycle · anxiety · syndrome · secondary gain · obstructive (aversive) responses

Differential diagnosis in learning theory terms
neurosis · psychosis · delusion · hallucination · alcoholism and drug addiction · phobia · anxiety attack · obsession and compulsion · hypochondria and psychosomatic illness · hysteria · malingerer · paranoia

Theory of cure

Psychotherapy as the teaching of labels and discriminations
talking versus performing phases · interpretation

The nature of insight
learning to stop and think · instrumental nature of insight · labeling not essential to cure

Relationship factors
practicing labels · transference · negative versus positive transference · resistance · countertransference

Normal behavior
sociologist's error · psychologist's error

Therapeutic techniques

The selection of patients

Free association, interpretation, and therapeutic suppression
free association · interpretation · successive approximations · interpretative prompting · dream interpretation · suppression

The termination of therapy

Notes

1. Thorndike, 1898. **2.** Thorndike, 1933, p. 66. **3.** Thorndike, 1943, p. 33. **4.** Ibid., p. 22. **5.** Watson, 1924, p. 6. **6.** Watson, 1913, p. 158. **7.** Watson, 1924, p. 8. **8.** Ibid., p. 15. **9.** Ibid., pp. 77, 79. **10.** Ibid., p. 11. **11.** Ibid., p. 82. **12.** Ibid., p. 216. **13.** Watson, 1917, p. 329. **14.** Watson, 1924, p. 84. **15.** Ibid., p. 220. **16.** McDougall, 1923a, p. 288. **17.** Tolman, 1960, pp. xvii–xviii. **18.** Ibid., p. 14. **19.** Ibid., p. 414. **20.** Ibid., p. 135. **21.** Ibid., p. 29. **22.** Ibid., p. 97. **23.** Hull, 1952, Ch. 5. **24.** Skinner, 1950, 1936b. **25.** Evans, 1968, p. 10. **26.** Ibid., pp. 19–20. **27.** Ibid., pp. 17, 19. **28.** Skinner, 1957, p. 460. **29.** Dollard, 1937. **30.** Dollard, 1942, 1943. **31.** Dollard and Auld, 1959; Dollard, Auld, and White, 1953. **32.** For a selective overview of Miller's work see: 1944, 1948a, 1948b, 1951, 1957, 1959, 1961, 1963, and 1964. **33.** Dollard, Doob, Miller, Mowrer, and Sears, 1939. **34.** Miller and Dollard, 1941. **35.** Dollard and Miller, 1950. **36.** Ibid., p. 187. **37.** Ibid., p. 277. **38.** Ibid., p. 270. **39.** Ibid., pp. 5–6. **40.** Miller and Dollard, 1941, p. 290. **41.** Dollard and Miller, 1950, p. 62. **42.** Ibid., p. 3. **43.** Ibid., p. 337. **44.** Ibid., p. 119. **45.** Ibid., pp. 146, 249. **46.** Ibid., pp. 216, 309. **47.** Ibid., p. 311. **48.** Ibid., p. 326.

49. Miller and Dollard, 1941, p. 59. 50. Dollard and Miller, 1950, p. 69. 51. Ibid., pp. 15, 50. 52. Miller and Dollard, 1941, p. 1. 53. Ibid., p. 16. 54. Dollard and Miller, 1950, p. 32. 55. Miller and Dollard, 1941, p. 22. 56. Dollard and Miller, 1950, p. 36. 57. Ibid., p. 37. 58. Ibid., p. 98. 59. Ibid., p. 56. 60. Ibid., p. 99. 61. Ibid., pp. 110–111. 62. Ibid., p. 37. 63. Ibid., p. 109. 64. Ibid., p. 53. 65. Ibid., p. 98. 66. Ibid., p. 105. 67. Ibid., p. 122. 68. Ibid., p. 101. 69. Ibid., pp. 56, 119. 70. Ibid., p. 100. 71. Ibid., p. 113. 72. Ibid., p. 119. 73. Ibid., p. 120. 74. Ibid., p. 103. 75. Miller and Dollard, 1941, p. 26. 76. Dollard and Miller, 1950, p. 220. 77. Ibid., p. 198. 78. Ibid., p. 250. 79. Ibid., p. 130. 80. Ibid., p. 122. 81. Ibid., p. 398. 82. Ibid., pp. 140–141. 83. Ibid., p. 9. 84. Ibid., p. 29. 85. Ibid., p. 30. 86. Ibid., p. 33. 87. Ibid., pp. 30–31. 88. Ibid., p. 78. 89. Ibid., p. 31. 90. Ibid., p. 40. 91. Ibid. 92. Ibid., p. 42. 93. Ibid., p. 187. 94. Ibid., p. 81. 95. Ibid., p. 55. 96. Ibid., p. 214. 97. Ibid., p. 117. 98. Ibid., p. 49. 99. Ibid., p. 51. 100. Ibid., p. 75. 101. Ibid., p. 63. 102. Ibid., p. 69. 103. Ibid., pp. 72–78. 104. Ibid., p. 30. 105. Ibid., pp. 318, 335, 412. 106. Miller and Dollard, 1941, p. 10. 107. Ibid., p. 11. 108. Ibid., p. 188. 109. Ibid., p. 197. 110. Ibid., p. 92. 111. Ibid., p. 149. 112. Dollard and Miller, 1950, p. 87. 113. Ibid., pp. 114, 219. 114. Ibid., p. 93. 115. Dollard, Doob, Miller, Mowrer, and Sears, 1939. 116. Lewin, 1961. 117. Dollard and Miller, 1950, p. 355. 118. Ibid., p. 363. 119. Ibid., p. 365. 120. Ibid., p. 221. 121. Ibid., p. 220. 122. Ibid., pp. 211–213. 123. Ibid., p. 200. 124. Ibid., p. 453. 125. Miller and Dollard, 1941, p. 164. 126. Dollard and Miller, 1950, p. 181. 127. Ibid., pp. 184–185. 128. Ibid., p. 177. 129. Ibid., p. 323. 130. Ibid., p. 132. 131. Ibid., p. 130. 132. Ibid., p. 131. 133. Ibid., p. 132. 134. Ibid., p. 133. 135. Ibid., p. 134. 136. Ibid., p. 136. 137. Miller and Dollard, 1941, p. 81. 138. Dollard and Miller, 1950, p. 138. 139. Ibid., p. 139. 140. Ibid., p. 141. 141. Ibid. 142. Ibid., p. 142. 143. Ibid., p. 143. 144. Ibid., p. 144. 145. Ibid., pp. 145–146. 146. Ibid. 147. Ibid., pp. 146–147. 148. Ibid., p. 149. 149. Ibid., p. 148. 150. Ibid., p. 150. 151. Ibid., p. 91. 152. Ibid., p. 36. 153. Ibid., p. 45. 154. Ibid., p. 36. 155. Ibid., p. 171. 156. Ibid., p. 337. 157. Ibid., p. 152. 158. Ibid., p. 7. 159. Ibid., pp. 13–14. 160. Ibid., p. 223. 161. Ibid., p. 281. 162. Ibid., p. 359. 163. Ibid., pp. 248, 306. 164. Ibid., p. 15. 165. Ibid., p. 169. 166. Ibid., pp. 224–225. 167. Ibid., pp. 385–386. 168. Ibid., p. 195. 169. Ibid., p. 238. 170. Ibid., pp. 127–128. 171. Ibid., p. 141. 172. Ibid., p. 130. 173. Ibid., p. 19. 174. Ibid., p. 225. 175. Ibid., pp. 266, 270. 176. Ibid., p. 399. 177. Ibid., p. 318. 178. Ibid., p. 425. 179. Ibid., p. 338. 180. Ibid., p. 237. 181. Ibid., p. 180. 182. Ibid., p. 181. 183. Ibid., p. 377. 184. Ibid., p. 158. 185. Ibid., p. 17. 186. Ibid., p. 190. 187. Ibid., p. 164. 188. Ibid., p. 17. 189. Ibid., p. 165. 190. Ibid., p. 167. 191. Ibid., p. 183. 192. Ibid., p. 7. 193. Ibid., p. 8. 194. Ibid., p. 25. 195. Ibid., p. 235. 196. Ibid., p. 331. 197. Ibid., p. 248. 198. Ibid., p. 281. 199. Ibid., p. 311. 200. Ibid., p. 333. 201. Ibid., p. 307. 202. Ibid., p. 362. 203. Ibid., p. 316. 204. Ibid., p. 319. 205. Ibid., pp. 332–333. 206. Ibid., p. 342. 207. Ibid., p. 235. 208. Ibid., p. 306. 209. Ibid., p. 304. 210. Ibid., p. 286. 211. Ibid., p. 299. 212. Ibid., p. 279. 213. Ibid., p. 300. 214. Ibid., p. 315. 215. Ibid., p. 317. 216. Ibid., p. 318. 217. Ibid., p. 321. 218. Ibid., p. 267. 219. Ibid., p. 276. 220. Ibid., p. 246. 221. Ibid., p. 334. 222. Ibid., p. 261. 223. Ibid., pp. 262–266. 224. Ibid., p. 273. 225. Ibid., p. 277. 226. Ibid., p. 274. 227. Ibid., p. 293. 228. Ibid., pp. 274–275. 229. Ibid., p. 431. 230. Ibid., p. 345. 231. Ibid., p. 419. 232. Ibid., p. 421. 233. Ibid., pp. 233–237. 234. Ibid., p. 241. 235. Ibid., p. 252. 236. Ibid., p. 254. 237. Ibid., p. 284. 238. Ibid., p. 6. 239. Ibid., p. 280. 240. Ibid., p. 253. 241. Ibid., p. 282. 242. Ibid., p. 256. 243. Ibid., p. 395. 244. Ibid., p. 350. 245. Ibid., p. 445. 246. Ibid., p. 448. 247. Ibid., p. 458. 248. Ibid., p. 317. 249. Ibid., p. 349. 250. Ibid., pp. 431–442. 251. Ibid., p. 431. 252. Ibid., p. 438.

Chapter 7

From the Laboratory to the Consulting Room: Skinner, Wolpe, Stampfl, and Bandura

Dollard and Miller set the scene for a dramatic shift in the way we look at and treat neurotic behavior. Though they did not speak of *behavior therapy*, their focus on the importance of changing client habits already contained the newer attitude.

Behavior theory emphasizes the great importance of being certain that the groundwork of new habit is laid while the therapist still has some influence. Perhaps most therapists already instinctively follow this injunction of behavior theory. If so, they should continue to do what they are doing and put this condition of therapy yet more consciously and systematically into effect.[1]

The systematic and conscious attempt to effect conditions was precisely the aim of the behavioral therapies.

As long as Dollard and Miller argued that "the direct removal of a symptom (without treatment of its cause) produces an increase in drive and throws the patient back into a severe learning dilemma," they could be merely transitional theorists, retaining that element of the Freudian outlook that held there truly was some independent cause of a symptom.[2] To the complete behaviorist a symptom can be taken literally as the *illness,* as the observable maladaptive behavior to be removed. Why then be concerned with supposed underlying causes (conflicts)? What does this add to the observed behavioral pattern (habit)? Furthermore, if stimulus-response psychology can subsume Freudian psychology and thereby account for all of those factors that psychoanalysis explained, why not take the next logical step and drop the psychoanalytical terminology altogether? Why not approach psychotherapy *strictly* on behavioristic principles? Most experts believe that Skinner and Lindsley (1954) actually coined the phrase *behavior therapy*. For those who dislike using *therapy,* R. I. Watson's (1962) phrase *behavior modification* has been substituted. There are many behavior therapists who have made important contributions to the area, but we can only take up a handful of the leading theoreticians in the limited space of an introductory text.

The tie that binds behavioral approaches together is their claim to scientific accuracy, that their findings have been drawn from empirical researches in the laboratory. There is no common formal personality theory, though there is a definite image of humanity reflected in the behavioristic outlook. There is a marvelous—and sometimes zealous—spirit of empirical flexibility among these theorists. The old therapy prescriptions have all been challenged and in large measure rejected. Nothing is sacred except the spirit of empirical investigation. Within a remarkably short span of time the behavioral approaches have become a major force in the field of (psycho?) therapy.

In the present chapter, we will take up four of the most widely cited approaches to behavior therapy: B. F. Skinner, Joseph Wolpe, Thomas G. Stampfl, and Albert Bandura.

The Technique of Operant Conditioning: B. F. Skinner

Biographical Overview

Though he is not a psychotherapist in the usual sense nor even a personality theorist, anyone who would study in these areas must understand the theory of B. F. Skinner for he has had an immense influence on modern thought going beyond the limits of psychology proper (see p. 384 for initial comments on Skinner). He must be considered the major spokesman for the behavioristic tradition in the latter half of the twentieth century. He has been admired and honored by a number of highly talented psychologists, and yet no psychologist since Freud has been more severely criticized by those who find his style of thought distasteful.[3]

He was born on 20 March 1904 and was reared in the small railroad town of Susquehanna, Pennsylvania, though his parents (of English-American lineage) later moved to the larger city of Scranton around the time he was attending college. Skinner's father was a lawyer, a cultivated and ambitious man who apparently felt that life did not give him the chance to show the talent he actually possessed. Though he wrote a widely used text on workmen's compensation law, he impressed his son as a bitter man who considered himself a failure.[4] Skinner's mother was an attractive, intelligent, emotionally strong woman who seems to have complemented her husband and established

B. F. Skinner

what many would consider an old-fashioned, hard-working family climate typical of the American Protestant family at the turn of the century. The Skinners named their first son Burrhus (maiden name of his mother) Frederic. A second son died of a cerebral aneurism at the age of 16. There were no other children. Skinner's childhood was characterized by much activity, a love for the outdoors, great interest in building and making things, and a love for school work.

Skinner attended Hamilton College in Clinton, New York where he majored in English. He did not take any courses in psychology as an undergraduate student. He did not consider himself a typical student of the times, for it seemed to him that few of his fellow students had interest in anything except typical fraternity activities and athletics. Though he joined a fraternity he did not enjoy the experience. He was also not a particularly talented athlete. Skinner resented the school's restrictive rules and the pressures to conform. Students were required to attend daily chapel, and Skinner had long since dismissed any belief in a God. By his senior year he was known as a rebel and had begun writing for student publications criticizing the school administration. One memorable editorial attacked the honorary scholarly society, Phi Beta Kappa.

Skinner was also working at his desired profession of novelist and poet, and he began submitting poems to literary magazines. After receiving a Bachelor of Arts degree in 1926, his plan was to give writing a serious effort. He built a small study in the attic of his parents' house and set to work. By his own evaluation, the results were disastrous for he could not discipline his creative spirit and frittered away his time. Within a year he took a writing assignment in which he abstracted court decisions for a year and published them as a volume dealing with labor-union grievances in the coal industry. There followed a brief stint of bohemian living in Greenwich Village, a trip to Europe, and then a return to the United States to enter graduate school in psychology at Harvard in the fall of 1928.

Through a Herculean effort, he made up for his lack of psychology background as he moved toward the Master's degree in two years (1930) and the Doctoral in another (1931). Skinner remained at Harvard for the next five years, doing various researches as a National Research Council fellow and then as a junior fellow in the Harvard Society of Fellows. He took his first teaching position at the University of Minnesota in 1936, where he worked until 1945, at which time he moved to Indiana University as chairman of the department of psychology. In 1948 he was invited to join the psychology department at Harvard, where he was to enjoy several decades of international recognition as one of the foremost psychologists of his time. Skinner married in 1936, the year of his first teaching position and fathered two daughters—the second of whom received considerable publicity for having spent her first 2½ years in the air crib designed by her father. This enclosed cabinet with transparent sides completely controls the environment of an infant so that clothing is unnecessary, temperature and humidity are kept constantly comfortable, and interesting toys are readily available for the child's amusement. Hundreds of children have since been reared in this fashion; it removes the necessity of constant care and frees the mother to spend time with her baby in happier contacts than diaper and tousled clothing changes.

We have already reviewed Skinner's primary constructs in Chapter 6 (see pp. 384); the following terms are the most significant in his outlook: *emitted responses, operants, contingencies, classes of responses,* the *shaping of behavior,* and the *method of successive approximations.* One of the most fundamental insights Skinner (1956) was to gain in his early years as researcher was that behavior does *not* require a reinforcement on every occasion (trial) in order for it to continue in the organism's (rat's, pigeon's, then man's) response repertoire. The drive-reductive behaviorists of this time were of the opinion that behavior could not be stabilized at some constant level unless reinforcements occurred following *each* performance of the conditioned response (100 percent reinforcement). Skinner was to find that even when responses are administered reinforcements less than 100 percent of the time in either *periodic* (regular) or *aperiodic* (irregular) *time intervals* or *response ratios,* the organism will continue its behavioral output. A stable level of responding can then be graphed as a standard against which we might measure the effects of any behavioral manipulations.

To prove his point Skinner invented various experimental devices. The apparatus that now bears his name (*Skinner box*) consists of a four-walled cage in which an organism can be placed; one wall has a bar (lever) protruding near a container into which food pellets (reinforcers) are ejected from an outside supply each time the bar is depressed. If we place a rat in the Skinner box and wait for a period of time, the rat will sniff about and eventually move the bar, thus ejecting a pellet of food into the adjoining container. Based on operant-conditioning principles, it will soon be possible to establish a bar-pressing response, particularly if we use 100 percent reinforcement (set our device to eject a pellet with each bar depression).

This frequency of food appearance in relation to the operant response (bar depression) is called a *schedule of reinforcement,* and we can then vary it into an interval or ratio schedule if we so desire. For example, we could set the device to eject a pellet every fifth depression (*fixed ratio*) or every fifth, then every third, then back to every fifth bar depression (*variable ratio*), effectively rewarding only some of the rat's operant responses. Similar manipulations could be made on a time schedule, having the device eject a pellet each minute (*fixed interval*) or every one minute, then two minutes, then back to one minute time intervals (*variable interval schedule*). Depending on the distribution of reinforcements, the rat will probably strike a level of responding so many times per unit of measured clock time (minute, hour, day). Moreover, altering the schedule of reinforcement will cause the rat to alter the level of responding accordingly.

Skinner could now define his concept of reinforcement entirely on such empirical grounds of changing behavior. "By arranging a reinforcing consequence, we increase the rate at which a response occurs; by eliminating the consequence, we decrease the rate. These are the processes of operant conditioning and extinction." [5] Skinner thus took issue with theories like Dollard and Miller's which distinguish between primary and secondary-drive learning. The internal drive is

an unnecessary addition to the empirical description of behavior. Regardless of what we name these presumed internal states of the organism, it is experimentally clear that *behavior is attached to stimulus consequences.* In time, Skinner increasingly emphasized what he called the *contingency* of an operant response which was another way of speaking about the consequences of an operant response—whether or not its emission will lead to reinforcement. A *program* is a series of such changing contingencies, resulting in the manipulation of behavior or the control of behavior. Tolman had used the phrase *contingent implications* in speaking about the means-end aspects of learning. Hull's anticipatory goal-response concept also carried this general meaning of the influences on behavior as a consequence of that behavior.

To clarify this, take the case of hiring a young person to do a job of some sort. If we were to ask, "Will you do this work for one hundred dollars?" we are essentially dealing in hypothetical contingencies. What are the conditions in this potential employee's response history that might cause him or her to see the sum of one hundred dollars as a reasonable reinforcement for the emission of work responses? Obviously, this would depend on past experience, which is another way of saying the typical operant level of work-responses and the financial amount to which the person has typically responded contingently in the past. Almost anything can serve as a contingent reinforcement. This is simply an empirical question (*empirical law of effect*). Some people work more for status than money, particularly when the salaries are all quite high in the kind of work they do (executives, for example). Others need signs of affection and care from their employer, in a dependent fashion. It is not our role as operant conditioners to speculate about why this or that reinforcement works for the individual. The point is, regardless of what reinforcement we may single out, the principles of operant conditioning remain unchanged.

Not every contingent reinforcement has literally to occur in the life of a person. For example, a woman learning to play bridge does not have to spend months and even years losing game after game until she finally works out a satisfactory style of card-playing behavior. She can read books on the subject and learn the probabilities of the game without literally working them out for herself.[6] Much of what we call the fruits of culture as contained in our libraries is nothing more than making clear what likely contingent reinforcers will be following various types of behaviors. Legal systems are based on the same principle. We know what the rewards and punishments are for certain behaviors as written into our laws.

Recall from Chapter 6 (p. 385) that Skinner interpreted a *negative reinforcement* as the removal of an aversive stimulus resulting in the increase of a response. This is not the same thing as *punishment*. "You can distinguish between punishment, which is making an aversive event contingent upon a response, and negative reinforcement, in which the elimination or removal of an aversive stimulus, conditioned or unconditioned, is reinforcing."[7] Thus, our legal systems control through punishment because they state essentially that "if you do behavior A, you will be given the penalty B." Skinner does not favor controlling behavior through *aversive stimulations* like negative reinforcement or punishment. Research across the animal kingdom has shown that it leads to negative side effects, making it inferior to controls through positive reinforcement. A much better approach is to manipulate behavior through extinction (removal of reinforcement) or the positive reinforcement of responses incompatible with the undesired responses.[8]

Over his long and highly successful career as researcher and teacher, Skinner put these principles and beliefs into practice—both in the practical world of education and child rearing and in the fantasy world of fiction. While teaching at Minnesota he wrote a utopian novel entitled *Walden Two* (1948). It is the story of a brilliant but somehow threatening genius—a psychologist—who is the main force behind the creation of a near-ideal subculture. The community of Walden Two is behaviorally engineered along operant conditioning lines; it features group dependence on a series of changing, empirically verified set of scientific findings and principles put into effect by highly trained planners and managers (who are themselves recruited from the residents of Walden Two). Skinner frankly admitted that the book was written as a form of self-therapy, in which he was striving "to reconcile two aspects of my own behavior represented by Burris and Frazier,"[9] the two major figures, a professor of psychology named Burris (Burrhus) who tells the story, and the founder of Walden Two, a psychologist named Frazier (Frederic?). These two are not exactly on good terms at the outset of the story, but by the book's close Burris has moved from visitor to resident of Walden Two.

Although Skinner never lost his conviction that Walden Two communities were within the realm of possibility[10] and he expanded on the design of cultures in other writings,[11] his ideas were never realized in the literal sense of founding a utopia. Other ideas were to be put into more or less concrete form. We have already mentioned the air crib, the prototype of which can be seen in *Walden Two* (1948). During the years of World War II Skinner designed a workable means of guidance whereby pigeons, trained operantly to peck at objects projected onto a screen (such as small ship models), could be used in an air-to-ground guided missile.[12] The pigeons were to be placed within a projective of this sort and to act as a homing device. Though never used operationally, it showed the willingness of a highly creative person to put what he later joked was a "crackpot idea" into operation.[13] Probably the most practical and productive innovation for which Skinner can be given major credit (though Sidney L. Pressey must be recognized as originator of the basic idea[14]) is the teaching machine. The practical strategy of the widely used *programmed instructions* based on operant conditioning principles has established a place of lasting honor for Skinner in the sphere of education.[15]

The following books comprise Skinner's major writings: *The Behavior of Organisms: An Experimental Analysis* (1938); *Science and Human Behavior* (1953); *Schedules of Reinforcement* (with Ferster, 1957); *Verbal Behavior* (1957); *Cumulative Record* (1959); *The Technology of Teaching* (1968); *Contingencies of Reinforcement: A Theoretical Analysis* (1969); *Beyond Freedom and Dignity* (1971); *About Behaviorism* (1974); and *Reflections on Behaviorism and Society* (1978). He received several honors in recognition of his work, including the Distinguished Scientific Contribution Award of the American Psychological Association and the President's Medal of Science. His many students have carried on his work, and his impact on psychology and the image of humanity it portrays has been tremendous.

Yet the curious aspect of this impact is that Skinner pointedly set out to avoid playing the theorist, much preferring to confine his activities to the control and manipulation of behavior. He once observed, "When

we have achieved a practical control over the organism, theories of behavior lose their point."[16] Why quibble over which drive is being reduced or what behavior is being repressed when one has direct operant control of the organism? The basis of Skinner's attitude here rests on the inside-versus-outside dichotomy of behavior that Watson introduced (see p. 379). For Skinner, the term *theory* often means "an effort to explain behavior in terms of something going on in another universe, such as the mind or the nervous system."[17] As a dedicated empiricist, he had to reject this kind of theorizing, and since stimulus-response psychology is heavily invested with this tactic, he could not consider himself an S-R psychologist.[18] On the other hand, Skinner did feel that he was a theoretician in the sense of formulating an overall theory of human behavior combining many facts into a general picture.[19] In this sense, it would be fair to say that the weight of history forced Skinner into a role as theorist and even social philosopher, and we can see this trend reflected in the book titles cited in the previous paragraph.

This necessity of having to expand his interests beyond the findings of experiments actually began in the immediate reaction to *Walden Two* (1948). Though he tried to express his strong sense of humanity in the work, some readers were appalled by the seeming mass manipulation of the human spirit. Skinner felt that he was being misunderstood, for he at no time viewed his utopia as a kind of brave new world.[20] The citizens of Walden Two were happy. Aversive stimulation was virtually nonexistent, and both the basic and the aesthetic needs of life were amply reinforced. Skinner felt that his critics had confused the democratic political ideals of America with the intent of the book; the only thing wrong with his utopia, as far as he could tell from criticisms, was that someone (Frazier) had "planned it that way." [21] The role of social philosopher was subsequently furthered, thanks to a series of debates he had with his friend Carl R. Rogers (Chapter 9). Rogers specifically reacted against the seeming disregard of the "person" in Skinner's outlook, and he also questioned the "control and manipulation" of people as the proper role for the science of psychology. The following passage from an article of Rogers's in which he speaks of an exchange he had with Skinner shows both Skinner's intellectual consistency and the extremes to which he was willing to go in order to defend his theory of behavior.

A paper given by Dr. Skinner led me to direct these remarks to him: "From what I understand Dr. Skinner to say, it is his understanding that though he might have thought he chose to come to this meeting, might have thought he had a purpose in giving this speech, such thoughts are really illusory. He actually made certain marks on paper and emitted certain sounds here simply because his genetic makeup and his past environment had operantly conditioned his behavior in such a way that it was rewarding to make these sounds, and that he as a person doesn't enter into this. In fact if I get his thinking correctly, from his strictly scientific point of view, he, as a person, doesn't exist." In his reply Dr. Skinner said that he would not go into the question of whether he had any choice in the matter (presumably because the whole issue was illusory) but stated, "I do accept your characterization of my own presence here." [22]

It is this side of Skinner that we must neither overlook nor misunderstand. Though he always spoke of the consequences of behavior and the contingencies of reinforcement, Skinner staunchly defended the anti-teleological position of behaviorism. He observed: "Operant behavior, as I see it, is simply a study of what used to be dealt with by the concept of purpose. The purpose of an act is the consequences it is going to have." [23] Would this not imply that rules could be abstracted from past behavior and used in the present as a means of self-direction (telic behavior)? Well, though rules may be abstracted and plans surely can be made (Frazier was a great planner), this does not establish the fact of a *self*-direction: ". . . when a man explicitly states his purpose in acting in a given way he may, indeed, be constructing a 'contemporary surrogate of future consequences' which will affect subsequent behavior, possibly in useful ways. It does not follow, however, that the behavior generated by the consequences alone is under the control of any comparable prior stimulus, such as a felt purpose or intention." [24]

Those who argue for self-direction must inevitably defend internal stimulation as the controlling factor in behavior. As a behaviorist, Skinner was unable to accept this. He was convinced that scientific research had proven beyond doubt that people respond to external, environmental stimuli. The claim that there is some form of self-identity—a person, ego, or whatever—directing behavior from the inside is simply the last-ditch stand of an outdated ideology. [25] As Skinner saw it: "Men will never become originating centers of control, because their behavior will itself be controlled, but their role as mediators may be extended without limit. . . . 'Personal freedom' and 'responsibility' will make way for other bywords which, as is the nature of bywords, will probably prove satisfying enough." [26] This does not mean that people will forgo progressive improvements in their life adjustments.

I take an optimistic view. Man can control his future even though his behavior is wholly determined. It is controlled by the environment, but man is always changing his environment. He builds a world in which his behavior has certain characteristics. He does this because the characteristics are reinforcing to him. He builds a world in which he suffers fewer aversive stimuli and in which he behaves with maximum efficiency.[27]

We might still wonder how it is possible for an organism to both be controlled by and yet be capable of changing its environment *without* a self-initiated purpose or intention. This seems a paradox. There is a kind of chicken-egg problem here, because Skinner's claim that the environment is *always* the originating source of control remains an unfounded assumption until he tells us *why* this is the case. Having admitted that there is also an influence in the reverse direction—from personal behavior *to* environmental circumstance—how can Skinner be so confident that one side takes precedence over the other? Skinner solved this problem in his later works by drawing a parallel between, and then actually, equating, the process of operant conditioning and Darwin's concept of *natural selection* (see p. 118 and p. 281). Thus he says: "The environment not only prods or lashes, it *selects*. Its role is similar to that in natural selection, though on a very different time scale, and it was overlooked for the same reason."[28]

In other words, just as Darwin explained the advances to be seen in physical structures over the centuries by saying this was an unplanned, nonintentional process of environmental selection, so too did Skinner suggest that behavior works according to its own type of "survival of the fittest." What is fit in behavior is that action leading to contingently reinforcing circumstances. We can even translate Darwinian theory into Skinnerian terms by suggesting that when animals in nature happened to evolve a certain type of hide or a particular type of claw, it was the physical environment that "contingently rewarded" them with survival, assuming this unintended change in structure was more adaptable than the hides and claws that existed to that point. And, as is sometimes said of the dinosaurs, when the environment was no longer the right one for certain bodily structures, contingent reinforcements in the form of survival were not forthcoming. In his book *About Behaviorism* (1974), Skinner made his thinking very clear on this matter.

There are certain remarkable similarities between contingencies of survival and contingencies of reinforcement. . . . Both account for purpose by moving it after the fact [of an occurrence on the time dimension], and both are relevant to the question of a creative design. When we have reviewed the contingencies which generate new forms of behavior in the individual, we shall be in a better position to evaluate those which generate innate behavior in the species.[29]

Having now made contingent causation the basic dynamic of change in all of nature, Skinner provided a solution to his chicken-egg problem. Stemming from its beginnings in organic evolution, the environmental selective process continues to be the *basic* source of even behavioral control in the higher forms of life. "As far as I'm concerned, the organism is irrelevant either as the site of physiological processes or as the locus of mentalistic activities."[30] This is what many take to be Skinner's black-box or empty-organism conception of the behaving animal, a way of expressing the external controls on behavior that Skinner disowned as having been attributed to him by others.[31] There are surely mediating processes at work in the organism, which is a physical reality, but they cannot be observed and hence are a poor choice as the basic data of psychology. Skinner stuck to his empiricism, and he won many battles simply by demonstrating the obvious role operant conditioning has in behavior at all levels of the animal kingdom. (See, however, emerging problems with the concept below, p. 474.) And here is where psychotherapy or behavior modification enters. Though he was not a therapist, Skinner's views have worked well in the clinical manipulation (cure) of patients. We now turn to some examples of operant conditioning in a therapeutic setting.

Theoretical Considerations

Theory of Illness and Cure

Though they do not deny the occasional physical-biological cause, by and large the operant-behavior therapists believe that maladjustment is no different from any other behavior, once we understand the learning principles that keep it going. The psychotic individual's behavior, based on past environmental shaping, is now considered incorrect or inappropriate by the broader social culture. This usually leads to a loss of reinforcement, behavior under the control of aversive stimulation (punishments, negative reinforcements), or the complete rejection of external stimuli by the psychotic person in favor of an imagined dream world (delusion). Social expectations then enter once again to damn the abnormal person as lazy, bad, crazy, or possessed by the devil, none of which helps in adjusting his or her operant level to life in a more realistic fashion. Once labeled as sick or a mental patient, the maladjusted person is effectively shaped into behaving in this very manner.[32] The so-called secondary-gain features of mental illness are part of this *behavioral shaping,* but there is much more as well.

The good patient is not troublesome but rather passive and willing to accept the direction and dependency-shaping manipulations of his or her caretakers.

The broadest phrasing of the operant therapist's view of maladaptive behavior is that two things have gone wrong: (1) adaptive behaviors have never been learned, and (2) maladaptive behaviors *have* been learned. The problem facing the therapist is therefore to identify maladaptive behaviors in an individual's repertoire and *remove* them through operant techniques. At the same time, more adaptive responses should be shaped into the repertoire. There is little or no need for an extensive review of the client's past life, though the more information a therapist has concerning the maladaptive patterns the easier it is to arrange a program of operant conditioning for the client. Psychological tests or interviews are used only in this pragmatic fashion of identifying the symptom picture as clearly as possible and then laying down a schedule for modifying this pattern. Though informal insights doubtless occur to the client, there is no attempt to make cure dependent on the extent of self-understanding a client may have.

Individual Treatment Cases

Let us assume that Mr. and Mrs. Greenfield bring their eight-year-old son, Jimmy, to Dr. Thomas, a behavior therapist, with the complaint that the boy's verbal pattern has deteriorated terribly since he began school a few years ago. At present, Jimmy is virtually mute. He was held back in first grade for another year because of his inability to communicate. The Greenfields are at their wits' end, because up until the time of entering school Jimmy's speech was completely normal. Physical examinations and consultations with medical specialists have not helped. Dr. Thomas might spend several sessions reviewing the case history with the Greenfields and then, after careful planning, institute a program of operant conditioning. First, he would ask the parents to take the pressure off Jimmy to speak, because all this does is attach aversive cues to the speaking situation. Next, he would ask that Jimmy be brought in to see him over a series of half-hour to one-hour sessions. Having determined from the parents what Jimmy prefers in the way of sweets, Dr. Thomas would have on hand in the therapy room (which might be equipped with several games, construction toys, and so forth) an ample supply of—let us say—chocolate candy. Now, therapy would begin.

At the outset of the first hour Dr. Thomas might or might not tell Jimmy something about what they hope to accomplish together. More than likely he would simply introduce the boy to the playroom and permit him to select any toy or game that struck his fancy as a means of passing the hour. If Jimmy seemed to want it, Dr. Thomas would enter into the play. At the first sign of vocalization—a throat clearing, a grunt, or possibly merely a movement of the lips—Dr. Thomas would slip Jimmy a chocolate. With each following approximation to speech, Jimmy would obtain the desirable reinforcer of chocolate candy (method of successive approximation). The chocolate candy pieces are small, but they can be increased in number, particularly if Jimmy increases his vocal sounds or actually emits a word (two pieces of chocolate). After a very few such meetings (three or four), most children with Jimmy's problem will begin saying a few words to their therapist.

Dr. Thomas might change the nature of the reinforcement after a time. For example, he might work out some arrangement whereby, instead of chocolates, little plastic chips can be collected over the therapy hour, the amount based on the number of words and sentences emitted. At the end of the hour, these chips can be turned in for prizes, such as model airplanes or picture books which Mrs. Greenfield reports are among Jimmy's most prized possessions at home. Dr. Thomas may now instruct the Greenfields in how to operantly reinforce Jimmy's behavior *in vivo*—that is, in the life setting. Rather than showing concern—hence attention and thereby reinforcement—for muteness, Dr. Thomas instructs the parents to ignore Jimmy when mute (*removal of reinforcement*) but to make every reasonable show of attention when he does speak, grunt, or even move his lips (*shaping*). In this way, the operant level of speech emission which has been raised slightly in the therapy session can be transferred to the life setting proper.

The final phase of therapy would then demand an environment in which reinforcement for speaking would be arranged for Jimmy. Friends who are supportive and nonthreatening should be brought into the home, with the same schedule of ignoring muteness and attending to speech efforts followed. Gradually, this circle of environmental manipulation can be extended. Dr. Thomas may wish to speak to Jimmy's schoolteachers and to make recommendations along the above lines to them as well. This "behavior mod" program has proven to be quite successful, even though no effort is made to provide the child with insight into the reasons why speech was discontinued in the first place. Behavior therapists emphasize that there is little or no evidence to support the claim that a *symptom substitution,* or replacement of one disorder (such as muteness) with another (such as bed-wetting), is likely to take place.[33] Hence, Skinner proposed that the claim that an underlying reason must be brought to light before lasting cures result is simply another one of those unfounded superstitions that therapists have accepted without proper follow-up studies on their clients.

Operant techniques can be used in the modification of much more serious behavioral problems. Let us assume that we were to visit a large all-female locked ward of some hospital (where patients are unable to manage for themselves without constant supervision and protection). Women would be sitting around in heavy wooden chairs, gazing blandly into space or looking anxiously about. Some would be lying on couches or on the floor. Others might be nervously pacing about, mumbling to themselves, making strange facial expressions, and waving their hands in the air. Hardly a likely source of patients for psychoanalysis! Assume that we were to pick one of these women as a potential therapy *subject* (the terms *client* and *subject* are used interchangeably by most behavior therapists). Martha, the woman we select, has been showing no signs of improvement in her behavior for over two years. She is forty years of age, has been diagnosed as schizophrenic, and has been hospitalized for over five years. Martha sits all day long, staring into space or gazing at the television set. This is the fourth and seemingly last admission to the hospital in her life, for it appears unlikely that she will ever be discharged as "in remission" again. Even her family has begun to give up hope that she will ever be able to return home. Martha has never married because her odd behavior began showing up just following pubescence and boys were leery of her.

What kind of therapy can we provide this wretched person? Skinner and his associates devised a procedure which has brought more than a score of such people back to a level of living they had not experienced for some time.[34] The principles involved are taken from research on lower animals in the Skinner box. The behavior therapist would bring Martha into a specially prepared cubicle. She would be seated in a comfortable chair, facing a panel on which from one to four levers would protrude (depending on how intricate the reinforcement program is). There would probably also be a row of lights, one for each lever, and a screen on which pictures could be flashed (possibly from within the apparatus, so it would have the appearance of a television screen). Finally, below each lever there would be a container box into which small items like bits of candy or cigarettes could fall. Martha might show little interest in this panorama of unlit lights, darkened TV screen, and slot-machine-like arrangement of levers all beckoning her to respond. She might just sit there unmoved and stare at her clenched fists or some such.

However, in time, out of curiosity—particularly if the therapist reaches over and pulls one of the levers and a bit of chocolate falls into one of the trays below—Martha will probably pull a lever. Of course, it may be necessary to place her hand on the lever and begin the process by depressing it for her. These early responses are rewarded, possibly on a 100 percent basis, but ratio schedules (reinforcing one of every three pulls) can also maintain an operant level. Variations can be introduced in the procedure. For example, instead of candy or cigarettes, Martha may find that pulling a lever causes a pretty picture to flash on the screen. Since there are several levers some form of problem solution can be introduced into the task. The lights can be made to flash and a different color occur with each lever. It might now be necessary for Martha to learn that only when red is followed by blue light flashes will a reinforcement be forthcoming. It is possible to devise problems of varying difficulty, and the therapist can even introduce a second patient into the procedure later on, having the two women work cooperatively to solve their joint problem.

Several investigators have used this behavioral modification technique, finding it remarkably effective in bringing an abnormal person out of a dream world and enabling him or her once again to function with fairly appropriate verbal contact.[35] Martha no longer sits around the ward and stares into space. She talks, listens to others, and makes her wants known. The behavior therapist now extends his operant tactic outward, into more and more of her daily routine. Nurses, psychiatric aides, and indeed the entire staff of the hospital is instructed to use praise and attention to reward her adaptive responses and to ignore the maladaptive. In time, with additional instruction given to her parental family members, it may even be possible for Martha to return to life outside the hospital. Just as with Jimmy's growing satisfaction in speaking to others, the self-reinforcements that accrue to Martha as she advances on life will work to sustain and enlarge the recovery so mechanically begun in the quasi-Skinner box of the hospital. Through behavioral manipulation we have "pump-primed" Martha's behavior and now hope to see her take over on her own.

The Therapeutic Community and Social Revision

Since the operant-behavior therapist believes that an individual's environment shapes his or her behavior, for the most effective outcome a total community approach to cure should be put into operation. Skinner noted that too often our institutions for the mentally ill are based on ineffective and even improper contingencies.[36] Aversive stimulation (threats, beatings, confinement) and poor tactics, like providing the troublemaker with all of the attention of the hospital attendants, are more the rule than anything else. A totally redesigned community—not exactly a Walden Two but with an overview approach in mind—is the obvious answer.[37]

One of the most interesting applications of Skinnerian thought to a large-scale treatment of this sort has sometimes been called a *token economy*.[38] Since a community cannot be put into a Skinner box, why not use the same principles in vivo? Why not make the good things of life in the mental hospital contingent on a patient's performance? By designing an appropriate token, either circular or rectangular like the modern credit card, and enlisting the cooperation of the entire mental hospital or at least one or two large wards, operant conditioners can begin a designed program of behavioral manipulation and improvement. The first step usually will involve determining the typical behavior of patients. Do they engage in activities, attend group functions, meet at scheduled times for meals, and so forth? What is the incidence of bed-wetting? Do any patients take weekend leaves? Naturally, the general rate of turnover—hospital discharge—would be a significant measure of overall efficiency as well.

Once these *base rates* are clearly measured, a therapist could begin reinforcing all those behaviors he or she takes to be generally oriented toward personal adjustment both within and outside the hospital social milieu. For example, each time patients make their beds, clean themselves, get through the night without bed-wetting, or show an interest in others, they are given a token. The level of reinforcement can be varied by having different colored tokens represent more or less value. When a patient now wishes to watch television, a token would have to be handed over before this privilege would be made available. If candy or cigarettes are desired by the patient, there would be tokens required in exchange. The limitations on what should be reinforced and for how much is left entirely to the ingenuity of the therapists who supervise the program. The psychologist does not walk about administering tokens to all patients, of course. He or she acts as a consultant to the hospital staff—nurses, attendants, and so on—who in turn administer the reinforcers (the tokens).

Verbal Conditioning as Psychotherapy

The final aspect of psychotherapy to which Skinnerian thought applies is that of talking therapy. Can we view spoken words as operants on a par with actions like reaching for a glass of milk? Skinner would answer yes to this question, with the proviso that strictly verbal behavior is "behavior reinforced through the mediation of other persons." [39] Vocalizing is not essential, since literally "any movement capable of affecting another organism may be verbal." [40] A *nonverbal operant response* operates on the behavioral environment in some way, such as when we put a glass of milk to our lips; a *verbal operant response* operates on the behavior of another person. Skinner worked out a series of technical terms to describe how verbal behavior in the form of word-units influences other people when we use them—such as the *mand* (stop) or the *tact* (hello)—but there is no need to elaborate on this scheme for our purposes.

More to the point for present considerations is that Skinner gave language a central role in behavior without acknowledging a truly *meaningful* side to it. It was essential that he as a behaviorist contend this, because if he were to accept language as truly expressive of meanings, he would be picturing the human as purposively saying something or intending that something be expressed. *To mean* takes Anglo-Saxon roots from "to intend" or "to wish." This usage clearly implies a teleology. Here is how Skinner dealt with the technical problem even as he recognized the common bond of purposiveness to meaning:

It is usually asserted that we can see meaning or purpose in behavior and should not omit it from our account. But meaning is not a property of behavior as such but of the conditions under which behavior occurs. Technically, meanings are to be found among the independent variables in a functional account [of verbal behavior], rather than as properties of the dependent variable. When someone says that he can see the meaning of a response, he means that he can infer some of the variables of which the response is usually a function. [41]

What is the result of this analysis? It confronts us with the picture of humans speaking, none of whom is under the stimulus control of what they are saying. There are words being vocalized leading to other words being vocalized, but the control of what is being said has nothing to do with the meanings the participants may think they are expressing. In the same way that emitted behaviors of a nonverbal nature are under the control of their consequences, verbal statements are under the control of the effects they have on other people—which is another way of saying the consequences are to be noted in interpersonal behavior. We can now better understand why Skinner was willing to put his behavior under the personless-object characterization in his exchange with Rogers (see above). He could not be intimidated by this characterization because this was his formal stand on *all* behavior, including that of Rogers.

Hence, according to Skinnerian theory, classical psychoanalysts are not providing insight through making meaningful interpretations to their clients. They are verbally manipulating the emitted responses of their clients because they have themselves been shaped to emit responses in a certain way. Their training has verbally conditioned them to say certain things when their clients say certain things in a kind of exchange of contingent reinforcements. They are *not* an originating source of control in the relationship any more than their clients are. Fortunately, the therapist has been shaped to change the class of responses being emitted (change the topic, bring out more healthy responses and extinguish the unhealthy client responses) or the rate of emission. Hence, the nature of psychotherapy like the nature of speech itself is identical to verbal conditioning. Effective therapy involves efficient manipulation of the verbal behavior of a client with the therapist acting as a "social reinforcement machine." [42]

The line of research that buoyed up this view of psychotherapy began in the now classic study of Greenspoon (1954). The basic design called for a period of time in which the subject is asked to emit verbal responses with no limitation placed on the class of responses emitted (that is, nouns, verbs, adjectives, and so on, are equally acceptable). For example, the subject sits with his or her back to the experimenter and states aloud all the words (singly, not in sentences) that come to mind spontaneously. It is possible after a period of time (let us say ten minutes) to

get a base-rate estimate of the classes of responses the subject typically emits. Of all words emitted, what proportion are nouns, adjectives, singular or plural references, and so forth? Electrical sound recording of a subject's responses makes this analysis of the words emitted a simple matter after data have been gathered. In the next ten-minute phase of the experiment, the therapist selects a class of verbal responses (Greenspoon used plural nouns) and operantly reinforces only these words as they are emitted. The reinforcer used by the experimenter might be a simple *mmm-hmm* or possibly the word *good*. Each time the subject says a plural noun, the experimenter follows it with the verbal reinforcer (reinforcement stimulus). Finally, a closing ten-minute period is recorded in which the subject relies again on his or her own devices, emitting words without the mmm-hmm reinforcer taking place.

What did Greenspoon find? The verbal class of plural nouns showed a significant increase in operant level between the first and third periods of study. He had effectively manipulated the subjects' behavior, and even more fascinating, he claimed to have done this without the subjects of his study being aware of what was taking place (see p. 475 for some later challenges to this claim). Asking the subject of his study afterwards what had happened made no difference to the findings as to whether the operant level was changed. It was no accident that Greenspoon had selected the mmm-hmm reinforcement, for during this period historically, the nondirective approach to psychotherapy advanced by Carl Rogers (Chapter 9) was receiving considerable attention in psychology. Rogers was claiming that he did *not* manipulate the lives of his clients in any way. His entire strategy was to turn over direction of therapy to the client, and one of the reassuring expressions he used in this regard was mmm-hmm (in the sense of "Yes, I see . . .

please go on"). Now, here was Greenspoon and several other operant conditioners who followed with variations on his design, claiming that the mmm-hmm was not so noncontrolling after all.

There is no need to go into the variations on the Greenspoon design which were to follow.[43] Suffice it to say that the operant view or model of psychotherapy became one of therapists—themselves operantly trained—manipulating the behavior of their clients through well-placed contingent reinforcements in the chain of verbal emissions (operants) made by the clients. Though this has tremendous implication for all forms of so-called insight (meaningful) therapies, in point of fact the technique of verbal conditioning as pseudo-insight is not widely used as a behavioral therapeutic tactic. The reinforcing of personal insights is not in the traditions of behaviorism, since what the client says about personal behavior may or may not be behaviorally tied to what he or she actually does in a real life performance. Any insights thus sent the client's way are pitched to some definite behavioral adaptation. Rummaging around in the past is bypassed in favor of laying down specific programs of action for today and tomorrow.

Techniques Based on the Principle of Reciprocal Inhibition: Joseph Wolpe

Biographical Overview

Joseph Wolpe's family immigrated from Lithuania to the Union of South Africa around the beginning of the twentieth century. He was born on 20 April 1915 and recalls the closeness of his early family life. His

people were orthodox Jews, and though they were not extreme in the keeping of religious observances, Wolpe was reared in a decidedly religious atmosphere. He was particularly close to his maternal grandmother, who encouraged him to read the Hebrew theologian and philosopher, Maimonides. His grandmother died when Wolpe was 16, and by his early university days the theistic orientation she had fostered began to leave her grandson. As Wolpe extended his reading from Kant through Whitehead, Moore, and Russell, and immersed himself in medical studies, he gradually lost his belief in God.

Wolpe's father was a bookkeeper. His mother was a very competent person who looked after her four children (two sons, two daughters) with the same efficiency that she looked after the family finances. The father was a man of great integrity, who developed increasingly liberal or left-wing political views as the years passed. One has the picture of a very stimulating household, with crosscurrents of old world religion and a growing emphasis on the need for change in the modern world.

Wolpe's childhood was a happy one. He enjoyed school, was a constant reader of books by the age of eight, and in his teenage years became fascinated with chemistry, a development he felt led him into the profession of medicine. He enjoyed music but did not regularly listen to classical music until he was past age twenty. As a boy he did not especially appreciate the natural scenery of his environment, but he did have an uncanny sensitivity to aromas. In his mature years he developed a great interest in painting, and he also came to love the beauty of sculpture and Persian rugs.

In 1948 Wolpe was married and in time fathered two sons. This was the year in which he took the M.D. degree from the

Joseph Wolpe

University of Witwatersrand, where he subsequently retained an association for the next decade as a lecturer in psychiatry. Although initially attracted to Freudian theory, Wolpe rejected psychoanalysis because of its lack of empirical support in scientific researches. Near the end of his medical school days he had begun a careful study of the works of Pavlov (see Chapter 6). Though he did not accept Pavlovian theory, he was impressed by the conditioning-research designs. At about this time a friend introduced

him to the work of Hull (see Chapter 6), and here Wolpe found a theoretical formulation within which he could work—even though in time he gave his unique interpretation to the empirical findings. Another source of influence was Jules H. Masserman (1943), who had studied conflict using cats as subjects. Wolpe dismissed the psychoanalytical interpretation of these studies, but adapted Masserman's experimental tactics to suit a more behavioral view of neurosis.

In the years 1946–1948 Wolpe studied the role of counterconditioning—which he called *reciprocal inhibition*—in cats who had developed an experimental neurosis and then were cured of the affliction.[44] This was actually a continuation of the thesis research he conducted for the M.D. degree (1948). Basing his work in large measure on the findings of these experiments, Wolpe took up the private practice of psychiatry as a behavior therapist in Johannesburg.

In the year 1956–1957 Wolpe was awarded a fellowship at the Center for Advanced Study in the Behavioral Sciences at Stanford, California. He used this time to pull together his ideas on behavior therapy in his now classic book, *Psychotherapy by Reciprocal Inhibition* (1958). Feeling the need for more time to pursue the experimental implications of his theories, Wolpe accepted an appointment in 1960 as professor of psychiatry at the University of Virginia School of Medicine. Coming to a new land had been a challenge, but Wolpe had found that he increasingly disliked the political climate of South Africa. His brother, a lawyer who had been imprisoned there for political reasons and effected a spectacular escape to England, had since taken up a new career as academic sociologist. Wolpe thus considered immigrating to England feeling that that was his natural environment. However, his position in America allowed him to contribute more to his area of interest, and he never joined his brother in England. In 1965 he again changed academic affiliations, to the Health Sciences Center, School of Medicine of Temple University. In the meantime, he had lectured on behavior therapy throughout the world, acquired many followers, and established himself as one of the leading figures in this school of thought. His book *The Practice of Behavior Therapy* (1973) summarizes his views on the complete subject.

Unlike Skinner, Wolpe's medical education and Hullian drive-reduction constructs kept his theorizing close to the physical structure of the body. He was more ready than

Skinner to speak of the *necessary* role of neurons in learning, and physiological terms enter into his writings regularly. Wolpe's theories focused on the observable or potentially observable aspects of the body. He was firmly nonteleological in the best traditions of rigorous behaviorism. Here is how he once dealt the death blow to mentalistic conceptions:

Between a stimulus and the responses that follow it there must be an unbroken network of causally related events, potentially observable by an outside beholder, no matter whether or not some of the neural events have correlates in the consciousness of the subject. Any contents of the subject's consciousness would be in parallel and not in series *with their neural correlates, and would in essence constitute the unique reaction of a specially placed observer (the subject) to these neural events. Thus, an image of which I am not conscious now will appear in my imagination if appropriate stimuli activate certain of my neurones. It can have no independent existence apart from the stimulation of these neurones. Within my nervous system, a potentiality which includes the evocation of this image may be said to exist, but only in the same sense as it may be said that my nervous system harbors the potentiality of a knee jerk given the stimulus of a patellar tap. If the relationship of images to the nervous system is so conceived, all talk of "mind structure" becomes nonsensical.*[45]

Theoretical Considerations

Learning Theory and the Principle of Reciprocal Inhibition

Wolpe considered *learning* to have taken place when "a response has been evoked in temporal contiguity with a given sensory stimulus and it is subsequently found that the stimulus can evoke the response although it could not have done so before."[46] Even if the stimulus could have evoked the response earlier but now does so with greater regularity and strength, learning has taken place. In this definition Wolpe took a Watsonian-Hullian view of responses as evoked and not emitted. The *response* is a behavioral event standing as consequent to a *stimulus* or pattern of stimuli.[47] And *behavior* is always a "change of state or of spatial relations to other things."[48] When such shifting relations freeze into what Hull once called a *"persisting state of the organism,"* Wolpe would say that a *habit* or a recurring pattern of response to stimulation has been learned.[49] Drawing on his biological theoretical preferences, Wolpe essentially dismisses the distinction between operant and classical conditioning, as follows:

The physiological basis of learning (conditioning) is the establishment of functional connections between neurons. . . . There is no reason to believe that there is more than one kind of learning. Variation depends on the identity of interconnected neuronal sequences. Thus, the distinction between respondent and operant conditioning is not in the nature of the conditioning, but in the fact that in the former "nonvoluntary," especially autonomic, behavior is predominantly involved, whereas in the latter the behavior is either motor or cognitive.[50]

The process of shifting relations between stimuli and the responses they evoke is dependent on *reinforcement* which Wolpe defined as the strengthening of functional relations (with the underlying neuronal connections mentioned in the above quote presumably making it all possible).[51] Reinforcements are the results of two circumstances: (1) a certain closeness or *contiguity* must exist between a stimulus and its response, with reinforcement following closely behind or concurrently with the response; and (2) a drive reduction must be involved. Wolpe distinguished between a *need* and the *drive* that mediates it as follows: "Whatever the mechanisms involved, need conditions, being antecedents of neuro-effector responses, are stimulus conditions to these responses. But between the stimulus conditions and the effector responses *there intervenes excitation of neurones in the central nervous system;* and to this excitation the term *drive* may usefully be applied."[52] Needs are thus the ways we have of speaking about sensory stimulations of various sorts. "Every sensory stimulus . . . has the essential characteristic of a need."[53] We can often show that certain needs are correlated with the amount of activity or motor discharge (drive) an organism exhibits, but this is not a perfect relationship by any means. So-called primary needs—for nourishment, sex, and so on—are different from other needs only in the sense that they tend to stimulate stronger responses when the organism is deprived of them.[54]

Since the drive is stimulated by a need, the nature of the drive is more like a response than a stimulus (which is the interpretation Dollard and Miller had given to it also). Though Wolpe did not state it precisely this way, the drive state is likened to a mediating series of electrical responses, carried by the neurons of the nervous system, the *reduction* of which stamps in the stimulus-response contiguities occurring in the animal's behavior. There is no intentionality (teleology) involved, but Wolpe was attempting to account for the actual processes within the organism that make for learning. He therefore did not dismiss these organismic, internal processes as irrelevant to his theory, as did Skinner.

The most important drive concept of Wolpe's theory was *anxiety,* which he defined as "the automatic response pattern or patterns that are characteristically part of the given organism's response to noxious stimulation."[55] The anxiety construct was used to explain the disruptive effects on learning of noxious stimulation, as well as the learning effect noted by Dollard and Miller (see p. 412) of a reduction in anxiety leading to the stamping in of a response because of the reinforcing qualities of such a reduction. Wolpe did make a slight disclaimer, as when he noted in his original work: ". . . the argument of this book will not be affected if it should turn out that the onset of anxiety is all-important to its learning and its reduction of no moment at all. There are some apparently undeniable instances of learning reinforced by conditions of drive increment [rising anxiety] instead of drive reduction."[56]

Wolpe found in his researches that the direct effects of noxious stimulation were enough to produce the symptoms of an experimental neurosis.[57] For example, a cat would be placed in an experimental cage and given five to ten severe grid shocks, each of which was immediately preceded by a hooting sound lasting two or three seconds. The animal soon developed signs of crouching, trembling, heavy breathing, and striving to escape; when blocked the cat urinated and defecated out of apparent terror. These symptoms were soon brought on when the hooting sound was presented even before shock could be administered (on the order of Pavlovian conditioning and Hull's fractional antedating goal reaction; see Chapter 6). Generalization of the neurotic pattern was noted in other situations and with other noises; when exhibiting anxiety, the animal's eating pattern was disrupted.

It is this inability to make one response

(eating) while another is actively taking place (anxiety) that lies at the heart of Wolpe's explanation of both neurosis and therapy. Hull had pointed out that behavior is not only learned or put into habit regularities through reinforced practice (repetition of response), but there also seems to be a natural *inhibition* of responsivity with repeated trials. Whenever we must repeat some behavior over and over again, even if it is pleasurable to begin with, in time a sense of fatigue or boredom sets in which motivates us to stop performing. Hull named this fatigue-associated state *reactive inhibition.* Wolpe theorized that it was probably due to some form of substance produced by the muscles which acted on the neurons at their synaptic connections to other neurons.[58] This form of inhibition is not what seems involved in the fact that Wolpe's cats could not both eat and reflect anxious behavior at the same time. To explain the latter form of behavior, Wolpe borrowed a construct from the neurologist Sherrington (1947) and wedded it to a concept used by Hull.

Hull had found a type of inhibition occurring that was not simply due to repetitive fatigue but seemed a matter of *conditioned inhibition.*[59] When a response is forced to stop by some competing response, the stimuli associated with the stopping of this response act as conditioned inhibitors. If a cat is hungry and about to approach the food tray when Wolpe sounds the hoot and then administers the shock, the anxiety responses brought on by these noxious stimuli become conditioned to the stimuli of the sound and the electrical discharge. Furthermore, the food responses that *cease* taking place as anxiety is underway are themselves *inhibited.* We have a response acquired (anxiety) and a response inhibited (eating), both of which have been learned through conditioning. It is this form of conditioned inhibition that Wolpe now employs as a principle of explanation.

However, as if to underscore his greater reliance on neurophysiological terminology, Wolpe adapted to his theory a physically based concept used by Sherrington, as follows:

The term reciprocal inhibition *was first introduced by Sherrington . . . in relation to the inhibition of one spinal reflex by another, such as occurs when stimulation of an ipsilateral afferent nerve causes relaxation of a vastocrureus muscle contracting to a contralateral stimulus. Its use may be expanded to encompass all situations in which the elicitation of one response appears to bring about a decrement in the strength of evocation of a simultaneous response.*[60]

Reciprocal inhibition thus deals with the weakening of old responses by the carrying out of new ones. "When a response is inhibited by an incompatible response and if a major drive reduction follows, a significant amount of conditioned inhibition of the response will be developed." [61] By not eating (inhibition) but seeking to escape from the aversive stimulation, the animal reinforces its neurotic pattern through the reduction in anxiety that follows. The trick is to reverse this process.

And so Wolpe reasoned that if he wanted to inhibit the anxiety responses, a reasonable program to follow would be to present food in a *less* anxiety-provoking situation than the original one, where the naturally competing response of eating might be more likely to be elicited. For example, experimenters might begin feeding the animal outside the experi-

mental room, where the strength of generalization (generalized anxiety) is weaker and the food response has a better chance of being elicited. Once the animal is capable of eating in this removed situation, it can be brought back into the actual experimental room, then brought closer and closer to the original cage as it comes to eat while under a steadily decreasing level of anxiety. The food-eating response is inhibiting anxiety responses at a gradual pace. Wolpe knew that as early as 1924, Mary Cover Jones, working under John B. Watson's guidance, had actually removed the fear of animals from a three-year-old boy's response repertoire, using a similar technique in which a small animal was brought closer and closer to him as he was eating his meals.[62] Wolpe named this technique of behavior modification *systematic desensitization.*[63] Neurotic conditions could be cured by systematically desensitizing the organism to the anxiety-provoking stimuli at their core.

Theory of Illness and Cure

Wolpe's clients have been predominantly non-psychotics. He defines *neurotic behavior* as *"any persistent habit of unadaptive behavior acquired by learning in a physiologically normal organism."* [64] Since all of us are under causal determinations which dictate how we behave through lawful processes, to speak of the neurotic as someone who wants to be sick or who derives secondary gain from illness strikes Wolpe as absurd.[65] There is no essential difference between anxiety and fear, both relying on autonomic nervous system activity in the formation of neurosis.[66] A neurotic's maladaptive behavior patterns may have sprung from conflicts in life or resulted directly from noxious (aversive) stimulations, such as punishments which triggered anxiety directly. Once underway as a free-floating state, anxiety can be attached to almost anything. For example, Wolpe told of a man who had eaten onions while anxious. The anxiety sensed at this time was contiguously attached to the feeling of a distended stomach. Later, whenever he would overeat or suffer intestinal "gas" he would feel anxious.[67]

Anxiety is also "additive," in that mild fears stimulated by one thing can add up with other fears stimulated by other things and snowball into something quite serious.[68] We are sometimes surprised over the minor things that make people very anxious, little realizing that this is just the last in a long string of fears that have piled up little by little. Anxiety is difficult to manage because it is not as subject to reactive inhibition as are responses that stem from central (as opposed to autonomic) nervous system activity. Finally, we have the feature of anxiety that acts as a drive, stamping in behaviors which reduce its force automatically. Denise has neurotic fears of illness; therefore she ignores some ominous signs of possible cancer, because the thought of seeing a physician is so anxiety provoking that some other thought that suggests she does *not* need a physical examination reciprocally inhibits any move to the physician's door. Anxiety feeds on itself over the short term like this, keeping people from making satisfactory resolutions of their serious, longer-termed problems. It literally stamps in neurotic habits of avoidance and self-defeating actions of all types. The theory of cure Wolpe invokes in opposition to the neurotic habit-formation thesis is as follows:

If a response antagonistic to anxiety can be made to occur in the presence of anxiety-evoking stimuli so that it is accompanied by a complete or partial suppression of the anxiety responses, the bond between these stimuli and the anxiety responses will be weakened.[69]

Three Steps in Behavior Therapy

Wolpe has discussed three steps in the process of behavior therapy. The *first* involves a careful study and clarification of the stimulus conditions that presumably acted as antecedents to the clinical picture.[70] Therapists must learn about the client's earlier experience not because they want to fill in the outlines of a personality theory, but because they have to know as clearly as possible the nature of the abnormal pattern, the kinds of stimuli that bring it about, and the circumstances under which it seems to vary. In a real sense, the therapist conducts a stimulus-response analysis of the client's behavior from the outset of their contact.[71] Wolpe typically uses a detailed interview at this point, including questions about parents, siblings, school performance, and developing sexual adjustment. Each of these areas has been shown to be relevant to the development of anxiety in neurotic patients. Of course, the presenting problem will usually dictate the direction this background history (anamnesis) will take.

It is essential to be accurate about what stimuli have been at work in the production of a neurosis, because the approach to take in curing the client will depend on what this turns up. For example, one of Wolpe's female clients complained of a powerful urge to flee a feeling of being closed in when engaged in conversation with others. On first blush this seemed to be some form of claustrophobic response to social situations, but upon more detailed questioning, Wolpe found that this woman felt trapped in an unhappy marriage.[72] This added information put a new interpretation on the case and dictated alternative therapeutic tactics. To assist his diagnostic efforts, Wolpe made use of various paper-and-pencil scales which provide information about typical neurotic symptoms, the kinds of situations that may cause a person to feel anxious, and the general level of self-sufficiency the individual habitually feels.[73] Another unusual way in which Wolpe assessed the emotional level of his clients was to teach them to use units of measurement he called a *sud,* which stands for a *"subjective unit of disturbance."* [74] This involved a 100-point scale, with the top score (100 suds) being the "worst" fear or anxiety imaginable and the lowest score (zero suds) representing "absolute calm." By using this measure routinely, the therapist in time can simply ask his client, "How many suds would you say are involved in that scary situation?" and the client responds with immediate clarity, "Oh, about 50." The client also usually gives spontaneous sud estimates of reactions as therapy proceeds.

The *second step* of therapy concerns the proper preparation of the client. People are likely to begin blaming themselves or others for the maladjustment from which they suffer. Some clients are fearful of being crazy. Wolpe insisted that the proper attitude for a behavior therapist is to be objective and nonjudgmental.[75] Since behavior is determined by circumstances in the neural and external environment, little is gained by trying to find the more obscure objects of blame for a behavioral problem. Of course, if someone in the *present* life circumstances is frustrating the client or in other ways involved in his or her neurosis, then action will have to be taken to change the nature of the relationship. But the more removed, dynamic case studies so typical of psychoanalysis are unnecessary in order to bring about a cure. It was not unusual for Wolpe to provide his clients with a brief discussion of the nature of reinforcement, using as an example the

burnt-child phenomenon.[76] A child who is burned while touching a big, black, hot stove will later generalize the fear of such stoves to the black bureau in the bedroom, and so forth. The point of this structuring is to teach the client that anxiety reactions are automatic and—whatever their cause—capable of being corrected by proper conditioning procedures. Wolpe might even tell his client something about the experimental studies on which his techniques were founded.[77]

Despite this preparation, some clients need to be told directly in clear-cut language that (1) they are *not* insane; (2) their neurotic responses are not all that unusual, and the therapist understands them quite well; and (3) there is no point in forcing themselves to face their fears because these concerns have nothing whatever to do with character building. Neurotic symptoms are forms of "penance unrewarded by blessings." [78] Wolpe did not believe that therapeutic benefits derive from the so-called *relationship* ties of client and psychotherapist. He was once treating a client and had to leave town for a time. A substitute therapist was arranged, and therapy proceeded quite satisfactorily during his absence.[79] If *transference* were an essential part of the curative process, this kind of interruption would have been harmful to continued progress. There is no denying that a relationship may form with the client along the lines of conventional psychotherapy. The point Wolpe was making is that the behavior therapist does not seek to make such ties more than, let us say, the usual doctor of internal medicine does. Whatever benefit accrues to therapy as a result of the client's faith in or affection for the therapist is taken as just so much additional benefit.[80] Wolpe would explain relationship benefits as being due to reciprocal inhibition in any case.

The *third* and final step of therapy is to design the proper strategy to counteract the neurotic pattern and then put this program of change into effect. We shall take up three therapeutic techniques used by Wolpe.

Assertive Training

Some clients need instruction in how to express their natural and appropriate feelings in the life situation. Wolpe referred to this as *assertive* behavior, which he defined as *"the proper expression of any emotion other than anxiety towards another person."* [81] Indeed, when we are feeling one emotion, such as anger, this can reciprocally inhibit another emotion, such as anxiety. Wolpe cited recent research evidence suggesting that there are separate and reciprocally inhibitory centers for aggression and anxiety in the midbrain of animals.[82] But assertive training includes the expression of friendliness and affection as well as irritation and hostility.[83] Certain people are brought up to consider themselves fair game to the intrusions of others. They overemphasize social niceties, so that when someone pushes in ahead of them in a line, though they sense hostility as we all do, they would never think of complaining. The woman who expressed an unhappy marriage through claustrophobic feelings of being closed in is a case in point. Wolpe found that he had to deal with her problems through assertive training. He had to reassure her that she could make just demands on her husband, and after the specifics of the case had been worked out in the interview, he made recommendations about what she might say or do in certain situations relating to her husband.

A useful technique here is that of *behavioral rehearsal,* by which Wolpe meant a kind of role-play situation in which he would take the identity of some person who had been giving the client difficulty through some form of interpersonal behavior.[84] For example, if a woman found herself going into a depression right after breakfast each morn-

ing and Wolpe decided that this was due to the husband's behavior during the meal, he might set up a behavior rehearsal scene. He would take the part of the husband and teach her how to be more assertive with her mate. It might be difficult for her to say something like "Well, for goodness sake, *must* you constantly grumble about every little item in the newspaper? I find this very annoying, morning after morning." The truth would be that she has been finding this emotionally upsetting, but has been unable to express her honest reactions. Wolpe would take this woman through a detailed study of her approach to the husband, rehearsing her repeatedly until she had a definite strategy which is then carried out in vivo. There is an important rule to follow in using assertive training. The therapist should *"never instigate an assertive act that is likely to have seriously punishing consequences for the patient."* [85]

Considered more broadly, assertive training can be thought of as the learning of interpersonal *lifesmanship tactics.*[86] Morris, an easygoing bookkeeper of twenty-six years, comes to behavior therapy because he is increasingly unable to be himself with others who constantly victimize him or dominate him interpersonally. He is bullied by his boss and on the verge of losing his girlfriend because he is so tongue-tied in her presence. He is becoming desperate, but does not know what to do. As one aspect of therapy, Wolpe would instruct Morris in certain lifesmanship tactics. To handle his bullying boss, Morris would be taught to avoid eye contact and stare at the boss's forehead every time they have an encounter. People find this loss of eye contact annoying, and Morris would in this case begin making the encounter uncomfortable for the boss as well as for himself. This would give Morris more of a sense of being at least partially in control of the interpersonal situation. To increase his sense of control, Morris would be rehearsed in saying such things to the boss when they first meet in the morning as "Good morning, Mr. Dixon. Are you feeling all right? You look a little tired today." At other times throughout the day, he might vary this tactic by saying, "Mr. Dixon, is there anything wrong? You seem a little upset (pale, depressed) today. Is there anything I can do?" By focusing the tension in their contact on the boss, Morris ensures that he will be more defensive and tentative in the contact than previously.[87]

Wolpe is not trying to make his clients over into insincere, manipulative people. He wants them to use such tactics only in self-defense and with a sense of full responsibility for what they do. When we turn to Morris's relationship with his girlfriend, an alternative and more complimentary tactic is called for. He must be given practice in saying things like "You look tremendous tonight" or "Have I ever told you how much I think about you every day?" Since neither of these statements is insincere—Morris does indeed find his girl attractive and he constantly has her in mind—there is no real manipulation going on when these honest feelings are conveyed. Over the years, Wolpe developed lists of the most common hostile and complimentary statements that he had found it necessary to teach clients. On the hostile side, we note common assertive responses like: Please don't stand in front of me; you have kept me waiting for twenty minutes; do you mind turning down (up) the heat; your behavior disgusts me; I can't stand your nagging; how dare you speak to me like that. On the more complimentary side, he listed such remarks as: You look lovely; that was a clever remark; I like you; I love you; that was brilliantly worked out; what a radiant smile.

Systematic Desensitization

Wolpe found that he could remove fears from his clients' behavioral repertoires by systematically increasing their anxiety responses while at the same time inducing antagonistic relaxation responses.[88] The relaxation responses reciprocally inhibited the anxiety responses. To carry out this behavior therapy, we need to know the specific stimuli—social situations, actually—that evoke the anxiety. We learn this from the detailed interview and the personality scales the client has submitted to at the outset of therapy. In the case of free-floating anxiety where there has probably been a subtle form of anxiety snowballing over time, the specific stimuli may be hard to point out. But usually the client can differentiate between *some* situations that are more upsetting than others. He or she can use suds to help the therapist rank-order a series of life situations which are more or less frightening. Let us assume that Jean, a twenty-year-old college sophomore, has come to Wolpe for treatment concerning the extreme fear she feels in taking examinations. Jean becomes so anxious that she blanks out during exams and her grades suffer terribly as a result. After a detailed clinical interview and the administration of the paper-pencil scales, Wolpe finds that this anxiety pattern is not limited to school examinations but extends to all kinds of evaluative situations. For example, Jean is afraid to see doctors and dentists. She is gripped with uncomfortable tension when a policeman looks her way. She does not like to be asked directions by a stranger, and simply having people look at her is mildly upsetting. Without going into the detail that Wolpe would at this point, a complete picture of the anxiety reactions would be worked out and then rated as to sud units.

Wolpe now has the anxiety responses identified as a first step, but what response antagonistic to them shall he induce in Jean's behavior? Wolpe found the relaxation exercises of Jacobson's *Progressive Relaxation* (1938) very useful in this regard. Jacobson had demonstrated that autonomic responses like pulse rate and blood pressure could be lowered through what he called *deep muscle relaxation*. In adapting these exercises to therapy, Wolpe found that roughly six interviews of thirty to fifty minutes duration are required. Jean is told that in order to counteract her emotional anxiety, she must master a skill in muscle relaxation. Wolpe might begin muscle training by having Jean grip the arm of her chair with one hand while leaving the other relaxed. Can she sense the difference between the tense hand and the one that is relaxed? Good, then they can proceed to other muscles of the body in this fashion. How limp can she make her arms if she places both hands in her lap and simply relaxes for a few minutes? From here, they may go to the muscles of the shoulder and the neck, for these are particularly important indicators of tension level.[89] Tenseness in the facial and tongue muscles are usually easy to identify as reflecting level of anxiety. From here, they might go to the larger muscles of the back, abdomen, and thorax, and then end with a consideration of the feet and legs. Through careful study and some practice at home between sessions, Jean can acquire the skill of relaxing her deeper muscles quite readily.

In some instances, Wolpe might prepare a client for *hypnotism* at this point. Hypnosis is closely related to relaxation, of course. Wolpe's approach to hypnosis is strictly empirical; he uses it only when a subject seems especially prone to direction by suggestion and it has immediate benefit. Hyp-

nosis is not essential for systematic desensitization to work, though Wolpe uses it in about 10 percent of such cases.[90]

The next step would involve constructing an *anxiety* hierarchy, based on the data of the interview, the objective instruments, and the help of the client. "An anxiety hierarchy is a list of stimuli on a common theme ranked in descending order according to the amount of anxiety they evoke."[91] Anxiety hierarchies can be arrayed as relaxation training is being carried out. When all of the sources of anxiety have been identified, the therapist arranges a hierarchy according to some central theme. For Jean, Wolpe might construct one around the "taking of examinations," but he might also array one around the theme of "being examined by physicians or dentists" and even one of "being stared at by others."[92] Here is a hierarchy built around examination fears, based on one of Wolpe's actual cases:

(Greatest Sense of Anxiety)
1. On the way to the university on the day of an examination
2. In the process of answering an examination paper
3. Before the unopened doors of the examination room
4. Awaiting the distribution of examination papers
5. The examination paper lying face down before [client]
6. The night before an examination
7. One day before an examination
8. Two days before an examination
9. Three days before an examination
10. Four days before an examination

(Least Sense of Anxiety) [93]

Not all clients would array precisely the same hierarchy of from most-to-least anxiety reactions in the taking of examinations. Some might find the situation of having the examination paper lying face down before them more anxiety-provoking than—as in this case —feeling upset on the way to the university to take the examination. After Wolpe had constructed a hierarchy for Jean he would ask the young woman to begin relaxation exercises by imagining herself in the *least* frightening situation (four days before an examination) and to make use of the muscle-relaxation training to reciprocally inhibit this lowest level of anxiety. Jean would sit with her eyes closed, imagining it was four days before an important examination and going limp in complete relaxation at the same time. She would continue doing so until she could imagine herself in this circumstance *without* anxiety.

Feedback from the client is important in these fantasied or hypnotically induced states. If the client were under hypnosis, Wolpe would have him or her lift a finger when there was still anxiety in a situation. If the finger were not lifted, this would tell the therapist that the client was completely relaxed, and for this stimulus situation, anxiety had been successfully inhibited. In the case of imagined scenes, the client might use this finger technique as well, but Wolpe found that even when the client stated sud units aloud while under relaxation, the effectiveness of therapy remained. Hence, when Jean says "zero suds" while imagining herself four days before an examination, we know that she is perfectly calm at point 10 on the hierarchy. Wolpe would then move her up to the next anxiety level (three days before an examination) where the process would be repeated, and so forth, until gradually the most anxiety-provoking situation (on the way to the university on the day of an examination) could be imagined without anxiety.

The therapist must exercise clinical skill in the application of this technique. The scenes cannot be experienced for extended periods. The usual practice is to have the patient relax for a period of fifteen seconds or so before inducing the scene for five to ten seconds.[94] This brief enactment of a particular scene may be repeated several times. The more anxiety experienced by the client the shorter the scene presentation. Wolpe noted that prolonged exposure to highly anxiety-provoking scenes (as in a phobia) can lead to worsening of a symptom.[95] The number of scenes presented during a desensitization session also varies. In some cases only one or two exposures seems justified. In others, particularly in the advanced stages of therapy, as many as thirty to fifty presentations of five to seven seconds duration each may be employed. Some patients can be moved up from one scene to another in the same session. Others require concentration on one scene per session. A desensitization session ordinarily can be completed in from fifteen to thirty minutes, and the length of therapy varies from as few as six to possibly one hundred or more sessions. Wolpe once administered one hundred sessions to a client who suffered a severe death phobia.[96]

An interesting feature of this technique is that spacing of sessions does not seem to affect outcome. As a rule, clients are scheduled for two or three sessions per week, but even when sessions are massed on the same day (when for instance a client must travel long distances to therapy on a weekend) or carried on once monthly positive results can be noted. Wolpe has shown that the rate of symptom removal follows a clear deceleration pattern in curves of learning, regardless of the time factor.[97] Very little improvement occurs between sessions. Occasionally a client is so upset that it proves extremely difficult to achieve complete relaxation during the session. In such cases Wolpe has prescribed a sedating drug to be taken by the client one hour before the interview.[98] It is also possible to reduce free-floating anxiety by having clients inhale various mixtures of carbon-dioxide and oxygen.[99] The precise mechanisms of improvement here are unknown, but as a physician Wolpe will make use of anything that is helpful as long as it has a proven record in this regard.

Occasionally a client is not a good subject for hypnotism or cannot imagine situations well enough for the usual procedure. In such cases the therapist may have to plan an anxiety hierarchy which can be desensitized in vivo. For example, airplane phobias can be worked out by systematically taking an individual closer to the airport and then onto a plane which could be rented and simply taxied about for a time, and so forth. Gradually, increasing approximations to flight might be engaged in on the airstrip, until an actual take-off and immediate return to earth is accomplished. Lazarus (1961) has extended the desensitization tactic to group administration, working with several people who suffer in common from such afflictions as claustrophobia, agoraphobia, or sexual phobia. One highly ingenious tactic used by Wolpe involved an electrical (faradic) shocking device, much on the order of commercial shocking machines in amusement parks. Carnivals often have such an attraction, where individuals can test their mettle and see how much electroshock they can bear. Wolpe had his clients take such a shock to the most painful level they could stand. At the height of their pain, he had them say "calm" and then immediately shut off the shock machine. The word *calm* conditioned to the feeling of relief. Subsequently, when in a life situation that was anxiety provoking, the clients would find that by saying "calm" the conditioned relaxation that followed reciprocally inhibited the anxiety they were sensing.

Wolpe's technique revolutionized the practice of psychotherapy in the 1960s and thereafter. Extensions and variations of the systematic desensitization tactic were to flower after Wolpe's initial efforts. Though the principles of so-called *counterconditioning* had been known for years,[100] it was Wolpe's example that more than any other fostered the development of the noninsight or nondynamic psychotherapies of modern times.

Aversion Therapy

The final technique we will consider as an example of reciprocal inhibition is not specifically a Wolpean innovation, nor was it especially popularized by him alone. He rarely considered it the first-choice treatment in his own practice, except possibly in a case of drug addiction.[101] However, Wolpe has given considerable space to a discussion of this technique of *aversion therapy,* and hence we include it here. Aversion therapy or *avoidance counterconditioning* was probably first used in the control of alcoholism by Voegtlin and Lemere (1942). The treatment consisted of giving the alcoholic a nausea-producing drug, such as emetine, followed by consumption of a favored alcoholic beverage. Vomiting as a response to the emetine was thus conditioned to the taste of alcohol, and after ten sessions of this nature, it was not unusual for an individual to become severely nauseous at the smell or taste of alcohol alone. Recasting this general strategy, Wolpe viewed the process of aversion therapy as one in which an undesired response (drinking, gambling, food obsessions, and so on) is presented following the stimulus of a strong avoidance response (in the example cited, avoiding nausea). The avoidance response thus reciprocally inhibits the undesired response (avoiding nausea means avoiding drinking). The avoidant (aversive) stimulus Wolpe used in his work was electric shock.

Thus, Wolpe once successfully treated a woman with rheumatic heart disease who was obsessed by the thought of certain particularly harmful foods. From time to time she would lose control and go on eating sprees which threatened her physical health. The therapy tactic here involved making a list of all of the items of food that figured into her obsession. Electrodes were then attached to her forearms, and the woman was asked to close her eyes and to imagine each of these foods in turn, signaling with her hand when she achieved a good mental image. Ten faradic shocks of rather uncomfortable intensity were then administered per session for a total of five sessions. Following the second session Wolpe noted improvement and when therapy was terminated after five contacts, the results were complete and lasting.[102] In another instance, a compulsive gambler was treated by Barker and Miller (1968) while actually participating in his favored game of chance. A special "one-armed bandit" (slot machine) was equipped for the man in the hospital, and, as was his practice, he played this machine for a three-hour period. He withstood one hundred fifty shocks over this period of time through electrodes attached to his arms. The shocks were administered during all aspects of the gambling activity from the insertion of coin discs to receiving pay-offs. By the end of twelve hours this patient was sufficiently cured of his gambling to refrain for eighteen months. A relapse at that time was easily corrected by six hours of booster treatment.

One of the more ambitious applications of aversion therapy has been its use with homosexuals. Both emetic substances and electrical shocks have been used as the avoidant-producing stimuli.[103] Assuming that a therapist were to treat a male homosexual, the first step would be to assemble a number of pictures of men—including nudes—and to have the client array them as to preference value (though a specific hierarchy is probably not necessary in all cases). The therapist might then have the client take an emetic substance just before being presented with the slide projections of the men he had found sexually stimulating. An alternative method would be to shock him as he observed the picture. The therapist might have a device whereby the patient would press a button to keep the picture of a male on the screen for a certain length of time; the longer he would gaze at this sexual object the more severe would the shock become. In time, the sexual response stimulated by the masculine nudes would be reciprocally inhibited by the avoidant response to shock.

Clinical experience has shown that such avoidant techniques will not be successful unless the client is *also* exposed to the pleasant stimulation of heterosexual stimuli. Hence, we would have a session in which the client would be shown seductive pictures of females in varying stages of dress, including completely nude presentations. Sometimes a behavior therapist will increase the likelihood of pleasurable sexual stimulation in gazing at females by injecting his clients with ten milligrams of a male hormone (*testosteronum propionicum*).[104] As attraction to the female increases, the client will be urged to practice masturbation in relation to female pictures, elaborating as much as possible through fantasied imagery. This combined tactic of aversion with strong approach training is a good example of how flexible the behavior therapist must be if he or she is to help the client.

Those who criticize behavior therapists for supposedly indulging sadistically in shocking clients do not properly understand or accept the ground rules on which they operate. In every instance, their measure of success rests firmly on the proven well-being of their clients.

The Role of Reciprocal Inhibition in All Forms of Psychotherapy

We have not covered all the techniques Wolpe and his followers use, by any means.[105] Taken along with all of the other approaches to psychotherapy, the variety of behavior techniques that result in successful cures forces us to wonder what all of these methods of cure have in common? It seemed to Wolpe, as he mulled this question over, that reciprocal inhibition was more the common denominator than the variant gimmick some took it to be. What the so-called insight therapies have in common is that a private interview is conducted in which patients confidentially express their innermost emotional reactions to a skilled expert, who shows an interest in them and then proposes certain explanatory information. Hence, claimed Wolpe, "If, in a patient, the emotional response evoked by the interview situation is (a) antagonistic to anxiety and (b) of sufficient strength, supposedly it will reciprocally inhibit the anxiety responses that are almost certain to be evoked by some of the subject matter of the interview, and therapeutic effects will occur." [106]

This brings us back to the matter of transference. Although Wolpe dismissed this factor as central, he noted that certain patients having a strong positive emotion toward him occasionally began showing improvement even before the specific techniques of cure were settled on.[107] Such quick forms of transference cure could easily be seen as the direct results of reciprocal inhibition. Cures noted among clients placed on waiting lists may well stem from the fact that they now feel something is going to be done, and this renewed emotional confidence can serve to inhibit anxiety.[108] Indeed, reciprocal inhibition can explain cures—even those induced by drugs—to greater theoretical satisfaction than can alternative theories explain the cures of behavior therapy.[109] Rather than being superficial and secondary, behavior therapy may be said to change personality if by personality we mean the totality of a person's habits.[110] Symptom substitution is rarely the result, and then only when improper consideration has been given to specific autonomic responses.[111] Hence, Wolpe leaves us with a confidently expressed challenge to consider the likelihood that reciprocal inhibition is an overriding principle of explanation in the cure of *all* neuroses.

The Technique of Implosive Therapy: Thomas G. Stampfl

Biographical Overview

Thomas G. Stampfl was born in Cleveland, Ohio, on 28 December 1923. He is of German-Austrian lineage, both of his parents having immigrated to the United States from Austria. Stampfl's father was a printer by trade, a strict disciplinarian but a devoted father. His mother was the warmer parent, very supportive of her children and a hard worker. The family religion was Roman Catholic, and Stampfl has maintained an association with the more liberal, progressive wing of this faith. Stampfl was the tenth child, with eight sisters and a brother preceding him; one sister died in infancy. The

Thomas G. Stampfl

brother was ten years his senior, an outstanding athlete whom Stampfl found himself trying to compete with despite the disparity in age.

As the youngest child Stampfl was the center of family attention. His youth spanned the Great Depression years of the 1930s, but fortunately his father's trade was in demand and the family remained economically self-sufficient. Stampfl rebelled against his father's authoritarian ways, causing some friction in the home, but no actual physical punishment resulted. He took up the hobby of magic and sleight-of-hand as a boy; he also

became a superior gymnast during high school years. But his main interests were intellectual pursuits.

The impact of the Depression years contributed to Stampfl's decision while in high school to become a printer, but events were to alter his life greatly. He graduated from high school in 1942 during the period of World War II. In March of 1943 he volunteered for the U.S. Army paratroopers, eventually earning the rank of staff sergeant in the 82nd Airborne Division. Stampfl was wounded in the Battle of the Bulge and hospitalized for three months in England before returning to America where he was eventually discharged.

With the help of the GI Bill (government-supported higher education) Stampfl was able to think seriously of a career in psychology, an interest that had slowly developed during his maturing years. He attended John Carroll University in Cleveland, receiving his B.A. in 1949, and then subsequently earning his M.A. (1953) and Ph.D. (1958) degrees at Loyola University in Chicago. While in Chicago Stampfl also took courses in Rogerian client-centered counseling (see Chapter 9). He was particularly inspired and helped by Elaine Dorfman and Eugene T. Gendlin. In the meantime, he had developed great interest in the learning theory of Clark L. Hull (see p. 382) and had also worked for a year in psychoanalysis, with special emphasis on Fenichel. His major clinical professor, Frank J. Kobler, convinced Stampfl of the necessity of basing clinical work on laboratory investigation. Later, he found intellectual stimulation in the two-factor theory of O. H. Mowrer and the general outlook on abnormality represented by the work of Maslow and Mittlemann (1951). His highly varied educational background therefore combined both the classroom and the consulting room in a uniquely integrative fashion.

From 1952 to 1954 Stampfl held the position of director of the Newman School for Severely Mentally Retarded Children (Chicago). It was there that he began to note how important the expression of emotion was to a child's personal adjustment. Over the years, working with various neurotic and psychotic children in play therapy, Stampfl found that children seemed to whip up emotion in their play. This often took on gruesome prospects, like boiling a parent in vats of acid, sending siblings off to burn in hell, and so forth. Therapeutic results were more likely to take place when such emotional displays were generated by the child than when they were not in evidence. Stampfl was fully aware of Freud's early abreactive techniques (see Chapter 1). He believed that the early

psychoanalytical efforts of the Breuer period were probably closer to what therapy really amounted to than were those of the later couch period—which became too involved with the more debatable question of insight concerning a specific theory of illness and cure.

Stampfl had married in 1950 shortly after beginning graduate school, and as he worked his way through the graduate years, he decided to return to his home town of Cleveland, where he accepted a position as chief psychologist in a Catholic child guidance clinic. He also began an association with John Carroll University as instructor, and over the next dozen years or so was to increase his clinical skills, take the Ph.D. degree, and formulate the essentials of what he would call *implosive therapy*. He fathered two children and eventually relocated in Milwaukee, Wisconsin, where he became professor of psychology and director of clinical psychology training at the University of Wisconsin (Milwaukee). During the 1960–1966 period he was in private practice as a psychotherapist.

As he perfected his therapeutic approach, Stampfl felt increasingly that he needed more empirical justification for its effectiveness. Partly because of this need Stampfl returned to academia on a full-time basis to take up further study of *avoidance conditioning,* with rats as his subjects of study. Stampfl has never denied the possibility that a dynamic in the client's history may trigger a symptom picture of neurosis; however, the strictly therapeutic principles on which his therapy rests do *not* require that the client obtain insight into these factors before a cure is achieved. Hence, Stampfl's belief is that the best source of evidence for implosive therapy is in experimentation on lower animals. Stampfl is toughminded on the question of research, though his broader outlook is flexible and open to alternative explanations of the neurotic process. One senses the honest effort to keep all sides of psychology open in his writings. The scientific base is clearly the laboratory, but the clinical setting has much to reveal as well.

Theoretical Considerations

Learning Theory and the Principle of Experimental Extinction

The principle of learning Stampfl used to explain his therapeutic effectiveness is *experimental extinction*. Though all behavioral therapists make use of this construct to some extent, Stampfl raised it to its highest level, building on the earlier work of O. H. Mowrer. Mowrer was one of Hull's students, and he more than anyone developed the theory that *reduction in anxiety* could serve as a reinforcement.[112] As the presentations of Chapters 6 and 7 have demonstrated, this concept has been of supreme value to the explanations of symptom formation. Mowrer's theory of neurosis and cure is well worth study in its own right.[113] Space allows consideration of only one small aspect of Mowrer's work relevant to Stampfl's, a classic paper entitled "Learning Theory and the Neurotic Paradox" (1948), in which he demonstrated his considerable ability to parallel animal study with human behavior in an instructive fashion.

Mowrer drew an analogy between various types of rat experiments and the form of vicious circle in which neurotics find themselves daily. One such experiment went as follows: picture a long runway type of cage in which there are three separate areas of floor space. Referring to the floor of the cage in left-to-right spatial terms we might speak of area A, area B, and area C. Additional features of the cage include electrical grids set into the floor of areas A and B so that a shock can be given to any rat in these areas of the runway. Area C, on the other hand, lacks a grid and thus can always be considered a haven area if the experimenter turns on the electricity over the floor areas A and B.

The experiment Mowrer designed involved placing a rat on the floor area A, and then after a brief period of time (during which the rat sniffed about the runway walls and so forth) electrifying the grids over areas A and B. The rat naturally responded with excited (anxious) moving about in an effort to remove the painful stimulation of the electrical shock. In dashing about, rats (several animals were put through the apparatus) quickly learned to find area C where relief from pain was forthcoming. The reduction in pain presumably acted as a *primary* reinforcement to the learning of the sequential responses "run from A to C by way of B." Additionally, reasoned Mowrer, there were surely *secondary* reinforcements which could have contributed to this learning sequence. Upon reaching the C area, there was probably a reduction in pain (primary reinforcement) but *also* a reduction in anxiety or fear (secondary reinforcement). If this was true, then possibly a rat would continue running "from A through B to C" in order to reduce anxiety even after the grid on the floor of area A had been turned off.

Mowrer tested this hypothesis, and sure enough, he found that his rats continued to run out of area A without shock, over area B with shock, and into area C which also lacked a shock. In other words, thanks to anxiety drive-reduction (secondary reinforcement) the rats were *bringing about their own shocks!* This paradoxical outcome was, said Mowrer, analogous to the behavior of neurotics who constantly keep symptoms alive through the recurring anxiety they create for themselves. Mowrer found that he could eliminate this self-punishing behavior only when he placed a block between the B and C areas in the second phase of the study. When blocked from proceeding to area C and hence forced to dash back to A, the rat rapidly discontinued its self-punishing behavior—usually on one trial. Why did this happen?—presumably because the response of running to anxiety *extinguished,* thanks to the barrier that forced a more realistic learning to proceed.

It was out of researches like these that Mowrer fashioned his *two-factor theory of learning.* He proposed that some forms of learning can be considered *problem-solving* activities, mediated by the central nervous system and tied to the skeletal musculature of the body making responses in this domain under what we usually call voluntary or conscious control. An alternative form of learning, however, is *conditioning.* In this instance, the responses are tied to the smooth musculature and visceral tissues of the autonomic nervous system. Conditioned responses are thus *not* under voluntary control. Fear or anxiety reactions, depressions, the pain of guilt or the delight of love—all such emotional reactions on which a lie detector (polygraph) relies to catch us up in spite of our voluntary efforts to deceive can be considered conditioned responses (literally, *conditionable* because they are part of our innate equipment). In Mowrer's study, the reason neurotic behavior is self-defeating or stupid (re Dollard and Miller, p. 412) is because it is mediated by the conditioned responses of the autonomic nervous system. Problem-solving behavior is called for but cannot take place until the autonomic responses are first extinguished in some fashion. Once we have removed the grip of the latter on our behavior, we can

expect the former to find a more suitable level of adjustment.

Theory of Illness and Cure

Stampfl then put together the two-factor theory of Mowrer with his observations of children in play therapy, whose behavior mounts to a frenzy at times and then seems to improve dramatically. He recalled the early successes of Freud and Breuer with the abreactive technique (see p. 43). An old truism among practicing clinicians holds that a therapy session has not gone well unless the client has actually invested some overt emotion in the hour. It makes no difference whether the emotion is love, fear, or anger, just so there is an investment of feeling. Taking this conviction further, Stampfl wondered: could the affective factors mediated by the autonomic nervous system run their course and eventually extinguish in emotionally provoking circumstances that do *not* lead to punishment? What if, instead of trying to calm the client, we were to encourage an expression of the pent-up feelings he or she is too terrified to feel?

An *implosion* is a bursting inwards, in contrast to the outward bursting of an explosion. Hence, implosive therapy implies that emotive reactions are erupting, but their expression is internal to the individual's fantasy life, that is, within his or her imagination. Emotion is displayed, but action is totally through imagery and talk about what is being imagined. In other words, *primary* reinforcements or punishments do not follow re-enactment of emotionally arousing scenes just as they did not follow Anna O.'s abreactive states (see p. 42). It is not unlike the play of children noted above. The child boils a parent in oil or thinks personally of being boiled "with a shudder" but nothing really happens. No one blames the child for killing off a parent; he or she is not really being burned to death in a vat of bubbling oil. When he defined his approach, Stampfl placed emphasis on its unifying potential for bringing clinic and laboratory together. "Implosive therapy (IT) is an approach which incorporates formulations inherent to dynamic systems of treatment retranslated and reapplied in terms of learning principles; dynamically oriented clinicians need not relinquish their fundamental conceptions of the human situation to use it." [114]

The core theory of illness on which *implosive therapy* rests is as follows: for any of a number of reasons—including all of the typically Freudian explanations—the individual has been emotionally conditioned (via autonomic nervous system) to some stimulus-pattern in his or her environment (like a social situation, life circumstance, and so on). Whenever this stimulus comes into view—through imagination, a dream, or actual experience—the person is gripped with a sense of mounting anxiety (fear). As this level of anxiety increases, it acts as an additional signal of the horrible things that might happen. Stampfl agreed with Freud's final formulation of anxiety in this sense, that it is a warning signal of a situation of danger (see p. 90). Rather than permitting the anxiety state to reach complete expression, the individual has learned to do something that will lower the level of anxiety before it has a chance to take over his or her complete state of awareness. This something is what we know as either a host of defense mechanisms or the *symptoms* of a neurosis. [115] Such behaviors are aimed at avoiding the impending doom the autonomic responses suggest are about to take place ("I just know something

terrible is going to happen to me"). Probably the most common defense mechanism is what Freud had called *repression*. [116] Neurotics have learned to forget what raises their anxiety level, and when this forgetting results in lowered anxiety, they find themselves in a state of continuing ignorance, much along the lines of Dollard and Miller's *stupidity*.

Symptoms, on the other hand, are simply the more dramatic and personally harmful extensions of this mechanism for reducing anxiety. Technically we would call them *conditioned avoidance responses*. [117] The person with a phobia sees the feared object—be it a high place, a closed-in space, a snake, or speck of dirt—and he or she is gripped with anxiety until a distance is put between the self and the feared stimulus. Or if this stimulus-pattern has come to mind, the person must get it out of mind by doing something to remove its upsetting influence. Compulsive neurotics must wash their hands to counteract their horror of dirt. Obsessives must hum a lucky tune or repeat some magic formula which seems to calm them for a time. Hysterical body tics and even paranoid delusions can all be learned methods of reducing such anxiety promptings. An interesting feature of Stampflian theory holds that the symptom may have symbolic ties to the origin of the neurosis. When the stimulus arises and a symptom reaction occurs, a host of unknown or forgotten (repressed) thoughts, memories, and images are *redintegrated*. [118] To redintegrate is to reopen or re-enliven past cues of an anxiety-provoking nature. This is the reason anxiety seems to snowball when the neurotic is placed in a threatening situation. The claustrophobic is responding not only to the present cues but to other long-forgotten cues as well. Tina is claustrophobic, and when she begins to suffer anxiety in riding an elevator, her mounting fears are not only to the four walls of the elevator but *also* to the fact that these symbolize the four sides of her baby crib, in which she was often placed and emotionally neglected as an infant.

This teaches us something about neurotic symptoms. The reason they are retained in a behavioral repertoire is because they effectively offset the return to mind of a number of other even more painful stimuli. Tina flees the elevator stimulus-pattern with its four walls pressing in on her long before she begins to recall the more dynamic memories of a fear that she is being abandoned by her loved ones and buried alive in the blankets of her crib (symbolically equated now with a coffin). Hence, the level of anxiety experienced by an individual in any given situation is a rough measure of the *relevance* of this situation to his or her neurosis. Relevant situations redintegrate more anxiety than irrelevant situations. This is why Stampfl felt that "the symptom usually tells us what the patient is avoiding."[119] If we press neurotics to face up to the signals contained in their area of symptom formation and block their attempts to flee, in time a series of meaningful cues will emerge to tell us more and more about what has provoked their neuroses in the first place. It is thus possible to distinguish between two types of cues in neurosis: first, the *symptom-contingent cues,* which might be something as simple as the sight of a tall building; and second, the *hypothesized conditioned aversive cues,* which relate to what we have been calling the symbolic or dynamic meaning tied to the neurosis. The former essentially redintegrate the latter.[120]

The fascinating dynamcis of symptom formation and redintegration can be demonstrated by reviewing one of Stampfl's earliest cases, concerning a young man—let us call him Daryl—who suffered from a compulsion to make certain his radio was turned off before going to sleep at night.[121] Daryl came to Stampfl, complaining that he found it necessary to check this fact as many as fifty times

per night before he could doze off. Pulling out the electric plug did not help, and the symptom seemed to be getting worse. When asked what he felt might happen if the radio were left on, Daryl replied that he experienced a subjective feeling that something terrible or catastrophic would happen—possibly a fire which would consume him in flames. Rather than reassure him or teach him to relax while close to radios, Stampfl instructed Daryl to go to bed that night imagining that the radio was actually on or to turn it on so that he was certain it was alive with electricity. Then Daryl was to lie in bed and imagine that a spark from the radio produced a tiny flame which would get bigger and bigger until the room was filled with snapping, popping flames several feet tall, which would burn his bed and body to a cinder in a horribly painful manner! Stampfl encouraged Daryl to imagine this entire scene as vividly as possible and to experience fully the anxiety it provoked.

In the next therapy session Daryl reported that he had followed Stampfl's instructions, and though the image of the fire and his burning body was terrifying, he had found great relief from his compulsion immediately following the imaginary exercise. He was able to fall asleep without the recurring round of radio checks. Further, he told of an interesting thing that happened during the height of the imagined fire. He "heard" his father's voice calling to him over the roar of the flames. He had not mentioned his father up to this time, and Stampfl was to learn on further questioning that Daryl's father had been a stickler for security measures in the home. Such things as lights left on, dripping faucets, or running electrical appliances sent the father into a rage which almost always ended in a spanking for Daryl or one of his siblings. At the very least, the father would devote much time lecturing his children on the potentially dangerous consequences of such carelessness around the home.

Though Stampfl did not feel that insight into such factors was essential for a cure, he did accept the likelihood that a Freudian or Adlerian analysis of this family structure could well account for his client's symptom. Daryl may have sensed a death wish on the part of his father; the father wanted his son dead but expressed it through an obsessive preoccupation with safety measures (reaction-formation). Even if this were the dynamic cause of the case, the practical factor that kept the symptom active today was the fact that by checking his radio, Daryl could gain a sense of protective relief from mounting anxiety ("I will not die"). This reduction in anxiety sustained the abnormal pattern and *also* prevented a redintegration of the broader clinical dynamics (father hostility, rejection, the need to defend the self, the need to make the father guilty for his hostility by killing oneself in a fire, and so on).

By encouraging Daryl to experience his anxiety when no punishment resulted—a fire did not start—Stampfl found that the autonomic reactions quickly extinguished. After a few such practiced self-destructions, Daryl lost his radio compulsion completely. There was no warning sign to begin the compulsion at bedtime because permitting anxiety full expression interrupted the triggering mechanism. We are reminded here of Mowrer's closing of the passageway between the B and C areas in the second phase of his study. Area A no longer heralded shock to the rats, once they were forced to fall back on problem solving. This mechanism is what Stampfl now emphasized in his *theory of cure.* "The fundamental hypothesis is that a sufficient condition for the extinction of anx-

iety is to re-present, reinstate, or symbolically reproduce the stimuli (cues) to which the anxiety response has been conditioned, in the absence of primary reinforcement." [122] *Extinction* follows, and the symptom is removed since it no longer has any role to play. Though insight into a symptom's origin is satisfying to clients like Daryl, it is not essential to the cure.[123] Stampfl realized that a certain amount of insight probably always occurs during behavior therapy. If Daryl hears his father's voice calling to him, regardless of what Stampfl may be doing in the way of behavior modification, this young man will doubtless be prompted to do a certain amount of soul-searching concerning his relations with the father.[124] This is bound to result in what is called insight of a sort, but whatever is learned here is completely separate from the learning principles that actually account for the removal of the symptom.

The Steps of Implosive Therapy

Out of his early successes of the sort described above and considerable experience with various types of clients, Stampfl worked out a procedure of therapy consisting of seven steps.[125] These are not to be followed mechanically, and deviations or additions are allowed according to client needs. But the steps do provide a framework for our understanding.

1. *Symptom Study.* The first step in therapy is to make a careful study of the symptoms. We must identify as many of the symptom-contingent cues as we can. What things frighten the client? When is he or she likely to feel most anxious? What sorts of things relieve this symptom? We are likely to learn that the client's symptom has been working for some time, and that only recently has a symptom failure led to the redintegration of conditioned-

aversive cues.[126] The collapse of this older defense system and the resultant development of a broader symptom picture is what usually brings the client in to see a therapist. Things are getting worse.

Stampfl did not believe that a therapist is limited to what the client reports about the nature of the symptom. Though the therapist focuses on symptom removal, he or she can make appropriate guesses about what is involved in the neurosis.[127] Even though the therapist is not interested in interpreting client behavior to provide insight, a hunch or two borrowed from the classical psychoanalysts might come in handy during the implosive process. For example, if an excessively prudish woman comes in with a hand-washing compulsion, the therapist might actively speculate about why this symptom arose in the first place. If clinical interviews in the early days of therapy suggest that this woman has had a sexual-adjustment problem in living, the therapist may suspect that her current concern about cleanliness may date back to a time when she manipulated her own genitals and felt the guilt of sin intermingled with the physical thrill of sexuality. She might even have been thinking of her father as sex object at the time. The therapist notes that each time they touch on the topic of sex, and especially masturbation, in the interview, this woman (she may be married or unmarried) becomes very uneasy. The therapist records this as one of the areas in which anxiety will have to be provoked, because the very fact that the topic increases anxiety is prima facie evidence that the area of sex is tied to the area of being clean.

2. *Training in Neutral Imagery.* Since imagined scenes will be crucial to therapy, it is desirable to spend some time training a client to frame images in his or her mind. Stampfl viewed images as hypothetical constructs which the therapist presumes the client is actually seeing and experiencing personally; that is, we cannot as observers directly see such psychological processes ourselves.[128] It is possible, of course, to check on the client's imagery through questioning, and one can also measure emotional changes by attaching galvanic-skin-response, heart-rate, and breathing-rate devices to a client. These instruments can prove empirically that an autonomic response is taking place consistent with the reported imagery. In fact, experiments have established this relationship between imagination and emotional display many times.

At this point a therapist is teaching the client to imagine pleasant or neutral stimulus situations, making sure that a good picture of events is attained mentally. Not everyone is skilled at imagining situations, and some people cannot be treated in this fashion at all. But for the majority of cases, having clients imagine scenes from their home town or the faces of friends and associates in their present or past life is enough to develop imagination skills. This procedure may take only a portion of one session or it may require several sessions to prepare the client for visual, sensory (touch), and even auditory imagination. It is not unusual for implosive therapy to begin with actual deconditioning procedures after two clinical interviews, a portion of one having been devoted to imagery preparation.[129]

3. *Introduction of the Avoidance Serial Cue Hierarchy* (ASCH). At this point, the therapist may arrange a hierarchy of avoidance images in ranked or serial order, based on the study of symptoms in the

clinical interview (Step 1). The technical term for this ordering is the *avoidance serial cue hierarchy* (ASCH). It consists of various scenes or possible outcomes in life which the client greatly fears might take place (such as the fire and self-destruction in Daryl's case, above). When the therapist completes the ASCH, it runs serially from the least to the most anxiety-provoking set of circumstances in the client's life.[130] The client need not be told about the particular steps of this hierarchy, since some highly upsetting scenes may be readied for presentation at its apex. For example, in the case of the woman with the hand-washing compulsion, a therapist might begin at a very low level of anxiety, introducing scenes of witnessing dirt, then muck and mire; gradually, the greater anxiety-provoking scene of putting her hands into the filth might be called out. Then she might picture her hands festering with sores from germs caused by the filth—possibly including gore—when implosion would be induced. At the very highest levels would be scenes of actual masturbation with horrified discovery by loved ones or neighbors, possibly including sinful denunciation by ministers or even supernatural figures (Judgment Day). At this point in therapy, the scenes are merely arrayed by the therapist for future reference. It is also possible that a scene will be suggested by subsequent events—as in the client's spontaneous reactions—while actual implosion is underway.

4. *Scene Presentation.* The next step involves taking a client up the hierarchy of aversive cues framed by the ASCH, trying as realistically as possible to make them come alive in the client's imagination. The main point the client must grasp is that in order to extinguish an emotion like anxiety, he or she must first experience it to the full extent. Hence, as the implosive therapist begins verbally to describe the least anxiety-provoking scene, the client is encouraged to live it fully and "to experience as much anxiety as possible."[131] Focusing on the anxiety sensations per se is important, because at least part of the reason anxiety snowballs is that each succeeding wave of anxiety acts as a mounting secondary cue to further the extent of emotion being felt. As a client comes to problem solve by understanding clearly what the anxiety sensation feels like, more personal control over the emotion is made possible as therapy proceeds. If a slight reduction occurs following the first (least upsetting) scene presentation, the client then knows it and will be less prone to fall back into the vicious-circle direction of anxiety feeding on itself. In other words, there is an assumption that as clients ascend the ASCH, a *generalization of extinction* is taking place from the least to the most anxiety-provoking situations. The fact that not *only* symptom-contingent cues are used in the ASCH is made plain in the following quote, which also adds some insight into what constitutes the most frightening scenes:

The cues found most anxiety eliciting usually center about the expression of hostility and aggression directed toward parental figures, retaliation for aggressive acts by the patient with cues depicting various degrees of bodily injury, and those related to experiences of rejection, deprivation, abandonment, helplessness, guilt, shame, and sex. Oedipal, anal, oral, sibling-rivalry, primal scene, and death-wish impulse themes are worked into the hypothesized ASCH, along with the introduction of "acceptance of conscience" cues and other areas somewhat neglected by psychodynamically oriented therapies.[132]

By *acceptance-of-conscience cues,* Stampfl refers to the nagging sense of sinfulness people feel for behaviors in which they have indulged. (Mowrer also develops this in his integrity-therapy approach, 1961.) Rather than reassure these guilt-laden patients and teach them that they are wrongfully upset about such superego problems, Stampfl places them squarely in the guilt-provoking situation and calls out the anxiety. Assume that Aimee, a devoutly religious person of middle age, has developed a neurotic agitation with overtones of depression because of some imagined wrongs she has done to members of her family. Her brothers and sisters claim that Aimee has not really wronged them, but she has managed over the years to magnify some minor indiscretions in the past and is now very guilty and obsessively anxious about what this will mean to her salvation. With proper preparation (Steps 1 through 3), Stampfl would trade on the guilty reactions and fears of humiliation that Aimee has brought on herself. He might, for example, place Aimee in a courtroom scene where she is brought to trial for these sins in the presence of all of her relatives, as well as a host of other important people in her life.[133] Her evilness would be fully documented (based on her own claims in the clinical interviews of Step 1). The court might then find Aimee guilty and punish her in some way, such as hanging, electrocution, or to carry the religious theme further, burning at the stake! But Stampfl would not necessarily stop at the point of death. He might choose to take Aimee further into an afterlife, when she comes under the judgment of God who, again following a confession and delineation of her sinful ways, casts her into hell. And Stampfl would marvelously detail the wretchedly horrible experience of an eternity in hell. By this time, Aimee would have been carried to the apex scenes of her personalized ASCH.

5. *Scene Repetition to Anxiety Reduction.* The role of therapist in this implosive process is to describe the scenes in as complete and realistic detail as possible. The naive observer might think that the therapist is simply trying to "scare the devil" out of the client—by any means. But this would be a great misperception since the point of the therapy is to deal with *relevant* scenes. The therapist has no desire to punish the client, only to help *extinguish the cues* that are clearly related (symptom contingent) and those that are peripherally related (conditioned aversive) to the vicious circle of neurosis.[134] If clients were being punished or lastingly upset by the procedure, they would not return. Actually, the relief obtained from the first few sessions is noticeably helpful to clients, so they continue the treatment as they continue painful dental or medical treatments.[135]

Scenes can be presented and elaborated for ten minutes or longer. The autonomic responsiveness (perspiration, breathing rate, and so on) dictates the success a particular scene is having in arousing anxiety, and each scene is presented until anxiety reduction is achieved. Let us consider another case, that of Max, a thirty-year-old insurance salesman who suffers from acrophobia (fear of high places). Max could be started in a course of implosive therapy by having him simply imagine that he is looking at a high building off in the distance. The therapist would emphasize the height of the building until Max visualizes it clearly and his tenseness and rising perspiration indicate that it is having the usual effect on him. Next, Max would be encouraged to walk toward the building, closer and closer, and then enter, ascend the stairs, higher and higher, until he comes to the very roof. Each scene along the way would be detailed to give him the greatest sense of realism, which in turn would be accompanied by a progressively rising sense of anxiety, to the point of terror. To encourage these emotional responses, our implosive therapist might say something like the following: "You feel that ripple of fright down your arms as you climb the stairs. It is getting harder to breathe as you go up, and your heart is beating so rapidly you think it will explode. You feel that wrenching in the pit of your stomach and the spit turns sour in your mouth as you are about to vomit. You stop, covered with perspiration, feeling dizzy. You grab for the banister, sure you are going to faint and tumble down the stairwell. Now you do vomit, and as you see the mucus and stomach contents spilling down the stairwell, you picture yourself falling, falling, down to the marble floor over twenty stories below. Your foot slips and dangles dangerously over the edge of the stairwell. You counterbalance and feel yourself pitching head-forward over the banister. You try to hold on, but your hands are slipping." And so it goes, an upsetting prospect to consider —even in imagination—for anyone, and for the acrophobic Max, it is sheer misery.

6. *Elaboration of the Symptom-Contingent Cues to Hypothesized Conditioned-Aversive Cues.* It is at about this point that psychodynamic material, or simply extravagant and unreal scenes, may be introduced. This is when Aimee was taken after death

to confront her Maker. Max might be taken up onto the roof of the high building, led to the edge, dropped over it, and after a horrid drop of over twenty stories, squashed on the pavement below in as gory a scene of bone-crunching, blood-spurting reality as the therapist can muster. Great attention must be paid to details in this description, since the client should experience emotion to its fullest *without* primary negative reinforcements (punishment) taking place.

7. *Training the Client in Therapeutic Self-Management.* A unique feature of implosive therapy is the practice of having the client work through the scenes of his or her ASCH at home between sessions with the therapist. This form of homework speeds up the process of extinction. A similar technique had been used by the existential therapist, Viktor Frankl (1960), who called it *paradoxical intention.* Thus, paradoxically, rather than intending to avoid having some symptom—such as an anxiety attack—the neurotic intends that it come about at predetermined times throughout the day (for example, 1 P.M., 3 P.M., and so on). In time, this psychological control over the symptom permits the neurotic to willfully decide *not* to have the symptom. This explanation is non-behavioristic, of course (see Chapter 10 for existentialistic theories). It is common today to refer to all techniques relying on the expression of emotion to achieve a cure as *flooding* therapy. The client's awareness is flooded with emotional release rather than systematically calmed as in the Wolpean tactic. As is true of all behavior-modification techniques, there have been a host of flooding therapies worked out over the years. Stampflian implosive therapy remains the finest example of these approaches and the one most carefully framed by learning theory.

Some Final Considerations

Although the clearest effectiveness of implosive therapy shows up in treating a phobia, an anxiety state, or possibly an obsessive-compulsive neurosis, Stampfl does not feel that his technique must be limited to such syndromes. The limitations of implosive therapy depend more on the skill of the therapist in isolating symptoms than they do on the inherent nature of the technique per se. For example, depressed clients may be experiencing a certain amount of anxiety reduction by avoiding upsetting memories (scenes) out of their past. They may feel guilt for something they did years ago: instead of doing something about the act itself, they repressed it and now suffer pangs of conscience over unrelated events. Or they may have sensed rejection by loved ones in their early years and repressed the feelings and the hostility it engendered. Now the hostility is turned inward in the form of self-depreciation. By having the depressed client confront an ASCH built around his or her self-degradation (the court scene for Aimee described above) or around scenes of hostility and killing, it is possible to extinguish the anxiety attached to these underlying reasons for the manifest depression. Stampfl once said that the following situational cues are the most common themes of dynamic importance in implosive therapy: aggression, punishment, oral, anal, or sexual involvements, rejection, bodily injury, loss of control, acceptance of conscience, and autonomic or central nervous system reactivity.[186] Hence, regardless of the actual diagnosed syndrome, any case involving these themes can be approached through the implosive technique.

Although Stampfl recommends that the therapist begin implosion by using a traumatic situation from the client's past or a recurring dream, it is not essential that every ASCH scene be of this type. Clients do not have to believe or accept that every scene is directly based on their life in order to benefit from the implosive experience.[187] Unlike Wolpe's hierarchy which is constructed with the client's assistance and judgment of relevance, the Stampflian hierarchy is arrayed and even altered spontaneously according to the therapist's clinical judgment. Scenes may last for several minutes or may be changed within a minute—possibly through the introduction of new features into the action that is taking place. As clients, we look at a fear-provoking snake in our first ASCH scene. Soon Stampfl has us moving toward the snake, picking it up, and placing it around our neck. The snake bites us and tears out our eyeball, and as the blood gushes down our cheek, the snake thrusts itself into our cranial cavity where it continues its assault on our being, all described for us by Stampfl in gruesome detail. The pain is unbearable . . . and so on. Precisely how rapidly the therapist develops the gruesome extensions of the scene depends on our physiological reactions (tenseness, perspiration, heavy breathing, and so on) as we burst inward emotionally without actually receiving punishment or pain in reality.

Overcoming *resistance* to therapy is rarely a major problem because the benefits of the procedure are immediately felt by the client. An implosive therapy series seldom lasts beyond thirty hours.[188] There are certain personality types, however, who find it difficult adjusting to the procedure. Stampfl notes that someone with an extremely rigid superego often rejects the imaginary scenes as a matter of principle. Others with various character disorders resist the procedure because they cannot bear any form of discomfort at all. Psychotic patients also prove to be difficult cases because their general disorientation detracts from proper cooperation.

Finally, implosion can be a helpful adjunct to otherwise successful insight therapy. It has been used successfully in cases where, after a year of insight therapy, some nagging symptom like an anxiety attack persists at a much reduced level. The client has improved dramatically, but still occasionally suffers from a remnant anxiety. Implosive tactics can be introduced even at this late date to extinguish self-sustaining or free-floating feelings of anxiety.

Eclectic Behaviorism in Social-Learning Theory: Albert Bandura

The behavioristic theorists we have reviewed to this point fall nicely on one side or the other of the instrumental or operant (Skinner) *versus* the classic (Dollard and Miller, Wolpe, Stampfl) interpretations of conditioning, the nature of a response, and reinforcement. Though few behaviorists are likely to flatly deny that both types of conditioning occur, we do find the leaders in the field emphasizing one or the other of these two viewpoints in their explanations. Albert Bandura is an exception to this rule. Not only does he freely use both operant and classical conditioning explanations in the same theoretical account, he employs terminology borrowed from the science of cybernetics as well. It is for this reason that we call Bandura's social learning theory an *eclectic behaviorism*. An *eclectic theory* is one that seeks to take the best, or most useful, ideas from several different theories and combine them in a helpful way. Bandura's eclecticism stems from his willingness to pay attention to some trouble-

some empirical evidence emerging in recent decades from studies of the conditioning process in human subjects. We will review the highlights of this evidence before turning to Bandura's solutions of the problems it generates.

Some Problems with the Concept of Reinforcement

One of the first problems to arise in operant explanations of behavior stemmed from the Greenspoon type of experiment (see p. 446). Critics suggested that when Greenspoon said "mmm-hmm" following a verbal noun, he was probably cueing the subject on the purpose of the study, in the sense of suggesting "That's right, say plural nouns." Greenspoon denied this charge, noting that he had held postexperimental interviews with his subjects and not enough of them knew the experiment's purpose to account for the findings. However, as later events were to demonstrate, his interviews were not sophisticated enough. For example, he overlooked the possibility that a subject may have been verbalizing according to an assumption that called for plural nouns but was not specifically aimed at producing plurals. Assume that a subject had heard "mmm-hmm" after saying "books" and then "pencils." He or she might well have jumped to the conclusion that the experimenter was looking for "things in a schoolhouse" and had gone on reciting words like "blackboards," "chairs," "students," and so on without really discovering the actual purpose of the study. The experimental findings might show that this subject had been "conditioned" to emit plural nouns, when in fact the subject was accidentally emitting things in plural form based on a specific, albeit incorrect, hypothesis. Looked at from the subject's (introspective) perspective, a specific idea-hypothesis had been learned, and it was this meaning that was being consciously furthered, *not* a sequence of disjointedly pronounced plural nouns.

In order to get at such correlated but incorrect hypotheses, as well as to encourage a subject to feel free enough to know the aim (hypothesis being tested) of a research experiment, some rather detailed and sophisticated postexperimental interview procedures had to be devised. After such investigators as L. Douglas DeNike (1964), Don E. Dulany (1962), and Charles D. Spielberger (1963) began refining such interviews, we began to learn a great deal about the important role *subject awareness* plays in the operant-conditioning experiment. It gradually became evident that the reason operant conditioning works on human beings is that those subjects who catch on to—are aware of—the connection between the correct response (plural noun) and the contingent reinforcer (mmm-hmm) make the graphed lines of the experimental group studied rise and fall, as observed in the experimental results. And those subjects who do not develop this awareness, who are completely at sea concerning the experimental purpose, *do not condition!*

There are occasional studies appearing in the literature that claim to achieve operant conditioning without subject awareness. The vast majority of evidence, however, is that operant conditioning *without* awareness either does not occur, or if it does, the kind of response that conditions is very limited and nonverbal—such as a minute thumb contraction.[139] Furthermore, there is no assurance that when a subject is aware of the response-reinforcement relationship, he or she will comply and do what the experimental procedure calls for. Some people know that a certain word is expected of them yet consciously *refuse* to verbalize it. Monte M. Page (1972) conducted the prime experiment demonstrating this fact. He devised a way in which to identify three types of subjects in the typical verbal-operant conditioning study:

(1) subjects who are aware and cooperating with the experimental purpose (getting conditioned); (2) those who are aware but uncooperative (not getting conditioned); and (3) those who are simply unaware of the response-reinforcement relationship altogether (also not getting conditioned).

After identifying these three types of subjects in the first phase of his study, Page, who used the reinforcer, good, instead of mmm-hmm, stopped the experiment for a moment during the middle phase and asked all subjects to make him do the opposite of what he was then doing. Thus, to the aware and cooperating subjects, he said, "Make me stop saying good," and to the aware but uncooperative as well as to the unaware subjects, he said, "Make me start saying good." This is all he said, and the operant-conditioning procedure continued as before. Immediately, with the very next trial, the operant graph lines of his aware-cooperative subjects and his aware-uncooperative subjects *crisscrossed* so that he did not even need to use statistical tests to prove that these subjects knew precisely what was going on and that they could get conditioned or not get conditioned at will. In the meantime, the unaware subjects who were challenged in midexperiment to make Page (the experimenter) say "good" fumbled on as before without increasing their operant level. It seems clear that subjects who might catch onto a response-reinforcement contingent relationship, thinking, "When I say a plural noun he [the experimenter] says 'good,'" may *still* refrain from complying, possibly adding to themselves, "Well, let's have some fun and just not go along with his 'game.'" We know from frank discussions with subjects following the experiment that such playful or even hostile manipulations of the experimental sequence take place. Yet because of its traditional distrust of verbal report, operant-conditioning theory has failed to take these intentional manipulations into theoretical account.

Another type of experiment that raises questions about the role of operant reinforcement on behavior involves having all subjects reinforced according to one schedule while leading them to believe that they are on different schedules.[140] For example, we might ask subjects to perform a manual task of some type (for example, turn a crank) and then give them a reinforcement (for example, money) for this response *approximately* once every minute (variable-interval schedule). Some of the subjects are told the truth about how often their responses will be rewarded, while others are told that their behavior is being reinforced *exactly* once each minute (fixed-interval schedule) or after they have performed a certain number of responses on the average (variable-ratio schedule). We would find in such a study that it is more important what the subject *believes* is taking place in reinforcement than what is *actually* taking place. Even if all subjects were on a variable-interval schedule, the (crank-turning) responses emitted over a measured unit of time will be significantly different, with the fewest responses observed by subjects who believe they are on a fixed-ratio schedule and the most by far recorded when subjects believe that they are on a variable-ratio schedule. Subjects believing they are on a variable-interval schedule (the true schedule) fall somewhere between these extremely different groups in the number of responses they make over the run of the experiment. Obviously, results like this challenge the theory that it is the reinforcement schedule that is controlling a subject's behavior. They suggest instead that it is the subject's cognitive (thought) processes based on assumptions about the reinforcement scheduling that determine the course of responsivity.

Turning to Pavlovian or classical conditioning, we find a similar reliance on cognitive awareness taking place when human beings are studied.[141] These subjects do not have to be aware of the particular response being studied (though often they are), because in some cases this is totally reflexive in nature. For example, the *galvanic skin response* or GSR is a measure of the resistance to electrical conductance in the skin brought on by autonomic nervous system reactions (that is, completely automatically). It is noticeable during states of emotion and can be induced by shocking a subject electrically. Were we to conduct such a conditioning experiment, the unconditioned stimulus would be an electroshock, the conditioned stimulus might be a light (which we flash just before shocking a subject), and the response to be conditioned would be the GSR (which in time would occur when the light flashed even before shock was administered). The results of numerous studies that looked into this problem made it clear that only those subjects who became aware of the relationship between the conditioned and unconditioned stimuli—who realized "Every time that light flashes I get shocked"—actually conditioned their GSR to the light. Subjects who did not make the connection did not get conditioned. As in operant conditioning, it is not necessary for a subject to have the precise relationship between a conditioned and an unconditioned stimulus in mind. The wrong hypothesis may be employed, but as long as it is close to what the experimenter is trying to accomplish, the desired experimental effects come about.

When the response to be conditioned is motoric rather than autonomic, the subject can easily prevent its taking place following conditioning. For example, instead of the GSR (autonomic), we might have conditioned a subject's finger-withdrawal response (motoric) to a light by using shock. The subject rests a finger on an electrified stand and once he or she knows that the light (occurring first) and the shock bear a meaningful relationship, the subject will be seen quickly removing the finger from the stand before the stand is electrified—using the flashing light as the conditioned stimulus. However, assuming that the shock is not extremely painful, the subject can also *stop* removing his or her finger at any time, given the suggestion to do so by the experimenter. Undoubtedly, subjects could do so at will, even without this suggestion. It is somewhat more difficult to prevent the conditioned response when the unconditioned stimulus is a puff of air aimed at the eye, causing it to blink following the flashing of a light (the conditioned stimulus). However, even in this case, many subjects can willfully keep their eyes open after classical conditioning has been established and suffer the puff of air blown into their eye.

Finally, on the other side of the coin, subjects who are told from the outset exactly what the unconditioned and conditioned stimuli are can begin showing this conditioning immediately. They do not need any shaping trials to get them fixed into an automatic pattern of cause and effect. Simply knowing what the experiment is aiming at is enough to fix the classical conditioning response. Putting all of the evidence together from both operant and classical conditioning studies, there is little doubt that the concept of reinforcement in learning is far from being clearly understood at this point in psychology's history. Surely the subject's role in being reinforced and sustaining the effects of reinforcement is more crucial to the process than early behavioristic psychologists realized (see pp. 379). Albert Bandura, to whom we turn now, has tried to put these challenging empirical findings on reinforcement into a consistent picture in his framing of social learning theory.

Biographical Overview

Albert Bandura was born 5 December 1925 in northern Alberta, Canada, where he subsequently matured in this ruggedly beautiful although frigidly cold region. Upon graduating from high school he set out for the University of British Columbia in search of a climate that was at once more temperate in the physical sense and stimulating in the intellectual sense.[142] After looking into potential career alternatives, he chose psychology because it seemed the most intriguing, unexplored, and challenging of the lot. He decided to specialize in clinical psychology, but had picked up a strong interest in Hullian learning theory as well. Since the University of Iowa in the United States was then one of the leading centers for the study of learning theory under the leadership of Kenneth W. Spence, Bandura decided to pursue his graduate education at this institution. He became a student of Spence's, who had worked directly with Hull at Yale.[143] Bandura was also influenced by the writings of Miller and Dollard, particularly their 1941 book, *Social Learning and Imitation.*

After he had taken the Ph.D. at Iowa in 1952, Bandura joined the faculty of psychology at Stanford University in Palo Alto, California. He began as an instructor and in the course of time was to assume the distinguished title of David Starr Jordan professor

Albert Bandura

of social science in psychology. Bandura's initial research interests centered on dyadic interactions in psychotherapy as well as on the familial patterns conducive to the development of hyperaggressiveness in children. The latter work profited from the encouragement and support of Robert Sears, who at that time was also studying child-reading practices. Working with Richard Walters, his first doctoral student, Bandura was impressed by the central role that modeling processes had to play in the learning of aggression. After observing children in the home setting, Bandura devised a research procedure enabling him to take the study of aggressive modeling into the laboratory. A host of experiments then issued having to do with many different aspects of this interpersonal phenomenon.

Bandura has received many honors over the years, including a Guggenheim fellowship, distinguished scientific awards from both the California and the American Psychological Associations, and the James McKeen Cattell Award for outstanding contributions to psychology. He was elected president of the American Psychological Association in 1974 and was named a trustee of this organization in 1975. He has become a leading spokesman for the behavioristic movement in modern times, challenging the Skinnerian and even the neo-Hullian formulations to take more interest in the self-regulative processes to be found in human behavior.

Theoretical Considerations

The Eclectic Behaviorist

Bandura's eclecticism seems to reflect his effort to be as comprehensive in explanations of learning as he possibly can. In reading his accounts one is struck by his willingness to combine terms, as when he discusses the preparation of a typical Skinnerian behavior modification. Assume that a third-grade boy has been disrupting the school day by misbehaving in various ways; now we are preparing to reshape his behavior through operant reinforcement. In describing the early steps of this reshaping program, Bandura would suggest, "First, the child is observed for a period of time to measure the incidence of the deviant behavior, the contexts in which it typically occurs, and the reactions it *elicits* [italics added] from teachers." [144] Now if we are true to Skinnerian theory, we would see this preliminary study of the child's behavior as one of assessing operant *emission* rates for everyone concerned—the teachers as well as the child. Our disruptive third-grader is probably maintaining a high operant level of misbehavior because of the punishment form of attention (positive reinforcement) he obtains from the teachers. The teachers, in turn, are maintaining a high operant level of punishing responses because following these aversive measures (scoldings, mild spanking, and so on) the boy stops misbehaving for a time.

In suggesting that the child's operant re-

sponses elicit reactions from teachers, Bandura glossed over the issue Skinner raised against the classical S-R explanation of behavior (see p. 384). We see another example of this eclecticism in the following, wherein Bandura was speaking more generally about behavior: "Each expression by one person elicits some type of response from the other participant, which inevitably creates a specific reinforcement *contingency* [italics added] that has a specific effect on the immediately preceding behavior." [145] Skinner held that an operant response operates on the environment to create contingent circumstances that can possibly increase the rate of this response's emission, but he at no time contended that the way in which this comes about is through *eliciting* certain types of responses in other people. *Everyone* is behaving operantly through emitting responses in the Skinnerian world view. In adapting the language of contingent circumstances to his own neo-Hullian view, Bandura both reflected his eclectic tendencies and also took liberties with Skinnerian theory. Critics of eclecticism frequently point out that in bringing diverse theoretical terms together into one explanation, some of the meanings must inevitably suffer from the combination; doubtless Skinner would agree in this instance. We will return to the unique way in which Bandura interprets contingent reinforcement below.

Another reflection of Bandura's eclecticism is his regular use of cybernetic terminology to complement learning-theory explanations of behavior. The word *cybernetics* was coined by the scientist Norbert Wiener from Greek roots meaning "steersman." [146] Cybernetics is devoted to the study of those actions in nature that keep distinctive patterns alive in opposition to what is called *entropy,* or the tendency for natural objects and events to deteriorate—essentially disappear—into an undifferentiated mass of sameness. We can think of this as related to the *constancy principle* which we studied in Chapters 1 (p. 52) and 3 (p. 198). If such a complete dispersal of energy were to take place in a closed system, the end result would be that all of the patterned forms would melt into sameness—much as the weather becomes bland when the high and low pressure points balance out perfectly. Such leveling processes go on all the time in nature, as when physical materials rust or rot, turning to earth, or distinctive species of plants and animals are lost to extinction in the struggle for existence. Anything that counters this steady entropic erosion, or wearing away, by steering a course to retain the distinctiveness of articulated patterns in nature is said to be a living process by the cyberneticist.

In the case of human behavior, one of the chief ways in which entropy is countered is through the use of language, which permits human beings to retain the order and pattern of what we call knowledge. Cyberneticists speak of this as the flow of *information* through *input, output,* and *feedback* (output that returns as input as a kind of check on what is taking place over time). In retaining knowledge or information by encoding, organizing, and storing it, the human being ensures that the leveling forces of entropy will be countered. If we humans did not organize information in this way, we would forget it and everything would disappear, melt into the sameness of ignorance. Behavior is on this cybernetic model because of the processing of information, and the significance of information depends on its being ordered into a controlling sequence. As a matter of fact, Wiener held that all information processing is a type of behavioral control, because when we control the actions of another person, we always communicate a message to him or her, and vice versa.[147]

This *cybernetic* or *information-processing model* has been used very successfully in the construction of electronic computers, robots, and related thinking machines that have so captivated the imagination of people in modern times. Psychology too has become increasingly drawn to explanations of behavior in terms of information-processing terminology. A major trend in recent decades toward what is called *cognitive psychology* is to be seen, particularly in those theories relating to verbal learning and psycholinguistics.[148] Historically, the term *cognitive* has not been compatible with behavioristic explanations. The gestalt psychologists (see Chapter 9) first used the term to mean a supposedly nonmechanistic process going on within the individual to render external stimuli unique and therefore unamenable to an S-R or S-mediation-R sequence of motion. However, in recent times more and more psychologists with behavioristic leanings have begun speaking of input-mediation (feedback, memory storage)-output as a cognitive sequence, by which they mean an active process going on someplace in the central nervous system. Occasionally a direct parallel is drawn to the electronic processes of a computer, but just as often the precise machinery of how information is moved along through central organizing structures is left undescribed.

It is in this latter sense that Bandura has incorporated the language of information processing into his explanations of behavior. Thus we find him referring to the central organization of input stimuli[149] as well as the effects of feedback on experience.[150] A fine example of his information-processing usage can be seen in the following: "Transitory experiences leave lasting effects by being coded and stored in symbolic form for memory representation."[151] Of course, it is true that many and possibly most of the psychologists in the behavioristic camp today make some use of cybernetic terminology in their theoretical descriptions. It is common to equate *stimulus* with *input, response* with *output,* and *mediation* with *storage capacities.* Bandura has been both influenced by this trend and influential in furthering it.

Another indication of Bandura's eclecticism is to be seen in his willingness to give equal weight to what have been traditionally considered secondary aspects of learning, equating their significance as principles of explanation with so-called primary factors. The tradition in Hullian behavioristic psychology has been to account for all higher-level learning by showing first how certain basic S-R patterns are learned and then, based on such primary factors, the secondary learnings take place. For example, a child is first satisfied in infancy by the mother who provides nourishment through breast feeding, reducing innate drive stimuli (hunger) as a basic drive reduction. Through this basic learning, the child acquires a learned drive to focus emotions of love on the mother. The mother acquires *secondary* reinforcing qualities, thanks to the *primary* reinforcing qualities which she provided the child during breast feeding.

As the child matures, these acquired drives toward the mother assume major importance because now what mother says and does influences the child. Mother, and then by generalization, father and other authority figures serve as both models for how the child is expected to behave and reinforcers of the patterns of behavior actually taken on by the child. The implication here is that the *ultimate* cause of the child's socialization by the parents and others is the primary drive reduction that occurred in infancy. Though trained as a Hullian behaviorist, Bandura was in time to deny the pecking-order dis-

tinction implied between primary and secondary sources of learning. We find him unwilling to reduce socialization processes like modeling to underlying drive reductions of a supposedly basic nature.[152] So far as he was concerned, when children learn by example, observing the behavior of others, they have *not* arrived at this cognitive process because of a long chain of secondary reinforcements and generalizations from their first learning experiences in the nursery. Observing and processing the information seen in the behavior of others is *just as basic* as being reinforced by literally taking in and digesting food.

The final example we have of Bandura's comprehensive eclecticism is his insistence on what he called *reciprocal interaction* in the explanation of personality. In speaking of interaction, Bandura was referring to how causal processes operate in the description of personality.[153] He has been critical of those theorists who oppose the person and the environment, as if these are two independently interacting sources of causal influence. Others disregard the person as a separate identity and speak merely of behavior interacting with the environment. Bandura stressed that: "From the social learning perspective, psychological functioning is a continuous reciprocal interaction between personal, behavioral, and environmental determinants. The term reciprocal is used in the sense of mutual action between events rather than in the narrower meaning of similar or opposite counterreactions."[154] Reciprocity demands that we think of causes as occurring in a two-way direction.[155] There are three touchpoints among which two-way causation takes place: the *person,* the *behavior* studied, and the *environment* within which action takes place. Though Bandura did not define what *person* means in so many words, it is clear from his total presentation that he was referring here to the cognitive (thought) processes of the individual.[156]

Thus, each of us has various behaviors which we enact, and we are not always cognitively clear on what we are doing, or sometimes we do things automatically or accidentally. Our environments are also important to whatever we *do* when behaving. If the weather is hot or if people we know begin to treat us in some irregular manner, our reaction to such physical or social environmental influences is predictably determined—at least up to a point. That is, we always have the alternative of changing our environmental circumstances. We can change locations in the hot weather or adjust to the unexpected behavior of others in some way. Our behavior in turn reciprocally influences the environments we would be subject to in the future. It is in this sense that Bandura will occasionally refer to the reciprocally reinforcing processes involved in the mutual influence of behavior on environment and vice versa.[157]

But to round out the picture, we must recognize the role the person's cognitive processes play on this interacting course of events. In separating the person from behavior, Bandura is taking account of those researches we reviewed above, in which it was suggested that reinforcement demands more than just two terms for an accurate description of human action. We have to consider the person's cognitive awareness in addition to environmental stimuli and behavioral responses. Bandura appreciates that there is a certain chicken-egg problem in trying to say which of the three continually interacting touchpoints comes about first to "really" determine the other. In the same way that he was unwilling to reduce observational fac-

tors in learning to primary drive reductions, he is reluctant to say that one of these three interacting factors is more basic than the other two. Whether or not he is completely successful in this endeavor is open to debate, and we shall point to some of his theoretical difficulties when we take up his use of self-factors in behavioral description (see below).

Vicarious Learning as Modeling or Observational Learning

As we noted in the biographical overview, Bandura's studies convinced him that much of learning takes place *not* as traditional S-R theory would have it—that is, directly experienced and shaped through literal practice of a response in trial-and-error fashion—but *vicariously*. A vicarious event is one that some other person lives through, but that we as observers can learn from—in the sense of "what leads to what?" If as children we see a playmate touch a stove and shrink back in pain because of a burned finger, we learn to be wary of stoves radiating heat. Thus, said Bandura, "Observed rewards generally enhance, and observed punishments reduce, similar behavior in observers."[158] Bandura was to extend the range of *vicarious learning* to include not only what Dollard and Miller had called imitation and he called *modeling*, but to role-playing, contagion (rumor, fad, mob behavior), stereotypy, and the learning of social rules and principles of moral action.[159] In fact, through his modeling conception, Bandura was to extend the role of vicarious learning to virtually every aspect of human experience.

This is how we arrive at *social learning theory*. There is no other alternative really, because human learning is essentially an interpersonal process. As Bandura made clear:

In the social learning view, people are neither driven by inner forces nor buffeted by environmental stimuli. Rather, psychological functioning is explained in terms of a continuous reciprocal interaction of personal and environmental determinants. . . . In actuality, virtually all learning phenomena resulting from direct experience occur on a vicarious basis by observing other people's behavior and its consequences for them.[160]

Other phrases used to convey the idea of vicarious learning include *perceptive learning*[161] and *observational learning,* with the latter usage the most frequently employed and defined as follows in cybernetic terminology: ". . . observational learning entails symbolic coding and central organization of modeling stimuli, their representation in memory, in verbal and imaginal codes, and their subsequent transformation from symbolic forms to motor equivalents."[162] Since we do not witness a person who is learning observationally actually practicing what is being acquired, Bandura has referred to this covert process as "no-trial learning."[163] He liked to point out that in certain kinds of tasks—for example, conceptual rather than motor—we sometimes learn more by observing others than by doing the tasks ourselves.[164] The old adage, "Learn from others' mistakes," was doubtless drawn from observational learning principles.

The term used by Bandura most frequently to describe vicarious learning is *modeling* or the *modeling effect.* It is this most important of all his constructs that Bandura expanded into a complete explanation of the learning process. One of the most obvious characteristics of modeling is that it is a process through which observers acquire new behaviors, thanks to the *stimulus control of other people* encountered in social relations.[165] But modeling is more than this, for it can *inhibit* behaviors an observer has previously learned, or in the reverse direction, it can *disinhibit* behaviors that had previously

been suppressed.[166] For example, Janet, a young college woman who uses poor grammar, may be shamed into inhibiting these verbal errors after joining a sorority in which the other women make an effort to speak correctly. However, when she returns to her home town far from the college, Janet quickly reverts to her former speech pattern in talking with old friends (disinhibition).

In order for modeling to occur, a person has to come into contact with some modeling stimulus (contiguity principle of learning), and then find something distinctive about it in order to take notice. Bandura referred to the latter factor as *discrimination.* Now in developing the modeling construct, Bandura was to extend its meaning beyond simply taking on the discriminated patterns of other people seen in the flesh. He was to suggest that "the basic modeling process is the same regardless of whether behavior is conveyed through words, pictures, or live actions."[167] Effective models are therefore effective *discriminative stimuli,* for they catch our eye and hold our interest. In advertising, for example, the effective model stimulus may depend on size of print, vividness of a picture, or novelty of the sales pitch. Simply because a teen-aged cinema idol gets into a taxi cab does not mean that the middle-aged taxi driver will begin modeling the idol's lifestyle, though the driver may take an interest in this celebrity otherwise. Factors like the age, race, sex, and social status of models must be taken into consideration to account for how the process works.[168]

Extending the modeling concept to words means that Bandura considered it a fundamental process in all learning. We do not ordinarily think of ourselves as modeling when we reason our way to an understand-

ing of a mathematical rule or a moral principle. We think that we arrive at such positions through an exercise of reason. However,
Bandura considered the learning of rules
and principles to be a special case of
abstract modeling.[169] As social beings, we
take on in our use of reason through language manipulation those positions and
teachings that our culture has to offer. Modeling is in this sense a kind of instruction, a
conveying of long-standing information
across generations but still between people.
Of course, we do not have to follow the reasoning of all the models we come into contact with, any more than we have to accept
the message of every advertisement we see.
It is possible to *avoid* certain potential modeling effects.[170] We must keep in mind that
Bandura's reciprocal-interaction view of personality allows for the person's cognitive
processes to enter into the total picture of
what will take place. Higher-level reasonings
are a reflection of these cognitive processes.

Our discussion of modeling to this point
has brought to light the fact that this process is concerned with two broad functions.
On the one hand we have the learning of
new behavioral responses through observing
others, but on the other we have the factor
of willingness to copy a model *whether or
not* this will require the learning of new responses. Bandura highlighted these two sides
to modeling by differentiating between *acquisition* and *performance*.[171] Many times we
learn how to do something by observing a
model, yet we never actually carry over this
behavior into overt action. We see on television many dramas in which the central theme
involves holding up a bank. We acquire a
certain knowledge (information) from these
dramatizations, but we would never literally

perform this antisocial act—or would we? In
answering this question, we move into the
area of *motivation* in personality, which Bandura approaches through his concept of reinforcement.

Reinforcement as an Informational and Motivational Process

Although he combines classical and operant
(instrumental) explanations of reinforcement
into his theory, Bandura did not give these constructs the same interpretation that our other
behaviorists did. We will first review his
critique of these traditional accounts and then
give his social-learning-theory interpretation
of reinforcement. Turning to classical conditioning first, we find Bandura objecting to
the *drive theory* on which such reinforcements are said to be based. A drive is something specific that supposedly rises in the
organism and then lowers only through performance of the behavior it is said to stimulate. An aggressive drive, for example, is
said to be raised by frustration and then
lowered through actual aggressive behavior.
Bandura rejected this simplistic view and
said instead:

*From a social-learning perspective, frustra-
tion is regarded as a facilitative rather than
a necessary condition for aggression. That is,
frustration produces a general state of emotional arousal that may lead to a variety of
responses depending upon the types of frustration reactions that have been previously
learned, and the reinforcing consequences
typically associated with different courses of
action.*[172]

Bandura typically referred to *arousal* rather
than *drive* when speaking of a more generalized state of heightened autonomic and
central nervous system activity.[173] Something
in life may occur to arouse us. We may feel

frustrated because we are unable to get our automobile started in the morning or an attractive member of the opposite sex commands our attention, but what we actually *do* in behavior is never specifically tied to *a* given (aggressive or sexual) drive. Bandura felt that classical-conditioning theories relied too heavily on the drive concept. "If drives are invoked for everything people find satisfying, the result is an immense proliferation of drives that have no greater explanatory value than the conditioned reinforcers from which they are inferred."[174] To take this tactic to its extreme, we might postulate different drives for watching specific television shows, so that those people who prefer westerns would be said to have one kind of drive and those who watch situation comedies another. Obviously, all we would be doing here is naming a superfluous drive for each of the reinforcers (type of show) we already know have a differential effect on television viewing.

Reinforcers always take place *following* some behavioral act, as when we see a person turning on a television set and then sitting down to enjoy a particular show rather than doing something else for that period of time. Bandura pointed out that this is common to all theoretical explanations of reinforcement—they are based on the observed fact that behavior is controlled by its consequences.[175] Now in the case of operant responding, we may recall that Skinner believed these are *emitted* actions which literally bring about such consequences as so-called contingencies, contingent circumstances, or contingent reinforcers (see p. 384). We noted above in discussing Bandura's eclecticism that he essentially rejected the emission-versus-emitted issue Skinner raised. Bandura made it clear that as far as he was concerned "instrumental [operant] responses must be activated by antecedent stimuli."[176] Though Skinner did not deny that antecedent bio-

logical factors may enter into the production of a response, he did believe that the consequences flowing from operant responses are *the* cause of base-rate behavioral emissions. Bandura, on the other hand, observed somewhat dubiously that "although there is ample evidence that reinforcing consequences can significantly alter the probability of future occurrence of preceding matching responses, consequent events can hardly serve as a precondition for the acquisition of responses that have already been performed."[177]

We are back to the acquisition-versus-performance issue. Bandura did not believe that operant responding can be learned through the action of contingent reinforcers. All operant responding reveals is that the person who has *already* acquired the responses observationally will now perform them in order to get the reinforcer that follows. Thus, after Eddie, a three-year-old child, has learned how to open cookie jars by watching his parents (models) do so, he will perform this already acquired response given the slightest opportunity. When Eddie tries to get a cookie in this way he is behaving on the anticipated or expected assumption that a *reinforcer* (cookie) *will follow* the instrumental (operant) response. What if the cookie jar is empty when Eddie opens it? A learned response will not have led to reinforcement, yet this does not mean it will be forgotten even if the cookie jar is repeatedly opened without having any contents inside. Indeed, even after Eddie stops opening the jar (extinction), this would not reflect on his learning (acquisition) but merely on the performance of an already known behavior.

When we consider performance in this way, we are coming upon what is usually called *motivation* or *incentive-formation* in the study of personality. Both reinforcement and motivation are *anticipatory* processes.

"Indeed, in most instances persons are motivated by, and work for, anticipated rewards rather than immediate reinforcing outcomes." [178] If we now equate acquisition with learning and performance with motivation, we can better understand how Bandura combined these factors into his overall theory of reinforcement. Bandura suggested that, insofar as it relates to learning, reinforcement is an *information process*. "Reinforcing consequences convey information about the type of behavior required in a given situation. Anticipation of desired rewards for performing the requisite behaviors can increase and maintain appropriate responsiveness even though presentation of the earned reinforcers may be delayed for a considerable time." [179] We see both learning and performance aspects in this quote. For example, a young man or woman may become a scientist and work for years in the laboratory on the mere chance that the knowledge being put to use will lead to an important discovery. Sometimes it does and sometimes it does not.

Now, the fact that the scientist enters the laboratory in the first place is more a performance than a learning feature of reinforcement. The required skills of scientific work have already been learned in the past, as modeled by professors and famous scientists of history whose works were studied (abstract modeling). There will be new learning taking place as the scientist keeps up with the relevant literature (abstract modeling), as well as learns from the experiments to be conducted. But in large measure, the fact of working on and on for goals that may never be achieved has to be seen as exclusively motivational, that is, relating to the performance aspects of reinforcement.

The scientist's research responses are not really being automatically strengthened by having the drive to do the work of science reduced. Bandura's attitude toward such theoretical statements is made clear in the following: "The dubious status of both automaticity and response strengthening, and the vestigial connotations of the term reinforcement, make it more fitting to speak of *regulation* than *reinforcement* of behavior by its consequences." [180]

We are regulated by reinforcements in three ways.[181] First, there are those extrinsic reinforcements that actually do happen to us in the external world—as when we are given special attention for something we do during childhood. Mother hugs us for picking up our toys and we acquire information in this process, for now we know how to get such affection in the future. Secondly, there are a vast number of reinforcements we obtain vicariously through observational learning. In such cases, a literal extrinsic reinforcement is not required because "observational learning occurs through symbolic processes during exposure to modeled activities before any responses have been performed and does not necessarily require extrinsic reinforcement." [182] We might have seen a brother or sister being hugged by mother for picking up after themselves and learned through vicarious reinforcement to do the same thing.

Finally, we are capable of administering self-reinforcements. "According to social learning theory . . . self-regulated reinforcement increases performance mainly through its motivational function. By making self-reward conditional upon attaining a certain level of performance, individuals create self-inducements to persist in their efforts until their performances match self-prescribed standards." [183] In this case, we would have taken on the standard or rule of "always pick up after yourself," and whether mother hugged us or not, from that time forward we would experience a feeling of self-reward each time we achieved this goal.[184] We can even arouse ourselves emotionally to meet such standards.[185] This latter form of reinforcement takes us into the self-regulatory processes that Bandura proposed to describe behavior.

Self-Regulation as a Mediational Process

Bandura, even more so than Stampfl, presents us with theoretical statements that occasionally seem nonbehavioristic, as in the following: "At the highest level of development, individuals regulate their own behavior by self-evaluative and other self-produced consequences."[186] When commenting on modeling at one point, he seemed to align himself with phenomenology (see Chapter 9), suggesting that ". . . observational learning emerges as an actively judgmental and constructive, rather than a mechanical copying, process."[187] Though he was willing to employ cybernetic terminology, Bandura had this to say about its comprehensiveness: "People are not only perceivers, knowers, and actors. They are also self-reactors with capacities for reflective self-awareness that are generally neglected in information-processing theories based on computer models of human functioning."[188] He even believed that the "behavioral approach and humanism have much in common,"[189] when the scope of description is broadened by reciprocal interaction.

Bandura took the findings on *awareness in conditioning* very seriously, frankly admitting that ". . . consequences generally produce little change in complex behavior when there is no awareness of what is being reinforced."[190] Skinner argued that ". . . when a person is 'aware of his purpose,' he is feeling or observing introspectively a condition produced by reinforcement."[191] Bandura

found this hard to accept because of the dramatic effect a *preliminary* awareness on the person's part has on subsequent conditioning. Thus, Bandura said:

The responses that get conditioned are to a large extent cognitively induced rather than directly elicited by external [extrinsic] stimuli. Response consequences similarly have weak effects on behavior when the relationship between one's actions and outcomes is not recognized. On the other hand, awareness of conditions of reinforcement typically results in rapid changes in behavior, which is indicative of insightful functioning.[192]

In other words, if awareness is produced by reinforcement as Skinner claimed, then we must believe that at some point early in life there is conditioning without awareness. Bandura found little empirical evidence for this claim, so he turned the tables and essentially said that "whenever" reinforcement occurs in life, awareness probably precedes rather than follows it. Since awareness is a cognitive process implying awareness of something, in the sense of "A signals B" over time, Bandura stressed the role of *anticipation* or *expectancy* in the flow of behavior. "The notion that behavior is controlled by its immediate consequences holds up better under close scrutiny for anticipated consequences than for those that actually impinge upon the organism."[193] We acknowledged something like this when we suggested above that a scientist can work on for years under varying states of frustration in hopes of finally achieving something of importance to humanity.

An even more fundamental form of *anticipation learning* takes place in everyone's behavior, thanks to what Bandura calls *predictive stimuli*. A predictive stimulus is one that clues the person on the likely consequences of a series of events. Predictive stimuli occur first in such a series of events and are themselves evocative factors in the events to follow. These stimuli are obtained through modeled learnings which are retained in memory as potential evokers of behavior.[194] Because of such stored memorial stimuli, the individual can actually become self-aroused through use of imagination.[195] For example, a person who wants to become sexually aroused can begin recalling (predictive) stimuli relating to erotic scenes. In time these sexy memories (stimuli) will evoke or arouse the person's sexuality without anything of an erotic nature being present in the external environment (extrinsic stimuli). Thus: "Predictive stimuli can acquire evocative potential on a vicarious basis, or by association with thought-produced arousal. . . . Once stimuli become evocative, this function transfers to other classes of stimuli that are similar physically, to semantically related cues, and even to highly dissimilar stimuli that happen to be associated in people's past experiences."[196] When athletes speak of getting themselves up for a contest, they are making use of predictive stimuli, seeing themselves in a favorable competitive situation leading to victory. Of course, anticipated outcomes like this in imagination are not always realized, but we fail to capture the true nature of behavior if we do not take this cognitive process into consideration.[197]

When we speak of imagined situations projected into the future as possibilities, we are ascribing a *mediating* capacity to the learner. Bandura reflected this neo-Hullian tactic in his effort to humanize behavioral theory. He told us that: "Originally, conditioning was assumed to result automatically from events occurring together in time. Closer examination revealed that it is in fact cognitively mediated."[198] The principle of contiguity is not just an automatic linkage system, hooking up behavioral events without cognitive events taking place between inputs and outputs. Bandura defined *cognition* as follows: ". . . cognitive events refer to imagery, to representation of experiences in symbolic form, and to thought processes."[199] The construct of cognition specifies the form that mediation takes in human beings. There is surely mediation in animal behavior, but whether lower animals have complex symbolic systems or higher-level thought processes is debatable. Bandura had no doubt that such cognitive factors enter into human learning and performance.

Thanks to his use of mediational conceptions, Bandura could give his theory emphases approaching those we find in psychoanalytical and phenomenological formulations. However, there is a central issue separating behaviorists from the more humanistic theories of personality, and, as we shall now demonstrate, when he came right down to this point of difference Bandura stood firmly with his behavioristic colleagues. We refer here to the emphasis placed on *self-factors* in the personality. The term *self* relates to an *identity* in the course of a continuing behavioral pattern, an identity that directs and keeps the personality style continuous over time. Nonbehavioristic theories usually allow for this direction by having the identity (self, person, ego) beginning even before there is a preliminary shaping underway by external circumstances. In psychoanalysis, for example, the infant is said to begin thinking about life events (unconsciously) even before consciousness arises to influence the course of thought (see p. 45). Bandura's emphasis was quite otherwise. ". . . Social-learning approaches treat internal processes as covert events that are manipulable and measurable. These mediating processes are extensively controlled by external stimulus events and in turn regulate overt responsiveness." [200]

Even though Bandura was employing reciprocal determination in such statements, it is clear that he viewed mediators as originating more on the effect than the cause side of a cause-effect sequential interaction. We see this preferential ordering in the following quote as well: "Many influences impinge on people and produce cognitive changes which, in turn, affect selection and symbolic processing of subsequent influences." [201] The phenomenological existentialists discussed in Part III of this volume did not think of self-factors as having first to be put into the mind (cognitive system) before they make their influence on behavior known. But this does seem to be Bandura's position, as it was Dollard and Miller's (see Chapter 6). As reflected in the opening quotes to this section, Bandura framed some of the most humanistic-sounding statements of behavior of any of the behaviorists, but whether or not he actually departed from traditional Hullian mediational theory is open to question. When the issue is narrowed to the fundamental *origins of human behavior,* Bandura was always willing to slip into traditional behavioristic explanations, as in the following:

The way in which beliefs and conscious recognition of environmental contingencies can enhance, distort, or even negate the influence of reinforcing consequences has already been amply documented and needs no further illustration. Cognitive events, however, do not function as autonomous causes of behavior. Their nature, their emotion-arousing properties, and their occurrence are under stimulus and reinforcement control. Analysis of cognitive control of behavior is therefore incomplete without specifying what influences a person's thoughts.[202]

It would appear that Bandura wanted to stress the partial independence mediating cognitive processes give to the person. In this sense he was willing to assign agency to the person, who can generate self-arousal in behavior through mediating predictive stimuli.[203] The person can cue himself or herself by saying, "I'm going to get myself feeling more up than I do now by playing my favorite records," and then via this mediation, a state of heightened mood is brought about. But when it comes to assigning agency to a *self-system* as is so frequently done in the nonbehavioristic theories, Bandura objected: *"In social learning theory, a self system is not a psychic agent that controls behavior. Rather, it refers to cognitive structures that provide reference mechanisms and to a set of subfunctions for the perception, evaluation, and regulation of behavior."* [italics added] [204] In the final analysis, *self-control* for Bandura is *cognitive control* through mediation[205] and the question of self-identity is explained as a special case of the latter process. That is, insofar as we have an idea of ourselves as identities (selves), it comes from mediated inputs we acquired through observational learnings in our past. "People learn to respond evaluatively to their own behavior partly on the basis of how others have reacted to it. Parents and other socialization agents subscribe to certain norms of what constitute worthy or reprehensible performances." [206]

We are taught such *values,* but whether we accept them as a basis for self-reinforcement or not is partially up to us as persons. We have a capacity for reflective thought, so that what is input can be considered reciprocally and furthered or not.[207] The more options open to us in behavior, the greater is our *freedom* to act.[208] As persons (see reciprocal-interaction concept, p. 481), we are therefore always in the picture, to maximize alternatives or not. We have cognitive control (self-regulation) over our behavior *to some extent.* Bandura was not greatly concerned about settling the question of ultimate control of behavior—if indeed this can ever be known. He was willing to rest with what he took to be the more sophisticated insight of reciprocal interactions between several controlling factors all at once. Thus he could conclude: "To be sure, the self-regulatory functions are created and occasionally supported by external influences. Having external origins, however, does not refute the fact that, once established, self-influence partly determines which actions one performs." [209] We might learn as children that it is socially proper to wear certain clothes and to keep ourselves tidy. But, as is easily established, everyone does not follow these prescriptions to the letter. Those who do have often arrived at their highly proper personal styles of dress and grooming more by self- than external-reinforcement.

As we have already suggested, it is not entirely clear that Bandura's mediational model of behavior really differed from the Dollard and Miller formulation. Mediation theory since Tolman (see p. 381) has attempted to counter the simplistic, S-R bonding conception that Watson used initially in framing early behaviorism. But mediation theory has remained true to the empiricism of Watson, acknowledging that all *mediators* (symbols, cue-producing responses, and so on) originate in and—as Bandura tells us above—are supported by the external environment of the behaving organism. Though Bandura's eclectic tendencies prompted him to frame his mediational views about as close to nonbehavioristic statements of personality as is possible without actually changing positions, he in the final analysis kept the *basic*

or original controls in the nonpersonal (environmental) aspects of experience. The central issue we noted above is still active and helps us place Bandura in proper alignment. Had he stressed that reciprocal interaction begins from birth, so that self-regulatory processes already are underway in the first psychological encounter with the environmental inputs, he would have taken a giant stride from behaviorism toward what would probably be a form of phenomenology (see Chapter 10). Though his theoretical statements frequently have the spirit of such humanistic viewpoints contained within them, a strictly technical analysis of Bandurian psychology leaves no doubt that he spoke from the behavioristic tradition. We close this section with a prime example of Bandura's overall description of mediated behavior, including cybernetic allusions.

Both complex behaviors and even relatively simple performances that have generally been assumed to represent direct linkages between external stimuli and overt responses are extensively controlled by symbolic processes. These higher level activities involve, among other things, strategic selection of the stimuli to which attention is directed, symbolic coding and organization of stimulus inputs, and acquisition, through informative feedback, of mediating hypotheses or rules which play an influential role in regulating response selection.[210]

Theory of Illness and Cure

Bandura's theory added to the behavioristic accounts of abnormality an emphasis on the role of observational learning. Through vicarious punishment, people can learn to behave maladaptively without ever having directly experienced an external reinforcement of any kind. In the learning of a phobia, for example, the child observes a parent's fear of spiders (modeling) and then, thanks to self-reinforcement in imagination, acquires an extreme fright reaction going far beyond anything the parent originally displayed.[211] In addition to such cognitively mediated symptoms, many people are rewarded for their abnormal patterns by the attention they receive from others. Bandura, like so many of his behavioristic colleagues, pointed out that abnormal behaviors are more likely to receive the attention of others than normal behaviors.[212] Given this likelihood, a person who feels worthless and ignored is likely to take the path of least resistance and get interpersonal visibility through abnormal behavioral displays.

To understand certain abnormal conditions we must consider the short-range benefits over the longer-termed, harmful effects. For example, in the case of alcoholism or drug dependence, the immediate consequences controlling this behavior are so positive that the person is unable to consider its longer-ranged, self-destructive aspects.[213] There is a kind of flight from the distant to the immediate future in these cases. Bandura also pointed to the striking differences in the use of alcohol among different ethnic cultures. Chronic alcoholism is notably high among the Irish but very low among Jewish people, suggesting that this is a socially learned pattern of behavior. After surveying the literature on the problem, Bandura concluded that ". . . alcoholism typically results from habituation after prolonged heavy social drinking acquired within the context of familial alcoholism."[214] Similar familial influences can be found in the expression of aggression and other antisocial behaviors. Children reared in permissive atmospheres are more likely to display aggression as a typical pattern than children who are discouraged from being aggressive.[215]

Often the neurotic person is caught up in a learned but personally regulated sequence which forces him or her to inflict self-punishment in the form of obsessive guilt reactions, or bouts of depression. Bandura explained how, in maturing, we all learn a kind of *punishment sequence* that goes as follows: when we do something wrong, we feel internally distressed until we have been punished and can feel relief.[216] We actually learn to anticipate punishment in this course of events, based on the (predictive) stimuli of the situation in which we have done something wrong. As a boy, Lou always knew what would happen next when he did something wrong—like break a window of his family's house. In due course, Dad would give him a whipping whether the window was broken accidentally or not. As he matured, Lou began developing depressions and haunting guilt reactions for any sort of mistake he made in life. When he misfiled a report at the office where he worked which merely delayed a conference for a few minutes until it was located, Lou returned home to confront his wife in a complete state of depression. The next morning he could not leave home and before long he was hospitalized in a state of agitated depression. People like Lou cannot always recall the stimuli that trigger their self-punishing processes, or they can do so only with great effort.

Bandura referred to the therapist as a *change agent*,[217] a descriptive label that reflects his basic attitude toward the value of all psychological theories. "The worth of a psychological theory must be judged not only by how well it explains laboratory findings but also by the efficacy of the behavioral modification procedures that it produces."[218] All of the traditional behavioristic therapeutic techniques we have studied to this point in Chapter 7 are discussed in terms of their relevance to social-learning-theory applications. We see Bandura's eclecticism reflected here once again, as in the following comment: "A social-learning approach does not rely upon a single set of conditions for effecting personality changes, but rather it provides, within a unified framework, diverse methods for modifying multiform psychological phenomena." [219] The Skinnerian operant techniques were given much emphasis, but so too do we find references to Wolpean and Stampflian forms of corrective learning. [220]

The first step in a social-learning program of cure calls for a clear statement of what it is we wish to change. Unless we have clear goals, it will be impossible to check our effectiveness as we work along. The more concrete our goals are, the more likely that both we and our clients will work more effectively to bring about change. [221] The second step of social-learning therapy is to do a causal analysis [222] of the troublesome behavior from which our clients suffer. Once we have found these determinants, we can then stipulate the changes called for to achieve the goals we have set ourselves. Bandura favored breaking down the therapeutic effort into steps, with increasingly complex goals being set as the client improves. Along the way to recovery we should also constantly check our advance by empirically assessing the gains made, step by step.

Bandura believed that clients should be given every opportunity to help set the directions in which their behavior is being modified. [223] The social-learning therapist does not think of himself or herself as automatically manipulating others, but invites them to share in the direction therapy takes. Given these two steps as a broad framework for ac-

tion, we could now review specific examples of operant conditioning, systematic desensitization, or implosion, much as we have already done in Chapter 7. The only difference might be that Bandura would try to maximize the beneficial effects of modeling in the therapeutic program wherever possible. For example, he noted how essential it is to *shape* client behavior from the hospital setting over into the community setting. [224] There are great differences in the social demands of the hospital and those of the community outside the hospital. If a program is to be effective, it must take the maladjusted individual right back into his or her pre-hospital environment. Social-learning theory therefore favors extensive use of the *halfway house* concept, as well as continuing client contact with appropriate models through organizations like Alcoholics Anonymous to keep the level of adjustment satisfactory.

To capture the essence of what takes place in successful therapy, Bandura introduced the concept of *self-efficacy*. [225] He meant by this a mediating cognitive process having the characteristic of an expectation of success in the situation facing a person. When Margaret senses the fact that the car she is driving is going into a skid on the wet pavement, she knows that in a case like this she will have to turn the vehicle slightly into the direction of the skid (when skidding to the right, turn to the right). Bandura calls this an *outcome expectancy*, because Margaret knows that a given behavior on her part (turn the wheel to the right) will lead to a certain outcome (an aligned automobile). However, Margaret may *not* have the proper *efficacy expectation* that she can achieve the required outcome ("I can't do this"). Thus, said Bandura, "An efficacy expectation is the conviction that one can successfully execute the behavior required to produce the outcomes." [226] To the extent that a person has the conviction that he or she can indeed do what is called for in a situation, to that extent does the person experience the cognitive sense of self-efficacy. In brief, self-efficacy is *not* a drive but an expectancy that we can do things, solve problems, and meet new challenges.

There are many ways in which to reach greater levels of self-efficacy. The best way is by actually achieving the outcome called for in a situation that challenges us. Bandura calls these *performance accomplishments*. In therapy, a client might successfully conquer the fear of being closed in (claustrophobia), and in getting over this problem, he or she will generalize this efficacy expectation to other aspects of personal behavior as well. It is also possible to gain self-efficacy through *vicarious experience,* as in watching others solve their problems or hearing them tell how they did it. This is undoubtedly what takes place in Alcoholics Anonymous, where people who have conquered their drinking problems explain how they did so in testimonials for the general membership. There is also an element of *verbal persuasion* in such testimonials, for the person is urged to make efforts to reform. Therapists often use verbal persuasion to get clients moving in the direction of coping with their problems. By beginning with simple coping mechanisms and building on these early successes, a broader sense of self-efficacy can be achieved by the client. Bandura would refer to the desensitization technique as an example of *emotional arousal,* whereby the person is taught a tactic that can be employed to reduce anxiety in any of a number of different situations.[227] In reducing anxiety like this, Bandura cautioned us to appreciate that we have *not* simply reduced or removed a drive level that caused some type of defensiveness in the client; rather, we have *raised* the client's efficacy expectations so that from now on, he or she will be up to coping with other problems as well.[228]

Bandura did not necessarily reject all of the techniques employed by traditional insight therapies as totally ineffective, but he does give their terminology a behavioristic reformulation. Obtaining *insight* is a form of mediation in which either the client has been socially persuaded to agree with the psychoanalyst's interpretations[229] or, considered in terms of operant conditioning, there is a sudden discovery of the correct reinforcement contingency, so that the client begins performing in a way assuring that reward will follow.[230] The concept of *resistance* is challenged as a groundless charge made by therapists who are upset by the fact that clients refuse to accept their often highly dubious interpretations of client behavior.[231] The *unconscious* is simply a theoretical device to justify making such questionable charges. Finally, the utility of *catharsis* was brought into question by Bandura, who saw this construct as related to drive-reduction conceptions of behavior (see p. 382). Rather than relieving the person of the supposed emotional drive that has gone unexpressed in the past, cathartic techniques probably stimulate even further expression of this emotion in the future.[232]

Summary

Chapter 7 looks into various behavioristic approaches to the description and treatment of behavior. In his operant-conditioning approach, Skinner viewed the organism as emitting various responses without agency and, assuming that certain responses do arrange circumstances following emissions that prove reinforcing, the level of these operant responses will be observed to increase per unit of time's passage. We can identify the reinforcers of these operant responses by observing what contingent circumstances do in fact lead to a rise in the level of operant responding. This theoretical outlook is essentially an empirical law of effect. Based on our knowledge of reinforcers that work on various organisms, we can then arrange schedules of reinforcement to shape the behavior of the animal or person in question. The design of the Skinner box is based on this approach; rats or pigeons are placed and administered reinforcers (food pellets) on fixed or variable schedules of (interval-versus-ratio) reinforcement. This sequencing of reinforcement to change the level of responding is termed a program. In most instances operant conditioners employ positive reinforcement, but it is possible first to administer an aversive stimulation (for example, electroshock), then remove it, and in the rise of behavioral emission that follows, to manipulate behavior through negative reinforcement. Punishment suppresses responses rather than enhancing them, and Skinner opposed such methods in the treatment of human beings.

Skinner applied the technology of operant conditioning to human beings in the use of programmed instruction (teaching machines) and was instrumental in coining the term *behavior therapy* for the application of operant techniques to human beings. Whether behavior is abnormal (theory of illness) or normal (theory of cure) depends on its shaping, on how well the person is molded by past experience to meet his or her ongoing reinforcement requirements. Therapy therefore comes down to raising the emission rate of operant responses that lead to reinforcement, and lowering those that lead to no reinforcement or to punishment. A program of reinforcement is designed and carried out in

which base rates of the target behaviors are first determined and then, through successive approximation, gradually modified to obtain the therapeutic goal. Whole groups of people in mental hospitals can be treated in this manner, by placing them on a token economy designed to contingently reinforce certain (healthy) behaviors and to extinguish others through nonreinforcement. In general, operant conditioning has worked best in the nonverbal type of therapy. The highly verbal, insight therapies have not been shown to be amenable to operant manipulation.

Wolpe's concept of reciprocal inhibition was based on Sherrington's biological theory and Hull's learning theory. Wolpe viewed behavioral habits as forming exclusively through contiguous stimulus-response relationships aligning over time, given only that a drive is in ascendance and the stimulus-response sequence in question reduces this drive level. The drive state that is most likely to be reduced when unhealthy habits are formed is anxiety. Thus, all of those aversive maneuvers that Dollard and Miller discussed can be attributed to Wolpe as well. The person flees rather than confront a threatening stimulus which leads to anxiety reduction, yet ensures that the next time this threatening stimulus is confronted, anxiety will be even greater. What we must do is inhibit the fleeing response by substituting another, incompatible response to the threatening stimulus. This is what reciprocal inhibition means. In his technique of systematic desensitization, Wolpe first trained his clients in the art of progressive relaxation. One cannot be both relaxed and anxious at the same time. He then had the client rank-order a series of disturbing (for example, phobic) life situations, from least to most anxiety-provoking. These situations are measured in suds (subjective units of disturbance), and then ordered into an anxiety hierarchy.

In the actual therapeutic contacts, the client

is asked to imagine the anxiety-provoking (stimulus) situation and then is encouraged to relax—reciprocally inhibit the resulting anxiety. Clients are begun at the lowest sud level (least anxiety provoking), and taken gradually to the highest level of anxiety-provoking stimuli. Wolpe disparaged all of the emphasis on relationship that psycho-analysis employs, often using surrogate therapists to administer systematic desensitization when he could not meet a therapy appointment. Occasionally, a client may be hypnotized to enhance the reality of the systematic desensitization technique. It is possible to take a client into the actual life situation that provokes anxiety (like air travel, fear of enclosed places) and encourage relaxation in vivo. Wolpe also used the technique of assertiveness training when clients were unable to manage being victimized by others. He instructed them in how to express themselves, both positively and negatively, through behavioral rehearsal (role play) of certain lifesmanship tactics. Occasionally, Wolpe employed aversion therapy, in which case avoidance counterconditioning was used to reciprocally inhibit an undesirable response (for example, using shock to inhibit eating responses in obesity cases).

Stampfl rested his theory of illness and cure on the two-factor theory of learning introduced by Mowrer. This view suggests that learning consists of (1) problem solving, an activity mediated by the central nervous system and under voluntary control; and (2) conditioning, mediated by the autonomic nervous system and therefore not open to conscious influence. Emotional responses like anxiety, depression, love, hate, and so on are tied to conditioning processes. In the case of neurotic behavior, the person is viewed as having been conditioned to avoid problem solution through a pattern of behavior that reduces autonomic responses but does *not* permit problem solution to take place. Akin to Dol-

lard and Miller's suggestion, the neurotic was viewed by Stampfl as being kept stupid by continually fleeing the expected punishment of some life circumstance because of its emotionally stimulating qualities. Symptoms of neurosis are essentially these kinds of conditioned avoidant responses. Stampfl reasoned that if clients were to remain in place, confronting their feared expectations and *not* obtain punishment, though they would express much autonomically mediated emotion, they would quickly extinguish the contiguous relationship between the feared stimulus situation and the emotional (avoidant) response.

An implosion is a bursting inward. This describes what takes place when the client is verbally encouraged by the Stampflian therapist to imagine any of a number of fear-provoking, hate-provoking, guilt-provoking—the specific emotion varies—life situations or even after-life situations. People are concerned about all sorts of even foolish things, and Stampfl accepted the fact that such fears, hates, and so on, may have their origins in Freudian dynamics. In bringing forward his or her idea concerning what the client fears, the implosive therapist may begin with symptom-contingent cues that are known to be causing the autonomic response, but in quick order move on to hypothesized conditioned-aversive cues of even a fantastic variety (such as dying and going to hell, and so on). Clients often redintegrate (recall from the past) memories of relevant circumstances relating to the avoidance-provoking situation. Therapy proceeds through certain steps: symptom study; training in neutral imagery; framing a hierarchy of avoidance images called the ASCH (avoidance serial cue hierarchy), which is based on the extent of fear the patient manifests; and then actual scene presentation and repetition to extinction (including elaborations on the scenes when called for). Therapy ends with a period of training the client in therapeutic self-management.

The final behaviorist presented in Chapter 7 is Bandura, whose social-learning theory was an effort to combine descriptions of behavior in both the classical and the operant sense with more recent cybernetic models of behavior to present an eclectic picture. In his concept of reciprocal interaction, Bandura also encompassed influences issuing from the person, behavior, and the environment. Social-learning theory is essentially a mediational model of behavior, but what Bandura did was to raise the role of vicarious learning in the description of behavior. His experiments demonstrated that people can learn through modeling the behavior of others. In this sense, he followed Dollard and Miller's earlier work on imitation, but introduced considerable sophistication to the area of perceptive or observational learning. Modeling effects are not always apparent, for a person can observe others, learn what they are doing, yet avoid doing what they have learned if they see that it leads to punishment. Bandura drew a distinction here between the acquisition of behavior and the performance of behavior. He also believed that the learning of rules and principles is a case of abstract modeling.

Bandura preferred to speak of arousal rather than drive, and he essentially dismissed the elicited-versus-emitted issue which has traditionally separated Pavlovian from Skinnerian conditioned-response explanations. Reinforcements like indeed all motivational processes are seen as anticipatory in nature. Bandura would prefer to speak of the regulation rather than the reinforcement of behavior by its consequences. Self-reinforcement or self-regulation plays a major role in social-learning theory, and Bandura viewed this as

a mediational process. Bandura took the findings on awareness in conditioning more seriously than other behaviorists, trying to adapt them to his explanations. He noted that there are certain predictive stimuli that clue the person as to likely consequences of a behavioral act, resulting in what he called anticipation (expectancy) learning. Though Bandura placed much stress on cognitive (mediating) factors in human learning, when it came to assigning agency to a self system, he was opposed to any such theoretical usage. In the final analysis, self-control for Bandura is cognitive control through mediation, taking into consideration past learning of values and options (mediating alternatives). Even so, Bandura's insistence that the person has some cognitive control over the course of behavior represented a liberalization of the behavioristic line of description. Problems arise when we get down to the basic origins of self-regulation, where Bandura seemed to revert to traditional, nonpersonal, or environmental (as well as biological) origins.

Social-learning theory accepts all of the traditional explanations of abnormal behavior and its modification, but adds an emphasis on the role of observational learning (modeling). People are taught a punishment sequence of behavior, so that when they do something wrong they expect to be punished. Hence, even when a behavior is not all that wrong—more a mistake than a bad behavior—this expectation leads to self-punishment of an unrealistic nature or worse. The therapist acts as a change agent to provide cognitive cues (insights), or in other instances, to plan a program of scheduled reinforcements. Halfway houses and other group therapy strategies may be used because people will model the successful behavior of others. What the therapist hopes to promote is self-efficacy, or the mediating cognitive process of expecting success in the upcoming social circumstances of life. Therapists want to give their clients an efficacy expectation that they can indeed meet the challenges of life, at least as well as most people can. Through performance accomplishments under the tutelage of a therapist, this self-efficacy can be achieved. As with the other behaviorists, concepts of unconscious resistance are challenged by Bandura as excess theoretical baggage.

Outline of Important Theoretical Constructs

The technique of operant conditioning: B. F. Skinner

Biographical overview
emitted responses · operants · contingencies · classes of responses · shaping of behavior · method of successive approximations · periodic versus aperiodic time intervals or response ratios · Skinner Box · schedule of reinforcement · fixed versus variable ratio schedule · fixed versus variable interval schedule · program · empirical law of effect · negative reinforcement versus punishment · aversive stimulation · Walden Two · programmed instruction · natural selection as contingent reinforcement

Theoretical considerations

Theory of illness and cure
behavioral shaping

Individual treatment cases
removal of reinforcement · shaping

The therapeutic community and social revision
token economy · base rates

Verbal conditioning as psychotherapy
verbal versus nonverbal operant responses · nonmeaningful interpretation of language

Techniques based on the principle of reciprocal inhibition: Joseph Wolpe

Biographical overview

Theoretical considerations

Learning theory and the principle of reciprocal inhibition
response, stimulus, habit · reinforcement via contiguity and drive-reduction · anxiety · inhibition of response · reactive inhibition · conditioned inhibition · reciprocal inhibition · systematic desensitization

Three steps in behavior therapy
sud: subjective unit of disturbance · relationship factors

Assertive training
assertive behavior · behavioral rehearsal · lifesmanship tactics

Systematic desensitization
progressive relaxation · deep muscle relaxation · hypnotism · anxiety hierarchy · desensitization *in vivo* · counterconditioning

Aversion therapy
avoidance counterconditioning

The role of reciprocal inhibition in all forms of psychotherapy

The technique of implosive therapy: Thomas G. Stampfl

Biographical overview
implosive therapy · avoidance conditioning

Theoretical considerations

Learning theory and the principle of experimental extinction
experimental extinction · reduction in

anxiety · primary versus secondary reinforcement · extinction of anxiety · two-factor theory of learning · problem-solving versus conditioning

Theory of illness and cure
implosion · implosive therapy · symptoms of neurosis · conditioned avoidance responses · redintegrate · symptom contingent cues · hypothesized conditioned aversive cues · extinction of anxiety

The steps of implosive therapy
ASCH: avoidance serial cue hierarchy · generalization of extinction · acceptance of conscience cues · extinction of cues · paradoxical intention · flooding

Some final considerations
overcoming resistance

Eclectic behaviorism in social learning theory: Albert Bandura

Some problems with the concept of reinforcement
subject awareness

Biographical overview

Theoretical considerations

The eclectic behaviorist
combining eliciting with emitting responses · cybernetics · entropy · information · input, output, feedback · information-processing model · cognitive psychology · reciprocal interaction · person, behavior, environment

Vicarious learning as modeling or observational learning
vicarious learning · modeling · social learning theory · perceptive learning · observational learning · modeling

effect · inhibition versus disinhibition · discrimination · discriminative stimuli · abstract modeling · acquisition versus performance of responses

Reinforcement as an informational and motivational process
drive state versus arousal · motivation as incentive-formation · anticipatory processes in motivation · reinforcer · information process · regulation versus reinforcement of behavior

Self-regulation as a mediational process
awareness in conditioning · anticipation and expectancy learning · predictive stimuli · mediating capacities · cognition · self-factors in learning · basic origins of human learning · self-control as cognitive control · values · freedom · mediators begin in environmental input

Theory of illness and cure
punishment sequence · change agent · half-way houses · self-efficacy · outcome expectancy · efficacy expectation · performance accomplishments · vicarious experience · verbal persuasion · emotional arousal · insight as mediation · resistance · unconscious · catharsis

Notes

1. Dollard and Miller, 1950, p. 350. **2.** Ibid., p. 168. **3.** Skinner, 1967, p. 412. **4.** Ibid., p. 387. **5.** Skinner, 1963a, p. 506. **6.** Ibid., p. 513. **7.** Evans, 1968, p. 33. **8.** Ibid., p. 35. **9.** Skinner, 1967, p. 403. **10.** Evans, 1968, p. 46. **11.** Skinner, 1961, 1971. **12.** Skinner, 1960. **13.** Ibid., p. 36. **14.** Pressey, 1926. **15.** Skinner, 1968. **16.** Skinner, 1956, p. 231. **17.** Evans, 1968, p. 88. **18.** Ibid., p. 20. **19.** Ibid., p. 88. **20.** Skinner, 1948, p. 53. **21.** Rogers and Skinner, 1956, p. 1059. **22.** Rogers, 1963, pp. 271–272. **23.** Evans, 1968, p. 19. **24.** Skinner, 1963a, p. 514. **25.** Skinner, 1957, pp. 458–459. **26.** Ibid., p. 460. **27.**

Evans, 1968, p. 107. **28.** Skinner, 1971, p. 18. **29.** Skinner, 1974, p. 40. **30.** Evans, 1968, p. 22. **31.** See esp. E. G. Boring, 1946, p. 179. **32.** Ullmann and Krasner, 1965, p. 22. **33.** Eysenck, 1952; Rachman, 1963. **34.** Skinner, Solomon, and Lindsley, 1954. **35.** Ullmann and Krasner, 1965. **36.** Evans, 1968, pp. 41–44. **37.** Ibid., p. 44. **38.** E.g., Atthowe and Krasner, 1968. **39.** Skinner, 1957, p. 14. **40.** Ibid. **41.** Ibid., pp. 13–14. **42.** Krasner, 1962. **43.** Krasner, 1965. **44.** Wolpe, 1958, p. 37. **45.** Ibid., p. 16. **46.** Ibid., p. 19. **47.** Ibid., pp. 3–4. **48.** Ibid., p. 3. **49.** Ibid., p. 5. **50.** Wolpe, 1973, p. 205. **51.** Wolpe, 1958, p. 20. **52.** Ibid., p. 8. **53.** Ibid. **54.** Ibid. **55.** Wolpe, 1960, p. 88. **56.** Wolpe, 1958, pp. 23–24. **57.** Ibid., p. 43. **58.** Ibid., p 26. **59.** Ibid., p. 28. **60.** Ibid., p. 29. **61.** Ibid., p. 30. **62.** Cover Jones, 1974. **63.** Wolpe, 1958, p. 139. **64.** Ibid., p. 32. **65.** Ibid., p. 33. **66.** Ibid., p. 34. **67.** Ibid., p. 35. **68.** Ibid., p. 63. **69.** Ibid., p. 71. **70.** Wolpe, 1969, p. 23. **71.** Ibid., p. 22. **72.** Ibid., p. 142. **73.** Wolpe, 1969, p. 28; Wolpe, 1973, p. 28. **74.** Wolpe, 1969, p. 116. **75.** Ibid., p. 55. **76.** Ibid., p. 57. **77.** Ibid., p. 58. **78.** Ibid., p. 60. **79.** Ibid., pp. 244–245. **80.** Ibid., p. 13. **81.** Wolpe, 1973, p. 81. **82.** Ibid. **83.** Wolpe, 1969, p. 61. **84.** Ibid., p. 68. **85.** Ibid., p. 67. **86.** Wolpe, 1973, p. 90. **87.** Wolpe, 1969, p. 70. **88.** Wolpe, 1958, p. 139. **89.** Wolpe, 1969, p. 103. **90.** Ibid., p. 123. **91.** Ibid., p. 107. **92.** Ibid., p. 118. **93.** Ibid., p. 117. **94.** Ibid., p. 127. **95.** Ibid. **96.** Ibid., p. 131. **97.** Ibid., pp. 134–135. **98.** Wolpe, 1973, p. 182. **99.** Ibid. **100.** Watson and Rayner, 1920. **101.** Wolpe, 1969, p. 200. **102.** Ibid., p. 204. **103.** Freund, 1960; Feldman and MacCulloch, 1967. **104.** Freund, 1960, p. 317. **105.** Wolpe, 1969, Chapter IX. **106.** Wolpe, 1958, p. 193. **107.** Ibid., p. 194. **108.** Ibid., p. 198. **109.** Wolpe, 1960. **110.** Wolpe, 1969, p. 277. **111.** Ibid. **112.** Mowrer, 1939. **113.** See esp. Mowrer, 1961. **114.** Stampfl and Levis, 1967a, p. 497. **115.** Stampfl and Levis, 1968, p. 34. **116.** Ibid. **117.** Stampfl and Levis, 1967b, p. 24. **118.** Ibid. **119.** Stampfl, 1966, p. 14. **120.** Stampfl and Levis, 1969. **121.** Stampfl and Levis, 1966. **122.** Stampfl and Levis, 1967a, pp. 498–499. **123.** Ibid., p. 499. **124.** Stampfl and Levis, 1968, p. 33. **125.** Stampfl and Levis, 1967b, p. 26. **126.** Stampfl and Levis, 1968, p. 32. **127.** Stampfl, 1966, p. 19. **128.** Stampfl and Levis, 1969. **129.** Stampfl, 1966, p. 15. **130.** Stampfl and Levis, 1967a, p. 500. **131.** Stampfl and Levis, 1967b, p. 26. **132.** Stampfl and Levis, 1967a, p. 501. **133.** Stampfl and Levis, 1969. **134.** Ibid., p. 101. **135.** Ibid., p. 100. **136.** Stampfl and Levis, 1966. **137.** Ibid., p. 10. **138.** Stampfl and Levis, 1967a, p. 502. **139.** Hefferline and Keenan, 1963; Hefferline, Keenan, and Harford, 1959. **140.** Kaufman, Baron, and Kopp, 1966. **141.** Brewer, 1974. **142.** Personal communication. **143.** Evans, 1976, p. 244. **144.** Bandura, 1969, p. 26. **145.** Ibid., p. 77. **146.** Wiener, 1954, p. 15. **147.** Ibid., p. 16. **148.** Neisser 1967. **149.** Bandura, 1969, p. 127 and p. 152. **150.** Bandura, 1977a, p. 96. **151.** Bandura, 1977a, p. 170. **152.** Ibid., p. 91. **153.** Ibid., p. 9. **154.** Ibid., p. 194. **155.** Bandura, 1973, p. 43. **156.** Bandura, 1969, p. 45. **157.** Ibid., p. 47. **158.** Bandura, 1973, p. 48. **159.** Bandura, 1973, pp. 85–86; Bandura, 1977a, p. 41. **160.** Bandura, 1977a, pp. 11–12. **161.** Ibid., p. 91. **162.** Bandura, 1969, p. 127. **163.** Ibid., p. 133. **164.** Bandura, 1977a, p. 122. **165.** Bandura, 1969, p. 120; Bandura, 1973, p. 68; Bandura, 1977a, p. 149. **166.** Bandura, 1969, pp. 192–193. **167.** Bandura, 1977a, p. 40. **168.** Bandura, 1969, p. 136. **169.** Bandura, 1977a, p. 41. **170.** Ibid., p. 67. **171.** Bandura, 1969, p. 128. **172.** Ibid., p. 381. **173.** Ibid., p. 424. **174.** Bandura, 1973, pp. 194–195. **175.** Ibid., p. 47. **176.** Bandura, 1969, p. 220. **177.** Bandura, 1969, pp. 129–130. **178.** Ibid., p. 224. **179.** Ibid. **180.** Bandura, 1977a, p. 21. **181.** Bandura, 1973, p. 184. **182.** Bandura, 1977a, p. 37. **183.** Ibid., p. 130. **184.** Ibid., p. 161. **185.** Ibid., p. 70. **186.** Ibid., p. 103. **187.** Bandura, 1974, p. 864. **188.** Bandura, 1978, p. 356. **189.** Bandura, 1977a, p. 206. **190.** Ibid., p. 18. **191.** Skinner, 1974, p. 57. **192.** Bandura, 1973, p. 50. **193.** Ibid. **194.** Bandura, 1977a, p. 69. **195.** Ibid., p. 72. **196.** Ibid. **197.** Ibid., p., 66. **198.** Ibid., p. 67. **199.** Ibid., p. 160. **200.** Bandura, 1969, p. 10. **201.** Bandura, 1977a, p. 199. **202.** Bandura, 1973, p. 53. **203.** Bandura, 1977a, p. 165. **204.** Bandura, 1978, p. 348. **205.** Bandura, 1977a, p. 70. **206.** Bandura, 1973, p. 207. **207.** Bandura, 1978, p. 356. **208.** Bandura, 1977a, p. 201. **209.** Ibid., p. 13. **210.** Bandura, 1969, p. 564. **211.** Ibid., p. 21. **212.** Ibid., p. 105. **213.** Ibid., p. 530. **214.** Ibid., p. 535. **215.** Bandura, 1973, p. 148. **216.** Bandura, 1977a, p. 152. v. **219.** Ibid., p. 80. **220.** Ibid., p. 402. and p. 430. **221.** Bandura, 1973, p. 248. **222.** Ibid. **223.** 430. **221.** Bandura, 1973, p. 248. **222.** Ibid. **223.** Ibid., p. 249. **224.** Bandura, 1969, p. 275. **225.** Bandura, 1977b. **226.** Ibid., p. 193. **227.** Ibid., p. 195. **228.** Ibid., p. 209. **229.** Bandura, 1969, p. 94. **230.** Bandura, 1977a, p. 165. **231.** Bandura, 1969, pp. 590–591. **232.** Bandura, 1973, p. 148.

Chapter 8

Theory Construction in the Empirico-Behavioristic Tradition

Now that we have completed the three chapters of Part II concerned with an empirical-behavioristic explanation of behavior, we can return to the question-answer format of the Introduction and Chapter 4. All that we have considered before relates to Part II as well, of course. But the behavioristic theoreticians have stressed certain aspects of personality study, and they have offered alternative explanations to those of the psychoanalysts. Chapter 8 poses the following five broad questions:

If we predict and/or control the course of behavior, does this mean we necessarily understand it?

How well does behavioristic theory account for mind and human agency?

What are the implications of the findings on "awareness in conditioning" for the study of personality?

Are there any dialectical themes hidden away in behavioristic writings or empirical psychological researches?

What motives to psychotherapy are primary in the empirico-behavioristic tradition?

Before turning to the first question, there is an interesting point to be made. That is, there are personologists who believe that behavioristic theories should not even be considered in the same context with personality theories. There are several reasons for this attitude. Personality theories are on the whole *discriminal* theories, whereas learning (S-R) theory is a *vehicular* explanation of behavior (see p. 28 of the Introduction). Learning theories are written at a high level of abstraction, with a resultant assumption that these vehicular constructs can *subsume* or "take under definitional range of meaning" the constructs of less abstract theories, thereby accounting for them. This is what Dollard and Miller claimed to have done in subsuming Freudian theory by S-R theory. It would seem that such efforts alone would qualify behavioristic or S-R theories for inclusion in the study of personality.

At an even more abstract level, however, we *also* have the question posed by the "image of humanity" which any theory claiming to describe human beings projects. This is surely a problem for the personologist. Although it may not be correct to say that every personologist is ipso facto a self-proclaimed teleologist, surely our study of personality to this point suggests that it is when a theorist tries to capture human behavior in human-like terms that trouble arises in psychology. The behaviorist is likely to call such theories *anthropomorphic,* and the personologist is likely then to retort with the charge that behavioristic theory is *not* a personality theory and so it has no right to be critical of the personological conceptions which are called for to explain human behavior. When we look more carefully at the crux of the argument— what makes a theory anthropomorphic?—we *always* find a telic issue arising in one guise or another. No matter what terms are used to describe the person teleologically—agency, consciousness, free will, wish, self-direction,

purpose, intention, and so on—the issue we come back to again and again is the one of whether it is proper to describe people in terms of final causation.

Moving up to a still higher level of abstraction, it is possible for us to analyze the issues that separate the mechanistic (behavioristic, cybernetic, and so on) theorist from the teleological theorist by *subsuming* them with our theory-construction constructs. Continuing in the vein of the Introduction and Chapter 4, we can employ the causal constructs, the Lockean and Kantian models, and the demonstrative versus dialectical interpretations of meaning to sort out and understand the reasons for the disagreements between the mechanist and the teleologist. We turn, therefore, to a series of questions that often arise when personologists consider behavioristic explanations of behavior.

If We Predict and/or Control the Course of Behavior, Does This Mean We Necessarily Understand It?

One of the most convincing reasons we have for believing a theory is to find that it can predict an event's outcome before it takes place. This predictive requirement is central to validation in the research method. *Psychology* is frequently defined as the science of "the control and prediction" of behavior, and this phrase is interpreted broadly enough by psychologists to include predicting people's behaviors from test scores, or predicting their behavior during an experiment, or even manipulating their behavior directly in psychotherapy or environmental engineering. Bandura reflected this attitude when he said, "If progress in the understanding of human behavior is to be accelerated, psychological theories must be judged by their predictive power, and by the efficacy of the behavioral modification procedures that they produce."[1] The key word here is *understanding*. It makes good sense (based on procedural evidence) to think that if we can predict what is going to happen or actually manipulate events to make an expected outcome happen, we have an understanding of what we have accomplished. But is this *necessarily* true?

We know that people have predicted weather and seasonal changes, as well as cured (controlled) physical and mental illnesses for centuries without understanding the causes of these events in the sense that we do today. And even more fundamentally, we learned in the Introduction (p. 26; see also Chapter 4, p. 306) that because of the *affirming-the-consequent* fallacy of an "if, then" line of reasoning, we can never hope to have that *necessary* sense of conviction that we get when we reason through affirmed antecedents. Experimental predictions from theory A can be duplicated from theories B, C, and so on. Framing a crucial experiment to decide which of these theories is true for all time is impossible. We simply must learn to live with the insight that empirical support (validation) for a theory does not *necessarily* rule out alternative explanations of the same fact pattern. Does this mean that by reasoning through affirmed antecedents we can arrive at certainty? There is no guarantee that this will occur either. For example, were we to reason "properly" about behavior, we might follow a syllogistic line from "All outspoken people are basically hostile in personality" (major premise) to "Sidney is outspoken" (a minor premise affirming the antecedent of our major premise) to "Sidney has a hostile personality" (conclusion). Though this logical sequence is correct, we could well have arrived at a totally invalid judgment of our acquaintance, Sidney.

The sense of conviction that we have in coming to this necessary conclusion does not compensate for the fact that, having begun with a doubtful first assumption (major premise), we have wronged poor Sidney, who may be verbally aggressive but not a hostile person. Or is he? How can we know? What factors are involved in arriving at a clear decision concerning whether or not people who are outspoken have basically hostile personalities? It seems clear that we can never hope to achieve complete certainty (necessary understanding), given our problems of (1) reasoning from major premises that may be (completely or partially) wrong and (2) the affirming-the-consequent drawback of validation which must always allow for a possible alternative understanding of a fact pattern. Even so, we should not despair, because to have absolute, unchanging knowledge would mean that perfection had been attained and there was nothing further to learn. Yet we know that knowledge must always change, broaden, be made possible through different ways of testing it, and so on. About all we can hope to do at any point is to minimize our distortions and perfect the alternatives that seem reasonably related to the evidence we have at hand. We next turn to some ways in which we can sharpen our thinking about the theoretical description and methodological validation of human behavior.

Principles of Falsification and Verifiability

One of the ways in which Sidney might have been spared the judgment of being considered a hostile person is for us to have had a sounder major premise to begin with. Rather than believing that *all* outspoken people are basically hostile in personality, we might have begun with the view that *some* outspoken people behave in this way. This still would suggest that a meaningful relation exists between outspokenness and hostility. What do we mean by *outspokenness?* How can we recognize this quality in the behavior of people? How do we measure this quality of personality? The same kinds of questions can be raised concerning the construct of hostility. To help us frame clear-cut, hence testable hypotheses, the philosopher of science Karl Popper has suggested that we follow a *principle of falsification,* which states, *"It must be possible for an empirical scientific system to be refuted by experience."* [2] In other words, if we begin using words like *outspokenness* and *hostility,* we had better begin thinking seriously about how we can measure the role of these concepts in actual, observable experience. At least, we better begin thinking about this empirical problem if we want to study personality in a scientific manner, which means that we will have to validate our claims via the research method.

A common criticism of psychoanalysis is that it presents us with a theory that *cannot* be falsified, or refuted by empirical experience. A construct like *libido,* for example, cannot be defined in a way allowing us to test its effects on observed behavior. When a scientist frames the steps to be taken in measuring a theoretical construct empirically, it is called an *operational definition.*[3] The word *operation* is roughly equivalent to a *step* in the sequence, so that to *operationalize* a theoretical construct is to take steps to put it into a methodologically testable form. Recall from the Introduction that we tried to operationalize "jolliness" by gauging the laughter of subjects on an electrical laugh meter (see p. 25). This falsifiability criticism of psychoanalysis is in general well taken, but the truth is, Jung *did* suggest an operational definition of his libido construct. That is, Jung suggested that libido was an energy which reflected itself in consciousness as a judgment of personal *value.*[4] As Jungians, we could assess libidinal cathexes in various objects, life activities, or even other people by simply having our subjects rate these items for personal value (liking, preference, taking an interest in, and so on).

There is another way in which the heavily dialectical nature of psychoanalysis (see Chapter 4) works against proper falsification of its theoretical claims. Popper teaches us that not only must a scientific statement be operationalized, but it must be framed in one meaningful sense and one sense only, so that it is very clear precisely what is being predicted. Thus, if we were to say, "It will rain or not rain here tomorrow," this would *not* be a scientific hypothesis because it could not be falsified (refuted).[5] To meet the principle of falsification we must say either "It will rain here tomorrow" or "It will not rain here tomorrow." Note the stress on *demonstrative reasoning* here with its *law of contradiction* (see p. 8). Whenever we move from theorizing to a scientific test of anything in the research method, we begin reasoning in exclusively a demonstrative, *unipolar* way ("rain" or "not rain"). If we continued to rely on *dialectical reasoning* in the research context, we might begin splitting hairs, asking possibly, "Who can say precisely when the moisture which is always in the atmosphere *is* rain, as opposed to a fog or drizzle?" and so on.

Though such hair-splitting is called for in working out our theoretical position, at some point when we get down to the essentials of validation, we simply have to settle on a "this, and only this" (unipolar) definition of our concept. Returning to the example of our acquaintance Sidney, we would have to clearly define in operational terms what we consider outspokenness and hostility to be. In conducting a study aimed at testing our major premise—now called an experimental hypothesis—we might work out a research design in which subjects would be classified as outspoken if they spoke up very frankly in an experimental situation calling for tact and verbal restraint. Hostility might be assessed independently by having subjects choose behavioral alternatives in various imagined social situations to see if they would select the most hostile possibilities. For example, a subject might be asked what he or she would do if, after having requested that some neighborhood children please keep off a lawn, these children persisted in riding their bicycles across it. Alternative answers could range from speaking to the children's parents through some form of physical threat to attack on the children directly. A number of such situations could be devised and presented to subjects as a test of the experimental hypothesis that "Verbal outspokenness is related to a hostile personality."

This hypothesis could now be falsified, which means it could be submitted to validation. The reason we call the principle now under consideration one of "falsification" is because all we can *ever* do following the experimental test is to say "the experimental hypothesis has not been supported (is false) by the data observed." Because of the affirming-the-consequent fallacy, we are unable to say "the experimental hypothesis is true." Sometimes, a psychologist will reframe his or her experimental hypothesis in what is called the *null-hypothesis* form, thereby permitting a rejection of the prediction it encompasses at some given level of statistical significance. In the present example it would be something like "There is no relationship between verbal outspokenness and the level of hostility in a subject's personality." If we now find a statistically significant level of relationship, we can reject the null hypothesis with this level of confidence—for example, that only five times out of one hundred would we be wrong to suggest that the null hypothesis is false. Even so, this does *not* permit us to say the reverse of the null hypothesis is true! We never accept the meaning of any experimental hypothesis as being necessarily true. What we have is an ongoing theory, which we accept as the truth based on procedural evidence. But we also acknowledge that there could well be other theories that equally predict what we have observed in the experimental data, not to mention several kinds of criticisms about how we conducted our research experiment.

For example, a critic of our theory might point out that there are many kinds of hostility, some of which relate to outspokenness and some of which do not. The latter, nonverbal, smoldering forms of hostility may be just as harmful to interpersonal relations as the overt variety. Looking at our experimental design, this critic might suggest that we had actually fostered selection of merely the hostile-outspoken person plus the nonhostile-outspoken person, and missed the nonoutspoken-hostile person altogether. Our hostility measure might also be attacked as tapping merely what people *fantasy* doing, but would never actually do in overt behavior. What could we say to this critic? Well, we could think up counterarguments of one sort or another, but in the final analysis, we would have to admit that the critic might be right—or, equally true, the critic might be wrong. The falsification principle itself does not tell us which theory is *necessarily* true, nor does it tell us which theory should be furthered by being put to succeeding empirical tests. In other words, this principle is exclusively concerned with questions of *method* (proof, evidence, and so on). The principle of falsification makes reference *solely* to how we go about testing our theories; it can *never* select the right theory for us to put to test. This principle has *nothing at all* to do with theoretical explanation.

Even so, many behaviorists charge that psychoanalysts are too ready to advance theoretical justifications in order to twist what an experimental finding suggests into its opposite. For example, a psychoanalyst who finds that outspokenness in a sample of subjects is *not* related to hostility (no matter how these constructs are measured)—that it may even bear a negative relationship, so that it is the least outspoken subjects who are the most hostile—could justify this nonpredicted outcome as an example of *reaction-formation* (see p. 61). The outspoken subjects could be said to be so threatened by their underlying hostility toward others that they turn such promptings into the opposite behavior and appear even *less* overtly hostile than the non-outspoken subjects. This kind of dialectical maneuver is not unheard of in psychoanalytical interpretations of empirical research data, and it is one of the reasons that psychoanalysis is called a theory that "damns you if you do and damns you if you don't" behave as expected (predicted). Because the analysts have both outcomes covered by their dialectical constructs, they are like the person who predicts "rain or no rain" on the morrow.

Another principle that has been very influential in the behavioristic tradition is the *criterion of verifiability*. This comes to psychology from the philosophical school of thought known as *logical positivism,* an outlook that Clark Hull was early drawn to and helped popularize in America.[6] Logical positivism is a heavily empirical point of view, one that aimed to settle philosophical problems by first deciding whether they made a real difference in the observations of experience or not. The logical positivist Alfred J. Ayer essentially defined the principle of veri-

fiability when he wrote, "We say that a sentence is factually significant to any given person, if, and only if, he knows how to verify the proposition which it purports to express—that is, if he knows what observations would lead him, under certain conditions, to accept the proposition as being true, or reject it as being false."[7] If a sentence (containing a belief, point of view, claim, and so on) cannot be verified, then it is not a properly philosophical assertion, and there is little point in spending time discussing it with an aim of proving it true or false. The logical positivists were able to drop a number of traditional philosophical topics by using their principle of verifiability. For example, they concluded that philosophy could never determine the validity of a system of ethics, because there was no way of naming the observations called for to prove one ethical judgment any truer than another.[8]

Even though the principle of verifiability is stated in a reverse direction to falsification—it speaks to what can be accepted (verified) rather than to what can be rejected (falsified)—the two rules of how to proceed methodologically get at the same thing. Once the philosopher attempted to use a scientific procedure to verify a statement, he or she would become immersed in falsification as well. Note that both principles turn our attention outward, in *extraspective* fashion, to look for evidence in observation. We accept the plausibility of these principles based on procedural evidence, but their utility is in what they suggest we do in order to test our theories empirically. An introspective theory, one that might not show up so readily in direct observation, would prove difficult to verify or to design an experiment for in order to falsify the hypothesis being advanced. Those psychologists who are less empirical in outlook—the psychoanalysts of Part One or the phenomenologists of Part Three—often feel that these methodological principles have become too important in psychology. Methodological principles are said to foster superficial theorizing, and imply that unless we can operationalize every idea we have as psychological theorists we are dealing in meaningless constructs. And yet it takes time before a sound theory can be put to methodological test. Thinking up a way of proving a hypothesis is a difficult job in itself, but this should never become the grounds for dismissing the hypothesis or considering it meaningless from the start.

For example, in the history of psychology, John Romanes (1848–1894) was severely criticized by Lloyd Morgan (1852–1936) and others for anthropomorphizing his accounts of lower animals.[9] Romanes seemed to accept the theory that animals below the human level could reason and possibly communicate their thoughts as human beings do (but less proficiently, of course). This seemed an impossible contention to psychologists during the first two-thirds of the twentieth century. But when the Gardners[10] around 1960 hit on the idea of teaching a chimpanzee to use "words" from the American sign language for the deaf, the previously meaningless theory suddenly took on verifiability and falsifiability. In like fashion, say those psychologists who theorize more introspectively about behavior, there are many worthwhile concepts about personality—including the unconscious —that make sense in the clinical context but that are not yet ready for investigation in the research context. To say that these constructs are therefore meaningless merely serves to limit speculative creativity in *both* the theoretical and the methodological spheres of psychology.

Lawfulness and the Function Construct

When behavioristic psychologists consider the question of behavioral prediction, they are likely to emphasize the *lawfulness* of behavior. Tied to this is the concept of *variables* (see p. 25), which are said to be functionally related to one another; such *functions* can be measured as *laws* of behavior. As extraspective theorists taking a realistic position in their theoretical descriptions, the behaviorists think of themselves as looking *at* a course of perfectly lawful events that are really taking place in the world of empirical observation (realism). Rain falls, leaves are blown about, and human beings move hither and yon—all by the same laws (see Hull's raindrop analogy, p. 263). Behaviorists tend to demean the role of theory in psychology. Thus, Skinner once defined theory as an "effort to explain behavior in terms of something going on in another universe, such as the mind or the nervous system."[11] He went on to suggest that when a psychologist has achieved control over the behavior of an organism, there is no longer any need to theorize.[12] What is the point in speculating when we have our hand on reality and therefore can make it do our bidding? In time, Skinner came reluctantly to admit that theories can be helpful, except "when they lead the scientist in the wrong direction."[13]

For behaviorists to admit a major determining role for theorizing in science runs counter to their fundamental theory of knowledge. They view behavioral determinism in exclusively hard, physical terms based on the meanings of material and especially efficient causation (see pp. 266–267). This is why behaviorists qualify as mechanists. Since theorizing implies thinking, which takes its meaning from the formal and final causes as psychic determinism (at least, in the common sense meaning of a dictionary definition of *thinking*), it stands to reason that such conceptions would not be welcomed by the behaviorists. Wolpe once said that "people are never able to act like gods detached from causality." [14] The causes referred to here are, of course, of a material- and efficient-cause nature. A teleological psychological theorist (henceforth we will call this type a *teleologist*) might agree and then add, "Human freedom from nature is not a detachment from all causation, but is simply the operation of formal-final causation in addition and/or opposition to material-efficient causation" (see our discussion of freedom, pp. 297–300). The behavioristic psychological theorist (henceforth we will call this type a *mechanist*) would probably remain unimpressed by this telic addition, saying instead to the teleologist: "If we can control and predict the behavior of people (as well as lower animals), then how can you go on believing that there are these formal causes in nature? Any scientist knows that behavior is just nature in motion, and that all natural things are moving about lawfully, all of the time. In controlling and predicting behavior, I am simply capitalizing on this scientific knowledge just as all scientists do."

Recall from Chapter 4 (pp. 270–278) that this idea of nature as being in a constant state of locomotion took many centuries to arise in the history of science, and it was helped along by the shift from a Euclidian to a Cartesian geometry, a view of mathematics that Sir Isaac Newton wrote into his laws of motion. The remarkable thing about Newton's laws of motion is that they are both mathematical principles or assumptions and *also* empirically proven facts.[15] As such their meaning has had a duality about it. Mathematical principles or laws are framed initially as any theoretical statement is framed and then put to test through a cognitive method employing procedural evidence. Once these laws predict empirical events through valida-

tion in the research method, a somewhat different sense of the word *law* emerges. In this latter sense, we are speaking of a stable observation, a repeatable regularity in events that can be expected to occur like clockwork. This latter meaning of law is more akin to a methodological usage.

We therefore see that it is possible to speak of laws in either a theoretical sense or in a methodological sense. Laws that are stated as propositions to be expected or followed as assumptions are not always demonstrably true when we put them to the test of validation. The amusing Murphy's law which holds that "If something can go wrong, it will" strikes us as all too true judging from unsystematic recollections of our past frustrations. But until it is empirically shown to take place *in fact*—that is, reliably or again and again—it is not a law in the methodological sense, but rather a lighthearted theoretical commentary on human frailty. It is especially important to keep this distinction between a theoretical and/or methodological usage of the word *law* in mind when we begin saying things like "All behavior is lawful." Does this mean "We assume behavior to be lawful" (theory) or "We find behavior to be lawful empirically" (method) or both?

In framing his laws of motion, Newton did not think that every motion occurs in an efficient-cause sense of one item thrusting another along. Causes arise when there is an interference in the naturally free motion of events moving lawfully—as when a freely moving point strikes another freely moving point, *causing* the two points to change direction or, assuming that the momentum of each is perfectly balanced, bringing both points to a balanced standstill. By speaking of freely moving points we are, of course, reflecting Cartesian geometry and essentially attributing it to reality as if it is natural for events to be moving from the outset of existence. Strictly speaking, Newton's theory is clearest and most readily visualized in the realm of mathematics, where we can have a mental picture of a moving point, tracing a circle by moving equidistantly from a center point.[16] If we now think of this motion as the earth moving around the sun, we can say that the earth is not necessarily being efficiently-caused by some thrust moving it along in space. It "just does" encircle the sun in this manner "by nature." We would be taking Newton's purely mathematical calculations and applying them as theoretical laws of motion to the motions of the planets. Now, whether there is such a motion as free motion in nature was hotly debated in science,[17] and practically speaking, it became customary in science to think of all events occurring in nature as having (material and/or efficient) *causes*. At least, this was true up to the turn of the twentieth century, when the physicist Ernst Mach[18] began to question the usefulness of the efficient cause as a basic description of everything in nature. Mach pointed out that when we observe the relationship between two events in nature and prove through the research method (validating evidence) that one event is lawfully related to another event, all we have proven is that a *correlation* exists between our two observations. Since the turn of the twentieth century it has therefore become common to hear that science deals in correlations between observed events and not in (efficient) causes.

A question suggested here is: what is a correlation if not a *pattern* of relationship between points or events, hence a formal cause? Thus, if we are willing to broaden our usage of the causal construct, then we can subsume the meaning of Newtonian mathematics and Machian correlations by the formal-cause construct. Mathematics is a theory of knowledge resting entirely on patterns of relationship seen plausibly to interrelate according to known steps and clear rules of combination. When Newton found that his law of gravity did indeed apply to the world of reality, he was delighted to see it predict external events and yet puzzled by the fact that he could not fill in the picture with constructs of a material- and efficient-cause variety. He was aware of the strictly formal-cause nature of his law and did not, like so many of his colleagues, place gravity *into* things, as if it were some kind of invisible material force holding things together and making them happen (this was proposed by others as the "ether"). In fact, in a letter written in 1725, Newton took a colleague to task for doing precisely this, as follows:

You sometimes speak of gravity as essential and inherent to matter. Pray do not ascribe that notion to me; for the cause of gravity is what I do not pretend to know. . . . It is inconceivable that inanimate brute matter should, without the mediation of something else, which is not material, operate upon, and effect other matter without mutual contact.[19]

This "action at a distance" in which two bodies were drawn to each other gravitationally seemed to take place without an apparent cause, and even though it all worked out beautifully in mathematical space—that is, formal-cause patternings—the "father of gravity" was left speechless to put gravity into the accepted material- and efficient-cause type of explanation then required of the scientist. Recalling our discussion of motion in Chapter 4 (see pp. 268–269), it would not be wrong to suggest that free motion for Newton was *not* locomotion, but the qualitative motion of changing patterns and points moving along patterned shapes as defined and employed in geometry.[20] Later, Mach would say this is all any scientist ever does—

describe the patterns of observed experience without knowing what *the* (efficient-) causes of the observed regularity may be. Mach was fully aware of the limitations of the falsification and verifiability principles as regards the affirming-the-consequent fallacy. He was the first "father of modern science" to draw a firm line between the *methodological context* and the *theoretical context,* as follows:

Different ideas [theories] can express the facts [methodological findings] with the same exactness in the domain accessible to observation. The facts [method] must hence be carefully distinguished from the intellectual *constructs [theory] the formation of which they suggested. The latter—concepts— must be* consistent *with observation, and must in addition be* logically *in accord with one another. Now these two requirements can be fulfilled in more than one manner, and hence the different systems of geometry.*[21]

The implication that we can draw from Mach's distinction is that, just because we find behavior to be lawful in the methodological context, it does not *necessarily* follow that the theory explaining this lawful behavior will be the same one for every psychologist who tracks the regularity. To return to the debate between our teleologist and mechanist, we might now hear the teleologist say: "Just because you (the mechanist) 'control and predict' behavior in your experimental researches does *not* mean that your mechanistic theory explaining these facts is the only one that could be used to understand them. According to Ernst Mach, as long as I think up a telic theory that is logical and consistent with the facts predicted and observed, I have as much right to 'account for' them as you do." At this point the mechanist would probably retort with: "Well, maybe so, but I can't for the life of me see why, when you have direct control over the organism and can ac-

tually see it behaving according to your predicted directions, you would worry about other causal meanings in this lawful behavior than the efficient-cause meanings. If I can shape a pigeon to walk in a figure eight through the method of successive approximations, using grains of food to mold this behavioral pattern, I have about as clear and direct evidence of the effects of my efficient causation as I could possibly get. It *must* be true without doubt that the pigeon's behavioral responses are a *function* of my (food-) stimulus control."

The word *function* employed by the mechanist seems first to have been used in the seventeenth century by the German mathematician and philosopher Gottfried Wilhelm von Leibniz, who was a contemporary of Newton's and a codiscoverer of the differential calculus. He used it in a general sense to refer to the mathematical relationship between two changing numerical values. If two numerical series of values increase or decrease in a constant ratio, one to the other, then there is a 1-to-1 functional relationship obtaining between them. As one numerical value increases by a single step, so does the other. There could also be a 1-to-2 *functional relationship,* so that as one numerical value goes up by a single step, the other value doubles, and so on. In the nineteenth century, the German mathematician Peter G. L. Dirichlet brought this concept of the function into line with the concepts of an independent and dependent mathematical *variable.* An *independent variable,* which is typically plotted along the abscissa of a graph and symbolized by X, is the one the mathematician assigns a value to arbitrarily (at will). The *dependent variable,* which is typically plotted along the ordinate of a graph and symbolized by a Y, is the one that automatically receives a value according to the functional or ratio relationship it bears with the X-variable. In a 1-to-2 functional relationship, if X is arbitrarily given the value of 10, then we know Y's value is 20; if X is 30, then Y is 60, and so on. Of course, the size of the numerical units of steps can vary, so that X might be in inches and Y might be in some fraction of an inch. But the concept of *function* gets at the systematic relationship that obtains between these two scales of numerical value.

Thus far we have been considering the X- and Y-variables purely in an abstract, mathematical sense, but what if we were now to use our functional concept to measure actual relationships between variables that we have measured in the real world? Could we show that the function construct has utility in describing something that actually exists? Let us say that we want to measure the effects of practice (X-variable) on word retention (Y-variable) in a learning task. We have a list of fifty words we want our subjects in this experiment to memorize in the proper order. A subject would thus be asked to read through the list once and then try to recall the words, then go ahead to a second trial, attempt to recall, and so on, until he or she had reached the learning criterion (recall all fifty words in correct order). If we were to do this and graph the findings relating our independent variable (X) to our dependent variable (Y) of the "number of correct words recalled," what would we find? Undoubtedly, we would find that as the number of trials increased so did the number of words recalled. We could then apply statistical techniques to describe the *functional relationship* that obtained between our X- and Y-variables, stated in terms of a correlation coefficient, slope of the line graphing this relationship,

and so on. Now, if our findings—not the exact graph line but the general direction of the functional relationship—were to cross-validate by showing up again in a second, third, and several other samples put through the same experimental procedure, we might begin referring to this reliable finding as a law.

We are using the word *law* and the concept of a functional relationship in what is undoubtedly the most appropriate sense—that is, as a *methodological* term (rather than as a theoretical term). Saying "Behavior is lawful" cannot be doubted if we mean by this that it can be shown to take on reliable tendencies when framed according to independent and dependent variables and then tested in the research (methodological) context. But once again, when it comes to explaining why these observed regularities take place—why practice facilitates retention—our knowledge of the scientific method as well as the insights of Mach teach us that we must *always* keep open the possibility of alternative explanations of the resultant behavioral laws. Indeed, since experimental predictions are rarely supported perfectly, so that there is usually as much or more in a study that is unpredicted or uncontrolled as there is that is controlled and predicted, it is plausible to say as a general theory that "Some behavior is unlawful." The scientific method does not require that we believe all behavior to be lawful. What we must believe is that the experimental method can falsify (within the limitations of affirming-the-consequent errors) propositions of all types—telic, mechanistic, and so on—without prejudice. Problems arise when we permit our methods to act as theories or to stipulate what sorts of theories can be put to validation. We turn to this confounding error next.

Theory-Method Confusions

It is easy to sympathize with our mechanist, who manipulates the independent variable

(IV) of putting down food grains to see the *direct* effect of this manipulation on the dependent variable (DV) of a pigeon's behavior (walking a figure eight). Who can seriously deny that we are seeing *the* controls of the pigeon's behavior? It is very difficult in a situation like this to remind ourselves of the limitations of falsification and the affirming-the-consequent fallacy. Being so close to our methodological evidence, it is reasonable to begin using causal meanings that are identical to the causal meanings of our IV-DV manipulations. It so happens that *both* the IV-DV sequence of validation and the stimulus-response (S-R) sequence of theoretical description are subsumed by the meaning of *efficient* causality. The IV and S are antecedent in time, too, and provide the impetus that brings about the consequent events known as the DV or the R. The later event in time (R, DV) is thus considered to be *a function of* the earlier event (S, IV), and since both of these events occur lawfully we might even begin crossing over the two lines of efficient causality and speak of an IV-R sequence or an S-DV sequence of events. This is precisely what happened in the history of behaviorism, which has been singularly devoted to the meaning of efficient causation in the description of behavior.

Thus, in the early 1930s we find a leading behaviorist saying that he: "conceives mental processes as functional variables intervening between stimuli, initiating physiological states, and the general heredity and past training of the organism, on the one hand, and final resulting responses, on the other. These intervening variables . . . [are] behavior-determinants." [22] In the 1940s two leading behaviorists were suggesting that "like every other science, psychology conceives of its problem as one of establishing the interrelations within a set of variables, most characteristically between response variables on the one hand and a manifold of environmental variables on the other." [23] And by the 1950s this tendency to mix theory terminology (response) with method terminology (variable) had become so common, it was actually written into a widely used psychological dictionary, which defines an independent variable as either a stimulus or an organismic variable, and the dependent variable in psychology as "always the response." [24] Skinner was therefore consistent with the behavioristic tradition when he said, "As an analyst of behavior, I want to relate the probability of response to a large number of independent variables, even when these variables are separated in time and space." [25] Bandura too, in discussing abnormal behavior, mixes terms when he observes that "an adequate causal explanation must specify clearly the independent variables that produce and maintain the observed schizophrenic behavior." [26]

What is the danger in referring to an experimental sequence as either an IV-DV or an S-R succession of events? The danger lies in the fact that we may render the principle of falsification useless. If all experimental data gathered in the IV-DV format are *by definition* S-R data, how can we hope to test a theory of behavior that is *not* an S-R (that is, an efficient-cause) theory? Assume that we held to a psychic determination of human behavior, and even though we did efficiently manipulate circumstances in an experimental format—control our IV to see what happened to the DV—we still believed that our experimental subjects (human beings) were *not* simply responding to stimuli in a hard-determinism sense, but that they were somehow responsible for their own behavior in a softly deterministic sense (see p. 203). An S-R theory does not accommodate this kind of explanation, and if we now see only S-R regularities in IV-DV regularities, it will be impossible *in principle* to put our softly deterministic theory to test. Even though an S-R explanation may be the best one to use in any given instance (such as explaining a pigeon's behavior), it is not always going to be the best one to use, and we know from our study of falsifiability that a good scientific method must be open to any of a number of theories in any case. When our method dictates the theory to be used to account for the data it makes possible, it is no longer an *objective* method. The job of a method is to test or prove theory, *not* to frame theory.

This is why we suggested above that the law concept is best used in a methodological sense (that is, relating exclusively to the context of proof). This leaves no doubt that what a law means is some kind of empirical relationship between the IV and DV of an experimental study, and that the question of accounting for this regularity is open to alternative theoretical explanations. To speak, for example, of S-R laws in psychology would therefore be another compounding of theoretical (S-R) and methodological (law) terminology. It was the behaviorist Kenneth W. Spence who did most to popularize the distinction between what he called S-R and response-response or R-R laws. Though he presented this distinction as if it were methodological, in point of fact he was framing a theory about how various types of laws arise in the flow of natural events. Here are some excerpts from his writings that frame the distinction he made:

. . . R = f(R) laws, describe relations between different attributes or properties of behavior; they tell us which behavior traits are associated. This type of law is investigated extensively in the fields of intelligence and personality testing, and the laws that have been discovered have formed the basis of much of our technology in the areas of guidance, counseling, and clinical diagnosis. These empirical R-R relations also form the starting point for theoretical constructs of the factor analysts. . . .

The second class of laws, R = f(S), relates response measures as the dependent variable to the determining environmental conditions. There are really two subclasses of laws here, one relating to the environmental events of the present and the second to events of the past. The first subclass includes the traditional laws of psychophysics, perception, reaction time, and emotions. . . . Insofar as the behavior at any moment is a function of environmental events that occurred prior to the time of observation one is dealing with laws of the second subclass. The most familiar instance of this kind of relation is represented by the so-called learning curve which relates the response variable to previous environmental events of a specified character.[27]

The Spencian distinction was given great credence in psychology, where it has also been called the difference between a *correlational* (R-R) and an *experimental* (S-R) approach to scientific psychology.[28] It essentially counters the Machian claim that *all* scientific observations are of a relational (R-R) type. The suggestion seems to be that when an S-R law is involved, the experimenter has a hand on the IV in such a way as to leave no doubt that antecedent triggering of an efficient cause is thrusting a consequent along *without* a contribution being made to the regularity by the organism under observation. (We will have reason to question this assumption when we discuss the awareness issue below, p. 539.) In line with Spence's Lockean approach to psychology, the *S-R law* is viewed as a more basic building block in behavior than the *R-R law*. Spence reflects this attitude when he says ". . . R-R laws represent only one small segment of the total framework of a science of behavior, and unfortunately not a very basic one at that." [29] It is this preferential arraying of the two types of lawfulness that demonstrates for us that Spence is actually forming a *theory* of lawfulness, framed along the lines of the Lockean model, in which the simple motions of nature (S-R laws) total up into higher-level combinations of increasingly complex motions (R-R laws plus mediated S-R laws). In order to get at *the* cause of behavior, we must *reduce* these higher-level observations to their underlying constituents. Thus, for Spence, basic psychology is S-R psychology.

Though it is perfectly acceptable to entertain a theory of lawful interrelatedness like this, the danger again arises of letting our theory be represented directly by our methodological findings of a lawful nature. An observed relationship between an IV and a DV, whether this means giving grains of food to a pigeon in shaping its behavior or predicting from children's IQ test scores to their classroom performance, is nothing more or less *than what it is*—that is, an observed relationship that can be reliably generalized but is *in principle* open to more than one theoretical explanation. Calling one IV-DV relation an S-R law and the other an R-R law does nothing to change this fact of the scientific procedure. This Spencian distinction as all *theories* (metaphysical assumptions, philosophical presuppositions, and so on) is therefore open to challenge. The Machian view of alternatives in scientific explanation would seem a sounder assumption on which to base an objective scientific method, for it would not result in a pecking order of higher and lower in the realm of valid knowledge.

Personality Tests

In the present volume we focus primarily on those theories of personality that have been tied to the practice of psychotherapy. There is an entire psychometric tradition of personality which space considerations do not permit us to address and to which Spence alluded in his definition of the R-R law. *Psychometrics* is the study and application of mathematical procedures to the problems of psychology.[30] The field of personality assessment through tests, questionnaires, or scales (all three terms have been used to describe these instruments) has followed two lines— one being more dynamic and *projective,* the other more strictly *psychometric.*

The field of projective testing was given its original direction by the now famous diagnostic instruments, the *Rorschach*[31] inkblot test and the *Thematic Apperception Test* (TAT).[32] The basic idea in both of these instruments is that the subject taking them is projecting his or her personality style into an interpretation of the amorphous inkblot or the scenes depicted by a number of pictures in the TAT. Hermann Rorschach, who was in training to become a Freudian psychoanalyst when he devised the inkblot test, believed that it was not important *what* a person saw in the inkblots but rather *how* the perception of the blot took place. The inkblots are mostly of black ink, with varying shades of gray resulting, but some are made by colored ink. To give an example of Rorschach's theory, it is assumed that a person with an open personality and emotional spontaneity will be more likely to use the entire inkblot in "seeing" something, and also be more sensitive to the colored portions than a person who is not of this personality style. Conversely, a person who is narrow in personality and emotionally dull will be expected to focus more on the details of the blots and ignore the livelier colors than a person without these personality characteristics. By carefully analyzing a subject's use of the blots in putting together a perception, the Rorschach expert can often find identical personality tendencies in two subjects who have "seen" different things in the inkblots. Thus, though Judy may see a colorful seascape and mountain range in the same inkblot in which Peggy sees a masquerade ball, the ways in which each young woman organizes her blot perceptually are identical. Hence, although they have seen different things, they are *still* similar in personality.

The TAT was devised and extensively used by the famous American personologist, Henry A. Murray. In the original construction of the TAT, Murray and his coworker Christiana D. Morgan made it clear that they were trying to devise a kind of short-cut method of free association. Rather than having subjects lie on a couch as in Freud's original procedure (see p. 107) and wait for ideas to occur spontaneously, what if we were to show subjects a series of ten or twenty artistically drawn pictures depicting human beings in interpersonal situations—some placid and positively toned, others suggesting tension and conflict? Still other pictures would show a dreamlike scene of abstract figures difficult to make out. If we were to ask subjects to think up a story about the scenes depicted in these pictures, could we not get some of the same insights that Freud got when he listened to free associations concerning a dream or an early memory? This was the fundamental reasoning behind the construction of the TAT as a projective instrument.

Although they are tests of a sort, the Rorschach and TAT were not really designed along psychometric lines. Psychometric tests are standardized instruments, which means that singular test items with a specific meaning (for example, "I would rather direct a play than act in it") are administered to large groups of subjects. The items that are found empirically to correlate highest with a criterion measure (for example, leadership in social situations) are specifically culled out and built into reliable scoring norms that will apply to all those who take the test in the same way. Psychometric personality tests are therefore based on the assumptions that they *sample* a subject's regular behavioral patterns in some way—on the order of an IV or predictor variable—and that they relate this sampling to a lawfully related measure of some type—on the order of a DV or criterion variable.

Now, projecting one's personality tendencies into the interpretation of an inkblot was never thought of as being sampled. This was a basic *presumption* made by the projective tester, a theoretical belief that everyone naturally behaves in a certain fashion—much as we might presume that, in the Adlerian concept of a "body language," people reveal themselves in the way they walk and talk no matter where they are walking to or what they are talking about. The "old-line Rorschacher" of the 1930s and 1940s actually thought of the inkblot perceptions as *being* the personality under observation, so that the depressed person picked the darker shades of the inkblot to frame a perception, and the negatively hostile person chose to use the white spaces *between* the blot's parts rather than the obvious black portions themselves. The TAT stories were taken as reflecting in bits and pieces the themes and moods of the person's past life or a hoped-for development in the future. In other words, the findings of projective tests were seen as a kind of running *theoretical analogue,* as if Freud had taken his clinical materials from inkblot interpretations and stories instead of from a recalled case history and dream memories. Thanks to this close parallel to the theoretical activity of a psychotherapist, projective tests were extremely popular and widely used from the early 1930s through the 1950s, and they are still popular (in forms other than inkblots or TAT cards as well). But they are *not* as centrally important in the overall science of personality study today as they once were. Why not?

Because, as with any theory, it is necessary to provide validation of the claims being made, and when the Rorschach was submitted to empirical test, it suffered from its very strengths. The alternative ways in which a subject could construe the inkblots and the multiplicity of interpretations by administrators led to findings of low statistical reliability and unsatisfactory predictive validity. Not all studies conducted on the Rorschach have been negative in predicted relationships, but most have been and since the 1950s there has been a steady decline in the research conducted on this instrument. And yet it continues to be used by most clinicians in the field because it serves as a ready *theory* of how to order one's thinking about another person's behavior. This theory is a mixed bag of psychoanalytical and gestalt-phenomenological conceptions, with a decided Kantian emphasis and prominent telic features. As such, it gives the Rorschach user a frame of reference within which to understand the person as a whole. The TAT has fared better than the Rorschach in the methodological context, for it is somewhat easier to standardize and the variability in response is not so great as with the Rorschach. But here too, as with all other forms of projective tests, the volume of research on the TAT has declined significantly since the 1950s. It remains popular with practicing clinical psychologists for the same reasons cited for the Rorschach.

When we turn to the more properly *psychometric tradition* we find a shift from a theoretical to a methodological emphasis. Control and especially prediction is the lifeblood of a psychometrician, who usually pictures personality testing entirely as a matter of sampling, arriving at reliable scores, and then predicting (forecasting) to a relevant criterion, along the lines mentioned above. This kind of practical prediction of behavior is called *actuarial* prediction when it is concerned with life expectancy, accident-proneness, and the like. An actuary working for an insurance company may ask several questions of a potential customer before selling this person a policy. The actuary knows from previous empirical study of large numbers of people that if an individual suffers from certain chronic illnesses, smokes, drinks liquor often or takes drugs, or has a history of many accidents in the past, he or she is a poor bet for living a long life. Such an individual would not be likely to get an insurance policy, or if one were granted it would carry high premium rates due to the added risk. In making this decision to sell or not sell a policy to an individual, the actuary does *not* have to understand the nature of the chronic illness, or why a person may drink, smoke to excess, take drugs, or be prone to accidents. None of this is relevant to the prediction, which is based solely on sampling theory and population statistics. Unlike our projective tester, who usually tries to frame *discriminal* theoretical constructs (see p. 28) to understand the client even when predictions break down, the psychometrician theorizes predominantly in the mathematical sphere of sampling procedures, measurement, statistical assumptions in the mathematics used, and so on. Such mathematical theorizing is totally *vehicular,* and insofar as it relates to the person being studied, it fills in the methodological context more properly than the theory of personality. The actuary needs no theory of personality. The understanding called for is not "Why do people do what they do?" but rather "How can I predict behavior from point A to point B over time's passage?"

Often a projective test analysis contains statements that Popper has taught us are unscientific propositions, such as, "The subject may or may not respond to authority figures with overt hostility, depending on his perception of the authority figure's threat to the subject's sense of masculinity." Even if this were true, how could we ever falsify such a statement? We could never predict a fixed outcome, but would have to wait until the person either behaved hostiley or did not in order to explain in post hoc fashion what had taken place. Because of such weaknesses in the projective testing approach to the study of personality, a shift began to take place to the psychometric side of the investigation. Both clinical-diagnostic and strictly personality scales were devised. The *Minnesota Multiphasic Personality Inventory* (MMPI)[33] is the leading example of a clinical instrument, and there are any number of personality instruments designed to get at different styles of normal behavior.[34]

As we noted briefly in our reference to the sampling of behaviors and prediction to a criterion, the psychometrician building a personality scale proceeds on the same statistical assumptions employed by the actuary. The first step involves settling on what the personality test will be measuring—extent of maladjustment, personality tendencies like dominance versus submission, distinctions between diagnostic categories like schizophrenia, manic-depression, psychopathy, and so on. Any of these topics may interest the psychometrician, who next will write— or have others write—a series of statements that seem to relate to the test's focus of interest. In the clinical context, these items

might read like "I prefer being alone" or "Sometimes I get tunes going in my head which I cannot stop." A personality scale aiming at dominance-submission might have items like "It is fun to make plans and decide on priorities" or "Everyone needs as much help from others as can possibly be gotten." After a great number of such items are written, the next step involves making sure that subjects will respond to them reliably as a pool with a common meaning, and that the scores obtained from either agreeing with or rejecting the conveyed meaning of test items actually relate empirically to an independent criterion. By *independent* we mean a measurement other than the test score itself. Here is where the prediction enters. First, a subject might check "agree" or "disagree" for between fifty and two hundred items. After totaling the "agree" items, the psychometrician has a score which can then be used to predict to the criterion. Thus, a subject agreeing with forty of fifty items aimed at measuring dominance could be given a score of 80 in that he or she had accepted 80 percent of the meanings conveyed by the items. Such psychometric tests are often called *paper-pencil* tests in opposition to *projective* tests.

In the case of our clinical test, we would probably want to see if items selected as reliably rated (that is, subjects get about the same score today as they got last week) can actually predict to or distinguish between one clinical diagnosis and another. Do people who are diagnosed by a mental hospital staff as schizophrenic score differently on our paper-pencil test than people who are diagnosed manic-depressive? Can we put together a number of items into a subscale that will tap schizophrenia and a second pool that will tap manic-depressive psychoses? If so, then maybe we can predict the diagnoses made by the hospital staff even before they are made. Maybe we can offer our scale to the staff, who could save time by having patients answer the items and be diagnosed according to their pattern of scores rather than having to conduct an extensive review of the case history before assigning a diagnosis. This is the general tactic of the MMPI, and it has been shown to be a remarkably valid instrument over the years. Turning to the personality scale of dominance-submission, we would have to find some criterion like the diagnoses of the hospital staff in the case of the MMPI. We might build our scale using high school students and taking as dominant subjects those who are clearly leaders in school activities, such as the football and cheerleader captains, class presidents, editors of the school paper, and so on. Such students should score higher in dominance than students who are inactive, generally unknown by their classmates, and rated as submissive by their teachers. Using this independent criterion, we could, through statistical selection procedures, put together a scale of dominance-submission that would select these two types of students based on their answers to our items. And in this case, selection means the test would *predict* a student's behavior from point A (test score) to point B (school behavior) over time, just as in the case of actuarial prediction cited above.

Having achieved this success, we can now use our personality or clinical scale to do various studies, such as relating our test scores to other empirically derived measures which might tell us why some people are dominant, others submissive, or why some become schizophrenic and others develop a manic-depressive psychosis. But note: simply because we can reliably identify dominant or submissive individuals and, for example, relate this measured score to the personality test scores of their parents to see if they take after their parental personalities, this does *not* mean that we have a *theoretical understanding* of (1) how personality differences arise in the first

place, (2) how they are sustained in the overall personality, or (3) what the process might be that brings about transmission of personality style from a parent to a child. Are these differences learned through modeling others, as Bandura might claim, or are they strategized uniquely and put down as life plans in the style of Adlerian explanations? Is there anything covert about personality style, requiring interpretations as Freud would claim, or is what we have measured and shown to predict overtly all that we have to worry about, as Dollard and Miller would claim? Simply finding subject differences on a test prediction to a criterion will not tell us which of these theoretical stances to take. Indeed, the test itself should *not* tell us which stance to take any more than our methods should tell us which theory to use in pursuing validating evidence. It would be a grave mistake to assume that the predictor variable of a test score (X-variable) which bears a statistically significant relationship to a measurable pattern of behavior (Y-variable), such as finding dominance scores related to school leadership, is evidence for an S-R relationship or an S-R law. Spence tried to head off such a claim by calling these R-R laws, but we have already seen that this kind of description is based on a confusion between theoretical and methodological conceptions.

In a sense, when we use psychometric tests, we are in the same position that Newton found himself (see p. 508). We usually have a construct that is shown to bear a mathematical relationship permitting predictions to be made, such as dominance being predictive of leadership. Newton had a construct called gravity based on such mathematical assumptions involving measurement and predictive calculations to observed events. Gravity proved remarkably predictive, but Newton did not really understand it in a theoretical way to satisfy his broader grasp of how nature works. Knowing that "dominance predicts leadership" does not necessarily increase our understanding of the basic nature of this personality style. Indeed, it is possible to ask whether such statistical predictions lend primary weight to the personality dimensions being studied or to the mathematical theory on which they are based? We know that statistical theories of probability and techniques of sampling and data analyses apply just as readily to predicting levels of crop growth, forecasting weather, or deriving the odds in games of chance. Statistics is a remarkably effective *vehicular* theory, applying to literally *anything* we wish to subsume by its constructs. How can we believe that it will provide us with a fundamental understanding of personality? To *control and predict* is essential to a science, but to *conceptualize and understand* is of equal importance. The telic theorist in particular is likely to emphasize such understanding in all descriptions of human behavior, and it is for this reason that teleologists are likely to be more friendly to projective than paper-pencil tests.

Since behaviorists are more ready to accept a direct parallel with natural science—recall Hull's use of the raindrop analogy in Chapter 4 (p. 263)—there is less concern in this camp about understanding the *total* personality. Many behaviorists do not even raise questions about the ultimate nature of behavior since they feel these are fruitless efforts. All that really matters is what we can accomplish practically (for example, change, improve, and so on) in behavior, and since the teleologist has nothing to add but so-called understanding, why bother with an issue having no practical bearing on the control and prediction of behavior? As to what a personality test may ultimately be getting at in its samplings, the behaviorist with a psychometric orientation and a desire to be theoretically comprehensive is prone to think of this in terms of some underlying genetic factor, taking its meaning from the material- and efficient-cause constructs.[35] The schizophrenic person is one who has inherited a gene or combination of genes with this behavioral weakness linked to it, or the dominant person has inherited such behavioral tendencies as a genetic parental strain. The test "samples" such underlying determinants. It is rare to find psychometric tests based on a telic image of the person, whereby freely chosen alternatives are considered the pool from which samplings are drawn. In Chapter 11 we will consider George Kelly's *Rep Test,* which is a rare exception to this rule.

What if the projective testers are correct, and people are indeed moved along in behavior not only by the collection of genetic substances that nature has handed them by chance, but also by purposive, intentional self-manipulations from out of an unconscious region? What if these unconscious purposes enter into the test-taking behavior of our subjects on the paper-pencil measures, but we simply do not recognize these factors and call them sampling errors when they are *not* really erroneous occurrences? Well, even if these possibilities were true, there is little we can do about them empirically, and depending on what we are attracted to in the study of personality, we would be concerned or unconcerned accordingly. A psychometrically oriented psychologist would doubtless feel it is pointless to be taking up valuable time with such unmanageable occurrences. A projective tester would probably entertain such ideas, working with one client and trying to understand behavior even when the idiographic variations on this behavior are not always predictable in an overt way.

Coming back to the question posed at the outset of this section, do we *necessarily* understand behavior if we predict and control it? The answer must surely be *no, we do not!* Absolute necessity of understanding in the scientific method is impossible, but this does not mean we are unable to be rigorous in our thinking and careful to put our ideas to test empirically in the research context—recognizing always the provisos of the affirming-the-consequent fallacy. We must simply acknowledge from the outset that our method and our theory are two separate and distinct aspects of science, and hence our IV-DV findings or laws are open to more than one theoretical explanation. And when it comes to the prediction of personality through tests, those instruments that often provide us with a theoretical language enriching our understanding of the person can *fail* to predict satisfactorily in the methodological realm of research validation. On the other hand, tests built to predict specific concepts effectively do not thereby provide us with a rich, overall understanding of a person's total behavior, pitched as they are directly at the methodological demands of reliability and empirical validation which must always restrict their descriptive scope.

How Well Does Behavioristic Theory Account for Mind and Human Agency?

A major goal of the behaviorists has been to provide a more accurate, scientifically valid description of behavior than other theories of human behavior have provided. As we have seen, this natural-science orientation with its belief in the functioning of physical laws—which do not require a final-cause description—gives behaviorism its unique quality in the study of personality. How satisfactorily have the behaviorists subsumed the meanings

of mentalistic or teleological constructs by their material- and efficient-cause constructs? We will consider this question in terms of three separate but related subtopics.

The Impossibility of Subsuming One Causal Meaning by Another

The presupposition on which Dollard and Miller's effort hinged is that it is possible to subsume the meanings of Freudian psychology by S-R theory. Since, as we have seen in Chapter 4 (p. 287), Freud encompassed telic constructs through his use of the dialectic, we have every right to ask how accurately Dollard and Miller have translated these meanings into their account of psychoanalysis. An impartial review of their efforts would surely conclude that Dollard and Miller found it quite impossible to capture the exact meanings Freud was dealing with in describing human behavior. Take the mental constructs of *repression* and *unconscious thought,* for example. Repression is accounted for as the inhibition of cue-producing responses that *mediate* thinking, which is believed to occur exclusively at the *conscious* level.[36] The unconscious is the unlabeled or unverbalized.[37] Lumping these two theoretical conceptions together, Dollard and Miller then stated, "According to Freud . . . the repressed, or unconscious, is the unverbalized."[38] Technically, this is incorrect. Freud would say that unconscious meanings may not be vocalized or vocalizable in that the person refuses to state or discuss what he or she understands completely at the unconscious level, where there *are* verbal labels—akin to cue-producing responses in behavioristic terms—functionally active! Freud could hardly believe that unconscious mental processes lacked verbal labels, for he held that *"the most com-*

plicated achievements of thought are possible without the assistance of consciousness." [39]

Dollard and Miller thus made repression a passive affair whereas Freud thought of this mental process as an active, intentional one.[40] The basic repressive process involves keeping something (memory, wish, and so on) from entering consciousness, both in the initial act of primal repression and then continually throughout life as repression proper.[41] It is also technically incorrect to equate the *unconscious* aspects of mind with the *repressed* contents of mind. Freud was careful to distinguish between these constructs, as follows:

We have learnt from psychoanalysis that the essence of the process of repression lies, not in putting an end to, in annihilating, the idea which represents an instinct, but in preventing it from becoming conscious. . . . Everything that is repressed must remain unconscious: but let us state at the very outset that the repressed does not cover everything that is unconscious. The unconscious has the wider compass; the repressed is a part of the unconscious.[42]

In other words, not only can the unconscious portions of mind hold back ideas that might have once been conscious but are too upsetting to be entertained in consciousness at present, but the unconscious *can itself think up new thoughts* at any moment. Indeed, this is where all mentation begins—in the unconscious!

Dollard and Miller look extraspectively *at* the person they are describing. If something is out of consciousness, then it would no longer be observed in overt (language or motor) behavior and to this extent it would be out of mind altogether. Neurotics become stupid because they lack knowledge. Freud,

on the other hand, introspectively construed the person's overt behavior as an instrumentality, as the result of some preceding mental formulation in the final-cause sense of *"that* idea, wish, cathexis, and so on, for the sake of which" overt behavior is being carried out. Freud saw meaning in all behavior, even when it is supposedly accidental (parapraxes). Rather than being stupid the neurotic is too wise. The neurotic is close to knowing consciously what we *all* know unconsciously but could never admit to ourselves—that is, we have had incestuous wishes for one of our parents and death wishes for the other. Freud observed:

The more important portion of the mind, like the more important portion of an iceberg, lies below the surface. The unconscious of a neurotic employs the conscious portion of the mind as a tool [instrumentality] to achieve its wishes. The convictions of a neurotic are excuses invented by reason to justify desires of the libido. The principles of a neurotic are costumes employed to embellish and conceal the nakedness of the unconscious desires.[43]

Dollard and Miller's use of the anxiety concept furthered their nontelic translation of Freudian mental conceptions—as when they suggested that the drive of anxiety, allayed or reduced by some abnormal behavior, stamps in this maladaptive pattern à la the stupidity-misery-symptom cycle (see p. 412). Drives are biological (material-cause) constructs, but as we may recall from Chapter 1 (p. 54), in Freudian theory the individual is motivated by libido, a purely mental energy. Though Freud did confuse his readers for some years by calling anxiety transformed libido, his final theory of anxiety left no doubt as to where he wanted the anxiety construct placed in his theory of motivation (see p. 90). What motivates neurotic behavior is the *memory* of an intolerable fixation, a poorly resolved Oedipal complex in which intended actions are being turned back with great psychological effort. And when these lascivious and murderous intentions get too close to conscious awareness (they are in *full awareness* unconsciously!), anxiety is brought to bear instrumentally to turn them back. The ego, which is the only portion of the personality that can even feel anxiety, allows itself to experience a slight amount of the anxiety consciously which would take place full force if the complete truth were known (see p. 91). The unconscious portion of the ego *intentionally* sees to it that the conscious portion of the ego is made anxious. Hence, it is what is known unconsciously but not known consciously that motivates neurotic behavior—*not* anxiety!

Saying that neurotics are motivated behaviorally to avoid anxiety is like saying the reason we step off a railroad track with a train bearing down on us is because of that feeling of fright we sense based on our awareness of the impending danger (this would be Freud's realistic anxiety). Is it really the anxiety that moves us or our capacity to reason "for the sake of" a possibility in our immediate future—the likelihood of dying a wretched death if we remain inactive? Freud, the introspective theorist who took a more Kantian view of mentation, stressed the latter factor, whereas Dollard and Miller, the extraspective Lockean theorists, put their emphasis on the former in this case.

The behaviorist is likely to say at this point: "Well, granted, my meanings may not be precisely those that Freud had originally proposed, but so long as I can account for the same behavioral observations in my theory which he accounted for in his, is this not proof that my theory is superior? Why not use a scientifically validated theory rather than a clinically supported theory, based on procedural evidence?" Though this argument is not without merit, and surely it is in the spirit of Machian alternativism (see above), we must ask ourselves whether learning theory as conceived by the behaviorists would have ever suggested the personality dynamics Freudian theory proposed? How could a Lockean model possibly suggest a dialectical formulation, such as reaction formation or "knowing and not knowing at the same time"? More to the point of Dollard and Miller's specific accomplishment, do we really *forget* the meanings of Freud's constructs when we translate these discriminal notions into the vehicular S-R theory which subsumes them? Is it not true that we first think of Freud's original meaning *and then* make the mental equations to Hullian theory?

It seems clear that not only would there have been no psychoanalytical image of human behavior without Freud or someone like him to give us this peculiar slant on things, but that Dollard and Miller would make little sense to us if we did not retain our understanding of Freudian terminology along with the S-R terminology they use to describe behavior. Just as certain idiomatic phrases cannot be translated from French to English without great loss, so too the fundamental meanings of psychoanalysis will ever elude the S-R conception. If this were not true, there would be little need to study the different meanings of the four causal constructs. We must accept it as given that it is impossible to say or express the meaning of one (for example, efficient) cause and yet communicate or convey the meaning of another (for example, final) cause. These highly abstract, vehicular causal conceptions are *on a par,* and so when we try to subsume a lower-level construct having the meaning of one by the other, we must forever be doomed to *change* the meaning of this lower-level conception. In Chapter 4 we identified this as *qualitative* change, as changing the pattern of relations defining the meanings that a construct embraces (see p. 274 for a discussion of such meaning changes in therapeutic insight). Once such changes in meaning occur it is no longer a question of accounting for what Freud had accounted for, but rather of proposing something totally different as a substitute for the original formulation.

Lockean versus Kantian Interpretations of Cognition

The term *cognition* devolves from Latin roots meaning "to become acquainted with" or "to get a knowledge of." Probably the most general meaning of *cognition* is the act or faculty of knowing, which suggests that there is a process going on mentally that permits a person to gain insights and understandings of experience. Although in the 1930s and 1940s this concept was used most often by phenomenological theorists (see Part Three), since roughly 1950 there has been an increasing reliance on the term by behavioristic theorists. We hear today of cognitive psychology as a new and distinctive movement within academic psychology, Although Skinner[44] and Wolpe[45] specifically challenged the need for a special cognitive psychology, Bandura has been more friendly to the idea of what he has referred to as "cognitive determination"[46] in behavior.

As we have seen in Chapter 7, Bandura's theoretical efforts were more comprehensive than either Skinner's or Wolpe's. Bandura is eclectical because he wants if feasible to account for as much behavioral description as possible, including the somewhat more mentalistic conceptions that personologists are likely to propose. And although behaviorism has had, at least since the time of Tolman, a tradition of explaining behavior

via *mediation* conceptions, the modern trend to cognitive psychology implies something even more inclusive, bringing in cybernetics or information-processing theory as well. Additionally, Bandura's vicarious-learning construct seems to need something like a cognitive process to explain it properly. Thus, we find him putting more emphasis on behavioral mediation than his colleagues. Wolpe states flatly that "thought obeys the same 'mechanistic' laws as motor or autonomic behavior."[47] Skinner says, "I see no evidence of an inner world of mental life relative either to an analysis of behavior as a function of environmental forces or to the physiology of the nervous system."[48] As traditional behaviorists, Wolpe and Skinner are totally unsympathetic with the modern efforts to bring telic-sounding terminology into behavioristic accounts.

Returning to the meaning of *cognition*, it should not surprise us to learn that there have been two main interpretations given to this construct in the history of ideas, one based on the Lockean and the other on the Kantian model of theoretical description. As we shall see in Part Three, the phenomenologists employ a Kantian interpretation whereas the behaviorists draw their precedents from the Lockean models of British Associationism. The question we are pursuing in light of these two different interpretations is, can one model subsume the other or is there a totally different image of human behavior conveyed depending on whether we use a Kantian or a Lockean definition of cognition in human mentation?

The Lockean interpretation of cognition was first clearly expressed in the writings of William of Ockham, a fourteenth-century theologian who was trying to clarify how we can know such things as the existence or nonexistence of God. Ockham was critical of the so-called Scholastic theologians who tried to prove God's existence through purely abstract, logical arguments like St. Anselm's argument from the so-called first cause. In brief, this argument hinges on the meaning of efficient causation and holds that if every effect is produced by an impelling cause, it follows that there must have been an initial or beginning thrust to get events moving across time. Only a deity could accomplish this feat; hence, God exists. Ockham was not much impressed by arguments like this, feeling that all they proved was the analytical ingenuity of the theologians who thought them up. Ockham was a toughminded, empirical thinker who argued that in the final analysis only those proofs that were based on concrete, observed evidence could be entertained as legitimate in theological debate. Proper evidence for Ockham would therefore involve the life of Christ, his teachings and miracles, and the fact that he rose from the dead and then was observed ascending into heaven. We might deny the validity of such claims centuries after they were observed. But as long as these events *did* take place, they were proper forms of evidence for the belief in an existence after life and a God.

In expounding these views, Ockham proposed an early theoretical explanation of how it is that human beings learn. He suggested that people first make use of an *intuitive cognition* by taking in through sensory receptors (eyes, ears, touch) a preliminary knowledge of their environmental experience. Such sensations are then stored in mind as memory. Once these stored experiences exist, the person can then employ what Ockham called an *abstractive cognition* to draw from this information various ideas and arguments. Proofs of God are therefore found at the level of abstractive cognition and they are no better than the information that has been made available by the intuitive cognition. It is clear that Ockham was thinking of reasoning in what Aristotle had called a *demonstrative* fashion (see p. 9). Just as Aristotle insisted

that we must begin from premises that are primary and true, so too Ockham was saying that we had better base our proofs on empirically sound facts. We see a Man-God walk on water or rise from the dead. If this information is correct à la intuitive cognition, then our arguments (conclusions, beliefs) concerning God at the level of abstractive cognition will be sound. Thinking up fanciful arguments at the level of abstractive cognition without fundamental facts at the level of intuitive cognition can *never* bring us the conviction of a belief based on empirical facts. Note that Ockham's cognitive psychology begins in the assumption that knowledge originates completely outside of mind. This presupposition was brought forward in the philosophy of British Empiricism and Associationism as reflected in the later writings of Hobbes, Locke, Hume, and the Mills.

We have tried to capture this empirical view in the Lockean model (once again, we use Locke and Kant to typify our models, but the style each model represents transcends history and is reflected in thinkers from all ages; see p. 16). Locke wrote extensively on the topic of how human beings learn and think, and his theory of ideas is a fine example of Ockham's fundamental distinction. Ideas begin with the first inputs to mind from experience (intuitive cognition). Locke called these *simple ideas,* which he suggested were subsequently combined into increasingly abstract *complex ideas*. For example, we first learn individual letters, then combine them into words, words into sentences, and so on, as our higher-level mental functions are constituted from the simple to the complex. Whatever is therefore *in* mind was put there by experience (the environment), or at least the original foundations for all ideas in mind come from experience. At birth the human mind is tabula rasa on which experience does the initial etching. Locke also used the metaphor of the mind at birth as an "empty cabinet," [49] which the senses furnish with informational input much as we furnish an empty china cabinet with tea cups. Locke's ideas are therefore atomistic building blocks which combine in the very beginnings of knowledge; they are indivisible and cannot be created, for as he said, "It is not in the power of the most exalted wit, or enlarged understanding, by any quickness or variety of thought, to *invent* or *frame* one new simple idea in the mind . . . nor can any force of the understanding *destroy* those that are there." [50]

Locke's empirical attitude was reflected in the efforts he made to counter any belief in what he called an *innate idea*. He meant by this certain assumptions that philosophers might make, such as holding that "what is, is" or "it is impossible for the same thing to be and not be." The so-called rationalist philosophers of his time used such statements as presumed universally true assertions which did not require empirical verification. Locke argued as Ockham had before him that *all* knowledge is based on sensory input, simple ideas combined in time and brought forward as complex ideas. Anything else would suggest that we are born with information already populating our mental cabinets. Finally, note that as with Ockham, according to the Lockean view, *only* demonstrative reasoning is possible. There is no way in which to conceptualize dialectical reasoning on this model, which is why a simple idea can be thought of as atomic—that is, an indivisible, *unipolar* unit of meaning that combines with other singularities of this type to generate higher-level thought in what is essentially a mathematical fashion.

According to Locke, the meaning "left" enters mind as a simple idea and the meaning "right" enters as a completely different simple idea; in time through frequent (habitual) association of ideas—left to right and vice versa—the person learns the concept of directionality as a complex idea. This input frequency is thought of as occurring automatically, according to mathematical laws in an efficient-cause fashion. Both the original input and the associative tie to other ideas in forming complexity is assumed to occur as an efficient-cause process. Because the input information is conveyed by a sensory apparatus —nervous tissue, receptors, and so on—we find that the Lockean model also makes good use of material-cause description. We can even view the patterning of more and more complex ideas as a kind of formal cause. However, the pattern qua pattern is never the *originating source* of meaning; it does not organize what is developing meaningfully below (at the level of intuitive cognition), but is merely the determinate end-result of the coalescing of these lower-order inputs. Because the pattern does not endow things with meaning, there is no real way in which to express human thought in final-cause terms, as behavior "for the sake of" this organization. Indeed, human judgment occurs automatically because of the probabilities nurtured by the frequency of "this or that" sort of input from the environment. As Locke said, "Probability . . . carries so much evidence with it, that it naturally determines the judgment, and leaves us as little liberty to believe or disbelieve, as a demonstration does, whether we will know, or be ignorant." [51] As a mathematical ordering, the concept of probability borrows meaning from the formal-cause interpretation of determinism (see Table 4 in Chapter 4, p. 265), but it is clear that Locke combined this with a mix of material- and efficient-cause determinations that have the person reasoning according to how his or her mental cabinet has been filled "from without." Indeed, the ordered filling *is* reasoning, for the individual never transcends to reason apart from what has been directly put in.

Since the Lockean model is based exclusively on demonstrative reasoning, how did Locke account for what might be considered dialectical mental states, such as doubt, distrust, rejection of an alternative in the face of evidence to the contrary, wavering between affirmation and negation, and so on? He claimed that such subjectively felt experiences, which we take to be the operation of our active intellects as agents, are in fact due to the kinds of frequency distributions currently nestled in our memories based on the frequencies encountered in our past experience. Moderate or considerable input on *this* side of a point is sensed as opinion, belief, or conviction. We believe our country is the best of all countries because we have in the past heard more positive things expressed about it than negative things. Should we have fairly equal inputs on both *this* and *that* side of an issue, we experience this psychologically as indecision or doubt.[52] As the newspaper headlines present us with increasing criticisms concerning our country, we begin to wonder if it is still the best in the world. This conception of reason does *not* picture the individual as an *agent* or *identity* in his or her mental activity. Ideas are copies of reality and do not from the outset of life contribute to or create the person's knowledge—not even to a slight extent. The resultant belief system is not uniquely or freely decided upon so much as it is constituted (calculated) according to a frequency principle of the number of past inputs. Judgment is limited to the drift of these stored probabilities and the person is not really able to decide against the odds of these tabulated inputs. The person believes and does what he or she has been habitually shaped to believe because of a hard determinism via past experience,

conceived basically in material- and efficient-cause forms of determinism.

Turning to our other model, Kant agreed that there are two sides to knowledge—one having to do with sensation and the other with something more abstractly mental—but he disagreed with the passive conception of ideas that Locke had proposed. Kant questioned the validity of believing that sensation was a completely outside-to-inside process of copying meaningful patterns and orders of knowledge already existing in the noumenal realm. We can never know the noumenal realm directly (the other side of the Kantian spectacles from the side we are looking through), so we can never know reality directly, not even *in principle* at a later time in the development of science. Kant began his analysis of mental ideas at the phenomenal level, thereby making the processes of mind more of an inside-to-outside affair, which we have captured in the Kantian spectacles (see p. 18). As Kantians we always think about what mind does from the introspective theoretical perspective, as if it were the mind that put on the spectacles to order sensory input which to that point is nothing but noise. The spectacles pattern meaning out of the input noise. It is incorrect to think of the Kantian spectacles as filters which weed out the noise of sensory input in order to clarify what is coming in. This would be a Lockean, information-processing interpretation of the spectacles. The spectacles symbolize Kant's belief—and the belief of many philosophers across history back to at least Plato—that ideas frame and *create* understanding at least as much as do the circumstances existing in the environment independent of mind. We see this creative view of cognition in Kant's opening statements of his famous *Critique of Pure Reason,* as follows:

That all our knowledge begins with experience there can be no doubt. For how is it possible that the faculty of cognition should be awakened into exercise otherwise than by means of objects which affect our senses. . . . But, though all our knowledge begins with experience, it by no means follows that all arises out of experience. For, on the contrary, it is quite possible that our empirical knowledge is a compound of that which we receive through impressions, and that which the faculty of cognition supplies from itself . . . (sensuous impressions giving merely the occasion). . . .[53]

By *faculty of cognition* Kant meant an innate ability which reason has to combine with experience and bring about that ordering into meanings which we think of as knowledge. Rather than being tabula rasa, mind was thought of by Kant as pro forma—capable of providing a structure at the phenomenal level in advance of what is taken in at the noumenal level. There are two points at which such structuring takes place. First, when sensations are taken in by the sensory receptors (eyes, ears), they are ordered according to a pro forma conception of time and space. In other words, we are born with a phenomenal ability to organize sensations according to an awareness of here versus there or sooner versus later. We do not know the meanings of the words *here, there, sooner,* or *later,* but we know from birth the phenomenal experience they signify.

Following this preliminary ordering at the level of sensation, Kant held that an additional ordering into understanding takes place by what he called the *categories of the understanding.*[54] Once again, these are purely mental spectacles (frames of reference, a

priori schemes, and so on) which enter into cognitive activity to create knowledge at least as much as knowledge is being created by the environment. The categories covered such things as knowing *from birth* the difference between a single thing (unity) versus many things (plurality) in experience. There is no sensory apparatus to tell us that "over here" we have one piece of fruit, whereas "over there" we have two or three pieces of fruit. The fruit simply exists in nature as it exists. It is the human mind that provides the relational qualities and numerical distinctions. Another category of the understanding involved a relation of "possibility-impossibility." Sensory input does not provide this for the infant, who may reach for the moon only to learn that it is impossible to grasp it. This phenomenal experience is brought to bear from the inside of mind to the outside (devolving "from above" as noted in the Introduction, see p. 18). The conceptualization of what is possible or impossible to accomplish is framed introspectively even before the child knows words like *possible* or *impossible.* Later, in maturing, the child will learn these words as well as those defining unity versus plurality. But the ability to know or understand these meanings is already with the child at birth, for this is how mind works.

This ordering of noumenal inputs at the phenomenal level represents a different interpretation of the idea construct. We can think of the Kantian model as suggesting that the idea is a pro forma frame on the order of the categories. This interpretation is generally acceptable, but to be more precisely in line with Kantian philosophy, we could not really say this. It is not our purpose to translate Kantian philosophy directly and totally into the Kantian model, since—as we have already stated about both of our models—we believe this general view of "mind contributing to the understanding of experience" has applied to numerous philosophers over the history of thought. However, in speaking more directly now to Kant's actual theory of ideas, we must introduce that important feature of his model dealing with *dialectical* reasoning, and we would not want to overlook this significant aspect. Unlike the Lockean model, the Kantian model permits us to describe cognitive processes that are *bipolar*. Kant's entire view of the mind is heavily colored by dialectic. Note, for example, that the categories of the understanding are dialectically framed, so that unity and plurality are complemented by totality as the thesis and antithesis are potentially combined into a synthesis, and so on. This dialectical view of mentation is also to be seen in Kant's specific theory of ideas.

Kant held that ideas are those aspects of mentation (reasoning) that go beyond and often depart from sensory intuition. As he said, "A conception formed from notions, which transcends the possibility of experience, is an *idea,* or a conception of reason." [55] Ideas do not have to be bound to those environmental inputs that Locke based his theory of ideas on. In contradistinction to Locke, Kant would say it *is* possible to frame new simple *and* complex ideas in mind. The transcending capacity of mind that Kant postulated allowed him to say that mentation or thought is *self-reflexive,* that is, ideas can reflexively turn back on the ongoing thought process at any time and put it to question through introspective examination. When we are thinking something, we know that we are thinking it and that we could be thinking *otherwise* by way of the opposite meanings implied directly in that which we now are thinking. For example, sometimes we can play our own devil's advocate and challenge what we now truly believe because we know that there are alternative implications we could and probably should confront. In the example cited above, believing our country to be the best or nonbest of all others, Locke would have the

negating arguments "input" by environmental factors, such as newspaper headlines. Kant, on the other hand, would say that with each thought, "My country is the best of all countries," we have the *immediate* suggestion, "My country is *not* the best of all countries," which in turn prompts us to ask ourself, "What makes you think your country is the best one in the world? Why do you say this? What are your facts, and are you forgetting some of the drawbacks and problems it faces?"

We get such immediate contradictory suggestions because of our dialectical reasoning ability (recall Freud's early use of precisely this theory of ideas in Chapter 1, p. 81). Indeed, anytime we use our free play of intellect to ponder things like this, we immediately become involved in dialectic because, as Kant noted, "speculative reason is, in the sphere of transcendentalism, dialectical *in its own nature*." [56] We possess a transcendental logic that permits us to analyze even our most basic presuppositions, such as the organizing concepts of space and time (something Einstein and modern physics actually accomplished) or the categories of the understanding (as many philosophers have also accomplished). Indeed, thanks to the operation of what Kant called a *transcendental dialectic* in mind, it is possible for the human being to become lost in illusion, totally removed from knowledge as organized phenomenally. Kant often cautioned against the readiness with which human speculative thought can take flight to arbitrarily disregard the "is" as perceived phenomenally to pursue the "is not" in imagination. Though creative speculation is often rewarded with hypotheses leading to new discoveries, it is equally rewarded with nonsense. Once free of the demands of empirical testing, human beings can dream up almost anything to believe in that they wish to. This is why Kant favored a scientific approach to knowledge in which creative hypotheses might be put to demonstrative test in validation.

We thus see that Kant saw the person as more of an agent in cognitive reasoning processes than did Locke. Ideas (broadly conceived) shape experience to some extent rather than being shaped by experience, and they do so *from birth!* Ideas are not *contents* but *conceptualizing frames.* The Kantian view of mentation rests on a formal- and final-cause interpretation of determinism, along the lines of the psychoanalysts (see pp. 264–266). There is a true "that for the sake of which" process in the Kantian interpretation of mind. The person must always "take a position on" experience because of the many alternatives it presents to a dialectical intelligence ("My country is best or not?" . . . "Should I do this or that?" . . . "Is what they say true or false?"). Input probabilities from out of the past do not automatically (efficiently-)cause the person to judge one way or another, as Locke contended, because on the Kantian model a person can choose dialectically against the odds of past experience —even when this is a harmful or stupid choice. People *do* behave illogically, or to be more precise, they behave according to a dialectical logic (as well as a demonstrative logic) that can lead to the formation of paradoxes and self-defeating courses of *intended* behavior which we then call mental illness.

It would not be difficult to show that, in the modern trends to a cognitive psychology, we have the Lockean and *not* the Kantian conception of cognition being employed. There is no doubt that the Lockean model has provided the presumptive background for behaviorism since John Watson's historic 1913

paper.[57] About all that seems to have happened in the modern trend to cognitive psychology is the addition of cybernetic terminology to the classical S-R image of behavior.[58] Bandura's cognitive psychology is therefore of no fundamental difference from the noncognitive psychology of Wolpe and Skinner. Thus, Bandura accepted the fundamental Lockean view that knowledge arises exclusively through an outside-to-inside progression, so that reciprocal interactions (determinisms) begin only *after* there is some initial input to the tabula rasa mind. This makes the mind an exclusively mediational process. We see this clearly in the following comment by Bandura: "External influences play a role not only in the development of cognitions but in their activation as well. Different sights, smells, and sounds will elicit quite different trains of thought. Thus, while it is true that conceptions govern behavior, the conceptions themselves are *partly fashioned* [italics added] from direct or mediated transactions with the environment." [59]

A Kantian theorist would never propose that the mental conceptions that govern behavior in the sense of the categories would *themselves* be "partly fashioned" by the environment. This empiricistic claim is precisely what the Kantian is trying to counter by proposing that cognition is an inside-to-outside affair. Due to such empiricistic assumptions, a Lockean theorist must first suggest that the mind "inputs" certain simple ideas through a form of intuitive cognition, which then combine through a form of abstractive cognition into more complex ideas, which can *then* serve as those conceptions governing behavior Bandura speaks about. These complex ideas enter into the efficient-cause flow of antecedents and consequents by *mediating* between them after having first been partially fashioned by initiating antecedents. A Kantian theorist, on the other hand, would suggest that behavior is being cognitively influenced *from birth!* Mind simply works this way naturally (natively). No initial pump priming, no partial fashioning is required in order for a reciprocal interaction—or what Kant called a "compound" in our earlier quote from his *Critique*—between cognition and experience to be underway following birth.

Finally, it is evident that efforts to subsume a Kantian interpretation of cognition by a Lockean interpretation of cognition or vice versa is doomed to failure. We are back to the problem faced by Dollard and Miller, being unable to express one meaning through another. The Kantian model is fundamentally telic and demands that both a final-cause and a dialectical meaning be conveyed in the theory which speaks through its assumptions. Since neither of these concept meanings is relevant to the Lockean model, it is simply impossible for a behaviorist *satisfactorily* to account for personality theories which rely on a teleological image of the person. We next turn to a consideration of the ways in which behavioristic psychologists and other nontelic psychological theorists have specifically referred to the conception of freedom or free will in human behavior.

Nontelic Interpretations of Free Will in Psychology

There are three general ways in which psychologists who do not accept teleology have attempted to account for the widely held belief of human beings that they have a free will making them at least to some extent an agent in their personal behavior. In Chapter 4 we discussed this concept in terms of the Kantian model as adapted by the psychoanalysts (see pp. 299–300). We now want to see how the more empirically and behavioristically oriented psychologists have sought to explain this concept. Three explanations have been advanced. One of these focuses on the *methodological* problems of predicting behavior experimentally or psychometrically through tests, and the other two are variations on the mediation *theoretical* conception. We shall discuss these three explanations in separate subsections.

(A) Free Will as Statistical Unpredictability. We have already discussed the psychometric use of tests in psychology. Much of so-called applied psychology is concerned with the practical problem of finding out what people are likely to do beforehand and then capitalizing on this statistical probability in some way. For example, a group of people may be administered an attitude survey concerning their food preferences, and the psychologist hopes to predict actual purchases based on this information. They then observe what these subjects actually select from the shelves of their grocery stores. Do they follow their test selections (scores)? In the main, they do but some do not, and the question then arises, why not? Is this unpredictability due to the unreliability of the testing and sampling process itself, or have some of the subjects merely changed their minds? Statistically oriented psychologists often believe that what teleologists mean by free will is some behavior like this which is to some extent unpredictable.[60] They also are likely to think that the teleologists are drawing erroneous conclusions here, because such unpredictability really stems from the various uncontrolled factors that enter into any sampling of variables from a parameter, including misunderstandings of the test item by the subject, errors in scoring the tests, and so on.

However, the statistical psychologist is wrong in thinking that teleologists must base their concept of free will exclusively on the unpredictability of a person's behavior. They can also view the *predictability* of behavior as being due to the willful self-direction (psychic determinism) that agency makes possible in human behavior. If people do first consider alternatives before they *will* (intend) a specific course of action in choosing "this" food product over "that" as a likely purchase when taking a test (see p. 297), and if they can always re-examine their willful choice (decision, selection, affirmed position), then it surely may happen that their behavior will be less predictable than if they had not re-examined their position. Mrs. Thompson, who has indicated on her test survey that she prefers brand X, may go to the market only to notice that brand Y has a newly colored box on which is printed the claim that it has been improved. These two additional items of experiential information may "cause" Mrs. Thompson to change her mind. But what kind of cause are we dealing with here? The teleologist would suggest that Mrs. Thompson's behavior is only unpredictable in this instance, because at the time the survey was administered, we were unaware of these different *grounds* "for the sake of which" she now proceeds to buy brand Y rather than the brand X our survey had predicted. As a result, we tested the old and now discarded grounds for her still quite willful behavior. On the other hand, if Mrs. Thompson had entered the store to find all things as before, she would confirm our predictions by acting on her initial (now old) grounds in willfully selecting brand X. And if she could do this, so could every subject tested by the survey, which is why the survey is found to predict in the first place! The teleologist would thus turn the tables on the behaviorist's indeterminism argument at this point, and rather than claiming credit only for the unpredictable (error) portion of the statistical variance, lay claim to *all* of it.

In trying to interpret free will on the basis of unpredictability, we are using the *methodological* context as a substitute for the *theoretical* context. What is needed is a clear theory of what something called free will can mean psychologically or behaviorally even before we get around to testing this theory empirically (where the question of unpredictability always arises). To argue from unpredictability places the teleologist in the untenable position of having to use the *error variance* of an experiment as positive evidence of something when it can never fulfill this role. We first need an interpretation of free will theoretically; *then* we can move to falsify this theory by doing what all scientists do in the methodological context—examine the central tendency of the predicted (not error) variance of our experiments. We next move to a consideration of the theories that have been proposed to account for free will in a nontelic fashion.

(B) *Free Will as Mediating Alternatives.* When we turn to a theoretical explanation of free will in the empirico-behavioristic tradition, we notice two things. First, the concept itself is generally denied as illusory,[61] as a mistake people make about their personal behavior. Some psychologists even suggest that this illusion has utility, and that people should be allowed to go on believing in free will because this belief has empirically demonstrable positive effects on their behavior.[62] The reason psychologists are so confident that free will is an illusion is because they generally believe as our psychometrists mentioned in the previous section do, that if behavior is predictable it cannot then be free. It does not occur to them that a free-will theory could make claims on the predicted portions of the variance in an experimental variable. They consider such lawfulness to be in diametric opposition to a theory of freedom in personal behavior.

The second thing we notice about theoretical accounts of free will in the empirico-behavioristic tradition is that they are always based on a Lockean explanation. John Locke is widely known as a champion of political freedom. His phrasings were adapted to the Declaration of Independence by Thomas Jefferson in the call for human rights to life and liberty. Locke also had a distinctive theory of what free will can mean, and it is this core idea we will now consider. He began with the assumption that there are always a number of *uneasinesses*[63] that impel the person's will (behavior) to action, as, for example, to prefer or choose one course in life over another. Today, we would call these motives. But as a mental action the will does not have to be carried forward immediately. It can delay or suspend the actions that might lead to a reduction in uneasiness.

The person feels hungry, but it does not follow that this uneasiness will be satisfied by the first item of food spied in the environment. The person can willfully select one food over another by hanging fire in considering the alternatives. Hence, said Locke, "This seems to me the source of all liberty; in this seems to consist that which is (as I think improperly) called *free-will*." [64] Taking this one step further, Locke noted that the person's choice will be determined on the basis of what is likely to maximize his or her sense of pleasure. Things that bring pleasure are good things; those that result in pain are bad alternatives to pursue.[65] People can even project the long-range outcomes of present pleasures or pains, as when an overweight person contemplates entering an ice cream parlor looking for immediate gratification, yet mindful of the long-term harmful effects a banana split can have on the physique. Summing things up, Locke concluded, "Liberty, it is plain, consists in a power to do, or not to do; to do, or forbear doing, *as we will*." [66]

Locke's explanation of free will hinged on the idea that behavioral causation takes place only efficiently, as an antecedent-consequent impulsion over time's passage. The person can delay the course of this motion and then *decide* to go one way rather than another after contemplating the alternatives. However, as we have already seen above in considering Locke's theory of ideas, the actual decision arrived at is not *itself* freely made but is always based on the frequency of past probabilities in the individual's memory. Furthermore, as his critics were to point out,[67] Locke had no way of accounting for why it is that the person hesitates or pauses in the first place. If an uneasiness is a motivation and behavior can occur *without* pause, then why should the person on *certain occasions* choose to stop and contemplate alternatives? It seems that we need here a second realm of motivation to account for the stopping and thinking. In one of his examples, Locke spoke of a man who was told how much better it is to be rich than poor, but, even so, he made no effort to work his way out of poverty because he felt no uneasiness (motivation) to change things.[68] Locke concluded from this that mental choice (stay poor) follows motivation (no uneasiness), but it is just as easy for us to conclude that motivation (no uneasiness) follows mental choice (preference for the poor way of life).

The Kantian teleologist would, of course, begin to invoke formal-final cause conceptions at this point, acknowledging that though there are various physical uneasinesses in life, there are also psychological uneasinesses. Furthermore, the way in which all uneasinesses are dealt with involves a continuing final-cause conception in which the person must affirm a life's course by premising one thing rather than another (see our discussion of dialectical alternatives, p. 290). If we were willing to think of uneasinesses as being framed by premises or beliefs the poor man has toward his world (akin to the phenomenologist's world-view construct; see Chapter 10), then simply because he was not uneasy in his economic status did not mean that no choices had been made. Locke is presuming that because a person is shown the "best" or "richest" way of behaving (according to other people's premises), he or she *must* select this alternative lifestyle. If we think it absurd to opt for a "poor way of life," then the view of choice determining level of motivation would never occur to us. But if we really want a concept of *free* will in describing behavior, then it must be possible to select any alternative open to the person—even a stupid or impossible one.

The style of explanation begun by Locke has come down to us in behavioristic psychology as *mediation* theory. Being able to delay and scan or otherwise review information received previously to select an alternative for the present is central to the idea of behavior as mediated. Though we have presented mediation theory in the behavioristic line as beginning with Tolman, there are those who have traced it straight back to John Watson,[69] and even Watson's major professor in graduate school, James Rowland Angell, can be seen using a mediation conception in his discussion of how consciousness functions in human thought.[70] What makes a mediated behavior more free than a nonmediated behavior? The central argument of the behaviorists is that when we mediate behavior, we make use of past inputs, past information which gives us certain alternatives in the present that someone without such a mediating bank of probabilities would be un-

able to capitalize on. Dollard and Miller summed up this view nicely in the following:

Through their capacity to mediate learned drives and rewards, verbal and other cue-producing responses enable the person to respond foresightfully to remote goals. They free him from the control of stimuli immediately present in the here and now, provide a basis for sustained interest and purpose, and are the basis for the capacity for hope and reassurance. With their removal all these capacities should be lost.[71]

Being free of controlling stimuli in the present does not mean the person is free of controlling stimuli out of the past, of course. The basic explanation still holds that the cue-producing responses have been converted from previously learned input, and that what alternative is then selected in arriving at a decision occurs completely automatically, based on the reinforcement history of the behaving organism. There is no final-cause reasoning of a "that, for the sake of which" dialectical alternatives are being contemplated, and hence the individual can never decide to behave *in opposition to* the probabilities nurtured by the reinforcement history. Decision becomes an instrumentality of such past reinforcements, so that it is not the decision-making process that is free—the range of alternatives freeing the organism from a singular course of behavior defines freedom. Dollard and Miller would thus contend that an organism behaving instrumentally—without mediating cues—is less free than an organism that behaves selectively through actively occurring cue-producing responses.

Sullivan appreciated that something like intentionality occurs in human behavior, and he tried to capture this by stressing that behavior is always future oriented.[72] People facilitate effective action by knowing *why* they are pointing themselves in a certain direction even before they overtly behave. Though such foresightful themes of behavior are prominent in Sullivan's writings, he specifically denied making up a teleological theory.[73] The way in which he tried to account for the seeming inconsistency was to suggest that through "cultural conditioning"[74] we are taught to think about our personal behavior in such future-oriented ways. This gives us the illusion of complete freedom, when in fact, ". . . we project the future by juggling with past symbolizations, understandings, and present formulations in terms of probable future events."[75] This is the description of a Lockean intelligence, mathematically combining the "primary and true" (that is, dialectically unexamined) inputs from out of the cultural shaping of the past into the best projection of a probable outcome in the future. Though he is more biological than Sullivan, Wolpe's discussion is completely in line with interpersonal theory.

The behavior therapist takes it for granted that human behavior is subject to causal determination no less than the behavior of falling bodies or of growing plants. For example, a man pauses at crossroads, undecided along which of two routes to proceed. The route that he eventually takes is the inevitable one, being the resultant of a balancing out of conflicting action-tendencies. The strength of each action-tendency is essentially a function of the incipient reactions evoked by impinging stimuli, internal and external, whose effects depend primarily on the character of previously established neural interconnections —that is, on pre-existing habit structures.[76]

Stampfl has not commented on the free-will issue directly, but since he believes that conditioning principles shape behavior over the life span, it is likely that he too would conceptualize free will as increasingly broad mediations of behavioral alternatives.[77] Ban-

dura was clearly in line with the traditional explanation, when he said: "Within the social learning framework, freedom is defined in terms of the number of options available to people and the right to exercise them. The more behavioral alternatives and prerogatives people have, the greater is their freedom of action."[78] Here again, however, the question of precisely who or what creates alternatives in behavior and at what point in the life of the organism this ability to influence upcoming events begins is open to debate in Bandura's theory (see above). If, as seems evident, his concept of determinism is exclusively an efficiently-caused succession of events, then he has not departed in any significant way from explanations based on mediation theory since Locke's original formulation. The basic issue, of course, is whether or not the human being is an agent in behavior *from birth*. If the person can alter input from the outset of life, then we are describing a contributory agent behaving *freely* over the full life span. If not, we have an organism that is not an agent to begin with but in time combines initial inputs into ever more complex mediators as life is acted out over time's passage. One of the most colorful accounts of free will in the latter sense was given by the eminent physiological psychologist, D. O. Hebb, who wrote as follows:

I am a determinist. I assume that what I am and how I think are entirely the products of my heredity [material-cause determination] and my environmental history [efficient-cause determination]. I have no freedom about what I am. But that is not what free will is about. The question is whether my behavior is entirely controlled by present circumstances. Heredity and environment shaped me, largely while I was growing up. That shaping, including how I think about things, may incline me to act in opposition to the shaping that the present environment would be likely to induce: And so I may decide to be polite to others, or sit down to write this article when I'd rather not, or, on the other hand, decide to goof off when I should be working. If my past has shaped me to goof off, and I do goof off despite my secretary's urging, that's free will. But it's not indeterminism.[79]

We might now define free will in the traditional (S-R) behavioristic sense as *the number and variety of past controls operating cumulatively through mediation over the life span in the ever discernible present.* A teleologist would complain that this is not a proper theory of free will, but rather is a theory of the complexity of behavioral control. Hebb is not personally responsible for the decisions to be polite or to write his article. He cannot reason to the opposite of what ideas present themselves to his mind and break free from his past reinforcement history. His so-called free behavior is simply once removed from the external stimuli efficiently-causing him to behave as he does today. He *as a person* is no more an agent in this sequence of motions called behavior than Skinner was an agent in giving his address at the conference where he debated Rogers (see p. 439). Before we can complete our summary assessment of the behavioristic interpretation of free will, we must look specifically at Skinner's account of this supposedly illusory human experience.

(C) *Free Will as Guided Natural Selection.* Though he is not a traditional S-R theorist, Skinner used the concept of mediation in specifying the form of determinism he employed. "As a determinist, I must assume that the organism is simply mediating the relation-

ships between the forces acting upon it and its own output, and these are the kinds of relationships I'm anxious to formulate."[80] This is obviously thought of as a form of efficient-cause determinism (see Table 4, p. 265). As we recall from Chapter 7 (see p. 440), Skinner's interpretation of the operant response has been equated with the kind of causality Darwin proposed in his concept of natural selection. Nature or the environment selects for the organism, even though it is the organism that first "does something"—operates on the environment—to produce the contingent set of circumstances. Well, if the environment does the selecting then the person does *not* do so. Hence, insofar as a person may have the impression of making decisions or choosing alternatives freely, this must be an *illusion.* The person is in fact being guided along by natural selection, and if a scientist can learn enough about the kinds of contingent reinforcers that prove reinforcing to the person, his or her behavior can be *shaped* accordingly.

Skinner's choice of the word *contingent* is interesting, because this term was coined by the medieval philosopher-theologian John Duns Scotus to single out a special type of efficient causation. Duns Scotus said that when an efficient cause is made dependent on an act of will, it becomes a *contingent cause* —the succession of events is done for a reason decided upon beforehand. If leaves are blown from our lawn by the autumn winds, we have derived a benefit from an exclusively efficient-cause sequence of events. However, if we purposively will that our yard be clear of leaves and go about raking them up, we have behaved contingently. We put up with the work of raking contingent on the expectation that the yard will look attractive when we have accomplished the task.

Skinner was aware of such precedents to his theory for he has said: "Operant behavior, as I see it, is simply a study of what used to be dealt with by the concept of purpose. The purpose of an act is the consequences it is going to have." [81] True enough, but the question remains whether the behaving organism foresees the consequences as mere possibilities and then brings them about intentionally, or whether the organism first acts and then finds these consequences occurring, without foreknowledge. We cannot learn from a bird beforehand whether its pecking at a tree branch is aimless or whether there is some hope of discovering insects beneath the bark. We can watch the bird, as Skinner does, and if we see the (basal) operant level of pecking rising after insects have indeed appeared, we can call this a contingent circumstance or a contingent reinforcer. But note: our theoretical usage of the term *contingent* is *extraspective*. It is used completely from our vantage point as observers and in no way addresses the question of the bird's (introspective) point of view. On the other hand, had anyone asked us beforehand, we could have told them that we intended to rake the leaves off our yard. This projection of ours cannot be observed as a contingency until after our task has been completed—unless, of course, the observer is willing to take our stated goals seriously. If so, then the meaning of contingency would shift to a more *introspective* phrasing. Indeed, we could equate an introspective contingency with the *reason* behavior is carried out.

We can now see that as a theologian, Duns Scotus was actually combining the meaning of final and efficient causation in proposing his concept of contingent causation. He was emphasizing the fact that some efficient-cause sequences are without forethought. People do not think of the moral (religious, ethical) implications of what they do. Were they to think ahead, then many immoral acts could be avoided. If Lorraine can see that her theft of a bracelet from a department store will contingently injure financially the merchant

offering it for sale, not to mention violate her spiritual relationship with her God, then she will *not* carry out this temptation, even though the shoplifting would be easy to accomplish. The mechanical act of reaching for the bracelet and dropping it unobtrusively into her handbag is an efficiently-caused succession of events, true enough. But the *intent* of the act removes it from just efficient causation. Duns Scotus asked that we all accept such responsibility for our acts whenever it is possible to do so, and as a result, to behave morally.

Duns Scotus's contingency construct could be subsumed by the Kantian model, as a predicating set of spectacles which are the "that for the sake of which" behavior was intended. We might frame this predication or premise as "Think about the consequences of your acts before you do them, and if they lead to harmful or immoral outcomes, do not carry them out." Skinner, on the other hand, would view this "that" (premise) as having itself been shaped into the person's verbal repertoire by the naturally selecting environment. The fact that Duns Scotus expressed a view like this and lived according to it was due to the contingent reinforcements he had received from his parents and teachers as well as others in his past life who happened also to have been shaped by a common cultural heritage. What the person reads is also important for, as Skinner has observed, ". . . many . . . responses would never have been emitted except under the special encouragement of the literary community, which . . . provides sensitive examples of verbal behavior." [82]

Such verbally expressible reasons for behavior are what foster a belief in freedom among human beings. Arguing similarly to the traditional S-R explanation of freedom,

Skinner said that the more alternatives that have been shaped into a person's repertoire of responses, a portion of which are the supposed reasons for behaving alternatively, the freer will the person feel. Skinner then added that there is a greater truth about such illusions: "Freedom is a matter of contingencies of reinforcement, not of the feelings the contingencies generate." [83] A dramatic example of Skinner's interpretation of free will is to be found not in his formal psychological writings, but rather in his novel *Walden Two* (1948). At one point in this fictional tale, the hero Frazier who planned and shaped the ideal society in which people have been operationally conditioned into a marvelous life without their being aware of how this was achieved or how it is being sustained, confronts a critic in the person of the philosopher named Castle:

> [*Castle has just said:*] "... I know *that I'm free.*"
> "*It must be quite consoling,*" said Frazier.
> "*And what's more—you do, too,*" said
> [*Castle has just said:*] "... I know *that dom for the sake of playing with a science of behavior, you're acting in plain bad faith. That's the only way I can explain it.*" He tried to recover himself and shrugged his shoulders. "*At least you'll grant that you* feel *free.*"
> "*The 'feeling of freedom' should deceive no one,*" said Frazier. "*Give me a concrete case.*"
> "*Well, right now,*" Castle said. He picked up a book of matches. "*I'm free to hold or drop these matches.*"
> "*You will, of course, do one or the other,*" said Frazier. "*Linguistically or logically there seem to be two possibilities, but I submit that there's only one in fact. The determining*

forces may be subtle but they are inexorable. I suggest that as an orderly person you will probably hold—ah! you drop them! Well, you see, that's all part of your behavior with respect to me. You couldn't resist the temptation to prove me wrong. It was all lawful. You had no choice. The deciding factor entered rather late, and naturally you couldn't foresee the result when you first held them up. There was no strong likelihood that you would act in either direction, and so you said you were free."
> "*That's entirely too glib,*" said Castle. "*It's easy to argue lawfulness after the fact. But let's see you predict what I will do in advance. Then I'll agree there's law.*"
> "*I didn't say that behavior is always predictable, any more than the weather is always predictable. There are often too many factors to be taken into account. We can't measure them all accurately, and we couldn't perform the mathematical operations needed to make a prediction if we had the measurements. The legality is usually an assumption—but none the less important in judging the issue at hand.*" [84]

Note that this exchange turns on three important points which we have been examining in Chapter 8. By suggesting that there are inexorable forces determining Castle's behavior, Frazier is surely thinking of efficient-cause determinism. Castle would view his orderliness in Kantian terms (psychic determinism), as a premise "for the sake of which" he intends his behavioral patterns in doing such things as picking up or dropping a book of matches. Frazier views such actions as having been patterned or shaped by past experience which has been input and is now mediated solely without intention on Castle's part. Secondly, note the Lockean theme in Frazier's claim that Castle was contemplating roughly equal probabilities in his upcoming behavior. According to Frazier,

Castle is not actively conceptualizing his future and making choices (qualitative change) but is at a kind of loosely focused operant point where alternative contingent reinforcers can take over rapidly as events quickly move along (locomotion). Finally, the discussion ends on the question of just how predictable behavior can be. As we have noted above, though statistical unpredictability enters into free-will explanations (including that of Niels Bohr, see p. 297), it cannot be the sole grounds for believing in free will. Skinner, who of course wrote both sides of the Castle-Frazier debate, obviously believes that to the extent behavior is predictably controlled it cannot be working on the basis of a telic process.

How then do we shape people into feeling free? By assuring that they have a variety in behavioral patterns so that there are many different ways in which to attain contingent reinforcers for doing different things. Skinner cautioned that: ". . . a culture which made people as much alike as possible might slip into a standard pattern from which there would be no escape. That would be bad design. . . . The only hope is *planned* diversification, in which the importance of variety is recognized." [85] Critics have suggested that there is a contradiction in believing that individuals do not make their own choices but that a behavioral scientist can make plans to change things at the cultural level. Is not all planning impossible, a hit-and-miss affair in the sense of natural selection whereby first something occurs and *then* it proves useful or not? Skinner answered that scientific planning is based on empirical findings already established as having this utility. Since the aim in cultural planning is to avoid all forms of control through aversive stimulation and punishment—the traditional enemies of freedom—there should be few objections from those who will be socioculturally manipulated. When asked "Who controls the con-

trollers?" Skinner answered by pointing to countercontrol measures. There is a joke retold by every class of undergraduate students who take psychology: one rat in a Skinner box says to a fellow rat, "Look, I've got Professor Skinner conditioned. Every fifth time I press this lever down he gives me a food pellet in that dispenser over there." Joking aside, said Skinner, the fact remains that the organism under control *does* have a countercontrolling influence on the controller. Skinner even referred to this as a *reciprocal control*,[86] reminding us of Bandura at this point. Hence, in a well-designed culture, there would be avenues of influence extending in more than one direction, so that the citizenry would have some feedback capacity to those assigned the job of planning and carrying out a cultural milieu of "freedom."

A teleologist would find this Skinnerian explanation of free will unacceptable, not because it requires a controller over people, but because of the interpretation given to how such control is achieved. People are indeed controlled daily by cultural controllers whom they influence in turn, so that a reciprocity exists between the citizen and his or her elected officials, the police, and so on. But is this solely efficient-cause control and manipulation, or can we discern some contingent manipulations going on in the original sense used by Duns Scotus? The teleologist would suggest that a good citizen obeys the law because he or she freely affirms the premise (Kantian spectacles) that it is "right and proper to obey the law" and *then*, in willfully behaving "for the sake of" this reason, becomes open to social control by the officers of the law (psychic determination). Other citizens who violate the law can be found to have different assumptions "for the sake of which" they are seen to behave. This means social control is due to final-cause determinism rather than to efficient-cause determinism (see Table 4, p. 265), because the good citizens will follow what their leaders ask them to do and they will model the behaviors of those who best represent what the culture in general accepts. Good citizens are not manipulated; they conform to what is expected of them.

Speaking more generally, the teleologist would judge all behavioristic efforts to account for free will as unsatisfactory. These accounts do not describe free will as a psychological process so much as they describe the subtleties of control that provide us with the illusion of free will. In a sense, freedom comes out as covert control. Although political freedom may properly be conceived in terms of alternatives, to say that a prisoner in jail is psychologically less free in willed behavior than a person outside of jail is like saying that a person who can afford the best steaks has a different digestive process than a person who must exist on cornmeal. Ordinarily, we think of our free will as being under the constraint of external factors, so that though we may will it, we are unable to walk through walls. Wealthy people have more alternatives to consider in deciding what they can or cannot do, but this does not change their basic psychological processes. The behavioristic interpretation of freedom also holds for animals. Is an animal with more mediating cues trained into it *psychologically* freer than an animal that has not had the benefit of such training? Behaviorists would tend to answer yes, but this is because, as we have seen, they equate free will with the multiplying of alternatives—leading at times to unpredictability—rather than to the *reduction* of alternatives in behavior.

And yet, if we were to live according to Duns Scotus's interpretation of efficient causa-

tion, we would constantly be *reducing* the possible alternatives in behavior open to us, *rejecting* those that had contingent circumstances we deemed beforehand to be immoral or harmful. It has been said that a saintly individual is in time *less* free to behave than a person who does not contemplate the "that, for the sake of which" he or she behaves. Recall from Chapter 4 (p. 294) that when a person freely opts to submit himself or herself to God, this very act of commitment turns over direction to a supreme authority which then "controls" the course of behavior according to rules of conduct advocated by the religion in question. Since the saint is always free to do as Mrs. Thompson did and (qualitatively) *change* the premises that have grounded his or her decision to follow a supreme authority, it would not be correct to say that free will is any *less* in saints than in sinners. Overt options may be minimized by the moral person, but psychologically the level of free will remains the same as in all people. It is this side of free will that the behavioristic interpretation will never quite capture, because here again we are speaking of two different causal meanings in the interpretation of freedom and determinism under espousal. We cannot express telic behavior in nontelic constructs.

Having now covered three different topics in light of the second question of this chapter, we might now try to answer it as follows: It does not appear that mediation and related explanations of behavior do a very precise and accurate job in accounting for such personological conceptions as mind and free will. If this conclusion is correct, where does it leave us as students of personality? That is, assuming we want to take the teleological theory seriously for the time being, can we point to any experimental proof that might support it? Can we actually put final-cause conceptions to the test of falsification? This interest brings us to our third question.

What Are the Implications of the Findings on "Awareness in Conditioning" for the Study of Personality?

We noted at the outset of this chapter that those personologists who debate with behaviorists over the human image are almost always involved with teleological questions, the most pervasive of which relates to the suitability of using final-cause meanings in the description of behavior. Whether the personologist would classify himself or herself as teleological in theoretical persuasion or not, this is what the debate comes down to. Assuming for now that we are correct in this assessment, the behaviorist has every right to put the following question to the teleologist: "You find the mechanist's efforts to rigorize psychological theory unsatisfactory. You seem to feel that only *your* way of describing behavior is suitable. What empirical evidence can you cite which might suggest that there is in fact something like a final cause operating in human behavior?"

In response to a question of this sort, the teleologist would probably remind us of the vast findings on awareness in the reinforcement experiments (see pp. 474–477). Rather than supporting an image of the person as mechanically moved along by blind manipulations, these findings tend to suggest that human behavior is based on strategizing for ends. Bandura has admitted as much, and added, "The notion that behavior is governed by its consequences fares better for anticipated than for actual consequences."[87] As noted in Chapter 7 (p. 476), it is more important what a subject believes is occurring in the upcoming contingent circumstances than what actually does occur in the schedule of reinforcement. If this is true, could it mean that Duns Scotus was correct in suggesting that human beings can contemplate ahead of time and thereby *predicate* a "that for the sake of which" their behavior is determined purposively? Would this not imply that the image of human behavior demands something more than simply efficient-cause manipulations to be accurately captured in a scientific description?

Skinner would answer no to this question, contending instead that ". . . the basic fact is that when a person is 'aware of his purpose,' he is feeling or observing introspectively a condition produced by reinforcement."[88] Awareness or consciousness is not fundamental to the human condition; rather: "A person becomes conscious . . . when a verbal community arranges contingencies under which he not only sees an object but sees that he is seeing it. In this special sense, consciousness or awareness is a social product."[89] Since he made no use of a dialectical construct, Skinner was unable to describe how "seeing that one sees" or "knowing that one knows" can occur even without cultural inputs in self-reflexive fashion (see our discussion of reflexivity in the Kantian model, p. 527). Hence, he must contend that awareness is itself (demonstratively) shaped into the person's behavioral repertoire by environmental contingencies just as everything else is. In referring to the basic fact that awareness of purpose is produced by reinforcement, Skinner made it appear that he was speaking from empirical evidence. However, the teleologist has every right to challenge this suggestion because when the role of awareness is studied directly and adult human beings are used as subjects, precisely the *reverse* basic fact emerges in the data—awareness produces reinforcement (except for a small number of experiments that find conditioning without awareness; see p. 475).

Skinner doubtlessly was thinking of evidence drawn from the conditioning of lower animals where it is impossible to falsify telic interpretations. Even so, the teleologist would suggest that when we can communicate with people (adults) in the conditioning paradigm, we find considerable support for the view that there is indeed a "that for the sake of which" form of behavior going on. Thus, if we were to record a subject's self talk during an ongoing experiment (as had been done[90]), we would first hear the subject in an operant-conditioning format saying to himself or herself, "I think the object here is to say a plural noun and then he [experimenter] makes that 'mmm-hmm' sound or says 'good,' so I'll give it a try" and *then*—thanks to the instrumentality of the subject voicing the plural noun—we would hear the experimenter making the sound called the contingent reinforcer. And for some subjects we would even hear the verbal operant, "I know he wants me to say plural nouns, but I'm going to have some fun and not go along." Here again, we find the operant verbal response *working* even though from the experimenter's (extraspective) point of view, there is no verbal shaping going on. In still other instances, we hear the subject saying, "I wonder what this is all about; maybe he wants me to use words beginning with the letter S." This verbal operant *also* leads to provable findings in the electrical recordings, where we find the subject voicing words like *stairs, silky, socks, suddenly,* and *sticks* without really finding the connection between some of them and the experimenter's verbal behavior.

From the point of view of a teleologist, there is absolutely no difference between these three kinds of human actions, but the operant conditioner would find significant differences here. For example, one of the first counters to the telic implications of the awareness findings by the operant conditioners was that since a fair number of admittedly aware subjects never changed their behavior to go along with the experimental manipulation, these statements of awareness made during the postexperimental interview were really not important to behavior.[91] The distinction we saw Bandura using between learning (involving awareness) and performance (involving measured operant level) was drawn, and the suggestion was made that all behavioristic psychology had to account for was literal performance. Findings, such as those of Page (see p. 475), were to demolish this claim, because they showed how at times a subject's *not* performing was just as much an aspect of behavior with awareness as was his or her observed performance. At any moment a subject can either carry out or *not* carry out what the experimental procedure logically calls for—assuming that such a subject is aware of this operant procedure (that is, the research design).

Another point the teleologist is likely to focus on stems from the way in which Skinner conceptualized the sequence of events in operant conditioning. In differentiating between his views and those of the traditional S-R sequence in which an antecedent elicits a consequent, Skinner had the following to say:

To distinguish an operant from an elicited reflex, we say that the operant response is "emitted." (It might be better to say simply that it appears, since emission may imply that behavior exists inside the organism and then comes out. But the word need not mean ejection; light is not in the hot filament before it is emitted). The principal feature is that there seems to be no necessary prior causal event.[92]

The operant response "appears" and then "produces reinforcing effects."[93] This kind of theory effectively *reverses* the S-R sequence into a kind of R-S sequence of events taking place over time. The antecedent in Skinnerian theory is a response, the level of which is said to be dependent on that which it literally creates. If pigeons depress bars which produce grain in a tray, then we can modify their rate of bar depressions by following their operant responses with the presentation of grain. If children will pick up their toys when this results in attention from mother, let mother show the children attention at the right time and she will have a house in better order.

Without denying the facts or the utility of such behavioral control, the teleologist would point out that it is difficult to see how an efficient-cause determination could be involved here (see p. 264). In an efficiently-caused sequence of events, the "effect" is always later in time. Skinner says there is "no necessary prior causal event" bringing on an operant response. Duns Scotus would hold that a contingent cause would be one in which the person had *freely*—that is, without prior necessity—arrived at a choice to behave one way rather than another, and *then* brought about what eventuated by intentional design. In other words, if we were to assume that animals and children *intend* that certain ends be realized, we could use Skinner's own evidence to argue for a telic theory of behavior! When we study subjects with whom we can communicate, the role of *earlier* predications (beliefs, values, assumptions, premises, and so on) on their *later* behavior becomes very clear. Indeed, some things in life are contingently reinforcing only because a human being has previously projected them as goals having an anticipated value. One person plays a game to win because it seems a fascinating pastime, whereas another plays it with indifference. If both these individuals should happen to win, it is the former one who will consider this contingent state of affairs a reinforcer. The significance of the reinforcer is thus a factor even

before the actions carried out to obtain it have begun.

Of course, the problem is that we cannot determine clearly whether children and especially lower animals may be intending anything in their behavior. It is only when we can talk to fairly adult human beings that we begin to feel the need as personologists to frame their behavior in terms of final-cause determinations. We can demonstrate this by taking Skinner as an example. He tells of a special clock affixed to his desk lamp, which works as follows:

The clock runs when I'm really thinking. I keep a cumulative record of serious time at my desk. The clock starts when I turn on the desk light, and whenever it passes twelve hours, I plot a point on a curve. My record begins many years ago. I can see what my average rate has been at any period. When other activities take up my time, like lecturing, the slope falls off. That helps me refuse invitations [to speak at various universities, and so on].[94]

Now, our problem here is to suggest what is a cause and what is an effect in Skinner's record of his hard-thinking time. The cumulative record per se is simply a statistical estimate of the time he spends at work. Such graphed data are like the actuarian's estimates for longevity or the probability of having an accident (see p. 515). They do not explain the specific causes of Skinner's behavior any more than Newton's mathematical conception of gravity explained how it is possible for bodies at a distance to influence each other without an intervening substance conveying the impact (see p. 508). We are strictly in the realm of formal-cause determinism when we track events empirically with the aid of mathematics. How to, in addition, account for Skinner the man within the statistical pattern is up to us.

Skinner would say that he was under the control of a contingent reinforcer—namely, the level of productive time he had been shaped into believing was good for him to be at. The teleologist, on the other hand, would suggest that Skinner was behaving "for the sake of" a premised strategy for how to keep himself active in scholarly work. As Mach has taught us (see p. 509), either of these theoretical explanations may be employed, as they are both consistent with the observed facts. Skinner would doubtlessly argue that he had earlier in life been shaped into believing that this strategy was a good one and *also* shaped into being aware of his supposed role in framing the strategy. He would contend that there was a time in his past life when his behavior was molded *without* awareness. The teleologist would suggest that though such a *theory* has every right to be entertained, it should not be advanced as if it had been empirically validated, or even as if it were highly consistent with the facts emerging in current researches on conditioning. We can infer that animals could not possibly be aware, and since they do get conditioned, Skinner's claims must be true. And since young children can be conditioned, though they are often unable to state the relationship between their operant responses and the contingent reinforcers, Skinner's claims again must be true. However, the teleologist would be on scientifically firm grounds in reminding us that neither of these arguments is a substitute for a *direct test* of conditioning without awareness. At the present time in psychological science, the evidence would —if anything—support the claim that *human conditioning demands awareness and coopera-*

tion more than it would support the claim that *human conditioning is automatic and achieved without awareness.*[95]

When Skinner said that there is "no necessary prior causal event" bringing the operant response about, he posed a difficult conceptual problem for the traditional behaviorist, whose commitment to the efficient cause makes it natural to think that "first" a stimulus appears and "second" a response does. It does not seem to bother Skinner that he has reversed this S-R succession into an R-S sequence of events. He apparently believes that a kind of efficient causality takes place in any case, albeit of a Darwinian nature (see p. 440). In order to salvage their more traditional S-R framework, we sometimes find operant conditioners resorting to the use of the *discriminative-stimulus* construct as if it were an earlier (efficiently-) causal agent of the operant response (see Bandura's use of this concept, p. 483). A discriminative stimulus is a cue the subject distinguishes in the process of operant conditioning that is something *other* than the reinforcement stimulus. For example, if we were to both deliver a food reinforcer and flash a light on certain of the lever depressions emitted by a rat in the Skinner box, this additional stimulus could facilitate the rat's learning. It would have the food stimulus as reinforcer and *also* the discriminative stimulus of a light to indicate something about the reinforcing circumstance. Skinner emphasized that though a discriminative stimulus affords us some control over the organism, "it does not then elicit the [operant] response as in a reflex; it simply makes it more probable that it will occur again. . . ."[96] Note that here again we are speaking only of observed probabilities and not specifically *how* this probability is caused within behavior itself. To make clear how a discriminative stimulus might be influential in human behavior, we can think of Sandra, a woman who emits sobbing behavior whenever she wants special consideration (a form of contingent reinforcer) from others. Since she is more likely to get such consideration from men than women, we observe Sandra in time turning on tears primarily in the company of men. Men are discriminated as stimuli from women; the operant level of sobbing is kept alive by the special consideration she receives from the men, such as words of encouragement, being helped to a chair, being looked after solicitously, and so on. Thus, it would be possible for us to control her sobbing behavior by managing the sex of those around Sandra when she faces a problem.

Because the discriminative stimulus, once established, always occurs before the operant response (Sandra first sees a man and then is likely to sob), it so happens that many operant conditioners permit themselves to think of this as an S-R sequence in the traditional sense. Then when they manipulate such discriminative stimuli to control behavior, they have the impression or sense of efficiently-causing the resultant behavioral manipulation—for example, *first,* they arrange to have men absent and *second,* they find Sandra's sobbing incidents declining. What they overlook here is the theoretical assumption that it is the operant response itself that causes the discriminative stimulus to come about in the first place. That is, if operant behavior is behavior that operates on the environment to produce reinforcing effects, then by the *same* form of causation, it must also produce the discriminative stimulus. Discriminative stimuli would be meaningless signals without their implicit ties to the contingent reinforcer. To therefore speak of controlling behavior based on stimuli that this behavior has itself controlled into existence strikes the teleologist as putting the cart before the horse. There has to be some basis for explaining *why* these discriminative stimuli were created in the first place. The teleologist proposes that a return to the original meaning of contingent causa-

tion used by Duns Scotus would greatly help the theory of behavior at this point. Sandra seems definitely to be orienting her behavior "for the sake of" an intended audience, so that, as Bandura suggested (see p. 486), her sobbing seems to be contingent on the possible presence of men even *before* actual tears are to be seen on her cheeks.

This anticipatory capacity to bring behavior forward *or not* depending on the succession of events faced by the person can also be seen in classical-conditioning experiments (see pp. 476–477). The pattern of relationship between the unconditioned and conditioned stimuli can be interpreted as a "that" (formal cause) "for the sake of which" (final cause) behavior is made conditional upon. Lacking the initial pattern, the person is unable to connect a response to the preceding succession of stimuli, and, knowing the initial pattern, the person can also *negate* the conditioned response called for. At least, this breaking off of the conditioned response is often possible (see p. 477). Whatever automatic reflexive controls there may be occurring in classical conditioning, the findings on awareness imply that there are also significant conceptual or cognitive controls going on as well. This, at least, would be the teleologist's summary conclusion in tying up the case against a strictly mechanistic explanation of the conditioning experiment.

Returning to the question on awareness posed by this section, we might now answer it as follows: we once thought that behavioristic conditioning procedures received little or no contribution from the person of the subject in the procedure, but the growing body of evidence on awareness belies this simplistic view. Subjects are seen to be active agents in the conditioning procedure, conceptualizing as best they can what has to take place in order for this phenomenon to take place and then *complying* with the experimental instructions to achieve this end, *or not*. It is now possible to begin giving behavioral explanations of conditioning in more telic terms, thereby humanizing the procedure as was never before possible. It would therefore be a serious mistake for personologists to dismiss behaviorism and its conditioning theories as something other than the study of personality. It should be possible in the future to introduce introspective, idiographic, final-cause, and even dialectical theories into the experimental design known as conditioning of behavior. Mention of dialectical theory takes us to our next question.

Are There Any Dialectical Themes Hidden Away in Behavioristic Writings or Empirical Psychological Researches?

An insight we have gained from our study of falsification and verifiability is that what the scientist learns in conducting research depends on the theory that he or she is willing to put to test in the first place. If more than one theory can account for the same fact pattern as Mach suggests (see p. 509), then possibly a satisfactory theory that might stand up to the test of falsification is unknown, *not* because it is invalid but simply because it has never been framed in a testable form and submitted to test. There is every indication that this is precisely what has happened to theories bearing a dialectical coloration. Modern students of psychology do not hear about the dialectic in human behavior because psychologists have never taken this construct seriously. Psychology was born and has been nurtured in the atmosphere of British Empiri-

cism. Behaviorists have been a major force in promoting this *exclusively* demonstrative identity for psychology, as have other psychologists who wanted to make their field an empirical science. Dialectical conceptions are sometimes taken as a threat to the values of empirical science, implying as they do that there are dualities and contradictions in events, and that often the tangible and overt is merely a pawn for the subtle and covert. How can rigorous science be built upon such obscure and slippery foundations?

The result is that no effort has been made by the empirico-behaviorists of this century to falsify a dialectical theory of any sort. Indeed, the presupposition has been that people are *not* constituted in this manner. H. S. Sullivan nicely reflected this demonstrative image of human nature in the following:

It is my opinion that man is rather staggeringly endowed with adaptive capacities, and I am quite certain that when a person is clear on the situation in which he finds himself, he does one of three things: he decides it is too much for him and leaves it, he handles it satisfactorily, or he calls in adequate help to handle it. And that's all there is to it.[97]

There is no internal wrenching or compromising in this image of humanity. The psychoanalytical complexities of a Freudian or Jungian theory have given way to the Yankee spirit of practicality and good sense.

According to behaviorism, whether or not people negate, qualify, or oppose contrasting meaning mentally today depends on what they have been trained to do in the past. Referring to a dialectical Freudian formulation, Dollard and Miller therefore said, "It seems possible that the responses involved in reaction formation are favored by the fact that our verbal training produces an especially strong association between words that are antonyms [opposites]."[98] Thus, when we are taught certain (unipolar) word meanings, such as *boy, up, right,* and *good* as children, we are virtually always being taught the (unipolar) word meanings of *girl, down, left,* and *bad* at the same time. When controlled word-association studies are done asking subjects to say aloud the first word coming to mind when a cue word is given, the common finding is that a word having an opposite is most likely to suggest that meaning to the subject (for example, *boy* suggests *girl* and vice versa).[99] Rather than seeing such findings as support for a dialectical process in human reason, Dollard and Miller interpreted them to mean that because of the frequency of past training wherein one word was fed in in contiguity (closeness in time) with the other, an automatic bonding occurred (that is, an efficient-cause connection took place). There is no implicit tie of bipolarity going on in people's cognitive processes here, bringing one meaning into its opposite as a dialectical one-among-many conceptualization.

Other examples of findings that could easily be seen as evidence for dialectic can be found in the research literature, dating back to the father of psychology Wilhelm Wundt, who conducted studies on his *tridimensional theory of emotion.* This theory held that all emotions can be subsumed by the dialectically framed dimensions of pleasant-unpleasant, strain-relaxation, and excitement-calm.[100] Bipolar conceptions of this nature have been used numerous times since in psychology, particularly in the study of personality where scales have been constructed to measure dimensions like ascendance-submission, introversion-extraversion, repression-sensitization, internal-external control of reinforcement, and so on. In a vast experimental effort, the behavioristic psychologist Charles E. Osgood has shown that human beings from every corner of the globe can take a word like *mother* (or its equivalent in other tongues) and reliably place it on a seven-point scale

between each of a number of bipolar adjectives, such as fast-slow, good-bad, and strong-weak.[101] These arrays are then factor analyzed and explained by Osgood in an exclusively demonstrative, mediational-model fashion without ever suggesting that dialectical reasoning might have entered into the process. The personologists Klaus F. Riegel[102] and James C. Mancuso[103] have shown how psychologists use dialectical conceptions in their research on scaling techniques, cognitive processes, and human development without giving due recognition to this seemingly basic human capacity.

Some of the most interesting allusions to what might easily be seen as dialectical themes occur in the writings of our behaviorists when they are writing about personal matters or elaborating their theories discursively or through the use of pertinent examples. As they introduce their reader to the stupidity neurotics suffer from, Dollard and Miller recount a fascinating vignette from the closing moments of the author Gertrude Stein's life.

We are reminded of a pertinent anecdote concerning the death of Gertrude Stein. It seems that she came out of a deep coma to ask her companion Alice Toklas, "Alice, Alice, what is the answer?" Her companion replied, "There is no answer." Gertrude Stein continued, "Well, then, what is the question?" and fell back dead. . . . The neurotic person also does not know the answer and, furthermore, he does not know there is a question. Eventually the therapist will supply the question and, if need be, the answer.[104]

It was plausible to Dollard and Miller, in light of their demonstrative, mediation-model of mind, that Gertrude Stein was simply reflecting a lack of mediators—questions and/or answers—in posing her queries. They did not perceive the question-answer dialectic as an active process of elaborating knowledge through a bipolar (Kantian) frame. Opposites are simply closely associated meanings, and poor Ms. Stein lacked meaning (that is, cue-producing responses) on both the question and the answer side of things.

In recalling how he worked out procedures to bring about reciprocal inhibition, Wolpe said, ". . . I made an effort to procure a response that was theoretically the diametric opposite of anxiety, in the hope that this would be a particularly effective therapeutic instrument." [105] Since the word *reciprocal* means an inverse relation or an *opposite,* it would not be a stretch of the imagination to admit some form of dialectical conceptualization into Wolpe's system. Bandura also used this concept of a reciprocity going on between person, behavior, and the environment. Some of his characterizations of human behavior are heavily laden with dialectical connotations, such as the following: "Humans . . . possess facile cognitive capacities for reconciling distressing conflicts. Devalued actions can be, and often are, justified so that losses in self-respect are minimized as long as the self-deception remains convincing." [106] Shifting grounds facilely to devalue certain actions and self-deception are behaviors easily construed in dialectical terms. In criticizing those psychologists who use the concept of *demand characteristics* as something that goes on only in the laboratory, Bandura observed:

Another questionable practice is to invoke "demand characteristics" as a cause of behavior in experimental settings. This type of explanation recognizes that people infer from cues the kind of behavior that may be expected in particular situations and act compliantly or oppositionally to the perceived "demand." It is true that cues guide conduct in the laboratory as they do in everyday life. People often behave on conjectures of what others want them to do, but when this happens outside a laboratory it is rarely dismissed as a "demand effect." [107]

Bandura would seem to be admitting that people can and do negate what is expected of them. This would easily accommodate a dialectical description, but thanks to the fact that he like the other behaviorists relies exclusively on the demonstrative Lockean model, Bandura must hold that the negative alternatives reflected in a person's behavior are themselves unidirectionally input through past experience (see p. 11). Since Stampfl was willing to use dynamic formulations, one would expect that he might find dialectical formulations to his liking. Yet, true to behavioristic form, when he recognized a potential role for dialectical reasoning, he translated this opportunity into a demonstrative premise. For example, in discussing dream distortion and the absence of (demonstrative) logic in dreams, Stampfl suggested that these irregularities are due to early conditioning (input) experiences which have been retained since the earliest, hence most sketchy, moments of self-awareness. [108]

The most extensive and fascinating examples of dialectic are found in the literary and biographical writings of Skinner. In *Walden Two* (1948), Skinner has his hero Frazier, who planned the ideal society, say at one point, "We take no pleasure in the sophistical, the disputative, the dialectical." [109] He was referring to the fact that in Walden Two humans are not set against their fellow human beings in competitive fashion. We might recall at this point the discussion between Castle and Frazier excerpted from this novel (see p. 536). The dialectician would see in the very fact that the novel is carried along by *clashes* of this sort evidence that drama—like life itself—is a dialectical affair.[110] Both Frazier and Castle can easily be described as reasoning dialectically. Castle says he is free (thesis). Frazier negates this belief (antithesis). Castle picks up a pack of matches and says he has at least two alternatives—to hold or to drop the matches. Frazier, falling back on the demonstrative tactic, claims he has just one (primary and true) alternative—and then, when Castle seems to go against his first tentative prediction, Frazier claims that very opposition as evidence for his unipolar theory of behavior (". . . that's all part of your behavior with respect to me"). Castle behaved in opposition to the prediction *not* because of a dialectical reasoning process, but because of the additional unipolar feedback information that this was Frazier's prediction and he was out (programmed) to prove Frazier wrong. Castle's change was one of locomotion and not qualitative shifting the grounds for the sake of which an argument was being waged.

Since Frazier has the advantage of explaining Castle's behavior, he is able to account for literally any type of dialectical maneuver that Castle might have attempted. For example, when Frazier predicted that the matches would be held or dropped, if Castle had instead tossed the matches up in the air negating the alternatives projected altogether, Frazier could still account for this behavior as being under the operant control of Castle's reactions toward Frazier. Since Frazier has the prerogative of the extraspectionist to call the shots as he presupposes them to be, there is nothing for Castle to do but fall back on the Machian insight that more than one theory can account for the same fact pattern. The dialectician would see great evidence in this exchange for his or her image of humanity. Yet, there is no convincing another theorist if the latter also has his or her concepts locked into place, and they meet the empirical flow

of events reasonably well. This goes for all theorists, teleologists as well as mechanists, of course.

There are other strictly biographical accounts of the dialectic in Skinner's writings. He told of an exchange he once had with the eminent philosopher and mathematician, Lord Alfred North Whitehead (1861–1947). The point of their exchange was quite similar to the fictionalized account just presented. It seems that Skinner once sat next to Whitehead at a banquet and naturally fell into conversation with him concerning the nature of science. This was in 1934, and the youthful Skinner was admittedly flushed with the excitement of behaviorism, arguing that in time man's behavior will be completely accounted for by the environmental factors that determine it. Whitehead apparently found some things lacking in this program for a science of behavior. Skinner gives us this account of their closing positions:

He [Whitehead] agreed that science might be successful in accounting for human behavior provided one made an exception of verbal behavior. Here, he insisted, something else must be at work. He brought the discussion to a close with a friendly challenge: "Let me see you," he said, "account for my behavior as I sit here saying 'No black scorpion is falling upon this table.'" [111]

How would we as dialecticians understand this exchange? We would be intrigued by the fact that Whitehead reached for an improbable something to have fall on the table—a black scorpion—not to affirm but to negate! The point of this sentence was made not by what was communicated, but by what was denied (dialectically negated). What Whitehead was doing was posing a convoluted argument which might be expressed as fol-lows: "Only a human being, with dialectical reasoning capacities to affirm or deny any proposition expressed, would feel it necessary to prove a point by saying what is obviously the case—that something highly improbable to begin with is *not* taking place." Yet, this is not what the demonstratively inclined Skinner was to make of this sentence. After mulling it over, Skinner framed what he pre-sumed *was said* and not what did not need saying! He thus analyzed the sentence to find the probability in it that the black-scorpion response was a metaphorical allusion to be-haviorism.[112] Hence, the demonstrative rea-soner finds Whitehead saying, "I'm afraid that behaviorism just isn't going to be ac-cepted at this table today." Either interpre-tation can be considered correct, of course, but the point to be made for present purposes is that a dialectical formulation cannot ap-pear if it is never presumed as a possibility in the first place. Surely the dialectical interpre-tation makes sense even as it offers us quite a different message based on Whitehead's in-tended meaning expression from the one Skinner received.

The final example we have is drawn from Skinner's childhood. He tells of a time when he lost a watch that he had just been given by his family. Feeling unhappy about the loss, Skinner went out into the woods along a creek, where he and his friends had built a clubhouse, in order to contemplate his situa-tion. As Skinner put it: "I was miserably un-happy. Suddenly it occurred to me that hap-piness and unhappiness must cancel out and that if I were unhappy now I would neces-sarily be happy later. I was tremendously re-lieved." [113] Though he tells us this in passing and goes on to describe how he eventually found the watch and even was moved to

consider this a religious life event for a fleet-ing period, the point of significance for the dialectician is this oppositional cast to Skin-ner's own reasoning processes. Down through the ages, human beings have responded simi-larly at low points in their lives, often going forward with renewed faith in their future to found political causes or religions. Is this a mere accident of natural selection in oper-ant conditioning, or does the oppositional side of the human's reasoning potential re-flect a *basic* capacity to think dialectically?

The demonstratively inclined theorist would probably scoff at the anthropomor-phization of a purely lawful act, observing that happiness and unhappiness do follow lawfully over time and that it made good sense (demonstrative logic) to reason as Skinner did. Here again, what emerges as an explanation of the—historical or experimental —facts is up to the theoretician doing the ex-plaining. Without a basic change in the model used to describe behavior we shall never see dialectical explanations arising in modern psychological science, dominated as it is by the empirico-behavioristic (demon-strative) traditions of its past. There are some current efforts underway to stimulate dia-lectical theorizing and research in psychology, but whether they will be influential in the future remains to be seen.[114]

Even so, we can answer the question posed by this section with "yes." There are indeed dialectical themes and empirical research findings that support the utility of a dialecti-cal conception of human behavior.

What Motives to Psychotherapy Are Primary in the Empirico-Behavioristic Tradition?

Scholarly Motive

There is a generally lower level of the schol-arly motive to be noted among the therapists of Part Two. Sullivan was quite sensitive to the fact that psychotherapy rests in large measure on what we have called procedural evidence, as noted in the following: "Utility of a [theoretical] conception may be said to hinge on its providing a ground for successful prediction of events, and for the construction of crucial experiments. Its plausibility of application to facts of observation already at hand is not a scientific sanction if the hypothesis cannot be *tested*. The therapeutic 'test' is no test at all."[115] The patient's acceptance of an insight in therapy is no proof that it is correct,[116] because there are always five other theories to explain and cure the same problem in living.[117] We therefore need *both* clinical and experimental study before we can arrive at a legitimate theory of human behavior.[118] This attitude separates Sullivan clearly from Freud, who viewed psychoanalysis as a scientific method of equal status to laboratory investigation.

Sullivan was not a naive or rabid empiricist, for he clearly appreciated the point of view the psychiatrist brought to the therapeutic contact as a kind of bias. "There is no such thing as 'objective' observation; it is participant observation in which you [that is, the psychiatrist] may be the significant factor in the participation."[119] Even so, Sullivan clearly wanted to move psychiatry away from the older case-history tactic of the classic analysts to a more modern, empirical, evidential approach. He once remarked that individuals who are philosophical types do not make good therapists, because they find the schizophrenic patient only too happy to philosophize (talk, talk, talk) rather than actively work to change his or her behavior.[120] Sullivan had little patience with the highly intellectualized analyst, who spent huge blocks of time looking for theoretical subtleties in the client's history.[121] He once said, "I have never felt entitled to torture patients by the month to find out something that in-

terested me but was of no special moment to them—if only because I do not think that anything can be learned by doing it."[122] This is the comment of a pragmatist, a man who is more interested in effectively removing a symptom than in learning supposed truths about why the symptom arose in the first place. He was well aware that a psychiatrist could effect cures without understanding everything that was happening in a scientific sense.[123] We therefore conclude that Sullivan's motives to therapy were not *primarily* scholarly.[124]

It is Dollard and Miller among our behaviorists who most strongly recognized a role for psychotherapy as a means of obtaining worthwhile knowledge about human behavior. They observed:

If psychotherapy were used only as a way of curing neurotic persons, it would have a real but limited interest to students of human personality. The psychotherapeutic situation, however, provides a kind of window to mental life. Advanced research students in psychology are taught the rudiments of the therapist's art so that they may sit at this window.[125]

Such observations are of behavior in its natural setting, outside of the artificiality of the laboratory, and hence they are uniquely important to personality study.[126] We have much to learn from people in their daily routines of living, including those who are judged abnormal in behavioral pattern.[127] This general acceptance of the consulting room as an extension of the laboratory was not to be seen in the behavioral theorists who followed in Dollard and Miller's wake.

Wolpe thus viewed his role as that of applied scientist. He established his principles of behavioral change and then moved to the clinical setting in order to put that knowledge into effect. Stampfl moved in the same direction. Though he was ready to admit that dynamic factors may have been involved in the origins of neurosis, he felt that the most effective way to remove symptoms once formed is to fall back on learning principles and animal experimentation.[128] The Skinnerians and social learning theorists took similar positions. Behaviorists thus do not view themselves as detectives, searching for clues to new insights regarding the human condition. They are *doing something* to their clients, effecting changes in their behavior as efficiently as their previous scientific researches have made it possible to do.

Curative Motive

This is clearly the major motive of the therapists of Part Two. Sullivan's major research efforts were pitched at his unique approach to the healing (improving interpersonal relations) of the schizophrenic. His research ward, his creative analysis of the hospital as a social milieu, the advocacy of halfway houses and early intervention—all point to what seems to be Sullivan's major motive, that of cure. We can see this motive assuming increasing importance in the 1930 period, when Sullivan had parted ways with classical psychoanalysis. He summed it up in a typically Sullivanian sentence, as follows:

Either you believe that mental disorders are acts of God, predestined, inexorably fixed, arising from a constitutional or some other irremediable substratum, the victims of which are to be helped through an innocuous life to a more or less euthanastic exit—perhaps contributing along the way as laboratory animals for the inquiries of medicine, pathology, constitution-study, or whatever—or you believe that mental disorder is largely preventable and somewhat remediable by control of psycho-sociological factors.[129]

Sullivan believed that patients should expect to improve when they enter therapy.[130] People are not in consulting rooms to further the selfish goals of the therapist. Speaking to therapists, Sullivan once said: "There is no fun in psychiatry. If you try to get fun out of it, you pay a considerable price for your unjustifiable optimism."[131] Those therapists who frequent cocktail parties and stroke their —often bewhiskered—chins with supposed wisdom as they make "profound" comments or who write up case histories for popular consumption to gain cheap prestige or notoriety were objects of scorn to Sullivan.[132] He felt there were entirely too many such "juveniles" sitting in therapists' seats.[133] Psychiatry cannot be indifferent to its clients. In the post–World War II years Sullivan was to pitch his by then internationally acclaimed school of psychiatry in the direction of helpfulness to those in need. ". . . That is what we strive for in psychiatry of the Washington School: a rational system as to what can be done about anyone anywhere who is not living as well as he seems capable of living with his fellow man."[134] This commitment to action is one of the clearest manifestations of the character of the man who once said, "I am very much more interested in *what can be done* than in what has happened."[135] The analytical study of humanity had moved into a new age, in a new land, with a Yankee tempo of movement (efficient causation), change (locomotion), and controlled improvement.

Most behavior therapists assume that they have been hired by the patient to do a job in therapy, and they hope to accomplish this goal as professionally and effectively as pos-

sible in as little time as necessary.[136] The behavior therapist does not need six months of
free associations leading back to a client's
earliest years in order to propose a program
of change. Behaviorists take cure as their primary role, and they are usually on the road
that leads to overt changes in the patient
within a half-dozen sessions. As Wolpe once
expressed it, "The *raison d'etre* of psychotherapy is the presumption that it can overcome certain kinds of human suffering."[137]
For a therapist to say, as Freud did (see p.
101), that his therapy would occasionally
make a client worse seems to the behavioral
therapist a contradiction in terms and an admission of failure.[138]

Ethical Motive

Ethical themes are prominent in Sullivanian
thought. In Chapter 5 we reviewed his theories on social revision, his desire to liberalize
attitudes toward sex, and his general feeling
that Western society in the World War II
years was a "profoundly sick society" needing
basic reorganization.[139] Problems of personal
conscience were ascribed to the culture and
not to the individual. That is, Sullivan felt
cultural values—often issuing from religious
beliefs—foist guilt on the individual actor.[140]
Religions are not so different from delusions,
said Sullivan, except that many people participate in them and thus help to systematize
such beliefs.[141] Much of religious mythology
can be traced to the autistic and preverbal
attacks on the problems of living suggested
by powerful historical figures. Religious leaders like Moses have introduced a certain degree of parataxic distortion into the flow of
cultural outlooks, which are then handed
down as consensually understood religious
myths.[142] These quasi-delusions are not themselves harmful, particularly since they are
often based on the call for intimacy in human
relations. But there is one aspect of religious

conviction that can prove harmful to humanity, "the illusion that we have a more-
or-less all-powerful . . . will."[143]

Sullivan thus followed Freud in viewing
the guilt generated by a belief in the power
of personal will to result in more trouble for
people than the gains achieved in trying to
take responsibility for one's life. He could not
convince himself that there was any such
force as a will in the personality,[144] and concluded, "There seems to be very little profit in
psychiatry from dependence on any such
idea as the mysterious power of the will."[145]
Sullivan therefore rejected teleological explanations of behavior in favor of explanations based on field forces, interpersonal vectors, and sociopsychological variables of all
sorts. He was convinced that modern humanity has to look for group solutions, extending
even to international relations, to solve the
problems in living faced by each of us as individuals. His views therefore took on an
ethical motive of some importance. Indeed,
Sullivan became a moralist and social critic
of great influence in the post–World War II
years. His untimely death doubtlessly cut this
phase of his career as healer-to-mankind short.

The question of ethics is very complex regarding behavior therapy, and we will need
to develop this general topic in some detail.
The behaviorist's logic in applying knowledge from laboratory findings to everyday
behavior runs something like this: (1) experimentation has established certain lawful
relationships between the independent variable (IV) and the dependent variable (DV)
in laboratory studies; (2) for all practical
purposes the IV is the stimulus (S) and the
DV is the response (R); (3) the S is what
ordinarily controls the elicited R, or Rs which
are emitted are controlled by their consequences; (4) all behavior is thus shown empirically to be controlled by extraindividual

factors (physical determinism), either in the present situation or mediated from earlier life situations via memory (that is, psychic determinism is an illusion); hence, (5) insofar as change is possible in psychotherapy, it too must be controlled change, initiated by the therapist, who essentially manipulates an IV or S, and impacted on a client who is always at the DV or R side of things (that is, efficiently-caused change or *locomotion*); (6) conclusion: therapy is a *process of means to ends* rather than a question of selecting ends per se. When ends come into the picture, they becloud the issue, for *any* therapist *must* control the behavior of the client along the lines of an IV-DV relationship or there will be no therapy to talk about.

Basing their work on this train of reasoning, the behavioral therapists focus on the removal of client symptoms, and they demonstrate empirically that this form of cure does not result in relapses, secondary symptoms, or otherwise harmful outcomes. Sometimes their willingness to introduce behavioral prompts to change client behavior makes them seem highly unconventional or even immoral by customary standards. At other times they are seen as fascistic—the charge Castle was to hurl at Frazier in *Walden Two* —or at least power hungry in their zeal to influence the lives of others. Thus, even though behaviorists do *not* consider their therapy to be involved with ethics, their critics have forced them to consider ethical questions of this nature. There are roughly three kinds of ethical questions that arise for the behaviorist, and we will take them up in turn.

1. Is it right to remove a symptom without confronting the issues that prompt it? A person's anxiety is often due to mistreatments suffered at the hands of unthinking or un-

caring parents. The accidents of life scar us all, and in a case like this where a client has been reared by unloving parents, we have no qualms about removing anxieties or guilt feelings. But what about other instances, in which the anxiety might have its source in an *improper* behavior the client has indulged in. What if the client is not blameless after all? Are we still to remove the unwanted emotions through systematic desensitization without confronting the ethicomoral issues that prompted them? Stampfl was the only behavior therapist who touched on this question formally, dealing with problems of conscience acceptance.[146] More fundamentally, we might ask how fair this ethical question is to the behavior therapist? Presumably, the dynamic theorist like Freud would, in exploring the compromise solutions and defensive maneuvers of the neurotic, provide a thorough insightful account of how guilt might stem from actual death wishes for a parent, and so forth. But the dynamic therapist too must inevitably take a position on the merits of this symptomatic reaction—as Freud did, in fact, viewing along with Sullivan the harsh superego as a major cause of neurotic behavior.

Dollard and Miller accepted the Freudian thesis, as indicated in the following:

It is hard to say whether a morbid conscience is a worse enemy of life than a disease like cancer, but some comparison of this kind is required to emphasize the shock produced in the witness when he sees a psychotic person being tortured by such a conscience. Enough is known now to convince us that we should make the humble-seeming matter of cleanliness training the subject of serious research.[147]

Undoubtedly, just as many behavior therapists discuss the ethical concerns of the client as do dynamic insight therapists, and just as much harm or good can result from the removal of symptoms through either procedure. Though their formal position does not embrace introspective concepts per se, the behavior therapists interpret moral or ethical training as an important source of labels for mediation in behavior. They can hardly be blind to the necessity of dealing with such matters as the source of the client's symptoms in an informal manner. Finally, therapists who are also physicians—as is Wolpe—emphasize that the doctor is there for the aid of his or her client. Refusing to treat a client's anxiety on ethical grounds would be like refusing to heal a syphilitic on moral grounds.

2. Is it correct to violate convention in effecting therapeutic cures? The behavioral therapists have been criticized for their readiness to design unusual or extreme methods of cure. In a sense, the Stampflian implosive techniques are an example of such extremes. Having people imagine horrible things happening to themselves or to others can be taken as potentially upsetting or demeaning. Wolpe has noted that some of his clients find it morally objectionable to use assertive tactics in vivo (in life outside the consulting room).[148] Is it proper to play the gamesmanship tactic of "one up on you" with fellow human beings (see p. 455)? Wolpe usually told his client at this point that there are three ways to approach life. In the first instance, we can run roughshod over everyone and not care what happens to our fellow human being. The other extreme would be to completely submerge ourselves in the desires of others. Finally: "The third approach is the golden mean, dramatically conveyed in this fuller quotation from the Talmud: 'If I am not for myself, who will be for me? But if I am for myself alone, what am I?' "[149] Thus, Wolpe reassured his clients that sticking up for their just rights does not make an immoral monster of them.

But Wolpe took his therapist role even

further than this. In treating cases of religious scrupulosity, he has given his clients books with an antireligious content.[150] Freud's dynamic explanation concerning the nature of religion could hardly be considered pro-religion, of course (see Chapter 1). But in a kind of behaviorally engineered spirit of change, Wolpe has even seen it as his role to encourage male clients with sexual problems to seek extramarital affairs with lovers or prostitutes when their wife is unable or unwilling to assist in the relaxation procedures of systematic desensitization. As he once put it:

Perhaps there will some day be a "pool of accredited women who will sell their services to men with sexual problems. At present there seems to be no other recourse than to seek out a regular prostitute—and it is usually no easy matter to find one who is both personally appealing and able to muster enough sympathetic interest to participate in the therapeutic program.[151]

This concept of a "therapeutic extramarital relationship"[152] is open to the criticism now under consideration. However, Wolpe is moved to such extremes only when the marital partner is unable to assist. Furthermore, who can honestly say that a marriage without sexual compatibility is worse than a marriage with sexual adjustment brought about by extramarital training in systematic desensitization?

We must also not forget that some of the clients of a psychoanalyst do carry out extramarital affairs during therapy, or they come to therapy in the throes of such complex human relationships. The analyst can use such case-history material in making interpretations. Though they do not go out and arrange sexual liaisons for their clients, psychoanalysts do put several restrictions on what the client may do—such as not to marry or change occupations (see Chapter 1)—and this can be viewed just as ethically questionable as the practices used by Wolpe. After all, Wolpe is not advising divorce as a routine solution to sexual maladjustment in marriage, a likely outcome when such problems are not corrected in the marital union. So, here again, we would not wish to differentiate clearly between the behavior and dynamic therapists on the matter of violating convention. Our last point, however, does bring up a clear theoretical divergence between the behaviorist and the dynamic therapist in what they consider to be their role in the control of a client's life.

3. Should all psychotherapists control the behavior of their client, and can they avoid doing so even if they try?   By far, the greatest sense of confusion over the ethics of psychotherapy enters when psychologists begin speaking of the *control* of human behavior. All of the theory-construction factors discussed in the Introduction and Chapters 4 and 8 to this point—especially those relating to determinism and the change of behavior—coalesce at this point to help us understand why this confusion arises. We traced the logic of behavioristic therapists in six steps, moving from the empirical findings of the laboratory to the practical application of behavioral manipulation in the life circumstance. The result here is that behaviorists sincerely believe that they like anyone professing to be a therapist *must* control and presumably predict the course of their client's everyday life. A classic phrasing of this attitude may be seen in the following:

A science of psychology seeks to determine the lawful relationships in behavior. The orientation of a "psychology of behavior control" is that these lawful relationships are to be used to deliberately influence, control, or change behavior. This implies a manipulator or controller, and with it an ethical and value system of the controller.[153]

Note that this behavioristic rationale is based on a fundamental confound of the IV-DV and S-R relationships, which in turn makes it plausible to believe that only locomotion can effect a change in behavior. After all, since it is the IV which is seen empirically to efficiently-cause (locomote) the DV up and down some scale of measured value change, then as applied scientists we must do the same thing to our therapy clients, whose behavior or responses are presumed to be always on the DV side. Note also that the behaviorist does not consider moving from the first sentence to the second—from the study of laws to their overt application—an *ethical* decision. Ethics do not come in for consideration until *after* the decision to control a person's life has already been made; then we must consider the ethical code of the controller. Yet there are many psychologists—Carl Rogers (Chapter 9) being a prominent example—who would consider this decision to be the *primary* ethical decision of the citation. Indeed, even the psychoanalysts did not picture themselves controlling a client's life, but rather working with the client to help the latter achieve insights which might then be used *by the client* to effect changes via qualitative change (insight) rather than via locomotion (behavioral manipulation).

The problem here obviously comes down to what is meant by *control of behavior*. Behaviorists clearly think of this as involving material and/or efficient causes, resulting in a physical determination of behavior, and changes therefore being due to quantitative and especially local motion (locomotion). Dynamic and telic therapists, who are likely to raise our third ethical question, view the person as moved by formal and final causes, leading to psychic determinisms of behavior and qualitative changes of behavior (see p. 269). The particular assumptions we make about human nature will determine (in a formal-cause, qualitative sense!) what we will believe is the best, or most properly good, way of relating to and dealing with people. The question of what is good for people is at the basis of all ethics, a term used by the Greeks to apply to the human's character as opposed to his or her intellect.[154] Throughout history there has been disagreement on the matter of what this good is and how it is to be known or who is to receive its benefits. Since we can see this historic conflict in our behavioristic versus humanistic disagreement over the control of behavior, it would be helpful to clarify the two sides of this dispute—usually said to be involved with the distinction between *intrinsic* and *instrumental* value. A value is an estimate of worth, but in speaking of *the good,* we address the grounds for making such an estimate.

On one side, we have had over the centuries ethical philosophers who believed that each person has the rational—sometimes called the intuitive—power to know the *good* implicitly and to carry out ethical obligations for their own sake as a matter of duty. There is no calculation from means to ends in this view; the *good* is not the pursuit of happiness so much as it is the fulfilling of a *premising duty* "for the sake of which" behavior is carried out. Happiness may arise in carrying out one's duty, but *not always.* When the intent is happiness rather than some considered duty to conduct oneself in an ethical manner, there will surely come a time when duty will be submerged to happiness. Kant reasoned in this tradition when he argued, "Act so as to treat humanity, in thyself or

any other, as an end always, and never as a means only."[155] Note that the strategy here is entirely on the side of qualitative change where the decision to act is *first* made, and then through a form of psychic determination, behavior is carried out to fulfill the end intrinsically decided upon. We have a clear teleology here.

On the other side, we have had ethical philosophers who believed that the only thing people seek is happiness—sometimes phrased as "pleasure rather than pain"—and that they decide on what is good in the particular case by referring to *this* end. We might say that the goal of general happiness for oneself and one's fellow human beings is what we base our decision on in any given question of how we ought to behave. The British utilitarians Jeremy Bentham and John Stuart Mill reasoned in this instrumental-value tradition when they argued that pleasure is what people pursue in life and that the greatest pleasure over pain for the greatest number of people is the foundation of ethical obligation. People do not have an intrinsic sense of moral intuition which guides them nor can they be counted on to do the *good* things through rational thought; it is the ultimate pleasure or pain associated with the observance or violation of moral rules that directs their behavior. Note that an extraspective theoretician who does *not* believe that behavior is telically directed could employ this instrumental theory of value quite nicely. It does not demand that we believe the human being is predicating his or her behavior according to some "that, for the sake of which" decision as to what is best or good for all.

Now, invariably, when operant conditioners speak of controlling behavior they presume an instrumental interpretation of value. They are out to provide the greatest good for the greatest number, so, as in *Walden Two,* they aspire to arrange a social milieu in which everyone is being positively shaped [156] into happiness—whether they are aware of this shaping or not. The question of self-direction is irrelevant to this ethical stance. Skinner is noted for his rejection of aversive controls, preferring to use positive reinforcement because of its proven utility—its tendency to make more people happy more of the time. He observed rather halfheartedly, "If we knew as much about negative reinforcement as we do about positive, I suspect we would find that it can be rather effective in shaping behavior, but at the moment it isn't very effective, and the negative by-products are still in evidence, so I am opposed to it." [157] This is a technical acknowledgement of the value of positive reinforcement, but it is clear that Skinner wants to maximize such controls more generally. [158] He speaks fondly of his followers in this vein: "When operant conditioners get together, there is never any criticism or bickering. Everyone tries to be helpful. They practice positive reinforcement, and it is a wonderful thing." [159]

Since he was using positive reinforcement and trying to bring about the greatest good for the greatest number of people, it stymied and confused Skinner to learn that others found his plans objectionable. The matter of intentionality, of the fact that a person is being controlled "for the sake of" another person's purposes, seemed to him quite beside the point since everyone controls everyone else all of the time anyhow. There was no appreciation for the possibility of formal-final causation in the determination of behavior, hence the possibility of a qualitative control (change) did not occur to Skinner. Yet, when he found his critics irritated over *Walden Two* (1948) and observed that the only problem seemed to be "that my good life was

planned by someone," [160] Skinner was unknowingly dramatizing the fact that people who consider themselves *agents* in their behavior do not want manipulation planned by others! People want to do their own planning, to have a say in their futures, and the only person in Walden Two with such a capacity is Frazier. So unless the reader identifies with him, the only other existence open is as one of the mob of controlled, unaware organisms enjoying the good life.

A related problem here is: what is the *good* life? How can Frazier or anyone else for that matter decide how all of us *ought* to behave without making certain intrinsic assumptions to begin with? Harking back to Skinner's operant conditioning, let us assume that we wish to manipulate the behavior of a pigeon. We are going to drop kernels of food each time the pigeon takes a step in some way and gradually, over time, through the method of successive approximations, teach it to walk a figure eight. This form of behavioral shaping has been achieved several times, and Skinner himself has taught pigeons to do remarkable things. An intrinsic ethical thinker might ask, why have we selected a figure eight to shape the pigeon's walk? Why not a circle or a diamond-shaped pattern? When it comes to human behavior, such questions are *not* irrelevant! People want to know the *grounds*—the "that, for the sake of which"—for making a decision of this sort. If we have the techniques to shape a person's behavior into group dependency or self-dependency, what course should we take in setting up our ideal society? Do we want people to be highly dependent on one another, to mix and spend time with one another? Or would we prefer a society in which people live more inwardly and individually (à la Jung), relying upon others for solace and support only during times of unusual difficulty? If Skinner or others have done research to prove that group dependency is a more satisfying way of life and then have proceeded to control us into believing and acting this way also, what do those of us who value individuality, social reserve, and solitude have to say? Had we conducted the experiments, might there have been evidence in our direction?

Well, why not leave it up to science like this? Cannot science empirically establish the *good* for us, even with the provisos of affirming-the-consequent? As we reviewed in the Introduction, the scale of measurement of an experimental test must be selected beforehand in order to arrive at validation. This means that when we turn to the test of an ethical proposition, we must agree at the outset on what will constitute a positive or negative outcome at the criterion end of our control-and-prediction sequence (validating evidence). We can then decide on an experimental design and test the hypothesis; for example, "group dependency is to be favored over self-dependency because it leads to a happier and more fruitful life for all concerned" (instrumental ethic). But here is the rub. By defining happiness and the essentials of a fruitful life, we must inevitably *rely on ethical considerations at the outset,* even before we have nailed down our criterion measurements operationally. This *criterion problem* is insurmountable, and it signifies that all attempts to validate ethical hypotheses must ultimately beg the question.

If a therapist tells us that he or she has empirical evidence on which to base decisions as to which way our behavior will be manipulated, we can be sure that this evidence itself rests on debatable value decisions. In short, value decisions cannot be circumvented by science and indeed science will never tell us what *ought* to be in behavior any more than the principle of falsification will tell us what theory *ought* to be put to test by it. The final point to be made here takes us back to the awareness issue. If we

know that we are under manipulation, then we can surely do something to change this if it is not to our liking. Skinner has observed, concerning what the individual can do in self-defense that: "The best defense I can see is to make all behavioral processes as familiar as possible. Let everyone know what is possible, what can be used against them." [161] This would seem to be a recognition that even positive shaping can be used to get people to buy automobiles they cannot afford, convincing them in the process that they are truly successful because everyone who is anyone has such an automobile and is in debt just as much as they are. Though Skinner does not discuss such outcomes, it seems entirely possible to shape "happy" people caught up in a materialistic rat race.

Of course, in judging materialism this harshly, we too are letting our values color our judgment. But surely the more aware we make our general populace in a society the more likely that people can decide questions of behavioral control for themselves. If this is the case, are we not acknowledging that intentionality and agency are involved in human behavior? The introspective theorist who presumes that individuals have an intrinsic valuing capability would say yes. The extraspective behaviorist who thinks of valuations as special instances of mediation or cue-producing responses would say no. There is no way to resolve this disparity in outlook. The student of personality must accept it, and understand the theory-construction issues that underlie it.

Summary

Chapter 8 begins by considering the principle of falsification, which asks that a scientific hypothesis be framed in such a way as to be capable of being disproven. Vaguely framed predictions or suggestions that events might go in an either-or direction are unscientific. This principle relies on demonstrative reasoning with its stress on the law of contradiction. It forces the theorist to translate his or her thinking into operationalized measurements or procedures leading to one (unipolar) outcome, and one only. We recognize in falsification that all scientists can do is say what is *not* true with logical certainty. We cannot say what *is* true with logical certainty, because in this case, we fall prey to the affirming-the-consequent fallacy. This is why scientists recast their experimental hypothesis in the null-hypothesis form and then reject or fail to reject it at a given level of probability. Logical positivism has proposed a principle similar to falsification, its criterion of verifiability. This criterion asks a philosopher to say what observations can lead us to accept a proposition as being true or reject it as being false. If such observations are not possible, the proposition is considered philosophically meaningless. Both falsification and verifiability ask us to take an extraspective perspective in looking for evidence. Ironically, though, we accept these principles on the basis of procedural evidence—an introspectively framed type of proof—they bias us to view things in light of extraspective theoretical explanations.

An important feature of behavioral prediction is its *lawfulness*—a term that takes us into the consideration of variables and the meaning of the function construct. If we look extraspectively at behavior and predict its outcome in terms of measurements called the independent and dependent variables, it is easy to think that the (antecedent) independ-ent variable mechanistically (efficiently-) "causes" the dependent variable to "happen." As the latter is a function of the former, we can confuse our theory being put to test with our method of testing (falsifying) it and draw this conclusion—which may be totally erroneous! It was Mach in physical science who clarified the fact that all of our observed laws are on the order of formal causes, correlational ties of antecedents to consequents. The scientific method relies on efficient-cause manipulations in that the scientist arranges a succession of events (independent and control variables) preliminary to making a prediction (to the dependent variable[s]). But this manipulative method can put other than efficient-cause theories to test. Serious problems arise when psychologists let their methods operate as theories, for this limits the scientific method's application to one theory and one only. An example of what results is discussed in terms of the widely cited distinction between S-R laws (efficient-cause laws) and R-R laws (formal-cause laws). The law conception is best limited to the methodological context.

Chapter 8 next takes up the use of personality tests or scales, contrasting the projective and the psychometric traditions. The Rorschach and Thematic Apperception Test are the leading projective instruments employed in psychology. These tests were developed within a tradition that viewed them as more theoretical analogues than actuarial sampling devices. They aimed at discriminal descriptions of behavior. In time, however, tests like the Minnesota Multiphasic Personality Inventory supplanted them as leading personality instruments. The latter type of scale follows assumptions about personality—as being sampled from parameters of behaviors ranging across the target population—and therefore seeks literal prediction. Relying on mathematical theory, which is fundamentally vehicular, the actuarial tests have moved personality theory from a theoretical to a more methodological context. As a result, today the empirical observation via prediction of actual behavior is considered more important than the understanding of a given person's behavior, even when it is completely unpredictable! Actuarial tests reflect the spirit of falsification, empirical lawfulness, and above all, extraspective explanations of behavior. Projective tests often strain against falsification, seek to identify a person's internal motivations of even an unconscious nature, and above all, frame their explanations from an introspective theoretical perspective. It is this extraspective-versus-introspective issue that is involved in the fact that we sometimes can predict something we fail to understand. This happens in physical theories as well as psychological theories. Hence, just because we can actuarially predict a person's behavior extraspectively, does not mean we necessarily understand what is taking place introspectively.

Chapter 8 next takes up the issue of how well behavioristic theories account for mind and human agency. The Kantian, pro forma interpretation of cognition is contrasted with the Lockean, tabula rasa interpretation of cognition. Just as we cannot express the meaning of one cause through the meaning of another—as in reducing final causation's meaning to the meaning of efficient causation—so too we cannot express what Kant said about cognition in Lockean terms and vice versa. Whereas Locke made use of the intuitive-to-abstractive cognition idea in order to view mind as constitutive, Kant's a priori categories of the understanding lent meaning to experience in a conceptualizing sense. Hence, the Kantian innate idea is nothing like what Locke would consider an innate idea to be. Innate ideas for Locke were *contents,* whereas for Kant they were *faculties* that lent order to experience. Furthermore, in his transcendental-dialectic conception, Kant intro-

duced a faculty of mind that ordered meaning oppositionally, making self-reflexivity possible.

Chapter 8 also takes up the various ways in which free will has been interpreted in psychology: as statistical unpredictability, mediating alternatives, and guided natural selection. Behaviorists tend to use one of these interpretations, which are typified by the fact that they are all nontelic theories. None of these views considers the person to behave "for the sake of" an intention. Yet the findings on awareness in conditioning suggest that subjects must understand what is expected of them and be willing to comply with the experimental instructions. They seem more *in compliance* than *under control* in conditioning experiments, for even the discriminative stimulus is something the person frames through action and then behaves "for the sake of" (or rejects it along with the demands of the experiment altogether). It is becoming increasingly clear that personologists require an interpretation of behavior enabling them to capture a subject's predication of the life situation. Logic is involved in human behavior, and this calls for more use of formal and final causation with a consequent de-emphasis on efficient and material causation in personality theories. This also means that dialectical logic is an important aspect of human description. Chapter 8 next reviews some of the dialectical theoretical usages which have been hidden away in behavioristic writings, ranging from the tridimensional theory of emotions proposed by Wundt to the dialectic of Wolpe's reciprocal inhibition and the verbal clashes in Skinner's *Walden Two.*

It is clear that behaviorists do not consider the therapeutic contact as the proper context for the learning of new things about human behavior. The laboratory is the proper place for such investigation, wherein controls enable the scientist to work out precise laws. Hence, the scholarly motive is not high on the behavior therapist's list of priorities. As behaviorists, we apply known laws in the therapy context, laws that have been discovered or delineated in the laboratory. This application naturally places the curative motive in a supreme position. Behavior therapists are very interested in keeping precise records demonstrating their success rate, the rapidity with which they manipulate behavior, and so on. Many of them would say that this is the *only* reason any therapist (behavior modifier) should have for meeting with clients, even if the clients may be prompted by scholarly or ethical motives. Behaviorists embrace an instrumental theory of value, so for them what is good is what brings the greatest benefit to the most people in the most efficient manner possible. Trying to define the *good* intrinsically is for them a fruitless exercise, because culture defines this for everyone based on instrumental considerations. Though some behaviorists seem to believe that it is possible to prove empirically what the *good* is in life, in point of fact there is a serious criterion problem involved in trying to validate ethical claims. We inevitably assume the very value system in defining our dependent variables (criteria) that we set out to study in the first place.

Behaviorism has had immense historical influence on psychology, shaping the nature of the discipline more than any other school of thought. Its disciplined approach to validation and the practical effects to be achieved in applying its techniques of cure have ensured a leading position for behaviorism in the future of psychology. Whether it has helped or hurt the personologist's efforts to frame an acceptable image of human behavior is not easy to answer without seeming biased. Certainly traditional personality theory, which placed telic considerations uppermost in human description, has been injured by the image of humanity behaviorism has promoted. The telic-versus-mechanistic interpretation of human behavior continues to divide psychology just as it divided psychiatry in Freud's beginning as the father of modern personality theory. The end has not yet been seen to this basic cleavage in how the human being thinks (theorizes) about the human being.

Outline of Important Theoretical Constructs

If we predict and/or control the course of behavior does this mean we necessarily understand it?

necessity versus alternatives · affirming-the-consequent fallacy · principle of falsification · operational definition · demonstrative reasoning · law of contradiction · unipolarity · dialectical reasoning · null hypothesis · criterion of verifiability · logical positivism · extraspection in falsification and verifiability · lawfulness, laws · variable · function · teleologist versus mechanist · correlations as formal causes · Machian distinction between theory and method · functional relationship as formal cause · theory-method confusions · S-R versus R-R laws · personality tests · Rorschach · Thematic Apperception Test (TAT) · psychometric tradition · actuarial prediction · Minnesota Multiphasic Personality Inventory (MMPI) · vehicular versus discriminal issues in prediction

How well does behavioristic theory "account for" mind and human agency?

causal meanings cannot subsume each other · Lockean versus Kantian interpretations of cognition · mediation theories · intuitive versus abstractive cognition · simple-to-complex ideas · tabula rasa · innate ideas · pro forma · categories of the understanding · a priori schemes · transcendental dialectic · free will as statistical unpredictability · free will as mediating alternatives · free will as guided natural selection · contingent cause · reciprocal control

What are the implications of the findings on "awareness in conditioning" for the study of personality?
predication · intention · discriminative stimulus · compliance in experiments

Are there any dialectical themes hidden away in behavioristic writings or empirical psychological researches?
tridimensional theory of emotions · opposition in reciprocal inhibition · demand characteristics · verbal clashes in *Walden Two*

What motives to psychotherapy are primary in the empirico-behavioristic tradition?

Scholarly motive

Curative motive

Ethical motive
intrinsic versus instrumental theories of value · grounds for decision-making · criterion problem in validating ethical claims

Notes

1. Bandura, 1969, p. 16. 2. Popper, 1959, p. 41. 3. Bridgman, 1927. 4. Jung, 1946, p. 356. 5. Popper, 1959, p. 41. 6. See, e. g., Hull, 1943. 7. Ayer, 1946, p. 35. 8. Ibid. 9. Boring, 1950, pp. 473–474. 10. Gardner and Gardner, 1969. 11. Evans, 1968, p. 88. 12. Skinner, 1950. 13. Skinner, 1974, p. x. 14. Wolpe, 1978, p. 441. 15. Newton, 1952, pp. 14–24. 16. Simon, 1970, pp 39–43. 17. Collingwood, 1940, p. 57. 18. Bradley, 1971, p. 44. 19. Wightman, 1951, pp. 101–102. 20. see Rychlak, 1977, p. 47. 21. Bradley, 1971, p. 83. 22. Tolman, 1967, p. 414. 23. Bergmann and Spence, 1941, pp. 9–10. 24. English and English, 1958, p. 578. 25. Evans, 1968, p. 12. 26. Bandura, 1969, p. 16. 27. Spence, 1956, pp. 16–17. 28. Cronbach, 1957. 29. Spence, 1956, p. 9. 30. English and English, 1958, p. 427. 31. Rorschach, 1942. 32. Morgan and Murray, 1935. 33. Hathaway and McKinley, 1951. 34. See Cattell, 1957; Eysenck, 1952. 35. Ibid. 36. Dollard and Miller, 1950, p. 10. 37. Ibid., p. 136. 38. Ibid., p. 198. 39. Freud, Vol. V, p. 593. 40. Ibid., p. 604. 41. Freud, Vol. XIV, p. 147. 42. Ibid., p. 166. 43. Freud and Bullitt, 1967, p. 106. 44. Skinner, 1978, pp. 111–112. 45. Wolpe, 1978, p. 441. 46. Bandura, 1969, p. 45. 47. Wolpe, 1978, p. 438. 48. Skinner, 1978, p. 111. 49. Cranston, 1957, p. 266. 50. Locke, 1952, p. 128. 51. Ibid., p. 369. 52. Ibid. 53. Kant, 1952, p. 14. 54. Russell, 1959, p. 241. 55. Kant, 1952, p. 115. 56. Ibid., 229. 57. Watson, 1913. 58. Neisser, 1967. 59. Bandura, 1978, p. 348. 60. Boneau, 1974, p. 308. 61. Immergluck, 1964. 62. Lefcourt, 1973. 63. Locke, 1952, p. 190. 64. Ibid. 65. Ibid., p. 195. 66. Ibid., p. 193. 67. Rickaby, 1906, p. vii. 68. Ibid., p. 90. 69. Goss, 1961, p. 288. 70. Angell, 1907, p. 85. 71. Dollard and Miller, 1950, p. 219. 72. Sullivan, 1956, p. 8. 73. Sullivan, 1953, p. 369. 74. Sullivan, 1940, pp. 13–14. 75. Sullivan, 1964, p. 202. 76. Wolpe, 1969, p. 55. 77. Stampfl and Levis, 1969, p. 88. 78. Bandura, 1977a, p. 201. 79. Hebb, 1974, p. 75. 80. Evans, 1968, p. 23. 81. Ibid., p. 19. 82. Skinner, 1957, p. 96. 83. Skinner, 1971, pp. 37–38. 84. Skinner, 1948, pp. 257–258. 85. Skinner, 1971, p. 162. 86. Ibid., p. 169. 87. Bandura, 1978, p. 356. 88. Skinner, 1974, p. 57. 89. Ibid., p. 220. 90. Kennedy, 1970. 91. Farber, 1963. 92. Skinner, 1974, pp. 52–53. 93. Evans, 1968, p. 19. 94. Ibid., p. 104. 95. Brewer, 1974, see pp. 28–29. 96. Skinner, 1974, p. 74. 97. Sullivan, 1954, p. 24. 98. Dollard and Miller, 1950, p. 184. 99. Ibid. 100. Boring, 1950, p. 330. 101. Osgood, Suci, and Tannenbaum, 1957. 102. Riegel, 1973. 103. Mancuso, 1976. 104. Dollard and Miller, 1950, p. 281. 105. Wolpe, 1958, p. 73. 106. Bandura, 1973, p. 49. 107. Ibid., p. 138. 108. Stampfl and Levis, 1969, p. 95. 109. Skinner, 1948, p. 112. 110. See Rychlak, 1968, Chapter XI.

111. Skinner, 1957, p. 457. **112.** Ibid., p. 458. **113.** Skinner, 1967, p. 391. **114.** see, e. g., Rychlak, 1976. **115.** Sullivan, 1962, p. 141. **116.** Ibid., p. 151. **117.** Ibid., p. 207. **118.** Ibid., p. 197. **119.** Sullivan, 1954, p. 103. **120.** Sullivan, 1962, p. 289. **121.** Ibid., p. 35. **122.** Sullivan, 1956, p. 270. **123.** Ibid., p. 368. **124.** Sullivan, 1953, p. 167. **125.** Dollard and Miller, 1950, p. 3. **126.** Ibid., pp. 6, 98. **127.** Ibid., p. 5. **128.** Stampfl and Levis, 1967a, p. 498. **129.** Sullivan, 1962, p. 270. **130.** Sullivan, 1954, p. 16. **131.** Ibid., p. 10. **132.** Ibid., p. 12. **133.** Sullivan, 1953, p. 295. **134.** Sullivan, 1964, p. 262. **135.** Sullivan, 1956, p. 195. **136.** Dollard and Miller, 1950, p. 275. **137.** Wolpe, 1969, p. 18. **138.** Wolpe, 1958, p. 204. **139.** Sullivan, 1964, p. 155. **140.** Sullivan, 1962, p. 232. **141.** Sullivan, 1964, p. 80. **142.** Sullivan, 1956, p. 348. **143.** Sullivan, 1953, p. 173. **144.** Sullivan, 1940, p. 191. **145.** Sullivan, 1953, p. 301. **146.** Stampfl and Levis, 1969, pp. 107–108. **147.** Dollard and Miller, 1950, p. 141. **148.** Wolpe, 1969, p. 19. **149.** Ibid. **150.** Ibid., p. 257. **151.** Ibid., pp. 77–78. **152.** Ibid., p. 77. **153.** Krasner, 1962, p. 201. **154.** Sidgwick, 1960, Chapter I. **155.** Ibid., p. 274. **156.** Evans, 1968, p. 42. **157.** Ibid., p. 34. **158.** Ibid., p. 72. **159.** Ibid., p. 111. **160.** Ibid., p. 47. **161.** Ibid., p. 54.

Part III

Kantian Models in the Phenomeno-logical Outlook

Chapter 9

Applied Phenomenology: The Client-Centered Psychology of Carl R. Rogers

Rogerian personality theory is based on phenomenology and gestalt psychology, and so we will want to familiarize ourselves with the major thinkers in these earlier points of view. There is also a tie between phenomenology and the philosophy of existentialism, which is surveyed in Chapter 10 (see pp. 619–630).

Background Factors in Rogerian Thought

Edmund Husserl (1859–1938)

Husserl is often called the father of phenomenology, though he was not the first to speak of phenomena nor was he the first philosopher to refer to his outlook as phenomenological (that distinction belongs to Hegel). Yet he did more to define the issues and to stimulate the general phenomenological point of view than any other theorist.

Recall from the Introduction (p. 14) that Kant had divided experience into two spheres: the *noumena* (what something is in itself, independent of our sensations of it) and the *phenomena* (our sensory knowledge of things or actions in the external world). Fay holds her favorite comb in her hand. She feels its heavy plastic weight in her palm and runs her fingers along its teeth. These feeling sensations are phenomenal experiences, but does Fay ever really know the comb as a reality independent of these sensations—know it noumenally? Though he believed that noumenal reality really exists, Kant argued that we can never know such "things in themselves" directly, and that, in fact, our mind through its categories of the understanding frames-in the *meaning* of the noumenal world for us.

Husserl's philosophy begins in this distinction between noumena and phenomena. Since meaning resides in the phenomenal realm, the only way for a science of psychology to understand anything is to see it from the person's subjective point of view. We cannot hope to find an independent noumenal reality existing objectively someplace; all it can mean is the agreement reached phenomenally by a number of subjects—individual people. Thus, even Fay cannot prove that her comb *really* exists unless she finds several other people to agree that they too see and feel its presence. Husserl called this approximation to general agreement *intersubjectivity*. Thus his formal position on psychology was idealistic, as suggested in the following:

Everything that in the broadest sense of psychology we call a psychical phenomenon, when looked at in and for itself, is precisely phenomenon and not nature [that is, noumenal existence]. . . . A phenomenon, then,

is no "substantial" unity; it has no "real properties," it knows no real parts, no real changes, and no causality; all these words are here understood in the sense proper to natural science.[1]

The physical scientist can properly define things materialistically as "really existing" and can see things in terms of antecedent events pushing consequent events along in mechanistic fashion. But can we as psychologists define the natural scientist *as a human being,* who must therefore behave from within a phenomenal understanding of reality in similar terms? Husserl said that we could not. Human beings are moved by intentions, by goals and aims which they strive to realize in a peculiarly nonmechanistic fashion. Husserl argued that we need a new language of description as well as a new *method* of scientific investigation if we are to capture this distinctively human course of action. What sort of method is this to be? Husserl devoted much of his life to working out a proper phenomenological method, one that would capture experience as known by the man or woman subjectively *within* phenomenal experience rather than from *without*, as science pretends to accomplish.

Since the question of independent, noumenal existence is irrelevant (who can know it?), Husserl argued that a phenomenological method must capture the *essence* of meaning. This essence is the conceptual significance of the words we use to describe our phenomenal world through an act of intuition; it involves the immediate, unbiased knowing of what is going on in our phenomenal experience.[2] This method is not precisely introspection, because the introspective psychologists of Husserl's time felt that they were studying the body's *real* or noumenal processes. *Phenomenology* focuses exclusively on the phenomenal aspects of experience.[3] If we were to have asked

Husserl, "What can phenomenology teach us?" he would have answered:

Phenomenology can recognize with objective validity only essences and essential relations, and thereby it can accomplish and decisively accomplish whatever is necessary for a correct understanding of all empirical cognition and of all cognition whatsoever: the clarification of the "origin" of all formal-logical and natural-logical principles (and whatever other guiding "principles" there may be) and of all the problems involved in correlating "being" (being of nature, being of value, etc.) and consciousness. . . .[4]

Scientists can only be objective through use of their subjective cognitions (thoughts); hence, they need a more personal method to complement the impersonal method employed when they study things other than themselves. This demands a study of consciousness, which always involves consciousness of something else.[5] Consciousness is fundamentally intentional; it seeks to know things beyond itself yet in patterned relation to the self. Phenomenology seeks to clarify how we become *conscious of* these related events in experience.[6] In the phenomenological method, we are not studying *that* but *this,* our very existence as conscious, meaning-creating beings. Hence, Husserl can say of his proposed science, ". . . we meet a science of whose extraordinary extent our contemporaries have as yet no concept; a science, it is true, of consciousness that is still not psychology; a phenomenology of consciousness as opposed to a natural science about consciousness."[7]

Kant was alert to the seeming fact that human beings are able to turn mental attention to themselves—to reflexively study their own mind as a process. If humans have machine properties, then unlike other machines in nature, they can turn back on themselves and observe their own parts and processes at work. To describe this ability Kant employed the term *transcendental*. We transcend when we go beyond the usual flow of our thoughts (cognitions) and see things as they happen from the vantage point of an observer outside this flow. This is more than simply feedback (see our discussion of cybernetics, p. 479); a machine that is feeding back portions of output as new input does not transcend and *know* that it *is* feeding back. It never gets outside of its processes to know that it is a process of knowing. Husserl borrowed Kant's construct of transcendence to speak of the new method of personal study as *transcendental phenomenology.*

The success that Husserl achieved in these phenomenological studies is debatable. His career seemed more a critical introduction to the possibilities of a phenomenological method than an actual demonstration of the fruits of that method. He presented insights into the nature of consciousness, particularly as it relates to the dimension of time, but we cannot point to a systematic body of knowledge in this area as we can point to a body of knowledge in gestalt psychology—an approach to psychology that acknowledged the role of phenomenological description.

The Gestalt Psychologists: Max Wertheimer (1880–1943), Wolfgang Köhler (1887–1967), and Kurt Koffka (1886–1941)

When psychology began as an independent branch of science, a major interest of its founders was sensation and perception. How does a person come to know his or her environment through the senses, and how can we explain the higher thought processes in light of these sensory receptors? John Watson's (see Chapter 6) emphasis on the observed motions of behavior was not in vogue during the last few decades of the nineteenth century and the first decade of this century. The founding fathers of experimental psychology, Wilhelm Wundt and Hermann von Helmholtz, were trained in physiology and physics. They assumed that their role was to explain human behavior in the general style of all natural scientists which meant finding the underlying (atomic) basis and source of the physical energies that were *really* the cause of overt behavior.[8] This actually became a search for the noumenal reality! Psychological study was therefore aimed at breaking down the structure and function of the nervous system and its receptors (eye, ear, skin, and so on) into the neurons and nerve impulses that supposedly make observable behavior happen in the first place.

Many young men entering the field of psychology could not accept this form of material reductionism which seemed bent on ignoring the totality of human experience, a totality that simply could not be found in the underlying building blocks of atomic energies. Looking back, Köhler spoke of the excitement generated when an alternative to the reductionistic approach was first suggested:

. . . it was not only the stimulating newness of our enterprise which inspired us. There was also a great wave of relief—as though we were escaping from a prison. The prison was psychology as taught at the universities when we still were students. At the time, we had been shocked by the thesis that all psychological facts (not only those in perception) consist of unrelated inert atoms and that almost the only factors which combine

these atoms and thus introduce action are associations forged under the influence of mere contiguity [contact]. What had disturbed us was the utter senselessness of this picture, and the implication that human life, apparently so colorful and so intensely dynamic, is actually a frightful bore.[9]

The man who was to father this new look was Max Wertheimer (1945).

In 1912, one year before Watson's epic call for a behaviorism, Wertheimer published his classic paper on *phenomenal movement,* or more simply, the *phi-phenomenon.* Essentially, this perceptual phenomenon accounts for our seeing motion solely as the temporal displacement of perceived objects in our visual field, even when no actual external movement is taking place. For example, in viewing a motion picture, what we "see" is a series of pictures *without motion* flashed in rapid succession, each of which shows a person or object in relatively different proportion to the background. The same thing applies to music, wherein melodies emerge as total impressions from individual notes combining into certain tempos. The point Wertheimer was making and the criticism his students and collaborators, Köhler and Koffka, were to continue throughout their eminent careers was that "we can never find these qualities of experience in reductive experiments." Thus, the meaning of *gestalt* is that of the "total, whole, essential nature of." Just as Husserl argued that an essence cannot be found in reality, so too the gestalt psychologists argued that the human being is an organizing animal, one who arranges an incoming physical (*distal* or removed) stimulus into a unique totality at the level of phenomenal experience (*proximal* or close-by stimulus). Humans therefore do as much to reality in shaping experience as reality does to them.

Thus the first major reaction to an elementistic psychology, or a mechanical psychology, occurred in the field of perception. Gestalt psychology takes root in perceptual study, though its founders were to extend their descriptions to higher mental processes, personality, and even social organizations.[10] And in doing so, they specifically advocated the use of phenomenology, which they defined as follows: "For us phenomenology means as naive and full a description of direct experience as possible."[11] This emphasis on naive (simple, unsophisticated) description is a typical phenomenological caution, that we as scientists not allow our assumptions regarding what is "good" science or "factual" description to get in the way of the human experience we are trying to understand.

For example, science teaches us that some things are sensations and other things are realities. A cloud may appear threatening to us as it approaches from across the sky, but this threat is not really being *seen*. The cloud is just a collection of liquid material particles. It has no intrinsic quality of threat. Yet, says Köhler, to the primitive mind a phenomenal experience of threat *is* perceived directly in the cloud.[12] Primitives have no science to tell them otherwise. They can only perceive (see, understand) what they perceive, and hence the natural environment is experienced in quite other terms than it appears to a modern person. Indeed, Köhler once suggested that modern people cannot be completely naive about their phenomenal understanding of life, so biased have their perceptions become, thanks to the influence of natural science.[13] The primitive belief in spiritual forces, such as mana (see Jung, Chapter 3), can thus be taken as a directly perceived *phenomenal* experience.

Making an analogy to physical science, the gestaltists spoke of a *field* of vision, organized into a *molar totality* (unitary mass) and acting as a gestalt. Though it is a constantly changing field, the relative properties within the field of vision remain somehow constant and obey certain *laws of organization*. The subparts of the total are *articulated*—that is, divided into distinctively recognizable suborganizations—but the overall effect of the molar totality cannot be predicted from a study of the separate parts. The whole is something uniquely different from or greater than the sum of its parts. We might say the whole transcends reduction to the parts. Over a period of years the gestaltists named a series of laws that describe how this *phenomenal field* is organized, as follows:

Law of unit formation and segregation. Uniform stimulation produces a cohesive (united) field, whereas inequality in level of stimulation produces articulation (division) in the field.[14] A circle or ring would be an example of the very cohesive field, unbroken by articulated inner parts. If we now begin drawing lines through the circle, making it into a cartwheel design, we are increasing the complexity of articulation. Generally, the geometric form having the most cohesive properties is the one that is most likely to be "seen" and the easiest one to remember. Thus, we can recall a circle easily, but in recalling the cartwheel, we might forget exactly how many spokes it had, and so on.

Law of closure. If we perceive a straight line, it remains as such until it may begin to curve and return to its point of origin—at which time there is great cohesive pressure to close the line into an actual figure of some sort.[15] Thus, a circular line that is not completely closed into a ring will be seen as a closed ring by the average person, especially if he or she merely glances at the incomplete figure. Closed areas are more stable than open areas because they have the cohesiveness of a uniform field or articulated subfield.

Law of good shape. The shapes that emerge perceptually—as in closure—will be those having the best balance and symmetry.[16] An unbalanced, asymmetrical figure is not cohesive and will not be perceived as readily as a nicely balanced figure. A blob, with its disbalanced, uneven edges, is difficult to picture or describe accurately, whereas a nicely proportioned outline like a teardrop shape is quickly recognized and readily recalled.

Law of good continuation. Straight lines or the contours of geometric figures seem to follow their natural or "internal" tendency to continue as they "are." A curve will proceed in the direction of its arc, an ellipse will continue as an ellipse, and so forth.[17] In addition, this principle can be discerned in a melodious tune which continues in the direction previous notes have taken it. There is a certain demand placed upon the melody to flow in the line of best continuation.

Law of proximity and equality. Items in the perceptual field that are equal or similar in nature will be grouped together, as will items that are simply placed close to one another.[18] In viewing this series of dots . . . . we are prone to see three groups of three dots, rather than nine dots in a row. So long as each articulated subpart of three dots is fairly close to the others, we tend to relate the total as a gestalt, because after all, they are all equally dots. However, if we extend the distance between the subparts, we would eventually see three different totals rather than three subparts of one total.

These laws of organization are not mutually exclusive categories of description. They can interact as, for example, when a good continuation either might combine with or might counter closure in order to bring a melody to a close or keep it going for several more notes. In the final analysis, all of the laws are referring to the *same* gestalt phenomenon. The gestaltists formalized this commonality by saying that a *law of pragnanz* subsumed or was the most general phrasing of all the other laws of organization. Pragnanz holds that "psychological organization will always be as 'good' as the prevailing conditions allow."[19] By *good,* the gestaltists meant regular, symmetrical, simplified, and perfect articulation of what they called the *figure*—that is, the content on which we fix attention when we perceive anything (what we see, hear, smell, touch, and so on). Furthermore, it is possible to speak of such figures only if we also consider the *ground* on which they rest. A closed circle, for example, closes a cohesive figure set against a background of cohesiveness, as when we draw a circle on a blackboard. The blackboard acts as the ground for the circle. The contour of the circle is defined inwardly, so that the only way we see *any* figure—the circle or a friend—is as a figure framed-in by a ground. We can thus name another all-embracing *law of figure-against-ground formation*: ". . . if two areas [of the perceptual field] are so segregated that one encloses the other, the enclosing one will become the ground, the enclosed the figure."[20] When we now add that this figure will tend to be as simple, well articulated, and cohesive as possible, we have rephrased the law of pragnanz in figure-ground terms.

The gestaltists now had these principles, plus several others which we need not go into, to oppose to the reductive explanations of their theoretical opponents. In fact, Wertheimer was to suggest that the actual motions of the molecules and atoms of the brain, insofar as they move about, conform to the patterns of gestalt laws. As molar processes, both the actions of physiological structures and the very way in which we go about thinking are *isomorphic*—that is, identical as to form.[21] This *principle of isomorphism* was the supreme gestalt response to the reductionistic theories of Wundt and Helmholtz. Isomorphism claimed an *identity in pattern* for the phenomena (thought) and the noumena (the swirling atoms and molecules in matter). In this sense, gestalt psychology takes on a nativistic tone. Experience following birth can influence figure-ground relations, of course, but this innate tendency to think and perceive in a certain patterned way is *given* by our very natures—much in the way that our hearts and livers function in a given way from the outset of life.[22]

When it came to describing personality, the gestaltists simply extended their laws to a description of the ego as a figure set within the ground of the social field. As Koffka said, ". . . the Ego seems to behave like any other segregated object in the field."[23] When disbalances occur in the total field, the ego does what is required to re-establish harmony (symmetry, balance, closure, and so on). Feelings of pleasure and pain, wishes, desires, and all such needs were considered articulated subparts of the ego organization. The ego, in turn, was viewed as in articulated relations with and a subpart of other divisions of the field, such as the family, neighborhood, social class, and so on. Each of these divisions of the total field has its own organization following the laws of organization. To gain some impression of how gestaltists discussed group formation, we might turn to Koffka:

Groups are more or less closed, with more or less defined boundary lines. Consequently, the more closed they are, the more difficult

it is to introduce new members into them. . . . It seems that the degree of closure and of resistance to innovations vary directly with each other. Thus the rural group is more conservative than the city group.[24]

Koffka went on to break down group formation into the articulated subunits of leader, follower, class levels in the social hierarchy, and so forth.[25]

Kurt Lewin (1890–1947)

Though he was not an orthodox gestalt theorist, Kurt Lewin, as the founder of field theory in psychology, received considerable stimulation from the work of Wertheimer, Koffka, and particularly Köhler—all of whom were his colleagues for a time at Berlin University.[26] Lewin took the concept of a perceptual phenomenal field and drew it out into a theory of the *life space,* the total psychological environment that each of us lives within. Everything that might be said to have an influence on our behavior is nestled within the articulated parts of the life space.[27] Lewin drew the equation $B = f(LS)$, or, behavior is a function of the life space. Rather than seeing behavior as an *incoming* process of stimulus-to-response in the manner of the behaviorists, Lewin emphasized that behavior takes on field properties as an outgoing process of organization and interpretation.

The life space is thus a phenomenal field.[28] In order to predict an individual's behavior accurately, we must know the patterned structuring of the total life space. In defining the articulation and resultant structure of the life space, Lewin did not fall back upon specific laws of organization as the orthodox gestaltists did. He and his many students worked out a number of alternative concepts, some of which directly overlapped the traditional gestalt theory, though others did not. One such concept was the *level of aspiration*.[29] Lewin's field theory emphasized that human behavior is directed toward goals and that people set their own expectations for what they will take to be success or failure in life. For some—even talented—students, a grade of C will be considered successful attainment, whereas others will be as crushed by this "low" grade as if it were an F. The former have acquired the habit of setting low levels of aspiration for themselves, whereas the latter have come to project high levels of aspiration—at least in this one sphere of possible achievement.

Lewin called the course of behavioral action carried out in the life space the *path* or *pathway*. When Juan makes his way from home to his job as a lathe operator, he follows a pathway from one articulated *region* of his life space (home) to another (job). Juan likes working on a lathe so this job goal has a *positive valence,* but he dislikes having to go into the main office and speak with his head boss. The main office bears a *negative valence* for Juan when he must direct his path of behavior to it as a goal. As we noted in Chapter 6 (p. 401), Neal Miller's researches on frustration and conflict were based on these Lewinian constructs of goals, pathways, and valences, as well as *barriers* to the attainment of goals. Of course, Lewin always kept the valence of a goal *in* the life space of the person who is essentially making the environment what it is. The negative meanings of the main office are in the final analysis due to Juan's psychological outlook. In his theory, Miller had these valences as stimuli nestled *in* the environment. Miller would have Juan under the control of these independent factors rather than somehow responsible for them.

If behavior is the result of a total life space functioning constantly in the present, combining features from the past, and projecting a directedness into the future, then figures within this field other than the person might influence the action taking place at any point in time. For example, if we pass by a mailbox on our stroll to our place of work each morning, that mailbox is *not* quite the same item in our life space each morning. On the morning when we have no letter to drop, it is merely a potential obstacle in our path like any other object—a tree, a post, or whatever. But on those mornings when we have a letter to mail—and especially when it is an important letter—the mailbox takes on quite a different figural status. Rather than being something to be stepped around, the box literally beckons us to use it (acquiring great positive valence). Phenomenologically speaking, it takes on what Lewin called a *demand character,* so that it would be as correct to say that the "box brought us to it" as it would be to say "we went to the box." We usually say the latter only because of our egocentricity, but the field forces of our life space play no favorites. The stresses and strains of disbalance when one aspect of the field beckons must be thought of as acting in a molar fashion "all at once" to re-establish harmony (pragnanz). The person is merely one figure among other figures set against an environmental ground.

Lewin hoped that one day a mathematical system could be adapted to measure the molar activities of the life space. He thought that the nonquantitative form of geometry known as topological geometry would have the best chances to handle the structural and positional factors in the life space. Actions in the life space were not always identical to those

State Childhood 17-12

internal dialogue
memoric thought
concrete ops.
morality of coop.
conservation

Adol:
general, abstract
hyp-deductive + propositional
hypothetical, decenter

Infancy – 0-2

reflexive behavior

sucking initial schema 4 sec. quart

circular reactions repeatative actn.

actn schemata, deliberate

impact of styles perm.

Early Childhood 2-7

moral parents to ego ideal

congo: thinking (animism, intuition, animilope

moral reason

ely - ver. start

of the *foreign hull,* which is what Lewin called the nonphenomenal, palpable reality (a derivative notion of the noumena). Sometimes the shortest phenomenal distance between two points is to move *away* from the desired goal, as any girl knows who has played hard to get with a potential boyfriend. But how to measure this kind of complex psychological behavior with mathematical precision was quite another matter; though Lewin pinned his hopes on topology for this purpose, it cannot be said that they were ever realized.

Lewin considered the articulated regions of the life space to be separated or *differentiated* by more or less permeable membranes, so that some are in contact with each other and some are isolated and cut off from influence. Someone who conducts an active religious life on Sundays but engages in unscrupulous business practices during the rest of the week would be a person with no internal *communication* between "work" and "church" regions. In moving from one life region to another, the person is said to *locomote*. We must also consider the person himself or herself as a region, because internal differentiations and articulations occur, such as motivations to achieve some goals and avoid others. There is a limit to the differentiation of the life space. Lewin called this the *cell,* but rather than viewing it as a building block of the life space in the reductive style of Wundt and Helmholtz, he considered the cell a cohesively stable organization which requires no further subparts.

At the upper reaches of organization, we can begin speaking of the social group entering the organization of our life space. Actually, during the last decade of his life, Lewin was moving away from personality theorizing toward the role of social theorist. He probably did more for the establishment and development of social psychology than any other theorist in the history of psychology.

In 1939 he coined the phrase *group dynamics,* and in the early 1940s he established the Research Center for Group Dynamics at the Massachusetts Institute of Technology (MIT) (later moved to the University of Michigan following his death). He and his students performed the first controlled studies of leadership, in which they contrasted democratic, authoritarian (autocratic), and laissez faire (indifferent, weak) types of group leadership.[30] The model that underwrote this new area of group dynamics featured the typical gestalt emphasis on totality, organization of social roles, and the resultant channeling of hostile tensions outward to scapegoats, and so forth. Lewin also worked on propaganda and the role of prejudice in the control of human relations. Indeed, his life work always bore the stamp of relevancy and practical application. Yet he was fond of saying, "There is nothing as practical as a good theory."[31]

Thanks to his open mind and practical approach, Lewin and his associates (Ronald Lippitt, Leland Bradford, and Kenneth Benné) initiated the interpersonal activity that has been called T-groups (Training groups) or sensitivity training or *encounter groups.*[32] In 1946 the researchers from MIT were holding a summer workshop aimed at training leaders to become more capable in the battle against racial and religious prejudice. The project was sponsored by the Connecticut State Inter-Racial Commission, and it eventually led to the creation in 1947 of the National Training Laboratories. The workshop brought together some forty-one hand-picked professional educators or social agency workers, about half of whom were minority group members from the black and Jewish segments of the population.

The strategy of the workshop was to begin with open discussion among participants and then to reach group agreement if possible on various social issues, such as the nature of prejudice, its causes, and how to counter it. A research staff observed and recorded these group discussions and then later that evening discussed their findings with Lewin in a kind of second group exchange. Apparently some of the subject-participants also attended these evening reporting sessions, which were conducted on the campus of Teachers' College, New Britain, Connecticut. When the point of view being expressed by the research psychologist conflicted with that of a subject-participant's memory of what had taken place that day, a kind of spontaneous group dynamic took place in the often heated discussion that followed.

Rather than discourage such commentary from his subjects and the debates that resulted, Lewin in typical spontaneous fashion pounced on the opportunity and literally began a second study of group interactions based on the feedback from earlier interactions. The discussion in these evening sessions became increasingly personal, and a participant necessarily gained insights concerning his or her impact on others in the group. In effect, the evening sessions had become group therapy, with tremendous potential for personality change among participants—subjects and researchers alike. Lewinian advocates were to refine this tactic of group confrontation into a device for the promotion of personal and social change. As we shall see below in this chapter, Carl Rogers picked up on the importance of such encounter groups for therapeutic purposes. Therefore, though he was not a psychotherapist, Kurt Lewin has left us with an extremely important legacy having far-reaching implications for the healing of social ills.[33]

Otto Rank (1884–1939)

Along with Adler and Jung, Otto Rank is generally considered one of Freud's most talented and important coworkers. Unlike them, however, Rank was not a physician. He joined the psychoanalytical circle while still a young man of roughly eighteen years. He served as the secretary to the Vienna Psycho-Analytical Society while attending the University of Vienna. He was to stay with Freud for approximately twenty years, until the appearance of his first major book, *The Trauma of Birth* (1922–1923). As he had been moved to do in other instances (see Chapter 1), Freud parted with his younger colleague—though the split with Rank was not nearly as bitter as were others. This separation between teacher and student became a symbolic manifestation of Rankian theory, for Rank's entire outlook was colored by the necessity for human beings to express their own will, to shift for themselves, and to be *independent* persons.

Rank left Vienna in 1926 for Paris, followed by several trips to America; in 1935 he moved to the United States permanently. He died in 1939. While in America Rank became quite influential in the area of social work, where he and his major student Jessie Taft helped promote what has been called the *functional* school—as opposed to the *diagnostic* school—of social case work. Essentially, in Rank's view, a social worker takes a dynamic approach to the client and through relatively short-term therapy contact, effects a cure by helping the client to exert his or her own will in assuming responsibility for life actions. Diagnosis or problem definition is thus secondary to actual change in living. It was while he was director of the Rochester Guidance Clinic that Carl Rogers came into contact with the philosophy of treatment advocated by Rankian social work, and we shall see definite parallels in the two outlooks.

It is essential that we grasp Rank's convictions regarding the purpose of psychotherapy. He never tired of saying that the therapy relationship is for the client and *not* the therapist. If a therapist insists on pressing a pet theory onto the client, generalizing from past clients to the human being now present, he or she can never cure what is wrong in the life of *this* neurotic. Rather, says Rank, "In each separate case it is necessary to create, as it were, a theory and technique made for the occasion without trying to carry over this individual solution to the next case." [34] The effective therapist always knows the client's individualized outlook on life and is able to discuss it in the client's own language. [35] Technical jargon is to be shunned. It is the spontaneity and the uniqueness of the therapeutic relationship which is the precious aspect of therapy—and that which cures—rather than the fanciful, high-blown theories of the therapist.

The central problem facing the neurotic is the problem of every one of us as we grow to maturity. We must learn to express our personal *will* and thereby take command of our own life. If we fail to attain this independence from mother and father, we will go through life defeated and miserable, hating those who repress us and hating ourselves for not willing positively. By giving up, the neurotic expresses a negative form of will, opting essentially for a flight from responsibility. After experiencing feelings of complete defeat, the neurotic person enters therapy and sees the therapist as a symbol of all that is positive in the sphere of willful behavior. This idealization occurs because the neurotic projects his or her positive will onto the therapist. Rank believed this is

what Freud meant by transference. But there is ambivalence in this transference, because the neurotic would like to become a positively willing person like the therapist and therefore resents the therapist to an extent. Being fundamentally afraid to will positively, the client puts this effort off and submits dependently to the therapist's will. One can see glimmerings of a client's more positive will when he or she stands up to the therapist and argues against this or that interpretation made in the course of the analysis. Freud incorrectly referred to this as resistance, [36] considering it frustration of therapy. For Rank, so-called resistance is the very heart of *successful* therapy, for it signals the fact that the client—long subjugated by the wills of others (parents, peers, teachers, and so on)—has finally begun to express his or her *positive* will.

Of course, the time it takes for a client to come to this stage of independence ("resistance") in therapy varies. If therapists assume that clients are slaves to their past, unable to shake off the mistakes of their childhood, so that much time is devoted to searching about for these long-forgotten fixations, then clients may never gain the maturity to do their own thinking in psychotherapy. Even worse, the client's occasional "resistances" are likely to be crushed as childish re-enactments by the authority of the therapist. Rank once observed that therapy is like a battle, a dynamic clash between participants, but it is a battle that *the client must win!* [37] The therapist simply aids in this process of finding independence. An innovation that is usually credited to Rank—at least in the sense that he developed this tactic to its fullest extent—is setting a definite time for the *termination of therapy*. A host of short-term therapy approaches have evolved from this general strategy. However, as a theoretical development,

Rank viewed the termination as the high point and most crucial phase of therapy. He drew direct parallels between the anxiety generated in the client at this point and the *separation anxiety* the child experiences in being born (*birth trauma*), in leaving mother to attend school as a child, in leaving the family to take up an independent life in young adulthood, and so forth.

These are the clear acts of commitment to life we all must make. In growing to adulthood by degrees and thus expanding our consciousness, we all take on the responsibility of self-direction, which means we exercise our positive will function. Rank found his clients reliving all of these separation situations during the end stages of therapy. In their dreams he saw birth symbols and came to view therapy termination as a form of *rebirth*—paralleling the religious acts of baptism which have for centuries been characterized as being "born again." As such, particularly since the client plays a major role in directing this rebirth, Rank considered it a *creative* act. In the Rankian world view, each person constantly creates his or her own reality. Here is a definite tie to phenomenology and existentialism. Just as a person must perceive things phenomenally and never know them directly, so too must he or she believe in some things that are illusory —points of view that are more or less socially acceptable opinions. Hence, said Rank, "The individual often lives better with his conception of things, than in the knowledge of the actual fact, perhaps is able to live only with his own conception of things." [38] Since life is fraught with opinions, what better than to live by *our own* opinions? It is therefore not important that we as therapists discover the real facts of how the client became neurotic. It is of secondary concern that we have a unifying, single theory of the neu-

rosis. What is important is the decision on the part of a neurotic to create his or her own cognitive-phenomenal world and to live within it with willful commitment from day to day. When this commitment is made, the neurosis ends.

There are other influences on Rogers's thought that could be detailed, such as Lecky's (1945) self-consistency construct or Snygg and Combs's (1949) view of the phenomenal self. However, the major drift of phenomenal theory has been captured in the positions reviewed to this point, and we can turn to Rogerian thought with sufficient background for a proper understanding.

Biographical Review of Carl R. Rogers

Carl Ransom Rogers was born 8 January 1902 in Oak Park, Illinois, a suburban community in the metropolitan area of Chicago. He was the fourth of six children, five of whom were males. His father was a civil engineer and contractor who achieved considerable success in his profession, so the family was financially secure throughout Rogers's childhood and young manhood. When he was twelve, Rogers's parents bought a large farm thirty miles west of Chicago, and it was in this essentially rural atmosphere that the founder of client-centered therapy spent his adolescence. Though the family was self-sufficient and dependent upon each other, one does not get the impression of actual joy and lightheartedness among its members. [39] For one thing, the parents, although sensitive and loving, were devoutly and rigidly committed to fundamentalist religious views—at least, the mother was. Rogers's parents seemed to foster independence and common sense in their children,

Carl R. Rogers

offering them opportunities which might stimulate growth whenever possible. Rogers could never recall having been given a "direct command on an important subject" over his span of maturing years.[40]

Rogers was a dreamy boy who loved books and spent much time in solitary pursuits. He could read before he attended grammar school which prompted the school authorities to start him in the second grade, and he remained a top student throughout his preparatory years. All of the children had farm chores, and Rogers was often up at 5 A.M. to milk several cows before breakfast. Summers were spent cultivating the fields and learning to be responsible; the family's most central belief was that hard work could straighten out any of life's problems. Rogers attended three different high schools and did little dating. He was apparently a rather lonely person who felt that

his next older brother was favored by their parents.[41] Even so, Rogers drew strength from and even sought a "very positive kind of aloneness" at times in his life.[42]

Rogers attended the University of Wisconsin, the school that both his parents and three siblings attended. He selected scientific agriculture as his initial field and roomed in the Young Men's Christian Association (YMCA) dormitory. He became active in various Christian youth groups. During his sophomore year, following a conference of young people who had as their motto to "evangelize the world in our generation," Rogers decided to drop agriculture and study for the ministry. A major event at this point changed the direction of his life: in his junior year he was selected as one of ten students from the United States to participate in a World Student Christian Federation Conference in Peking, China. He was gone for more than six months and had an opportunity to witness a broad range of human behavior in cultures far different from his own. The experience liberalized his outlook, and on the ship enroute, he first seriously entertained the thought that "perhaps Jesus was a man like other men—not divine!" [43] From this point onward his letters home carried a different tone, one that was to upset his parents; but partly because of the geographical distance between parents and their son, the emancipation was achieved with a minimum of emotional upheaval.

Though his religious views had altered, Rogers was still drawn to Christian work. He had, in the meantime, begun corresponding with a young lady whom he had known since childhood in the Oak Park area. By the time of the voyage to China a decided romance had blossomed. Upon graduation from college Rogers opted to attend Union Theological Seminary, a liberal religious institution quite at variance with the fundamentalism of his youth. Against the advice of both their parents, he and Helen Elliott were married in August of 1924, just before setting off for New York City and a life of their own. It was in a course at Union Theological Seminary that Rogers was first extensively exposed to psychiatrists and psychologists who were applying their skills to individuals needing help. Realizing the commonality of the ministry and the mental health professions, Rogers began taking psychology courses at Teachers College, Columbia University, which was located across the street from Union Theological Seminary. His entire outlook on life began to change. In

about his second year of graduate study, a group of students put together a seminar on "Why am I entering the ministry?" in which instructors were not permitted to influence the directions taken. As a result of this early group experience and the soul-searching that followed, most of the participants including Rogers "thought their way right out of religious work." [44]

He then turned to psychology and over the next few years managed to keep himself, his wife, and their first-born child together on modest fellowship stipends. There was no single, outstanding figure in his education, and Rogers was to look back somewhat thankfully that he never had a mentor to defend or to react against as he came to intellectual maturity. [45]

After taking the Ph.D. in clinical psychology in 1928, Rogers accepted a position with the Rochester Society for the Prevention of Cruelty to Children. He remained in Rochester, New York, for the next twelve years, a highly productive time in which he developed his approach to the treatment of both children and adults in what was then called *nondirective therapy* and is better known today as *client-centered therapy*. It was there that he came into contact with social workers who were greatly influenced by Otto Rank. He heard Rank speak in a workshop and, though not impressed at first, gradually began to see the value of these new conceptualizations. Educated in an eclectic theoretical atmosphere with fairly heavy doses of Freudian theory, Rogers needed a few years to find that therapist insights—even when acceptable to the client —often failed to help the client materially alter his or her lifestyle. The Rankian emphasis on shifting creative self-definition to the client began to cement with Rogers's heavy personal commitment to the ideals of individual choice and freedom.

Rogers found the typical brand of psychology reported on in the professional meetings of the American Psychological Association (APA) too far removed from his interests as a clinical psychologist to become active in that organization. Consequently, he turned to the professional organizations of the social workers and held both state and national offices in this wing of the helping professions. Later, he was to be very active in the American Association for Applied Psychology (AAAP), a splinter group of psychologists who had organized to press their interests in a more practical form of psychology. He became president of AAAP, and later he played a central role in bringing the APA and AAAP together into a single organization which is known today as simply the APA. Rogers served as the president of the APA and received its Distinguished Scientific Contribution Award in 1956. He also played a leading role in forming the American Board of Examiners in Professional Psychology (ABEPP), a group commissioned by the APA to protect the public from malpractice in the areas of clinical, counseling, and industrial psychology. Rogers tired of professional activities per se and withdrew from them as his interests ranged beyond psychology to education, industry, and social issues of all sorts.

While in New York, Rogers founded a new Rochester Guidance Center and had his first experience with interprofessional tension with psychiatry over the fact that he—a psychologist—was to direct what appeared to be a medical facility. Working with children and their parents in psychotherapy seemed no more medical than psychological to Rogers—and to thousands of psychologists since—so a professional confrontation came about which Rogers "finally won." [46] In the closing years of the 1930s Rogers published a book on the *Clinical Treatment of the Problem Child* (1939), and as a result of this highly successful work,

he was offered a position as full professor at the Ohio State University. Though reluctant to accept because of his affection for the new guidance center, Rogers had always found the idea of an academic affiliation very attractive. He had lectured at Teachers College for a summer and found the experience rewarding and broadening. Hence, with the encouragement of his wife, he moved to Columbus, Ohio.

It was while he was at Ohio State that Rogers achieved his initial worldwide recognition. He brought to the academic setting a new kind of practicality and direct study of what clinical psychologists do as psychotherapists. He was one of the—if not *the*—first clinicians to work out a scheme for the study of the interpersonal relationship that evolves during therapy. He attracted numerous talented students, and a series of breakthroughs in clinical research began to issue from Ohio State University. To order his thoughts concerning a proper client-therapist relationship, Rogers wrote the manuscript of *Counseling and Psychotherapy* (1942), a clear and thorough statement of how the therapist should proceed if he or she hopes to bring about changes in the client. By this time he had also completed his family—a son and daughter—and life seemed to be settling into another phase of successful achievement.

In 1944 Rogers spent the summer teaching a course at the University of Chicago, and out of this contact came an unusual offer. He was given the opportunity to establish a counseling center at the University of Chicago, using those practices and procedures he felt were necessary without concern about interference from other sources of influence in the academic or professional community. Rogers took up these duties in the autumn of 1945 and established a center in which professional staff, graduate students, clerical help, and related faculty members worked as complete equals. Rogers was then working out the details of what he has called the helping relationship, and in his major work, *Client-Centered Therapy* (1951), he provided a first statement of the theory underlying his approach to interpersonal relations. This book and a paper written subsequently[47] provide the two primary theoretical statements of his career, although there are many less technically oriented papers which add to these fundamental statements. A collection of the latter papers were published under the title *On Becoming a Person* (1961). The Chicago period was once again highly successful, as the nondirective approach was being shown empirically to be as effective a method of psychotherapy as any other approach.[48] Rogers not only had an outlook on therapy and a theory of personality, but he constantly sought to prove the merits of his thought empirically. It was this interest in research and a desire to extend his approach to the highly abnormal person that took him away from Chicago to the University of Wisconsin and an unpleasant period of his professional life.

Returning to his undergraduate university in 1957 was naturally a sentimental occasion for Rogers. A seemingly excellent position was arranged for him which carried joint appointments in the departments of psychology and psychiatry. Unfortunately, things did not turn out as he had hoped. He initiated a large-scale research project on the schizophrenic patient which involved a staff of two hundred and extensive arrangements with a local state hospital, but problems developed among the staff—not all of whom

had a point of view amenable to client-centered philosophy. Data mysteriously disappeared, and considerable tension mounted, but after much heartache among all concerned, the project was completed.[49] It was not an entirely successful piece of research. The abnormals showed little improvement, and there was little evidence to support the contribution of a course in client-centered therapy over and above the typical hospital routine (which was modern and efficient in its own right).[50] However, other aspects of the study supported the fact that therapists with the proper client-centered outlook facilitated more improvement in their patients than did therapists who lacked the proper outlook.[51]

It was not such tepid research findings that discouraged Rogers at the University of Wisconsin. What destroyed his confidence in that school's psychology department and in all such "typical" programs of education in that period of psychology's history was the narrowly restrictive and punitive approach taken to the education of aspiring doctoral candidates. Rogers found that graduate students in psychology were given an extremely detailed form of preliminary (predoctoral) examination, which usually meant that they had to devote themselves entirely to so-called scientific courses which in fact required them to memorize vast amounts of useless information. As a result, some of the most talented clinicians and creative individuals left the program in disgust. Rogers claimed that only about one graduate student in seven ever attained the doctoral degree under this rigid, laboratory-oriented program.[52] In a "passionate statement" of dissent from the then-current trends of graduate education in psychology, Rogers fired his parting shot and resigned from the department of psychology at Wisconsin.[53] Shortly thereafter he resigned from the department of psychiatry as well, and in 1964 he took a position with the Western Behavioral Sciences Institute (WBSI) of La Jolla, California. He was once more out of an academic setting—forgoing his professorship and tenure at a university for the third time in roughly two dozen years.

The WBSI acted as a bridge for Rogers, since, after a few years of affiliation with this organization which was devoted to humanistic studies of the interpersonal relationship, he helped found a new group which is called the Center for Studies of the Person, also located in La Jolla. A developing interest in the needs of the group, organizations, school systems, and indeed, the common problems of humanity were to preoccupy him. He became a major spokesperson for the use of encounter groups in resolving human tensions.

Personality Theory

Structural Constructs

Mind-Body, Phenomenal Subjectivity, and the Wisdom of Organic Evidence

Rogers avoids separating mind from body by having both forms of experience united in his conception of the *phenomenal field*. Figure 22 contains a schematization of the Rogerian phenomenal-field construct. The phenomenal field proper is at the right; at the left we have an expanded version of it with certain forms of experience listed from top to bottom. Arrows direct our attention from left to right because we are suggesting that all of the things listed in the enlarged version of the phenomenal field are present in the phenomenal field proper.

A dotted plane separates the experiential processes in the upper half of the figure that are usually called *mental* (thoughts, con-

sciousness, and so on) from experiential processes in the lower half, usually called *bodily* (feelings, biological processes, and so on); all of these processes are shown via the arrows to be related to the phenomenal field proper (the right-hand side). What we are demonstrating in this coned-shaped figure is that though we might single out *mind* versus *body* distinctions (on the left), when it comes to the phenomenal field (on the right), no such distinctions are possible. The organismic experience summarized at the right-hand side of the figure combines *both* mind and body experiences into a single gestalt organization. Of course, the actual firing of the neurons in the central nervous system or the chemical reactions taking place in ongoing biological processes like digestion are *not* part of the phenomenal field.[54] This is why they are placed outside, to the left of the enlarged version of the phenomenal field. We sense the satisfaction of a delicious meal as it is being digested, but never literally know the chemical reactions that make this satisfaction possible.

Rogers hoped to avoid the pitfalls connected with reducing behavior to some underlying physical determinant, even as he hoped to preserve a central role for the biological organism in his theory. He did not want to lose the meaning of phenomenal experience in the mechanisms of the organic body. Those theorists who seek atomistic physical causes of behavior rarely provide us with a satisfactory understanding of personality.[55] The reason a physicalistic theory is almost useless to the phenomenologist is that physical processes *bear* phenomena. A physical illness like an upset stomach indicates malfunction, and to that extent it is represented in the phenomenal field (see "biological processes" in Figure 22). But the person cannot through introspective effort become aware of the

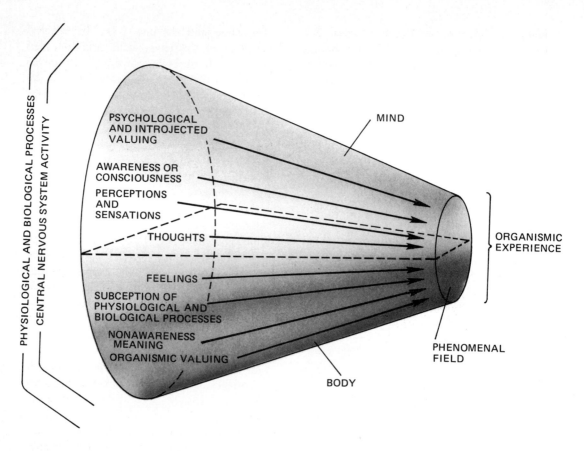

Figure 22   Rogerian Uniting of Mind-Body in the Phenomenal Field

physiological processes that have malfunctioned. He or she can only report the effects of the malfunction and submit to proper medical treatment. It is quite another thing when we speak about phenomenal fields, for now we are dealing with not the bearer of behavior but literally with the internal meanings of this behavior as known (or potentially known) by the person. This is not unlike moving from the noumenal realm (chemical malfunction) to the phenomenal realm (feeling of stomach pain). And as we do so, our values enter in to compound the picture all the more, as in the case of a person

who will not accept medical treatment because of religious convictions.

Though it may be impossible to experience the noumenal-like physical actions of neurons firing or chemicals reacting, this does not mean that everything in phenomenal experience forms into conscious awareness. As Rogers said, the phenomenal field: ". . . includes all that is experienced by the organism, whether or not these experiences are consciously perceived. . . . only a portion of that experience, and probably a very small portion, is *consciously* experienced. Many of our sensory and visceral sensations are not symbolized." [56] A *symbol* is a cognitive (mental) reflection of some state of affairs in the ongoing life of a person. We can think of it as a word or image having meaning for the person, as when we either use the word *hate* or see ourselves mentally in a state of extreme irritation caused by another person's actions toward us. We symbolize hatred when we are aware of this state in our phenomenal field. But sometimes we have physiological *feelings* of hatred that go unsymbolized in our phenomenal field.

Each time Lisa enters the room, Karen feels a tension of irritation flow through her body, because Karen has symbolized the fact that she dislikes (hates) Lisa. Karen has symbolized her attitude accurately, but it would be possible for her to feel her irritation organismically (that is, running through her body) and yet fail to symbolize the emotion actually being sensed. The raw feeling would be phenomenally experienced, but its *meaning* or the significance of its pattern would not. Thus, Karen might complain to friends that Lisa "makes me feel uncomfortable." As a physical being, Karen's biological processes—the firing of her neurons and the release of her hormones into her blood stream—would be identical, whether she had symbolized what was taking place in her relations to Lisa or not. Thus, in a sense, Karen's bodily reactions are always in line with the proper attitude toward Lisa, but her consciousness or mental awareness may be out of kilter with what is actually taking place. Hence, the feelings we have in relation to all aspects of life are very important in defining what its various situations and circumstances *mean* to us (potential symbolization).

Indeed, the phenomenal field defines the person's *subjective reality.*[57] "Man lives essentially in his own personal and subjective world, and even his most objective functioning, in science, mathematics, and the like, is the result of subjective purpose and subjec-tive choice."[58] Behavior is always goal oriented, organized by the phenomenal field and carried out as a total gestalt.[59] What we call objectivity in science is merely a special instance of *intersubjectivity,* in that individuals called scientists have agreed to use a common terminology and means of observation which makes sense to each of them *subjectively.* The agreement is intersubjective and never truly objective, if we mean by the latter some kind of realm of knowing that is independent of the individuals concerned. It is literally impossible for us to know another person's phenomenal field or to know anything free and clear of our own phenomenal field. As already noted above, we have trouble enough getting to know our own phenomenal field completely. The more open and unafraid we are to experience all that we feel in relation to the changing circumstances of life, the more likely that we will know ourselves—that is, our phenomenal field—and feel free to communicate this genuine state of being to others.[60]

The only way we can learn about ourselves this genuinely is to do what Karen may not have been able to do when she complained of Lisa making her feel uncomfortable: we have to turn our attention to our feelings and really get in touch with their meaning! We do this because, as we noted above, our feelings are always what they *are.* Feelings define our (necessarily subjective) reality. The trick is to symbolize feelings accurately if we are to know who we really *are.* Symbolization is more a mental act, whereas feelings seem to be completely organic or physical. How do we cross the bridge from one (organic) realm to the other (mental) realm? Rogers had these two realms interfusing in the phenomenal field, but what is the process by which he describes how we can know our true feelings? As a neogestaltist, Rogers fell back on the construct of differentiation or discrimination here. He suggested that people have the ability to *subceive,* a process that enables the person to know something emotively which is not yet distinctive enough to be a full-blown perception.[61] This is akin to seeing something before it is a clearly differentiated and articulated figure on the ground. We can feel things before they are good perceptual figures in our phenomenal field. Rogers defined *subception* as "a discriminating evaluative physiological organismic response to experience, which may precede the conscious perception of such experience."[62]

Thus, our very organic processes as feelings can instruct us, often dealing in subtleties of which our intellect falls short. In his first book on the nature of emotive, organismic learnings in psychotherapy, Rogers sounded the note he would continue to express over his long career: "They are learnings with deep emotional concomitants, not learnings of intellectual content, and hence may or may not find clear verbal expression."[63] We cannot always state the reasons for our feelings. Karen will not know immediately why it is that she feels hostility for Lisa. But in mulling over her relations with Lisa in light of her new understanding, in time these reasons will be found. The important thing for Rogers is that our total being includes an "organismic valuing process."[64] We can and do judge our relations with others in terms of our "personal organic evidence."[65] And what is most important of all, there is *wisdom* in such *organic evidence.*[66] To be a fully functioning person we

have to take stock of such evidence and profit from the understanding that results.

The Self as a Conscious Articulation of the Phenomenal Field

Rogerian theory is sometimes referred to as self-theory because of the importance placed on coming to know oneself accurately and thoroughly as a complete person. The terms *self-concept* and *self-structure* are both used to describe the self, with slightly different emphases. The *self-concept* refers to the conscious self-definition we give to ourselves when we speak of *I,* or *me.*[67] The term *self-structure* is a more technical concept, used when speaking about individuals from an external frame of reference. As a conscious or potentially conscious aspect of the phenomenal field, we can think of the self as a differentiated and articulated figure on the ground of the phenomenal field.[68] We are not always aware of ourselves as an identity as we go through the day; we may lose ourselves in work, for example. But given the right circumstance, we can always fix attention on self-identity and come up with a rough estimation of who we are or what we are doing at the moment. This is not always the case with an abnormal (psychotic) person.

But when the self emerges into awareness, we have a figure on the ground of experience, just as any life experience now in awareness may be said to take on figural properties. ". . . most of the individual's experiences constitute the ground of the perceptual [phenomenal] field, but they can easily become figure, while other experiences slip back into ground."[69] Thus, as Joel strolls down the street feeling quite pleased with the fact that he has the time to enjoy the beautiful weather, this self-awareness heralds the fact that his self has emerged as a figure on the ground of experience. When he now

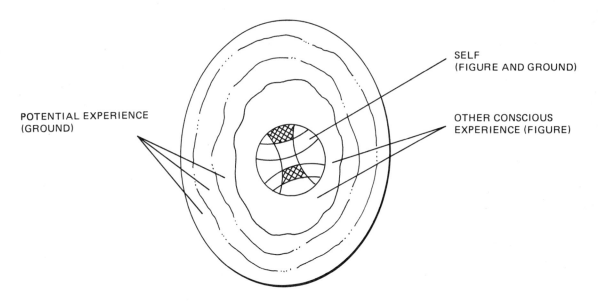

POTENTIAL EXPERIENCE
(GROUND)

SELF
(FIGURE AND GROUND)

OTHER CONSCIOUS
EXPERIENCE (FIGURE)

Figure 23 The Self as a Conscious Aspect of the Phenomenal Field

sees Camille strolling by across the street and begins to make hurried steps in her direction, this heralds the fact that she too has emerged as a figure on the ground of his phenomenal experience. Figure 23 presents a schematization of the self as an organized subportion of the phenomenal field. Note that we have taken the tip of the cone-shaped figure in Figure 22 (what we call the phenomenal field proper on the right-hand side) and turned it outward in Figure 23, so that the phenomenal field now takes on an elliptical shape.

In the very middle of Figure 23 is the self, which is also an organized (differentiated and articulated) configuration of subparts, set within the broader context of experience known as the phenomenal field. Note that this self is also differentiated and articulated into subregions, each of which can be seen as other figures on the ground of the total self. There are two heavily cross-checked (articulated and differentiated) subregions within the self. These might rep-

resent two important (strong, cohesive figures) preoccupations of Joel as a self (I, me). One of these regions might represent his self-image as a doctor someday, which is why he is currently attending medical school, and the other might reflect his desire to marry Camille someday. He literally identifies himself as her future husband. Each of these subregions is itself a figure on the ground of the total self-concept. That is, we could remove the inner circle and consider it as a separate configuration with inner regions. Note further that the self nestles within a region of the phenomenal field defined by a continuous line labeled "other conscious experience." This too would be a generalized figure in Joel's experience, representing possibly the nice weather he is experiencing on his walk. The other large circular areas with broken lines symbolize "potential experience," which Joel may have as he continues his

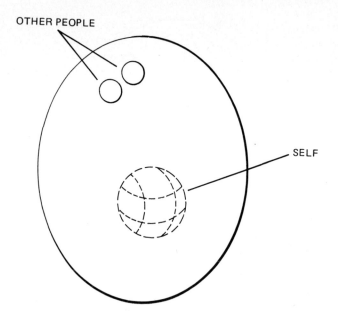

OTHER PEOPLE

SELF

Figure 24 The Self as Ground, as a Potential but Absent
Aspect of Conscious Experience

walk. We then have a firm outer line to define the limits of phenomenal experience.

If something were to turn up in the outer regions of the phenomenal field, such as Joel's seeing Camille or even more emotionally arousing, Camille in conversation with Marshall—a rival for her affection!—Joel would suddenly lose himself as figure and focus attention very specifically on the newly emerging figures in his phenomenal field. Figure 24 schematizes this circumstance. Note that the "self" has become an indistinct pattern, withdrawing more into the ground of the phenomenal field, and the "other people" have emerged from the ground of potential experience to rivet Joel's attention. He is no longer aware of the attractive weather. He forgets about himself as a person. He has one preoccupation now and one only. What to

do? Should he walk over to Camille and Marshall, who have not yet seen him? Should he keep his distance unobserved and follow them to see how friendly they really are? What to do?

Joel will eventually make a goal-oriented decision and act accordingly. His self-concept will also reappear as he brings himself back consciously into the deliberations and recommended course of action. In judging what to do, it is almost certain that Joel will have to consider himself as a potential suitor and mate to Camille. In a real sense, his self-concept is a series of hypotheses about himself, his strengths and weaknesses in relation to Marshall and other young men, the likelihood that he can actually succeed in obtaining the M.D. degree, and so on. Only in the sense that such hypotheses take on organization phenomenally is it possible to speak of a structural construct in Rogerian theory. Actually, Rogers was diametrically opposed to all personality theories that see humans as fixed by typologies and related personality structures. He preferred to think of human behavior in fluid, process terms. Yet, in the sense that we now consider the term, we find Rogers saying, "We may look upon this *self-structure* as being an organization of hypotheses for meeting life—an organization which has been relatively effective in satisfying the needs of the organism" [70] [italics added]. We may think of this organization as a *self-gestalt.*[71]

Motivational Constructs

Organismic Enhancement as Life's Master Motive

Rogers took it as a basic assumption that all living organisms strive to maintain, further, and actualize their experience.[72] He found from his earliest days as therapist that when given a chance the client would spontaneously begin a positive course of action to correct some life problem.[73] People just naturally want to know more about themselves and their world, including a knowledge of others. This comes down to a single, master motive—to enhance their phenomenal field by enriching its range, articulation, and differentiation. Rogers termed this motive *organismic enhancement,* a goal-directed activity,[74] which he described as follows:

The directional trend we are endeavoring to describe is evident in the life of the individual organism from conception to maturity, at whatever level of organic complexity. It is also evident in the process of evolution, the direction being defined by a comparison of life low on the evolutionary scale with types of organisms which have developed later, or are regarded as farther along in the process of evolution.[75]

This evolutionary concept is a subtle but important point in Rogerian thought which we must keep in mind.

Rogers made use of a *need* construct, which he defined as "physiological tensions which, when experienced, form the basis of behavior which appears functionally (though not consciously) designed to reduce the tension and to maintain and enhance the organism." [76] Our subjective feeling of need is therefore rooted in our physiology, but what is specifically need-generating in our lives is influenced by our unique experiences and personal understandings. For example, hunger is not experienced identically by all people. Some people view any sensation of hunger as very uncomfortable, even threatening. Others care little for food and eat primarily to keep their energy level up in order to do other things. A drive theory as employed in behaviorism (see Chapter 6) would simply not be able to capture these important phenomenological differences in what it *means* to be hungry. It is this meaning in the *current* and *ongoing* processes of the phenomenal field that determines the behavior of a person.

Behavior is not "caused" by something which occurred in the past. Present tensions and present needs are the only ones which the organism endeavors to reduce or satisfy. While it is true that past experience has certainly served to modify the meaning which will be perceived in present experiences, yet there is no behavior except to meet a present need [77] [emphasis added].

This currency emphasis means that we do not have to dig back into a distant past in order to find out why a person behaves as he or she does. The meaning of the behavior is current and knowable if we but relax the pressures on the person and let him or her express what is there for the expressing. Rogers emphasized that emotional tones always go along with need-satisfaction efforts, and they can be used to achieve this goal if we are but sensitive to our feelings in an open and honest way.[78] The more intense an emotion is, the more important is the goal being sought by the individual. There are both pleasant and unpleasant emotions, reflecting the contrasts of satisfaction or frustration in ongoing behavior. A complicating factor in human behavior is the fact that the needs that have been taken on by the self-concept or the self of Figures 23 and 24 are not always in agreement with the needs as felt directly in the body—or as we might now call it, the organism.

Rogers would therefore say that the *needs of the organism* are not always consonant with the *needs of the self*.[79] The organized subportion of the phenomenal field we know as the *I* or *me* may not have it as a goal to enhance the organism by moving in the directions spontaneously felt (emotions) to be the natural, correct ones. Darleen is with a group of popular neighborhood girls with whom she would like to be identified, when they begin poking fun at another girl, Martha. Martha is being painted as a drudge and a bore. Darleen does not really agree with this assessment, and she feels uncomfortable making fun of others in any case. But she goes along with the ridicule and overlooks the fact that she feels terribly ingenuine and even guilty in playing the game of popularity. Her *self needs* to be popular have come into conflict with her *organismic needs* to be true to herself. If she were genuine in this instance (organismic need), she would risk her opportunity to be known as one of the popular girls in her neighborhood (self need).

This takes us into what Rogers calls the *valuing process*. In defining his or her self-concept, an individual differentiates certain preferences articulated with ideals and feelings of commitment to certain ends.[80] Often a value is sensed directly by way of "sensory or visceral reactions."[81] We know instinctively or intuitively that "this I like" or "I have never really felt right doing that sort of thing." Many of our formal values as encompassed in our self-concept are handed to us by our culture as reflected in the attitudes of our parents. We are taught what is right and what is wrong in behavior. We come to value certain religious and political views. The trouble is, sometimes what we sense viscerally (deep, in our internal organs or guts) does not coincide with what we tell ourselves consciously. When this happens, we witness a confrontation of the needs of the organism with those of the self. Faced with personal inconsistency, we are forced to ask ourselves, "What do I really believe in anyhow?"

The reason we invariably ask ourselves this question is that, along with a need for organismic enhancement and growth, the individual has a need to be *self-consistent*. "The only channels by which needs may be satisfied are those which are consistent with the organized concept of self."[82] In other words, in organizing the configuration of the self-concept, we do not simply accept and articulate within it all of the evidence available to us. A person who considers himself or herself brave may have a fleeting sense of fear in a dangerous situation which he or she does *not* articulate and combine into a self-concept. This sincere organismic reaction is therefore ignored because it is not consistent with the self-concept being furthered. Any such self-inconsistency is experienced as a *threat* by the individual.[83]

Rogers noted how we like to think of ourselves as a finished product, complete and unified through a reliable outlook on life. If we change in any way, this completed structure alters to some degree over time. To think of ourselves as a fluid process of continuous change is upsetting, especially since these changes when they come on us often contradict what we have assumed our completed identity to be. Yet Rogerian theory is saying precisely this: the self is never finished, it is a constant process of change within spells of sameness. Hence, it is correct to say that *both* the organism (biological being) and the self (psychological being) are pitched toward actualization—that is, growth, enlargement, enrichment, and diversity.[84] They may not always agree on *the* goal of importance, but both sides to our being are agreed on the gestaltlike necessity to develop into a totality. One does not move in this enlarging direction without sensing ever-recurring periods of inconsistency in that totality. When this happens, new tensions develop and a sense of needing to be whole—self-consistent—once again is renewed. This is exactly comparable to the way in which *pragnanz* operates, and so it is not wrong to suggest that this principle underwrites Rogers' fundamental theory of motivation.

Congruence versus Incongruence and Positive Regard

It is freedom from inner tension that indexes the extent of psychological adjustment a person has achieved. As Rogers expressed it in his first theoretical statement, "We may say that freedom from inner tension, or psychological adjustment, exists when the concept of self is at least roughly congruent with all the experiences of the organism."[85] If Stanley tells us that he enjoys a marvelous life and we can see in his general mood that he is vibrant and alert, we tend to admire him for the good personal adjustment he has achieved. But if Stanley tells us this and we

see in his general mood that he is depressed and defeated, we begin to suspect that he has a picture of himself (self-concept) which is at variance with how he is actually living organismically. There is a lack of *congruence* between his emotional life (organism) and his psychological outlook (self). Congruence is defined as follows: ". . . when self-experiences are accurately symbolized, and are included in the self-concept in this accurately symbolized form, then the state is one of congruence of self and experience."[86] A more personalized definition would be: "The term 'congruent' is one I have used to describe the way I would like to be. By this I mean that whatever feeling or attitude I am experiencing would be matched by my awareness of that attitude."[87]

To be *incongruent* is thus to be out of kilter with what one truly is as a human being. This condition can come about entirely accidentally, as in the case of growing up with parental values which one never truly commits himself or herself to; one just goes along because it is expected. Or one might actually bring on this state personally by refusing to be open to experience, by playing a role with others, by never being sincere with oneself, and so on. There is a range of congruence-to-incongruence, so that the extent of inner tension (*psychological maladjustment*) can vary. In its more extreme form the state of incongruence can be quite harmful. "This state is one of tension and internal confusion, since in some respects the individual's behavior will be regulated by the [organismic] actualizing tendency, and in other respects by the self-actualizing tendency, thus producing discordant or incomprehensible behaviors."[88]

Thus, in a real sense, the directionality taken by the self-concept strains against the spontaneous organismic actualizing tendency.

A depressed Stanley is bravely trying to be the optimistic person his mother taught him to be, but the deception is beginning to break down completely for everyone to see. Intuitively, Stanley has the organismic capacity to turn his life around and admit to various frustrations and hostilities which he has been suffering through with a phony smile and pretended optimism. It would be best for him to admit to these sincere feelings, and motivated by their negative prompts, set a course in his life that could realistically correct things. If he actually would do this, then we would all notice a *change in his personality,* a change Rogers would call a *growth* because now, rather than working at cross-purposes, his total phenomenal being (his personality gestalt) would be congruent. It would still have problems to work out in relation to the world, of course, but it would be underway again. What has changed in cases like this is the inner alignment. A fixed structure has not been altered. Rather, a process has once again begun to flow forward to accomplish goals, including difficult ones.

In his studies of what it takes to be congruent, Rogers hit on the factor of *positive regard* in human relations. This is defined as follows: "If the perception by me of some self-experience in another makes a positive difference in my experiential field [that is, phenomenal field], then I am experiencing positive regard for that individual. In general, positive regard is defined as including such attitudes as warmth, liking, respect, sympathy, acceptance." [89] Drawing on the work of one of his students,[90] Rogers was to add to his enhancement principles and the need for self-consistency, a "need for positive regard" which each person is said to possess.[91] We cannot have a feeling of self-regard—a sense of personal acceptance—unless we feel positively toward our entire organism and accept

it for *what it* is, rather than merely what someone has told us it is. Before we can sense congruence we must first sense "I am worthy" or "I can be what I feel myself to be without shame or apology." At heart, Stanley's incongruence is due to the fact that he has not come to accept himself as a unique person. His pretended optimism is therefore a defensive act, done to appease others and earn their positive regard. As in the case of most defenses, the brittle adjustment they permit for a time tends to break down.

Defensiveness versus Spontaneity in Human Behavior

Defensiveness is brought on by a growing sense of *anxiety,* which in turn indicates that there is a disparity between the concept of self and the total organismic experience pressing through to awareness.[92] An attitude at variance with the symbolized belief system is differentiated as a figure from out of the ground of the phenomenal field. In order to maintain the picture of self as symbolized, the individual now begins several maneuvers which are comparable to the classical defense mechanisms. Thus, Rogers is likely to speak of *introjection* when he is referring to the fact that we take in values from others, usually our parents, and thus make it appear that these are our personal values when in fact they may or may not be.[93] He also used *repression* but gave this defense or adjustment mechanism a uniquely Rogerian interpretation. ". . . it would appear that there is the organic experience, but there is no symbolization of this experience, or only a distorted symbolization, because an adequate conscious representation of it would be entirely inconsistent with the concept of self." [94]

This notion of a *distorted symbolization* is central enough to be considered a Rogerian mechanism of defense. It is closely related to what Rogers sometimes called *denial,* and both of these concepts rely somewhat on the phenomenon of subception (see p. 584). A good summary definition is, "When an experience is dimly perceived (or 'subceived' is perhaps the better term) as being incongruent with the self-structure, the organism appears to react with a distortion of the meaning of the experience (making it consistent with the self), or with a denial of the existence of the experience, in order to preserve the self-structure from threat." [95] For example, if Cora, a college sophomore, thinks of herself as a poor scholar but earns an unexpected A on an examination, she can retain her low level of positive self-regard by distorting the symbolized conceptualizations of this success experience and saying, "The professor is a fool" or "It was pure luck." Rogers would occasionally refer to such distortions as *rationalizations*. [96]

The final Rogerian mechanism that can be used defensively deals with *locus of evaluation*. Each person acquires values in life; the locus of this valuation bears directly on the responsibility an individual will take for his or her behavior. What is the source of a person's values? Rogers observed: ". . . an internal locus of evaluation, within the individual himself, means that he is the center of the valuing process, the evidence being supplied by his own senses. When the locus of evaluation resides in others, their judgment as to the value of an object or experience becomes the criterion of value for the individual." [97] A "mama's boy" who never manages to untangle himself from mother's apron strings would be putting his locus of evaluation into her identity. He would think as mother thinks and value what mother values. Though it would be difficult to see how organismic enhancement or self-enhancement might be achieved in this flight from independence, the young man would attain a short-term advantage by shifting his locus of evaluation from his self to his mother. She

would be deciding things for him, freeing him from the responsibility of making choices in life. To that extent, this maneuver would represent a type of defense.

Running through Rogerian theory on the matter of defensiveness is an opposition between the status quo and spontaneity. Individuals caught up in defensiveness are not truly free to be spontaneous. They live by distorted preconceptions of themselves. A preadolescent boy may subceive "I would like to 'punch' my younger brother" but deny this potential symbolization from awareness—that is, fail to differentiate and articulate as a figure on the ground of the self—because he already thinks of himself as a good boy. He is therefore too rigidly fixed to accept the new understanding of what he is truly like. This distorted symbolization need not involve only negative behaviors like striking others. It would be just as possible for this boy to subceive the warmly emotional feeling of "I want to tell baby brother that I love him" and yet fail to do so because of his self-concept as a "tough little boy who does not act sissified." The repression of a positive experiential prompting proves, said Rogers, that it is not *only* evil promptings that are denied to awareness. [98] Indeed, the relative goodness or badness of an experiential prompting is irrelevant. It is the consistency or inconsistency of an experience with the self-concept that determines whether it will be made conscious (symbolized) or not (denied or distorted symbolization).

Time-Perspective Constructs

Although Rogers did not theorize in detail about development, he did try to sketch the process of maturing in terms of his personality constructs. He stressed the fact that a human infant is a valuing organism. The child begins life with a "clear approach to values." [99] Hunger is negatively valued, and food is positively valued as are security and an urge for new experience. Pain, bitter tastes, and sudden loud noises are negatively valued by the infant. This *organismic valuing process* is never fixed into a rigid routine. Children can shift their value judgments from positive to negative or vice versa as they mature. In time, some foods will be disliked and certain levels of pain in vigorous play may well be liked. The growing organism is constantly responsive to experience, promoting whatever tends to actualize it and halting that which fails to do so. The valuing process is a kind of regulatory system which keeps the organism on the proper course of need satisfaction.[100]

In a true sense, we all create our own world beginning in our infancy. Someone may have picked us up from our cribs intending to cuddle us and show us love, but if for some reason we perceive this action as hostile, we may respond with fright. This fright is for us *reality,* and from that point onward our expected relations with this person and others will be colored by our unique perception of the phenomenal realm. As Rogers said, ". . . the effective reality which influences behavior is at all times the perceived reality." [101] Rogers believed that it is pointless to catalogue the supposed behavioral equipment a child brings into the world, such as the various reflexes. He considered these to be secondary factors in the understanding of personality, because no matter what inborn structures may be present they all serve the master motive of organismic enhancement in any case.

Out of a general tendency for organismic enhancement and actualization, the child gradually differentiates a self-concept. Self-identity is grasped along with a personal locus of evaluation in the interpersonal relations carried on with parents, siblings, and other people. Precisely what the nature of this interpersonal style will be—whether shy and uncertain or bold and outgoing—is up to the child's unique subceptions and perceptions in the articulation and differentiations being organized into the total gestalt of the phenomenal field. Each life is subjectively unique. In Rogerian terms, the *personality* would include this unique totality of the phenomenal field—self-concept, style of relations with others, important goals differentiated as figures toward which behavior is oriented, and so on. Personality involves one's entire life, the developing changes that result and the present changes that are called for in this continuing process of evaluation and fluid movement to the next, most enhancing situation or state.

If all goes well, self-enhancement will parallel and be congruent with organismic enhancement, resulting in what Rogers called the *fully functioning person.*[102] This is an unlikely probability for most individuals. As self-awareness emerges, the child develops a need for positive regard, which may be learned or may be innately given to all humans.[103] Children need such positive regard from others, but also from themselves in assessing their own worth. Just as we can frame a hostile environment when people pick us up from the crib, so too can we look at ourselves negatively. With such poor self-regard, it becomes difficult for us ever to sense the values of real achievement when we accomplish things, or acceptance when others show us attention. Many problems for maturing children stem from the fact that they try to keep their self-concept in line with the projected positive regard of others. Derek's father wants him to excel in athletics and so the boy makes every effort to do so with only bad results for he is simply not well coordinated. Derek's excellent talent as a scholar does not bring much sincere praise from father, however. As a result, we see the development of a boy who foolishly devalues himself for not being what he really does not want to be in any case. Too often, Rogers noted, adults make their positive regard for the child *conditional*—that is, depending on whether the child will first do something or achieve something the adults want accomplished or conformed to. They are unable to provide the young person with *unconditional positive regard,* which requires an acceptance of the individual exactly as he or she is.

Language enters here as well. As he moves from infancy to early childhood, Derek must symbolize (name, develop a system of ideas about) his experience. In line with our discussion of the defense mechanisms, he is likely to symbolize only those valued behaviors and attitudes his parents and other adults consider valuable. He will necessarily think of himself as a failure in life because he cannot fulfill his father's phenomenal-field expectations, even though if he had been left to his own spontaneous phenomenal differentiations and articulations, he would have found positive self-regard in his good school work. This incongruent state of affairs, in which the valuation process has been repressed organismically in favor of an inaccurate self-estimation, is called distorted symbolization. Instead of symbolizing what he really *is*, Derek has distorted the self-concept which he now carries through life and which ensures his low self-regard.

Rogers is a great believer in the superiority of learning by actually experiencing things, rather than by simply being told or taught them. A parent who expresses his or her own views of things yet allows the child leeway to test out a position at variance with the parental view will—in the long run—

facilitate a congruent adjustment for the offspring. This is where Derek's father has been short-sighted if not actually selfish. He is unable to change his perspective on what is or is not a successful "son," probably because he was never given the chance by his own father to be himself and do his own thinking and evaluating. Rogers once described the correct approach for a parent to take who has an offspring misbehaving in some way and who therefore needs talking to:

I can understand how satisfying it feels to you to hit your baby brother (or to defecate when and where you please, or to destroy things) and I love you and am quite willing for you to have those feelings. But I am quite willing for me to have my feelings, too, and I feel very distressed when your brother is hurt (or annoyed or sad at other behaviors), and so I do not let you hit him. Both your feelings and my feelings are important, and each of us can freely have his own.[104]

Note the consideration given to the child in this free and open exchange, wherein each side can negotiate further as the discussion continues. By behaving in this manner a parent would not allow a phony relationship to develop with the child. Derek's father would give the boy a chance to express his feelings about baseball and football in relation to school work, and in the sincere exchange that would follow, a more genuine self-concept would emerge for the boy, as the father would now know his son in a new way. Having a competent scholar, a sensitive and insightful young man as offspring has its positive features too. On the other side of the coin, once Derek really understands what his father's feelings mean in their relationship, a new perception of athletics might arise on his part. Derek enjoys pleasing his father, and it is possible that he has overestimated what his father expects of him. Possibly he could be less than a star in one of his favorite sports and still earn dad's respect.[105] Note that when Derek came to this point, he would be taking over the locus of evaluation. No longer would he routinely be doing what he thinks dad insists that he do. He would now be working through an alternative more pleasing to himself and yet acceptable to his father. Rogers believed that this type of sincere, open, interpersonal exchange encourages the taking of responsibility on both sides and thereby furthers the growth-as-enhancement that human development always is.

Individual-Differences Constructs

Rogers is opposed *in principle* to pigeonholing people into personality classifications of any sort. He once said, "The client is the only one who has the potentiality of knowing fully the dynamics of his perceptions and his behavior."[106] In a sense, Rogers permits each individual to write his or her own personality theory in order to describe the unique nature of the person's phenomenal field. To force our concepts on others is to do violence to the fundamental Rogerian outlook on interpersonal relations. This is why nondirective or client-centered theory has always treated lightly the need for a fixed series of personality constructs. In his first book on individual therapy, Rogers avoided the question of a personality theory altogether, only to be criticized later because his views failed to proceed from a coherent formulation of this sort.[107] This interested and amused

Rogers, who felt that such formulations are unnecessary until and unless clear phenomena call for explanation.

One therefore looks in vain for a series of technical theorotypes in Rogerian psychology. At the same time, however, generalized commentaries on certain types of adjustment, and even descriptions of definite personality traits, can be found in Rogers's writings. With full appreciation for his theoretical position, we will now review a handful of the more informal constructs used by Rogers to account for individual differences.

Dependent versus Independent. A clear theme in Rogerian writing deals with the matter of whether or not the person takes on an independent or a dependent pattern of behavior. We can see decided Rankian influences emerging here. Speaking about the most difficult client to deal with through his therapy approach, Rogers noted:

The attitudes which most frequently seem to be ineffectively handled are those which might be called "aggressive dependence." The client who is certain that he is incapable of making his own decisions or managing himself, and who insists that the counselor must take over, is a type of client with whom we are sometimes successful, but not infrequently unsuccessful.[108]

When he discussed the kind of client best suited for his therapy, Rogers suggested that he or she should have achieved a reasonable level of independence.[109] It seems clear that this dimension of personality held great significance for Rogers, and it related to the question of locus of evaluation. A dependent person surely does not, and often cannot, assume responsibility for the locus of evaluation that has been framed internally. Dependent people look outward for standards to introject uncritically.

Self-Ideal versus Self. In some of his researches, Rogers used a concept of the ideal self or self-ideal, which he defined as "the self-concept which the individual would most like to possess, upon which he places the highest value for himself."[110] The ideal self is essentially a goal toward which the person would aspire if all things were equal in the sense of opportunities being available to achieve the valued level of behavior. Unfortunately, people often have differentiated and articulated various barriers to the attainment of their ideal selves. Sometimes their ideals are not really theirs, and they can in time change this side of the ledger as well. But in the main, Rogers assumed that people have a reasonable understanding of what they would "like to be like" if all things were equal.

Rogers and his students have made use of a sorting procedure adapted from Stephenson's Q-technique (1953) to measure the extent of relationship between perceived self ("how I am") and self-ideal ("how I would like to be"). The procedure followed is quite simple. Clients about to enter therapy sort several statements which may or may not describe them accurately as individuals. Each statement is printed on a separate card, and it might read "I feel pleased to meet other people" or "Rather minor things tend to upset me." There is no fixed type of statement. The main point is that a client must sort these cards according to certain statistical assumptions (approximating a normal distribution), usually on a seven-point scale from "like me" to "not like me." Having completed this sorting (taken as the conscious self-concept), the client re-sorts the same cards into a scale of "most like an ideal person" and "least like an ideal person." The definition of what *ideal* means is of course made clear to the sorter ("someone you think would be near perfect and like whom you would want to be"). The two sortings can then be statistically intercorrelated and even factor analyzed. Rogers's studies usually employed a simple correlational measure indicating to what extent a self-concept and an ideal-self concept were identical. The assumption is that the greater the positive correlational value, the more highly a person thinks of himself or herself. Clients have been shown to acquire higher correlations following psychotherapy than before therapy.[111] Rogers therefore used this scale as a measure of therapeutic improvement.

Vulnerability. "Vulnerability is the term used to refer to the state of incongruence between self and experience, when it is desired to emphasize the potentialities of this state for creating psychological disorganization. When incongruence exists, and the individual is unaware of it, then he is potentially vulnerable to anxiety, threat, and disorganization."[112] Hence, just as we can draw distinctions between people on the basis of how similar they are to their self-ideals, so too can we speak of differences among people in degree of vulnerability to maladjustment.

Mature Behavior. It is also possible to think of individuals as more or less mature in their behavior.

The individual exhibits mature behavior when he perceives realistically and in an extensional [that is, flexible and alert] manner, is not defensive, accepts the responsibility of being different from others, accepts responsibility for his own behavior, evaluates experience in terms of the evidence coming from his own senses, changes his evaluation of experience only on the basis of new evidence, accepts others as unique individuals different from himself, prizes himself, and prizes others.[113]

This abstract conception gives us a succinct picture of what Rogers's personal ideal type might represent.

Fully Functioning Person. This phrase is a special case of the maturity construct. However, since Rogers did name the ideal person as a worthwhile goal for humanity, we could do no better than end our consideration of his individual-differences concepts by citing his definition. "It should be evident that the term 'fully functioning person' is synonymous with optimal psychological adjustment, optimal psychological maturity, complete congruence, complete openness to experience, complete extensionality, as these terms have been defined. . . . The fully functioning person would be a person-in-process, a person continually changing."[114] Further, the fully functioning person is:

. . . more able to live fully in and with each and all of his feelings and reactions. He makes increasing use of all his organic equipment to sense, as accurately as possible, the existential situation within and without. He makes use of all of the information his nervous system can thus supply, using it in awareness, but recognizing that his total organism may be, and often is, wiser than his awareness.[115]

Psychopathology and Psychotherapy

Theory of Illness

Maladjustment as the Clash of Organismic versus Self-Actualization

To actualize in Rogerian terms means to grow, enhance, or enrich. We tend to believe that only our selves are capable of actualizing, but Rogers insisted that our organisms—our physical beings independent of our self-concepts—also seek such actualization.[116] Indeed, as we have already suggested, thanks to their tie to our physical feelings, our bodily organisms are literally more in touch with who we are and what we want from life than are our self-concepts. However, if a person's self-concept is incongruent with the organismic valuing process, so that he or she holds to a self-concept that is not truly reflecting the underlying organic feelings, then we find increasing tension developing in the personality structure. Lorie feels surprisingly unenthusiastic and confused about herself. Her mood should be one of excitement and satisfaction because she leaves for the big city next week to take up her new job. She has always said she wanted to go off to the city like her older sister. This is her chance to do so. What could be wrong? Rogers defined *psychological maladjustment* as arising when the personality system "denies to awareness, or distorts in awareness, significant experiences, which consequently are not accurately symbolized and organized into the gestalt of the self-structure, thus creating an incongruence between self and experience."[117]

Given the proper circumstances and enough time, Lorie could examine her feelings in light of what she is thinking about at the moment and come through subceptions and eventually perceptions to find out what is really going on in her personality. Since behavior is always current, we can find out what it means by taking the proper attitude of openness and genuineness. But what usually happens is that a person like Lorie who believes that her self will be actualized in the big city and who senses thereby incongruence between her self-aspirations and her spontaneous feelings about these aspirations, begins to develop an overlay of threat. Rogers defines *threat* as a state of anticipation ("Something's coming that I won't like") that is due to the subception of an incongruence between the self-structure and life experience.[118] The person cannot say what it is that is anticipated, but he or she knows that it will not be anything good. When the underlying incongruence approaches awareness —is close to being a perception—the person moves from threat to outright anxiety. *Anxiety* is a heightened state of fear with an emphasis on anticipation of disaster. Lorie is sensing threat in the present, but on the day when she is scheduled to leave home, feelings of anxiety will pass like waves through her body.

This anxiety, however, is likely to pass, and in time Lorie will work out her adjustment problems, either coming to like the city after all or, more probably, returning home to build a life in the smaller community. In the case of a more serious maladjustment, the person will not examine the underlying reasons for feelings of threat or anxiety. Instead, defenses will be tightened and symbolization will be distorted even more. The young man who subceives a homosexual impulse becomes touchy about jokes implying he is sexually interested in his male friends or reacts with disgust at the effeminacy of certain men, and so forth. As long as a defensive separation of emotion from conscious intellect can be sustained, the young man will go on functioning reasonably well. However, it is likely that in time so much insincere deception will take place that profound psychological maladjustment will develop.

It is when the person begins to sense (subceive) that he or she cannot resolve the growing *tension of incongruence,* so that neither self *nor* organismic actualization is taking place, that help is sought in the form of psychotherapy.[119] The extent of behavioral disorganization (symptoms) varies, but one thing all neurotic people have in common is this sense of ineptness or low positive self-regard. With each passing day they find it more difficult to understand what is taking place in their lives. It is almost as if one were living with a stranger but in this case the stranger is oneself. Put another way, the individual has lost communication within his or her personality system, and this breakdown affects interpersonal relations as well. As Rogers summed it up, "The emotionally maladjusted person, the 'neurotic,' is in difficulty first because communication within himself has broken down, and second because, as a result of this, his communication with others has been damaged."[120] Internal incongruence always breeds external incongruence.

The Irrelevancy of Diagnostic Distinctions

In the same way that Rogerian theory dismisses categorizing people into preselected, hence arbitrary and unnatural, designations of personality, so too does it argue that diagnosis is unnecessary. Since our behavior is presumably caused by the ever-recurring present of the phenomenal field, how can anyone really tell us what we have as a problem in the way that a physician can tell us what our biological sickness is? As Rogers said: "Behavior is caused, and the psychological cause of behavior is a certain perception or a way of perceiving [present circumstances]. The client is the only one who has the potentiality of knowing fully the dynamics of his perceptions and his behavior."[121] Any changes in perception that result from therapy must be brought about by clients themselves.[122] So, why diagnose, categorize, and run the risk of once again distorting what the client can spontaneously know if he or she simply turns inward to re-establish proper communication between feelings and conscious ideas? Anything that might pressure or control a psychotherapy *client*—the term Rogers preferred to the more passive designation, *patient*—is thus to be shunned.

Rogers did speak in broad terms of neurotic and psychotic behavior. A *neurosis* can actually begin organismically as a prompt to accept an attitude in contradiction to the self-attitudes consciously accepted. Randy enters psychotherapy and says, "I don't know what has come over me. I just can't concentrate on my studies, yet I know how important they are to me. All my life I have wanted to be an engineer, just like dad." The question is: are these consciously accepted engineering goals congruent with the organismic valuing process (feelings), or are they introjected and distorted values pressed onto the self-concept by others? Randy is merely aware of a symptom: he cannot concentrate, he cannot sleep, and so on. The thought that he should work at cross-purposes with what he wants stymies him. As Rogers noted, ". . . the neurotic behavior is incomprehensible to the individual himself, since it is at variance with what he consciously 'wants' to do, which is to actualize a self no longer congruent with experience."[123] At other times, a neurosis may represent the defensive maneuvers of the individual to avoid becoming aware of his or her lack of self-consistency. All of the defense mechanisms discussed above may enter here.

When efforts to keep up incongruence in the personality lead to *excessive* distortions in reality, then we can begin speaking of a *psychosis*. An example of a mild distortion of reality might be when the individual refuses to accept responsibility for a misadventure in life which was clearly his or her fault. The person senses this guilt organismically (via feelings) but denies it, asserting that "that was not due to anything I did." If this insincerity continues and extends into all aspects of life, rather than preserving the brittle structure of the self, in time a complete split from reality might result. Now the person says, "Other people are always blaming me. Everyone seems to be out to get me, maybe to kill me" (paranoid delusion). Other forms of escapist fantasies can then intrude, so the thoroughly disjointed personality now takes refuge in some preposterous insight: "They want to capture and torture me because I'm really the reincarnated Jesus."

An individual who has slipped over the brink of rationality to this extent might begin hearing voices or seeing images as well (hallucinations). Since the phenomenal field is organized by all factors active from moment to moment, it follows that perceptual distortions can become great if the falsification somehow holds things together. If we inwardly feel that things are about to explode with terror, then "seeing" an evil figure lurking about with clearly hostile intentions helps us to account for our extreme anxiety.[124] During this entire course of deterioration, the individual's relations with others suffer. One cannot speak of neurosis and then psychosis without thereby speaking of interpersonal relationships. Rogers made quite clear that, to the extent one individual in an interpersonal relationship is incongruent, the relationship suffers in that it encourages incongruity in the other; it distorts the nature of the true interpersonal experience, and it seriously handicaps any form of genuine communication emerging.[125] Once again, internal incongruence breeds external incongruence. Fortunately, through proper interpersonal relations, this process can be reversed.

Theory of Cure

The Nature of a Healing Relationship: The Client-Centered Hypothesis

From the first, Rogers approached counseling and psychotherapy with the view that a therapist's responsibility is to provide a climate that furthers the personally directed change of the client. It is the client who must change, and the therapist must trust him or her to do so. In his earliest phrasing of what he then called the *therapist's hypothesis*, Rogers wrote, *"Effective counseling consists of a definitely structured, permissive relationship which allows the client to gain an understanding of himself to a degree which enables him to take positive steps in the light of his new orientation."* [126] The key word in this statement of therapist values is *relationship*. Rogers made clear that the most essential ingredient in therapy is the creation of a free and permissive relationship having the characteristics of warmth, acceptance, and freedom from coercion. [127] Certain limitations had to be placed on the client, of course. The therapist could not be assaulted or office furniture broken. But all such restrictions in the structuring of the client-therapist relationship were to be kept to a minimum. Rogers expanded this therapist hypothesis into what he called the *client-centered hypothesis*, as follows:

. . . we may say that the counselor chooses to act consistently upon the hypothesis that the individual has a sufficient capacity to deal constructively with all those aspects of his life which can potentially come into conscious awareness. This means the creation of an interpersonal situation in which material may come into the client's awareness, and a meaningful demonstration of the counselor's acceptance of the client as a person who is competent to direct himself. [128]

Over the years, since first expressing this client-centered hypothesis, Rogers moved gradually to espouse the therapist's growing openness in revealing himself or herself as a person. There was good reason for his change in approach, and we want now to capture those reasons. In the earlier formulations, the relationship was pitched entirely in the direction of the client's identity.

. . . the relationship is experienced as a one-way affair in a very unique sense. The whole relationship is composed of the self of the client, the counselor being depersonalized for purposes of therapy into being "the client's other self." It is this warm willingness on the part of the counselor to lay his own self temporarily aside, in order to enter into the experience of the client, which makes the relationship a completely unique one, unlike anything in the client's previous experience. [129]

Rogers was careful to emphasize that there should be no evaluation of the client by the therapist (to parallel his dislike for diagnosis in general), no probing, no interpretation of what the client is supposed to be doing, and "no *personal* reaction by the counselor." [130]

The relationship is thus *client*-centered because it is the client who needs to reopen an inner communication between organismic and self-evaluations of what is worthwhile and important in life and what is not. The therapist begins by simply accepting the client as he or she *is*, which in turn prompts the client to re-evaluate things. [131] There is no effort made by the therapist to control the client or to positively reinforce behaviors made by the client. As Rogerian therapists, we simply ask of our clients to be completely natural, to assume responsibility for being who they *are* and not who we might wish them to be. We trust our clients to know organismically—based on their genuine feelings as they explore themselves—what is best for them in life. Although it is not the whole answer, part of the therapeutic cure stems from the fact that a client is likely to introject our accepting attitude.[132] Rosa, a stammering teen-aged girl with many fears and expressions of helplessness, finds the therapist's attitude totally different from what her parents and teachers display toward her. In time, the idea will occur to her, "If this 'doctor' can accept me as I am, even with my obvious shortcomings, why can't I accept myself *as* myself?" This attitude is often the first step toward change.

As Rosa increasingly puts herself in touch with her organismic values (reflected in feelings about the various things considered) and rejects those values of the self that are distorted and ingenuine, she will promote congruence. She might think, "Some of what I can't accept about myself is what mother always expected of me. She wants me to be letter-perfect in my speech and to always make a good impression. I've never felt comfortable trying to be in the spotlight. So what if I am a little awkward with others? I'm a shy person. At least I am sincere with others and never phony." As this corrective process is taking place, we might think of it as the congruence *in* the relationship between therapist and client leading to congruence *within* the client's personality. In fact, Rogers was to take this general theory of change and raise it to a *law of interpersonal relations* which he felt had relevance to *all* human interactions, inside of therapy or out.

Assuming a minimal mutual willingness to be in contact *and to receive communications,*

we may say that the greater the communicated congruence of experience, awareness, and behavior on the part of one individual, the more the ensuing relationship will involve a tendency toward reciprocal communication with the same qualities, mutually accurate understanding of the communications, improved psychological adjustment and functioning in both parties, and mutual satisfaction in the relationship.[133]

This interpersonal prescription has occasionally been termed the *helping relationship,*[134] and it is also a significant aspect of what is called the *process equation* of psychotherapy.[135] The basic idea is that one person in a relationship—be it therapeutic or simply social—intends that there should come about in another person "more appreciation of, more expression of, more functional use of the latent inner resources of the individual."[136] The Rogerian world view has every person a therapist for every other person. Therapy is life and life is therapy, both involving a succession of relationships with others—relationships that can either make or break the participants who enter into them. Indeed, it is better to speak of a *facilitator* than a therapist in interpersonal relations when speaking of the helping relationship.

An interesting question that arises is, if a therapist-facilitator is 100 percent congruent, without facade and completely accepting of personal organismic values, how can he or she avoid expressing strong feelings that *naturally* arise in the relationship? How can the Rogerian therapist keep from intruding in the relationship in a personal way? The therapist really cannot avoid this eventuality, of course, and so it is that we witness in the development of Rogerian thought an increasing willingness to permit personal expressions from both ends of the therapeutic relationship. One can see this gradual shift in Rogers's writings, and it is especially prominent in his later work with the basic encounter group. "When a young woman was weeping because she had had a dream that no one in the group loved her, I embraced her and kissed her and comforted her." [137] He also noted, "If I am currently distressed by something in my own life, I am willing to express it in the group. . . ." [138]

This change in manner over some thirty years as therapist did not make Rogers inconsistent. He frankly admitted that his manner in the group differed from that in the individual psychotherapy session, but he quickly added, "In no basic philosophical way, so far as I can see, does this approach differ from that which I have adopted for years in individual therapy." [139] The basic philosophical outlook remains one of genuineness, openness, congruence, and a client-centered focus of concern. The therapist remains a facilitator of client growth through congruence.

Insight and Transference

One of the clear implications of the client-centered approach as first conceived was that clients have to find their own explanations for why they suffer from psychological maladjustment. As subjective identities, clients are basically responsible for what occurs in their phenomenal fields. Rogers defined therapeutic *insight* as "the perception of new meaning in the individual's own experience." [140] An insight permits the client to understand new relationships of cause and effect or to see the pattern of his or her behavior in a new light. But there are also many things to learn at the emotional level where, though insights may not be easily put into words, they are taking place if the therapeutic relationship is a good one. Hence, "insight is a highly important aspect of counseling treatment, and as such deserves the closest scrutiny." [141]

Since the classical analytical theories make much of the relationship in terms of transference and countertransference, Rogers had to take a position on these topics. The caressing and kissing of clients could easily be taken as an instance of countertransference. Because Rogers rejected—even in principle—the pressing of what he considered arbitrary theories of personality onto clients, he did not have to concern himself with such questions on an abstract level. However, on the more practical plane, Rogers discussed the issue of *transference* in terms of client-centered counseling. He admitted that transference phenomena seem to come up in client-centered therapy but at a much reduced level when compared to that of psychoanalysis. As he put it in 1951: "Thousands of clients have been dealt with by counselors with whom the writer has had personal contact. In only a small minority of cases handled in a client-centered fashion has the client developed a relationship which could in any way be matched to Freud's terms." [142] Rogers meant that surely infantile attitudes are not transferred onto a therapist who presents himself or herself as another human being of equal status in face-to-face contact with the client. [143] There is plenty of feeling expressed in the relationship, but the realistic approach and equal status of client and therapist prevent the sort of distortion, regression, and projection that so typifies psychoanalysis, with its therapist as authority and client reclining on a couch approach to therapeutic change.

If Dolores is being counseled by a Rogerian therapist and somehow develops a transformed neurosis (see p. 98), Rogers would say that this has occurred because the therapist she was seeing mishandled the case.

The therapist may have been too authoritarian, forgetting that only Dolores can know her subjective feelings, which in turn help her to differentiate and articulate her phenomenal field through the organismic evaluations she makes. The therapist may have unknowingly supported value statements issuing from the self-concept, a body of attitudes and beliefs that are not congruent with the spontaneous feelings that Dolores is having about her life. Rather than accepting feelings of love or hostility from Dolores for what they were—honest reactions in the here and now which could be explored to see what they mean—her therapist probably tried to relate these to past figures in her life, such as her father or mother.[144]

Emotional displays toward a therapist are often just what they are. Assuming that Dolores had a male therapist, his manner in the relationship may have been sexually attractive or even seductive. By taking the authority role, such a therapist could invite through a display of power all kinds of subservient and sexually flirtatious behaviors from a female client. If the therapist was a woman, it could be that she had mannerisms which *in fact* were like Dolores's mother, and that a parallel between therapist and mother was perfectly natural and in no way a repetition of the past. Rogers liked to point out that so-called negative transference is often used as an excuse by ineffective therapists who refuse to take responsibility for the irritation and frustration they have brought about in their client. As Rogerian therapists, we fix on the present relationship, make all feelings and attitudes clear, avoid incongruence, and in time things begin falling into place for Dolores who essentially constructs her *own* theory of why she has certain problems and what seems called for to correct them.

Just how much a therapist should reveal himself or herself as a person was a slowly developing position for Rogers. In 1941 he thought of counseling primarily in terms of a one-way emphasis on the client. This had changed by 1959 to the view that sometimes the therapist has to speak out personally in the relationship. This is especially called for when certain emotions are pressing onto the therapist's subjective awareness.[145] In this case, to ignore the feelings generated by the organismic valuing process would be to promote interpersonal incongruence. The therapist might be feeling something like "You sadden (surprise, shock, and so on) me by your attitudes," but would not communicate this to the client. How could satisfactory therapy take place in a context of such insincerity? By 1970 Rogers was prepared to be as open as his organismic valuing process spontaneously suggested, to the point of venting great anger and irritation to other members of the encounter group.[146]

Psychotherapy as a Process of Change

An interesting outcome of the fact that Rogers desired to keep therapy free and open is that his writings contain much more about a theory of the therapist than a theory of the client. As client-centered therapists, we do not wish to judge or evaluate the client, but we have rather decided ideas about the proper manners and *attitudes* a *therapist* should hold to and display in behavior. In the early writings, the emphasis is on a selfless style of therapist interaction. "In client-centered therapy the client finds in the counselor a genuine alter ego in an operational and technical sense—a self which has temporarily divested itself (so far as possible) of its own selfhood, except for the one quality of endeavoring to understand."[147] Therapists behave like the clients' other selves, helping them to differentiate and articulate their phenomenal fields more openly and accurately.[148] Summing up this process, Rogers essentially defined *psychotherapy* as follows: "Psychotherapy deals primarily with the organization and functioning of the self. There are many elements of experience which the self cannot face, cannot clearly perceive, because to face them or admit them would be inconsistent with and threatening to the current organization of the self."[149]

The therapist acts as a companion, as an acceptant alter ego who helps the client work his or her way through a dark forest of misunderstanding and confusion.[150] In making this passage, clients come to experience themselves in new ways even as they reject the older ways of self-definition.[151] In a very real sense, psychotherapy is a "learning of self."[152] Of course this learning will not take place if the proper relationship is not formed. From the outside, psychotherapy might be defined as the "alteration of human behavior through interpersonal relationship."[153] It was when he attempted to name the essential elements in this relationship that Rogers made it most clear that he put more trust in attitudes than formal theories. One cannot teach psychotherapy in textbooks. Every research study he did convinced Rogers more that "personality change is initiated by *attitudes* which exist in the therapist, rather than primarily by his knowledge, his theories, or his techniques."[154] The true *facilitator* achieves therapeutic ends by approaching interpersonal relations with the nondirective attitude that permits others to be themselves.[155]

Figure 25 schematizes the *process of change* taking place in a client's self-concept (removed from the phenomenal fields of Figures 23 and 24) as he or she progresses through nondirective therapy. Let us think of this in terms of a specific client: Jesse is a young man who did not finish high school, has had a poor work record, and is at present very undecided about what to do in life. He has moved through various personality phases in the past, playing the lady's man and the tough guy, including a few scrapes with the police. He has recently lost his driver's license through an arrest following a minor automobile accident in which he was discovered driving while intoxicated. He enters nondirective therapy expecting to hear another series of lectures from authority. This does not happen, of course, and in time, thanks to the permissive therapeutic climate, Jesse begins to talk more and more about himself. At point 1 of Figure 25 we see Jesse's self-concept upon entering psychotherapy. It is a poor gestalt, with pieces that do not fit together well, as they are distortions of the real organismic valuations he was making years ago. Jesse is not as tough or as sure of himself with the opposite sex as he has pretended to be in the past. He is actually uncomfortable with these pretenses, as symbolized by the poorly differentiated and articulated self-gestalt at point 1. Note also that there are some potential aspects of Jesse's self-concept which have never been brought out into a clear figure; these are symbolized by the dotted subparts of the self.

As he goes along in therapy, Jesse quite naturally takes himself apart, looking over his personality from different angles. The therapist is essential here, encouraging self-exploration and supporting Jesse when admissions become difficult. Point 2 of Figure 25 symbolizes this sorting out and specific examination of portions of the self. Jesse's self-concept is like a poorly put-together picture puzzle, and now he is moving the pieces apart again to see if there is not a better fit, including the discarding of some pieces. Elements of the phenomenal ground that have been denied symbolization as figures in

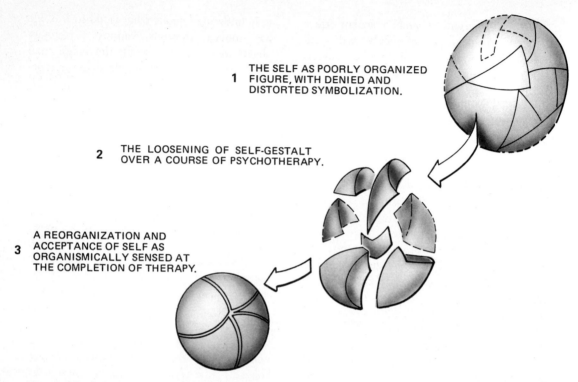

1 THE SELF AS POORLY ORGANIZED FIGURE, WITH DENIED AND DISTORTED SYMBOLIZATION.

2 THE LOOSENING OF SELF-GESTALT OVER A COURSE OF PSYCHOTHERAPY.

3 A REORGANIZATION AND ACCEPTANCE OF SELF AS ORGANISMICALLY SENSED AT THE COMPLETION OF THERAPY.

Figure 25   The Process of Change in Figure-Ground Terms

the past may now be differentiated clearly and examined in great detail. Jesse will come to admit that he has sensed the idiocy of his ways wherein he has let his life slip by aimlessly, but he has been confused about what it means to grow up and be a man.

When things went wrong in the past, he blamed others, but deep down he always knew that he was the only person to blame for his frustrations in life (organismic valuing processes have been repressed). He has been running away from a responsible life for some time now, making jokes about those who live conventionally, and yet it was only his deep feeling of inadequacy that supported his sarcastic and flippant manner. Actually, he envied those who have their lives pulled together. The therapist's acceptance of him *as he is* reassures Jesse, who in time, if therapy is successful, will come to know and accept himself as he genuinely feels himself to be. He will now admit to his drawbacks and weak points, but he will also accept responsibility for some strong points and potentials for growth. Point 3 of Figure 25 symbolizes the better gestalt organization achieved by Jesse's self-concept if therapy proves successful. We see a well-articulated self now, one that is congruent with the organismic values with which Jesse has now been put in touch. He is no longer fooling himself.[156] He accepts the locus of evaluation as within himself and leaves therapy with an honest sense of personal responsibility for his future life, which he now has tied to certain realistic goals he has set for himself.[157]

The process of change taking place across Figure 25 is even more detailed than we have pictured it. Actually, Rogers and his colleagues worked out a scale measuring *seven stages of movement* in therapeutic cure.[158] The specific points on this scale are not relevant for our purposes, but we might note the general scheme as an example of Rogers's theory of cure. The first stage is fixity and remoteness of experience, like our client Jesse who is not even sensitive to his feelings. He is rigid and unbending at this point, unwilling to admit to personal problems of any sort. Here is where other people are blamed for his plight. Gradually, in stages two and three, Jesse begins to become aware of himself as a feeling organism, sensing his evaluative reactions in relation to life's experiences. At stage four, Jesse's outlook on life is more relaxed and objective, enabling him to become aware of the contradictions existing between his feelings and his everyday experience. He is amazed at the greater understanding achieved by honestly letting his feelings point the way. As a result of the confidence stemming from the accuracy of his feelings, Jesse begins to trust his spontaneous emotional sensations more and more. By the fifth stage, feelings of great importance are beginning to well up in Jesse's awareness, surprising him and teaching him a great deal about himself. He is fascinated by this process of spontaneous change and tries to understand the meanings of these feelings. Once he has an understanding of the feelings, he also has an idea of what must be done about them, what they are suggesting to him as a course for the future.

Occasionally a feeling tone fails to make itself known clearly to Jesse. He has a "kind of" feeling about his high school principal which is not clear as to its meaning. A working-through of such partially known feelings is necessary at this point until, along about stage six, they break loose and flood Jesse's awareness with insight. This is about the time when Jesse begins putting things together again, reorganizing his self-concept in the process. He is now fully aware of the locus of his feelings and of the evaluations they imply. He no longer thinks of himself as an object to be moved about by others or by circumstances, but takes responsibility for self-direction. Subjectivity is no longer a threat. In the final or seventh stage, Jesse becomes a fully functioning person.

There are a half-dozen or so essential ingredients that must be present if Rogerian therapy is actually to work like this. First, two people must be in *contact,* which means that there is communication between them. One of them, the client, must be *incongruent* though he or she may experience this incongruence as anxiety and not see the actual problem. The other person, the therapist, must be *congruent* in the *relationship.* Further, the therapist must be experiencing *unconditional positive regard,* which is defined as follows: ". . . if the self-experiences of another are perceived by me in such a way that no self-experience can be discriminated as more or less worthy of positive regard than any other, then I am experiencing unconditional positive regard for the individual."[159] This is essentially the attitude of nonjudgmental acceptance Rogers always insisted upon in the therapist's behavior. Another requirement is that the therapist genuinely feel an *empathic understanding* of the client from the latter's frame of reference. Empathy is seeing another person's point of view without forgetting that his or her subjective feelings in their entirety can never be known. Finally, for therapy or the process of change outlined above to be successful, the client must personally perceive the unconditional positive regard and the empathic understanding of the therapist, "at least to a minimal degree."[160]

Mental Health: The Characteristics of a Therapized Individual

Over the years, Rogers wrote extensively about the benefits of counseling or therapy for the individual. However, because of the extent of this literature, we will only consider selected aspects of his writings as examples of what Rogers understood to be mental health.

In his earliest papers, as he was working out the essentials of a therapeutic relationship, Rogers stressed the necessity for the individual to be more objective in self-perceptions.[161] This does not mean seeing oneself as an object, something acted upon and manipulated without internal control. Rather, it implies a more willing, honest, and open acceptance of whatever our feelings indicate. Another characteristic of mentally healthy people is that they lose their self-consciousness as they develop greater self-awareness. We are self-conscious when we are out of touch with our genuine being. Once we accept who we are, there is no reason to be concerned about ourselves in self-conscious fashion.[162] Neurotics are symptom-laden because they are continually on guard and sensitive to the reactions of others. Their symptoms are their defensive shields. A healthy person is not concerned with the rigid requirements that others hold out as bait or reward for what they want done. Healthy interpersonal relations are not achieved by such unyielding manipulations of one person by another.

A healthy person is not entirely without defenses, of course. Threats will naturally arise, and even the most self-enhanced individual will from time to time exhibit a certain defensiveness.[163] But the mentally healthy person is more aware of this protective maneuver when it arises, and in most cases, will drop its use as soon as possible. If more openness in life were the rule, it would be easier for all of us to drop our defensiveness. As long as we recognize when we *are* being defensive, we have not slumped to the level of the first stage of the process of change, wherein the individual is unaware of feelings altogether. Hence, in defining mental or psychological adjustment, Rogers was to say, "Optimal psychological adjustment exists when the concept of self is such that all experiences are or may be assimilated on a symbolic level into the gestalt of the self-structure."[164]

Awareness thus continues to be the central concept in Rogerian definitions of mental health. Mentally healthy people are open to experience, trusting of their organism, accepting of their subjectivity as evaluators of their phenomenal experience, and willing to be a process of change.[165] Taking a phrase from the existential philosopher Sören Kierkegaard, Rogers said that to be fully functioning is "to be that self which one truly is."[166] This state necessitates dropping facades, moving away from rigid compunctions, meeting experience as it is and not doing things simply to please others, accepting responsibility for self-direction, and moving always toward new aspects of life with an acceptance of others and a trust in one's self.[167] These are the essentials of what Rogers was finally to call *existential living,* a concept that combines his phenomenological approach and his emphasis on the changing processes of life. *Existential living* is thus to live with "a maximum of adaptability, a discovery of structure *in* experience, a flowing, changing organization of self and personality."[168] An individual following this advice would live fully, "in the moment,"[169] and from moment to moment as a fully functioning person.

An Evolutionary Theme and a Natural Ethic

Rogers had us evaluating our lives spontaneously and, through considering our feelings in relation to various alternatives, opting in a direction that will inevitably promote the welfare of everyone. Yet, can we really trust our feelings like this? Rogers would seem to need additional theoretical justification for this optimistic view of people, who supposedly fall back on subjective feelings to opt unselfishly for the betterment of all. Interestingly, though it was not given prominent emphasis in his earlier writings, we can indeed find a theoretical justification for this positive outcome of the organismic valuing process in Rogers's theorizing. This justification stemmed from an *evolutionary view of human nature,* in which values are carried by the organic processes of life. We might even say that these processes are the essence of life, the truest reflection of what we are as human beings, because they are closest to nature.

Hence, as in his wisdom-of-the-organic assumption discussed above (see p. 584), we find Rogers essentially contending that when we are mentally healthy, our tie to physical organic nature is closest. Congruity is a genuine tie to *natural* processes, a tie that is never made or shaped or controlled into existence by cultural (made by people) artifacts. There is no way for human beings to manufacture congruity, because it can only arise naturally, as a process of being in touch with and consistent with one's organic totality. This unity with perceived experience is what Rogers meant when he wrote in 1951, "From an external point of view the important difference [following reorganization of the self] is that the new self is much more nearly congruent with the totality of experience—that it is a pattern drawn from or perceived in experience, rather than a pattern imposed upon experience."[170] There is no way in which to create a sense of congruence artificially. Congruence is the very opposite of artificiality. It is actually a movement back into nature as spontaneously experienced by an organic being. Rogers brought this point home as follows: "Thus the therapeutic process is, in its totality, the achievement by the individual, in a favorable psychological climate, of further steps in a direction which has already been set by his growth and maturational development from the time of conception onward."[171]

Client-centered therapy is thus not a form of human engineering nor a method of controlling nature to meet an arbitrary end. The only end acceptable to Rogers is that spontaneous state of uncontrolled—literally natural—living. In 1959 he stated, ". . . psychotherapy is the releasing of an already existing capacity in a potentially competent individual, not the expert manipulation of a more or less passive personality."[172] We now begin to see what Rogers considered the human's capacity for self-enhancement. As congruence is fostered both intrapersonally and interpersonally, the potentials for a broadened experience are of necessity enhanced since people do not need to act defensivly, to turn off sincere promptings. If nature prompts, why should we deny this prompting? Drawing on more than thirty years of experience as therapist and consultant, Rogers in his mature statements began to see that *all* people move in the same general direction of enhanced experience, provided that they are allowed to be free in their relationships. ". . . There is an organismic commonality of value directions." [173] These common-value directions are of such kinds as to enhance not only the individual and the members of his or her community but also *to make for the survival and evolution of his [or her] species"* [174] [italics added].

Rogers has seen clients in many different countries and engaged in therapy or encounter groups with therapists of quite differing personalities, all moving toward the common organismic values he outlined in such detail. Putting this commonality in natural terms, he observed, "I like to think that this commonality of value directions is due to the fact that we all belong to the same species—that just as a human infant tends, individually, to select a diet similar to that selected by other human infants, so a client in therapy tends, individually, to choose value directions similar to those chosen by other clients." [175] When people are free to choose, they choose alike, and the valued goals selected are goals that make for their "own survival, growth, and development, and for the survival and development of others." [176] This is to say that *in any culture, at any time in history,* the mature individual would opt for these very same values. [177] Thus, Rogers defended a *universal natural ethic,* rooted in the very fabric of organic life and transcending cultures. He makes this plain in the following excerpt:

Instead of universal values "out there," or a universal value system imposed by some group—philosophers, rulers, priests, or psychologists—we have the possibility of universal human value directions emerging from the experiencing organism. Evidence from therapy indicates that both personal and so-cial values emerge as natural, and experienced, when the individual is close to his own organismic valuing process. The suggestion is that though modern man no longer trusts religion or science or philosophy nor any system of beliefs to give him values, he may find an organismic valuing base within himself which, if he can learn again to be in touch with it, will prove to be an organized, adaptive, and social approach to the perplexing value issues which face all of us. [178]

Techniques of Therapy and Life Processes

The Early Technique Emphasis: Nondirective Therapy

Thanks to the great interest he took in the nature of a relationship and the resultant attention paid to the therapist's manner, Rogers frankly admitted that his early writings were heavily technique oriented. [179] This emphasis was a paradox of sorts, because the value system on which his approach was based *rejected* all attempts to manipulate or control the lives of clients. Yet the great stress placed on a therapist's approach (avoiding making decisions for clients, turning the discussion lead over to the client at all times, and so on) seemed to impress some of Rogers's colleagues as shrewd "how to" steps of client manipulation. Rogers was merely trying to demonstrate the essentials of an effective therapeutic relationship, and he had developed some scoring procedures on the basis of which recorded interviews could be coded and analyzed for empirical study. It was therefore possible to operationally define the difference between a *directive* and a *nondirective therapist.* Table 5 lists the characteristics of these two types of therapists, as found by Rogers in his experiments.

When we list such points as Table 5 contains, it is always possible to view either side

Directive Counselor-Therapists	Nondirective Counselor-Therapists
Most Frequent	*Most Frequent*
1. Asks highly specific questions, delimiting answers to yes, no, or specific information.	1. Recognizes in some way the feeling or attitude the client has just expressed.
2. Explains, discusses, or gives information related to the problem or treatment.	2. Interprets or recognizes feelings or attitudes expressed by general demeanor, specific behavior, or earlier statements.
3. Indicates topic of conversation but leaves development to client.	3. Indicates topic of conversation but leaves development to client.
4. Proposes client activity.	4. Recognizes the subject content of what the client has just said.
5. Recognizes the subject content of what the client has just said.	5. Asks highly specific questions, delimiting answers to yes, no, or specific information.
6. Marshals evidence and persuades the client to undertake the proposed action.	6. Explains, discusses, or gives information related to the problem or treatment.
7. Points out a problem or condition needing correction.	7. Defines the interview situation in terms of the client's responsibility for using it.
Least Frequent	*Least Frequent*

Table 5 Frequency of Techniques Used by Directive and Nondirective Approaches[180]

—directive or nondirective therapist approaches—as simply alternative techniques to be used in bringing about (controlling, shaping, manipulating) changes in our clients' behaviors. This is what seems to have happened to Rogers and why at one point in his career he was known as the "mmm-hmm therapist." One of the least directive or leading statements a therapist can make is simply to nod his or her head or murmur an encouraging "mmm hmm" as if to say, "yes, go ahead, I am listening" to the client. Although most of Rogers's advocates stressed the nonauthoritarian values underlying this nondirectiveness, some viewed the tactic as a cleverly subtle way of controlling the client's topics of conversation. As we have already seen in Chapter 7 (p. 446), the classic study by Greenspoon (1955) was done to prove that a therapist could indeed verbally condition a client through something as subtle as a nod of the head or an "mmm

hmm." The awareness issue was to enter in the years following Greenspoon's original work (we have covered this question in Chapter 7).

Rogers believed that by taking the non-directive approach to people, we are more likely to *validate* them as human beings. By this is meant that the therapist responds to others with questions or comments that show immediately his or her respect for their presence, their view, and their problems.[181] Only when the therapist can *trust* others is this kind of interpersonal validation possible.[182] If as Rogerian therapists we nod our head and say "mmm hmm" or make a more extensive comment bearing on the problems of the person, we are not covertly trying to manipulate events to some preconceived solution that we have in mind. We are simply being as spontaneous and natural in the situation as possible. We always avoid interpreting client behavior via our pet theories, and we try to learn from the client—a valid factor in our phenomenal field—what he or she would prefer to see as the problem and its eventual solution.

Generalized Principles for Interpersonal Behavior

The interpersonal concern for the "other" should not be limited to therapy. Rogers extended his view of the relationship to all manner of interpersonal and even institutional situations. An effective facilitator in the classroom sets an open climate, helps the class choose its goals, trusts the students to direct their own self-actualization, and becomes a participant learner within the total process.[183] Rather than filling the heads of students with facts, as in the mug-and-jug view of learning, Rogers saw the teacher working as a resource person for the student body. Effective teachers share themselves with their students, recognize and accept their own limitations, and encourage the expression of emotions as well as intellectual insights in the classroom. They organize and help make things available, but do not forfeit trust in others in favor of a kind of military regime or obstacle course. Learning is another natural process, and it will be entered into spontaneously if the learner is given the right climate in which to grow.

Rogers emphasized that material must be relevant if we expect people to learn it. Engaging the person's interest is easy if what we have to offer is seen as a potentially enriching phenomenal experience. One of the poorest tactics for a teacher to use is to threaten a student. All this does is promote rigid defensiveness. By reducing threat and encouraging spontaneity, new experience can

be differentiated and articulated. Learning is greatly enhanced when students share in the responsibilities of the classroom, including selection of topics and decisions concerning their final grades.[184] Self-evaluation is one of the most important things we must learn in life, and yet how many teachers view this as one of the skills they must develop in their students? Rogers felt deeply that effective education like effective therapy must teach the person about life as a continuous process of change. Hence, he drew this parallel: *"To my mind the 'best' of education would produce a person very similar to the one produced by the 'best' of therapy."* [185]

This would seem to make every teacher a therapist. Yet an even more fundamental truth is that *every person is a therapist!* Many of Rogers's later papers are taken up with discussions of how congruence can be promoted in various interpersonal settings. For example, parents must be congruent in their relations with their children and acquire that sense of trust that will permit the child at a certain time in life to be a separate person.[186] Every member of a family must be allowed the dignity of separation from time to time, with the freedom to have solitude and his or her own preoccupations. Rogers was not seeking a world of hand-holders with smiling faces who place the group above the individual. In fact, his view was that one cannot be creative unless he or she has the capacity to accept the feeling, "I am alone." [187] The creative individual hopes to communicate with others in time, but in order to be capable of independent thought, he or she must retreat to a psychological if not literal corner in life from time to time.

Rogers proposed a few rules which might facilitate congruence in interpersonal relations. For example, what if a family discussion or a labor-management arbitration were to follow the rule, "Each person can speak up for himself only *after* he has first restated the ideas and feelings of the previous speaker accurately, and to that speaker's satisfaction." [188] If all group participants honestly followed this rule (given the limitations of subjective phenomenal fields), Rogers believed that improved communication would necessarily result. Not that an easy solution would then follow; but at least one side would not be manipulating the other, forcing it to support predetermined prejudices, and so forth. Each side would validate the other. Rogers felt that even organizations and nations might consider some such principle in facilitating change.[189] It is unfortunately true that sometimes the individual person changes, but the institutional framework within which he or she lives and works *does not*.[190] This is one of the reasons that Rogers became heavily involved in the encounter group, a technique that he felt could change (cure?) institutions.

The Basic Encounter Group

As we have noted above, Rogers's approach is more personally revealing and open in the encounter group than it is in individual psychotherapy. The basic philosophy of congruence and relationship remains the same, but encounter groups have demands of their own which require special techniques.

There is really no adequate definition of an *encounter group*. Recall that the first such groups were essentially post-mortems on Lewinian researches (see p. 573). These evolved into an attempt to treat several individuals together in what is tantamount to group therapy. The number of clients in a contemporary encounter group can vary from three or four up to as many as fifteen or twenty, but the usual size is from six to ten. Some group therapists have taken strictly Freudian views of illness and cure, and the level of interpretation in such approaches is virtually identical to interpretations in individual therapy. Other group therapists have relied more on gestalt psychology or Lewinian small-group theory to provide the rationale for what goes on when people get together, motivated by an interest in self-knowledge and greater facility for relationships. Rogers found himself trying to maximize everyone's freedom in the groups he conducted. "In an encounter group I love to give, both to the participants and to myself, the maximum freedom of expression. . . . I do *trust* the group, and find it often wiser than I in its reactions to particular situations." [191]

Encounter groups are customarily held at a somewhat removed hotel, motel, or resort area. They may continue for a few days or as long as a week. The group sessions may take up a half-day or an entire day; it is not unusual for so-called marathon groups to last for twenty-four and more hours, with participants taking catnaps along the way to termination. There are many different rationales given for each of these approaches, but the essential point is that in time a peculiar phenomenon emerges in which the identification among members is strengthened, and the false faces come off or at times are ripped off by fellow participants. Coretta tells Lennie, "You always hide behind that 'I'm so defenseless' mask of yours, but you aren't fooling anybody in *this* group. You are about as defenseless as a cobra. You use other people's pity like some people use alcohol." This would be termed a *confrontation* between group members. Many times the exchanges between members are positive, expressing love and concern as in the case of Rogers's embracing and reassuring the woman who felt rejected.

Rogers did not believe in leading groups

by assigning the members tasks or lecturing them (unless asked about something as a resource person); everyone shares responsibility for what is accomplished.[192] He opens the group with a minimum of structure and then listens to others—validating each in turn.[193] He hopes to make the climate of the group psychologically safe, so that no one will feel threatened and real learning can proceed. It is vital to accept the group and each individual within it as they now *are*. Effective facilitators never push the group, but neither do they go along with the group when no real effort is being made to work toward the therapeutic goal by having sincere interactions. Rogers has been known to walk out of a therapeutic session and go to bed when the group members are relating superficially.

Though he devoted little space to the topic of *resistance* in his writings on individual therapy, Rogers did take up this phenomenon in regard to groups. "Silence or muteness in the individual are acceptable to me providing I am quite certain it is not unexpressed pain or resistance."[194] It would appear that if a group facilitator does sense resistance in a group member and then expresses this feeling to the member, he or she would essentially be *interpreting* or providing *insight* of sorts to the client. Rogers would have no argument with this suggestion. He would merely stress that the focus of his interpretative comments is always on the ongoing behavior of group members, specifically as these behaviors impinge on his personal phenomenal field. He is also cautious when it comes to the use of more aggressive confrontations with members. He is prepared to say, "I don't like the way you chatter on" to a participant, but this does not mean he will try to pull down a person's typical defensive style. "To attack a person's defenses seems to me judgmental."[195] By focusing on a specific behavior and the present relationship, he makes points concrete for the participant and avoids the distortions in symbolization that often result when interpretations become subtle and abstract.

The approach that entails discussing how the group as a whole is functioning can also be overdone. The Lewinians called this dynamic interaction *group process* and studied it in great detail. Rogers said: "I make comments on the group process sparingly. They are apt to make the group self-conscious; they slow it down, giving members the sense that they are under scrutiny."[196] Rogers does not schedule *group exercises* beforehand or think that he simply has to use certain techniques if the group is to work. This attitude is too mechanical and gimmicky for Rogers's taste. But if a facilitator spontaneously thinks of trying role playing, bodily contact, psychodrama, or various other exercises aimed at promoting group interaction, then such exercises are likely to flow into the process naturally and prove beneficial. Rogers has used all of these group exercises.[197]

When a group begins to settle down to its task and people loosen up enough to say what they honestly feel, a number of problems may arise as certain members find this frankness and openness unbearably threatening. The skills of the facilitator enter at this point to know exactly when an encounter is getting out of hand, and so on. Many psychologists oppose the encounter-group movement because of the harm such experiences can have on people, sometimes even with the most experienced facilitators present. Rogers admitted that he had known people who developed psychotic breaks following their encounter experience.[198] However, he felt that these were rare enough occasions to be worth the risk, considering the thousands of people he had seen helped by their encounter experience.

Rogers cited several characteristics of certain encounter-group facilitators as *nonfacilitative*.[199] In general, Rogers was suspicious of the person who appears to be exploiting the purposes of the group, using it for his or her subjective needs. Facilitators who manipulate the group, make rules for it, or covertly direct it toward preconceived ends are *not* recommended. The histrionic facilitator, who judges success by how many participants weep, is also to be avoided. Rigid facilitators, who have some one thing to achieve like "drawing out the basic rage in everyone," are not going to help a group become what it otherwise could. Rogers would not recommend facilitators who have such severe personal problems that they constantly turn the center of attention on themselves. He also did not favor the type who doles out dynamic interpretations at every turn. Finally, Rogers did not advocate facilitators who withhold themselves from personal emotional participation in the group—which would be the other side of completely dominating the group with personal hang-ups. It is often the expert type who keeps aloof, feeling that he or she can analyze the group processes or the dynamics of the participants by remaining on the sideline.

Summary

Chapter 9 begins with a review of the gestalt-phenomenological school of thought that Rogers was to base much of his theory on. It was Husserl who coined the term *phenomenology*, taking his lead from the Kantian distinction between noumena and phenomena. The first area of study in which phenomenology had an impact was in the sensory investigations of the gestaltists—Wertheimer, Köhler, and Koffka—who with their colleagues were to provide empirical justification for a number of laws of organization: unit formation and segregation (via articulation), closure, good shape, proximity and equality, and good continuation. The law of pragnanz held that the figure-ground relations will always be as good, symmetrical, and stable as the prevailing conditions will allow. It is this figure-against-the-ground conception that personologists were to borrow from the gestaltists, making the person a figure on a field of interacting factors, all obeying gestalt laws. Though not a strict gestaltist, Lewin used a similar idea in his construct of the life space—a region which he saw as differentiated and articulated within the person's phenomenal awareness and within which the person both communicated and locomoted. Even more removed from traditional gestalt psychology was Rank, who influenced Rogers through concepts like separation, independence, and the need to become one's own person in maturing to adulthood.

Rogerian personality theory therefore begins on the assumption that each of us lives within our own phenomenal field, which combines unique mental and bodily experiences into an overall understanding of subjective reality. We have important physical reactions—feelings, moods, emotions—which define this reality and with which we may or may not be in touch. When we are cognitively aware of a feeling, Rogers would say we have symbolized it. Sometimes we can subceive a personalized emotion—a meaningful indication of how we are framing a life circumstance—even before we have given it symbolical form, or symbolization. The identity of the person in Rogerian theory is termed the self, and our subjective self-concepts or self-structures are differentiated and articulated from out of the total mass of our subjective phenomenal fields. It is impossible in principle for anyone else to know our selves the way *we* know our selves, because to do so, the other person would have to *be* in our subjective reality. Hence, even so-called objective descriptions of behavior are in reality intersubjective accounts. The self-concept emerges from the phenomenal field as a figure from the ground, and when we are not focused on our selves, it can lose articulation and become an undifferentiated aspect of the ground. We can lose ourselves for a time as we focus on other figures of interest in our subjective phenomenal fields.

There is a single, master motive in life which Rogers called organismic enhancement. This is a desire on the part of all living organisms to extend the range of their phenomenal fields and to enrich them through further articulations and differentiations—much as we enrich diamonds by cutting more facets into their totality. A problem arises, however, in the fact that this enhancement takes two forms. There are needs of the organism and needs of the self which must be satisfied. The former are essentially natural and personal, whereas the latter are taught to us by important figures in our lives—parents, teachers, and the society in general. The person organizes his or her self-concept according to a valuing process which strives to be acceptable to others and internally (self-) consistent. Feelings that may be genuine and accurately reflect the organismic valuing process may be denied in favor of a societal value that implies that the person should not be experiencing such emotions. This results in threat, and the person may then distort the symbolization of the accurately perceived emotion. Ideally, there should be a matching up or congruence of the organismic (emotional, feeling) and the self-concept (psychological, social) aspects of phenomenal experience. However, a certain amount of incongruence is usually experienced, and when this disbalance is excessive, we can even speak of psychological maladjustment.

Unfortunately, human beings often lack positive regard for each other, so that when one person deviates from a traditional way of behaving, even though this injures no one else, there is a certain amount of pressure to bring this deviant back into line. Parents in particular are likely to ignore a child's individuality and press upon him or her values the child does not sincerely or organismically feel in tune with. According to Rogers, repression occurs when such unacceptable feelings are not symbolized. Such denial can be rationalized away for a time, but eventually the internal locus of evaluation shifts to what others think and feel rather than what the person thinks or feels. The person is now essentially victimized by others, who move him or her about like an automaton. In order to mature properly and become what Rogers called a fully functioning person, the individual must bring back the locus of evaluation to an internal frame of reference, relying on organismic enhancement. In achieving this internal congruence, the person would effectively become more independent in behavior. The mature person in Rogerian terms has achieved independence from parental pressures.

Rogers's theory of illness stems from the incongruence construct and the distortion in symbolization it invariably results in. The person is vulnerable to attacks of anxiety, threat, and disorganization because he or she does not feel up to the events that seem to throw life into one conflict after another. There is also a continuing tension of incongruence leading to lowered confidence in general. Rogers disliked labeling people through diagnosing a symptom picture, but he did refer to moderate incongruence as neurosis and extreme incongruence as psychosis. Rogers devoted considerable attention to his theory of cure which was based on what he called nondirective or client-centered therapy. The client-centered therapist assumes that a client can deal constructively with all those aspects of his or her life that can potentially come into conscious awareness. The climate of the therapeutic contact is all-important here. Rogers called this a helping relationship, an interest by one person with empathic understanding of and unconditional positive regard for the problems of another person. Effective therapists are congruent individuals who create a process equation in the therapeutic contact which intends that there be more open expression and functional use of the client's inner resources. The client must be encouraged to rely on organismic feeling tones, which reflect sincere values and preferences that would set life on a healthy track if they were only taken into account. Hence, the therapist is a facilitator of this genuine acceptance of what the person *is* rather than an individual striving to mold or shape the person according to some preconceived image or plan. This emphasis on the spontaneous and genuine gives Rogerian theory a decidedly existentialistic flavor.

Rogers considered insight to be the perception of new meaning in the client's own phenomenal experience. He did not dwell on transference in the Freudian sense, feeling that if the person does indeed transfer feelings meant for another onto the therapist, it is the behavioral manner and attitude of the therapist that has invited this transference. The client-centered relationship focuses on congruence—both in the behavior of the therapist and it is hoped, as time passes, in the behavior of the client as well. Psychotherapy is a process of change in which the self-concept comes more into line with the organismic valuing process, thanks to the open, accepting, positive regard of the therapist in the therapeutic relationship. Rogers broke down this process of change into seven stages of movement. He also conducted extensive empirical studies of these stages. In the final analysis, awareness was the central concept in Rogers's definition of mental health. Psychologically well-adjusted people are open to experience, trusting in their organism, accepting of their subjectivity as evaluators of their phenomenal experience, and willing to be a process of change. The emphasis on organismic trust led Rogers to envision what we have termed a universal natural ethic in human relations. That is, he came to refer to a wisdom in organic feelings, leading to natural valuations made of life which are beyond the social order as such. Organisms that react naturally to their feelings about things enhance their survival chances, and particularly so when considered as a member of a species. The species is likely to survive if its members take organismic valuations into consideration.

This growing emphasis on naturalistic bases of valuation paralleled Rogers's own development as therapist, moving him from a one-to-one therapist in individual therapy to a facilitator of the encounter group. Since Rogers always held that congruence in one person promotes congruence in another and vice versa, in the final analysis, every person becomes a therapist. Hence, even in an encounter group where only one facilitator is present, several individuals may promote through healthy interpersonal relationships of a congruent nature the psychological adjustment of all the members. Rather than focusing on how to be nondirective in therapy, Rogers in his later years focused on the problems of the encounter group, including the development of trust, the overcoming of resistance in certain members, protecting the individual, and the use or nonuse of certain group exercises. Rogers's lasting influence on psychology will doubtlessly stem from his image of the person and his attitude toward how people develop and change their behavior. His technical theory is more a borrowed product than his own creation. He is, however, a great humanist and a leading innovator in therapeutic technique in the history of psychology.

Outline of Important Theoretical Constructs

Background factors in Rogerian thought

Edmund Husserl
noumena versus phenomena · intersubjectivity · essence of meaning · phenomenology · transcendental · transcendental phenomenology

The Gestalt psychologists: Max Wertheimer, Wolfgang Köhler, and Kurt Koffka
phenomenal movement, phi-phenomenon · gestalt · distal versus proximal stimulus · laws of organization · articulation · law of unit formation and segregation · law of closure · law of good shape · law of good continuation · law of proximity and equality · law of pragnanz · law of figure-against-ground formation · principle of isomorphism

Kurt Lewin
life space · level of aspiration · path, valence, barrier · demand character

· foreign hull · differentiation · communication · locomotion · group dynamics · T-groups, encounter groups

Otto Rank
birth trauma · independence · positive versus negative will · separation anxiety · termination of therapy

Biographical overview of Carl R. Rogers

Personality theory

Structural constructs

Mind-body, phenomenal subjectivity, and the wisdom of organic evidence
phenomenal field · consciousness · symbol · subjective reality · intersubjectivity · subception · wisdom of organic evidence

The self as a conscious articulation of the phenomenal field
self-concept · self-structure

Motivational constructs

Organismic enhancement as life's master motive
organismic enhancement · need · needs of the organism · needs of the self · valuing process · self-consistency · threat

Congruence versus incongruence and positive regard
congruence · incongruence · psychological maladjustment · positive regard

Defensiveness versus spontaneity in human behavior
anxiety · introjection · repression · distorted symbolization · denial · rationalization · locus of evaluation

Time perspective constructs
organismic valuing process · personality · fully functioning person · conditional versus unconditional positive regard

Individual differences constructs
dependent versus independent • self-ideal versus self • vulnerability • mature behavior • fully functioning person

Psychopathology and psychotherapy

Theory of illness

Maladjustment as the clash of organismic versus self actualization
psychological maladjustment • threat, anxiety • tension of inconguence

The irrelevancy of diagnostic distinctions
client versus patient • neurosis • psychosis

Theory of cure

The nature of a healing relationship: the client-centered hypothesis
therapist's hypothesis • client-centered hypothesis • helping relationship • process equation • facilitator

Insight and transference
insight • transference

Psychotherapy as a process of change
therapist attitudes • psychotherapy • facilitator • seven stages of movement • contact • congruent relationship • unconditional positive regard • empathic understanding

Mental health: the characteristics of a therapized individual
awareness • existential living

An evolutionary theme and a natural ethic
evolutionary view of human nature • values of survival and evolution of species • universal natural ethic

Techniques of therapy and life processes

The early technique emphasis: nondirective therapy
directive versus nondirective therapy styles • validating others

Generalized principles for interpersonal behavior
every person is a therapist

The basic encounter group
encounter group • trust • confrontation • resistance • interpretation, insight • group process • group exercises • nonfacilitation

Notes

1. Husserl, 1965, p. 106. 2. Ibid., p. 110. 3. Ibid., p. 116. 4. Ibid. 5. Ibid., p. 90. 6. Ibid., p. 91. 7. Ibid. 8. Rychlak, 1968, pp. 222–223. 9. Köhler, 1961a, p. 4. 10. Koffka, 1935. 11. Ibid., p. 73. 12. Köhler, 1961b, p. 209. 13. Ibid., p. 10. 14. Koffka, 1935, p. 126. 15. Ibid., p. 150. 16. Ibid., p. 151. 17. Ibid., p. 153. 18. Ibid., pp. 164, 166. 19. Ibid., p. 110. 20. Ibid., p. 192. 21. Ibid., p. 62. 22. Ibid., pp. 209–210. 23. Ibid., p. 319. 24. Ibid., p. 665. 25. Ibid., p. 666. 26. Marrow, 1969, p. 8. 27. Lewin, 1935. 28. Marrow, 1969, p. 37. 29. Lewin, Dembo, Festinger, and Sears, 1944. 30. Lewin, Lippitt, and White, 1939. 31. Marrow, 1969, p. 128. 32. Ibid., pp. 210–214. 33. See especially Lewin, 1947. 34. Rank, 1968, p. 3. 35. Ibid., p. 4. 36. Ibid., pp. 104–105. 37. Ibid., p. 179. 38. Ibid., p. 172. 39. Rogers, 1967. 40. Ibid. 41. Ibid., p. 345. 42. Ibid., p. 376. 43. Ibid., p. 351. 44. Ibid., p. 354. 45. Ibid., p. 376. 46. Ibid., p. 360. 47. Rogers, 1959. 48. See Rogers and Dymond, 1954. 49. See Rogers, Gendlin, Kiesler, and Truax, 1967. 50. Ibid., pp. 79–81. 51. Ibid., pp. 83–85. 52. Rogers, 1967, p. 370. 53. See Rogers, 1970e. 54. See Rogers, 1959, p. 197. 55. Rogers, 1951, p. 487. 56. Ibid., p. 483. 57. Ibid., p. 485. 58. Rogers, 1959, p. 191. 59. Rogers, 1951, p. 491. 60. Ibid., p. 496. 61. After McCleary and Lazarus, 1949. 62. Ibid., p. 507. 63. Rogers, 1942, pp. 174–175. 64. Rogers, 1951, p. 522. 65. Ibid., p. 524. 66. Rogers, 1970f, p. 53. 67. Rogers, 1959, p. 200. 68. Rogers, 1951, p. 491. 69. Ibid., p. 483. 70. Ibid., p. 191. 71. Ibid. 72. Ibid., p. 487. 73. Rogers, 1942, p. 18. 74. Rogers, 1951, p. 491. 75. Ibid., pp. 488–489. 76. Ibid., p. 491. 77. Ibid., p. 492. 78. Ibid., pp. 492–493. 79. Ibid., p. 493. 80. Ibid., p. 498. 81. Ibid.,

p. 501. **82.** Ibid., p. 508. **83.** Ibid., p. 516. **84.** Rogers, 1959, pp. 196–197. **85.** Rogers, 1951, p. 513. **86.** Rogers, 1959, p. 206. **87.** Rogers, 1961, pp. 50–51. **88.** Rogers, 1959, p. 203. **89.** Ibid., pp. 207–208. **90.** Standal, 1954. **91.** Rogers, 1959, p. 208. **92.** Ibid., p. 204. **93.** Rogers, 1951, p. 523. **94.** Ibid., p. 505. **95.** Rogers, 1959, p. 205. **96.** Ibid., p. 228. **97.** Ibid., p. 210. **98.** Rogers, 1951, p. 508. **99.** Rogers, 1970c. **100.** Rogers, 1959, p. 222. **101.** Ibid., p. 223. **102.** Rogers, 1961, p. 191. **103.** Rogers, 1959, p. 223. **104.** Ibid., p. 225. **105.** Ibid. **106.** Rogers, 1951, p. 221. **107.** Ibid., p. 15. **108.** Ibid., p. 213. **109.** Ibid., p. 228. **110.** Rogers, 1959, p. 200. **111.** Rogers and Dymond, 1954. **112.** Rogers, 1959, pp. 203–204. **113.** Ibid., p. 207. **114.** Ibid., p. 235. **115.** Rogers, 1961, p. 191. **116.** Rogers, 1959, p. 203. **117.** Ibid., p. 204. **118.** Ibid. **119.** Rogers, 1951, p. 192. **120.** Rogers, 1961, p. 330. **121.** Rogers, 1951, p. 221. **122.** Ibid., p. 222. **123.** Rogers, 1959, p. 203. **124.** Ibid., p. 227. **125.** Ibid., p. 236. **126.** Rogers, 1942, p. 18. **127.** Ibid., pp. 87–89. **128.** Rogers, 1951, p. 24. **129.** Ibid., p. 208. **130.** Ibid., p. 209. **131.** Ibid. **132.** Ibid., p. 518. **133.** Rogers, 1959, p. 240. **134.** Rogers, 1961, p. 40. **135.** Rogers, 1970a. **136.** Rogers, 1961, p. 40. **137.** Rogers, 1970f, pp. 58–59. **138.** Ibid., p. 55. **139.** Ibid., p. 45. **140.** Rogers, 1942, p. 174. **141.** Ibid., p. 175. **142.** Rogers, 1951, p. 201. **143.** Ibid., p. 200. **144.** Ibid., p. 203. **145.** Rogers, 1959, p. 214. **146.** See Rogers, 1970f, p. 55. **147.** Rogers, 1951, p. 40. **148.** Ibid., p. 208. **149.** Ibid., p. 40. **150.** Ibid., pp. 112–113. **151.** Ibid., p. 222. **152.** Ibid., p. 519. **153.** Rogers, 1953, p. 48. **154.** Rogers, 1970a, p. 202. **155.** Rogers, 1970d, p. 470. **156.** Rogers, 1951, p. 77. **157.** Ibid., p. 210. **158.** Rogers, 1961, pp. 132–151. **159.** Rogers, 1959, p. 208. **160.** Ibid., p. 213. **161.** Rogers, 1951, pp. 40–41. **162.** Ibid., p. 135. **163.** Ibid., p. 195. **164.** Rogers, 1959, p. 206. **165.** Rogers, 1961, pp. 115–118. **166.** Ibid., p. 166. **167.** Ibid., pp. 169–175. **168.** Ibid., p. 189. **169.** Ibid., p. 285. **170.** Rogers, 1951, p. 194. **171.** Ibid., p. 196. **172.** Rogers, 1959, p. 221. **173.** Rogers, 1970c, p. 439. **174.** Ibid., p. 441. **175.** Ibid. **176.** Ibid., p. 440. **177.** Ibid. **178.** Ibid., p. 441. **179.** Rogers and Hart, 1970, p. 520. **180.** From Rogers, 1942, p. 123. **181.** Rogers, 1969a, p. 63. **182.** Ibid., p. 75. **183.** Ibid., pp. 164–165. **184.** Ibid., p. 91. **185.** Ibid., p. 279. **186.** Rogers, 1961, p. 325. **187.** Ibid., p. 356. **188.** Ibid., p. 332. **189.** Ibid., p. 180. **190.** Rogers, 1970f, p. 72. **191.** Rogers, 1969a, p. 73. **192.** Ibid., p. 144. **193.** Rogers, 1970f, p. 47. **194.** Ibid., p. 50. **195.** Ibid., pp. 54–55. **196.** Ibid., p. 57. **197.** Ibid. **198.** Ibid., p. 70. **199.** Ibid., pp. 66–68.

Chapter 10

Existential Analysis or Daseinsanalysis: Binswanger and Boss

Existential Philosophy

Existentialism as a movement in philosophy dates from the first half of the nineteenth century, when Sören Kierkegaard (1813–1855) began to criticize the heavily intellectualized or rational philosophy of Georg Wilhelm Friedrich Hegel (1770–1831). Kierkegaard believed that human existence is not accurately represented when we leave out the spontaneous and emotional side of life in our philosophies. The spirit of this movement was then advanced by Friedrich Nietzsche (1844–1900), but it was not until a series of brilliant people, most of whom read, admired, or actually studied with Husserl (see p. 565), began speaking of *being, ontology* (the study of being), and *existence* that the movement really took shape. These were individuals, such as Karl Jaspers (1883–1969), Martin Heidegger (1889–1976), and Jean-Paul Sartre (1905–1980). There were other important thinkers like Gabriel Marcel (1889–1973) who advanced existentialism, but we will focus on those philosophers having a direct relevance for psychology.

Existentialism as a view of the world is *not* a uniform philosophy. Although central to the development of this view, both Jaspers and Heidegger specifically denied that they were existentialists. These men disagreed on major points, and meanings for the same terms change when we read each of them. Yet existentialism is a peculiarly *modern* philosophy which speaks for large segments of the world's populace; it has something to say about our contemporary *predicament* (a term often employed) as we advance into the twenty-first century. Will we make it? Is it all worth it? Do we really have the answers, philosophical or scientific, to enrich life as we once dreamed was possible? Can we discover or create that which we must know to "truly be"? These are the questions existentialism addresses.

The writings of Kierkegaard and Heidegger are probably more relevant to personality and psychotherapy than those of the other men. These two thinkers had the most direct influence on modern psychology. In the remainder of this introductory section, we will review a half-dozen conceptions which best reflect the thrust of existential philosophy and which we will see as prominent themes in the psychology of Binswanger and Boss.

Alienation

As the last philosopher who tried to write an all-encompassing account of our human nature, including our historical development as a people across the ages, Hegel played an important role in the birth of existentialism. An important idea he advanced in his writings was that those things that human beings

create can actually have a "life [existence] of their own." For example, an artist's painting or the writings of an author are really *there* in existence independent of his or her control. If the artist and author change their views—their judgments of what is beautiful or worthy of literary mention—their creations remain as originally conceived. In fact, the creations may take on meanings never intended by the creators! More than one creation has been known to bring pain to its creator as in the fictional case of Frankenstein's monster. Not only the works of major artists and authors but even the most humble statements and activities of everyday life can have a similar effect—like a letter written in haste, an act of seemingly justified revenge, and so forth.

Hegel referred to this independent life of our creations—a kind of existence that is basically foreign to us—as *alienation*.[1] Aliens are foreigners. Kierkegaard used this idea of being alienated from certain aspects of our existence to describe the way in which Christians of his period practiced their faith. Too many Christians, said Kierkegaard, repeated meaningless prayers and nodded in agreement to dogmas of their religion which they never understood, much less put into practice. Religion was no longer a living force in their lives. People had become alienated from their faith. Nietzsche had a similar criticism to make of the established philosophies of his time. The philosopher who mouthed what others had said instead of following the promptings of his or her own reason had become alienated from that very reasoning capacity.[2] How can thinkers answer today's problems by repeating solutions offered for yesterday's problems?

Heidegger showed how words can be alienated from the meanings they are supposed to convey so that people can twist things to suit themselves in violation of what is known in immediate experience.[3] We behave cowardly in a time of threat—then point out later that everyone is cowardly at some time in life, hence our actions were perfectly understandable and not unusual. We can actually live out a lifetime of untruth, making our alienated understandings "real" in the sense that we enact them. Marlene is a wretchedly sad and unloved person, who turns all signs of affection into humorous taunts. She belittles what she wants most. Sartre said that psychology as a science of behavior has become alienated from its subject matter because, rather than capturing phenomenal reality in its theories, it has turned human beings into machines.[4] Sartre also strongly developed the idea first suggested by Kierkegaard—that group pressures like national identities (being an American, German, and so on) have become so great in our time that everyone lives in self-alienation. We cannot be who we spontaneously and phenomenally are because of the many subtle pressures to conform, to be as others would have us be and as everyone around us is.

Authenticity

Kierkegaard was the first philosopher to point out that we become inauthentic if we let the group or culture define who we are (self-alienation). Modern concepts of the mass person, who sells out by submitting to what the system says he or she ought to be, have their roots in Kierkegaard's attack on the lifeless rituals of the Christian church.[5] Nietzsche spoke of the *will to power* (see p. 135) as being the human person's fundamental capacity to be self-creative and hence authentic (real, genuine, spontaneous, and so on). As long as we base our lives on what we *are*—what we think, feel, desire—then we cannot be self-alienated or self-estranged. Our conscience urges us only to be free, to be ourselves as we constantly experience life

unafraid; *guilt* is that feeling we suffer when we do not assume this responsibility but let others define who we are.[6]

Jaspers' philosophy dealt with the opposition between authentic and inauthentic living. He referred to *Dasein* as *being-there,* or literally, the objective fact that we do materially exist.[7] Nature automatically determines that we exist in this sense. But another realm of existence that Jaspers termed *being-oneself* demands personal action before it is realized (created). To be oneself requires effort, personal decision, and the selection of alternatives that might not prove popular. The group cannot provide this being-oneself for us. It can, however, set limits on what we might be. The point is not to reject all of its views about what is good and/or proper in life, but to realize that only individual effort can bring about being-oneself.

For Heidegger, authenticity was fulfilling one's possibilities.[8] That is, we can become what we aspire to be. As humans we can see a "potential being" ahead of us and work to become that unique self. The term *Dasein* as used by Heidegger includes this possibility, this tentative projection of what "might be" in the future. We also realize that our possibilities are not unlimited. Other human beings have established certain prescribed ways of doing things, as codified in our laws. We can go along with this established routine without question—which would make us inauthentic—or we can evaluate, accept, discard, and affirm our own ways of possible living—which when realized in our lifestyle would make us authentic.[9] No one can be completely free of group pressures. The authentic person thus synthesizes the imposed and the self-willed to reach a pattern of existence (*Dasein*) that is uniquely his or her own. We admire Aaron, for though he is a conventional person, he has a style all his own which he obviously has carved out for himself and within which he feels at home. Aaron is authentic, more genuinely alive than the unorthodox people with whom he comes into contact because he is self-created and they are merely conforming to the latest fad in eccentricity.

Subject versus Object

The person who lives inauthentically, said Kierkegaard, who lets others define his or her identity, begins to think of that identity as an *object* and not as a *subject*.[10] Objects are things to be factually described, manipulated, and put in their place because they are passive. The subjective side to life, on the other hand, involves action, a desire to create that which is not yet factual but a mere possibility. In morality, for example, we project an "ought" as a possibility and then make it a reality in our life. We say "A man and woman who marry ought to be faithful to each other," and then create this pattern in our own, subjectively determined pattern of behavior. If we merely express this moral principle objectively, it remains a mere possibility and hence we never make it so.[11] To bring moral precepts alive, we must first think of ourselves subjectively, recognizing thereby that we have a unique responsibility to do something more than just pay lip service to what is being stated.

Jaspers made a similar point in speaking about the error of letting modern science define who we are as persons. Science *levels* everything on earth into a common form of description and analysis, confounding thereby the objective realm of being-there with the subjective realm of being-oneself. Since the former can never arrive at the latter, Jaspers asked that we transcend (rise above) mere objectivity and think of ourselves subjectively.[12] Heidegger referred to the inauthentic form of existence that results when we consider each other to be objects rather than subjects as *nothingness*. To the objectivist, a person is "anyone" or "everyman" or a "plastic person." The danger is that we allow ourselves to become a part of this objective mass, this faceless crowd of objects which move about like ants conforming to the manipulations of science, church, and country without subjectively examining and creating our lifestyles for ourselves. To *be* is to emerge from the background of nothingness as a figure emerges from the ground (see p. 570).

Commitment, Action

The essence of the human spirit according to existentialism is *activity*.[13] It takes active effort to become a subjective person. As Kierkegaard once put it, "To be human is not a fact, but a task."[14] Nietzsche said that we must leap into life with passion and, above all, a sense of *commitment* to that which we are bringing about. This passion does not mean that the committed person is irrational. Reason and emotion are not antithetical.[15] Only an automaton is without passion, and if we simply go through the motions of life, we are not existing but simply enacting what someone else has determined we should be doing. When we are alive, we will *feel* alive.

What we commit ourselves to will be influenced to an extent by the historical time in which we live, as well as by our strictly personal set of circumstances. Much has gone before us in our country's history. Our parents have been living and creating their existence for some time as well. Jaspers cautioned that the wise person does not arrogantly reject all that has gone before, but selects to affirm that which a subjective examination establishes is correct and good to live by.[16] Heidegger showed how some people run away from this need to make a subjective examination and a personal commitment by fleeing into mass movements and other popular fads.[17] Millard becomes a revolutionary, not out of a real examination of the issues he is opposed to, but because he obtained a quick sense of identity by becoming part of a powerful movement with an aim to achieve. But this is still not Millard's subjective aim. Randal may have entered the priesthood on equally unreasoned grounds—to obtain the same cheap solution to a life problem that faces all of us. Sartre called this self-deception *bad faith,* by which he meant letting ourselves down and not really fulfilling the possibilities open to us in life.[18] The thrust of existentialism is thus to put the individual at the center of life, personally responsible for what then takes place in that life. We cannot sidestep this responsibility and claim that we behave as we do because of our parents, our society, or our racial inheritance. We must recognize that even when we refuse to *choose,* to act, to commit ourselves to a direction in life, *we have already chosen.* There is no escaping the existential predicament of *having to be.*

Anxiety, Dread, Despair

The existentialists use words like *anxiety, dread,* and *despair* to describe inauthentic living. Kierkegaard spoke of anxiety as the "sickness unto death,"[19] resulting from self-alienation (inauthenticity) and giving the person nothing but despair to look forward to. Nietzsche considered fear or anxiety to be the result of negating or refusing to use one's will to power.[20] Not everyone who suffers the dread of inauthenticity appears to be anxious overtly. We look at Rita as she works feverishly to organize the local Parent-Teacher's Association chapter, and we never realize that her heightened tempo and breathless commitment to the PTA masks an underlying sense of emptiness in her personal life. Rita really does not know who she is, but as her mother was an active person in PTA, she too now tries to solve her problem of existence through her mother's solutions. Sometimes a person living through an inauthentic existence masks the underlying anxiety with overt boredom. Everything in life bores Charles. He tends to blame others for this sense of boredom, but the truth is he is personally unable to commit himself creatively to life. Hence, as Heidegger said, his anxiety reflects his nothingness, which in turn manifests itself as boredom.[21] Anxiety can be a constructive factor in life, for as both Kierkegaard and Heidegger stressed, out of anxiety is born the motivation to conquer indecision and self-deception. Anxiety is in one sense the beginning of self-affirmation. We are afraid, but this means we "are," and in our being, we can as identities alive to the possibilities in things bring about a tomorrow that is more authentic than today.

Absurd

The last concept we will consider as typical of existentialistic philosophy is *absurd.* This word has been used in both a positive and a negative sense by the existentialists. Kierkegaard used it in the more positive sense, as a basis for belief. For something to be true, we have to believe it, and, said Kierkegaard, when we come right down to it, all belief is subjective in nature. This makes all truth subjective as well. Well, it is clearly absurd to think of a God who was born, grew up, and died, exactly as other human beings have done and are doing. Yet when we think about this subjectively, it is the very absurdity of this sequence of events that lends it believability.[22] Paradoxes and absurdities always seem to bring us up short, make us think about what they are driving at; in this way they carry great weight as evidence. When we honestly look at some things privately and openly, as subjects, we are moved to think, "That is just so unusual, so odd, so different that there must be some truth to it. It is absurdly true."

Sartre, on the other hand, used the term *absurd* in a more negative sense. He tended to view absurdity as a way of talking about human existence. The human drama is full of absurdities. We have the absurdity of death, bringing to an end nature's highest creation.[23] We have the absurdity of clashing moralities, where opposed sides are drawn along a line of armed conflict aiming to demolish one another in the name of their God (Who is often the same). We have the absurdity of birth, in which material advantages are partitioned according to class or race. And the more complex modern life becomes, the more absurd it becomes. The implications of Sartre's rather pessimistic summation is that if we would each contemplate these absurdities in our own subjective state of existence, we could in time remove them through individual commitment and action.

Existential Themes in Oriental Philosophy

In recent times there has been much interest shown in the philosophy of the East by Westerners, particularly in the world view of Zen Buddhism. Oriental philosophers and historians stress the style of thought among Indian, Chinese, and Japanese peoples.[24] The remarkable thing about Buddhistic thought is that, although it differs from existentialism on the active-passive dimension (see below), this religiophilosophical world view shares many ideas with existential philosophy. Many of the pop (popular) philosophies of the 1960s and 1970s in the West have combined existential themes of authenticity and subject-object with the themes of Buddhistic writings, so that today we often hear Kierkegaard and Sartre being wound into conversations centering on some wise Indian guru or Japanese Zen master. In this section, we will try to capture the essential themes of Oriental philosophy, and to show how they relate to existential-phenomenological thought.

The Quest for Unity

Buddhism took root from the even more ancient religion of Hinduism, which traces its lineage back to the ancient sacred writings of the Vedic literature in India (about 1500 B.C.).[25] These writings placed great stress on the interrelatedness of everything in lived experience, so that a state of alienation would be considered very unnatural and even immoral.[26] This theme—of searching for the unity that exists in nature, which must not be violated by introducing false dichotomies or intellectualizing about nature—remains foremost in Buddhistic philosophy. We see here a parallel to existentialism's authenticity in that what is most authentic, real, and natural is what lives spontaneously and free of what must always be arbitrary and forced distinctions.

Western science teaches us that to know anything, we must first break it down into its presumed parts (reduce the one to the many pieces that make it up). Buddhistic philosophy runs counter to such reductionism, challenging us to remember what the gestaltists taught us (see p. 569), that we can never find the whole by merely summing up its parts. The concept of complete totality in all things is captured by the Hindu conception of the *Brahma* or the Buddhistic conception of *Buddha*. These concepts symbolize both a deity and also the ultimate in unity we all can find if we will but make an internal search, finding within our personal identity a kind of universal soul to which we can relate. Each person makes this internal search individually, and it involves an active commitment similar to what we saw occurring in the Jungian individuating (balancing) process (see p. 206). Jung, of course, relied on Buddhistic writings to support his theory of the centering of the personality.

According to the traditions of Hinduism and Buddhism, all theories about reality or the nature of life are equally true.[27] Westerners presume that one point of view must be right and the others wrong, hence they search for a single account of reality by looking outward, empirically testing this and that in hopes of finding *the* truth. Truth is interpreted as something split off from error, and what is erroneous is therefore useless, to be tossed aside onto a slag heap of meaningless experience. The Eastern philosophy strives to liberate the person from this outward search and replace it with a kind of internal examination of the question-answer, proof-finding process itself. As a counter to the splitting-up process in knowledge seeking, early Buddhistic philosophy proposed a *negation* of the dualities being proposed by other philosophies of that time. The great Buddhistic philosopher Nāgārjuna (*c.* A.D. 100–150) proposed a widely cited Eightfold Negation. In doing so, he claimed there was neither birth nor death, neither coming nor going, neither permanence nor extinction, and neither unity nor diversity.[28]

This denial sounds strange to our Western ear, but the point involved is that when we first pose dichotomies like life versus death or coming and going, we of necessity force ourselves to say where we *are* in relation to them. Are we dead or alive? What is death? What is life? Is nature dead or alive? When we die, are we no longer a part of nature? Are we coming or are we going in life? In relation to what? If we are going, then what direction ought we to take? If we are coming, where have we been and why did we leave? All of these ridiculous questions, said Nāgārjuna, spring to our minds only because we first split up our existence needlessly.

What Nāgārjuna sought was the "middle path" of existence, or as it is called, *nirvana*. By rejecting such dichotomies placed onto nature, we avoid the tension of extremes (either-or) and attain a balance combining both sides into a unity, totality, or "middle path." Once again, Jung's centering process in individuation best captures the meaning here of how we can find our complete selves inwardly and attain a more balanced midpoint (see p. 231). It is clear that Buddhistic philosophy is heavily dialectical and that it contrasts dramatically with the more demonstrative emphasis given to logical reasoning in the West (see p. 11). The Indian Hindu, for example, would not reason as a Western scientist and say that we can see what is *there* on a table or see nothing at all; instead, the Indian mentality has it that "looking at the table, we can say that there is no cat there, just as we can say that there is a book there."[29]

It is when we affirm (express a belief in) our own body, our own mind, our own personal egos that we separate ourselves from Brahma (or Buddha). Through *meditation,* it is possible to employ a dialectical tactic of dismissing each of these antithetical (contradictory) affirmations in order to arrive at oneness (unity). Once achieved, and all separation from the unity of Brahma is removed, we can speak of the person as having attained *enlightenment*.[30] This process begins in knowing who we *are,* and then by negating our customary separateness as individuals, we become what we *are not* ordinarily—that is, a unity. Once the focus of our search for knowledge has shifted from *are* (self) to *are not* (unity, Brahma), we rise to a level of harmony (balance, centering) that transcends all our previous experience and where dichotomies are unnecessary and the striving for certainty is pointless because a direct knowledge of nature is achieved by becoming one with it. Knowledge (enlightenment) is immediate and enriching, spontaneous and certain.

It is this dialectical reverse logic of seeing what is not there and negating what one is to become what one is not that prompts Westerners to view Oriental philosophy as mysterious. It also appears to the Westerner that the Buddhistic philosophy achieves enlightenment by denying the validity of a question put to nature. Though this is true, we must appreciate that the Easterner has traditionally sought to live with and in the natural order, rather than seeking to alter it or even destroy it, as our fears today about pollution and catastrophic warfare surely imply can take place. In a sense, Western thought has emphasized the thesis-antithesis schism of dialectic, whereas Eastern thought puts its emphasis on the synthesis.

Probably the most famous of dialectical concepts of Oriental philosophy is the *yin-yang principle,* which can be traced to the ancient collection of writings known as the *Tao Te Ching* (c. 600 B.C., probably of multiple authorship). This principle attempts to explain the actions of all things in nature and might be contrasted with the demonstrative principle of constancy which Freud wrestled with as a tool of explanation (see p. 53). The *yin* force or element is described as passive, receiving, and meek (on the face of things); yet, like the female or mother, *yin* represents the potential for infinite creation in the world. In this sense, *yin* is closer to *tao* or the *way*—that is, the creative principle that patterns the growth and development of everything in nature. The *yang* force is more active and bold, showing its power openly in a more masculine sense. Harmony as a kind of dialectical balance between *yin* and *yang* is most desirable, although it is traditional in Buddhism for the enlightened person to hide the more aggressive *yang* forces and thus appear overly passive to the Western intellect. Yin and yang thus interact dialectically to bring forward the creativity of *tao*. We can see this exchange of active and passive in all things, as in, for example, the developments of the weather in which wind and storm (yang) are followed by sunny calm (yin) to encourage growth (tao) in all vegetation.

The Buddhistic ideal of the strong (yang) person appearing passive (yin) has even been incorporated into the martial arts of the Orient, such as jujitsu or kung fu. The preferred style in these encounters is to use the opponent's aggressive moves (yang) as a self-defeating act. For example, by deftly grasping the arms of a person who lunges for us, we can fall backward and, using our legs as a lever, carry this lunge through to catapult the aggressor behind us. The deftness and style of our action is effortless (yin), but the outcome can be devastating nevertheless.

Not all Chinese philosophy is dialectical. Confucianism is more demonstrative in tone, oriented to tradition and parental authority.[31] Confucius (551–479 B.C.) was critical of the rulers of his time, whom he felt were unconcerned for the welfare of their citizenry. He

was a great teacher and tried to influence subsequent generations by stressing the character
of the Chinese people. His sayings are still
quoted as guidelines for the right, proper,
and humane way in which to live. He believed that there is a right and a wrong way
in which to behave, and it was absolutely essential to respect one's parents as supreme
authorities. The demonstrative flavor of his
approach is clear, and we would look in vain
to find a dialectical contradiction in his
writings.

But the more characteristic spirit of Chinese thought is dialectical, and there was even
a dialectician school of philosophy founded by
Mo Ti which represents one of those unbelievable parallels in the history of thought.
Mo Ti lived from *c*. 470 to 391 B.C., a span of
years which is almost identical to the life of
the great Greek dialectician, Socrates (who
lived *c*. 470–399 B.C.). There was no possibility
of cultural contact here. The fact that two
human beings of such diverse backgrounds
could frame a world view around the play
of dialectic surely argues that there is something basic to human nature in this oppositional, contradictory, paradoxical manner of
thought. It was not until 1227 that Dogen
brought the Soto Zen sect of Buddhism to
Japan. We find in his writings the paradoxical
statements of this philosophy, such as the
often cited query "What is the sound of one
hand, clapping?" Such paradoxical statements
are called *koans,* and they are frequently used
as the focus of attention in meditation exercises (see below). Muso (or Soseki) followed
Dogen, and the general style of master-stu-
dent instruction in Zen was perfected under
his leadership and example. As we have noted
above, Zen Buddhism is the specific school
of thought that was popularized in America,
beginning in the 1950s and continuing to the
present day (influenced to a great extent by
the writings of Alan W. Watts[32]).

Thus far we have seen many similarities

between the philosophy of existentialism and
Oriental philosophy. Both approaches call on
the individual subject to become authentically balanced and in tune with the world as
experienced phenomenally. Both approaches
stress the alienation that results when we try
to press onto nature our theories rather than
listening to nature sensitively and accepting
what we hear without bias or prejudice. They
each value sincerity and tranquil acceptance
of life *as it is*. But there is a major difference
between Eastern Buddhistic precepts and
Western existential precepts, having to do
essentially with the notion of commitment.
As we have seen, the existentialist stresses
the need for action, for putting one's values
to action in some concrete way rather than
accepting the status quo. The Zen Buddhist,
on the other hand, views such commitment
as an inward action, a coming to terms with
oneself rather than with the external world.
The external world is not to be acted upon so
much as accepted for what it is. Existentialistic arguments were used to justify civil dis-
obedience in America during the 1960s Viet-
nam War period. Believing in what they
were committed to, certain individuals took
a Nietzschean leap into the situation and
burned draft (conscription) cards, demonstrated illegally, destroyed records and property, and so on. The stress here on yang over
yin is not consistent with Buddhistic precepts,
where presumably a more passive resistance
would be the style followed.

This contrast between East and West can
also be seen in a comparison of Socrates as
dialectician with the typical Zen master's
method of instruction.[33] Though both methods of seeking insight, knowledge, or enlightenment are based on a dialectical exchange between teacher and student, the
manner in which this instruction is carried
out differs tremendously. In his dialogues

with students, Socrates always took the initiative (yang) to keep the exchange moving along, following up a student's answer to his question with another question. The Zen master, on the other hand, is always pictured in a passive (yin) role, and it is the student who must take the initiative in asking questions. When the student does this, the Zen master responds in a most unusual manner by Western standards. He might give an answer that is completely unrelated to the question; he might simply raise a finger or a fist as a kind of reply; or he might pick up a small stick and throw it at the student. Often he remains silent. If the student prods for knowledge long enough, the master might ask the student to meditate by focusing on some koan ("What is the sound of one hand clapping?").

In the literature of Zen, one routinely reads of students going from one master to another, trying various questions out on them, getting assorted replies or queries of the paradoxical type mentioned, all the while suffering a sense of almost unbearable frustration. Students have even been known to strike their Zen master, but to no avail because a conventional answer was still not forthcoming.[34] Socrates at times frustrated his students, but this was due to the sense of confusion his involved questioning sometimes brought on. The Socratic dialogues did not always end in clear-cut answers, and occasionally they led to unexpected paths that created more problems for the student than they solved. But the Zen student's irritation stemmed from the frustration of not even getting started on the road to knowledge—or so it seemed!

What students had to learn, of course, was that there *is no such road*. All of the questions they put to the Zen master could not satisfy their hunger for knowledge in any case. Knowledge must lead somewhere, it must find that focus or nodal point at which oneness (Buddha) is grasped, understood, and accepted. Questions do not lead to such unity. They break up the totality of experience, posing those dichotomies that we pointed out above detract from unity. When they attain *perfect enlightenment,* Zen students no longer raise questions. The Hindus call this understanding of the unity of nature *nonattachment*. This does not mean that the Zen student forgoes life or loses interest in the commitments of everyday experience. Emotions are a vital aspect of this totality, and pleasures can be taken so long as they do not come between the person and the experiential totality.[35] Someone who would pursue pleasures in a selfish manner, for example, would destroy the unity of experience which knows no selfishness. Nonattachment merely signifies that the person can experience all sides to life, feeling both positively and negatively on the same experience without fearing that this somehow violates the logic of life. Life is dialectical and admits of contradictions within its overriding unity.

Psychotherapy and Zen Buddhism

Zen Buddhism is sometimes considered in the context of psychotherapy, and before leaving this section on Oriental philosophy, we should address this possibility. Actually, a person who entered a relationship with a Zen master would not be getting "therapized," if we mean by this having one person somehow cure or readjust the lifestyle of a second person. Zen Buddhism is a way of life, one that has been mastered by the teacher and that must in turn be mastered by the student.[36] The teacher is a very special person in this relationship, one who teaches entirely by exemplifying (modeling) that which the student-disciple seeks to understand.[37] What is sought might be best termed a *re-evaluation of life*. As we have seen, the Zen master would have no formal ideology—no theory—to offer. Distinctions between conscious and unconscious would not be accepted. In time, the point would be demonstrated that rational considerations—the verbal questions and answers we discussed above—only get in the way of the person's liberation from the problems of his or her past life. We have to forgo our dependence on rational concepts, on the explicit, demonstratively precise explanations we assume must be present in life to account for why things are as they are.[38]

In a sense, Zen would consider such intellectualized efforts at explanation to be a form of defense mechanism, a way we have of dismissing immediate phenomenal experience in preference to some way we want to think, believe, or justify what is taking place. We can turn off our real feelings and go on intellectualizing. Zen practices are quite similar to Rogerian therapy in this sense (see Chapter 9). But there is more to Zen, particularly in regard to the meditative experience.

Zen masters since Dogen have distinguished between *thinking, not-thinking,* and *nonthinking*.[39] Thinking involves categorizing things, naming them, applying arbitrary schemes in questions, answers, and so on. Not-thinking refers to a rejection of this process, a refusal to conceptualize anything. But nonthinking is neither of these things. Nonthinking is a preconceptual state of mind, a purely spontaneous phenomenal state of being which is fundamental to both thinking and not-thinking. When the Zen master *meditates* in a seated posture, the aim here is to attain the state of nonthinking. This state is said to transcend time (*transcendental meditation*). That is, the meditator steps out of time's unilinear (demonstrative) flow for brief periods to fix his or her attention on a koan, a *mantra* (richly flowing word), or a *mandala* (graphic, usually circular image). The focusing of consciousness here immerses the person in the present and also removes him or her completely from the customary state of seeking to conceptualize (name, know, question) things or negate such conceptualizations.

When the person is able to achieve a state of nonthinking, Zen advocates contend that he or she has arrived at the virtual root-source of all thought. Harking back to our discussion of gestalt psychology in Chapter 9 (see p. 567), we might say that nonthinking is like a generalized *ground* on which mind must build. Once we achieve this state, we do not need to review our past lives in that freely associated sense that Freud employed to find the causes of today's problems. We have gone beyond such mental conceptions to the basic flow of life as ground to all else. This capacity to transcend the fixed figures of the mind (that is, conceptions, ideas) and melt into the ground of a unified totality (Buddha) sets the person free from so-called unconscious forces, fixations, hang-ups, or whatever.

Functioning in the present the person can now return from the meditative interlude to begin a new middle path to living without dichotomizing it at every turn. This is not simply a return to normalcy, it is a positive elevation, an advance to supernormalcy. There is no longer any need for resistance or defense because there is nothing to defend against. If unconscious conflicts existed before, they only did so because the person had not yet transcended the unnatural divisiveness of his or her psyche to live a more balanced life of nirvana. Once again, the closest parallel we have to Zen therapeutic change in the West is Jung's individuation process,

Ludwig Binswanger

a fact that has been acknowledged by experts in Zen Buddhism.[40] The major difference is that, whereas Jung had each person framing his or her unique way in which to individuate, the Zen Buddhists framed a common course of individuation, a *tradition* of how to achieve this balanced state of enlightenment which is then handed down from master to student by example.

Biographical Overview of Ludwig Binswanger and Medard Boss

Two men have taken the lead in applying existential philosophy to personality and psychotherapy. Both men were Swiss in national origin, Heideggerian in philosophical outlook, and initially trained in classical (Freudian, Jungian) approaches to psychoanalysis. In the chapter sections to follow, we will review the customary topics by interchanging the

Medard Boss

thought of these two men, providing contrasts where called for. The actual founder of existential analysis or *Daseinsanalyse* (after Heidegger) was Ludwig Binswanger, who was born in Kreuzlingen, Switzerland on 13 April 1881. There was a tradition of medicine in his family, and Ludwig decided to follow it, taking the M.D. degree from the University of Zurich in 1907. He studied under Jung for a time and also took an internship with Eugen Bleuler (see p. 177).

In 1911 Binswanger succeeded his father as director of the Sanatorium Bellevue at Kreuzlingen, a position he held for over four decades during which he earned an international reputation. Although he studied with Jung, the major therapeutic interest among the Swiss in the first decade of this century was Freudian

psychoanalysis. Binswanger became active in this area of psychiatry and gradually cemented a personal friendship with Freud—who visited him in 1912 when Binswanger was ill.[41] Gradually, however, Binswanger became disenchanted with Freud's seeming need to explain human behavior in essentially dehumanizing terms—as being due to energies, psychic systems, and the like. Somewhere in this translation, Binswanger felt Freud was losing the phenomenal reality of human experience. There followed a period of reading and study during which Binswanger became interested in the philosophy of Heidegger. By the 1920s he had worked out a view of human behavior which he felt was more accurate than Freud's. Binswanger delivered a lecture in Vienna on the occasion of Freud's eightieth birthday in which he attempted to contrast psychoanalysis with a more existential view.[42] The paper was not well received by the Freudians, and not until recent times has existential thought made inroads on the classical analytical position.[43] Binswanger and Freud remained on good personal terms through all of their disagreements.[44] In 1956 Binswanger stepped down from his directorship of the Sanatorium Bellevue, though he continued to study and write until his death in 1966.

Our second existentialist, Medard Boss, also graduated from the medical school of the University of Zurich. He was born in St. Gallen, Switzerland, on 4 October 1903 and is currently professor of psychotherapy at the University of Zurich Medical School, as well as the director of the Institute of Daseinsanalytic Therapy there. Boss also studied Jung, Bleuler (his former teacher), and, of course, Freud. Though he was to disagree with the founder of *Daseinsanalyse* (translated as "Daseinsanalysis") on certain points, Boss acknowledged that he was initially stimulated to study Heidegger by the writings of and then personal contacts with Ludwig Binswanger.[45] Boss became a close personal friend of Martin Heidegger as well. He has written more extensively than Binswanger and has also lectured in the United States and South America. For many years Boss was the president of the International Society for Medical Psychotherapy. Boss uses the term *Daseinsanalysis,* but we can consider this translation interchangeable with *Daseinsanalyse,* both of which are synonymous with "existential analysis."

Personality Theory

Structural Constructs

The Centrality of Phenomenal Meaning for the Person as a Body-Mind Gestalt

Phenomenologists believe that the only reason the so-called problem of how body can interact with mind arises in psychology is because we have split the person up into these two sides in the first place. When experience is studied phenomenally, Binswanger noted, the person "is and remains a unit."[46] Body and mind are always found to be two sides to the same thing—*being!* This is what interests the existentialists, the study of being, or to use the technical term meaning the same thing, *ontology.* When we look at the problem of mind versus body ontologically, we find that it does not exist. People live out their lives without drawing such distinctions; they know themselves as living beings primarily and only consider a mind-body issue when it is raised for them by scientists as a theoretical issue. Psychological scientists would like to solve this problem of their own making, but it is of course unsolvable because it is based on a phenomenologically untrue division of our being.[47]

Since scientific explanations must be based on what *is there* (bodily substance) and not on what is *not there* (substanceless thought), psychologists conclude that they must reduce the phenomenal to the physical.[48] Existence is viewed as what *really* exists, and in the process of scientific explanation, we find the person being turned from a *subject* into a material *object.*[49] Yet Boss noted: "Without a subject nothing at all would exist to confront objects and to imagine them as such. True, this implies that every object, everything 'objective'—in being merely objectivized by the subject—is the most subjective thing possible." [50] Phenomenally considered, we *are* our experience. We do not have ideas about things; we *are* our ideas.[51] When we stand before a beautiful tree, we do not face it with our consciousness or perceive it with our eyes or brains. The tree is simply there in phenomenal awareness, it presents itself to us as we experience it for what it is.[52]

This is not to deny that brain processes go on as we come to know the tree. The tree's image surely appears on our retina, and nervous impulses can be measured as they move toward certain areas of our brain. But what has this to do with the *meaning* we experience in our relations with the tree? Very little, said Binswanger, who added concerning the role of such biological processes, "What we perceive are 'first and foremost' not impressions of taste, tone, smell or touch, not even things or objects, but rather, meanings." [53] Boss enlarged this theme by noting that ". . . man cannot see, hear, and smell because he has eyes, ears, and a nose; he is able to have eyes, ears, and a nose because his very essence is luminating and world-disclosing." [54] To suggest that the eye "causes" the meaning of tree through vision is to completely overlook the phenomenal realm.

Hence, as existentialists, we may speak of the "body," but we recognize in this merely a partial realm of existence, one that has no real significance for phenomenal experience. The scientific truths about brain function, the chemical actions of the nervous system, and so on, may well be valid, but the subjective meanings of existence are not to be found in chemical substances or biological processes; indeed, the concepts of instinct, libido, and drive are considered equally meaningless as descriptive terms for experience—regardless of their *facticity* (the *given fact* that a person *has* instincts as he or she *has* ears).[55] Binswanger referred to the bodily sphere of experience as the *eigenwelt* (see below).

Existence, Being-in-the-World, and Dasein as Endowed or Disclosed

The core theoretical constructs used by our existentialists are *existence, being-in-the-world,* and *Dasein.* All these terms refer in one way or another to *being,* and we can actually think of them as synonyms. Being is central to existence, and it transcends in importance all other qualities of experience, such as colors, the size and weight of materials, the feelings we may experience as emotions, and so on. Being *is* something in phenomenal existence, even though it *is not* something that can be captured by the usual terms we employ to say what something *is.* To clarify what we are driving at here, we can review an argument that was first advanced by Hegel and later adapted by Heidegger concerning the nature of being.[56] It runs as follows: suppose we were to explain the being-ness of one of nature's most common items, the chunk of earth known as a *rock.* If we now ask, "Is the rock's being-ness due to its color?" the answer would be, "No, its being is not due to its color." Comparable questions about the rock's shape, its material substance, its weight, and so forth would also be answered in the negative. A rock's being or not-being is not quite any of these qualities—even when we put them into combinations (gestalts). Stripped of all its qualities, therefore, we would still have failed to capture the is-ness of the rock. Even more paradoxical, after all of the qualities have been removed from the rock, we would have *nothing.* Heidegger as Hegel before him thus concluded that being and nothingness are closely related. Hegel considered these as opposites and Heidegger viewed these as independent though partially identical states of existence.[57]

One might say: "But this is surely nonsense. For all practical purposes and insofar as it is possible to prove anything, a rock *is* the sum of its qualities, which I perceive and name as a 'thing.' When the properties are not there, the rock does not exist and there is no such concept as 'being' to be concerned about." Granting this retort for a rock, what does one say in response to a person's *self-examination?* If we simply and honestly look into our own *phenomenal* experience, what do we learn about *our* being? Is it not true that even as we grow to adulthood and change coloring, size, personal attitudes, and ambitions, we somehow sense a continuity of having-been, of being-now, and of being-in-the-future? And is there not (for some) a spiritual sense of continuing on with this identity even beyond the grave, a compulsion to feel this futurity even though we may know scientifically that it is unlikely? [58] What do we learn about *our* being? Is it not true experiences of being? Are we to dismiss them as quaint illusions, or are we to attempt an ontological study of them in their pure form?

The existentialists have obviously decided on an ontological course of study. But Binswanger and Boss do not come at this study in exactly the same way. Binswanger emphasized the ways in which phenomenal experience is made possible or *endowed* with meaning by the human being's most basic ways of looking at and thinking about it. To endow is to furnish something which in turn makes something else occur. Boss, on the other hand, emphasized the meaning *disclosed* to the human being by existence, as if it were not so much how we look at existence that matters but how existence reveals itself to us. A disclosure is an opening up or a making known. Returning to the example of phenomenally perceiving a tree, Binswanger would suggest that our phenomenal frame of reference lent (endowed) meaning to the tree, whereas Boss would say that the tree simply presented (disclosed) itself to our phenomenal awareness. This contrast in views will become clearer as we move through the more technical terms of the theories.

Turning to Binswanger first, a major structural construct employed in his version of existential analysis might be called the *a priori ontological structure.* [59] *A priori* means "coming before," and *ontological structure* refers to the kind of beginning frame of reference the person has in coming at life. Binswanger also called these basic assumptions about life *world-designs.* We say that Melissa is an optimist because she greets each day with an expectation that everything will go well. Greta, on the other hand, is called a pessimist because she always expects the worst to happen. These are the attitudes that Melissa and Greta *endow* their existence with daily—beginning assumptions of a positive or negative variety. Examples like these are rather complex and far removed from the a priori ontological structures that we all bring to bear as infants and young children. Binswanger held that we all begin very early in life making certain assumptions, given our very narrow and poorly formed understanding of things. One such example of a primitive world-design might be the belief by an infant that the world is something to be sucked and tasted, since this is the extent of his or her experience in the first weeks of life.

These a priori structures are not to be thought of as inherited ideas, nor was Binswanger interested in trying to find out how many ontological conceptions a person carries about at any one time—though he did mention this point in his theory of illness. [60] What Binswanger wanted to convey in this construct is that human beings begin to frame a matrix of meaning within which they continually know their ongoing experience.

There are various ways in which the existential analyst can come to recognize a person's most basic presumptions. "Language [that is, what a person says about life], the poetic imagination, and—above all—the dream, draw from this basic ontological structure." [61] Optimism or pessimism would surely be easy to identify in how a person speaks about life or the sorts of poetry he or she would write. Dream themes are full of such attitudes as well.

Boss was none too pleased with Binswanger's explanation of how our being-in-the-world supposedly takes place—as if it were framed in by an overriding abstraction coming before concrete experience is possible. [62] For Boss, existence is not predicated on anything; it simply happens. Being is a concrete happening that needs no preliminary structure to lend it meaning. "Fundamentally, 'being' always means 'coming forth and lasting.' How could any such coming forth and lasting be possible without a lightened realm into which this happening can take place?" [63] In other words, if we let Melissa and Greta tell us phenomenally about their lives, they will in no sense tell us about assumptions, world-designs, or ontological structures. These are conceptions that Binswanger used, but they are *not* part of the immediate experience of our two women. Melissa's life simply happens in optimistic fashion, whereas Greta's life continually discloses itself to her in pessimistic fashion.

Boss viewed life as if it were constantly emerging under the rays of a torch or flashlight, carried by the living person. The rays are actually the person's awareness of concrete experience, the structured phenomena of life. As Boss noted, "The very word 'phenomena' . . . is derived from *phainesthai,* i.e., to shine forth, to appear, unveil itself, come out of concealment or darkness." [64] Hence, for Boss, a *phenomenon* is "that which shows itself." [65] Binswanger would say that the phenomenon

is found most directly in the language expressions of an individual as a world-design. [66] There is a kind of chicken-egg problem developing here, for according to Binswanger, the world-design helps frame the meanings to follow in phenomenal experience. Boss, on the other hand, pointed out that it could well be that the world-design itself has been shown to the person out of a more primitive (original) form of being. [67]

Both men stressed the importance of *meaning* to existence. They also were in agreement that existence consists of a *being* (sein) *there* (da) that is always immediate and ongoing, a right-now happening that must be studied in its own terms and not taken out of context or otherwise contorted by theory. Hence, we can think of the *Dasein* (there-being) as being-in-the-world or existing concretely. There is also the idea here of the human being as an aspect of nature different from, for example, subhuman creatures or inanimate structures like rocks. Binswanger noted the "distinction between human existence (*Dasein*) or being-in-the-world, on the one hand, and nature on the other." [68] Boss defined *Dasein* in terms of his light analogy, which he called *lumination,* and emphasized that the there (da) of Dasein is a luminated happening. [69] We can essentially equate *lumination* with *disclosing,* as the following definition by Boss makes clear: "*Dasein,* thus being essentially and primordially of a disclosing, i.e., luminating, nature, shines forth at any given time. But—as with every kind of 'light'—its lumination varies as to color and brightness." [70]

The fact that lumination varies underscores the fact that Dasein (existence, being-in-the-world) takes on different features. Binswanger thought that Dasein is experienced in both a temporal and spatial sense. Our existence passes through time, and it extends outward in various directions. Even though we have a memory of the past, Binswanger would say that the primary emphasis in the temporalization of Dasein is on its pitch toward the future.[71] This is sometimes called *futurity* and it refers to the fact that human beings always frame their upcoming life in an intentional manner. We are not simply shaped by what has gone before. We intend that certain things come about in our lives, and then maneuver circumstances as best we can to attain our ends.

Sometimes we are unable to maneuver or otherwise change things about and hence must direct our behavior according to what already exists or must be carried out. For example, we are born into this world with certain physical equipment, into cultural environments with already established beliefs and laws. We cannot become outstanding athletes if we lack the physical stature, and it hardly seems reasonable to object to every law now on the books in our society. The existentialists would say we are *thrown* by such circumstances.[72] Related to this concept of being under the constraints of our physical and cultural heritage is the concept of *historicity*.[73] Binswanger would be more likely to use this concept, by which he would mean the world-designs and related assumptions that have been worked out and brought to life by our ancestors. Our Dasein is in this way continuous with the Dasein of our forebears. Historical precedents are thus one way of speaking about the thrownness of Dasein; there is a facticity about the history of a people which any one person born into the group must recognize and appreciate if he or she is to feel adjusted. We tend to call influences from out of our past social norms or social values, but they are in fact simply the historicized aspect of our *present* Dasein.

Dasein is at all times a gestalt totality. Boss said, "There are *myriads* of *different*

modes of human relationships and patterns of behavior toward what is encountered, all of them constituting man's *one* fundamental nature, i.e., his unique way of being-in-the-world as the disclosing, luminating realm of world-openness."[74] As a totality there is always the communal or social aspect to consider. Though we can speak of the individual's Dasein, we must not forget that an aspect of "being there" is "being with" others.[75] We are not cutting up existence into individual private worlds when we speak of the Dasein. Binswanger condsidered the Dasein to be a gestalt total consisting of three differentiated aspects or "worlds" (*welts*): (1) *eigenwelt*, the self-world of inner feelings and affections, including all of those experiences we think of as *within* our bodies; Andrew feels love or anxiety in his eigenwelt; (2) *umwelt*, the environment or world around us, including both animate and inanimate features of existence; Andrew perceives trees and city streets with people walking along them in his umwelt; and (3) *mitwelt*, the social world, the interpersonal world of people as psychological rather than physical beings, including all of those things we mean by *society;* Andrew meets others, argues, flirts, and feels an allegiance to causes in his mitwelt.[76] This last aspect of existence has been highlighted by Boss, who noted that "the world of *Dasein* is essentially *Mitwelt*."[77] We live primarily in relation to other psychological human beings.

If our Dasein is to some extent thrown by the intentions of people in earlier times (as in our legal systems, and so on), then it must be possible for us to project *possibilities* for fulfillment into our future and the future of others who come after us as well. Binswanger called this *being-able-to-be* and added that the human being achieves greatest *authenticity* through actualizing such potentials or possibilities.[78] Indeed, the very notion of temporalization—Dasein moving across time—

demands that we all try to frame and then achieve a better tomorrow. We live *inauthentically* when we are simply thrown by circumstances and do not try to improve things.[79] Thus Boss warned how easy it is for us to fall prey to the anonymous, unauthentic mentality of tradition or to the authoritarian commands of a superior in the hierarchy of social power.[80] The person who does something less than human and then says, "I was only following orders" is not excused by existentialism. There is always a dialectical interplay between the thrown features of Dasein and the possibilities open to the person in the future. It is in this future that we modify the past by which we are being thrown. The existentialists speak of *care* (caring) when they discuss the willingness a person has to commit himself or herself to change and growth by way of fulfilling possibilities.[81] It takes courage to grow, for we must *transcend* the familiar and the accepted to put ourselves at *risk* in the henceforth (future) of our life existence.

Dasein and Identity

Now that we have reviewed the nature of being and the global view of Dasein which existentialists advocate, we might ask, "Is there a concept of self or personal identity which is used to explain personality?" This question may be answered with both a no and a qualified yes. That is, strictly speaking, the existentialist, like any convinced phenomenologist, is opposed to categorizing experience according to some arbitrary preconception (see pp. 755–758). To name a self in the personality means we must speak about the self versus the environment, or the external world confronting the self. This structural split is *not* acceptable. Freud was thus taken to task by the existentialists for having split up the unity of experience into an id, ego, and superego.[82]

Technically speaking, no *formal* construct of self has been proposed by the existentialists, even though the word *per se* is used descriptively as an *identity* concept.[83] Hence, we can for the purposes of discussion use the general term *identity* to refer jointly to that aspect of Dasein that other theories mean by references to the *self, person, human being, I, Me, man, woman*, and so on. All of these words can be found in the writings of the existentialists as symbols of identity. In considering identity according to existentialism, we must also keep in mind the endowing versus disclosing distinction which Binswanger and Boss have drawn in their outlooks. Figure 26 presents a schematization of the Dasein and identity, as modified according to meaning-endowing or meaning-disclosing features of the Dasein.

Point 1 of Figure 26 is a figure-on-ground arrangement, with the global figure labeled "identity" and the entire complex (of darkened global figure and dashed-line arrows) labeled the "Dasein." It is not unusual for the existentialists to speak of the self as a form of emergent (that is, figure) on the background of the Dasein, so we begin with this tactic.[84] Assume that we think of the global-identity figure as Andrew, who confronts life daily by way of the three worlds of Dasein. Andrew cannot be passive in this confrontation. He must act, decide, and commit himself to the facticity of his existence and to the necessity of fulfilling his possibilities if he is to live authentically.

Point 2 in Figure 26 is a side view of the Dasein, with the identity portion arbitrarily pulled out away from the gestalt complex as a whole, stretching the fabric of Dasein without disturbing the totality of point 1. Once again, the *identity* aspect of Dasein is not *other than* the Dasein. Andrew is always one

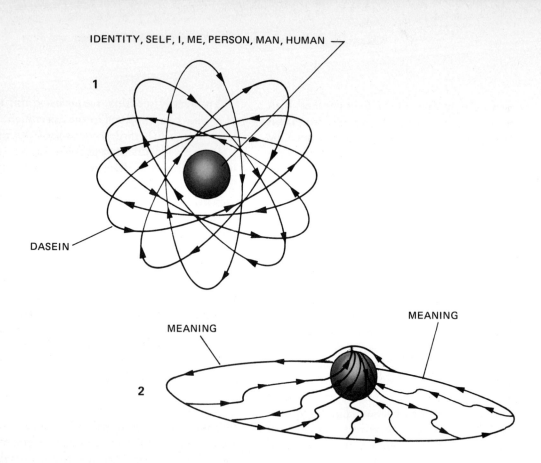

IDENTITY, SELF, I, ME, PERSON, MAN, HUMAN

1

DASEIN

2

MEANING

MEANING

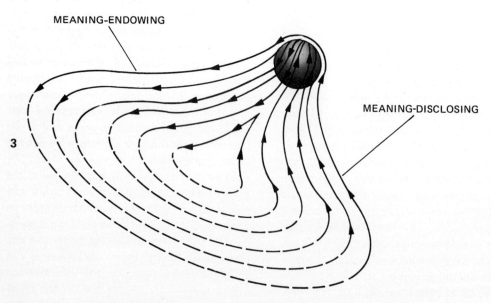

MEANING-ENDOWING

3

MEANING-DISCLOSING

Figure 26 The Dasein and Identity Terms

as a being-in-the-world. The only thing distinctive about Andrew as an identity is the fact that he is the locus of meaning relations within the differentiated eigenwelt, mitwelt, and umwelt. In other words, whether we want to say that Andrew's world-designs (assumptions) endow Dasein with meaning or the Dasein discloses meaning to Andrew, the *point* to which meaning flows or is anchored is the I, self, Me, or whatever term Andrew might use to describe his identity. We have tried to capture this idea of meaning either flowing outward from Andrew's identity or flowing inward to it by the use of several lines with arrows indicating a direction.

At point 3 we can see the different emphases placed on the role of meaning in the stretched Dasein (that is, assume we had taken hold of the identity as if it were a marble in a liquid mass and simply pulled it away from the center without removing it from the total mass, which simply stretched). Note at point 3 that the moving outward, away from identity arrows are labeled "meaning-endowing." This symbolizes Binswanger's view of the a priori ontological structures which lend meaning to the worlds of Dasein. Andrew would be sending his assumptions outward, finding always in life what his frames of reference meaningfully express. Boss, on the other hand, thought of the meanings of the Dasein as flowing inward *toward* Andrew. Thus we have labeled the arrows moving inward, toward identity as "meaning-disclosing." Rather than seeing the person as projecting subjective inner perspectives onto the world, Boss argued that: ". . . the 'essence' of a human being, as phenomenological investigations of dream phenomena have shown time after time, is of quite a different kind: man 'ex-ists' in the very literal sense of the word. He is always 'outside'; he is with the people, animals and things of the world he meets; just as a light can appear as such only through the things it happens to reveal." [85]

The concept of *lumination* is central to the differences between Binswanger and Boss on how the Dasein has meaning—whether it is endowed or disclosed. To illuminate something like the Dasein is to light it up. If we build on this metaphor of a shining light, it is possible to think of it as shining forth from one of two vantage points. We can think of it from the point of view of the source from which it is being emitted, or we can think of it from the point of view of that onto which it is being projected. We use the vantage point of the source when, after gaining a new insight on some question, we say, "Well now, that throws a new light on the matter." Our thought has shifted its stance and now endows the matter at hand with a new light. This is how Binswanger thought of lumination.[86] On the other hand, we can describe this process of acquiring a new insight in terms of being given a flash (of light) from out of the blue. Sometimes we get an "Aha, now I see the light" reaction which is like standing in a darkened region and observing the light coming toward one. This is how Boss thought of lumination.[87]

The existentialists do not accept the dichotomizing of personality into conscious and unconscious realms of behavior. This would be another one of those arbitrary distinctions on the order of dividing the person into body and mind.[88] Freud could arrive at this theory because he had an a priori view of existence as being a matter of being contained within separate, nonopen structures.[89] He did not see the person as living outwardly, in a world openness. Thus Freud could break up the gestalt totality of human experience into an unconscious person and a conscious person, since two things can be contained within one structure (the psyche).[90] The rejection of psychoanalysis on this point does not mean the existentialists deny that behaviors like those that Freud considered unconscious actually take place. For example, if a person is being thrown to some degree, we might think of these often rigid patterns of behavior as being unconscious.[91] Such a person is not directing his or her own futurity and to that extent strikes the psychoanalyst as being less conscious than another person.

Unconscious behavioral tendencies probably also stem from what the existentialists call a *constricted* (too narrow, limited) world-design or world-outlook.[82] Sometimes the existentialists speak of this constriction as the person's relying on a *key* or *key-theme* to an exaggerated extent (we are referring now to meaning-endowing themes).[93] For example, one of Binswanger's clients viewed the world as either entirely harmonious at any point in time or as on the verge of complete collapse. One day, as she was skating, the heel on her shoe gave away, and interpreting this as a collapse of her entire world, she fainted. She had relied too much on an either-or key-theme in which a moderating ontological category—for example, of the unexpected or chance event—did not exist. The cause of the fainting was not some repressed and hence unconscious conflict or wish but the even more basic factor of a constricted Dasein.

Motivational Constructs

Motivation as Thrownness, Pitch, and the Fulfilling of Possibilities

Since mind cannot be reduced to body, it follows that motivation as a human experience within Dasein cannot be reduced to physical energies or libidos. All such physical substrates to human behavior are said by the existentialists to be an aspect of the thrown-ness of Dasein.[94] They make no attempt to reduce the more psychological aspects of Dasein to such elements, although occasionally the term *energy* may be used in the sense of putting forth effort to achieve some end.[95] Boss spoke of a person's mood, passion, or affect as coloring his or her Dasein. This can alter a person's existence noticeably. Boss spoke of such moods as the *pitch* of Dasein, as follows:

An individual's pitch at a certain moment determines in advance the choice, brightness, and coloring of his relationships to the world. In a mood of hunger, for instance, he perceives totally different things than when he is in an anxious mood, or when he is in love. He also discloses quite different qualities and meaningful connections of the things he perceives in these respective moods.[96]

We do not *have* emotions any more than we *have* ideas; we *are* our emotions just as we *are* our ideas. *Emotions* therefore reflect the state of attunement, or being-in-tune with our existence as a whole; they also reflect the special manner in which we are experiencing Dasein at the moment.[97] Invariably, this means we experience emotions in relation to others in our interpersonal contacts. Boss would say our emotions present themselves to us just as anything else in the Dasein presents itself to us. We find our emotions in our interactions, in what we are doing and in what others are doing, and not in the biological processes of blood chemistry or the nervous system. Lynette feels an emotion coursing through her body, but it has meaning only because this feeling is in fact a sense of irritation with the way in which she has been treated by her parents. Without the interpersonal context (mitwelt) of Dasein, the flow of biological feeling would be dismissed as a fleeting malfunction.

The primary motivational concept used by

the existentialists stems from their view of the human being as future-oriented. As a result, it is held that we human beings are constantly drawn to the *possibilities* Dasein offers, so that we are always seeking to grow by transcending what now exists and creating a better future for ourselves as well as others. We do not have to explain Ron's current interest in entering law school and the hard work he is putting into his studies so that he might be accepted to the bar by reducing his motivation to some underlying drive. All we need know in order to understand Ron's present efforts is that he sees a career in law as a possibility, luminated in his Dasein, and he is now working to bring this possibility into facticity. This creative ability is what distinguishes the human being from the lower animal. Binswanger said, "The [subhuman] animal has its environment by the grace of nature, not by the grace of freedom to transcend the situation." [98] A person, on the other hand, can be many things—a student, marital partner, business person, artist, and so on—all in one span of time or at various times over his or her life. [99] Indeed, we human beings are probably always more "about to be" something we are not quite yet than we are anything fixed and "given." Boss reflected this emergent theme when he said, "In reality, man exists always and only as the myriads of possibilities for relating to and disclosing the living beings and things he encounters." [100]

If Dasein is thrown and assumes a pitch from time to time, how can we suggest that the human being is free to choose one manner of behavior over another? The existentialists have probably devoted more time to this question of freedom and choice than any other group of thinkers in modern times. Essentially, the answer to our question is that each person must face up to the fact that Dasein *is* thrown. This is the facticity of Dasein, and to deny it would be to deny our very existence. Our freedom begins "in the

commitment of the Dasein to its Thrownness." [101] Having accepted the facticity of Dasein's thrownness, we can then oppose ourselves to the *seeming* rigidity and fixity of the past, and, using these set ways of doing things as a point of departure, oppose ourselves to them. We can say no to certain forms of thrownness and, instead of allowing them to continue unchallenged, project a possibility that will negate them. This is effectively what happens when we challenge a law that is on the books. If the law has now been outmoded, we call for a re-examination of the grounds on which it was based and, through this *possible* basis for a change, sometimes effect a new legal statute. The civil rights changes that have come about in recent American history reflect this kind of turning the thrownness of the past into the facticity of the present by actualizing a possibility. Not all possibilities are realized, of course.

Boss emphasized that to recognize and accept the disclosed possibilities of one's Dasein and bring them to facticity in a unique and free manner is the very heart of authentic living. [102] Too many people are so invested in the views and lifestyles of others that they cannot see real possibilities for themselves. Hence, they live other people's lives, they live inauthentically! It takes courage to live authentically. The pitch of Dasein makes claims on us. We feel this way or that about what we are doing, who we are relating to, and what sort of person we are. Feeling this way, what is suggested in our mood? A change? Can we change our occupation, turn our backs or at least say no to our so-called friends, and become the sort of person that we now are not? This is the beckoning challenge of Dasein, the claim that it makes on us through suggested possibilities at every turn. And Boss concluded, "Man's option to respond to this claim or to choose not to do so seems to be the very core of human freedom." [103]

Existential versus Neurotic Forms of Anxiety and Guilt

Though the last section ends on a positive note, the truth is that not all people opt for freedom or try to transcend their current circumstances to achieve a future possibility. Even those who do can see yet another possibility that was not attempted, a further possibility beckoning from tomorrow's Dasein. In speaking about why possibilities are or are not achieved or furthered by the individual, Binswanger and Boss emphasized the concepts of anxiety and guilt, respectively, even though at a certain level, these constructs seem identical.

Binswanger thus distinguished between what he called *existential anxiety* and what we may term *neurotic anxiety*. All anxiety stems from difficulties in the world (mitwelt, umwelt, eigenwelt) as experienced by the individual.[104] Rosa is flooded with anxiety at the prospect of having now to actually take charge of her life, to leave her parental home, find a job, and seek her own circle of friends. Her world seems to have disintegrated as she now faces the prospects of living authentically for the first time in her life. This authentic living is still merely a possibility. Whether it will be actualized remains to be seen. The existentialists note that anxiety often begins with a feeling of *uncanniness,* such as when things begin happening that seem unfamiliar to our previous experience.[105] Something unnatural or weird is taking place, but we are in the dark about why this is happening. In time, our level of apprehension and confusion grows to a level of *dread*.[106] And when we fix

this dread upon something definite—we realize that our work performance may have slipped below acceptable standards—then our emotional state has moved into *fear*. Anxiety (*angst*) thus moves from an amorphous quality through uncanniness to a heightening level of dread and then into a state of fear.

How does anxiety arise in the first place? Binswanger pointed out that part of *being* in a *world* is concerned with the likelihood that this world will fade into *nothingness*. It is this basic loss of world that he calls *existential anxiety*. This form of anxiety is not an emotion, it is not felt in a heightened, tremulous state of terror with perspiring hands and quaking voice. Binswanger once described a bland, soft-spoken client of few words as "a burned-out crater" and added that this state was not a feeling or an affect: "but an expression of *existential* anxiety, that is, of the draining of the existence, and of its progressive loss of 'world.' Of course, loss of world is accompanied by loss of self. Where the existence is no longer in a position to design the world freely, it also suffers the loss of the self." [107] Existential anxiety is thus the reason why some people feel bored, empty, and void. Melanie does not seem to be suffering from anxiety, since she is constantly moping about, complaining about how bored she is. But Binswanger would say that she is actually suffering from the "nothingness of anxiety," which has petrified Melanie's Dasein, narrowing its horizons and negating all chances that she will be sensitive to the possibilities for growth in the future.[108] Recall that being and nothingness are related concepts. Hence, everyone is motivated to enrich Dasein and thereby avoid the nothingness of existential anxiety.

The other form of anxiety, which is *neurotic* in tone, is also likely to be experienced by all of us from time to time, but it is more an unpleasant sensation we usually identify as feeling uptight, jumpy, shaky, and so forth. Those individuals who develop a neurosis invariably arrive at this level of derived anxiety by way of their world-designs. A common reason for this is *constriction of world-design.* "The emptier, more simplified, and more constricted the world-design to which an existence has committed itself, the sooner will anxiety appear and the more severe will it be." [109] Healthy people have a broad-ranging world-design. If one aspect of their world does not go well, they can move on to another for they have alternatives at hand. The constricted person, however, like the young woman who fainted while skating, must surely sense a loss of world (that is, anxiety) more readily.

Although Boss referred to anxiety as a mood, or the pitch of Dasein, he developed the themes we are now considering under the construct of *guilt.* [110] That is, we can distinguish between an *existential guilt* and a *neurotic guilt* on almost the same grounds that we have distinguished between these two forms of anxiety. By existential guilt, Boss meant a primary or basic *debt* the person has, to carry out possibilities in existence that keep presenting themselves and that would allow the person to further his or her potentials, enrich life in some way, improve things, and so on. [111] If we think of all of those things that need doing in life, that have to be accomplished in order for Dasein to be enlarged and enriched in meaning-openness, then we must surely recognize that all human beings sense a basic indebtedness to their future. We feel a sense of responsibility for our futures because that is where we are always creating ourselves. Think of all those things we know —deep in our hearts—that we should have done or could have done in our past lives that would have enriched our existence today! And in the present, we know that with every act, with every choice we make, we must of necessity close out other possibilities that might be open to creation if we had chosen

them instead of the alternative we opted for. This too puts us behind the flow of events as we ponder "Have I done the right thing?"

For this reason, Boss viewed the human being's basic life situation as being one of guilt. If being and nothingness are two inevitable aspects of existence, then being and guilt are also necessary aspects. And here we can speak of the *conscience* in existentialism. "Man is aware of existential guilt when he hears the never-ending call of his conscience. This essential, inevitable being-in-debt is *guilt,* and not merely a subjective *feeling* of guilt." [112] As existential anxiety is not *simply* an emotion, existential guilt is not *simply* a feeling. We are down to the basics of existence here. Neurotic guilt, on the other hand, is a form of derived guilt in which the individual has suffered the misfortune of having been reared in a given environment. [113] This is the result of historical accident, an unlucky development which might have been otherwise in this person's life. But existential guilt is something we all *must* experience as we commit ourselves to the possibilities of our Dasein, and woe to the psychotherapist who fails to distinguish between these two fundamentally different manifestations of guilt. Neurotic guilt can sharpen and worsen existential guilt, but the reverse is not true.

Psychodynamics and the Adjustment Mechanisms

If Dasein cannot be split into conscious and unconscious regions or into the subdivisions of ids, egos, or superegos, then surely it cannot be made into a *past* which now psychodynamically influences the *present.* [114] For Boss, *defense* meant that the individual is unwilling to become aware of a certain world-relationship which is under lumination. [115]

The more Alvin tries to defend himself against the lumination in his Dasein that he is relating to others in a childish, dependent manner, the more certain it is that he will go on acting in this fashion. He really cannot escape this behavioral pattern no matter how much he looks past the lumination which is there for the seeing if he but looks. We cannot hide the real character of our behavior from its world-openness.

The theories of Freudian adjustment mechanisms all presuppose some arbitrarily reductive, divisive breakdown of existence. Take, for example, Freud's concept of *introjection.* Boss saw an entirely different phenomenon here. "Wherever so-called introjection is observed, nothing has been taken *in.* On the contrary, a human existence has not yet taken itself *out* of and freed itself from the original being-together undividedly and undiscriminatingly with somebody else." [116] Freud seemed incapable of looking directly at the phenomenal reality of experience to describe what was luminated directly. Rather than our calling something *repressed,* we would be more accurate if we said that an aspect of existence is unable to become engaged in an open, free, authentic, world-disclosing relationship. [117] A person does not *project* into Dasein, but finds there what experience means as he or she luminates existence. [118] Who is to say that a subject's Dasein is a projection of something else?

Although Binswanger agreed with Boss in this general matter of defense and so-called mechanisms of adjustment, he was more likely to use language that smacked of these meanings—often in an informal sense and occasionally with apologies. [119] So-called defenses are merely one way of speaking about world-designs. For example, if a person endows Dasein with the meanings of solid certainty versus holes of uncertainty, then he or

she might well take in meaningful patterns from others in order to fill the areas (holes) of phenomenal uncertainty. [120] Such filling-in or taking-in can be termed *introjection* or *identification* for a practical clinical purpose. [121] But we must never forget that it takes a more basic assumption (a priori structure) to be in operation before the defense mechanism is possible. Binswanger made informal references in his writings to regression, repression, and progression, each of which were interpreted differently from Freud. [122] He had rather severe reservations concerning *sublimation,* however, since it implies that something higher literally comes out of something lower—and this is essentially the reverse form of the reductive explanation that existentialism has found unsuitable. [123]

One genuine mechanism (in the sense of a stylized behavioral tactic) can be laid at the feet of the existentialists, and that is what might be termed *trusting to fate.* To believe that *fate* will somehow enter into one's existence and decide alternatives for one is an escapist device that many people use. [124] Such individuals relieve themselves of existential anxiety by saying, "Oh well, no need to feel guilty or worry about how things are going. It was my destiny to be here and you can't argue with your fate."

Time-Perspective Constructs

Dasein's Historical Development

The existentialists have not worked out a detailed scheme for the description of human development. Their feeling is that Freud and others stressed development based on biological assumptions, [125] which calls for such notions as growth, physical stages of maturation, and so on. We do not have to believe that biological forces bring about differences in life experience over time. Since Dasein is a historical totality which includes the past, present, and future (temporalization), extensions across time are to be expected in the life experience of the person. At birth, each of us is thrown into existence with certain givens, such as our sex and possible strengths or weaknesses in physical structure.[126] The first meaningful relationship established in the mitwelt is with our mothers. Children come to know existence in its fundamentals through their relation with their mothers. If she is not open and luminating—conveying love and modeling behavior for the child—then the child will be likely to frame narrow and constricted world-designs.[127]

The existentialists frankly admit that we cannot really say what the original world-designs of an individual were like, since they were preverbal. Of the earliest a priori structures of one client, Binswanger observed, "If we knew the infantile arch-form of the father theme, we would probably recognize in it the seeds of all possibilities which we found developed and utilized in the later variations."[128] This suggests that our world-designs build on each other over the years, modifying through extension but always having a common theme. The main difference from Freud here is that Binswanger would insist that we cannot find *the* meaning of today's world-designs in these earlier formulations. We cannot reduce today to yesterday, even though we can find threads of similar meanings across time. It is possible for the person to form impermeable boundaries between the eigenwelt, umwelt, and mitwelt of Dasein.[129] For example, a baby might begin sensing anxiety (uncanniness) early in life. Even though this originates in the relationship with mother (mitwelt), the child begins to separate himself or herself (eigenwelt) from the rest of world that is *not* self (umwelt) by stopping the ingestion (sucking) of milk. If the relationship in the mitwelt (with mother) does not improve, the child can become seriously ill and, even

following treatment, can retain an unnatural splitting up of Dasein into worlds that fail to influence each other with ease. The more normal developmental progression is for the eigenwelt, umwelt, and mitwelt to act as a totality and maintain an openness to each other as the child learns about these three aspects of existence over the years.

The Task of Life

If there is a central theme in the existentialist's view of what life development is all about, it is that we as individuals must advance on life actively and assume the responsibility of meeting our possibilities to enrich and extend Dasein. Each of us must attain *independence* from the thrownness of rigid nature, paternal direction, and those related social forces that take decision and choice out of our hands. The major life theme and challenge of existence is thus *dependence-independence*. Though they referred to stages merely informally,[130] ample evidence suggests that a mature-versus-immature existential life pattern[131] was being used by both Boss and Binswanger in their assessment of life's developmental aspects. Boss reflected this attitude when he observed that ". . . the child's world must die and give way to ever more grown-up ways of behavior."[132]

Major shifts in the nature of Dasein take place at important points in life. Probably the first and most general change in Dasein occurs during that period when language is being learned. The very concept of phenomena in existentialism rests upon language capacity, for as Binswanger has observed, ". . . it is in language that our world-designs actually ensconce [settle into] and articulate [clarify] themselves. . . ."[133] Of course, many thrown aspects of Dasein are already *given* in the language structure which the child is taught. Eskimo children are taught several words for *snow* that have meanings different from the one concept of *snow* that a non-Eskimo child is taught. Eskimo children therefore recognize and relate to many different nuances of snow, which is not simply one phenomenon but many. Even so, the existentialists point out that language is a preverbal possibility of Dasein, a possibility that need not be actualized, but that the infant does have open in life, for "understanding something *as* something, marking it, spotting it, denoting it, indicating it, necessarily presupposes language, even though the perceived characteristic of the thing cannot be named as yet by audibly perceptible names." [134] Hence, the existentialists would reject any suggestion that experience is the result of language or that language is "input" to make Dasein possible. Language is vital to phenomenal experience, but Dasein contains a basic and primary possibility for language expression.

Another major change (development?) in Dasein occurs at the time of school. The possibility of forming friendships increases at this point, and henceforth the mitwelt increases in importance. As we noted above, Boss liked to emphasize that *being* means primarily *being with* others, as well as things. [135] At puberty, there is a fantastic extension of horizons as Dasein holds the possibilities for sexual and love relationships. Identity problems are quite common during adolescence, and it was in this sense that Binswanger was likely to use the term *identification* to say that a meaning relation to peers is cemented during the teen-age years. [136] This gradual shift from family to complete independence is furthered over adolescence until adulthood. Adolescents have by now elaborated their world-designs and luminated existence in their own subjective fashion. So-

called fixations would represent the inability for Dasein to move forward (reminding us here of Jung's theory, see p. 211). This is called a *stuck Dasein,* in the sense that it is not moving forward to mature properly, which in turn amounts to a constriction. The Freudian Oedipal conflict is viewed as an immature pattern of a stuck Dasein, in which extreme dependency on a parent is the major feature. [137] The existentialists do not agree with the sexual interpretations of Freud. Sex is a possibility which arises at one point in life, and by adulthood a well-adjusted person has usually made his choice and acquired a sexual role. However, if an adult were to choose a life of religious celibacy, this would not necessarily mean the person had taken an abnormal course. [138] Freud greatly simplified things in his overly sexualized accounts of behavior.

The Role of Religion

Binswanger and Freud had one of their most fundamental disagreements over the human being's religious inclinations. Freud thought of religion as an adult type of dependency. People were trying to extend their paternal affections into a cosmic principle—a father in the sky. Binswanger argued that this seemed to be another one of those reductions that Freud was so fond of, reducing one thing (religion) to another (paternal fixation). Binswanger tells us of his retort to Freud.

. . . *I found myself forced to recognize in man something like a basic religious category; that, in any case, it was impossible for me to admit that "the religious" was a phenomenon that could somehow be derived from something else. (I was thinking, of course, not of the origin of a particular religion, nor even of religion in general, but of something that I have since learned to call the religious I-thou relationship).* [139]

Freud dismissed such talk as essentially an emotional and personal wish on the part of Binswanger to defend religion. Whatever the case, though existential analysis may view other behaviors as immature and dependent, the cultivation of religious I-thou unions with others and even a phenomenally sensed supreme being is *not* considered an immature adult pattern.[140]

Individual-Differences Constructs

Since the existentialists are particularly sensitive to the alienating possibilities of categories that supposedly capture why Dasein is as is, they naturally are reluctant to name a type of theorotypes. What one means by types, such as anal, oral, and so forth, is that a given and restricted world-design has taken hold of an individual.[141] Anality, for example, may be true of miserly people, compulsive people, and so forth. This world-design is probably one of viewing the world as a hole, to be filled up.[142] This filling premise makes possible the eventual clinical picture of anality, since the former preoccupation frames and hence shapes the latter. Subsequent fillings may also take place, and we may call the person a compulsive hoarder of money, affection, ideas, and so forth.

Of course, in order to apply their theories to all people, the existentialists have to generalize their concepts. We have already seen how they speak about what is essentially a dependent-versus-independent Dasein pattern in the growing child. They also speak of tradition-bound people who are thrown by the attitudes and beliefs of the inauthentic *everybody* rather than living by the authentic views peculiar to themselves.[143] We might therefore accuse the existentialists of doing precisely what they find objectionable in Freudian theory. However, the thrust of their theory is clearly to keep their general concepts

more abstract than those of classical analysis, leaving thereby a broad range of detail for the subjective description of any one person's case history. Hence, their very concept of individual differences is more individual than is the case in classical analysis.

Psychopathology and Psychotherapy

Theory of Illness

Constricted Dasein

The personality system that advances on life with only a few a priori ontological structures is most vulnerable to abnormality.[144] Dwight has grown up thinking that people are either good or bad, and that one either succeeds perfectly in what one attempts or fails completely. Given this set of life assumptions, it is no wonder that Dwight ends up one day feeling paranoid, that he experiences people as evil and desirous of making him suffer miserably. With only one or two world-designs to fall back on, our world must inevitably shrink. The more constricted it becomes, the more likely it is that a situation will arise that cannot be understood—leading in turn to that sense of uncanniness that signals the onset of anxiety (refer above). In a sense, a person with limited world-designs suffers an *unfreedom* to act, because not enough alternatives are open to him or her.[145] Dwight's problems stem from wanting things to be too perfect in life, and this is a frequent cause of difficulty for people. We tend to idealize things in our Dasein, confusing what *ought* to be in life with what *is*. This is an example of finding the eigenwelt (self beliefs) to be incompatible with the mitwelt (people's actual behavior).[146]

The constriction of Dasein also takes place across time, resulting in a temporally stuck existence.[147] Dwight's problems with others may have surfaced in his teen-age years, and now we find him at the age of thirty-five still recounting and reliving failures from his high school years. He cannot experience a sense of achievement or advance today because his world is always a replay of yesterday —again and again.[148] Rather than extending and growing, Dwight's being-in-the-world is being thrown by this replay.[149] He is not living authentically and has become totally alienated from the potentials for successful living that he once enjoyed. Former friends and associates describe him as a very disturbed, highly immature, and resentful human being. He does not know quite what to make of himself, but feels certain his problems are due to other people and not himself.

Lack of Autonomy and Independence

Dwight's beliefs about who is at fault for his miserable existence, in which he merely sits about the house and lives off his parents since being fired from his last job, is typical of the abnormal individual. If we study abnormals, we learn that they have actively surrendered themselves to the thrown aspects of existence. When things go wrong for a long period of time, an abnormal person may reject the mitwelt in preference to a fantasy life, but at least in the beginning, the abnormal adjustment accepts direction from others only too willingly. The existentialists do not blame this so much on the modeling (shaping) capacities of parents and other external influences in the child's life as they do on the individual's own actions. Dwight is the cause of his own difficulties, for, as Boss has observed: ". . . in the strict sense of the term, no event in the life history of a person can ever be the 'cause' of neurotic symptoms. Personal experiences merely initiate inhibitions against fully carrying out all possible interpersonal and interworldly relationships."[150]

This attitude places the major responsibility on Dwight's shoulders to move beyond the difficulties of his environment, where because of a harshly demanding parent, he might have indeed felt that things were either perfect or totally unworthy. But as he came to find other people having other points of view, he was not forced in any necessary way to go on limiting his Dasein to the characterizations of his parent. By constantly focusing on his past and blaming his parent for the latter's overprotectiveness and unrealistic standards, all Dwight accomplishes is further constriction, because his problem is *not* in the past but in the present and the future. Dwight has never been willing to commit himself to authentic living by first accepting responsibility for remaining where he is now at in life. For this reason the existentialists would describe Dwight as living—like all abnormal individuals—in a state of *self-chosen unfreedom*.[151]

The point of growing up is that we must learn to transcend, which includes rising above the difficult experiences of life, and to carry out our potentials by authentically committing ourselves to the new avenues the future opens up. Some people have more difficult times than others, but if we clinically examine the life histories of abnormals, we often find that they have permitted minor life setbacks to defeat them. It is the subjective interpretation of setbacks that counts, of course.[152] Dwight's serious problems began the first day of his high school attendance when he tried to have a course changed but was denied. He never got over this rebuke, as he considered it. As with most abnormals, he could never understand the grounds for this rejection, but childishly insisted in his own mind that he was being punished unfairly.[153] Often, the abnormal person is unable to accept authentic feelings when they arise. Boss once analyzed a nine-year-old boy who was terrified of police dogs and concluded that the boy "could not achieve a free relationship to his own impulsive and sensual possibilities of relating, nor to the realms of being which show themselves in the light of these possibilities."[154]

Binswanger has noted that many abnormals vary the fixing-on-fate defensive maneuver by projecting a certain amount of inauthentic futurity. Thus, through emphasis on superstition, luck, and magic, the immature person hopes to offset doom by performing some rite, saying certain words, carrying a potent charm, and so forth. Normal manifestations include knocking on wood or believing in lucky numbers or rabbit's feet, but an overreliance on such devices suggests that an *existential weakness* has developed. "By existential weakness we mean that a person does not stand autonomously in his world, that he blocks himself off from the ground of his existence, that he does not take his existence upon himself but trusts himself to alien powers, that he makes alien powers 'responsible' for his fate instead of himself."[155] The various forms of mental illness are thus extensions of a tendency to surrender the self to others, to circumstance, to a world-design that limits authentic growth.

Differential Diagnosis

Since the existentialists are critical of the classic medical model of disease as reductive, they are reluctant to diagnose their patients in the style of this model.[156] On the other hand, they do not deny the legitimacy of clinical pictures and over the years they have

offered a number of explanations of the so-called clinical entities.[157] *Symptoms* are viewed as forms of communication, announcing the existential problem in which the person feels himself or herself trapped.[158] Often the symptom is just as much a possibility as is any other form of behavior. It may offer a way out of an intolerable life circumstance.[159] By settling on a paranoid delusion, Dwight can stay in his parent's home and avoid having to face the humiliation of failing on his jobs again and again. The symptom often conceals a world-relation the individual does not wish to be open about.[160] Dwight's hostility toward his harshly dominating parent comes through as a severe stammer which he displays each time he must speak to his parent. In the final analysis, said Boss, the diagnostic picture always emerges in a *social* context. ". . . No psychopathological symptom will ever be fully and adequately understood unless it is conceived of as a disturbance in the texture of the social relationships of which a given human existence fundamentally consists, and that all psychiatric diagnoses are basically only sociological statements."[161]

The existentialists view *neurosis* as an increasingly serious constriction of Dasein with the accordingly self-surrender of autonomy and independence. This self-chosen unfreedom moves into *psychosis* when the degree of surrender is so complete the individual lives entirely within fantasy, which means that literally a "new *form* of being-in-the-world" has come about.[162] In other words, when a psychotic person *hallucinates* something that is not *there* in our Dasein, this does not mean it does not exist in his or her Dasein. We should not call these hallucinations unrealistic or figments of imagination, because to the psychotic person they are just as real as anything we consider to exist in our Dasein.[163] In most cases, a person has the hallucination because he or she is finding some reason for being thrown. Thus, a figure appears to tell the psychotic what to do and to pass judgment on these actions once they are carried out. The self-surrender of abnormality comes back in this literal form with a vengeance.

To further round out the picture, psychotics usually concoct some kind of *delusional system*. Here again, though false from our vantage point, these belief systems must be considered as genuine aspects of the Dasein within which the psychotic is living. Binswanger suggested that a delusion—especially of persecution—is always lurking somewhere in the psychotic state. Because of this central dynamic of feeling persecuted, the psychotic inevitably comes to hate those whom he or she considers to be enemies.[164] There is always a good deal of hatred in psychosis, and by so directing hatred to others, the psychotic individual can take the spotlight off his or her personal responsibility. Indeed, this is how self-identity is eventually lost in psychosis. As Binswanger noted: "Where there is delusion there can no longer be any genuine self. To speak of a 'delusional self' would be a contradiction. . . ."[165] In time, the psychotic loses all sense of distinction between inside and outside, between what he or she is as a self-identity in existence and what the world is as another aspect of that existence.[166] When this occurs, the psychotic individual has slipped completely into a thrown state. Neurotic anxiety is compounded by existential anxiety, and the future is bleak indeed.

We will next examine some of the classic clinical syndromes which the existentialists have mentioned in order to illustrate their approach to diagnosis.

Ulcer cases. The world-relation typical of an ulcer patient emphasizes seizing, overpowering, and taking possession of the environment, so that everything is robbed of its individuality.[167] The considerable concealment of this demolishing pattern among ulcer patients renders its manifestation inward. The person may appear to be unaggressive, even passive, but the somatic (bodily) realm behaves in the style that typifies the Dasein's true structure. Food is grasped, cut up by the teeth, and plunged into the stomach and intestine, where it is literally demolished by an overabundance of motility, hydrochloric (digestive) acid, pepsin, and the enzymes of the pancreas.[168] As a by-product of this world-disclosing pattern, the symptoms indicate the actual intestinal damage known as a peptic ulcer.

Hysteria. The hysterical patient is far more open and straightforward in showing a symptom of neurosis than is the ulcer case. Hysterics invariably show us an extremely immature, passive world-design.[169] Valerie smiles weakly and snuggles closer to her husband as she tells the doctor that the pain in her bowels feels as though a hot poker is being shoved right through her body. She then coughs softly and looks at her husband as a child looks at a parent. It is far more obvious in hysteria than in almost any other disorder that the patient in making physical complaints is seeking to be cared for. Usually we find, as in the case of Valerie and her husband, that the hysterical patient has formed an almost organic bond with another person —usually a parental substitute. Symptoms tend to be dramatic, including various tremors, limp extremities, even blindness. We note in these symptoms the fact that the hysteric no longer feels capable of carrying his or her Dasein forward in authentic living. A not infrequent solution for the hysteric is to suffer amnesia, which is a kind of total collapse of responsibility for the self.

Phobia. Phobias (unnatural fears) guard against an individual's losing hold of his or her world completely. As long as Luke can focus his anxiety on dirt, he can at least keep a certain order in his life as he plans his routine and maneuvers through the day, making certain he stays clear of filthy things and the germs he presumes they carry. Without this phobic concern, Luke's world would reveal its nothingness and precipitate in turn a really traumatic existential predicament.[170] Luke also uses various magical rituals and lucky charms to keep his world in order, a not infrequent accompaniment of the phobic symptom.

Sexual Abnormality. In most instances, a person with a sexual abnormality is finding it difficult to affirm and make real the possibilities that Dasein is luminating in the sexual sphere.[171] The peeper cannot participate in sex but wants desperately to observe acts of sexual copulation. It is relatively safe to observe from afar, even though a threat is posed by the fact that a law is being broken in trespassing and window peeping. The homosexual cannot give himself or herself to an opposite-sex partner; the essence of this pattern is to continue a lower level of masturbatory sexual activity by entering into a same-sex relationship. In every instance of an abnormal sexual tendency, we can find a time in development when the afflicted person did not accept the responsibility of committing himself or herself to possibilities a maturing physical status had brought.

Obsessive-Compulsive Neurosis. Obsessive individuals invariably have world-designs that are highly intellectualized.[172] That is, everything is expected to fall into line with pure, conceptual thought. Life is like a huge conceptual puzzle that does not require emotional commitment so much as accurate, logical thinking. The strategy here is clear, for the obsessive-compulsive person finds in this world-design a kind of defense against having to form close interpersonal ties in the mitwelt. People can be dealt with on an affectless plane, as if they were logical machines. The existentialists do not deny the Freudian anality tie-in to this syndrome, but they see in this relation a fear developing of one's creature, emotive, nonintellectual side. In other words, anal tendencies of neatness and precision develop because the person is denying his or her basic humanness. Just as logical machines do not produce organic waste nor invite disorder, so too the obsessive-compulsive individual likes to have a life free of human frailty, including fecal matter, filth, or disorder of *any* variety. Fearing to be quite that human, the person denies possibilities and approaches life in a more idealistic, superhuman, intellectual vein.

Schizophrenia. Binswanger called this disorder a complete "emptying of the personality."[173] The schizophrenic patient retreats from mitwelt into *autism,* so that there is a complete split with the world of others.[174] But even in this dreamlike world, the person has no true self-direction or competent identity. The delusions and hallucinations that direct the schizophrenic make his or her world a nightmare of thrownness. Binswanger pointed to two general steps in the schizophrenic process.[175] In the first phase, this person begins sensing many types of inconsistencies arising, which is due of course to the fact that he or she is not in control of life. When we allow circumstances and/or other people to direct us, it is inevitable that such inconsistencies will arise because there is no unifying point of view (world-design) to keep things flowing consistently. In the second phase of the illness, these inconsistencies are split into what is right and what is wrong, or what things are like and what things should be like. Following this split, the schizophrenic tries to attain what he or she considers right or what should be done. As these rightful "shoulds" are defined subjectively and with a poor grasp on reality, we have the seriously ill individual trying to achieve good ends which are completely bizarre from our perspective.[176] Thus we have the madman lurking about a large city, shooting people in the name of some deity in order to cleanse the world, or some such. A psychosis this dramatic is extremely rare, of course. In most cases, the schizophrenic is hospitalized without serious incident, although as the rigid and inaccurate delusional systems crumble, these individuals go through some personally difficult periods of confusion and terror.

Manic-Depressive Psychosis. The manic-depressive person jumps from one world-design to another, thrown into each one, yet never freely committed to any.[177] This is a type of inconsistency slightly different from the one experienced by the schizophrenic. The manic-depressive person seems to be on the verge of finding a perspective, a world-design that would put his or her existence into order. There are periods of clarity, and yet in each period, there seems to be another alternative suggested, so that the manic-depressive seems always to be moving between two worlds. And there are mood changes accompanying these shifts, so that we see euphoria (elation) on the one hand and melancholy (depression) on the other. The melancholy seems to come on when things projected in a state of euphoria do not work out as expected; these

possibilities are not realized because in fact the person is being thrown. At times of failure, the manic-depressive person is likely to blame others for his or her frustrations.[178] Not infrequently, those receiving the blame are the very ones who direct the abnormal person's life, but what is required is not recrimination or fault-finding. The manic depressive must begin living authentically. When he or she cannot do so, there are often severe guilt feelings, sometimes taking the form of self-destructive tendencies (suicide attempts, and so on).[179] Suicide, however, is another of those avoidant behaviors wherein, rather than solving life problems, the person is defeated most finally by them.

Theory of Cure

The Search for Authenticity and View of Insight

There are probably three points which the existentialists would make about what it means to be well-adjusted. The mentally healthy person is *free to choose* and hence transcend,[180] *mature* in outlook,[181] and *independently responsible*.[182] The goal of psychotherapy is therefore to help the unfree and childishly dependent person become a genuine human being. Boss spoke of this as a debt owed to one's existence, because in the poorly adjusted lifestyle, we have a depleted Dasein, one probably not yet bankrupt but in need of replenishment (enrichment).[183] Psychotherapy is a process of phenomenological study, helping the patient to understand his or her *present* circumstances as thoroughly and honestly as possible. Binswanger's goal as therapist was to find "the particular world-design, the being-in-it, and the being-self corresponding to it."[184] Boss was seeking the "immediately accessible essential meaning and content of all immediately perceptible phenomena."[185]

The focus of existential analysis is thus on self-understanding or insight, but this is of an immediate, current nature. "How am I existing in the present? What are my assumptions about life and how do I see them in operation 'right now'? What does my experience disclose to me if I am open and just 'let it happen'?" These are the kind of questions we would be putting to ourselves, not some far-removed obscurity like "Where are the fixation-points in my life history?" The existentialists see little use for such Freudian genetic examinations.[186] This does not mean that Boss or Binswanger would avoid going over a client's life history in therapy. They make a very thorough analysis of the client's Dasein from the earliest years, including fantasy products like favorite daydreams and so on. But what is being sought is not *the* explanation for what now exists but rather the historical grasp of Dasein. We can only understand a person's Dasein through a review of the complete historicity of the total organization of experience. In this search and review, the existential analyst always stays within the language usage of the client.[187] We want to understand things in the client's own words, so technical jargon should be avoided.

Several factors account for a cure. First of all, the person gains a more genuine perspective of his or her Dasein, knowing for the first time in life how the three worlds interrelate and summate to present possibilities for the future. This *future orientation* is important, for if the person now begins actualizing possibilities, the Dasein is more likely in time to become unstuck.[188] The therapist assists the client to begin taking charge of life (we will return to this important role in the next section). A client is not cured simply because these first steps to independence are taken, of course.[189] But this is an important beginning and we must encourage the process to continue. Binswanger

noted that we can usually count on the client's conscience for some help at this point. The client invariably feels guilty about forgoing responsibility for life and self-direction. Conscience is thus a kind of calling back to authenticity.[190]

Hence, the existentialist may not be too ready to dismiss or explain away the client's guilt feelings. As we have noted above, to feel guilt is normal. Existential guilt is a major experience of all human beings. If we now confuse this form of guilt with guilt over something far removed from the existential predicament of the present—a fixation or unresolved Oedipal complex—we effectively teach the client that he or she should *not* be feeling this guilt. It is removed from the ongoing present and cannot be relevant to what is now taking place. The existentialists feel that the Freudians arbitrarily decide on which of the phenomenal experiences to take seriously in this fashion, distorting the client's Dasein in the process. Existential analysts take *all* phenomenal experience at its face value, seeking the meaning for present existence of all moods and emotions.

As clients begin to respond to their feelings, see possibilities in their future, and make attempts to achieve these possibilities, they steadily increase their independence and sense of well-being in lifestyle. The existentialists insist that behavioral changes must take place outside of the consulting room if we are to speak of successful therapy outcomes. Merely talking about the same old life in new dynamic terminology would not impress Boss as a successful therapeutic endeavor.[191] When growth takes place in behavior outside the therapy hour—and we cannot fix a definite time period for when this will come about—existential analysis has been brought to a successful conclusion.[192]

Relationship, Transference, and Resistance

The existentialists believe that an essential ingredient in therapy is the sense of trust a patient has in his or her relationship with the therapist. Binswanger spoke of the therapist as "the post to which existence clings while adrift in the whirlpool, from whom it expects aid and protection as a sign that some inter-human relationship is still possible." [193] The severely disturbed person needs to be rescued by someone else.[194] Boss emphasized that these are *genuine* relationships between two human beings, and any love expressed by the client for the analyst is therefore "love of the analyst himself, no matter how immature and distorted it may appear because of the limitations of perception imposed on the patient by his earlier relationship to his real father." [195] In other words, existential analysis would not want to detract from the present situation by reducing it to the past experience of the client.

The existential analyst is at all times kind and reassuring, respectful of all that emerges from a client's Dasein, and above all, *permissive* in the relationship.[196] Of course, this permissiveness does not mean that the existential analyst is passive, allowing the client to direct therapy entirely to his or her whim. Permissiveness encourages clients to be open, so that now, for possibly the first time in their lives, they can live out their true being in relation to their therapists.

The existentialists accept the clinical facts of *transference* and *resistance,* but they interpret them differently from the Freudians. The client truly loves the therapist, who is after all a source of last-ditch help in meeting the client's problems. Of course, the nature of such loving may indeed be colored by the past, particularly since Dasein is stuck in the client's life pattern. As a result, we begin to see the client's love expressed as if it were still the kind of love being sent forward to a parent. But this is only because the client is immature.[197] Nothing is being transferred in this expression of love. If the therapist accepts the role of a parent and somehow—possibly through distortions in his or her own Dasein—encourages such a pattern in the client-relationship, the therapist is sure to generate hostility in the client. This is what the Freudians have done, although they mistakenly interpret this natural irritation with their method of relating to the client as *negative transference.*[198]

Boss observed that if a male analyst is aware of the childlike nature of the female neurotic's Dasein, he will never confuse the erotic demands she makes on him with "grown-up sexuality." [199] He will appreciate that these demands arise from a childlike longing to be loved and cared for as a small daughter. The therapist must appreciate that in psychotherapy clients have to at some point live out or "act out" those world-designs that are ever active in their Dasein. The existential analyst makes these known through proper interpretations and thereby encourages the client to begin advancing on life through a more appropriate world-design—which is worked out through phenomenal self-study. The therapist might say to a female client at some point, "You seem to express your love to me as if I were your father. Have you ever thought about this? Are there times, for example, when you can love other people in some other way than a daughter-father way?"

The client naturally finds it difficult to make this phenomenal study and often feels a certain degree of resentment in being encouraged to do so. Some clients are literally terrified by the threat of having to face their Dasein openly, and at this point we are likely to see signs of *resistance.*[200] It is here that the therapist must demonstrate his or her greatest compassion and skill in order to help the client overcome this resistance—that is, a flight from responsibility. The therapist encourages the client to begin in a small way, looking openly at first at the luminations of Dasein. As more confidence is achieved in this vein, the therapist can help the client set modest goals for actualizing those possibilities that have a high probability of being realized outside the consulting room in life proper. The existential analyst is completely committed to the client, even to the extent of going to the latter's home during times of crises to provide support and encouragement.[201] A classical Freudian analyst would never do this, feeling that this would suggest countertransference on the part of the therapist.

In fact, many critics of Daseinsanalysis charge that the approach formalizes countertransference into a technique of therapy. Boss rejected this criticism and observed that a decided healing agent in the relationship must necessarily be what he called *psychotherapeutic eros*. This is not like any other love relationship in human experience, not like a parental, romantic, friendship, or even a religious love for others. It has a quality completely its own. "Genuine psychotherapeutic eros . . . must be an otherwise never-practiced selflessness, self-restraint, and reverence before the partner's existence and uniqueness."[202] Therapists who cannot feel this love for certain clients should remove themselves from the case in question. Boss frankly admitted that he had done this on more than one occasion.[203]

Therapeutic Techniques

Comparison to Classical Psychoanalysis

Since Binswanger and Boss began their professional careers as orthodox Freudian-Jungian psychoanalysts, it is appropriate for us to compare their present techniques with the classical procedures from which they took leave. In the strict sense, existentialistic therapists do not like to use doctrinaire techiques, because they fear these stylized steps of how to do therapy may alienate the client from his or her true phenomenological experience.[204] For example, the methods of free association (Freud) or amplification (Jung) tend to take the client away from what is immediate or current in the Dasein to some other or earlier locus of concern, which is then said to be the important or real cause of the problems in living. This often twists a true symbolical manifestation into meaning something it does not—such as when the analyst finds sexual objects behind fantasies by waiting until the patient suggests something sexual in free association.

At the outset of therapy the client is required to be absolutely and unreservedly open in the relationship.[205] Honesty and candidness are valued in this approach as they are in classical analysis. If the patient prefers, he or she may lie down, but this position is not essential.[206] Existentialists follow most of the customary procedures of classical analysis; the therapist generally listens silently and tries to enter into the meaning-disclosing relationship of the client.[207] Free association may be used but never in a rigidly doctrinaire fashion. This is merely a convenient way in which clients can begin reviewing their world.[208] As the client goes along, the therapist may question in order to clarify; gradually the clinical history begins to take shape.[209] It is at this point that interpretation is employed to further client insight.

The point of the *interpretation* is to clarify a world-design, although it may be some time before such insights are possible. Existential analysis can take anywhere from one to five years, although presumably there are shorter contacts with some clients.[210] But when an interpretation is advanced, it may just as likely refer to the current life activity of the client as to his or her past.[211] In line with their de-emphasis of genetic explanations of neuroses, the existentialists do not feel that some *one* dynamic must be confronted with each client—like having to analyze the unresolved Oedipal conflict. Furthermore, the so-called deep interpretation is not likely to be made by an existentialist therapist, because he or she sees these depth efforts as reductive attempts. Hence, the interpretations are probably more at the level of common sense. A good example of Boss's interpretation, made to a female patient and bearing content that a classical analyst would consider Oedipal, is as follows:

Perhaps those feelings toward me that came over you, and that you had for your father in that dream, and your wish to have pretty clothes and to be attractive, are still far too big and unmanageable for you. I don't think the little girl, who you really are, can yet even begin to cope with such feelings. Perhaps it will be best if you don't do anything, or start wanting to do anything, without first asking the little girl within you if it's all right with her.[212]

This is a particularly good example because we can see the immaturity view of neurosis reflected in the little-girl reference. There is no intricate superstructure of personality theory here to bring into an interpretation. We are concerned as existentialists with the person's ever-present world, hence interpretations are made in terms of the present life setting. There is also a form of challenge put to the client to begin meeting the possibilities revealed in the Dasein.[213] Boss

observed: "The Daseinsanalyst often asks his patients, 'Why not?' thereby encouraging them to ever greater tests of daring. 'Why is it that you don't dare to behave in such-and-such a manner during the analytic session?' is a question which is often asked in place of the usual analytic 'Why?' " [214] Of course, we should not put the "why not" question to a client too early in the analysis, for this would place undue pressure on him or her to act. But it is apparent that given the great commitment they have to the client and the gentle pressure they are willing to put on their clients, the existential analysts take a highly active role in therapy.

Dream Interpretation

The existentialists make use of dream interpretation, and in fact, Boss wrote two books (1958, 1977) on the topic. Consistent with their broader view, the dream is seen as a legitimate aspect of Dasein. Binswanger viewed it as somehow entangled in the eigenwelt, reflecting a certain amount of confusion and self-forgetfulness there.[215] In our dreams we mean to act, but seem immobilized by the passing of visual events.[216] Binswanger added, "To dream means: I don't know what is happening to me." [217] Boss was critical of Binswanger on this point, feeling that he was differentiating unnecessarily between wakefulness and dreaming, and that he assigned much too passive a role to the dreamer.[218] Boss emphasized the totality of Dasein when he said, "Waking and dreaming, as but two different modes of carrying to fulfillment the one and the same historical human existence, belong fundamentally together in that one existence." [219] When we are awake, our Dasein presents itself as more alert, but otherwise there is no basic difference between being asleep and dreaming and being awake.[220]

Boss emphasized that "we *have* no dreams; we *are* our dreaming state. . . ." [221] The dream state is a completely subjective experience which can, for example, present us with new perspectives on the experience of time and space.[222] Events change rapidly, and we move backward and forward in time; there are distortions, but this does not make the dream a product of some unreal other world (Dasein). Our waking and dreaming worlds are opposite sides of the same coin.[223] We do not take dream contents and call them symbols of something else. We take them in the phenomenal reality at their own level and then explore the meaning as expressed for the individual *with* that individual.[224] Boss called this unbiased study of phenomenal reality *phenomenological observation.*[225]

For example, assume that Ivan comes to us for therapy and that in the course of treatment he tells of a dream in which his teeth are being removed or otherwise tampered with. Boss noted that Freud would have considered such a dream to be involved with masturbation—as the wish to masturbate, guilt over masturbating, or whatever.[226] Why would Freud think that teeth somehow symbolized masturbation? Because in the slang Viennese dialect of his time, to "rip one out" (as a tooth) referred to onanism (penis removed before ejaculation during intercourse) or to masturbation.[227] Boss showed how Freud's interpretation completely overlooked the fact that teeth *actually* serve us in the realm of seizing, gripping, capturing, assimilating, and gaining power over things. The existentialistic therapist would never limit himself or herself to the single and clearly arbitrary symbolic interpretation of the Freudian analyst. To be fair to the Freudians, we are not entirely certain an analyst would be this routine in making interpretations today, either. But Boss was addressing Freud's writings, and his main point was that when something appears in a dream, we should consider it more openly than he felt Freud did. Freud seemed to Boss to have been more

interested in advancing a theory than in observing and capturing the phenomenal truth.

Boss distinguished between objective and subjective dream interpretation.[228] Freud approached the dream objectively, hoping to isolate a theme common to all dreamers. Hence, if Ivan went on from his teeth dreams to dream that he was plowing a field, Freud's sexual bias would suggest ipso facto that the plow was really a penis and the furrow it parted was really a vagina.[229] Once again, Freud would be overlooking relevant alternative interpretations, such as that it might reflect a prompting to pick up life again, to forge ahead and break new ground by meeting responsibilities and affirming possibilities, no matter how much effort might be required. Boss said that *dream interpretation* comes down to two main questions.[230] First, to what phenomenon is the person's Dasein sufficiently open, so that it shines forth in the dreaming state? Second, upon awakening, can the person recognize features in existence that are identical in essence with the dream phenomena? In drawing the latter parallels, Boss referred to this as *explication.*[231] To explicate is thus to enlarge on the meanings of dreams, relating them to the Dasein as a whole—including the waking state. Thus, Boss would ask Ivan if he could see any parallel in his current life situation with the theme of plowing through or forging ahead? He would refrain from *telling* Ivan what the dream meant and always phrase his statements as questions. This would ensure that Ivan would not be put in the role of a subordinate or infant, and that he would feel free to agree with the thrust of a question or not.[232]

Most of what Freud and Jung called *symbols* Boss would view as reflections of the luminating Dasein, visual contents reflecting a given world-design. For example, a person might dream that he or she was a thing, rather than a person. This would suggest existentially that the person was being made aware of a certain inability to act or commit in the waking state.[233] The dream would suggest that the person was an inanimate, inert something rather than a human being. The terror dreams of children often involve wild animals or strange creatures. We can view these existentially as fearful reactions to certain newly discovered sensuous or hostile possibilities that the child is just becoming aware of. As such, the strange creatures do not symbolize anything needing covering up. The creatures rather capture precisely what is going on in the conscious aspect of Dasein. A man dreams that he sees his brother lying dead in a casket, having been killed in a traffic accident. Boss would interpret this *not* as a covert (hidden) death wish for a sibling but as the projected softer, loving side of life, a side this man had been turning his back on in his egotistical devotion to business matters.[234] The dream is telling him that he is killing off his humane side in the vain pursuit of material wealth.

Note the uncomplicated approach to dream interpretation here. There is no claim made of a dream censor, distorting what is into what is not.[235] Dreams merely supplement the rest of our experience. In a true sense, they alert us to possibilities developing in life.[236] This is where their use in therapy is particularly relevant. We can, as existential therapists, base our "why not?" questions to the client on material and behavioral directions suggested by dreams. The person's childishness can be brought out in a dream,[237] but also the person's better side can be suggested in the dream content.[238] By discussing the dream content and drawing implications therefrom,

existential analysts can usually find something vitally meaningful to their clients from which to begin a new approach on life.

Summary

Chapter 10 begins with a survey of the major themes that have issued from the philosophy of existentialism: alienation, authenticity, subject versus object, commitment, action, anxiety, dread, despair, and absurdity. Philosophers who have been important in this school of thought include Kierkegaard, Nietzsche, Jaspers, Heidegger, Sartre, and Marcel. In recent times, the themes of existentialism have been paralleled with similar concepts in Oriental philosophy, and Chapter 10 reviews in broad outline the essentials of this Eastern outlook. Beginning in ancient Hinduism and extending into Buddhism—particularly Zen Buddhism—these concepts of living in unity with nature have enjoyed great popularity along with existentialism. It would not be incorrect to say that the second half of the twentieth century has been an age of existentialism, providing that we understand the parallels across Western and Eastern philosophies.

The two personologists discussed in Chapter 10—Boss and Binswanger—have both drawn from the writings of Heidegger. Their approach is based on a study of being, or as it is called, ontology. The German word *Dasein* has the meaning of "being there," hence analysis of immediate experience is what Daseinsanalysis attempts to do. Existential analysis (Daseinsanalysis) focuses on the phenomenal experience of a person as it is immediately experienced. Binswanger stressed the way in which phenomenal experience is *endowed* with meaning by the human being's most basic ways of looking at and thinking about existence. Boss, on the other hand, emphasized the meaning *disclosed* to the human being *by* existence, as if it were not so much how we look at existence that matters but how existence luminates or reveals itself to us.

Binswanger viewed the person as bringing to bear certain a priori ontological structures, or world-designs, which function at the phenomenal level and make experience what it *is* to the individual. These phenomenal frames are what endow Dasein with meaning. Boss, on the other hand, felt that Dasein is not framed by a priori structures, but rather shines forth or luminates the phenomenal realm with meaning. Dasein was said by both Boss and Binswanger to be pitched toward the future. There is also a historicity to Dasein, a past that reflects the commitments and actions of earlier human beings who have pitched their Dasein into their futures and in the process thrown the current Dasein of people in one direction rather than another. Binswanger distinguished three worlds (welts) in the totality of Dasein: (1) the eigenwelt, or world of inner feelings and affections; (2) the umwelt, or the physical environment around us, including both animate and inanimate things; and (3) the mitwelt, or the social world of people, including all those things we mean by society.

To avoid being completely (100 percent) thrown by the intentions of others, we must behave authentically, assume responsibility for our commitments, and exhibit care in furthering the possibilities that come up in the futurity of our lives. We must occasionally transcend the familiar and routine ways of doing things and put ourselves at risk by making new commitments. Though there is no formal *self* concept in existentialistic personality theory, there is an emphasis on the identity of the person, who comes at life phenomenally and opens it up to alternative possibilities. If this is not done, the Dasein can constrict. Emotions reflect the unique

pitch of Dasein that a person may experience at any point in time. Binswanger discussed the difference between existential anxiety and neurotic anxiety. The former is a sense of alienation, a loss of world that might be captured in the idea of nothingness. It can be experienced as boredom and emptiness. Neurotic anxiety stems more from a constricted world-design, a simplistic and unrealistic framing of the world which makes the person vulnerable to collapse in the face of a challenge.

Boss makes a comparable distinction between two kinds of guilt. Existential guilt arises from the basic sense of indebtedness that the person bears, since it is not possible to fulfill every option in life. Affirming one alternative, we forgo many others. This kind of guilt is borne by all of us, and it reflects a realistic assessment of existence. Our conscience prompts such existential guilt, and this is not a sickness as Freud sometimes made it appear to be. Neurotic guilt, on the other hand, is the result of having been reared in an unhealthy environment. Commitment always brings about existential guilt of one sort or another. But neurotic guilt can spring from a lack of commitment, or it can sharpen the pain of existential guilt. Even so, we should keep these two types of anxiety and/or guilt separate. Psychotherapy aims at removing the neurotic forms but not the existential forms of anxiety and/or guilt.

Rather than speak of repression, the existentialists suggest that an aspect of Dasein has remained closed and inauthentic. Most of Freud's defense mechanisms are said to be due to underlying world-designs (Binswanger) or inauthenticity (Boss). The existentialists criticize both psychoanalysis and behaviorism for attempting to reduce the Dasein to something else. Rather than taking Dasein as it is, these schools of therapy reduced it to underlying S-R units, or place it under the compulsion of repeating what has gone before. One genuine defense mechanism the existentialists might be said to recognize involves trusting to fate. To believe that fate will somehow enter into one's existence and decide alternatives is an escapist device which ultimately denies authentic living. The existentialists do not accept clear-cut stages in life, but they do recognize that Dasein always has an historical development. The task of life is essentially to gain one's independence from the thrownness of others—or at least reduce the extent of such dependency. If the Dasein does not move forward and become enriched in maturing, the existentialists speak of a stuck Dasein, much in the vein of the Jungian conception. The existentialists are also much more accepting of a role for religion in the life of people. The existentialists do not wish to categorize people into typologies, but take a very individualized view of each personality as a unique product of the identity concerned. To be overly tradition-bound is to live an inauthentic life of "everybody."

The theory of illness employed in existentialism follows the themes of a constricted Dasein, a stuck Dasein, or the self-chosen unfreedom leading to a kind of existential weakness for the individual, which then collapses altogether. Neurotics are people who have created their own seriously constricted Dasein, surrendering their autonomy to others and eventually paying the price of inauthenticity. Psychotics in their delusions and hallucinations reflect a completely new form of being-in-the-world, one in which supposed, independent forces taunt, threaten, and then actually direct what will take place. Each of the classic syndromes—ulcer cases, hysterias, phobias, sexual abnormalities, obsessive-compulsives, schizophrenias, and manic-depressives—reflect their own unique form of this existential weakness and constricted Dasein. It is not the specific diagnosis that is important, but an historical understanding of the unique Dasein framed by or illuminated to the identity concerned.

The mentally healthy person is said to be free to choose, hence transcend the given of life to affirm possibilities, assume a mature outlook, and be independently responsible. Daseinsanalysis is an insight therapy which seeks to aid a person to achieve these three broad goals in life. The future is stressed because the person must let the past stand and begin building a better life in the henceforth. It is important for the client to trust the therapist, and existentialistic therapists take quite an active role in the establishment of a genuine, permissive relationship. Boss felt that an important healing agent in the relationship is psychotherapeutic eros, that is, a unique kind of selfless reverence for the client's existence and uniqueness. We are reminded of Rogerian writings at this point. If the therapist cannot feel this commitment for the client, he or she should discontinue the therapy contact. Though something like positive or negative transference arises in therapy, the existentialists refuse to accept this as the literal transferring of anything. There is either some immature, groping attempt to cement a bond to the therapist (positive transference), or probably there is a well-deserved feeling of irritation for the fruitless procedure (negative transference) of observation and misinterpretation by the psychoanalysts. Resistance is a flight from responsibility and not some kind of interpersonal warfare waged by the client against the therapist.

The existentialists follow most of the techniques used by the psychoanalysts, though they naturally give dreams and free associations a completely different kind of interpretation. Interpretations are aimed at clarifying the world-design predicating the person's phenomenal experience. Many of these interpretations bring out the stuck Dasein, the unwillingness people have to mature and assume responsibility in life. Boss referred to the study of dreams as phenomenological observation, which means that he tried to understand the dream at its own level, rather than making it fit some preconceived scheme. In a manner similar to Jung, the existentialists reject Freud's manifest-versus-latent-content theory of dream formation. A dream presents an aspect of the Dasein to us as framed by the dreamer; it reflects his or her unique situation at the time. Another term used in the description of dream analysis is *explication*.

Outline of Important Theoretical Constructs

Existential philosophy
  being · ontology · existence

Alienation

Authenticity
  guilt · Dasein · being oneself

Subject versus object
  object · subject · being-there · nothingness

Commitment, action
  activity, action, to act · commitment · bad faith · choice in non-choice

Anxiety, dread, despair

Absurd

Existential themes in Oriental philosophy

The quest for unity
  Brahma · Buddha · negation · nirvana · meditation · enlightenment · yin-yang principle · *Tao Te Ching* · tao · koan

· perfect enlightenment · non-attachment

Psychotherapy and Zen Buddhism
  re-evaluation of life · thinking, not-thinking, and non-thinking · transcendental meditation · mantra · mandala

Existentialism as a theory of personality and psychotherapy: Binswanger and Boss

Biographical overview
  Daseinsanalyse or *Daseinsanalysis*

Personality theory

Structural constructs

The centrality of phenomenal meaning for the person as a body-mind gestalt
  being · ontology · subject versus object · meaning · facticity

Existence, being-in-the-world, and Dasein as endowed or disclosed
  existence = being-in-the-world = Dasein · phenomenal self-examination · endowed phenomenal experience · disclosed phenomenal experience · a priori ontological structure · world design · lumination of Dasein · futurity · thrown, thrownness · historicity · eigenwelt, umwelt, and mitwelt · possibilities · being-able-to-be · authenticity versus inauthenticity · care · transcendence · risk

Dasein and identity
  identity · constricted Dasein · key, key themes

Motivational constructs

Motivation as thrownness, pitch, and the fulfilling of possibilities
  pitch · emotion(s)

Existential versus neurotic forms of anxiety and guilt
existential anxiety · neurotic anxiety · uncanniness · dread · fear · angst (anxiety) · nothingness · constriction of world-design · existential guilt · neurotic guilt · conscience

Psychodynamics and the adjustment mechanisms
introjection · repression · projection · identification · sublimation · trusting to fate

Time perspective constructs

Dasein's historical development

The task of life
dependence versus independence · stuck Dasein

The role of religion

Individual differences constructs everybody

Psychopathology and psychotherapy

Theory of illness

Constricted Dasein
unfreedom

Lack of autonomy and independence
self-chosen unfreedom · existential weakness

Differential diagnosis
symptoms · neurosis · psychosis · hallucination · ulcer cases · hysteria · phobia · sexual abnormality · obsessive-compulsive neurosis · schizophrenia · autism · manic-depressive psychosis

Theory of cure

The search for authenticity and view of insight

free to choose · mature outlook · independently responsible · future orientation

Relationship, transference, and resistance
genuineness · permissiveness · transference · resistance · negative transference · psychological eros

Therapeutic techniques

Comparison to classical psychoanalysis
interpretation

Dream interpretation
phenomenological observation · dream interpretation · explication · symbol(s)

Notes

1. Heinemann, 1958, p. 10. **2.** Kaufmann, 1956, p. 70. **3.** Blackham, 1959, p. 93. **4.** Ibid., p. 143. **5.** Heinemann, 1958, p. 35. **6.** Kaufmann, 1956, p. 213. **7.** Heinemann, 1958, p. 64. **8.** Ibid., p. 91. **9.** Blackham, 1959, p. 98. **10.** Heinemann, 1958, p. 36. **11.** Blackham, 1959, p. 9. **12.** Heinemann, 1958, p. 65. **13.** Blackham, 1959, p. 19. **14.** Heinemann, 1958, p. 39. **15.** Kaufmann, 1956, p. 203. **16.** Blackham, 1959, p. 58. **17.** Ibid., p. 91. **18.** Sartre, 1956, p. 48. **19.** Heinemann, 1958, pp. 36–37. **20.** Kaufmann, 1956, p. 163. **21.** Heinemann, 1958, p. 98. **22.** Ibid., p. 43. **23.** Ibid., p. 116. **24.** Nakamura, 1964. **25.** Raju, 1967, p. 44. **26.** Saksena, 1967, p. 31. **27.** Moore, 1967a, p. 14. **28.** Takakusu, 1967, p. 113. **29.** Datta, 1967, pp. 129–130. **30.** Nikhilananda, 1967, p. 147. **31.** Kuo, 1976. **32.** Watts, 1957. **33.** Plato, 1952. **34.** Suzuki, 1962, p. 40. **35.** Ibid., p. 84. **36.** Fromm, Suzuki, & DeMartino, 1960. **37.** Kasulis, 1977. **38.** Ibid., p. 71. **39.** Ibid., p. 69. **40.** Ibid., p. 88. **41.** See Freud, 1960, p. 286. **42.** Binswanger, 1963, pp. 149–181. **43.** See Freud, 1960, p. 431. **44.** Binswanger, 1957. **45.** See Boss, 1958, p. 10. **46.** Binswanger, 1958, p. 231. **47.** Binswanger, 1963, p. 209. **48.** Binswanger, 1958, p. 200. **49.** Ibid., p. 193. **50.** Boss, 1958, p. 51. **51.** Boss, 1963, p. 82. **52.** Ibid., p. 83. **53.** Binswanger, 1963, p. 114. **54.** Boss, 1963, p. 140. **55.** Binswanger, 1963, p. 99; Boss, 1963, p. 230. **56.** See Rychlak, 1968, pp. 286–287. **57.** Boss, 1963, p. 36. **58.** Binswanger, 1963, pp. 2, 183. **59.** Ibid., p. 250. **60.** Ibid., p. 119.

Ibid., p. 41. **64.** Ibid., p. 28. **65.** Ibid., p. 70. **66.** Binswanger, 1958, p. 200. **67.** Boss, 1963, p. 218. **68.** Binswanger, 1958, p. 232. **69.** Boss, 1963, p. 39. **70.** Ibid., p. 183. **71.** Binswanger, 1963, pp. 5–6. **72.** Ibid., pp. 130–131. **73.** Ibid., p. 174. **74.** Boss, 1963, p. 233. **75.** Ibid., p. 55. **76.** Binswanger, 1958, p. 224; 1963, p. 72. **77.** Boss, 1963, p. 55. **78.** Binswanger, 1958, p. 303. **79.** Binswanger, 1963, p. 116. **80.** Boss, 1963, p. 68. **81.** Binswanger, 1963, p. 213; Boss, 1963, p. 45. **82.** Binswanger, 1963, p. 171. **83.** Ibid., p. 67. **84.** Ibid., p. 100. **85.** Boss, 1958, p. 183. **86.** Binswanger, 1963, p. 174. **87.** Boss, 1958, p. 108. **88.** Boss, 1963, p. 89. **89.** Ibid., p. 92. **90.** Binswanger, 1958, p. 326.. **91.** Binswanger, 1963, p. 219. **92.** Ibid., p. 31. **93.** Binswanger, 1958, p. 223. **94.** Binswanger, 1963, pp. 99, 311. **95.** Ibid., p. 117. **96.** Boss, 1963, p. 41. **97.** Ibid., pp. 113–114. **98.** Binswanger, 1958, p. 198. **99.** Ibid., pp. 197–198. **100.** Boss, 1963, pp. 182–183. **101.** Binswanger, 1963, p. 116. **102.** Boss, 1963, p. 47. **103.** Ibid., p. 271. **104.** Binswanger, 1958, p. 205. **105.** Ibid., p. 280; Boss, 1963, p. 121. **106.** Binswanger, 1958, p. 280. **107.** Binswanger, 1963, p. 337. **108.** Ibid., p. 299. **109.** Ibid., p. 112. **110.** Boss, 1963, p. 100. **111.** Ibid., p. 270. **112.** Ibid. **113.** Ibid., p. 271. **114.** Ibid., p. 108. **115.** Ibid., p. 97. **116.** Ibid., p. 127. **117.** Ibid., p. 120. **118.** Ibid., p. 126. **119.** See, e.g., Binswanger, 1963, p. 250. **120.** Ibid., p. 323. **121.** Binswanger, 1958, pp. 280–281. **122.** Binswanger, 1963, pp. 250, 321, 324. **123.** Ibid., p. 175. **124.** Ibid., p. 300. **125.** Ibid., p. 196. **126.** Binswanger, 1958, p. 271. **127.** Boss, 1963, p. 35. **128.** Binswanger, 1958, p. 225. **129.** Ibid., p. 270. **130.** See Boss, 1963, p. 250. **131.** Ibid., p. 126. **132.** Ibid., p. 266. **133.** Binswanger, 1958, p. 200. **134.** Boss, 1963, p. 215. **135.** Ibid., p. 245. **136.** Binswanger, 1958, pp. 280–281. **137.** Boss, 1963, p. 200. **138.** Binswanger, 1963, p. 183. **139.** Ibid. **140.** See Boss, 1963, p. 260. **141.** Binswanger, 1958, p. 318. **142.** Ibid., pp. 218, 310. **143.** Boss, 1963, p. 96. **144.** Binswanger, 1963, p. 112. **149.** Binswanger, 1958, p. 194. **146.** Binswanger, 1963, p. 254. **147.** Ibid., p. 116. **148.** Boss, 1963, p. 178. **149.** Binswanger, 1963, p. 115. **150.** Boss, 1963, p. 248. **151.** Binswanger, 1963, p. 118. **152.** Boss, 1963, p. 173. **153.** Ibid., p. 242. **154.** Ibid., p. 179. **155.** Binswanger, 1963, p. 290. **156.** Binswanger, 1958, p. 230. **157.** Ibid., pp. 330–331. **158.** Ibid., p. 213. **159.** Binswanger, 1963, p. 260. **160.** Boss, 1963, p. 145. **161.** Ibid., p. 56. **162.** Binswanger, 1958, p. 201. **163.** Boss, 1963, p. 85. **164.** Binswanger, 1963, pp. 263–264. **165.** Ibid., p. 336. **166.** Ibid., p. 311. **167.** Boss, 1963, p. 144. **168.** Ibid. **169.** Ibid., pp. 143–145. **170.**

Binswanger, 1958, p. 205. **171.** Boss, 1963, p. 186. **172.** Ibid., p. 183. **173.** Binswanger, 1958, p. 363. **174.** Binswanger, 1963, p. 288. **175.** Ibid., pp. 252–254. **176.** Ibid., p. 254. **177.** Ibid., p. 143. **178.** Boss, 1963, p. 209. **179.** Ibid., p. 210. **180.** Binswanger, 1963, p. 218. **181.** Boss, 1963, p. 160. **182.** Ibid., p. 210. **183.** Ibid., p. 271. **184.** Binswanger, 1958, p. 327. **185.** Boss, 1963, p. 285. **186.** Binswanger, 1958, pp. 334–335. **187.** Ibid., p. 330. **188.** Ibid., p. 295. **189.** Ibid., pp. 224–225. **190.** Binswanger, 1963, p. 318. **191.** Boss, 1963, p. 254. **192.** Ibid., p. 210. **193.** Binswanger, 1963, p. 292. **194.** Ibid., p. 348. **195.** Boss, 1963, p. 125. **196.** Ibid., pp. 198, 234, 253. **197.** Ibid., p. 124. **198.** Ibid., p. 240. **199.** Ibid., p. 258. **200.** Ibid., pp. 79, 150. **201.** Ibid., p. 20. **202.** Ibid., p. 259. **203.** Ibid., p. 260. **204.** Boss, 1958, p. 119. **205.** Boss, 1963, p. 19. **206.** Ibid., p. 62. **207.** Ibid., pp. 61–64. **208.** Ibid., p. 192. **209.** Ibid. **210.** See Binswanger, 1963, p. 272; Boss, 1963, p. 147. **211.** Binswanger, 1963, p. 30. **212.** Boss, 1963, p. 22. **213.** Ibid., p. 196. **214.** Ibid., p. 248. **215.** Binswanger, 1963, p. 231. **216.** Ibid., p. 319. **217.** Ibid., p. 247. **218.** Boss, 1958, p. 129. **219.** Boss, 1977, p. 190. **220.** Ibid. **221.** Boss, 1963, p. 261. **222.** Boss, 1958, pp. 47, 89. **223.** Ibid., pp. 80, 127. **224.** Ibid., p. 158. **225.** Boss, 1977, p. 141. **226.** Ibid., p. 226. **227.** Ibid. **228.** Boss, 1958, p. 120. **229.** Ibid., p. 158. **230.** Boss, 1977, pp. 26–27. **231.** Ibid., p. 32. **232.** Ibid. **233.** Boss, 1958, pp. 155–156. **234.** Boss, 1963, p. 265. **235.** Boss, 1958, p. 103. **236.** Ibid., p. 130. **237.** Boss, 1963, p. 200. **238.** Ibid., p. 204.

Chapter 11

Two Kinds of Constructive Theories: Jean Piaget and George A. Kelly

We depart from our usual organization in Chapter 11, because in this instance, we will be reviewing the theory of Jean Piaget, which is *not* specifically aimed at abnormal behavior or psychotherapy. There are two reasons for taking up Piaget even though he is not a psychotherapist. First, his theory has become increasingly important in recent years and many personologists feel that it should be considered by everyone concerned with human behavior, whether engaged in psychotherapy or not. Second, and more germane to our purposes, Piaget has helped to popularize the widely used term *construction,* a term also used, but in a different sense, by the second theorist of this chapter, George A. Kelly. Because Kelly was a psychotherapist-personologist of wide influence, it is important to clarify the meanings employed in these related but still different theories of human behavior.

The Evolutionary Rationalism of Jean Piaget

Jean Piaget considered himself a scientist engaged in the study of *genetic epistemology,* which has to do with "both the formation and the meaning of knowledge."[1] We will return to this phrase below, after first familiarizing ourselves with some basic Piagetian terminology. Because of the central role he assigns to evolution in his concept of development, and because of his great emphasis on the developmental stability (he called this *equilibrium*) of higher-level cognitive conceptions, we have chosen to characterize Piaget's theory as *evolutionary rationalism*. This meaning will be clarified as we move through Piaget's thought.

In a sense, Piaget is to the phenomenological-existentialistic school of thought (see Chapters 9 and 10) what Bandura (see Chapter 7) is to the behavioristic school of thought. That is, Piaget has tried to be comprehensive in his explanations of human behavior; in doing so he rivals Bandura's eclecticism. However, where we saw Bandura uniting behavioristic with cognitive terminology having less of a mechanistic sound to it (see p. 487), we will find Piaget moving in the reverse direction, so that his fundamentally nonmechanistic theory embraces terminology taken from cybernetics; he is willing to draw parallels between his explanations and those of clearly mechanistic theorists.[2] Even so, Piaget is a decidedly individualistic theoretician who has much to say about human behavior that is unique.

Biographical Overview

Jean Piaget was born on 9 August 1896 at Neuchâtel, Switzerland and died on 16 September 1980 at Geneva. His father, a teacher and scholar of medieval literature, set the pattern for Piaget's own lifestyle in which a devotion to the study of factual matters is uppermost. Piaget tells us that he has always "detested any departure from reality,"[3] and this attitude takes on even greater significance when we realize that his mother apparently suffered from pronounced neurotic tendencies. For a time his mother's maladjustments spurred an interest in psychoanalysis and abnormal psychology, but after he had achieved independence from his parents, Piaget lost all interest in such topics, preferring, as he tells us, "the study of normality and of the workings of the intellect to that of the tricks of the unconscious."[4] Piaget was a child prodigy. At the age of ten, he submitted a one-page article on the albino sparrow to a journal of natural history, and it was accepted for publication. He then obtained permission to study after hours at the museum of natural history in Neuchâtel, specializing eventually in land and soft-water shells. He was on his way to becoming a naturalist and almost all of his free time was spent in collecting mollusks.

Piaget continued to publish in natural history throughout his teen years, and an amusing outcome of his growing reputation in the scientific literature was that he received a letter offering him a position as curator of a mollusk collection in another town while he was still in secondary (high) school. Piaget experienced his share of the usual problems confronting adolescents, especially those having to do with religion. He was given a traditional education in this regard, but eventually he worked free of religious dogma, preferring a completely scientific outlook. In his mid-teen years, an uncle, worried about Piaget's narrow interests in mollusks, encouraged him to read Henri Bergson, the philosopher who espoused creative evolution. The basic idea here is that evolution is not

Jean Piaget

merely a series of static structures that are fixed like so many points along the way, but involves also a flow of change between such points which must be given proper consideration and emphasis. Organisms that exist in nature are living beings in a *constant* state of change, a creative motion which is just as much a part of their total being as the part-structures that evolve. Piaget was impressed by this idea, but he also felt that Bergson failed to provide an experimental basis for his theories, and therefore, they were open to easy rejection.

After he had taken the baccalaureate degree in 1915, Piaget threw himself into the reading of a broad range of scholars, including Kant, Spencer, Comte, Fouillée, Lachelier, Boutroux, Lalande, Durkheim, Tarde,

Le Dantec, James, Ribot, and Janet. An important teacher of this period was A. Reymond, a logician who introduced Piaget to the study of psychology and scientific methodology. Piaget learned from Reymond that "logic stems from a sort of spontaneous organization of acts."[5] This idea of an organization of acts into logic would combine with the Bergsonian conception of evolution as a dynamic, creative movement and remain with Piaget forever after. We will see its mature development in Piaget's conception of increasing stages of equilibration in development, culminating in the stability of mathematical formulations (refer below).

In 1918 Piaget took his doctoral degree from the University of Neuchâtel, with a dissertation on the mollusks of Valais. He had by this time acquired an interest in psychology, which promised to combine his biological and philosophical interests. He went to Zurich hoping to work in a psychology laboratory, but found nothing satisfactory. In the autumn of 1919 he went to Paris, where he was to spend two years studying pathological psychology at the Sorbonne. Piaget learned to interview mental patients here, which was important to his later work, because he always considered his research style to be an adaptation of the clinical method.[6] He also studied more philosophy of science and was notably influenced by the historical-critical method of Brunschwieg. This is important to our understanding of Piaget, for in his subsequent approach to the study of genetics, we have more than biology reflected, we have a decidedly historical interpretation of development being employed as well.[7]

His career as genetic epistemologist really began when Piaget was asked to standardize some reasoning tests on Parisian children. He was given the right to use Alfred Binet's laboratory at the grade school of the rue de la Grangeaux-Belles in Paris. Binet, who was then deceased, had achieved fame for devising the first effective means of assessing intelligence through the use of (IQ) tests. Rather than simply standardizing the reasoning test he was given, Piaget engaged the children in discussions patterned after the psychiatric questioning he had learned in the clinical method. He found that children up to the age of eleven or twelve have difficulties unsuspected by the adult in identifying such things as the part common to two wholes. For the next few years, he continued his study of both normal and abnormal children, which in time convinced him that here was that method of studying developmental-evolutionary processes that he had found wanting in Bergson. He could actually study the laws of mental development empirically. For example, he found that logic is not inborn but rather develops little by little over the childhood years. Concepts of cause-effect are not understood by children until they have reached a certain stage of development. Piaget interpreted this development as an evolution of mental structures. In a sense, he found himself studying an "embryology of intelligence."[8]

The next career move by Piaget established him professionally and fixed his life's course thereafter. In 1921 he was offered and accepted the position of director of studies at the Institut J. J. Rousseau of Geneva. His responsibilities involved guiding and associating with students working on advanced degrees, including the direction of their work on studies of Piaget's choosing. Piaget had by now decided to study the development of thought for itself, using his new interview method which would take him in directions he could not necessarily predict but was willing to follow. He and his students did their work at the primary school of the Rousseau institute and the local public schools. The data on which his first five books were based issued from this extensive research effort. One of the graduate students at the Institut Rousseau was Valentine Châtenay, who was to become Piaget's wife and coworker.

Piaget's thesis that logic follows a genesis, an evolution over the years of maturation in childhood, found immediate popularity among scholars all over the world. He was widely read and invited to many different countries where he presented his researches and theories of development. As the years passed, Piaget broadened the scope of his investigations, studying not only language and the verbal expression of ideas but the manipulations and experiences young children have with objects even before they have learned their native tongues. He also worked to perfect his theoretical formulations, noting in later years that sometimes his colleagues took more interest in his empirical findings on the stages of development than they did in the basic theory on which the researches were based.[9] This is a distinctive characteristic of Jean Piaget—a desire to advance *theory* as well as *method* (empirical research findings). We will in this chapter emphasize his theory and deal in less detailed fashion than is customary in books on Piaget with his developmental studies per se.

In 1925 his former teacher, A. Reymond, vacated the chair of philosophy at the University of Neuchâtel, and Piaget was given a portion of this appointment. Later he was appointed to the science faculty of the University of Geneva, where he taught child psychology. Piaget has also taught courses on the philosophy of science, and we see in his mature writings a genuine concern with the problems of scientific investigation and explanation. Much has been said of Piaget's children, two daughters and a son born between the years 1925 and 1931. With the help of his wife, Piaget carefully studied and recorded the development of his children, so that in some of his writings, he refers not only to subjects selected from the local school system, and so on, but also to observations made on his own children from cradle to school years. Over his long career, Piaget has worked with many colleagues and friends, but two who should be specifically mentioned are A. Szeminska and B. Inhelder. His publication rate of articles and books relating to genetic epistemology has been astonishing, and today he is cited in the writings of colleagues with a frequency second only to Freud. His worldwide appeal has remained constant, and his books are regularly translated into many other languages.

In 1929 Piaget became a professor of the history of scientific thought at the University of Geneva; within a few years he was also named a codirector of the Institut Rousseau, which eventually affiliated with the university. In 1939 Piaget was made professor of sociology at the University of Geneva, and a year later, moved to a chair in experimental psychology. He was also named director of the university's psychological laboratory. After World War II ended, Piaget was named president of the Swiss Commission to UNESCO and later served on its executive council. In 1952, he became a professor of child psychology at the Sorbonne. In 1955–1956 Piaget founded an international Center for Genetic Epistemology at the University of Geneva. Here, he assembled a staff which studied various aspects of mental development from an interdisciplinary perspective, employing knowledge from the biological sciences, psychology, sociology, mathematics, and cybernetics, to name only a few of the sources Piaget is willing to tap.

Piaget has been given many signs of recognition over his long and distinguished career. He was awarded honorary doctoral degrees from many leading schools, such as Harvard University, the Sorbonne, the University of Brazil, and the University of Brussels. In 1969 he was the first European to received the Distinguished Scientific Contribution Award of the American Psychological Association. Piaget's findings and theoretical interpretations are clearly among the most important items of knowledge in the study of personality, and we will now consider his outlook in terms of our usual organization of theoretical constructs.

Personality Theory

Structural Constructs

Construction of Patterns Among Related Actions

Piaget's lessons from Bergson and Reymond left him as unwilling to focus on static, unchanging structures as are the phenomenologically oriented theorists of Part III. Living organisms may take on patterned shapes, as all things in experience take on patterns, but we must always appreciate that the basic nature of reality is change, movement, and development. In the case of human learning and personality development, this begins early in life as a form of reflexive, sensorimotor action.[10] As infants, we learn by essentially copying the early automatic movements we make in our cribs. We first reach automatically in a direction, observe that we are reaching, and then copy the action by practicing it over and over again in our play (shaking rattles, clenching our fists, poking our fingers here and there, and so on). Now, there are two kinds of things here we can learn as a pattern. We can observe or see ourselves doing things, and we can also sense ourselves doing what we are doing in our

motions. At first, we reach reflexively, but as we practice our reaching, we are learning in a way that is no longer reflexive nor simply observational.

To understand Piaget, we must first grasp that he distinguishes between the copying of an action by *internalizing* (or *interiorizing*) its actual pattern of motion and the copying of an action by internalizing an image of what needs to be done or how it is to be carried out.[11] We do not learn about life by first forming an image of what needs doing or what we wish would happen and then carrying this action forward to overt action. The analysts of Part I looked at the infant's mind (psyche) in this way and Piaget disagreed with them. We must *first* act and then gradually learn what we can or cannot do over our life's ever-changing course. Piaget emphasizes that "as regards action itself, we have time and again seen that it plays a far more fundamental role than does the image."[12] To interiorize is thus to take in a cognitive awareness of the patterned action by abstracting from our play in the crib. As we grow older, we can, of course, copy the behavior of others by simply observing them and forming an image of their behavior, as in Bandura's modeling conception (see p. 483). But there is a long period of development between the crib and this adult stage of behavior.

The most basic structure of action in Piaget's theory is called the *scheme* (also referred to as *schema*). A scheme may be defined as "what there is in common among several different and analogous actions."[13] For example, one such scheme might concern the understanding of distance. Infants learn, through reaching and moving about and through others moving in relation to them, that things and/or people may be close to them or farther away. This knowledge permits the maturing child to generalize from one action situation to another. Moving toward the kitchen sink is similar to reaching for a toy that is away from our side. Even so, Piaget does not consider a *scheme* to be identical to a *concept* of the understanding. Concepts are broader, taking into consideration both what is common and what is different about not only actions but all sorts of things (see George Kelly's definition of *construct,* p. 713). A scheme is what is common among different actions carried out at different times—like our moving about to close distances between ourselves and other people or things in many different situations. Though each person frames his or her scheme individually, it is also true that, because life is similar for everyone, the schemes we all make up share common meanings, by analogy if nothing else. It is such shared schemes that make the learning of language possible.[14] We can communicate through words because we have begun our understanding of things in schemes which permit us to grasp words, as the specific word *distance* is learned after we have already formed a scheme of this life experience.

When Piaget looks at the human mind as a totality, he thinks of the *schemata* (plural for *schema*) as interlacing parts of this much broader structure—reminding us of the field theories of gestalt psychology (see p. 571). Piaget does not consider himself a gestaltist, but he admits that had he read Wertheimer or Köhler early in his career, he probably would have become a member of this school of thought.[15] But he is surely within the theoretical traditions of Part III on the matter of looking at behavior globally rather than reductively. The whole-pattern is not just the sum of its part-patterns. The part-patterns (schemes) interlace and are in constantly shifting relations both internally and externally with other part-patterns to form in turn a whole-pattern. When we as children put together schemes of distance with other schemes like "resting upon," we can achieve a whole-pattern, enabling us to move toward something (for example, a table) to place something upon it (for example, a cup). Two schemes—"distance" and "resting upon"—combine into a more complex structure of action. The resulting whole-pattern is created not as two singles adding up to a double but as a *new pattern of relationship,* a distinctive singularity unique unto itself. Piaget is careful to point out that in the formation of patterns, it is "the relations among elements that count."[16]

The term Piaget uses to speak generally about patterned relationships like this is *structure.* Structures must have a reliably distinctive form (pattern) which is capable of being abstracted and recognized again and again. A mere heap of things piled together in haphazard fashion is not a structure.[17] Because structures have this reliable form making them capable of abstraction and recognizability, we are likely to think of them as fixed entities, but Piaget cautions that they are also *systematic* processes. A *system* is a regularly interacting or interdependent group of items (for example, schemata) forming a unified whole. In defining *structure,* Piaget therefore notes that it involves a distinctive pattern "which presents the laws or properties of a totality seen as a system."[18] Such structures can change, grow, and develop—tendencies Piaget captures in his concept of *transformation.* "Whereas other animals cannot alter themselves except by changing their species, man can transform himself by transforming the world and can structure himself by constructing structures; and these structures are his own, for they are not eternally predestined either from within or from without."[19]

Piaget seems to have first used the concept of transformation in his study of the development of concepts of number and related mathematical understandings in children. There are several transformations a mathematician can make on the same group of number relations without necessarily changing the fundamental meaning of the structural totality. For example, the group $x(yz)$ can be transformed to $(xy)z$, so that the equation $x(yz) = (xy)z$ is both different in organization on either side of the equation yet retains a basic identity. This is called associativity in mathematics, and there are other transformations that could be cited, such as closure, unity, and inversion. However, for present purposes, all we need grasp is the fact that patterned relations can be changed within a structure even though the overall systematic form remains identifiable. It is in this sense that Piaget can say "transformation and identity are forever inseparable."[20] This reminds us of the Heraclitian insight that we never step in the same river twice, even though there is a constant riverform (logos) moving before our eyes each day (see p. 4). The river transforms itself as an ongoing system even as it retains its identifiable pattern.

Referring to the transformation of physical objects like this is not inappropriate. Piaget notes that "a structure would lose all truth value if it did not have this direct connection with the [physical] facts."[21] As a genetic epistemologist, Piaget is primarily interested in the structures that relate to the formation and meaning of knowledge, but knowledge would have no validity if the structures of the mind failed to match up to the structures of physical reality. The reason our mental structures do coincide to our experience of reality is because they actually begin in the physical patterning of real events.[22] As suggested in the quote above regarding animals changing their species, the very survival of organisms in nature depends on their capacity to structure physical patterns favoring adjustment to reality. Thus, Piaget notes, "The organism adapts itself by materially constructing new forms to fit them into those of the universe, whereas intelligence extends this creation by constructing mentally structures which can be applied to those of the environment."[23] Thus, the physical body of any animal represents a structure having both an identifiable form and also a constantly changing process of interaction with the environment in which it takes on chemical nutrients and gives off wastes to carry on the survival actions of life.

From these basically physical exchanges, a higher-order organization occurs which is also physical; the structures involved, however, permit that creative interplay with nature that Piaget referred to above as "transforming the world" in human behavior. These higher-order structures also develop through transformation of earlier forms. "Actually the whole process of development, starting out with perception and culminating in intelligence, demonstrates clearly that transformations continually increase in importance, as opposed to the original predominance of static perceptual forms."[24] This idea of moving from the static and unchanging to the fluid and flexible structure is important in Piagetian developmental theory. We may as children look at things concretely and literally, so that we fail to analyze our schema and the structures within which we relate them in helter-skelter fashion. A child slips on the wet pavement while playing in the rain and for a period of time thereafter presumes that water or wet means harm, hurt, or something of the sort. Now, a wet surface that becomes slippery can indeed signify potential harm (danger), but this is merely one aspect of the total structure of what rain, water, or wetness actually means. When children (or adults for that matter) think in such personal, vague, or unanalyzed schematic structures, Piaget calls this *syncretic thought*.[25] We all begin with syncretic thinking, but thanks to our maturing capacity to transform structures of a primitive, sensorimotor (reflexive), schematic nature to increasingly abstract structures, we can promote our cognitive understanding. In doing so, we construct *structures* by our own design.

This brings us to the central theoretical term employed by both theorists of this chapter. Piaget dramatizes its importance to his structuralist theory when he states, *"There is no structure apart from construction, either abstract or genetic."* [26] Unlike George A. Kelly (see below, p. 713), who viewed construction as a purely cognitive (mental) process, Piaget suggests that we have both a *material construction* of bodily adaptations in organic evolution (generating new species, and so on) and also a more abstract, cognitive *construction of structures* which the human being uses to transform his or her world (see earlier quotes in this section). We might say that for Piaget, the general term *construction* means to bring about a structure (schema, and so on) in the ongoing, systematic processes of both organic and mental life. In general, this takes place through either *combination* and/or *differentiation* of part-structures (schemata) or whole-structures.[27] In organic evolution, an animal might differentiate by evolving a unique appendage (fin, claw, and so on), making possible motions that better adapt it to reality than another animal. In the case of human beings, a structure might have been created by combining two seemingly unrelated schemes in an unusual way. For example, the discovery of the wheel might have occurred when the human animal put together the scheme "rolling" with the scheme "unmoving" in a unique way by having a stable bed of wood undergirded with poles and slices of logs that could rotate.

The outcome of both (organic and cognitive) constructions is a new structure, and in Piagetian theory, it is usually assumed that such changes are advances or progressions over what had existed to that time. An animal better adapted to the physical world is improved over one not so endowed, and a reasoning human being who can reconstruct the world of natural forms can transform it to his or her liking. The essential point in both *organic* and *cognitive construction* is that the animal is actively involved in what comes about. Piaget dislikes the British Associationistic account of behavior which merely assumes that the newborn child is a reactive mechanism having the capacity to know that when a stimulus occurs, it is spatially located either "over here" or "over there." [28] To the contrary, says Piaget, "the perception of space involves a gradual construction and certainly does not exist ready made at the outset of mental development." [29] The physical environment does, of course, impinge upon the developing person to influence what organic or cognitive structures will be formed, but there is also a reciprocity of structural formation. Reminding us at this point of Bandura (see Chapter 7), Piaget says: "Knowledge does not begin in the I, and it does not begin in the [physical] object; it begins in the interactions. . . . there is a reciprocal and simultaneous construction of the subject on the one hand and the object on the other." [30]

Cognition as Equilibrating Operations

Since mental activity (cognition) is a systematic process of constructing experience (making structures) through an interaction with the physical world, Piaget must now propose terms that enable us to describe how this mutual interdependence of the subject (person) and object (environment) takes place. This is somewhat of a chicken-egg problem, difficult for all theorists to deal with. Few theorists of this volume (including Jung) have wanted to say that a person is born with all of his or her knowledge structured into understanding (innate ideas). Obviously, we all learn from living. The behaviorists of Part II are prone to emphasize the environment, but even they recognize that the organism must somehow process (pattern, order) the stimuli that are input, and Bandura in particular insisted upon the role of an active organism in reciprocal interaction with the environment. The phenomenologists of Part III have tended to put their emphasis on the person's conceptualizations, which are essentially what is meant by the phenomena, in preference to the independent reality, which is more on the side of the noumena. The phenomenal field of Rogers (Chapter 9), the world design of Binswanger (Chapter 10), or the personal constructs of Kelly (see below) all point to a kind of person-over-environment (phenomena over noumena) emphasis on the source of knowledge and understanding. Piaget is no real exception to this rule. He focuses on the person as actor and conceptualizer, but unlike the other phenomenologists, he insists on studying the biological basis of construction.

That is, the patterns of structure that the other phenomenologists of Part III accept as given in the phenomenal realm are said by Piaget to be derived from organic development. It is pointless to speak of a phenomenal field as ordered spatially in the newborn child, when, so far as Piaget is concerned, experimental evidence proves that children must construct their life space over a period of time. They achieve this by *beginning* with material or organic constructions and only later accom-

plish the structures known as the phenomenal field in their cognitive (mental) constructions. This heavy reliance on the physico-biological basis of phenomenal understanding sometimes leads to confusion among those who study Piaget. He seems to be saying that mind reduces to body, and therefore it is a kind of secondary phenomenon. Though one might argue that this is the practical outcome of his theory, Piaget at least does not want to suggest that mind or cognition reduces to the physical body. Mind has legitimacy in its own right, and through his uniting conception of construction, Piaget attempts to show how patterned structures occur at both the organic and the cognitive levels of existence. All he wants to do is remind the phenomenologists that their cognitive conceptions are not given at birth, but must in fact begin in the constructive capacities of the body as foreshadowed in the reflexive movements, the sensorimotor actions that we all bring with us biologically when we are born. The developmental course of construction is thus from body-to-mind *as a matter of fact!* What is important is to recognize the structuralism of this constructive process and not to try reducing one level (mind) to the other (body).

How then are we to think of the interaction between the person on the one hand and the environmental factors on the other? Piaget employs two concepts at this point, one of which frames on the person's influence on an understanding of the environment, and the other of which captures the environment's influence on the person. The first of these is *assimilation,* or the taking-in of the surrounding environment on the basis of an existing scheme or the more complex (whole-)structures they make up.[31] From this point forward, we will refer simply to the schemes or schemata that people construct, recognizing but not mentioning that these more basic structures can be combined into the larger whole-structures or structures proper discussed in the previous section. All organic life tends progressively to assimilate more and more of the surrounding environment as growth proceeds (for example, the chemical substances in foods and water are assimilated during development). In constructing structures at either the organic or the cognitive level, the organism is assimilating. Babies suck their thumb because they have assimilated this appendage to the schema of their mother's breast.[32]

As children mature, they can assimilate all kinds of actions of others by drawing a sort of analogy between their schemata and the observed behaviors. Piaget calls this *prehension,* which is an early form of imitation that can occur without the use of language.[33] Another form of assimilation occurs, called the *circular reaction,* which Piaget describes as follows: "A circular reaction is a reproductive assimilation. It is the mechanism by which a scheme is developed. The child performs an action, is interested in the result, and repeats the same action again. . . . It is this repetition that engenders the scheme."[34] By repeating an action such as picking up a toy, the infant gradually differentiates the specific movements, structuring or constructing the schema of "picking up" as something distinctive from the schema of "reaching." Assimilation is, therefore, another way of talking about the construction process, a process that has two sides.

On the other side of the person-environment interaction we have *accommodation,* or the "remodification of behavior as a result of experience."[35] In this case, rather than making the environment fit the scheme already constructed, the person modifies the scheme to fit the environment. This is when a new differentiation or combination is called for, because the person discovers that a scheme no longer fits the demands of reality too well. For example, a baby may observe someone's eyes close and open wide once again, and in trying to assimilate this, the baby may open and close his or her mouth.[36] The assimilation here is in error, and in order for the action to be imitated properly, the child will have to differentiate between a visual-action scheme and a mouth-action scheme. In making this accommodation, the child is drawing an analogy between mouth action and eye action, but the point is that through experience, a behavior has had to be modified and reschematized. In like fashion, throughout life we are forced to modify or transform our schemata in the face of new experience, as we learn that we cannot grasp the moon or that everything we place on water does not float.

Life is a continuing interplay of assimilation and accommodation in our growing cognitive understanding, and in order for our lives to be reasonably well adjusted, it is good for these two processes to be well coordinated.[37] There is a reciprocal interaction going on here, and if it is not balanced off reasonably well, the person can become rigidly fixed in schemata that are no longer reality-oriented, or conversely, can be readily swayed by irrelevancies in the environment. Piaget calls such reciprocal balancing relations *equilibrium,* which in this instance he would define as the compensatory adjustments made in personal action in response to intrusions from the external environment.[38] However, he has a much broader referent in mind in his equilibrium concept, one that covers both the physical and the psychological aspects of existence.

. . . Equilibrium is . . . an intrinsic and constitutive property of organic and mental life. A pebble may be in states of stable, unstable,

or indifferent equilibrium with respect to its surroundings and this makes no difference to its nature. By contrast, an organism [that is, living being] presents, with respect to its milieu, multiple forms of equilibrium, from postures to homeostasis.[39]

Even so, Piaget places greatest emphasis on the equilibrium of assimilation and accommodation in his personality theory, because this is what he takes to be the course of improvement occurring in development. Thus, he can say, ". . . [the] developmental theory necessarily calls upon the concept of equilibrium, since all behavior tends toward assuring an equilibrium between internal and external factors or, speaking more generally, between assimilation and accommodation."[40] In other words, as the maturing individual experiences *disequilibria*[41] between the internal (assimilation) and the external (accommodation) relations of its functioning schemata, a *motive* is generated to rectify the disbalance. We will take up Piaget's motivational constructs below, but for now we merely wish to demonstrate that, according to Piaget, in resolving the disequilibria successfully, the individual *necessarily* progresses, advances, that is, *develops* higher and higher levels of structure. Furthermore, according to Piaget, the equilibrations (acts bringing about equilibrium) that have been achieved in the past remain with the person, so that as life proceeds, the person who develops successfully should be more advanced than the person who does not. In general, adults, because of the very fact that they have *equilibrated* for years, are more advanced cognitively and emotionally than children.

Put another way, as we go along living our lives, we gradually work out a set of useful notions and points of view that fit our understanding of reality pretty well. We call this our knowledge or our intelligence. The four-year-old child has a shaky grasp of what

the concept of school or schooling means, but as the person develops over the years through elementary and secondary school education, an increasingly stable and also complex and sophisticated understanding of school develops. As we saw in the transformations of mathematics discussed in the previous section, higher-level thought always has this quality of being able to change relations without losing the identifiable structure (recall Heraclitus' *logos* and the ever-changing river).

As noted in the introduction to this chapter, Piaget's entire approach to the study of cognition has borrowed heavily from the terminology used and reasoning processes followed by mathematicians. In fact, it is impossible to understand equilibrium fully without appreciating that the highest-level, most equilibrated structures in existence occur as the abstract concepts of mathematics. In discussing anything having to do with thought, we are, of course, referring to cognitive rather than organic constructions. We have left the realm of physical structures and are speaking of what are often called in psychology higher-level mental processes. Piaget employs four terms which will help us understand what he is driving at in suggesting that equilibration is a process of greater and greater stability even as shifting relations occur within the structure of the process. We shall take up in order these concepts of *transduction, reversibility, decentration,* and *operation.*

Ordinarily, in thinking, we employ cognitive processes known as *induction* and *deduction.* To induct is to move from a particular meaning to a general meaning—that is, make a generalization from a series of specific points. We induct when we find it difficult to hit a tennis ball, stumble awkwardly in running after a soccer ball, and gasp with fright in trying to swim, then conclude from these particulars that "I am not athletic." Later, when someone asks us to try golf, we may deduct from our generalization ("I am not athletic") to a judgment on the particular prospect facing us and conclude, "I will be terrible on the golf links." The question of accuracy is not at issue here. We may indeed be a poor athlete, or it may be that we have not yet found our sport. But in reasoning as we do, we are in effect moving up and down a hierarchy of levels of abstraction (see p. 20). We move from the particular (less abstract) to the general (more abstract) in inducting and vice versa in deducting. However, Piaget has found that early in life we also move from the particular to the particular, unable somehow to abstract in our more syncretic style of thought to construct a hierarchy of from lesser to more abstract meanings. Piaget calls this reasoning at the level of particulars *transduction*.[42]

We would reason transductively if we played golf and found ourselves doing well at this sport, and concluded thereby that our tennis, soccer, or swimming skills had also improved. In other words, we would not have differentiated within the structured class of athletics the one sport in which we did well from the others in which we did not. Improving in one (particular), we assumed we improved in another (particular). Except for the brain-damaged or the mentally retarded, adults do not ordinarily reason transductively, but children always begin reasoning this way before they think more hierarchically by way of induction and deduction. Piaget gives as an example the case of a child who reasoned that if a hunchback had influenza and was cured of it, the first affliction would disappear as well.[43] Another way in which Piaget has defined *transduction* is as "reasoning without reversible nestings of a hierarchy of classes

and relations."[44] The core word here is *reversible* for it relates to a concept Piaget framed very early in his studies on the development of cognitive constructions. Reversibility is another way of speaking about equilibrium, for when there is a permanent reciprocity existing between accommodation and assimilation so that distortion in a construction does not take place, we can speak of reversibility.[45] In other words, it would not matter whether we were looking at a construction from the point of view of the subject (assimilation) or the object (accommodation); both structures would work equally well.

Young children who think transductively cannot reverse in this fashion (the same is true for syncretic thought in general). They are unable to shift their point of view from what they perceive to be going on in their experience and think about the reverse possibilities that might be involved. Our child does not see a hunchback with a cold (two schemes) but merely a sick person (single scheme). In order for a more accurate understanding of the circumstances to arise, the child must be able to move beyond what he or she perceives—the sick-person schema —and look at it from another perspective. The child must move from assimilation to accept the possibility that an accommodation is called for, that something besides a sick-person schema is involved. Piaget refers to this breaking free from what we literally perceive in order to cognize, to *think* about the various aspects of what we perceive, as *decentration* (or the act of *decentering*). To be glued concretely to merely what is perceived (schematized) is called *centration* (or the act of *centering*). To be creative in reasoning, we have to decenter and lose our simplistic understandings of our external reality. When we decenter, we can improve our level of adjustment, because "decentration . . . results in equilibrium between assimilation and accommodation, an equilibrium which of necessity tends towards a reversible structure." [46]

When a reversible structure exists in thought, this means we can turn it around in mind and look at it from all sides. Our child can essentially say, "Wait a minute. I have been thinking [assimilation] that 'sickness is sickness' but maybe looked at from that person's problems over there [accommodation], this is too simple. My point of view just may not fit the facts over there." This would be an example of *reciprocal reversibility*,[47] with the reciprocity (inverse relationship) taking place between assimilation and accommodation. Piaget also refers to *negational reversibility*.[48] In this case the person is capable of questioning his or her own viewpoints by essentially negating their certainty ("I could be wrong, maybe a hunchback isn't an illness like a cold after all") or by bringing the facts into question by negating them ("How do we know these so-called influenza symptoms aren't due to an allergy?"). Once we are able to do this, an important development occurs in cognition. "It is this freeing from perception that marks the beginning of operations properly so called, which are thus seen to be the result of the progressive reversibility of thought." [49]

The concept of the *operation* or *operational thinking* summarizes in a way all of the cognitive constructs that have been advanced to this point in Chapter 11. This is as close as we get to saying "thought in action" or "cognition" in Piagetian theory. There are four characteristics of an operation.[50] It is an interiorized action, so that it can be carried out in thought as well as executed materially in physical behavior (that is, we are talking about cognitive as well as organic structures in referring to operations). An operation is a reversible action, so it can be enacted in opposite directions. Operations also have an invariant structure about them, retaining the identifiable characteristic of the system even

though they change relations through reversibility. Finally, no operation exists alone; it is always related to a system or total structure. This latter point is important because it tells us that operations are more than schemata and always involve a "co-ordination of differentiated actions within the framework of a single whole." [51]

As we shall see, operational thought begins at what Piaget will call a *concrete* level, one that is above transductive reasoning but that is still not very advanced (developed). The child will begin to interrelate different parts of a total pattern under consideration without yet attaining the definite mobility and complete reversibility of the more rational operations of the adult.[52] The more rational thought becomes and the more it attains equilibrium (including the Heraclitian identity of form), the more *abstract* it becomes. And with this abstraction we witness an ever-increasing stability of organizational structure; in effect, thought becomes increasingly systematic. The highest levels of such abstraction occur in the operations of formal logic and/or mathematics.[53] The person can now think of multiplication as an "addition of additions," reflecting a beautifully reversible construction in which multiplication and addition are one, even though they are also kept separate in schematic organization. The critic might object that mathematical reasoning is not based on the motions of an action, but Piaget's fundamental assumption is that all mathematics arises from action patterns.

Mathematics for Piaget is simply the higher stages of biological evolution, a purely "man-made" [54] construction that defines relations among inanimate actions and provides a set of universal structures of great stability and reversibility. We human beings have come by way of our structured beginnings in the organic constructions of life to this most abstract of all rational constructions, operating cognitively but in a remarkably transpersonal manner to give the best picture not only of inanimate reality, but of ourselves as human beings. Piaget's fundamental assumption about human nature, and the reason we have called him an evolutionary rationalist, may be seen in the following summation: "Hence the universe is known to man only through logic and mathematics, the product of his mind, but he can only know how he constructed mathematics and logic by studying himself psychologically and biologically, that is, in terms of the entire universe." [55]

The Dynamics of Human Operations

We now have an understanding of Piaget's highly fluid conception of patterned orders (structures) taking form across all levels of life, beginning in the organic and evolving to ever-higher stages of stable identity and reversibility through equilibration. With this background, we can now review a number of concepts bearing on the higher-level operations—remembering always that when we speak of an operation, we are speaking of an interiorized structure, hence a *mental* organization of some pattern. Now, patterns exist independently of mind in physical reality. When the person has knowledge of an object from direct contact with it, Piaget calls this *perception*.[56] We perceive something like a house by constructing its image mentally through the act of interiorizing. Piaget has referred to *mental images* as "imitative schemata," [57] in that they copy the structures of experience by actively rehearsing them again and again. We do not look and then take in a carbon copy of the world in our perceptual images (the same goes for hearing,

smelling, feeling, and so on). We actively construct a mental image, bringing it into greater stability and reversibility as we come to understand that which we perceive.[58] We think about houses. We picture ourselves going into and coming out of houses, both as we actually *do* enter and leave, but also later in our imagination.

The fact that we can think about things like houses even when we are not perceiving them (no house is directly present) signifies that we have *represented* these schemata in mind. *Representation* or imagination is not only active when we are away from houses, of course. To represent an object in mind when it is present is the same operation as representing an object in mind when it is absent.[59] Here is where we find a decidedly phenomenological emphasis in Piagetian theory. He does not want to say that we use our active imagination in thoughts *only* when we are not in direct contact with environmental objects (people, things, weather conditions outside, and so on). We constantly use our imaginations in constructing our knowledge of the perceived world. Of course, being able to represent this world allows us to go beyond the present situation facing us, extending our cognitions (thoughts) out into both space and time.[60] We can place ourselves into the past or the future, jump over in mind from where we *are* to where we *might be* in location.

Since representation tends to bring in (interiorize) the external world to the cognitive sphere of understanding, we can also see it as a form of accommodation.[61] That is, even though there is always the equilibrating interaction of assimilation and accommodation going on, the basic thrust of representation is to accommodate the mental schemata to *something else*. A representation represents something else. Piaget would say that as representation becomes increasingly abstract, we can begin speaking of *concepts* taking place in mind, rather than images.[62] That is, as we begin to equilibrate at higher levels of thought, our operations lose that tie to perception that they once had. We have perceived many houses, but now in thinking about the concept "house," we might begin getting all kinds of ideas about what a house might be someday. We might even redesign the typical house and come up with something that does not even look like the actual houses we have perceived in the past. In order to do so, we would have to decenter and, through higher-level conceptions based on reversible operations, dream up an alternative in our mind which is entirely creative. To the extent that we center on perceptions, our representations remain very rigid and concrete, and therefore they are unlikely to be very creative or innovative.

Representations thus make intelligent *thought* possible, and in turn: "It is operations that are the essence of thought . . . it is of the nature of operations continually to construct something new." [63] Operations copy not the form of objects per se, but rather the form of our actions on objects. Thought is a continuous series of constructions in which the hierarchical classes, groupings, and systems of knowledge gradually evolve over the years of maturation from childhood to adulthood.[64] *Mind* is therefore a continuing process of constructive activity with a large amount of self-construction involved.[65] We will discuss the role of self below, as an aspect of the motivational constructs in Piagetian theory. As we shall see, Piaget does accept the role of an identity factor in human behavior. People construct their worlds, and they construct a picture of themselves within this complexity of interlacing factors. The natural attitude of the mind is to be credulous, that is, to believe everything that is perceived and constructed as basically true.[66] Young children demonstrate this most clearly. It is not until later that doubt creeps in (via reciprocal or negational reversibility), and it is some

time before the young person can understand what it means to look at things hypothetically.

Having seen how Piaget accepts a phenomenological theme, we might now demonstrate the reverse instance. This arises when Piaget tells us: ". . . there are no innate structures in the human mind which simply come into being . . . all our mental structures must be constructed." [67] This position would directly contradict what some existentialists call the *a priori ontological structure* (see p. 634). The gestalt laws of organization are also interpreted by many psychologists to exist mentally as an aspect of human nature from birth (see p. 568). Though Piaget realizes that assimilation must come before accommodation in all circular reactions—because to accommodate means a previous schema exists and this "implies assimilation" [68]—he also contends that the very *first* time a scheme is organized (in early life), this process is based on the copying of a *biological structure*. Mind begins by accommodating bodily constructions which assimilate at the organic level. For example, a common organic assimilation is that of taking in food nourishment. We might say that the infant accommodates this taking-in organic scheme to an interiorized mental assumption by credulously believing all that is perceived is true ("taken-in" as perceived without doubt).

There *are* innate bodily structures in the form of sensorimotor actions called reflexes. The sucking response is one such example, and so from birth, the child begins to suck at the mother's breast automatically and then later assimilates to this action (as we have noted above) his or her thumb. Looked at this way, the mind may be said to imitate or learn from the innate structures of the body. Mind qua mind has no innate structures of its own, but the body in turn has no operations. Bodily constructions are not operational. They lack the reversibility and the stability of form that we have seen characterizes abstract levels of thought. Hence, in time as we mature, we all literally create a sphere of cognitive understanding which makes us more than strictly organic organisms. Indeed, our mental operations take on greater importance in our personal lives and for humanity as a whole than the innate organic structures on the basis of which they have been patterned.

This treatment of how mind organizes from the innate structures of body is unique and stamps Piaget as a theorist apart from the mainstream of the phenomenological-existentialistic school—a school to which he is nevertheless closer than either psychoanalysis or behaviorism. When Piaget uses the term *behavior,* he couches it in light of the basic terminology we have been considering. Thus, he observes that "every behavior . . . has two poles: assimilation to earlier schemas and accommodation of these schemas to new situations." [69] Behavior is action, and it therefore bears a necessary relation to the entire process of beginning life in sensorimotor construction and moving through development to the cognitive operations of mind. Behavior also involves motives and valued goals, but as these are properly motivational conceptions, we will put them off for consideration below.

Piaget would say that what is generally called *intelligence* consists of establishing permanent relations between schema that cover greater and greater spatiotemporal intervals. Our representations extend across various perceptions and organize into a stable, permanent understanding of what seems related to what, or how one event bears an implication

for another event.[70] Implications reach for the future and therefore we call intelligent those actions that order future lines of behavior. We can plan our actions and anticipate their outcomes before they even take place when we behave intelligently. Piaget has no faith in so-called IQ tests, feeling that though statistical findings of a person's performance on various tasks in relation to other people's performances may have a practical benefit in prediction, they never tell us anything about the operations involved in doing these IQ tasks.[71] This interest in how the person actually accomplishes a task, remembers, organizes, and so on, is what got Piaget started on his long career as genetic epistemologist.

The emphasis on permanence in relations among schema in Piaget's view of intelligence is important, because this is what he means by *conservation,* a characteristic of operational thought he has studied in great detail. Piaget reminds us that every notion we have in common sense of a lasting value presupposes a fixed or set structure, a permanence in definition.[72] For example, when we discussed the constancy principle in Chapter 1 (see p. 52), its fundamental idea was that something (force) remains permanent in a closed system. If we look at other widely accepted scientific principles like that of inertia or consider moral precepts like the Golden Rule, what gives them meaning is the fact that we can all grasp a permanent, unchanging given that retains its structure, even though we may apply this organization to different specific instances. We may speak of inertia as it affects the rolling wheels of a racing automobile or the tumbling of a rock down a sloping hill. Treating others as we would have them treat ourselves may serve as a principle in relating to people of all ages, races, and sexual identities. The principles do not change. Piaget believes that it is this tendency for thought to take on such permanent conceptual organizations that gives the existentialistic-phenomenological theorist the impression that there are a priori organizations in thought.[73]

For example, in the history of mathematics, it so happened that both Newton and Leibniz discovered the differential calculus independently of each other. We might be tempted to conclude from this that there were a priori organizations in mind necessitating such a discovery, no matter who did the thinking. Piaget, on the other hand, would hold that it was because of the developmental evolution of higher-level operations that this common discovery was possible. Both Newton and Leibniz, beginning as children and following the leads of other thinkers who had already constructed certain stable (conserved) mathematical structures, carried this evolutionary process forward to its natural and necessary end state. This development was not an *effect* of an a priori structure but rather a *point of arrival* following a long period of construction. More than one mind could make the journey to arrive where it did, but the end state of *permanent* (conserved) mathematical order was evolved nevertheless.

We have now seen Piaget both agree and disagree with aspects of the phenomenological-existentialistic theoretical line. We have also suggested that Piaget is clearly not a behavioristic theorist, since he believes that stimulus input would never directly influence behavior until after it had been constructed and equilibrated. This would seem to remove Piagetian theory from any hint of being mechanistic. However, as we noted in the introductory comments to this chapter (p. 668), it so happens that Piaget does embrace cybernetic theory, a point of view that many personologists believe is not truly compatible with his otherwise more humanistic orientation. The feature of cybernetics that attracts Piaget is the *feedback loop*. Recall from Chapter 7 (p. 480) that feedback occurs when a

portion of the output from a computer returns as input to the computer, so that there is a possibility for adaptation to changing circumstances.

For example, a robot employing the mechanisms of cybernetics might have its core electrical computer send output to its "legs" indicating a move to the left. Now, part of this output message would also return as input to the core computer, so that if the legs bumped something while underway, this new message of "getting bumped" in conjunction with "moving left" would combine as new input to the computer. In this case, thanks to the computer's program, a new output could be sent to the legs, like "back up and move ahead to the right" or some such. Without the additional feedback of "moving left," the computer might have continued sending the legs to the left in an ineffective effort to get past whatever the obstacle was. Feedback is essential information if an ongoing process is to modify or regulate its course while continually underway.

Piaget has concluded that feedback is essentially the same thing he had earlier called the circular reaction of the equilibration process, and the reason he holds out hope of uniting his theory with cybernetics is because he believes that both approaches deal with the question of self-regulation in an ongoing process. In discussing his construct of equilibration, Piaget once said:

Now I did not use cybernetic terminology when I began talking of this factor, but nonetheless since the beginning I have insisted that it was not a balance of opposing forces, a simple case of physical equilibrium but that it was a self-regulation. And of course today cybernetics is precisely that, the study of self-regulating models.[74]

Piaget does not delude himself into thinking that human beings are identical to robots or computers, of course: ". . . even if we could build a maximally complex computer and keep using it over and over again, this computer will never change. But the human mind with all its complexity continues to actually grow with use. It becomes more complicated." [75] Computers cannot invent problems as the human being can. Even so, as a description of the underlying mechanisms of both organic and cognitive constructions—interacting assimilations and accommodations—the feedback model is helpful, and therefore Piaget intends to use it. [76]

Genetic Epistemology as Evolutionary Rationalism

We can now look in more detail at what Piaget means by *genetic epistemology*, beginning with the dictionary definitions of the two words making up this phrase. The adjective *genetic* refers to the origins, development, and antecedents of something. For example, if we were to study the biochemical determinants of hereditary transmission from parent to child, we would be studying the genetic code. The noun *gene* refers to such a determining element in the germ plasm, controlling hereditary transmission like this. The noun *epistemology* refers to the study or theory of the nature and grounds of knowledge, including such topics as the limits and validity of what we know. Putting these two terms together, we can understand why Piaget defines *genetic epistemology* as the study of "both the formation and the meaning of knowledge." [77]

Piaget's specific definition of *genesis* combines the meanings of antecedents, transformations, and increasing stability, as follows:

We can define genesis as a relatively determined system of transformations comprising a history and leading in a continuous manner from state A to state B, state B being more stable than the initial state and constituting an extension of it. For example, in biology, ontogenesis leads to the relatively stable state of adulthood. [78]

We have discussed ontogeny in Chapter 1 (see p. 65); it relates to the developmental study of an organism through stages, from conception through *in utero* maturation, and after birth, through childhood to adulthood (maturity). Piaget holds that the course of this development is one of moving from structure to structure, in which there is a *formative transition* from an unstable, weaker to a more stable, stronger structure. [79] It is therefore correct to say that for Piaget, development is synonymous with progress.

We see a heavy biological emphasis in Piaget's theory of development, but this is not precisely an emphasis on the physical matter being transmitted from one human generation to the next—like germ plasm, for example. Though we find Piaget saying in one context that his aim is to "uncover the psychogenetic and biological roots of thought," [80] in another context he emphasizes that "knowledge is not predetermined in heredity; it is not predetermined in the things around us—in knowing things around him the subject always adds to them." [81] In other words, though human beings have organic structures which undoubtedly have evolved and which are influenced by genetic codes carried by the very protoplasm of parent to offspring, the structures of thought—knowledge—are *not* so transmitted. Even though the thought of children bears a resemblance to the thought of primitive peoples and the thought of adults bears an identity to the thought of the ancient Greeks, and so on, this is not proof that we have inherited our thought processes or that children are re-enacting a primitive time of the race (ontogeny recapitulating phylogeny; see p. 65). Piaget suggests that quite the reverse is true, because "since all men, including 'primitive men,' started by being children, childhood thinking preceded the thought of our most distant ancestors just as it does our own!" [82]

The study of genetic epistemology must be seen as a scientific study in its own right, calling for interdisciplinary contributions but never fully accounted for by related fields, such as biology. Since, according to Piaget, mind begins its development by interiorizing the structures of the body, it is here that the biological roots of thought may be said to occur. Biology has a contribution to make to genetic epistemology, but it is a vain hope to expect that thought can be explained in terms of physical matter. Genetic epistemology teaches that the mind is constructed by its own actions, primitive and unstable at first, but in time increasingly stabilized, conserved, and reversible—made better and better, thanks to the actions of the person on the source of knowledge in the environment. The person constructs mind like the artist constructs a work of art. Beginning with malleable clay, an artist continually molds and shapes, modifies and reworks the form of his or her artistic production, adding details, looking at it from all sides, and in time completing it by achieving the best (strongest, most stable, and so on) form of the work possible. The clay is then baked and in time, a bronze statue is cast, further strengthening the artist's conceptualization. In like fashion, the evolution of mind is an active process of shaping and reshaping knowledge until that stability in abstraction we outlined above is achieved.

Piaget refers to his style of theorizing as *constructivism*. He has a *constructive theory* of cognitive structure.[83] We have called his approach an *evolutionary rationalism* because of the unique way in which he rests mind on body, *not* as a direct outgrowth of physical matter, but as a developmental patterning over and beyond the physical structures to achieve the reliability and reproducibility of rational thought. The highest form of rationality is achieved in logic and/or mathematics, and for Piaget these are the virtual end points of a lifelong evolutionary process reproduced in the thinking of every person, whether or not the fruits of such thinking are codified and recorded in textbooks. Of course, not everyone would evolve an understanding of higher mathematics, but presumably the potential for such development is "there" for the developing in all human beings. It is always to some extent up to the person.

In fact, Piaget's conception of evolution allows for the possibility that changes in physical structure might be affected by the actions of the behaving organism and genetically transmitted. Piaget once studied a pond snail (*Limnaea stagnalis*) which he found making certain movements during growth that resulted in an altered physical structure (phenotype), which combined with its genetic species characteristics (genotype) to be transmitted through heredity to succeeding generations.[84] This Lamarckian theme in Piaget's work has been supported by the writings of the eminent naturalist and evolutionary theorist E. H. Waddington, who refers to such interactions of heredity and what the organism does in actually adapting to the environment as *genetic assimilation*.[85] Waddington has also demonstrated that in documented cases, animals have been known to change environmental locations *not* because of any pressing need to migrate (such as hunger, temperature extremes, and so on) but simply because they "chose" to do so.[86]

Though Piaget has theoretical reservations about using words like *choice* in his theory (see our discussion of his self construct, below), this view of an organism interacting with its environment to bring about changes is very helpful to his constructivist position. Evolution or development becomes a two-way street, influenced by physical (hereditary) genesis but also by cognitive (behavioral) genesis. Lower animals construct their physical structures by assimilation and accommodation just as higher animals construct their rational cognitive structures by assimilation and accommodation. Piaget's theoretical constructs can hold "up and down" the levels of animal evolution. And when we look more closely at the constructions of mind, we find Piaget standing against the behavioristic type of explanation in which it is said that mind "inputs" schematic structures from reality in ready-made fashion. Though Piaget may use the language of cybernetics in trying to capture the self-regulatory nature of human thinking, he never forgoes that phenomenological insistence upon the mind as having the capacity to organize its *own* schemata.

This is why Piaget can say that "development is more fundamental than learning"[87] in the construction of schemata. The person does not learn cognitive operations in the same way that language is learned. *Learning* is a concept that characterizes the ongoing equilibrations of the ever-improving schemata over the years.[88] There would be no learning possible unless the organism did not already possess this native or innate capacity to structure experience. The structures that result are not innately programmed, of course, which would mean that we are back to a heredity explanation. What is innate is strictly the active process of construction. Evolutionary de-velopment then takes off from here to wend its progressive way upward to the abstract levels of rational thought. Piaget rejects theories of behavior like Dollard and Miller's (see Chapter 5) that suggest that we learn to reason rationally or logically as we are being taught our native language.[89] Language is the content of mind, mere verbal instrumentalities that we use to express knowledge. Logical reasoning on the other hand reflects the active patterning of this knowledge, quite aside from the specific content that is being ordered and conveyed.[90] Even a person reared in the wilds of nature who had never learned a language would reflect a logic in his or her crudely unstable cognitive operations. Hence, just as we will not find the roots of mind exclusively in the protoplasm of hereditary transmission, so too will we not find it exclusively in the input shapings of sociocultural instructions. As genetic epistemologists we must fashion our own theory rather than borrowing quick and ready explanations from other bodies of knowledge in the scientific community.

Motivational Constructs

Behavior as Teleonomic

Piaget uses the term *behavior* to cover all those instances in which an organism is seeking to change the outside world in some way or to change its own position in relation to surroundings.[91] Such adjustments are seen across the full range of equilibrating developments. "At the lowest level, behavior amounts to no more than sensorimotor actions (perceptions and movements in conjunction); at the highest, it embraces ideational internalizations, as in human intelligence, where action extends into the sphere of mental operations."[92] The more complex behavior becomes the more it presupposes intelligence, and above all, the more it implies that a motive and/or a goal will be involved in the observed action.[93] Piaget uses the adjective *teleonomic* to describe the fact that behavior is goal oriented. It is a mistake to believe that because the body suffers from a biochemical lack, this insufficiency can bring about behavior. Not until this disequilibrium is both sensed physiologically and oriented toward a goal can we speak of the actions occurring as genuine *behavior*.

Behavior is not centered on survival; to the contrary, it has decentered from the aim of "just getting by" both to expand the environmental range within which the organism behaves and to facilitate the organism's mastery of this environment.[94] Behavior is action par excellence. Whether we think of the wild animal roaming through the forest in search of food or the human being coming alive intellectually in going to school, all behavior moves outwardly to assimilate more and more experience. As long as this mastery occurs without a hitch, we can speak of *adaptation* or adjustment in the organism's behavior.[95] In this case, equilibration is moving along nicely as development proceeds. If a disequilibrium occurs in behavior, then we can consider this a *need* of the organism.[96] This term is used when the disequilibration is not severe or chronic. Marie is not presently liked by her peer group in school. As a new student who has just moved into the school district, she has yet to prove herself to the other students. Marie is *disequilibrated* and needs to accommodate to the fact that the other children expect her to do more than simply be polite to them. She has to relate more personally to them, play with them, and reveal herself as a regular person. If she does indeed make this accommodation, Marie's need for acceptance will be resolved. If she does not, if she is for some reason unable to adapt, then her disequilibration will become chronic, and we could refer to Marie as *maladapted* or maladjusted.

Personality as a System

Thus far we have made it appear that emotional schemata do not occur, but this is not true. Piaget uses the term *affection* rather than emotion, but he makes it quite clear that all thinking is shot through with the interests and biases of emotional schemata, and that we must always consider the ongoing actions of affective equilibration in human behavior.[97] Affective schemes are harder to generalize than intellectual schemes. There is an energic quality about affective schemata, which makes them distinctively different from the purely structural role intellectual or cognitive schemata play in thoughts.[98] Affections get us going and orient our teleonomic behavior in relation to the ends we seek. As Piaget summarizes it:

Affectivity is the motor of any conduct. But affectivity does not modify the cognitive structure. Take two school children for example. One who loves mathematics, who is interested and enthusiastic, and anything else you wish; and the other who has feelings of inferiority, dislikes the teacher, and so forth. One will go much faster than the other, but for both of them two and two makes four in the end. It doesn't make three for the one who doesn't like it and five for the one who does. Two and two are still four.[99]

We see here Piaget's clear distinction between the structural demands of purely logical operations like arithmetic and the affective operations of how much these necessary patterns are liked or disliked by the individual who must at some point confront them. If we add to these two schemata the sensorimotor patternings that take place early in life, we have pretty well covered the range of operations we are likely to see in a person's total behavioral pattern. This is what Piaget means by the *personality* in general—that is, the total system of interrelating schemata and operations thereby which occur across the sensorimotor, intellectual, and affective levels.[100] Piaget also uses the term *personality* more specifically to mean a person's character, that is, the capacity the person has to willfully pursue a valued course of action when tempted to disregard it. We will return to this specific usage below, when we discuss Piaget's theory of development and in particular his self construct (see p. 702).

We come now to a problem in the understanding of Piaget's theory, which stems from the general way in which he uses the concept of construction. In suggesting as he does that there are material (organic) as well as psychological (cognitive) constructions, we are left with the problem of wondering what perspective to take in thinking about this constructive process. Do we think about it as happening *to* the organism (extraspectively; see p. 21)? Or do we think of the constructive action as occurring from the point of view of the behaving organism (introspectively), who brings it to bear in the sense of Binswanger's world-designs (see p. 634) or Kelly's personal constructs (see p. 713)?

Our problem here is like watching the growth of a tree versus a person. The tree matures and grows branches with leaves which assimilate nourishment from the sun even as the tree's roots assimilate nourishment from the earth. These physical processes may indeed be patterned and active in constructive organization, because trees must accommodate to weather and soil conditions even as they assimilate nourishment according to already established structures like leaves and roots. But the growing person, who patterns mental operations on the physical constructions of his or her body, is doing so in a different sense.

To understand what is taking place, we must necessarily look *through* the cognitions of the actively constructing intellect in a way that is impossible to do in understanding the equilibrating processes of trees or human (physical) bodies. We may use a single word like *construction* to describe both physical (organic) and mental (cognitive) processes of equilibration through the construction of structure, but this does not alter the fact that there are major differences in how we must understand what appears to be taking place. Without denying that both forms of construction do take place, we are still left with this puzzle.

A major difference between trees or bodily physical actions (like digestion) and what we call the person or personality is, of course, the possibility of *self-direction* in behavior. Common sense suggests that people are agents directing their behavior, and by using the word *teleonomic* to describe behavior, Piaget certainly implies that he considers people to be agents. This is a central tenet of the phenomenological outlook of Part III. And yet, Piaget is not really sympathetic with an *agency* interpretation of human behavior. He does not want to hypostatize (make real) something he considers to be a construction by the person moving from *organic* to *cognitive constructions*. That is, a *self*, or *cognitive self*, as Piaget sometimes calls it, is itself a schema framed by operational thinking. At birth, Piaget believes the baby and the physical environment are not yet differentiated, so that there is no sense of I versus the world in the cognitive processes of the infant.[101] In order to gain some sense of a self—a continuity of I-ness—the child must in time come to construct this self-concept, and this can only occur through the usual processes of assimilation and accommodation. Earliest thought is said to be *egocentric,* by which is meant the fact that children cannot differentiate between their thoughts and themselves as thinkers nor can they grasp what is make-believe and what is real, much less the difference between their point of view and the viewpoints of others.[102]

The fact that the child's earliest thought is egocentric does not mean that he or she has an ego in the sense suggested by Freud's theory. This concept of egocentricity is more the observer's term, applied to the child's cognitive style in capturing its essentials. Of course, as already noted, in time children construct a cognitive self-image, a picture of themselves in relation to others. But since this self-concept is the *result* and not the cause of assimilation-accommodation in equilibration, we have difficulty assigning true agency to the personality of the individual. Construction in assimilation and accommodation leading to equilibrations over childhood maturation take place automatically, even though they are not mechanical in the sense of behavioristic theory. It is as if, in describing the processes of self-regulation in feedback and equilibration or disequilibration, Piaget has kept a true self-directedness out of his theory whether he intended doing so or not.

We can think of a robot as teleonomic in that everything it does—its behavior—is goal oriented. But in achieving its equilibrations, does the robot know that *it* as an identity (self) exists and that it is carrying forward intentional actions? Obviously not. Robots lack such self-reflexive intelligence even when we program them to make statements "sounding" like they are aware of "themselves." The same can be said of Piagetian personality theory, particularly in light of the following wherein the term *organs* is used to describe mental equilibration as essentially a mechanism:

The organism has special organs of equilibrium. The same is true of mental life, whose organs of equilibrium are special regulatory mechanisms. This is so at all levels of

development, from the elementary regulations of motivation (needs and interests) up to will for affectivity and from perceptual and sensorimotor regulations up to operations for cognition.[103]

At a more subtle theoretical level, Piaget's attitude regarding the use of anything smacking of a finalistic (final-cause) explanation in science is quite negative. For example, in his study of children's understanding of causation, he found again and again that they attributed intentions to inanimate structures, so that they would say the sun was causing the rain today much as their mothers might water potted plants. Piaget interprets these anthropomorphic explanations as not true causal explanations; that is, he will not accept final causation as a legitimate construct (see p. 5). He prefers to call such explanations *precausal,* which he interprets as a "primitive" view of reality in which the person has not yet differentiated psychological motivations (à la egocentric thought) from the natural causation of a scientific form of description.[104] Unlike Adler, Piaget does not wish to be considered a theorist who uses finalistic explanations.[105] It is this continuing commitment to the traditional explanations of hard science that keeps Piaget from introducing more decidedly teleological concepts into his theory. Behavior is always seated in the interacting equilibrations of assimilation and accommodation which, according to basic Piagetian tenets, occurs with or without a self identity in the personality structure.

Conscious versus Unconscious Cognitions

Piaget states flatly that "all thought, even the most rational, is both conscious and unconscious."[106] *Consciousness* arises in personality when the environmental situation in which the person finds himself or herself blocks some ongoing activity. Children act in accordance with their needs and everything takes place without conscious awareness of the equilibrations going on until there is a frustration arising (see a comparable theme in Piaget's treatment of will below, p. 699). Food is wanted and mother is not there to provide it, or a toy is reached for but it is too far outside the playpen's confining limits to grasp. Each of these frustrating circumstances serves to focus the child's attention on the reasons for the disequilibration rather than simply on the desired goal (food, toy). This in turn generates a sense of consciousness and as the behaviors of life extend in maturation, a growing sense of consciousness will occur because of the inevitable frustrations life brings about.

When reasons for the frustration are examined, the child must eventually recognize that something like a self "over here" wants to obtain something else "over there." These preliminary schemata are what begin ordering into a system of what we then call consciousness. The self-image therefore parallels development of consciousness. In line with what we discussed in the previous section, Piaget does not really place much emphasis on the role of consciousness in behavior. He does not believe that consciousness is an essential focus of concern for psychology because: ". . . the task of psychology is not the explanation of the working of the nervous system in terms of consciousness of behaviour, but rather the analysis of the evolution of behaviour. That is to say, the way in which a perception, for example, depends on past perceptions and conditions subsequent ones."[107]

Piaget rejects psychoanalytical interpretations of *unconscious symbolism*, believing that Freud confused the contents of symbols with the primitive, egocentric schemata that children were constructing when they framed these so-called symbols.[108] Indeed, Piaget presented a paper on this very point at the 1922 conference of the International Psychoanalytical Association,[109] at which Freud was present. Piaget argued that his studies found all childish thinking to be syncretic and prelogical, and therefore so-called unconscious symbols could be found in a child's statements even while awake. Piaget views the *symbol* as a special form of scheme, in which the *signifier* (name of a thing) has been differentiated from the *object signified* (the thing named).[110] When this occurs, the person uses the object as a means of symbolic adaptation to reality. For example, Monique might use a little box to symbolize a cat in her play. She has differentiated the image of the thing we call a box (signified object) from the word *box* (signifier) and can now use the former as a symbol for a cat walking across the floor. Piaget would call this a *primary symbol* because Monique is conscious of her playful representation.[111]

However, in another context, Monique might employ a *secondary symbol,* in which case she would be unconscious of its role in her behavior. Assume that Monique had been made jealous by the birth of a younger sister and is playing one day with two dolls of unequal size. In her play, we observe that Monique has the smaller doll go away on a long journey while the larger doll stays home with mother (Monique may pretend that she is mother). The larger doll may then be made to pet the cat as represented by the box, demonstrating as Piaget contends that conscious and unconscious thought goes on side by side. The distinction between conscious and unconscious behavior is always a matter of degree, and consequently, it is also true that "symbols cannot be classified once and for all as either primary or secondary."[112]

As for the Freudian construct of *repres-*

sion, Piaget would say that this occurs when the person refuses to accept what reality demands in the way of an accommodation and persists in assimilating reality to an egocentric schema which is unadaptive. For example, Marcel soon learns upon going to school that he can no longer have things entirely his own (egocentric) way. He cannot always have first turn in kicking a soccer ball, but must share this advantage with the other boys. If he does not accommodate to this demand of reality, but instead loses interest in soccer and begins to occupy his time in bullying younger children on the playground, pretending egocentrically that he has real leadership ability and even popularity, we would witness a case of repression taking place. Piaget does not see why we need to believe there is a censor within the personality to understand such unconscious behavior. The dynamics are clear enough. "A repressed tendency is by definition deprived of accommodation, and therefore dissociated from the conscious ego. If, in spite of this, it seeks support, it can only be by way of egocentric and unconscious assimilation, i.e., by means of a symbolic substitute." [113]

Another type of unconsciousness that may be seen in behavior stems from the fact that cognitive operations are based on physical constructions, and the latter may be at work without benefit of the former. Children will often know something in action as a *sensorimotor* kind of *intelligence,* yet not know it cognitively in awareness. [114] Andrea, a kindergartner, has outstanding ability to jump rope. She has a knack of moving into and leaving the rope area which ensures that she will almost never be caught by it, no matter how quickly it is rotated by the other girls. Andrea is unable to describe her technique of rope-skipping because she is totally unaware of the fact that she has one. Her behavior has been constructed at the sensorimotor level, but it has not yet been made operational.

When it is, Andrea will be able to offer an opinion on what she does to avoid being caught by the rope. Such "unconscious" sensorimotor learnings take place in adulthood as well, although they do not represent nearly the proportion of total behavior that they do in childhood. Sometimes the course of learning is in the opposite direction from operational thought to sensorimotor construction. Driving an automobile is a case in point. At first, we learn by concentrating on every move, but in time, as sensorimotor intelligence (motoric construction) takes over, we are able to drive the automobile without really thinking about it.

Piaget is distrustful of the analytical method of discovery and proof, whereby a patient recalls past occurrences and assumes that they are true. He tells of a very precise, detailed, and lively personal memory he still has of an attempted kidnapping in his early childhood. He can see in his mind's eye his nurse struggling with the kidnapper, the arrival of a passerby, and the eventual appearance of the police. It was not until he was fifteen years old that his former nurse wrote to his parents and confessed that the story was a hoax, made up to account for some scratches on Piaget's forehead which occurred because she had been derelict in her nursing duties. How did this clear memory arise? Piaget suggests:

. . . About the age of five or six, I must have heard the story of this kidnapping which my parents then believed and, using this story, I invented a visual memory which today still remains. This then is a matter of reconstruction, although false, and if the event had really occurred and consequently if the memory were true, it is quite probable that I would also have reconstructed it in the same manner, for no memory of evocation

(*but only one of recognition*) *exists for a baby in its carriage.*[115]

We are always interacting with our past in this way, so that *memory* is never a matter of holding fixed contents in mind, like carbon copies of what really occurred. Memory is an active reconstruction, bringing alive past constructions into ever-new constructions.[116]

Piaget views the *dream* as comparable to symbolic play, but with the additional proviso that the self or ego consciousness is lost.[117] Games are more deliberately controlled, whereas dreams carry the person beyond the point to which consciousness would ordinarily want to go. Almost anything is fair game to the dream. Piaget does not object to the view that dreams may be *wish fulfillments,* as long as we appreciate that a wish is nothing more than the person's effort to assimilate reality to the self or the ego (the two terms mean roughly the same thing). Wishing is like hoping that something desired really will happen, and in dreams we occasionally pretend that these desired goals really *do* happen. In certain cases, those accommodations that have been turned aside as so-called repressions may turn up as assimilations in the dream. Marcel might dream that he and only he is kicking the soccer ball around the playground as the other boys watch and applaud his skill. In having this wish fulfilled, Marcel is assimilating without regard for reality accommodations, because the boys would never permit him to do this nor would they applaud his clumsy kicking efforts.

Time-Perspective Constructs

Piaget is probably best known for his empirical studies of the development of various physical and mental characteristics, such as sensorimotor intelligence; the knowledge of space, number, and chance; moral concerns; play patterns; dreaming; imitation of others, and so on. In each of these researches, Piaget may be seen breaking development down into a series of stages and substages, ranging usually from three to six in number. Piaget insists that before we speak of a *stage of development,* four characteristics must be evident: (1) there must be a constant and orderly succession of acquired behaviors over time; (2) an integration of these behaviors must take place across succeeding levels; (3) this integration must have the quality of a completion of earlier development but also a preparation for further development; and (4) there must be a sense of totality as a whole structure rather than there being simply piecemeal or minor changes taking place.[118] Keeping these criteria in mind, we can consider Piaget's overall theory which can be said to have three major periods of development—infancy, childhood, and adolescence. Childhood is broken down into early and later stages so that on occasion, students of Piaget will refer to his developmental theory as containing four major stages.[119] The main point for our purposes is to catch the continuing flow of action across the three or four levels of development to which we now turn.

Infancy: Birth to Age Two Years

This first major stage of life is sometimes called the prelanguage period, and it could be broken down into as many as six substages if we wanted to follow each specific nuance. We will, however, follow the drift of Piaget's explanations of his experiments in terms of three succeeding substages which he has on occasion used in his writings to capture the main characteristics of infancy. Keep in mind that at each level equilibration and (physical) construction is taking place.

Reflex Action. At birth, the infant's behavior is completely unconscious and limited to the exercises of *reflexes,* the major one of which is sucking. Piaget notes that considered mentally, for the infant "the world is essentially a thing to be sucked."[120] Sucking action is therefore used schematically to assimilate other objects to it, such as the thumb in place of mother's breast, and so on. There is no proper mental life going on in this period, because only the basic motor schemata are active. Of course, as Piaget reminds us, the reflex is the "forerunner of mental assimilation"[121] because the mind will be patterned on such structures as constructions move from the organic to the cognitive.

Every realm of sensorimotor reflex organization is the scene of particular assimilations extending . . . physicochemical assimilation . . . [and] these behavior patterns, inasmuch as they are grafted on hereditary tendencies, from the very beginning find themselves inserted in the general framework of the individual organization [that is, organic scheme]; that is to say, before any acquisition of consciousness, they enter into the functional totality which the organism constitutes.[122]

Organization of Percepts and Habits. Gradually, the child learns to thumb-suck in a more systematic way and also to turn his or her head in the direction of a sound. From about the fifth week on, children begin smiling in response to interpersonal prompts from their parents, and in time during this substage, the child will come to recognize certain persons as distinct from others. Piaget calls the equilibrating assimilations and accommodations taking place over these early months of life *reflex cycles.*[123] Such reflex cycles will develop into circular reactions because the child develops an interest in some activity and repeats it automatically. Thus, the infant of a few months of age finds that

the head-turning action is workable and begins repeating it; or the child may look about to recognize people again and again. Piaget calls such beginning practice of actions based on reflexive patternings *reproductive assimilation,*[124] because in reproducing the action, the child is assimilating the environment to it in an active way—as well as accommodating for environmental changes. For example, the child learns that head-turning is easier to do in some positions rather than others only because of the effort he or she has given to reproductive assimilation in the first place. In practicing looking at people and then at things in general, the child comes to organize *percepts* (things seen), and the practice of actions like head-turning lead to stable mannerisms of behavior called *habits.* It is not until about nine months that children begin actively looking for specific percepts like a rattle on which to center attention.

Sensorimotor Intelligence. The child in the second year of life is sometimes said to be living in a period of *practical intelligence* because he or she knows things without yet having internal thoughts.[125] That is, the child through circular reactions is continually expanding his or her range of understanding concerning how the world is patterned, how hands work and where the mouth is located, and so forth. All such schemata are differentiated completely at the level of organic construction. Piaget refers to the structures of this period as *action* schemata because they are all based on the active manipulation of objects rather than on the use of words or concepts. For example, at about the age of eighteen months, children are able to grasp a stick and use it to draw a toy toward themselves which had been placed out of reach.[126] Children have no operations (words or mental concepts) to use in reasoning through such coordinated movements, but rely totally on sensorimotor action schemata.

In addition, this stage of development reflects what Piaget has called *reciprocal assimilation,* by which he means a form of coordination that takes place among the separate action schemata of the child.

For example, a baby presented with a new object successively incorporates it into each of his "action schemata" (shaking it, stroking it, balancing it, etc.), as though he could come to know the object by perceiving how it is used. . . . It is natural, then, that these various action schemata should become assimilated with one another, i.e., coordinated so that some serve as a goal for action as a whole, while others serve as a means.[127]

There is no differentiation of a self at this time of life, so everything the baby perceives is centered on himself or herself. Psychoanalysis has called this the period of *narcissism.* Piaget says he would not quarrel with this designation, as long as it is appreciated that this is a "narcissism without Narcissus"[128] because the child has no *personal* awareness at all. Whereas Freud placed ego identity in the unconscious, for Piaget egocentricity early in life is a state of unconsciousness *without* what will later be termed self-identity. Like most of the phenomenological-existentialistic theorists, Piaget places emphasis on consciousness in the workings of what are often called the higher mental processes. Lower, automatic, sensorimotor "mental" habits of the sort we witness in infancy are nothing like what Freud believed took place, because operational thought has not yet evolved (developed). There really is no mind in that self-reflexive sense of reasoning around things,

trying to get one's wishes expressed or enacted through strategies like the parapraxes (Freudian slips), until *after* operational thought begins.

It is out of the centering of narcissism (on our own person) that the next stage of development becomes possible. Because the child does indeed consider his or her own bodily processes (satisfactions, activities, and so on) as being everything in life, there is a natural tendency to focus on them and reproduce them. Building on natural-reflex cycles, this narcissistic egocentricity will in time lead to constructions of what in the next stage of development we will call the concrete operations. This occurs by interiorizing the patterns of reflex cycles through assimilation and then by way of further circular reactions, evolving the basis for thought itself. In the second half of the first year of life, children begin to imitate the actions of others. These imitations are all of the physical variety, of course, such as reaching for what others are holding, opening the mouth when parents do, and so on. In this way, sensorimotor intelligence widens as the child is creating and reciprocally assimilating more and more schemata to the ongoing store already constructed.

By the end of the second year of life, the child has evolved four important action schemata which form the basis of *sensorimotor intelligence:* (1) a sense of the distribution of surrounding space; (2) the perception of objects (including the body) in this space; (3) a notion of causal sequence in which something brings something else about; and (4) a beginning sense of time's passage.[129] To know that objects exist, the child must first grasp the idea of permanence. Early in life, infants who fixate on an object (for example, a toy) which is then covered by a handkerchief make no effort to find it. By the end of the second year, they are seen to do so. Piaget found a direct relationship between the development of a sense of space and that of sensorimotor intelligence. To realize that objects can be nearer or farther away from our bodies is essential to our getting what we want or avoiding what we do not want. Causality is linked first of all with the child's own egocentricity. Children naturally assume that everything that happens does so because of the same motives we all have in wanting to satisfy our needs. We shall return to this point below. Finally, children have some idea of delay, waiting, happening, and all similar states that we associate with the passage of time.

Early Childhood: From Ages Two to Seven Years

Piaget has discussed this major substage in light of four topics, and we will follow his breakdown.

Socialization of Action. Early childhood reflects the groping beginnings of social life, even though as we shall see there is no real interpersonal action taking place in much of what the child does. By age two, children are conversing with some regularity so that parents are in constant verbal communication with them. Imitation is facilitated by such exchanges, as the child tries to talk like and be like mother and father. Piaget refers to the parental and other adult models as *ego ideals* for the child.[130] But the basic tenor of life during early childhood remains that of egocentricity. Children still do not have a self-awareness, although it will begin to be laid down during this preparatory period. In his studies of language development, Piaget found that until the age of seven years, children scarcely know how to have a discussion among themselves. They speak as if playing at words in a way that has no real focus on communicating ideas to another person. We see children gathered around the same table

coloring pictures, and as they jabber away in what Piaget calls a collective monologue,[131] real ideas are not being conveyed or exchanged, even though each individual participant seems to believe that he or she understands and is being understood by others. In time this interpersonal jabbering will mature into true social relations, but in early childhood it is difficult to see how language inputs from the environment have much effect on actual behavior.

The Genesis of Thought. Piaget refers to early childhood as a *preoperational stage* in the development of thought.[132] This means that there is not yet complete interiorization achieved in the patterning of organic schemata to mental levels of schematization. In essence, early childhood is a transitional and preparatory substage during which the child is moving from complete reliance on sensorimotor intelligence to the beginnings of operational intelligence. This does not begin until about age seven when use is made of *concrete operations*. "We will call concrete operations those [which] we bear on manipulable objects (effective or immediately imagineable manipulations), in contrast to operations bearing on propositions."[133]

We cannot really consider early childhood to be a truly operational substage because, though preliminary schemata are being gradually interiorized, they are not yet reversible, so they cannot be used to actively think one's way from point A to B and back again. The child's grasp of reality remains narrow and rigid, even though steps are being taken in the right direction by interiorizing the action schemata of sensorimotor intelligence through circular reactions. This often occurs during play. For example, the child may facilitate interiorization of schemas of motions, such as "moving toward" or "moving away," by having two dolls actually come together or be separated in some little drama like "Daddy go work. Mommy stay home." Although thought is being assimilated to action here, the child has not yet interrelated *go* and *stay* in a reversible sense (*going* means *not-staying,* and so on), so that true operations are not yet being "thought." [134]

From the age of three (sometimes earlier) to the age of seven, a question that occurs with increasing frequency among children is the well-known "why?" A child will ask, "Why does it rain?" or "Why does my marble roll?" If an adult tries to answer these questions with the usual scientific-mechanical explanations of atmospheric moisture and temperature or the effects of an inclined plane on gravity, these explanations will not be understood. It is impossible *in principle* for them to be understood. Children at this level cannot understand cause-effect in the abstract way required to explain rain or the workings of gravity. As we noted in a previous section (see p. 687), Piaget defines *precausality* as a primitive structural relation "in which causation still bears the marks of quasi-psychological motivation." [135] In other words, what the child wants to hear from us is that the sun made the rain fall or the marble rolls because it is fun to roll.

Such anthropomorphic explanations can be assimilated to the child's schemata because this is how he or she egocentrically understands the world. The child can make water spill by toppling over a glass, and it is certainly true that rolling down a slope is fun to do. This belief that inanimate things like the sun or a marble have intentions like we do is called *childhood animism,* which is another way of referring to the general question of anthropomorphization (see p. 11). Piaget notes that most children at this age ". . . are

practically unanimous in believing that the moon accompanies them on a walk, and their egocentricity impedes them from thinking what the moon would do in the presence of people strolling in the opposite direction." [136] Along with believing in the humanlike (anthropomorphic) nature of physical reality, children also assume that everything that takes place has a point to it, an end (*finalism*) or a purpose which must be accepted as a kind of moral law. In fact, no distinction is drawn between natural and moral laws, so the child assumes that what occurs in the world should occur, because mother, father, other important adults, or God made things the way they are and that is how they should always be.

Children cannot abstract, so they never understand the spirit of a law, but always demand that the letter of the law be observed. This is termed *moral realism,* a tendency we see merging late in this substage at about six years of age and carrying over into later childhood: ". . . moral realism induces an objective conception of responsibility. . . . For since he takes rules literally and thinks of good only in terms of obedience, the child will at first evaluate acts not in accordance with the motive that has prompted them but in terms of their exact conformity with established rules." [137] The combined effect of precausality, childhood animism, and moral realism on the psychology of the child is to present a world of intentional beings and objects, all focusing on the child, doing things for the child, and yet conforming to a set of rules that have no special justification but exist merely to be obeyed. Out of this egocentric and literal grasp of reality the child constructs a series of schemata, which is unstable and poorly systematized at first; but the very simplicity and rigidity of such preliminary understandings ensures that a stable pattern will eventually be interiorized as childhood is lived through.

Intuition and Semilogic. If operational thinking is not occurring in early childhood, then what do we call this early cognitive effort on the part of the child? It is an in-between kind of activity, not totally sensorimotor but not yet up to concrete operations either. In some of his earlier writings, Piaget referred to the first efforts at operational thought during early childhood as intuitive reasoning or simply *intuition*. He defined this concept as follows: "Primary intuition is no more than a sensorimotor [action] schema transposed into an act of thought so that it naturally inherits the characteristics of the sensorimotor schema."[138] For example, a child of four or five years may be shown a series of eight blue discs aligned in a row with little spaces between each, and then be asked to reproduce the series by selecting red discs from a pile. The child will intuitively construct an arrangement of red discs in a row of exactly the same length as the blue discs but without bothering to keep the number of discs identical and without considering the matter of spacing between discs.[139] Piaget points out that this child has thought of the task solely in terms of quantity, that is, of the space occupied as a unit by the blue series in the perceptual field. It is as if a global impression as an action scheme is taken over uncritically and used whole hog without accommodation.

A more detailed examination of the task would have required the child to reason with reversibility. That is, the child would have needed to mull the task over, looking at it from different perceptual angles ("Let's see, what is that blue bunch really like? Is it just those discs all together or is there another thing about them?") and asking questions once a copy had been made ("Now, is the red bunch just like the blue bunch? How are they alike and are they different at all?"), and so on. This more abstract reversibility in reasoning has yet to be constructed by the child. Piaget first called all such preoperational thought intuition, but as he did further work, he began to see that there was a certain degree of half logic (half operationality) in these crude understandings, and in time, he called this *semilogic*.[140] Here is another example: Paul, a five-year-old boy, has a brother Etienne, and when asked, he correctly states that he (Paul) has a brother, but Etienne *does not*. The semilogic reflected here is in Paul's premise that "one boy plus a brother makes two." Hence, as there are only two children in the family and Paul is unable to reverse perspectives, if he has *the* brother, then Etienne cannot.[141] Thanks to Paul's egocentricity, the concept of "brother" can mean only "in relation to me."

Affectivity and Expanding Motivations. Affectivity continues its maturation along with the development of semilogical thought. Piaget places emotions on a par with strictly intellectual cognition, as follows: "There is never a purely intellectual action, and numerous emotions, interests, values, impressions of harmony, etc., intervene [with each other]—for example, in the solving of a mathematical problem. Likewise, there is never a purely affective act, e.g., love presupposes comprehension."[142] There are many challenging sources of affection at this time of life, sources that create the disequilibria of needs and motivate the child to restore equilibrium—which in turn spurs further development because this is never a matter of settling things or quieting them down. With every need met, a further step is taken along the road of life bringing on the possibility of further needs being generated.

Some of the major feelings experienced at this age relate to the interpersonal. Feelings of sympathy and antipathy (dislike) are important. To feel in sympathy with another person, we must share certain basic values or preferences. Ordinarily, there is no problem here in most families because children at this stage are quite literal in accepting whatever the adult wishes, often taking via moral realism each parental request or show of interest as a command. Feelings of dislike occur when the child comes into conflict with the values of others, and sometimes this arises from the unusually high standards generated by moral realism. A child of six or seven might severely criticize a younger sibling for not following some home rule—such as wiping one's shoes before entering the family dwelling—and generates considerable interpersonal hostility in the process. Slight changes in familiar patterns during this age may provoke anxiety in the child, who much prefers keeping the world as it is. Along with enjoying the same fairy tale told to them night after night, children like to have the same routine followed on special occasions, such as holidays or birthdays. It is as if the predictable routine of these events is reassuring, something to be looked forward to and counted on as completely known and understood.

Near the end of early childhood, an important affective event takes place in what Piaget calls the act of *self-evaluation*.[143] This refers to the relative feelings of worth a child senses in relation to his or her emerging identity and touches upon what Adler was getting at in his constructs of inferiority or superiority feelings. As the child is beginning to frame some understanding of a self, moving to later childhood where this sense of identity will be even more important, it is essential that a proper equilibration occur in relation to mastering environmental challenges of both an interpersonal and impersonal nature. In addition to getting along

with others, children must feel competent to dress themselves, handle their food utensils, color with a crayon, and so on. Piaget notes that all of us have our failures and successes in early childhood, and that in time, we frame a scale of worth concerning ourselves which is fairly accurate. Some of us form higher opinions of ourselves, some lower, but as long as they meet reality, this is as it should be. Sometimes, however, children get distorted pictures of themselves. Mother must neither minimize frustrations or shortcomings for the child nor escalate the importance of every challenge or setback in the broader scheme of things. It is especially harmful when children begin imagining plusses or minuses in their personality which do *not* exist. If there is mutual love in a family, such extreme disequilibrations will normally be avoided.

Late Childhood: From Age Seven to Twelve

In considering late childhood, we will repeat the same four-part breakdown we used in looking at early childhood.

Progress in Behavioral Development and Socialization. Many changes take place when children reach the age of seven or eight years, the most important of which is that social and intellectual egocentricity is being left behind.[144] Egocentrism has permitted the child to detach the processes of adaptation from reality in favor of make-believe experience.[145] With the loss of such nonreality orientations, children in later childhood begin to concentrate better on the tasks of life; they also begin working more effectively in collaboration with others.[146] In a sense, children help construct each other's grasp of reality, thanks to their individual behavioral gains. There is a reciprocal process going on—one in which each individual child begins to see that he or she has a viewpoint distinctly independent from and often contrary to the viewpoints of others.

The continuing socialization process also helps alert the child to his or her internal processes through a rudimentary *self-reflection.* Piaget observes, "Reflection is nothing other than internal deliberation, that is to say, a discussion which is conducted with oneself." [147] This *internal dialectic in self-dialogue* serves to further a sense of selfhood as the child comes to affirm (believe in, agree with) *a* point of view rather than holding to all points of view without concern for contradiction.[148] Having a point of view and sticking to it permits clearer social relations to occur as children align themselves on one side or the other of various issues and reputations for believing this or that are established. The practice of internal discussion is helpful in resolving interpersonal disagreements, because each child can now see that there is more than one outlook on a question. Whether to play a game following one set of rules or another set can be negotiated and changed if necessary to meet the needs of all participants. By and large, children tend to cooperate at this stage of life because in many cases a logic of fairness is suggested.[149] By pleading for fairness, most children in later childhood can influence the course of a disagreement as long as a good case can be made for what they are recommending to their playmates. We will return to this point below in discussing morality.

Progress of Thought: Development of Conservation. Piaget and his colleagues conducted numerous experiments to establish the fact that reversibility emerges in late childhood. These studies are called *conservation experiments,* because what they aim to find out is whether a child can grasp that quality of change within stability (permanence) that typifies the more abstract schemata (see p.

680). Can the child appreciate that concepts like mass and weight are constant even though we manipulate their *perceived* appearance by pouring liquids from glass to glass or slice wholes into portions? For example, assume that we have two identical glasses, A and B. Bridget, a four-year-old girl, and Annette, a seven-year-old girl, are both asked to place equal numbers (a dozen or so) of blue beads in glass A and red beads in glass B. We next ask both girls to pour the blue beads from glass A into glass C, which is taller and narrower so that the level of beads is stretched out in glass C, thanks to its more tubelike shape. Even though they have poured the blue beads from A to C themselves, when asked which glass, B or C, now has more beads, Bridget will say C and Annette will say that neither has.[150]

Annette has constructed a stable conception of volume (schema) to interrelate with her conception of shape (schema), enabling her to abstract operationally and not rely solely on what is seen (perceived) but on what is *known.* Bridget is still very concrete in operational thought, more sensorimotor in her schematic understanding, so that she cannot abstract conceptions like volume and shape but must instead report what she sees (perceives in a literal sense). And what she literally sees is one glass much taller than another with beads piled in it almost to the top, whereas the shorter glass is not nearly so filled up. Annette is able to take her thinking forward from the original comparison of glasses A and B and then bring it back after we have manipulated her visual field by bringing in glass C. This is why Piaget defines *conservation* as "the possibility of a rigorous return to the point of departure." [151] This flexibility enables her to decenter her egocentricity and view things in a reversible fashion, thereby enabling logical thought to proceed to even higher-level constructions of rational thought.

The Rational Operations: Concreteness. As soon as a child's intuition or semilogic is transformed into reversible thought, we can begin speaking about true operations taking place. Piaget explicitly states that the age of seven or eight is the point where *concrete operations* first appear.[152] This means that in late childhood we still witness schematic organizations which relate to manipulable things rather than to abstractions. The average child cannot therefore follow discussions in which hypothetical or relativistic propositions are being considered. It would be pointless to make a list of the concrete operations employed during this stage. Almost anything relating to thought or cognition is an operation. About the only distinction we see Piaget making is that of separating affective operations from what we might call intellectual operations. The main point needing emphasis is that *rational thought* is evolving, maturing, developing, but it is doing this in an actively *constructive* fashion.

A distinctive feature of rational thought is that it takes two initially separate schemata and combines or *groups* them to create a new structure. This constructive process of *grouping* is essential to the development of rational thought, to the creation of even more stable— hence abstract—cognitive operations. Grouping also includes the processes of reversibility, of course. Indeed, *four characteristics of grouping* are necessary preliminaries for further evolution of rational (logical) thinking in the child. Using mathematical examples, Piaget summarizes these four characteristics as follows:

We may draw a general conclusion: a child's thinking becomes logical only through the organization of systems of operations which obey the laws common to all groupings: (1) Composition: two operations may combine to give another operation of the grouping (e. g., +1 +1 = +2). (2) Reversibility: every operation can be inverted (e. g., +1 becomes inverted to −1). (3) The direct operation and its inverse gives rise to an identical or null operation (e. g., +1 −1 = 0). (4) Operations can combine with one another in all kinds of ways.[153]

Once these four characteristics have been constructed, the child will be moving into the higher-level cognitive operations of adolescence and adulthood.

Affectivity in Morality and Willful Behavior. The gradual loss of egocentricity in later childhood has great relevance for the development of morality. Piaget distinguishes between the *morality of constraint* and the *morality of cooperation.*[154] All morality, according to Piaget, "consists in a system of rules,"[155] and hence this morality distinction has to do with how children look at the following of rules. As we have seen, in early childhood, moral realism rests upon a literal rule-following pattern in which the child feels constrained to behave as expected simply because "that's the way it is." The world is set up with strict laws and the child follows them as understood without regard for their (abstract) rationale. This morality of constraint begins to give way to a morality of cooperation in later childhood, as the growth of reversibility in thought makes it better understood that things are not *always* "precisely so" or that the natural order of lawfulness is not identical with a moral order of how things "ought" to be in every case.

Piaget has conducted many interesting studies on rule-following behavior. Using games like marbles, he has shown that young children find it upsetting to be arbitrary in following rules once they have been learned. "For very young children, a rule is a sacred reality because it is traditional; for the older ones it depends upon mutual agreement."[156] Younger children also are much harsher in assigning punishment to those who break the rules. They seem to want to emphasize the punishment for its own sake, whereas older children use punishment more to show the transgressor that a bond has been broken between people when a wrongdoing takes place. Piaget's value system considers rule by cooperation a more satisfactory equilibration in human relations than rule by authority. In order for a *rule* to work without authority pressures, there must be feelings of mutual respect among the persons who subscribe to the rule.[157] This necessarily brings affectivity into considerations of morality. Authoritarian constraint rules through feelings of anxiety and fear, but when mutual respect exists among people, a morality of cooperation can occur. Just as logic is the sum of rules that intelligence makes use of to control behavior, so too is morality the sum of rules that our affective life makes use of to control behavior.[158]

Affections (emotions) are therefore closely aligned with *self-control,* filling thereby not only an energizing but a selective role in behavior. We do things that make us feel pleasant or good (including morally good) and avoid things that make us feel unpleasant or bad. Affective operations are therefore important to self-emergence and willful behavior because:

. . . to the extent that the emotions become organized, they emerge as regulations whose final form of equilibrium is none other than the will. Thus, will *is the true affective equivalent of the operation in* reason. *Will is a late-appearing function. The real exercise of will*

is linked to the functioning of the autonomous moral feelings, which is why we have waited until this [late-childhood] stage to discuss it.[159]

Not until the child has left the egocentric-moral-realism stage of seeing rules as unquestionable and progressed to the stage of seeing rules as demanding personal judgment and commitment can we speak of the will emerging in the personality.

Piaget thinks of willfulness as occurring when the person must regulate his or her energy expenditure. If a person has a single, firm intention to do something like eat an ice cream cone, then there is no point in speaking of willful behavior in this action. Piaget describes the origins of will much as he described the origins of consciousness (see p. 687), that is, as entering when there is a conflict in behavioral tendencies. The nine-year-old boy who is struggling with the temptation of watching television rather than doing his homework is involved in a willful decision-making process. At the precise moment of temptation the boy's morally superior tendency (to study) is *weaker* than the more pleasurable albeit inferior tendency (to watch television). "The act of will does not consist of following the inferior and stronger tendency; on the contrary, one would then speak of a failure of will or 'lack of will power.' Will power involves reinforcing the superior but weaker tendency so as to make it triumph."[160] In this way, when a duty is momentarily weaker than a specific desire, will re-establishes values according to the hierarchical order that was initially constructed by the boy in assigning values to his various behaviors. If he had not constructed a value system placing study over television viewing, there would not have been a conflict to begin with. Will is therefore an operation that permits reversibility to take place in returning fleeting interest values that arise as feelings of pleasure (watching television) to their proper place lower in the systematic hierarchy of values (studies come first).

The will waits on two important earlier developments to occur: (1) *self-identity* must begin, because intentional behavior is impossible without self-awareness;[161] and (2) disequilibrations in the form of *moral conflicts* must arise. Thus, as we noted earlier when discussing Piaget's reticence concerning finalism (see p. 686), even though he describes behavior as teleonomic,[162] this does not mean it is thought of as being under freely intended direction by the individual. Self-identity and intentionality in behavior are late-born developments that spring from earlier (unconscious, reflexive) equilibrations and the resultant constructions which were fashioned concerning the self and others. In the final analysis, there is a kind of impersonal evolutionary flow to behavioral events which carry them from origins in bodily patterns to the abstractions of high-level thought without benefit of selfhood, although later in life when a self-image has been constructed, this contributes to the forward-moving, improving, evolutionary process.

Adolescence

The final stage of development is adolescence, which carries the person forward into adulthood. As we know, dramatic physical and physiological changes take place in the body at this time. Piaget notes that the maturation of the sexual instinct results in a degree of disequilibration for the young person, so that in accommodating this new factor and as-

similating it to ongoing schemata, there is a "characteristic affective coloration"[163]—namely, a preoccupation with emotional display and heterosexual contacts. There are also dramatic changes taking place in operational thought. We will consider these two sides to the adolescent's experience, beginning with the intellectual and moving to the affectional.

The Formal Operations of Mature Thought. Beginning sometime betwee eleven and thirteen years of age, we witness the developing person beginning to use *formal operations,* which means that he or she employs "the form of general ideas and abstract constructions"[164] rather than relying on the perception and/or manipulation of concrete objects. Adolescents can therefore begin taking an interest in problems that are totally removed from everyday reality. We might say that adolescence is the period of life in which theorizing is born. "Formal thought is 'hypothetico-deductive,' in the sense that it permits one to draw conclusions from pure hypotheses and not merely from actual observations."[165] All of the typical adolescent characteristics the Freudians and others have explained as sublimations of sexuality—intellectualism, desire to improve the world, asceticism, religiosity, and so on—are reflections of this newly evolved ability to "think about conceptual thought" and not merely to deal with concrete reality. Adolescents can see what "is" and aspire to achieve what "might be" because their thinking is no longer "practical"; indeed, it is often idealistically impractical.

Formal operations of abstract thought are like concrete operations in the sense of reversibility and a logical ordering of what is understood in their use. But in reasoning formally, reversibility moves up a notch, so that now the person can be more arbitrary and consider not only alternative courses of action but also the advisability of pursuing alternatives in the first place. This thought turning back on itself is what is meant by *reflexivity,* or *self-reflexivity.* The person can think about the form his thought is taking as a series of propositions, so that rather than merely planning a course of action, he or she can frame a "representation of a representation of possible action."[166] When we reason *propositionally,* we are essentially taking an "as if" or a "let's assume" or even a "let's pretend" attitude about the most stable structures of our perceived experience. In order for Einstein to challenge concepts like time and space, he had to think about assumptions, about how physicists before him had affirmed unchallenged premises (propositions) regarding their study. It is this key ability for self-reflexivity that truly separates formal from concrete operational thought. "Formal operations engender a 'logic of propositions' in contrast to the logic of relations, classes, and numbers engendered by concrete operations."[167]

In his later writings, Piaget was to refer to this capacity of thought to pair off contrasting or conflicting propositions as a *dialectical* form of reasoning (see p. 9). However, when he did so, he was usually referring to the developmental synthesis to be achieved, so that his conception of dialectical mental processes is tied closely to his idea of progress in thought achieved by resolving differences and moving ahead to a new level. Thus, we do not find Piaget referring to the contradictory style of thought used by children up to ages seven or eight as dialectical, presumably because no synthesis is achieved moving thinking as a constructive process along.[168] Dialectic should be reflected in the progressive flow of events, events that do not move in a linear fashion but evolve to higher levels nonetheless. Piaget says, ". . . dialectic over and over again substitutes 'spirals' for the linear or 'tree' models with which we start, and these famous spirals or non-vicious circles are very much like the genetic or interactions

characteristic of growth."[169] As we shall see below in this chapter (see p. 713), Kelly frames his process of construction as a dialectical understanding of how two items are alike and yet contrasted oppositionally to a third; but he does not relate this process to a developmental progress, to higher and higher levels of structured thought.

Piaget, on the other hand, seems to place construction at the heart of the evolutionary process, as in effect bringing about dialectical advance. "It is often construction itself which begets the negations along with the affirmations, and the syntheses whereby they are rendered coherent as well."[170] We can see this in logical or mathematical reasoning, wherein dialectic is reflected as a "construction by negation."[171] Dialectic allows the developing person to abstract by understanding that whatever he or she is thinking about, alternative meanings are generated by the opposites suggested. Believing that "My neighborhood is the best one in the whole city" may be accepted quite literally by the child reasoning according to concrete operations. But with formal operations, the child begins to understand that this is simply a statement of opinion, one needing support and justification in some manner, and that its validity might depend on the grounds we arbitrarily select to judge this blanket statement. There is a decentering in such a self-reflexive examination, a loss in the authoritative conclusion which was reached. But in understanding things this way, the child necessarily constructs a higher-order schemata, form, and so on, making possible a much broader and more sophisticated grasp of what knowledge is all about. Thus it is that dialectic must be seen as essential to the equilibrating process of assimilation-accommodation, reversibility, and so on: ". . . the dialectical attitude seems essential to the full working out of structures;

dialectic is both complementary to and inseparable from analytic, even formalizing, reason." [172]

Even though *egocentricity* in the childhood sense is over by adolescence, we should not get the idea that it stops occurring during this period, or even later in life for that matter. Egocentricity is a certain style of thought people use—predominantly in early life, but later as well. Adolescent egocentricity is reflected in the often simplistic schemes young adults have for improving the world. They have their point of view, and even though they are capable of seeing alternatives, they may decide with great genuineness and/or arrogance that this is the *only* answer to the problem at hand. As Piaget says, "Adolescent egocentricity is manifested by belief in the omnipotence of reflection, as though the world should submit itself to idealistic schemes rather than to systems of reality." [173] Accommodation is called for here, and in time with increasing experience, the young adult will gradually achieve an equilibration between his or her formal thought and the realistic possibilities of reality. Even so, there are times when the exuberance of adolescence effects a significant change in society. Young people have made important contributions by thinking the unthinkable or by serving as the conscience of their country to bring about a change in its national policy.

Affectivity as Personality in Adult Society. Paralleling the evolution of formal operations in thought, Piaget sees a rise in adolescent affectivity in the completion of personality and its injection into adult society.[174] We are now considering personality in the more specific (nonsystematic) sense referred to above (see p. 686). Personality began to emerge in middle to late childhood (eight to twelve years) along with the development of will

and the formation of a value system. Piaget draws a distinction between the *self* and the *personality* in overall behavior. The self is a more primitive aspect of the person, so that it is closer to egocentricity of either a conscious or unconscious variety than is the personality.[175] The person constructs a schema of identity, but this is still centered on the self in a "selfish" manner because of the continuation of at least some egocentricity. Piaget's concept of personality now comes in to counter this egocentric selfishness in the sense of the person's *character* (see p. 27). Thus, personality is the capacity to submit oneself to some form of discipline. "For example, a man is not said to have a strong personality when everything is egotistically determined and he remains incapable of dominating the self. He is said to have a strong personality when he incarnates an ideal or defends a cause with all his activity and will." [176]

Personality therefore implies "a kind of decentering of the self," [177] which subordinates the more egocentric tendencies to a disciplined course of action. Piaget does not believe that such value-directed behavioral patterns are "input" from the environment. The person must construct his or her own personality (character). Consistent with what we have already said of the egocentricity of idealistic thought in adolescence, there is a paralleling sense of affective egocentricity during this stage of life. Piaget believed that the adolescent: ". . . wants to surpass and astound them [his or her elders] by transforming the world. That is why the adolescent's systems or life plans are at the same time filled with generous sentiments and altruistic or mystically fervent projects and with disquieting megalomania and conscious egocentricity." [178]

Adolescents therefore inject themselves into adult society by means of projects, theoretical systems, and ideas of political or social reform. Their hypothetico-deductive thinking—that is, from presumed propositions to deduced implications—may depart from reality in that their hypotheses may be debatable, but their emotional feelings of commitment to the values they embrace are real enough. The gradual movement into higher education or a job will tend to help restore the equilibrium as the older adolescent comes to focus emotions on a more structured, realistically oriented goal once again.[179] At this point, we often witness the young adult's true genius as creative innovations are made a reality. In the final analysis, Piaget puts his trust in reason to calm the turbulent waters of adolescence. "In reality, the most profound tendency of all human activity is progression toward equilibrium. Reason, which expressed the highest form of equilibrium, reunites intelligence and affectivity." [180] This is precisely where we would expect him as an evolutionary rationalist to place his trust. Human beings are rational animals who have evolved in body-to-mind fashion a higher intelligence which serves them in the affective sphere as well.

Commonalities and Variations in Development

Piaget's contention is that all human beings pass through the stages of intellectual and affective development we have just reviewed. They do so *not* because they have been preprogrammed by heredity but because there is a kind of logico-epistemological *necessity* for all human beings—given their natural endowment—to develop in this fashion, once interactions with reality are begun following birth. It is easy to confuse the biological necessity of heredity with the logical necessity of higher and higher levels of thought. Our biological structures frame certain beginning limits on how we will think and what we can normally think about. But in time, logic of

both a dialectical (oppositional) and a demonstrative (linear) type (see pp. 6–9) will allow the person to move beyond biological determinism yet *also* proceed in an evolutionary way to develop common thought and emotional patterns. There is a logical necessity over and above the biological necessity, which is why systems of mathematics have been worked out by different cultures and by different people within the same culture with no direct contact between them. The specifics of a logical system might even differ from one point of view to the next, but the form all thought takes as regards conceptions of space, succession, order, and so on, will be common. It is as if each person relives the same process in each individual life (ontogeny recapitulating a phylogeny of logical development).[181]

This does not mean that everyone makes it to the highest levels of abstract thought, of course. Some people do not construct things clearly; they make errors in judgment or fail to progress beyond a certain level. This is what Piaget would call a *fixation* in development—a failure to evolve. He also offers some interesting observations on the possibility of only limited development in operational thinking, as follows:

. . . There can be fixations at certain stages; there can be delays and accelerations. But I would even go further. Within the formal operational level, it is entirely possible that some people, for instance those in manual professions, specialized laborers of various sorts, may reach the formal operational level in the particular professional domain, but not right across the board.[182]

Here again—since it is always up to the person to construct what will eventuate in cognition—Piaget is making allowances for the fact that there will be variations in the development of higher-order operations. But there is no talk of regression in his theory. He follows more the theory of Jung concerning fixation than that of Freud (see p. 211). People do not regress to an earlier stage; they simply fail to progress completely to the next level or do so in only a limited sense.

Individual-Differences Constructs

Becoming a Person: Interiorization via Imitation

Piaget obviously leaves much room for the person as actor in constructing not only his or her self schema but also the affective schema which, as a system of values, holds the more selfish side of behavior in check as the personality (character). The specific contents of these schemata are naturally influenced by the people with whom the child is reared and the society in which the rearing takes place. But it is up to the person to do the actual constructing of self and personality. It is true that people pattern themselves after others, interiorizing those aspects of another person's behavior which they *imitate*. Piaget defines *imitation* as the "primacy of accommodation over assimilation." [183] Of course, assimilation is always primary to accommodation and imitation probably grows out of reproductive assimilations which have a beginning schema already patterned. As Piaget notes, "The child imitates an aeroplane or a tower because he understands their significance, and he is only interested in them when they have some bearing on his own activities." [184]

In time, however, as the child imitates more and more things, he or she finds the accommodation side of the circular reactions

that result quite fascinating, particularly because in the act of imitation, there is always more to be learned about the self. Imitating others, we also learn how we might differ from others and to this extent we know more about our selves. Affection plays an important role as well, because children are more likely to imitate liked than disliked people. [185] Piaget would suggest that so-called *identification* with a parent is tied closely to the accommodations based on affective schemata. We interiorize our parents' behavior and values because we have emotional schemata to which we assimilate their identities and then accommodate that which they believe in. [186] Piaget has no series of personality theorotypes to which he alludes in his writings. What the particular self-identity and personality-related value system will be like depends entirely on the uniquely developing individual, the equilibrations achieved in the continuing circular reactions of adjustment, and the peculiar patterns accommodated through imitation. We would have also to take into consideration any fixations or partial fixations in development, as discussed in the previous section. It follows that the range of *individual differences* in Piagetian theory is great indeed. He, like the other theorists in the phenomenological-existentialistic tradition, is loathe to categorize people.

Language as a Means of Personality Influence: Pros and Cons

Piaget has never been of the opinion that language structures thought. His studies of egocentric language convinced him that verbal usage is not patterned by the environment but is rather constructed from within the child's internal mental activity. Sensorimotor constructions and action schemata are patterning behavior even before the child has a language to use. Thus, says Piaget, ". . . prior to any language, more or less complex systems of representation can be formed." [187] Once it is learned, language can influence what we think, but it cannot be said to shape thought itself as the behaviorists would claim.

In using language, the child's imitative capacities are being extended, but the point of importance is that the child does actively make use of words as an instrumentality to gain a desired goal (teleonomic behavior). Language is an accompaniment to action, beginning mainly in the form of orders and expressions of desire by the child. Once it is being used, the child is also able to reconstruct past actions in memory by verbalizing about them; this would be the beginnings of representation (imagination). [188] In time, the word used to describe an action begins to function as a sign, so that rather than just being a part of the action, it can evoke the action or bring it to mind. Then and only then is the verbal scheme detached from the sensorimotor scheme and used in imagination as a memory. The child begins by grasping the teddy bear reflexively and, in time after imitation-prompts from parents, learns to say "teddy" while fondling the beloved toy. The word would never be related to the toy if the child did not already possess a sensorimotor scheme of the fluffy plaything. Later, each time the child plays with the toy, the word "teddy" will be part of the action, but also a verbal scheme will be under construction. Once it is constructed, the child will be able to ask for "teddy" and/or recall playing with the toy bear (representation).

Even after the child has constructed a series of verbal schema (words tied to perceived objects, persons, and so on), there is no assurance that by using them a genuine communication is being attempted. During the period of collective monologue, "words have no social function" [189] as the child is playfully assimilating them to action schemata. Piaget would say that a true *dialogue* does not occur until the child responds to a state-ment expressing a proposition by talking about something that was in that proposition. [190] If Paul offers an opinion on why the swimming-pool water is so cold only to have Louis "respond" by laughing and saying that he is going to throw his toy duck into the water, a dialogue has *not* been joined. When it does emerge, it will be because both children make an effort to cast their language in a mutually understandable way. Piaget suggests that children probably learn the importance of this by first getting in an argument over some point of mutual interest. [191] For example, if Louis jumped into the water and claimed it was *not* cold, then in the quarrel with Paul over this issue, a lot could be learned by both boys in how to communicate. As in the case of the development of will, so long as a statement goes unchallenged, the child simply *says things* to accompany the more important fact that he or she is *doing things*. Language thus evolves from a playful endeavor to the serious business of making our wants and opinions known.

Once this bridge has been crossed, language becomes an important factor in social influence. The child can through representation make a better estimate of what is taking place in life and can more clearly negotiate circumstances to his or her preference. With the acquisition of the skills of reading, the maturing person will greatly extend representations, take on various interests, and eventually construct those important schemata known as the self and the personality. Even though language plays such an important role in development, Piaget must be considered a critic of personologists who explain behavioral style in terms of environmental shaping through language acquisition. Language does not shape the person; it is the other way around. Indeed, Piaget has reservations about those explanations of personality that rest upon social influence.

The Limitations of Social Explanations

In the final analysis, Piaget's message is that mind and those related factors entering into personality are created (constructed) independently not only of language shapings but of *any* form of social or cultural influence. There is a patterning of behavior constantly underway in development, but the logical order of this pattern is not done *in* the environment and then placed *into* the person. The person as an organically developing but also logically developing organism does the patterning, the *constructing* of what he or she will be like as a finished product in adulthood. *Society* is not something apart and different from the individuals who make it up. All members of society learn to be who they are in a similar fashion, and although there are interpersonal factors to consider in each individual's life, these factors do not explain how this learning is achieved.[192] Learning is rooted in human nature, in the biologically based sensorimotor actions on which mind is then constructed. Society is in this sense closer to biology than to a supraindividual force of a group mind or some such. Humanity is the reflection of the single mind of any one human being.

Piaget's views are nicely summarized in the following: " 'Society' is neither a thing nor a cause, but a system of relationships, and it is for the psychologist to classify these relationships and analyse separately their respective effects."[193] Now these relationships are not simply *there,* in reality from the beginning of time. *Social norms* are constructed over historical time and bind people to them,[194] but in the final analysis, they exist only because they have been so structured by individuals. In this sense, ". . . *all* the social sciences yield structuralist theories since, however different they may be, they are all concerned with social groups and subgroups, that is, with self-regulating transformational totalities."[195] As social scientists, we study these stable structures called societies, structures that have evolved through construction in the same way that higher mental reasonings have evolved within the skulls of each of us. Just as we do not reify *mind* as existing independently from body, we do not reify *society* as something existing independently from the individuals who gave it birth and now sustain its existence by mutual consent.

Having now put the matter of society's origins straight, we can recognize that the normative structures of the historical past serve a constraining influence on the present. Society is not transmitted from generation to generation internally, as is the case of instinctive behavior in lower animals. Only through the external pressure exercised by individuals upon each other can the weight of society be felt.[196] In this sense, society can be seen as "a series (or rather many intersecting series) of generations, each exercising pressure upon the one which follows it. . . ."[197] If we look at the history of societies, we find a gradual lessening of this pressure brought to bear on one generation by an earlier generation. "The more complex the society, the more autonomous is the personality [of its members] and the more important are the relations of cooperation between equal individuals."[198] In a complex society, it no longer becomes possible to press just one point of view in an authoritarian, constraining sense. People must at this more advanced stage of societal evolution cooperate and compromise in order to maintain the integrity of the culture.

Looked at from the point of view of the individual person evolving beyond the sensorimotor influences of biological reflexes to a higher order of reasoning, the major role of society is to further consciousness among its individual members. For the individual, left to himself or herself, would remain unconsciously egocentric.[199] It is in the comparison of oneself to others—attempting to convey an idea through language or observing some disparity in behavior between oneself and other people—that more and more awareness is generated. Also the resulting competitions when we compare ourselves to others stirs greater achievements as well as cooperative endeavors. All of the problems of interpersonal relations then enter to greatly complicate the picture of what human nature is *really* like. Piaget's basic image of humanity stresses the biological beginnings and the individuality of construction in genetic epistemology. The child is parent to the adult, and children develop from an organic reality which must not be forgotten in our zeal to explain behavioral patterns interpersonally.

Implications for Abnormal Behavior

Though Piaget does not have a formal theory of illness or cure, there are many points in his writings at which we can see implications for these aspects of personality study. First of all, we must get a general definition of what abnormal behavior or maladjustment means to Piaget. Recall that Piaget defines learning as taking place when a *durable equilibration* is achieved via some behavioral action.[200] The person who has learned has constructed a behavioral pattern that lasts because it is successfully answering needs via the circular reactions of assimilation and accommodation. On the other hand, Piaget notes that ". . . durable disequilibria constitute pathological organic or mental states." [201] In other words,

when we have a lasting (learned) pattern of behavior that fails to meet the person's needs, we have *abnormality* taking place. It is not "natural" for evolution to develop *disequilibria,* of course. But since the individual person is a factor in the construction of schemata and the operations of thought that employ these conceptual frames, it is inevitable that serious problems will arise. We might now review some of the possible sources of difficulty.

First of all, Piaget notes that the very inadequacy of being a child among adults has within it the possible seeds of a serious problem. Children are constantly surrounded by adults who not only know more than they do, but who are capable of anticipating the thoughts and desires of children. This leads to some children thinking that adults (and later, other people in general) can read their minds. This may even be the reason egocentric children do not make the effort to talk clearly, convinced as they are that adults know what they are thinking about anyhow. Piaget suggests that some of the delusional symptoms to be seen in adult psychotic disorders like schizophrenia may stem from this early experience.[202] This may come about especially if the child is reared in a home where control through constraint rather than through cooperation and mutual respect is practiced. Though children construct their own self-identities and the affective schemata of personality, they are obviously influenced by the kinds of interpersonal relations (love, trust, and so on) they encounter in their family setting.

We have already noted in our discussion of development that it is essential for a child to acquire a realistic self-estimate. Children who grossly overrate or underrate themselves are doomed to maladjustments of one form or another. Piaget is fundamentally a *realist* in theoretical persuasion (see p. 14). The point of evolution is to actively adapt the person to both the physical and the social environment.[203] If the maturing child fails to accommodate to the realities of existence but instead represses those aspects that are not assimilable, then maladjustment is sure to follow. Probably we all have a certain degree of such denials of reality. We all live somewhat in a dream world, assimilating to our self-images those things we find admirable and repressing those things we dislike. But if this lack of realistic adaptation to the realities facing us gets too extreme, we will essentially construct our own problems because it will be us and not reality that is out of adjustment. Affective schemata in particular are likely to distort reality in this essentially unconscious fashion.[204]

We must also recall that Piaget's recognition of fixation allows for abnormal thought patterns to develop, because if a child retains egocentricity and continues thinking about reality in syncretic and other prelogical ways, it would be increasingly likely that his or her social adjustment would suffer in maturation to adulthood.[205] Many of the bizarre behaviors witnessed among psychotic individuals can be understood as being due to the confused perceptions and operations that result from fixated, narrow, syncretic thought. The rigidity of paranoia, for example, suggests a lack of reversibility as noted in the intuition of semilogic of early childhood. It is not that the paranoid has regressed to early childhood, but merely that he or she has fixated at this level. Partial fixations can also be seen in restricted problems of narrowness of the sort that Jung called one-sidedness. To the extent that the schemata are narrow and thought lacks reversibility, the individual may be seen to compensate by pressing schemata that really do not fit onto reality. When this happens, Piaget tells us that "assimilation is distorted." [206] It is a combination of all these factors—durable disequilibria, feelings of weakness, repression, and fixation—which provides the basis for explanations of abnormal behavior in Piagetian theory. In order to cure these difficulties, Piaget would doubtlessly put his trust in an honest facing-up to the realities of life. The well-adjusted (adapted) person in Piagetian theory is self-accepting, willing to accommodate, and above all, realistic about life.

George A. Kelly's Psychology of Personal Constructs

We next move to a constructivism of another variety in the psychology of personal constructs proposed by George A. Kelly. Though he shares certain phenomenological precedents with Piaget, as a psychotherapist interested in viewing the world from the (introspective) point of view of his clients, Kelly had a purely cognitive or conceptual interest in the constructive process. He did not have that biological or material form of construction in his theory that we found so central to Piaget's views.

Biographical Overview

George A. Kelly was born in America's heartland, the flat, expansive state of Kansas on 28 April 1905. Kelly was an only child, and his mother doted on him. His father was a Presbyterian minister and farmer who was forced to give up his ministry for reasons of health but did occasionally follow his calling over the years. Kelly was born in a farm home and began his education in a one-room elementary school. He later attended high school in Wichita, Kansas, living away from home much of the time after he was thirteen years old. Kelly's parents were devoutly religious in a fundamentalist sense, and they were always working to help the needy in any possible way. His mother made pastoral calls on the sick, and his father was active in his faith, even when he was not leading a church congregation of his own. The family was hard-working and frowned on the less serious aspects of life like dancing or card-playing. However, as the only child, Kelly was given much attention by his parents, and his school attendance away from the family home provided him with a broadened outlook on life which he might not otherwise have had.

Kelly attended Friends University for three years, where he was active in debate and music. His last year of undergraduate work was spent at Parke College, where in 1926 he received the B.A. degree in physics and mathematics. Kelly was not certain what he wanted to do with his life at this point. He first considered a career in aeronautical engineering and even worked in this new field for a brief time before he found his interests turning to education.[207] In rapid succession, he worked at a labor college in Minneapolis, taught speech for the American Bankers Association, and then conducted an Americanization class for future citizens. It was while he was teaching at a junior college in Sheldon, Iowa, during the winter of 1927–1928, that Kelly met Gladys Thompson, who later became his wife. Mrs. Kelly was teaching high school English, but both she and George coached dramatics in the same building. This work in theater was to prove extremely important to Kelly's eventual theory of behavior.

Kelly's professional development took a major turn in 1929 when he was awarded an exchange scholarship. He spent a year studying under Sir Godfrey Thomson—an eminent

statistician and educator—at the University of Edinburgh. Kelly earned a Bachelor's degree in education during this period, but in the process he developed an interest in psychology. He returned to the United States from Scotland in 1930 to enter the State University of Iowa as a graduate student in psychology. In 1931, working under Lee Travis, Kelly was awarded the Ph.D. based on a dissertation dealing with common factors in speech and reading disabilities. He had, in the meantime, begun work in physiological psychology and developed a speculative theory on the nature of what he called transient aphasia.[208]

The stock market collapse and subsequent depression had settled on America by this time, and Kelly's career did not seem especially promising as he took up a position with the Fort Hays Kansas State College. He had recently married. Times were difficult, and though Kelly's home life was a source of personal happiness—he was to father a daughter and a son—he soon decided to "pursue something more humanitarian than physiological psychology."[209] Kelly threw himself into the development of psychological services for the state of Kansas. He was the major force in establishing a program of traveling psychological clinics which not only served the entire state but permitted his students to obtain practical field experience. Kelly never distinguished between what in psychology was science and what was application. His early writings dealt with such practical issues as training and treatment, but Kelly was a confirmed experimenter and creative thinker. He was beginning to piece together his innovative approach to personality and therapy.

Kelly first turned to Freud when he dropped physiological psychology.[210] He had to admit that Freudian interpretations often helped his clients understand themselves, but

George A. Kelly

he also noted that other theoretical explanations worked as well to provide insight and thence a cure for some disturbance.[211] He was also reading Moreno and Korzybski during this period, theorists who emphasized language and the importance of the human being's dramatic or role-playing capacities. By 1939 he had begun using a form of role play in his therapeutic approach as well as a technique of fixed-role therapy.[212]

Kelly often said that a major influence on his life was the onset of World War II. He entered the Navy as an aviation psychologist and was placed in charge of a program of training for local civilian pilots. Later he went to the Bureau of Medicine and Surgery of the Navy in Washington, D.C., and remained in the Aviation Psychology Branch until the war's end. In 1945 he was appointed associate professor at the University of Maryland. The war had brought considerable demand for the training of clinical psychologists as U.S. veterans were returning en masse with all forms of personal problems. Indeed, World War II was doubtlessly the single most important factor in evolving the profession of clinical psychology. Kelly was to become a major figure in this development—working with medicine, psychiatry, and related professions to spell out a proper role for psychology in the healing sciences. In 1946 he moved into national prominence as professor and director of clinical psychology at Ohio State University. Carl Rogers had already left Ohio State for Chicago, and Kelly, along with his brilliant clinical colleague Julian B. Rotter, during the next twenty years built this program in clinical psychology into one of the best in the world.

Kelly completed his major theoretical work at Ohio State. His students helped to refine his thought, conducting supportive experiments; at the end of a decade of hard work, the *Psychology of Personal Constructs* reached print (1955a & b). The only other volume of Kelly's work appeared posthumously under the editorship of a former student, Brendan Maher (1969). Kelly spent the last decade of his life applying his theories to various aspects of psychology. He held visiting professorships at several universities in the United States and lectured at various research congresses and institutions of learning all over the world. He acquired followers and admirers on both sides of the Iron Curtain. In 1965 Kelly left Ohio State to take the Riklis Chair of Behavioral Science at Brandeis University. He was in the process of putting his many papers together into a volume when he died in March of 1967.

Personality Theory

Structural Constructs

Body-versus-Mind Theoretical Formulations and Constructive Alternativism

Kelly based his approach to psychology on a single philosophical assumption: *"We assume that all of our present interpretations of the universe are subject to revision or replacement."* [213] He did not mean to frame a complete philosophical system concerning the universe but called this attitude *constructive alternativism.* For Kelly the world in which we live is one of continually changing *interpretations* or points of view rather than a world of frozen meanings. It is not that we make up the world to suit our fancy, for we do not live in a dream world. Events must be handled in such a way that our interpretations fit what is actually present.

The universe is real; it is happening all the time; it is integral; and it is open to piecemeal interpretation. Different men construe it in different ways. Since it owes no prior allegiance to any one man's construction system, it is always open to reconstruction. Some of the alternative ways of construing are better adapted to man's purposes than are others. Thus, man comes to understand his world through an infinite series of successive approximations. [214]

The distinction between mental and physical events troubles theorists only because they think of the problem in these terms at the outset. Yet, literally, "any event may be viewed either in its psychological or in its physiological aspects." [215] Events in the real world do not belong to any one discipline or any one scientist. The physician cannot claim the mind as his or her province simply because a physical theory underwrites brain function. Nor can the psychologist claim the mind as an area of study completely out of the realm of physical theory. Kelly did not feel that a genuine solution to this divergence could be achieved by simply uniting the realms of mind and body, nor did he think that a dualistic assumption placing these two theories of events side by side made much sense.[216] He thought it most useful simply to admit that these are two different ways in which human beings have tried to make sense of their experience. As meaningful alternatives, each interpretation can be used independently of the other—at least for the time being. Kelly left open the question of whether it is possible to frame a *single* theory of reality—arguing that *if* this were to take place it would happen at a very distant point in the future.[217] Even so, Kelly, like Piaget (see p. 708), essentially accepted a realistic view of the world.

It made the best sense to Kelly to proceed for the foreseeable future with theories of an intermediate, even "miniature" nature, theories that did not profess to be capturing the single or ultimate nature of reality. He spoke of his psychology of personal constructs in these terms, expecting that it would one day give way to better formulations which might say more sweeping and lasting things about the reality of experience.[218] Kelly asked his students to try his theory on for size to see how instructive it might be, and he always added that if after ten years or so the theory was found to be unfruitful, he would toss it aside and try something else. Thus for Kelly, the issue of mind versus body is a pseudo-problem, one that disappears when we properly understand the nature of theorizing in psychological science.

Every Person a Scientist: The Human Organism as a Process

Kelly was opposed to those theories of behavior that viewed the human being as fundamentally passive and inert, as a fixed and finished structure being moved by forces outside of human nature per se. Too many psychologists have accepted the view that human evolution has ceased.[219] For Kelly, what human nature "is like" must still be seen as an open question, for we continue to alter, change and develop *by definition*. "For our purposes, the person is not an object which is temporarily in a moving state but is himself a form of motion." [220] Hence, the person is a behaving *organism* steeped in the *process of movement* which is pitched toward the ever-recurring future events taking place in life. Kelly stated flatly that "all behavior can be construed as anticipatory in nature." [221] Behavior is the person's way of posing questions about life.[222] Human beings come at life with an active intellect, one that is not under control by events but that puts events under control by posing questions of experience and then seeking answers to them.[223]

As people find these answers and pose new questions, they constantly change their outlooks. That is, they do so spontaneously if they have not cut off such flexibility initially by freezing into a single outlook which is no longer open to questions and answers. Human beings can *learn* or they can *avoid learning*.[224] There is nothing special about our capacity to learn. This is simply another way of speaking about ourselves as *processes of organismic functioning*. A *person* is thus an organismic motion, a network of posed questions and answers sought along various pathways into future experience.[225] For this reason Kelly could say that ". . . every man is, in his own particular way, a scientist." [226] Kelly once remarked that he was amazed to see the contrast between personality theories employed by psychologists to explain their *own* behavior and those they employed to explain the behavior of their experimental subjects.[227] Psychologists describe themselves as designing experiments and framing hypotheses which they put to test at will and with a clear knowledge of where they are going. Subjects, on the other hand, are described in terms of a blind determinism, a reinforcement history which pushes them onward like some unwilling and unthinking blob of protoplasm.

Running through the very heart of Kellyian psychology is this continuing polemic waged against those theories of personality that deny the subject or therapy client the same organismic status afforded the scientist. Kelly insisted that a personality theory *must* account for *all* people—those under study and those who study and report on the findings of psychological science. For his part, *personality* was defined in terms of the organismic processes already mentioned, as "a course of events that keeps flowing along." [228]

The Basic Nature of Construing and Constructs

The person looks at life, notes a series of recurring events which seem repetitive, and then "places an interpretation" upon this *predictable* aspect of his or her experience.[229] This process of interpretation and prediction is termed *construing*. It bears the meaning of an abstraction from events and also involves conceptualizing subsequent events according to this abstraction. These events or the facts of experience are real enough, but each person sees them from his or her own particular slant. Different people do not always see the same meanings in the same fact pattern. Shirley pokes fun at Lori in an effort to be friendly, but Lori finds this humor offensive. Not only has Shirley failed in her effort to be friendly, she has alienated Lori altogether. Neither young woman is at fault here. Shirley might indeed have intended to be hostile in making a joke about Lori's behavior. In point of fact, she was not. But also in point of fact, Lori construed the joking behavior as intentionally hostile and this is what will require change if this interpersonal relationship is to improve.

Kelly emphasized that the construing process is temporal, so that "to construe is to hear the whisper of the recurrent themes in the events that reverberate around us." [230] This process is uniquely *bipolar*. That is, when a person affirms the commonality of events that recur over time, he or she must *also* negate some other aspect of that experience. To say "Redheads tend to be hotheads" is *also* to say "Nonredheads tend to be levelheaded." Construing is *never* a unidimensional process.[231] Indeed, said Kelly, *thought* is only possible because we humans can and must dichotomize experience into *similarities* and *contrasts*.[232] Meaning always takes on this bipolar nature, for when we speak of what something means, we are always referring to a *relationship* between what things seem *like* and also *different from*. Lori undoubtedly feels that Shirley's jokes are like those of another associate's, Margot—and everyone knows how hostile Margot is! On the other hand, Stephanie is never hostile like this and she is one of Lori's dearest friends. In contrasting how two people are alike and yet opposite in behavior from a third, Lori has effectively given us one of her *personal constructs*. Kelly defined the *construct* as follows: "In its minimum context a construct is a way in which at least two elements are similar and contrast with a third. There must therefore be at least three elements in the context. There may, of course, be many more." [233]

Constructs are like transparent patterns or templets which human beings create (construe) in order to fit over the recurring realities of life.[234] They begin in abstraction and generalization, but they are also imposed on subsequent events, so that in a sense we all create our personal experiences at least as much as they create us.[235] Lori's (mis)construction of Shirley's behavior might become a self-fulfilling prophecy if she begins to respond in kind, and overt hostility does in fact emerge in the relations between these young women. Constructs are always the end product of that organismic process discussed in the previous section—a process we may now call *construing*. Kelly used several different terms and phrases to refer to constructs over the years, including "working hypotheses," [236] "interpretations," [237] "predictions," [238] "pathways of movement," [239] and even "appraisals." [240] His point is that the construct is an identifiable, patterned structure or style of viewing life experience which we, as students of personality, can point to in others and in ourselves. It is not essential that a construct be named.[241] Kelly presumed that children begin formulating constructs even before they can speak. Some of our constructs are so difficult to put into words that we may find it necessary to pantomime them. For example, poking a forefinger under a nose to slightly raise the head can signify "being uppity" or "stuck-up." This is a construct, even though we might not add the symbol (word) *uppity* to the visual act.

Of course, just saying "uppity" makes it appear that we have named our construct in terms of a commonality of behavior—as seen in people with inflated self-conceptions, for example. This would not quite capture what Kelly meant by a construct. To be specific, we must name *both* ends of the construct dimension in order to define it properly. Kelly once put it in terms similar to our example, as follows:

We do not explicitly express a whole construct if we say, "Mary and Alice have gentle dispositions but neither of them is as attractive as Jane." We would have to say something like this, if we were to express a true construct: "Mary and Alice are gentle; Jane is not." Or we might say, "Jane is more attractive than Mary or Alice." [242]

Kelly referred to these two ends of the construct dimension as the *poles* of a construct. Each construct thus must have a *similarity pole* and a *contrast pole*.[243] A construct always says how two things are alike (similar) and also different (contrast) from a third thing. Kelly rejected the term *concept* because he felt that it merely considered the similarities among things, and he never wanted to overlook that saying what something *is* implies what it *is not*.

When we come to name our constructs, we are free to choose the most secret, cryptic, and even vague designations we might spontaneously arrive at. This is what Kelly meant by the *personal* construct, combining the meaning of *private, unique,* and even *peculiar* into its designation. We never know what a person's language actually means until we have a fairly good understanding of his or her personal constructs in light of this verbal usage.[244] This is not to say that we lack group constructs or common constructs which everyone grasps quite clearly (objectively). But as a personality theorist, Kelly was trying to show how individuals arrive at their (subjectively) unique interpretations of things. Constructs are usually named on the basis of their similarity pole. In Kelly's example above, for instance, "the construct of *Mary-like-Alice-unlike-Jane* is likely to be symbolized in the person's thinking simply as *Mary* or *Maryness*." [245] Our construct of "uppity" suggests that we see people commonly (similarity pole) as having this characteristic but that there are others who are *not* seen this way. Of course, just what the contrast pole may be named is up to the individual who is doing the construing. One person may contrast "uppity" to "just plain folks," whereas an-

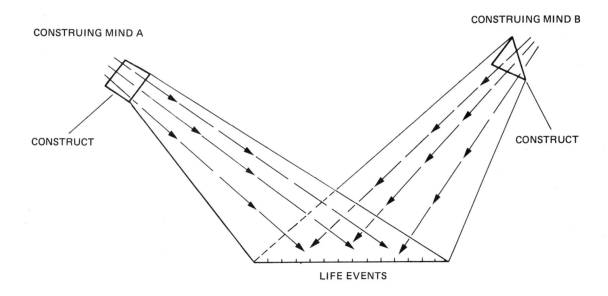

Figure 27 Alternative Constructions of the Same Life Event

other may contrast "uppity" to "poor folks." The point of a psychology of personal constructs is to find what the individual personally (subjectively) means when he or she brings a construct to bear in life.

Figure 27 presents a schematization of two construing minds, A and B, ordering identical life events from different perspectives. Note that one templet or construct is stylized as a square (mind A) and the other as a triangle (mind B). This symbolizes the fact that the specific constructs may vary, yet the events brought under consideration or framed by the constructs may be identical—which is essentially what occurred when Shirley viewed her jokes (life events) one way (let us say, as mind A) and Lori viewed them quite another way (mind B). In most instances of the sort depicted in Figure 27, the two people concerned would find it difficult to communicate because they would literally be viewing the world from two different perspectives. On the other hand, other constructs can come into

play to facilitate communication, or the constructs presently employed can always be *reconstrued* (changed) in order to bring into alignment their conflicting alternatives (circles can become triangles or vice versa).

Kelly always stressed that the human being is not locked into a fixed construct system unless he or she believes that this is true. The square thinker can take on a triangular slant for variety or in a "let's pretend" sense. When this takes place, the kinds of meanings that will issue from the life events under construction will have changed somewhat. The person will see things differently. A *reconstruction* will have taken place. Indeed, if each mind symbolized in Figure 27 assumes the other's perspective, we might end up with, rather than a square and a triangle, two circular constructions of the same life events as a meeting of the minds comes about. This is what *constructive alternativism* is all about. People should constantly seek to find a better fit between their perspectives and the demands of life—which invariably include the points of view of others.

Common Characteristics of Constructs

Since constructs are not only abstracted from but imposed upon life events—ordering them and determining the meanings of one's experience—they can be called *controls*.[246] A construct can lock us into a fixed course of action. Constructs are real, and they capture real events. Although the reality of a construct is not necessarily the reality of a factual element under construction, the person behaves in terms of his or her controlling construct and *not* in terms of the factual elements.[247] A divorce lawyer hearing a husband and wife recount the "facts" of their declining marital relationship soon realizes that people are not simply lying about what happened. With each hurt, a predicted recurrence of the offending partner is put to test again and again, convincing the husband or wife of the other's loss of devotion. Neither seems to see that by not accepting the viewpoints of each other, they have effectively doomed their relationship. A reconstruction is required, but the time seems past when it might have been possible.

Life would be an intolerable series of inconsistent events if the human being could not perceive regularities and thereby formulate constructs. We also have the capacity to systematically order our constructs into what Kelly called *construction systems*.[248] We do this by overlooking inconsistencies in the use of our constructs, so that even if a construct does not fit exactly in each recurring life event, we keep its general order intact. We cannot make allowances for every little nu-

ance of change that we notice in one rainstorm to another. There are changes, but the consistencies are what count. Cultural stereotypes are negative examples of our tendency to systematize our constructs. We do not analyze those times when a black person is industrious, a Catholic is flexible, or a Jew is shy and suggestible. We allow our prejudiced (controlling) views to freeze us into the stereotypes of lazy blacks, rigid Catholics, and aggressive Jews, despite the many contradictions we confront daily. Even such fixed constructs can help us anticipate events, of course, as long as our predictions are not always invalidated. If it is possible to see laziness, rigidity, and aggressivity in *any* person —to some extent, at least—then finding these qualities in our ethnic prejudices should not be too difficult. Furthermore, how we behave in relation to blacks, Catholics, and Jews could easily bring about the kind of behavior we predicted from the outset. As we have noted above, constructs can become self-fulfilling prophecies.

Constructs are not all framed (construed) at the same level of abstraction, so that some of them have a broad reference in our lives, whereas others refer to very limited and specific life events. Kelly referred to this higher- or lower-order ranking in abstractness as the *ordinality* of constructs.[249] A *superordinate* construct is said to *subsume* (include the meaning of) a *subordinate* construct. The former is more abstract than the latter, and it thus can take the latter into its *range of convenience* (its scope of referential meaning).[250] For example, a construct such as "loyalty" may be superordinate to the less abstract concepts of "working unselfishly" and "doing what's asked." The range of convenience a construct has also delimits the relevance its meaning has to the person. Going beyond the range of convenience means a construct is no longer relevant or applicable to life events. In Figure 27 the life events subsumed by the square or triangle would define the range of convenience for these constructs. Those life events that fall outside a construct's range of convenience are *not* opposites of the construct but are simply irrelevant to the dichotomous meanings being applied.[251] Thus, a person may apply his or her loyalty construct *only* to the family sphere. Family members should be loyal to one another. Once it is outside of parental and sibling relations, the range of convenience for this construct ceases and we no longer need exhibit loyalty even to our friends.

A construct can move up or down the ordinal ladder of abstraction, subsuming other contexts of the construction system by extending its range of convenience or by delimiting a narrow range by constricting and specifying only a few life events to which it applies. For example, we can *dilate* our construct by broadening the perceptual field within which we make it applicable (spread out along the life events of Figure 27 more and more).[252] The loyalty construct can be extended beyond the family setting. Sometimes this extension of a construct's range of convenience is *loose,* so that the meaning is unclear because of its tentative fit to the range of life events being included.[253] If we extend loyalty to people beyond the family, when do we stop? Can a boss be loyal to a worker, particularly during times of economic recession when a cutback in the work force is necessary? Is it possible to lay someone off work and yet be loyal to that person? Such questions arise for all of us as we attempt to make sense of our lives, and we all have these more or less *loose* constructions in our hierarchy of personal constructs. To loosen construct meanings is not always bad, since it leads to creative insights at times.[254] When we loosen, we apply a "rubber-sheet templet" to experience and thereby shift our frame of reference.[255] The best way in which to do this is consciously, dealing with a construct's

meaning in an experimental fashion and looking for the new insights a changing meaning might provide us with. Once again, the construing process is one of raising and answering questions about our life events.

It is also possible to *tighten* constructs, to freeze them into rigid definitions. Tight constructs lead to unvarying predictions, which can in turn have either a positive or a negative impact on the fit of our construct system.[256] Assume that Vernon has a stereotype about redheaded people being hotheads. If he were now to tighten this construct when confronting a redheaded man, he would say to himself something like this: "Now, let's see, if it's true that redheaded people are hotheaded, then this redheaded guy talking with me will lose his temper if I press him on a point. Let's see if he does!" Here is a clear-cut prediction in which the outcome will put the construct system to test. Had Vernon persisted in using a loosened construction of his stereotype, he would have simply chatted along with the man and then later "recalled" certain things said as being hostile in tone. Or he might have gone through the conversation with the idea, "I had better be careful in talking to this guy or he'll fly off the handle." In behaving like this, Vernon never puts his loose construction to risk. Tightening stabilizes constructs and facilitates their organization. Superordinate constructs are difficult to develop if the lower-order constructs they subsume continue to be vague and unstable (loose).[257] If every person is a scientist, then tightening is obviously an important aspect of experimentation—making thinking clear, projecting a hypothesis that can be confirmed or denied, and so forth.

Tightening also relates to the *permeability* of constructs. By this Kelly meant the relative capacity for a construct to take on new elements.[258] A permeable construct is not necessarily loose. If a construct of "loyalty" could not be applied beyond the family context, it would be *impermeable,* but this would not necessarily mean it was loose. We could have a very tight conception of loyalty limited to the family context. A good example of a tight, impermeable construct occurs when someone says, "That is clearly a chair and all one can do is use it as a chair." A person like this would be unlikely to see the myriad possibilities of chair functions, such as ladders for reaching, props against doors, or barricades for children's games. The impermeable thinker reasons like this, rigidly asserting that "You are either right or you are wrong, now which is it?" In contrast to such impermeable constructions, Kelly noted, "A construct is permeable if it is open to the addition of new elements, or elements beyond those upon which it has been explicitly formed." [259] The permeable construct admits situational differences. A ladder is not a chair, but given certain situations in which no stepladder is available, we can substitute a chair or even a table for a ladder. Here is the beginning of supple thought, responsive to circumstance in a creative fashion. Like anything else, it can lead to difficulty if constructs are too impermeable and hence interfuse with one another to a great extent. Here permeability may shade into looseness.

Kelly termed a highly impermeable construct that freezes its elements into *only* its unique range of convenience a *pre-emptive construct.*[260] The black-or-white form of thinking so typical of the rigid person reflects this extreme form of impermeability. On the other hand, a construct that permits its elements to belong to *other* realms concurrently (at the same time), even as it fixes definite

qualities for present purposes, Kelly called a *constellatory construct.*[261] For example, assume that Marty is called Jewlike even though he is a Christian; the qualities of a Jewish stereotype would be immediately constellated to him: if Jewlike, then aggressive, pushy, materialistic, and so forth. The preemptive thinker would say, "Only Jews are Jewlike," whereas the constellatory thinker can generalize a construct or use it in an analogical sense without diminishing its fundamental meaning. A construct that leaves its elements open to construction in all other respects is termed a *propositional construct.*[262] The propositional thinker is likely to engage in conscious elaboration of a permeable construction system, for he or she would reason that "it is conventional to view all Catholics as rigid and authoritarian, but let's see if things can be this uniform and simple." The propositional thinker is thus open to new evidence, willing to take an altered view on an experimental basis, and to this extent, he or she represents an opposite end of the continuum from pre-emptive and constellatory thinkers.[263]

There are other terms of descriptive importance used by Kelly. A *comprehensive construct* is one that subsumes a wide variety of events, whereas the *incidental construct* has a much narrower range of convenience.[264] Mildred reflects a comprehensive construct when she says, "Life is mostly a matter of good or bad luck," but her construct is more incidental when she says, "Once in a great while I seem to let what other people say or don't say get to me." Constructs can be made more comprehensive through dilation, of course, which broadens their range of convenience. The opposite tendency to focus a construct and thus restrict or narrow its range of convenience is called *constriction.*[265] It is possible so to constrict the range of convenience that it will apply to a very limited aspect of life. Presumably, something like a profound religious experience that has taken place only once in life might be delimited by a highly specific, constricted construct. The feelings and impact of this single experience might not be applicable anywhere else in life. A *regnant construct* is a form of superordinate construct which subsumes many other constructs and helps to color their meaning.[266] This kind of regnancy is reflected in Herman's suggestion that "People are either for me or they are against me." As he goes through life, Herman will be letting this superordinate construction color all of his interpersonal relations. When they are impermeable, such constructions are likely to become pre-emptive and constellatory.[267] At some point in life, Herman might begin seeing more and more others against him, which in turn suggests the development of a paranoid delusion.

Conscious, Unconscious, and the Self as a Core-Role Construct

We have already noted that not all constructs are verbalized. Kelly accounted for the conscious-versus-unconscious-mind conceptions of classical analytical theory in terms of this capacity for people to formulate templets which are not put into words. So-called unconscious mental contents, as seen in dreams, represented preverbal constructs which continue to exert an influence on experience.[268] Strictly speaking, Kelly did not want to use this distinction.

We do not use the conscious-unconscious dichotomy, but we do recognize that some of the personal constructs a person seeks to subsume within his system prove to be fleeting or elusive. Sometimes this is because they are loose rather than tight. . . . Sometimes it is because they are not bound by the symbolisms of words or other acts. But of this we are sure, if they are important in a person's life

it is a mistake to say they are unconscious or that he is unaware of them. Every day he experiences them, often all too poignantly, except he cannot put his finger on them nor tell for sure whether they are at the spot the therapist has probed for them.[269]

Kelly was opposed to thinking of an entity called self or ego, but he did say that we all have some construction label in terms of *self-identity*. ". . . It is quite appropriate to refer to a given person's self-construct, or to a class of constructs which can be called personal self-constructs."[270] Here again, we are likely to formulate our *self-construct* around what we see as a core of similarity about our behavior transcending a series of life events. We are "sincere" or "athletic" or "nice" in all of life's circumstances; at least, we believe ourselves to be consistent across many time-bound life events like this. It might surprise and even hurt us to discover that what we consider nice behavior another person calls passivity, but that is how life goes. The point is: we do formulate constructions of our own behavior based on our experience, and these self-constructs exert the typical *control* on what we do as we move through life.

Why do we formulate a self-construct in the first place? It happens spontaneously as we mature, passing through interpersonal relations. Indeed, to construe another person is often to construe oneself.[271] We tend to see ourselves as *like* others yet *different* from people at the opposite end of our self-construction. Sometimes we place ourselves at the *different* end of a construct dimension. Certain people are "dirty" or—more positively framed—"confident" and we are different from them in that we are "clean" and/or "unconfident." The particular meaning that enters into our construct issues from our interpersonal impressions as we frame the behavior of others. Kelly called this tendency we have to relate ourselves to others the *role relationship,* and he was so taken by this conception that he even toyed with the idea of calling his approach to personality study "role theory."

Kelly's use of the term *role* should not be confused with the usage often employed by sociologists and social psychologists. A *role* in the latter sense refers to a series of behavioral prescriptions (how to behave), laid down by the culture and then enacted by all those people who play the role of father, physician, mother, teacher, and so forth. Kelly viewed the *role* as a pattern of behavior defined by the individual rather than as a cultural product. It is a *process* whereby we as individuals construe the construction processes of other people, and basing our actions on what we uniquely understand is taking place *in relation to us* with these other people, carry out an interpersonal activity.[272] In a manner of speaking, we each write our own scenario for how our interpersonal relations will be going with other people. We make an *interpretation* of what they are thinking about us, and then we frame a *role construct* based upon this assumption.[273] This role construct guides the role relationship we have with these other people. Clayton suspects that his teachers find him boring, and basing his actions upon this personal construct of boring-interesting, relates to his teachers in a certain way. Kelly emphasized that a role construct must be "based upon one's interpretation of the thinking of the other people in relation to whom the role is enacted."[274]

Now, the interesting thing about such role relations is that the other people with whom we relate do not necessarily have to be thinking about us in the way that we assume they are![275] Clayton's teachers are not necessarily finding him boring, and even if some do, they all do not. This teaches us that role constructs may include gross distortions of the interpersonal truth.[276] The beautiful young woman who finds one day that her pleasantries spoken to a rather innocuous young man down the block have led the latter to construe an intricate and involved love affair between them finds herself the victim of the unfortunate lad's colorless and lonely life. Yet insofar as this fantasied love affair entered into the young man's behavior—eventuating in a highly embarrassing scene when he sees his "girlfriend" on the arm of another—we can speak of his delusional system as a kind of role relationship (predicated on erroneous role constructs). In most cases, of course, the role relations of people are more realistic and interpersonally accurate than this. Most of us learn to read the intentions of others more correctly.

Now, when we speak of the *self* as a construct or a *self-construct* (self-concept, and so on), we actually refer to a special case of the role construct. Kelly noted that there are unique *core-role constructs* which define our relationship to other people.[277] We behave in relation to these as if our very life depended on them—as in one sense, it does. The early Christians, for example, who went to their deaths rather than renounce their faith were behaving in terms of their core-role constructs, viewing their cobelievers as brothers and sisters in God. A more mundane example might be the case of Dennis, who thinks of himself as an individualist. This is his core self-image, and he invariably arrays people along this comprehensive and superordinate construct of individualism versus collectivism. If Dennis senses that others are—in their construction of him—putting him into a mold, he might react quite angrily and stubbornly to any suggestion that he compromise or accommodate his views to those of the group.

Motivational Constructs

The Person as a Problem-Solving Animal: Freedom versus Determinism in Behavior

Since Kelly began with the assumption that human beings are processes in constant change, he did not think of motivation as a form of propulsion added to a personality structure in order to get it moving. There is no frozen psychic structure to move. Hence, we need no mental energies to run the personality system.[278] Kelly specifically rejected such terminology, as well as the drive construct which has been used so widely by the learning theorists.[279] He was not sympathetic with the views of learning being advanced in the academic centers of his time, which he felt saw the person as little more than the tail end of an unplanned reinforcement history.[280]

Rather than seeing people as behaving according to some hedonistic principle based on the satisfactions of energic expenditure or instinctual reinforcements, Kelly said that people find their rewards in the successful anticipation (prediction) of events.[281] It is not the reward but the *solution* that brings the person satisfactions.[282] There is nothing special about this sequence of "construe in prediction and solve." All behavior is like this. Motivation is not a special topic for the psychologist, who could as readily dismiss it from the professional vocabulary as retain it.[283] If we look to the person as a problem solver engaged in an active process of construing events in order to predict and control them, then both learning and motivation fall into line without special treatment. For Kelly, *change* was always a question of *reconstruction*.[284] When an individual's construction system confronts new life events and yet is not helpful or applicable, a change is called for. When newly formed constructs are inconsistent with older constructs, a change is called for.[285] Of course, we human beings do not always change. We develop *habits*, which Kelly defined as "a convenient kind of stupidity which leaves a person free to act intelligently elsewhere."[286] Or we literally avoid changing because of the secondary factors operating on us, such as the lack of understanding that change is possible or the threatening possibilities that changing our behavior implies.

It was on the basis of constructs as controls that Kelly developed his conceptions of *choice, freedom,* and *determinism.* Since a construct projects its meaning onto reality, the range of convenience and the significance of the construct are important controls. If these constructs prove to be impermeable, the individual becomes locked into their meaningful import in an unvarying, controlled, inflexible—literally determined—sense. Superordinate constructs are naturally the most significant determiners of behavior, for they subsume many lower-level constructs and thus have a broader range of convenience and influence.[287] To become free of this superordinate control, the individual must either reconstrue his or her circumstances or otherwise alter the most superordinate constructions. Once we have placed a new determining control over our outlooks like this, we can speak of a freedom taking place. Freedom and determination are not two different things, but rather are opposite sides of the same coin. ". . . Determinism and freedom are two complementary aspects of structure. They cannot exist without each other any more than *up* can exist without *down* or *right* without *left*. Neither freedom nor determination is absolute. A thing is free *with respect to something;* it is determined *with respect to something else.*"[288]

If we are to see behavioral change, we must alter the "respect to something" that freezes a person into his or her present pattern. As we have noted, this amounts to some form of construct alteration. Kelly was sensitive to the charge that his theory of freedom and determinism as a relationship between superordinate (controlling) and subordinate (controlled) constructs might be seen as an overly "intellectual" account of human behavior.[289] His typical response to this criticism was that the person's construing of events is *not* limited to verbalized symbols. Furthermore, conative (active doing) as well as cognitive (passive knowing) behaviors fall under the range of convenience of one's construct system. Behavioral conations like all overt actions are not something *other than* our cognitions. Intellectual explanations would seem to be limited to verbalized (symbolized in language) and cognitive explanations, which is clearly *not* the tactic selected by the psychology of personal constructs.[290] Actually, Kelly did not like to think of his view as a cognitive one.[291] He did not believe the term signified anything worthwhile for the personality theorist.

The C-P-C Cycle and the Creativity Cycle

Two important concepts used by Kelly clarify how constructs and construction systems can change. The first is the *C-P-C Cycle,* which involves a sequence of construction in which *circumspection, pre-emption,* and *control* follow in that order and lead to a choice which precipitates the person into a particular situation.[292] By *circumspection,* Kelly meant that the individual deals with the issues facing him or her as regards some problem in a propositional fashion. Recall that a propositional

construct leaves its elements open to construction in all other respects. It is "open to alternative hypotheses." Hence, at the outset of the C-P-C Cycle, individuals mull over the various possibilities facing them and look at the problem from different slants, until they finally *pre-empt!* Pre-emption means that one and only one alternative is taken on as *the* definition of the problem under consideration. And as the old saying "A problem defined is a problem half-solved" suggests, once this pre-emption occurs, a course of action in the service of its resolution is undertaken.

When Hamlet mulled over his life situation, including his father's death, his mother's behavior, his uncle's attitude, and so forth, he was dealing circumspectively with a gnawing issue. However, when he finally settled on the question "To be, or not to be?" Kelly argued that Hamlet had pre-empted other possibilities, other middle grounds short of his murderous construction (kill versus don't kill).[293] A definite control (determination) was fixed to Hamlet's future behavior once he decided which of the pre-emptive alternatives open to him he would follow. Kelly notes that the final C of the C-P-C Cycle could just as well be termed a *choice* as a *control* feature of the cycle.[294] Because of the dichotomous nature of thought, people are always free to choose in the direction of a construct pole that they believe will further their construction system as a whole—and the subsequent prediction of events this system makes possible.[295] Once the choice has been made, then the control settles in and an act of behavior is *determined.* And so it happened in the gloomy "destiny" of Hamlet that he was to kill his uncle.

Kelly termed the second way in which we can observe a sequence of events taking place in the process of construction leading to change the *Creativity Cycle.* In this case, the succession of events follows a loosening-to-tightening of constructs.[296] People with tight constructs find it difficult to be creative, for they cannot go beyond the bounds of their rigid frames of reference. Creative people, on the other hand, can allow their constructs to stretch or bend. They can often play with constructs or, as Kelly liked to phrase it, "try them on for size." We do not always have to take ourselves seriously or believe everything we think or say. It is this "what-if?" or "let's-assume-this-for-the-heck-of-it" attitude that differentiates the Creativity Cycle from the C-P-C Cycle. In the latter case, we are always engaged in a process that will *bring us to an action* of some personally construed variety.[297] We are not fooling around but are engaged in a search that will be a mere preliminary to some action. We are committed to act, even though the specific directions of this action are not worked out yet at the outset of the C-P-C Cycle. In the Creativity Cycle, there may be no appreciable personal commitment to an eventual action, although it is true that when something new is construed, an action does often follow.

Emotive Terms and the Psychology of Personal Constructs

Kelly thought of *emotion* as behavior that was either loosely defined[298] or was not a word-bound but a preverbal or nonverbal construction.[299] A person's *feelings* are inner events needing construing (for example, "What's happening to me? Why do I have this mood?").[300] Sometimes what the individual calls an emotion is the other side of some consciously known and expressed construct. How we *feel* is in this sense the other side of what we *know*. By and large, however, in the psychology of personal constructs, emotional expression is considered *loose* construction.[301] Emotional people are essentially unable to say clearly what their attitudes are toward some aspect of their lives. We only make sense of emotional behavior after we

have clarified what is taking place in the construction system.

Kelly had many creative things to say about those aspects of behavior that are typically associated with the emotions. Take *humor,* for example. *Jokes* were interpreted by Kelly as neat reconstructions of ongoing experience associated with quick movements and unexpected outcomes because of a reversal in our constructive expectations (predictions).[302] The arrogant and pompous general stumbles on his way to the rostrum and in his subsequent blushing and stammering proves to his snickering troops that he is a human being after all. If we analyze our favorite jokes, we are struck by the fact that, as Kelly said, their punch lines invariably rest upon a twist (reconstruction) which rapidly rearranges our expectations of what is taking place.

Kelly defined *threat* as awareness of an imminent comprehensive change in one's core-role constructs.[303] We are threatened to the extent that what we feared might take place looks as though it is really coming about. Threats are unhappy predictions we make. We do not want these predictions to come true, but we expect them to anyhow. We are fearful that we have some terrible disease, so we arrange to see our physician. With each solemn look on the physician's face, we grow increasingly apprehensive, for we continually predict that she is finding what we are fearing she will indeed find—usually quite in error, of course. *Stress* is a more removed psychological state, a kind of awareness of potential threat.[304] Stress moves into threat when the person becomes convinced that something is about to happen which will upset the ongoing construction system.[305] As this begins to happen, as the constructs begin to lose their grip on our personal reality, we are likely to say that things look shaky, or scary, or simply incomprehensible.

At times like these, we witness *signs of emotion*. The person may tense up, perspire, act erratically, and possibly in time, actually flee from the threatening situation in a headlong panic. Flights into states of amnesia which leave the person completely unable to recall anything about his or her past life are also possible. In fact, a spotty memory is characteristic of the threatened state. Because it is difficult to hold in memory that which is unstructured (poorly, loosely construed), people have a hard time remembering what is happening to them when under various levels of threat.[306] Here is where abnormal states termed *unconscious behavior* are likely to be seen. One of the main reasons we fail to construe properly under states of threat is because we have the feeling that our ready-made constructs cannot help us. We are essentially waiting to see what will happen in our life, thereby forgoing the important role we must personally play in structuring the future course of that life.

Kelly considered the resultant "loss of structure" to be *anxiety*.[307] He used to refer jokingly to this psychological state as being *caught with our constructs down*.[308] When we are anxious, we cannot predict; hence, it is impossible for us to solve our problems. The emotional state of *fear* is at least a more focused experience. Fear occurs when some imminent incidental construct has loomed up in one's path to suggest that impending change is likely to take place.[309] In our earlier example, we suffered anxiety as we watched our physician, knowing not what she might find but predicting that whatever it was, it would be terrible. When she now fixes a specific diagnosis (incidental construct) which is serious and demands immediate treatment, we begin to suffer *fear*. The advantage of fear

is that with the stipulation of a given illness we have already begun a process of reconstruction. We can now set about following our physician's directions for cure, read up on our disorder, lay new plans for health care, and so on. Of course, if our illness is incurable, our anxiety will never turn to fear. Here is something—death—so incomprehensible that nothing within our present construction system subsumes it properly. At this point, what problem solution we arrive at depends on many factors, including our views on the meaning of existence and afterlife.

Another aspect of emotional life having great relevance to personality is what might be termed *aggression* or *hostility*. Although these terms are often used interchangeably by psychologists today, Kelly had a unique way of viewing what he took to be two distinctive emotional states. For him, *aggression* was tantamount to an active elaboration of a perceptual field.[310] Nate is an aggressive person. He is constantly trying to broaden his horizons, to extend the scope of his construction system. We see him relying on the Creativity Cycle a lot as he plays with new ideas, reads new books, and looks for alternative courses of action. He is also a bit stubborn, reflecting the end state of the C-P-C Cycle, at which point he has put down a plan of action and is now committed to put his ideas into practice. Nate is always willing to put his ideas on the line, devising experiments which put his thinking to risk. Larry, on the other hand, is a *passive* individual. Larry dislikes having to put his ideas on the line. He tends to put this off, or he expects conditions to be perfect before he is willing to try anything out. Of course, we are all a little like Nate in some areas of life and a little like Larry in others. But the point is: for Kelly, aggressive-passive as a construct describing behavior related to how actively we elaborate our construction system from day to day. Unfortunately, because the aggressive person does seek to know and to do things actively, he or she is likely to upset the gentle routine and construction systems of other people, who then misconstrue this aggressivity and consider it hostility!

We are only *hostile* in Kelly's terms when we insist upon finding true the predictions we have made in the face of contradictory evidence.[311] As Kelly observed: "The trouble with hostility is that it always attempts to make the original investment pay off. It is unrealistic." [312] The hostile individual freezes his or her constructs into impermeability. Garret "knows" what is taking place in his job situation, where he has been having a lot of trouble with his coworkers. He "knows" what others are thinking, and why they are giving him all the trouble he is experiencing. No amount of explanation or alternative recommendations by his coworkers will change his mind. It is the same thing at home with his children, where Garret never spares the rod. His children had better do what is expected of them, and he allows no excuse making. There is no effort on his part to understand a child's construction of events when things go counter to what Garret demands. As is true of all hostile people, Garret really does not care what other people think. If he were simply an aggressive person, Garret would take an interest in other people's viewpoints, even though he might dispute them. But Garret always punishes, frustrates, or somehow injures others when they fail to behave in the way his construction system predicts they ought to be behaving. He can even do this injury in a passive way, by not hearing what others say to him, by forgetting an appointment or a birth date, or by overlooking the positive aspects of life in preference for the negative in all things.

Another emotional tone often emphasized in personality theories is *guilt*. Kelly defined this as perception of apparent dislodgment from one's role structure.[313] The guilty person

is thus one who has done something which either is or seems to be in direct contradiction with his or her self-image around which the core-role constructs order themselves. Here is where the psychology of personal constructs would place *conscience* or *superego*. Note that this dislodgment of guilt still represents threat. We are threatened by guilt just as readily as we are by anxiety—and indeed it is sometimes difficult to separate anxiety from guilt. In general, however, a guilty person can identify the specific source of the emotional upset. The guilty individual feels that he or she has transgressed a core-value system, which, if religious in nature, represents a *sin*.[314] When we violate our core-role constructs, we often feel alienated from others, because it is here that our interpersonal relations take root. The once-faithful husband who "slips" from his role and has an affair with another woman while on a business trip finds himself unable to relate to his wife upon his return home. By dislodging his self-construct, this man both feels guilt and finds that he can no longer relate to his wife on the same grounds as before. What to do? If confession is eventually made of the infidelity, it is because the husband wants to reconstrue his self-image (as no longer perfectly faithful but a repentant "sinner") and regain a sense of relatedness with his wife. Of course, the marital bond itself might be reconstrued by the wife, resulting in divorce or a much less affectionate relationship, and so forth.

The Defense Mechanisms

Kelly did not favor a defense-mechanism approach to the description of behavior, though he did comment on some of these Freudian conceptions. He considered *repression* to be a suspension or stopping of the construing process, occurring most probably when a person could not come to grips with the threat of an imminent change in the construction system or possibly saw unresolvable contradictions in the system.[315] *Incorporation* was described as a person's willingness to see other people like himself or herself.[316] *Identification* or *introjection* results when we take over constructs our group—including family members —have already been using.[317] *Regression* is due to behavior that is predicated upon either preverbal or at least very immature constructions of life.[318] *Projection* would be a special form of hostility, in which the person insists on naming what another's motives are despite all evidence to the contrary. Note the implicit tie here between hostility and projection! *Reaction-formation* is an attempt to put the "opposite" construct pole in effect when it is the other pole that bears the significance for a person.

Time-Perspective Constructs

Development as the Dispersion of Dependency

Kelly did not formulate many time-perspective constructs, feeling that the *present* is what counts in behavior. The psychology of personal constructs also turns our attention forward in time. Even so, some things can be said about development from birth to maturity.

Essentially, this question of maturing construction extends the human being's dependencies from one or a few to several persons. Kelly did not favor calling people either dependent or independent, since he believed that everyone is both. We cannot exist without relying on others. In the earliest months of life, children presumably focus their relatively crude attention capacities on their mothers. They frame a *dependency construct*

at this stage of life, by which Kelly meant a preverbal figure construct signifying that some one person (mother) is essential to personal survival.[319] By *figure* we mean the image (mental picture) of a mother or surrogate (stand-in) mothering-one. Kelly noted, "When the child uses a figure in this manner he actually develops two levels of meaning for *Mother*: the one referring to the actual behaviors of his mother, the other referring to *motherliness*." [320] Such preverbal constructs relying on images tend to be impermeable and are what we usually find popping up in dreams and other so-called unconscious behaviors. They are not very effective in determining interpersonal relations because they fail to consider the other person to be a construing organism. In other words, they are *not* role constructs.

The task of maturing now becomes one of making such basic dependency constructs more permeable, extending the child's reliance for existence to others besides mother. We can be fairly certain that in their initial contact with them, children assess other people in terms of preverbal mothering constructs. They will begin seeing how other adults (father, uncles, aunts, visitors) are alike and yet different from mother. Language enters in time to increase the complexity of this construing process. Kelly defined *language* as "a device for anticipating the events that are about to happen to us." [321] Verbal constructs allow a sense of growing awareness (consciousness) to develop, including the insight that other people are construing our behavior even as we construe theirs. The net effect here is that role construction takes place, and children extend their dependencies onto others even more as they form *friendships* during their school-attending years.

Another important development in everyone's life is the ability to experiment, to predict and control events in order to find avenues for extending the range of one's construct system. In childhood, this is the function of *play*. Kelly observed: "Play is adventure. Its outcomes are always veiled in some delightful uncertainty."[322] Children develop skills in their play even as they are putting down some of their primary constructs. Even in later adulthood, we can get some idea of what a person considers most important in life by observing recreational selections. Some people are very social in their recreations, whereas others prefer solitary pursuits.[323] To understand the person, we would do well to observe his or her free-time activities.

If the child matures properly, we will in time begin seeing a development away from the rigidly simplistic construction system toward greater use of propositional constructs and more permeable dependency constructs. The range of dependency expands as the person comes to understand life in a more complex fashion. Children move from whole-figure constructs—in which the mother image is rigidly framed as *only* such-and-such a person—to more flexible trait attributions that recognize alternatives in the behavior of a single person. Mothers are motherly at times but they can also be quite *un*motherly at other times. Thus as we grow to adulthood, we can confirm or disconfirm our constructs *in part* rather than in their entirety.[324] We do not totter on an all-or-none brink of construct application so that with each failure in prediction we are flooded with threat. Rather, we mature to adulthood knowing that some lack of predictability is normal in any construction system.

Society and Culture as a Validational Backdrop for Individual Prediction

Our personality styles are drawn out along lines that tie into the patterns of our *society* and *culture,* so that we tend to behave like other people on many important dimensions. Southerners in the United States speak in a dialect which stamps them as regional residents quite different from New Englanders. The question naturally arises: is not our behavior entirely determined by our culture and society? Kelly could not accept an affirmative answer to this question, preferring to focus on the individual person rather than on such "in common" descriptions of behavior.[325] Thus, he insisted that "social psychology must be a psychology of interpersonal understandings, not merely a psychology of common understandings."[326] Society exists, *not* because it is some form of external power dictating social roles for people to fill, but *rather* because people do construe one another as fellow construers and hence can enter into role relationships.[327] We must not be tricked into assigning the responsibility for our behavior to an impersonal society any more than we must be tricked into assigning it to an impersonal nature.

Of course, society's cultural values and rules are important. A *cultural norm,* for example, may be thought of as "the eyes of society," and it is the unusual person who can ignore the evaluation of such eyes completely.[328] Kelly believed that cultures arise in the first place because people just happen to "construe their experience in the same way."[329] This means that a group of people can agree on what will *validate* their construction systems, their individual predictions as to life experience, and so forth.[330] Hence, as we are the initial construers of culture, we human beings can only submit to cultural controls by construing things in this way—believing that we are merely pawns being moved about by cultural forces.[331]

The best way to think about culture is as a kind of background against which we can put our constructions to test. For example, in growing to adulthood, the individual selects a career or job vocation. But the work situation is fraught with a number of cultural practices which enable the individual to test out or validate what this vocation really means.[332] In fact, the person begins to construe the entire culture through the eyes of his or her profession. Farmers have one view of what is right or wrong about their society and truck drivers have another. Communistic theories have made it appear that it is a culture's means of production that determines the person's construction system, because of this tendency for people to see things by way of their occupational validations. Kelly found the communistic analysis wanting, and he was also critical of the tendency to break society down into upper-, middle-, and lower-class levels.[333] Though such breakdowns do tell us what advantages large groups of people enjoy, they sidestep the fundamental issue of how the individual person can come to view the world independently of his or her class norm. Kelly thought that too often sociocultural analyses of behavior oversimplify descriptions of human behavior. Furthermore, they tend to downplay the responsibility the individual has for his or her behavior. "Just as we have insisted that man is not necessarily the victim of his biography, we would also insist that man is not necessarily the victim of his culture."[334]

Individual-Differences Constructs

Personality differences arise because different people take on different constructs in coming at their life events. To understand the person, we have to know how he or she typically approaches life. Since people are essentially alike in many ways, it is possible for us as students of personality to abstract commonalities between them, call them dimensions or traits, and then begin aligning people along these constructs according to what *we* consider individual differences. Kelly was not opposed to psychologists doing this, and in fact he said that psychotherapists must have an ability to construe their cases in some such fashion so that they can organize their knowledge.[335] Yet, he also stressed that such professional constructions must always be propositional and permeable, open to invalidating evidence, and adhered to only speculatively rather than rigidly.

If we now wish to capture the typical drift of a person's construct system, we may do so—calling the person dependent[336] or aggressive[337]—but Kelly was not much interested in promoting such common designations. He developed a means (Rep Test) for identifying the unique constructions people make for themselves, recorded from their own unique slant. Kelly could see little profit in pigeonholing other people. What the psychology of personal constructs aims for is to grasp the unique slant of each individual human being. This means that by definition advocates of this approach have entered into a role relationship with these individuals and thus can carry out the purposes for which the theory has been laid down. As far as Kelly was concerned, the major purpose of his theory was to further professional activity in the clinical area, particularly as regards psychotherapy.[338]

Psychopathology and Psychotherapy

Theory of Illness

Personal Constructs in Abnormality

Kelly defined *psychological disorder* as "*any personal construction which is used repeat-*

edly in spite of consistent invalidation." [339] The construction system is thus not accomplishing its purpose.[340] The person's experiments are not coming out as predicted, but he or she insists upon using them anyway. Amy is convinced that her problems in life are due to the fact that everyone in her home town has been jealous of her family name. Her forebears were always leading citizens of the community, and ever since her youth, Amy has found people blocking out of pure jealousy her attempts to take a leadership role. Amy never examines the evidence that her leadership efforts have been of low quality, or that when others have tried to work out differences with her, she has bluntly turned them aside as covering up their jealousy of her family background. In fact, so intricate have Amy's rationalizations become that when she first entered into psychotherapy at the age of forty her therapist had difficulty understanding her behavior. This is one of the signs we have of a serious abnormality in a personality—when we as therapists cannot predict our client's behavior.[341] Of course, therapists have a professional construction system which should always permit prediction of client behavior to some extent.[342] But Amy is skirting the fringes of a delusional system at this point and there is much that is unpredictable in her behavior as she departs more and more from common sense in order to maintain her inadequate construction system.

Amy reflects the basic attitude of all abnormal individuals, in that they feel their troubles stem from the *facts* of their life events rather than from their *interpretation* (construction) of these factual events.[343] Often, the abnormal person will begin retreating to earlier constructions of life, resulting in so-called *regression* taking place.[344] Abnormals turn to their parents, marital partners, or physicians for support and assistance in the validation of their distorting constructs.

When regression is severe and an activation of preverbal constructions is pronounced, we are likely to perceive what the analysts call acting-out behavior in which the person is unable to verbalize the reasons (constructs) for his or her unusual behavior.[345] This is usually the point at which a maladjusted individual is likely to enter therapy.

The *presenting complaint* of a client in psychotherapy will usually provide us with a reference point for beginning our understanding of the maladjustment process. Kelly would have his clients elaborate on their presenting complaint so that he could grasp the conceptual processes within which the maladjustment developed originally and is now being sustained.[346] What does Amy really mean by *family name* and *jealousy?* These are two important constructs, but are we sure that we understand how she is using these meanings? As she makes her thinking clearer to us regarding the complaint, we are bound to learn how Amy has approached life in general.[347] We learn from her elaboration that by *family name* Amy means something more like *respect,* and *jealousy* has the distinct connotation of *nonacceptance* about it. Amy is telling us that she has been unable to gain respect from others, and that they do not accept her as a person. Kelly did not favor a professional construct of "conflict," saying that this really does not capture what the client is experiencing.[348] Amy is anxious because her construct system is not working, she is *not* "conflicted" about anything in her life.

A normal reaction to the sense of anxiety that heralds the fact that a construction system is not working—that it is failing to structure life events helpfully—is to *reconstrue* these events. The normal person relaxes the superordinate constructs and rearranges the more permeable aspects of his or her total construction system.[349] The increasingly disturbed person, on the other hand, does a poor job of reconstruction and hence the system is not improved; in fact, it is made worse. Were we to know more about Amy's jealousy construct, we would learn that early in life she properly understood that other children were *not* accepting her because of certain selfish mannerisms in her behavior. Rather than reconstrue her self-construct at this point and behave less selfishly, she fixed the impermeable and unrealistic construct of jealousy on others. Henceforth she could dismiss all self-examination when others rejected her by saying, "They are just jealous of my family name." Her family name provided her with a —highly distorted—sense of respect and hence she could continue on as she did for years in a vulnerable psychological state, using a brittle construction system which was to put her on the brink of paranoia.

Amy will be helped in her therapy, for she has not allowed her mental organization to deteriorate completely before seeking help. In cases of severe deterioration, the person has often loosened rather than tightened the construction system, dilating his or her constructs to some bizarre extreme of plausibility. As this occurs, it becomes obvious that the person has a loss of structure known popularly as loss of a grip on reality. Kelly held that no one loses the patterning structure of his or her construction system *entirely*.[350] Even the most regressed psychotic has some remnant of construction in operation. In fact, we can view the *symptom* of a disorder as one form of this remaining structure. Kelly defined the symptom as "the rationale by which one's chaotic experiences are given a measure of structure and meaning."[351]

Symptoms are, therefore, inappropriate ways of adapting to problems.[352] Rather than meet a life challenge, an individual gets sick or gets drunk feeling that his or her inability to meet challenges is somehow now more acceptable. The illness developed need not be free of an organic involvement, for just as an element of a construct is used as a referent for that construct in symbolic form (the "name" of a construct), so too can a bodily organ become the symbol of a construct. "When the client talks about the pain in his chest he may be expressing in his own language a far more comprehensive construct than the psychologist at first suspects."[353] Preverbal constructs are based on the raw experience of bodily sensation without labels, and so-called psychophysiological disturbances are likely to be expressions of such beginning attempts to construe experience.

In addition to providing a rationale (reason, excuse) for present behavior, a symptom is also the way a client asks questions about the future.[354] The person is often asking, "Must I go on in this wretched state, being hounded and manipulated by people who do not understand what a good person I really am?" From an external reference, this might be viewed as a delusional thought pattern. But from the client's viewpoint, it is an admission that he or she is unable to enter into satisfying role relationships and to have a free interpersonal contact with the give-and-take all of us hope to experience with others.

Diagnosing Personal Constructs: The Rep Test

Kelly could find no real use for the Kraepelinian system of categorizing clients into what often become impermeable constructions of a disease entity.[355] He considered *diagnosis* to be the "planning stage of therapy."[356] In diagnosing the client, we as therapists are trying to get a better understanding regarding which way the client will move, given that certain circumstances will arise either in the consulting room or outside. By diagnosing, we are experimenting, making predictions which, if supported by a client's subsequent behavior, establish that we do really understand him or her.[357] The therapist needs a set of coordinate axes as reference dimensions within which client behavior can be plotted and predicted.[358] These professional constructs should be propositional and permeable. Most important of all, the professional-construct system of the clinician must be capable of subsuming the personal-construct system of the client. In order to facilitate this process of coming to know how the client is viewing his or her world, Kelly designed what he called the *Role Construct Repertory Test,* or simply the *Rep Test.*[359]

Let us assume that we have a client named Marco who has come to us with complaints of losing confidence in meeting challenges, and we want to increase our understanding of his construction system by administering a Rep Test to him. The logic of this test involves getting Marco to use and then name his personal-role constructs by having him compare and contrast several people with whom he has had to deal in his life to date.[360] Various figures can be drawn from life, as for example: "a teacher you liked," "the most successful person whom you know personally," "the most threatening person whom you know personally," or "the most ethical person you know personally." In addition, the test taker's parents and siblings are used, and there is usually a self figure as well. Through the use of individual cards for each test figure or a specially prepared test form combining all figures on one page, Marco is then taken through a number of sorts in which he states how person X and person Y are alike and yet different from person Z. For example, he might be asked, "Compare your mother and your favorite teacher, and tell me (or record

in writing) how they are alike and yet *different* from your best friend."

The characterization that emerges here—let us say it is "competent"—is considered only one pole of the construct actually involved. After a series of other comparisons and contrasts of this type, Marco will be taken back through his list of descriptive words (*competent, sneaky, moral, threatening,* and so on) and asked to name the other pole of the underlying constructs. Assume that Marco would write down "questioning" as the opposite pole for "competent." Kelly would say that one of the basic dimensions along which Marco relates to other people is in terms of this construct of "competent versus questioning." Whereas Marco's therapist might have assumed that the opposite of competence was *in*competence, Marco has now revealed that he believes that competent people are likely to be a little close-minded and unquestioning in their approach to life. An open, questioning attitude may not suggest competence to Marco, and as therapy proceeded, this interesting usage might become a central point of consideration as his feelings of lowered confidence came into the discussion. Maybe because he does tend to question things and is open to other people's viewpoints, he assumes that he is *not* a competent person! There are many such hypotheses to be gleaned from a study of the client's construction system, and the point of the Rep Test is to bring therapists into the world of the client's personal construction system.

Kelly also devised a method for *factor analyzing* the construct matrix of the Rep Test.[361] In the test form, for example, Marco would have provided us with twenty-two constructs, having sorted some nineteen different persons (test figures) as outlined above (that is, how are X and Y alike and different from Z). Through the (nonparametric) factor analysis of these sorts, a therapist can arrive at a much shortened list of basic constructs presumably used by Marco in his actual construct system, but which he essentially renames several times in going through the Rep Test. Rather than his having twenty-two constructs, we learn that Marco has only four or five construct dimensions that he *actually* uses in coming at life. This *core* of meaningful conceptions is what we must get at if we are really to understand Marco and help him to change by reconstruing at this most basic of all levels.

Constructs are not always stated in single words. Test subjects often describe their role constructs in brief phrases like "I feel good with them" or "I don't like being with her." Prepared with such a list of constructs, the therapist can now (1) appreciate the client's slant on life; (2) adapt the language used in therapy to that of the client's level of understanding; and (3) begin framing hypotheses about which way the client's construction system will take him or her, given the changing events that arise over the course of therapy. This is the proper scientific attitude, the one Kelly wanted all advocates of personal-construct theory to follow.

Clinical Syndromes and the Psychology of Personal Constructs

Although Kelly did not feel we need to retain the classical syndromes of personal maladjustment, he did make some effort to subsume these well-known Kraepelinian distinctions. He took a quantitative view of the differential diagnosis between neurosis and psychosis, feeling that the same individual could pass through both patterns of living.[362] The essential difference between these two states cen-

tered on the level of anxiety and the kind of solution made to the problems in living. The *neurotic* is likely to manifest anxiety more consistently and to show greater variation in pattern because of the fact that he or she is constantly trying to frame a new construction of events.[363] The *psychotic* has passed through this fumbling phase and, after possibly going to the heights of anxiety, has now settled on some delusional or hallucinatory solution to the problems of living.[364]

The neuroses are variations on this idea of trying to frame new constructions to justify the growing maladjustment. The *hysterias* are typified by converting problems from one area (psychological) into another (bodily).[365] Hysterical and other *psychosomatic* patients are often people who have construed their worlds dualistically and pre-emptively—that is, in terms of either a body or a mind sphere.[366] Having accepted this predicate assumption, they can easily symbolize their mental problems in terms of a chest pain or an immobile hand. *Obsessive-compulsive* clients use tightening as a defense against the failure in prediction they are beginning to sense in their construction systems.[367] When their compulsions begin to trip them up, locking them into some ritualistic performance, we witness the end stage of a tightly drawn, impermeable construct. Anxiety neuroses or *panic* states come about when a sudden comprehensive construction is suggested with no escape in sight.[368] The person in a state of panic is probably as low in predictive power as the human ever gets, and we often see these states popping up just before a psychotic solution is arrived at. Kelly saw the *psychopath* as a person whose style of construction is not truly of a role-relationship variety.[369] That is, a psychopath is interested in manipulating others rather than relating with them in a spontaneous fashion. Psychopaths are very selfish individuals, thinking only of themselves in any interpersonal encounter.

Kelly felt that *suicide* is attempted for various reasons—as a dependency reaction, for example—but that in every instance, it is a form of problem solution, even if it means escape from the responsibility of having to go on predicting.[370]

We have already noted that *delusions* and *hallucinations* are forms of problem solution. Delusions of grandeur ("I am the most powerful person on earth") or persecution ("Everyone is out to do me harm") are forms of construct dilation.[371] Delusions of world destruction would suggest imminent collapse of the construct system ("My world is falling apart"), and a constricted solution might well lead to delusions of self-worthlessness ("I can't find a way out of my problems because I'm useless"). The *depression* psychotic often takes the latter solution to his or her problems.[372] We all construct our fields of action when under pressure to solve some life problem. Depressed cases simply take this tactic to its extreme, severely limiting their alternatives to act. Suicide is always a danger here, but sometimes the depressed person swings to the opposite tactic and dilates his or her construction system into what is then termed a *manic* phase of the same disorder. Delusions of grandeur are then likely to appear, and the person's loosening of the construct system can also be seen in the phenomenon known as *flight of ideas*. The *schizophrenic* individual also reveals such flights, but these are of a long-standing nature and they reflect a much looser form of construction (usually called schizoid thinking). Kelly did not wish to label people as schizophrenics.[373] Too often such labels could not be wiped from a client's record after therapy had been successfully completed. Besides, schizoid thought could be helpful in the beginning of the Creativity Cycle, and it was Kelly's view that creative people loosen in this fashion without moving into a psychotic state.[374] Some forms of schizophrenia reveal considerable withdrawal, suggesting a constriction as well as a loosening of thought patterns.[375]

The *paranoiac* reaction, or some less systematized *paranoid* variation on the schizophrenic diagnosis, was seen by Kelly as involving more permeable construction systems than most psychotics. The paranoid has a highly systematized construction system, and the superordinate constructs are sufficiently permeable to account for changes in experience.[376] This is what makes paranoids so difficult to treat. They can successfully counter virtually anything we think of to shake their delusional systems. There is considerable threat in a paranoid case, probably more so than in any other mental disorder.[377] Finally, the *hebephrenic* and *catatonic* variations of schizophrenia may be seen in terms of highly regressed or preverbal construction systems.

Theory of Cure

Cure as Reconstruction and the Nature of Therapy

People are mentally healthy to the extent that they can solve the problems they encounter in life.[378] Kelly was fond of speaking of this process of solving life's problems as the rotating of "the axes on life." [379] A new set of dimensions comes into play which opens freedom of movement. Kelly once considered calling his therapeutic approach *reconstruction* rather than *psychotherapy,* and he was never happy with the latter term.[380] He finally settled for a definition emphasizing that "psychotherapy is a reconstruing process." [381]

The therapy relationship is viewed as a kind of running psychological experiment or a laboratory for the testing of ideas and feelings.[382] As therapists, we ask our clients to join us in a controlled investigation of their lifestyles.[383] Experiments will be performed and field studies will be carried out (at home), with proper validation sought for the predictions both the therapist and the client will make. Kelly did not believe that therapy was confined to the four walls of the consulting room.[384] Since reconstruction cures, the therapy will not be successful unless a client begins his or her reformulations in the actual life setting. Therapy involves the dual task of reviewing present constructs and then either altering them in some fashion or formulating entirely new ones which might serve the process of life more adequately.

Kelly liked to speak of this process of change in therapy as *movement*. It is a good prognostic sign if clients enter therapy with some preliminary construct of movement of their own;[385] for example, if they see themselves as already changing in some way— even getting worse—this is better than seeing themselves as frozen into a situation which somehow changes around them. Such clients recognize that they are participating in the flux of events, and hence we can work with them to direct their movement productively. One of the first types of movement to be seen in a therapy series is *slot movement*.[386] This involves simply moving over to the contrast end of one's constructs, as when the woman who sees her neighbors all as kindly begins to think of them as mean. Kelly considered this a superficial change but a process of movement worthy of note. We can as therapists build on this change, extending the client's alternative constructions to a more comprehensive level. Whether neighbors are kindly or mean can then be tested in a series of experiments—such as asking the client to predict what will happen at the next church social or block party.

Following a statement of the opening complaint by the client, the therapist usually asks for more information on the circumstances surrounding such difficulties. Kelly viewed this preliminary as a fundamental task of the therapist, one he called *elaboration*.[387] The point is: in elaborating the complaint, the therapist encourages the client to extend the range of convenience of his or her constructs and usually to bring other constructs into play as well. Reconstruction often begins in the loosening that such elaboration encourages. That is, as clients date the onset of their problems and move backward or forward in their recollections, they naturally begin to loosen their terms.[388] The therapist assists in this loosening process, encouraging a tightening at the proper moment so that, in effect, the Creativity Cycle or the C-P-C Cycle may operate. The therapist's goal is to help the client develop a set of constructs which are permeable and comprehensive.[389] As these are psychological activities, Kelly can sum up his definition of the therapeutic contact as follows: "Psychotherapy is the intelligent manipulation and organization of various psychological processes."[390]

Interpretation, Insight, and the Client's Viewpoint

The most vital point of Kellyian therapy is that in the final analysis, the client always cures himself or herself. This is why the therapist considers the client to be a coinvestigator in a running series of experiments. Kelly never tired of telling his therapy students, *"If you don't know what's wrong with a client, ask him; he may tell you!"* [391] To be effective, the therapist must have (1) a permeable, nonpre-emptive set of professional constructs within which to construe the client, and (2) a talent for making use of the client's construct system in its own sense.[392] Kelly did not expect his clients to learn the professional constructs of his approach. He did not force interpretations onto clients that were cloaked in the terminology of personal-construct psychology. Kelly was not doctrinaire in making interpretations, and in fact, he held that *insight* in the classical sense was not always necessary for a cure to result.[393]

Kelly defined *insight* as "the comprehensive construction of one's behavior."[394] Note that the vantage point of this definition is the client's. The same goes for *interpretation*. " 'Interpretation' is a term for which we have no particularly limited definition. . . . The therapist does not so much present interpretations as attempt to get the client himself to make helpful interpretations."[395] The therapist says such things as "Is this what you mean when you say that you feel people are ignoring you?" or "Let's try this on for size and see if it helps us organize our thinking about the problem." In saying these things, the therapist is not directing the client toward any single area of knowledge called insight. Clients always provide the focus of therapy because of personal constructions they introduce, and whatever change takes place is similarly going to take place only on the basis of their personal efforts to reconstrue their lives. Kelly would take his clients through a review of their past lives, but not because this was required by his theory of personality or therapy cure. Indeed, the past is only relevant because it can shed light on the present and the future life into which the client is moving.[396] Therapy serves a primarily anticipatory function.[397]

Kelly liked to think of the therapist as a source of validation for the client.[398] In reconstruing their experience, clients must necessarily begin with their perception of the therapist. They try out their old and new constructs on the therapist at one time or another—framing the relationship in light of their changing perspectives and looking in turn for some kind of reaction in the therapist's behavior. Kelly liked to use these client experiments as the focal point for insightful comments, or as he preferred to think of it, as *organized instruction*.[399] By either validating or not validating the client's constructions, the therapist—through his or her personal reactions—is effectively teaching the client which constructs fit and which do not. This process of adjusting constructs to experiential reality is then extended beyond the therapy room to the client's real world. Therapy proceeds, like any other scientific venture, through successive approximations.[400] The client does not need *one* insight but a host of increasingly predictive insights to formulate and reformulate the construction system. Some of these insightful experiences with the therapist will be unique, whereas others may fall under the constructs of the better known personality theories like the Freudian or Adlerian theories.[401]

By saying that insight is not always necessary, Kelly meant that the individual does not have to learn any doctrinaire theoretical explanations of behavior. Some problems are not worth mulling over. Kelly sometimes thought it is better to *encapsulate* an old problem rather than try to work it through and master it via insight.[402] This can be accomplished through a *time-binding* technique, in which the therapist takes the position: "Well, that was a very tough period in your life all right, and I suppose we might be able to find out more about it if we spent several months in a search. But maybe we can consider that past and begin our search for a happier and more productive time in the present and the future. What do you say?" With an attitude of this sort, the therapist turns the client's attention away from those intricate, soul-searching efforts in which classical analysis seems to become engulfed.

There are other ways in which psychologists use the term *insight* which Kelly would not greatly quarrel with. For example, if the psychologist feels it is desirable for a client to name—that is, assign a symbol to—some new construct which is emerging in his or her repertoire of constructs, then Kelly would consider this action a form of insight.[403] Too many therapists seem to want this more for their own needs—as proof of their effectiveness rather than as a necessary aspect of cure—but Kelly was willing to accept the necessity on occasion. If a highly rigid, religiously devout man who has become more propositional and permeable in his thought is made aware that his thinking has loosened up, he might be spared some later threat when this more liberal outlook now appears in conflict with his religious convictions. This is surely a kind of insight.

Relationship Factors: Acceptance, Transference, and Resistance

When we take up relationship factors in the theory of personal constructs, we begin dealing specifically with *role constructs*. Since therapists are major validators of client constructs, they begin to take on great importance as therapy progresses. This is why therapists, working through their professional constructs, must have greater sensitivity to and knowledge of relationship factors than clients. As Kelly put it, "A therapist-client relationship is one which exemplifies greater understanding on the part of one member than on the part of the other."[404] Thus, to be effective as a therapist, one must understand and utilize the constructs of clients—see with their eyes and talk their language. This is what Kelly meant by *acceptance*.[405] By accepting the client's construction system

in this way, the therapist conveys a sense of *support* to the client.[406] This does not mean the therapist approves of the client's value system, nor does it commit the therapist to going along with everything the client does. Acceptance merely signifies to the client that the therapist truly understands why things are taking place—right or wrong, good or bad things—from the client's perspective on life. This understanding *reassures* the client and makes it more likely that he or she will undertake the experiments therapy will call for.

This brings us to the factor of *rapport* or relationship in therapy. Kelly interpreted rapport in terms of his role theory.[407] Rapport is established when the therapist subsumes a part of the client's construction system and thereby enters into a role relationship with him or her. It is not unusual for the client to establish a comparable rapport with the therapist sometime later in the consulting sessions. Signs of rapport in clients include increased relaxation, greater spontaneity, flexibility, and the willingness to loosen a construction.[408] Kelly believed that therapists can help promote client rapport by taking on a *credulous attitude* regarding what is being communicated in the therapy hour.[409] A credulous person is ready to believe whatever is told him or her. Kelly was not suggesting that effective therapists have to be gullible. What he meant by the credulous attitude is that we must take in everything the client says, understand it correctly from his or her personal slant, and above all, never discard information because it fails to fit with our own conceptualization of the case history. Credulity in this sense is openness. When clients perceive us as open to their complete construction of events, we establish in them the proper expectancy for *communication*.[410] We cannot begin to communicate until we believe that the person to whom we send information is actually open to it. The effective therapist is always open to such information.

Some of the constructions that enter into the relationship are preverbal and hence often distortions of what is taking place. This is how Kelly viewed the phenomenon of *transference*, which especially involves those early dependency constructs that were mentioned above as having been framed in infancy and childhood. Since these are always formulated around parental figures, Kelly viewed transference in the following manner:

The psychoanalytic use of the term [transference] seems altogether too loose for our purposes. We have therefore tightened up our use of the term to refer precisely to the tendency of any person to perceive another prejudicately as a replicate of a third person. In this sense, "transference" is not necessarily pathological, nor is the prejudgment necessarily pathological, nor is the prejudgment necessarily antipathetic.[411]

The dependency construct that underwrites transference is what we must understand, for it is invariably pre-emptive and often constricted—focused on some one type of person in life, such as a rejecting mother or a hostile father. Kelly did not believe that the therapist's task was to make clients *non*dependent. The task was rather to encourage through reconstruction a greater dispersion of dependency. People need one another and must depend on one another if mental health is to be enjoyed by all. Dependency is not a one-way street. It is a mutual give-and-take.

Kelly called the type of transference we have been considering thus far—based on a kind of replay of role constructs from out of the past in terms of parental dependencies—*secondary transference*.[412] It is secondary because nothing in the therapist's personality or physical appearance can account for why the client brings these constructs to bear in the relationship. However, a *primary transference*

can also develop in the relationship, in which case a special construct is framed pre-emptively by the client to be applied to the person of the therapist.[413] The client may idealize the therapist, turn him or her into a hero figure, and consider the therapy hour the high point of any day. Kelly felt that primary transference is a great hindrance to effective therapy, for it limits construction to the conference room (as opposed to life outside the relationship), distorts reality, and is if anything a kind of smokescreen the client throws up in order to avoid true experimentation. He insisted that when primary transferences arise, the therapist must behave in ways that will disconfirm them.[414] If the client flatters the therapist for "being nice," the therapist might begin acting a bit more aggressively and threaten the client to some degree (all of this is ultimately discussed as therapy proceeds, of course). The worst thing that can happen is for a therapist to begin accepting the adulation and using the power of primary transferences in the relationship; this would be taken as a sign of *countertransference*.[415]

Therapists who follow personal-construct theory do not make themselves completely open in a personal sense during psychotherapy—at least, not until therapy has gone on for some time. They are very sensitive to the fact that clients use their person as a source of construct validation, and what Kellyian therapists want above all is to promote these validation efforts *outside* the consulting room. Clients must learn that they can find many ways in which to validate their constructs, and that it is absolutely essential for them to assume personal responsibility in this regard. Hence, at times the therapist must begin to play a role in opposition to the role the client has written for him or her in the idealization of primary transference. Kelly even suggested that acting skills can be helpful to a prospective therapist.[416] Since cure does not issue from some emotive bond of genuineness any more than it issues from detailed insights, Kelly did not feel that a therapist has to become involved in the relationship *literally* as a personality—revealing himself or herself as if to a close friend or confidant. On the other hand, the therapist *does* have to apply constantly a properly professional set of constructs, for "the therapist who cannot adequately construe his client within a set of professional constructs runs the risk of transferring his own dependencies upon the client." [417]

Kelly found that his clients did not move through only one or two phases of transference, but that often the process went on throughout their contacts. Frequently what was taking place in transference depended on his or her attitude at the time. Hence, Kelly began to speak of *transference cycles* in psychotherapy.[418] Transference cycles typically begin in the secondary sense of attributing dependency constructs onto the therapist, which may then develop into the idealizations of primary transference, before the cycle swings downward again as the client turns his or her attention elsewhere in life and the therapist takes on minor importance. However, a cycle can then be repeated, particularly if for some reason the therapist becomes the focus of a discussion or decision-making process. If countertransference enters, cycles can be drawn out or restimulated as well. Kelly defined *resistance* as a downward swing of the transference cycle, where we are likely to find clients countering their therapists, striking out to do more construing on their own outside of the consulting room, even if this goes against what the therapist might prefer.[419] Therapists can also encourage resistance. For example, by interpreting too early, the therapist might threaten

the client, bringing about a rapid constriction in the latter's loosening processes which might then be seen by the therapist as an act of resistance.[420]

Kelly would consider such resistances normal tightening reactions in the face of threat, and he would chalk them off to errors of therapeutic interpretation. However, the notion that a continuing resistance to the therapist must always take place if therapy is to proceed to a successful conclusion was construed by Kelly as arising from the fact that dependencies are being extended to more and more people. The therapist's lowering in the eyes of the client is also the therapist's gain, because this means the client is establishing role-relationships outside the therapy hour.[421] All therapists want their clients to be resistive in this sense, even though the actual experience of being taken out of central focus by the client may prove personally threatening at times. No one enjoys losing adulation, even if that idealized respect is not earned. Even so, Kelly insisted on his students accepting resistance as a natural course of therapy. If a therapist spoke of *negative transference,* Kelly interpreted this to mean something felt by the therapist and *not* the client.[422] All moves away from exclusive dependence on the therapist toward distributing dependency to other people was taken by Kelly as a *positive* occurrence.

When a transference cycle has settled and remained stable for some time, the therapist considers termination of therapy. At the very mention of termination, the client may revert to a more dependent pattern, wanting to rekindle another transference cycle, but the therapist should have by this time acquired the confidence that this is not necessary and thus carry out plans for ending the sessions. The therapist never, on the other hand, breaks off therapy at the height of a transference cycle, leaving the client stranded without alternative sources of validation (that is, other people!).

Therapeutic Techniques

Enactment

Personal-construct therapists like to bring their sessions alive by setting up *role-play* situations with their clients, designed to elicit the latter's construction of life events. Kelly defined role playing in the following terms: "The therapist may tentatively present a carefully calculated point of view in such a way that the client, through coming to understand it, may develop a basis for understanding other figures in his environment with whom he needs to acquire skill in playing interacting roles."[423]

Assume that Harry, a client in psychotherapy, complains at one point that his boss is always picking on him. A Kellyian therapist would be very likely to enter into a spontaneous role play with Harry, probably by abruptly saying something like, "When you say your boss picks on you, what do you mean? He says, 'Haven't you got that work finished yet?' or something to that effect? Well, when he talks that way what do you say? Answer me in your typical way— 'Haven't you got that work finished yet?'" We introduce such on-the-spot acting without fanfare so as not to threaten Harry, who might get tied into knots when told that he will be expected to re-enact his past life in therapy or some such. Gradually, Harry will be brought deeper into the technique as the role-play situations grow longer and more involved. Kelly would also insist that when the roles became anything more than simply a clarifying example of the sort just presented, Harry and his therapist should play both roles. This is called *role reversal*. In playing his boss after first portraying himself, Harry will get a different perspective on the role relationship under study, and the reverse is true for the therapist. As constructive alternativists, we are always ready to see things from more than just one perspective.

The technical term for role-playing is *enactment*.[424] In training to become a Kellyian therapist, enactment is very important, because only if a therapist is at ease in role play will the client feel comfortable. Enactments are usually very brief, not lasting more than a few minutes in ordinary therapy. It is also important to avoid enacting caricatures of people. The more lifelike we can make the role play the greater are the chances that the client will benefit. Of course, there is room in working out a role play for the client to experiment and thereby depart from his or her typical approach to others. The therapist can also enact the client in a somewhat altered manner, providing grounds for reconstruction in this manner as well.

Self-Characterization and Fixed-Role Therapy

Although a certain insight can be obtained from enacting roles with the therapist during the regular session, a far greater potential for experimentation and reconstruction lies outside the consulting room in the life sphere itself. Kelly believed that clients should approach their daily lives with a construct system that is not of their usual choosing—all with a sense of "let's pretend."[425] This can be done by first rewriting the client's customary constructs, giving the person an essentially new scenario regarding life, and then encouraging him or her to experiment by living according to the modified construction system. The Rep Test can help here, but in addition, Kelly relied on what he termed a *self-characterization sketch*. After Harry has been in therapy for several weeks, his therapist might say to him, "I want you to write a character sketch of Harry Brown, just as if he were the principal character in a play.

Write it as it might be written by a friend who knows him very *intimately* and very *sympathetically,* perhaps better than anyone ever really could know him. Be sure to write it in the third person. For example, start out by saying, 'Harry Brown is . . .' " [426]

Harry will produce a statement running anywhere from a few paragraphs to possibly several pages of self-description. The next step is for the therapist—usually with the help of other professional therapists—to write out a *fixed role* based on what Harry has said about himself, as well as what has already been learned of him in therapy to this point. What this comes down to is a role written *in contrast* to the role that Harry has written for himself in the self-characterization. [427] Kelly suggested that the new role should always remove impermeable constructions, consider available validation for the constructs introduced, and include a framework for construing others to aid in establishing role relationships. Roles that include notions of financial wealth for a client living in near-poverty conditions or other wildly unrealistic suggestions are pointless. Finally, Harry must be made aware that this is a make-believe experimental effort, and that no matter how he may find other people responding to his contrived change in behavior, he has the protection of experimental fantasy to reassure him. He is, in the final analysis, the person in charge of what is taking place during the fixed-role experiment.

Harry's role would probably involve a more assertive pattern of speaking up when being victimized by his boss or other dominant people. If directly speaking up is not suggested, then possibly some alternative form of behavior might be framed, such as appearing relaxed and inviting criticism in relation to the boss rather than cowering as he now does. Possibly the role would have Harry begin criticizing himself and/or other people—beating his superior to the punch, so to speak. Whatever role would eventuate, it would be written broadly enough to enable Harry to move permeably within alternatives. That is, we do not want the client to follow specific instructions, but rather to get the general theme of a different approach to life in which he or she could then spontaneously create variations.

It is clear from everything that Kelly wrote on the topic that fixed-role therapy is *not* a manipulative device to subtly and covertly control client behavior. [428] Harry is not being encouraged simply to act more assertively in the fixed role, and when he is through with this experiment, he may well return to *exactly* the same sort of person that he was at the outset. As long as he has come to view life from the opposite side of the behavioral street, however, and to see what it is like to be a more critical, bossy person himself, he will have gained something of vital importance from the experiment performed. He can grasp the impact of his manner on others more clearly now for he has taken the role of the "other," a capacity that is essential to understanding and healthy role relationships. In fixed-role therapy, the client writes the first script, the clinician-therapist the second, and the final life plan remains to be worked out. Hence, Kelly defined this technique as follows: *"Fixed-role therapy is a sheer creative process in which therapist and client conjoin their talents.* Any attempt to make it a *repair* process rather than a *creative* process seems to result in some measure of failure." [429] His hope was that a fresh personality, of the client's own choosing, would emerge. [430]

Fixed-role therapy is ordinarily conducted for an eight-week period, though there is no hard and fast rule to follow here. [431] Clients are often fascinated by the impact their changed roles have upon others. This can be very upsetting to a spouse or other important figures in a person's life, of course. As Harry reports back on what his wife or boss did in reaction to his altered pattern of behavior, the therapist focuses on these issues and through further role play helps him work through difficult situations. Harry finds some marvelous opportunities in this process for making propositional and permeable constructions of his life events. The first sign of progress will probably occur when Harry informs the therapist that new elements are falling into place in his construction system. He sees now why such-and-thus seems to happen, or he feels in empathy with his boss for doing what he does at times.[432] Though we have not written his role for this manipulative purpose, it would be possible for Harry to find himself in the new role and take it over fairly completely in time. This is not the usual outcome, however. Occasionally roles need to be rewritten after a few weeks, and here again Kelly thought it advisable to consult with peers in the therapy profession.

Controlled Elaboration

We have already seen above that a major task of the therapist is to help the client elaborate the presenting complaint. However, Kelly further refined this general therapeutic role into a technique he called *controlled elaboration*. In using controlled elaboration, we take up large sections of a client's construction system and try to make the contents internally consistent so that they can be put to experimental test. The C-P-C Cycle might be used in this effort. A therapist using controlled elaboration might say to the client, "Let us think through how this would be done and how it would turn out in the end."[433] In laying plans for the future, we of necessity must pull our thoughts together in anticipation of what will lead to what, how

we will react if things go this way rather than that way, and so on. All of our constructs necessarily come into play when we frame such broadly ranging plans. Although elaborations of this sort could be done in considering an interpretation of the past, Kelly usually tried to orient the client's thinking forward in time, trying to anticipate and predict the future, and this in turn usually clarified and reorganized the construction system.[434]

The Use of Dreams

Dreams were viewed by Kelly as "the most loosened construction that one can put into words,"[435] and they are often prompted by preverbal constructs.[436] Kelly thought it pointless to believe that something as vague as a dream can have a *single* meaning.[437] Freud's so-called latent dream content is probably the *submerged pole* of a construct. Of course, dreams can sometimes make sense if we interpret their imagery in an oppositional sense.[438] This is similar to slot movement in that a person is likely to try the other side of the conceptual street when in a dream or even a conscious reverie (daydream). This is the reason we are sometimes shocked by what we spontaneously "think of," even while awake. We picture our beloved parent full of life, and in the next instant we see the same loved one dead and lying in a coffin. Dreams skip about like this because they play both ends of our construct poles off against each other.

Kelly did not have a formal role for the dream in his therapy, except in this sense of taking it as a sign of the possible beginnings of loosened thinking. Sometimes this loosening suggested the beginnings of movement. Kelly did not routinely ask the client to report dreams, but he felt that if it were of sufficient impact on the client to be brought up spontaneously, he would at least want to hear the dream story out. He was interested in the loosened construction and not the content of the dream per se. He was opposed to those approaches which see dreams as reflecting symbols.[439] If a dream heralded some movement, Kelly would interpret this to the client in light of their ongoing discussion as a form of controlled elaboration. For example, a female patient who was beginning to wrestle with her passive approach to life might begin dreaming that she was bound and gagged. This would be a loosening extension of her generally quiet and ineffective manner with others, and Kelly would so inform her.

Procedural Details

Kelly sometimes found it necessary to get clients moving by threatening them or aggravating their anxiety.[440] He never attacked their construct system directly, of course; the therapist who accuses a client of not having good ideas or lacking insight makes a mistake. But Kelly had a way of bringing the client around to discussions of life areas in which his or her construction systems were simply not working well. This was enough to motivate such clients to begin movement. When it came to opening up new areas for consideration, Kelly always made certain that the client had a foundation construct on which to build his or her understanding.[441] We do not want to send people into areas where they have no frame of reference at all. Kelly advised his students to sharpen their understanding by predicting what their clients would do from one therapy hour to the next.[442] In working with children, Kelly ad-

vocated bringing the parents into the treatment program.[443]

Kelly favored *group therapy* whenever a problem area bringing people together with a common dilemma might be arranged.[444] He considered role-play (enactment) techniques particularly well-suited to group therapy. Occasionally he found it necessary to *confront* a client sharply, to challenge his or her construct system in no uncertain terms.[445] We have already mentioned the techniques of encapsulation and time-binding. Kelly also spoke of *word-binding,* by which he meant tying the client down to some specific term for each of his constructs.[446] This is an aspect of tightening, and it can prove useful in making some item impermeable, as when we wish to encapsulate a paranoid idea with something like, "Yes, that's probably another example of those strange happenings which we spoke about last week as things which we all experience but can't explain. Let's chalk it up to that and move on to this next point." We can dismiss the significance of the experience by binding it in the already-discredited construct bound by the words *strange happenings.* This cuts down rumination and turns the client's attention to the more propositional and permeable aspects of his or her construction system.

Kelly said that he had never taken a *fee* from a client in over thirty years of therapeutic practice.[447] We can only guess what this can mean to the form which his therapy was to take on. It is important to note that Kelly's attitude toward taking payment for psychological services was somewhat negative. Here is an excerpt from his writings on the point.

The psychologist because he operates within a psychological rather than an economic framework, cannot allow himself to be caught up in such a system of values. As a psychologist he is committed to a more comprehen-

sive viewpoint with respect to human relations. If he makes his fee system the universal basis of his psychotherapeutic relations, he abdicates this more enlightened position at the outset. One cannot always insist upon a monetary exchange as the primary basis of his relations with his client and at the same time hope, as a therapist, to represent values which transcend crass materialism.[448]

Summary

Piaget's genetic epistemology bridges the gap between body and mind by suggesting that a scheme can be interiorized (cognitively) of the physical motions made (reflexively) by the organism, and that subsequently this patterned relationship can combine into increasingly abstract structures or structured systems. Human beings can therefore transform themselves and their environments intellectually and not only organically through changes in species. As used by Piaget, the term *construction* means the creation of a structure (scheme) through ongoing processes of both an organic and cognitive nature. Thanks to the offsetting cognitive processes of assimilation (taking-in of environmental factors) and accommodation (remodifying behavior due to experience), a reciprocal influence is possible in cognition leading to equilibration. When assimilation brings about a disequilibration, the organism is motivated to bring accommodation into play to thereby achieve a new level of equilibrium. This balancing process effectively results in new learning. Piaget discusses many cognitive processes in light of their contribution to this equilibrating process, such as induction, deduction, and transduction. Centered thought is glued concretely to merely that which is perceived, whereas more creative thinking calls for decentrations.

An important cognitive process described by Piaget is reversibility, which refers to the fact that higher-order thought can be reciprocally examined or turned around, without losing its original meaning. Reciprocal and negational reversibility enables the maturing child to think reflexively, to bring thought into examination self-critically. Another important construct in Piagetian theory is that of the operation. Operational thinking summarizes all that can be said about cognition. Operations are interiorized actions having the property of reversibility, but also retaining an identifiable structure that can be related to other operations. Operations never exist entirely alone in thought. Operational thinking begins at a concrete level and then gradually develops (evolves) to increasingly abstract levels of cognitive thought. Piaget refers to imagination as representation, an operation that is identical whether we are presently looking at an object (perception) or recalling it mentally (memory). Very abstract representations are what we mean by "concepts," and by using these, we "think." Mind is therefore a continuing process of constructive activity, with a large amount of self-construction involved. Intelligence arises when we establish permanent relations between schema that cover greater and greater spatiotemporal intervals. This ability for mind to take on permanent conceptual organizations is what Piaget means by conservation. Mathematical insights exist as fixed structures with great conservative value, no matter who it is that reasons them out. Piaget interprets the feedback loop of cybernetics theory as a means of retaining structure within change, a self-regulatory process akin to equilibration which also retains the integrity of the structured process. Human beings differ from computers, however, in that they can transform themselves and become more complex.

Piaget notes that all behavior is teleonomic, that is, goal-oriented. Personality is the total system of interrelating schemata and operations that are made possible by these structures, occurring across the sensorimotor, intellectual, and affective (emotional) levels of behavior. Though he accepts the fact that human beings are self-directing actors, Piaget is not sympathetic with theories of agency such as we find in Jung, Adler, Rogers, Boss, or Binswanger. The self or cognitive self (image) that we are aware of as human beings is itself a schema framed by operational thinking. Earliest thought is egocentric and anthropomorphic, or precausal, in nature, so that children confuse their personal constructions with the objects they see around them— attributing humanlike characteristics to clouds, trees, and so on. Consciousness arises when the environmental situation blocks the person from continuing some ongoing activity. Piaget rejects the psychoanalytical interpretation of unconscious symbolisms. He would say that so-called repression occurs when the person refuses to accept what reality demands as an accommodation, but instead persists in assimilating reality to an egocentric schema which is unadaptive. Piaget does not object to the view that dreams may be wish fulfillments, as long as we appreciate that a wish is nothing more than the person's effort to assimilate reality to the self.

Piaget is probably best known for his detailed study of the stages of development. Infancy is the period of life from birth to age two, dominated by reflexive behaviors. Sucking is the first major reflex, providing the child with an initial schema for cognitive growth. Reflex cycles move into circular reactions as the child practices actions like head-turning, assimilating experience to such actions and accommodating them in turn. Piaget calls these early efforts reproductive assimilations. Percepts and habits are structured in time. Children in the second year of life have a practical, sensorimotor intelligence. Action schemata dominate cognitive life as the child learns how hands work, where the mouth is located, and so on. The schemata are also related to each other via what is called a reciprocal assimilation. By the end of the second year, the child's sensorimotor intelligence includes a sense of surrounding space, the perception of objects in space, a notion of how one event brings another about, and a beginning sense of time's passage.

Early childhood covers the ages of roughly two to seven years. This is the time of early gropings for a social existence, moving out of the egocentricity of infancy. Children model their parents as ego ideals. This is still a period of preoperational thinking, however, in which the person relies on childhood animism, intuition, and semilogic. Moral realism typifies this period, so that rules are followed concretely and without insight into the principles lying behind them. Self-evaluation begins in early childhood.

Late childhood extends from age seven to twelve years. The child becomes more cognizant of self factors through internal dialogue. Conservation reflects development in the child's cognitions during this period, as the child's thought is progressing from intuition and semilogic to reversible thought. Piaget specifies the age of seven or eight as the time of life in which concrete operations first appear—that is, those that bear on manipulable objects (things) rather than on propositions (abstractions). Over the period of late childhood, rational thought continues to evolve, as reflected in a growing capacity to group items and examine them conceptually through reversibility. The morality of constraint (rule-following) of the earlier period begins to develop to a morality of cooperation, in which justice supplants routine.

Because of this, the first moral conflicts arise in late childhood.

The final stage of development is adolescence, which carries the person forward to adulthood. Beginning sometime between eleven and thirteen years of age the development of formal operations occurs. The person can now use general ideas and abstract constructions. Thought becomes self-reflexive and propositional, thanks to the reversibility and dialectical features of such abstractions. Whereas the self is a primitive, hence egocentric schema of identity, the personality that emerges in adolescence takes into account ideals and aspirations beyond just the self. Piaget's conception of personality borrows from the notion of character—that is, an evaluation of behavioral tendencies. Piaget would view fixation in the Jungian vein, as a failure to progress beyond a certain level, resulting usually in errors in judgment when the person behaves in relation to others. Imitation of others' behavior is viewed as the primacy of accommodation over assimilation, and the adolescent is often prone to imitate in the so-called gang age. Identification is a similar idea. There are many behavioral patterns possible in life, so that Piaget accepts a broad range of individual differences, even though he dislikes categorizing people. He also dislikes tracing the differences in people's behavior to explanations relying on language acquisition and the shaping of the person through social pressures. Piaget's theory of abnormality would combine his constructs of disequilibration and fixation over the years of development.

In George Kelly, we find a different—more clearly and totally Kantian—constructivist. Construing is viewed by Kelly as a process of framing interpretations about life, trying in a sense to capture that which recurs in a dichotomous frame known as the construct. In a construct, there are at least two elements that are similar and they contrast with a third.

Constructs are thus relationships between things that seem alike (similarity) and yet differ from something else (contrast). They are like transparent patterns or templets through which the person makes predictions about life's continually unfolding future. Constructive alternativism (Kelly's philosophy) suggests that there is always more than one way to slice the pie of experience. We can always reconstrue a set of circumstances and thereby place an alternative construction on what we know about things.

Constructs form into interlocking relations known as the construction system. This system is ordinal, so that there are superordinate (more abstract) and subordinate (less abstract) constructs. The former can subsume or take the latter under their range of convenience—that is, their definitional meaning. Constructs can dilate or extend their range of convenience, as they can constrict and focus in on a narrow referent. Constructs can be said to loosen or tighten. Permeable constructs readily take on new elements of meaning, whereas the impermeable constructs do not admit of new possibilities. Pre-emptive constructs fix rigid, either-or distinctions, and the constellatory construct permits its elements to belong to more than one realm of meaning at the same time. A construct that leaves its elements open to new construction—as in accepting new evidence—is termed a propositional construct. There are comprehensive constructs that subsume a wide variety of events, and there are incidental constructs that are more limited in their referent.

We human beings form self-constructs, which is what we mean when we speak about our identities. Kelly was more accepting of an identity conception than Piaget, just as he was purely a psychological constructivist. There is no mention of organic constructions in the psychology of personal constructs. Personal constructs enable us to control what we do as we move through life. Interpersonal relations encourage the person to frame role relationships. The role is a pattern of behavior defined by the individual such that one person construes the construction processes of another person. We make an interpretation of what others are thinking about us, and then working on this assumption, we frame a role construct. We may err in this interpretation, but our behavior will depend on it even so. The most central conceptions of this type which define our relationship to other people Kelly termed the core-role constructs.

Kelly did not like drive-reduction theories of learning. He, like Adler, saw the person as a process, as behaving and changing through reconstruction when necessary, but always contributing to his or her determination of behavior. Freedom to behave is just another way of talking about the alternative construction people can always place on events. Change in construction systems is said to follow one of two courses. First, we have the C-P-C Cycle, in which the person begins circumspectly by looking at all sides of an issue, using propositional constructions. After considering possible alternatives, the person pre-empts one and only one course of action. This alternative then controls behavior in the course of events to follow. The second method of changing behavior follows a loosening-to-tightening process of employing constructs, which Kelly termed the Creativity Cycle. Kelly thought of emotional behavior as either loosely defined construction or some preverbal construction which has persisted in the construction system. The feelings of threat and stress signal that one's core-role constructs are not working completely and hence might require change. Anxiety is the extreme result of being caught in life

with one's core constructs inadequate to the task of predicting and controlling (understanding and anticipating) the course of life events. Kelly thought of aggression in much the same way that the existentialists think of commitment, that is, as an active elaboration of the construction system. He favored this style of behavior over the passivity of an individual who does not seek to extend the range and diversity of the construct system or does so only tentatively. Kelly drew a distinction between aggression and hostility. Hostile persons insist on using the same bankrupt constructs even though they do not predict and control life well. The emotion of guilt occurs when the person feels dislodged from his or her role structure. This is where conscience or superego would be placed in Kellyian theory.

Though Kelly did not care much for the Freudian defense mechanisms, he did offer alternative definitions in light of his theory. Repression is the suspension or stopping of the construing process. Incorporation is a willingness on the part of a person to see other people like himself or herself. Identification occurs when we take over constructs that our group—including family members—have already been using. Regression is due to behavior that is predicated on preverbal or immature constructions of life. Projection is a special case of hostility in which the person forces his bankrupt constructions onto others. Reaction-formation is an attempt to put an opposite construct pole into effect when it is the other pole that bears significance for a person. Kelly did not propose a stage theory of development, though he did emphasize the importance of other people to proper maturation. He disliked the Rankian-Rogerian talk of seeking independence from others, feeling instead that early dependency constructs framed around parents had to be extended to more and more people with development. He had something in mind like the Adlerian social interest here, though he called it a dispersion of dependency. This is why societies arise in the first place, because people are dependent on each other, and cultural norms arise because a group of people come to construe existence in a common way. Kelly shared a dislike for categorizing people with other theorists in the phenomenological tradition. Personality styles of either a type or trait variety can always be seen to depend on the unique construction system fashioned by the person in question.

Kelly's theory of illness holds that people who repeatedly bring to bear invalid constructions of life eventually become maladjusted. For whatever reason, the abnormal person is wracked with anxiety or projecting distorted views of reality or behaving in a hostile manner, and so on, because of an unworkable construction system which he or she cannot reconstrue. Symptoms of disorder reflect the rationale the person accepts for this inability to control or predict life—due to strange physical losses (hysteria), terrifying fears (phobias), or intruding forces of unknown origins (schizophrenic delusions). Kelly fashioned a Role Construct Repertory Test (Rep Test), which could help the therapist understand the client's construct system, reducing, through a special form of factor analysis, the various reference frames to a few core constructs. Neurotics reflect much anxiety but are trying to frame new constructions of events (reconstrue). Psychotics have settled on a bizarre delusional or hallucinatory solution to their problems of living. Hysterics convert their psychological problems to a physical rationale. Obsessive-compulsive clients use tightening as a defense against their failing construction system. Psychopaths fail to frame genuine role relationships with others. Depressed clients tend to constrict and manic clients dilate their constructs. Schizophrenic constructions are the loosest of all.

Kelly's theory of cure builds on the idea of reconstruction, for to the extent that people can control and predict their lives they can solve their problems by themselves and achieve mental health. Kelly saw his therapeutic role as helping clients to "rotate the axes" on life and come at things anew with alternative constructions that work better. He spoke of the process of change in therapy as movement, beginning in an elaboration of the presenting complaint and going on to the more involved aspects, using the C-P-C and Creativity Cycles. Interpretations are made by the client, assisted by the organized instruction of the therapist who helps the client know what his or her construction system is, how it is failing, and how it might be improved. Sometimes old problems cannot be solved, and it is best to encapsulate them through a time-binding technique. Kelly always took a credulous attitude with clients, accepting and supporting them in every way so that through such reassurance they would begin reconstruction. So-called transference is due to distortions in the client's constructions, stemming from earlier life (secondary transference) or from the actual regard the client has for the therapist (primary transference). The latter form of transference hinders therapy. Kelly saw therapy as a series of transference cycles, in which the client moves from being highly drawn to the therapist to a period of increasing conflict or resistance as the client tightens construction in the face of threat. Kelly did not really accept the idea of negative transference, feeling that if it occurs, it is probably brought on by the therapist rather than the client.

Kelly used the technique of enactment or role play extensively. He also employed a self-characterization technique preliminary to fixed-role therapy, in which a client was asked to live according to a different construction system for a period of several weeks. Controlled elaboration was another technique in which the meaning of the presenting complaint and other meanings that occurred over therapy were enlarged upon in the hope of systematizing them to a greater extent; this would point in turn to what the meanings suggested concerning the future course of the client's life. Kelly occasionally used a client's dreams for insightful understanding, believing that they were often prompted by significant preverbal (infantile) constructs. He felt that so-called latent content is nothing more than the submerged pole of a bipolar construct—that is, the other side of what is being used consciously in life all of the time.

Outline of Important Theoretical Constructs

The evolutionary rationalism of Jean Piaget

genetic epistemology · evolutionary rationalism

Biographical overview

Personality theory

Structural constructs

Construction of patterns among related actions
internalizing (interiorizing) · scheme, schema · structure · system · transformation · syncretic thought · construct, construction · organic versus cognitive construction · combination · differentiation

Cognition as equilibrating operations
assimilation · prehension · circular reaction · accommodation · equilibrium · disequilibrium · motive · equilibration, equilibrate · induction · deduction · transduction · reversibility · decentration · centration, centering · reciprocal reversibility · negational reversibility · operation, operational thinking · concrete versus abstract operations

The dynamics of human operations
mental · perception · mental image · representation · concept · thought, thinking · biological structure · behavior · intelligence · conservation · feedback loop

Genetic epistemology as evolutionary rationalism
genetic epistemology · genesis · formative transition · constructivism, constructive theory · evolutionary rationalism · genetic assimilation · learning

Motivational constructs

Behavior as teleonomic
behavior · teleonomic behavior · disequilibration · adaptation versus maladaptation

Personality as a system
affection · personality · self-direction · agency · organic versus cognitive construction · self, cognitive self · egocentric thought · precausality

Conscious versus unconscious cognitions
consciousness · unconscious symbolism · primary symbol · secondary symbol · repression · sensorimotor intelligence · memory · dream · wish-fulfillment

Time perspective constructs
stage of development

Infancy: birth to age of two years

Reflex action
reflex

ordinate · subsume · subordinate
· range of convenience · dilate, dilation
· loose, loosen · tight, tighten · permeability · impermeability · pre-emptive
construct · constellatory construct
· propositional construct · comprehensive construct · incidental construct
· constriction · regnant construct

*Conscious, unconscious, and the self as
a core role construct*
self-construct · role relationship · role
· role construct · core role construct

Motivational constructs

*The person as a problem-solving animal:
freedom versus determinism in behavior*
change as reconstruction · choice
· freedom · determinism

The C-P-C cycle and the Creativity Cycle
C-P-C = circumspection, pre-emption,
control · determination · Creativity
Cycle

*Emotive terms and the psychology
of personal constructs*
emotion · feelings · humor · threat
· stress · anxiety · fear · aggressivity
· passivity · hostility · guilt

The defense mechanisms
repression · incorporation · identification, introjection · regression · projection · reaction-formation

Time perspective constructs

Development as the dispersion of dependency
dependency construct

*Society and culture as a validational back-
drop for individual prediction*
society · culture · cultural norm

Individual differences constructs

Psychopathology and psychotherapy

Theory of illness

Personal constructs in abnormality
psychological disorder · regression
· presenting complaint · reconstruction
· symptom

Diagnosing personal constructs: the Rep Test
diagnosis · Role Construct Repertory
Test = Rep Test · factor analysis
· core constructs

*Clinical syndromes and the psychology
of personal constructs*
neurosis · psychosis · hysteria
· psychosomatic disorders · obsessive-
compulsive disorders · panic · psychopathy · suicide · delusions · hallucinations · depression · mania · flight of
ideas · schizophrenia · paranoia
· hebephrenia · catatonia

Theory of cure

*Cure as reconstruction and the nature
of therapy*
reconstruction · movement · slot movement · elaboration

*Interpretation, insight, and the client's
viewpoint*
insight · interpretation · organized
instruction · encapsulation · time-
binding

*Relationship factors: acceptance, trans-
ference, and resistance*
acceptance · support · reassurance
· rapport · credulous attitude · communication · transference · secondary
transference · primary transference
· countertransference · transference
cycles · resistance · negative transference

Therapeutic techniques

Enactment
role play · role reversal · enactment

Self-characterization and fixed role therapy
self-characterization sketch · fixed-role
· fixed-role therapy

Controlled elaboration
controlled elaboration

The use of dreams
submerged pole

Procedural details
group therapy · word binding · fees

Notes

1. Piaget, 1970b, p. 12. 2. See Evans, 1973, p. 45 and p. 50. 3. Ibid., p. 106. 4. Ibid., p. 107. 5. Ibid., p. 113. 6. Piaget, 1955, p. 15. 7. Piaget, 1967, p. 144. 8. Evans, 1973, p. 120. 9. See his comments in Flavell, 1963, p. viii. 10. Piaget & Inhelder, 1967, p. 452. 11. Piaget quoted by Rotman, 1977, p. 111. 12. Piaget & Inhelder, 1967, p. 452. 13. Evans, 1973, p. 18. 14. Piaget, 1955, pp. 133–134. 15. Evans, 1973, p. 115. 16. Piaget, 1970a, p. 9. 17. Ibid., p. 36. 18. Piaget, 1967, p. 143. 19. Piaget, 1970a, pp. 118–119. 20. Piaget, 1971, p. 37. 21. Piaget, 1970a, p. 112. 22. Ibid., p. 41. 23. Piaget, 1952, p. 4. 24. Piaget & Inhelder, 1967, p. 15. 25. Ibid., p. 192. 26. Piaget, 1970a, p. 140. 27. Ibid., p. 25. 28. Piaget & Inhelder, 1967, p. 447. 29. Ibid., p. 6. 30. Evans, 1973, p. 20. 31. Piaget, 1970a, p. 71. 32. Piaget, 1962, p. 171. 33. Ibid., p. 141. 34. Evans, 1973, p. 22. 35. Piaget, 1967, p. 18. 36. Piaget, 1962, p. 201. 37. Piaget, 1952, p. 32. 38. Piaget, 1967, p. 101. 39. Ibid., p. 102. 40. Ibid., p. 103. 41. Ibid., p. 102. 42. Piaget, 1962, p. 235. 43. Ibid., p. 235. 44. Ibid., p. 234. 45. Ibid., p. 240. 46. Ibid., p. 243. 47. Evans, 1973, p. 27. 48. Ibid. 49. Piaget, 1965a, p. 84. 50. Piaget, 1970b, pp. 21–22. 51. Piaget & Inhelder, 1967, p. 296. 52. Piaget, 1962, p. 291. 53. Piaget, 1967, p. 104. 54. Evans, 1973, p. 49. 55. Piaget, 1971, p. 118. 56. Piaget & Inhelder, 1967, p. 17. 57. Ibid., p. 455. 58. Piaget, 1962, p. 70. 59. Piaget & Inhelder, 1967, p. 17. 60. Piaget, 1962, p. 273. 61. Ibid., p. 5. 62. Ibid., p. 67. 63. Piaget, 1965a, p. 202. 64. Ibid., p. 180. 65. Piaget, 1970a, p. 70. 66. Piaget, 1962, p. 167. 67. Evans, 1973, p. 32. 68. Piaget, 1962, p. 51. 69. Ibid., p. 83. 70. Piaget & Inhelder, 1967, p. 418. 71. Evans, 1973, pp. 32–33. 72. Piaget, 1965a,

p. 3. 73. Ibid., p. 4. 74. Evans, 1973, pp. 45–46. 75. Ibid., p. 50. 76. Piaget, 1978, pp. 47–48. 77. Piaget, 1970b, p. 12. 78. Piaget, 1967, p. 144. 79. Piaget, 1970a, p. 141. 80. Ibid., p. 53. 81. Evans, 1973, p. 46. 82. Piaget, 1967, p. 27. 83. Piaget, 1970a, p. 106. 84. Piaget, 1978, p. xvi. 85. Ibid. 86. Ibid., p. 5. 87. Evans, 1973, p. 9. 88. Piaget, 1967, p. 102. 89. Piaget, 1970b, pp. 18–19. 90. Piaget, 1970a, p. 28. 91. Piaget, 1978, p. ix. 92. Ibid. 93. Piaget, 1967, p. 15. 94. Piaget, 1978, p. 8. 95. Piaget, 1967, p. 102. 96. Ibid., p. 7. 97. Ibid., p. 101 and p. 151. 98. Piaget, 1973, p. 32. 99. Evans, 1973, p. 7. 100. Piaget, 1962, pp. 188–189. 101. Piaget, 1952, p. 415. 102. Piaget, 1962, p. 160. 103. Piaget, 1967, p. 102. 104. Piaget, 1955, p. 188. 105. Piaget, 1962, p. 153. 106. Ibid., p. 171. 107. Piaget & Inhelder, 1967, p. 14. 108. Piaget, 1962, p. 156. 109. Ibid., p. 170. 110. Ibid., p. 123. 111. Ibid., p. 171. 112. Ibid., p. 172. 113. Ibid., p. 203. 114. Piaget, 1973, p. 38. 115. Ibid., p. 44. 116. Evans, 1973, p. 5. 117. Piaget, 1962, p. 202. 118. Piaget, 1973, pp. 50–52. 119. Evans, 1973, p. xxxix. 120. Piaget, 1967, p. 10. 121. Ibid. 122. Piaget, 1952, p. 409. 123. Piaget, 1967, p. 10. 124. Piaget, 1952, p. 411. 125. Piaget, 1967, p. 11. 126. Ibid. 127. Ibid., p. 12. 128. Ibid., p. 16. 129. Ibid., pp. 13–15. 130. Ibid., p. 20. 131. Ibid. 132. Piaget, 1970b, p. 50. 133. Piaget, 1973, p. 56. 134. Ibid., p. 52. 135. Piaget, 1955, p. 188. 136. Piaget, 1967, p. 26. 137. Piaget, 1965b, p. 111. 138. Piaget, 1967, p. 32. 139. Ibid., p. 30. 140. Piaget, 1970b, p. 50. 141. Piaget, 1967, p. 52. 142. Ibid., pp. 33–44. 143. Ibid., p. 35. 144. Ibid., p. 41. 145. Piaget, 1962, p. 161. 146. Piaget, 1967, p. 39. 147. Ibid., p. 40. 148. Piaget, 1955, p. 91. 149. Piaget, 1967, p. 39. 150. Piaget, 1971, p. 34. 151. Piaget, 1967, p. 46. 152. Piaget & Inhelder, 1967, p. 406. 153. Piaget, 1967, pp. 53–54. 154. Piaget, 1965b, p. 197. 155. Ibid., p. 13. 156. Ibid., p. 102. 157. Ibid., p. 362. 158. Ibid., p. 398. 159. Piaget, 1967, p. 58. 160. Ibid., p. 59. 161. Piaget, 1952, p. 47. 162. Piaget, 1978, p. x. 163. Piaget, 1967, p. 60. 164. Ibid., p. 61. 165. Ibid., p. 63. 166. Ibid. 167. Ibid. 168. Piaget, 1955, p. 91. 169. Piaget, 1970a, p. 125. 170. Ibid., p. 123. 171. Ibid., p. 124. 172. Ibid. 173. Piaget, 1967, p. 64. 174. Ibid. 175. Ibid., p. 65. 176. Ibid. 177. Ibid., p. 66. 178. Ibid. 179. Ibid., p. 69. 180. Ibid., p. 70. 181. Evans, 1973, p. 71. 182. Ibid., p. 27. 183. Piaget, 1962, p. 5. 184. Ibid., p. 73. 185. Ibid. 186. Ibid., p. 211.

187. Ibid., p. 69. 188. Ibid., p. 222. 189. Piaget, 1955, p. 39. 190. Ibid., p. 42. 191. Ibid., p. 83. 192. Piaget, 1962, p. 68. 193. Piaget, 1962, p. 68. 194. Piaget, 1970a, p. 79. 195. Ibid., p. 97. 196. Piaget, 1965b, p. 186. 197. Ibid., p. 336. 198. Ibid., p. 336. 199. Ibid., p. 400. 200. Piaget, 1967, p. 102. 201. Ibid. 202. Piaget, 1955, p. 116. 203. Piaget, 1978, p. 28. 204. Piaget, 1962, p. 208. 205. Piaget & Inhelder, 1967, p. 194. 206. Piaget, 1952, p. 413. 207. Kelly, 1955a, p. 361. 208. Kelly, 1969, p. 49. 209. Ibid., p. 48. 210. Ibid., p. 51. 211. Ibid., p. 52. 212. Kelly, 1955a, p. 363. 213. Ibid., p. 15. 214. Ibid., p. 43. 215. Ibid., p. 11. 216. Kelly, 1955b, p. 613. 217. Kelly, 1955a, p. 15; 1969, pp. 299–300. 218. Kelly, 1955b, pp. 908, 943. 219. Kelly, 1969, p. 29. 220. Kelly, 1955a, p. 48. 221. Kelly, 1955b, p. 744. 222. Kelly, 1969, p. 21. 223. Kelly, 1955a, p. 127. 224. Ibid., p. 75. 225. Ibid., pp. 48–49. 226. Ibid., p. 5. 227. Kelly, 1969, p. 62. 228. Kelly, 1955a, p. 453. 229. Ibid., p. 50. 230. Ibid., p. 76. 231. Ibid., p. 304. 232. Ibid., p. 62. 233. Ibid., p. 61. 234. Ibid., pp. 8–9. 235. Kelly, 1970, p. 40. 236. Kelly, 1955a, p. 72. 237. Ibid., p. 109. 238. Ibid., p. 120. 239. Ibid., p. 128. 240. Kelly, 1969, p. 219. 241. Kelly, 1955a, pp. 16, 110. 242. Ibid., p. 111. 243. Ibid., p. 63. 244. Ibid., p. 116. 245. Ibid., p. 139. 246. Ibid., p. 128. 247. Ibid., p. 136. 248. Ibid., p. 56. 249. Ibid., p. 57. 250. Ibid., p. 68. 251. Ibid., p. 69. 252. Ibid, p. 476. 253. Kelly, 1955b, p. 816. 254. Ibid., p. 1031. 255. Ibid., pp. 854, 1038. 256. Kelly, 1955a, p. 483. 257. Kelly, 1955b, p. 1065. 258. Kelly, 1955a, p. 80. 259. Ibid., p. 229. 260. Ibid., p. 153. 261. Ibid., p. 155. 262. Ibid. 263. Ibid. 264. Ibid., pp. 477–478. 265. Ibid., p. 67. 266. Ibid., p. 480. 267. Ibid., p. 482. 268. Ibid., p. 466. 269. Kelly, 1969, p. 92. 270. Kelly, 1955a, p. 114. 271. Ibid., p. 133. 272. Ibid., p. 100. 273. Kelly, 1969, p. 221. 274. Kelly, 1955a, p. 503. 275. Kelly, 1969, p. 178. 276. Kelly, 1955a, p. 99. 277. Ibid., p. 503. 278. Ibid., p. 35. 279. Ibid., p. x. 280. Ibid., p. 37. 281. Ibid., p. 68. 282. Kelly, 1955b, p. 888. 283. Kelly, 1969, p. 68. 284. Kelly, 1955a, p. 78. 285. Ibid., p. 83. 286. Ibid., p. 169. 287. Ibid., p. 21. 288. Ibid., p. 78. 289. Ibid., p. 130. 290. Kelly, 1969, p. 9. 291. Kelly, 1970, p. 36. 292. Kelly, 1955a, p. 515. 293. Ibid., p. 516. 294. Ibid. 295. Ibid., p. 62. 296. Ibid., p. 528. 297. Kelly, 1955b, p. 1060. 298. Kelly, 1955a, p. 89. 299. Kelly, 1955b, p. 803. 300. Kelly, 1969, p. 54. 301. Kelly, 1955b, p. 1049. 302. Ibid., pp. 643, 699. 303.

Kelly, 1955a, p. 489. 304. Kelly, 1955b, p. 792. 305. Ibid., p. 717. 306. Kelly, 1955a, p. 473. 307. Kelly, 1955b, p. 1032. 308. Kelly, 1955a, p. 14. 309. Ibid., p. 484. 310. Ibid., p. 508. 311. Ibid., p. 510. 312. Kelly, 1955b, p. 881. 313. Kelly, 1955a, p. 502. 314. Kelly, 1969, p. 186. 315. Kelly, 1955a, p. 473. 316. Kelly, 1955b, p. 768. 317. Ibid. 318. Ibid., p. 887. 319. Ibid., pp. 668–669. 320. Kelly, 1955a, p. 297. 321. Kelly, 1969, p. 148. 322. Kelly, 1955b, p. 998. 323. Ibid., p. 721. 324. Kelly, 1969, p. 223. 325. Kelly, 1955a, p. 94. 326. Ibid., p. 95. 327. Kelly, 1969, p. 28. 328. Kelly, 1955b, p. 779. 329. Kelly, 1955a, p. 94. 330. Ibid., p. 176. 331. Kelly, 1955b, p. 700. 332. Ibid., p. 750. 333. Ibid., p. 694. 334. Ibid., p. 700. 335. Kelly, 1955a, p. 40. 336. Ibid., p. 463. 337. Kelly, 1955b, p. 877. 338. See Kelly, 1955a, pp. 185, 319. 339. Kelly, 1955b, p. 831. 340. Ibid., p. 835. 341. Ibid., p. 781. 342. Ibid., p. 780. 343. Ibid., p. 889. 344. Ibid., p. 760. 345. Ibid., p. 804. 346. Ibid., p. 789. 347. Ibid., p. 797. 348. Kelly, 1955a, p. 118. 349. Kelly, 1955b, p. 896. 350. Ibid. 351. Kelly, 1955a, p. 366. 352. Kelly, 1955b, p. 759. 353. Ibid., p. 763. 354. Kelly, 1969, p. 19. 355. Kelly, 1955a, pp. 26–27, 193. 356. Ibid., p. 203. 357. Kelly, 1955b, p. 829. 358. Ibid., p. 836. 359. Kelly, 1955a, Chs. 5 and 6. 360. Ibid., p. 219. 361. Ibid., p. 302. 362. Ibid., p. 456. 363. Kelly, 1955b, p. 895. 364. Ibid., pp. 895–896. 365. Ibid., p. 1081. 366. Ibid., p. 872. 367. Kelly, 1955a, p. 498. 368. Kelly, 1955b, p. 918. 369. Kelly, 1970, p. 55. 370. Kelly, 1955b, p. 846. 371. Ibid., p. 840. 372. Ibid., p. 904. 373. Ibid., p. 866. 374. Ibid. 375. Ibid., p. 858. 376. Kelly, 1955a, p. 482; 1955b, p. 938. 377. Kelly, 1955b, p. 840. 378. Ibid., p. 887. 379. Kelly, 1955a, p. 134. 380. Kelly, 1955a, p. 187; 1969, p. 185. 381. Kelly, 1955b, p. 937. 382. Ibid., p. 683. 383. Kelly, 1969, p. 60. 384. Kelly, 1955b, p. 622. 385. Kelly, 1955a, p. 348. 386. Kelly, 1955b, p. 938. 387. Ibid., p. 967. 388. Ibid., p. 850. 389. Ibid., p. 912. 390. Ibid., p. 1071. 391. Kelly, 1955a, p. 201. 392. Kelly, 1955b, p. 673. 393. Ibid., pp. 834–835. 394. Ibid., p. 917. 395. Ibid., p. 1102. 396. Ibid., p. 833. 397. Ibid., p. 649. 398. Ibid., p. 575. 399. Kelly, 1955a, p. 417. 400. Kelly, 1955b, p 1085. 401. Kelly, 1969, pp. 82–83. 402. Kelly, 1955b, p. 890. 403. Ibid., p. 1002. 404. Kelly, 1955a, pp. 96–97. 405. Kelly, 1955b, p. 587. 406. Ibid., p. 1160. 407. Ibid., p. 1099. 408. Ibid., p. 1105. 409. Kelly, 1955a, p. 322. 410. Kelly, 1955b, p. 1089. 411. Ibid., p. 1100. 412. Ibid., p. 674. 413. Ibid., p. 675. 414. Ibid., pp. 684–685. 415. Ibid., p. 620. 416. Kelly, 1955a, p. 399. 417. Kelly, 1955b, p. 671. 418. Ibid., p. 681. 419. Ibid., p. 1101. 420. Ibid., p. 1053. 421.

Ibid., p. 1050. **422.** Ibid., p. 665. **423.** Kelly, 1955a, p. 97. **424.** Kelly, 1955b, p. 1025. **425.** Kelly, 1955a, p. 369. **426.** Ibid., p. 323. **427.** Ibid., p. 376. **428.** Ibid., p. 369. **429.** Ibid., p. 380. **430.** Ibid. **431.** Ibid., p. 391. **432.** Kelly, 1955b, p. 1092. **433.** Ibid., p. 585. **434.** Ibid., p. 938. **435.** Ibid., p. 1037. **436.** Kelly, 1955a, p. 465. **437.** Kelly, 1955b, p. 1037. **438.** Kelly, 1955a, p. 470. **439.** Kelly, 1955b, p. 1041. **440.** Ibid., pp. 583, 844. **441.** Ibid., p. 917. **442.** Ibid., p. 635. **443.** Ibid., p. 625. **444.** Ibid., p. 1155. **445.** Ibid., p. 967. **446.** Ibid., p. 1074. **447.** Kelly, 1969, p. 54. **448.** Kelly, 1955b, p. 610.

Chapter 12

Theory Construction in the Phenomenological Outlook

Now that we have gone over representative theories in the phenomenological outlook, we can complete our theory-construction analysis of personality description by returning to the question-answer format of the Introduction, Chapter 4, and Chapter 8. The themes and constructs of these earlier portions of the text will continue to have relevance to what we will be taking up in this chapter, which poses the following five questions:

Can a phenomenological theory be objectively validated?

How do the phenomenal and noumenal realms interact, interrelate, or otherwise combine in the formation of knowledge?

Is it essential to describe behavior as taking place over time?

Does psychology have adequate terminology to account for teleological behavior, and if not, what is called for?

What motives to therapy are primary in the phenomenological outlook?

Can a Phenomenological Theory Be Objectively Validated?

If there is one point we have seen emphasized in the phenomenological theories, it is that people have a unique slant on their experience, and that in order to understand what their personal experience means to them, we have first to grasp things from *their* (introspective) perspective. Phenomenologists are always ready to point out that behaviorists and psychoanalysts alike are so anxious to develop their own theories of experience that they regularly *distort* the very experience they are supposedly trying to explain. This kind of—what we might now call—*purity criticism* was once defined for us by Hegel (see p. 619), who noted that a philosopher might erroneously bring "reason to bear on the object [of his or her description] from the outside and so tamper with it [distort its pure meaning]." [1] Oddly, Kierkegaard (see p. 619) once accused Hegel of doing precisely this by confusing reality with his speculative theories. [2] We can see Rogers using a purity criticism when he suggested that since its field is the extraspective study of *objects,* "science transforms people into objects." [3]

Though he did not level his criticism in theory-construction terminology, it is clear that Rogers was saying that science reduces the more humanizing meanings of formal- and final-causation in behavior to the presumed underlying material- and efficient-cause meanings of the inanimate (object-like) universe. Our claim in Chapter 8 (see p. 520) that Dollard and Miller's mediation conceptions failed to subsume Freudian telic meanings because they necessarily forced a final-cause meaning into an efficient-cause meaning is also a purity criticism. But note: Rogers was implying that science as now conceived *must* bring about a mechanistic (object-like) interpretation of human behavior because of its very method of study which cannot encompass the unique phenomenal experience of each subjective person.

There is a theory-method confound in Rogers's thinking here, one which is to be noted in the arguments of many phenomenologists who want to change scientific *method* (validating evidence) because they think it cannot capture spontaneous (pure) phenomenal experience. [4] If we are clear on what *phenomenal experience* means, then we appreciate that this is a phrase having *theoretical* relevance. Phenomenologists look at experience one way, and behaviorists or psychoanalysts look at it another. The phrase has nothing directly to say about *method*— about the "means or manner of proving a theoretical proposition to be true or false." We have maintained in Chapter 8 (see p. 505) that scientific method can remain theory free—in the sense of not dictating which personality theory will be put to test through its use. Phenomenologists obviously reject this claim, and in so doing they run the risk of undermining psychology's commitment to science. It is the position of this text that though the phenomenologists have a legitimate criticism, they have misplaced their attack on the problem. The problem exists in the traditional natural scientist's penchant for reducing formal- and final-cause theories to material- and efficient-cause theories of what is being *objectively* studied in the methodological (experimental) context. The problem is *not* with the method of *scientific* validation but with the limited range of theory being put to test in the experiments following this method.

We can trace this developing confound of theory and method in Rogers's reasoning, as he first gives us his conception of what *reality* means: ". . . reality is basically the private world of individual perceptions, though for social purposes reality consists of those perceptions which have a high degree of commonality among various individuals."[5] This would seem to sound a note for idealism, for the view that it is phenomenal experience and not noumenal reality which is important in human understanding. However, Rogers presumably did not wish to be considered an idealist because this would imply that his theory referred to things that do not exist (are not real). Rather than admit to idealism, the phenomenologically oriented theoretician is likely to speak of *intersubjectivity*. This is what Rogers meant by the "commonality among various individuals" in the above quote. Each single person is a subject and it is only when subjects can agree between themselves (intersubjectively) that it is proper to speak of *a* reality taking place.

If we were idealists, we could accept this characterization of how people know things and still consider the so-called intersubjectivity—more properly, "interpersonally understandable"—to be a reflection of objectivity in knowledge! In other words, using the terminology of the Introduction (see p. 14 and p. 15), we could embrace an *objective-idealism* and subsume Rogers's viewpoint without difficulty. Each person is a *singular* identity, whose knowledge or personal understanding may indeed be totally private— that is, *subjective*—or it may also be shared by others in an *objective* manner. To be an individual person is not necessarily to be 100 percent subjective in the grasp of knowledge about experience. But Rogers does not take an objective-idealistic theoretical position. He replaces idealism with subjectivity, and once having done so brings into doubt whether we can *ever* hope to capture objec-

tivity in our scientific methods: "To put it more briefly, it appears to me that though there may be such a thing as objective truth, I can never know it; all I can know is that some statements appear to me subjectively to have the qualifications of objective truth."[6] If all Rogers means here is that we each must give our individual, singular affirmation to objective truth, he is most certainly correct. But if he means (as it appears) that because he individually (as a person) must affirm what is objectively (or subjectively) the case, then it necessarily follows that objective truth *can never be known,* he is surely open to challenge.

It is common in psychology to confuse idealism with subjectivity and also realism with objectivity. Phenomenologists are too ready to believe that just because psychologists strive for objectivity in the methodological context (that is, in doing experiments), they must be assuming a realistic theory of what is being studied (turn their data into palpable objects). There is an assumption that all natural scientists believe they are studying the noumena (the reality) directly, so that they will give the phenomena inadequate consideration. Actually, we can find many examples of phenomenal insights in science (for example, Heisenberg's indeterminacy principle, Bohr's principle of complementarity, and so on). In fact, Ernst Mach (see p. 509) referred to his entire approach as that of a phenomenological physics precisely because he realized that the noumena is alway capable of being construed phenomenally—and objectively so!—from more than one theoretical viewpoint.[7] To have a phenomenological psychology which is perfectly objective and open to validation is therefore not only possible, but entirely appropriate.

It is not difficult to see idealistic themes in existentialistic theories, particularly those like Binswanger's which propose that the a priori

ontological structures (world-designs) literally create or make experience possible. As
we have seen in Chapter 10 (see p. 638), Boss
objected to this meaning-endowing emphasis, calling it an unwarranted revision of
Heidegger's philosophy.[8] Boss contended that
neither Heidegger's philosophy nor existentialism in general is an idealistic philosophy.
The reality as well as the subjectivity of
Dasein is revealed to the person as a lumination. Boss noted that Sartre developed an
idealistic brand of existentialism that was
more in line with Binswanger's outlook than
was Heidegger's.[9] Boss was therefore taking
a *realistic-subjectivistic* position on the nature
of Dasein. In doing so he arrived at the same
impasse concerning phenomenal study in
science that we have noted in Rogerian
thought. The following purity criticism
nicely sums up Boss's attitudes concerning
the natural sciences and their methods of
empirical validation:

*It is fortunate that Daseinsanalytic think-
ing does not require us to accept a ready-
made conceptual framework and to learn it
by heart. On the contrary, analysis of Dasein
urges all those who deal with human beings
to start seeing and thinking from the beginning, so that they can remain with what they
immediately perceive and do not get lost in
"scientific" abstractions, derivations, explanations, and calculations estranged from the
immediate reality of the given phenomena.
It is of paramount importance to realize
from the start that the fundamental difference which separates the natural sciences
from the Daseinsanalytic or existential science of man is to be found right here.*[10]

Though Piaget would not accept the characterization of natural science as somehow
opposed to the aims of a humanistic psychology, he would agree that his study of behavior is based on a realism. Indeed, knowing

reality in his view involves constructing systems of transformation which grow increasingly isomorphic (identical in pattern) to
the transformations of (noumenal) reality.[11]
In learning about his or her reality, the child
reduces perception to a fixed schema. We
might say that the phenomenal for Piaget
is an intellectual stylization of the perceived
(noumenal) reality. As Piaget says, "In this
sense . . . [the child's] realism is not visual,
but intellectual."[12] As we have seen in Chapter 11, Piaget's conception of construction
begins in the very processes of inanimate
matter, being patterned according to evolutionary laws which in time work their way
up through equilibrating operations to the
highest reaches of abstract (mathematical)
thought. But the constructive process clearly
begins in the palpable reality of lived experience and can therefore be examined empirically by natural science. Though he
shares certain Kantian emphases with Rogers
and Boss, Piaget differs from them in his
confidence that objective—including phenomenal—knowledge can indeed be attained
by scientific investigation.

Kelly was generally in line with Piaget on
the matter of science's ultimate potentials for
obtaining objective knowledge. Though he
did not express this in terms of individual
phenomenal experience, Kelly considered the
person to be "an inveterate collector of paradigms."[13] We might easily think of this as a
process of aligning phenomenal hypotheses
(paradigms) with the patternings of noumenal
reality in the style of Piaget. In fact, Kelly
was more clearly Kantian than Piaget because in personal-construct theory, we always think of construction as taking place
from the introspective perspective. Piaget
has his constructions occurring both extraspectively (early in life via biological pro-

cesses) and introspectively (later, when mentation per se is underway; see our discussion of this issue on p. 686). We might now ask Kelly if he believes that there is an order in noumenal reality that our constructs match up with to a greater or lesser degree. Consistent with Piaget on this point, Kelly answers, "For my part, I am quite ready to assume—indeed it seems important to assume—that there is a reality out there, or, if you prefer, a truth deep inside all of us." [14] The "reality out there" is what the noumena (things in themselves) is typically considered to be. The next question for Kelly to answer would seem to be: will we ever agree on what this "reality out there" is like? If so, we would seem to be realistic in theoretical stance. Once, when Kelly was taking up the question of two constructs being in conflict over the nature of reality, he essentially answered our second question as follows: "I prefer the . . . cosmic view which supposes these two progressions [the conflicting constructions of reality] may ultimately join hands, though that auspicious moment may prove to be an infinity of years away." [15]

It would therefore appear that Kelly and Piaget are more hopeful in their assessment of science, believing that a thorough knowledge of phenomena is objectively possible, based on the reality of noumenal experience which underwrites phenomenal "reality." Boss saw no necessary tie between phenomenal and noumenal experience, so he like Rogers was more oriented to studying the uniquely subjective meanings of the phenomenal realm. But Rogers also seemed to believe that there is a way in which science can at least suggest objective knowledge, though he was unable to resolve the fact that it takes unique subjects to understand this knowledge.

How Do the Phenomenal and Noumenal Realms Interact, Interrelate, or Otherwise Combine in the Formation of Knowledge?

Theories that propose two realms of explanation (see p. 43)—such as the noumenal and the phenomenal or the body and the mind—are called *dualisms* (duo = two). Theories that try to explain everything in terms of a single realm of explanation—all is noumena, all is body—are called *monisms* (mono = one). Once we have taken on the dualistic position, a problem that arises is "How do these two aspects interact, interrelate, or come to influence each other?" The classic example here is the mind-body interaction, which Descartes once suggested takes place in the pineal gland at the base of the brain (see p. 279 for a discussion of the mind-body problem). Fundamental to a consideration of this question is our understanding of the concept of knowledge. We might have framed this question more simply as "How does knowledge come about?" This is the crux of the issue. Whether one, two, or even more realms of explanation are to be considered, what we are ultimately after is an understanding of how organizations may be patterned into meaning that can be written down, expressed mathematically, or pictured directly as knowledge. In other words, we want to know about knowledge.

The Meanings of Interaction

A word that is often used in personality and/ or behavioral theories is *interaction*. In Chapter 7 (see p. 481), we discussed Bandura's use of *reciprocal interaction* between behavior, environmental influences, and cognitive mediators. *Reciprocity* refers to a mutual determination of some outcome, where one side of an issue or a line of behavior is of equal importance in determining outcome as the other. In discussing knowledge, Piaget gives us a fine example of this mutuality when he observes, "Knowledge does not begin in the I [that is, phenomenal experience], and it does not begin in the object [that is, noumenal experience]; it begins in the interactions . . . [and] then there is a reciprocal and simultaneous construction of the subject on the one hand and the object on the other."[16] Though he is equating idealism with subjectivity and realism with objectivity, Piaget is suggesting here that phenomenal understanding is of equal importance to our knowledge of anything as are the objects, the things in themselves, that is, noumenal experiences. A complete (100 percent) idealist would suggest that the noumenal aspects of experience are unnecessary assumptions to make and that insofar as we know anything, knowledge is completely phenomenal. This seems to be Boss's view, although he spoke of Dasein (phenomenal experience) as being real (see previous section).

We might now ask ourselves more specifically what this concept of interaction means and whether everyone who uses the concept has the same meaning in mind. Actually, it is easily shown that there are three primary ways in which the concept of interaction (interdependence, interrelationship, and so on) is used in psychology. The first usage may be termed *conceptual interaction*, because the point being conveyed is that an interdependence is taking place between a mental scheme or frame *and* some independent set of circumstances which must be put to order but which may not be completely schematized or framed by mentation (thought). Immanuel Kant took the position of conceptual interactionism when he originally proposed the noumena-phenomena duality. In discussing how we human beings might know anything, he observed:

That all our knowledge begins with experience there can be no doubt. For how is it possible that the faculty of cognition should be awakened into exercise otherwise than by means of objects which affect our senses, and partly of themselves produce representations, partly rouse our powers of understanding into activity, to compare, to connect, or to separate these, and so to convert the raw material of our sensuous impressions into a knowledge of objects, which is called experience? In respect of time, therefore, no knowledge of ours is antecedent to experience, but begins with it.[17]

This is the opening paragraph of Kant's monumental work on pure reason, and it is clear that he was trying to say we are *not* born with knowledge already contained in mental pockets or containers. We have to begin our knowing of things in experience following birth. Given this truism, Kant added:

But, though all our knowledge begins with experience, it by no means follows that all arises out of experience. For, on the contrary, it is quite possible that our empirical knowledge is a compound [emphasis added] *of that which we receive through impressions, and that which the faculty of cognition supplies from itself (sensuous impressions giving merely the occasion), an addition which we cannot distinguish from the original element given by sense, till long practice has made us attentive to, and skilful in separating it.*[18]

In speaking of a compound of that which comes to us through the senses and that which we bring to bear through our faculty of cognition, Kant was suggesting that a conceptual interaction takes place between the noumenal and phenomenal realms. Sensory inputs are sheer noise until we organize them on the basis of our innate frames of reference, which he called the categories of the understanding but which we have seen the existentialists call the a priori ontological structures. What is innate here is *not knowledge* but a *way of knowing,* a way of coming at sensory experience—input from the noumena—to conceptualize it meaningfully. Piaget's claim that a child can take the schema of sucking from observing himself or herself nursing reflexively at mother's breast and then assimilate it to other aspects of life would be for Kant an example of such categorical understanding.

Piaget argues that there are no innate structures in the human mind,[19] but Kant would counter that a child could only grasp the relational tie of one experience (mouth action) to another experience (assimilation of milk) because of an *innate* conceptual schema to begin with. One of Kant's categories of the understanding was, in fact, relation, and he believed that causal relations of dependence in which we know that one event (assimilating milk) depends upon another (sucking) is *not learned* but is conceptually possible *from birth.*[20] Just as our hands work to flex fingers inwardly or our eyes focus to keep a sharp image on our retina, so too does our cognitive reason (thought, mentation) work to grasp causal ties of one event relating to another when they occur as a patterned order. Now, the child cannot assimilate—to use Piaget's terminology—just anything imaginable to the category of relation. Sucking a finger does not result in milk being ingested, hence, an accommodation is called for in the knowl-

edge of what a finger means. Knowledge is therefore a compound of that which the child initially brings to bear and that which the environmental experience provides as content for knowledge. We do not create our realities—even subjectively create them—without some consideration for noumenal *givens* (those things that exist but that we never know directly). We have to adapt and adjust that which we imagine or hope might occur with what does in fact prove to be the case in unfolding experience.

A second interaction usage may be termed *evolutionary interaction,* for it is based on the Darwinian idea that human beings act on and are in turn acted upon by the "organic and inorganic agents of this earth, like every other animal."[21] This environment-versus-organism view of interaction has been historically very important in psychology. We see it reflected in the old *nature-versus-nurture* arguments, for example, where it was put in terms of heredity's influence as opposed to the influence of learning. Darwin did not think of evolution as a unidirectional a priori law unfolding within heredity over time. He actually thought of developing organisms as separate from the environmental milieu and as often resistant to environmental pressures of one sort or another.[22] Sometimes the organism was far from perfectly adapted to circumstances because of this resistiveness.

Interactions between certain species of animals and the milieu within which they lived were pictured as irregularly intersecting branches of a tree which unpredictably brought about changes in structure when they did not in fact connect with each other smoothly. Darwin was also more open to a view of mind influencing the course of evolution than were the early behaviorists who adapted his arguments to their cause.[23] Classical (Pavlovian) conditioning theory took an evolutionary-interaction position in suggesting that animals are acted upon or determined by heredity on the one hand and environmental stimulations on the other. Learning theories of the Hullian variety replaced heredity with the drive concept, retaining the essential idea of an internal (feelings) versus an external (environmental) source of stimulus determination on behavior. Finally, we may recall from Chapter 8 (see p. 440) that Skinner drew a direct parallel between operant behavior and organic evolution.

The third and last usage for interaction we can identify stems from the nature of mathematical comparisons among empirical measures and may be called *statistical interaction*. Assume that we wanted to study the kinds of people who might be apt to voice their personal irritation, frustration, or hostility in a life situation likely to provoke any of these emotions. Assume that we have designed an experiment in which we first identify subjects on the basis of a personality scale as either aggressive or nonaggressive in personality. Then we have them stand in line to obtain some kind of prized reward—say, a free ticket to a musical that we know is highly attractive to our subjects but is already sold out except for our supply of tickets. As there are only "so many" (unspecified) tickets available and not everyone can hope to get one, there is a certain element of chance about the time spent standing in line. This could prove to be time wasted. Now in this experiment, we will first simply observe our subjects to see how many statements of frustration they make in having to stand in the *very* slow-moving line. Next, we will thicken the plot by having a few of our stooges begin pushing into line ahead of our targeted experimental subjects. What will we learn?

We will probably find that the aggressive person makes more frustration statements in the line even when no one is trying to cheat —there will be grumbling about the likelihood of standing for a long time only to learn that the tickets are gone, and so on. We will also probably find that the nonaggressive person is likely to grumble aloud when he or she sees people pressing into the line ahead. Finally, and this is the point of importance for present considerations, we will almost certainly find that the combination of (1) aggressive personality and (2) the frustration of having others press into the line unfairly will lead to the greatest number of frustration statements by our experimental subjects. This combination of factors (combined independent variables) will show up in the measured variance of our frustration statements (dependent variable) as *statistical interaction,* a purely mathematical characteristic of our measured experimental manipulations. In most studies like this which combine groups of subjects divided according to personality level (aggressive versus nonaggressive) and levels of situational influence (no one pushing ahead versus stooges pushing ahead in line), we find that the lion's share of the findings occurs in this interaction variance.[24]

Even so, is it clear from such empirical findings that one and only one type of interaction is taking place in the subjects under observation? Obviously not, since if we wanted to account for the observed statistical interaction theoretically, we could—and, indeed, would probably have to—fall back on either a conceptual or an evolutionary interaction to explain the results. A complex theory of behavior might even include both of these latter forms of interaction. Piaget's conception of development, for example, begins in reflexive (evolutionary) actions, moves to (conceptual) schemata based on these biological assimilations, and then is tested empirically through measurements that enter into various interdependent (statistical) relationships in the calculations performed. Statistical interaction seems clearly to be more on the side of method than on the side of personality theory per se—although in cybernetic models of behavior, they virtually coalesce with theoretical explanations (that is, behavior is mathematized).

It is also clear that our three types of interaction can be readily subsumed by the meanings of the four causes. Conceptual interaction surely has the meanings of formal and especially final causation wound into it, for the person is said to frame conceptual patterns (formal-cause meaning) "for the sake of which" (final-cause meaning) understanding is made possible and brought forward. Evolutionary interaction is interpreted in psychology, if not entirely so by Darwin, as blindly combining hereditary (material-cause meaning) and environmental stimulations (efficient-cause meaning) to direct behavior without self-awareness or agency. Cybernetic formulations have dropped the heredity emphasis but they retain the environmental inputs versus the mediated stimulus-bank (cues) emphasis and—as we have suggested—weave such factors very closely into the mathematized complexities of statistical interaction. Considered strictly by itself, statistical interaction is pure mathematical abstraction, relying on the interlacing patterns (formal-cause meaning) of metric values. Statisticians may reason in ways calling for final-cause description, but strictly mathematical accounts take meaning exclusively from the formal-cause construct.[25]

The lesson to be learned in this analysis of three types of interaction is that simply because we find interactions taking place in the data analyses of our experimental studies does *not* end our theoretical challenge in understanding that which we have measured and found interacting. We must still decide which type of factor may be involved—final-cause meanings of a conceptual sort, efficient-cause meanings of an evolutionary sort, and so on—in the observed behavior that shows statistical interactions in our empirical data. Finding that hostile people are especially likely to become frustrated in a frustrating situation does not in itself provide us with an understanding of *why* this may occur. As we learned in Chapter 8 (p. 502), because of the presence of the affirming-the-consequent fallacy in scientific method, our job as theoreticians is not completed simply because we have proven factually that something interacts statistically with something else. Facts can never speak for themselves entirely free of a theoretical frame. The greatest danger arises if we assume that simply because we can show predictable interactions between person variables and situation variables in the methodological context, we have therefore proven evolutionary interactions in the behavior under observation. This has happened too often in psychology, where clear distinctions are not always drawn between the methodological context of proof and the theoretical context of explanation (see p. 512).

Sensory versus Logical Phenomenology

We have made it appear in the discussion thus far that Kant had *only* the categories of the understanding, operating at the level of higher or pure reason, interacting with noumenal inputs and conceptualizing this noise (unpatterned signals) into an understandable message. Actually, this is not correct. At the level of immediate sensory input (eye, ear, and so on), even before the categories per se are brought to bear, Kant held that we organize sensation according to space (location of things) and time (sooner, later). Though he might have done so, Kant did not consider space and time to be categories of the understanding, but philosophers like Bertrand Russell have since noted that these concepts are "somewhat akin to the categories." [26] They are brought to bear conceptually and interact with noumenal experience to order it concomitantly with the interacting categories. Meaningful order is brought to bear from above and not taken in from below (see our contrast of the Kantian versus Lockean models on pp. 16–18). For Kant, sensory receptors like the eye or the ear do not filter out noise to bring in a clear message. Sensory receptors make this noise over into something structured and thereby literally create to some extent the message received.

This dual-level interpretation of how noumenal experience is translated into phenomenal knowledge has interesting implications for psychology, because we have the same issues arising that any dualism generates. Is the pattern of meaning (words, symbols, signs) *first* ordered by the environment and *then* input by the organism which merely mediates through the senses that which is fixed by this noumenal referent? This is the position taken by Lockean theorists, who see human reason beginning as a blank tablet which, following birth, receives input etchings (patternings of meaning) bearing signals for use in behavior forever after (via mediation). Phenomenology as an approach to human study reacted against this model of mind to take its lead from Kant, who suggested that the external world is not the *only* source of patterning into meaning. The internal world provides at least as much of the order as the external world. But at what level is this order set into place internally? Does meaningful order

emerge at the level of entry, where our eyes, ears, sense of touch constructs the patterns that we will come to know as experience? Or does meaning emerge at an even higher level of cognition or conceptualization—at the level of Kantian understanding? Where is the ordering of Kantian spectacles to be thought of as taking place? We find our Kantian theorists placing different emphases on the precise means whereby the noise of sensory input is organized and made knowable as meaningful knowledge.

Historically, phenomenologists fall into two broad groups based on their approach to this matter of precisely where the patterned order of meaning called knowledge is actually framed. The first group may be called *sensory phenomenologists;* they take their lead from the gestalt psychologists, Wertheimer, Köhler, and Koffka (see pp. 567–571). These gestaltists were active at a time in history when psychology was focusing on how human beings can be said to know things through the senses—a program of study laid down by founding fathers of experimental psychology like Helmholtz and Wundt who were influenced by the philosophy of British Empiricism. As a result, in reaction to the reigning British philosophy, the gestaltists brought their Kantianism to bear at the level of sensory receptors—with vision playing a major role in their theories and researches. We can see their anti-Lockeanism nicely reflected in their figure-ground conception, which effectively suggests that the ground always frames or orders the figure, whereas the reverse is never true. A stimulus that enters the organism cannot define the ground within which it is perceived because contour (the outline of a stimulus) works inwardly to differentiate what is perceived. It is impossible for a stimulus to "be there" as an input. Out of an indistinct or uniform *ground* the organism differentiates and articulates (constructs) a figure.

The laws of organization we reviewed in Chapter 9 (pp. 569–570) were all said to operate at the level of proximal stimulation (that is, the phenomenal stimulus) and *not* —as British Empiricism assumed—at the point of distal stimulations (that is, the noumenal stimulus, which is noise until ordered by the person). Having now framed a number of gestalt laws operating at the level of sensory input—proximal stimulation of the retina of the eye, for example—the gestaltists *then* claimed that the central or higher-level mental processes worked according to the *same* laws. This is what the principle of isomorphism (see p. 571) comes down to: the lawful processes ordering things at the level of sensation also order things at the level of cognition (thought, mentation). The sensory phenomenologists did not have a use for dialectic in their theory because, in the final analysis, the person is just as much under the unidirectional control of sensorily organized inputs in their theory as is true in the Lockean theories of behaviorism. The meaning of experience (knowledge) is ordered by the person's phenomenal perceptions, but there is no way in which it can be said that the person can *transcend* this stimulation once it is ordered at the point of proximal stimulation. It is, of course, possible to think of unique and even bizarre (distorted) forms of differentiation and articulation.

When certain personality theorists later borrowed from traditional gestalt psychology, they took the approach of a *sensory phenomenology,* basing their explanations on an analogy to the differentiation and articulation of the sensory (visual, auditory, tactual) phenomenal field. Lewin, Rogers, and Boss were clearly following this style of explanation. Piaget has leanings in this direction but has also made efforts to encompass what we will be calling below logical phenomenology, and hence we cannot place him here without reservation. All sensory phenomenologists hold that behavior takes place in a field or space, spread into differentiated and articulated regions of a formal-cause nature. This holds even for the organization of self-identity. Precisely how this articulation and differentiation comes about is not generally made clear. It seems as though having the gestalt experiments to point to in evidence is enough for the phenomenological psychologists to rest their case. Though the phenomenological-existentialistic tradition has favored explanations centering on agency, choice, and personal responsibility for the course of behavior, precisely how these self-selections come about is never made clear.

What does *lumination* really mean, and how can something shine forth to disclose itself? Boss did not confront these challenging questions. And as if to complicate things even further, Rogers in his wisdom-of-the-organism conception seemed almost to be *reducing* personal decisions not only to biological underpinning but to extraindividual group processes as well. Here is an excerpt from Rogers's later writings in which he argued for the utility of encounter groups:

To me the group seems like an organism, having a sense of its own direction even though it could not define that direction intellectually. This is reminiscent of a medical motion picture which once made a deep impression on me. It was a photo-micrographic film showing the white blood corpuscles moving very randomly through the blood stream, until a disease bacterium ap-

peared. Then, in a fashion which could only be described as purposeful, they moved toward it. They surrounded it and gradually engulfed and destroyed it, then moved on again in their random way. Similarly, it seems to me, a group recognizes unhealthy elements in its process, focuses on them, clears them up or eliminates them, and moves on toward becoming a healthier group. This is my way of saying that I have seen the "wisdom of the organism" exhibited at every level from cell to group.[27]

Aside from what this might mean for therapeutic change—an issue we will discuss in relation to our final question of this chapter—it is clear that knowledge emanating from cellular or group interactions in some patterned way is no longer simply a conceptual explanation of events. Rogers was moving here from conceptual to evolutionary interactionism, whereby sensations known as feelings are more important to knowledge than higher-level reasoning. It is this fundamental commitment to sensory phenomenology that prompted Rogers to say: ". . . I have learned that my total organismic sensing of a situation is more trustworthy than my intellect. . . . I have found that when I have trusted some inner non-intellectual sensing, I have discovered wisdom in the move."[28]

The second broad group of phenomenologists—who emphasize conceptual understanding over sensory organization—we can call *logical phenomenologists.* Jung was this type of theorist. His construct of the archetype is as close to a Kantian category as one could hope to find in modern personality theory. Archetypes are formative agents which can conceptualize alternatives not yet active in the person's life, but which can potentially or possibly be adopted and carried out. We might say they hold wisdom which is not organic but psychic! Although Kant employed *primordial image,* a phrase Jung

equated with *archetype,* it appears that Jung took this usage from Jacob Burckhardt.[29] Even so, the phenomenological line of theory is uniform here, and it is therefore not surprising to find Jung saying, "Although I have often been called a philosopher, I am an empiricist and adhere as such to the phenomenological standpoint."[30]

Binswanger and Kelly were also logical phenomenologists, whose respective concepts of world-design and personal construct are conceptual organizers of knowledge, brought to bear continually in life, orienting the person toward the ever-arising future. As Binswanger expressed it, "The primary phenomenon of the original and authentic temporality is the future, and the future in turn is the primary meaning of existentiality, of the designing of one's self 'for-one's-own-sake.'"[31] Kelly spoke of self-control as involving successful prediction of behavior, putting one's course sequentially toward a desired end; hence, ". . . in the case of [self-] control, to make it follow upon intent, and, in the case of prediction, to envision outcomes before they happen."[32] Note the theoretical emphasis on premising or predicating one's life in these more logical than sensory formulations. People can create themselves or attain their own ends because they first frame their course according to meanings they *intend* to further—that is, the meanings premised in the world-designs and/or personal constructs. They may not be aware of these intentions consciously, but nevertheless the course of life is endowed with or enriched by the meanings assumed, induced, deducted, predicted, and so on, from the outset. We get a much clearer teleological image of behavior from the logical phenomenologists than we do from the sensory phenomenologists.

The meanings framed in human reason need not follow only a demonstrative form of logic; that is, logical phenomenologists are willing to encompass *dialectical logic* in their formulations (recall that Jung was a self-proclaimed dialectician; see p. 293). It is therefore not surprising to find Binswanger speaking of the dialectical movement that occurs between freedom and nonfreedom during the course of life.[33] Dialectical formulations can also be seen in Binswanger's treatment of shame, a human emotion that reveals to others precisely what the individual wishes to hide.[34] Kelly early noted that he was ascribing a dichotomous quality to all human thinking,[35] and he later added, "Whatever one says about any event gathers its meaning from what contrasting things could otherwise have been said about it, as much as from the other events of which the same might have been said."[36] As we have seen in Chapter 10 (p. 624), this is beautifully consonant with the dialectical views of Oriental Philosophy.

If we turn to Piaget, we find that though a Kantian formulation is evident in his view of human knowing beyond the first few months of life, we cannot be so certain about his view of the newborn child. As noted above, there is a certain element of sensory phenomenology in Piagetian thought, and it stems from the way in which he interprets the constructive process. We end our consideration of the second question of this chapter by contrasting Piaget and Kelly on this matter of constructivism in human knowing.

Piagetian versus Kellyian Constructivism

When Kelly thought of constructivism, he was always describing behavior from the introspective perspective. He found the extra-spective account, couched as it is in efficient causation, to be unacceptable. To understand the person, we must introspectively grasp what he or she is bringing-to-bear in life from "this" point forward (that is, the point at which we first look through the Kantian spectacles being worn by the person involved). Hence, Kelly said, "In specifying *ways of anticipating events* [that is, personal construing style] as the directive referent for human processes we cut ourselves free of the stimulus-response version of nineteenth century scientific determinism."[37] This is a final-cause determinism (see p. 265), in which the person as agent plays a selective role from the outset of life. There is room for arbitrariness (see p. 723) in Kelly's theory, because he considered the individual person—the "inveterate collector of paradigms"[38]—to be the creator, the selector, the user or nonuser of the constructive frames he or she will be involved with.

If we could equate Kelly's use of paradigm with a cybernetic program—both are ordered, hence formal-cause conceptions—we might say that in constructive alternativism, the person is always the *programmer* who thinks up the program and never merely the machine, that is, the *processor* of programs conceived by others. Cybernetic machines reason only demonstratively. They never sense what the human being senses in contemplating why a program is being used in the first place: "Why am I doing this? What convinces me this is really the right way of looking at things? What else might I be doing about what I'm doing?" Thinking in this self-reflexive fashion, the person can always change programs by dialectically reasoning to alternatives (see our discussion of free will, p. 529). Kelly minimized past influences in his theory, *not* because they are irrelevant to present constructions, but because psychologists erroneously assume that what has taken place in the past must necessarily bear an efficiently-caused (unidirectional, blind) *effect* on the present: "We have intentionally avoided saying that the raw events of the past have themselves [efficiently-]*caused* the individual to become the person that he is. Events may be the mile posts in reference to which the individual's progress is timed, yet it is the *construing* that weaves impersonal events into personal experience." [39]

Piaget does not have this commitment to future-oriented or finalistic theories,[40] and in his use of construction, he does not focus exclusively on what the person brings forward in life as a predication "for the sake of which" behavior is then intended. At least, we do not see this emphasis in his theory from the outset of human life, at which point the construction process is pictured more extraspectively, as a material construction that only later becomes psychological (see p. 686). Children do not appear to be logicians at birth, conceptually interacting by constructing schema from the outset. The initial constructions are being done biologically, and only at some time later does the child schematize the reflexive patterns already underway constructively as reflexes. It is as if, in describing the process of self-regulation through concepts such as equilibration, disequilibration, and feedback, Piaget has lost that self-reflexivity and arbitrariness called for in true self-directedness. Unlike Kelly, he seems more accurate in his portrayal of the processor, the machine that brings forward information rather than the programmer of the machine. Of course, his analysis is not mechanistic.

We can pinpoint this difference between Kelly and Piaget by looking at their use of *subsumption* and *assimilation,* respectively. Each of these terms act as a further description of the constructive process, but they rest on dramatically different metaphors. To subsume is to encompass a meaning by a more comprehensive, abstract meaning. Kelly's logical phenomenology is made evident here, for

in logic we say that the major premise of a syllogism (for example, All human beings are mortal) subsumes the meaning of the minor premise (This is a human being) in arriving at the conclusion (This human being is mortal). Meaning is extended or brought forward here from the premising beginnings to the conclusion arrived at (called deduction, of course). Returning to a favorite Piagetian example, if an infant while sucking at mother's breast construes this reflexive process, the personal construct framed (things to be sucked versus not sucked, and so on) subsumes not only mother's breast but later possibilities as well—such as trying to suck fingers or toes to receive food nourishment. What happens when fingers or toes fail to provide milk nourishment? The infant would then reconstrue certain items in relation to others and gradually extend the range of his or her personal constructs.

Turning to Piaget's metaphor, to assimilate is to take in. Assimilation has the meaning of absorption, which is essentially opposite to the Kellyian stress on encompassing and/or extending something. In nature, living cells at all levels absorb liquids through their membranes by a process known as *osmosis*. The disequilibration of dehydration in bodily tissues can be rectified through the osmotic assimilation of liquids through the membranes of the cellular wall. Thus, Piaget can speak of the equilibrium of plants on the one hand,[41] and then on the other say that:

. . . all behavior is an assimilation *of reality to prior schemata (schemata which, in varying degrees, are due to heredity) and all behavior is at the same time an* accommodation *of these schemata to the actual situation. The result is that developmental theory necessarily calls upon the concept of equilibrium, since all behavior tends toward assuring an equi-*

librium between internal and external factors or, speaking more generally, between assimilation and accommodation.[42]

Piaget would therefore say that the baby assimilates the finger or toe to a scheme of the mother's breast.[43]

And right here we begin to understand that unlike Kelly's interpretation of construction as a framing or bringing-to-bear of a conceptual scheme, Piaget's interpretation of construction is as the adding-to, becoming-more-complex, developing organization of a conceptual scheme. Kelly is speaking of how things are set in a context and Piaget is speaking of how things are "built." Kelly always thinks of the constructive process from the introspective theoretical perspective, whereas Piaget tries to maintain an extraspective point of view. Mollusks take in nourishment and develop patterned structures of behavior in equilibrating, and human beings take in nourishment and develop patterned structures (schemata) of behavior in equilibrating. Both Piaget and Kelly are in the final analysis realists (see previous section), but Kelly's view of mental construction has the person more a central agent in the *making* of that reality. In other words, even when we would someday all agree on the nature of reality and use a common set of constructs to describe it, Kelly would expect that our uniform psychological processes of construction would play a role in the creation of that reality. This is what he meant by "a truth deep inside all of us" when referring to reality (see quote on p. 758). Reality will always be internally constructed in the psychology of personal constructs. Piaget, on the other hand, in stressing the role of accommodation *to* reality rather than constant reconstruction *of* reality, has in mind—or appears to have in mind—

something totally independent from and external to human cognition (the real) which must be copied or conformed to as accurately as possible if an equilibration is to be achieved.

Kelly was always ready to admit that scientific knowledge itself was constructed, hence could be given ready alternative explanations. Piaget, on the other hand, cautions us as follows: "Structures [that is, the fruits of construction] are not simply convenient theoretical constructs; they exist apart from the anthropologist[-scientist], for they are the *source* of the relations he observes; a structure would lose all truth value if it did not have this direct connection with the facts."[44] It seems clear that "facts" are assimilated or taken in as objects to be accommodated, rather than themselves brought into understanding constructively by an intellect which "makes them up." In the final analysis, Piaget's Kantianism is muted and we might even suspect that he has a mixed Lockean-Kantian model at work in his theorizing. Genetic epistemology borrows much from evolutionary interactionism, although after the initial constructions are schematized, there is considerable similarity between Piaget and Kelly. Kelly simply leans in the direction of the phenomenal realm and, like Kant, cannot bring himself to deny the reality of a noumenal realm altogether, whereas Piaget leans in the direction of the noumenal realm and cannot bring himself to deny that purely phenomenal factors also enter into the determination of behavior.

Is it Essential to Describe Behavior as Taking Place over Time?

Carl Rogers was once asked to draft a detailed presentation of his theory for a publication being sponsored by the American Psychological Association. The editorial policy for this volume asked that contributors use a *common* style of presentation, in which the theories would be presented in terms of independent, intervening, and dependent variables. Rogers found it impossible to express his theory in these terms, noting that they: "... smack too much of the laboratory, where one undertakes an experiment *de novo,* with everything under control, rather than of a science which is endeavoring to wrest from the phenomena of experience the inherent order which they contain."[45] What he was objecting to here, of course, was the confounding of methodological terminology (variables) with theoretical terminology (his phenomenal field construct, and so on). Rogers went on to say that only after we first put a theory together may we then translate our constructs into the variables of an experiment in an effort to validate them.

What difference does all of this make? Well, if we do not keep clear in our minds what is our theory and what is our method, it is extremely easy for the method to become our theory (see p. 512). Rogers was leveling a purity criticism at the editors, because their policy stacked the cards against a theory that *did not* rely on local motion to explain change of behavior, but might wish to explain behavior via qualitative motion (see p. 269). If we force a theorist to break up his or her concepts into "independent, intervening, dependent," we make it appear from the outset that behavior moves *across time*—from "left to right" with antecedents efficiently-causing consequents to come about. Viewing events as in motion across time was central to the Newtonian mechanics, and we noted in Chapter 4 (p. 270) how this view was underwritten by Cartesian geometry. But subsequent developments in science culminating in Einstein's theory of relativity were to take time out of the equation as a *necessary* grounding for explanations of natural events.

Thus, it was shown how Newton's assumptions concerning the passage of absolute time were not possible to demonstrate. Ultimately, what we mean by time is the changing pattern of items within the total constellation (pattern) of the planets. In other words, local motion is said to occur across time because in moving from point A to point B an object or person changes relative location to some unchanging point of comparison. As everything in the universe can therefore be shown to be moving relative to something else, the final standard becomes the *overall pattern* or constellation of heavenly bodies that *does not* change. Though the universe may be expanding, we can still identify the precise location of certain heavenly bodies in the constellation we know as the universal field. This kind of field theory is what the neogestaltists like Lewin and Rogers attempted to bring into psychology by way of their *life space* and *phenomenal field* constructs. Rather than thinking of time as the flow (locomotion) of efficient causes, from past to present to future, this explanation frames time as a formal-cause, qualitative change. Some psychologists believe that their empirical studies somehow prove that time does in fact flow or locomote from antecedents to consequents. But here again, Einstein in his general theory of relativity showed that the hypotheses upon which Cartesian geometry is founded are *not* fixed into such rigid linearity in nature. This is so because the rigidly mechanistic features of measuring rods, watches, and light rays are themselves subject to varying observed values of measurement in the space-time continuum.

Physicists in the twentieth century have become increasingly convinced that the human being as conceptualizer (conceptual interaction) always is a factor in the relativity of all factual information. Nowhere is this more evident than in subatomic physics, where, rather than finding that reliable material- and efficient-cause substrate Bacon had pointed to, we find reality slipping away from our understanding. Sounding very much like a constructive alternativist, we find one of the fathers of subatomic physics, Niels Bohr, saying in 1927 that:

> . . . the quantum postulate implies that any observation of atomic phenomena will involve an interaction with the agency of observation [that is, the person as agent] not to be neglected. Accordingly, an independent reality in the ordinary physical sense can neither be ascribed to the phenomena nor to the agencies of observation. After all, the concept of observation is in so far arbitrary as it depends upon which objects are included in the system to be observed.[46]

Bohr's conceptual interactionist position carried forward Mach's phenomenological interpretation of the physical world. In psychology, it was the gestaltists and related phenomenologists who were trying to bring about the same revolution in the way behavior is to be explained.

Put in theory-construction terms, the phenomenologists were trying to replace the efficient-cause determinism of locomotion with a formal-cause determination of changing patterns of meaning, set within a field of interlacing meanings that did not change *across time* but qualitatively changed *within time*. Behaviorism, which relies on efficient causality to explain things, cannot *in principle* explain behavior with time left out of the account. How did the phenomenologists accomplish this theoretical revision? Figure 28 diagrams the distinction we are now considering.

Note that Figure 28 is framed around two time lines, with the upper line (I) representing stimulus-response psychology and the lower line (II) representing gestalt-phenomenological psychology. Taking up the stimulus-response position first, note that the various things to be said about behavior below time line I all rest on an efficient-cause meaning in which time is essentially pictured as being thrust along from left to right. Whether we use the stimulus-response, stimulus-mediation-response, independent-dependent variable, or independent-intervening-dependent variable ideas, everything falls into line as a before and an after across time. There is no other way in which to express these meanings except through use of an efficient-cause conception.

Dropping down now to time line II in Figure 28, note that we have a series of tubular slices or pieces lined up, one following another in an order that stretches across the expanse of the time line. Think of this tubular figure as "all the time that ever existed." We are looking at the whole length and breadth of time when we look at the figures of II-A and II-B. In order to focus more on the individual pieces, we might think of them as a series of poker chips stacked up and turned on end. Each poker chip has a different design on it. Note II-B, where one poker chip might be said to have been pushed out of the stack: it has a unique design. If we are willing to think of the pieces of our figure as potential slices which are not yet cut, we can think of the entire tubular figure as a time sausage of materials packed into a skin with different hues of meats and contrasting organizations of meat and fat stuffed throughout the entire length. Just as each poker chip has a different design, each slice of the time sausage presents us with a completely unique *pattern* of meat, fat, gristle, flecks of seasoning, and so on, all forming into a whole. Now, what we are after here is a way of suggesting that the design on each poker chip or the contents patterned by a slice of the time sausage matches up to and

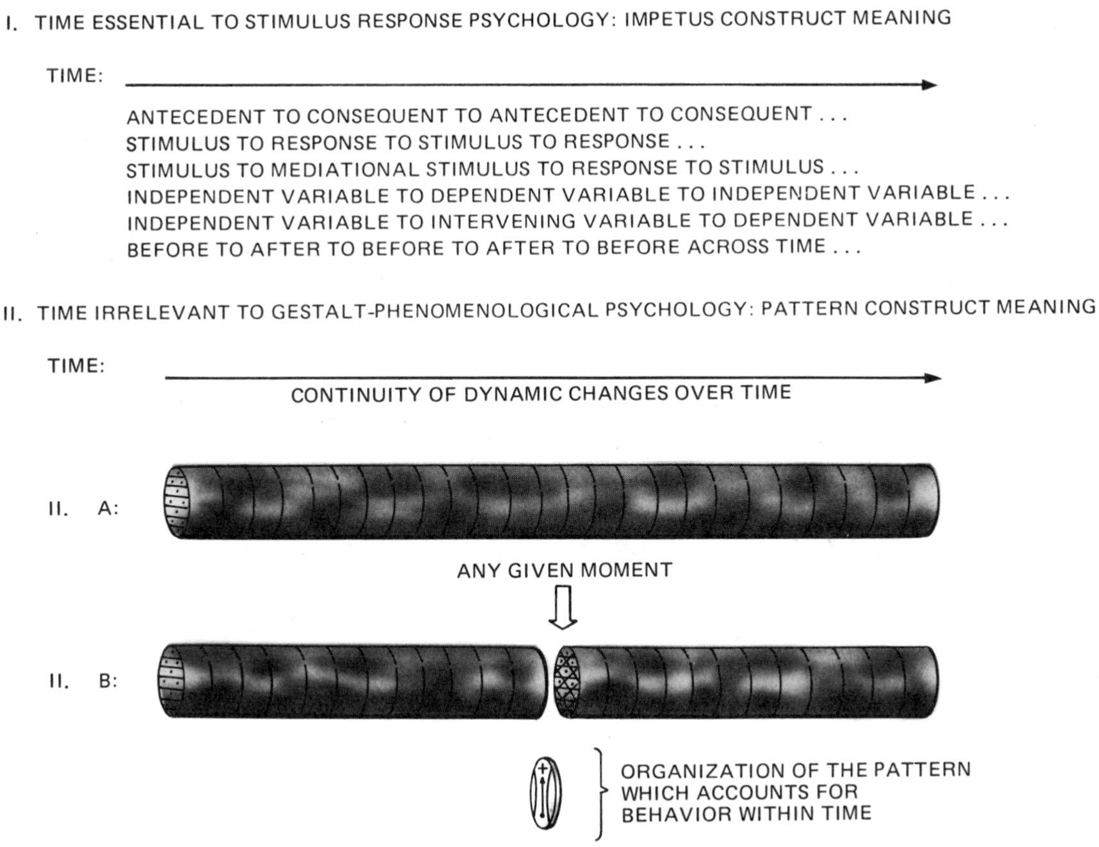

I. TIME ESSENTIAL TO STIMULUS RESPONSE PSYCHOLOGY: IMPETUS CONSTRUCT MEANING

TIME: ⟶

ANTECEDENT TO CONSEQUENT TO ANTECEDENT TO CONSEQUENT . . .
STIMULUS TO RESPONSE TO STIMULUS TO RESPONSE . . .
STIMULUS TO MEDIATIONAL STIMULUS TO RESPONSE TO STIMULUS . . .
INDEPENDENT VARIABLE TO DEPENDENT VARIABLE TO INDEPENDENT VARIABLE . . .
INDEPENDENT VARIABLE TO INTERVENING VARIABLE TO DEPENDENT VARIABLE . . .
BEFORE TO AFTER TO BEFORE TO AFTER TO BEFORE ACROSS TIME . . .

II. TIME IRRELEVANT TO GESTALT-PHENOMENOLOGICAL PSYCHOLOGY: PATTERN CONSTRUCT MEANING

TIME: ⟶

CONTINUITY OF DYNAMIC CHANGES OVER TIME

II. A:

ANY GIVEN MOMENT
⇩

II. B:

ORGANIZATION OF THE PATTERN
WHICH ACCOUNTS FOR
BEHAVIOR WITHIN TIME

Figure 28 The Role of Time in Stimulus-Response versus Gestalt Psychology

coordinates with that chip or slice *before* it and *after* it in order. We have a continuing pattern running through our tubular chunks of time, much as marble has a continuing pattern carrying through any chunks we happen to remove from the earth. As a result, when we slice a given area of our sausage, there is a similarity of one slice with the one immediately before it that might have been sliced as well as the one following it. Now, think of this flowing succession of changing patterns as following *gestalt laws,* such as good continuation, closure, and so on (see pp. 569–570). The organization of each slice is

not caused by the slice preceding it any more than it is caused by the slice following it. Everything is of a single piece across our total expanse of time. If we now equate our poker chip or sausage slice with a formal-cause conception of field, we can begin to understand what the phenomenologists are driving at in their view of qualitative changes in behavior.

Suppose at point II-B of Figure 28 we were to slice a piece of our sausage or poke one of our chips away from the stack, turning it face up to observe the pattern (**design,** organization) at *that* point in time. We have placed a gestalt organization on this sliver of time, with a positive valence ($+$) suggested according to Lewinian field theory (see p. 571). It is the organization on *this* phenomenal slice of the life space that causes behavior in the gestalt-phenomenological line of theorizing. Since the changing relations within the stacked poker chips of time (or the time sausage) follow gestalt principles and *not* S-R principles, we cannot find gestalt in S-R. The antecedent field organization does *not* impel the consequent field organization. Time's passage is irrelevant to these changing field organizations, which can be thought of as being due to conceptual interactions alone—to the ways in which we look at things, including dialectical understandings of the very opposite to what is taking place at any given point in time. If our point of view can influence what we see at the subatomic level, as Bohr suggests, then our point of view may also enter into what we see in our everyday world as well. We might shift from one position to another, from one life premise to another, quite instantaneously, as a dialectical change rather than a linearly arrayed, demonstrative change.

Modern physics has effectively made time a formal-cause conception, interpreting it as a qualitative change in the relative standing any item has in the fixed outline of a field—ultimately, to the field outlining the fixed constellation of the stars. Patterns *as such* exist within events, and time does nothing to influence this formal-cause organization of things, except to pass as the order is being brought out in some fashion. In the same way that a stack of IBM computer cards already contains within its pattern of keypunched scores the *F*-tests or correlation coefficients that a subsequent run-through in a computer will print out for us to read, so too can

we think of behavioral organizations as already plotted out before time enters in as a secondary factor. Time does *not* shape behavior unless the behavior we have in mind is enacted according to efficient causation exclusively. But behavioral efficient causes can also be seen as mere instrumentalities, put into motion in order to complete or copy a pattern that was initially *the* reason for the course of action carried out in what is then an *intentional* manner. Though a robot behaves by moving its efficiently-caused mechanical legs, it never *intends* to bring about the end framed by its program. It cannot intend because it cannot *conceive* of an alternative to what its program dictates. But note: even the program cannot be captured in efficient-cause terminology. It is a fixed pattern —like our *F*-test in the IBM cards or the fixed constellation of the stars—operating within time which uses mechanical steps of the robot to instrumentally carry out its effects.

The reason that we find theorists in the phenomenological tradition (for example, Kelly, the existentialists) reluctant to speak of motivation is because the behaviorists have so firmly identified learning as something taking place exclusively along a time dimension. Learning is change, change is time, hence learning *must* involve time. True, an unseen motivational factor may enter in secondarily to get the organism going across time by some drive or empirical law of effect; but only what is observable behaviorally over time can be thought of as learning. For the gestaltist, the Kantian a priori is like the stack of data cards before they enter the computer. Time brings out the order already there. Hence, time catalogues change, but what learning is need not be tied to a time factor. Look for the patterns *within* time, argues the gestaltist. Since these patterns are often concerned with valences, judgments of what the individual wishes to do, accomplish, achieve, it would seem that motivational factors are not secondary but *basic* to learning. Knowing the perceptual organization, we know the behavior to follow without doubt. Actually, the phenomenologists do *not* wish to order motivation as primary and behavior as secondary in importance. They simply wish to drop the question of motivation altogether—at least this is true of Boss, Binswanger, and Kelly.

And so, if we were to answer finally the question heading this section, we would—as phenomenologists—say no, it is *not* essential to describe behavior as taking place over time. Behavior is more than simply observed action. It is, in the case of human beings, *predicated* action, and the premises framed are not themselves determined by antecedent thrusts of influence across a time dimension. This takes us to the next question.

Does Psychology Have Adequate Terminology to Account for Teleological Behavior, and if Not, What Is Called for?

We come now to a question which has vast implications for the future of personality theory. We have seen over the course of this text a number of images of the person represented by our psychoanalytical, behavioral, and phenomenological traditions. A persistent desire on the part of personality theorists is to somehow group together if not eclectically unite these currently diverse images of what behavior is like. The position of this text is that we need not ever expect to frame a *single* personality theory to which everyone will subscribe. However, it is still possible for certain theories to share a basic image—a metaphor, possibly—of what fundamental human nature is like without thereby agreeing on the specific terminology to be used in fleshing out the image or metaphor.

An obvious and fundamental way in which to group our various theories is according to whether or not they conceptualize human behavior as telic in nature. We could phrase this issue alternatively as whether or not a personality theory should be expected to encompass the meanings of final causality. As we have documented in many different contexts over the theory-construction sections, in order to capture a human teleology, we absolutely have to suggest theoretically that the person (identity, agent, ego) creates (frames, construes, predicates) and then behaves "for the sake of" this created factor (wish, end, reason). And to understand this kind of behavior, we also must assume the introspective theoretical perspective. This is where the intention is being brought to bear, whether we call it a Freudian wish, an Adlerian life plan, or a Kellyian personal construct. None of these concepts are capable of being understood in an exclusively extraspective sense. Behaviorism and its modern derivatives, such as cognitive psychology, *always* assume the extraspective theoretical perspective in accounting for behavior.

In thereby evolving its rigorous extraspective terminology, psychology never really made it possible for an introspective conception like telic behavior to be brought into the laboratory and be put to test. To this very day in its history, psychology lacks a meta-conception which is technically equivalent to response but conveys the meaning of a *cause* (initiator of behavior) rather than an *effect*. Responses are always effects, even when they are mediators (former responses now acting as stimuli). This single issue of behavioral cause-effect description is what most clearly separates the traditional applied or clinically based theories of personality from the basic or laboratory-based theories of personality. It would therefore be instructive to show in diagram form how the most widely used *technical constructs* describing behavior fail to allow a satisfactory test of telic descriptions and then to propose an alternative that promises to do so. There are essentially four technical constructs (with certain subvariations) describing behavior that have been used by psychologists in the laboratory (behaviorists as well as gestaltists). We could easily call these models of behavior, but as such, they are less abstract and comprehensive than our basic theory-construction conceptions (that is, Lockean-versus-Kantian models, the causal conceptions, and dialectical-versus-demonstrative meanings). Our first technical construct is the fundamental conception of *stimulus-response* (1), which we can diagram as follows:

havioristic theories, such as the view of Piaget that higher-order schemes can be abstracted from the hereditarily determined reflexive behavior of an automatic stimulus-response nature. This material-cause emphasis is also retained in drive-reduction theory.

So, we might say that the stimulus-response technical construct as initially framed combined material- and efficient-causes into a reflex-arc conception as literally built into the nervous tissue of the body. The next step in the evolution of this construct occurred when psychologists found it necessary to admit a greater chain of complexity in the left-to-right flow of behavior over time, including factors

STIMULUS ————————————————————————————▶ RESPONSE

Figure 29   (1)

This is the most basic effort on the part of rigorous psychologists to frame behavior amounting to a single unit of efficient causation whereby an assumed antecedent cause connects with, impels, determines, cues, and so on, an observed consequent. Theoretical debates concerning this technical construct centered around whether anything but sheer contiguity (the nearness of the stimulus and response over time) accounted for the pairing up of the antecedent to the consequent, and what if anything was needed to cement this bond, such as a drive, the number of repetitions (trials) it took for the bonding (habit) to take place, and so on. In the earliest formulations, the S-R unit was viewed as essentially built-in to the reflex-arc apparatus of the body. We still have such conceptions active in psychology, even in nonbe-

that were not easily tied into the nervous-tissue reflexes of the body. Though it was still assumed that some form of biological action took place in the brain tissues of the body and that drives might well be an aspect of this action, the emphasis came to be more on the patterning of past experience into an influence on current experience. This raising of the formal-cause meaning to be more important than the material-cause meaning, but still secondary to efficient causation, resulted in the technical construct of *mediation* (2) (see p. 775).

The essential point here is that something of importance takes place *between* the antecedent and the consequent that is as important to the final outcome as is the basic drift of earlier factors determining later factors in the demonstrative sense, which we schematized in the upper half of Figure 28 (see p. 771). There are several variations of the mediation model. In fact, it has been

Figure 30   (2)

argued and with good reason that the original stimulus-response conception (1) used by John Watson had within it a mediating conception in the sense of implicit vocal responses (voice-box muscular actions), which in turn acted as stimuli for subsequent overt responses (walking, writing, and so on).[47] Even more basic to this is the fact that the Lockean model, on which behaviorism was based, held to the view that the initial etchings on the tabula rasa intellect combined to total up to higher and higher levels of complexity (see Figure 1, p. 16). Simple ideas combined to form more complex ideas.[48] If this is the case and if these more complex ideas in time enter into the course of behavior, then it follows necessarily that the Lockean model is a mediational model of mind.

This highlights an interesting feature of the meaning of *mediation*. To mediate is to occupy a middle position in relation to two or more sides. It also bears the meaning of an intervening factor, one that can exert an indirect influence on the flow of cause-effect. There is no necessary suggestion here that the *direction* of this influence need be "stimulus-to-response" or "left-to-right" as the technical constructs (1) and (2) usually imply. In fact, mediation subsumes the meanings of negotiation, reconciliation, and compromise. Dialectical formulations could be seen as mediating (compromising) mental factors, as in the sense of Freudian symptom-formation where both the repressing and the repressed wishes are brought into the manifestation of illness (see p. 85). This reciprocity between stimulus and response was not stressed in early behaviorism. One of the first variations of technical construct (2) was Tolman's mediation model (2a):

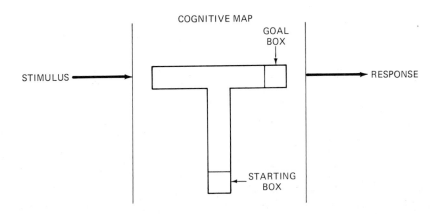

Figure 31   (2a)

Recall from Chapter 6 (p. 381) that Tolman proved empirically that animals in a T-maze could frame a visual image (significate) of the relationship between the starting box in which they were placed and the goal box to which they had to run in order to be fed even though they were not under a drive state at the time. Around this same time, Woodworth (p. 381) was referring to the organismic (0) variables in behavior, and hence the technical construct (2ₐ) can also be thought of as the S-O-R model of behavior. Tolman and Woodworth badly confounded methodological terminology (intervening variables) with theoretical terminology (visual mediators, cognitive map, and so on), but the essential point for present considerations is that they raised the relative importance of a formal-cause patterning in S-R theory even as they kept the drift of influence (determination) strictly left to right in their technical account of antecedents bringing about consequents. Dollard and Miller next proposed their highly influential mediational construct (based on Hullian theory), as follows (2ᵦ):

(effects) can become in time stimuli (causes) for even later responses. Note that the drift still remains essentially from left to right in (2ᵦ). Our next adaptation begins to alter this uniform direction. Cybernetics brought something new to the mediation technical construct in its notion of feedback, as in (2ᵧ).

The specific names for the boxes pictured in (2ᵧ) are not important for our purposes. We would find them being labeled with words like *selective filter, limited capacity decision channel, short-term memory store, long-term memory store,* and so forth. Note, however, that the arrows we have depicted begin to turn back on themselves, so that in mediating, our cybernetic adaptation begins now to reflect a reciprocity that the earlier mediation models do not capture. One of the major forms of this reciprocal influence we have labeled is *feedback*. Recall from our discussion of cybernetics in Chapter 7 (p. 429) that feedback occurs when a portion of the output returns as input. Feedback always refers to what was *literally* done or carried out by the series of information processed as

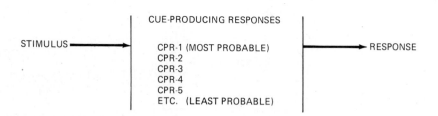

Figure 32   (2ᵦ)

This is a more detailed example of the basic conceptualization we presented in Chapter 6 (p. 392) of the fact that earlier responses

output. Feedback informs the process as to what *is happening* and never what might *possibly* be taking place. Though there is a certain reciprocity in this cybernetics conception, there is no true dialectic involved, as the

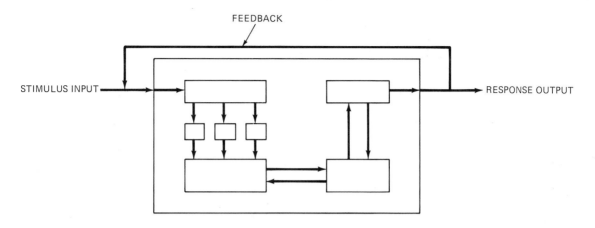

Figure 33   **(2$_c$)**

information processed is exclusively demonstrative in meaning.

What have the mediation technical constructs (2, 2$_a$, 2$_b$, 2$_c$) added to Watson's original stimulus-response construct (1) in the sense of our theory-construction terminology? It is clear that they have raised the formal cause as a principle of explanation, giving it roughly equal emphasis to the efficient cause. The material-cause meaning remains as a kind of background conception, because obviously any mediational process is likely to be taking place in some palpable structure of the organism—the brain, or whatever. But the point of importance is that in the rise of modern theories of experimental or laboratory psychology, we have a clear trend to the explanatory power of patterns, orders, encodings, or structures per se. The stimulus input is no longer simply *there*. It has first to be recognized as a pattern, filtered through various mechanisms, and encoded according to existing structures before we can speak of *the stimulus*.[49] Indeed, even the concept of a reciprocal relationship between two focal points (boxes) of the mediating information process implies a patterning that is not *ex-*

clusively due to the input. The person's long-term memory enters in to shape (order, pattern) the input occurring at present.

Of course, when we come right down to it, the *first* inputs from reality on traditional mediational models are either said to be ordered exclusively by the external environment, or there is some concession made to constructing at the level of sensory input similar to the sensory-phenomenological emphasis. That is, the stimulus image is said to enter the organism as a response, and so what is constructed is this stimulus input as a sensory response.[50] Information so input is then processed, stored, and retrieved without in any way representing the sort of conceptual, meaning-endowing, subsuming capacities of the logical phenomenologist. If a genuine sensory phenomenologist like Rogers were to speak of the stimulus input, he would *not* consider it a response. The meaning of the input would be constructed from the inside out, from phenomenal-to-noumenal, and not vice versa as is the case in cybernetics. Con-

Figure 34   (3)

structions are not taken in from the environment and then processed. Constructions are put on the environment in the sense of the Kantian model (see p. 18).

Nevertheless, the information-processing or cybernetics adaptation of the mediation construct highlighted the reciprocity of one action being modified in turn by another action, and it is therefore not surprising that we find in recent years psychological theories taking on our next technical construct, of *reciprocity*. Above is the actual schematization proposed by Bandura (3):[51]

In this case, B signifies behavior, E represents the external environment, and P stands for the cognitive and other internal events that can affect perceptions and actions.[52] The letter P is used in the latter case because this means essentially all of the *personal* or *person-determined* factors in behavior. Note that in this case, rather than having *two* arrows connecting each of the three points of the reci-

procity technical construct—one going in each direction (see the 2_c mediation model for an example of this type)—we have a *single* double-pointed arrow connecting B with P, P with E, and E with B. This means that our drift of from left to right in the stimulus-response and mediation constructs has been dropped. Of course, Bandura is not conceptualizing the S-R relationship in a reciprocal manner. He is not extending reciprocity to this traditional unit of behavioral analysis, to suggest that the R is reciprocally determining the S as the S is determining the R. Recall from Chapter 7 (p. 490) that Bandura accepts a standard mediation conception, with cybernetics involved as well.

What the reciprocity construct does is draw our perspective back more globally from strictly the S-R relations of behavior to look at the *context* of interacting elements that determine its eventual outcome. We can see that P represents mediational factors on this scheme, whereas B refers to the responses people overtly make in various situations, which in turn are located in the *E*. Rather than stimulus—mediation—response, we have environment—person mediators—behavior, with the left-to-right drift dropped in favor of reciprocity. But this is a very important change in traditional behavioristic description, because now the *person* can be said to have an equal role in behavior's eventual outcome equal to that of environmental input. If this extends to birth, it is clear that Bandura has left the Lockean model. That is, if children *from birth* reciprocally interact with the environmental etchings entering mentation, then it cannot be said that we have a tabula rasa account under development. Kantian categories of the understanding would be at the level of *P*, and if they have equal weight to *B* and *E*, we have a totally different behaviorism underway. When specifically asked whether children can indeed influence their knowledge of external events *from birth*, as opposed to the traditional Lockean view of initial etchings upon the tabula rasa intellect that act in time as mediators for later behavior, Bandura had the following to say:

Social learning theory does not assume a blank passive organism at birth. Infants display attentional selectivities and some capacity for organizing experiences. Microanalyses of spontaneous infant-adult interactions reveal that far from being merely passive receptors of external inputs, infants reciprocally influence their social environment from birth *[emphasis added]. . . . With further development they bring their conceptions more heavily to bear on the world around them. Cognitive competencies and perceptual sets affect what information people extract from the environment and how they organize and interpret what they see and hear. Conceptions thus give meaning to experiences and are in turn altered by them. Conceptions of oneself, of generative skills, and of the physical and so-*

cial environment are not simply yesterday's passively imprinted stimulus inputs acting unidirectionally as today's internal efficient causes.[53]

If Bandura means in this statement that infants influence their social environments in the sense of *P* from birth and not only in the sense of *B*, then he has written here a scenario for any Kantian theorist to embrace. Bandura takes here the position of *conceptual interaction* which Kant early espoused (see p. 759). The phenomenologists of Part III could readily accept this statement. In fact, Bandura seems to have gone beyond Piaget's theory of how schemata are framed. Recall that Piaget would have reflex actions under *B* acting as the unidirectionally influential basis for the framing of schemes at the *P* level. The patterns of *B* in this instance act as initial structurings for *P* without any reciprocity. Bandura would seem to be suggesting that a purely conceptual interaction takes place, so that even reflexive patterns are open to influence. One child's conception of sucking at mother's breast may be unique in comparison to a second child's conception (scheme) of the same experience.

There are other aspects of Bandura's presentation that lead us to suspect that he may not be using a conceptual interpretation of interaction after all. This suspicion arises through his use of self-reflexive or reflective thought—a concept that is entirely compatible with the Kantian model because of its reliance upon *transcendental dialectic*. Recall from the Introduction (see p. 20) that Kant believed there was a dialectical capacity in free thought for reason to turn back on itself in a reflexive manner. If we were to schematize this conceptual reflexivity using Bandura's two-headed arrow we might do it as follows (a):

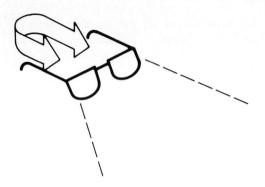

Figure 35   (a)

What we are symbolizing here is the fact that even though a person might ordinarily look through the Kantian spectacles, it is also possible to reciprocally *not* look through them or to bring to bear an alternative set of spectacles. We might have symbolized this as follows (b):

Reasoning dialectically, the person might be thought of as looking through one pair or *its dialectical opposite*. Let us say that we ordinarily understand the world we perceive phenomenally through our spectacles as falling into order in a certain way. As we know from our discussion of logical versus sensory phenomenology, we might first order it according to space and time at the level of sensation and then bring to bear a conception, such as cause-effect, at the level of understanding. Given this ordering of noumenal—*assumed* noumenal!—experience, we could still in our freely speculating thoughts challenge these assumptions. We could say to ourselves "Maybe space and time are illusions" and "I don't really believe in causes of things. Thing's just happen, they aren't caused." Now, having dialectically negated what our senses and our understanding imply directly does not mean we necessarily have an alternative understanding of that which we now imply. Saying something happens may simply be another way of saying it is caused. But we at least have this built-in capacity to challenge *any* idea we have concerning our ex-

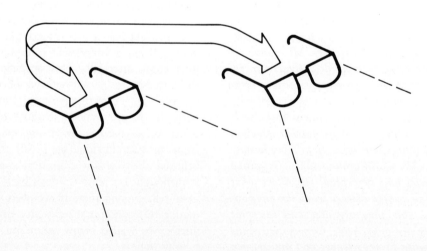

(b)

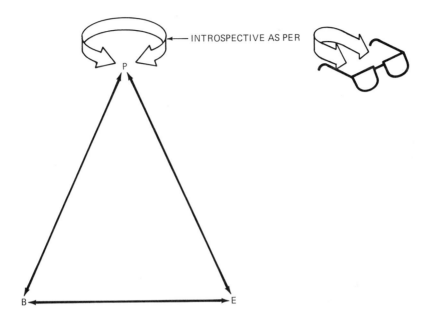

INTROSPECTIVE AS PER

Figure 36   (3ₐ)

perience. Kant held that this turning back on what we know to negate it, or to suggest its dialectically opposite meaning, is basic to free thought. This is what is meant by reflexive thought, and it would be the *P* of Bandura's technical construct where it would be brought to bear. A Kantian adaptation of (3) would look like the above (3ₐ).

Note that we have combined the Kantian spectacles with transcendence depicted by a looping double-headed arrow from the introspective perspective at *P*. This adaptation of (3) would enable us to say that the internal (phenomenal) factors of experience are capable of being brought to bear *or not*. The child may not question assumptions regarding phenomenal experience early in life, but the potential to do so is not something that is learned following birth, as the Lockean model would have it. This transcending capacity to bring premises, assumptions, constructs, and so on, to bear is part of the human being's

conceptual equipment *from birth*. The (3ₐ) adaptation could easily subsume a logical phenomenology.

How well does the introspective adaptation in (3ₐ) mesh with what Bandura had to say? First of all, we should be assured that Bandura did in fact sprinkle his writings with references to reflective thought. He said that people "engage in reflective thought for innovative action" and that people are self-reactors with capacities for reflective self-awareness.[54] When asked specifically what the term reflective meant to him, Bandura answered: "Reflective thought refers to thoughts about one's thoughts. By operating on what they know, people can derive knowledge about things that extend beyond their experiences and generate innovative courses of action."[55] In further explicating his theory of reflective thought, it becomes clear that Bandura was *not* thinking in the introspective Kantian vein concerning these "thoughts about one's thoughts." Referring to the interactive schematization we have numbered (3) above, Bandura said:

In the social learning view, behavior, cognitive and other personal factors, and environmental influences all operate as interlocking determinants of one another. . . . Within each of the triadic factors there exist, of course, many reciprocal processes. In the action domain, particular movements reciprocally activate other movement patterns. Similarly, there exist reciprocal spiraling processes in thought-produced affective reactions. The occurrence of an environmental event likewise reciprocally affects other environmental events.[56]

Bandura went on to refer to the "many reciprocal subprocesses that operate within each of the three constituent factors [that is, *B*, *P*, and *E*]." [57] If we were to schematize his elaboration of technical construct (3), it would look as depicted in (3b).

Note that in this case the looping double-headed arrows at each of the three components of the reciprocity construct are to be thought of extraspectively. It is obvious that Bandura equated reflective thought (or self-reflexivity) with reciprocal interaction, so that it seems perfectly natural for *B* and *E* to have—shall we say—reflections in on themselves. A child skipping rope (that is, *B*) brings many movements into coordination, so that as one action (twisting the rope) is undertaken, a second is automatically coordinated (leaping from the ground). In this sense, we can think of *B* reciprocally interacting with itself. A railroad diesel train, as it approaches a crossing, triggers mechanisms to lower a gate so that we are unable to drive across the railroad tracks at a certain crossing in our path. This would be a case of *E* reciprocally interacting with itself. And returning to our original point, a businessperson who spends time thinking about the filing system can in time concoct some improvements in how these records are kept. This would be a case of *P* reciprocally interacting with—reflecting thought on—itself.

Bandura can view all of these interactions in common because he—like Piaget in his view of assimilation (see p. 767)—retains an extraspective perspective across *B*, *P*, and *E*. He never takes the phenomenal perspective of the person, which would mean looking through the spectacles being worn at *P* (see 3a). Hence, he finds nothing different between the three types of reciprocity that are possible. Yet, the phenomenologist, who means by self-reflexivity a transcendent thought process turning back on itself to challenge its own assumptions or to recognize that it is, after all, simply taking a position on things and hence not irrevocably fixed into the viewpoint, could never agree with Bandura. How can behavior once it is enacted overtly transcend its assumptions? How can the impersonal environment turn back on its point of view and be prepared to see what *is* occurring as having a possible alternative that *might* take place? Obviously, transcendence and reflexivity interpreted via the introspective perspective make no sense at all when applied to conceptions that are best thought of in exclusively extraspective terms. Behavior, as muscular instrumentalities like jumping rope, or environment, as the effects of railroad trains on crossing gates, are not framed in a way calling for the phenomena-noumena distinction. We cannot say the same for the ruminations of a person considering alternative ways to keep records.

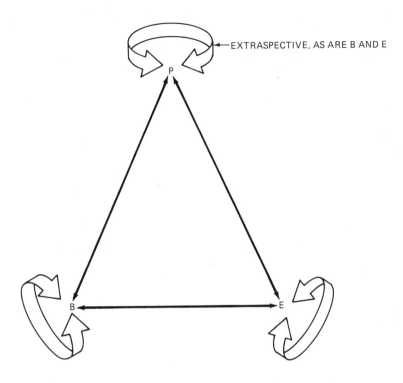

EXTRASPECTIVE, AS ARE B AND E

Figure 37   (3ᵦ)

It is when he elaborates on the technical construct of reciprocity in the sense of (3ᵦ) that we realize Bandura is *not* dealing in conceptual interaction, for this is clearly an instance of statistical interaction. Bandura is saying that what we observe taking place over there as human activity is always a highly complex interaction between what people think, as they come into the environmental circumstances they confront from moment to moment, and what it is realistically possible for them to do, given these constantly changing circumstances. Measurements must be taken at these three touchpoints of observation, but to assign *the* cause to any one of them is unrealistic. Bandura is *not* arguing for a telic addition to this interlocking triad of statistically interacting fac-

tors. His basic image of how *P* functions is as a variation of the mediation-cybernetic technical construct (see p. 490). We must keep in mind that the reciprocity technical construct does not rule out use of a mediational construct at the level of *P* any more than our analysis shows that it need rule out a truly phenomenal self-reflexive process, given that we confine this exclusively to *P* as in (3ₐ). But Bandura is not interested in framing a telic theory of agency. As he put it:

There is a difference between analyzing cognition as a contributing factor in the reciprocal determination of events and concep-

tualizing cognition as a psychic agent that orchestrates behavior. Understanding of how people exert some influence over their actions is more likely to be advanced by delineating and exploring the nature of self-regulatory mechanisms than by simply ascribing behavior to a psychic agent.[58]

We are back to the question posed in this section. Though Bandura's writings carry the ring of teleology, it is clear that he like other psychologists who consider themselves rigorous scientists (including Piaget!) finds it either demeaning or at least scientifically improper (unfruitful?) to posit telic human behavior. As it is then impossible to put telic experimental hypotheses to test, there is no way to investigate scientifically the soundness of this theoretical stand. The reciprocity technical construct carries the formal-cause emphasis of the mediation construct a step

further, because rather than focusing on the role of patterns of past inputs operating in the present to direct behavior as delayed efficient causes (mediators), we are looking from a greater extraspective distance at a whole complex of mutually interacting factors. There was an attempt earlier in the history of psychology to capture this global effect of many patterned factors working in concert to bring about behavior. We refer here to gestalt psychology, which was based primarily on the technical construct of *figure-ground,* as schematized below (4).

Note that now we have an arrow, directing our attention from the realm of phenomenal to the realm of noumenal experience, and that it takes direction through a figure set on a ground. The arrow is *not* symbolizing efficient causation, for there is no flow of from left to right on this model. The arrow merely symbolizes the fact that it is the framing order of the figure-ground relations that pattern behavior or pattern the meanings on the basis of which behavior takes place. The ge-

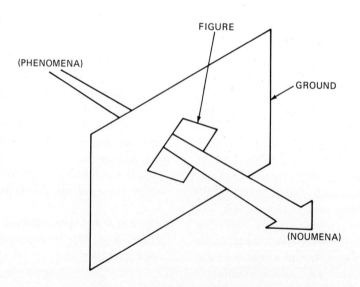

Figure 38   (4)

staltists were interested in the fact that, phenomenally speaking, we all sense a certain agency in our behavior, the behavior of others, and sometimes even in the actions of inanimate events. They questioned whether it is entirely proper to reduce such immediate experiences of agency to supposed underlying principles of explanation which take this meaning out of these experiences. Köhler tells of a time when this phenomenal perception of intentionality reverberated through his psyche, balanced only by the fact that he was, after all, a twentieth-century person and to that extent no longer entirely natural (or pure à la the purity criticism):

While climbing once in the Alps I beheld, on stepping cautiously around a corner of the rocks, a big dark cloud which moved slowly and silently towards me along the slope. Nothing could look more sinister and more threatening. Genetically this might have been a case of empathy; but for my awareness the menace was certainly in the cloud. I could perhaps persuade myself that a cloud as such is an indifferent percept. If, however, I had been a primitive, no reason whatsoever could have given me such sober consolation. The threatening character of the cloud itself would have remained just as "objective" as its ugly dark color.[59]

Thanks to his training in science, Köhler could reduce the perceived threat the cloud seemed to be *intending* to carry out to a formula for condensation of liquids in the atmosphere and so forth, but had he not known or not accepted such scientific reductionism, his behavior would most surely have been determined by a factor that this very science finds unacceptable as a descriptive explanation of behavior. There is something more than mediators taking place in such experiences, said the gestaltists, and in looking for it they settled on the organization of field forces according to figure-ground relations of differentiation and articulation (see our review of their laws on pp. 569–570). For example, Koffka suggested that *willful* or intended behavior occurred because of field forces emanating from an individual ego in the phenomenal field.[60] Lewin gave will this same interpretation in terms of the life space.[61] In his book on productive thinking, Wertheimer's treatment focused on the directed features of thought in what is clearly an intentional manner: "In real thinking the *functional* meaning of an item, of a proposition, that meaning which changes as thinking advances, is of the utmost importance—without it thinking gets sterile; without realization of that change one does not grasp the line of progress. For statements, etc., have a *direction* in their context." [62]

The direction of gestalt psychology is always forward, because the phenomenal frame of reference is what we essentially look through as we confront life daily. This is why we have the arrow of the figure-ground technical construct running from the phenomenal inside to the noumenal outside. It is the formal-cause frame *right now* that makes the difference and not how many times in the past we have been shaped through efficient-cause motions to behavior one way rather than another (see Figure 27, p. 771). Thus, in the figure-ground technical construct (4), we have dropped the efficient-cause meaning altogether. On this point of how behavior is determined—whether by efficient-cause or formal-cause determinism (see p. 265)—Wertheimer properly concluded that what separated gestaltists from behaviorists was their respective emphasis in explanation on the "question of repetition." [63] Are people merely shaped by frequent influences out of their past lives or is there some other factor going on even as these so-called influences are being repeated? Wertheimer answered:

. . . the role of past experience is of high importance, but what matters is what one has gained from experience—blind, un-understood connections, or insight into structural relatedness. What matters is how and what one recalls, how one applies what is recalled, whether blindly in a piecemeal way, or in accordance with the structural requirements of the situation.[64]

By referring to the "insight into structural relatedness," Wertheimer is placing emphasis on the formal-cause patternings of meanings over the efficient-cause connections of blind (nontelic, non–forward looking, and so on) stimulus-response links over time. Much of his writing on the higher mental processes reads as a logical phenomenology.

Unfortunately, the basic figure-ground conceptions of gestalt psychology were drawn from experiments that emphasized sensory phenomenology, for example, the seeing of things, the patterned recognition of sounds, and the organized sense of touch. Gestalt laws took much from such purely sensory experience, and the resulting technical construct of figure-ground seems to have borne this emphasis ever since. This emphasis on sensation and perception has served to obscure the *logical* phenomenology emphasis in gestalt psychology. The reasons for this de-emphasis of the logical side of knowledge can be seen in examples taken from Koffka's writings. Basing his position on the distinction between the *distal* (environmental, external, or noumenal) and *proximal* (retinal, internal, or phenomenal) stimulus, Koffka could say, "Things look as they do because of the field

organization to which the proximal stimulus distribution gives rise."[65] It is not the antecedent distal stimulus that causes the proximal stimulus as we see a tree in the distance. The tree becomes a tree at the level of the proximal stimulus, thanks to the organizing (formally-causing) role of gestalt laws. So far, we are clear on the primary role of formal causation in the gestalt analysis. But now, if the field is under organization at the level of proximal stimulation, where does the ego—which, as noted above, supposedly provides the source of willful behavior—come into play? Koffka answered, ". . . the Ego seems to behave like any other segregated object in the field."[66] If we remember now that according to gestalt theory an isomorphism exists between the laws of organization operating at the level of the sensory apparatus *as well as* the central nervous system—that is, we not only see but we *think* according to gestalt laws—it is difficult to know how we can have a telic explanation in this account.

That is, if the ego is segregated by these laws *in the field,* how can the ego also be *looking through* to bring about the organization of the field in the sense of agency? Put another way, does the ego willfully influence the direction of differentiation and articulation in the field, or does the field organization beginning at the level of proximal stimulation differentiate and articulate the ego? If the latter is being contended as it appears to be, then the ego comes out just as much an effect as it does in the behavioristic theories using the stimulus-response technical construct. The problem here stems from the difficulty of placing the ego in two places on the figure-ground technical construct. Wertheimer, who leaned in the direction of logical phenomenology, seems to have wanted the ego to be *behind* the figure-ground per se, in the region we have labeled phenomena in (4). Here is where Kelly would place the construer of events, who then construes the figure-ground framework through which the noumenal realm is organized. By referring to the ego as a segregated aspect of the field, Koffka has set the ego onto the figure-ground organization *itself*—that is, on the oblong ground that comes between the phenomenal and noumenal realms. In doing so, he loses the *introspective* perspective implicit in the construct and makes it into the following (4a):

In (4ᵦ) we have the familiar field explanations of behavior in which the ego or organism is said to emerge as a figure from the ground, and acting in concert with all of the *field forces* summating in total according to gestalt laws, works its way across the differentiated and articulated *regions* of the phenomenal field (life space, and so on) according to gestalt laws. Furthermore, now that

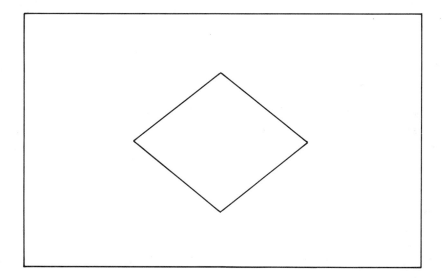

Figure 39   (4ₐ)

This shifts our attention to the diamond-shaped figure from an *extraspective* perspective, so that now we can talk about how all of the forces in the total grounding field work together to influence the figure—which at this point might symbolize Koffka's ego concept. This kind of shift in perspective can be seen in the Lewinian and Rogerian theories, where the organism is depicted as enacting behavior in a life space of phenomenal field, as schematized on p. 788 (4ᵦ).

isomorphism has us thinking of physical matter in motion according to gestalt principles as well, it is easy for us to assume that these so-called field forces are energic expenditures of a material- and efficient-cause nature. Hence, our theory now encompasses three of the four causes, but do we have a meaningful teleology here? In order to account for telic behavior on this construct, the gestaltists had

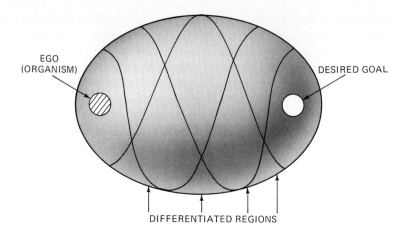

EGO
(ORGANISM)

DESIRED GOAL

DIFFERENTIATED REGIONS

Figure 40   (4ᵦ)

to think of intentional behavior as being pointed toward a region of the phenomenal field at which a desired goal was differentiated and articulated. Returning to Koffka on will (see above), it is then those field forces emanating from the region of the total field known as the ego that bring about what we know in common sense terms to be willful behavior. The ego, on the left side of (4ᵦ), would emanate forces that would in time take it to the goal region on the right side of the field (Lewin called this locomotion). It is not possible to see how a true "that for the sake of which" action is being carried out here. The ego seems to be at the mercy of the gestalt forces, acting completely within time in a gestalt fashion (see Figure 28, p. 771), but acting *upon* the ego nevertheless. The ego seems incapable of transcending this influence or to behave in any way arbitrarily.

If we are to have a genuine teleology in personality theory, we must propose a technical construct which is unequivocally a final cause. That is, the agency postulated must clearly act as a cause which in turn brings about an effect in behavior. It must be possible for this agent to behave *for the sake of* alternatives *at any time,* regardless of the number of past inputs that dictate one and only one direction to be taken in the everrecurring present. This technical construct must also allow us to speak of self-reflexivity, of knowing that one knows, and of behaving in both an arbitrary and a contradictory manner at times. We must, in short, have a technical construct that can hope to subsume the *human* nature we saw depicted in both the psychoanalytical and the phenomenological traditions and, at the same time, demonstrate its utility in the understanding of the behavioristic tradition as well. The technical construct that promises to do all these things is *telosponse,*[67] which is schematized in (5).

Note that we have retained the general perspective of the figure-ground technical construct (4), with our attention drawn to the arcing arrow labeled A, pointing essen-

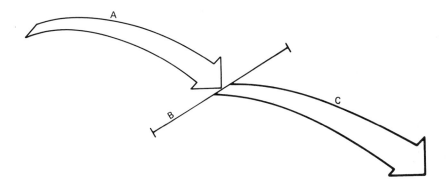

Figure 41   (5)

tially at a straight line B, and then continuing on as C. We do not have the figure-ground spatially represented at B because our emphasis is now on the act of *predication* rather than on the formal-cause patterns which predication may entail. By predication, we mean the act of taking on or *affirming* (assuming, presuming, believing, knowing) a meaning at B "for the sake of which" behavior is then intentionally carried forward at C. This meaning at B may be called a *premise*. In affirming, we actively predicate meanings encompassed in premises. To affirm some one premise at B does not mean another premise could not have been affirmed. We might next focus on just affirmation and demonstrate this selection of a given premise over others as schematized on p. 790 (5_a).

In this case, the affirmation actually made was merely one from among several possible alternatives. We have symbolized this by showing premise 3 being affirmed (brought forward from among the alternatives open). Note also that we do not put a limit on the number of premises that might have been *possibly* affirmed. At least in principle, if not in fact, we can think of telosponsive actions as open to any number of alternative affirmations (N). Let us make concrete what we

have said thus far with an example. Assume that we are trying to understand the reasoning processes and decision-making steps of Joe, a young man presently trying to decide on a college major and the work career this will entail in his future life. First of all, it should be noted that in deciding to go to college, Joe has already considered and discarded other alternative premises that might have been affirmed and carried forward in his life, such as not going to college at all in preference for a career in the armed forces of his country—which is what his brother opted for. Or he could have gone to work at the local foundry where his father made a decent living for thirty years. But Joe thought it best to get an education, so he capitalized on a football scholarship to attend college. Now he is trying to decide what he wants to do in life. Our schematization at (5_a) depicts four alternatives he considered: coaching (physical education), accounting, prelaw, and library administration. Joe finally decided after many switchings back and forth that he would try the "hardest" of the four alternatives—pre-

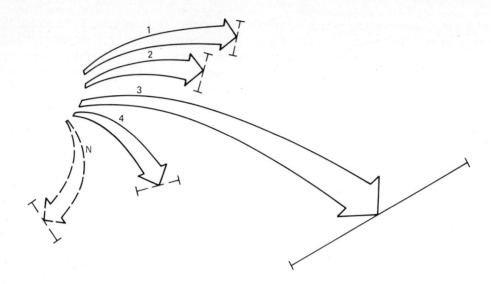

Figure 42   (5ₐ)

law. He considered alternative 3 the most difficult because it committed him to not only undergraduate preparation but to three years of law school as well.

Once affirmed, this alternative becomes the premise B "for the sake of which" Joe is now attending college. It took Joe some time to come to this decision, but time's passage is not what mattered in the final outcome, any more than it matters in the organization and reorganization of the phenomenal field (see Figure 28, p. 771). Joe reasoned through his alternatives by picturing himself in the various professions/occupations, but—thanks to his orderly approach—he did much more than this. He actually sat down and drew up a table of the pros and cons which each of these career alternatives held for him. He liked all of them, but when he had focused carefully on every detail, it became obvious to him that law was his only choice. Whether

this will remain true or not is still an open question. There have been other "Joes" who as late as their senior year in college suddenly find themselves switching majors because of an altered view of what they value in life. But at least for now, Joe is sure what he wants to do. He has a plan now, and this is not so different from the plans he has memorized as plays in his sport of football. There too an alternative is selected, affirmed, and then *brought forward* intentionally on the field of competition.

It is entirely proper to compare Joe's lifestyle game plan with the game plan of his football coaches, because in both cases the planning is nestled in a *patterned* order. In other words, a coach of any sport that has strategic plays to be enacted by the contestants can always diagram these on a strategy board. Every participant can look at this pattern and see immediately what his or her job is if the play is to be carried out successfully. If we were to think about this total play as gestaltists, we might say that it takes on figure-ground significance, because each person on the team is an interlocking element which "creates" the total "as of a piece." Football, soccer, or basketball plays are not designed as *effects* but as *causes* of a totally integrated (gestalt) outcome. And when each of the players understands the design of a play, he or she creates it on the field of competition by *personally* (introspectively considered) extending the meaning at B forward to become the region of the arrow symbolized as C.

Athletic plays are obviously formal-cause conceptions. And the same applies to Joe's extensive examination of his alternatives for a career, his picturing of himself in the various work roles, his totaling up the pluses and minuses of the alternatives; these are all formal-cause patterns of meaning "for the sake of which" Joe now projects himself into his future life. We might therefore say that the B line of our telosponse technical construct is *always* involved with a formal cause. A premise is always some kind of patterning of meaning which can stand alone, just as the coach's game plan (plays) can be sketched on the strategy board and stand alone. We can look *at* a premise that is written down or a play sketched on a strategy board in extraspective fashion. But once we take on this premise for ourselves and behave for its sake, the psychological process taking place can only be understood introspectively. Telosponsivity makes no sense from the extraspective perspective. Note that we could refer back to the figure-ground construct at (4) and say that the framing rectangular ground surrounding the diamond-shaped figure could easily be combined into the telosponse construct as a B content. This would give us a logical phenomenology. We could not, however, go on to the refinements at (4_a) and (4_b), because, as we noted above, they tend to remove the introspective perspective from the account.

It is absolutely essential to appreciate that telosponsivity occurs *only* in the sense of an introspective theoretical description. What we are driving at in our schematizations of telosponsivity is *not* the specific content of the premise at B—not the organization of the phenomenal field at B—but the fact that an agent (Joe) has affirmed and brought forward *this* premise rather than *that* premise. Joe has taken alternative 3 rather than 1, 2, or 4. He could also have concocted a fifth or sixth alternative to contemplate, because Joe is an *active agent* or a cause in his behavioral line and not simply a responder, an effect of previous stimulation or previous inputs. Once Joe as an agent in the selection (choosing) process had affirmed prelaw, he was under a final-cause determination (see p. 265), which in turn means that he enacted those behaviors that will ensure an entrance to law school in time. He took certain courses and worked hard to achieve a good grade-point average, strategizing all the time according to a personal life plan which would take him to his goal. We can diagram his projected course of action, and hence there is a formal-cause meaning encompassed in the telosponse. But the essential point is that Joe as an agent framed and now brings the premise affirmed forward into the reality of his life. We might symbolize Joe's agency with an exclamation mark (!), as depicted on p. 792 (5_b).

The life plan framed by Joe (!) has a purpose and Joe *intends* to bring it about; he behaves "for its sake." The terms *purpose* and *intention* are widely used today as synonyms.[68] We can be somewhat more technical and draw a distinction as follows: (1) *Purpose* is the "aim of the meaning" of a premise, focusing more specifically on the formal-cause aspects of telosponsivity (the fact that there is always something patterned at B). Joe's official plan of study over his under-

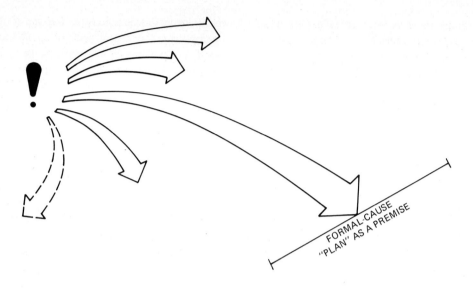

Figure 43 (5_b)

graduate years has a purpose. It shows his advisers where he is heading. It can be filed and his progress monitored over the semesters as he works toward his goal. But there is no psychic life in this plan. It is simply a sheet of paper on which there are tracings of ink imprinted by a typewriter. It is strictly and only at the B point of telosponsivity. (2) *Intention* gets at the other major ingredients of telosponsivity, the A and C arrows suggesting that Joe (!) as agent has framed this plan and now behaves for its sake. Intentional behavior is thus behavior "for the sake of" what has been premised purposively. It would be carried out in the C portion of construct (5), based on the affirmation of a meaningful premise (plan, purpose, reason) at B.

To use an even simpler example, let us analyze the way in which we pick up a pencil in order to write a note to someone. Pencils have *a* purpose. They are writing instruments which have been carefully designed to serve this useful end. But the pencil is not alive to its purpose. The pencil we use is actually a concrete example of the *concept* we carry about in our minds bearing the meaning of this writing instrument. This concept is brought to bear at B, just as any other premise is brought to bear when we think, "I have to send a note to my friend." The pencil is never alive to its purpose—to the "aim of its meaning." It is we, as human agents, who desire to intend the meaning of the pencil, who bring the pencil's purpose to life by picking it up and jotting off a note to our friend. We behave intentionally by extending the meaning of pencil, paper, and the point of our written message in our behavior. The pencil as a concept has a purpose, and we as telosponding organisms have intention(s). Given these background definitions we can now provide a specific definition of the telosponse, as follows:

A telosponse *is a mental act whereby the person affirms and thereby predicates a meaningful premise encompassing a purpose* for the sake of which *behavior is then intended.*[69]

It can now be seen more clearly that the C portion of telosponsivity signifies that whatever meaning is premised (framed, assumed, believed in) is extended in a logical way rather than impelled along in a motile fashion. That is, in completing his college preparation for law school, Joe will be seen walking about the campus, attending classes, taking examinations, and so on. All of these behaviors flow from his purely mental plans which require him to carry out the plan of study he has affirmed. But these behaviors are mere instrumentalities on the side of *effects* done to accomplish the goal as framed in his premise. The premised (or predicated) meanings are the *cause(s)* of Joe's behavior. As in the case of all logical phenomenologies, the explanation of Joe's behavior is *not* related to time per se.

To round out our understanding of how meaning is extended and brought forward in behavior, we need some way of describing C without relying on an efficient-cause meaning. Rather than using the antecedent-consequent phrasing which traditional S-R psychology has used to describe events taking place one after the other, we will use the terms *precedent* (pre-cēē-dent) and *sequacious* (se-quā-shus) to capture the same progression, *but only on the C side of the telosponse conception* (5). Precedent-sequacious sequences refer to the *order* of meanings, with particular emphasis on the extension, development, or furtherance of a meaning in the logical sense of a syllogism.[70] Thus, a *precedent meaning* is one that goes before others in order or arrangement, as the major premise always precedes the minor premise in a syllogism framing its general meaning, so that the minor premise can only extend the mean-

ing of that which has gone before. If the major premise is "All people are mortal" and the minor premise is "This is a person," then we have a *necessary* extension to the conclusion of "This person is a mortal." In Chapter 4 we learned to call this kind of *necessary* outcome an instance of final-cause determination (p. 265). If we had said "This is an antelope" instead of "This is a person," we would not have expressed a minor premise at all. The original statement "All people are mortal" would therefore have failed to serve as a precedent meaning in the order of what is called deduction in logic.

While we are on this point, it should not be thought that precedent meanings are relevant only to deductions in human reasoning. We find similar circumstances obtaining in so-called induction, where by looking at many individual cases, we can abstract a commonality and frame some general precedent meaning that has even further implications for what might then take place. An epidemiologist, looking for the causes of some kind of disease in a particular area of the world, might look about carefully and isolate certain factors which, once they fall into place, imply through induction that some one factor is always present and hence might be a cause of the disease—an insect, a certain form of air pollution, or a manner of preparing certain types of foods. In looking for these various possibilities, the epidemiologist would be hypothesizing alternatives (1, 2, 3, 4, . . . N) on the A side of telosponsivity, but once he or she affirms "This is probably due to an infection from an insect," a precedent meaning is affirmed, which will *then* be brought forward in subsequent studies with a certainty. That is, the scientists who investigate this preliminary hunch will most certainly put it to test again and again.

This necessity in following out what is

framed by the premise B is what the term *sequacious* is driving at. A *sequacious meaning* is one that follows or flows from the meanings of precedents, extending them in a necessary sense (telic or final-cause determination). *Sequacious* bears the meaning of slavish compliance to what has gone before. In logic, it has been used to describe *logical necessity*. Recall from Chapter 4 (p. 264) that a logical proposition can be broken down into antecedent and consequent terms, as follows: "If a person (antecedent term), then a mortal being (consequent term)." There is no *necessary* relationship involved here, except only in the sense that "person" and "mortal" are tied together conceptually. We might have said "If a person, then a liar" or some such, and this obviously would not follow. Of course, no matter what we express

as a major premise, as long as we believe it —affirm it!—we can arrive at *necessary* conclusions. Assume we really believed "If a person, then a liar," and now confront a person standing before us. What follows? This person must also be a liar! It is this slavish compliance which certain meanings have on precedently held-to meanings that the word *sequacious* gets at. Given that the epidemiologist really believes that insects are involved in the illness, we can predict with certainty what he or she will be doing in the way of follow-up experiments. Given that Joe has really settled on a career in law, we can predict with certainty what sorts of courses he will be taking in undergraduate school. We may not be precise in these predictions, but we will narrow down the possibilities notably. We might now schematize the course of precedent-sequacious meaning-extension as follows:

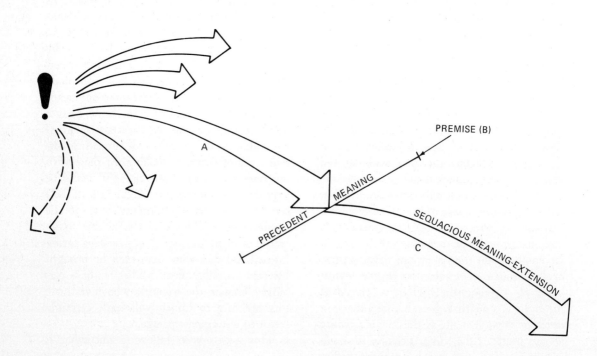

Figure 44   (5$_c$)

This refinement (5_c) permits us to appreciate that once the agent (!) has in fact affirmed a precedent meaning, it *follows necessarily* that this meaning will be brought forward into lived experience. We might say that before affirmation, on the A side of telosponsivity we have free selection of alternatives, but that following affirmation, on the C side we have 100 percent *psychic determinism* arising. Describing this sequence in terms of the popular telic conception known as *free will*, we could say that psychological freedom is on the A side and willful determination is on the C side of premise affirmation B. But even (5_c) does not clarify all that is required of a teleological construct. In order for a true final cause to be in operation, it must be possible for the agent (!) to (1) behave *arbitrarily,* and (2) *repredicate.* Both of these psychic actions must be capable of being done *at will*. If arbitrariness and repredication are not possible, then all we have here is another mediation conception. Predication is *not* mediation.

To behave arbitrarily means behaving according to shifting grounds. A person who claims one principle (reason, purpose) is in operation only to shift grounds in the face of some whim or other preference is behaving arbitrarily. The employer who claims that everyone in the company has an equal chance of promotion only to promote an unqualified son-in-law over others having the required skills and experience has behaved arbitrarily. This does not mean *without grounds*. A premise encompassing helping one's own or some such has taken precedence in this instance over a premise of open competition. This may be the only time the employer shifts grounds like this. But the arbitrariness of the action remains. In time, the employer may even repredicate the completely open-competition premise by modifying it to read "open, given certain special considerations for minority groups." In order to redress for past

wrongs in hiring practices, the employer may acknowledge that minorities like females, blacks, and so on, may be given certain advantages for a period of time. This would not be an arbitrary shift in grounds, but it would be a form of repredication "for the sake of which" people would be hired in the future.

The natural question arises: how do such mind-changings come about? Are they not the *effect* of changing circumstances in the social environment of the employer? Though the environment does indeed provide content meanings for our premises B, the way in which such changes come about need *not* be thought of in demonstrative terms—as being due to stimulus inputs causing these changes unidirectionally, as the effects of efficient causation. In line with Kant's original theory of cognition, we can view the telosponse as a conceptual interaction in which there is always a *transcendental dialectic* at play. This is schematized on p. 796 (5_d).

The (5_d) adaptation depicts that fact that with each affirmation B the agent (!) makes, there is an opposite meaning implied (not-B, non-B) *by definition*. In using *by definition,* we do not imply that this has to be framed in words. The person might essentially picture a course of action in the sense of "I'll do this" (B) yet have an immediate contradiction implied of the sort "I can't do this" or "I'll do [why not do] that [?]" (not-B). Thanks to this transcendent, self-reflexive capacity, the human telosponder has a constant sense of "decisions, decisions" to be made, and this in turn leads to considerable attention being devoted to the grounds or premises actually affirmed. The human ponders "Is this right?" or "What should I do?" and looks to various sources for a reliable sense of conviction on which to base a predi-

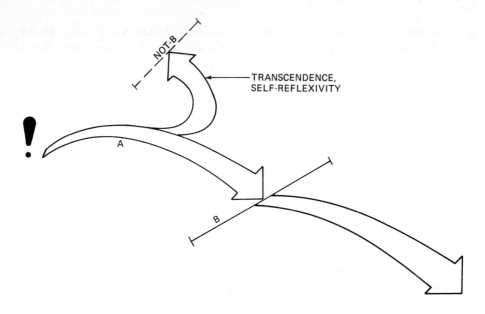

Figure 45   (5ₔ)

cation. Young children look to parents. Religionists look to their God. Scientists look to the hard facts of reality. Much of life becomes a quest for certainty in which grounds are sought that might give the best advantage to the telosponding organism. Social relations are obviously an important source of reassurance in this regard. It is comforting to look at things the way others do.

Viewed in this manner, human beings are not comfortable with change. Change or the chance occurrence is not something people naturally prefer. As Kelly taught us, people like to predict things with certainty and this means getting their grounds right. Mechanistic psychology's commitment to demonstrative formulations prejudices our thinking in the direction of "How do people change?" rather than "How do people remain so constant, given that they see alternatives so readily?" If we begin thinking of people as telosponders, we are at least equally interested in the latter question.

It is important to appreciate that the transcendence and self-reflexivity depicted in (5ₔ) is *not* the same thing as the feedback loop depicted in the (2ₑ) adaptation of the mediation model. Note in (2ₑ) that feedback returns as input that has in fact been output! The organism receiving input is being instructed as to what it is *literally* doing, which effectively keeps the drift of behavior from antecedent-to-consequent in an efficient-cause sense, because feedback is akin to any other type of stimulus input concerning what is *now taking place* in the environment or the social situation. We do not need an agent to decide, because there is never any "possibility" in this literally behaving succession of events. The robot does what it does and never ponders what it might possibly be doing otherwise.

The dialectically framed loop in (5ₔ) depicts a *possibility*—a transcendent alternative that is not now framed but that might be used as grounds in place of what is being affirmed. The fundamental decision in affirmation is always—as Hamlet put it—what will be (premised) and what will not be (premised). There are, of course, many possible ways in which *not* to do something that is about to be done or not to think something that is about to be thought. The (3$_a$) adaptation of the reciprocity construct could easily be combined with (5$_d$). That is, (3$_a$) is a kind of all-inclusive way of looking at behavior, and (5$_d$) is a detailed schematization of what could be taking place introspectively at P in the reciprocity construct. Self-reflexivity is not, as Bandura suggested, merely thoughts about thoughts. Self-reflexivity involves a deep recognition that we as human reasoners are a factor in what will be thought, believed in, and enacted behaviorally.

How well does the telosponse technical construct meet the needs of our personality theorists? Can we subsume meanings within it that the nontelic conceptions discussed above have been unable to encompass without distortion? Surely telosponsivity is what Freud had in mind as he framed his very first theory of ideas (B) and antithetic ideas (not-B), adapted later into the compromise models. The Freudian wish can only be stated in a telosponsive manner because it is something that the person wants to happen yet often does not want to happen, or fears that it will not really happen. The fact that Freud spoke of three points within the human psyche from which telosponses may be extended (id, ego, superego) does not disturb us if we are aware of the dialectical multiplicity that can be generated. There is nothing *dialectically illogical* about Freud's theory of mind. Adler's concept of the life plan or prototype depicted in Figure 8 (p. 130) is obviously an attempt to describe a lifelong premise "for the sake of which" behavior is sequaciously determined. It is true that Adler was not as dialectically oriented in his theories (especially later) as the other major psychoanalysts, but he did have room for the dialectic in his theory and would undoubtedly have welcomed the notion of telosponsivity.

Jung's treatment of the shadow side of mental life is very consonant with telosponsivity. The "not-B" meanings of life do not simply disappear. They coalesce into a total and live a life of their own as an alter ego in dialectical contrast to consciousness. Indeed, the very concept of unconscious behavior follows from a view of human reason as telosponsive, because there are always more alternatives to entertain in affirmation than can be brought to bear. It would be highly inefficient and even destructive to life for a person to be constantly reviewing every one of the possibilities open to him or her as life progresses. Even so, for various reasons that the psychoanalysts attempt to name, alternatives not considered, or considered and rejected, *do* continue to exert an influence in the psychic sphere. Finally, it should be appreciated that all *insight* therapies in the tradition of psychoanalysis rely on a telosponsive conception of the human being *as an agent* reframing or repredicating his or her life by reflexively turning back on what is now being premised to frame an alternative possibility and then in time making this a reality in lived experience.

This is equally true in the phenomenological-existentialistic outlooks. Surely Binswanger's world-designs and Kelly's personal constructs are best captured (subsumed) by the telosponsive technical construct. The case of Piaget is not quite so clear, but even he seems to be suggesting that the person uses initially reflexive patterns of behavior as grounds for framing other aspects of experience in a telosponsive fashion. Rogers and Boss also want to view the person as a telosponder, though their fundamentally sensory-phenomenological emphasis puts them into an extraspective frame of reference at one point in their theoretical development, which loses the explanatory power of telosponsivity (see p. 764). *Telosponsivity cannot be described extraspectively!* Of course, the basic thrust of the purity criticism on which Rogers and Boss rely to criticize the behaviorists and others is that modern science insists on premising the human being in precedent terminology suited to scientific requirements, but sequaciously forcing this reductive and/or mechanistic image onto people when it is inappropriate to do so.

Turning to the behaviorists, note that we have not proposed a technical construct for Skinner's operant-conditioning model. This is because it seems clear that he is *in fact* relying on the telosponse to describe behavior without knowing it. Skinner does not believe in agency, and he therefore dismisses as irrelevant all that takes place on the A side of the telosponse. But his theory of so-called operant responses issuing forward to create contingent circumstances of a positive or negative variety is marvelously well-suited to the notion of telosponsivity. Indeed, as we noted in Chapter 8 (p. 534), Skinner's contingency construct was taken from the theology of John Duns Scotus who was without doubt conceptualizing behavior telosponsively. Contingent circumstances, said Duns Scotus, arose because the person—in thinking about various possibilities before affirming an alternative—sequaciously *made them happen.* The moral person gave thought to what *ought* to be done and then enacted what he or she first premised as a moral line of be-

havior. More generally, we can say that *all* of the behavioristic theories must today confront the findings on awareness in conditioning (see pp. 474–477) and resolve the question, what does awareness really signify, and what better way than telosponsivity is there in which to conceptualize it?

If psychology were to adopt a concept of telosponsivity, thereby bringing the final cause back into the description of human behavior, it would surely benefit the science of humanity in the long run. Rather than trying to account for the telic themes of our personality theories in technical conceptions that simply *must* take away their basic meaning (like turning Freud's *wish* into a *cue-producing response*), we would legitimize the telic conception at its own level of description. For psychology to continue to grow as a science of human behavior, we will surely need to admit telosponsivity—or a concept like it—into our theoretical arsenal. Teleology was dismissed from traditional natural science for a good and proper reason. It was attributing unfounded and unprovable characteristics to natural phenomena, which were totally unnecessary to a scientific description of these phenomena. But psychology has been finding it quite impossible to capture all that there is to the human experience with teleology left out of the account. It is surely time for the legitimate concerns of an earlier century to be set aside in the interests of the equally legitimate concerns of our age.

What Motives to Therapy Are Primary in the Phenomenological Outlook?

The Scholarly Motive

Rogers does not think of therapy as the proper place in which to be testing hypotheses about human behavior. In therapy, we give ourselves over to our subjectivity. We allow the spontaneous patterns to emerge without feeling that they must fit some predetermined scientific scheme (purity criticism). Of course, this does not mean that science has no relevance to therapy. Speaking of the therapeutic experience, Rogers observes:

. . . I can abstract myself from the experience and look upon it as an observer, making myself and/or others the objects of that observation. . . . I make use of all the canons of science [in so abstracting myself]. A deeper understanding of therapy . . . may come from living it, or from observing it in accordance with the rules of science, or from the communication within the self between the two types of experience.[71]

Note Rogers's implicit understanding of theory versus method in this insightful statement. The main danger, Rogers is reminding us, is to confuse the extraspective *observation* of therapy with the introspective happening of therapy. Hence, though Rogers did considerable work of a scholarly nature on the process and outcome of client-centered therapy, he never considered the therapeutic relationship itself to be a proper methodology in the sense of Freudian psychoanalysis.[72]

Though the existentialists were critical of the Freudian reductive explanation, they were not as reluctant to think of therapy as a methodology as was Rogers. Binswanger noted that: ". . . in the mental diseases we face modifications of the fundamental or essential structure and of the structural links of being-in-the-world as transcendence. It is one of the tasks of psychiatry to investigate and establish these variations in a scientifically exact way."[73] Binswanger argued that there were really two types of scientific knowledge. The *discursive inductive* variety describes, explains, and controls natural events, whereas the *phenomenological empirical* variety critically and methodically ex-

plores phenomenal contents in their own realm.[74] It is typical of natural science to separate experience, breaking it up into pieces rather than capturing it as a phenomenal totality. In doing so, the natural scientist fails to appreciate that phenomenological empirical knowledge is distorted when it is made to conform to discursive inductive principles. The greatest error of natural science is that of *"interpreting existence as natural history."*[75]

To force an inappropriate terminology onto Dasein in this fashion can only result in the poorest form of scientific knowledge, a distortion of cataclysmic proportions. The lower animal will never transcend experience in the way that we human beings do; hence, what is the use of describing our behavior as the behaviorists do?[76] Animals are *in* nature and can never remove themselves from the natural science description. The human being is often above or beyond nature, bending nature to the willful aspirations of his or her transcending possibilities. We see in this line of argument a reflection of the purity criticism, which plays such a central role in existential philosophy as well as in existential analysis. Here is an excellent example of this polemic, taken from Boss:

It is fortunate that Daseinsanalytic thinking does not require us to accept a ready-made conceptual framework and to learn it by heart. On the contrary, analysis of Dasein urges all those who deal with human beings to start seeing and thinking from the beginning, so that they can remain with what they immediately perceive and do not get lost in "scientific" abstractions, derivations, explanations, and calculations estranged from the immediate reality of the given phenomena. It is of paramount importance to realize from the start that the fundamental difference which separates the natural science from the Daseinsanalytic of existential science of man is to be found right here.[77]

Despite such worthy criticisms of the biases of natural science, the existentialists do not escape a heavy reliance on procedural evidence in their theory of knowledge.[78] To speak of a phenomenal reality is to speak of the plausible assumptions, biases, and so forth, that guide thought. A world-view or world-design is nestled into place by procedural evidence. The existentialists might argue that a belief in something like procedural evidence is itself a world-design and hence requires further explication to see what a priori ontological structures frame this view of experience.

But all this serves to demonstrate is that ultimately the *basis* for deciding what is *the* beginning of thought, vision, awareness, and so on, must ever rest on *someone's* plausibility. And just how pure can anyone be in this regard? When one of his male clients spoke of feeling ashamed every time he sensed a gentleness in his nature, Boss retorted as follows: ". . . each time he confessed to his shame of these gentler feelings, we confined ourselves to asking him whether there was any need actually to feel so ashamed of them."[79] Is not Boss here—dialectically via qualitative motion—challenging the phenomenal truth of the client's Dasein? He *does* feel shame. It is of course possible for him *not* to feel shame. By asking him questions in this fashion, do we not raise possibilities for him to consider, turn over in his mind, and eventually embrace as an alternative phenomenal reality (reconstrue, repredicate, and so on)? Boss goes on to say that the stern attitude of this client had been taken over

from his father, but "it took weeks for him to realize, under the consistently kindly and reassuring guidance of the analyst, that the dislike of and contempt for feeling which dominated his parents' world was not universally valid."[80] Without in any way challenging the truth of this statement, we might ask of Boss just how far has he alienated this client from *his* subjective, phenomenal reality?

This, of course, is the reason for science. It is flatly unacceptable to rest with plausibilities of this nature—even if they are subjectively true. Science speaks beyond the individual, true enough, but this in itself does not demand that its terminology be destructive of phenomenal truth (see our analysis of telosponsivity above). Variations on the common or objective themes of knowledge will always occur, and they must be appreciated as worthwhile items of knowledge. What science aims to do is to decide what are the common factors and what are the variations. It should also appreciate that variations may become the common trend over time and vice versa. Scientific knowledge is alienated knowledge only when that openness that is an integral part of science has been closed. New data, new ideas: these are the essentials of a vital science. This may require adaptations in thought, the reintroduction of teleologies, and so on, as the existentialists themselves call for. But only if we assume from the outset that *the* subjective truth exists someplace—in a phenomenal Garden of Eden unique to each person's Dasein—can we presume that *all* objective knowledge must of necessity become alienated (purity criticism) from subjective description.

Kelly spent the major part of his career trying to bring clinical psychology as a profession into the realm of knowledge known as science. Clinical psychology was thus to be considered a basic science.[81] Kelly emphasized that so far as he was concerned: "I have very little interest in applied psychology. . . . for me the most exciting experimental situation is the therapy room." [82] If every person is a scientist and a theorist, then it would follow that life—even a life fouled by neurosis—would lend itself to study in terms of how the human being enacting it perceived and predicted events.[83] It was therefore important for all therapists practicing in the name of the psychology of personal constructs to prepare themselves in the fundamentals of science. "It seems to me that the extensive training of therapists in theory and technique only, and failing to demonstrate scientific methodology as an actual interview-room procedure, is itself unethical." [84]

Kelly's scholarly motive was therefore rather prominent in his approach to the client, though it was not of paramount importance. Kelly believed with great conviction that in order to know people we must get intimately close to them and this in turn is most possible in a therapeutic contact.[85] The greatest mistake one could make is to feel that the therapy room and the experimental room were based on mere analogy: "We believe there is a fundamental similarity. The discoveries one makes in therapy are similar to the discoveries one makes in the laboratory or in the field." [86]

In pressing his case so adamantly and colorfully, Kelly inspires admiration in those of us who would prefer a more humanistic psychology. Yet in terms of theory-construction factors, it seems clear that he, like the existentialists, confounded procedural with validating evidence. Kelly's definition of validation is as follows: "A person commits himself to anticipating a particular event. If it takes place, his anticipation is validated. If it fails to take place, his anticipation is invalidated. Validation represents the compatibility (subjectively construed) between one's prediction and the outcome he observes. Invalidation represents incompatibility (subjectively construed) between one's prediction

and the outcome he observes." [87] This definition of validation would fit our control-and-prediction definition (see p. 25) if it were not for the fact that controls in the life situation are always less certain than controls in the laboratory, and it is always possible for the person in the life situation to recall past "predictions" in a way suitable to his or her present desires (intentions, hopes, purposes). Kelly actually said it most succinctly himself, although he seemed little concerned about this very likely outcome to validation in the life setting:

One's anticipation of a future incident is scarcely more than a plotted position within a system of personal constructs. If subsequent observations made within the same system seem to coincide with the forecasted plot, one may say, within the referents of his system, that his anticipation has been confirmed. Later, of course, he may devise other reference axes against which the occurrence may take on new meaning. Then he may wonder if what happened is what he would have anticipated if he had been using the new reference axes at the time he made his original forecast. But this is a question he can scarcely hope to answer. The best he can do is make another forecast, this time in terms of his augmented dimensional system.[88]

Since it is up to the individual to decide what his or her past predictions "really were" and since it is no great problem for us to shift the grounds on the basis of which we now evaluate or to realign our constructs with the evidence now emerging, this process described by Kelly is surely fraught with potential error. Procedural evidence plays a much greater—often exclusive—role in the validations of the life setting than it plays in the validations of the laboratory. Kelly has noted that "group expectancies operate as validators of personal constructs."[89] In the laboratory or any similarly well-designed experiment, what the group expects—even if this group is the scientific community—is of no consequence to the outcome of the hypothesis under test. Hence it is of questionable value to draw such direct parallels as Kelly does between the laboratory and the consulting room.

The Ethical Motive

Rogers is above all an ethical thinker. He makes his strongest case and leaves the greatest impression when he speaks of the interpersonal phoniness, insincerity, and manipulation among people. The emphasis on values, the subjectivity of experience, and the absolute necessity for allowing people the freedom to be what they are all add up to an ethical philosophy of life, one that we might term the ethics of existential freedom. This is why Rogers focuses so on the therapist rather than the client. He does not wish to tell people what they ought to be like in order to find the good life. He *does* wish to find out and then tell therapists what is required of them in order to facilitate the good life in their clients' experience. Invariably, this instruction in how to cure comes down to a series of ethical pronouncements: accept, show regard for others, be congruent, and so forth.

Note that Rogers insists that one cannot simply "affect" these prescriptions. These are not instrumentalities or techniques for the more efficient manipulation of a client. One either *is* this sort of person intrinsically or one *is not*.[90] And if not, then one will never prove a helpful therapist. Recall from Chapter 9 that Rogerian ethics are intrinsic and not instrumental (p. 599). In a sense, it is more

true for client-centered therapy than any other approach that therapists are either spontaneously made—they acquire the proper attitudes through living—or they are simply not therapists. Rogers could not teach others to be accepting or congruent; he could simply show through studies that attitudes like these promote constructive changes in neurotic clients seeking to be cured of nagging conditions.

The well-publicized debate with Skinner in 1956 centered on this issue of intrinsic versus instrumental values.[91] Is not the therapist's attitude merely one of the intervening factors (variables, when studied empirically) that come between the client and his or her environment and that can therefore be used as a manipulative technique? Do we not as therapists subtly and covertly influence our clients to talk the way we want them to talk by reinforcing (operantly or whatever) what we want in our show of interest, the nodding of our head, or our saying of "mmm hmm"? Rogers staunchly denied these allegations, and his denial takes on particular relevance because if he *were to manipulate* a client in this manner, he would be *violating* his intrinsic ethic of existential freedom. Hence, we find him arguing as follows:

Here is the answer to those who question, "Isn't client-centered therapy really directive, because the counselor selects the elements he will respond to, and thus subtly guides the client toward certain areas and certain goals?" As indicated here, if the attitude of the therapist is to follow the client's lead, the client not only perceives this, but is quick to correct the counselor when he gets off the track, and comfortable in doing so.[92]

In short, Rogers argued that though he might indeed influence his client through subtleties, by keeping the relationship open and without facade, he could make this control *two-way*. Not only the therapist but the client can contribute to the controls being exerted in the relationship. And not only the client but the therapist will be affected by such controls. We might make this view clearer by imagining one therapist proceeding on the following value basis: "It is right and good that I, as a psychotherapist, with certain knowledge and training, make decisions for others, and consciously, deliberately influence others' behavior in ways that my researches tell me are good ways, correct ways, or at the very least, usual ways of behaving." A behavior therapist might take such a view, and this would be a good example of an *instrumental* ethic. But another therapist, possibly a Rogerian, would proceed on the following value assumption: "It is right and good that I should try, as best I can, to refrain from making decisions for my clients, even though I realize that social conventions, the force of my personality, and my personal values may very well exert a selective influence on them as we move along; in fact, when appropriate, I intend to bring up all of this and talk it over with them." [93]

Now, when critics ask "Doesn't the client-centered therapist have *goals* in mind, which he or she specifically aims for?" a psychologist of this approach can freely admit to an intrinsically ethical goal of existential freedom. There are goals, and then there are goals! By striving to attain this form of open, free, self-enlarging relationship, client-centered therapists need not press their selective goals on the client anymore than clients press goals onto them. There is no covert manipulation in this goal-striving attempt of the therapists. We can speak of controlling the client here only in the sense of a language of description or possibly as a theory of knowledge. But control as a method of social influence has been specifically negated in this intrinsically ethical pronouncement (see pp. 599 and 600).

The existentialists emphasize the ethical motive to therapy, as witnessed by their call for a commitment to life and a willingness to accept responsibility for one's behavior. Boss probably leaned a bit more in this direction than did Binswanger, who probably leaned more toward the scholarly motive. It is no accident that Kierkegaard studied for the ministry, was a very devout human being personally, and was primarily responsible for founding a philosophy of personal commitment and responsibility. These themes have remained with the existential thinkers, even those who have since lost a belief in a Supreme Being. Hence, like Adlerian psychology, existentialism has struck some readers as excessively moralistic.

The insight of existentialism is that the person, being capable of formulating a possibility in light of what now exists, must of necessity be capable of *evaluating* which of the present circumstances needs improving in Dasein. We humans can sense immediately what is best or right or proper in awareness because this is our nature. And with this judgmental evaluation, the "oughts" begin taking form in our Dasein: things ought to be improved, we ought not treat other people in this or that fashion, we ought to do our best, and so on. Here we have the nagging of conscience. The existentialists, however, view the conscience as coaxing people to their greatest acts of humanity, rather than enslaving them in throes of guilt. Freud and the behaviorists would have our ethical values being deflected into our identity following birth by way of toilet-training routines or the reinforcement schedules of parental figures, but the real truth is that our morality is based on an a priori capacity to judge all that comes into our awareness. "Mankind's ethics becomes self-evident on this basis of such an understanding of man's essence. No so-called ethical values need be added *a posteriori*." [94]

Hence, the existentialistic cure of neurosis is heavily tinged with ethical considerations. The neurotic is a person who has given in to a narrowed existence, a thrown Dasein in which possibilities open to him or her are not being affirmed. Therapists help their clients to regain a foothold in life. Through the relationship, the client begins to exercise those "oughts" which have slipped by unaffirmed in the past. He or she looks at this side and that side of existence, reasons to the opposite of a maladaptive given of today and projects the counterbalancing pattern that can set things straight tomorrow. The client begins to live again, to grow again, and to accept the succeeding beckoning goals of the forward-pitched Dasein, reaching into the future where life is constantly unfolding.

Kelly's commitment to ethical considerations was probably the least of his reasons for entering the consulting room. He was not deaf to the obvious role that guilt, feelings of sin—that is, loss of role factors—played in the etiology of mental illness. He once said of those who rely exclusively on disease models of abnormality that they were avoiding: ". . . moral judgments where their patients are concerned. They end up making medical judgments instead!" [95] Nor did Kelly reject religious devotion and belief as one aspect of a person's perfectly normal and healthy behavioral side. [96] What he did reject in religious observation was what he took to be its magical features. [97] Any person who accepts the challenges of life runs the risk of sinning, of falling out of role and suffering guilt as a consequence. [98] Kelly felt that too often a nonsinner is nothing more than a flaccid personality, an individual who lacks

the personal courage to take risks and to engage in life aggressively.

The problem with moralistic theory is that it begins to pre-empt and to reify moral behavior, so that it eclipses the spontaneous side to life. Kelly had observed the chest-beating confessions of both Catholic and communist peoples in his time, and he found that all such efforts were suppressive of individuality and basically counterproductive. [99] In the final analysis, the search for good and evil is a personal quest, not something to be dictated by doctrinaire, impermeable formulations. This is why it is so important to think of the human being as controlling rather than as controlled. Those who wish to manipulate behavior, no matter how scientifically, invariably fall into the impermeable trap of the moralists. They must choose *for* their subjects of control. Kelly said that it took him a long time to realize that his clients were just as capable of deciding for themselves as he was of deciding for them how they might conduct their lives. [100] He thought only a psychopathic person could take the behavior-manipulation thesis seriously. [101] Though he did not state it as such, this is surely an ethical question and just as relevant for Kelly as it was for Rogers and the existentialists.

The Curative Motive

The motive to help others, to remove their self-distortions, and to help set them back on the spontaneous, natural track in life is surely quite prominent in Rogerian theory. However, there is a definite way in which this must be accomplished. Hence, strictly speaking, the Rogerian curative cannot be divorced from the ethical motivation we have already considered. The same goes for the existentialists. Once a man has begun affirming his possibilities and meeting the "oughts" of existence, he is on the way to health. For both Rogers and the existentialists, this client achieves his own cure, and will continue to take over the reins of his life when he leaves therapy.

Kelly attached more significance to the curative motive per se in his writings. He once said that he specifically invented his theory in order to assist psychotherapists.[102] We would conclude that this motive was probably on a par to the scholarly in his thinking about therapy. As he said of the client: "When a client comes to a psychologist for assistance he usually, though not always, believes there is a chance that he can be helped. The psychologist, in accepting him as a client, necessarily concurs in this hope."[103] We enter therapy to accomplish things for our clients.[104] Kelly was not even opposed to a symptomatic approach to therapy, feeling that often basic changes in personality will flow after we have alleviated the presenting symptom.[105] Unfortunately, the therapist sometimes becomes more interested in the details of his or her professional constructions than in the personal constructions of the client, leading to an ignoring of complaints and consequent misery for the client.[106] Kelly's feelings about such egocentric therapist practices speak for themselves. He greatly appreciated curative motives—possibly more than the scholarly at this point—when he observed that: ". . . the clinical psychologist is in the process of developing hypotheses as he goes along, and . . . the emphasis of the method is on formulating appropriate questions whose answers may have relevance to the client's difficulty, rather than on extracting definitive answers to irrelevant questions [that is, trying to prove one's own professional construction system]."[107]

Summary

A common objection raised by phenomenologists against other personologists is that they tend to distort the very phenomena they have set out to explain by bringing to bear questionable assumptions in their explanations. The psychoanalysts want to bring everything back to childhood, and the behaviorists want to reduce phenomenal awareness to underlying chemical or motoric forces. This tendency to bring questionable assumptions to bear which in turn distort a pure description of phenomenal events is called the purity criticism. Phenomenologists always seek to capture the subjectively unique in behavior, and rather than use the term *objectivity,* they would prefer to emphasize the fact that all agreed-upon knowledge is actually based on intersubjectivity. Because of such criticisms, it is believed by many in psychology today that phenomenological theories cannot be validated. Chapter 12 dispels this erroneous belief, noting that objective-idealistic views are just as amenable to the research method as objective-realistic views. Phenomenology has a large measure of idealism in its conceptualizations. Of course, some existentialists like Boss do effectively arrive at a subjectivism, and in this case, it is difficult to see how it would be possible to validate their claims. But the other phenomenologists— Rogers, Binswanger, Piaget, Kelly—presented theoretical constructs that are amenable to empirical definition and hence are surely capable of being validated.

Chapter 12 next considers the construct of interaction, with a view to understanding the ways in which phenomenal and noumenal experience may be said to interrelate. It is soon clear that there are several ways in which the construct of interaction has been used in psychology. There is a conceptual form of interaction, in which an interdependence is said to occur between a mental scheme and some independent set of circumstances which can both take influence from and yet influence the framing scheme. The second usage concerns an evolutionary inter-action, drawn from the Darwinian idea that human beings act on and are in turn acted upon by their physicobiological and social milieus. The third and last usage is statistical interaction, which combines two or more variables as measured and tracked in an em-pirical investigation to show that the effects of one on the other(s)—and vice versa—varies in a unique fashion. The lesson to be learned in this breakdown of interaction con-cepts is that, even though we may find sta-tistical interaction taking place between two or more variables of our experiments, this does *not* mean that we have found either a conceptual or an evolutionary interaction in the experimental results. Our theoretical in-terpretation of these findings, which must take the course of either a conceptual or an evolutionary interaction, is not itself ac-counted for by the purely statistical interac-tion which is observed.

Chapter 12 next draws a distinction be-tween sensory and logical phenomenology. Sensory phenomenology, as witnessed in ge-stalt psychology, focuses on how knowledge is constructed out of the inarticulated sensory input. Noumenal experience is noise until it is articulated and differentiated via the laws of organization into a patterned gestalt. Tran-scendence is not an obvious feature of sensory phenomenology. Field-theory explanations as witnessed in Lewin or Rogers reflect a sen-sory phenomenology. Boss's suggestion that the Dasein luminates spontaneously is also suggestive of this interpretation of phenome-nology. Beginning with the same Kantian as-sumptions used by sensory phenomenologists, the logical phenomenologist focuses more on the conceptualizing role of a priori factors than on the ordering of initial input at the level of sensory receptors. Kant had sensation

ordered according to time and space. But then, in the major thrust of Kantian con-ceptual theory, a logical (ordered, patterned) conceptualization was brought to bear in the sense of a conceptual interaction. Jung's archetype, Binswanger's world-designs, and Kelly's personal constructs all reflected a logical phenomenology. Logical phenome-nologists are more likely to accept dialectical reasoning, hence transcendence and self-re-flexivity are naturally encompassed in their views.

Chapter 12 next contrasts Piaget's with Kelly's use of constructivism. Kelly always clearly placed construction on the side of the human being as selector, chooser, program-mer of the process that goes forward in logi-cal development. Kelly's future orientation and introspective concept of subsumption give us a clear, logical-phenomenological in-terpretation of construction. Kelly had the construct framing and hence lending mean-ing to experience from above (that is, from overriding mental conception *to* what is be-ing conceptualized). Piaget lacks this com-mitment to finalistic theories, and he does not focus specifically on what the person brings forward as a predication "for the sake of which" behavior is intended. Piaget uses the idea of assimilation instead of subsump-tion. Assimilation can be thought of extraspec-tively, and its tie to a logical phenomenology is uncertain. Assimilation merely highlights the process of taking-in, and this can be conceived of extraspectively as a completely automatic (nonintentional), essentially pas-sive process. Piaget's emphasis in construc-tion is on the "adding to" or "becoming de-velopmentally more complex" intonation of constructivism. Kelly is thus emphasizing how things are set in a context and Piaget is emphasizing how things or thoughts are built-up. This is why we suggest that Piaget has an element of Lockean constitutive ex-planation in his approach which distinguishes him somewhat from the purer Kantianism of Kelly.

The question of time is analyzed to show that the gestaltists were trying to explain behavior without consideration of time's passage—*within* time, so to speak. Time conceptions rely on efficient causation, conceived of as an antecedent event impelling a consequent event along in the sense of a locomotion. But gestalt and related phenomenological viewpoints conceive of behavior as being due to formal-cause factors—that is, altering patterns in the sense of qualitative change. Modern physics makes use of such formal-cause explanations as well. Kelly's constructs and Binswanger's world-designs are also patterns existing *within* time, and when acted on—that is, behavior is carried out "for the sake of" (final cause) these patterns—can lead to changes in behavior of a telic nature.

The matter is discussed of whether or not psychology has used theoretical terminology which is adequate to a description and explanation of teleological behavior. A series of five technical constructs are schematized and discussed in light of the book's contents: stimulus-response, mediation, reciprocity, figure-ground, and telosponse. The telosponse is introduced by the author as a viable alternative to the other four constructs, all of which are nontelic conceptions. A telosponse is a mental act in which the person takes on (predicates, premises) a meaningful item (image, language term, judgment, and so on) relating to a referent acting as a purpose "for the sake of which" behavior is then intended. Telosponsive behavior is done "for the sake of" grounds (purposes, reasons) rather than "in response to" stimulation. The grounds act as a precedent meaning in that they occur first in logical order. Meanings that flow from such assumptive grounds are said to extend in a sequacious manner—that is, following logical necessity in the same way as psychic (hard) determinism was described

by Freud as taking place. Telosponsivity contrasts with responsivity in that there is always a recognition through the use of transcendental dialectical reasoning that something *other* than what is taking place could possibly be taking place. Whereas responsivity lacks such arbitrariness, the telosponding human being can in fact see Kellyian alternatives in life's choices. Though not every alternative can be enacted, mentation always presents the human being with more possibilities than he or she might prefer having to contemplate. Hence, telosponsivity lays the groundwork for active agency in the description of behavior, and enables the basically telic nature of concepts like Adler's prototype, Jung's archetype, or Binswanger's world-design to be expressed at their own level. No reduction to or distortion of these useful personality terms is required if we but accept the possibility that human behavior is telosponsive as well as responsive.

Chapter 12 ends with a consideration of the motives to therapy in the phenomenological tradition. Rogers did not think of therapy as the proper place to be testing hypotheses about human behavior. Research on therapy itself may be appropriate, but Rogers was more concerned with curing the client, and more than any other of the phenomenological therapists, with doing so by way of a certain ethical stance in relation to the client. Rogers's naturalistic ethic surely ranks first in his hierarchy of motives to therapy. The existentialists too are distrustful of using the therapy hour as a scholarly medium, since invariably the client seems to be wound into the premised assumptions of the therapist (purity criticism). Though Kelly was as committed as the other phenomenologists on the curative dimension, he felt that the nature of the curative process could be similar to the process followed in any scientific investigation. Hence, he had the highest scholarly motive of the phenomenologists. He probably had the lowest ethical motive. The existentialists are heavily committed to the ethical motive, which they relate more closely to curative motives than Kelly did, but probably less so than Rogers. Overall, the leading motive to therapy in the phenomenological tradition is probably the curative, with ethical a close second, and (except for Kelly) scholarly taking the lowest position.

Outline of Important Theoretical Constructs

Can a phenomenological theory be objectively validated?
purity criticism · intersubjectivity as objectivity · objective idealism · realistic subjectivism

How do the phenomenal and noumenal realms interact, interrelate, or otherwise combine in the formation of knowledge? dualism versus monism · reciprocal interaction · conceptual interaction · evolutionary interaction · statistical interaction · sensory versus logical phenomenology · Piagetian versus Kellyian constructivism · subsumption versus assimilation

Is it essential to describe behavior as taking place over time?
life space · phenomenal field · time as pattern

Does psychology have adequate terminology to account for teleological behavior, and if not what is called for?
technical constructs · stimulus-response · mediation · cognitive map · cue-producing responses · feedback · reci-

procity · introspective versus extraspective reciprocity · figure-ground · introspective versus extraspective figure-ground relations · telosponse · predication · affirmation · premise · active agency · intention versus purpose · precedent meaning · sequacious meaning · precedent-sequacious meaning-extension · logical necessity · psychic determinism · free will · arbitrariness · re-predication · transcendental dialectic · self-reflexivity · possibilities in mentation

What motives to therapy are primary in the phenomenological outlook?

The scholarly motive

The ethical motive

The curative motive

Notes

1. Hegel, 1952, pp. 19–20. **2.** Rychlak, 1968, p. 390. **3.** Rogers, 1961, pp. 212–213. **4.** See, e.g., Giorgi, 1970. **5.** Rogers, 1951, p. 485. **6.** Rogers, 1959, p. 192. **7.** Cassirer, 1950, p. 93. **8.** Boss, 1963, p. 51. **9.** Ibid., pp. 52, 84. **10.** Ibid., pp. 29–30. **11.** Piaget, 1970b, p. 15. **12.** Piaget, 1955, p. 189. **13.** Kelly, 1969, p. 47. **14.** Ibid., p. 210. **15.** Ibid., p. 25. **16.** Evans, 1973, p. 20. **17.** Kant, 1952, p. 14. **18.** Ibid. **19.** Evans, 1973, p. 20. **20.** Russell, 1959, p. 241. **21.** Gruber, 1974, p. 459. **22.** Ibid. **23.** Ibid., p. 235. **24.** Bowers, 1973. **25.** See Rychlak, 1977, p. 36. **26.** Russell, 1959, p. 241. **27.** Rogers, 1970f, p. 44. **28.** Rogers, 1961, p. 22. **29.** Jung, Vol. 7, p. 64. **30.** Jung, Vol. 11, p. 5. **31.** Binswanger, 1958, p. 302. **32.** Kelly, 1969, p. 40. **33.** Binswanger, 1963, p. 313. **34.** Binswanger, 1958, p. 338. **35.** Kelly, 1955a, p. 109. **36.** Kelly, 1969, p. 11. **37.** Kelly, 1970, p. 37. **38.** Kelly, 1969, p. 47. **39.** Kelly, 1955b, pp. 752–753. **40.** Piaget, 1962, p. 153. **41.** Piaget, 1967, p. 102. **42.** Ibid., p. 103. **43.** Piaget, 1962, p. 171. **44.** Piaget, 1970a, p 112. **45.** Rogers, 1959, p. 189. **46.** Bohr, 1934, p. 54. **47.** Gross, 1961 p. 288. **48.** Locke, 1952, p. 128. **49.** Neisser, 1967.

50. Ibid., p. 116. **51.** Bandura, 1978, p. 345. **52.** Ibid. **53.** Bandura, 1979, p. 440. **54.** Bandura, 1978, p. 345 and p. 351. **55.** Bandura, 1979, p. 439. **56.** Ibid., p. 440. **57.** Ibid. **58.** Ibid. **59.** Köhler, 1961b, p. 210. **60.** Koffka, 1935, pp. 417–421. **61.** Marrow, 1969, p. 77. **62.** Wertheimer, 1945, p. 215. **63.** Ibid., pp. 11–12. **64.** Ibid., p. 62. **65.** Koffka, 1935, p. 98. **66.** Ibid., p. 319. **67.** Rychlak, 1977, see esp. Chp. 7. **68.** Ibid., p. 285. **69.** Ibid., p. 283. **70.** Ibid., p. 288. **71.** Rogers, 1961, p. 278. **72.** Rogers, and Dymond, 1954; Rogers, Gendlin, Kiesler, and Truax, 1967. **73.** Binswanger, 1958, p. 194. **74.** Ibid., p. 192. **75.** Binswanger, 1963, p. 175. **76.** Binswanger, 1958, pp. 197–198. **77.** Boss, 1963, pp. 29–30. **78.** Ibid., p. 201. **79.** Ibid., p. 198. **80.** Ibid. **81.** Kelly, 1955a, p. 400. **82.** Kelly, 1969, p. 154. **83.** Kelly, 1955b, p. 605. **84.** Kelly, 1969, p. 53. **85.** Ibid., p. 215. **86.** Kelly, 1955b, p. 1123. **87.** Kelly, 1955a, p. 158. **88.** Kelly, 1969, p. 32. **89.** Kelly, 1955a, p. 176. **90.** Rogers, 1951, pp. 21–22. **91.** Rogers and Skinner, 1956. **92.** Rogers, 1951, p. 113. **93.** Rychlak, 1968, pp. 143–144. **94.** Boss, 1963, p. 271. **95.** Kelly, 1969, p. 171. **96.** Kelly, 1955a, p. 127. **97.** Kelly, 1955b, p. 1076. **98.** Kelly, 1969, p. 11. **99.** Ibid., p. 187. **100.** Ibid., p. 18. **101.** Kelly, 1970, p. 55. **102.** Kelly, 1955a, p. 12. **103.** Kelly, 1955b, p. 611. **104.** Kelly, 1969, p. 221. **105.** Kelly, 1955b, pp. 995–996. **106.** Ibid., p. 831. **107.** Kelly, 1955a, pp. 192–193.

Glossary

Abstractive Cognition based on Ockham's writings, this is the higher-order mental process that takes information from the lower-order, intuitive cognition in order to create ideas and thoughts. This style of explanation is compatible with the Lockean model. *See also:* Intuitive cognition, Lockean model.

Accidental Change Aristotle's term for changes due to progressive differences or degrees of change called locomotion, qualitative, or quantitative change. *See also:* Local motion, Qualitative motion, Quantitative motion.

Actuarial relating to statistical predictions. An actuary is one who calculates probabilities of occurrence based on empirical samplings of behavior, incidence of some characteristic in a population, etc.

Affirmation to accept as the case, or fix as grounds, some meaning in the act of predicating or premising. Affirming something is essentially saying "this is what we know to be taking place" or "this is given and no longer open to doubt." *See also:* Affirming the consequent, Ground, Predication.

Affirming the Consequent a logical error growing out of an "if, then" course of reasoning. It takes place when we reason "If A then B" and subsequently affirm B to conclude "Therefore A." In science, it arises when we reason "If my theory is true, then my experimental data will array as predicted" and subsequently affirm "My experimental data array as predicted" to conclude "Therefore, my theory is [necessarily] true." The latter conclusion is technically incorrect: the theory is "true" with the proviso that an alternative theory might *in principle* also be validated by the observed data. *See also:* Affirmation.

Agent, Agency the view holding that an identity factor enters into behavior, so that the individual may be said to direct (determine) his or her own behavior—at least to some extent. Agency theories are framed from the introspective perspective and rely on final-cause descriptive terminology. As such, they are teleologies. *See also:* Final cause, Introspective perspective, Teleology.

Antecedent in traditional stimulus-response psychology, this is the event occurring first in time—usually said to be the stimulus but also confounded with the independent variable—that supposedly efficiently caused the consequent event. This is not to be confused with the antecedent term of an "if, then" proposition. *See also:* Antecedent term of "if, then" proposition, Consequent, Efficient cause.

Antecedent Term of "If, Then" Proposition in any "If A then B" proposition or course of reasoning, the A term is called the antecedent. *See also:* Affirming the consequent, Consequent term of "if, then," proposition.

Anthropomorphize to frame a theory in humanlike (teleological) description when it is wrong or at least questionable to do so. When we see humanlike tendencies in our household pets, we are anthropomorphizing. *See also:* Teleology.

Antithesis the statement, position, point of view, argument, etc., advanced in opposition to a thesis. *See also:* Dialectical meaning, Synthesis, Thesis.

Antithetic Idea(s) a concept employed by Freud in his first theory of the neuroses. It is readily subsumed by a dialectical metatheory. *See also:* Dialectical meaning.

A Priori meaning(s) that is (are) presumptive, coming beforehand, and therefore taken as ground for subsequent understanding without question or proper examination. *See also:* Affirmation, Ground, Pro forma.

Arbitrary, Arbitrariness shifting at will the grounds "for the sake of which" behavior is intended or an item of understanding is known. Arbitrariness can result in contradiction and inconsistency, but it is also how creative alternatives are made possible. *See also:* Ground.

Arguments from Definition logical cases that flow necessarily or sequaciously, once we accept the precedent meanings as framed by our definitions. If withholding funds is akin to withholding fecal matter in toilet-training and hence suggestive of anal traits, then anyone who behaves conservatively in the expenditure of funds is reflecting anality. If we accept the definition of anal behavior, we must accept an example that is encompassed by these definitions. *See also:* Sequacious.

Awareness, of Experimental Subjects the widespread finding that psychological experiments, such as conditioning procedures, do not lead to positive results unless the subjects being studied perceive the experimental design and thereby intentionally comply with what is called for.

Behavior a global reference to the overt and covert activities of organisms, including the various physiological and biological functions of life. Behavioral descriptions in psychology vary: some employ predominantly material- and efficient-cause meanings, and others introduce the formal- and final-cause as equally important.

Bipolarity the view that some meaningful relations are dual by nature, as in the case of opposite meanings. Rather than being two separate meanings united, opposites may be thought of as intrinsically bipolar so that *left* necessarily implies, hence means at one point, *right*. We cannot understand one pole (left) without understanding the other (right). *See also:* Dialectic, Meaning, Multipolarity, Unipolarity.

British Empiricism a philosophical school of thought emphasizing that all knowledge must be based on observable things and events. Psychology has been primarily shaped by this philosophy, which is virtually identical to the meanings subsumed by the Lockean model. *See also:* Lockean model.

Cartesian Geometry and Locomotion defined the geometric patterns (formal-cause conceptions) in terms of moving points as opposed to the fixed points of Euclidean geometry. This paved the way for Newtonian mechanics. *See also:* Locomotion.

Categories of the Understanding in Kantian philosophy, the a priori mental patterns brought to bear in pro forma fashion to organize noumenal experience into cognizable meanings. *See also:* A priori, Pro forma.

Causal-Mechanistic vs. Final-Energic the language Jung selected to differentiate between efficient-cause theories and the more telic style of explanation in which he was interested.

Cause(s) concept originating with Aristotle to account for the nature of things and behaviors. There are four basic types of causes

—that is, material, efficient, formal, and final —and by using meanings as universal models, we can better understand the common knowledge we have of everything in our experience, including the behavior of people. *See also:* Efficient cause, Final cause, Formal cause, Material cause.

Character a theoretical description of personality placing emphasis on our final-cause judgment of another person's behavioral style. The implication is that some people are better than others in personality pattern: "You can count on good old Charlie; he is a trusted and true member of the community." *See also:* Personality, Temperament.

Choice another term for the selection of a given affirmation when confronted by dialectical alternatives. *See also:* Affirmation, Dialectical alternatives and choice.

Cognitive or Conceptual Method a manner of testing theoretical propositions to determine their consistency or coherence with the already accepted, common sense understanding of a body of knowledge. We judge something to be true if it makes immediate sense. This kind of proof is sometimes called *face validity. See also:* Method, Procedural evidence, Research method.

Coherence Theory of Truth a philosophical principle which holds to be true that which coheres plausibly or logically with some already accepted or proven body of knowledge. Procedural evidence is predicated on a coherence theory of truth. *See also:* Correspondence theory of truth, Procedural evidence.

Conceptual, Conceptual Model a method of behavioral description and analysis that assumes that an actively formative process is underway, so that rather than being shaped by circumstance, the organism is viewed as a shaper of circumstances. The patterns, shapes, and orders we know as meaning are not reducible to underlying building blocks, but are the actual source of understanding. The Kantian model and related phenomenological models like the gestalt laws of organization rely on conceptual descriptions. *See also:* Constitutive, Kantian model.

Conceptual Interaction a form of reciprocal interdependence or interrelationship obtaining between a mental scheme or frame and some independent set of circumstances which must be put to order but which may not be completely schematized or framed by mentation. Immanuel Kant took the position of conceptual interactionism when he proposed the noumena-phenomena duality. *See also:* Evolutionary interaction, Reciprocal, Statistical interaction.

Connotative Meaning, Connotation refers to the less specific ties that an item (concept, word, image, etc.) has with other items, as through implication. The word *milk* can connote reassurance, safety, and love to any one person who has been satisfactorily mothered. *See also:* Denotative meaning, Meaning.

Conscious Determinism limitations placed on behavioral alternatives with full awareness that a choice is being made as a reason "for the sake of which" a given course of behavior is then being intentionally carried out. *See also:* Determinism, Unconscious determinism.

Consequent in traditional stimulus-response psychology, this is the event occurring second in time—usually said to be the response but also confounded with the dependent variable—that is supposedly efficiently-caused by the antecedent event. This is not to be confused with the consequent of an "if, then" proposition. *See also:* Antecedent, Consequent term of "if, then" proposition, Efficient cause.

Consequent Term of "If, Then" Proposition in any "If A then B" proposition or course of reasoning, the B term is called the consequent. *See also:* Antecedent term of "if, then" proposition.

Constitutive, Constitutive Model a method of behavioral description and analysis that assumes that complex habits are "made up" of from smaller to larger units. The pattern we observe in the shape of things is always reducible to smaller and smaller units until what we have left is a "given" unit, a singular building block. The Lockean models, such as various reductive, atomic, etc., models, are essentially constitutive. *See also:* Conceptual, Lockean model, Reductionism.

Construct essentially a synonym for mental or theoretical *concept,* which is usually a schematic label used to describe (explain, analyze, account for) something in experience. Technically, the Kantian theorist would *construct* or *construe* these schematic labels from the disordered noise input from reality, whereas the Lockean theorist would *abstract* these patterned meanings from the already ordered reality. *See also:* Construction, Kantian model, Lockean model.

Contingent Cause a telic conception, introduced by theologian John Duns Scotus to describe an efficient cause that was also based on a final cause—i.e., a willful decision. If the person can look ahead and evaluate contingent circumstances—i.e., those that follow or will happen given that a behavior is carried out—then his or her behavior is *not* simply efficiently caused; it has a "that, for the sake of which" characteristic as well. The person can decide, come to a grounding choice of the reason for his or her behavior to follow. *See also:* Free will, Teleology, Telosponse.

Control Variable potential measurements the scientist ignores or holds constant in a research experiment so that he or she may observe more clearly the relationship between the independent and dependent variables. *See also:* Dependent variable, Independent variable, Research method, Validating evidence.

Construction, To Construe refers to active mentation in which the person literally brings about or constructs meaning on the basis of which his or her understanding is then predicated. *See also:* Predication.

Correspondence Theory of Truth a philosophical principle which holds to be true that which corresponds with some independent standard of comparison. Realists assume that empirical validation checks the correspondence of a theory with reality. However, it is possible to be an idealist and still want an independent experimental test of a theoretical proposition. In either case, validation clearly rests on a correspondence assumption. *See also:* Coherence theory of truth, Validating evidence.

Counterwill a concept employed by Freud in his first theory of the neuroses. It is readily subsumed by a dialectical metatheory. *See also:* Dialectical meaning.

Criterion Problem, in Validating Ethical Claims the fact that in order to do an empirical study to test an ethical belief, we must already make a judgment as to what is the good or bad effects of that which we are studying. Our dependent variable must inevitably be prejudiced by an ethical decision as we design our experiment aimed at testing an ethical course of action. We can never put ethical claims to validation without a circularity of this type developing.

Critical Realism the view held to by Kant, who argued that naive realism—i.e., assuming reality to be exactly as perceived—was too simple in conception. As critical realists, we accept the fact that there is a realm of independent (noumenal) experience that can be called reality, but we also recognize our personal (phenomenal) contributions to this experience of reality. We never perceive reality naturally or naively. We therefore must be critical of our naive perceptions, analyzing them in light of our personal contributions to the nature of reality.

Curative Motive   a reason for entering psychotherapy in which therapist or client seeks to rectify an abnormal condition in the most efficient and direct manner possible, usually by applying techniques of cure that have been perfected outside the walls of the consulting room. *See also:* Ethical motive, Scholarly motive.

Cybernetics   the science of communications and controls that counter entropy (undifferentiated sameness) in nature. These are nontelic forms of control. *See also:* Information-processing theory.

Data   measurements gathered in research. *See also:* Method.

Deity Teleology   believing that everything in existence is under the direction of a Creator's hand, that a God has a divine plan which is unfolding in the course of time. *See also:* Human teleology, Natural teleology, Teleology.

Demand Characteristic(s)   a phrase used to describe the observed fact that subjects form an hypothesis of their own concerning the intent of a psychological experiment. Furthermore, they frequently take on the role of being cooperative subjects in order to make certain that the intended outcome actually takes place. This concept is easily viewed in teleological terms, but it has not been so interpreted by most psychologists to date.

Demonstrative Meaning   a way of describing meaning in which meaning relations are said to bear the characteristics of singularity, linearity, unidirectionality, and noncontradiction. The demonstrative reasoner presumes

that his or her premises are "primary and true," hence not open to question or alternatives. *See also:* Dialectical meaning, Law of contradiction, Meaning.

Denotative Meaning, Denotation   refers to the specific ties that an item (concept, word, image, etc.) has with other items. The word *milk* denotes a specific liquid with clearly discernible properties which can be named. *See also:* Connotative meaning, Meaning.

Dependent Variable   the value of a measurement that records the observed effects of prearranging an independent variable, with control variables held constant. Dependent-variable measurements are what we call the results or findings of a research experiment. *See also:* Control variable, Independent variable, Research method, Validating evidence.

Determine, Determinism   refers to the limitation or setting of limits on events, including behavior. Framed in terms of antecedents (or precedents) and consequents (or sequacious events), *four* types of determinism can be described, depending on which of the causes we wish to emphasize in our account. *See also:* Cause.

Dialectic, Dialectical   see Dialectical meaning.

Dialectical Alternatives and Choice   a recognition of the fact that for a dialectically reasoning organism, the possibilities that arise because of bipolarity constantly require that a choice be made regarding what premise to affirm. *See also:* Affirmation, Bipolarity, Dialectical meaning.

Dialectical Change   oppositional alternation of the pattern of precedent events, thereby affecting changes in meaning "for the sake of which" sequacious events occur. This can be contrasted with the linear, unidirectional change of efficient causation. Dialectical change thus relies on the formal- and final-cause meanings, introducing the *vehicle* for a reconstruction through its capacity for oppositional reasoning. *See also:* Dialectical alternatives and choice, Precedent meaning, Sequacious meaning.

Dialectical Meaning a way of describing meaning in which meaning relations are said to bear the characteristics of oppositionality, duality, relationality, contradiction, and arbitrariness. There is often a uniting of opposites or contradictions into a new totality, described most frequently as the synthesis of a thesis and an antithesis. *See also:* Antithesis, Demonstrative meaning, Dialectical alternatives and choice, Dialectical change, Meaning, Synthesis.

Discriminal Theory theory that tries to distinguish (discriminate) between certain behavioral sequences and other behavioral sequences, resulting in an emphasis on individual differences. Discriminal theories are written at a lower level of abstraction than vehicular theories and hence they do not have the range of explanation that the latter theories do. Traditional personality theory always tends toward the discriminal level of explanation. *See also:* Vehicular theory.

Discriminative Stimulus a cue that the organism under operant conditioning distinguishes to make its response more likely to occur than otherwise. One could readily give a telic interpretation to such a stimulus, but the behaviorists have used this concept to retain the integrity of efficient-cause control in their theories.

Dualism a theory that proposes two realms of explanation to account for the observed facts. Freud's theory of a psychic and a somatic realm is an example of a dualism. *See also:* Monism.

Dynamic Mental Phenomena a concept used by Freud to describe the active, often contradictory nature of mentation.

Efficient Cause any concept used to account for the nature of things (including behav-

ior) based on the impetus in a succession of events over time. Explanations of behavior based on energy pushes, gravity attractions, and the machinelike flow of motion are usually thought of in efficient-cause terms. *See also:* Cause(s).

Empiricism, Empirical basing knowledge solely or as much as possible on what can be observed. The more empirical a theorist is, the more likely he or she is to be a realist. *See also:* Idealism, Realism.

Ethical Motive a reason for entering psychotherapy in which therapist or client seeks to rectify past injustices which were due to improper or immoral interpersonal relations, seek heightened awareness, or attain a new level of self-realization. *See also:* Curative motive, Scholarly motive.

Evolutionary Interaction a form of reciprocal interdependence or interrelationship obtaining between the biologically developing organs of an animal and its environment. Classical conditioning took an evolutionary interactionist point of view in proposing drive-vs.-external stimulation views of learning, and Skinner later analogized his operant view of conditioning to the "natural selection" processes of biological evolution. *See also:* Conceptual interaction, Reciprocal, Statistical interaction.

Experiment, Experimental Design a trial run arranged by a scientist to see whether his or her theory can meet the rigors of validation in the research method. An experiment describes the specific relations obtaining between an independent, dependent, and certain control variables which the scientist manipulates according to plan (design) and then steps back to observe an outcome which is predicted to take place in a certain manner from the outset. This always results in validating evidence. *See also:* Control variable,

Dependent variable, Independent variable, Research method, Validating evidence.

Extraspective Perspective, of Theory framing theories of things and/or events in the third person from the convenience of an observer. Extraspective theory describes "that, it" rather than "I, me." Extraspection is the natural outlook for validation, but it is always possible to test introspective theory through validation. *See also:* Introspective perspective, Perspective, Validating evidence.

Fact a meaningful relationship between constructs which is no longer disputed. Usually, facts emerge when reliable relationships between independent and dependent variables are achieved. Thus, *fact* is primarily a methodological concept, though its content is framed by theory. We explain facts theoretically. *See also:* Construct, Method, Theory.

Falsification, Principle of Falsification states that it must be possible for an empirical scientific system to be refuted by experience. This means that a theoretical proposition must be phrased in such a way as to be capable of being true or false. If we say, "It will or will not rain tomorrow," this is not a falsifiable statement and hence is not scientific. We must put the statement in terms of "It will rain tomorrow" or "It will not rain tomorrow" if we hope to test it scientifically. *See also:* Verifiability.

Feedback a mediational concept used in information-processing theory to capture the fact that early events can be used as information to direct later events over time. In feedback, we have the return to the input of a part of the output, so that the machine corrects itself based on what it *literally* is doing. There is never a possibility being considered in feedback. Feedback is a literal

form of control, fitting the organism to the actual environment.

Figure-Ground the general view and technical construct holding that meanings occur only because of the framing ground that defines a figure or "centering" point. Figure-ground theory grows out of sensory phenomenology as elaborated by the gestalt psychologists. It has been used widely in personality theory to describe a phenomenal field or life space within which the person is said to behave according to gestalt principles. *See also:* Sensory phenomenology.

Final Cause any concept used to account for the nature of things (including behavior) based on the assumption that there is a reason, end, or goal "for the sake of which" things exist or events are carried out. Explanations that rely on the person's intentions, aims, or aspirations are final-cause descriptions of behavior. *See also:* Cause(s), Teleology, Telic.

Formal Cause any concept used to account for the nature of things (including behavior) based on their patterned organization, shape, design, or order. Explanations of behavior emphasizing the style or type of behavioral pattern taken on are formal-cause descriptions. *See also:* Cause(s), Personality.

Freedom, Free to be without constraint, open to alternatives, and not bound by the singularity of a fixed course. In a sense, this is the opposite of determination because the latter state fixes limits on alternatives. However, it is possible for the organism to be *both* free and determined. *See also:* Determine, Free will, Telosponse.

Free Will means it is possible to arrange the premises "for the sake of which" one is determined. This is a nontechnical way of referring to the capacity telosponding organisms have dialectically to alter meanings which they affirm as predications in the course of behavior. Before affirmation, we can speak of freedom, and, after affirmation, we can speak of will (-power) in the meaning-extension to follow sequaciously. Free will and psychic determinism are opposite sides of the same coin. *See also:* Affirmation, Psychic determinism, Telosponse.

Free Will as Guided Natural Selection   a view advanced by Skinner which holds that operant control of behavior is identical to (but on a different time frame than) the form of control discovered by Darwin in his study of natural selection. This is tantamount to a mediation conception, but as the operant response is not technically mediated, we classify this differently from free will as mediating alternatives. *See also:* Free will, Free will as mediating alternatives, Free will as statistical unpredictability, Freedom.

Free Will as Mediating Alternatives   a view held in psychology that what we experience as our free will is actually our early input experiences which today direct us without real agency but give us an illusion of control. Dollard and Miller's cue-producing responses acting as mediators would give the behaving person a sense of agency, self-direction, and freedom to direct his or her course of behavior. But this would be an illusory sensation, for the control of behavior would continue to be exclusively on the basis of efficient causes (i.e., S-R units). *See also:* Free will, Free will as guided natural selection, Free will as statistical unpredictability, Freedom.

Free Will as Statistical Unpredictability   a view held in psychology based on methodological shortcomings in the prediction of behavior to a perfection. That is, since we never have all of the information to predict with certainty what people will do, we can, if we like, call this unpredictable aspect of behavior free will. Actually, it is clear that this is not a *theory* of free will, for it has no real definition of freedom except as a form of error variance in actuarial prediction. *See also:* Free will, Free will as guided natural selection, Free will as mediated alternatives, Freedom.

Freud's "Project for a Scientific Psychology"   Freud's single Lockean venture in the explanation of behavior, in which he tried unsuccessfully to use material- and efficient-cause reductionism. He never completed this work and tried to have it destroyed when a draft turned up in his later years.

Function   a term that describes the relationship obtaining between the independent and dependent variables of an experiment. As originally coined, the dependent variable is said to be a function of the independent variable. This concept is based on the meaning of formal causation in that it is a *pattern* of relationship. It has been unfortunately identified with efficient causation, so that psychologists sometimes think the independent variable (as an antecedent event) is an impetus or force bringing about changes in the dependent variable (as a consequent event). When S-R theory is mixed in here, a serious problem arises because the experimental method is then believed to validate *only* S-R theory. *See also:* Dependent variable, Experiment, Independent variable, S-R bind, Variable.

Grace   a concept used by theologians to capture their assumption that human beings are unable to earn their own salvation but must rely on divine assistance. God bestows grace on the human being who gives himself or herself to His divine direction.

Ground(s), for Decision Making   the basis, case, plausible reason, etc., for belief or action, entering either clearly or through implication into premises which are then predicated by the individual. A ground is the "that for the sake of which" behavior is intended. The ground per se is essentially a formal-cause conception (meaning, plan, reason, etc.), but the use of this ground to intend its meaning telosponsively takes us into final causation. *See also:* Final cause, Formal cause, Predication, Premise, Telosponse.

Hard Determinism any view holding that 100 percent of the actions that took place in a sequence of events had to take place exactly as they did, so that *no* indeterminism is possible. That is, even if we could wind back the course of events, at any point along the way what took place would have to take place again in exactly the same way. Chance is an illusion in this view. *See also:* Determinism, Soft determinism.

Homunculus the "little person" who supposedly must be concocted to explain how agency can occur in human behavior. Teleologies are criticized for putting this smaller being within the human being in order to steer or run the psychic mechanism. This criticism rests on the invalid assumption that only "blind" efficient causes take place in human behavior. Telosponsive organisms need no homunculus to direct them, but can run themselves. *See also:* Agent, Telosponse.

Humanism a theory of behavior in which—knowingly or unknowingly—the theorist employs telic constructs. This is purely a technical theory-construction matter to be decided on by analysis of the theory under consideration. *See also:* Humanitarianism, Mechanism, Teleology.

Humanitarianism theories of *either* a mechanistic or a humanistic cast that seek to improve the lot of humanity in some way—e.g., by viewing people as positively endowed with potentials, or by somehow improving their material status through behavioral manipulations of one sort or another.

Human Teleology believing that human beings behave "for the sake of" purposes, reasons, goals, etc., *whether or not* inanimate nature does so (natural teleology) or a Supreme Being is directing things to an intended end (deity teleology). *See also:* Deity teleology, Final cause, Natural teleology, Teleology.

Idealism the philosophical view holding that the contents of our minds, i.e., the things and events that we know, are all that there is in experience. When we see a rose, touch it, and smell its fragrance, these experiences are created by mind and hence it is futile to try to discover the existence of an independent reality from which they have been drawn. *See also:* Realism.

Identity refers to a continuity in mentation over time, and may be considered a variant definition of *self*. *See also:* Self.

Idiographic an approach to the description of things (including behavior) based on what is distinctive and unique about a single country, individual, etc. The idiographic approach (*idios* = "one's own") always tries to capture what is uncommon and individually different about its subject matter. The study of history employs idiographic description. *See also:* Nomothetic.

Independent Variable the value of a measurement which a scientist pre-arranges or manipulates in order to see what impact this prescribed succession of events has on measurements taken at the dependent-variable half of the research experiment. *See also:* Control variable, Dependent variable, Research method, Validating evidence.

Individual Differences the variations in personality style to be seen taking place in any sample of people. *See also:* Discriminal theory, Nomothetic, Vehicular theory.

Information-Processing Theory a phrase that has devolved from cybernetics, and that can be thought of as a synonym for the word *cybernetics*. In essence, an information-processing theory is one using a form of mediation theory in which the concepts of input, output, and feedback are given prominence. *See also:* Feedback, Input-output, Mediation theory, Subjective theoretical construct.

Innate Idea a term of derision, used by the empiricists of psychology who deny that the mind can have a pro forma, conceptualizing capacity which is not itself learned. This would imply that human beings are born with ideas already underway, hence that they would have innate ideas. Actually, the Kantian conceptions of a priori categories of the understanding are formative organizers rather than idea contents. As such, they cannot be learned for they make learning possible. *See also:* A priori, Pro forma, Tabula rasa.

Input-Output information-processing or cybernetic concepts which capture the unilinear, efficient-cause flow of information as contained in electronic messages flowing in from the environment, processed according to a program, and sent outward as problem solutions, instrumental acts, etc. *See also:* Feedback.

Insight the benefits of psychotherapy which are easily construed as a form of qualitative motion or dialectical change. *See also:* Dialectical change, Qualitative motion.

Intention behaving "for the sake of" purposive meanings as encompassed in images, language terms, affections, emotions, etc., all of which are encompassed as premises in the act of predication. When purpose and intention combine, we have telosponsivity. Intentionality is as pure an expression of final causation as possible. *See also:* Final cause, Predication, Purpose, Telosponse.

Intersubjectivity as Objectivity certain phenomenological psychologists find it difficult admitting that any item of knowledge is completely objective, because they view each person as a subject ordering knowledge personally. Hence, so-called objectivity to them is merely intersubjectivity—i.e., a common agreement among subjects rather than anything really transcending the unique subject. *See also:* Objective theoretical construct, Subjective theoretical construct.

Intervening Variable a term introduced by Tolman whereby he confounds his theory of mediation with his methodological concept of variable(s). The assumption is that there is something going on *between* the independent and dependent variables, carried along by the organism (person, animal), but capable of measurement by the extraspective observer. For all practical purposes, this is synonymous with *mediator,* i.e., a prior supplementary stimulus acting currently as part of the efficient causes of observed behavior. *See also:* Efficient cause, Mediation theory, Method, Variable(s).

Intrinsic Theory of Value holding that the worth of something or some action can be shown to be due to its intrinsic merits. Duty and obligation are placed above pleasure and pain as grounds for positive value preferences. *See also:* Ground, Instrumental theory of value.

Introspective Perspective, of Theory framing theories of things and/or events in the first person, from the outlook of an identity acting within them. Introspective theory refers to "I, me" rather than to "that, it." *See also:* Extraspective perspective, Perspective.

Instrumental Theory of Value holds that a judgment (valuation) of worth should be based on the pleasure that results when some action is carried out. Actions leading to pleasure are good and those leading to pain are bad. *See also:* Intrinsic theory of value.

Intuitive Cognition based on Ockham's writings, this refers to the preliminary knowledge of external experience we obtain through our sensory receptors (eyes, ears, touch, smell, etc.). These sensations are then stored in mind for use in higher-order cognitions. This style of theorizing is compatible with the Lockean model. *See also:* Abstractive cognition, Lockean model.

Kantian Model a view of human behavior stressing dialectical as well as demonstrative reasoning, pro forma intellect, noumenal versus phenomenal experience, meaningful understanding, transcendence, and predication rather than mediation. Kantian models are closer to logic than to mathematics, dealing more with the orders (*logos*) mind brings to bear as meaning than with a tabulation of the ordered bits of meaning taken in by mind á la the Lockean model. *See also:* Conceptual, Lockean model.

Lawfulness, Law(s) stable and generalizable relations between independent and dependent variables. *See also:* Experiment, Method, Variable.

Law of Contradiction (or Noncontradiction) the view that "A is not non-A" or that something cannot both be and not be. This assumption predicates demonstrative reasoning. *See also:* Demonstrative reasoning, One and many principle.

Local Motion Aristotle's term for the movement of a thing from one place (location) to another, as when a rock rolls down a hill. Today we call this locomotion. *See also:* Qualitative motion, Quantitative motion.

Lockean Model a view of human behavior stressing demonstrative reasoning, unipolarity in meaning, tabula rasa intellect, simple-to-complex ideas in mentation, constitutive mentality, mediation, and empirical determination of all that mind represents. Lockean models are building-block conceptions in which little (atomic) unities make up or constitute bigger totalities in quasi-mathematical fashion. *See also:* Constitutive, Kantian model.

Logic an area of study in which order (*logos*) is primary, hence the emphasis is on patterned relationships between meanings of various propositions, premises, inferences, deductions, conclusions, and so forth. Logic is not subsumable by material and efficient causality. We have to use formal and final causality to describe the nature of logic.

Logical Necessity a synonym for the line of precedent-sequacious meaning-extension we witness in telosponsivity. *See also:* Meaning-extension, Precedent meaning, Sequacious meaning, Telosponse.

Logical Phenomenology placed its emphasis on the Kantian suggestion that a priori categories of the understanding serving as logical premises (predicated assumptions, etc.) ordered sensory input after it had been preliminarily framed in terms of time and space. Existentialists and theorists like Jung and Kelly took this approach, viewing the realm of phenomenal thought as the most important locus of organization, taking precedence over sensory organizations per se. *See also:* Sensory phenomenology.

Logical Positivism a philosophical school of thought which subscribes to verifiability as grounds for judging whether or not a question or issue has meaning. In essence, if we cannot name the empirical observations that would help us to solve a problem we raise, then our problem is *not* a philosophical one, though it may have emotional or psychological significance. Psychology has embraced logical positivism along with British Empiricism to limit its range of "scientific" investigations. *See also:* British Empiricism, Verifiability.

Material Cause   any concept used to account for the nature of things (including behavior) that assumes that things are comprised of underlying, unchanging *substances.* Explanations of behavior based on genetic transmission or chemical elements are examples of material-cause description. *See also:* Cause(s).

Meaning   a relational tie of one item to another, extending in time to form a concept within a host of interlacing relationships. Meaning can be given a symbolical or a signalizing interpretation. *See also:* Sign, Symbol.

Meaning-Extension   the precedent-sequacious flow of meaning in the conceptualizations of telosponsivity, commonly referred to as the inductive and deductive knowledge of experience. As meaning-extension proceeds, the knowledge framed by the premised meanings of telosponsivity extends its range. *See also:* Meaning, Precedent meaning, Sequacious meaning, Telosponse.

Meaningfulness   the extent of significance, import, or general understanding that an item (word, image, concept, idea, etc.) or its referent (that to which it relates) has for the individual. Meaningfulness is thus a measure or metric of the extent of meaning— that is, clarity, centrality, import, value, etc. —the item holds for the individual. *See also:* Meaning.

Mechanism   an explanation of behavior based predominantly on efficient causality, with occasional use of material causality. In no case is a final-cause concept employed. Hence, mechanism is essentially the opposite of teleology. *See also:* Efficient cause, Material cause, Teleology.

Mediation Theory   a theory of behavior in which all those things attributed to a self or an identity are said to occur *between* the incoming stimuli or input and the outgoing responses or output. Behaviorism employs mediation theories of one sort or another. *See also:* Information-processing theory.

Mentation   the act of thinking, knowing, cognizing.

Metaphysics   highly abstract philosophical study of the metatheoretical assumptions and points of view that guide our understanding and knowledge but cannot be put directly to empirical test. *See also:* Metatheory.

Metatheory   a highly abstract assumption, position, model, paradigm, point of view, etc., having meaningful relevance for many less abstract, even commonplace ideas. In philosophy, these abstract conceptions are often called universals because their meanings enter into so many understandings. The causes are an example of metatheoretical assumptions, as are the Kantian-versus-Lockean models, and demonstrative-versus-dialectical meanings. *See also:* Cause(s), Demonstrative meaning, Dialectical meaning, Kantian model, Lockean model.

Method   the means or manner of determining whether a theoretical construct or statement is true or false. There are two general types of method: (1) cognitive or conceptual method, which makes use of procedural evidence, and (2) research method, which uses validating in addition to procedural evidence. *See also:* Procedural evidence, Theory, Validating evidence.

Mind   a humanistic psychologist might define mind as the innate capacity to telospond in relation to ("for the sake of") patterns of meaning in experience as well as to create these patterns anew through dialectical reasoning. *See also:* Telosponse.

Mixed-Model Theories   refers to theories that have taken from two or more traditions of explanation. For example, Freud's libido theory is Lockean in tone, whereas his broader conceptions of mentation are closer to the Kantian model. *See also:* Kantian model, Lockean model.

Monism a theory that proposes a single realm of explanation to account for the observed facts. Behavioristic theories reducing everything to efficient causation in the material reality are examples of monisms. *See also:* Dualism.

Morality behavioral decisions made in line with what a Supreme Being would have chosen had He made the affirmation. Ethical behavior is concerned with the same questions of doing what is right and good, but unlike morality, ethics makes no claims regarding its assumptions being based on divine inspiration or intention. *See also:* Affirmation, Choice.

Motivation a general term referring to the desire, aspiration, drive, etc., that an organism has to bring something about, attain an end, or achieve a satisfaction. There are telic and nontelic interpretations of motivation.

Multiordinality, of Theory the fact that the meanings encompassed by a theoretical construct or proposition can change when the level of abstraction changes. A concept like response can mean an eye-blink reflex at one level and the reaction of an entire nation to a threat from some enemy nation at another level of abstract description. We have one word—response—but two different meanings arising from the change in abstractness.

Multipolarity a general term signifying many meaningful poles joined into relationship. The issue that is debated centers on whether these complexes of polar relations are made up of unipolarities or whether they also engage bipolar meanings. *See also:* Bipolarity, Meaning, Unipolarity.

Natural Teleology belief that nature works toward a purposive end, although no assumption is made that this end is under the direction of a Supreme Being. *See also:* Deity teleology, Human teleology, Teleology.

Nomothetic an approach to the description of things (including behavior) based on what is generally the case. The nomothetic approach relies on common laws (*nomos* = "law") which describe everything exactly the same way for all time. Individual differences are minimized and common trends are focused on. The study of astronomy employs nomothetic description. *See also:* Idiographic.

Noumena, Noumenal Realm of Experience experience as it presumably "is," independent of the sensory equipment of the phenomenal realm. This term was used by Kant to emphasize that we never know the noumenal world directly, but must always order it meaningfully at the phenomenal level. Kant accepted on faith that "things in themselves" —i.e., noumenal things—really existed. *See also:* Critical Realism, Kantian model, Phenomena.

N Theories to Explain Any One Fact Pattern because of the inescapable logical fallacy of affirming the consequent in science, it will always be true *in principle* that for any observed fact pattern or research finding, there can be an unlimited (*N*) number of possible explanations. However, this does *not* remove the responsibility of any theory having to meet such evidence—and the more wide-ranging the evidential tests the better. Because an alternative theory is possible *in principle* does not mean that *in actuality* there is even one alternative that does meet the range of evidence. *See also:* Affirming the consequent.

Null Hypothesis the statement of no relationship between the independent and dependent variables of an experiment. *See also:* Experiment.

Objective Idealism a theoretical outlook that would contend that it is possible to be objective about purely mental phenomena. If all people think essentially alike, then they might share completely objective meanings not rooted in a reality. For example, the objective idealist might contend that there is no *one* reality on which we will all agree someday, but that we can still be objectively clear regarding those idealistic conceptions we do frame as independent contributions to empirical knowledge.

Objective Theoretical Construct, Objectivity refers to constructs with meanings that transcend the individual who frames the relationships intended; hence they may be grasped or understood by all individuals who expend proper effort. Objective meanings can be understood by anyone who sincerely examines the contents at issue. *See also:* Construct, Objective idealism, Subjective theoretical construct.

One and Many Principle the view that all events are united (ordered meaningfully) and thus must necessarily be arbitrarily distinguished one from the other. This assumption predicates dialectical reasoning. *See also:* Dialectical meaning, Law of contradiction.

Operational Definition occurs when we stipulate the operations or empirical steps we must take in order to measure a theoretical construct which we are using. We operationalize an "aggressive personality" when we have people take a test of aggression and then, using the test scores, define a certain score above which we will consider the person "aggressive." If we cannot operationalize a construct, then so far as this view of science is concerned, it *lacks* meaning. Hence,

Freud's libibo construct would be considered a meaningless concept because it cannot be measured empirically. *See also:* Falsification, Verifiability.

Organon a way of coming to know truth, based on certain philosophical assumptions and styles of reasoning that eventuate in knowledge.

Parameter a statistical measurement, such as mean, of the population of any given variable. Assuming that there are a finite number of apples in the state of Washington during any given year, the parameter would tell us what the average or "constant" number of apples has been over any year we would like to single out for consideration. Since it is impractical if not impossible to take measurements of all the apples, we sample from this population and then estimate through mathematical calculations the "constant" value describing this total. We never count all the apples in any one year, but estimate this total statistically.

Periodic Cycles Fliess's biological-clock theory of behavior which influenced Freud to some extent.

Personality the style a course of behavior takes on. Considered just by itself, personality is a formal-cause conception, but in bringing out theories of personality, two or more of the causes are used. *See also:* Cause(s), Formal cause.

Personologist a scientist (usually a psychologist) who specializes in the study of the individual person—that is, behaviors that capture a single person rather than a "sample" of people. *See also:* Idiographic.

Perspective the stance, point of view, or slant a theorist takes in relation to the subject matter he or she has set out to describe, analyze, or explain. The theorist can take the point of view of the subject matter and write a first-person theory, or he/she can take the point of view of an observer looking *at* the subject matter to write a third-person theory. *See also:* Extraspective perspective, Introspective perspective.

Phenomena, Phenomenal Realm of Experience experience as known by the individual from a personal vantage point through his or her unique sensory equipment. Each of us has our own phenomenal understanding of the things and events in experience. This term was popularized by Kantian philosophy to emphasize the fact that we as individuals order experience into meaning and do not simply respond to it. *See also:* Critical realism, Kantian model, Noumena.

Physical Determinism limitations on behavioral alternatives due to material-cause and related efficient-cause conceptions. Gene theories and similar biological conceptions of behavior rely on physical determinisms. *See also:* Determinism, Psychic determinism.

Piagetian-versus-Kellyian Constructivism refers essentially to a difference between Kelly's completely introspective theoretical explanation of constructivism versus Piaget's confounding of extraspective with introspective constructivism. Piaget's use of *assimilation,* which bears the meaning of a taking-in on the order of osmosis, may be contrasted with Kelly's use of *subsumption* on this matter. Subsumption demands that we consider a reasoning intelligence bringing a conception to bear which can take other meanings under its range of convenience *or not.* Assimilation as an osmotic process does not require such active conceptualization by a reasoning intelligence. Kelly's usage can employ dialectical meanings, whereas Piaget's passive-input conception cannot.

Polarity, Poles of Meaning a recognition that meaning is relational and hence it always occurs by uniting referential points or items in experience. A pole merely refers to one, the other, or both ends of a meaning relation. Saying "John is lucky" unites a person with an evaluation. John is at one pole of the meaning relation and luck at the other. *See also:* Demonstrative, Dialectical, Meaning.

Precedent Meaning refers to the ordering of meaning without regard for time's passage; i.e., a precedent meaning is one that goes before others in order or arrangement, as the major premise always precedes the minor premise of a syllogism, framing its general meaning so that the minor premise can only extend the meaning contained therein. *See also:* Sequacious meaning.

Predication bears the same meaning as premise, except that the emphasis is more on the act of premising by an identity who has already affirmed some meaning. *See also:* Identity, Premise.

Premise an assumption that has been affirmed by the individual, so that granting the meaning contained therein, certain understandings occur and other implications follow. In logic, the major premise frames generalities (All people are mortal) and the minor premise specifies (This is a person). *See also:* Precedent meaning, Predication, Sequacious meaning.

Principle of Constancy a principle coined by Mayer, popularized by Helmholtz, and taught to Freud by Brücke. Essentially, this principle relies on locomotion and quantitative changes of forces in a closed system to explain the nature of behavior. Freud analogized to it when he framed his libido theory, but never really found it sufficient to understand human behavior.

Procedural Evidence the kind of evidence that issues from the cognitive or conceptual method. We rely on procedural evidence (proof) when we believe in something because of its plausibility or consistency with common sense. This is sometimes called theoretical proof, but it is best not to mix theory and method language. *See also:* Cognitive or conceptual method, Validating evidence.

Pro Forma for the sake of form, i.e., bringing patterns to bear so that meaningful relations are put onto experience by the person's mentality. This is the opposite of tabula rasa. The Kantian a priori categories of the understanding act in a pro forma sense. We do not teach people to use the categories, any more than we teach them to close their hands in grasping an object. The categories grasp—lend order or a pattern to—experience analogically to the hands grasping objects. *See also:* A priori, Innate ideas, Kantian model, Tabula rasa.

Program in cybernetics and its computer technology, this refers to a logical series of steps which have been prearranged to solve some problem and which are carried out electronically. In behavior modification, this refers to a series of steps aimed at changing behavior in a definite manner.

Project see Freud's *Project for a Scientific Psychology*.

Psychic Determinism limitations on behavioral alternatives that are due to final-cause choices of "this" rather than "that." Telic theories are psychic determinisms. Freud's approach relied on psychic determinism, in that he held that everything that occurs in mind has an intended meaning expression, a kind of formal-cause pattern that is being enacted by a finally-caused organism. *See also:* Determinism, Physical Determinism, Teleology.

Psychometrics the use of tests or scales to measure psychological constructs. Psychometricians effectively operationalize psychological theoretical constructs by devising em-

pirical instruments purporting to measure them. *See also:* Operational definition.

Psychotherapy an interpersonal relationship involving two or more people in which the motives of the participants are scholarly, ethical, and/or curative. *See also:* Curative motive, Ethical motive, Scholarly motive.

Purity Criticism the charge that theoretical constructs sometimes force their descriptive referents into arbitrary and distorted meanings, losing the essence of that which is under description (explanation). Purity criticisms range from mere cautions of this possibility to highly aggressive rejections of all theory in favor of a spontaneous illumination sent to the unprejudiced observer by the data qua data.

Purpose the aim or point of a meaning. When this aim is incorporated as an intention by a telosponding organism, we witness telic behavior taking place. A pencil has a purpose as a concept—a writing tool—but this purpose is not made manifest until a person intends that this purpose be recognized or put to use. When the person does behave for the sake of a pencil's purpose, we witness telosponsivity. *See also:* Intention, Telosponsivity.

Qualitative Motion Aristotle's term for the alteration of a thing's attributes, as when leaves turn color in the fall. *See also:* Local motion, Quantitative motion.

Quantitative Motion Aristotle's term for the alteration in size (mass, bulk) to be noted when things either develop or decline, such as grapes first growing to a plump size and then shriveling and reducing in size if left unpicked when ripe. *See also:* Local motion, Qualitative motion.

Rationalism a view holding as a universal assumption or metatheory that there is a plausible order in the universe. In general, a rationalistic theorist believes that only through the use of our understanding can we arrive at knowledge, even knowledge that is observed. *See also:* Empiricism, Idealism, Metatheory.

Realism the philosophical view holding that the contents of our minds, i.e., the things and events that we know, exist independently of our mind. When we see a rose, touch it, and smell its fragrance, these experiences are not created by mind but are abstracted from an independent reality. *See also:* Idealism.

Realistic Subjectivism a theoretical outlook contending that there are meanings rooted in the reality of a personally subjective experience that cannot be conveyed to others in an objective manner. For example, the subjective realist might contend that there are unique physiological reactions no two people share exactly; hence, though *really* taking place, these feelings cannot be understood objectively because there is no common basis for conveying the meaning of these unique experiences. *See also:* Objective idealism.

Reciprocal, Reciprocal Interaction refers to an interdependence or interrelationship obtaining between two or more sides to an outcome. There are three major types of reciprocal interaction which psychologists have used to interpret behavior: conceptual, evolutionary, and statistical. *See also:* Conceptual interaction, Evolutionary interaction, Statistical interaction.

Reciprocal Control mutually influencing controls, so that as one side is influenced, the other side is also influenced. *See also:* Reciprocal.

Reductionism the philosophical assumption holding that we have rendered a better understanding of anything (including behavior) after we have broken down formal- and final-cause theoretical conceptions to underlying material- and efficient-cause theoretical conceptions. Reductionists are likely to be realists and empiricists who believe in a Lockean substrate to all things—which make them up and to which they can therefore be reduced. *See also:* Cause(s), Lockean model.

Repredication to reframe, reformulate, reconstrue a set of circumstances.

Research Method a manner of testing theoretical propositions which is based on an empirical correspondence with circumstances that have been prearranged to support or not support the theory in question. We judge something to be true if it corresponds to the observed sequence of events as originally predicted. *See also:* Cognitive or conceptual method, Experimental design, Method, Validating evidence.

Scholarly Motive a reason for entering psychotherapy in which therapist and/or client is seeking to know more about human nature per se, with psychopathology merely one aspect of a broader picture. *See also:* Curative motive, Ethical motive.

Self bears the meaning of consistency or identity. Theories of agency make use of self-concepts to convey the idea of a sameness in the succession of behaviors a person is seen manifesting from one set of circumstances or situation to another. *See also:* Agent.

Self-Reflexivity, Reflexivity the capacity human mentation has to turn back on itself and therefore to know that it is knowing. *See also:* Transcendental dialectic.

Sensory Phenomenology placed its emphasis on the Kantian suggestion that sensory receptors organized inputs from the environment according to time and space. The gestaltists took this approach and devised a sensory phenomenology in which the laws of organization worked initially at the level of proximal stimulation and then were said to be isomorphic with (identical to) mentation itself. *See also:* Logical phenomenology.

Sequacious Meaning refers to the ordering of meaning without regard for time's passage; i.e., a sequacious meaning is one that follows or flows from the meanings of precedents, extending these in a *necessary* sense (telic determination). Metaphors and analogies are sequacious extensions of precedent meanings, as when we say "John is solid as a rock," extending thereby the similarities between a rock and our friend John. *See also:* Precedent, Telosponse.

Sign, Signalizing Meaning a nontelic formulation holding that words are associated stand-ins for environmental items bonded together according to the frequency and contiguity of past experience as input to mind totally without intention. *See also:* Mediation theory, Symbol.

Soft Determinism the view holding that although most events occurring are the only ones that could have occurred, a certain number are indeterminate. Thus, chance events do occur and alternatives would be possible if we could but wind back the course of events and start over again. *See also:* Determinism, Hard determinism.

Sophistry the art of weaving specious arguments to confuse and win points through guile. Socrates held that sophistry occurs because the individual uses dialectical strategies ingenuinely to bring about a predictable end, rather than being completely open to new discovery in discourse.

S-R Bind limiting one's theoretical conceptions to an efficient-cause frame. This is especially harmful to psychology when a theorist fails to distinguish between his or her theory and the method used to test the theory. In this case, it is common to see the independent variable being equated with the stimulus, and the dependent variable equated with the response. As a consequence, objectivity is lost because the *only* theory that can then be validated is S-R theory.

S-R versus R-R Laws can be seen as a theoretical distinction between efficient-cause (S-R) and formal-cause (R-R) interpretations of observed (lawful) relationships.

Stationary State the formal-cause atomic theory of Bohr, in which the overall pattern of orbits remain stationary but electrons continue to move within these orbits. In order to understand Bohr's theory of change, we must add qualitative motion to locomotion as a principle of explanation. *See also:* Qualitative motion.

Statistical Interaction refers to an interdependence or interrelationship obtaining between two or more variables measured and analyzed mathematically following data collection in an experiment. This form of interaction is more a methodological than a theoretical conception in the style of conceptual or evolutionary interactionism. It is likely to arise in any experiment we perform that measures aspects of behavior that have relevance for each other. *See also:* Conceptual interaction, Evolutionary interaction, Reciprocal.

Stereotype a stylized, popular view of certain people—usually minority group members—that may detract from their image, but also can be flattering. Believing that all blacks are lazy or Poles are stupid is a stereotypical form of either-or thinking. So is believing that all ministers are altruistic and all soldiers are brave. *See also:* Type.

Subjective Theoretical Construct, Subjectivity refers to constructs with meanings that are somehow private, difficult or impossible to circumscribe (vague), and hence are incapable of being extended beyond the behavior of the individual who has framed the meaningful relationship intended. Subjective meanings cannot be understood even when we sincerely examine the contents at issue. *See also:* Construct, Objective theoretical construct.

Subsumption, Subsume to take a meaning expressed at a lower level of abstraction under the definitional range of a more abstract meaning. Metatheories can always subsume those theories that come under their range of definition. Metaphysics is a study that subsumes many other, often seemingly unrelated concepts because of the abstractness and universality of metaphysical conceptions. *See also:* Metaphysics, Metatheory.

Syllogism a logical form of meaning-extension in which, given a certain order of (major and minor) premises, certain conclusions, deductions, etc., follow in precedent-sequacious fashion. *See also:* Affirming the consequent, Precedent, Sequacious.

Symbol, Symbolizing Meaning a telic formulation which holds that words express the intentions of ideas that have been formulated independently. *See also:* Sign, Telosponse.

Synchronicity Jung's formal-cause conception which he employed to account for paranormal experience.

Synthesis the combining of meanings from both the thesis and its antithesis into a new statement, position, point of view, argument, etc., which then acts as a new thesis. Syntheses take meaning from both sides and frame an emergent, alternative, or new thesis—which can then immediately imply its (dialectically framed) antithesis. *See also:* Antithesis, Dialectical meaning, Thesis.

Tabula Rasa meaning "smoothed tablet" or "blank sheet," the phrase was introduced by St. Thomas Aquinas and popularized by John Locke. It refers to the view that at birth the mind is completely empty, and that whatever role mentation has in life is shaped by the inputs from the environment, which essentially writes on a blank sheet what the person will know. The mind is basically passive, a collator and storage unit for influences from the environment. *See also:* Pro forma.

Technical Constructs a series of five distinctive conceptualizations (models, schemes, formal-cause notions, etc.) which personologists have employed to describe behavior: (1) stimulus-response; (2) mediation; (3) reciprocity; (4) figure-ground; and (5) telosponse.

Teleologist any theorist using telic (teleological) explanations. In rough terms, the opposite of a mechanist. *See also:* Teleology, Mechanist.

Teleology, Telic the view that events are predicated according to plan, design, or assumption—that is, based on purposive meanings—and therefore are directed to some intended end. Teleologies can be natural, deity, or human in formulation. *See also:* Deity teleology, Final cause, Human teleology, Natural teleology, Telos, Telosponse.

Telos Greek word for end, goal, or grounding reason "for the sake of which" behavior is taking place. *See also:* Final cause, Ground, Teleology, Telosponse.

Telosponse a mental act in which the person takes on (predicates, premises) a meaningful item (image, language term, a judgment, etc.) relating to a referent acting as a purpose "for the sake of which" behavior is then intended. This is a final-cause (technical) construct. Telosponsive behavior is done "for the sake of" grounds (purposes, reasons, etc.) rather than "in response to" stimulation. *See also:* Ground, Intention, Purpose.

Temperament a theoretical description of personality placing emphasis on the material cause. The implication is that we are as personalities what our genes and related biological structures make us out to be: "She is a Smith, and is easygoing like all the Smiths."

Theologian one who studies theology, i.e., the origins and teachings of God.

Theorotype a stylized, professional view of certain personality types based on clinical evidence or empirical studies. Freudian (oral, anal, etc.) types or Jungian (introversion, extraversion, etc.) types are examples of theorotypes. In a sense, the theorotype is a sophisticated stereotype, employed objectively and with no intention to demean or elevate the people under description. *See also:* Stereotype, Type.

Theory a series of two or more schematic labels (words, visual images that we name, etc.) that have been hypothesized, presumed, or even factually demonstrated to bear a meaningful relationship, one with the other(s). *See also:* Fact, Meaning, Method.

Thesis any given statement, position, point of view, argument, etc., that is put forward as a given or worthwhile outlook. *See also:* Antithesis, Dialectical meaning, Synthesis.

Time as Pattern the recognition that once we have removed efficient causality from our accounts of time's passage, we are left with a formal-cause explanation of time.

Tracking an attitude common in psychology and traceable to Newtonian mechanics, whereby it is assumed that we somehow understand a thing or event better if we can trace its course of locomotion and come to predict its directions even before they occur. Tracking suits validation's prediction emphasis, and hence many empiricists are fundamentally drawn to a tracking of behavior in extraspective fashion. *See also:* Extraspective perspective, Local motion, Validating evidence.

Trait a theoretical construct that is intended to capture that which is common to everyone —or almost everyone—to a greater or lesser degree. If we say that everyone is more or less aggressive in behavior, we are employing a trait description. Trait theories usually devolve from type theories. *See also:* Type.

Transcendental Dialectic, Transcendence in Kantian philosophy, the capacity all humans have to rise above their customary understanding of experience and—by thinking in opposition to it—bring it into question, analysis, and reinterpretation. *See also:* Dialectic, Self-reflexivity.

Type a theoretical construct which is intended to capture the total person all at once. Freud's oral personality is an example of a typological construct. *See also:* Stereotype, Theorotype, Trait.

Unconscious Determinism limitations placed on behavioral alternatives without full awareness that a choice is being made as a reason "for the sake of which" a given course of behavior is then being intentionally carried out. *See also:* Conscious determinism, Determinism.

Unipolarity the belief that the poles united into meanings are separate and distinct units. *See also:* Bipolarity, Meaning, Multipolarity.

Universal a highly abstract assumption, position, model, paradigm, point of view, etc., having meaningful relevance to many less abstract, even commonplace ideas. Since there are far fewer universals than there are lower-level ideas which they subsume, we sharpen issues by finding the universal meanings on which our ideas are based. The Aristotelian causes are an excellent example of universals in knowledge because they relate to literally anything that can be known. *See also:* Metatheory.

Validating Evidence, Validation believing in something only after it has been put to test in a prearranged course of events designed specifically to show what it relates to meaningfully. This is how scientists prove things, relying on the control of events and the prediction of an outcome. *See also:* Control variable, Dependent variable, Independent variable, Meaning, Procedural evidence, Research method.

Valuation the telic (final-cause) process by which values are framed. *See also:* Value.

Value the relative worth of a thing or an action in comparison with alternatives in kind. Not all values are clearly delineated, but many are and become incorporated into a group's mores. Fundamentally, there are two theories of value usually put forward—instrumental and intrinsic. *See also:* Instrumental theory of value, Intrinsic theory of value.

Variable literally anything in existence that can take on varying degrees of measurement. Technically, this term refers to methodological factors we employ in designing an experiment. Three types of variables may be distinguished: independent, dependent, and control. Some psychologists speak of an intervening variable, which is essentially a theoretical and not a methodological concept. When so-called intervening variables are studied, they are treated as independent variables. *See also:* Control variable, Dependent variable, Experiment, Function, Independent variable, Method, Theory.

Vehicular Theory theory that is aimed at abstracting descriptions that can subsume many different forms of lower-level theories. Stimulus-response explanations are vehicular because they use the same concepts to explain everything, as in the assumption that all behavior is a matter of responding to certain stimuli based on reinforcements. Hence, Dollard and Miller could subsume Freud's lower-level theory. *See also:* Discriminal theory.

Verbal Report experimental data based on what the subject says rather than what he or she does. Traditionally, rigorous empirical psychologists have dismissed verbal report as a satisfactory source of data, reflecting in this disdain for what the subject says an antiteleological bias. *See also:* Awareness, of experimental subjects.

Verifiability, Criterion of Verifiability suggests that a theoretical proposition is factually significant only if the person expressing it can tell us what observations would lead us to accept it as being true or reject it as being false. The logic of verifiability is related to the logic of falsification. *See also:* Falsification, Logical positivism.

Vitalism a type of deity teleology introduced by Galen which held that there are formless, undiscoverable forces acting on brute matter to bring about life. Not all teleologies are vitalisms. *See also:* Deity teleology, Teleology.

Will a telic conception that relies on the necessity of a sequacious meaning-extension brought forward in behavior as an intention. A willed action has the suggestion of a psychic determination, an intended end (telos) which the person really wants to take place. *See also:* Free will, Intention, Sequacious, Teleology, Telosponse.

References

Adler, A. (1930) *The education of children.* London: George Allen & Unwin, Ltd. Reprinted with the permission of the Estate of Alfred Adler. From *The education of children* by Alfred Adler. Copyright © 1930 by Alfred Adler.

————. (1954) *Understanding human nature.* New York: Fawcett World Library.

————. (1958) *What life should mean to you.* New York: Capricorn Books. Reprinted with the permission of the Estate of Alfred Adler. From *What life should mean to you* by Alfred Adler. Copyright © 1931, renewed 1959 by Kurt A. Adler.

————. (1963) *The problem child.* New York: Capricorn Books.

————. (1964a) *Problems of neurosis.* New York: Harper & Row. Quotations by permission of the publisher.

————. (1964b) *Social interest: A challenge to mankind.* New York: Capricorn Books. Reprinted by permission of the Estate of Alfred Adler. From *Social interest: A challenge to mankind* by Alfred Adler.

————. (1968) *The practice and theory of individual psychology.* Totowa, N.J.: Littlefield, Adams, & Co. Reprinted by permission of Humanities Press, Inc., New Jersey 07716, and Routledge & Kegan Paul, Ltd.

Alexander, F. G., and S. T. Selesnick. (1966) *The history of psychiatry: An evaluation of psychiatric thought and practice from prehistoric times to the present.* New York: Harper & Row.

Allport, G. W. (1946) Personalistic psychology as a science: A reply. *Psychological Review, 53,* 132–135.

Angell, J. R. (1907) The province of functional psychology. *Psychological Review, 2,* 61–91.

Ansbacher, H. L. (1959) The significance of the socio-economic status of the patients of Freud and of Adler. *American Journal of Psychotherapy, 13,* 376–382.

Ansbacher, H. L., and R. R. Ansbacher (Eds). (1956) *The individual psychology of Alfred Adler.* New York: Basic Books, Inc. Quotations by permission of Basic Books, Inc. Reprinted with the permission of the Estate of Alfred Adler. From *The individual psychology of Alfred Adler* by H. L. and R. R. Ansbacher, copyright © 1964, 1970 by Heinz L. and Rowena R. Ansbacher.

————. (1964) *Superiority and social interest.* Evanston, Ill.: Northwestern University Press. Quotations by permission of the publisher.

————. (1978) *Cooperation between the sexes: Writings by Alfred Adler on women, marriage, and sexuality.* Garden City, N.Y.: Doubleday & Co., Inc.

Aristotle. (1952a) *Physics.* In R. M. Hutchins (Ed.), *Great books of the western world* (Vol. 8). Chicago: Encyclopaedia Britannica, pp. 257–355.

————. (1952b) *Topics.* In R. M. Hutchins (Ed.), *Great books of the western world* (Vol. 8). Chicago: Encyclopaedia Britannica, pp. 143–223.

Atthowe, J. M., and L. Krasner. (1968) Preliminary report on the application of contingent reinforcement procedures (token economy) on a "chronic" psychiatric ward. *Journal of Abnormal Psychology, 73,* 37–43.

Ayer, A. J. (1946) *Language, truth and logic.* New York: Dover Publications.

Bacon, F. (1952) *Advancement of learning.* In R. M. Hutchins (Ed.), *Great books of the western world* (Vol. 30). Chicago: Encyclopaedia Britannica, pp. 1–101.

Bandura, A. (1969) *Principles of behavior modification.* New York: Holt, Rinehart and Winston, Inc.

———. (1973) *Aggression: A social learning analysis.* Englewood Cliffs, N.J.: Prentice-Hall, Inc.

———. (1974) Behavior theory and the models of man. *American Psychologist, 29,* 859–869.

———. (1977a) *Social learning theory.* Englewood Cliffs, N.J.: Prentice-Hall, Inc.

———. (1977b) Self-efficacy: Toward a unifying theory of behavioral change. *Psychological Review, 84,* 191–215.

———. (1978) The self system in reciprocal determinism. *American Psychologist, 33,* 344–358.

———. (1979) Self-referent mechanisms in social learning theory. *American Psychologist, 34,* 439–440.

Barker, J. C., and M. B. Miller. (1968) Recent developments and some future trends in the application of aversion therapy. Unpublished Manuscript.

Bennet, E. A. (1961) *C. G. Jung.* New York: E. P. Dutton & Co., Inc.

Bercel, N. A. (1960) A study of the influence of schizophrenic serum on the behavior of the spider Zilla-x-notata. In D. D. Jackson (Ed.), *The etiology of schizophrenia.* New York: Basic Books, Inc., pp. 159–174.

Bergmann, G., and K. Spence. (1941) Operationism and theory in psychology. *Psychological Review, 48,* 1–14.

Binswanger, L. (1957) *Sigmund Freud: Reminiscences of a friendship.* New York: Grune & Stratton.

———. (1958) The existential analysis school of thought: Insanity as life-historical phenomenon and as mental disease: The case of Ilse; The case of Ellen West: An anthropological-clinical study. In R. May, E. Angel, and H. F. Ellenberger (Eds.), *Existence: A new dimension in psychiatry and psychology.* New York: Basic Books, Inc., Chs. VII, VIII, and IX.

———. (1963) *Being-in-the-world* (translated and with a critical introduction by J. Needleman). New York: Basic Books, Inc. Quotations by permission of the publisher.

Blackman, H. J. (1959) *Six existentialist thinkers.* New York: Harper & Row.

Bohr, N. (1934) *Atomic theory and the description of nature.* Cambridge: The University Press.

Boneau, C. A. (1974) Paradigm regained? Cognitive behaviorism restated. *American Psychologist, 29,* 297–309.

Boring, E. G. (1946) Mind and mechanism. *American Journal of Psychology, 59,* 179–192.

Boss, M. (1958) *The analysis of dreams.* New York: Philosophical Library.

———. (1963) *Psychoanalysis and daseinsanalysis.* New York: Basic Books, Inc. Quotations by permission of the publisher.

Bottome, P. (1957) *Alfred Adler: A portrait from life.* New York: The Vanguard Press.

Bowers, K. S. (1973) Situationism in psychology: An analysis and a critique. *Psychological Review, 80,* 307–336.

Bradley, J. (1971) *Mach's philosophy of science.* London: The Athlone Press of the University of London.

Brewer, W. F. (1974) There is no convincing evidence for operant or classical conditioning in adult humans. In W. B. Weimer and D. S. Palermo (Eds.), *Cognition and the symbolic processes.* Hillsdale, N.J.: Lawrence Erlbaum.

Burtt, E. A. (1955) *The metaphysical foundations of modern physical science (rev. ed.).* Garden City, N.Y.: Doubleday & Co.

Cassirer, E. (1944) *An essay on man.* Garden City, N.Y.: Doubleday & Co.

Cattell, R. B. (1959) *Personality: A systematic, theoretical, and factual study.* New York: McGraw-Hill.

Collingwood, R. G. (1940) *An essay on metaphysics.* London: Oxford University Press.

Combe, G. (1851) *Lectures on phrenology.* New York: Fowler and Wells.

Conant, J. B. (1952) *Modern science and mod-*

ern man. Garden City, N.Y.: Doubleday Anchor.

Cranston, M. (1957) *John Locke: A biography.* New York: Longmans, Green and Co.

Cronbach, L. J. (1957) The two disciplines of scientific psychology. *American Psychologist, 12,* 671–684.

Darwin, C. R. (1952a) *The descent of man.* In R. M. Hutchins (Ed.), *Great books of the western world* (Vol. 49). Chicago: Encyclopaedia Britannica, pp. 251–659.

———. (1952b) *The origin of species.* In R. M. Hutchins (Ed.), *Great books of the western world* (Vol. 49). Chicago: Encyclopaedia Britannica, pp. 1–250.

Datta, D. M. (1967) Epistemological methods in Indian philosophy. In C. A. Moore (Ed.), *The Indian mind: Essentials of Indian philosophy and culture.* Honolulu: University of Hawaii Press, pp. 118–135.

DeNike, L. D. (1964) The temporal relationship between awareness and performance in verbal conditioning. *Journal of Experimental Psychology, 68,* 521–529.

Descartes, R. (1952) *Rules for the direction of mind* and *Discourse on method.* In R. M. Hutchins (Ed.), *Great books of the western world* (Vol. 31). Chicago: Encyclopaedia Britannica, pp. 1–40 and pp. 41–67.

Dollard, J. (1937) *Caste and class in a southern town.* New Haven, Conn.: Yale University Press.

———. (1942) *Victory over fear.* New York: Reynal & Hitchcock.

———. (1943) *Fear in battle.* New Haven, Conn.: Yale University Press.

Dollard, J., and F. Auld. (1959) *Scoring human motives.* New Haven, Conn.: Yale University Press.

Dollard, J., F. Auld, and A. White. (1953) *Steps in psychotherapy.* New York: The Macmillan Co.

Dollard, J., L. W. Doob, N. E. Miller, O. H. Mowrer, and R. R. Sears. (1939) *Frustration and aggression.* New Haven, Conn.: Yale University Press.

Dollard, J., and N. E. Miller. (1950) *Personality and psychotherapy: An analysis in terms of learning, thinking, and culture.* New York: McGraw-Hill Book Co. © 1950, by the McGraw-Hill Book Co., Inc., Quotations by permission of the publisher.

Dulany, D. E. (1962) The place of hypotheses and intentions: An analysis of verbal control in verbal conditioning. In C. W. Eriksen (Ed.), *Behavior and awareness: A symposium of research and interpretation.* Durham, N.C.: Duke University Press.

Dunham, A. M., Jr. (1938) The concept of tension in philosophy. *Psychiatry, 1,* 79–120.

English, H. B., and A. C. English. (1958) *A comprehensive dictionary of psychological and psychoanalytical terms.* London: Longmans, Green, & Co.

Euclid (1952) *Elements.* In R. M. Hutchins (Ed.), *Great books of the western world* (Vol. 8). Chicago: Encyclopaedia Britannica, pp. 1–396.

Evans, R. I. (1964) *Conversations with Carl Jung.* Princeton, N.J.: D. Van Nostrand, Co., Inc.

———. (1968) *B. F. Skinner: The man and his ideas.* New York: E. P. Dutton & Co.

———. (1973) *Jean Piaget: The man and his ideas.* New York: E. P. Dutton & Co., Inc.

———. (1976) *The making of psychology.* New York: Alfred A. Knopf.

Eysenck, H. J. (1952) The effects of psychotherapy: An evaluation. *Journal of Consulting Psychology, 16,* 319–324.

———. (1953) *The structure of human personality.* New York: John Wiley & Sons, Inc.

Farber, I. E. (1963) The things people say to themselves. *American Psychologist, 18,* 185–197.

Feldman, M. P., and M. J. MacCulloch. (1967) Aversion therapy in the management of homosexuals. *British Journal of Medical Psychology, 1,* 560–594.

Ferster, C. B., and B. F. Skinner. (1957) *Schedules of reinforcement.* New York: Appleton-Century-Crofts.

Flavell, J. H. (1963) *The developmental psychology of Jean Piaget.* New York: D. Van Nostrand Co.

Frank, P. (1957) *Philosophy of science.* Englewood Cliffs, N.J.: Prentice-Hall.

Frankl, V. (1960) Paradoxical intention: A logotherapeutic technique. *American Journal of Psychotherapy, 14,* 520–534.

Freud, S. (1954) *The origins of psycho-analysis: The letters to Wilhelm Fliess: Drafts and notes: 1887–1902.* New York: Basic Books, Inc.

————. (1960) *Letters of Sigmund Freud* (edited by E. L. Freud). New York: Basic Books, Inc.

————. *The standard edition of the complete psychological works of Sigmund Freud.* London: Hogarth Press:

Vol. I. *Pre-psycho-analytic publications and unpublished drafts,* 1966. Acknowledgment is made to Sigmund Freud Copyrights, Ltd., The Institute of Psycho-Analysis, and the Hogarth Press for permission to quote from Vol. I of the Standard Edition of the Complete Psychological Works of Sigmund Freud, revised and edited by James Strachey.

Vol. II. *Studies on hysteria,* 1955 (coauthor J. Breuer).

Vol. III. *Early psycho-analytic publications,* 1962.

Vol. IV. *The interpretation of dreams* (First part), 1953.

Vol. V. *The interpretation of dreams* (Second part), 1953.

Vol. VI. *The psychopathology of everyday life,* 1960.

Vol. VII. *A case of hysteria and three essays on sexuality,* 1953.

Vol. VIII. *Jokes and their relation to the unconscious,* 1960.

Vol. IX. *Jensen's "Gradiva" and other works,* 1959.

Vol. X. *Two case histories: "Little Hans" and the "rat man,"* 1955.

Vol. XI. *Five lectures on psycho-analysis and Leonardo da Vinci,* 1957.

Vol. XII. *The case of Schreber and papers on technique,* 1958.

Vol. XIII. *Totem and taboo and other works,* 1955.

Vol. XIV. *On the history of the psychoanalytic movement, papers on metapsychology, and other works,* 1957. Acknowledgment is made to Sigmund Freud Copyrights, Ltd., The Institute of Psycho-Analysis, and the Hogarth Press for permission to quote from Vol. XIV of the Standard Edition of the Complete Psychological Works of Sigmund Freud, revised and edited by James Strachey, and to Basic Books, Inc., Publishers, New York, 1957.

Vol. XV. *Introductory lectures on psycho-analysis* (Parts I and II), 1963. James Strachey (Ed.). Reprinted by permission George Allen & Unwin Publishers and W. W. Norton & Co.

Vol. XVI. *Introductory lectures on psycho-analysis* (Part III), 1963.

Vol. XVII. *An infantile neurosis and other works,* 1955.

Vol. XVIII. *Beyond the pleasure principle, group psychology and other works,* 1955.

Vol. XIX. *The ego and the id and other works,* 1961.

Vol. XX. *An autobiographical study, inhibitions, symptoms and anxiety, the question of lay analysis, and other works,* 1959.

Vol. XXI. *The future of an illusion, civilization and its discontents, and other works,* 1961.

Vol. XXII. *New introductory lectures on psycho-analysis,* 1964.

Vol. XXIII. *Moses and monotheism, an outline of psycho-analysis, and other works,* 1964.

Freud, S., and W. C. Bullitt. (1967) *Thomas Woodrow Wilson: A psychological study.* Boston: Houghton Mifflin Co.

Freund, K. (1960) Some problems in the treatment of homosexuality. In H. J. Eysenck (Ed.), *Behaviour therapy and the neuroses*, New York: Pergamon Press, pp. 312–326.

Fromm, E. (1959) *Sigmund Freud's mission.* New York: Harper & Bros.

———. (1963) C. G. Jung: Prophet of the unconscious. *Scientific American,* September, 283–290.

Fromm, E., D. T. Suzuki, and A. DeMartino. (1960) *Zen Buddhism and psychoanalysis.* New York: Harper and Row.

Furtmüller, C. (1964) *Alfred Adler: A biographical essay.* In H. L. Ansbacher and R. R. Ansbacher (Eds.), *Superiority and social interest.* Evanston, Ill.: Northwestern University Press, pp. 330–393.

Gardner, B. T., and R. A. Gardner. (1969) Teaching sign language to a chimpanzee. *Science, 165,* 664–672.

Gayley, C. M. (1965) *The classic myths in English literature and art.* New York: Blaisdell Publishing Co.

Giorgi, A. (1970) *Psychology as a human science: A phenomenologically based approach.* New York: Harper and Row.

Goss, A. E. (1961) Early behaviorism and verbal mediating responses. *American Psychologist, 16,* 285–298.

Granit, R. (1977) *The purposive brain.* Cambridge, Mass.: MIT Press.

Greenspoon, J. (1954) The effect of two nonverbal stimuli on the frequency of members of two verbal response classes (Abstract). *American Psychologist, 9,* 384.

———. (1955) The reinforcing effect of two spoken sounds on the frequency of two responses. *American Journal of Psychology, 68,* 409–416.

Gruber, H. E. (1974) *Darwin on man: A psychological study of scientific creativity* (transcribed and annotated by Paul H. Barrett). New York: E. P. Dutton & Co., Inc.

Harms, E. (1946) Carl Gustav Jung—Defender of Freud and the Jews. *Psychiatric Quarterly, 20,* 199.

Hathaway, S. R., and J. C. McKinley. (1951)

Minnesota multiphasic personality inventory: Manual. New York: Psychological Corporation.

Hebb, D. O. (1974) What psychology is about. *American Psychologist, 29,* 71–79.

Hefferline, R. F., and B. Keenan. (1963) Amplitude-induction gradient of a small-scale (covert) operant. *Journal of the Experimental Analysis of Behavior, 6,* 307–315.

Hefferline, R. F., B. Keenan, and R. A. Harford. (1959) Escape and avoidance conditioning in human subjects without their observation of the response. *Science, 130,* 1338–1339.

Hegel, G. W. F. (1952) *The philosophy of right.* In R. M. Hutchins (Ed.), *Great books of the western world* (Vol. 46). Chicago: Encyclopaedia Britannica, pp. 1–150.

Heinemann, F. H. (1958) Existentialism and the modern predicament. New York: Harper & Row.

Hilgard, E. R., and D. G. Marquis. (1940) *Conditioning and learning.* New York: Appleton-Century-Crofts.

Hobbes, T. (1952) *Leviathan.* In R. M. Hutchins (Ed.), *Great books of the western world* (Vol. 23). Chicago: Encyclopaedia Britannica, pp. 49–283.

Hofstadter, R. (1955) *Social Darwinism in American thought.* Boston: The Beacon Press.

Horne, H. H. (1912) *Free will and human responsibility: A philosophical argument.* New York: The Macmillan Co.

Hull, C. L. (1937) Mind, mechanism, and adaptive behavior. *Psychological Review, 44,* 1–32.

———. (1938) The goal-gradient hypothesis applied to some "field-force" problems in the behavior of young children. *Psychological Review, 45,* 271–299.

———. (1943) *Principles of behavior.* New York: Appleton-Century-Crofts.

———. (1952) *A behavior system.* New Haven, Conn.: Yale University Press.

Husserl, E. (1965) *Phenomenology and the crisis of philosophy* (translated by Q. Lauer). New York: Harper & Row Torchbooks.

Immergluck, L. (1964) Determinism-freedom in contemporary psychology: An ancient problem revisited. *American Psychologist, 19,* 270–281.

Jacobson, E. (1938) *Progressive relaxation.* Chicago: University of Chicago Press.

Janet, P. (1920) *The major symptoms of hysteria* (2nd ed.). New York: The Macmillan Co.

Jones, E. (1953) *The life and work of Sigmund Freud* (Vol. 1). New York: Basic Books, Inc.

———. (1957) *The last phase* (Vol. 3). New York: Basic Books, Inc.

Jones, M. C. (1974) Albert, Peter, and John B. Watson. *American Psychologist, 29,* 581–583.

Jung, C. G. (1946) *Psychological types.* London: Kegan Paul, Trench, Trubner & Co., Ltd., and New York: Harcourt, Brace & Co. (This work appears in the Bollingen Series as Vol. 6.)

———. (1963) *Memories, dreams, reflections.* New York: Pantheon Books, and London: William Collins Sons, Ltd.

———. *The collected works of C. G. Jung* (Ed. H. Read, M. Fordham, and G. Adler). Bollingen Series. New York: Pantheon Books, and London: Routledge & Kegan Paul.
Vol. 1. *Psychiatric studies,* 1957.
Vol. 3. *The psychogensis of mental disease,* 1960.
Vol. 4. *Freud and psychoanalysis,* 1961.
Vol. 5. *Symbols of transformation,* 1956.
Vol. 6. *Psychological types,* 1971. (See Jung, 1946).
Vol. 7. *Two essays on analytical psychology,* 1953.
Vol. 8. *The structure and dynamics of the psyche,* 1960.
Vol. 9i. *The archetypes and the collective unconscious,* 1959.
Vol. 9ii. *Aion,* 1959.

Vol. 10. *Civilization in transition,* 1964.
Vol. 11. *Psychology and religion: West and east,* 1958.
Vol. 12. *Psychology and alchemy,* 1953.
Vol. 13. *Alchemical studies,* 1967.
Vol. 14. *Mysterium coniunctionis,* 1963.
Vol. 15. *The spirit in man, art, and literature,* 1966.
Vol. 16. *The practice of psychotherapy,* 1954.
Vol. 17. *The development of personality,* 1954.

Kant, I. (1952) *The critique of pure reason.* In R. M. Hutchins (Ed.), *Great books of the western world* (Vol. 42). Chicago: Encyclopaedia Britannica, pp. 1–250.

Kasulis, T. P. (1977) Zen Buddhism, Freud, and Jung. *Eastern Buddhist, 10,* 68–91.

Kaufman, A., A. Baron, and R. E. Kopp. (1966) Some effects of instruction on human operant behavior. *Psychonomic Monograph Supplements, 1,* 243–250.

Kaufmann, W. (1956) *Nietzsche: Philosopher, psychologist, antichrist.* New York: Meridian.

Kelly, G. A. (1955a) *The psychology of personal constructs. Volume one: A theory of personality.* New York: W. W. Norton & Co., Inc. Quotations by permission of the publisher.

———. (1955b) *The psychology of personal constructs. Volume two: Clinical diagnosis and psychotherapy.* New York: W. W. Norton & Co., Inc. Quotations by permission of the publisher.

———. (1969) *Clinical psychology and personality: The selected papers of George Kelly* (Ed. Brendan Maher). New York: John Wiley & Sons, Inc. Quotations from *Clinical Psychology and Personality: The Selected Papers of George Kelly,* Ed. Brendan Maher. © 1969 by John Wiley & Sons, Inc. Reprinted by permission.

———. (1970) A summary statement of a cognitively-oriented comprehensive theory of behavior. In J. C. Mancuso (Ed.), *Readings for a cognitive theory of personality.* New York: Holt, Rinehart and Winston, Inc., pp. 27–58.

Kennedy, T. D. (1970) Verbal conditioning without awareness: The use of programmed reinforcement and recurring assessment of awareness. *Journal of Experimental Psychology, 84,* 487–494.

Kety, S. S. (1960) Recent biochemical theories of schizophrenia. In D. D. Jackson (Ed.), *The etiology of schizophrenia.* New York: Basic Books, Inc., pp. 120–145.

Koffka, K. (1935) *Principles of gestalt psychology.* New York: Harcourt, Brace & Co.

Köhler, W. (1961a) Gestalt psychology today. In M. Henle (Ed.), *Documents of gestalt psychology.* Berkeley, Calif.: University of California Press, pp. 1–14.

———. (1961b) Psychological remarks on some questions of anthropology. In M. Henle (Ed.), *Documents of gestalt psychology.* Berkeley, Calif.: University of California Press, pp. 203–221.

Korzybski, A. (1921) *Manhood of humanity.* New York: E. P. Dutton & Co.

———. (1924) *Time-binding.* New York: E. P. Dutton & Co.

———. (1941) *Science and sanity: An introduction to non-Aristotelian systems and general semantics* (2nd ed.). Lancaster: Science Press.

Krasner, L. (1962) Behavior control and social responsibility. *American Psychologist, 17,* 199–204.

———. (1965) Verbal conditioning and psychotherapy. In L. Krasner and L. P. Ullmann (Eds.), *Research in behavior modification.* New York: Holt, Rinehart and Winston, Inc., pp. 211–228.

Kuhn, T. S. (1970) *The structure of scientific revolutions* (2nd ed.). Chicago: The University of Chicago Press.

Kuo, Y. (1976) Chinese dialectical thought and character. In J. F. Rychlak (Ed.), *Dialectic: Humanistic rationale for behavior and development.* Basel, Switzerland: S. Karger AG, pp. 72–86.

Lazarus, A. A. (1961) Group therapy of phobic disorders by systematic desensitization. *Jour-*

nal of Abnormal and Social Psychology, 63, 504–510.

Lecky, P. (1945) *Self-consistency: A theory of personality.* New York: Island Press.

Lefcourt, H. M. (1973) The function of the illusions of control and freedom. *American Psychologist, 28,* 417–425.

Leff, G. A. (1958) *Medieval thought: St. Augustine to Ockham.* Chicago: Quadrangle Books.

Lewin, K. (1935) *A dynamic theory of personality.* New York: McGraw-Hill Book Co.

———. (1947) Group decision and social change. In T. M. Newcomb and E. L. Hartley (Eds.), *Readings in social psychology.* New York: Henry Holt & Co.

———. (1951) Field theory in social science: selected theoretical papers (Ed. D. Cartwright), New York: Harper & Row.

———. (1961) Environmental forces in child behavior and development. In C. Murchison (Ed.), *A handbook of child psychology.* Worcester, Mass.: Clark University Press.

Lewin, K., T. Dembo, L. Festinger, and P. S. Sears. (1944) Level of aspiration. In J. McV. Hunt (Ed.), *Personality and the behavior disorders* (Vol. I). New York: The Ronald Press, pp. 333–378.

Lewin, K., R. Lippitt, and R. White. (1939) Patterns of aggressive behavior in experimentally created "social climates." *Journal of Social Psychology, 10,* 271–299.

Lippmann, W. (1946) *Public opinion.* New York: Penguin Books.

Locke, J. (1952) *An essay concerning human understanding.* In R. M. Hutchins (Ed.), *Great books of the western world* (Vol. 35). Chicago: Encyclopaedia Britannica, pp. 85–395.

McCleary, R. A., and R. S. Lazarus. (1949) Autonomic discrimination without awareness. *Journal of Personality, 18,* 171–179.

McDougall, W. (1923a) Purposive or mechanical

psychology? *Psychological Review, 30,* 273–288.

———. (1923b) *Outline of psychology.* New York: Charles Scribner's Sons.

McGuire, W. (Ed.). (1974) *The Freud/Jung letters.* Bollingen Series XCIV. Princeton, N.J.: Princeton University Press.

Mancuso, J. C. (1976) Dialectic man as a subject in psychological research. In J. F. Rychlak (Ed.), *Dialectic: Humanistic rationale for behavior and development.* Basel, Switzerland: S. Karger AG, pp. 113–125.

Marrow, A. J. (1969) *The practical theorist: The life and work of Kurt Lewin.* New York: Basic Books, Inc.

Maslow, A. H., and B. Mittlemann. (1951) *Principles of abnormal psychology: The dynamics of psychic illness* (rev. ed.). New York: Harper and Row.

Masserman, J. H. (1943) *Behavior and neurosis.* Chicago: University of Chicago Press.

Meyer, A. (1910) The dynamic interpretation of dementia praecox. *American Journal of Psychology, 21,* 385–403.

Miller, N. E. (1937) Analysis of the form of conflict reactions. *Psychological Bulletin, 34,* 720.

———. (1944) Experimental studies of conflict. In J. McV. Hunt (Ed.), *Personality and the behavior disorders* (Vol. I). New York: The Ronald Press, pp. 431–465.

———. (1948a) Studies of fear as an acquirable drive. 1. Fear as motivation and fear-reduction as reinforcement in the learning of new responses. *Journal of Experimental Psychology, 38,* 89–101.

———. (1948b) Theory and experiment relating psychoanalytic displacement to stimulus-response generalization. *Journal of Abnormal and Social Psychology, 43,* 155–178.

———. (1951) Learnable drives and rewards. In S. S. Stevens (Ed.), *Handbook of experimental psychology.* New York: John Wiley & Sons, Inc., pp. 435–472.

———. (1957) Experiments on motivation: Studies combining psychological, physiological, and pharmacological techniques. *Science, 126,* 1271–1278.

———. (1959) Liberalization of basic S-R concepts: Extensions to conflict behavior, motivation, and social learning. In S. Koch (Ed.), *Psychology: A study of science* (Vol. II). New York: McGraw-Hill Book Co., pp. 196–292.

———. (1961) Analytical studies of drive and reward. *American Psychologist, 16,* 739–754.

———. (1963) Some reflections on the law of effect produce a new alternative to drive reduction. In M. R. Jones (Ed.), *The Nebraska symposium on motivation* (No. XI), pp. 65–112.

———. (1964) Some implications of modern behavior theory for personality change and psychotherapy. In P. Worchel and D. Byrne (Ed.), *Personality Change.* New York: John Wiley & Sons, Inc.

Miller, N. E., and Dollard, J. (1941) *Social learning and imitation.* New Haven, Conn.: Yale University Press.

Moore, C. A. (1967) Introduction: The comprehensive Indian mind. In C. A. Moore (Ed.), *The Indian mind: Essentials of Indian philosophy and culture.* Honolulu: University of Hawaii Press, pp. 1–18.

Moore, T. V. (Dom) (1921) The parataxes. *Psychoanalytic Review, 8,* 252–283.

Morgan, C. D., and H. A. Murray. (1935) A method for investigating phantasies. *Archives of Neurology and Psychiatry, 34,* 289–306.

Mowrer, O. H. (1939) A stimulus-response analysis of anxiety and its role as a reinforcing agent. *Psychological Review, 46,* 553–566.

———. (1948) Learning theory and the neurotic paradox. *American Journal of Orthopsychiatry, 18,* 571–610.

———. (1961) *The crisis in psychiatry and religion.* New York: D. Van Nostrand.

Nakamura, H. (1964) *Ways of thinking of Eastern peoples.* Honolulu: East-West Center Press.

Neisser, U. (1967) *Cognitive psychology*. New York: Appleton-Century-Crofts.

Newton, I. (1952) Mathematical principles of natural philosophy. In R. M. Hutchins (Ed.), *Great books of the western world* (Vol. 34). Chicago: Encyclopaedia Britannica, pp. 1–372.

Nikhilananda, S. (1967) Concentration and meditation as methods of Indian philosophy. In C. A. Moore (Ed.), *The Indian mind: Essentials of Indian philosophy and culture*. Honolulu: University of Hawaii Press, pp. 136–151.

Nunberg, H., and E. Federn (Eds) (1962) *Minutes of the Vienna psycho-analytic society: 1906–1908* (Vol. I). New York: International Universities Press.

Oppenheimer, R. (1956) Analogy in science. *American Psychologist, 11*, 127–135.

Osgood, C. E., G. J. Suci, and P. H. Tannenbaum. (1957) *The measurement of meaning*. Urbana: University of Illinois Press.

Page, M. M. (1972) Demand characteristics and the verbal operant conditioning experiment. *Journal of Personality and Social Psychology, 23*, 372–378.

Park, R. E., and E. W. Burgess. (1921) *Introduction to the science of sociology*. Chicago: University of Chicago Press.

Pavlov, I. P. (1927) *Conditioned reflexes: An investigation of the physiological activity of the cerebral cortex* (Trans. G. V. Anrep). New York: Oxford University Press.

Penfield, W. (1975) *The mystery of the mind*. Princeton, N.J.: Princeton University Press.

Piaget, J. (1952) *The origins of intelligence in children*. New York: International Universities Press, Inc.

———. (1955) *The language and thought of the child*. New York: Meridian Books, Inc.

———. (1962) *Play, dreams and imitation in childhood*. New York: W. W. Norton & Co.

———. (1965a) *The child's conception of number*. New York: W. W. Norton & Co., Inc.

———. (1965b) *The moral judgment of the child*. New York: The Free Press, a Division of Macmillan Publishing Co.

———. (1967) *Six psychological studies*. New York: Random House.

———. (1970a) *Structuralism*. New York: Harper & Row.

———. (1970b) *Genetic epistemology*. New York: W. W. Norton & Co.

———. (1971) *Psychology and epistemology: Towards a theory of knowledge*. New York: The Viking Press.

———. (1973) *The child and reality: Problems of genetic psychology*. New York: Grossman, a Division of The Viking Press.

———. (1978) *Behavior and evolution*. New York: Pantheon Books.

Piaget, J., and B. Inhelder. (1967) *The child's conception of space*. New York: W. W. Norton & Co., Inc.

Plato. (1952) *Dialogues*. In R. M. Hutchins (Ed.), *Great books of the western world* (Vol. 7). Chicago: Encyclopaedia Britannica, pp. 1–799.

Popper, K. R. (1959) *The logic of scientific discovery*. New York: Basic Books.

Pressey, S. L. (1926) A simple apparatus which gives tests and scores—and teaches. *School and Society, 23*, 373–376.

Rachman, S. (1963) Introduction to behaviour therapy. *Behavioral Research and Therapy, 1*, 3–15.

Raju, P. T. (1967) Metaphysical theories in Indian philosophy. In C. A. Moore (Ed.), *The Indian mind: Essentials of Indian philosophy and culture*. Honolulu: University of Hawaii Press, pp. 41–65.

Rank, O. (1968) *Will therapy and truth and reality*. New York: Alfred A. Knopf, Inc.

Rickaby, J. (1906) *Free will and four English philosophers*. London: Burns and Oates, 1906.

Riegel, K. F. (1973) Dialectic operations: The final period of cognitive development. *Human Development, 16*, 346–370.

Rivers, W. H. R. (1920) *Instinct and the unconscious: A contribution to a biological theory of the psychoneuroses.* Cambridge: Cambridge University Press.

Rogers, C. R. (1939) *The clinical treatment of the problem child.* Boston: Houghton Mifflin Co.

———. (1942) *Counseling and psychotherapy.* Boston: Houghton Mifflin Co.

———. (1951) *Client-centered therapy.* Boston: Houghton Mifflin Co.

———. (1953) The interest in the practice of psychotherapy. *American Psychologist, 8,* 48–50.

———. (1955) Persons or science? A philosophical question. *American Psychologist, 10,* 267–278.

———. (1959) A theory of therapy, personality, and interpersonal relationships, as developed in the client-centered framework. In S. Koch (Ed.), *Psychology: A study of a science. Study I. Conceptual and systematic. Vol. 3: Formulations of the person and social context.* New York: McGraw-Hill Book Co., pp. 184–256. © 1959 by the McGraw-Hill Book Company, Inc. Quotations by permission of the publisher.

———. (1961) *On becoming a person.* Boston: Houghton Mifflin Co.

———. (1963) Learning to be free. In S. M. Farber and R. H. L. Wilson (Eds.), *Control of the mind, Vol. 2: Conflict and creativity.* New York: McGraw-Hill Book Co., pp. 268–288. Quotations by permission of the publisher.

———. (1967) Autobiography. In E. G. Boring and G. Lindzey (Eds.), *A history of psychology in autobiography* (Vol. V.). New York: Appleton-Century-Crofts, pp. 343–384.

———. (1969a) *Freedom to learn.* Columbus, O.: Charles E. Merrill Publishing Co.

———. (1969b) Self-directed change: An answer to the educational crisis? Talk given to the Council of Chief State School Officers, Phoenix, Arizona, Nov. 17.

———. (1970a) The process equation of psychotherapy. In J. T. Hart and T. M. Tomlinson (Eds.), *New directions in client-centered therapy.* Boston: Houghton Mifflin Co., pp. 190–205.

———. (1970b) The process of the basic encounter group. In J. T. Hart and T. M. Tomlinson (Eds.), *New directions in client-centered therapy.* Boston: Houghton Mifflin Co., pp. 292–313.

———. (1970c) Toward a modern approach to values: The valuing process in the mature person. In J. T. Hart and T. M. Tomlinson (Eds.), *New directions in client-centered therapy.* Boston: Houghton Mifflin Co., pp. 430–441.

———. (1970d) The interpersonal relationship in the facilitation of learning. In J. T. Hart and T. M. Tomlinson (Eds.), *New directions in client-centered therapy.* Boston: Houghton Mifflin Co., pp. 468–483.

———. (1970e) Current assumptions in graduate education: A passionate statement. In J. T. Hart and T. M. Tomlinson (Eds.), *New directions in client-centered therapy.* Boston: Houghton Mifflin Co., pp. 484–501.

———. (1970f) *Carl Rogers on encounter groups.* New York: Harper & Row Publishers.

Rogers, C. R., and R. F. Dymond. (1954) *Psychotherapy and personality change.* Chicago: University of Chicago Press.

Rogers, C. R., E. T. Gendlin, D. J. Kiesler, and C. B. Truax. (1967) *The therapeutic relationship and its impact.* Madison, Wis.: University of Wisconsin Press.

Rogers, C. R., and J. T. Hart. (1970) Looking back and ahead: A conversation with Carl Rogers. In J. T. Hart and T. M. Tomlinson (Eds.), *New directions in client-centered therapy.* Boston: Houghton Mifflin Co., pp. 502–534.

Rogers, C. R., and B. F. Skinner. (1956) Some issues concerning the control of human behavior: A symposium. *Science, 124,* 1057–1066.

Rorschach, H. (1942) *Psychodiagnostics.* New York: Grune & Stratton.

Rotman, B. (1977) *Jean Piaget: Psychologist of the real.* Ithaca, N.Y.: Cornell University Press.

Russell, B. (1959) *Wisdom of the west.* Garden City, N.Y.: Doubleday & Co., Inc.

Rychlak, J. F. (1968) *A philosophy of science for personality theory.* Boston: Houghton Mifflin Co.

———. (1970) The two teleologies of Adler's individual psychology. *Journal of Individual Psychology, 26,* 144–152. (Paper read at the 78th Annual Convention of the American Psychological Association, Miami Beach, Florida, Sept. 7).

———. (1976) (Ed.), *Dialectic: Humanistic rationale for behavior and development.* Basel, Switzerland: S. Karger AG.

———. (1977) *The psychology of rigorous humanism.* New York: Wiley-Interscience.

Saksena, S. K. (1967) Relation of philosophical theories to the practical affairs of men. In C. A. Moore (Ed.), *The Indian mind: Essentials of Indian philosophy and culture.* Honolulu: University of Hawaii Press, pp. 19–40.

Sapir, E. (1921) *Language, an introduction to the study of speech.* New York: Harcourt, Brace & Co.

Sartre, J. P. (1956) Being and nothingness. New York: Philosophical Library.

Schur, M. (1972) *Freud: Living and dying.* New York: International Universities Press, Inc.

Sheldon, W. H. (1944) Constitutional factors in personality. In J. McV. Hunt (Ed.), *Personality and the behavior disorders* (Vol. 1). New York: The Ronald Press, pp. 526–549.

Sheldon, W. H., C. W. Dupertuis, E. McDermott. (1954) *Atlas of men: A guide for somatotyping the adult male at all ages.* New York: Harper & Bros.

Sheldon, W. H., E. M. Hartl, and E. McDer-

mott. (1949) *Varieties of delinquent youth: An introduction to constitutional psychiatry.* New York: Harper & Bros.

Sheldon, W. H., and S. S. Stevens. (1942) *The varieties of temperament: A psychology of constitutional differences.* New York: Harper & Bros.

Sheldon, W. H., S. S. Stevens, and W. B. Tucker. (1940) *The varieties of human physique: An introduction to constitutional psychology.* New York: Harper & Bros.

Sherrington, C. S. (1947) *The integrative action of the central nervous system.* Cambridge: Cambridge University Press.

Shock, N. W. (1944) Physiological factors in behavior. In J. McV. Hunt (Ed.), *Personality and the behavior disorders* (Vol. I). New York: The Ronald Press, pp. 582–618.

Sidgwick, H. (1960) *Outlines of the history of ethics.* Boston: The Beacon Press.

Simon, Y. (1970) *The great dialogue of nature and space.* Albany, N.Y.: Magi Books.

Skinner, B. F. (1938) *The behavior of organisms: An experimental analysis.* New York: Appleton-Century.

———. (1948) *Walden two.* New York: The Macmillan Co. © 1948, by B. F. Skinner. Quotations by permission of the publisher.

———. (1950) Are theories of learning necessary? *Psychological Review, 57,* 193–216.

———. (1953) *Science and human behavior.* New York: The Macmillan Co.

———. (1955) The control of human behavior. *Annals of the New York Academy of Science, 17,* 547–551.

———. (1956) A case history in scientific method. *American Psychologist, 11,* 221–223.

———. (1957) *Verbal behavior.* New York: Appleton-Century-Crofts. Reprinted by permission of Prentice Hall, Inc., Englewood Cliffs, N. J.

———. (1959) *Cumulative record.* New York: Appleton-Century-Crofts.

———. (1960) Pigeons in a pelican. *American Psychologist, 15,* 28–37.

———. (1961) The design of cultures. *Daedalus, 90,* 534–546.

———. (1963a) Operant behavior. *American Psychologist, 18,* 503–515.

———. (1963b) *Behaviorism at fifty. Science, 140,* 951–958.

———. (1967a) Autobiography of B. F. Skinner. In E. G. Boring and G. Lindzey (Eds.), *History of psychology in autobiography* (Vol. V). New York: Appleton-Century-Crofts, pp. 387–413.

———. (1968) *The technology of teaching.* New York: Appleton-Century-Crofts.

———. (1969) *Contingencies of reinforcement: A theoretical analysis.* New York: Appleton-Century-Crofts.

———. (1971) *Beyond freedom and dignity.* New York: Alfred A. Knopf, Inc. © 1971 by B. F. Skinner. Quotations by permission of the publisher.

———. (1974) *About behaviorism.* New York: Alfred A. Knopf.

———. (1978) *Reflections on behaviorism and society.* Englewood Cliffs, N.J.: Prentice-Hall, Inc.

Skinner, B. F., and C. Ferster. (1957) *Schedules of reinforcement.* New York: Appleton-Century-Crofts.

Skinner, B. F., and O. R. Lindsley. (1954) Studies in behavior therapy, status reports II and III, Office of Naval Research Contract N5 ori-7662.

Skinner, B. F., H. C. Solomon, and O. R. Lindsley. (1954) A new method for the experimental analysis of the behavior of psychotic patients. *Journal of Nervous and Mental Diseases, 120,* 403–406.

Snygg, D., and A. W. Combs. (1949) *Individual behavior: A new frame of reference for psychology.* New York: Harper & Bros.

Spielberger, C. D., A. Berger, and K. Howard. (1963) Conditioning of verbal behavior as a function of awareness, need for social approval, and motivation to receive reinforcement. *Journal of Abnormal and Social Psychology, 67,* 241–246.

Spielberger, C. D., and L. D. DeNike. (1966) Descriptive behaviorism versus cognitive theory in verbal operant conditioning. *Psychological Review, 73,* 306–327.

Stampfl, T. G. (1966) Implosive therapy: The theory, the subhuman analogue, the strategy, and the technique. In S. G. Armitage (Ed.), *Behavior modification techniques in the treatment of emotional disorders.* Battle Creek, Mich.: Veterans Administration Publication, pp. 12–21.

Stampfl, T. G., and D. J. Levis. (1966) Implosive therapy. Unpublished Manuscript.

———. (1967a) Essentials of implosive therapy: A learning-theory based psychodynamic behavioral therapy. *Journal of Abnormal Psychology, 72,* 496–503.

———. (1967b) Phobic patients: Treatment with the learning theory approach of implosive therapy. *Voices, 3,* 23–27.

———. (1968) Implosive therapy—a behavioral therapy? *Behavioral Research and Therapy, 6,* 31–36.

———. (1969) Learning theory: An aid to dynamic therapeutic practice. In L. D. Eron and R. Callahan (Eds.), *The relation of theory to practice in psychotherapy.* Chicago: Aldine Publishing Co., pp. 85–114.

Standal, S. (1954) The need for positive regard: A contribution to client-centered theory. Unpublished doctoral dissertation, University of Chicago.

Stephenson, W. (1953) *The study of behavior.* Chicago: University of Chicago Press.

Stevens, S. S. (1935) The operational definition of psychological concepts. *Psychological Review, 42,* 517–527.

Storch, A. (1924) *The primitive archaic forms of inner experience and thought in schizophrenia: A genetic and clinical study of schizophrenia* (Trans. Clara Willard), New York and Washington, D.C.: Nervous and Mental Disease Publishing Co.

Sullivan, H. S. (1924) Schizophrenia: Its conservative and malignant features. *American Journal of Psychiatry, 4,* 77–91.

——. (1940) *Conceptions of modern psychiatry.* New York: W. W. Norton & Co., Inc. Quotation by permission of the publisher.

——. (1953) *The interpersonal theory of psychiatry* (Eds. H. S. Perry and M. L. Gawel). New York: W. W. Norton & Co., Inc. Quotations by permission of the publisher.

——. (1954) *The psychiatric interview* (Eds. H. S. Perry and M. L. Gawel). New York: W. W. Norton & Co., Inc.

——. (1956) *Clinical studies in psychiatry* (Eds. H. S. Perry, M. L. Gawel, and M. Gibbon). New York: W. W. Norton & Co., Inc. Quotations by permission of the publisher.

——. (1962) *Schizophrenia as a human process.* New York: W. W. Norton & Co., Inc. Quotations by permission of the publisher.

——. (1964) *The fusion of psychiatry and social science.* New York: W. W. Norton & Co., Inc. Quotations by permission of the publisher.

Suzuki, D. T. (1962) *The essentials of Zen Buddhism* (edited and with an introduction by B. Phillips). New York: Dutton.

Takakusu, J. (1967) Buddhism as a philosophy of "thusness." In C. A. Moore (Ed.), *The Indian mind: Essentials of Indian philosophy and culture.* Honolulu: University of Hawaii Press, pp. 86–117.

Thomas, W. I. (1951) The behavior pattern and the situation. In E. H. Volkart (Ed.), *Social behavior and personality: Contributions of W. I. Thomas to theory and social research.* New York: Social Science Research Council, pp. 14–36.

Thorndike, E. L. (1898) Animal intelligence: An experimental study of the associative processes in animals. *Psychological Review Monograph Supplement,* No. 8.

——. (1933) *An experimental study of rewards.* New York: Bureau of Publications, Teachers College, Columbia University.

——. (1943) *Man and his works.* Cambridge, Mass.: Harvard University Press.

Tolman, E. C. (1960) *Purposive behavior in animals and men.* New York: Appleton-Century-Crofts.

Ullmann, L. P., and L. Krasner. (1965) *Case studies in behavior modification.* New York: Holt, Rinehart and Winston, Inc.

Voegtlin, W., and Lemere, F. (1942) The treatment of alcohol addiction. *Quarterly Journal of Studies on Alcoholism, 2,* 717–723.

Watson, J. B. (1913) Psychology as the behaviorist views it. *Psychological Review, 20,* 158–177.

——. (1917) The place of the conditioned reflex in psychology. *Psychological Review, 24,* 329–352.

——. (1924) *Behaviorism.* New York: W. W. Norton & Co., Inc.

Watson, J. B., and P. Rayner. (1920) Conditioned emotional reactions. *Journal of Experimental Psychology, 3,* 1–16.

Watson, R. I. (1962) The experimental tradition and clinical psychology. In A. J. Bachrach (Ed.), *Experimental foundations of clinical psychology.* New York: Basic Books, Inc., pp. 3–25.

Watts, A. W. (1957) *The way of Zen.* New York: Vintage Books, A Division of Random House.

Wertheimer, M. (1945) *Productive thinking.* New York: Harper & Bros.

Whitehead, A. N., and B. Russell. (1963) *Principia mathematica* (3 vols., 2nd ed.). Cambridge: The University Press.

Wiener, N. (1954) *The human use of human beings.* Boston: Houghton Mifflin Co.

Wightman, W. P. D. (1951) *The growth of scientific ideas.* New Haven: Yale University Press.

Wittels, F. (1924) *Sigmund Freud: His personality, his teaching, and his school.* New York: Dodd, Mead.

Wolpe, J. (1948) An approach to the problem of neurosis based on the conditioned response. Unpublished M.D. Thesis: University of Witwatersrand.

———. (1958) *Psychotherapy by reciprocal inhibition*. Stanford, Calif.: Stanford University Press. Quotations by permission of the publisher.

———. (1960) Reciprocal inhibition as the main basis of psychotherapeutic effects. In H. J. Eysenck (Ed.), *Behavior therapy and the neuroses*. New York: Pergamon Press, Inc., pp. 88–113.

———. (1969) *The practice of behavior therapy*. New York: Pergamon Press, Inc.

———. (1973) *The practice of behavior therapy* (2nd ed.). New York: Pergamon Press, Inc.

———. (1978) Cognition and causation in human behavior and its therapy. *American Psychologist, 33,* 437–446.

Woodworth, R. S. (1929) *Psychology*. New York: Holt, Rinehart, & Winston.

Index of Names

Index of Subjects

Photography Credits